PACIFIC
ISLANDS
YEARBOOK

EDITED BY NORMAN & NGAIRE DOUGLAS

16TH EDITION

Published in association with Nationwide News Pty Ltd

ANGUS & ROBERTSON PUBLISHERS
in association with NATIONWIDE NEWS PTY LTD

Unit 4, Eden Park, 31 Waterloo Road,
North Ryde, NSW, Australia 2113;
94 Newton Road, Auckland 1,
New Zealand; and
16 Golden Square, London WIR 4BN,
United Kingdom

16th edition first published in Australia
by Angus & Robertson Publishers
in association with Nationwide
News Pty Ltd in 1989

Copyright ©

ISBN 0 207 16114 3
ISSN 0078-7523

Typeset in Plantin by Best-set Typesetter Ltd
Printed in Australia by Australian Print Group

Foreword

The Pacific Ocean is the greatest single geographical entity on earth, extending over nearly a third of the planet's surface, or about half the area covered by water and one-fifth more than all the land area put together.

Small wonder that when the sheer immensity of the Pacific became known through Magellan's crossing of 1521, it captured the imagination of mankind as probably no part of the globe, and certainly no ocean, has done before or since. "This serene Pacific," wrote Herman Melville, "once beheld, must ever be the sea of his adoption."

But Magellan told us little of what this vast ocean contained and it was not until Cook's three voyages that the western nations realised that the Pacific was not only the greatest unit of the hydrosphere but an ocean of a thousand and one islands inhabited by generally friendly and hospitable people.

The result was a spate of literature on what came to be known as the South Seas. Much of it was fiction: the escapist romances of Paradise which made J. C. Furnas complain that "more thousands of words of swill have been written per square mile of dry land about the Islands than about any other geographical entity".

With the commencement of commercial ventures, however, there grew up an increasing demand for reliable factual information on what was becoming the world's ultimate frontier – where the European cultural streams moving west via America met those moving east via Australia.

At first those who needed a reference work or guidebook to the Pacific Islands had to be content with the compendiums prepared from the accounts of the explorers, early missionaries and trading captains, of which Reinzi's three-volume *Oceanie*, Meinicke's *Die Inseln des Stillen Ozeans* and Cheyne's *Description of Islands in the Western Pacific Ocean* were the best known.

The growth of commerce, however, led to the founding of the port towns of Levuka, Apia, Honolulu, Papeete, Nukualofa and Avarua. These attracted increasing numbers of Europeans: a hierarchy ranging upwards from the remnants of the former beachcombers, through the carpenters, masons, pubkeepers, chandlers and other skilled workers, to the apex of missionaries, heads of the larger business firms and consuls.

It was the development of an economic infrastructure that led to a demand for a specific reference work to cover the new but still geographically limited worlds of commerce and small-scale industry. This was met by the publication of the *Cyclopaedia of Samoa, Tonga, Tahiti and the Cook Islands* and the separate *Cyclopaedia of Fiji* in 1907, sumptuous, well-illustrated but expensive works containing all the information likely to be required by the island residents and visitors, including biographical sketches of the leading local notabilities.

Their success led to the production of the first edition of *Stewart's Handbook of the Pacific Islands: a reliable guide to all the inhabited Islands of the Pacific for Tourists, Traders and Settlers* the following year, the publishers being McCarron, Stewart and Company, of Sydney.

This work appeared annually, except for the war years, and was edited by the island authority Percy Allen, who compiled for the 1922 and succeeding editions the bibliography of works on the Pacific Islands which became the standard documentary source for island researchers. Its 8th edition was the only book I took with me on my voyage from England to the islands in 1929, and I had read every page before we reached the Red Sea.

When Percy Allen retired, *Stewart's Handbook* ceased to exist, leaving a gap which was eventually filled by R. W. Robson, who in 1930 had commenced publication of the *Pacific Islands Monthly*, and two years later followed it by publishing the *Pacific Islands Year Book*, the first nine editions being compiled and edited by himself, for by then his knowledge of the islands was unrivalled.

With the end of World War II the colonial powers who had political control over the Pacific Islands bowed out one by one, with the exception of France, leaving an assemblage of independent mini-states, some in association by agreement with their former metropolitan powers, with only the three French territories and a few isolated and for the most part uninhabited islands still under European or American control.

The small size of these new island nations has led to the growth of a unique variety of regional organisations for specific purposes, among the most important being the South Pacific Commission (the sole legacy from the colonial era); the South Pacific Forum; the South Pacific Bureau of Economic Co-operation; the University of the South Pacific; the Pacific Council of Churches; the South Pacific Air Transport Council; the Pacific Islands Tourism Development Council; the South Pacific Creative Arts Society; and by now over 200 others, including such exotics as the South Pacific Coconut Tree Climbing Championship.

The constant inter-island exchanges by governments, religious bodies, business organisations, professional groups, workers' associations, cultural, sporting and other groups, and the visits of many thousands of tourists, are now facilitated by an intricate network of air services linking the island world for the first time in a close-knit regional web of communications.

When I bought my first edition of the *Pacific Islands Year Book* in 1932 I regarded it as a self-indulgence, for like most residents in the South Seas I had never journeyed beyond the confines of my island territory and did not expect to. Today the whole region has for many purposes become a unit; and an increasingly complex one in which a reliable and up-to-date Year Book is no longer an indulgence but an absolute necessity which nobody – resident, visitor or interested spectator of the island scene – can afford to be without.

It is indeed a new island world, and the new publishers of the Year Book have wisely decided to completely revise the 16th edition in a new format which will provide all the information we require on the Pacific Islands of 1989; no longer the sleepy hollow of the colonial era but a vital, independent but inter-dependent association of nations in which change and progress are the keynote.

H. E. MAUDE
Canberra

Contents

Introduction

Although not yet over, the 1980s have already seen some of the most tumultuous political events of the Pacific's modern period, beginning with the uncertain birth of independent Vanuatu in 1980, an event that served as a reminder that the process of decolonisation which began for the Pacific Islands with the independence of Western Samoa in 1962 was far from over. Other events which stamp the decade as one of tremendous — if troubled — significance include the assassination of Palauan president Haruo Remeliik, the sabotage of the Greenpeace flagship *Rainbow Warrior* and the signing of the Treaty of Rarotonga (South Pacific Nuclear Free Treaty) all within a few months of each other in 1985.

The previous year, the decolonisation movement which seemed to have gone into suspended animation following Vanuatu's independence, kicked violently as Melanesian frustrations and French fears on the subject of self-government collided in New Caledonia, setting off a series of hostilities that culminated in the tragic events of April 1988. Much more surprising, even to close observers, were the two military coups which took place in Fiji in 1987 and resulted in an eventual declaration of republican status for the disturbed nation. Political uncertainties in Vanuatu, New Caledonia and even Fiji were made worse by the ever present bogy of Libya's Colonel Gaddafi, whose effect on the Pacific Islands has been minimal, but whose grip on the region's media is apparently unrelenting.

These and other events of recent years, not all of them necessarily political, such as the disquieting incidence of crimes of violence and against property in many parts of the Pacific but especially in Papua New Guinea, or the growing tendency of Island nations to move outside their circle of historical associations and seek trade and diplomatic relations with new acquaintances, not all of them condoned by the major powers of the Pacific rim, have led a number of commentators to reach for their clichés and phrases such as 'the end of the age of innocence' or 'paradise lost' have become predictable.

But well before Europeans imposed their own notions of order and disorder on the Islands, Pacific peoples intrigued, conspired and fought among and against each other. Politics, political rivalry and power games, despite the curious views of some writers, were not products of the post-colonial era: they have been an essential part of Pacific societies for centuries, and those of us who seek to understand the Pacific Islanders would be doing them and ourselves a service if we began by expunging the term 'paradise' from our vocabularies. Despite the perennial myth which surrounds them, the islands have never been Edens. Paradise, since it never was, cannot possibly be lost.

This is an appropriate place to draw attention to these matters although it is not the place to attempt an analysis of them. They are among the thousands of facts and details which make up the 16th edition of the *Pacific Islands Yearbook* which the editors hope will be as widely and as well used as its previous editions have been. Those facts and details are presented as far as possible without editorial comment. The profounder truths behind them can be left for others to disclose.

Users of previous editions of the *Pacific Islands Yearbook* will notice some changes in this one. A few may require comment. The alphabetically arranged directory of islands, which is the real meat of the *Yearbook*, has been brought to the front, while the descriptions of regional organisations and similar entries now occur in the second half of the volume. One or two have gone, to be replaced by others that seemed more pertinent, although the long-standing chronology of the Pacific War remains. Within the directory the demise of the US Trust Territory is celebrated by separate entries devoted to its one-time components: the Federated States of Micronesia, the Marshall Islands and Palau.

The individual entries still have their recognisable shape, although the long, sometimes almost interminable, lists of names of

'personalities' have been reduced to a few major office holders. In today's volatile Pacific, there is very little assurance that this week's Minister of Finance in, say, Papua New Guinea, is going to occupy the position next week, let alone in another three years, which is supposed to be the effective life span of this volume. In place of the names of personalities the reader will find the names, addresses and telephone numbers of the most important government offices, diplomatic representatives and regional or international organisations, details which are somewhat more durable. Also absent from this edition are the 'trade directories' which were at best incomplete and inconsistent in previous editions. Seekers after this kind of information are now catered for by a number

SUMMARY OF ISLANDS

	Status
AMERICAN SAMOA	Unincorporated US territory
COOK ISLANDS	Self-governing in free association with New Zealand
EASTER ISLAND	Territory of Chile
FIJI	Independent republic
FRENCH POLYNESIA	Overseas territory of France
GALAPAGOS	Province of Ecuador
GUAM	Unincorporated US territory
HAWAII	State of the US
IRIAN JAYA	Province of the Republic of Indonesia
KIRIBATI	Independent republic, member of Commonwealth of Nations
KOSRAE	Member, Federated States of Micronesia
MARSHALL ISLANDS	Self-governing republic, in association with US
LORD HOWE ISLAND	Dependency of New South Wales, Australia

* *At last census or estimate*
** *French Pacific Franc*

of publications, including the official trade directories of several countries, which contain far more detailed information than can possibly be summarised in these pages. The trade directory for Papua New Guinea alone runs to 384 pages, that for Fiji to 120. However, the increasing importance of tourism and travel in the Islands is reflected in the extensively revised accommodation listings which are perhaps more comprehensive than can be found in any other single source.

Many people and institutions helped to provide information for this volume, far more than can be individually acknowledged, although the editors greatly appreciate the assistance of all of them. However, particular thanks should go to Polynesian Airlines, the Fiji Visitors Bureau in Sydney and Suva and Vanuatu's National Office of Tourism. Thanks are also due to the many contributors to previous editions of the *Yearbook*, some of whom may still recognise their words.

Every attempt has been made to ensure that the facts and statistics contained herein are as accurate and up-to-date as possible, but the present editors will not accept liability for errors or omissions in text, maps or tables. Monetary values in each section are given in the currency of that particular country unless otherwise noted. Maps are not intended for navigational use.

Norman and Ngaire Douglas

Capital or Administration Centre	Land Area (sq. km)	Population*	Local Time (GMT ±)	Currency
Pago Pago	197	36,260	−11	$US
Avarua	240	17,185	−10.30	$NZ
Hanga Roa	180	2060	−3	Chilean Peso
Suva	18,272	715,735	+12	$F
Papeete	4,000	172,080	−10	CFP**
Puerto Baquerizo	7,700	6000	−5	Sucre
Agana	549	118,000	+10	$US
Honolulu	16,641	1,053,900	−10	$US
Jayapura	410,660	1,424,800	+9	Indonesian Rupiah
Tarawa	726	63,883	+12	$Aust.
Kosrae	109.6	6462	+10	$US
Majuro	171	43,355	+10	$US
—	14.5	270	+10	$Aust.

SUMMARY OF ISLANDS

	Status
NAURU	Independent republic, associate member of Commonwealth of Nations
NEW CALEDONIA	Overseas territory of France
NIUE	Self-governing in free association with New Zealand
NORFOLK ISLAND	Territory of Australia
NORTHERN MARIANA ISLANDS	Commonwealth of the US
OGASAWARA ISLANDS	Japanese territory
PALAU (BELAU)	Self-governing republic, in association with US
PAPUA NEW GUINEA	Independent state, member of Commonwealth of Nations
PITCAIRN	Dependency of Britain, administered by British High Commissioner in NZ
POHNPEI (PONAPE)	Member, Federated States of Micronesia
SOLOMON ISLANDS	Independent state, member of Commonwealth of Nations
TOKELAU	Dependency of New Zealand
TONGA	Independent monarchy, member of Commonwealth of Nations
TORRES STRAIT ISLANDS	Australian possession administered by Queensland
TRUK	Member, Federated States of Micronesia
TUVALU	Independent State and member Commonwealth of Nations
VANUATU	Independent republic, also member of Commonwealth of Nations and Association de Co-operation Culturelle et Technique (France)
WALLIS AND FUTUNA	Overseas territory of France
WESTERN SAMOA	Independent state, member of Commonwealth of Nations
YAP	Member, Federated States of Micronesia

* *At last census or estimate*
** *French Pacific Franc*

Capital or Administration Centre	Land Area (sq. km)	Population*	Local Time (GMT ±)	Currency
Yaren	21	8042	+12	$Aust.
Noumea	19,103	145,368	+11	CFP**
Alofi	258	2532	−11	$NZ
Kingston	34.5	1880	+11.30	$Aust.
Saipan	475	20,350	+10	$US
Chichi-Jima	100	1804	+9	Yen
Koror	500	12,250	+10	$US
Port Moresby	461,690	3,483,360	+10	Kina
Adamstown	4.5	58	−8	$NZ
Kolonia	345.4	28,902	+10	$US
Honiara	29,785	285,796	+11	$SI
—	12.1	1703	−11	$NZ
Nuku'alofa	696.71	96,592	+13	Pa'anga — $TP
Thursday Is.	673	4837	+10	$Aust.
Moen	118	46,159	+10	$US
Funafuti	25.9	8364	+12	$Aust.
Port Vila	12,189	140,154	+11	Vatu
Mata Utu	124	12,391	+12	CFP**
Apia	2,934	162,220	−11	Tala — $WS
Colonia	121.2	10,948	+10	$US

Pacific Chronology

c. 35,000–25,000 BC — Settlement of New Guinea; much later settlement of Island Melanesia.

c. 3500–2000 BC — Much of Western Micronesia settled.

c. 1500 BC — Ancestors of present-day Polynesians reach Fiji.

c. 1200 BC — Proto-Polynesian colonising of Tonga; subsequent movement into Samoa.

c. 300–500 AD — Marquesas colonised; subsequent settlement of Eastern Pacific including Hawaii.

c. 750 AD — Settlement of New Zealand.

1506 — Alvaro Telez (Portuguese) visits Sumatra.

1509 — Diego Lopez de Sequeira (Portuguese) visits Sumatra and Malacca.

1511 — Antonio d' Abreu (Portuguese) sails as far east as Aru Islands and Irian Jaya, then to Moluccas. This is first visit to Spice Islands.

1513 — Vasco Nunez de Balboa (Spanish) crosses the Isthmus of Panama and sights the Pacific.

1517 — Fernando Perez de Andrada (Portuguese) in China.

1520–21 — Ferdinand Magellan (Spanish) discovers Magellan Strait and crosses Pacific to Guam and Philippines in ships *Victoria* and *Trinidad*. After Magellan's death in Philippines, Juan Sebastian Elcano returns to Spain in *Victoria* with cargo of spices, reaching Seville on 9 September 1522.

1521 — Spanish conquest of Mexico.

1525–26 — Spanish monarch sends expedition under Garcia Jofre de Loaisa to East Indies for spices. Four ships enter Pacific, but are separated by storm. Only the flagship reaches Moluccas. Expedition becomes fiasco. One ship, caravel *San Lesmes*, lost.

1526 — Jorge de Meneses (Portuguese) lands on Vogelkop (Irian Jaya) and names region Ilhas dos Papuas.

1527–29 — Alvaro de Saavedra (Spanish) sent from Mexico to trade with Spice Islands and ascertain fate of Loaisa expedition. Two of his three ships lost after becoming separated in the Marshall Islands. With cargo of spices, Saavedra makes two attempts to return to Mexico from Moluccas, but is defeated by contrary prevailing winds.

1529 — Spain cedes Moluccas to Portugal by Treaty of Zaragoza.

1531–35 — Spanish conquest of Peru.

1537–42 — Spaniards explore Pacific coasts of North and South America, reaching as far north as San Francisco.

1542–45 — Ruy Lopez de Villalobos (Spanish) crosses Pacific from Mexico to Philippines, where attempt to found colony fails. Villalobos' flagship *San Juan* fails in two attempts to return to Mexico. On one, Inigo Ortiz de Retes skirts northern coast of New Guinea and names it Nueva Guinea.

1564-65 — Spanish colony founded in Philippines by Miguel Lopez de Legaspi. Two of Legaspi's ships return to Mexico by running north to 40th parallel and skirting North American coast. These voyages establish Spain's galleon route, in use between Mexico and Philippines for next 250 years.

1567-68 — Alvaro de Mendana crosses Pacific from Peru and discovers Guadalcanal, San Cristobal, Malaita and other islands in the Solomons.

1577-80 — Francis Drake enters Pacific and sails up coasts of South and North America, looting Spanish towns and capturing treasure ships. After crossing Pacific to East Indies, he becomes first British circumnavigator.

1595 — Mendana leaves Callao with four ships to colonise Solomon Islands. In May, he discovers group now known as Marquesas Islands. Later, one of his ships disappears near Santa Cruz Island (Ndeni), where settlement is established. However, after Mendana's death, expedition leaves for Philippines. Second and third ships disappear en route, leaving flagship alone.

1598-1600 — Beginnings of Dutch exploration of Pacific. Mahu and Van Noort expeditions.

1605-06 — Pedro Fernandez de Quiros, pilot on Mendana's second voyage, sails from Callao in search of supposed southern continent. After passing through the Tuamotu Archipelago, Quiros reaches the Duff Islands (north of Ndeni) and then sails south past the Banks Islands to the island which he calls La Austrialia del Espiritu Santo (now simply Espiritu Santo or Santo). After an abortive attempt to found a colony in Big Bay, Quiros heads northward for the standard route home to Mexico. Eventually the second-in-command, Luis Baez de Torres, reaches the Philippines through Torres Strait and the Spice Islands.

1606 — Willem Jansz (Dutch) reaches southern coast of Irian Jaya from East Indies.

1616 — Willem Cornelisz Schouten and Jacob Le Maire (Dutch) round Cape Horn for first time and cross the Pacific in search of the southern continent. They discover northern outliers of Tonga, Futuna and Alofi (which they called Hoorn Islands), and some of the New Guinea islands.

1642-43 — Abel Tasman (Dutch), on voyage from Java and Mauritius, discovers Tasmania, New Zealand, Tonga, some of the Fiji Islands. New Ireland, New Britain, etc.

1648 — Fedot Alexeev and Semen Dezhnev discover Bering Strait on voyage from Kolyma River, Siberia. (See also 1728.)

1700 — William Dampier (British) discovers strait between New Britain and New Ireland, and sights southern end of New Ireland.

1722 — Jacob Roggeveen (Dutch) discovers Easter Island and Samoa.

1728 — Vitus Bering (Russian) rediscovers Bering Strait.

1742 — Commodore George Anson (British) captures Spanish treasure galleon.

1765 — Commodore John Byron crosses Pacific on first British attempt to discover the southern continent.

1767 — HMS *Dolphin* (Captain Samuel Wallis) and *Swallow* (Captain Philip Carteret) on new voyage in search of southern continent. After separation near Strait of Magellan, Wallis discovers several Tuamotuan atolls, Tahiti and Wallis Island (Uvea). Carteret discovers Pitcairn Island, crosses Pacific to Ndeni, and lands at Buka and New Britain.

1768 — Louis Antoine de Bougainville visits Tahiti; subsequently sights and names islands in Samoa and Western Pacific.

1769-78 — Captain James Cook makes three voyages to the Pacific. On the first, he observes transit of Venus at Tahiti, charts and names the Society Islands, circumnavigates the North and South Islands of New Zealand, and skirts Australia's east coast. On the second voyage, which establishes beyond doubt that no southern continent exists, he discovers and/or explores several islands in the Cook group: Niue, Tonga, Norfolk Island, Vanuatu,

New Caledonia, Easter Island and the Marquesas. On his last voyage, he finds more islands in the Cook group, and adds the Hawaiian Islands to his list of discoveries before being killed at Kealakekua Bay, Hawaii, 1779.

1785–88 — La Perouse (French) explores Pacific in ships *Astrolabe* and *Boussole* which are both wrecked at Vanikoro. La Perouse's fate remains unknown for 37 years.

1788 — First British settlement in Australia — at Port Jackson (Sydney).

1789 — Mutiny on the *Bounty* in Tongan waters.

1791 — Captain Ingraham (American) discovers northern Marquesas Islands.

1791–92 — Vancouver and Broughton (British) discover Chatham Islands and Rapa, and visit Hawaii and north-west coast of America.

1792–93 — D'Entrecasteaux (French) visits many Pacific islands in searching for La Perouse.

1797 — London Missionary Society establishes stations in Tahiti and Tongatapu.

1810 — Kamehameha I achieves unification of Hawaii.

1815 — Christianity adopted in Tahiti and nearby islands. Pomare II establishes control over Tahiti.

1820 — Bellingshausen (Russian) makes extensive survey of Tuamotu Archipelago.

1823 — Rev. John Williams (LMS) takes Polynesian missionaries to Rarotonga and other islands in Cook group.

1830 — Williams takes Christianity to Samoa.

1834 — French Catholic missionaries occupy Mangareva.

1840 — British sovereignty proclaimed in New Zealand with Treaty of Waitangi.

1842 — French annex Marquesas and proclaim protectorate over Tahiti.

1845 — Taufa'ahau Tupou I achieves unification of Tonga; extends 1839 code of laws.

1853 — French annex New Caledonia.

1856 — Representative of J. C. Godeffroy und Sohn, of Hamburg, arrives in Samoa.

1874 — Fiji ceded to Britain.

1875 — Tupou I of Tonga signs constitution guaranteeing freedom to all Tongans.

1876 — First LMS missionaries reach Papua.

1877 — Western Pacific High Commission created by Great Britain to deal with British affairs in parts of the Pacific having no established governments.

1883 — British Government repudiates Queensland's annexation of Papua.

1884 — Germany annexes New Britain, New Ireland, and north-east coast of New Guinea. Britain declares protectorate over Papua.

1888 — Cook Islands declared under British protection. Chile annexes Easter Island.

1892 — Britain declares protectorate over Gilbert and Ellice Islands.

1893 — British protectorate established over southern Solomon Islands.

1894 — Republic set up in Hawaii.

1898 — Philippines and Guam ceded to United States following war with Spain. US also annexes Hawaiian Islands.

1899 — Spain sells Caroline and Marshall Islands to Germany. Western Samoa becomes German colony. Eastern Samoa becomes a US territory. Phosphate discovered on Ocean Island and on Nauru, a German colony.

1900 — Niue declared a British possession.

1901 — Ocean Island added to Gilbert and Ellice Islands Protectorate.

1906 — Australia accepts control of Papua from Britain. New Hebrides becomes an Anglo-French condominium.

1914 — German New Guinea and Nauru occupied by Australians; Western Samoa by New Zealanders, and Caroline, Marshall and Mariana Islands by Japanese. Otherwise, World War I has little effect on Pacific affairs.

1915 — Gilbert and Ellice Islands Colony created.

1919–20 — Former German colonies in Pacific become mandated territories of League of Nations — New Guinea to be administered by Australia, Western Samoa by New Zealand, Caroline, Mariana and Marshall Islands by Japan, and Nauru by Australia, Great Britain and New Zealand jointly.

1932 — Japan annexes Caroline, Marshall and Mariana Islands.

1935 — Philippines created a semi-independent commonwealth by the United States, to become independent republic in 1946.

1941–45 — War in Pacific between United States, the Netherlands and British Empire on one side and Japan on the other. Japanese occupy Netherlands East Indies, Guam, Nauru, Gilbert Islands, Solomon Islands and some parts of New Guinea until driven out.

1946 — Former mandated territories of League of Nations become trust territories of United Nations under same administering countries, except that United States takes over Mariana, Marshall and Caroline Islands as the Trust Territories of the Pacific Islands from Japan. Holland surrenders East Indies to Javanese nationalists.

1947 — Agreement creating South Pacific Commission signed in Canberra, Australia.

1949 — Australia approves administrative merger of Papua and New Guinea.

1950 — Independent state of Indonesia established.

1958 — Referendum in French territories returns majority vote for continuing control by France.

1959 — Territory of Hawaii becomes 50th state of USA.

1962 — Western Samoa becomes independent.

1963 — Dutch New Guinea (Irian Jaya) handed over to Indonesia.

1965 — Cook Islands attain self-government.

1968 — Nauru becomes independent.

1970 — Fiji becomes independent.

1971 — South Pacific Forum established.

1974 — Niue attains self-government.

1975 — Papua New Guinea becomes independent.

1976 — Gilbert and Ellice Islands Colony becomes two colonies, Gilbert Islands and Tuvalu. Northern Mariana Islands becomes a Commonwealth of the United States.

1978 — Solomon Islands and Tuvalu become independent.

1979 — The Gilbert Islands become an independent republic under the name of Kiribati. The United States signs treaties of friendship with Tuvalu and Kiribati and abandons claims to islands in both groups. Marshall Islands and the Federated States of Micronesia (Truk, Ponape, Yap and Kosrae) become technically self-governing.

1980 — The New Hebrides becomes independent under the name of Vanuatu (Our Land).

1981 — The Micronesian state of Palau becomes technically self-governing as the Republic of Palau. Pacific Forum of Trade Unions inaugurated in Vanuatu.

1985 — Palauan President Haruo Remeliik assassinated. Treaty of Rarotonga (South Pacific Nuclear Free Zone Treaty) signed by nine Forum countries. Greenpeace flagship *Rainbow Warrior* sunk in Auckland harbour by French agents.

1986 — Marshall Islands and Federated States of Micronesia implement Compact of Free Association with US.

1987 — Two military coups occur in Fiji; Fiji declares republic. Referendum in New Caledonia returns majority vote for continuing French control.

1989 — (May) Kanak leaders Jean-Marie Tjibaou and Yeiwene Yeiwene assassinated in New Caledonia.

American Samoa

American Samoa consists of five principal islands and two atolls in the Samoan group east of the 171st meridian of west longitude. It is an unincorporated and unorganised territory of the United States of America with a land area of 197 sq. km. Population is about 36,260.

The main island is Tutuila (135 sq. km), which is about 3700 km south-west of Honolulu and 2575 km north-east of New Zealand. The other islands are Aunu'u, Tau, Ofu, Olosega, Swains Island and the small, isolated atoll Rose Island, in reality two small islets which are uninhabited. The administrative centre is Pago Pago on Tutuila. Local time is 11 hours behind GMT.

The currency is that of the United States and the National Anthem is also the American National Anthem but there is an official song, *Amerika Samoa* and two flags, the US Stars and Stripes and the territorial flag adopted in April 1960, when a new constitution was approved. This flag consists of a large white triangle bordered in red and containing a white-headed eagle, all on a blue field. The American national bird bears in its claws a yellow 'uatogi' (a war club representing the power of the state) and a 'fue', or fly switch (signifying wisdom, and the 'fono', the traditional Samoan council). The motto on the Territorial Seal is 'Samoa Muamua le atua' (Let God be first).

Public holidays include all US national holidays and 17 April (Flag Day), commemorating the first raising of the US flag.

THE PEOPLE. In 1900, just after the US took over American Samoa, its Samoan population was 5698. The Samoans are Polynesians, the majority of whom still live in rural communities and nearly all of them on the main island of Tutuila, with the biggest proportion of these around Pago Pago, the seat of government.

The people are the same as those in Western Samoa, speaking the same language, and Polynesians have been in the Samoan Islands for over 2500 years. Total population of American Samoa in the census of 1980 was 32,395, an increase of 3205 on the census figure for 1974. Population density per square mile was 421. In 1986 the population numbered 36,260.

The growth rate of the population peaked in 1970 when the increase was 3.10 per cent per annum. Since 1980 the increase has settled to 1.8 per cent per annum. There were 1368 births in 1984, representing a live birth rate of 39.14 per thousand of the population. Deaths at all ages in 1984 were 150, or 4.29 per cent of the population.

The sexes are almost equally divided in numbers, and almost half the population is under the age of 15, and more than half under 19.

Migration. There are more American Samoans abroad than in Samoa. There are an estimated 65,000 on the US West Coast, and 20,000 in Hawaii. This continuous outmigration is an important reason why the population in the islands has remained fairly constant.

Nationality. The American Samoans are nationals of the US, and have free entry to the US. After meeting the necessary requirements, they may become citizens of the US. Many have achieved that status by service in the US Armed Forces.

Language. The Samoan language is closely related to Hawaiian and other Polynesian

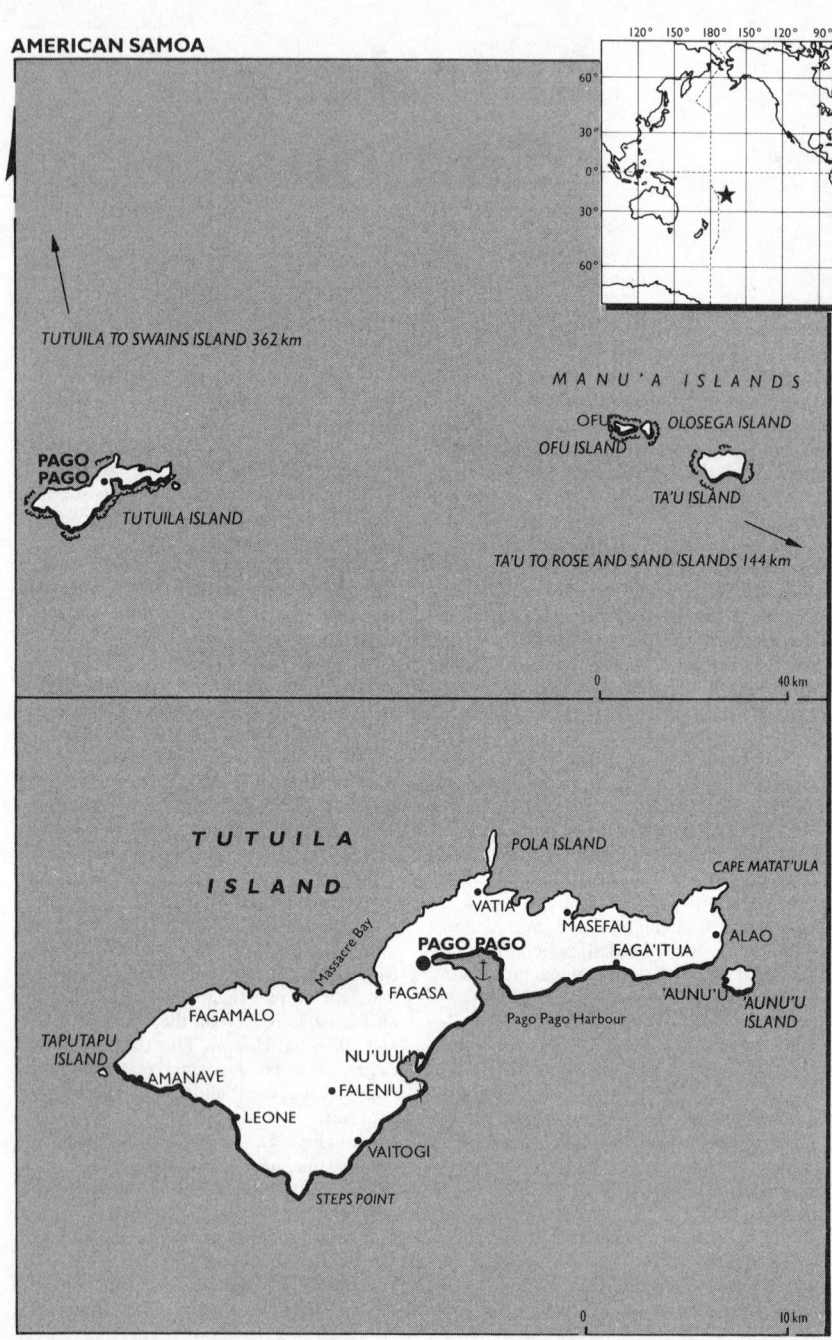

AMERICAN SAMOA

TUTUILA TO SWAINS ISLAND 362 km

MANU'A ISLANDS

OFU
OFU ISLAND   OLOSEGA ISLAND

TA'U ISLAND

TA'U TO ROSE AND SAND ISLANDS 144 km

**PAGO
PAGO**

TUTUILA ISLAND

0   40 km

*TUTUILA
ISLAND*

POLA ISLAND

CAPE MATAT'ULA

VATIA

PAGO PAGO

MASEFAU

ALAO

Massacre Bay

FAGASA

FAGA'ITUA

Pago Pago Harbour

'AUNU'U

FAGAMALO

'AUNU'U
ISLAND

TAPUTAPU
ISLAND

NU'UULI

AMANAVE

• FALENIU

LEONE

• VAITOGI

STEPS POINT

0   10 km

languages, however most American Samoans also speak English as bilingual education has been in effect for the greater part of this century.

In Samoan, the 'g' is pronounced 'ng' as in 'English', 'Pago' is pronounced as 'pahng-o'.

Religion. Religious institutions in American Samoa are an important influence in the community. The major denominations are Catholic, Congregational, Mormon and Methodist. More than half the islanders are members of the Christian Congregational Church, and about 19 per cent are Catholics.

A priest or minister is accorded a privileged high position in the village community and is equal in status to a high chief. They may make village rules that affect the conduct of the villagers on Sunday, e.g. no one may swim in the sea on Sunday, and no one may cause a disturbance while the church is in service.

The church is also a landowner by reason of gifts and purchases of real property. The amount of influence of the church is highly dependent on the personality of the priest or minister.

Lifestyle. 'Fa'a Samoa' means the Samoan way and is frequently used in describing the lifestyle of both American and Western Samoa. 'Fa'a Samoa' has inherent flexibility which has allowed the people to withstand or absorb the influences of foreign cultures. As American Samoa's contact with western ways has accelerated with increased travel and education coupled with a decreasing satisfaction with the subsistence lifestyle 'Fa'a Samoa' is increasingly tested.

The Samoan way of life is structured around a social system of clans, or extended family ('aiga') and their chiefs ('matai'). A village may have any number of chiefs, depending on the number of related families in the village. The 'matai' is chosen by the family members and is responsible for the well-being of the 'aiga', for the maintenance of family lands and the communal economy which still prevails in village life.

Recreation. Pastimes include many sports such as cricket, played Samoan style, and long boat racing, and Samoans are keen supporters of American football and baseball. Results of games in mainland USA are followed closely. 'Fiafias' (feasts accompanied by traditional songs and dancing) are also an important part of Samoan recreation.

GOVERNMENT. The government of the territory is divided into three branches: executive, legislative and judicial.

Executive. The executive branch consists of the Governor, Lieutenant Governor and departmental and office heads. The Governor is popularly elected and exercises his authority under the direction of the Secretary of the Interior. The Lieutenant Governor is also elected and assists the Governor in administering the territory; he also serves as Secretary of American Samoa. Both the Governor and Lieutenant Governor serve a four-year term. The executive branch department and office heads are appointed by the Governor and confirmed by the legislature ('Fono') and are responsible to the Governor.

Legislature. American Samoa has a bicameral legislature. The Senate consists of 18 senators chosen in accordance with Samoan custom ('matai') by county councils of each of the 12 established senate districts for four-year terms. The House of Representatives has 20 voting members elected by popular vote from the 17 established house districts for two-year terms. There is also one non-voting delegate from Swain's Island, elected at a meeting by the island's adult permanent residents. Senate and House members serve four-year and two-year terms respectively.

JUDICIARY. The judicial power of American Samoa is vested in the High Court of general jurisdiction, District Court of limited jurisdiction and village courts with jurisdiction only over violation of their respective village regulations. There are three divisions of the High Court: the Appellate, Trial and Land and Titles. The judicial branch, independent of the executive and legislative branches, is administered and supervised by the Chief Justice of American Samoa. The Chief Justice and an Associate Justice are appointed by the Secretary of the Interior. Associate judges and district court judges are appointed by the Governor upon the recommendation of the Chief Justice, and confirmed by the Senate.

Washington representative. American Samoa has a representative in the US Congress, with all congressional privileges except the right to vote. This position replaces that of American Samoan Delegate-at-Large in

Washington. The position was held from 1980 until September 1988 by Fofo Sunia who resigned after being indicted on counts of payroll fraud.

Local government. The Office of Samoan Affairs, also known as the Office of Local Government, supervises operations carried out at the district, county and village level. The office is a link between the Samoan people and territorial government officials.

Within the Samoan administration are three district governors, 14 county chiefs and 53 'pulenu'us' (village mayors), six village police officers and three district clerks. The Office of Samoan Affairs conducts elections and concerns itself at the local level with village problems, such as water systems, roads, sanitation, agriculture, schools and land disputes.

Public service. Out of a total public service of 3960 employees in 1985, 3661 were recruited in American Samoa, 281 were contract employees mostly from the United States, and 18 were part time.

JUSTICE. The judicial branch consists of a High Court having territorial jurisdiction throughout the islands, a district court for each of the five judicial districts into which the islands are divided, a small claims court, a traffic court and a 'matai' title court. The small claims, traffic and 'matai' courts are presided over by Samoan judges.

A law requiring that all disputes regarding 'matai' titles and land registrations be arbitrated by the Office of Samoan Affairs has helped cut down the court's case-load in those areas.

High Court proceedings on the trial level are generally conducted in Samoan and English before a panel composed of the chief justice or the associate justice and two associate judges. 'Matai' cases are heard exclusively by a panel of three associated judges. Traffic courts are conducted by a single associate judge. Legislation was passed by the Fono in 1978 expanding membership of the Court of Appeal to include judges from other United States territories.

Another important innovation has been the introduction of the right of an accused to trial by jury in serious criminal cases.

LEGAL AFFAIRS. The Attorney-General's office functions as chief prosecutor and legal adviser for the government, but also handles immigration and serves as territorial registrar. In an election year, the Attorney-General acts as electoral commissioner.

In 1985 crime reports listed a total of 1960 adult offences, 952 in the major categories. Of these, assault accounted for 425 and theft for most of the remainder. In addition there were 54 listed juvenile offences.

Public safety. The Department of Public Safety is responsible for protection and security of citizens and property, fire services, disaster control, rescue services including search and rescue services previously performed by the US Coast Guard, prison control and rehabilitation, vehicle registration and driver licensing.

LIQUOR LAWS. Persons must be over 18 to purchase alcohol.

DEFENCE. Until 1951 the territory had, from its inception in 1900, been under the control of the US Navy Department, administered by a naval officer. Pago Pago was a naval base. But in 1951 administrative responsibility was transferred to the Department of Interior and the naval presence was phased out. A Coast Guard service was stationed there but that has gone and the Coast Guard functions are now handled by the Port Administration.

There are no naval or military forces stationed in American Samoa.

EDUCATION. Total school enrolment in American Samoa in 1986 was 12,919. There are five public high schools, 22 elementary schools, 95 early childhood centres and a special education school, with a total enrolment of 11,012 and nine private schools with a total enrolment of 1907.

The early childhood education programme, which reaches about 1764 children, involves preschool education for Samoans under the age of six who get 2½ hours a day five days a week. This training is done within the village by Samoan parents who are given special training. The teaching is in Samoan.

There are 6355 elementary school pupils in grades 1 to 8, and 2827 secondary school pupils. The special education school (enrolment 66) is for the benefit of pupils with learning difficulties or other handicaps.

The largest private schools are the Marist elementary school at Atu'u and the St Francis' girls' school at Lepua.

In 1986, 57 Samoan students graduated from colleges in the US under a Government of America Samoa scholarship programme. There were 295 scholarship recipients that year. Samoa has one college, the Samoa Community College, which provides among other courses trades, business, teaching, communication, clerical and nursing instruction. The college also provides additional adult education training.

In 1986 there were 725 school teachers and 427 other personnel in the public school system.

School food programme. The School Food Service provides nutritional meals to Samoan schoolchildren. All schools have their own kitchens and serve breakfast every school day. For private schools and ECE village centres without kitchens, breakfast is delivered. Lunch is also provided. Over 90 per cent of the food is provided by the Federal Department of Agriculture.

LABOUR. The government is the biggest employer in American Samoa followed by the tuna canning industry. Tourism and a few other enterprises account for most of the rest of the workforce. Total labour force in 1985 was estimated at 12,001 persons, of whom 10,516 were in actual employment and 1500 (or 12.5 per cent) unemployed.

Total public service was 3960, or 33 per cent of the work force; 3356 (or 28 per cent) were employed in the fish cannery; and 3200 (or 26.6 per cent) distributed in other employment.

Minimum wage. The US Department of Labor sets minimum hourly wage rates for American Samoan enterprises with gross revenues in excess of $250,000 a year. In 1985 the hourly rates varied from $1.77 an hour in the laundry and dry cleaning industry, to $2.05 in retailing and warehousing, $2.38 in construction, $2.56 in finance and insurance, and $2.82 in fish canning and processing and can manufacture. Some rates are well above these minimums, particularly in the skilled trades.

Average income. Latest income analysis available is for 1980, when 8446 people were employed out of a total population of 32,297. Median household income for 1980 was $9241, and average income of all persons in employment was $3850.

Social security. The Old Age and Survivors

FIGURE 1 LABOUR FORCE AND EMPLOYMENT: AMERICAN SAMOA 1978–1984

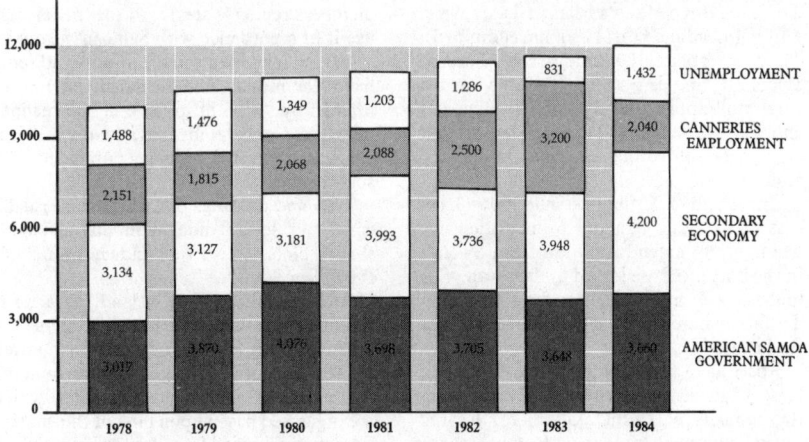

Insurance provisions of the US Social Security Act are handled in American Samoa just as in the US mainland. The US Social Security Administration maintains an office in American Samoa.

HEALTH. The Lyndon B. Johnson Tropical Medical Center is Samoa's general care hospital in the fields of general surgery, internal medicine, obstetrics, pediatrics, TB and leprosy, ophthalmology, dental care and ambulance services. Specialised treatment not available there is provided in Hawaii at the Tripler Army Medical Center. Dispensary services are available throughout American Samoa, together with dental care, school and home health services.
Diseases. The main health problems are venereal disease, influenza, diarrhoea and heart disease. Cancer is a significant cause of death. According to statistics, tuberculosis and filariasis have ceased to be health problems. In 1985 the crude death rate remained at 4.4 per thousand of population, as against 4.1 in 1979. The crude birth rate was a record in 1985 at 43.0 per thousand.

THE LAND. The total land area of American Samoa is 197 sq. km. Tutuila, largest of the seven islands in the group, is almost bisected by the harbour at Pago Pago and has an area of 145 sq. km. Aunu'u is a small island off the south-eastern tip of Tutuila. There are three Manu'a islands: Ta'u (39 sq. km), Olosega and Ofu (11 sq. km combined). They are about 100 km east of Tutuila. Swain's Island is a small, privately-owned coral atoll approximately 2 km in diameter and 450 km north of Tutuila. Rose Island, 400 km east of Tutuila, is a tiny uninhabited atoll.

The island of Tutuila extends 30 km from east to west and is about 6 km wide. The whole group extends 500 km from Swain's in the north to Rose Island in the south. The highest peak is Mount Matafao (702 m) on Tutuila, where Mount Pioa, known as 'The Rainmaker', is 563 m.

Apart from the coral atolls of Swain's and Rose Islands, the territory is formed from the remains of extinct volcanoes, leaving central mountain ranges with only limited coastal plains.
Soil. Some 70 per cent of the group is forest. Of the remaining 30 per cent suitable for agriculture, about 4,800 ha are under cultivation.
Climate. Trade winds and frequent rains give American Samoa a pleasant climate. Pago Pago usually receives about 5000 mm of rain a year, most of it falling between December and March. The average temperature ranges from 21 to 32°C. Humidity averages 80 per cent.
Fauna and flora. The mountainous regions are characterised by rain forests with tall ferns and trees such as the Barringtonia.

LAND TENURE SYSTEM. American Samoa has three kinds of public land ownership: native or communal land, freehold land, and individually owned land.
Native or communal lands. These include more than 90 per cent of all lands in American Samoa, are held under Samoan customs and are subject to the authority of the 'matai'. The 'matai' at the head of an 'aiga', a family group, has been elected to at least one title and sometimes to several. Each title bestows authority over family lands.

Assignments of land by a 'matai' for a house or plantation for a family member is for that person's lifetime and cannot be revoked except for good cause, i.e. refusal to render services to the 'matai'. The permission to use family lands given or assigned to family members continues as long as family members render a service to the 'matai' and use it in accordance with Samoan customs.

'Matai' may use produce, profits and rents from communal land in which he has an interest by virtue of his title in any manner he wishes, and members of a family may not claim an interest in property purchased with such profits.

The land holdings of each 'matai' usually consist of several noncontinuous and odd-shaped plots and are well-known throughout the village.

An interesting aspect of land character is the village 'malae', which is equivalent to a green or town plaza. The 'malae' is located in the centre of the village and is surrounded by the 'matai' guest houses or 'fales' which are organised based upon rank of the 'matai'. The 'malae' is used for village social activities and for sports events, and is maintained by all the families in the village.

Alienation of communal land must be reviewed by the Land Commission and approved by the Governor. Alienation of communal land to anyone who is not a full-blooded Samoan is prohibited unless that person was born in American Samoa, is a descendant of a Samoan family and lives with Samoans as a Samoan, and has lived in American Samoa for more than five years and officially declared intent of making American Samoa home.

Leases of communal lands are limited to 55 years, including options to renew or extend, and are reviewed by the Land Commission and must be approved by the Governor also.

Freehold land. Freehold lands are lands created by the court grants prior to 1900 under the German administration. Freehold lands, however, represent a very small portion of the total land area of American Samoa.

Private ownership of freehold land is comparable to fee title. It is alienable freely, and leases are not restricted to specific terms of years. Neither alienation nor lease is subject to review by the Land Commission or approval by the Governor.

Individually owned land. Other lands, commonly called individually owned land, but again a small portion of the total land area, are also recognised. This title to land can result from the land title registration process, affidavits curing title defects, or adverse possession of 30 years or more. The occupancy and use of 'virgin' land, previously unestablished native land in general, is often involved. Individually owned land is similar in character to fee ownership. However, alienation is limited to persons of at least one-half Samoan blood. Leasehold terms of years are again not specifically limited.

Leasehold security interests. Improvements to communal or individually owned land may become the personal property of individuals by recorded separation agreements. As already indicated, leaseholds may also be created in both native and individual owned lands. These legal interests may be used in turn as collateral or security interests in construction and business loan financing.

Government, church, and school lands. All lands, including native or communal lands, may be conveyed freely to the American

Samoa Government or US Government for governmental purposes, or upon the Governor's approval to an authorised and recognised religious society for a church or pastor's dwelling. Reconveyance must be to native Samoans only and is subject to the Governor's approval. The American Samoa Government may also acquire any lands by eminent domain. Native or communal lands may also be leased to any organisation for school purposes for up to 30 years. Renewals for like periods are permissible indefinitely. However, the Governor must approve both lease and any renewals, and may require regular teaching of the English language in the school.

Corporate interests in land. Corporate land acquisitions are subject to several special limitations. Except as indicated above for religious organisation, corporations may not acquire any interest in native or individually owned lands other than leasehold interests approved by the Governor. The 55-year restriction, including options to extend or renew, is applicable to native or communal lands. Leases of government land, particularly at the Industrial Park in Tafuna, are limited generally to a similar period. Corporations may purchase or lease freehold lands, but again the Governor's approval is required.

PRIMARY PRODUCTION. American Samoa's thriving fish industry and its by-products such as fish meal is the territory's major industry, and other primary production is comparatively small, but growing. The government, in 1980, made a survey of all villages in an effort to estimate the extent and potential of subsistence and commercial farming, and developed a five-year agricultural plan.

Commercial agricultural sales for vegetables, taro and bananas at the main Fagatogo markets have increased steadily in volume and dollar value each year from 1978 (when they totalled 411,472 kg, worth $520,554) to 1981 (when they were 1,058,480 kg, worth $1,653,760). The increases were 158 per cent in volume and 218 per cent in money value. However by 1984 there had been a considerable decline in sales figures through this channel. A total of 670,380 kg of produce (vegetables, bananas and taro) was sold compared to a 1982 record figure of 1.1 million kg. In 1984 bananas constituted 44 per cent of the market volume, taro 34 per cent and vegetables 23 per cent. The Department of Agriculture concluded that a considerable portion of local production was being sold through alternative local business outlets such as restaurants, fishing fleets and within villages.

Feasibility studies done for a feed mill, abattoir and egg-laying production resulted in these facilities being established commercially, contributing to import substitution.

An economic report to the Governor published by the Economic Development and Planning Office in 1982 identified the major constraints on agricultural development as inadequate extension services to farmers, inadequate marketing systems, 'misdirected' commercial agricultural subsidies and incentive programmes, relatively inexpensive import alternatives, and limited land, capital and labour.

Fishing. Local fishermen supply a negligible amount of tuna to the canneries, which depend on foreign off-shore sources. Competitive entry into tuna fishing requires substantial initial capital and difficulties in local financing have restricted entry by locals. Only one locally-owned long-line tuna vessel supplies tuna to the cannery (and this production is in addition to that of the local fishermen). Total fish production by local commercial fishermen in 1985 was estimated at 120 tonnes valued at $439,000 gross.

Local fishing. There were 49 local fishing boats registered in 1985, employing 104 people.

TOURISM. The government encourages tourism, but it is not yet strong, partly because of the cost of air fares and a dearth of air services, from the US particularly.

Cruise ships are calling into Pago Pago for visits of a few hours during the summer season. The majority of passengers go on prepaid, organised tours, ensuring that very few tourist dollars find their way into the local economy.

Table 1 shows the rapid decline in tourism since 1980. Figures for the first quarter of 1986 indicate a turnaround in visitor arrivals of nearly 14 per cent over the previous year.

MANUFACTURING. Fish canning is American Samoa's major manufacturing industry. The Van Camp and Star Kist canneries are located side by side in Satala, across Pago Pago Bay from Fagatoga. Value of exports from the canneries in 1984 was $202,405,051 achieved with 8,190,499 cases. Canned tuna made up 95.5 per cent of the country's exports in 1984.

In 1984 the Van Camp Seafood Cannery announced the conclusion of an agreement with the American Samoan Government for a 10-year tax exemption in exchange for the company's investing $US3.5 million in plant expansion. Under the agreement full tax is to be paid on the first 25,000 tonnes of annual production, but no tax on the next 25,000. By 1986 it was expected that 60 purse seine boats would be operating out of Pago Pago harbour. A large percentage of workers in the two canneries come from Western Samoa.

The government's industrial park at Tafuna was expanded from 10 ha to 14 ha in

TABLE 1 ARRIVALS IN AMERICAN SAMOA

	1980	1981	1982	1983	1984	1985
Tourists	13,478	8505	7280	5183	4437	5875
Business	5698	5263	5212	5484	6337	4370
Transit	22,293	14,291	13,220	10,878	7640	6948
Visiting Relatives	24,107	27,338	21,879	20,281	25,504	1044*
TOTAL	65,576	55,397	47,591	41,826	43,918	18,237

* *This figure excludes American Samoans returning from the United States where, in fact, the majority of them reside.*

1983 to accommodate the increased demand for sites from industrial and commercial users. Twelve companies are established there and another eight have pending leases. Those established or pending include machinery, electrical and automotive workshops, a roofing iron manufacturer, a drink bottler, and aluminium recycling and sandal factories.

LOCAL COMMERCE. Local commerce is not large nor strong, acting as a support group around the tuna canneries, which together with the public service generate most of the incomes in American Samoa. Most of the commerce is centred around the Pago area, but there is a growing commercial area in the west of Tutuila, towards the airport. An industrial estate is also there.

There are a number of supermarkets and larger stores, but the majority of businesses are small retail stores and vendors. Of the total number of 1108 businesses registered in 1985, the largest group, 300, were retail stores and vendors, 158 were involved in commercial transport (taxis, trucks and buses), 80 were import/export and 40 wholesaling businesses. Among other businesses, there were 34 restaurants and taverns, 16 motor repair shops, 12 bakeries, 9 pool halls and 12 tour and travel agencies. In the professions, there were 10 accountancy firms registered, 11 firms of attorneys and two banks. A shopping centre and office complex opened in Nu'uuli in late 1985 at a cost of $US4 million.

OVERSEAS TRADE. In 1985 virtually all exports from American Samoa were accounted for by tuna and fish products, including pet food, a by-product. Other exports amounted to only $320, all in banana chips.

For a five-year period up to 1978 major exports also included watches and clocks assembled in Samoa to take advantage of duty-free export incentives, but this ceased. Tuna canning remains the backbone of the economy.

Customs tariffs. American Samoa is a duty-free port. But some items, alcoholic beverages, tobacco products, motor vehicles and parts, firearms and ammunition, petroleum products, sub-standard construction materials and soft drinks are subject to special excise taxes. Virtually all capital equipment imports and intermediary goods intended for final processing in American Samoa are duty free.

Products manufactured, processed or assembled in American Samoa are eligible for duty-free entry into the US provided that 30 per cent of the value of the finished product is added in American Samoa. American Samoa is also eligible for favourable duty treatment under the general system of preferences of Australia, New Zealand, Japan and the US.

Business tax incentives. Exemptions from the payment of all or some taxes may be granted for a period of up to 10 years for the established or expansion of a qualifying industrial or business enterprises under the industrial incentives act. Tax exemptions may be extended for additional periods to encourage new types of business or significant expansion of an existing business. Tax exemptions are generally transferable upon the sale or transfer of ownership of the exempted business.

To qualify for tax exemptions, an industrial or business enterprise must satisfy a number of conditions, including an undertaking to employ American Samoan residents to the extent of 75 per cent of the enterprise's work force.

The Development Planning Office provides basic economic data to investors, and is the main agency responsible for the promotion of industrial development in the territory.

Approved industries are given the option for a tax holiday or investment through the deduction of capital investment amount from taxable income.

Dividends paid by several wholly-owned subsidiaries of US parent companies, presently operating in American Samoa, are not taxed.

Business losses can be carried forward for tax purposes up to seven years. Long-term funds for promoting private enterprise and meeting the needs of a developing economy are available from the Development Bank of American Samoa. The bank is also empowered to guarantee industrial or commercial loans of other banks and financial institutions for development projects in American Samoa.

**TABLE 2 DOLLAR VALUE OF MAIN EXPORTS
IN COMPARATIVE THREE-YEAR PERIODS**

	1978	1981	1984
Watches & clocks	318,209	—	—
Fresh vegetables	20,837	—	—
Sharks fins	—	699,968	3075
Fresh fish	57,077	n/a	386,539
Fish meal	533,709	1,241,493	2,435,889
Canned meat	9400	10,228	—
Pet food	5,584,315	6,385,008	6,777,231
Jewellery	806,389	336,403	—
Canned tuna	96,822,867	190,382,039	202,405,051
Wearing apparel	—	—	3011
Dried sea cucumber	—	12,600	—
TOTAL	104,155,656	199,075,687	212,010,796

**TABLE 3 DOLLAR VALUE OF MAIN IMPORTS,
FISCAL YEARS 1980–1984**

Item	1980	1981	1982	1983	1984
Mineral products	39,631,621	52,419,844	48,054,604	47,428,281	50,116,625
Building materials	6,177,567	8,419,066	18,276,801	13,835,034	28,265,773
Foodstuffs, tobacco	9,264,550	12,420,514	12,026,090	11,629,603	17,525,355
Machinery, electrical appliances	5,456,263	5,608,642	7,757,081	6,835,744	13,359,371
Miscellaneous manufactured articles	12,696,022	10,608,336	7,089,138	7,793,696	13,154,642
Animals, animal products	5,037,518	5,045,135	5,479,202	5,500,099	9,469,022
Vegetable products	2,740,948	3,947,468	4,302,776	3,372,522	8,304,026
Textiles & textile articles	2,314,074	2,420,054	3,265,380	3,924,894	6,453,950
Vehicles & transport equipment	3,650,245	4,457,332	3,105,067	3,986,737	6,294,235

TABLE 4 BALANCE OF TRADE IN $(MILLIONS)

Year	Imports	Exports	Trade balance
1981	234.38	199.08	−35.30
1982	197.74	186.78	−10.96
1983	227.12	177.22	−49.90
1984	284.07	212.01	−72.06
1985	296.20	200.64	−95.56

Note: Summary of imports includes Government imports and estimates of fish landed for processing.

Investors can obtain industrial sites on long-term (up to a maximum of 99 years) lease at the Tafuna Industrial Park. The park is divided into lots of various sizes although final size may be adjusted to fit specific business needs.

FINANCE. Samoa's economic development is firmly linked to that of the US. Its per capita income is several times higher than those of surrounding island groups, its minimum wage is higher, it relies on financial assistance from the US Government, and its goods have duty-free access to the American market. The public service is the biggest employer.

Between 1980 and 1984 the average annual budget was $US75 million. The overall static growth since 1981 is largely attributable to reduced Department of the Interior funding levels and relatively static Federal Grant Assistance, plus the Territory's relatively narrow local tax and revenue base.

The 1988 levels of Federal assistance will be maintained at the 1987 levels. $US20.7 million will be appropriated for government operations and $US3.4 million for capital improvement projects. Of the increase in capital projects, $US1 million will be for a housing loan programme and $US500,000 to assist relocating residents living near the unsafe dock in Pago Pago.

TABLE 5 GOVERNMENT OPERATING EXPENDITURES BY FUNCTION 1985

Function	$1000	% of total
General expenditures	71,877	79.8
General Government	26,749	29.7
Education & culture	21,012	23.3
Health	11,171	12.4
Economic development	2571	2.9
Public safety	2353	2.6
Transportation	1627	1.8
Conservation & environment	1480	1.6
Capital projects	4915	5.5
Total expenditures	**90,023**	**100.0**
International airport	1340	1.5
Tafuna industrial park	57	0.1
ASPA (electric utility)	12,239	13.6
Communications	4215	4.7
Public market	113	0.1
Lava Lava Golf Course	182	0.2
Enterprise operations	**18,146**	**20.2**

Of the overall budget about 49 per cent comes from local revenues, 26 per cent from the Department of the Interior and 25 per cent from other Federal agency grants.

The budget for 1984 was $US76.5 million. Local revenue was $19.4 million with another $US17.5 million from local commercial enterprises. Department of Interior grants were $US20.2 million, direct Congressional Appropriation $US0.7 million and other Federal grants $US18.7 million.

Income Tax. The income tax laws applicable to citizens, residents or non-residents of American Samoa are the same as the US laws. The wages of US citizens residing in American Samoa and working for the American Samoa Government or for private industry are subject to withholding of Samoan income tax. The tax rates are the same as those in the US.

A non-resident is subject to tax on Samoa source income only and may use itemised deductions only if they pertain in American Samoa. An individual who is not a citizen of American Samoa and who is living in Samoa temporarily will generally be classified as a non-resident for tax purposes.

A US citizen is not required to pay taxes to both the US and American Samoa on the same income.

Currency. Official currency is the US dollar.

Banking. The Amerika Samoa Bank and the Bank of Hawaii maintain full services in American Samoa. The Development Bank of American Samoa specialises in housing and small business loans.

TRANSPORT. Most of the formed roads are on Tutuila, the main island. They are continuously being extended or upgraded.

TABLE 6 PERCENTAGE OF MAJOR ITEMS OF EXPORT BY FISCAL YEAR 1977–1984

Year	Canned tuna	Pet food	All others	Total
1977	90	6	4	100
1978	93	5	2	100
1979	96.5	2	1.5	100
1980	94.6	2.8	2.6	100
1981	95.6	3.2	1.2	100
1982	97.3	1.9	.8	100
1983	94.1	3.1	2.8	100
1984	95.5	3.2	1.3	100

TABLE 7 COMPARATIVE STATEMENT OF RECEIPTS BY FISCAL YEAR FOR AMERICAN SAMOA GOVERNMENT, 1980–1984

Fiscal year	Local appropriation	Direct Congressional appropriation	Department of Interior grant-in-aid
1980	14,900,800	680,000	17,108,700
1981	17,537,250	680,500	25,749,800
1982	20,057,000	720,000	24,427,000
1983	22,462,050	681,000	30,337,000
1984	19,446,100	678,000	20,222,000

The major road is between Pago Pago harbour and the airport and it is sealed as are a growing number of other roads. The main island has a high ratio of vehicles for the population, including an ever-increasing number of privately-owned buses which provide cheap and fast transport. Most are not buses in the strict sense, but are multi-passenger vehicles built up on commercial truck bodies, gaily painted and equipped with loud-speakers blaring out music from tapes or radio. Timetables can be erratic or non-existent, but there always appears to be something going somewhere in daylight hours. There are also adequate taxi services. **Vehicle registration.** There were 4754 vehicles registered in 1985, 4472 of them com-

mercial and private and 346 government. There were 29 motorcycles in the total.

Of the commercial vehicles there were 139 buses, 56 taxis and 172 cargo vehicles registered. Total number of private vehicles registered was 3981.

AIRLINES. International services from Pago Pago are operated by Polynesian Airlines, Hawaiian Airlines and Air Nauru. Services have been constantly changing in the 1980s, a major reason for the decline in tourism. The Apia connection is important to American Samoa, as it allows frequent connections to and from Australia, New Zealand, Fiji and other islands such as the Cooks and Tahiti. Apia-based Polynesian

FIGURE 2 PERCENT OF SIGNIFICANT IMPORTS BY NOMENCLATURE (CCCN) SECTION CLASSIFICATION AMERICAN SAMOA 1984

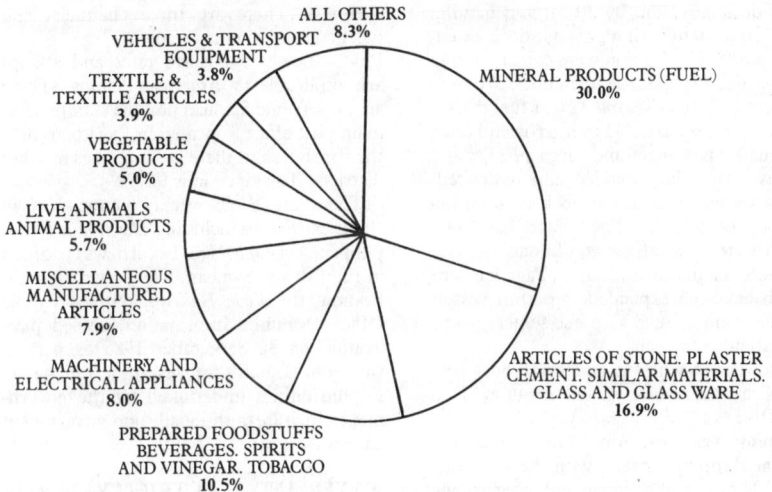

Other Federal grants	Sub-total	Receipts by ASG industrial commercial operations	Grant total (all sources)
16,943,500	49,633,000	10,985,500	60,618,500
14,431,977	58,399,527	14,116,373	72,515,900
14,237,000	59,441,000	15,655,000	75,096,000
15,495,379	68,974,429	21,558,536	90,532,965
18,770,983	59,117,083	17,449,000	76,566,083

Airlines services the Apia–Pago route.

Local airfields. The excellent international airport at Tafuna is about 15 km from Pago by a good sealed road. The major runway, built partly across the reef, is 2700 m long, and the airport has a modern terminal building, including duty-free facilities. There are small airstrips on the islands of Ta'u and Ofu in the Manu'a group.

Port facilities. Pago Pago has one of the best natural deepwater harbours in the Pacific. Depths of 77 metres have been recorded at the harbour entrance and the channel has never required dredging. Harbour depths range from 12 to 48 metres. The harbour has a right-angled bend which provides the inner harbour with natural protection from ocean swells. High mountains surrounding it protect it from winds and make it a popular yacht refuge during the December to March hurricane season. The main dock is 121 m by 20 m, and handles ships up to 10 m in draught, but dock extensions worth $6.5 million were constructed in 1983 which brought the main dock 570 m to connect it to the existing 121 m fuel dock.

There is a separate 42 m inter-island dock for smaller passenger and cargo vessels, and this is also to be extended and renovated, and a second inter-island dock is to be developed outside the Pago Pago bay area. Fresh water is available at all docks.

There is a marine railway in Pago harbour which has been expanded to permit vessels of 3000 tonnes, such as purse seiners, to be hauled out for repair.

Inter-island wharves and small-boat harbours are located at Auasi, Aunu'u, Ta'u and Ofu.

Shipping services. American Samoa has regular shipping services with the US, Australia, New Zealand, Japan and other Pacific islands. Much of it is containerised, and the official policy of the government is to encourage trans-shipping services to other islands. As an incentive, normal charges and dues are waived for 30 to 60 days.

Among the international lines are Farrell Lines, Warner Pacific Lines, Pacific Forum Line, General Steamship Corp, Kyowa, Nauru Pacific Line and China Navigation's Bali Hai service. A regular ferry service operates between Pago Pago and Apia with the *Queen Salamasina*.

COMMUNICATIONS. The territory has up-to-date communications built around the COMSAT satellite system, and is in direct touch with many countries for telephone, telex, telegraph, facsimile and television services. Samoa can receive live television by satellite. There are telex services to more than 125 countries. The telephone service which includes ISD, is automatic and there are more than 5000 phones installed.

Radio and TV. Radio WVUV broadcasts Samoan and English programmes, providing news and entertainment. American Samoa has had television services since 1964 when KVZK began operating with a transmitter on the top of Mt Alava, overlooking Pago harbour. The signal can be picked up throughout Samoa, and also in Western Samoa and parts of Tonga. The television service is operated for school use during the day and for news and entertainment in the evenings. There are three channels, and most transmission is in colour.

Post office. US postage rates and stamps are applicable in American Samoa. There are no separate Samoan postage stamps. The main post office is located in Fagatogo, near the harbour, and there are branches in other districts. The zipcode is 96799.

There are three weekly newspapers in American Samoa including *The Samoa News*, published in Pago Pago. Local news is printed in English and Samoan. The only daily publication, the *News Bulletin*, put out by the Office of Public Information, ceased publication on 30 September 1985 as part of Governor Lutali's moves to terminate all responsibilities undertaken by the government which are traditionally non-government enterprises.

WATER AND ELECTRICITY. In many areas of American Samoa water is from roof catchment, but on the main island the government has water storage capacity of 7.75 million gallons and a reticulated system. There are sewage treatment plants and septic systems. The tuna processing industry consumes about one third of the water supply.

American Samoa generates its own power which on the main island of Tutuila is adequate for present needs. It depends entirely on imported petroleum products for its power. It will have to be expanded before the territory can put fully into effect its plans to widen the economy through manufacturing plants.

Electrical failures are common due to maintenance problems. In 1983 the US Department of the Interior granted $2.1 million for repairs to electrical equipment in Pago to solve short term problems, and a full study of the power problem was conducted mid-1983 in the hope of finding a permanent solution.

At the beginning of 1983, the American Samoa Power Authority had 18 power engines with a total capacity of 36,200 kW, but only 10 units were serviceable with a combined capacity of 17,600 kW — and these were not capable of carrying full loads because 'the loading systems were inadequate. Power line systems were officially described as 'basic', with manual controls.

The two major power plants are at Satala (seven engines with a total of 14,700 kW), and Tafuna (five engines with 12,500 kW). There are in addition power stations at Faleasao and Ofu in the Manu'a Islands. Power is 110 volts.

MAJOR OFFICE HOLDERS

Governor:
   Peter Tali Coleman
Lieutenant-Governor:
   Galea'i Poumele
US Congress Representative:
   Eni Hunkin Jr.
Chief Justice:
   Michael Kruse

GOVERNMENT DEPARTMENTS

Administrative Services Dept. Utulei, Tel.: 633-4155; Divisions: Director's Office, Grants Management Division, Tax Division, Information System Division, Systems Division, Accounts Payable, General Accounting, Revenue, and Material Management
Agriculture Department, Fagatogo, Tel.: 633-1834; Divisions: Director's Office, Marketing Division, Quarantine, and Extension Services
American Samoa Legislature, Fagatogo, Tel.: 633-4565; Divisions: Senate, House, and Legislative Counsel
Communications Office, Fagatogo, Tel.: 633-1121; Divisions: Director's Office,

Directory Information, Radio and Teletype Maintenance, and Telephone Business Office
Education Department, Utulei, Tel.: 633-5237; Divisions: Director's Office, Federal Grants Coordinator, Financial Aid — Scholarship, Student Records and Information, Elementary, Secondary, Early Childhood Education, Facilities and Transportation, Supply and Publications, Testing/Evaluation, and Libraries
Governor's Office, Utulei, Tel.: 633-4116; Divisions: Governor, Lt. Governor, Red Cross, Records Management Services, Veterans Affairs, Insurance Commissioner, Museum, Territorial Auditor, Office of Traffic Safety, Criminal Justice Planning Agency, and US Coast Guard
High Court of American Samoa, Fagatogo, Tel.: 633-1261; Divisions: Chief Justice, Chief Judge of Land and Titles, Juvenile Commissioner, Probation Officer
Legal Affairs Department, Fagatogo, Tel.: 633-4163; Divisions: Attorney General and Immigration Office
Local Government Department, Fagatogo, Tel.: 633-5201; Divisions: Samoan Affairs, Eastern District, Manu'a District, and Western District
Manpower Resources Office, Utulei, Tel.: 633-4485; Divisions: Director's Office, Classification and Pay, Personnel, Contract, Data Control, Records, Retirement, JTPA and Training, Vocational Rehabilitation, Credit Union
Medical Services Department, Faga'alu, Tel.: 633-1222; Divisions: Director's Office, LBJ Tropical Medical Center, Public Health Office, Family Planning, Physical Therapy, Mental Health Office, Health Planning and Development Office, and Laboratory
Office of Economic Planning and Development, Fagatogo, Tel.: 633-5156; Divisions: Economic Analyst-Planner, Statistician, and Tourism
Office of Marine Resources, Fagatogo, Tel.: 633-4456
Parks/Recreation Department, Fagatogo, Tel.: 633-1195; Divisions: Director's Office, Recreation Division, and Tafuna Compound
Port Administration Department, Fagatogo, Tel.: 633-4251; Divisions: Director's Office, Harbor Division, and Airport Management

Program Budget and Planning, Utulei, Tel.: 633-4201

Public Defender Office, Fagatogo, Tel.: 633-1286

Public Information Office, Utulei, Tel.: 633-4191; Divisions: Community TV, Engineering, Instructional Television, Production, and News

Public Safety Department, Fagatogo, Tel.: 633-1115; Divisions: Police Protection, Fire Protection, and Correction

Public Works Department, Utulei, Tel.: 633-4141; Divisions: Director's Office, Administration and Finance, Civil, Engineering, Design, Water Utility, Sewer, Motor Pool Operation and Maintenance

OTHER AGENCIES

American Samoa Community College, Mapusaga, Tel.: 699-9155

American Samoa Power Authority, Satala, Tel.: 633-5251

Territorial Administration on Aging, Pago Pago, Tel.: 633-1251

Territorial Emergency Management Coordination Office, Fagatogo, Tel.: 633-2331

Territorial Energy Office, Tafuna, Tel.: 699-1325

HISTORY. No archaeological research has yet been carried out in American Samoa, but excavations in Western Samoa have revealed Lapita pottery dating back to about 800 BC. It can probably be assumed that the Samoan Islands have been inhabited for more than 2500 years.

In the centuries immediately preceding European contact, Tutuila, American Samoa's main island, was subordinate to the Atua district of Upolu, and was a place of banishment for troublesome Upolu chiefs. The people of Manu'a lived largely to themselves, under the leadership of a powerful chief, the Tui Manu'a.

The islands of American Samoa first became known to the Western world in 1722 when the Dutch navigator Jacob Roggeveen sighted Ta'u, Ofu and Olosega in the Manu'a group, and had brief contact with the islanders. Forty-six years later, Bougainville, the French explorer, also touched at Ofu and Olosega and bartered trinkets for fresh food. At these and other islands in Western Samoa Bougainville was struck by

the islanders' skill in handling their canoes, and he accordingly named the two groups the Navigator Islands. In 1787, Bougainville's countryman La Perouse anchored near Aasu on the northern side of Tutuila. His second-in-command, de Langle, and 11 of his men were massacred when they went ashore for water. Four years later, Captain Edward Edwards of HMS *Pandora* called at Tutuila twice during his search for the *Bounty* mutineers.

For nearly 40 years after news of the de Langle massacre reached Europe, most European navigators gave Samoa a wide berth. However, from about 1803 onwards runaway sailors and escaped convicts from New South Wales began to reach Samoa from Tonga and elsewhere. By 1830 several score had settled there. Some of these men, as well as a well-travelled Samoan named Siovili, introduced a form of Christianity to the Samoans. In addition, converts from Tonga and a Tahitian who drifted to Ta'u from Tubuai began teaching.

Missionaries arrive. The Samoans were therefore well prepared for the arrival in 1830 of the first Christian missionaries, John Williams and Charles Barff of the London Missionary Society, who left Tahitian teachers ashore. In 1836, the Rev. A. W. Murray of the LMS settled on Tutuila where he remained for many years. He arrived only a few months after Captain Cuthbert of the British whaler *Elizabeth* had discovered Pago Pago harbour. Most Tutuilans were soon under firm missionary influence and within a year Island teachers had also carried the Gospel to Manu'a.

Meanwhile, word about Pago Pago's commodious harbour had spread, and soon it was a popular port of call for whaling vessels. However, Pago Pago never experienced the activity that occurred in neighbouring Apia, particularly after the German firm of J. C. Godeffroy and Son began trading there in 1857. On the other hand, American shipping interest foresaw that Pago Pago could be of value to a proposed trans-Pacific steamship service and they took steps to obtain a foothold there. In 1872, Commander R. W. Meade of the USS *Narragansett* signed a treaty with High Chief Mauga of the Pago Pago area which gave the exclusive right to build a naval station in return for US

Government protection. Meade's treaty was never ratified, but in 1878 certain harbourside lands were transferred for a coaling depot.

The Big Powers are involved. During the next 20 years, the US, Germany and Great Britain were deeply involved in the turbulent events that were played out in Western Samoa. The upshot of these events was that in 1899 a commission of the three powers recommended that the only means of providing stable government was to partition the islands. Germany thereupon annexed Western Samoa, the US accepted Tutuila and Manu'a; and Great Britain withdrew from the group in return for German concessions elsewhere.

The American territory was placed under the jurisdiction of the US Department of the Navy and designated a naval station. Commander B. F. Tilley, USN, became the first officer in charge. The US flag was formally raised on Tutuila on 17 April 1900, following the receipt of a deed of cession from the chiefs of that island. The Manu'an chiefs signed a deed of cession in 1904. The US did not formally accept the two deeds until 1929, but even after it did so the Samoans still had only the status of American-protected persons — not that of US citizens.

From 1905 onwards, commanders of what was then called the Tutuila Naval Station received appointment as governor rather than commandant, and in 1911 American Samoa was adopted as the name of the territory. Swain's Island, 320 km north of Tutuila, which had been acquired by an American citizen, Eli Jennings, in 1876, was made an administrative part of American Samoa in 1925. The territory remained under naval administration until 30 June 1951, when it was transferred to the jurisdiction of the US Department of the Interior. The Hon. Phelps Phelps became the first civilian governor.

First constitution. In 1960, after six years of discussion, a constitutional convention of American Samoans approved the territory's first constitution. This contained a bill of rights, granted law-making authority to the territorial legislature, and stated that it would be territorial policy 'to protect persons of Samoan ancestry against alienation of their lands and the destruction of the Samoan

way of life and language contrary to their best interests'. At a ceremony commemorating the 60th anniversary of the raising of the American flag, the first flag of American Samoa was hoisted. The governor's report for that year stated that American Samoa was still an 18th century society, but that it was 'trying to meet 20th century hopes and aspirations'. The report warned that the people needed to exercise effort and restraint in trying to accomplish in a few years what Europe had achieved in 400.

In 1961, however, all ideas of administrative restraint were seemingly abandoned. With the appointment of Governor H. Rex Lee, it was decided to start forthwith on what was officially described as 'a complete rehabilitation and development program to correct the lagging economic and social development'. Special funds were obtained from the US Congress, and a dynamic programme began that rocketed American Samoa into the 20th century. Governor Lee's term of office lasted six years. When it ended, American Samoa had many new roads, new harbour facilities, new houses, a new hospital, the Lee Auditorium, widespread electric light and sewerage schemes, fine schools, a luxurious hotel in Pago Pago, a jet airport with attractive terminal buildings, a growing tourist industry, thriving fish canneries and a TV system of education with programmes transmitted in English.

The tourist boom initiated under Governor Lee (and the accompanying Westernisation of the territory) surged on during the next few years. But the many Samoans who had been persuaded to invest in the hotel saw little in the way of dividends because of the massive cost of running it. Meanwhile, some of the magnificent enterprises of the Lee era began to falter. Frequent power and water shortages caused heavy losses to business people as well as irritation and inconvenience to tourists; the idea of trying to educate the Samoans in English rather than Samoan was abandoned as a failure; and TV education itself had to be curtailed because of its high cost and the inability to transmit lessons without power. Finally, in early 1975, many Samoans in government employment had to be laid off as funds from Washington dried up.

Governor John M. Haydon, who resigned

in August 1974 after five controversial years in office, had hoped to be American Samoa's last appointed governor. But during his term the Samoans voted decisively against electing a governor from their own ranks.

However, after two further referendums resulted in rejection of Washington's attempt to bring some autonomy to territorial rule, the voters changed their minds and voted 'yes' with the fourth referendum. American Samoan Peter Tali Coleman, the first Samoan to be an appointed governor, and who held office for over four years (15 Oct. 1956 to 24 May 1961) and later served with distinction in Micronesia, won the contest for the first elected governor. He took office on 3 January 1978 from H. Rex Lee, who was brought back from Washington as caretaker governor on 28 May 1977. Tufele Li'a, Mr Coleman's running mate, became lieutenant-governor.

In the elections of 1984, A. P. Lutali became the new governor with Eni Hunkin as his lieutenant-governor. Lutali claimed that his administration was looking more towards the Pacific for support than towards the US.

Civil governors
Governor Phelps Phelps
    23 Feb. 1951–20 June 1952
Governor John C. Elliott
    16 July 1952–25 Nov. 1952
Governor James Arthur Ewing
    28 Nov. 1952–4 Mar. 1953
Governor Lawrence M. Judd
    4 Mar. 1953–5 Aug. 1953
Governor Richard B. Lowe
    1 Oct. 1953–15 Oct. 1956
Governor Peter Tali Coleman
    15 Oct. 1956–24 May 1961
Governor H. Rex Lee
    24 May 1961–31 July 1967
Governor Owen S. Aspinall
    1 Aug. 1967–31 July 1969
Governor John M. Haydon
    1 Aug. 1969–15 Oct. 1974
Lt. Gov. Frank C. Mockler (*Acting*)
    15 Oct. 1974–6 Feb. 1975
Governor Earl B. Ruth
    6 Feb. 1975–30 Sept. 1976
Governor Frank Barnett
    1 Oct. 1976–27 May 1977
Governor H. Rex Lee
    28 May 1977–3 Jan 1978
Governor Peter Tali Coleman
    3 Jan. 1978–Jan. 1985

Governor A. P. Lutali
    Jan. 1985–Jan. 1989
Governor Peter Tali Coleman
    Jan. 1989–
Further information: J. A. C. Gray, *Amerika Samoa*, Annapolis, Maryland. 1960.

MAIN ISLANDS IN DETAIL
Tutuila. Tutuila is about 30 km long, and ranges from about 3 to 9 km wide. A broken mountain range runs almost the whole length of the island, with numerous deep fertile valleys running down to the coast. The main villages are scattered along the level land near the west and south coasts and on the southern slopes. The settlement on the northern side of the island, which is rough and precipitous, is very small. The whole island, even to the tops of the peaks, is densely wooded. There are several outstanding peaks, notably Matafao (702 m) near the centre of the island; northward and westward are Mount Alava (520 m) and Mount Pioa; in the western part of the island is Mount Olotele (486 m). The best-known mountain is the Rainmaker (Mt Pioa), a truncated cone seen across Pago Pago harbour from the Rainmaker Hotel frequently wreathed in cloud.

There are several harbours in Tutuila apart from Pago Pago, with villages of some importance. Leone, on the south coast, is the only harbour besides Pago which can accommodate other than small ships, but is little used.

Fagatale Bay, 12 km south-west of Pago Pago, has been designated a national marine sanctuary. The bay, formed when the seaward wall of a volcanic crater collapsed, is the habitat of a large variety of plants and animals including the Green Sea Turtle and the Hawksbill Turtle which are protected in the sanctuary under a 1972 law.

The Pago Pago Bay area is the centre of Tutuila (and, indeed, American Samoan), activity. The town itself is scattered along several kilometres of foreshore on the deeply indented harbour, with the hotel and high school at one extremity, the Government offices, banks and businesses in the centre, and other stores and the canneries etc. at the other extremity.

Between 1961 and 1966 there was considerable building activity in Pago Pago in connection with the tourist hotel and the introduction of TV education. The aerial tramway was installed at this time from Solo Hill across the harbour to Mt Alava.

The territory's international airport at Tafuna takes Boeing 747 jet aircraft. There is much development along the road from the harbour to the airport, including shopping centres, which at one time were confined to the harbour area, and in recent years Pago has begun to spread.

Manu'a group. Ta'u, the chief island of the Manu'a Group, is conical in shape and rises to a central mount (1000 m). The southern and eastern coasts are precipitous, but the land slopes gently to the westward and northward. The principal settlement is at Luma, on the west coast. The population of Ta'u is about 3500. An airstrip of 716 metres is near the village of Fitiuata.

Olosega and Ofu are small islands about 11 km NW of Ta'u with a population of about 400 each. They are separated by a very narrow strait and both are enclosed by the same reef which dries out at low tide and obstructs the channel between them for anything but very small boats. Both islands have precipitous hills with small areas of flat land where soil is very fertile. Highest points are 500 m on Ofu and 600 m on Olosega. There is a small airstrip on Ofu. On 18 January 1987 the group was battered by hurricane Tusi, leaving 2000 people homeless. The Manu'a Islands were declared a disaster area.

Swain's Island. Swain's Island, which lies 450 km north of Tutuila, is an atoll about 2 km long by 1.7 km wide. The greatest elevation of the land is about 6 m. There is no entrance into the lagoon, which has brackish water.

The atoll was once thought to have been discovered in 1606 by the Spanish explorer Quiros and named Gente Hermosa because of its attractive people. However, recent research has established that Gente Hermosa was Rakahanga in the northern Cook Group, and that Swain's Island remained unknown to Europeans until well into the 19th century. It was named by Captain W. L. Hudson of the United States' Exploring Expedition who learned of it in Samoa in 1841 from a whaling captain called Swain. Shortly afterwards, some islanders from Fakaofu (now in

Tokelau) formed a colony on the atoll, and three Frenchmen began exploiting it as a coconut plantation. The atoll is known to the Tokelau people as Olosenga.

In 1856 Eli Jennings, an American with a Samoan wife, claimed title to the island from Englishman Captain Turnbull, and took over the plantation and its Tokelauan labourers. The plantation has remained in the Jennings family ever since.

Because of its proximity to Tokelau (about 175 km) and its cultural affinities with them, Swain's Island was included with those islands then called the Union Group when Britain incorporated them into the Gilbert and Ellice Islands Colony in 1916. However, in 1925 the island was annexed by the US and placed under the administration of American Samoa. Control was more or less nominal until 1953–54 when labour disputes between the Jennings family and Tokelau copra cutters resulted in a resident government representative being stationed on the island by US executive order. In 1983 US sovereignty over Swain's Island was confirmed in a treaty with New Zealand, which also confirmed New Zealand's possession of the Tokelau Islands. The treaty was ratified by the US Congress in June. By traditional custom, the islanders choose a delegate to the House of Representatives in Pago Pago, but he has no vote. The population at the 1980 census was 27 compared with 74 in 1970.

FOR THE TOURIST. Although American Samoa and its near-neighbour Western Samoa are separate politically, they are the same people. But with their modern development there are now many contrasts in lifestyle although the two Samoas still share a common language and customs. Visitors will find it interesting to make comparisons. Thus any visitor to Apia, Western Samoa, should take the opportunity to board one of the frequent air services between the airports serving Apia and Pago and see at least some of American Samoa; and visitors to Pago should take the same opportunity for at least a quick visit to Apia.

There are a number of tour operators in Pago who arrange sightseeing tours, some of the more popular packages being day trips to the eastern and western districts, village feasts and kava ceremonies, and special trips to the island of Aunu'u and to the Manu'a group. Hire cars are also available.

The Office of Tourism is at the convention centre next to the Rainmaker Hotel. Travellers' cheques should be endorsed for local use, and international credit cards are not widely accepted in American Samoa.

ENTRY FORMALITIES. No visas are required to enter American Samoa for a stay of up to 30 days. Persons wanting to stay longer must contact the Immigration Officer to receive special permission for a stay of up to 90 days. For longer periods visitors must obtain a sponsor and receive the approval of the Immigration Board. US citizens or nationals must have proof of citizenship and onward passage. All other visitors must have a valid passport or certificate of identity and onward passage. No vaccinations are required except for visitors arriving from an area infected with yellow fever. For further information contact Director of Public Health, LBJ Tropical Health Center, Pago Pago.

Sightseeing. Pago Pago harbour area is full of interest, from the business and administrative centre at Fagatogo, to the tuna canning factories on the north side of the harbour. Around Fagatogo there is the 'malae' or public green, with a cluster of small shops and cafes pressing towards the hills behind them, the white colonial style courthouse, the museum, markets, and Sadie Thompson's hotel (of Somerset Maugham's 'Rain'), now used as a Valupac store.

There are a number of vantage points around the mountainous perimeters of the harbour for taking photographs, but easily the most spectacular is the 'tramway', or cable car, which crosses the harbour from Solo Hill above the old and historic Government House on the point near the Rainmaker Hotel, to the television tower on the top of Mt Alava, 520 m. It takes only five minutes one way. Unfortunately, it has been out of operation frequently over recent years.

The Tourist Office or local tour companies will provide details of walks or climbs around the hills of the harbour, some of them suitable only for the very fit, such as the climb to the top of the Rainmaker. Outside the bay area there are trips available to other spots including Fagasa Bay or the 'Forbidden

Bay', and to historic Leone village with its fine old church.

Near Vaitogi Village is the home and workshop of Mary Pritchard, a part-Samoan whose efforts have ensured that the art of 'siapo' (tapa) making will remain an important part of Samoan culture. She has run summer schools and organised exhibitions of siapo for students from all over the world as well as writing a very informative book on the subject. She welcomes visitors by appointment to her magnificent fale, built in the traditional Samoan manner and decorated with 'siapo' pieces old and new.

Festivals. There are three special festivals of interest to tourists. Flag Day on 17 April is a major holiday with plenty of activity, including long boat racing on Pago harbour. White Sunday — the second Sunday in October — is Children's Day, with Samoan children leading church services and acting out religious plays. And some time in October or early November there is the rising of the palolo, the eggs of the mating coral worm, with the Samoans wading to the reefs to scoop up the delicacy.

ACCOMMODATION. There is not a great deal of accommodation. During the 1970s the Intercontinental Hotel chain obviously thought that tourism was on the rise and financed the building of the Rainmaker Hotel, right on the waterfront in Pago Pago harbour. Samoan-style architecture was used to construct the huge fales which made up the various buildings required in an international hotel, however tourists did not come in sufficient numbers to retain the interest of a multi-national company and the government took over the administration of the hotel. In 1985 the hotel was sold off as part of the government's privatisation programme and it was purchased by a group of local businessmen. It is now in need of a good facelift.

Accommodation listed here is in alphabetical order:

Apiolefaga Inn: 9 rooms, restaurant, bar, pool, close to airport. PO Box 366, Pago Pago, 96799. Tel.: 699-9124.

Don and Ilaisa's Motel: 5 rooms, 1 aircon, located on Olosega. PO Box 932, Pago Pago, 96799.

Herb and Sia's Family Style Motel: 15 rooms, some private facilities, centrally

located. PO Box 430, Pago Pago, 96799.
Tel.: 633-5413.
Rainmaker Hotel: 184 rooms and suites,
aircon, restaurant, bar, shop, beach, major
credit cards accepted. PO Box 996,

Pago Pago, 96799. Tel.: 633-4241,
Telex 782511.
Vaoto Lodge: Ofu, Manu'a. 10 rooms.
Contact Majorie Malae, Ofu, Manu'a.

Clipperton Island

Clipperton Island, a lonely coral atoll at 10 deg 18 min N latitude, 109 deg 13 min W longitude, north-west of the Galapagos and 2900 km due west of the Panama Canal, is a dependency of France. Clipperton was under the authority of the Governor of French Polynesia until 1979. Under a ministerial decree gazetted on 2 February, jurisdiction was transferred direct to Paris.

Its status was again called into question in 1983 when Senator Daniel Millaud, representing French Polynesia in the Parliament in Paris, asked that the island be annexed to French Polynesia because its 200-mile economic and fisheries zone offers promising opportunities.

Clipperton has a strange history. John Clipperton was mate on a ship of the English

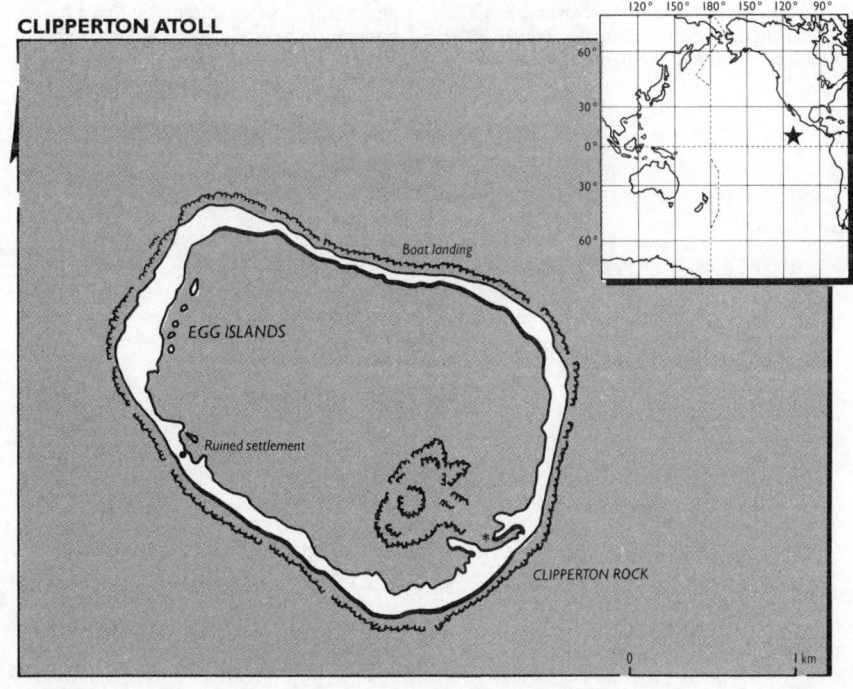

CLIPPERTON ATOLL

Boat landing

EGG ISLANDS

Ruined settlement

CLIPPERTON ROCK

0   1 km

navigator, William Dampier. In 1704 he quarrelled with Dampier in the Gulf of Nicoya and, with 21 other mutineers, seized a barque and roamed the eastern Pacific as a pirate. They made the isolated atoll — originally discovered by the Spaniards — their hide-out in 1705, and the island thus was named after the pirate.

A reef about 8 km in circumference encloses a lagoon where small ships may once have sheltered, but which now is closed by the coral reef. It was listed as one of the United States Guano Islands under the Guano Act of 1856; but it was not occupied by Americans.

France had already annexed it in 1855, and in 1897 it was seized by a Mexican garrison. Mexico kept a garrison there for years. The opening of the Panama Canal gave the atoll new importance, and France asserted her prior claim. The question of ownership was submitted to the arbitration of King Victor Emmanuel of Italy, and on 31 January 1930 he declared in favour of France. Mexico, announcing to the world that the Monroe Doctrine was being flouted, handed over the atoll to France in November 1932.

Lieutenant Gauthier in the *Jeanne d'Arc* took possession in the name of France on 26 January 1935.

A British firm (Pacific Islands Company) worked phosphate deposits on Clipperton between 1906 and 1917. About 100 people, the phosphate settlers and a Mexican army garrison, regularly received supplies by ship from Mexico; then, at the outbreak of war in 1914, Clipperton was forgotten by the Mexican authorities.

During the next three years most of the people died from starvation and sickness. The garrison commander, Captain Ramon d'Arnaud, and a few others set out in a small boat to intercept an imaginary passing ship, but were never heard of again. When most of the men had died, the keeper of the lighthouse murdered the remainder; he, in turn, was killed with an axe by one of the young women he tried to enslave. This happened on 18 July 1917, only a day before the US Navy vessel *Yorktown* called at the island and rescued the surviving three women and eight children.

During World War II the US Navy maintained a small base on the island. The waters around Clipperton have enormous fish stocks and in 1987 France announced that a fishing base was to be established on the island, and work began in 1988.

Cook Islands

Located between 156 and 167 deg W longitude, and between 8 and 23 deg S latitude, the 15 islands of the Cooks are an internally self-governing state in free association with New Zealand. The population in December 1986 was 17,185 (provisional).

The main island is Rarotonga (a little over 67 sq. km) which is 3000 km north-east of Auckland. The administrative centre is Avarua. Local time is 10 hrs behind GMT but 'daylight saving' from 1 January to 31 March reduces that by one hour.

The flag comprises the Union Jack in the top left quarter and a ring of white stars on a royal blue background. The stars represent the islands of the group. The National Anthem is *God Save the Queen*, but there is also a Cook Islands national song *Te Atua Mou'e* (God is Truth). New Zealand currency, together with Cook Islands coins, are legal tender.

Public holidays include: 1 January, Good Friday, Easter Monday, 25 April (ANZAC day), early June (Queen's birthday), early August (Constitution Day), late October (Gospel Day), Christmas and Boxing Day.

THE PEOPLE. The Cook Islands Maori is Polynesian and several tribes trace their ancestry back to Samoa and Raiatea (French Polynesia). By tradition there are also connections between the Rarotongans and the New Zealand Maori. The Cook Islands census of 1 December 1981 recorded a total population of 17,754, compared with 18,128 in 1976 and 21,323 in 1971. The southern islands have the most population (86.8% in 1981). The most populous islands are Rarotonga (9530 in 1981), Aitutaki (2335), Mangaia (1364) and Atiu (1225).

Nationality. Cook Islanders are British subjects and citizens of New Zealand through the New Zealand Citizenship Act 1948, and by the Constitution adopted in 1965.

Language. Most islanders are bilingual, using their own Polynesian dialect and English. The languages of Polynesia are all closely related and are of the Malayo-Polynesian family. There is a strong similarity between the dialects of the NZ Maori, the Cook Island Maori and the Tahitian. If a NZ Maori speaks Maori in the Cook Islands he is readily understood. If he goes to Tahiti and speaks Maori without pronouncing his k's, he can still be understood.

Migration. Hundreds of Cook Islanders go to New Zealand to seek employment. In 1982 there were about 24,500 in New Zealand compared to about 20,000 in 1977 and 4499 in 1961. The largest communities of islanders are in Auckland and timber mill towns.

Religion. The London Missionary Society was the pioneer in educational and missionary effort in the Islands. Evangelisation began at Aitutaki in 1821 and, with some setbacks, spread through the group, guided by Rev. John Williams. For many Cook Islanders the most respected early Christian teacher was Papeiha, a Raiatean, who introduced the gospel to Aitutaki in 1821, and Rarotonga in 1823. Many Cook Islanders were sent away in the early days as native pastors to Samoa, the New Hebrides, Papua and elsewhere. The church is still a powerful influence.

About 69 per cent belong to the Cook Islands Christian Church (formerly the LMS); about 15 per cent are Roman Catholic and the remaining 16 per cent Seventh-day Adventist, Latter Day Saints, etc.

Lifestyle. Generally, the outer islanders

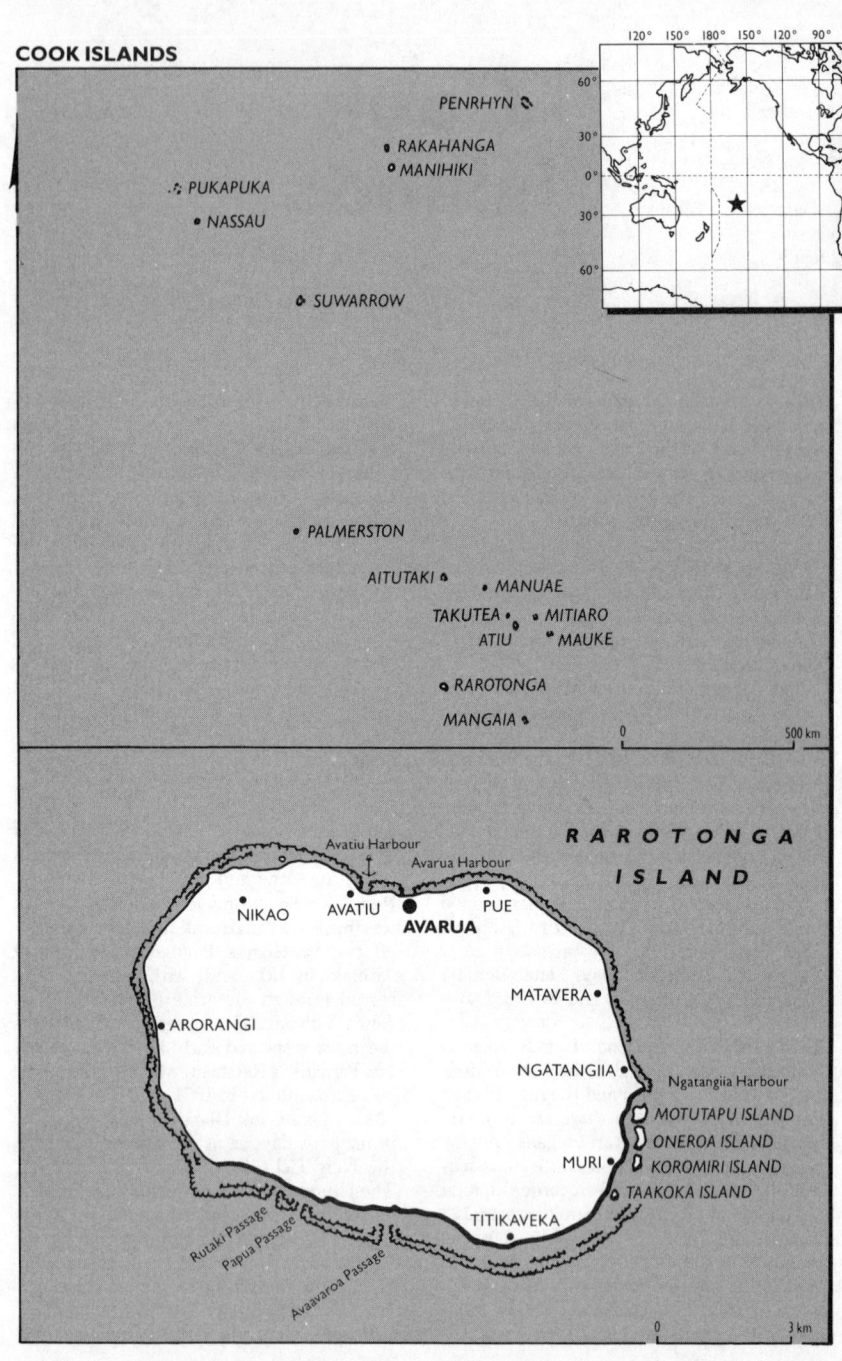

COOK ISLANDS

PENRHYN

RAKAHANGA
MANIHIKI

PUKAPUKA

NASSAU

SUWARROW

PALMERSTON

AITUTAKI
MANUAE
TAKUTEA
MITIARO
ATIU
MAUKE

RAROTONGA

MANGAIA

0   500 km

RAROTONGA
ISLAND

Avatiu Harbour
Avarua Harbour

NIKAO   AVATIU   PUE
AVARUA

MATAVERA

ARORANGI

NGATANGIIA
Ngatangiia Harbour

MOTUTAPU ISLAND
ONEROA ISLAND
MURI   KOROMIRI ISLAND
TAAKOKA ISLAND

TITIKAVEKA

Rutaki Passage
Papua Passage

Avaavaroa Passage

0   3 km

continue to live in extended families with the traditional communal pattern of living. In Rarotonga, lifestyle more closely follows a European style.

Recreation. Favourite pursuits follow Polynesian tradition and include feasting, musicmaking and dancing. There is also frequent participation in church meetings. Sports include cricket, tennis, rugby, lawn bowls, netball, boxing, golf, sailing and athletics. There is also a fishing club.

GOVERNMENT. The islands formally became part of New Zealand on 11 June 1901. They gained internal self-government in 1965, and after the first general elections held in April 1965 voted to remain in free association with New Zealand. The latter, with the Cook Islands government, assumes responsibilities in external affairs and defence.

Legislature. The Parliament of the Cook Islands established under a written Constitution consists of 24 members each representing a separate constituency. The constituencies are Rarotonga 9; Aitutaki 3; Mangaia 3; Atiu 2; one each in Manihiki, Mauke, Mitiaro, Penrhyn, Pukapuka and Rakahanga. Under amendments to the Constitution in 1981, which extended the life of Parliament from four to five years, a constituency was created in New Zealand to give Cook Islanders living there representation in Parliament. The Constitution is the supreme law and Parliament alone has power to amend or repeal it upon a two-thirds majority vote.

Executive. Executive authority is vested in the ruling monarch of Great Britain. The Queen's Representative (at present a former Education Minister, Sir Tangaroa Tangaroa) is appointed upon the advice of the Cook Islands Government. Previously, the New Zealand High Commissioner was also Cook Islands Head of State. New Zealand is now represented at the diplomatic level by a Representative.

Executive Government lies with a Cabinet of Ministers comprising the Prime Minister and six other Ministers chosen by the Prime Minister.

Elections. A general election, by universal suffrage, is held every five years. Governing party, elected in the March 1985 General Elections, is the Democratic Party with the Cook Islands Party in opposition.

Local government. Island councils exist on each of the outer islands. They were reconstituted by the Local Government Act 1966 which provides for the chairman to be elected from among council members, instead of having the island Chief Administration Officer in this post as previously. The councils meet regularly to supervise various local activities, collect minor taxes and carry out various island works and services. In addition, most villages have a committee which helps to maintain roads and does other local work.

House of Ariki. The House of Ariki of the Cook Islands consists of up to 15 Ariki, representing all islands in the group, and is required to meet at least once every 12 months. The House acts in an advisory capacity only and considers traditional matters such as customs and any matters submitted to it by Parliament in relation to the welfare of the people. The Ariki are hereditary chiefs.

DIPLOMATIC MISSIONS. The New Zealand Government maintains a permanent office in Rarotonga with the chief officer known as the New Zealand Representative. The Republic of Nauru has a permanent Consulate. Other countries have their New Zealand representative accredited to the Cook Islands.

JUSTICE. The High Court has three divisions: Civil, Criminal and Land. There are two permanent judges, both appointed from New Zealand, who conduct the Court in regular sessions. Justices of the Peace have lesser jurisdiction in criminal, civil and land matters. A Children's Court deals with juvenile crime.

Appeals from all divisions of the High Court are to the Cook Islands Court of Appeal which comprises three judges, one of whom must be a judge of the New Zealand Court of Appeal or the High Court of New Zealand Appeals from the Court of Appeal go to the Privy Council in London.

Liquor laws. The manufacture of intoxicating liquor without a licence is illegal. Liquor is imported by the government and sold through the Cook Islands Liquor Supplies and various authorised stores. There are several licensed hotels, restaurants and bars in Rarotonga, as well as various sporting clubs which may serve members and guests. Aitutaki has two licensed hotels. It is an offence to drink in public places such as outside dance halls.

Gambling. Licences are issued under the Gaming Act 1967, to permit gambling by totalisator, housie (bingo), small raffles and lotteries. A local totalisator covers betting on some New Zealand horse races.

DEFENCE. Under the Cook Islands Constitution Act 1964, New Zealand has retained responsibility for the defence of the Islands.

EDUCATION. Schools are operated by the government, the Roman Catholic Mission, and the Seventh-day Adventist Mission. Under the Education Act 1966 education is free and compulsory between the ages of six and 15.

There are 38 schools, including nine colleges, 26 primary schools and a teachers' college. Pre-school centres are established on most islands. There is also an apprentice training scheme.

The Roman Catholic mission operates two primary schools, and Nukutere College at Avarua, Rarotonga. The Seventh-day Adventists operate two primary schools, Papaaroa Junior College at Titikaveka, Rarotonga, and a college on Aitutaki.

Schools in 1984 recorded a total of 6421 pupils (including pre-school). In government schools, there were 3148 in primary (grades 1–6), and 2746 in secondary (forms 1–6). In the Seventh-day Adventist schools there were 142 in primary and 98 in college. In the Roman Catholic schools there were 241 in primary and 203 in college.

The Teachers College completed at Tereora in 1970 had 32 students in 1981. Teacher trainees at local and overseas institutions average 30 annually. The University of the South Pacific has an extension centre at Avarua.

Students enrolled overseas are mainly in New Zealand and Fiji, with some in Western Samoa, Papua New Guinea and Australia. Up to 100 students and trainees receive education or vocational training each year under various aid programmes.

LABOUR. In the northern atolls, people subsist largely on coconuts and fish. There is little economic opportunity other than making copra. In the Southern Group, many people work on their own plantations although in recent years there has been a noticeable shift into other forms of paid labour.

In 1985 the distribution of wage earners on Rarotonga was:

Commerce, hotels and restaurants 32.12%, Manufacturing 23.64%, Community, social and personal services 15.30%, Transport and communication 12.12%, Construction 8.86%, Other (including agriculture and fishing) 7.96%

The government is a major employer with 80.6 per cent of all salary earners, most of these in service departments. Most private sector employees work in commerce, hotels and restaurants, small manufacturing and financial services.

Wages. The minimum wage rate in 1988 was $NZ2.09 per hour for adults. Construction workers received the highest rate at $2.54 per hour.

Unions. Unions do not play a very significant role. Main unions are the Cook Islands Industrial Union of Waterside Workers and the Airport Workers Union. The Public Service Association is fairly influential and received a 6.5% pay increase for members in early 1987.

Social security. Many Government employees have retained membership of the New Zealand Public Service Superannuation Scheme. A compulsory universal scheme has been promoted since early 1981, but no legislation to establish the scheme has been enacted. There is an old age and destitute persons scheme, and a child benefit scheme for children under 5. In early 1988 old age pensions were $NZ66 per month.

HEALTH. Free medical and surgical treatment is available for all Islanders. School and pre-school children also receive free dental treatment.

A general hospital equipped with dispensary, X-rays and laboratory facilities is maintained in Rarotonga, on Sanitorium Hill. In addition an outpatient clinic at Tupapa and at Akaoa district caters for minor ailments six days a week.

The office of the division of Public Health

Foreign Minister:
  Norman George
Chief Judge of the High Court:
  Sir Graham Speight

GOVERNMENT MINISTRIES AND DEPARTMENTS

Prime Minister, Rarotonga Tel.: 29-451.
Parliament, Rarotonga Tel.: 26-500
Ministry of Agriculture and Lands, Rarotonga Tel.: 21-511
Ministry of Education, Rarotonga Tel.:23-900
Ministry of Economic Planning and Management, Rarotonga Tel.: 23-111
Ministry of Finance, Rarotonga Tel.: 23-700
Ministry of Foreign Affairs, Rarotonga Tel.: 21-250
Ministry of Health and Medical Services, Rarotonga Tel.: 23-600
Ministry of Home Affairs and Provincial Government, Rarotonga Tel.: 21-621
Ministry of Immigration, Rarotonga Tel.: 22-585
Ministry of Natural Resources, Rarotonga Tel.: 21-521
Ministry of Police and Justice, Rarotonga Tel.: 21-181
Ministry of Ports and Telecommunications, Rarotonga Tel.: 21-281
Ministry of Labour and Commerce, Rarotonga Tel.: 29-363
Ministry of Transport Works and Utilities, Rarotonga Tel.: 21-141
Cook Islands Tourist Authority, PO Box 14, Rarotonga, Tel.: 29-435
Statistics Office, PO Box 125, Rarotonga
Cable and Wireless P.L.C., Rarotonga Tel.: 26-171
Cook Islands Broadcasting and Newspaper, Rarotonga Tel.: 29-460

HISTORY. The Cook Islands did not exist as a political entity until European times. Although the people today are all of a common Maori ancestry, when the first Europeans arrived most islands were very much places unto themselves. Each island should be examined separately, particularly before New Zealand annexation in 1901 when the boundaries of what are now the Cook Islands were laid down. The history of each island is set out in the 'Islands in Detail' section.

From 1823 most of the islands came under the spiritual and, to a large extent, temporal control of the LMS missionaries, who were stationed on Rarotonga and supervised the Hervey Islands Mission of the London Missionary Society.

During this time the mission-inspired 'blue' laws were codified on the islands, with many of their features remaining to this day in practice, if not by legal sanction. F. J. Moss, the British Resident in 1893, described the police appointed by the Church on Rarotonga: 'This police, irresponsible and under no direct control, incessantly spied upon and harassed the people. The fines they could extract from the people formed their sole pay and were divided at stated times between the Ariki, the Judge and the police.' The missionaries also sought to protect the islanders from the 'evil' influences of Europeans by controlling the entry upon islands of traders and men from the ships, especially the whalers. The ariki in many cases also tried to stop young men from joining ships as crew members.

Protectorate declared. In the 1880s there was increasing concern about the possible intrusion by the French into the area and New Zealand began to take an interest in the group. A British Protectorate was declared on Rarotonga in October 1888 by Captain Bourke, of HMS *Hyacinth*. The protectorate was extended to include all the islands in the southern Cook group, and they became known as the Federation of the Cook Islands. During this period an elected federal parliament came into being and made laws for the whole group, although each island had the right of self-government. A system of public schools was set up, a hospital board was established and postage stamps were issued.

Frederick J. Moss was appointed by the New Zealand Government to be the British Resident in the Cook Islands. In 1897, Moss drafted a bill to create a court having exclusive jurisdiction over cases involving foreign residents, with the British Resident to be the judge. The Cook Islands parliament refused to pass the bill and Moss dissolved the parliament, with the result that the ariki petitioned the Governor in New Zealand to remove Moss. Sir James Prendergast, the Chief Justice of New Zealand, conducted an enquiry into Cook Islands affairs and subsequently Moss was withdrawn and replaced by Lieutenant-Colonel W. E. Gudgeon.

New Zealand annexation. Annexation by New Zealand became an immediate goal and in 1900 the Rarotongan ariki were persuaded to petition New Zealand to annex the Cook Islands, and on 11 June 1901 the Cook Islands formally became part of New Zealand, the boundaries being extended to include the northern islands. The British Resident became the Resident Commissioner and the old laws of the Cook Islands continued in force subject to the provisions of the Cook Islands Act, which was passed in the same year.

In 1915, an act of the New Zealand Parliament consolidated the laws concerning the Cook Islands and provided for the appointment of a Minister for the Cook Islands, with the Resident Commissioner being responsible to the minister. The functions of the minister were later assumed by the Minister for Island Territories.

During World War I many Cook Islands men served overseas, and most of the islands have honour boards which list their names. In World War II, the New Zealand Government decided not to recruit Cook Islanders and only a handful served.

In 1946 a Legislative Council was set up, with the Resident Commissioner as President and with the members of the council representing all the islands and government departments. 1957 saw the creation of a Legislative Assembly with extended powers and in 1962, as a first step towards self-government, an Executive Committee of the Legislative Assembly, to advise the government, was set up. The purpose of the Executive Committee was to advise on policy matters and to draw up proposals for the annual appropriations of funds.

In December 1962 New Zealand's delegate to the United Nations told the Trusteeship Council that the Cook Islands would have internal self-government within three years. 1964 was marked by the withdrawal of the Resident Commissioner and all official members from the Legislative Assembly and the Executive Committee, under a Leader of Government Business, became a fully operative Cabinet. Provision was also made for the election, under universal suffrage, of a new Legislative Assembly of 22 members.

Self-government approaches. The New Zealand Parliament passed legislation in November 1964 granting a new constitution to the Cook Islands. Observers from the United Nations supervised the first general election for the Legislative Assembly on 20 April 1965, with the Cook Islands Party led by Mr (later Sir) Albert Henry winning a substantial majority. However, although Mr Henry led the party, he could not stand as a candidate because of residential qualifications.

One of the first acts of the new assembly was to amend the constitution by deleting the clause relating to the length of residence of electoral candidates. In June 1965 Mrs Marguerite Story, the sister of Mr Henry, resigned from her newly-won place in the assembly, a by-election was held and Mr Henry upon his election became Premier of the Cook Islands. Mrs Story became Speaker.

The Legislative Assembly had been offered the choice of four forms of self-determination for the Cook Islands: full independence; integration with some other Pacific Islands nation; full integration within New Zealand; and internal self-government. The assembly chose the last alternative and the Constitution as amended came into force on 4 August 1965, giving the Cook Islands full responsibilities for internal affairs. New Zealand assumed responsibilities for external affairs and defence. New Zealand undertook to provide the Cook Islands with financial support and Cook Islanders remained New Zealand citizens with unrestricted rights of entry into New Zealand.

In 1965, the constitution was also amended to provide for the establishment of a House of Ariki — an ariki being a paramount chief, there being several ariki on Rarotonga and a paramount ariki on each of the outer islands. The one exception is Penrhyn, where there is now no ariki, the line having been broken by the raid made upon the population there by Peruvian slave-raiders. The House of Ariki has no legislative powers — it considers any matters relating to the welfare of the people which the Legislative Assembly (now Parliament of the Cook Islands) puts before it, and it gives its opinion and recommendations to the assembly. The House of Ariki also makes recommendations to the Parliament on the customs, traditions and land tenure. In short, it is a consultative body.

Under the constitution, the position of High Commissioner to the Cook Islands was created. The High Commissioner was to represent New Zealand and, as the representative of the Queen, he also filled the role of Head of State. It requires a two-thirds majority of the Legislative Assembly to amend the constitution. However, the office of New Zealand High Commissioner was discontinued in 1975. In 1974, Sir Albert Henry called a snap election with the intention of increasing his majority in the assembly, thereby ensuring himself of the numbers required to carry through amendments. In the result, the ruling Cook Islands Party lost one seat, thereby failing to achieve the required number of seats to bring into being any amendment.

The Cook Islands Party won its fifth successive election on 30 March 1978, but was unseated the following July by Chief Justice Gaven Donne for electoral corruption and the Democratic Party members, elected in March, became the government with Dr Thomas Davis as Premier. Sir Albert Henry and seven of his fellow party politicians were arraigned on the corruption charges. Subsequently, the Queen deprived Sir Albert of his knighthood. He died on 1 January 1981.

Substantial changes to the Constitution were enacted in the Constitution Amendment (No. 9) Act 1980–81. The 'Legislative Assembly' became the 'Parliament' and the 'Premier' the 'Prime Minister'. The term of Parliament was extended from four to five years. The number of seats in the Parliament was increased to 24, providing an additional seat for the island of Mangaia and one seat representing voters resident outside the Cook Islands. The previous multiplicity of seats in certain constituencies was abolished with the new constituencies established to provide one member for each constituency throughout the Cook Islands.

A Bill of Rights and a new Court structure were established.

General elections were held on 30 March 1983, and resulted in a return to power of the Cook Islands Party (CIP) led by Mr Geoffrey Henry, a cousin of its founder and former Premier. The CIP won 13 seats and the Democratic Party 11 seats. Mr Geoffrey Henry was elected Prime Minister. The

incumbent Prime Minister, Sir Thomas Davis, and Iaveta Short, Minister of Justice and Minister for Tourism in the last government, lost their seats. A third party, the Unity Movement, led by Dr Joe Williams, a former minister in the Albert Henry Government, did not win a seat. The winner of the newly-formed Overseas Constituency, Ms Fanaura Kingstone, was appointed Minister of Internal Affairs and Postmistress-General, becoming the first woman cabinet minister and first woman MP since self-government in 1965.

Only a few months later parliament was dissolved on a constitutional technicality. After new elections in November 1983 the Democratic Party, led by Dr Thomas Davis, was returned to office. A coalition was formed with opposition leader Geoffrey Henry as Deputy Prime Minister.

The coalition was short-lived and was replaced 12 months later with another in which Dr Terepai Maote was named Deputy Prime Minister.

Although Dr Thomas Davis retained the leadership following the election of 1985, by mid-1987 it was evident that his popularity was declining. In late July he was dropped as leader after a 23-nil vote of no-confidence and replaced as Prime Minister by Dr Pupeke Robati.

Population outflow. Since the end of World War II Cook Islanders have been migrating to New Zealand in large numbers, a process accelerated by the establishment of a new international airport on Rarotonga in the early 1970s. They have generally been able to find employment in hospitals, as drivers and in large industries, especially timber-milling. Since they are citizens of New Zealand, they are exempt from the immigration restrictions which cause so much concern to other Polynesian Islanders in that country. The Cook Islands Government, however, has become very concerned about the effects on the economy and social life of the country and especially of some outer islands which show evidence of gradual depopulation.

FURTHER INFORMATION. Richard Gilson. *The Cook Islands 1820–1950*, Wellington, 1980, is a detailed history. Ron Crocombe (ed.), *Cook Islands Politics — the Inside Story*, Auckland, 1979, is a close examination of the politics of the Albert Henry era by a number of contributors. Tom and Lydia Davis, *Doctor to the Islands*, London, 1955, is an early view of life and work in the Cook Islands by the man who was to become a Prime Minister. Norman and Ngaire Douglas. *Cook Islands — a guide*, Sydney, 1987, includes an up-to-date history as well as details of every island.

MAIN ISLANDS IN DETAIL
Rarotonga.   Rarotonga is circular in shape, about 30 kilometres in circumference and has a total land area of a little over 67 sq. km. In most places the fringing reef is close to the shore and the lagoon is shallow. At Muri the lagoon widens out. There is a narrow band of coral debris beyond the beach. This is backed by fertile land, which is used for growing crops, or for commercial citrus plantations.

Ancient taro beds, still in use, are to be found in several of the valleys which penetrate into the interior with several streams, notably the Avana and Avatiu, making their way to the sea. Fresh water from the streams inhibits the growth of coral and has formed the openings in the reef at Avatiu, Avarua and Ngatangiia. In earlier times ships were able to enter the lagoon at Ngatangiia, but the entrance is now silted up. Legend has it that some Polynesians sailed to New Zealand from Ngatangiia to form part of the Maori population there.

There are exciting climbs to be made in the hills, which rise to 652 metres at Te Manga, 638 metres at Te Atukura, 509 metres at Maungfaroa and 485 metres at Ikurangi, an isolated and dominating peak behind Avarua.

Avarua was previously extensively used as a harbour for the lighters which worked overseas ships but now the harbour at Avatiu has been dredged, sheet piling walls installed and wharf sheds built. Sizeable vessels now tie up at the wharf in Avatiu harbour, also a favourite haven for cruising yachts. There are facilities available on the wharf for the crews of visiting yachts.

For many years the LMS missionary, Rev. John Williams, was credited with being the first European to 'discover' Rarotonga on 25 July 1823. However, historical reconstruction has shown that the mutineers on the *Bounty* were at Rarotonga in 1789, but did not land.

The Sydney schooner *Cumberland*, Captain Philip Goodenough, was at Rarotonga in 1814, seeking a cargo of sandalwood. Violence broke out between the Maoris and the crew and several people from the schooner were killed.

When John Williams was off Rarotonga on the *Endeavour* in 1823, Papeiha, who had previously worked as a Christian teacher on Aitutaki, volunteered to swim ashore and he is now revered as the first man to preach the doctrine in Rarotonga.

A tar-sealed coastal road encircles the island and inland a second round-the-island road, the Ara Metau, is considered to have been built under the leadership of the chieftain Toi about the 11th century AD.

During World War II an airstrip was constructed at Rarotonga and this has been progressively upgraded and is now the international airport.

According to legend, the present Rarotongan Maori population are the descendants of two Polynesian chiefs, Karika from Samoa and Tangiia from Raiatea, who arrived at Rarotonga about the end of the 12th century and combined forces to conquer the earlier Polynesian inhabitants. The two invading parties were united through marriage of Tangiia to Karika's daughter. It is from these two parties that the present Rarotongan tribal divisions, each with its paramount ariki, trace their descent. The ownership of land in Rarotonga remains in the hands of Rarotongans, but many of the people who live on the island today are from the outer islands and few have land tenure rights.

When the missionaries came to Rarotonga, the people were domiciled in the house-sites spread throughout the island and the missionaries were able to coerce the people into moving into villages which were set up around the early churches. The people still retain land rights in their tapere, or land-holding units, but land rights have become very complex because of the registration of multiple inheritance.

Various export crops have been grown on Rarotonga since the mid 18th century, including cotton, copra, limes and oranges. The island once received many visits from whaling vessels seeking provisions or recruits for their crews.

It is estimated that in 1823 the population of Rarotonga was about 6000, but as a result of introduced diseases and other causes, by 1893 F. J. Moss, the British Resident, estimated that the population was probably less than 2000.

Since World War II emphasis has been placed on revitalising the citrus industry with most fruit being processed at the factory at Avarua. Although the citrus industry is still promoted by the government, it is in decline. The opportunities created by regular airfreight have brought diversification of crops as well as very significant increases. Pawpaw, beans and bananas are among the popular fresh exports.

There are three clothing factories, all of which have had substantial increases in size in recent years. Smaller factories include manufacturing in electronics, furniture, handicraft, building materials and milk reconstitution; and grading of sausage casings.

Tourism has created new opportunities for employment in Rarotonga with The Rarotongan Hotel the single biggest employer after the Cook Islands Government. The restaurants and bars built as a response to tourism are spread around the island except for the eastern side of Muri-Ngatangiia. Avarua has most, followed by Arorangi.

There is a modern hospital situated on the site of the former tuberculosis sanitorium on the hill overlooking Black Rock. There are eight primary schools in the villages and Tereora College and the Nikao Teachers' College are located at Nikao. The Catholic Church has St Joseph's Primary School and Nukatere College at Avarua and the SDA Church has a small school at Titikaveka. The buildings of the Cook Islands Library and Museum Society occupy a most beautiful site near the old Avarua Church.

In the main settlement at Avarua the large stores supply almost all requirements from stock. A daily newspaper is published in Avarua, which is also the site of Radio Cook Islands.

Each village is marked out by its coral limestone church of the Cook Islands Christian Church. Most of these buildings are over 100 years old and have been constructed in an intriguing variety of architectural styles. In each village there is a large meeting hall, where dances and various meetings and ceremonial occasions take place.

Electricity and a continuous telephone service are available in all inhabited areas of the island. There are many sporting facilities and the Rarotonga Golf Course is unique in that its greens and fairways are scattered among the many masts and stays of the wireless station.

The people of Rarotonga and Palmerston Island are represented by nine members in the Parliament of the Cook Islands.

Mauke. London Missionary Society missionary, Rev. John Williams, on his voyage of exploration in 1823 in what is now the southern Cook Islands, on the British vessel *Endeavour* (Captain John Dibbs), landed on Mauke on 23 July 1823 and began the work of converting the inhabitants to Christianity. The people of Mauke, together with those of Mitiaro, had suffered over the years from raids by the warriors of Atiu. The Atiuans had established a form of sovereignty over Mauke, and after the appearance of the Europeans the Maukeans were able to enlist their aid to resist the incursions of the Atiuans.

Mauke is low-lying, with a land surface of 2032 hectares, situated 241 kilometres north-east of Rarotonga. The geological formation of the island is similar to that of Atiu and Mangaia, with some fine caves located in the cliffs of the makatea.

Since the mid-1950s efforts have been made to expand the agricultural production of Mauke with plantings of citrus. Trial plots of peanuts, tobacco and ginger were also made but none of these led to further large-scale commercial exploitation. The ownership of land on part of Mauke has been consolidated and a small herd of shorthorn beef cattle is run there.

Landing on Mauke is difficult, as open boats have to use a boat passage or at times land upon the open reef. The island has a 914 m airstrip.

Most of the peope live in Areora, which has a school, hospital, government offices and store. There are two churches, belonging to the Catholic Church and the Cook Islands Christian Church. The latter church building is of great interest as, when it was built, the two principal groups in the congregation could not agree about the style of construction. As a consequence it was built in two distinct styles at either end, with the pulpit straddling the midpoint between the contending sides.

In the past, the children of secondary school age attended the Junior High School at Atiu, or Tereora College on Rarotonga. In 1975, Sir Albert Henry announced that in future most Mauke children would receive their secondary education on their home island. The people of Mauke are represented by a member in the Cook Islands Parliament.

The author Julian Dashwood (pseudonym Julian Hillas) lived on Mauke for many years and describes life there in his *South Seas Paradise* (1964).

Mitiaro. The first European to visit this island was Rev. John Williams, on the *Endeavour* (Captain John Dibbs) on 19 July 1923. The island, which has an area of 2455 hectares, is 229 kilometres north-east of Rarotonga. It is low-lying and much of the surface is taken up with a cliff of old coral, up to about six metres in height. The interior of the island is largely swampy and there is a brackish lake in which are found the itiki, or Mitiaro eels, which are regarded as a great delicacy in the Cook Islands. There are a few patches of fertile soil in which the people grow bananas, which form the principal source of carbohydrates in the Mitiaro diet.

There has been little European exploitation of the island. Its commercial potential is very small. Attempts to establish cash crops such as copra, pepper and allspice, have failed.

Landings are made by open boat through the boat passage in the reef near the settlement. The island has a 914 m airstrip.

The life style of Mitiaro is dominated by the food cycle. The men spend much time at sea in one-man canoes catching tuna and other large fish, or bringing bunches of bananas to their homes along the causeway which has been constructed across the swamp. Among the Cook Islanders, the people of Mitiaro are renowned for the manufacture of piere, or dried bananas, which are tightly packed in a wrapping of banana leaves.

There is a school on Mitiaro, a dispensary, a wireless station and government offices. Mitiaro is represented by a member in the Parliament of the Cook Islands.

Takutea. Unihabited, Takutea is a small island of 125 hectares about 41 kilometres north-west of Atiu. James Cook sighted Takutea and landed on the island on 31 March 1777. In 1903, Ngamaru, Ariki of Atiu, presented the island to the Crown. W. E. Gudgeon, the Resident Commissioner, proposed that Takutea be made a penal colony for the Cook Islands. However, there were numerous claims by Atiuans to rights on Takutea and the Land Court of the Cook Islands awarded the island to the people of Atiu as a whole. An elected committee administers the island and, since 1955, parties of Atiuans have visited the island at about yearly intervals to gather copra and the red tail feathers of the frigate birds which nest there.

Takutea has no safe anchorages. The waters near the islands are a bountiful fishing ground.

Palmerston Island. Palmerston Island is a small coral atoll of about 225 hectares, 434 kilometres north-west of Rarotonga. It was uninhabited when it was discovered by James Cook on 16 June 1774 during his second voyage of discovery. There is evidence of a previous occupation by Polynesians.

Several islets are situated on the fringing reef, with the present inhabitants residing on Home Islet. Several attempts were made to exploit Palmerston Island during the first half of the 19th century and one of these, set up by Captain Michael Folger of the Sydney vessel *Daphne* in 1811, resulted in violence and murder among the Europeans placed on the island.

In 1862 an Englishman, William Marsters, established his family, by three Polynesian wives, there. He divided his family into three clans, the 'head', the 'middle' and the 'tail', and drew up family laws which forbade members of a clan marrying within the clan. The Marsters family, who speak a local form of English, have remained in occupation of the island.

In 1953 the licence issued in 1888 to William Marsters, confirming his rights of occupation, expired and was not renewed. Instead, an amendment to the Cook Islands

Act in 1954 vested the island in the inhabitants (that is, the Marsters family) as customary land, except for 4.45 hectares set aside for administration purposes.

Over the years a number of ships have been wrecked on Palmerston Island, and several of the major buildings, including the meeting house and church, are largely built of shipwreck timbers.

The Palmerston Island men are noted boatmen and boat-builders. Many of the Marsters people have moved away from their home island, and there are colonies of the family on Rarotonga, Aitutaki and Penrhyn islands.

The island is included in the Avatiu-Ruatonga constituency in Raratonga for the purposes of representation in the Cook Islands Parliament.

Suwarrow. Lieutenant Mikhail Lazarev, of the Russian vessel *Suvarov*, discovered the uninhabited coral atoll now known as Suwarrow on 28 September 1814. H. B. Sterndale, who spent some time on the island later in the century, reported the existence of former coral limestone buildings, and this has led to debate as to whether or not Polynesians or earlier Europeans had been on Suwarrow before Lazarev landed.

There have been several shipwrecks on the atoll and stories have been generated of buried pirate treasure and loot from shipwrecks. Various attempts were made to find treasure on Suwarrow during the 19th century and outbreaks of assault and murder ensued. The Auckland trading company of Henderson and Macfarlane used the island as a trading post during the latter part of last century.

The island was declared a British Protectorate on 22 April 1889, and part of Anchorage Island, the principal islet, is still an Admiralty reserve. It was occupied for some time by Lever Bros. Company, when experiments with Torres Strait shell were carried on without success. There is some pearl-shell of good quality in the lagoon, but only sporadic diving is done. Until the 1930s, A. B. Donald Ltd (Auckland) leased the island for copra-making but the ravages of termites have made it necessary to prohibit the export of copra.

Suwarrow has suffered severely from the effects of hurricanes and much of the atoll has been eroded away. During the 1942 hurricane, the group of Europeans on the atoll were able to survive only by climbing into the branches of a large Barringtonia tree.

In more recent times Suwarrow has received some prominence because of the interest taken in the lifestyle of the late Tom Neale, who lived there for long periods often as a hermit. His adventures are told in the book *An Island to Oneself*. He died at Rarotonga in December 1977.

The atoll is a bird sanctuary and there are great flocks of tropical sea-birds, including terns, frigate birds and bosun birds.

Vessels may go through the passage and anchor in the lagoon near Anchorage Island, but this is not safe in northerly weather.

Nassau. The first European sighting of Nassau appears to have been made by Captain Louis Coutance, in the ship *Adele*, owned by the Mauritius firm Merle, Cabot and Company, in 1803. The island, about 45 kilometres south-east of Pukapuka, is a coral outcrop of about 225 hectares, which has no lagoon. There are no safe anchorages and boat landings are made across the open reef.

The island was annexed for Great Britain in 1892 by Captain Gibson, of HMS *Curacao*. On his third visit, in 1881, Rev. W. Wyatt Gill (LMS) of Rarotonga found the island to be occupied by John Ellacott, an American, in charge of a few Pukapukans. Ellacott had registered, in 1873, a claim of protection of his occupation of the island with the US Consul in Tahiti. He sold Nassau to H. G. Moors in 1892, and Moors in turn sold it to Messrs Rye and Stunzer; it later passed from them to Burns Philp and Co.

There is evidence that in pre-contact times the Pukapukans made the occasional visits to Nassau and in 1945 the island was purchased on behalf of the people of Pukapuka by the New Zealand Government for £2000; the Pukapukans then raised £2000 from the sale of copra from Nassau and repaid the amount.

It was intended that the people from Pukapuka would spend limited periods on Nassau, before being returned to the home island. However, many of the colonists expressed a desire to remain on Nassau and a permanent population has now been established, although fears have been expressed about the food resources available there.

A school has been built, wireless links are established with Rarotonga and a medical dresser attends to health matters. Nassau is represented in the Cook Islands Parliament by the member for Pukapuka.

Manihiki. The first European report of the existence of Manihiki is credited to Captain Patrickson, of the ship *Good Hope* on 13 October 1822, who named it Humphrey's Island. The atoll was declared a British Protectorate in August 1889.

Manihiki has many motu, or islets, strung along the reef which fringes the lagoon. The total land area is about 140 hectares. Two settlements, Tauhunu and Tukao, have been set up since the advent of the missionaries, who discouraged the people from making frequent boat passages to Rakahanga, some 40 kilometres to the north. The people are said to be descendants of migrants from Rarotonga, 1675 kilometres to the south.

During the 19th century the population suffered from the activities of blackbirders and Peruvian slave-raiders. It was fitting, perhaps, that Captain 'Bully' Hayes, Pacific blackbirder, was shipwrecked on Manihiki.

The New Zealand Government blasted boat passages through the fringe reef opposite both villages and these are used for the handling of passengers and cargo. The island produces copra, and at various times has been a wealthy source of pearl-shell. However, the pearl-shell trade has fallen away because of reduced prices for shell and over-exploitation of the oyster-shell beds. Manihiki men are skilled divers, both without artificial aids and with the conventional brass helmeted diving suit.

For a number of years the Royal New Zealand Air Force maintained a landing area on the lagoon for its Sunderland flying-boats, and this island played a vital role in many search and rescue missions in the Pacific.

On a number of occasions, boatloads of Manihikians have been blown away from their island and there have been some remarkable survival voyages. In 1965 four survivors out of a crew of seven men reached Erromanga in the New Hebrides after 65 days at sea with virtually no provisions.

The lagoon abounds with the paua (clam)

and the Manihiki people send supplies of the salted shell-fish to friends and relatives on Rarotonga. Experimental programmes with cultured pearls have been conducted in the lagoon for several years.

There is a hospital at Tauhunu, where the government offices and wireless station are situated, and there are primary schools in the two villages. The people are represented by a member in the Cook Islands Parliament.

Rakahanga. The first European to reach Rakahanga was Spaniard Pedro Fernandez de Quiros on 2 March 1606. One of the chroniclers of the expedition, Torquemada, was so taken with the appearance of the Rakahangans that he called it 'Isla de Gente Hermosa' (Island of the Handsome People). There were no further European visitors until the Russian, Thaddeus Bellingshausen, called at Rakahanga on 7 August 1820, and called the island Grand Duke Alexander Island. Rakahanga was declared a British Protectorate in 1889 by Commander A. C. Clarke, of HMS *Espeigle*. The island, which has a land surface of 1085 hectares, lies about 1120 kilometres north-west of Rarotonga.

In pre-contact times the Maoris lived on Rakahanga and made occasional visits to Manihiki, about 40 kilometres to the south, to gather food and other items. The passage between the two islands has always been chancy and frequently boats have been lost. The missionaries were able to persuade some of the Rakahangan people to take up permanent residence on Manihiki.

The atoll is unusual in that the shallow lagoon is almost land-locked. The main boat passage is at the south-west corner, near the settlement. The main cash crop is copra, and the women of Rakahanga, like their kins-women on Manihiki, are noted for their skill in weaving fine Panama-style hats and mats from rito, the young leaves of the coconut palm. The people use coconuts and fish as their main food and they also have plantings of puraka, a coarse variety of taro. Some attempts have been made to establish pearl-shell beds in the lagoon, but these have been largely unsuccessful.

The burial grounds on Rakahanga are of interest as some of the dead have been placed in grave houses, that is, graves which have been roofed over and which have in them items such as sewing machines and kerosene lamps which would be of use to the departed in the hereafter.

The island has a school, government offices and a dispensary. Secondary school age pupils attend either the Junior High School at Aitutaki or Tereora College on Rarotonga. The Catholic priest at Manihiki uses any vessels travelling between Manihiki and Rakahanga to visit his congregation on the latter island. Rakahanga is represented by a member in the Cook Islands Parliament.

Pukapuka. Pukapuka was the first island in the Cook Islands sighted by Europeans, the expedition of the Spaniard Alvaro de Mendana on 20 August 1595. Mendana called the island San Bernardo. The position of the atoll was confirmed by Commodore Byron on HMS *Dolphin* on 21 June 1765, when he named it Isle of Danger.

The atoll, which has a surface area of about 45 hectares, lies about 1150 kilometres north-west of Rarotonga. It consists of three motu, or islets, Wale, Moto Ko and Motu Kotawa, each of which is situated at one of the corners of the triangular-shaped lagoon. The atoll has suffered severely from hurricanes and a long submerged reef leads to the west to the Toka (sand bank), which appears to have been once part of the main island.

Christianity was established on the island about the time of the visit, in 1857, of the LMS missionary Rev. Aaron Buzacott. Peruvian slave raiders abducted about 100 men and women in 1863. The Pukapukans are closely related to the Tokelauans and Samoans and there are marked dialectic differences between the Maori language spoken on Pukapuka and that of the other islands in the Cook group.

The three main tribal subdivisions all live on Wale, but each has planting and other rights to one of the motu, the planting lands being worked at times decreed by the elders of the island. Life is communal and work tasks and food are shared according to a person's status as a man, a woman or a child. Over the centuries the Pukapukans have created an extensive taro swamp on Wale, and all work in the swamp is reserved for the women. The main source of cash income is from the sale of copra and again the proceeds are shared on a communal basis. The Pukapukan men are skilled canoe builders

and still use large canoes made from a number of small pieces of wood lashed together with sennit (braided cordage).

An American expedition conducted solar eclipse observations on Motu Kotawa in 1958.

On the island there is a school, hospital, wireless station and government offices. The Catholic church is remarkable for its decoration in religious motifs formed by the use of thousands of cowrie shells. This was a labour of love carried out by the Dutch priest, Father Benetio, who was stationed on Pukapuka for many years.

The LMS barque *John Williams* was wrecked on Pukapuka on 15 May 1864. The American author, Robert Dean Frisbie, lived on Pukapuka for many years, and has written about life there in *The Book of Pukapuka*, *Mister Moonlight's Island* and *The Island of Desire*.

Pukapuka has a representative in the Cook Islands Parliament. Many Pukapukans have migrated to Rarotonga and most are concentrated in the settlement at Pue, near Avarua.

Mangaia. Mangaia, the southernmost of the Cook Islands, lies about 177 kilometres east by south-east of Rarotonga and has a total land area of 5714 hectares. Its highest point, Rangimotia, is 169 metres above sea level. The island is surrounded by a narrow fringing reef, backed by formidable cliffs of makatea, or coral limestone, which reach heights of 60 metres with breadth varying between 60 and 1500 metres.

Much of the makatea is bare rock, which slopes into areas of sharp, closely packed pinnacles, which are almost impenetrable. Beyond the makatea the land is of red volcanic soil formed into rolling hills, with several swamps and a small lake situated near the inner wall of the makatea.

In the old days the people had to make their way inland by means of steps cut into the makatea but there is now a road to Oneroa which passes through a cutting blasted through the makatea. The land on Mangaia has not been surveyed nor have land titles been registered with the Cook Islands High Court (Land Division), and land is distributed among the Mangaian population according to traditional practices.

There are three villages, at Oneroa, Ivirua

and Tamarua, linked by a road which encircles the perimeter of the island.

James Cook was the first European visitor, on 29 March 1777. He did not land as the people gave him a hostile reception. The LMS missionary Rev. John Williams failed also in his initial attempts to land Polynesian teachers during his first visit there on 13 July 1823. H. E. Maude, in his reconstruction of the voyages of the *Bounty* after the mutiny, suggests the ship called at Mangaia. Whaling ships called at Mangaia frequently during the early part of the 19th century to obtain provisions and to recruit crew.

In earlier times the principal exports were copra, citrus fruits and tomatoes, but since the mid-1960s the emphasis has been on pineapples. The industry flourished in the early 1970s but went into decline in the late 1970s. In 1982 the uneconomic government-owned cannery in Rarotonga announced that it would no longer purchase pineapples, leaving the growers with the fresh fruit market as their only outlet. However, towards the end of 1982, the establishment of a major dehydrating project in Mangaia was commenced. This is being run by Californian interests with infrastructure being financed by aid from the Asian Development Bank and the New Zealand Government, in addition to funds from the Cook Islands Government. Mangaia has a 792 m airstrip.

The work load imposed by growing and harvesting the pineapples has restricted opportunities to grow other crops, such as coffee, or to engage in traditional subsistence tasks like taro growing and fishing.

Deposits of manganese have been found on the island but are not in sufficient quantity to warrant commercial exploitation. The makatea contains an extensive system of limestone caves, with stalactites and stalagmites and ancient subterranean burial sites. The Mangaians use the limestone from the stalactites and stalagmites to make multi-coloured food pounders. The women make gaily coloured hat bands and other decorative items from pupu, a small land snail, which emerges from the makatea after rain.

The Cook Islands Christian Church has a church at Oneroa of great artistic interest because of the intricate bindings in sennit which adorn the rafters and other interior timbers. The Mangaians cling to many traditional customs, such as those which accompany the choosing of a new paramount ariki, the ceremony combining elements of the traditional Polynesian practices and the pomp and circumstance of a coronation of British royalty.

The main government offices, stores, hospital, a primary school, and the Mangaia Junior High School are at Oneroa. There are also primary schools at Ivirua and Tamarua. Mangaia has three representatives in the Cook Islands Parliament.

Manu'ae. Captain James Cook on HMS *Resolution* was the first European to visit Manu'ae on 23 September 1773. He named the atoll Hervey's Island in honour of Captain Hervey, one of the Lords of the Admiralty. The name Hervey Islands came to be used for what is now the southern Cook Islands for most of the 19th century.

Manu'ae is the only true coral atoll in the southern Cook Islands. It has a surface area of 680 hectares, and is 200 kilometres north-north-east of Rarotonga.

When Cook visited Manu'ae it was inhabited by Aitutakians, who had seized it from the Atiuans. The island was abandoned in the 1830s. Several Europeans were domiciled there under arrangements with the Aitutakian leaders until a legal lease for John Strickland was created in 1893.

The lagoon at Manu'ae encloses two islets, Manu'ae and Te Au o Tu. About 85,000 coconut palms have been planted on the two motus and for much of the present century the plantation was worked by Manu'ae Plantations, for whom A. B. Donald and Co. acted as managing agents.

More recently the plantation was worked by first the Cook Islands Co-operative Bank and then Mitiaro Trading Co Ltd, both of which maintained plantation workers on the island. The lease of the island has now been purchased by a local company comprising representatives of the Aitutakian landowners.

In 1965 an international expedition carried out solar eclipse observations on Manu'ae commemorated by a special Cook Islands stamp.

Atiu. Atiu, which has an area of 1483 hectares, lies 187 kilometres north-east of Rarotonga. It is of volcanic origin and beyond the cliffs of makatea the red volcanic soil is formed into rounded and flat-topped hills. The people all live in what appears to be one settlement at the centre of the island, but which is in fact seven contiguous villages representing the precontact organisation of the people into seven land-holding tapere. Each tapere was traditionally headed by a person of the chiefly rank of mataiapo or ariki.

James Cook was the European discoverer of Atiu, on 31 March 1777. The Rev. John Williams was at Atiu on 20 July 1823 when the work of converting the Atiuans to Christianity began. At the time of European contact the ariki of Atiu had established sovereignty over the neighbouring islands of Mauke and Mitiaro, and the three islands are collectively known as Nga-Pu-Toru.

The cliffs of makatea on Atiu are noted for some extensive limestone caves, which contain stalagmites and stalactites.

The traditional leaders of the island retain much of their former powers and have been largely instrumental in encouraging the people to improve conditions on the island. The co-operative movement has played a significant role in the Atiuans' work of re-housing themselves. The citrus replanting scheme has enabled the growers to greatly reduce their indebtedness to the Cook Islands Government.

In recent years the Atiuans have consolidated ownership of some of the planting land and a valuable pineapple plantation been established. As the production of export crops has increased so have the problems multiplied in transporting the fruit to the processing plant on Rarotonga. Formerly, cargo was landed through very difficult reef passages, but in 1974 and 1975 New Zealand Army engineers built a small harbour for the lighters that work the ships standing off the Atiu reef. The island has an 825 m airstrip.

Dr Dennis McCarthy, a retired New Zealand doctor, has been responsible to a great extent for the implementation of a programme to control the incidence of filariasis and its advanced stage, elephantiasis, on the island. The disease has now been virtually eliminated.

The island has a primary school, junior high school, hospital, wireless station, government offices, stores and a three-unit motel. Atiu has two members in the Cook Islands Parliament.

Aitutaki. The first European to discover Aitutaki was William Bligh, on HMS *Bounty*, on 11 April 1789. Captain Edward Edwards, of HMS *Pandora*, was there on 14 April 1791, while searching for the mutineers. The Rev. John Williams visited Aitutaki in 1821, when he put ashore the Raiatean teachers Papeiha and Vahapata, this being the first work of Christian conversion in the Cook Islands.

The LMS missionary Rev. Henry Royle, who arrived there in 1839 and remained until 1876 was an influential figure. Many whaling ships called at Aitutaki to obtain provisions and to recruit crew.

The island is about 225 kilometres north of Rarotonga and has a total land area of 1991 hectares. Its geological structure is unusual in that it is part volcanic island and part coral atoll. Its lagoon, generally considered to be one of the most beautiful in the Pacific, was previously a stopover for the flying-boat service operated by Tasman Empire Airways Ltd (now Air New Zealand). There is no deep boat passage into the lagoon and ships land their passengers and cargo through a reef passage opposite the settlement of Arutanga.

During World War II an American construction battalion was stationed on Aitutaki and a causeway was built to the edge of the reef near Arutanga, but this has been eroded away. The Americans also built an airstrip, which is still in use.

Earlier this century Hansen's disease (leprosy) on Aitutaki was a serious problem and quarantine measures were enforced, but these were abandoned in the 1960s.

The Aitutakians are noted for the precision and vigour of their dancing. Their dancing teams have had much success in the Bastille Day celebrations in Tahiti.

A successful banana industry was established in Aitutaki in the mid-1960s. This particularly flourished in the late 70s (after recovering from Sigatoka disease) and in recent times.

Primarily because of its magnificent lagoon, Aitutaki is regarded as a great attraction for tourist development. The government built the first hotel, and now private enterprise has established a 25-unit resort hotel on an island in the lagoon.

A marine beacon was erected in 1954 on Maina Island, at the south-western end of Aitutaki, and it serves as a navigational aid. Aitutaki has an annual rainfall of about 2350 mm, but there are long periods of dry weather when public supplies come from government tanks.

Aitutaki has a public electricity supply, primary schools, a junior high school, hospital, wireless station, government offices, stores and two hotels. The Aitutakians have three representatives in the Cook Islands Parliament.

Penrhyn. The *Lady Penrhyn* was one of the ships in the first fleet which took convicts to Botany Bay, in the first settlement of Australia. On departure she set sail for China, and on 8 August 1788 Captain William Sever sighted and named an atoll Penrhyn's Island. The Maori name for the island is Tongareva, which has been translated as meaning either 'floating Tonga' or 'away from the south'.

The atoll encloses a lagoon of 280 square kilometres, one of the largest in the Pacific. 1170 kilometres north-east of Rarotonga, Penrhyn has a total land area of 600 hectares, much of which carries little vegetation.

With Suwarrow, Penrhyn is the only coral atoll in the Cook Islands where quite large vessels are able to enter the lagoon. There are three entrances, the most frequently used being that of the Taruia Passage near the village of Omoka. Te Tautua is the only other settlement, being on the opposite side of the lagoon from Omoka. Prior to the arrival of Europeans, the Penrhyn people lived on most of the motu on the fringing reef. There is a depth of about 6.5 metres of water in the Taruia Passage and inter-island vessels tie up at the wharf at Omoka.

Maori LMS pastors from Rarotonga introduced Christianity to the island in 1854. Peruvian slave-raiders were largely responsible for depopulating Penrhyn during the 1860s when many of the people, including the Maori LMS pastors, were transported to South America, most to work in the saltpetre mines. It is estimated that there were about 2000 people on Penrhyn in pre-European times and this figure fell to 326 in 1916.

The island was annexed by Britain in 1888. At the turn of the century, several European traders had set themselves up at Penrhyn and the Maori people owned their own trading schooners. The island was exploited for its pearl-shell beds and the Penrhyn men are noted for their prowess as divers. The production of shell has declined and is now of little relative importance. The island's principal export is copra. The people sail about the lagoon in English-style cutters about 6 metres long.

During World War II the American forces built an airstrip on Penrhyn and it was re-activated in post-war years in connection with the American and British nuclear testing programmes. The airstrip is still maintained. A Liberator bomber crashed on the island during the war and the duralumin from the wreckage is still used in the manufacture of artifacts such as combs and the barbs on fishing trolling hooks.

There are primary schools at Omoka and Te Tautua, with a hospital, wireless station and government offices being located at Omoka.

There have been several shipwrecks on Penrhyn, the most well-known being that of the *Chatham* in 1853. E. H. Lamont, who survived the wreck and spent about 18 months on Penrhyn, wrote one of the Pacific classics, *Wild Life Among the Pacific Islanders*, about his adventures on Penrhyn.

Earlier in this century, stern measures were imposed to control the spread of Hansen's disease (leprosy) which had been contracted by some Penrhyn Islanders, and some of the people were isolated on a motu at Penrhyn or sent to the leper station at Makogai, Fiji.

The people of Penrhyn are represented in the Cook Islands Parliament by one member.

FOR THE TOURIST. The Cook Islands provide many delights for visitors who enjoy walks, horse and buggy rides or travelling to outer islands. Detailed information is provided by the Cook Islands Tourist Authority, Air New Zealand and Cook Islands International. Visitor accommodation spans a good range, from a major hotel to small, self-contained units.

Duty free facilities. There are several duty-free stores in Avarua, offering a variety of imported goods. In addition, there are local handicrafts including woodcarvings following traditional patterns, delicately worked pearl shell, woven hats, baskets and broad mats as well as embroidery which has been popular since missionary days. A novel item is the ukelele made from a coconut shell by island craftsmen.

Entry formalities. Entry permits are not required by local people, permanent residents of the group, and visitors (other than those on business) whose stay does not exceed 31 days, provided they hold valid travel documents and ticket with a confirmed booking for the outward or return journey. A passport is required for all visitors, except Cook Islanders who hold a certificate of identity.

For stays over 31 days application must be made to the Principal Immigration Officer. This can be done after arrival in Rarotonga but 14 days' notice must be given and a fee of $20 paid with each application. Extensions are granted on a monthly basis up to a maximum of three months over the original 31 days. Persons intending to stay for more than four months must apply for a permit before arrival in the Cook Islands to the Principal Immigration Officer, Ministry of Labour and Commerce, Rarotonga, Cook Islands; the Cook Islands Government Office, Cook Islands House, Parnell, Auckland NZ, or to any New Zealand Embassy or Consulate.

Visitors are not required to have vaccinations unless arriving from an infected area. Persons arriving in Rarotonga from a stopover in Samoa, Fiji, Tahiti or any area where rhinoceros beetle is prevalent may be required to have their baggage fumigated.

Airport tax. There is a $20 departure tax for adults and $10 for children (2–11 years).

Sightseeing. The coral reef and lagoon waters are a centre of interest for those who enjoy snorkelling and shell collecting, especially in guided groups on the reef at night.

On land, the island may be toured along the Ara Tapu 33 km sealed road which encircles Rarotonga. The visitor can see the green tropical growth which begins beside the beach and stretches across the coastal plain to the hills, broken by lines of citrus trees and small villages.

The Ara Metua is an historic road which still survives in broken stretches, slightly inland from the Ara Tapu. The origin of its stone paving is shrouded in legend dating back to about 900 AD. Stone seats of earlier councils may be sighted near this road. Many are sacred to the descendants of the early warriors.

Other touches of history can easily be seen during a walk around Avarua, including the main Cook Islands Christian Church (1853), the Mission College, the small but well-maintained museum and the ruins of 'Queen' Makea Takau's palace. Elsewhere around Rarotonga, churches are also of great historical interest as are their graveyards, which contain a wealth of historic identities famous and infamous, from early missionaries to more recent figures like Tom Neale and the controversial Prime Minister Albert Henry. The cemetery of the Roman Catholic Church at Nikao is colourfully decorated with flowers for All Souls festivities in early November.

Other occasions of festive interest are the Constitution celebrations which last for about 10 days in early August; Gospel Day on 26 October, which commemorates the arrival of the first Christian missionaries with exuberant religious plays in every district, and various floral, dance, fashion and other cultural festivals.

Race days on Muri Beach are popular with bareback riders of less than professional jockey standard competing on mounts of less than thoroughbred standard. A totalisator betting system operates and the atmosphere is much closer to Polynesia than to Epsom. Race days are usually advertised well in advance.

'Umukai' — traditional Polynesian feasts with food cooked in an earth oven (umu) — are held frequently by the leading hotels, and in villages on special occasions. They are usually accompanied by superb singing and dancing.

Detailed information may be obtained from the office of the Cook Islands Tourist Authority, PO Box 14, Rarotonga; the Cook Islands Government Information Office, Parnell, Auckland, NZ or from offices of Air New Zealand, Polynesian Airlines or Cook Islands International (Ansett).

ACCOMMODATION
RAROTONGA

Rarotongan Resort Hotel: 12.1 km from Avarua on white sand beach, 150 rooms with ensuite, 4 beachfront suites, tea/coffee-making facilities, fans, pool, water sports, tennis, shops, 3 restaurants, conference facilities, motor scooter, push bike and car rental, tour desk, credit cards. PO Box 103, Rarotonga. Tel. 25 800, Telex RG62003.

Tamure Resort Hotel: 2.4 km from Avarua, ocean frontage, 35 rooms with ensuite, tea/coffee-making facilities, fans, pool, tennis, shop, tour desk, restaurant, entertainment, rental bikes, credit cards. PO Box 17, Rarotonga. Tel. 22 415, Telex RG62007.

Lagoon Lodges: 11.6 km from Avarua, opposite beach, 10 self-contained units, full kitchen facilities, pool, tennis, BBQ, rental cars and bikes. PO Box 45, Rarotonga. Tel. 22 020, Telex RG62076.

Little Polynesian Motel: 12.2 km from Avarua on white sand beach, 9 fully self-contained units, full kitchen facilities, pool, rental cars and bikes arranged. PO Box 366, Rarotonga. Tel. 24 280, Telex RG62065.

Muri Beachcomber Motel: 13 km from Avarua on Muri Lagoon, 12 fully self-contained units, full kitchen facilities, pool, BBQ, water sports equipment, rental vehicles arranged. PO Box 379, Rarotonga. Tel. 21 022, Telex RG62055.

Puaikura Reef Lodges: 10.8 km from Avarua, opposite beach, 12 fully self-contained units, full kitchen facilities, pool, BBQ, rental cars and scooters. PO Box 397, Rarotonga. Tel. 23 537, Telex RG62045.

Rarotongan Sunset Motel: 8 km from Avarua, lagoon frontage, 20 fully self-contained units, full kitchen facilities, pool, BBQ, water sports equipment, rental cars and bikes. PO Box 377, Rarotonga. Tel. 28 028, Telex RG62074.

Moana Sands Resort: 12 km from Avarua on white sand beach, 12 fully self-contained units, full kitchen facilities, cafe and house bar, activities desk, rental vehicles arranged, credit cards. PO Box 1007, Rarotonga. Tel. 26 189, Telex RG62044.

Beach Motel: 8 km from Avarua on lagoon, 20 fully self-contained units, full kitchen facilities, beach bar, Sunday entertainment, rental vehicles arranged, credit cards. PO

Box 700, Rarotonga, Tel. 22 461, Telex RG62060.

Edgewater Motel: 7 km Avarua on lagoon, 84 fully self-contained units, full kitchen facilities, pool, BBQ, squash, beach bar, rental vehicles, credit cards. PO Box 121, Rarotonga. Tel. 25 437, Telex RG62059.

Raina Village Motel: 14 km from Avarua opposite beach, 6 fully self-contained units, full kitchen facilities, spa, BBQ. PO Box 1047, Rarotonga. Tel. 20 197, Telex RG62026.

Palm Grove Lodges: 15.3 km from Avarua opposite white sand beach, 4 fully self-contained units, full kitchen facilities, pool, rental scooters. PO Box 23, Rarotonga. Tel. 20 002, Telex RG62045.

Moana Sunrise Motel: 7.3 km from Avarua, ocean frontage, 8 fully self-contained units, full kitchen facilities, shop, motor scooter hire. Depot 8, Ngatangiia, Rarotonga. Tel. 26 560, Telex RG62044.

Ariana Bungalows: 2 km from Avarua, rural garden setting, 10 fully self-contained units, full kitchen facilities, pool, BBQ, bush walks, transport daily to beach. PO Box 434, Rarotonga. Tel. 20 521, Telex RG62072.

Kii Kii Motel: 1.5 km from Avarua, ocean frontage, 20 fully self-contained units, full kitchen facilities, pool, BBQ, rental vehicles arranged, credit cards. PO Box 68, Rarotonga. Tel. 21 937, Telex RG62008.

Arorangi Lodge: 8.5 km from Avarua on lagoon, 8 fully self-contained units, full kitchen facilities. PO Box 51, Rarotonga. Tel. 27 379, Telex RG62034.

The Paradise: on edge of Avarua township, 16 fully self-contained units, cooking equipment, fans. PO Box 674, Rarotonga. Tel. 20 544, Telex RG62062.

Orange Grove Lodge: 15.4 km from Avarua, garden setting, 2 fully self-contained units, full kitchen facilities, fruit in season provided, rental vehicles arranged. PO Box 553, Rarotonga. Tel. 20 192, Cables 'Anani'.

Tiare Village Motel: 3 km from Avarua, rural setting, 3 fully self-contained chalets, 3 rooms with shared facilities, full kitchen facilities, rental vehicles, fully equipped ham radio 'shack'. PO Box 489, Rarotonga. Tel. 23 466, Telex RG62017.

Whitesands Motel: 10 km from Avarua on

sandy beach, 6 fully self-contained units, full kitchen facilities. PO Box 115, Rarotonga. Tel. 25 789, Telex RG62058.
Mana Motel: 3 km from Avarua, ocean frontage, 2 fully self-contained units, full kitchen facilities. PO Box 72, Rarotonga. Tel. 26 485, Telex RG62026.
Onemaru Motel: 11.7 km from Avarua opposite beach, 4 fully self-contained units, full kitchen facilities. PO Box 523, Rarotonga. Tel. 24 770, Cable 'Witta'.
Airport Lodge: adjacent to airport, 2 fully self-contained units, full kitchen facilities. PO Box 223, Rarotonga. Tel. 20 050.
Are Renga Motel: 8.5 km from Avarua, 6 fully self-contained units, full kitchen facilities. PO Box 223, Rarotonga. Tel. 20 050.
Rutaki Lodge: 12.2 km from Avarua, 2 fully self-contained units, 1 beachfront, 1 inland, full kitchen facilities. PO Box 170, Rarotonga. Tel. 22 115.
Atupa Orchid: 2 km from Avarua, rural setting, 2 fully self-contained units, full kitchen facilities. PO Box 64, Rarotonga. Tel. 28 543.
Matareka Heights: 3 km from Avarua, rural setting, 3 rooms with ensuite, communal kitchen facilities and lounge, 3 fully self-contained units, rental bikes. PO Box 587, Rarotonga. Tel. 23 670, Telex RG62050.
Dive Rarotonga Hostel: 11 km from Avarua, rural setting, 9 rooms with communal bathroom, kitchen and lounge facilities, rental bikes. PO Box 38, Rarotonga. Tel. 21 873, Telex RG62046.

AITUTAKI
Aitutaki Resort Hotel: situated on Aitutaki Lagoon, 25 bungalows with ensuite, tea/coffee-making facilities, fans, pool, restaurant, bar, shop, water sports, golf nearby, entertainment, rental vehicles arranged, credit cards. PO Box 342, Rarotonga. Tel. 20 234, Telex 62048 Oceania.
Rapae Cottage Hotel: 1.6 km from main village, on white sand beach, 12 rooms with ensuite, 2 fully self-contained units with kitchen facilities, tea/coffee-making facilities, restaurant, bar, rental vehicles arranged. Cook Islandair, PO Box 65, Rarotonga, Telex Sita RARRMKH. Or Air Rarotonga, PO Box 79, Rarotonga. Tel. Aitutaki 77, Telex RG62026.
Tiare Maori Guesthouse: adjacent to main village, 6 rooms with shared facilities, bed and breakfast only. Cook Islandair, PO Box 65, Rarotonga, Telex Sita PARRMKH. Or Air Rarotonga, PO Box 79, Rarotonga. Tel. 26 300 (Cook Islandair), Telex RG62026.
Josie's Lodge: 6 rooms with shared facilities, bed and breakfast. PO Box 320, Rarotonga. Tel. Aitutaki 111, Telex 62058.
Aitutaki Guest House: 8 rooms with shared facilities, tariff includes bed, breakfast and evening meal. PO Box 1, Aitutaki. Tel. Rarotonga 25511.

ATIU
Atiu Motel: 4 km from main village, rural setting, 3 fully self-contained chalets, full kitchen facilities, foodstuffs suplied on 'pay as you use' system, rental motor scooters. Air Rarotonga, PO Box 79, Rarotonga. Tel. 22 888, Telex RG62026.

MAUKE
Tiare Holiday Cottage: on Mauke Island, 250 km north-east of Rarotonga, 2 rooms with communal kitchen and bathroom facilities. Tiare Cottage, Mauke, Cook Islands.

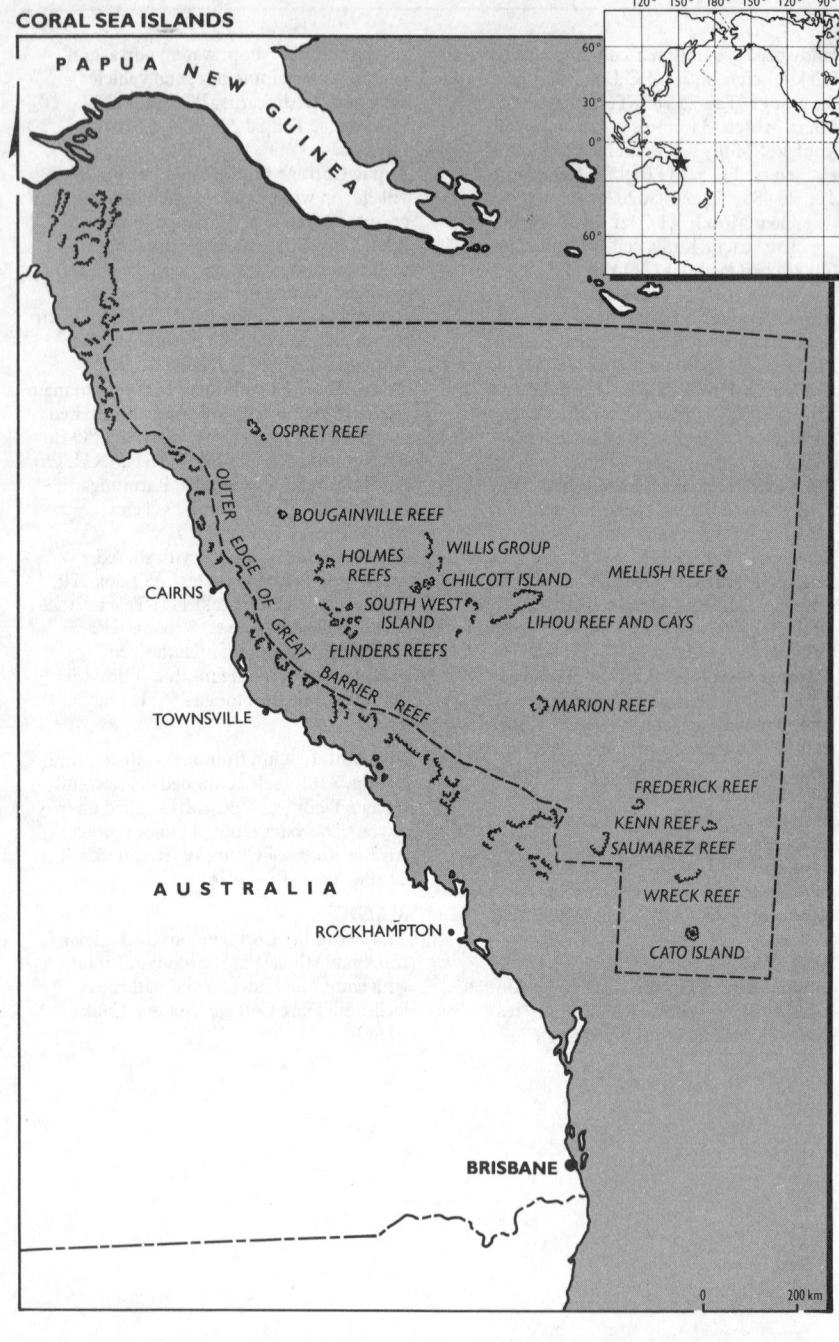

CORAL SEA ISLANDS

PAPUA NEW GUINEA

OSPREY REEF

BOUGAINVILLE REEF

HOLMES REEFS   WILLIS GROUP

CHILCOTT ISLAND   MELLISH REEF

CAIRNS   SOUTH WEST ISLAND   LIHOU REEF AND CAYS

FLINDERS REEFS

OUTER EDGE OF GREAT BARRIER REEF

MARION REEF

TOWNSVILLE

FREDERICK REEF

KENN REEF

SAUMAREZ REEF

AUSTRALIA   WRECK REEF

ROCKHAMPTON   CATO ISLAND

BRISBANE

0   200 km

Coral Sea Islands Territory

The Coral Sea Islands Territory is an Australian external territory. It comprises scattered reefs and islands, often little more than sandbanks, spread over a sea area of 780,000 sq. km with only a few square kilometres of actual land area. The territory lies to the east of Queensland between the Great Barrier Reef and longitude 156 deg 6 min E and latitudes 12 deg S and 24 deg S. There are no permanent inhabitants.

The islands were declared to be Australian territory by the Coral Sea Islands Act of 1969. This followed an exchange of letters between the governments of Australia and the United Kingdom in November 1968, in which Britain recognised Australian control over the islands. Laws of the Australian Capital Territory apply to the Coral Sea Islands Territory.

Some of the better known islands are Cato, Chilcott Islet in the Coringa group, and the Willis group. Others are Bird Islet, West Islet and others forming part of Wreck Reef: Herald Beacon Islet and others forming part of Mellish Reef; the Frederick Reef, Bougainville Reef and Lihou Reef islands.

There is no administration on the islands, but they are visited regularly by Royal Australian Navy vessels and Australia has control over the activities of any visitors.

There is a manned weather station on Willis Island, about 483 km east of Cairns. A number of unmanned facilities, including a lighthouse on Bougainville Reef, weather stations on Cato Island, Flinders Reef, Holmes Reef, Marion Reef and Lihou Reef and beacons on Fredrick Reef and Saumarez Reef, are also operated by the Australian Government.

Two areas of the territory were declared National Nature Reserves on 3 August 1982 — the Coringa-Herald Reserve and the Lihou Reef Reserve. The reserves include the islands, reefs and cays and surrounding waters. The whole of the Coral Sea Islands Territory is an important nesting area for many species of sea birds and for turtles. Thirteen of the approximately 24 bird species in the territory are protected under an Australian–Japanese agreement on endangered and migratory species.

The Minister for Territories and Local Government, Canberra, is responsible for the administration of the territory. The Department of Territories and Local Government liaises with other interested bodies such as the National Parks and Wildlife Service, which administers the reserves, and the Bureau of Meteorology.

Easter Island

Easter Island, a territory of Chile, lies between the west coast of South America and Pitcairn Island, its nearest inhabited neighbour. It is situated in approximately 27 deg 10 min S lat. and 109 deg 30 min W long. Santiago, the Chilean capital, is 3790 km eastward; Pitcairn is about 1600 km westward. The official Spanish name for the island is Isla de Pascua. It is also known as

Rapanui, a Polynesian name dating back to the 1860s, and as Te-Pito-O-Te-Henua (The navel of the world). The French call it Ile de Paques.

The island has an area of about 180 sq. km. There are about 2060 residents. The coastline is generally rugged and the interior is chiefly composed of low hills and plateaus. Hanga Roa, on the west coast, and adjoining

EASTER ISLAND

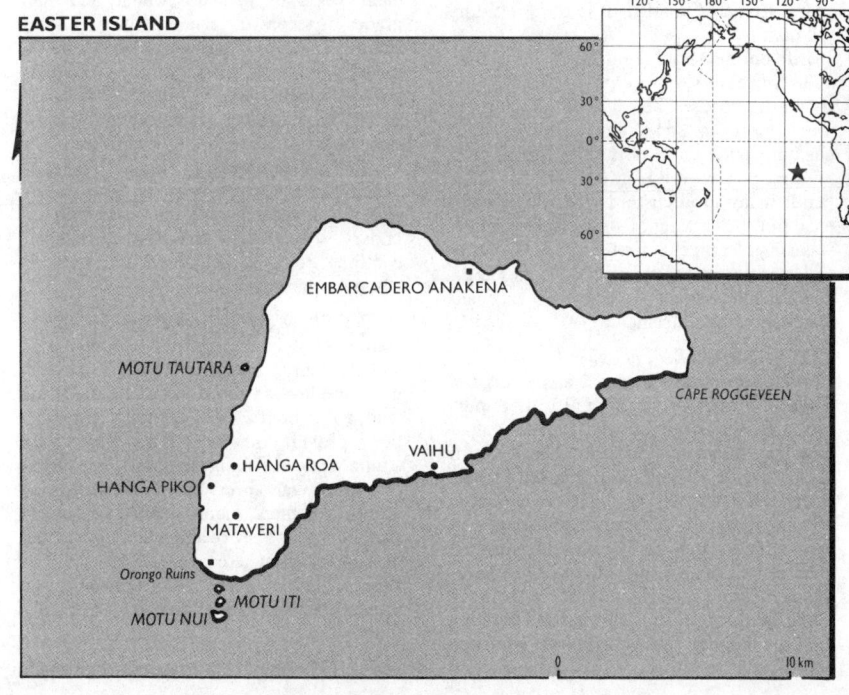

Mataveri are the only settlements. The island is administered by a governor appointed by the Chile Government. The Chilean peso is the official currency. The coat of arms, national anthem, flag and public holidays are also those of Chile. The only variation is that on 9 September, the day when Chile annexed the island in 1888, a special Rapanui or Policarpo Toro Day is commemorated.

THE PEOPLE. Of the 2060 residents (1986), about 800 are temporary residents from Chile — government and airline officials, members of the Chilean Air Force, Navy, hospital workers, police, nuns, etc. The remainder are native Easter Islanders, a Polynesian people speaking a language known locally as Rapanui. The islanders also speak Spanish, the official language. Residents of all descriptions in contact with tourists usually speak some English.

Citizenship. The islanders have Chilean citizenship. Almost all islanders over 15 have visited Chile, and some have lived there to go to secondary school or to work for several years. Roman Catholicism is the prevailing religion.

Life on the island is informal. More than 400 vehicles of various types are used on the rough dirt roads. Their houses and clothing are Chilean in style, and many of their customs, such as tea-drinking, the 'abrazo' (embrace), etc., are identical. On the other hand, many local customs are still in evidence but the making of string figures which was a popular diversion is dying out. Tamure-style dancing has been imported from Tahiti. The islanders make a variety of excellent wood and stone carvings.

GOVERNMENT. The island is administered by a military governor and a corps of Chilean officials. For administrative purposes, Easter Island is included with Valparaiso and Vina del Mar. Frequently, even minor details of administration have to be referred to Chile for decision. A local mayor appointed by the governor has a voice in local affairs, but his powers are limited because he has no means of raising revenue.

Justice. The legal system is the same as in Chile operated on an island basis. There is a Chilean judge at the courthouse, who also acts as civil registrar and performs all legal functions. The National Police or 'Carabineros' patrol the island and maintain the small gaol.

Liquor and gambling. Liquor laws are the same as in Chile, though liberally interpreted. There is no formal gambling, but many invest in the weekly Chilean national soccer pool. There are no restrictions on the amount of liquor that can be brought in by visitors, and bottled liquor is very expensive.

DEFENCE. The Chilean Air Force maintains a small base on the island at Mataveri, site of the airstrip. A Chilean warship or the Chilean naval training vessel *Esmeralda* usually pays an annual visit to the island. The Chilean Navy has a small base. However, the largest armed force is the National Police.

EDUCATION. The Regional Department of Education in Valparaiso is responsible for education on the island. There is one school with just over 700 students run by the government under the same Regional Department and a kindergarten. There are eight years of primary school and four grades of secondary school, which is being extended. Pupils attend in two shifts, morning for grade 5 (primary) and secondary grades and afternoon for primary grades 1 to 4. The kindergarten has morning and afternoon sessions with different children. The nursery has 25 pupils.

Scholarships from various sources are available to enable children to attend secondary school in Chile. Some islanders continue to post-secondary education in colleges and universities.

LABOUR. Work opportunities for the islanders exist in the Chilean administration and the tourist industry. About 80 government employees from Chile are on the island who, with about a third of the local population, provide the workforce. Most local adults work in fishing, agriculture, tourism or commercial stores. However, a growing number of more highly-qualified islanders join the Public Service and seek employment in Chile or elsewhere.

Wages. These are fixed according to Chilean standards, and in 1980 were about $US150 a month.

HEALTH. Maternity patients or others

needing surgery or casualty treatment are accommodated in a hospital with a capacity of 40 beds, opened in 1976, in Hanga Roa village. There are two doctors, a dentist, chemist, midwife, two nurses and auxiliary staff. There are two ambulances.

THE LAND. The island is 22 km long by 11 km wide, with an area of 180 sq. km. It is almost triangular in shape, having an extinct volcano near each corner. The highest of these is Mt Terevaka (506 m) in the NW. Its crater is called Rano Aroi. Lava flows from Terevaka spread over much of the island in ancient times to the other volcanoes. These have left the surface of the island exceedingly stony. There are numerous caves below the surface. High black cliffs, battered by a strong surf, make access to the island difficult from the sea. There are only three or four small sandy beaches. The main one is at Anakena, the legendary landing place of the culture hero of the Rapanui, 'King' Hotu Matu'a.

The island has a semi-tropical climate, with trade winds blowing from the east and SE during most of the year. It can on occasions get very cold. The annual rainfall varies considerably and there are occasional droughts. However, precipitation of 1250 mm, mainly in winter (June–July), is about the average. The only surface water is in the crater lakes of the extinct volcanoes.

Grasses flourish on the island which was once treeless, but trees planted in recent years are now flourishing. The trees include pines, eucalypts and fruit trees. Seabirds, a small lizard and insects are the only indigenous fauna.

Hanga Roa is the centre of population — all Easter Islanders live there.

PRIMARY PRODUCTION. Plants cultivated by the pre-European inhabitants of the island are still cultivated today. They include bananas, sweet potatoes, yams, sugar cane and gourds. Food plants introduced since then include corn, melons, potatoes, beans, tomatoes, grapes, avocados, squash, pineapples, and fruit trees. Many islanders bring seeds and cuttings back from their travels and many of these have prospered.

Livestock in ancient times consisted of only the chicken and a native edible rat, the 'kio'e', now extinct. Sheep, horses, cattle,

pigs, cats, dogs, pigeons, quail and ducks have been introduced in the past century or so. Sheep, first brought from Australia by John Brander of Tahiti in 1872, provide Easter Island with its only significant export, wool.

Livestock. Due to serious soil erosion, the sheep population of 60,000 in the early 1950s had to be drastically reduced. There are now about 10,000. Most are corriedales but there are some merinos. At the annual shearing, each clip is about 2.8 kg and all wool is sent to Chile. The sheep also provide meat for local consumption.

There are also about 2000 horses on the island which are mostly wild but are useful for keeping down the grass. About 280 farmers have mixed breed cattle which provide beef. Late in 1976, 600 cows and 32 Hereford bulls were imported from Punta Arenas, southern Chile. They are maintained at a government station and bred with bulls from Australia and New Zealand.

Fish and lobsters are caught locally including tuna and a local delicacy, 'nanue'.

TOURISM. With an extension of LAN Chile flights, the number of tourists is growing, with 2624 visitors recorded in 1985. There are frequent all-inclusive tour parties from North America particularly, staying for a few days at a time. Passengers between Santiago and Papeete frequently stop over between flights, but tourism is still in its infancy on the island due to the high cost of air fares and living costs on the island.

LOCAL COMMERCE. The two supermarkets obtain supplies from Chile and stock canned and frozen foods, wines and soft drinks. A small range of clothing and cosmetics can be bought from about 20 general stores. Fresh fruit and vegetables can be obtained at the local market.

FINANCE. The island is a financial drain on Chile, which spends much more on the island than is obtained from the sale of wool and from tourism, the only industries. Government support per capita is greater here than in any other part of Chile. The Banco del Estado de Chile (the Chilean State Bank) has a branch on the island.

TRANSPORT. There are no bitumen roads, but over 200 families have vehicles, usually with 4-wheel drive. Horses are numerous and everything in Hanga Roa is within walking distance. Horses may be rented daily or weekly. A car with driver can also be rented. There are also more than 250 motor cycles on the island.

Depending on the season, ships may anchor at almost any time in one or other of several indentations round the coast. The one most commonly used is Hanga Piko, on the west coast, a short distance south of Hanga Roa. Cruise ships call occasionally. Facilities include a stone quay, cranes, warehouses and electric light. The pier takes three 16 m landing craft used for unloading ships which anchor offshore. Other landing places are: Hanga Roa or Cook Bay; La Perouse Bay, NE coast; Hotuiti, SE coast; and Vinapu, SE coast. Two cargo ships provide non-perishable foods, goods, machinery and equipment. They are supported by the Chilean Government.

The Chilean airline LAN-Chile, using a Boeing 707, calls at Easter Island on flights from Santiago to Tahiti and return, twice weekly. Flying time from Santiago is about five hours, and to Tahiti, four hours. Mataveri Airport, in the SW corner of the island, is of jet standard. A passenger terminal was completed in 1982.

COMMUNICATIONS. Telephones are installed in all public offices and in several dozen private homes. Calls to Chile may be made with little difficulty. International calls are made by satellite. Radio contact is maintained daily with Valparaiso by the government radio station. All day radio programmes are transmitted from the local station radio Manukena maintained by the Chilean Air Force. TV programmes on videotape from Chile are broadcast at night from 1800 to 2400 hours. Over 100 households have television, and many now have video. Short wave and medium band radio reception is good. Chilean newspapers and magazines arrive each week. The local priest, Father David Reddy OFM, is the only licensed amateur radio operator. His call sign is CE 0 AE.

WATER AND ELECTRICITY. Water is obtained from cisterns collecting from roof run-offs and also from wells pumped to Hanga Roa from the north slope of Rano Kau. It is safe to drink. Electricity is 110 volts at the Hotel Hanga Roa. Elsewhere, the voltage is 220 (2-pin round plug).

MAJOR OFFICE HOLDERS.
Governor:
　Sergio Rapu Haoa
Mayor:
　Samuel Cardinale
Chief of Police:
　Aliro Escudero
Judge:
　Orasmin Gillies Gil

HISTORY. Recent research has shown that Easter Island was probably inhabited as far back as AD 400. Over the centuries, the islanders built large numbers of stone statues, temple platforms or 'ahus' and other stone works. These were distributed over much of the island. The tallest statue is about 10 m high; some are 6 to 9 m; most are from 3.5 to 6 m; and some are smaller. They were carved out of volcanic rock, and represent the upper portion of the human body. The latest theory is that they represent stylised portraits of significant ancestors.

The quarry and carving site for the statues was the crater slopes of the most easterly volcano, Rano Raraku. The sculptors apparently worked on them until they were attached to the living rock by only a slender keel running down the back. When freed, they were slid down the slopes and were stood up to be finished, then dragged by manpower to be erected on the 'ahu'. Many were crowned with topknots of red volcanic tuff. The statues were called 'moai', and about 1000 of them were carved. The carving seems to have gone on for 1000 years until, suddenly, it ceased. Work on some 'moai' at Rano Raraku was never completed; others were abandoned half-way down the slopes or en route to their platforms.

Roggeveen's arrival. One theory suggests that the carving era ended when a war broke out between two groups of islanders known as the Hanau Eepe (usually called the Long Ears) and the Hanau Momoko (Short Ears). This war apparently began just before or just after the arrival of the European discoverer of the island Jacob Roggeveen. Roggeveen, a Dutchman, came upon the island on Easter Day, 1722, and named it accordingly.

His three ships remained off the island for three days, but he and his men made only one excursion ashore.

In 1770, a Spanish expedition under Captain Felipe Gonzalez visited the island from Peru and took possession of it for the King of Spain. A document was drawn up, and several of the islanders signed it with 'certain characters of their own form of script'. This was the first time that a version of the celebrated 'rongo-rongo' writing of Easter Island was seen.

Four years after the Spaniards' departure, Captain Cook visited the island briefly. Other explorers to call there over the next 60 years were: La Perouse (1786), Lisiansky (1804), Kotzebue (1816), Beechey (1825), and Du Petit-Thouars (1838). In 1806, Captain Benjamin Page took an islander to London where he sponsored his baptism in 1812. Nearly 50 ships, mostly whalers, visited the island from 1792 onwards, but on average probably never more frequently than once every two years.

Peruvian blackbirders. In 1862, when the island's population probably stood at about 3000, a flotilla of Peruvian ships raided the island to get much-needed labour for Peru. There was a second raid in 1863. From 800 to 1000 islanders are estimated to have been carried off. However, protests by diplomats and missionaries soon forced the Peruvian government to insist on the islanders being repatriated. Many died before arrangements could be made to send them home; others died on the way. Some of the few who did see their homeland again carried smallpox and tuberculosis germs with them which quickly wiped out many of those who had remained behind.

In 1864 while smallpox was still raging, a French religious missionary, Brother Eugene Eyraud of the Order of the Sacred Hearts, settled on the island. Two priests with assistants from Mangareva arrived with him on a second visit. These missionaries did all they could to alleviate the islanders' misery, but their numbers fell away rapidly during the next few years. Meanwhile, the missionaries discovered that many of the islanders had inscribed wooden boards called 'rongo-rongo' in their houses, and they succeeded in obtaining a few examples of this unique Polynesian writing before the

tablets were all hidden or destroyed with the adoption of Christianity.

By 1868, when Eyraud died, the missionaries had baptised all the remaining islanders. In that same year a French adventurer, Dutrou-Bornier, settled on the island. In an arrangement with John Brander, a merchant in Tahiti, Dutrou-Bornier began buying up the islanders' land with a view to establishing a sheep ranch. Conflict soon arose with both the islanders and the missionaries. The upshot was that the missionaries withdrew to Mangareva in 1871 taking some of the islanders with them, and other islanders were persuaded to leave the island to work on Brander's plantations in Tahiti. Six years later, Dutrou-Bornier was murdered, apparently because of brutality and overbearing conduct. By then Easter Island's population had fallen to a record low of 110. All modern Easter Islanders are descended from 15 couples among those 110 people, plus a few outsiders who arrived on the island afterwards.

Chilean annexation. Until Chile annexed the island in 1888, Brander's sheep-raising interests were managed by a part-Tahitian, Alexander Salmon. Those interests were then taken over by a Chilean company, Compania Explotadora de la Isla de Pascua, a subsidiary of Williamson, Balfour Co., of London and Valparaiso. About 18,000 sheep had the run of the island, and the few islanders were confined to a small region round Hanga Roa on the west coast. Except that the islanders gradually increased in numbers, there was little of note in the island's history until World War I when, in October 1914, the German Pacific Squadron used Easter Island as a rendezvous and revictualling base.

While the squadron was at the island an English archaeologist, Mrs Katherine Scoresby Routledge, was making the first serious attempt to unravel some of the mysteries of the island's past. She remained there nearly 17 months, and subsequently wrote a book, *The Mystery of Easter Island*. Another important scientific expedition arrived in 1934 comprising a Belgian ethnologist, Henri Lavachery, a French archaeologist, Alfred Metraux and a Chilean scientist, Israel Drapkin. The following year saw Father Sebastian Englert. He lived there until just before his death in 1969, and worked incessantly to improve the lot of the islanders and to record what he could of their language, history and traditions. In 1955 a large-scale scientific expedition under the leadership of the Norwegian explorer Thor Heyerdahl visited the island and carried out extensive archaeological research.

Recent history. Meanwhile, the island was under the administration of the Chilean Navy, which appointed a naval officer as governor. Apart from the occasional visits by scientists, and sporadic calls by yachts and liners, the islanders' only contact with the outside world was an annual visit by a Chilean naval vessel. However, about 1950, with the aim of opening the island to aviation, a rough 600 m airstrip was built at Mataveri at the SW corner of the island. A Chilean Catalina amphibian aircraft piloted by Roberto Parrague of the Chilean air force landed there in 1951, but could not take off again with a load of fuel. When the plane attempted to take off from the sea it crashed. Shortly afterwards an Australian airman, the late Sir Gordon Taylor, called at the island on a trans-Pacific west-to-east survey flight in a Catalina flying-boat. Thereafter there were no significant developments in the aviation field until the 1960s.

In 1954, the Chilean government terminated its lease to the Compania Explotadora and turned the sheep ranch over to the naval administration. Its aim was to improve conditions for the islanders. However, as time passed the islanders grew increasingly discontented.

In 1965, their leaders wrote an open letter to the President of Chile complaining of the naval governor's treatment of them, of restrictions on their movements, and of their lack of a vote in Chilean elections. Soon afterwards the naval administration was superseded by a civil administration, and the islanders obtained all the rights provided by Chilean citizenship.

In the early 1960s the airstrip at Mataveri was lengthened and improved and new plans were afoot to bring Easter Island into the modern world. With a view to recording all they could about the physical conditions of the islanders before their age-old isolation was shattered, a Canadian medical expedition visited the island for two months in 1964 and examined every island resident.

In 1965 and 1966, Roberto Parrague made further proving flights to the island from Santiago and Tahiti. At the time of his second flight, the Mataveri strip had been lengthened to more than 1800 m and had been sealed. A fortnightly service between Santiago and Easter Island was inaugurated by LAN-Chile in April 1967 with a DC6B aircraft. The flight took nine hours. The service was extended to Tahiti at the beginning of 1968. By March 1970 the Mataveri airstrip had been further upgraded and LAN-Chile was able to begin a weekly jet service to Easter Island and Tahiti using 707 Boeing jets. This was later extended to two or three times weekly, depending on seasons.

The link with Tahiti placed Easter Island within relatively easy reach of passengers from Australia, New Zealand and North America, as well as Chile and the Pacific Islands.

In 1983, 1200 Easter Islanders, virtually the entire non-Chilean population, petitioned the United Nations Committee on Decolonisation for assistance in securing a referendum on independence for Easter Island. Chilean authorities in Santiago dismissed the petition as the work of 'foreign agitators'. At the same time a three-man scientific team from NASA found that the island was actually moving closer to South America — geologically if not politically.

In late 1987 an emergency landing strip for US space shuttles was opened on Easter Island, following negotiations between the governments of the US and Chile. The runway, built at a cost of $US8 million by NASA, is an extension to an existing airstrip. US and Chilean authorities were insistent that there would be no risk to the island's statues.

Origins of the people. The most hotly debated question of Easter Island history in recent years has been the origins of the people who inhabited the island when Roggeveen encountered it in 1722. The orthodox view has long been that the islanders of Roggeveen's time were Polynesians of South-East Asian origin who had reached the island, probably from the Marquesas, in the last phase of their exploratory voyages eastward. However, Thor Heyerdahl, of

Kon-Tiki fame, and some other scholars believe that the islanders of 1722 were a mixed people — that before the Polynesians arrived from the east the island was settled by South American Indians and that it was they who were responsible for the statues and other stone works.

In 1975, Australian historian Robert Langdon gave the debate a new twist when he suggested in his book *The Lost Caravel* that the islanders were actually an amalgam of three racial types: from South America, Polynesia and Europe, the latter including a Basque element from the Spanish caravel *San Lesmes* which was lost in the eastern Pacific in 1526. Langdon and Dr Darrell Tryon argued in a book in 1983, as a result of studying the Rapanui language, that Easter Island was an important dispersal centre for people moving westward in the Pacific.

In 1983 the University of Chile began an accelerated series of archaeological investigations on the island, with student parties arriving almost every month to help in the work.

Further information. Most of the ample literature on Easter Island is concerned with its ancient history rather than recent times. Among the few books in the latter category are Helen Reed's *A World Away*, Toronto, 1965, which tells of conditions at the time of the Canadian medical expedition's visit in 1964, and Bob Putigny, *Easter Island*, Papeete, 1976, an excellent tourist guide. A comprehensive account of the contact of Easter Island with Europeans and of contemporary life is to be read in *Reaction to Disaster* by Grant McCall, New York, 1977. A more recent book, Michel Rougie's *Rapa Nui*, in English, Spanish and French (Editions Delroisse, Paris, 1979), explores the island's archaeology, history and tourism, adding some beautiful photographs. Other books dealing chiefly with the island's prehistory include: Alfred Metraux, *Easter Island*, London, 1957; Thor Heyerdahl, *Akuaku*, London, 1958; Thor Heyerdahl and Edwin Ferdon, (eds), *Archaeology of Easter Island*, Stockholm, 1961; Sebastian Englert, *Island at the Centre of the World*, London, 1972; Peggy Mann, *Easter Island, Land of Mysteries*, Holt, Rinehart & Winston, New York, 1976. Beautiful descriptions and illustrations of ancient and modern stone and wood artifacts from the island are in *The Art of Easter Island*, Thor Heyerdahl, London, 1976. William Mully and Gonzalo Figueroa's *The Ahu Akivi-Vaiteka Complex and its Relationship to Easter Island Architectural Prehistory*, Hawaii, 1978, is a recent book on the island's treasures. *The Language of Easter Island: Its Development and Eastern Polynesian Relationships* by Robert Langdon and Darrell Tryon (Hawaii, 1983) discusses the origins of the islanders.

FOR THE TOURIST. The huge statues and other archaeological remains are the chief features most tourists wish to see. There are several organised day and half-day tours to the most interesting sites. Visitors may also fish, swim and ride horses. Because of the stony ground, sturdy walking shoes are advisable. The standard of food at hotels and private guest houses is high. Seafood, beautifully served, is a specialty. Souvenirs for sale include small stone 'moai' (statues), straw hats, shell necklaces, wood carvings and similar handicrafts.

Hotel Hanga Roa, the leading hotel, has 60 twin rooms (some triples). Facilities include room service, swimming pool, bar and lounge, and several shops. Hotel Hotu Matu'a has a bar and restaurant.

There are over 40 guest houses, including that of Rosita Cardinale. They are clean, have about six double or triple rooms and hot water. To experience the real island atmosphere, a stay at a guest house is recommended. Tariffs include meals. Larger establishments apply the 20 per cent government hotel tax.

There are several primitive, but interesting restaurants and night spots, such as 'Piditi' near the airport, and 'Toroko' adjacent to the fishermen's dock at Hanga Roa.

Islanders control local tours and can arrange excursions, 'curantos' (feasts and parties) and other activities. The largest firm is Mahina Tours but similar facilities are offered by Martin Rapu, Daniel Tepano, Mana Ika Aku Aku Tours and Archaeological Travel Service.

As it can get both cold and wet at some times of the year, some warm clothing and a raincoat are recommended. As clothing is expensive on the island, islanders are usually happy to trade clothing instead of cash for local artifacts. Artifact traders are at the airport to meet every plane and brisk business is done.

The authorities are strict about the export of genuine artifacts from the stone quarry sites, which is illegal without authority, and passenger baggage is usually inspected carefully before airport departure.

Entry formalities. For visitors staying less than three months, a current passport is required for most nationalities, as is a tourist visa. For further information contact the nearest Chilean Embassy or Consulate.

Airport tax. A tax of about $US5 is charged to visitors who make a stopover on the island on flights from Santiago.

Sightseeing. Visits are usually made to Ahu Tahai, a reconstructed ceremony centre where three ahus have been restored and where Ko Te Riku, the only standing moai with a red top-knot, can be seen. Work of reconstruction is continuing. During reconstruction of an 'ahu' at Anakena in 1978 under the supervision of the museum curator, Sergio Rapu Haoa, pieces of shaped white coral were discovered. It was found that they fitted into the eye sockets of the 'moai'.

They also discovered three layers of 'ahus', one on top of the other, coming from three civilisations.

Regarded as the leading archaeologist of Easter Island, Dr William Malloy, of the University of Wyoming, USA, died in 1978 and his ashes have been buried at Ahu Tahai on the island.

Other musts are: Akivi, where seven standing statues on the 'ahu' were restored in 1960; Rano Raraku, where the statues were quarried and where many still lie on the slopes; Togariki, which had the biggest 'ahu' of all and where 15 'moai' once stood, but which was destroyed by a tidal wave in 1960; Poike, where two factions, the Long Ears and the Short Ears, are supposed to have fought their last battle in which the Long Ears were virtually exterminated; the crater, reed-covered lake in the middle of Rano Kau; and Orongo ceremonial village where there is an area of rock outcroppings covered with petroglyphs in high relief. Anakena, a very beautiful beach and the site of the residence of the ancient kings, exhibits an extraordinary, well-preserved 'ahu' which was restored in 1978. Its statues have 'pukao' or top-knots of red volcanic tuff.

Federated States of Micronesia

The Federated States of Micronesia (FSM), associated with the USA in a compact of free association, occupy the major part of that group of Micronesian islands called the Carolines. There are four states: from west to east they are Yap, Truk, Pohnpei and Kosrae. The remaining part of the Caroline Islands forms the Republic of Palau (Belau). (See separate entry.) The FSM consists of hundreds of islands and atolls though only about 40 are of significant size and even several of these are unpopulated.

The state of Kosrae consists of one large island. The islands of the FSM extend from 0 deg to 14 deg N latitude and from 136 deg to 166 deg E longitude. Distance from east to west in the scattered FSM is over 2500 km. Geography is extremely varied, ranging from isolated reefs and atolls rising barely above sea level to dramatic peaks of several hundred metres on the high islands of Pohnpei and Kosrae. Total land area of the FSM is only 700.8 sq. km, with almost half of this taken up by the state of Pohnpei. Major islands in the FSM are: Pohnpei (345.4 sq. km, population 28,902), Kosrae (109.6 sq. km, population 6462), Yap (121.2 sq. km, population 10,948), Truk group (118 sq. km, population 46,159). After these the land area of individual islands rapidly decreases although population densities are high in many cases.

The FSM flag consists of four white stars (for the four states) on a pale blue field, and is based on the Trust Territory flag adopted by the UN in 1962.

Public holidays are mainly those of the US, with some specifically national ones added including: 10 May (Constitution Day), 12 July (Micronesian Day) and 25 October (United Nations Day).

THE PEOPLE. The people of the FSM are in the broad sense Micronesian (perhaps an even less useful term than Polynesian or Melanesian) and in a narrower sense Carolinian — an ethnic distinction recognised by the US Census. But local affinities rather than national or ethnic ones are strong and people are likely to consider themselves Yapese, Trukese, Pohnpeians, etc. As is the case with most other Pacific Islanders, the Carolinians are thought to have originated in South-East Asia. The remarkable colonial history of these islands, however, has resulted in degrees of acculturation from Spain, Germany, Japan and the US, a history reflected in personal names and language. Ancient Carolinian society was matrilineal, a form of organisation common throughout Micronesia. Social stratification was so pronounced that five of Yap's original nine social classes are still recognised today, despite the historical influences from outside. In 1985 the total population of the FSM was 91,440. In 1983 the crude birth rate averaged 23.8 per 1000 with the death rate 3.4 per 1000, but there are wide variations between states. In 1984 totals of 2601 live births and 242 deaths were registered.

Citizenship. FSM people are citizens of the Federated States of Micronesia, since the signing of the Compact of Free Association with the US. The first FSM passports were issued in late 1986.

Language. Carolinian languages are branches of the great Malayo-Polynesian (Austronesian) family, although there are dialectical variations from island to island. In their written form the languages use the Roman script, as do all Pacific Islands languages. English is the official language and is taught in all the schools but many of the older people can speak at least conversational Japanese.

Religion. The people of the FSM are overwhelmingly Christian, with Protestant and Catholic faiths in rough equilibrium although Kosrae is over 98 per cent Protestant (Congregationalist). The ubiquitous Church of Jesus Christ of Latter-day Saints is also represented, but in a small way, as are the Seventh Day Adventists, Jehovah's Witnesses and the Assembly of God. Despite outward appearances, traditional religious beliefs are still quite strong in some areas. The United Church Board of World Ministries maintains regional headquarters on Pohnpei, while the Catholic Vicariate of the Marshall and Caroline Islands is headquartered on Truk. There are no recent statistics

on religious affiliation available, but a de facto census in 1973 listed 50.1 per cent of the population as Roman Catholic, 47.4 per cent as Protestant and 0.2 per cent as traditional religion.

GOVERNMENT. The FSM is headed by a President elected from the 14-member National Congress of the Federated States of Micronesia. A vice-president is similarly elected, but cannot be from the same state. Capital of the congress is Pohnpei, but each of the four states (Pohnpei, Yap, Truk and Kosrae) elects its own legislature and governor and has executive, legislative and judicial branches. A national judicial branch is headed by a Chief Justice of the Supreme Court, and the national executive branch is composed of various departments headed by secretaries.

Like the other components of the Trust Territory, the FSM came into existence only after a protracted series of negotiations on

FEDERATED STATES OF MICRONESIA

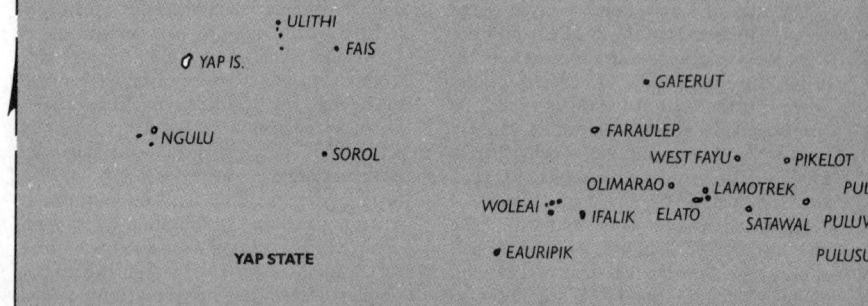

political status with various US administrations which began in 1969. Almost 20 years later, the negotiations were finalised and in late 1986 the Compact of Free Association, defining the political status of the FSM and its relationship with the USA, was implemented and the Trusteeship terminated by the UN Trusteeship Council.

JUSTICE. The Supreme Court of the Federated States of Micronesia was established pursuant to Article XI of the FSM Constitution. It became operational in 1981, with the appointment of Edward C. King as the first Chief Justice. The Court consists of a trial and an appellate division, with two judges now permanently assigned to the Court. Chief Justice King handles trials in Pohnpei and Kosrae and Associate Judge Richard Benson in Truk and Yap. When a decision is appealed, whichever judge did not hear the trial will sit with two designated judges on the appellate panel. All four states now have

their own state supreme courts certified and functioning.

Support services afforded the Justices of the FSM Supreme Court can be categorised as follows: (1) Chief Clerk of the Court: schedules the court calendar, prepares transcripts and statistics; (2) Administration: provides all administrative services required by the national judicial branch; and (3) Justice Ombudsmen: carry out traditional court functions as probation officer and also provide the essential service of keeping the FSM Supreme Court in touch with the local communities that the Court services. A Justice ombudsman has to be a citizen of the state where the case is heard and keeps the court informed of customs and traditions in that area.

At present there are 12 trial counsellors and 132 attorneys admitted to practice before the FSM Supreme Court. Since the inception of the Court in July 1981 until September 1985, cases filed and disposed of

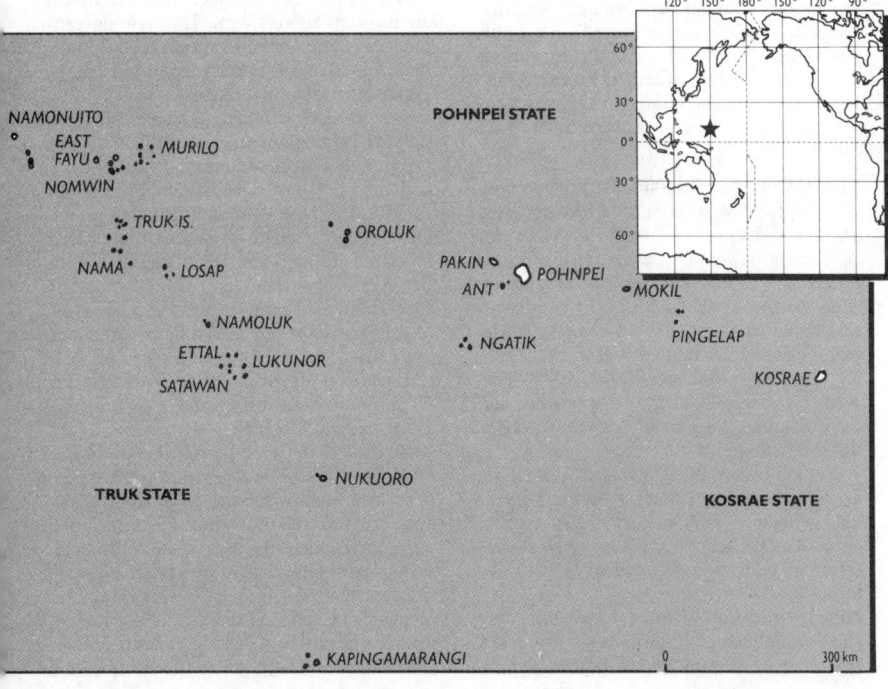

were as follows: civil cases — filed 390, disposed 313; criminal cases — filed 486, disposed 457; juvenile cases — filed 91, disposed 84.

Attorney-General. The office of the Attorney-General comprises four divisions: law, litigation, immigration and security and investigation. The divisions of law and litigation, through the Attorney-General, provide legal services to the President, his staff and to the departments and offices within the executive branch of the national government.

Public Defender. The Office of Public Defender is one of the major offices in the executive branch of the Government of the FSM. The Public Defender is a Presidential appointee and his appointment is subject to confirmation by the FSM National Congress. The office is responsible primarily to its clients. The Public Defender's executive office is in Pohnpei, with branch offices in the other states. There is at present a staff of 21 throughout the Public Defender system. The office is seen as playing a vital role in the protection of human rights and assuring that accused persons are accorded the rights guaranteed them under the FSM constitution.

Criminal cases represented by the Public Defender in 1985 amounted to 1992 throughout the FSM: 1916 of these were in state courts.

EDUCATION. The administrative responsibilities for education in the FSM are based on the Constitution, which provides for concurrent power between national and state governments. State governments are responsible for the actual provision of education, instruction at primary and secondary levels, planning and development and teacher training. The responsibility of the national government is essentially that of supporting and co-ordinating educational services throughout the nation.

Available enrolment statistics (for 1985) are as follows: elementary school enrolment (all schools), 23,636; secondary school enrolment (all schools), 4780; public expenditure on education per student in 1985 was $682.

Higher education. Until a decade ago, only small numbers of high school graduates from the FSM went on to post-secondary

education with scholarships. Since 1972 when Micronesia became eligible for US federal grants for post-secondary education in the US the number of FSM students enrolled in colleges and universities has risen sharply and now totals 1200. Annual current level of US support for students in post-secondary education on Guam, Hawaii or mainland US is estimated to be between $4 m and $5 m.

The College of Micronesia, established in 1972, maintains a Community College on Pohnpei, currently with 170 full-time students. In addition, there are numbers of part-time students in the four states. Courses in general business, education, liberal arts, home economics and marine science are offered.

HEALTH. With the emergence of the constitutional governments in Micronesia, all provisions related to the co-ordination, administration and delivery of health care services have been transferred to the new governments, leaving the Trust Territory Office of Health Services in a technical advisory status to them. The new governments — Republic of Palau (Belau), Republic of the Marshall Islands, and the FSM — remain the sole providers of comprehensive health services although religious missions provide varying amounts of medication and care for their own personnel. Private dental and medical practice exists on Pohnpei in the FSM. Physicians and dentists in the Government's health programme are often recruited through the US National Health Services Corps and the United Nations Development Programmes. A variety of health, nutrition and sanitation programmes are carried out under the auspices of such international organisations as World Health Organisation, South Pacific Commission, UNICEF and UNDP.

In 1984 there were four hospitals in the FSM (one in each state) with a total of 325 beds; two super-dispensaries (both in Truk) and 110 field dispensaries. Most facilities were operational. Diseases of the respiratory system and those caused by intestinal parasites are the most frequently reported. The incidence of venereal diseases is apparently low. Major causes of death are: heart disease (30 deaths in 1984); cancer (24 deaths) and tuberculosis (31 deaths). Suicide claimed the next largest group with 13 deaths.

Some 698 people are employed in the Division of Health Services, including 36 physicians, 227 nurses of various kinds and 13 dental officers.

As is the case elsewhere in Micronesia, water borne diseases, resulting from contaminated supplies, are a considerable problem in the FSM. In 1982 an outbreak of cholera in Truk State needed an additional $1.59 m in operational funds for its control. In 1985 people in the FSM served by a protected water supply and an excreta disposal system numbered only 2850. Such refinements are usually available only to housing areas for government employees, hospitals and to a few schools. Forty years after the establishment of the Trusteeship no unchlorinated water supplies, except those at the Kwajalein Missile Range in the Marshall Islands, can be considered safe for consumption.

THE LAND. Total land area of the FSM is 700.8 sq. km, scattered over hundreds of thousands of sq. km of ocean and distributed among hundreds of islands and islets. Land on the many coral islets is sparse and generally infertile — only coconuts and pandanus will grow without considerable effort, while land on the high volcanic islands, though fertile, is often steep and inaccessible. Agricultural productivity, therefore, is rather low, although in traditional times subsistence agriculture was the economic basis of society.

Population tends naturally to be concentrated on the larger high islands (Yap, Pohnpei, etc.), though some quite small islands are still supporting relatively large populations — Nama in Truk State, for example, has 1021 people on 0.7 sq. km of land. Many other small islands, however, no longer have populations and many of the very small ones never did. Distances between the main administrative centres of the states are great.

Significant peaks include Mt Finkol on Kosrae (629 m), Nahnalaud or Big Mountain (772 m) on Pohnpei and Mt Tonachau (229 m) on Moen island in Truk. On the high islands streams, originating in the tall mountains, are numerous and swift, and cascades and waterfalls are frequent and quite spectacular.

CLIMATE. The Caroline Islands are wet, though more so in the eastern than the western islands. Pohnpei receives rain on an average of 300 days each year, but most of it falls between March and December. The western islands are among the most cyclone prone parts of the Pacific. The 'dry' season tends to be brief — January to March is a generous estimate. From about November/ December to April/May the north-east trade winds prevail; for the rest of the year south-west winds bring frequent heavy rains. Temperature variations are slight — from about 24–30°C — and hours of daylight vary little throughout the year.

FLORA AND FAUNA. Vegetation varies from high island to low atoll, although some trees — coconut, breadfruit, pandanus — are common to both. The high islands often have mangrove swamps on the tidal flats, a surprise to visitors who expect every Pacific Island to be ringed by white sand beaches. There are few beaches on Pohnpei, for example; its attractions lie elsewhere. In the valleys of the high islands vegetation is of the dense tropical rainforest type. Land fauna is scant, in common with many other Pacific islands, though there are rats in impressive numbers. The variety of marine fauna almost makes up for this and includes numerous species of fish, crustaceans, bivalves and sea mammals such as porpoise. Whales are uncommon. The dugong occurs, although rarely, in the western Carolines.

Land tenure. Land use and ownership are to a great extent still governed by traditional systems. It is, therefore, not possible for non-Micronesians to buy land, although they may lease it from the traditional owners or the appropriate government agency.

PRIMARY PRODUCTION. Primary production in the FSM is low, for reasons which are not entirely clear. Critics of the US Trust Territory administration have accused it of imposing a dependency mentality upon the Micronesians which has resulted in the forsaking of traditional agricultural pursuits in favour of employment by the state or US handouts. Others have suggested that the scattered, fragmented nature of the islands makes a national agricultural programme difficult, if not impossible, to achieve. Certainly agricultural production statistics are not encouraging. There is only one agricultural commodity of any export consequence — copra, which is exported to Japan — although at various times bananas, betelnut and trochus shell have been exports. In fiscal year 1985 total FSM production of copra amounted to about 4700 tonnes, more than half of which came from Truk State. The copra industry is regulated by the Coconut Development Authority, which is also seeking ways to manufacture other products from the coconut tree.

Small farm enterprises include black pepper production and poultry egg raising, but no figures are available. In 1985 the FSM Development Bank approved loans amounting to $305,976 for 32 agricultural projects throughout the country.

Fishing. Management of the FSM's 200-mile marine economic zone is by the Micronesian Maritime Authority (MMA), which has a full-time staff of eight. Fisheries in the FSM are said to be in a state of flux due to a decrease in tuna prices and a general stagnation of worldwide markets. However, the MMA has concluded fishing agreements with Japan, Taiwan, Korea, Mexico and the US. In 1985 Japanese fishing fleets maintained 85 pole and line vessels and 32 purse seiners. Figures for local fishing in the FSM are incomplete, but in 1985 Yap State recorded local catches of 25.2 tonnes valued at $37,000, enough to halt fish imports and export small quantities.

TOURISM. Tourism in the FSM can be fairly said to be undeveloped, even though there are Offices of Tourism within each state and a number of hotels in the main centres. With the cessation of the Trusteeship and the relative paucity of natural resources, however, it is likely that more emphasis will be placed on tourism as a revenue earner. The FSM boasts a number of attractions for visitors not found elsewhere in the Pacific and although the infrastructure cannot at present support large numbers of tourists, there is evidence of a gradual increase in visitor numbers. Tourism is co-ordinated by the National Tourism Office which provides assistance to the state

governments on request.

Estimates of tourist expenditure per day vary between $60 and $100 depending on the state. Average length of stay is three to four days. In 1985 Yap State's 1316 visitors contributed $237,000 to local revenues.

MANUFACTURING. This aspect of the economy is even less developed than primary production, though development plans speak of increases in the manufacturing sector. Such activity as there is tends to be very small scale concentrating on 'those which utilize our natural and human resources'. These include coconut oil extraction, garment manufacture and soap making. There are plans for small canneries in at least one state. It is hoped that foreign investment will be able to boost the very limited manufacturing sector. Not always included in manufacturing data are traditional handicrafts which brought $1000 in export earnings in 1984.

OVERSEAS TRADE. Figures are available only from Yap State which in 1985 had exports amounting to $185,000 in value, $165,000 of which was in copra exports to Japan. In 1984 Yap imported goods to the total value of $3.6 million.

FINANCE. Funding for government operational support and capital improvement programmes in the FSM (and other Trust Territory countries) was derived from three major sources: (1) an annual grant provided from funding appropriated to the Secretary of the Interior of the US; (2) federal categorical grants provided on a matching or outright grant basis. In effect the Trust Territory was treated as a state of the US for participation in federal programmes; and (3) tax revenues levied by the government of the FSM.

In 1986 the Department of the Interior grant to the FSM was $38.76 million, compared with $40.34 million in 1985.

The termination of the Trusteeship and the implementation of the Compact of Free Association will result in more than $1.4 billion in US assistance to the FSM over a 15-year period.

Currency. Official currency is the US dollar.

Banking. FSM residents have access to banking institutions in Guam, Hawaii and mainland US in addition to branch banks in all the FSM states. The headquarters of the Bank of the FSM are in Pohnpei; its first branch opened in Kosrae in 1986. FSM citizens own a majority of shares.

FSM Development Bank. This is a statutory body chartered by the FSM Congress in 1979. It commenced business in 1982. Headquarters are in Pohnpei State, with branch offices in the other states. The Development Bank has the responsibility of mobilising available financial resources for development and providing medium and long-term loans and equity capital for high priority and financially sound projects in the FSM. The bank is managed by a board of directors consisting of seven members appointed by the President of the FSM. It has a staff of 17.

In fiscal year 1985 the bank's equity was $3.5 m, compared with $1.7 m in the previous year. As of September 1985 the bank's total loans were $3.6 million with real estate development accounting for $1.4 million of that figure, commercial projects for another $763,000.

TRANSPORT. International sea transport services in the FSM have stabilised with an average frequency of every 30 days from East Asia, the US West Coast and the South Pacfic to the major ports of Yap, Pohnpei, Kosrae and Truk. Carriers include Tokyo Senpaku Kaisha, Saipan Shipping Company, Palau Shipping Company, Orient Navigation Company and Nauru Pacific Line.

Road conditions are generally poor in the FSM, although improvements are constantly being made. The FSM's first five-year development plan acknowledges the need for infrastructural development and is devoting an average of over 50 per cent of plan funding in each of the four states to this purpose.

Major airports in all four states can accommodate 727 aircraft or those of similar size. International airports in all four states are serviced by Continental/Air Micronesia from Hawaii and Guam. Internal services are largely the province of Pacific Missionary Aviation.

COMMUNICATIONS. The FSM Telecommunications Corporation operates as the sole provider of all national and international telecommunication services. The Corpora-

tion has a station in each state, with headquarters in Pohnpei. Revenue collection from subscribers amounts to about $118,000 per month.

Post office. A national postal service was established in July 1983 and is an independent agency of the national government. The FSM issues its own postage stamps, designs of which are chosen for philatelic sales possibilities as well as relevance to national culture and history. There are post offices and/or agencies throughout the four states. In 1985 revenues derived from postage and philatelic sales exceeded $550,000.

Radio and TV. Estimates indicate that most homes in the FSM have radios and home videos. Each station broadcasts local and state news in both English and the local vernacular. Public announcements are also made in at least two languages. There are four state-operated radio stations and one which is privately owned. Yap State has the only state-run television station (WAAB-TV), while Pohnpei has a private television and FM radio station.

Newspapers. No private newspapaer exists in the FSM, although there are four official publications: the national government's *National Union* (in English); Yap State's *Mogethin* (in English); Truk State's *Us Me Aus* (in Trukese and English) and Kosrae State's newsletter (in Kosraean and English). Newspapers and magazines from the US and the South Pacific are widely circulated throughout the FSM.

WATER AND ELECTRICITY. Water supply in the FSM is plentiful on the high islands as a result of the many fast-flowing streams. On the low islands there is often an absence of ground water and water must be obtained from roof catchment. Throughout the FSM, however, water is considered to be of doubtful quality unless properly chlorinated.

Electricity is supplied by diesel-generation equipment, much of which is reaching the end of its service life and is being gradually replaced throughout the four states. During 1985, using funds made available through the US Department of the Interior, eight 2000 kW generators for the states of Pohnpei, Truk and Yap were purchased from a utility company in Canada. In Pohnpei a completely new power station is planned. Rates charged to consumers have tended to be below the cost of production and distribution, a situation not expected to endure.

In 1985 a US funded 1700 kW hydroelectric project on Pohnpei's Nanpil River was commenced. It is expected to produce 4,000,000 kW hours per year, a quarter of Pohnpei's needs. Power in the FSM is 110 volts.

MAJOR OFFICE HOLDERS
President:
  John R. Haglegam
Vice President:
  Hiroshi Ishmael
Chief Justice:
  Edward King
Governor of Truk:
  Erhart Aten
Chief Justice of Truk:
  Soukichy Fritz
Governor of Yap:
  John A. Mangefel
Chief Justice of Yap:
  John Tharangan
Governor of Pohnpei:
  Resio Moses
Presiding Judge of Pohnpei:
  Resio Moses
Presiding Judge of Pohnpei:
  Carl Kohler
Governor of Kosrae:
  Yosiwo George
Chief Judge:
  Harry H. Skilling

GOVERNMENT OFFICES AND DEPARTMENTS

FSM GOVERNMENT
Office of the President/Vice President, Kolonia, Pohnpei, FSM 96941; Tel: 228
Disaster Control Office, Kolonia, Pohnpei, FSM 96941; Tel: 822
Office of the Attorney General, Kolonia, Pohnpei, FSM 96941; Tel: 644/608
Office of Budget, Kolonia, Pohnpei, FSM 96941; Tel: 823
Office of Personnel, Kolonia, Pohnpei, FSM 96941; Tel: 642
Office of Public Defender, Kolonia, Pohnpei, FSM 96941; Tel: 648
Office of Public Information, Kolonia, Pohnpei, FSM 96041; Tel: 548

Office of Planning and Statistics, Kolonia, Pohnpei, FSM 96941; Tel: 820/821
Department of External Affairs, Kolonia, Pohnpei, FSM 96941; Tel: 641
Department of Resources and Development, Kolonia, Pohnpei, FSM 96941; Tel: 646
Department of Social Services, Kolonia, Pohnpei, FSM 96941; Tel: 647
Department of Finance/Administration, Kolonia, Pohnpei, FSM 96941; Tel: 640
Supreme Court, Kolonia, Pohnpei, FSM 96941; Tel: 357
FSM Congress, Kolonia, Pohnpei, FSM 96941; Tel: 337

FSM GOVERNMENT AGENCIES
Micronesian Maritime Authority, Kolonia, Pohnpei, FSM 96941; Tel: 700
FSM Coconut Development Authority, Kolonia, Pohnpei, FSM 96941; Tel: 892
FSM Development Bank, Kolonia, Pohnpei, FSM 96941; Tel: 840
FSM Telecommunication Corporation, Kolonia, Pohnpei, FSM 96941; Tel: 740
Office of Public Auditor, Kolonia, Pohnpei, FSM 96941; Tel: 863
FSM Banking Board, Kolonia, Pohnpei, FSM 96941; Tel: 701
FSM Post Master General, Kolonia, Pohnpei, FSM 96941; Tel: 615
College of Micronesia, Kolonia, Pohnpei, FSM 96941; Tel: 479
FSM Social Security, Kolonia, Pohnpei, FSM 96941; Tel: 706

FSM OVERSEAS OFFICES
FSM Washington Office, 706 G. St SE, Washington DC 20003; Tel: (202) 544-2640

KOSRAE STATE GOVERNMENT
Office of Governor/Lt Governor, Lelu, Kosrae, FSM 96944; Tel: 3002
Department of Public Affairs. Lelu, Kosrae, FSM 96944; Tel: 3009
Office Of Planning and Budget, Lelu, Kosrae, FSM 96944; Tel: 3170
Ofice of Employment and Labor Services, Lelu, Kosrae, FSM 96944; Tel: 3161
Department of Finance and Treasury, Lelu, Kosrae, FSM 96944; Tel: 3004
Department of the Attorney General, Lelu, Kosrae, FSM 96944; Tel: 3043
Department of Education, Lelu, Kosrae, FSM 96944; Tel: 3008

Department of Health Services, Lelu, Kosrae, FSM 96944; Tel: 3198
Department of Public Works, Lelu, Kosrae, FSM 96944; Tel: 3011
Department of Economic Development, Lelu, Kosrae, FSM 96944; Tel: 3044
Judiciary (Chief Judge), Lelu, Kosrae, FSM 96944; Tel: 3033
Kosrae State Legislature, Lelu, Kosrae, FSM 96944; Tel: 3177

POHNPEI STATE GOVERNMENT
Office of the Governor/Lt Governor, Kolonia, Pohnpei, FSM 96941; Tel: 235
Office of Legislative and Municipal Relations, Kolonia, Pohnpei, FSM 96941; Tel: 633
Office of Program and Budget, Kolonia, Pohnpei, FSM 96941; Tel: 238
Department of Administration, Kolonia, Pohnpei, FSM 96941; Tel: 634
Department of Education, Kolonia, Pohnpei, FSM 96941; Tel 102/103
Department of Community Services, Kolonia, Pohnpei, FSM 96941; Tel: 611
Department of Health Services, Kolonia, Pohnpei, FSM 96941; Tel: 215
Department of Conservation, Kolonia, Pohnpei, FSM 96941; Tel: 735
Department of Legal Affairs, Kolonia, Pohnpei, FSM 96941; Tel: 703
Judiciary, Kolonia, Pohnpei, FSM 96941; Tel: 353
Pohnpei State Legislature, Kolonia, Pohnpei, FSM 96941; Tel: 752
Community Action Agency (CCA), Kolonia, Pohnpei, FSM 96941; Tel: 575
Economic Development Authority, Kolonia, Pohnpei, FSM 96941; Tel: 775

TRUK STATE GOVERNMENT
Office of the Governor/Lt Governor, Moen, Truk, FSM 96940; Tel: 234
Office of Personnel, Moen, Truk, FSM 96940; Tel: 236
Office of Planning Office, Moen, Truk, FSM 96940; Tel: 237
Office of Property and Supply, Moen, Truk, FSM 96940; Tel: 247
Office of Attorney General, Moen, Truk, FSM 96940; Tel: 397
Department of Treasury, Moen, Truk, FSM 96940; Tel: 515
Department of Education, Moen, Truk, FSM 96940; Tel: 202

Department of Health Services, Moen, Truk, FSM 96940; Tel: 212
Department of Public Affairs, Moen, Truk, FSM 96940; Tel: 347
Department of Public Safety, Moen, Truk, FSM 96940; Tel: 223
Department of Resources and Development, Moen, Truk, FSM 96940; Tel: 755
Department of Public Works, Moen, Truk, FSM 96940; Tel: 785
Department of Transportation, Moen, Truk, FSM 96940; Tel: 718
Judiciary Branch, Moen, Truk, FSM 96940; Tel: 718
Truk State Legislature, Moen, Truk, FSM 96940; Tel: 668
Truk Housing Authority, Moen, Truk, FSM 96940; Tel: 665

YAP STATE GOVERNMENT
Office of the Governor/Lt Governor, Colonia, Yap, FSM 96943; Tel: 2108
Office of the General Attorney, Colonia, Yap, FSM 96943; Tel: 2106/2107
Office of Planning, Budget & Statistics, Colonia, Yap, FSM 96943; Tel: 2167
Department of Administrative Services, Colonia, Yap, FSM 96943; Tel: 2270
Department of Public Affairs, Colonia, Yap, FSM 96943; Tel: 2168
Department of Resources and Development, Colonia, Yap, FSM 96943; Tel:2182
Department of Health Services, Colonia, Yap, FSM 96943; Tel: 2110/2115
Department of Public Utilities and Contracts, Colonia, Yap, FSM 96943; Tel: 2175
Department of Education, Colonia, Yap, FSM 96943; Tel: 2150
Office of Land Commission, Colonia, Yap, FSM 96943; Tel: 2164
Yap State Court, Colonia, Yap, FSM 96943; Tel: 2162
Yap State Legislature, Colonia, Yap, FSM 96943; Tel: 2260

HISTORY. The early history of the group now known as the Federated States of Micronesia is inseparable from that of the Caroline Islands generally, while its development from 1947 to the early 1980s is closely associated with the rest of the Trust Territory of the Pacific Islands. This account, therefore, makes reference to islands in Micronesia other than those which now comprise the Federated States. For the sake of convenience, much of the history of the Caroline Islands contained in the section on Palau is also given here.

From the little that is yet known of the prehistory of the Caroline Islands, it appears that some parts of the archipelago have been inhabited for more than 4000 years. The chief archaeological work carried out so far has been in Palau, Yap, Pohnpei and the Polynesian outlier, Nukuoro but there has been considerably more work done in recent years. Not all the results have been published, or they are still at the preliminary stage. Excavations in Palau have revealed extensive agricultural terraces, trade beads, pottery and shell artifacts resembling those of the Marianas. The trade beads indicate links with South-East Asia dating back some 200 years before the Christian era. On Yap two types of pottery have been discovered, the earlier of which is thought to have been in use from at least the second century to 847. On Pohnpei stone structures with walled and unwalled burial sites have been investigated as well as stone and coral platforms. The chief artifacts found have been of shell. Radio-carbon dates obtained have ranged from AD 1180 to 1430. At Nukuoro, excavations have suggested human occupation since about AD 1300. Early in 1979, an ancient living site was found on Mt Tonachau overlooking Truk Airport on Moen. Tradition has it that the great leaders Soukachaw and Souwooniiras had a meeting-house on the mountain.

The history of European contact with the Carolines has much in common with that of the Marshalls. After some of the islands had been discovered by the first European navigators to cross the Pacific in the 16th century, the archipelago remained largely unvisited until the end of the 18th century. Ulithi and Fais, in the north-western corner of the group, are thought to have been the first islands to be discovered, as their description seems to match that of the Spanish explorer Villalobos in 1543. On his way from Mexico to the Philippines, Villalobos called at two islands which he named Matelotes (Sailors) and Arrecifes (Reefs).

Galleon trade. After the galleon trade between Acapulco and Manila began in the mid-1560s, the captains of the galleons were instructed to cross the Pacific from east to west in the latitude of the Mariana Islands and they thus avoided both the Marshalls and Carolines. However, occasionally a galleon would be driven out of its way and some new island would be discovered. In 1686, Francisco Lazeano, commanding a westbound galleon, chanced on the high island of Yap, which he called La Carolina, after Charles II, the Spanish king of the time. The name was later applied to the archipelago as a whole. Another island, Faraulep, was discovered by a Manila ship in 1696. It was at about that time that the Spaniards were also made aware of the existence of the Carolines by the arrival of islanders in the Philippines and Guam who had drifted from there in storms. In 1710, the Spaniards made an exploratory voyage to the archipelago which resulted in the discovery of Palau and Sonsorol. Two years later, a second ship went to Palau and Ulithi; and in 1731 yet another Spanish ship went to Ulithi with a party of missionaries headed by Juan Antonio Cantova. Although Cantova had taken a close interest in the welfare of some Carolinians who had drifted to Guam several years earlier, he and his party were murdered within three months, apparently in retaliation for some imagined misdeeds. This setback dissuaded the Spaniards from any further efforts to Christianise the Carolines for the time being.

Wreck of the _Antelope_. In 1783, an event occurred which was to bring the Palau islands to the notice of people in Europe for the first time. This was the wreck of the East India Company ship _Antelope_ at Palau, and the subsequent escape of the crew to the Philippines in a much smaller vessel which they had built. The crew took with them the second son of the island's principal chief — a young man of 20 who eventually reached London where he was much feted as Prince Lee Boo of the Pelew Islands. A book compiled by George Keate from a journal kept by the _Antelope_'s commander, Captain Henry Wilson, was one of the most popular books on the Pacific of the late 18th century.

A few British ships sailing to China from New South Wales began passing through the Carolines in the 1790s. At about the same time, an occasional Spanish ship also ventured there en route from the Philippines to Peru. Almost every voyage resulted in the discovery of new islands. Captain James Wilson of the *Duff* discovered Satawal, Lamotrek, Elato, Ifaluk and Woleai in 1797. Juan Ibargoitia discovered Pulusuk, Pulawat and Oran in 1800, and his countryman, Juan Baptiste Monteverde, added Nukuoro to the charts in 1806. Meanwhile, in 1804, Luis de Torres, vice-governor of Guam, paid a visit to several of the Carolines in the American ship *Maria* of Boston.

Trading posts. A surveying voyage by the French exploring vessel *Coquille* under Captain L. I. Duperrey in 1824 greatly increased European knowledge of the Carolines; and the Russian explorer Lutke in the ship *Seniavine* added further details to the charts in 1828. At about this time, American whalers and traders began frequenting the archipelago; and by the middle of the century the high islands of Palau, Yap, Pohnpei and Kusaie (now Kosrae) were all known. However, evangelists' visits to Truk were uncommon until the 1880s. Protestant missions were established on Pohnpei and Kosrae by American evangelists in 1852; and in the next few years British, American and German companies established trading posts there and elsewhere and became rivals in the copra trade. One of the leading figures was David O'Keefe, an American, who built up a trading empire on Yap.

In 1869, Germany acquired 1215 ha on Yap for use as a way station between Samoa and Cochin to serve as a centre for her Caroline-Marshalls-Marianas trade. Later, Germany's increased presence in the area was seen by Spain as a threat to her interests in the Philippines. In 1873, Spain demanded that all merchant ships bound for the Carolines should stop in the Philippines to receive permission to trade there and to pay customs and licensing fees for the privilege. The Germans refused to comply, and Britain later took Germany's side. Both nations declared that they did not recognise Spanish sovereignty over the Carolines because the islands had never been occupied by Spain.

Spanish sovereignty. In 1885, Spain sent a warship to take possession of Yap. But the Germans anticipated it and ran up the flag first. When the Germans also occupied Truk, Pohnpei, Kosrae and some of the lesser islands, Spain protested, but later agreed that Pope Leo XIII should arbitrate in the matter. On 22 October 1885, the Pope declared in favour of Spain; but Germany was given liberty to trade and fish in the area, and to establish settlements and coaling stations. Spain thus gained sovereignty over the archipelago with all the attendant expenses and responsibilities, while Germany was given the privileges without responsibilities.

In 1886, Spain sent two warships to the Carolines to raise the flag and bring the islands under the control of the Philippines government. Pohnpei was made the administrative centre and an agency of the administration was opened at Yap. At the same time, Capuchin priests established missions and schools in Yap, Pohnpei and Palau. The arrival of the Spaniards at Yap produced little change; but difficulties arose on Pohnpei. A Protestant missionary, E. T. Doane, was arrested and sent to Manila in June 1887; native Protestant teachers were removed; and the islanders generally were forced to work like convicts. In an uprising against the Spaniards, the governor and some of his men were killed and the priests fled. Three Spanish warships later called at Pohnpei and arrested a few islanders, but on being tried in Manila they were acquitted. Another party of Spaniards was killed on Pohnpei in 1890. When news of this reached Madrid, a punitive expedition was sent to the island. But the transport vessel carrying the Spanish troops ran aground on a reef and the Pohnpeians killed 1500 men.

During the Spanish–American war in 1898, Germany made a secret provisional agreement with Spain whereby it secured a lien on Kosrae, Pohnpei and Yap in any future disposal of Spain's insular possessions. Later that year, Spain agreed to give Germany the right to purchase all the Caroline and Mariana Islands, other than Guam, which the Americans had captured. A German – Spanish treaty of 12 February 1899 transferred the Carolines and Marianas to Germany for 25 million pesetas.

German administration. With the establishment of German administration in the Carolines, German Catholic missionaries arrived to replace the Spanish Capuchins, and

German Protestants moved into the islands where the American Protestants had been working. The Germans governed the eastern Carolines from Pohnpei and the western Carolines, including Palau, from Yap. The Germans introduced strict sanitary measures to control epidemics of diseases the islanders had no immunity to. By 1900 the pre-contact population of Palau of perhaps 40,000 had dropped to 4000. Relations between the islanders and the German administration were mainly peaceful. However, in 1910, a German overseer was killed after striking an islander with a whip, and when the governor hastened out to restore order he was shot dead. The ringleaders in this incident were later executed and 200 islanders were deported to Angaur to work in the phosphate deposits.

Japanese administration. The Japanese, who had had commercial interests in the Carolines from 1893 onwards, were quick to occupy the islands in World War I. Having declared war on Germany on 23 August 1914, the Japanese captured Yap on 7 October, and less than three weeks later all islands in the Carolines were under their control. The islands were mandated to Japan by the League of Nations in 1921 and administered from 1922 as an integral part of the Japanese empire. Administrative headquarters were at Koror, a small island off Babelthuap, and there were district offices at Yap, Truk and Pohnpei. Following the arrival of the Japanese civilian administrators, Spanish Jesuit missionaries replaced the German Catholics and pastors from the Congregational Church of Japan replaced the German Protestants.

As in the other islands of its Micronesian territory, Japanese policy was to develop the resources of the Carolines to the full. Japanese immigration was encouraged. In Palau, the biggest centre of Japanese interest, there were more than 25,000 Japanese civilians in 1935, four times as many as the local population of the group. The Japanese introduced modern conveniences such as electricity, sewerage and good roads, and improved the standard of living. Harbour facilities were developed in Palau; production was stepped up from the Angaur phosphate deposits; the copra industry was expanded; and the growing of tapioca, rice and oil palms was introduced to some

islands. After Japan withdrew from the League of Nations in 1935, Palau and Truk were developed for military purposes and other islands were fortified. The islands became a closed military area. When Japan entered World War II, Palau was used as a base to attack the Philippines and the Netherlands East Indies, and Truk was a key to the Japanese thrust into the South Pacific.

World War II. American fleet aircraft attacked Truk early in 1944 and destroyed 23 ships and 201 planes at a cost of 17 American planes. However Ulithi Atoll was the only island in the Carolines to be occupied by the Americans before the Japanese surrendered in September 1945. After the Caroline Islands became part of the United States Trust Territory of the Pacific Islands in 1947, the archipelago was divided into four districts — Palau, Yap, Truk and Pohnpei — with headquarters for each district on the islands named. Kosrae, which was a sub-district of Pohnpei, became a separate district in 1977. The five districts developed into separate entities of today through the constitutional developments described below.

Trust Territory. The Caroline Islands, like the rest of Micronesia, remained under US military occupation for two years after the war. In 1947 the United Nations, responding to considerable pressure from the US, agreed to create the only Trusteeship based on strategic factors. Thus was born the United Nations Trust Territory of the Pacific Islands, to be administered by the US. The legal status of the Territory was based on the Trusteeship Agreement between the US and the UN Security Council which came into force on 18 July 1947. In the view of the Trusteeship's many critics, Micronesia became little more than a colony of the US for a period of over 30 years.

The US President delegated authority for the civil administration of the territory to the Secretary of the Navy on an interim basis. Subsequently, Admiral Louis E. Denfeld was commissioned as the first US High Commissioner of the Trust Territory (with headquarters in Hawaii) and Rear-Admiral Carleton H. Wright was appointed Deputy High Commissioner (with headquarters in Guam). On 1 July 1951 adminitration of the territory passed from the Navy to the US Department of the Interior and Mr Elbert

D. Thomas became the first civilian high commissioner. But in 1953 all islands in the Marianas, except Rota, were returned to the control of the Navy Department for a special security purpose. This situation prevailed until mid-1962 when control reverted to the Department of the Interior and the Northern Marianas became the Mariana Islands District of the Trust Territory. At the same time headquarters for the entire territory were transferred from Guam to Saipan. Beside the Mariana Islands, five other districts were established — Palau, Yap, Truk and Pohnpei (Carolines) and the Marshall Islands.

Congress of Micronesia. The Micronesians were given a voice in their own government in January 1965 when the first elections were held for a bicameral Congress of Micronesia, consisting of a House of Representatives and a Senate. The Congress held its first meeting in the following July. In 1967, the Congress established a Future Political Status Commission, comprising six of its members (later increased to 10), to investigate ways in which the territory might develop politically. The commission visited Washington and Puerto Rico in 1968 and American and Western Samoa, Fiji and Papua New Guinea in 1969, besides studying the political systems in the Cook Islands and Okinawa. When it eventually reported to the Congress of Micronesia, the commission recommended that the territory should either become a self-governing state in free association with the US, or it should have complete independence. The US, for its part, offered the territory commonwealth status, like that of Puerto Rico. Talks between US representatives and the commission in 1970 and 1971 resulted in impasse. But in 1972 there was a breakthrough when the US agreed to guarantee the four basic requirements of the Micronesians. These were: the right of self-determination; the right to decide their own constitution and laws; the right to control their own land; and the right, unilaterally, to terminate any compact with the US. However, the 1972 negotiations did not cover the future status of the Marianas which, it was agreed, should be decided through direct dialogue between Marianas leaders and the US.

Northern Marianas opts out. From the beginning of the negotiations the people of the Northern Marianas had made known their long-standing desire to integrate permanently with the US and become US citizens. In 1972, after it became obvious that the different future political status aspirations of the people of the Northern Marianas and the remaining peoples of the Trust Territory were irreconcilable, the elected representatives of the Northern Marianas and the US began separate negotiations for territorial status.

Those negotiations were completed in 1975 and resulted in the 'Covenant to Establish a Commonwealth of the Northern Marianas in Political Union with the United States'. The covenant was approved by the people of the Northern Marianas in a United Nations-observed plebiscite on 17 June 1975 by a margin of 79 per cent and was subsequently approved by the US Congress. A separate constitution and government were proclaimed on 9 January 1978.

Separate states emerge. The negotiations for free association continued throughout the 1970s under three American administrations and were based on principles put forward by the Micronesian negotiators. In 1978, as the result of action by the remaining districts of the Trust Territory on a draft constitution for a unified Micronesia, three separate political groupings emerged: Palau, the Marshall Islands, and the Federated States of Micronesia (FSM).

The US had agreed to respect the outcome of the constitutional referendum and therefore negotiated with each of them for a free association relationship, the provisions of which would be set forth in a single Compact of Free Association.

Meanwhile the Congress of Micronesia, which had been elected in July 1965, fell apart when it became obvious that there would be no unified Micronesia.

The Compact and several of its related agreements were initialed, but not signed, by the US Government and by the governments of Palau, the Marshall Islands and the Federated States of Micronesia in October and November 1980. By this time each of the three groups had approved a locally enacted Constitution. Constitutional governments were installed in the Marshall Islands and the Federated States of Micronesia on 1 and 10 May 1979, respectively, and in Palau on 1 January 1981.

The 13 years of negotiations were concluded with the signature of the Compact and its related documents by the US and the Marshall Islands on 30 May 1982, Palau on 26 August 1982 and the Federated States of Micronesia on 1 October 1982. A plebiscite held in the Federated States the following year gave the Compact overwhelming approval, although the Trusteeship was not terminated in the Federated States until 1986.

Further information. Micronesian Archaeological Survey, *The European Discovery of Kosrae Island* (Saipan, 1982). David Lobby, *The Demystification of Yap* (Chicago, 1976). John L. Fischer, *The Eastern Carolines* (New Haven, 1970). See also book listings for Palau and the Marshall Islands.

FEDERATED STATES
OF MICRONESIA IN DETAIL

There are four states — Yap, Truk, Pohnpei and Kosrae.

Yap State consists of nine inhabited atolls, two single islands and four normally uninhabited islands and atolls. They are scattered over a distance of about 1120 km.

Yap is a group of four islands (Yap, Map, Rumung, Gagil-Tomil), separated by narrow channels. It is hilly and covered with magnificent forests of coconut and areca palms, bamboos and crotons, and is one of the most beautiful and picturesque of the Caroline Islands. Although all tropical fruits and vegetables are grown there is mainly a subsistence economy augmented by some copra production. The main centre of the State, Colonia, is located on Yap, which has a land area of about 100 sq. km. The combined land area of the outer islands is only 21 sq. km. Most people live on Yap, although there is population scattered thoughout the islands.

Yap is known as 'the land of grass skirts and stone money'. The women prefer their bulky grass skirts, although Western clothing is now worn when visiting the main centres. Betel-chewing is widespread.

The famous stone money — discs, some of them very large, hewn out of coral stone with holes through their centres — were brought by sea from Palau, and represent hoarded wealth.

The Germans built stone paths, causeways and retaining walls around these islands. They also dug the Tageren canal, which bisects the main island in the north-east.

The Americans cleared Yap harbour of coral heads, so seaplanes could use it. Roads extended several kilometres north of Colonia along the east coast of the main island and are being improved continuously.

Colonia is not to be confused with Kolonia, FSM headquarters in Pohnpei.

Yap Island is in the north-west section of the State. Highest point is Mt Tabiwol (178 m) in the north-centre of the main island. Southwards, about 200 km from Yap, lies Ngulu Atoll (a string of 12 islets, some inhabited).

North-east of Yap are Ulithi (with nearly 40 islets, it has the largest land area of any atoll in the Carolines — 8 sq. km) and Fais, south-east of Ulithi, an inhabited raised atoll with some phosphate deposits. Sorol, with five other islets in an elongated grouping of two clusters is well south of Ulithi. The only island in Yap captured by the Americans before the surrender of Japan in 1945 was Ulithi which subsequently was used by Allied naval forces as a staging area.

Although in pre-European times the peoples of Ulithi and Woleai were vassals of the Yapese, they differ in several respects, including language. The atoll people are generally lighter skinned and look more like Polynesians.

These atolls, like all of Yap State, are subject to typhoons and severe storms.

Between Sorol and the boundary of Truk State are a dozen small groups of atolls and islets, the only one of importance being Woleai.

Truk State, about 1440 km east of Yap, lies roughly in the centre of the long, east-west chain of the Caroline Islands. It consists of 15 island groups with a total land area of 118 sq. km scattered over an ocean area some 480 km by 960 km.

Truk proper is a complex group composed of 14 mountainous islands of volcanic origin, with a combined area of 72 sq. km, surrounded by a great coral ring which forms a lagoon of over 2000 sq. km. The outer islands of the State are all low islands or atolls.

Moen, Tol, Dublon, Fefan and Uman are

the most populous islands of Truk group. State headquarters is on Moen Island.

According to some authorities the Trukese acted as predators on Polynesians who moved along this corridor and into Polynesia proper. The first European sighting is credited to Alvaro Saavedra in 1528. The Dublon lagoon did not become known until the early 19th century when the navigator Dublon visited it in 1814. Duperry mapped the lagoon island of Truk in 1824, but Dumont d'Urville, 14 years later, was the most thorough explorer of Truk.

After the Germans acquired the area they established trading stations and encouraged the people to plant more coconuts and produce more copra. The Japanese who followed invested large sums in commercial fisheries and plant for drying the fish. Early in World War II there were 35,000 Japanese (including Okinawans) on Truk.

The Japanese chief port and administrative centre was on the eastern side of Dublon. The modern headquarters is on Moen.

Most people live in small villages scattered along the shores of all the green islands, which are in an area about 48 km by 19 km.

The most northerly atoll of the district is triangular Namonuito (the world's second largest atoll), with 10 small islets. Eastwards lie East Fayu and the Hall Islands (Nomwin and Murilo).

Westwards from Truk are Pulap and Puluwat; while directly south is Kuop (Royalist) Atoll, with its four islets. Continuing south are Nama, a single low island and Losap, a small atoll with a narrow reef. Laol, Pis and Talap, the largest of its eight islets, are inhabited.

To the south-east, near the State boundary, are Namoluk Atol (triangular, with a reef opening in the south-east) and the Mortlock (or Namoi) islands. They consist of some 100 islands arranged in three groups — Etal, Lukunor and Satawan.

Pohnpei State consists of the high volcanic island of Pohnpei and eight atolls.

Pohnpei, the main island, is surrounded by a barrier reef and by more than 25 small islands, half of them volcanic.

It is 19 km long and 37.6 km wide with Mt Totolom (791 m) being the highest peak.

Kolonia is the main town and also headquarters of the FSM government. It has a good airport and harbour close by. There are building relics of both Spanish and German times in the town.

This island is fertile and in places very beautiful, with luxuriant forest covering the slopes that rise from the beaches to the mountain tops. There are many freshwater streams, some of considerable dimensions. The people live on the coastal lands — the interior is practically uninhabited.

In early times Pohnpei was ruled by the Saudeleurs, who lived on Nan Madol, a group of 92 artificial islets spread over 60 ha of reef flat of the south-east coast of the island. Ruins of the canals, temples and walls, built with enormous crystals of basaltic rock may still be seen and are of considerable interest to visitors. They are reached by boat at high tide.

German traders operated in Pohnpei while it was still nominally Spanish, and during this time Protestant missionaries also established themselves. However, after the Papal decision in favour of Spanish sovereignty, the Spanish built a walled town in the Bay of Ascension (Kolonia) and dislodged the Protestants. The town was named Kolonia by the Germans who reorganised the copra industry.

Later, the Japanese had a manioc flour-processing plant at Metalanim and planted sugar cane in the hitherto unused upland. A sugar mill was completed just before World War II and the cane was used to make alcohol for military use.

Near Pohnpei are the small islands known as the Ants, and Pakin Groups and Ngatik (or Raven's Island). The Ants, 19 km west of Pohnpei, consists of two large and 12 small islands. Pohnpei, Ant and Pakin are collectively known as Senyavin Islands after the *Senjanin* in which Lutke, a Russian, surveyed the Carolines in 1828.

Oroluk, isolated in the north-west of the state, has a large lagoon but its islets are very small. Except for a handful of people on Oroluk island in the atoll's north-west corner, the atoll is uninhabited.

About 160 km south-east of Pohnpei is the Mokil Group — Urak, Manton and Mokil. There are several hundred on these islands, and the main village is on Mokil. The islands, though small, are well-wooded and very beautiful.

South-east from the Mokils is the Pingelap group — three small islands (Pingelap, Takai and Tagulu) close together on the one reef. The land area is about 715 ha and population is dense.

Kapingamarangi and Nukuoro, two isolated atolls in the south-west corner of Pohnpei State, are inhabited by people whose physique, language and culture are Polynesian.

Kapingamarangi (known also as Greenwich) is 1 deg north of the equator, on 154 deg E longitude; it has about 30 islets, all on the east of the pear-shaped atoll. The population of a few hundred is mostly confined to the tiny islet of Touhou, although a few people live on Werua and Taringa, flanking islets separated by narrow water channels.

Three hundred and twenty kilometres to the north-east is Nukuoro Atoll, on 155 deg E longitude. It is nearly circular, with a completely enclosed reef, and has 40 islets, on each side except the west.

Kosrae State, formerly known as Kusaie, is the most easterly state in the FSM. It is one of the most beautiful islands in the Pacific. It has an area of 109.6 sq. km and is mountainous and broken in the interior, but possesses four good harbours — Okat in the north-west and Lelu on the east coast and Taf and Utwe in the south. It is forest-clad, well-watered and is so fertile that almost any tropical product can be grown there. It is noted for valuable timbers which are used for shipbuilding and similar work. The large population of pre-European discovery times, dwindled to 200 by 1880. It was 5588 at the 1980 US Census, and increasing thanks to the provision of an airstrip and development following the Compact of Free Association arrangements.

More than half the population is under the age of 18.

Highest peak, Mt Crozer or Fenkol (634 m), is near the centre of the island; others are Matanti (583 m) on the north-east, Tafeayat and Wakapp. A fringing reef surrounds and is narrow and close to the shore in places.

The four main villages of Takunsak, Lelu Malem and Utwe are placed around the circumference of the island and connected by a single unpaved road. Lelu is on an island on the north-east coast attached to the mainland by the reef. There are four municipalities, but the Lelu area is the main centre.

The charm of the life on Kosrae has been described by well-known Pacific writers including Louis Becke. With others, he added much to the atmosphere of romance which surrounded Pacific islands in the early part of the 20th century. The harbour of Lelu was once a notorious rendezvous for American whaling ships and wild orgies took place there among the natives. Lelu was also notorious in 1874 as the base of 'Bully' Hayes, who was one of the last of the Pacific Ocean buccaneers. Hayes lost his vessel on the reefs in this vicinity, and settled in Kosrae with his swashbuckling crew of islanders.

Stone ruins similar to those of Nan Madol, in Pohnpei, are to be found at Lelu, but in a worse state of preservation.

The last few years have accelerated changes on Kosrae as returning youths, improved education, and closer contact with outsiders bring new ideas.

Regular air services by small aircraft connect Kosrae with Pohnpei and a larger airstrip built in 1983 permits bigger aircraft to land on more direct flights.

FOR THE TOURIST. Tourist facilities in the FSM are minimal, although since the states have few economic resources, tourism is a significant part of development. Despite the relative lack of sophisticated hotels and restaurants, the FSM contains a number of 'attractions' for visitors which are quite distinctive. Chief among these are the ruins of Nan Madol in Pohnpei, a complex of the structural remains of a civilisation which is said to have flourished about the 13th and 14th centuries. It is on the eastern side of Pohnpei, built on and among some 90 artificial islands. Tours from Kolonia can be arranged, but usually these take in other features of Pohnpei besides Nan Madol.

Elsewhere in the FSM, Truk is well-known to the international diving fraternity for its splendid lagoon, additionally remarkable for the number of sunken Japanese ships it contains. Yap, probably the most tourist-inclined of the four states, is best known for its stone money; huge circular carved pieces of limestone which were obtained from Palau and signified accumulated wealth in traditional times.

Travellers to the FSM must begin their journey in Guam or Honolulu. From these ports, Continental/Air Micronesia has services to Truk, Pohnpei, Yap and now Kosrae, following the completion of Kosrae's new runway. The outer islands of the FSM are served by 10-seaters operated by Pacific Missionary Aviation.

Entry formalities. US citizens are required to produce proof of citizenship as well as return or onward tickets. Non-citizens of the US must possess a valid passport and a US visa. Visitors who wish to remain longer than 30 days must obtain an entry permit in advance from the Chief of Immigration, Kolonia, Pohnpei, FSM 96941.

Further details may be obtained from the FSM Public Information Office, Kolonia, Pohnpei, FSM 96941.

ACCOMMODATION
YAP STATE

Rai View Hotel: 10 rooms, some with private facilities, a/c, some TV, bar, restaurant, tours arranged, PO Box 130, Colonia, Yap, FSM 96943. Tel. 2279, Telex 7296857 WAAB.

Esa Hotel: 16 a/c rooms, private facilities, restaurant, tours arranged. PO Box 141, Colonia, Yap, FSM 96943.

TRUK STATE

Truk Continental Hotel: a/c rooms with private facilities, restaurant. PO Box 340, Moen, Truk, FSM 96942.

Christopher Inn: rooms with fan or a/c, private facilities, bar, restaurant, conference room, car rental, tours arranged. PO Box 37, Truk, FSM 96942. Tel. 652.

POHNPEI STATE

Cliff Rainbow Hotel: a/c rooms, private facilities, bar, restaurant, tours arranged. PO Box 96, Kolonia, Pohnpei, FSM 96941. Tel. 415.

Palm Terrace Hotel: a/c rooms, TV, bar, restaurant, rental cars, tours arranged. PO Box 310, Pohnpei, FSM 96941. Tel. 119/392, Telex 7296811.

Village Hotel: 10 km from Kolonia at Uh, bungalow units, private facilities, scuba diving arranged. PO Box 339, Pohnpei, FSM 96941.

Ifumi Hotel: PO Box 811, Kolonia, Pohnpei, FSM 96941. Tel. 382.

Hotel Pohnpei: PO Box 430, Kolonia, Pohnpei, FSM 96941. Tel. 330.

KOSRAE STATE

Sandy Beach Hotel: at Tafunsak, 2 km from airport, cottages on beach, private facilities, refrig. in units, car rental. PO Box 6, Tafunsak, Kosrae, FSM 96944.

S. S. Hotel: at Tofol on east coast, 4 rooms with shared facilities. PO Box 62, Tofol, Kosrae, FSM 96944. Tel. 3076.

Skilling's Hotel: at Tofol on east coast. PO Box 296, Lelu, Kosrae, FSM 96944.

Noda Inn: at Lelu on east coast, 4 rooms, kitchen facilities. PO Box 4, Lelu, Kosrae, FSM 96944.

Fiji

Fiji became a republic on 7 October 1987. Some authorities on Fiji say there are 320 islands in the Fiji archipelago (18,376 sq. km), but others say this figure does not include the many islets, some of them in rivers. One list of names of islands in Fiji is said to contain almost 1000 names (not counting alternatives), and a more accurate figure of islands may be 800.

The group is located between 15 and 22 deg S latitude and 177 deg W and 175 deg E longitude. The capital, Suva, is on Viti Levu and is about 3160 km north-east of Sydney and 2120 km north of Auckland. Population of the group at the August, 1986 Census was 715,375. Local time is 12 hours ahead of GMT.

Fiji's first national flag, flown for the first time on Independence Day, 10 October 1970, consisted of the Union Flag of Britain in the top lefthand corner and the shield with the Fiji Coat of Arms in the fly, all on a light blue background. Ensigns flown on vessels were similar but with varying backgrounds — government ships with dark blue, merchant ships red and naval squadron white. The Governor-General's flag was the dark blue Commonwealth flag with a centre crest of a crown with lion and the word 'Fiji' below the crest. The National Anthem, by Michael Prescott of Suva, was *God Bless Fiji*, which begins 'Blessing grant, oh God of Nations, on the Isles of Fiji'. A new anthem and national flag are to be selected from entries to a competition held by the Government. The competition apparently did not consider the currency, which features the British monarch on both notes and coins. The currency is the Fiji dollar, divided into 100 cents.

POPULATION. The indigenous Fijians are racially classed as Melanesians but they have a considerable admixture of Polynesian blood. At the time the first Europeans arrived in Fiji, this Polynesian influence was greater in the Lau Islands (nearest to Tonga) and on the windward sides of the largest islands, while those people in the interiors of the large islands were more purely Melanesian.

The Fijians are outnumbered by the Indians, the first of whom came from India as indentured labourers in 1879. The indenture system was abandoned in 1916 but by then 40,000 elected to remain as free settlers, and they have long since become part of the community as farmers, business or professional men, public servants, clerical workers, transport workers, etc.

The Europeans came first to Fiji in the early 19th century in search of sandalwood. They were followed by missionaries and by settlers who wanted land and trade.

Many of the 'other islanders' who now show up in the census figures are people such as the Banabans who originally came from Ocean Island and settled on Rabi Island, which was purchased for them before World War II; or the people from Kioa Island where several hundred Ellice Islanders have been resettled. The people of Rotuma, which became a dependency of Fiji in 1881, are Polynesian.

The Rotuman population in 1986 was more than 8000, with more than half of them living in Fiji proper, the majority of these being in the Greater Suva area.

The Chinese were comparative latecomers to Fiji, the first census to record them being in 1911 when there were 305, with males

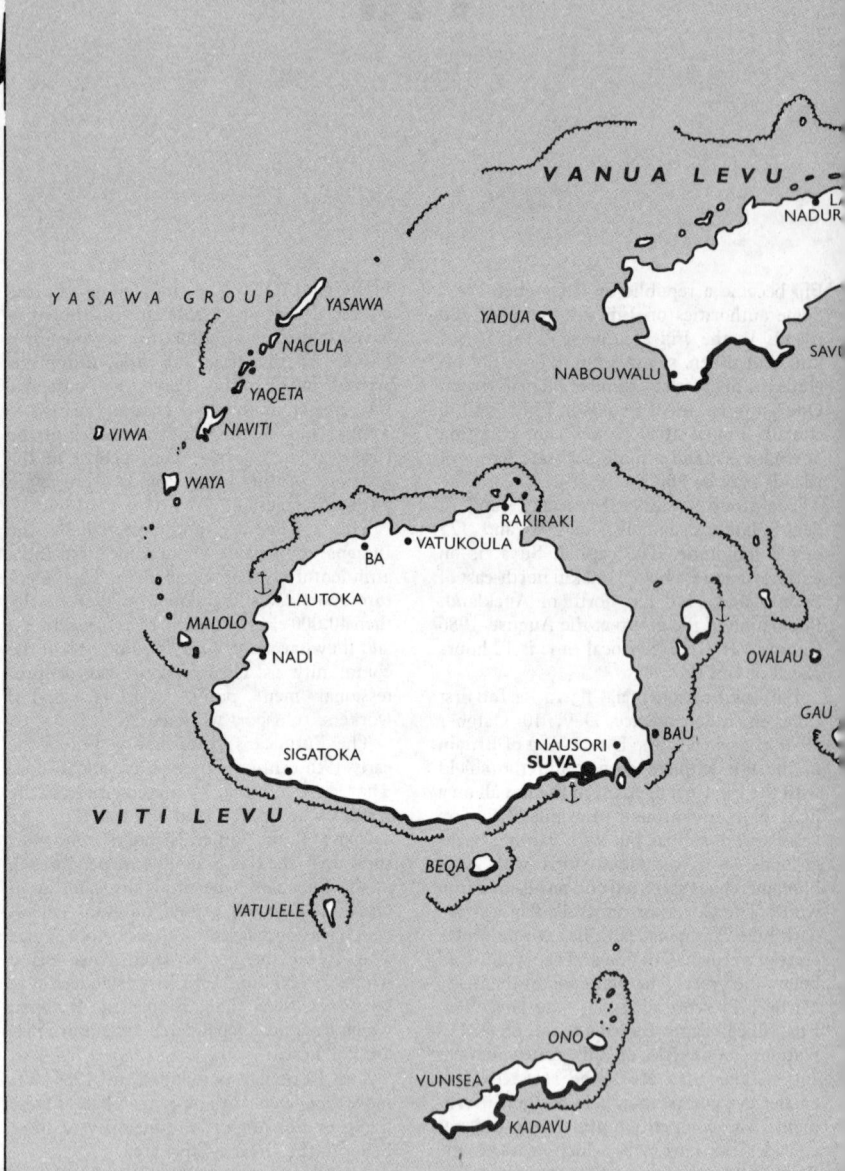

VANUA LEVU

NADUR

LA

YASAWA GROUP   YASAWA

YADUA

NACULA

SAVU

YAQETA

NABOUWALU

VIWA   NAVITI

WAYA

RAKIRAKI

BA   • VATUKOULA

LAUTOKA

MALOLO

NADI

OVALAU

GAU

NAUSORI •   BAU

SIGATOKA   SUVA

VITI LEVU

BEQA

VATULELE

ONO

VUNISEA

KADAVU

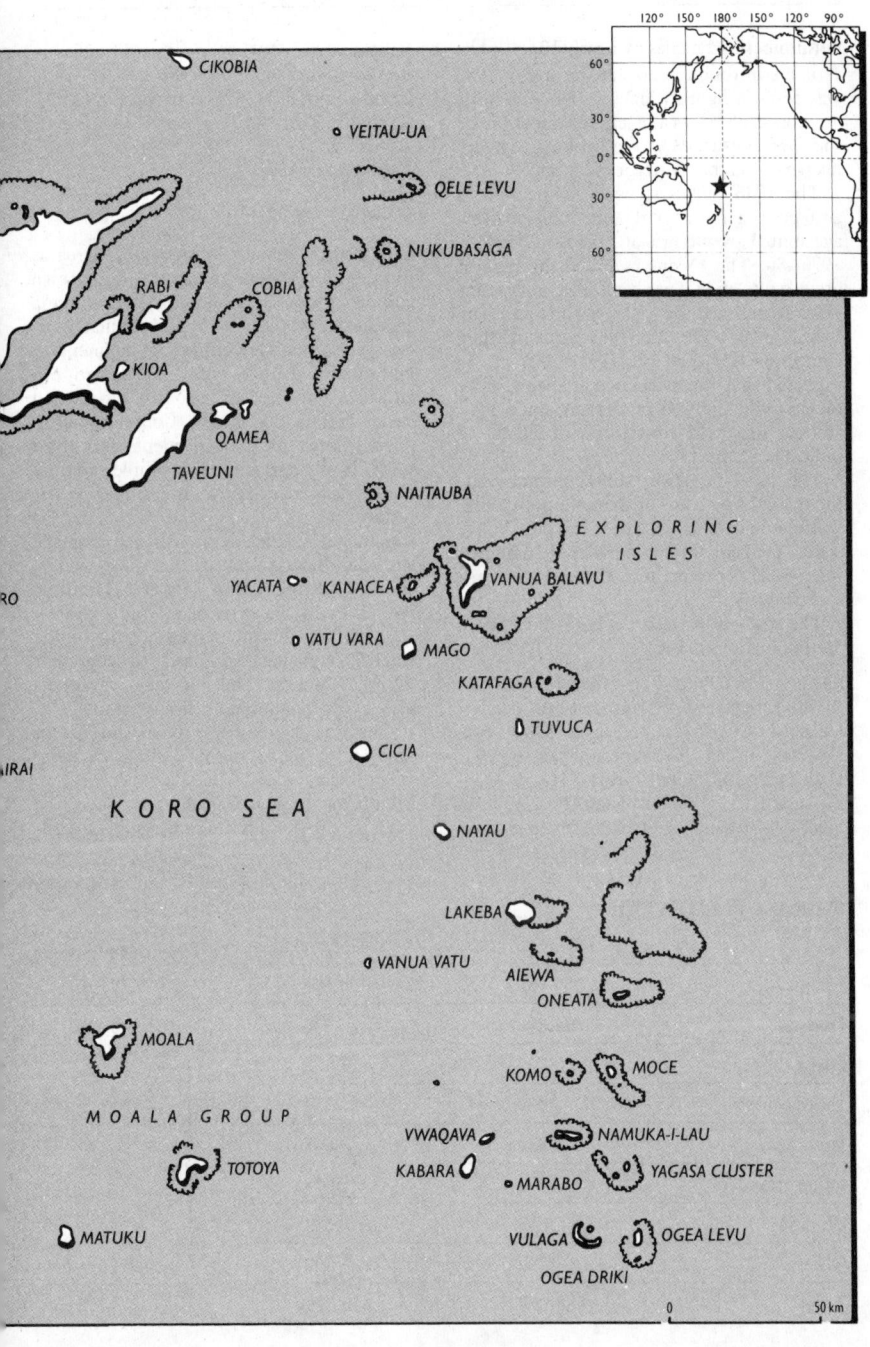

outnumbering females by nearly 10 to 1. The estimate in round figures at the end of 1986 was 5000, a figure which, so far as records are concerned, has not altered much since the 1966 census. Most are working as shopkeepers, merchants, tradesmen, etc.

The 1986 census showed an increase of 21.6 per cent in the total population; an average annual growth rate of 2 per cent between 1976–86. The Fijians recorded the highest growth rate of 26.7 per cent. They now comprise 46 per cent (329,305) of the total. The Indian growth rate was 19.1 per cent; they comprise 48.7 per cent (348,704). It is expected that this balance will change with increased emigration of Indians since 1987 and the increased growth rate of Fijians as indicated in the 1986 census.

The rural to urban shift continues, although 61.3 per cent of the total population still lives in rural areas. The urban population is 38.7 per cent of the total. The 1976 figures were 62.8 per cent and 37.2 per cent respectively.

The main urban centres have the following populations (1986):

Suva: urban 69,665, peri-urban 71,608
Lami: urban 8597, peri-urban 8110
Nausori: urban 5242, peri-urban 8740
Lautoka: urban 28,728, peri-urban 10,329
Nadi: urban 7709, peri-urban 7511
Ba: urban 6515, peri-urban 3745
Sigatoka: urban 2097, peri-urban 2633
Labasa: urban 4917, peri-urban 11,620
Savusavu: urban 2179, peri-urban 693
Levuka: urban 1106, peri-urban 1789
Rakiraki: 3361
Tavua: 2227
Vatukoula: 4789
Navua: 2775
Korovau: 340

(The census defines the peri-urban area as those built-up areas contiguous to the town and city statutory boundaries, and where a significant proportion of the population is engaged in non-agricultural employment.)

Nationality. People born in Fiji are Fiji citizens. Others may acquire citizenship under certain conditions. Commonwealth-born citizens must be residents for seven years. Non-Commonwealth people can only obtain Fiji nationality after nine years' residence.

Language. English is the official language and the Bau dialect is the most widely adopted of the Fijian tongues. Hindi is spoken by the majority of the Indians.

In writing Fijian, certain letters of the English alphabet are used to represent different sounds. The five main variations are: 'c' is pronounced as 'th' (as in that), 'b' as 'mb' (as in number); 'd' as 'nd' (as in sand); 'g' as 'ng' (as in ring); and 'q' as 'ng-g' (as in linger).

Migration trends. Canada has been the main destination for emigrating Fiji Island-

TABLE 1 POPULATION

	1976 Census	1981 Estimate	1986 Census
Fijians	259,932	290,496	329,305
Indians	292,896	326,346	348,704
Part Europeans	10,276	11,128	
Europeans	4929	3554	
Rotumans	6822	8008	
Other Islanders	7291	5675	37,366
Chinese	4652	4692	
Others	1270	490	
Total	588,068	650,389	715,375

ers, particularly for Indians and Chinese. Changes in Australian and New Zealand migration policies have slowed the flow to those countries to a large extent. However, both continue to accept skilled tradesmen and investors. Because of increased Fiji population and a shortage of employment, migration into Fiji is strictly controlled. Generally, permission to work in Fiji is given to non-Fijian citizens only when there are no qualified local personnel capable of doing the job.

Religion. The principal religious groups are Methodist (36.7 per cent); Hindu (38.1 per cent); Roman Catholic (8.8 per cent); and Moslem (7.8 per cent). Other groups include Anglican, Seventh-day Adventist, Latter Day Saints (Mormon), Presbyterian, Sikhs and Ba'hai.

LIFESTYLE. Of the Fijian people, 61 per cent still live in villages in a largely subsistence economy and with the obligations of communal life. However, under modern economic pressures life for the people, particularly the Fijians, is changing, with increasing numbers of Fijians working for wages or looking for work in cities such as Suva, living far away from their family villages. The drift from the rural areas is creating problems.

The growth of urban areas has associated problems. Lack of housing, employment, education facilities and basic infrastructures have all contributed to a rapid growth in crime rates, which is recognised by the authorities but, as with similar rural-urban migrations around the world, solutions cannot catch up with the problems.

Recreation. Fiji offers a wide variety of sporting activities, including cricket, hockey, basketball, squash, tennis and bowls. The winter sports, Rugby football and soccer, easily command the biggest followings, both for players and spectators. Water sports are popular throughout the group. Golf has made spectacular advances in recent years through private sponsorship of tournaments that have attracted leading overseas players. The new regulations governing Sunday activity have affected many sporting fixtures.

GOVERNMENT. Since independence was gained on 10 October 1970, Fiji had been independent within the Commonwealth. It had a bicameral parliament consisting of a nominated Senate and an elected House of Representatives, with a Cabinet presided over by a Prime Minister. The constitution contained a statement of fundamental freedoms and rights. The Cabinet was directly responsible to parliament and consisted of the Prime Minister and other Ministers appointed on the PM's recommendation.

The 1970 constitution provided for the House of Representatives, in the first instance, to have 52 members — 12 Fijian, 12 Indian and three general members elected from communal rolls; and 10 Fijian, 10 Indian and five general members elected from national rolls. (The national rolls had members of all races who vote together.) A new constitution will change the composition of parliament to give ethnic Fijians a permanent majority. The proposal is for a 71-seat assembly, with 36 for ethnic Fijians, 22 for Indians, eight for other races, one for Rotuma and four to be nominated by the Prime Minister. It is unlikely that the new constitution will be adopted before 1989. In the meantime the country is being governed by a 21 member cabinet appointed and headed by Ratu Sir Kamisese Mara.

The Queen was Head of State and Queen of Fiji, and was represented in Fiji by the Governor-General. His position no longer exists and has been replaced by a President.

The first general election after independence took place in April 1972. The Alliance Party was returned to power, taking 33 seats. The National Federation Party won 19.

A Royal Commission on the electoral system reported in 1976 that the communal system should be retained for some time but with a reduction in the number of communal seats and an increase in the number of national seats. This report was rejected by the Alliance Party.

An election was held in March–April 1977 and the National Federation Party gained 26 seats, the Alliance 24 with a seat each to the Fijian Nationalist Party and an independent. The NFP was unable to form a government and the Alliance was reappointed as a minority government. Another election was held in September 1977 and in this, the Alliance regained power with 36 seats. The NFP had 15 and one was taken by an independent.

The fourth general election since independence was held in July 1982, and the Alliance Party was returned to government, but with a greatly reduced majority, winning 28 seats. The National Federation Party won 22 seats and the new party, the Western United Front, formed by some Fijian chiefs in West Viti Levu, won two seats. The National Federation Party and the Western United Front formed a coalition in January 1982.

Another coalition, of the recently formed Fijian Labour Party and the Federation Party, successfully contested the elections of April 1987, their victory setting off an unprecedented series of events that culminated in Fiji's being declared a republic in October 1987. Fiji's new republican constitution, published in draft form in September 1988, provides for a single chamber parliament with 71 seats, 59 to be elected and 12 nominated. Indian voters will elect 22 representatives and general electors 8. Fiji's 14 provinces will elect 28 representatives. The Great Council of Chiefs will nominate eight Fijians and the Prime Minister will have the power to appoint another four to his Cabinet. Rotuma will elect one representative. The interim government expressed confidence that elections under the new constitution would be held within two years.

Local government. The district administration was retained when Fiji became independent. The four districts, each in the charge of a commissioner are: Central (headquarters at Nausori), covering Tailevu, Naitasiri, Rewa, Serua and Namosi; Eastern (Levuka) covering Lau, Lomaiviti, Kadavu and Rotuma; Northern (Labasa) covering Bau, Macuata and Cakaudrove; and Western (Lautoka) covering Ba, Nadroga/Navosa and Ra.

The Fijians, while still subject to the central government, have their own administration based on the village ('koro'). The head of the village, usually nominated by the people, is the 'turaga-ni-koro', who directs the village's activities. Several 'koros' are grouped to form a 'tikina' (district), while a number of 'tikina' in turn form a 'yasana' (province).

There are 14 provinces: Nadroga/Navosa, Ba, Ra, Tailevu, Naitasiri, Rewa, Serua, and Namosi are all on Viti Levu and take in

some islands adjacent to the coast. The others are Bau and Macuata (Vanua Levu), Cakaudrove (part of Vanua Levu, Taveuni, and adjacent islands), Lau (the Lau Islands), Kadavu (the island of Kadavu and adjoining islands) and Lomaiviti (a number of islands in the Koro Sea).

Each province is governed by a council and a 'roko tui'. The 'roko tui' is executive head of the council and his appointment has to be approved by the Fijian Affairs Board. The councils deal with all matters affecting Fijians, impose rates and make bylaws that must have approval of the Fijian Affairs Board. Each year the annual meeting of the Great Council of Chiefs discusses proposed legislation that has a direct bearing on Fijians. The council is regarded as the keeper of Fijian tradition. A new function for the council is to elect eight senators.

Fijian Affairs Board. This is the authority under which the Fijian administration system functions. The board comprises the Minister for Fijian Affairs and Rural Development, eight members elected by the Fijian members of the House of Representatives, and two members elected by the Great Council of Chiefs. The board has a number of expert advisers. One of the board's main functions is to make recommendations to the government on matters it feels will benefit Fijians. It sees also legislation that affects Fijians before it is submitted to Parliament.

Rabi Island administration. This island is administered internally by the Rabi Island Council. The island is owned by the Banabans as a freehold property but is otherwise part of Fiji, and the islanders are Fiji citizens. In 1975 the Banabans announced that they wanted their original home, Ocean Island, to be granted independence from the Gilbert Islands as an associate state of Fiji, but this has been rejected by Kiribati with the agreement of Britain.

Town councils. Suva and Lautoka city councils and eight town councils are regulated by the Local Government Act. The town councils are at Nadi, Ba, Sigatoka, Nausori, Labasa, Savusavu, Levuka and Lami. Lami, just to the west of Suva, was declared a town in 1977. All council members are elected from common rolls.

Public service. In 1985 the Fiji civil service totalled 27,461. Of these, 18,080 were salaried workers while the balance were employed on an hourly rate, mainly by the Public Works Department.

Justice. Under Fiji's new constitution justice will be administered by a High Court, the Fiji Court of Appeal, the Supreme Court and the magistrates' courts. The judiciary comprises a Chief Justice, appointed by the President after consultation with the Prime Minister and up to eight puisne judges presided over by the Chief Justice, who have jurisdiction to hear and determine appeals from the Supreme Court, which itself is an appellate court for decisions by magistrates' courts. The Supreme Court is the superior court of record, with unlimited criminal jurisdiction to hear and determine any civil or criminal cases including those involving interpretation of the Fiji constitution.

Police. The strength of the Fiji Police is 1408 (1372 males, 36 females) plus 96 civilian employees. The police force is also assisted by a very active dog section trained in tracking and drug detection. There is also a Special Constabulary to augment the regular force, organised on the same lines as the Fiji Police coming under the supervision of the Deputy Commissioner.

Liquor laws. All liquor outlets are closed on Sundays, though hotel guests may still obtain service. Licensed nightclubs can operate but hours of trading were constrained by the emergency regulations. Most private social clubs have liquor licences for the benefit of members and guests. Consumption of liquor in public places is an offence in most Fiji towns.

Kava drinking. In Fiji 'kava' is known as 'yaqona'. The drink is prepared from the root of the 'yaqona' plant and usually served from a large wooden bowl. 'Kava' drinking is one of the most ancient and honoured customs of the islands of Fiji, where it is probably taken more seriously than anywhere in the Pacific. It is associated with most of the religious and state functions, and also popularly drunk at feasts, etc. The effect of 'kava' drinking has been much misrepresented and exaggerated. Unless taken in enormous doses, it has very little if any effect on the mind or body. 'Kava', or 'yaqona', is not an intoxicant but a soporific and after a long drinking session an individual may appear heavy-headed and dull.

Gambling. There is generally tight control on gambling in Fiji. Poker machines are illegal. Some dice games are also illegal. Betting on horses, etc., is legal and there are about 20 betting shops in the country. Betting is mainly on the results of Australian races. Lotteries can be conducted by charity and club organisations on permits obtained from the police. The Fiji Government has rejected propositions for the opening of gambling casinos in Fiji; however, it is possible to play roulette and similar games at club and charity functions.

DEFENCE. A defence agreement with New Zealand is under renewal. Men of the Fiji Military forces (FMF) have trained in Australia, New Zealand and Sandhurst Academy in England. They have also received valuable training in jungle warfare when NZ and British Army units, including Gurkhas from the Hong Kong Regiment, came to Fiji for military exercises.

The nominal strength of the FMF, which has its headquarters at the Queen Elizabeth Barracks in Suva, is nearly 2600 men in the regular and territorial forces, including engineers, and a naval squadron of 160 men, three ex-United States Navy minesweepers and a former Marine Department survey ship. The FMF has two battalions of more than 1100 officers and men serving in the Middle East. One has been serving with the United Nations Interim Forces in Lebanon since 1978, and the other with the Multi-National Force and Observers in the Sinai Desert since 1982. The latter force was recruited from volunteers, mostly unemployed, and was regarded as a means of reducing the growing number of unemployed. Several soldiers have been killed in the Middle East. Fiji also supplied soldiers for the UN force supervising the elections in Zimbabwe in 1980.

The Fiji Naval Squadron is doing valuable work in surveillance of the country's 200-mile economic and fisheries zone to curb illegal operations by unlicensed fishing vessels. Under an agreement with the Australian Government, Fiji is to receive a number of patrol boats to assist the FMF in its surveillance programme. The first of these was handed over by the Australian Government in May 1987.

EDUCATION. The great majority of schools in Fiji are operated by local committees, and tend to be uni-racial. So while there is no government policy of racial segregation in schools, considerable racial segregation has resulted because of the committee school system encouraging individual groups of people to establish schools.

At the end of 1985 there were 668 primary schools, 139 secondary schools and 42 technical vocational schools. There were also 244 preschools. The majority are operated by committees, most of them in Indian communities and more than 100 of them maintained by the churches, but all receive assistance of one kind or another from government grants. The government decided some years ago to hand over the running of its primary schools to local committees and by the end of 1985 five of the 19 primary schools in the programme had been handed over.

There were 127,286 primary enrolments in 1985, 4206 preschool pupils and 41,505 secondary students. Primary school teachers totalled 4396 while there were 2721 secondary teachers, 88.6 per cent of whom were trained but only 37 per cent of whom had graduate qualifications.

The government introduced a Free and Partly Free Place system based on parental income in 1957. In 1985, all children in classes 1 to 8 received free education and in secondary schools the average fee was $36 per annum. Students whose parents are unable to pay the fees are subsidised and in 1985 the government paid out $875,746 in remission of fees to assist low income families. School attendance is not compulsory, but in 1985 97.3 per cent of children at primary level were at school. The teacher-student ratio has reached the national target of 1:30.

Technical education. The government gives special attention to increasing the provision of technical and vocational training at all levels and to encourage secondary and higher education. Full time vocational training is available from the Fiji Institute of Technology, the School of Maritime studies for Seamen and the School of Hotel and Catering Services, all in Suva. The Western Division Technical Training Centre at Ba, which opened in 1978, enables apprentice training to be decentralised. Fiji's Development Plan for 1986–90 recognises the relationship between technical and tertiary education and middle level manpower requirements. Courses will be directed toward meeting demands; computer education is to play an important part at all levels of education. The overall directive of DP9 is 'twelve years of education for every child who so desires'. Voluntary organisations such as the Montfort Boys Town together with the government industrial training centres will continue to provide training in skills such as construction, farming and animal husbandry for young school leavers who will live in a mainly rural environment.

Teacher training. Teacher training is available from the Lautoka Teachers' College (government), the Corpus Christi Teachers' College (Roman Catholic) and the Fulton Missionary Teachers' College (Seventh-day Adventist). Secondary teachers are encouraged to do degree courses at the University of the South Pacific. After graduating they will be re-directed to a locally organised secondary teachers' training course that will be more relevant and more specific to Fiji's needs.

In-service awards are offered to teachers to enable them to undertake further academic and professional studies both in Fiji and overseas.

University of the South Pacific. The university, at Laucala Bay, Suva, occupies buildings previously used by the Royal New Zealand Air Force and donated by the NZ Government when the university was established. Other, more modern buildings have been added since. The first preliminary courses began in 1968 as a preparation for islanders in the region wanting to proceed to degree and diploma courses. It has an enrolment of about 2500 students and offers six first degree courses, two postgraduate courses, eight diplomas and six certificate programmes. In 1985 the Fiji Government awarded 100 scholarships for the university and 46 overseas scholarships. Scholarships are also awarded by some of the leading commercial interests in the region and others are provided by memorials such as the Adi Laisa Memorial and Narsey Memorial. Countries represented on the University Council are Western Samoa, New Zealand, Australia, Fiji, Solomon Islands, Cook Islands, Kiribati, Tuvalu, Nauru, Vanuatu, Tonga and the United States of America. The South Pacific Commission is also represented.

The university has four schools — the School of Social and Economic Development and the School of Natural Resources, both of which provide a three-year degree course; the School of Education, which provides a three-year degree course as well as a four-year degree course, and the School of Agriculture at Alafua, Apia (Western Samoa), which provides a three-and-a-half year Bachelor of Agriculture course. There are residential places for about 750 student at the Laucala campus and 25 at the Alafua campus. Under its extension programme, USP has established extension centres in nine regional areas. The university requires a current budget of $12–13 million per annum. Funds are provided by the 11 member countries: Fiji makes a special grant in respect of economic advantages derived from having the University in its territory.

The Fiji School of Medicine. The Fiji School of Medicine, in Tamavua, Suva, was established in 1886. It is actually based on two campuses — the pre-clinical school at Tamavua Heights and the clinical school at the CWM Hospital. The school has enrolment of about 200 students from Fiji and many other Pacific islands. More than 100 students are taking the 5–6 year Degree of Bachelor of Medicine and Bachelor of Surgery (MBBS) programme. The University of the South Pacific awards the MBBS as an external degree to students completing their programme. In addition to the medical programme, the school offers 10 other para-medical courses. They are Pharmacy, Health Inspectors, Dental Assistant, Dental Technology, Dental Therapy, Physiotherapy, Radiography, Medical Laboratory Technology, Laboratory Assistant and Dietitics. There is also provision for overseas students to take elective training at the School on request.

Fiji College of Agriculture. This was established at Koronivia in 1954 and has approximately 72 students.

The Pacific Theological College. Located in Suva, this college was established in 1956 and has 44 full-time students.

Fiji School of Nursing. The school at Suva and Lautoka has an intake of about 80 students a year for a three-year course. The School provides 95 per cent of required nursing staff. A new campus is being funded by a Japanese grant.

Education Budget. In 1985 the total recurrent and capital expenditure by the Ministry of Education was $72.6 million and $1 million respectively. The University of the South Pacific received grants of $6.7 million from the Fiji Government.

LABOUR. The employment status of the economically active population shows that one third, 81,000 (33.6 per cent) are own Account Workers, 38,102 (15.8 per cent) Employed Public, 63,553 (26.4 per cent) Employed Private and 39,231 (16.3 per cent) Unpaid Family Workers (1986 Census). Industry classifications include 106,305 (44.1 per cent) in Agriculture, 1345 (0.5 per cent) in Mining, 18,106 (7.5 per cent) in Manufacturing, 2145 (0.9 per cent) in Electricity, 11,786 (4.9 per cent) in Construction, 26,010 (10.8 per cent) in Trade, 13,151 (5.4 per cent) in Transport, 6016 (2.5 per cent) in Finance and 36,619 (15.2 per cent) in Service Industries. 19,668 were classified as unemployed. These figures account for an active work force of 241,160.

Wages and hours. Fiji has established an employment pattern similar to that in the more developed countries, mainly through bargaining processes established by law and custom and recognised as being as sophisticated as those in the developed countries. Working hours are now clearly defined and, in most industries, there is a five-day week of 40 to 44 hours, with paid overtime. Inflation has pushed up wages, a condition not confined to Fiji, and in the decade 1975/85 wages almost doubled. In 1985 the lowest paid workers were those in agriculture at $1.04 per hour and the highest, electricity workers, at $1.87 per hour. In 1980, mean hourly wage rates for respective industries were: agriculture $1.04; mining $1.31; manufacturing $1.52; construction $1.53; electricity $1.87; commerce $1.42; transport $1.65; financial services $1.42; and community services $1.60.

Industrial relations. In 1985 there were 46 trade unions with 45,000 unionised employees. Most other workers are not covered by a trade union but are covered by their respective wages councils. Wages councils regulate the following trades: building, civil engineering and electrical; wholesale and retail; hotel and catering; road and transport; sawmilling.

**TABLE 2 NUMBER OF PERMANENT EMPLOYEES
AND AVERAGE ANNUAL SALARY**

	1983		1984		1985	
Agriculture, forestry and fishing						
Wage	2113		1825		2135	
Salary	405		442		442	
Total	2517	$6203	2577	$5426	2577	$6310
Mining and quarrying						
Wage	1057		986		974	
Salary	169		253		240	
Total	1226	$5422	1239	$8624	2577	$8288
Manufacturing						
Wage	12,514		12,382		12,095	
Salary	2188		1802		1962	
Total	14,702	$7447	14,184	$8541	14,057	$7669
Electricity, gas and water						
Wage	1846		1732		1665	
Salary	385		333		486	
Total	2231	$7612	2065	$7512	2141	$7397
Construction						
Wage	6267		5664		6252	
Salary	457		390		604	
Total	6724	$8506	6034	$10,134	6856	$7875
Wholesale and retail trades, restaurants and hotels						
Wage	10,986		11,094		10,960	
Salary	3902		3810		3845	
Total	14,888	$5995	14,904	$6363	14,805	$6645
Transport, storage and communications						
Wage	3628		3675		3936	
Salary	4070		3905		3875	
Total	7698	$7070	7580	$7355	7811	$8180
Finance and business						
Wage	1667		1192		1313	
Salary	3390		3479		3578	
Total	5057	$7907	4671	$8064	4891	$8110
Community, social and personal services						
Wage	6975		6071		7433	
Salary	18,057		19,616		19,297	
Total	25,032	$6195	25,687	$6741	26,730	$7536
Total employment						
Wage	47,053		44,601		46,753	
Salary	33,022		34,001		34,329	
Total	80,075	$6192	78,602	$7055	81,082	$7577

Fiji's legislation governing industrial relations is probably the most enlightened in the region and includes the Trade Dispute Act (1973), enacted for the settlement of disputes in certain situations through compulsory arbitration; giving the minister power to declare a strike or lock-out unlawful; and requiring a union covering workers in an essential service to give 28 days' notice of withdrawal of labour. Special legislation contained in the Sugar Industry Act governs disputes in the sugar industry separately from all other industries, because of the dependence of Fiji's economy on sugar production.

Another Act, the Recognition Act, came into force in 1976. It entitles a union to compulsory recognition for the purpose of collective bargaining if that union's membership constitutes more than 50 per cent of the persons eligible for membership. However, the creation in December 1976 of the Tripartite Forum under the chairmanship of the Prime Minister has probably had the greatest influence on industrial relations of any one instrument. Its stabilising effect on industrial relations and the economy is generally recognised. The Forum consists of representatives of the Fiji Trade Union Congress, to which most unions belong, the Fiji Employers Consultative Association and the Government. It is a voluntary organisation and has done much to settle disputes and claims through a common understanding. It has 10 committees, the Consultative Committee, the Guidelines Committee, Investment, Taxation Review, Productivity, Industrial Relations, Redundancy, Ability to Pay, Price Justification and the Economic Development Board. The last-named has greatly widened its sphere of activities to take in all sectors of economic development including the organisation of 'Invest in Fiji' seminars abroad.

After independence, Fiji became a full member of the International Labour Organisation (ILO) and an ILO regional office was opened in Suva in 1975. The ILO helped draft social security legislation, helps with seminars and organises training in rural areas in the field of vocational rehabilitation.

Other organisations active in the field of industrial relations are the Chamber of Commerce, the Retail Association, the Master Builders Association and the Fiji Hotel Association.

Fiji National Provident Fund. To provide social security for employees, the Fiji National Provident Fund was set up in 1966 to pay members on retirement a lump sum, a pension, or a combination of both. Provision is also made for pension payments to widows. Since 1971 a members' insurance scheme is included in the fund, and in 1976 the government offered housing finance for fund members on condition that loans were repaid. Employers are responsible for paying into the fund for the employees at the rate of 12 cents in the wages dollar, half of this payment being deducted from the employees' wages.

The fund had 143,622 contributors in June 1986, and contributions for the year ending 30 June 1986 totalled $59,039,116. The fund is now the largest single source of finance in Fiji. Total investment by the FNPF in June 1986, was $559,515,156. Fiji Government securities amounted to $232,582,015. On loan to the Housing Authority was $75,743,676; on loan to various statutory authorities $140,429,984, and investments in the private sector totalled $110,759,481. The overall gross rate of return was 10.4 per cent.

Fiji National Training Council. Created in 1974 this organises training programmes for commercial, industrial and technical workers throughout the country. From 1976 new schemes include overseas study grants and grants to employers in setting up training courses. Funds are obtained from employers who can each contribute 1 per cent of their annual payroll.

HEALTH. Medical services in Fiji are in the charge of a Ministry of Health, and the permanent head of the Medical Department is Secretary for Health. Medical and dental treatment can be obtained at low charges from government hospitals and clinics covering most areas of Fiji.

Health standards in Fiji are high compared with other countries with similar backgrounds and circumstances, and the country is free of most tropical diseases including malaria, though there has been a large increase of the 'social' diseases with growth of the tourist industry and transport links. Such diseases increased from 1501 in 1980 to 2191 in 1984. The most common illnesses are influenza, dengue fever, infantile diarrhoea, measles and chicken pox, but the main causes of death have become the diseases associated with highly developed countries; heart disease, cancer and diseases of the respiratory and circulatory systems.

Fiji budgeted for $35.9 million for health services in 1984. The government provides most of the medical care facilities and, in 1984, there were 25 hospitals, 46 health centres and 94 nursing stations operating in both rural and urban areas. Each of the four administrative divisions has a major hospital, the chief hospital, the Colonial War Memorial Hospital (CWMH), in Suva having 379 beds plus a new 100-bed maternity unit, Lautoka 305, Labasa 129 and Levuka 47.

Fiji had a total of 1801 hospital beds in 1984. Specialist hospitals are Tamavua (tuberculosis) St Giles and P. J. Twomey Memorial Suva (leprosy). In 1984 the Ministry of Health employed 351 doctors and medical assistants, 1226 nurses and 151 dentists. In private practice were 93 doctors, and 14 dentists.

The doctor population in 1984 was 1:1553. The crude birth rate and crude death rate were 29.8 and 5.2 per 1000 population respectively. Fees for medical services provided by the Ministry of Health are heavily subsidised. A charge of 50 cents is made for general outpatient attendance in the major hospitals, and 20 cents at health centres and subdivisional hospitals. Admission to general wards is 50 cents per day, which covers all medical care. Treatment at nursing stations is free, as is all treatment for the destitute and for all children under 15 years, who comprise 37 per cent of the total population.

The ministry is exploring the feasibility of setting up a National Health Insurance Scheme. Life expectancy rate is 68 years.

Family planning. These services are available at all government and private health facilities and contraceptives are subsidised. Statistics show that Indian women of child-bearing age are more likely to accept birth control methods than their Fijian counterparts. In 1984, the percentages using some method of contraception were 33.4 and 16.3 per cent respectively.

The crude birth rate was 32.6 per 1000 for Fijians and 27.7 per 1000 for Indians. Of live births, 93.2 per cent are in general hospitals, 4.4 per cent are attended by district nurses and 2.4 per cent are attended by traditional birth attendants.

Medical research. Fiji Medical Department hospitals have laboratories that conduct research on local health problems. The Fiji School of Medicine does limited research, mainly in the form of surveys. The Colonial War Memorial Hospital in Suva also contains the Wellcome Virus Research Laboratory, set up by the Wellcome Trust of New Zealand. This concentrates on filariasis and other mosquito-borne diseases and works closely with Otago University, New Zealand.

Development plan. 'Health for all by the Year 2000' has been the aim of development plans since independence. During DP9 (1986–1990), the Health sector will be particularly directed toward providing effective medical services to low-income earners and rural dwellers. The government also hopes to encourage increased involvement in provision of health care services by the private sector. Community and voluntary groups will also be encouraged to be active in preventive and primary health services. The birth rate will also be a target as it is hoped to reduce it to 25 per 1000 by the end of the plan period.

The National Food and Nutrition Committee, working through the Ministry of Health, will continue to promote the production of local foodstuffs and the reduction of reliance on imported foodstuffs. Malnutrition is a growing problem in Fiji, affecting a cross-section of the population.

THE LAND. Though there is general agreement that Fiji comprises about 320 islands, some people (mainly those whose work involves them in land matters or in surveying) estimate that, if islands in rivers and all the unnamed islands in the many scattered groups were included, the total would be around 800. Fiji has a total land area of 18,376 sq. km. The largest island is Viti Levu (Big Fiji) which covers 10,390 sq. km. The second largest is Vanua Levu (Big Land) of 5538 sq. km. About 150 islands are inhabited.

The distance from the Yasawa Group in the north-west to the Lau group in the south-east is about 480 km. The islands of Fiji have an obvious strategic importance for airlines, shipping and telecommunications.

The highest peak in the country is Mount Victoria, at 1424 m. There are several other mountains in the vicinity of 1000 m. The larger islands, especially Viti Levu, Vanua Levu, Taveuni, Kadavu and the Lomaiviti Group are mountainous and of volcanic origin, rising more or less abruptly from the shore to a height of from 1300 to 1400 m. The hills are generally of a grand and picturesque outline, being composed for the most part of old volcanic lavas. The south-eastern or windward sides of the islands are covered in dense forests.

Natural features. The country is well watered. Frequent rains keep alive the thousands of small streams feeding the main rivers. Of these rivers, the Rewa (on Viti Levu) is the biggest. It is navigable for 130 km from its mouth, with several large streams running into it. Beside these, the Sigatoka, Nadi and Ba Rivers, with many others, drain the principal watersheds of Viti Levu. On Vanua Levu the rivers are not so large, though they are nearly as numerous. The largest is the Dreketi River.

The lower lands are more lightly timbered, and have apparently been under cultivation at some distant period. On these flats the soil is almost everywhere deep, easily worked, and especially rich in humic acid. The northern and north-western sides or leeward sides of the larger islands are characterised by a comparative absence of forest lands; hills or plains are covered with long reeds or grass and dotted with clumps of casuarina and pandanus.

Fiji is as rich in harbours and roadsteads as it is in rivers. Each island is surrounded by a barrier reef of coral and, with few exceptions, is accessible through passages usually found opposite a river or a large valley from which water drains into the lagoon.

Climate. The climate is of the tropical oceanic type, but with the tempering influences of the prevalent south-east trade winds that control it. The hot months are December to April, when humidity is high.

In rainfall, clear demarcation is shown. The windward sides of the large islands are extremely wet, while on the lee sides sheltered by the mountains the annual precipitation may be 1640 mm more or less, with a well marked dry season favourable to sugar grow-ing. But there is no month without some rain, while the abundant running streams assist both communications and cultivation. Strong winds, excessive rainfall and hurricanes occasionally prove destructive to crops.

Flora and fauna. Fiji wildlife extends from 68 species of land and freshwater birds (including brilliantly coloured parrots) to flying foxes, a tree python and chameleon. Fiji's most unusual animal is the mongoose, introduced from India to keep down the rat population in the cane fields. It has multiplied to pest proprtions and its feeding habits have taken a drastic toll on the native lizard and bird populations.

Flora in Fiji ranges from the mangrove swamps to grasslands (talasiga) and rainforest, which still covers almost half the total land area. More than 3000 species of plants have been identified, one third of them native to Fiji. Probably the most famous is the fuchsia-like 'tagimaucia', which blooms on the high slopes of Taveuni Island.

Resources. Fiji's main agricultural crops are sugar, coconuts and root vegetables. The forest lands possess a wealth of hard and soft wood timbers.

Land reclamation. DP8 provided for 83,000 ha to be brought under cultivation, some of it reclaimed land from mangrove swamps. DP9 allows for the consolidation of this project. The government is well aware of the value of the tens of thousands of hectares of mangroves in the ecology of the country and as a food source for Fijians whose traditional fishing rights incorporate them.

Land tenure. The arrival of European and Indian settlers with their desire for land has prompted various measures to protect Fijian land ownership. Before cession to Britain in 1874, Europeans gained title to a considerable proportion of the easily cultivated land. Then, when the chiefs of Fiji ceded the territory to Britain, one condition was that Fijian land rights should be protected. Shortly after, about 160,000 ha of land were granted and registered as freehold while further alienation of Fijian land occurred in sales during 1905–1909. Since 1909 there has been no further land alienated. Land holdings in 1986 were as in the accompanying table:

	Hectares
Fijian communally owned land	1,520,775
Freehold (other than Crown)	181,035
Crown, freehold	35,640
Crown, Schedule A	59,940
Crown, Schedule B	31,185
Rotuman communal	4455
Total	1,833,030

Crown land shown in the table has been purchased by the Crown from time to time. Some of this is land that has reverted to the Crown when the Fijian 'mataquali', or landholding unit, has died out. Other Crown land is that for which no Fijian owners could be found at the time of cession. At the end of 1984, 370,388 ha of Fijian land was leased principally to non-Fijians.

Land Sales Act. A 1973 Land Sales Act aimed at defeating speculation by restricting purchases of freehold land by non-residents. A resident is classed as a citizen or person who has lived in Fiji for at least seven years. Generally the consent of the Minister of Finance is needed before a non-resident can buy a large undeveloped parcel; if this is obtained and the land is subsequently resold at a profit without development, the seller is liable to tax on the profit at income tax rates.

Native Land Trust Board. With the agreement of the Fijian people, the government created the Native Land Trust Board in 1940 and gave it control of all native land on behalf of the Fijians. The board has three duties: to protect the interests of native owners by reserving ample lands for their present and future needs; to provide suitable land for settlement; and to secure continuity of policy and security of tenure. Certain land classified as native reserve may not be leased or otherwise disposed of, while all other native lands may be leased by the board to people of any race.

In 1975, the Native Land Trust Board set up a Native Land Development Corporation as a public company to develop Fijian land with maximum involvement of Fijian landowners as shareholders, managers, and businessmen. The company also takes an interest in general business ventures, has bought into several local businesses and manages the Seaqaqa sugar-cane estate on Vanua Levu.

In 1984 the Native Land Trust (Leases and Licences) Regulations were revised. At the expiry of a lease, the lessee has the right to request a new lease and if he does so is then entitled to a new lease for the same use or fair and equitable compensation for all improvements to the land. There are certain restrictions on who may apply for renewal and a copy of these regulations can be obtained from the NLTB, PO Box 116, Suva. The board has also established tourist policy objectives for native land. These include the offering of native land for development as an alternative to the development of freehold land and the promotion of Fijian participation in tourism enterprises. The Yasawa chain of islands, once regarded as inaccessible for tourism projects, has been re-examined by the board and parts of it are now considered suitable for such development. Details are available direct from the NLTB.

The Department of Lands, Mines and Surveys administers Crown Lands and its leasing. Since 1940, persons wishing to acquire land in Fiji must either (a) buy or lease from the owners of alienated, or freehold, land; or (b) lease any available land from the Native Land Trust Board or from the Department of Lands, etc.

Landlord and Tenant Act. The Agricultural Landlord and Tenant Ordinance has operated since 1967 to help overcome the problem that most agricultural developments in the country are on leased land. The legislation initially provided for tenancy over renewable 10-year periods as well as five-yearly rent assessments if desired.

As a result of a committee appointed to review this ordinance, in 1976 an amendment raised the minimum period for an agricultural lease to 30 years. This gave tenants of Fijian land much greater security of tenure. Leasehold disputes can be decided by an independent tribunal and rent revisions may be considered through an independent authority.

PRIMARY PRODUCTION. Fiji's chief export-earning industries are sugar, fishing, gold and copra. Banana exports, once a big earner of overseas exchange, ceased in 1974. Ginger became a new export and surpassed the value achieved by bananas. Industries that produce the most for home consumption are dairying, rice, fruit and vegetable growing.

Sugar. Sugar was grown commercially in Fiji as far back as 1870 around what is now Suva. The industry was weakly based until the Australian Colonial Sugar Refining Co. became interested in Fiji and built the first sugar mill at Nausori, by the Rewa River, about 22 km from Suva in 1882. The same company established mills at Rarawai, on the 'dry' side of the island, at Labasa on Vanua Levu, and at Lautoka in the north-west of Viti Levu.

At about the same time that CSR was establishing itself on the Rewa, several other smaller mills were set up, but by 1926 the Australian company was the only sugar miller in the colony. The company closed down its Nausori mill in 1959. Originally sugar was grown on large estates in Fiji, mostly with indentured Indian labour, but when the indentured system ceased after 1916, the larger sugar estates were gradually broken up and Fiji's sugar industry began to be worked on the present system of small holdings by tenant farmers.

Over the years there was a number of industrial disputes, and in the 1960s there were two important inquiries into the sugar industry. CSR established a local subsidiary, South Pacific Sugar Mills Ltd, to operate the Fiji industry, but after the second inquiry in 1969 CSR announced that it was unprofitable for it to remain in the industry in Fiji and that it would withdraw after the 1972 crushing season.

The Fiji Government purchased the CRS Company's 36,199,300 shares in South Pacific Sugar Mills Ltd on 31 March 1973 at 27.625 cents a share. In addition, the Fiji Government purchased CSR Company's freehold land for $3.75 million.

On 1 April 1973 the Fiji Sugar Corporation Ltd (FSC) took over the assets of South Pacific Sugar Mills Ltd except for the CSR freehold land, which came under direct Fiji Government administration. Sir Vijay Singh is the Chief Executive of the Sugar Growers' Council.

FSC was formed by the government as a public company to run milling on commercial lines. All but 2.2 per cent of its shares are owned by the government. The company has a board appointed by the government. Part of the agreement with CSR provided that CSR should continue as marketing agents for Fiji sugar, but in 1975 the government decided to undertake its own marketing. The Fiji Sugar Marketing Co. Ltd was formed in 1976. In 1979 a new FSC subsidiary company, South Pacific Distillers Ltd, was formed to manufacture rum, gin, vodka, whisky, brandy and industrial alcohol with a factory at Lautoka. Chairman of the Fiji Sugar Corporation is Mr Lyle Cupit.

At the end of 1984 the sugar industry was restructured to enhance a sense of equal partnership between millers, growers and employees; to provide an effective machinery for the settlement of disputes; to establish a forum to determine future policy; and to provide representation for growers in industry policies. This restructuring has involved the formation of the Sugar Commission, with representatives from the Fiji Sugar Corporation, the Sugarcane Growers Council, Government, employees of the Fiji Sugar Corporation and the Sugar Industry Tribunal.

The 1985 cane production of 2,975,000 tonnes was 29 per cent less than the all-time record of 4,289,929 tonnes achieved in 1984. Cyclones Eric and Nigel in January 1985 caused extensive damage to both the cane crop and the Lautoka crushing mill. In 1985 the total sugar production was 341,011 tonnes. The 8:98 ratio of tonnes of cane to tonnes of sugar was the worst ever realised. Despite the crises in 1987, however, Fiji exported 423,844 tonnes of sugar, the second highest amount on record.

Sugar cane contract. This is a contract between the FSC and the growers that sets out conditions for the sale and purchase of cane and regulates the relationship between the two parties. Each contract stipulates a Farm Harvest Quota. The price received by the farmer for his cane is based on a division of the total net proceeds of the sale of sugar and molasses during the season. The share paid to growers and millers in any one season depends on the total sugar production: up to a production of 325,000 tonnes, growers receive 70 per cent and millers 30 per cent; above that figure the grower's share becomes greater. The present contract system, negotiated in 1980, is expected to continue until the end of the decade.

Sugar marketing. Following the expiry of

the Commonwealth Sugar Agreement and United States Act in 1974, Fiji in 1975 concluded an agreement with the European Economic Community that ensured continued minimum sales of about 170,000 tonnes of sugar a year to the EEC (effectively Britain) at a guaranteed minimum price. Fiji also has long-term sugar supply agreements with New Zealand, Malaysia and Singapore. In 1977, under a new International Sugar Agreement, Fiji was given a world quota of 125,000 tonnes. As that did not include the EEC quota, Fiji was able to sell all the sugar it produced.

In 1985 these contracts accounted for approximately 60 per cent of sales, and helped protect the industry from being further depressed by falling world prices.

Copra. The preparation and export of copra was Fiji's earliest industry, commencing with the first white population and now ranks fourth as an export earner after sugar, gold and fish. The industry is centred on Vanua Levu and outer islands — initially because coconuts on the mainland of Viti Levu were completely controlled by a pest peculiar to Fiji, the purple moth (*Levuana iridiscens*), and no attempt was made to cultivate coconut plantations there.

Annual production since 1975 has been as follows:

	tonnes
1975	23,496
1976	26,510
1977	30,646
1978	26,092
1979	21,729
1980	22,525
1981	20,493
1982	22,033
1983	23,566
1984	24,545
1985	25,000

The Coconut Industry Ordinance provides for the development and control of the copra industry. It also provides for a Coconut Industries Board and a Coconut Advisory Council: the board is not a marketing organisation as in some other Pacific islands and does not compulsorily acquire all export copra, but controls the industry by licensing buyers, processors etc.

About 50 per cent of Fiji copra is pro-

TABLE 3

	1980
Contract area (ha)	86,153
Area harvested (ha)	65,639
Cane (tonnes)	3,360,275
Sugar (tonnes)	396,157
Molasses (tonnes)	158,839
Tonnes cane/ha harvested	51.2
Tonnes cane/tonnes sugar	8.48
Tonnes sugar/ha harvested	6.0

TABLE 4

	1980
Exports:	
Sugar (tonnes)	441,000
Molasses (tonnes)	161,000
Export Value:	
Sugar ($m)	157.67
Molasses ($m)	10.65
Total ($m)	168.32
Employment:	
Farmers	19,567
Cane cutters	19,300
FSC employment	3951
Total	42,818
Cane price: $/tonne	35.19
Income:	
growers $m	118.25
FSC $m	48.91

Note: e = estimate

duced from Fijian native groves and subsidy payments for rehabilitation work and new plantings have in the past been big incentives for plantation improvements, but when the subsidy scheme started to tail off in 1969 most of this work tailed off also.

PERFORMANCE OF THE SUGAR INDUSTRY 1980–85:
PRODUCTION AND EFFICIENCY

1981	1982	1983	1984	1985ᵉ
88,338	90,220	91,499	91,998	92,197
65,888	69,270	59,171	69,282	71,593
3,931,329	4,074,727	2,202,667	4,289,929	2,975,000
469,972	486,679	275,877	480,106	350,000
151,824	150,049	83,955	88,475	15,000
59.7	58.8	37.1	61.9	41.6
8.37	8.37	8.00	8.94	8.5
7.1	7.0	4.7	6.9	4.9

PERFORMANCE OF THE SUGAR INDUSTRY 1980–85:
ECONOMIC INDICATORS

1981	1982	1983	1984	1985ᵉ
408,000	411,000	343,000	379,513	335,000
141,000	157,000	93,000	150,153	111,000
136.94	142.99	87.73	122.06	98.44
7.93	5.56	2.94	7.90	4.97
144.87	148.55	90.67	129.96	103.41
21,015	22,091	20,500	21,796	22,146
19,411	19,911	11,295	16,244	15,500
4000	3708	3521	3871	3400
44,426	45,710	35,316	41,911	41,046
26.24	28.60	29.00	22.37	23.60
103.17	108.99	65.30	98.26	75.43
41.30	43.37	27.99	39.16	32.05

In addition, because of the combined effects of a series of hurricanes and droughts, which damaged palms in the main coconut areas (coupled with the fact that more than half the palms are estimated to be well past their best bearing age), copra production remains low and it seems unlikely that the peak production of 1977 will be attained again. The Development Plan aims to maintain production at the 1985 level.

Efforts are being made to replant ageing trees and to introduce a hybrid plant with a higher yield. The government realises that for the industry to maintain its viability, it must increase productivity. Fiji has no control over copra pricing, which in turn has led to income instability for growers and associated insecurity. In an effort to stabilise the industry the Government introduced a support price of $190 per tonne in the mid 1970s: this was raised to $280 per tonne in 1980, and DP9 has undertaken to keep this support mechanism in place.

Coconut Products. As the demand for copra and coconut oil in world markets declines, other products are being examined. Tests have been made to find uses for the timber of the coconut tree as well as coir products from the coconut husk. Coconut cream is a successful canned product for both international and local consumption.

Rice. Fiji hopes to achieve 90 per cent self-sufficiency in rice by the end of DP9. Main growing areas are Central division in Viti Levu and Northern Division in Vanua Levu. In 1985, about 11,653 ha were planted, with some under rainfed rice and production from this was 24,075 tonnes of paddy, equivalent of 7092.4 tonnes of polished rice. Rice imports in the same year amounted to 14,418 tonnes of polished rice worth $5.8 million.

In April 1983, the government adopted measures to control rice imports. All imports had to be through Rewa Rice Ltd, a private company wholly owned by the government. Other importers were allowed to nominate their overseas suppliers and to fix the quantity and species they wanted to import. A surcharge is levied on all imported rice to support the price of local rice. The scheme is designed to support the local rice industry and to help Fiji to become self-sufficient in rice, a staple food of the Indian community.

To achieve the objects of greater self-sufficiency and increased employment, an additional 5200 ha will be brought under cultivation in the Northern and Central Divisions in the DP9 period. Farmers in cane areas will also be encouraged to grow more rice as a diversification crop. Priority is to be given to technologies that can easily be adapted to conditions faced by the majority of farmers, including gravity-fed irrigation systems rather than costly pump systems.

National Rice Week is held at the beginning of the year to increase public awareness and to provide organised activities and demonstrations for growers.

Ginger. Ginger has rapidly become an important export crop. Exports of fresh ginger began in 1964, about 10 years after the industry became established on a few farms, and the first consignments sold overseas earned $34,000. In 1985, 2056 tonnes were produced from 95 ha were valued at $2,229,786. This was 17 per cent lower than the 1984 production. The United States and Canada account for 90 per cent of ginger exports, but competition is increasing from Brazil and Hawaii. With the growth of the industry have come problems and these, together with competition, have attracted the attention of the Fiji Economic Development Board (EDB), which carried out a survey of the industry in 1983. The survey recommended better marketing practices by ginger exporters. It said there was an assured market

TABLE 5 RICE PRODUCTION, IMPORTS AND SELF-SUFFICIENCY (PADDY EQUIVALENT)

	1981	1982	1983	1984	1985^e
Production (tonnes)	16,972	20,302	16,160	22,246	27,400
Imports (tonnes)	21,623	23,245	27,517	20,665	18,300
Import value ($m)	7.4	6.4	7.5	6.2	5.5
Total Consumption (tonnes)	38,595	43,547	43,677	42,911	45,700
% Self Sufficient	44	46	37	52	60

Source: MPI — Rice Commodity Profile
Note: e = estimate

TABLE 6 TARGETS FOR FRESH GINGER PRODUCTION 1986–1990

	1986	1987	1988	1989	1990
Area (ha)	110	110	110	110	110
Production (tonnes)	4500	4480	4400	4400	4570
Export (tonnes)	2700	2800	2900	3000	3200
Export Value ($000)	2160	2240	2320	2400	2560
Employment (Total)	238	238	238	238	238

in Canada and the United States because of the high quality of the ginger. All Fiji ginger could be sold as long as quality remains high, supplies are consistent and prices reliable. The EDB's Agricultural Commodities Development Committee formed a sub-committe to identify problems in the industry.

Cocoa. Although it has been grown in Fiji since 1890, a constant battle with disease has made cocoa growing a frustrating experience for farmers. In 1967 a canker-resistant variety was introduced to small holdings in the Wainibuka Valley, Natewa Bay and Buca Bay areas, which helped to revive interest in cocoa as a cash crop. However, despite good prices and other incentives available to farmers, the rate of cocoa development has been somewhat slower than expected. Landowners in areas considered suitable for the crop have been indecisive about moving from coconuts and 'yaqona' crops. The cyclones of 1985 also had a heavy effect on the crop and consequent production figures have been lower than in previous years. The government has attempted to assist the industry by building new roads with the aid of $3.3 million in EEC funds. These 'cocoa roads' will be completed in the DP9 period.

To date most of Fiji's cocoa has been sold on the London Cocoa Exchange. However, it is hoped an Australian market will be developed.

In 1985 the total yield was 224 tonnes, 221 tonnes of which were exported to the United Kingdom and West Germany; 404 ha of new crops were planted, bringing the total to 4375 ha. Foreign exchange earned from cocoa in 1985 was $0.54 million, compared with $0.57 million in 1984.

Passionfruit. In 1985 passionfruit plantings were reduced by 50 per cent by the time the cyclones had passed through, and 33.43 ha of passionfruit were reduced to 17 ha. This remaining planting yielded 109 tonnes of fruit compared with the 217 tonnes produced in 1984. The number of farmers handling this crop was reduced to 220 from a record high of 457 in 1983/84. South Pacific Foods (SPF) is the sole buyer of all passionfruit grown in the Sigatoka Valley, the primary growing area. As an incentive to growers the company offers a bonus per kilogram for those producing more than 61 kg per vine.

SPF processes the fruits into pulp and juice, then exports the products to its parent company in Australia. From 1985 local winemaker Lester Stocks purchased the pulp for the production of his fruit wines, making this another interesting outlet for SPF. Export earnings for 1985 were $26,715 from 21,826 litres of juice and $28,665 from 22,292 kg of pulp. Total earnings of $55,370 were 50 per cent down on those of the record year of 1983, when earnings reached $100,562.

On Vanua Levu, Fiji Citrus Products processes fruit from its own orchard at its Batiri factory as well as fruit from the Seaqaqa Research Station's 61 vines. It is hoped this operation will expand in the DP9 period.

Citrus. Since the inception of the Batiri citrus scheme in 1978, 133 ha of oranges and lemons have been established. Initially, the intention was to run two 81-ha orchards, one by Fiji Citrus Products Limited (FCPL) and the other by Ministry of Agriculture unit farm holdings. During 1982 the two estates were merged and FCPL took over the citrus orchards developed by MAF for continued cohesive development and management.

Of the initial planting of 170 ha, 37 have

been lost because of lack of water prior to the installation of an irrigation system. In 1985, 125.5 ha were planted with valencia oranges and 7.5 ha with lemons. Actual production in 1985 amounted to 1034 tonnes, of which 861 tonnes were of acceptable quality. The loss was due to a fruit-piercing moth and brown rot disease. The fresh fruit market took 74 tonnes, while the balance was processed into juice, yielding 314,800 litres of single strength juice — a decline of 24 per cent on the 1984 figure.

Pineapples. The Department of Primary Industry is trying to make growers more aware of the need to spread the ripening time of pineapples more evenly throughout the year in order to avoid the regular seasonal glut. The use of fruiting hormones can achieve this.

An estimated 383 ha were planted with fruit in 1985, a slight decrease over the 1984 figure because of cyclones and inconsistent planting. Production was estimated at 3000 tonnes from the 220 ha actually producing.

265 tonnes were processed by the three canning and juice factories — an increase of 102 per cent over the 1984 figure, due to better farmer response. Future expansion it is hoped will produce 12,000 tonnes of fruit per year along with the development of the export market to New Zealand.

Tobacco. The total area under tobacco in 1985 was 179 ha, grown by 610 farmers. The main tobacco growing areas are the Sigatoka Valley and Sabeto-Votualevu in Nadi. Production of cured leaf in 1985 was 317 tonnes, a 30 per cent increase over the 1984 figure. Tobacco is grown principally for the local market, with small quantities being exported to other islands in the region. The industry has now reached saturation point and the Southern Development Company is involving itself in crop diversification.

Poultry. Fiji is self-sufficient in both eggs and poultry meat. Egg production for 1985 exceeded 3,000,000 dozen; broiler meat production exceeded 3558 tonnes. Local hatcheries produced in excess of 167,000 day-old chickens. There are minimal imports of day-old chickens, mainly for use as breeding stock, and special types of poultry meat. Such imports are under licence control. Cyclones Eric and Nigel caused extensive damage to all areas of the industry in 1985, but major

recovery programmes managed to maintain production for the year. The number of slaughterhouses was reduced to five, two having decided not to rebuild after the cyclones.

Local feed millers are protected against imports and feed prices are controlled to restrict unjustified price rises.

Pork. Fiji had achieved self-sufficiency in pork prior to the cyclones of 1985 and the high cost of feed in that year, which resulted in the closure of at least four piggeries. Total production for 1985 was 575 tonnes, 165 tonnes or 22.3 per cent less than the previous year.

To make up the shortfall in production, imports increased significantly and the level of self-sufficiency dropped from 99.9 per cent to 85.1 per cent. These figures only account for pigs killed in registered abattoirs and do not include the large number killed by individual families.

Dairy. In 1985 there were 194 registered dairy farmers, compared with 187 in 1984. Milk and cream received at the Rewa Co-operative Dairy Company showed an increase in production of 10.9 per cent over 1984. Cream production increased by 51.4 per cent. An estimated local non-factory production of ghee and raw milk recorded an increase of 9.4 per cent.

Imports of full cream milk powder, ghee, cheese and curd increased by 5.8 per cent, ghee being the major contributor. Fiji is only 22 per cent self-sufficient in dairy products and the Department of Primary Industries is placing emphasis on improved dairy hygiene, better husbandry techniques and improved pastures in an effort to increase overall production.

Beef. Fiji is striving for self-sufficiency in agricultural products, but imports of farm produce are still high. There has been a drive to increase beef production and two large beef development projects promise good results: the Uluisaivou Corporation scheme, on 40,470 ha on Kadavu, and the Yalavou project on 25,092 ha of hilly country along the upper reaches of the Sigatoka River. However, Fiji has a shortage of female breeding cattle, a slow rate of development and competition from imported beef, comparatively cheap and of good quality. A private cannery, Hygrade Meats

Ltd, produces corned beef.

Local production at registered abattoirs in 1985 was 2239 tonnes of boneless beef.

Total imports of 780 tonnes of boneless beef equivalent was 40 per cent lower than in 1984, due mainly to restrictions placed on canned beef imports since the local cannery commenced operation. Canned beef imports dropped from 1039 tonnes in 1984 to 10 tonnes in 1985, while imports of fresh beef increased by 193 per cent from 263 tonnes to 770 tonnes. Nearly 95 per cent of the raw material for the locally canned beef was imported.

Overall per capita consumption declined from 5.1 kg to 4.3 kg, but the local content rose from 63 per cent to 74 per cent.

The Agriculture Department has concentrated much of its effort on cattle farming. The Uluisaivou project, which involves 2500 'mataqali' landowners who have leased their land to the government, is the fruit of a New Zealand aid scheme. Large numbers of cattle have been imported, most from Australia. They are Brahman–Hereford crosses and there is a large cattle yard with all handling facilities, large stretches of pasture and an extensive roading system. The ranch is consolidated on 2600 ha of land and runs around 1325 head of cattle.

The Yalavou scheme, which is financed partly by Australia, opened in 1979. Seventy-four of the farmers in the project have been funded by the Fiji Development Bank. Supervision is provided by management consultants from Australia. In 1985 there were 99 farms in the project, including 74 beef farms, 21 goat farms and four crop farms; 5496 head of cattle were run in 1985.

Yalavou is expected to produce at least 10 per cent of the country's needs by 1990. Another beef project, at Nabukelevu in Serua/Namosi, will cover 2400 ha of native land at the outset. A ranching scheme at Yaqara on Viti Levu, also government-owned, supplies pure-bred and commercial bulls.

Goats. Per capita consumption of goat meat in 1985 was 1.2 kg, the figure having remained fairly consistent since 1980. Official records show that only 2 per cent of production of goat meat comes from registered slaughterhouses, which in 1985 killed only 1044 animals. However, the major method of marketing continues to be on the hoof direct to consumers, and it is estimated that in 1985 63,000 goats were slaughtered by this method. Goat meat imports rose by 27 per cent to 173 tonnes in the same year.

The Fiji Development Bank, encouraged by the wish of the government to develop goat farming on a greater scale, has undertaken loans to about 254 farmers and extension services assist with improved husbandry techniques. Major goat projects are at Yalavou and the Koroboya Project.

Sheep. The Fiji and Australian Governments are partners in a $1 million sheep breeding project on Makogai Island in the Koro Sea, a leper colony until its closure in 1969. In an attempt to develop a new breed suitable for Fiji's tropical conditions, the tropical Barbados black bellied sheep (from America) are crossed with poll Dorsets from Australia and the local Corriedale variety.

During the DP9 period further research will take place on both Makogai (currently running 1260 sheep) and Nawaicoba (576 sheep) to improve the quality of the crossbreeds for Fijian conditions as well as training programmes for shepherds and managerial staff.

Per capita consumption is 3.3 kg and this continues to rise because of the comparatively low cost of mutton compared to other meats.

In 1985, 5049 tonnes of carcass and 2285 tonnes of boneless lamb and mutton were imported. Self-sufficiency in mutton would save Fiji over $7 million per year in imports.

Commercial fishing. An increasing number of people are being involved in commercial fishing for the local market, and the government continues to encourage participation for both subsistence and commercial purposes. Three programmes assist the establishment of fishing ventures.

The Rural Fisheries Development Programme runs courses in local areas and assists in boat-building for subsistence fishing. In 1985, around 500 people attended courses and an estimated 180.7 tonnes of fish were sold commercially for $256,940. Subsistence production estimates totalled 15,000 tonnes. Infrastructure including collection vessels, trucks and ice plants worth $1.8 million have been established for this programme.

The Commercial Artisanal Fisheries programme assists commercial fishermen, particularly with suitable boats and distribution methods. In 1985 the total volume sold through wholesale and retail outlets was 4083.7 tonnes, valued at $8.1 million.

An estimated 1599 tonnes of aquatic non-fish products valued at $1 million were sold through municipal markets, NMA and other outlets.

The Industrial Fisheries Programme aims to consolidate skipjack tuna processing by assisting the Ika Corporation to catch sufficient quantities of fish for the Pacific Fishing Company (PAFCO).

A fourth programme, the Rural Fish Farming Project, advises on the establishment of fish ponds as commercial ventures. About 40 fish ponds have been established but their success is limited.

Other fishery products exported in 1985 include trochus (274 tonnes, valued at $534,000), 16.1 tonnes of mother of pearl shells valued at $56,000, 62.2 tonnes of beche-de-mer valued at $660,000, 42 kg of frozen crab valued at $183 and 10.82 tonnes of shark fin valued at $108,000.

Tuna industry. In partnership with the Japanese in a fish freezing and canning factory at Levuka, the government is the largest exporter of fish products in the South Pacific islands. The Pacific Fishing Co. (PAFCO), owned by two Japanese companies, has operated a tuna freezing factory at Levuka since 1964. Fiji became a significant shareholder in 1975 when a canning factory was built for $1.3 million. This was followed by the opening of a can manufacturing plant. In 1987 the government had 96 per cent of PAFCO shares.

Another partner in the industry is the Ika Corporation, a government statutory authority. It was established after Fiji was assured by a UN/FAO feasibility study in 1974 that there was sufficient skipjack tuna in Fiji waters to support a commercial fishery. The corporation was launched in December 1975 with one fish catcher chartered from the Hokuku Marine of Tokyo and including 10 Japanese key officers in its complement.

In 1985 the Ika Corporation had a fleet of seven vessels, three Ika-owned, two Japanese-chartered Hokuku Marine vessels and two other privately owned pole and line. A total of 3252 tonnes was landed and sold to the Pacific Fishing Company for $497,400.

A total of 10 long-line vessels was contracted by PAFCO during 1985, landing 2105.6 tonnes of fish valued at $3.75 million. This was an increase of nearly 15 per cent over 1984 figures. In total PAFCO received 8424 tonnes of fish in 1985; 36.6 per cent of this catch was by pole and line vessels, 8.2 per cent from purse seiners, 24.9 per cent from longliners and the remainder imported.

The Pacific Fishing Company continues to operate at about 50 per cent capacity, employing some 300 people. The main reason for under-utilisation is contraints on the supply of fish.

In 1985 about 391,047 cartons of canned fish were produced using 6820 tonnes of fish. A total of 55,554 cartons of tuna valued at $12.5 million were exported and 7400 cartons valued at $106,509 were sold locally.

Timber. Fiji has been self-sufficient in sawn timber, plywood and veneers for some years, and generally speaking limits timber imports to those types of boards or panels for which no local substitutes are available. Paper products are also imported. Exports of timber have increased substantially in recent years, and in 1984 indigenous logs were exported for the first time. Exports consist of sawn timber, veneer and plywoods.

The Forestry Department expects to plant approximately 5000 ha per year until 1989, mainly in mahogany, which will account for 60 per cent of the planted area. Other species will include cordia, cadamba, pine, dakua and even some sandalwood, the timber that helped change the history of Fiji. An additional 1000 ha of pine per year to extend the Department's established 10,000 ha will also be planted.

In 1984 with the lifting of the ban on the export of indigenous timber, logs worth $1 million were traded. Sawn timber exports amounted to 12,015 cubic metres, almost double that of 1983, and were worth more than $3.3 million. There was also a modest increase in the volume and value of veneers and plywoods. Total value of timber exports in that year was $7,763,440.

Imports are subject to licensing under the Customs (Prohibited Imports) Order. In 1983 the total value of imports (mainly chipboard, particle boards and improved wood from New Zealand) was $2,353,962. In 1984 imports had declined to $1,459,985. New Zealand and Australia are main import-export destinations under SPARTECA, while other markets include the UK, Japan, Taiwan and the USA.

At Fiji Expo 86 in Sydney, displays of furniture, furniture components and timber samples resulted in orders valued at $3 million. In mid-1987 pine trees worth about $7 million were destroyed by fire at Nabou.

Mining. The ownership of all minerals in Fiji is vested in the Crown under legislation enacted in 1908. A Mining Board today has oversight of the industry, and there is also a Department of Mineral Resources.

The most valuable mining in Fiji to 1987 has been goldmining, now confined to the mine operated by Emperor Gold Mining Co. Ltd in the Vatukoula area near Tavua, in northern Viti Levu. Until the fishing industry became fully operative in 1978, gold was Fiji's second highest export earner—$8.584 million in 1975, $7.250 million in 1976 and $6.599 million in 1977.

Then came a slump: in January 1978 about 600 of the 1300 workers lost their jobs at Vatukoula and there was uncertainty about the mine's future. But with gold prices rising, a new era of prosperity loomed. Though production in 1980, at 778 kg, was 226 kg less than in 1979, it earned $12.410 million in exports compared with the 1979 figure of $6.492 million for 904 kg.

Production in 1981 was 951.6 kg of gold, valued at almost $12 million, and 250.6 kg of silver valued at almost $70,000.

There was a significant advance in 1982, with production rising to 1456.3 kg of gold earning $15.579 million in export income; 594.3 kg of silver were worth $1.32 million. Figures for 1983 were 1246.2 kg of gold, earning $17.006 million, and 411.6 kg of silver worth $1.46 million.

In 1984, production increased further to 1675.5 kg of gold worth $20.704 million, and 519.7 kg of silver worth $1.38 million. Peak production was 3691 kg in 1941, with later peaks at 3236 kg in 1949 and 3501 kg in 1966.

There were important changes in the gold-mining industry in March 1983, when Emperor Gold Mining Co. and a newcomer,

Western Mining Corporation of Australia, formed a consortium that was granted new mining leases, to which was attached a condition that the consortium could not retrench staff without consulting the government. The consortium was also granted a special prospecting licence, renewable annually, with an agreed $3.13 million exploration programme over 6123 ha in the Tavua basin near Vatukoula. Emperor and Western Mining may establish another mine with the partners having equal shares.

In 1985 the partners began to sink a new shaft south of the existing mine. In 1986 they announced that they planned to invest $30 million over the next three years to increase Vatukoula's output to 54,000 ounces a year of gold.

Copper. In 1975 interest was centred at Namosi, about 40 km inland north-west from Suva, where the giant Amax group, working with the Anglo-American group of South Africa, CRA and the Preussag group of West Germany were exploring copper deposits. In 1977 they announced they would intensify work on the prospect, which looked most promising. However, optimistic statements by Fiji Government ministers at the time indicated that a major copper mine was a strong possibility by the end of the 1970s. Amax was working in an area pinpointed by the Barringer group of Canada, whose Fiji interests it purchased.

Most of the areas licensed to Barringer had been surrendered by it in 1975, but several pinpointed areas, including Namosi, were being investigated more closely. Released areas were being taken up by other companies.

There was disappointment at the end of 1979 when the company reported that the deposits probed appeared to be marginal. While work in this area has ceased, the government continues to advertise the availability of this resource so other developers may submit proposals.

Oil. Fiji has no known deposits of oil or gas. The country possesses large offshore platforms with water depths of less than 250 metres, and these have been the focus of sporadic oil exploration since about 1970. During the five-year tenure of the initial leases about $40 million was spent on exploration. Preliminary geological, geophysical and related activities led to the drilling of five deep wells, three of them offshore, but no petroleum discoveries were made. However, the findings have not been regarded as conclusive and exploration will continue. During 1984 three licences were renewed. Oil searches are controlled by the Petroleum (Exploration and Exploitation) Act 1978, which is designed to cope with the conditions now prevailing, especially the fact that the main areas of interest are offshore. The three licensed exploratory areas are the Yasawas, Bligh Water (north of Viti Levu) and the Great Sea Reef, west of Vanua Levu. A fourth, in the Lomaiviti group east of Viti Levu, had not had its licence renewed by 1986. Each of the four areas comprises approximately 8000 sq. km.

MANUFACTURING. Since independence in 1970, Fiji has produced a range of manufactured products. The processing of raw materials from primary resources has been the most significant form of manufacturing — sugar milling, gold extraction, coconut oil extraction and fish canning. Apart from these, most other manufactured products have been for local consumption rather than export: they usually also have a high import content. Under the terms of SPARTECA export market are being examined for such products as garments, nails, matches, confectionery, alcoholic beverages, paint and processed ginger. The manufacturing industry is largely controlled by local entrepreneurs and is supported by a range of government incentives and concessions to facilitate the establishment or expansion of such industries. In 1988 the government was anxious to increase incentives, especially for overseas investment.

Three industrial subdivisions have been developed at Suva and industry is tending to move out in the direction of Nausori as land becomes scarce in the city area. Other industrial estates are at Lautoka, Nausori, Ba, Tavua, Labasa, Savusavu, Taveuni, Rakiraki and Levuka. The government has plans for estates in rural areas.

The Fiji Trade and Investment Board serves as the first point of contact for investors and the private sector in general. The Development Plan DP9 hopes to maximise Fiji's access advantages under SPARTECA and LOME III; to develop local potential exporters and to continue trade protection policies.

TOURISM. With what was described as phenomenal growth, beginning in the late 1960s, faltering around 1974 and showing an improvement from 1975 onward, Fiji's tourist industry occupies an important position in the country's economic structure. In the early 1960s, the Fiji Visitors Bureau had a difficult task to persuade the government to give it more financial support. The tourist season was almost confined to the winter months; there was only one resort hotel catering for tourists, and few aircraft landed at Nadi Airport. Today there are about 110 tourist resorts, hotels and apartment blocks and visitor totals have risen from 44,561 in 1966 to a record 275,000 in 1986. Cyclones in 1985 had damaged many hotels but recovery was rapid, many resorts taking the opportunity to refurbish.

In 1986 Fiji had a total of 3865 rooms within the tourist industry. Three hundred were added in December 1987, with the opening of the Sheraton Fiji Resort at Nadi. Others planned over the next two years include a $3 million luxury resort on Vatulele Island, south-west of Suva, a Sheraton development on Vomo Island, the $1.5 million Tokoriki Island Resort in the Mamanuca Islands, the $2.5 million Liku Beach resort on Yasawa Island and the $26 million waterfront hotel on reclaimed land in Suva.

Employment within tourism, both directly and indirectly, accounted for 17,823 people in 1985: if development predictions made in 1986 occur, the industry will have the potential of absorbing 300,769 people by 1990. Events of 1987 may have some effect on these predictions.

In 1986, 257,824 tourists came to Fiji: Australia was the biggest market, with more than 86,000 tourists, the USA was next with 69,000 tourists, followed by New Zealand and Canada with 23,000 each. Other markets included the United Kingdom, Japan, continental Europe and other Pacific islands.

After May 1987 tourist arrivals declined rapidly and · monthly statistics for June showed a decline of 76 per cent for Australian arrivals and a massive 87 per cent for arrivals from the US. Other markets showed a similar decline. The introduction of cheaper air fares from Australia and New Zealand and cheaper package tours did something to redress the balance. A greatly devalued Fiji dollar was another attraction toward the end of 1987. However, with the exception of Australia, all visitor markets were significantly down in late 1987 and early 1988. Visitor numbers for 1987 amounted to 189,866, an overall decline of 26.4 per cent from 1986. Gross tourism receipts have increased from $23.4 million in 1970 to $168.7 million in 1986.

The Fiji Government recognises the need to ensure the retention of the 'tourism dollar'; currently two-thirds of tourism receipts flow out of the country. Local people are being encouraged to participate in small scale development in rural areas.

Government also acknowledges that duty-free shopping, once a major attraction for visitors, no longer has the appeal for tourists as dollar values decline in their own countries and the restructuring of home markets often means prices are better there. Merchants are being encouraged to diversify into specialised tourist goods over 'traditional' duty-free items.

The Fiji Visitors Bureau (FVB), the marketing and promotions organisation responsible for selling Fiji abroad and for looking after visitor interests in the country itself, has its headquarters in Suva. It has a branch at Nadi International Airport as well as international offices in Sydney and Melbourne, Auckland, Los Angeles and Tokyo. The FVB is financed largely through the Ministry of Tourism, Civil Aviation and Energy. In 1985 the National Department of Tourism was created and in 1986 the contribution of the government to the FVB was $1 million with additional finance from the private sector.

A hotel turnover tax of eight per cent is levied on all hotel turnover, other than cash bar sales. There is also $10 departure tax paid by all departing air travellers.

HOUSING. The Housing Authority, which was established in 1958, had completed 9014 housing units by the end of 1985. DP9 aims to build 5750 home units in the period. It plans to make available at reasonable cost 7300 serviced land sites for low-income housing.

Basic policy of the Housing Authority is to provide houses at a cost of from 25 per cent to 33 per cent of a person's income. Rental Flat Scheme tenants pay only 15 per cent of their gross weekly wage as rent, the difference between the actual rent and the amount paid being subsidised by the Government. With the Home Purchase Plan, a variety of houses and superior quality flats are sold to people on mortgage after they have served a satisfactory probationary period to determine their acceptability as a tenant of the estate. Repayment is from 20 to 30 years and the amount of monthly repayment depends on the type of house and the amount of the purchaser's deposit.

Under a Site Provision Scheme, fully serviced sites are allocated to people without residential lots who wish to build homes to preferred designs. People aided by this scheme can also obtain cash loans from the Authority to build homes of their own choice. The Authority also encourages self-building by individuals in this scheme to minimise labour costs.

The Housing Authority is financed by government grants and loans, expected to be worth $98 million in the DP9 period. The government also provides Crown land at little or no cost to the Authority to develop into serviced sites.

There are an estimated 4000 to 5000 families defined as squatters. Those who are unemployed or very low income earners are assisted by the Housing Assistance Relief Trust (HART), funded by public appeals, donations and government grants. It is hoped these squatters can eventually be resettled in proper housing areas.

LOCAL COMMERCE. Before they can engage in any business, individuals or companies must take out a licence and pay the necessary fee, ranging from a few dollars to hundreds of dollars. Persons engaging in the professions must also take out a licence and pay an annual fee. From 1977, all businesses in towns and cities had to pay an annual business licence fee to the municipal council. The amount of this fee depended on the classification of each business. Other fees are paid to the Registrar of Titles, for the registration of companies. Forms of enterprises recognised in Fiji are incorporated companies, branches of foreign companies, partnerships, sole proprietorships and trusts.

Types of companies allowed under the Companies Act are limited liability companies, limited either by shares or by guarantee; these can be public or private companies; unlimited liability companies and no-liability companies.

The most common form is the limited liability company, where the members' liability is either limited to the amount unpaid on their shares or to a guaranteed nominated liability in the case of the company winding up. A minimum of two persons is required to form a private company with an upper limit of 50 shareholders. A private company has to appoint a minimum of two directors, one of whom must be resident in Fiji. A public company is formed by seven or more people, with a minimum of three directors, one of them resident in Fiji.

Company registration. To form a company two or more persons subscribe their names to the memorandum and articles of the proposed company. At least one share has to be taken by every subscriber. The memorandum, articles, and declaration of companies are then filed with the Registrar of Companies. After registration, a Certificate of Incorporation is issued, from which date the company may commence business. After incorporation, the following additional documents have to be filed with the Registrar: particulars of directors; return of allotment; location of registered office; later, annual return; as well as, in the case of a public company, statutory report of a statutory meeting; and a prospective or equivalent statement.

Companies incorporated outside Fiji must register within one month after establishment in Fiji and file the relevant documents with the Registrar of Companies. In addition to the documents to be supplied by a local company, the name and address of person(s) resident in Fiji acting as agents for the firm have to be provided. In case the original of the memorandum and articles are not in English, a certified English translation has to be filed. Registration fees range from $38–$303 depending on share capital.

Partners and sole owners. Registration is only necessary where the business name differs from the name of the owner(s). For registration, the name of the business, general nature and principal place of the business and proprietors' names must be filed with the Registrar.

Business licences. Business licences have to be obtained from the respective city or town councils, or for rural areas from the commissioners of the relevant division (Central, Western, Northern, Eastern). A general business licence is issued if the applicant fulfils such conditions as health and zoning regulations and has the landlord's approval for the enterprise. Fees vary depending on locality and type of business, ranging between $20 and $2000.

Special licences. A special licence is necessary from the appropriate authority if a company wishes to engage in a business covered by specific legislation such as banking, insurance, liquor and transport.

OVERSEAS TRADE. Fiji's main exports are sugar and molasses, gold, fish, coconut oil, lumber (including veneer sheets) and ginger in that order of value, but in reality tourism is competing with sugar for first place. It is a 'hidden export', however, and hard figures cannot be quoted.

Tables 7 and 8 illustrate the struggle Fiji has had to make its way in the commercial world. Its exports have more than quadrupled since 1971 but its imports have also quadrupled. So has the trade deficit. It was $49.84 million in 1971 and $184.3 million in 1986. Fiji has attempted to reduce the deficit by import substitution. It has succeeded with eggs, poultry, meat, flour and sharps, fresh beef and lumber—cold comfort when compared with other competitive imports, especially rice, in connection with which Fiji entertained hopes many years ago of becoming self-sufficient. In 1987 largely as a result of economic cut-backs following the May coup, there were significant decreases recorded in such imports as machinery, mineral fuels and manufactures. The provisional trade deficit was thus lower than it had been for many years.

Australia is the dominant supplier of Fiji's imports, accounting for $133.5 million or 28.7 per cent in 1987. New Zealand followed

TABLE 7

PRINCIPAL EXPORTS ($000)	1982	1983	1984	1985
Sugar	125,076	111,935	109,955	111,828
Coconut oil	6165	10,579	18,467	7636
Gold	15,579	16,864	20,520	21,821
Cement	10	127	395	714
Fish (prepared & canned)	9130	14,824	14,362	10,885
Lumber	1643	1812	4362	3052
Ginger	2894	1937	2004	2230
Bakery products	885	1131	1204	1090
Paints	465	509	402	512
Veneer sheets	1762	2179	2873	2785
Molasses	5082	3171	6678	6468

PRINCIPAL IMPORTS ($000)	1982	1983	1984	1985	1986
Food	70,764	78,098	74,736	80,057	77,720
Beverages and tobacco	4030	3623	3560	4299	3469
Crude material ex. fuel	3686	5194	3508	3303	2930
Mineral fuels	136,873	114,753	107,051	115,365	82,101
Animal & vegetable oils	5174	6840	9371	10,478	5867
Chemicals	34,999	39,063	44,286	38,835	41,311
Manufactured goods	78,933	91,480	90,984	100,782	106,278
Machinery, transport equip.	82,010	93,040	86,512	91,625	116,199
Misc. manufactured articles	46,585	47,416	51,256	50,050	44,494
Misc. transactions	12,573	13,677	15,718	13,199	16,361
Total	475,591	493,185	486,983	507,993	496,729

with $78.8 million (16.9 per cent), Japan $56.4 million (12.1 per cent) and Singapore $51.6 million (11.1 per cent). Other imports came from the USA, Britain, Hong Kong, Taiwan and the People's Republic of China.

The main destinations for Fiji's exports were the United Kingdom, worth $138.3 million (41.4 per cent), Australia $67.8 million (20.3 per cent) and Malaysia $30.2 million (9 per cent). New Zealand, Japan, the US, Taiwan and Canada also were small export markets.

In 1987 Fiji's total exports to the EEC were worth $142.9 million while imports from EEC amounted to $38.1 million.

Regional trade agreement. Fiji and the other countries in the region, as member countries of the South Pacific Forum, have

TABLE 8 BALANCE OF TRADE—ALL ITEMS ($000)

	Imports	Exports of local products	Re-exports	Total exports	Trade deficit
1981	539,907	193,735	75,233	268,968	−270,939
1982	475,591	181,199	86,358	267,557	−208,034
1983	493,185	177,875	67,139	245,014	−248,171
1984	486,983	197,869	82,272	280,141	−206,842
1985	507,993	190,630	80,797	271,427	−236,566
1986	493,605	242,049	70,403	312,451	−181,154
1987	465,583	334,173	74,642	408,815	−56,768

TABLE 9 BALANCE OF TRADE BY MAJOR PARTNER COUNTRIES 1986 AND 1987

Country	January–December	Imports	Domestic exports	Re-exports	Total exports	Trade deficit (−) surplus (+)
Australia	1986	166,501	50,623	2864	53,487	113,014 (−)
	1987	133,528	67,798	7583	75,381	58,146 (−)
Canada	1986	4945	4720	218	4938	7 (−)
	1987	3085	5498	117	5615	2530 (+)
China-Taiwan	1986	13,293	3238	44	3282	10,011 (−)
	1987	18,101	10,284	43	10,326	7775 (−)
People's Rep. of China	1986	10,476	6030	8	6038	4438 (−)
	1987	11,892	12,911	6	12,917	1025 (+)
Japan	1986	71,303	4930	486	5416	65,888 (−)
	1987	56,445	11,720	636	12,356	44,089 (−)
New Zealand	1986	82,987	14,864	6071	20,935	62,052 (−)
	1987	78,740	16,428	7335	23,763	54,977 (−)
Singapore	1986	16,091	88	34	122	15,969 (−)
	1987	51,623	149	41	190	51,434 (−)
United Kingdom	1986	21,628	108,153	556	108,709	87,081 (+)
	1987	21,897	138,270	521	138,790	116,894 (+)
United States	1986	23,832	12,999	1763	14,762	9070 (−)
	1987	24,438	17,656	3235	20,891	3547 (−)
Other	1986	82,549	36,404	58,359	94,763	9090 (+)
	1987	65,834	53,459	55,125	108,586	42,752 (+)
TOTAL	1986	493,605	242,049	70,403	312,451	181,154 (−)
	1987	465,583	334,173	74,642	408,815	56,768 (−)

Totals subject to rounding of figures.

TABLE 10 EXPORTS TO EUROPEAN ECONOMIC COMMUNITY ($000)

	1983	1984	1985	1986
Total domestic exports	70,667	75,451	83,449	110,184
Major items				
sugar	60,514	61,944	72,696	90,541
canned fish	8539	10,092	8564	12,035
coconut oil	551	—	310	2666
cork and wood	292	207	232	130

TABLE 11 EXPORTS UNDER SPARTECA ($000)

	1983	1984	1985	1986
Destination Australia	7045	11,762	9532	9427

begun to improve their export trade with Australia and New Zealand through the South Pacific Regional Trade and Economic Co-operation Agreement (SPARTECA), which they signed with Australia and New Zealand on 14 July 1980 at Tarawa (Kiribati). Under the agreement Australia and New Zealand permit certain scheduled goods free and unrestricted entry provided they originate in and are imported from Forum countries.

The list began with a wide range of products and, on several occasions, new items have been included. One important addition on the Australian list was plywood and this was enlarged in 1983 to include pine timber.

An amendment to the Agreement in 1986 meant that from July 1986 all exports from Fiji with the exception of clothing, textiles, footwear, motor vehicles, steel and sugar are allowed to enter Australia duty-free and quota-free providing they meet the Rules of Origin requirements.

Australian Joint Venture Scheme. This scheme has been established under the administration of the Australian International Development Assistance Bureau. It is designed to provide assistance in the form of loan funds to enable business concerns or individuals in Fiji to acquire equity in joint business ventures with Australian partners. Such ventures should be development related and contribute to the creation and expansion

of income and employment in Fiji. The Fiji Trade and Investment Board, in co-operation with Fiji Development Bank Nominees Ltd, is responsible for the implementation of the scheme in Fiji.

Fiji co-operatives. About 1203 co-operative societies of all types operated in Fiji in 1986, providing services to about 30,000 rural families. Most small towns and agricultural settlements have one or two for the purpose of marketing copra, and there are co-operative land, fishing and other ventures. The Fiji Co-operative Association has been developed as the central wholesale supplier for retail co-operatives throughout the country.

Co-operatives are supervised by the Department of Co-operatives. A co-operative training centre at Lami, Suva, is attended by co-op officials from many other Pacific Island countries. Most towns have a municipal market where local farmers sell vegetables, fruit, eggs and fish. Saturday is the main market day.

The FCAL is directing its activities toward the marketing of agricultural produce, developing close working strategies with the National Marketing Authority.

Customs tariff. Fiji uses the Brussels Nomenclature schedule for import duties. This is a very detailed system and breaks down the schedule into more than 1200 individual items. Fiji also now uses the single-line system. The tariff rate is divided into fiscal duty and customs duty. There is an export tax on some primary products and minerals.

The import duties range from free on several staple food lines to more than 75 per cent on some lines. A new schedule for import duties was introduced in the 1986 Budget to protect local industries and to help conserve foreign exchange. On the other hand, some items were added to the duty free list aimed at promoting the tourist industry. Suntan oils now attract 10 per cent duty (as compared with 57.5 per cent previously).

A detailed list of duties may be obtained from the Comptroller of Customs, c/- Ministry of Finance, Government Buildings, Victoria Parade, Suva (Tel. 22831).

FINANCE. For budget purposes, Fiji divides its revenue and expenditure into 'recurrent' and 'capital'. Its recurrent revenue comes from taxation, customs and excise duty, post office receipts, licence fees, etc. Its capital revenue comes mostly from raising loans; from grants and from appropriations from general revenue.

The 1986 Budget estimates were $463.325 million on total expenditure and $378.306 million in total revenue and grants. Actual figures were below original estimates, with a negative impact on both the government's operating and overall deficits. The actual operating deficit in 1986 was $22.8 million, while the overall deficit of $94 million was

$17 million greater.

The total government expenditures for 1986 amounted to $454.8 million, representing a 10.2 per cent increase over the corresponding figure for 1985 ($402.6 million). Actual revenue for 1986 was $360.8 million, compared with $349.9 million in 1985.

Inland revenue receipts declined in 1986 by 1.9 per cent from the 1985 receipts ($143.7 million and $146.5 million respectively). Customs and excise revenue increased only slightly — $124.3 to $125.9 million; non-tax revenue increased by 13.4 per cent ($73.7 to $83.6 million) and grant aid increased from $5.4 to $7.6 million.

Overall, the 1986 Budget revenues showed a 3.1 per cent increase over the 1985 figures; actual revenue was only 95.4 per cent of original estimates.

The 1987/88 Budget was delayed by the coups until late December 1987, and provided for expenditure of $421 million and a deficit of $83 million.

Tax system. The Department of Inland Revenue administers the laws relating to income taxation, estate and gift duties, and assesses and collects those duties. Both individuals and companies are liable to income tax. The tax year is the calendar year.

Income tax. The 1974 Income Tax Act came into force on 1 January 1974, replacing the Income Tax Ordinance of 1965. It introduced a new scale for the taxation of incomes, but retained the pay-as-you-earn and pro-

TABLE 12 COMPARATIVE STATEMENT OF EXPENDITURE 1983–85 ($000)

	1983	1984	1985
General administration	71,486.6	75,829.1	89,162.2
Social services	31,107.7	35,910.5	34,556.5
Education/USP	81,494.5	88,317.0	82,983.0
Economic services	27,710.1	32,786.1	43,149.4
Infrastructure	61,562.1	60,182.5	55,516.4
Miscellaneous	87,283.1	100,558.3	98,185.4
Total operating	310,614.3	344,188.0	349,323.4
Total capital	50,291.8	49,395.5	53,229.5
Grand total	360,901.1	393,583.5	402,552.9

TABLE 13 FIJI — RECURRENT BUDGET ($ millions)

	1984	1985	1986^P
Operating expenditure	344.188	349.323	398.680
Capital expenditure	49.395	53.229	56.157
Total expenditure	393.583	402.552	454.837
General revenue	325.619	338.975	348.195
Capital revenue and grants	12.038	10.958	12.619
Total revenue	337.658	349.933	360.814
Overall budget deficit	55.925	52.611	94.023

P = Provisional

TABLE 14 AID GRANTS FOR 1985

	Estimate	Actual
Australian Development Import Grants	2,500,000	92,985
Australian South Pacific Assistance Programme	4,388,500	2,050,030
New Zealand Bilateral Assistance Programme	1,525,900	1,960,354
United Nations Development Programme	—	40,336
European Economic Community	3,086,000	699,610
Other grant aid	2,753,600	563,083
Total	14,254,000	5,406,398

visional tax systems. Amendments were made in 1986 raising the ceiling of income at which only basic tax is paid from $1500 to $2000. The 1983/84 Budget introduced a new 5 per cent surcharge on all those paying above the basic tax.

Basic tax is levied at a rate of 2.5 cents on every dollar of income less personal allowances, and on every dollar of chargeable income derived during the year by every company, except non-resident shipping companies. In addition to basic tax, normal tax is levied on chargeable incomes: after deduction of main allowances such as those for single people, widows and widowers with dependent child, non-employed spouse, working wife, child allowance, education, dependent blood relative, life insurance and provided fund payments, professional membership, subscriptions and journals.

In 1985 the Estate and Gift Duties Act was amended to discontinue payment of duties in respect of people who died after September 1984 or gifts made after that date. Per-

sonal income tax rates were also reduced. After the devastating effects of four cyclones in 1985 and resulting problems with insurance claims, the government introduced a deduction for cyclone reserve accounts subject to certain limitations.

Composite rates for companies non-resident in Fiji are higher than for resident companies. New rates were introduced in 1985 and details are available from the Commissioner of Inland Revenue, 5th Floor, Fiji Development Bank Building, Victoria Parade, Suva.

Other taxes. Fiji citizens and residents pay a 5 per cent tax on company interest and dividends, and non-residents are liable to a 15 per cent dividend withholding tax. Dividend tax is not payable by non-resident companies on branch profits repatriated out of Fiji, and dividend tax is not payable on dividends paid to a Fiji resident company.

All Fiji employers are required to pay a levy of 1 per cent of their annual payroll to the Fiji National Training Council but can claim grants from the council for the training of employees.

Fiji has arrangements for relief from double taxation of income with several countries including Britain, Japan and New Zealand. Negotiations are also taking place with Australia and India for similar agreements. In 1985 an amendment to the Income Tax Act allowed staff at the USP under the AUIDP and any other staff on programmes paid for by the Australian Government to be exempt from Fiji taxation laws, providing they are subject to tax in Australia.

Currency. Fiji's decimal currency has notes in denominations of $1, $2, $5, $10 and $20. Coins are 1c, 2c (bronze), 5c, 10c, 20c and 50c (cupro-nickel).

In 1974 the Fiji dollar's link with the pound sterling was broken and attached to the US dollar for the purposes of exchange transactions. In 1975 the government also ended the tie with the US dollar and in mid-1975 the Fiji dollar was 'floating'. The rate for exchange purposes is calculated daily by the Reserve Bank of Fiji and is based on prevailing rates of currencies of several countries having major trade with Fiji. Fiji is a member of the International Monetary Fund, World Bank and various other international finance agencies. In 1987 the currency was devalued twice, amounting to a total devaluation of 34 per cent.

Banks. Banks in 1987 were: National Bank of Fiji, Bank of New Zealand, Westpac, Bank of Baroda, Australia and New Zealand Banking Group Ltd and the Fiji Development Bank.

Fiji's banking system is controlled by the Reserve Bank of Fiji, which grew from the previous Central Monetary Authority (CMA) established in 1973, itself an outgrowth of the earlier Currency Board. The Reserve Bank is banker and fiscal agent of the government and banker to certain statutory corporations and the commercial banks. The bank's headquarters are in Pratt St, Suva.

The National Bank of Fiji provides savings bank facilities at all post offices and postal agencies; there are also branches in most commercial centres. It is a state-owned trading bank. Banking hours are 10 am to 3 pm Monday to Thursday and 10 am to 4 pm Friday; closed weekends. Head office and main branch are in Victoria Parade, Suva.

Fiji Development Bank. This is a statutory body set up as a source of credit for agricultural, industrial and commercial ventures. Funds come from the government as grants and loans and from the Asian Development Bank. At the end of 1985 outstanding advances by it totalled $73 million. The bank also operates a stock exchange, which opened in June 1979.

Fiji Trade and Investment Board (FITB). This was created by the government to create employment by generating more vigorous investment activity and to achieve national development objectives; to promote investment in and the development of industries, ventures or enterprises that enhance employment opportunities; increase exports; reduce imports or otherwise benefit Fiji's economy. The board comprises representatives of government, employers and trade unions.

It is the first point of contact for potential investors, foreign and local, and will provide information to investors on all aspects of industrial investment and development, as well as facilitating investors' dealings with ministries and departments.

As an investment promotion body, the FITB provides guidelines on priority sectors for investment in accordance with overall government policy, and on available incentives and concessions; identification of product lines and projects based on natural and manpower resources; preparation of schemes/profiles on product lines already identified; pre-feasibility studies; marketing research; survey of domestic and export markets and expansion programmes; information to entrepreneurs on choice of industry, size of investment and plant; sources or raw material and equipment; information on Fiji's economic and investment conditions; information for foreign investors seeking local investors; information on appropriate technology; extension services such as assistance to local and foreign investors and in the co-operation of local and foreign investors for joint ventures; assistance to entrepreneurs for all administrative, commercial, financial, technical and management problems during the starting period. Prospective investors and firms or companies should apply to the Director, Fiji Trade and Investment Board, PO Box 2303, Government Buildings, Suva.

Investment incentives. Fiji welcomes investment in manufacturing industries and offers many incentives to foreign investors. But the government has a priority list and the Ministry of Economic Development's policy is to see local participation in any foreign-sponsored undertaking when possible. Concessions include income tax concessions (up to five years tax free); reduced rates of withholding tax on interest and dividend paid to non-residents; accelerated depreciation relief; permit for primary industries to write off certain development costs in the year when they occur and to carry losses forward until they have been fully recouped; duty concessions on imported plant, machinery and equipment and raw materials; and, protection against imports.

Special tax relief is available for mining companies if the minister is satisfied the enterprise is expedient for the economic development of Fiji. New agricultural projects receive special tax attention, as do any developments concerned with tourism.

The Australian Joint Venture Scheme assists foreign investors and local entrepreneurs to set up projects; it is administered by the Fiji Trade and Investment Board.

The government prefers local and foreign borrowing for setting up a new industry to be in the same ratio as the local and foreign shareholding in the company. Finance is available from the Fiji Development Bank, Fiji National Provident Fund, and normal local sources. Potential investors seeking information about regulations and incentives covering foreign investment should contact the Director, Fiji Trade and Investment Board, PO Box 203, Government Buildings, Suva (Tel. 31 5988).

Development plans. Fiji is currently working through its Ninth Development Plan (DP9), which covers the period 1986–1990. The total allocated for capital expenditure is $439.9 million, during the plan period, although development fundings, in common with every other aspect of the economy, is expected to be affected by the consequences of the military coups.

TRANSPORT. Fiji is well supplied with public transport. Virtually every road has a bus service and there are well over 300 operators, with 1280 vehicles. In addition there are about 2218 taxis and 2736 rental

and hire cars. All bus and taxi fares are fixed by the Road Transport Authority, but some taxis in country areas do not have meters installed.

Roads. The longest road in the country is that around Viti Levu of 510 km. From Suva to Lautoka, west-about, it is called Queen's Road; and from Suva to Lautoka, east-about, it is King's Road. At the end of 1986 Fiji had about 2600 km of roads maintained by the government with about 600 km being all-weather roads. The multi-million dollar highway between Suva and Nadi (Queen's Road) is completely tar-sealed.

Vehicles. At the end of 1986 there were 68,654 vehicles of all kinds registered in Fiji, compared with 66,287 in 1985. The total includes 28,646 private cars, 22,443 goods vehicles, 4450 tractors and 3924 motor cycles. 'All other vehicles', totalling 2957, includes trailers, cranes, loaders and forklifts.

Overseas airlines. Fiji is well serviced by international airlines. Nadi, on the western side of Viti Levu, is the main entry point though Air Pacific and Air Nauru land at Nausori Airport, near Suva on the eastern side of Viti Levu, from Tonga and Nauru. Air Caledonie, Air New Zealand, Canadian Airlines, Continental Airlines, Fiji Air, Polynesian Airlines, Airlines of the Marshall Islands, and Qantas all fly into Fiji.

Air Pacific is currently being managed by Qantas Airlines in a three-year contract signed in 1985, following a widely publicised series of management difficulties. The contract is regarded as an important instrument for returning Air Pacific to profitability.

Flights arrive and depart 24 hours a day and there is a departure tax of $10, to be paid at time of check-in.

Domestic airlines. Fiji Air Limited operates all domestic routes in Fiji with the exception of Nadi-Nausori-Labasa and also flies to Tuvalu. It has a fleet of DHC Twin Otter 200s and an amphibian. The company is private, but the government holds about 16 per cent of issued stock.

Pacific Crown Aviation Ltd operates helicopters from Lami. Charter work is undertaken for the mining industry, the Fiji Electricity Authority, government departments and private interests.

Turtle Island Airways Ltd operates amphibian planes from Nadi Airport on charter flights to island resorts and other destinations in Fiji.

Sunflower Airlines flies regularly between Nadi and Savusavu Taveuni and Pacific Harbour. Sun Tours Air flies between Nadi and island resorts in the Mamanuca group.

Airport. Fiji's international airport is at Nadi, about 200 km from Suva by road. A multi-million dollar scheme to upgrade the airport for use by jumbo jets was completed in mid-1975. Improvements included an enlarged terminal building, strengthened runways and more parking aprons.

Apart from Nadi, the most important local airport is at Nausori, 22 km from Suva. It was, like Nadi, built during the war. It is subject to occasional flooding because of its proximity to the Rewa River. The 1969 m main runway is sealed and has a flare path for night landings. A secondary runway is grass over gravel.

Domestic airstrips are at Ba, 730 m long; Bureta (Ovalau), 790 m; Bua, 1060 m; Deuba, 760 m; Gau, 760 m; Koro, 760 m; Lakeba, 760 m; Labasa, 1070 m; Laucala Island, 820 m; Malololailai Island, 640 m; Matai, 910 m; Natadola, 595 m; Rabi, 660 m; Rotuma, 700 m; Savusavu, 915m; Vanuabalavu, 920 m; Vatukoula, 745 m; Wakaya Island, 730 m; Ono-i-Lau, 760 m; Moala, 700 m.

Aircraft arrivals at Nadi Airport in 1985 totalled 2645, carrying 250,337 passengers and departures were 2737 with 256,409 passengers. Nausori Airport arrivals in 1985 totalled 490 with 14,503 passengers. Departures were 385 with 10,859 passengers. Domestic aircraft carried 267,268 passengers in 1985 on 3122 domestic flights. Ground-handling operations at Nadi Airport were taken over from Qantas on 1 September 1981 by government-formed Air Terminal Services (Fiji) Ltd.

Ports. The three ports of entry in Fiji are Suva, Lautoka and Levuka. All ports and wharves are under the jurisdiction of the Ports Authority of Fiji, which also assumes responsibility for stevedoring and the supply of cargo-handling machines. It is concerned with developing and expanding harbour and shore facilities to cater for the needs of overseas shipping.

Water and fuel oil can be obtained at all three ports. At Lautoka and Suva ships can be connected to telephone services. None of the ports has cranes: all cargo is discharged by ships' derricks. At Suva harbour tugs are available; they are of an ocean-going class, also suitable for salvage work.

Wharves. The main Suva wharf, Kings Wharf, has a face of 495 m and can take vessels up to 42,000 tonnes. Flanking the main wharf are the Walu Bay face of about 183 m and Princes Wharf of 152 m. The Port Lautoka is the second largest port in Fiji. Most of the sugar exports pass through Lautoka. The wharf has three faces, Queens West of 139 m, Queens North 78 m and Queens East 122 m, with a sugar-loading pier of 76.2 m. The Levuka wharf on the east coast of Ovalau was opened in May 1980. It has two faces, Kings North of 171 m, and Kings South of 175 m. Its main traffic is the fishing fleet, which serves the Pacific Fishing Company's factory.

There are smaller wharves at Vatia and Point Ellington on Viti Levu, at Labasa and Savusavu on Vanua Levu and at Rotuma.

At Suva there are slipping facilities for ships up to 1000 tonnes. Engineering facilities for a wide range of repairs for much larger ships also exist at Suva.

There are three ship repair and building yards at Suva, one government-owned and equipped with a gantry crane. IMEL (Industrial and Marine Engineering Ltd) has the largest shipyard in the region. Charles Whippy & Co. Ltd operates the other shipyard.

Harbour masters are located as follows: Suva Harbour Master's office, Kings Wharf, Suva; Lautoka — Lautoka Harbour Master's office, Queens Wharf, Lautoka; Levuka — Harbour Master and Chief Customs Office at Customs Office, Levuka jetty, Levuka.

Shipping services. Fiji receives a number of shipping lines, both cargo carriers and cruise boats.

The following lines operate out of Australia on a regular basis: PACE Line (ACTA Shipping), Sofrana-Unilines (Fiji Express Line), Pacific Forum Line, Australia Pacific Islands Line, Sitmar Cruises, and P & O. Kyowa Shipping sails ex Singapore to Suva. New Zealand Unit Express (NZUE) sails ex Manila to Fiji and Nedloyd sails ex Surabaya to Fiji.

From Honolulu, State Shipping Associates

sails to Fiji. From Japan to Fiji the services are provided by Kyowa Shipping and Bali Hai. Reef Shipping connects Auckland and Fiji, as does the Blue Star Line.

As with airline schedules, these connections change with demand and enquiries should be made direct to shipping agents.
Inter-island shipping. Local shipping plays an important role in Fiji and provides services to scattered outer islands. In Suva the largest part of the trade to other islands is handled from Princess Wharf. The Walu Bay wharves are used by barges and vessels with shallow draft. Shipping services between the two main islands have increased considerably in recent years with the introduction of two roll-on-roll-off ferry services. Main shipping agents are Wong's Shipping, Patterson Bros and North West Shipping, all in Suva.

COMMUNICATIONS. Internal telephone and radio telephone services are being continually extended in Fiji. Practically all inhabited islands can be contacted by telephone or radio telephone services. There are automatic exchanges in most large towns on Viti Levu with direct dialling between Suva, Lautoka, Nadi, Ba, Nausori, Deuba, Labasa, Levuka, Navua, Rakiraki and Sigatoka.

Fiji is a telecommunications centre for the South Pacific region and is linked by the Commonwealth Pacific Telephone Cable (COMPAC) with Australia, New Zealand, and the international telecommunications network. Fiji International Telecommunications Ltd (FINTEL) operates the earth station at Wailoku near Suva, which connects Fiji with the artificial satellites relaying messages around the earth.

The telex system, with international subscriber dialling to most worldwide destinations, is now a familiar part of the country's commercial life and is used extensively. Its development was rapid, following upon the concentration of many diplomatic and international agencies in Fiji after independence.
Radio. Radio broadcasts are in English, Fijian and Hindi. Under the call Radio Fiji, the Fiji Broadcasting Commission provides all broadcasting services in Fiji apart from the introduction in 1985 of FM96, Fiji's first independent commercial radio station, which provides a 24-hour service to the

south-east corner.

Radio Fiji 1 broadcasts in English and Fijian and Radio Fiji 2 broadcasts in English and Hindi. Radio Fiji 3FM broadcasts in English. As radio is often the only source of news and information for people in outer regions, considerable emphasis is placed on news, current affairs and rural interest programmes.
Television. The start of commercial television broadcasting was planned for 1987, based on negotiations between the Australian media group Publishing and Broadcasting Ltd (PBL) and the Fiji Government with PBL controlling 80 per cent of the service, but the political situation has upset all plans and in 1988 there were no signs of a start to TV transmission. Video is already widely used in Fiji.
Newspapers. Newspapers are available in all three languages — English, Fijian and Hindi. The _Fiji Times_ (1869) and _Fiji Sun_ (1974) were the English dailies. The _Sunday Times_ and the _Sunday Sun_ were the Sunday papers published by the Fiji Times and Herald Ltd and Newspapers of Fiji Ltd respectively. Following the first coup and the imposition of press censorship, both the _Times_ and the _Sun_ closed. The _Times_ recommenced publication shortly after, with an assurance that nothing detrimental to stability and public order would be published. The _Sun_ remains closed.

Nai Lalakai in Fijian and _Shanti Dut_ in Hindi are weekly papers. _Islands Business_ is a monthly business and news magazine. There are also several newspapers directed at the tourist market. These include the _Fiji Beach Press_ and _Fiji Funtastic_.

ARCHIVES, LIBRARIES, MUSEUM. The National Archives of Fiji are housed in the Thurston Gardens, Suva. The documents preserved there mainly concern the British administration of Fiji, but there are other important collections, such as the records of the Methodist Church in Fiji. Attached is the Sir Alport Barker Library, an extensive collection of books on the Pacific bequeathed to Fiji by a former owner of the _Fiji Times_.

The Fiji Museum is in the same area and has an extensive display of Fiji and Pacific artifacts, including war canoes and the rudder from the _Bounty_.

WATER. Water supplies are provided to all main towns. Vatukoula has a private supply. The Suva, Ba, Lautoka, Nadi, Nausori and Tavua supplies are fully treated. The Labasa, Levuka, Navua, Savusavu, Sigatoka and Vaileka supplies are partly treated or just chlorinated. Many villages, schools, hospitals and government stations in rural areas have untreated supplies. Special treated supplies go to the tourist areas at Korotogo and Pacific Harbour.

More than 75 per cent of Fiji's population has access to piped water. The Vaturu Dam in the Nausori Highlands, constructed at a cost of more than $80 million, has greatly eased supply problems in the Nadi and Lautoka areas. Water supplies are currently heavily subsidised and DP9 aims to make provision of water supplies more cost-effective and efficient.

ELECTRICITY. The Fiji Electricity Authority (FEA), created in 1966 with a small building in Lautoka, a staff of 210 and income of $400,000 a year, owns all power stations and made a big stride forward in September 1983 with the opening of the $230 million Manasavu hydro-electricity project, which took five years to construct on Nadrau Plateau in the centre of Viti Levu. It is expected to save Fiji $22 million a year, much of it in oil imports which, it is hoped, will be cut by more than 60 per cent. There are 367 towers to carry the aluminium conductor wires. The 17 km-long lake covering 470 hectares is cradled in the Nadrau Plateau (1000 m above sea level) where average rainfall is about 360 cm a year. The dam wall across Nanuku Creek is 82 m high. The turbines on the Wailoa River 625 m below the lake can produce double the power needs of Viti Levu in the 1980s. There is a 5.4 km tunnel from the lake to Wailoa power house which houses four 20-megawatt generators. The national control centre is at Vuda, near Lautoka, and there are substations at Vuda, Wailoa and Cunningham Road in Suva.

The FEA's total income in 1985 from the sales of electricity and fees charged amounted to $39.53 million.

MAJOR OFFICE HOLDERS
President:
   Ratu Sir Penaia Ganilau
Prime Minister, Minister for Foreign Affairs
and Minister for the Civil Service:
   Ratu Sir Kamisese Mara
Minister for Home Affairs, National Youth Service and Auxiliary Army Services:
   Brigadier Sitiveni Rabuka
Minister for Finance and Economic Planning:
   Josefa Kamikamica

GOVERNMENT MINISTRIES AND DEPARTMENTS
Parliament, PO Box 2352, Gvt Bldgs, Suva Tel.: 211-652
Cabinet, PO Box 2353, Gvt Bldgs, Suva Tel.: 211-207
Judiciary (Supreme and National Courts), PO Box 2215, Gvt Bldgs, Suva Tel.: 211-335
Attorney General and Minister of Justice, Government Bldgs, Suva, Tel.: 211-580 Divisions: Crown Law, Fiji Law Commission, Public Prosecutions, and Judicial Department
Communications, Transport and Works Ministry, Ganilau House, Suva, Tel.: 315-133 Divisions: Post and Telecommunications, Public Works, Road Transport, and Marine Department
Cooperative Ministry and National Marketing Authority, Fiji Development Bank Bldg, Suva, Tel.: 312-566 Divisions: Consultancy and Development, Administration and Accounts, Fiji Cooperative Training Centre, Central Division, Eastern Division, Audit Division
Education Ministry, Headquarters Bldg Suva, Tel.: 314-477 Divisions: Research, Training and Development, Curriculum Development, Education Resources Centre, Library Services, Fiji Institute of Technology, Nasinu Residential College, Department of Youth and Sports
Employment and Industrial Relations Ministry, Fiji Development Bank Bldg, Suva, Tel.: 211-640 Divisions: Tripartite Forum, Permanent Arbitrator, Central/Eastern Division, Employment Services, Factories
Fijian Affairs Ministry, 61 Carnarvon St, Suva, Tel.: 22-971 Divisions: Fiji Affairs Board, Fijian Education, Business Opportunity, Fijian Development Fund, Native Lands and Fisheries Commission,

Fijian Dictionary Projects
Finance and Economic Planning Ministry,
Government Bldg, Suva, Tel.: 211-425
Divisions: Budget, Statistics, Customs and
Excise, EDP Computer Services,
Government Supplies, Inland Revenue,
Printing and Stationery
Forest Ministry, 91 Gordon St, Suva,
Tel.: 313-439 Divisions: Resources and
Development, Timber Production,
Educational Services, Forest Park and
Nasinu Timber Research Unit
Health and Social Welfare Ministry,
Government Bldg, Suva, Tel.: 314-564
Divisions: Hospital Services, Health
Planning, Primary and Preventive Health
Services, Dental Services, Fiji School of
Medicine, Social Welfare Department
Home Affairs Ministry, Government Bldg,
Suva, Tel.: 211-401/211-210 Divisions:
Emergency Operations, Fiji Military
Forces, Fiji Police, Prison Services,
Immigration
**Housing and Urban Development
Ministry,**
Government Bldg, Suva,
Tel.: 211-310/211-416 Divisions: Housing,
Urban Affairs, Town and Country Planning
Indian Affairs Ministry, Government
Bldg, Suva, Tel.: 211-370
Information Ministry, Government Bldg,
Suva, Tel.: 211-700
Lands and Minerals Ministry, Mead
Road, Suva, Tel.: 381-611 Divisions:
Lands and Surveys, Minerals, and Energy
Primary Industries Ministry, Rodwell
Road, Suva, Tel.: 22-993 Divisions:
Economic Planning and Statistics, Animal
Health and Production, Quarantine,
Fisheries, Drainage and Irrigation, Farm
Management Cooperative Association of Fiji
Primary Minister's Office, Government
Bldg, Suva, Tel.: 211-201 Divisions:
Cabinet, Fiji Institute for Fijian Culture,
Government Archives, Public Service
Appeals Board, and Public Service
Commission
**Rural Development and Rural Housing
Ministry,** Government Bldg, Suva,
Tel.: 314-286
**Tourism, Civil Aviation and Energy
Ministry,** Reserve Bank Bldg, Pratt St,
Suva, Tel.: 312-788
Trade and Commerce Ministry,

Government Bldg, Suva, Tel.: 211-327
**Women's Affairs and Social Welfare
Ministry,** Qtrs 5A and 5B, Clark St,
Suva, Tel.: 312-681
Youth and Sports Ministry, Selbourne St,
Suva, Tel.: 315-800

FIJI REPRESENTATIVES OVERSEAS

Australia: Fiji High Commission, 9
Beagle Street, Red Hill, ACT 2600,
Canberra, PO Box E159, Tel.: 959-148,
Tlx: 62-345, Cable: FIJIREP Canberra,
Accredited to Malaysia and Singapore
Fiji Consul-General, 225 Clarence Street,
Sydney, NSW 2000, Tel.: 290-1615,
Tlx: 70-342
Fiji Visitors Bureau, 38 Martin Place,
Sydney, NSW 2000, Tel.: 231-4251
Belgium: Embassy of Fiji, 66 Avenue
de Cortenberg, Boite Postale 7, 1040
Brussels, Tel.: 736-9050, Tlx: 26934,
Cable: FIJIREP BRUSSELS,
Ambassador to the EEC, France,
Belgium, Netherlands Luxembourg and
Italy
Canada: Fiji Honorary Consul, 1437 West
64th Avenue, Vancouver, BC, V6P 2NS
Japan: Embassy of Fiji, Noa Building (10th
Fl.), 3-5, 2-Chome Azabudai, Minato-
Ku, Tokyo 106, Tel.: 033872038,
Tlx: FIJIREP J32150, Accredited to the
People's Republic of China and the Republic
of Korea
Pacific Islands: Roving Ambassador, PO
Box 2220 Govt Bldgs, Suva, Tel.: SUVA
211-702, Roving Ambassador to Pacific
Island countries in Fiji
Papua New Guinea: Fiji Honorary Consul,
PO Box 1457, Boroko, Tel.: 258-811
New Zealand: Fiji High Commission, 2nd
Fl. Robert Jones House, Jervois Quay,
Wellington, PO Box 3940, Tel.: 735-401,
Tlx: FIJIREP NZ 31406
Fiji Visitors Bureau, Rm 605, Tower Block,
Canterbury Arcade, 47 High Street, PO Box
1179, Auckland, Tel.: 732-133
United Kingdom: Fiji High Commission,
34 Hyde Park Gate, London, SW7, 5BN,
Tel.: 584-3661, Tlx: 22408, Cable: FIJIREP
London, Accredited to West Germany
(Federal Republic of Germany), Egypt,
Israel and the Vatican Marketing Services
(T&T) Ltd, 52-54 High Holborn, London
WCIV 6RI, Tel.: (01) 242-3131

United Nations and USA. Permanent Representative of Fiji to the United Nations, One UN Plaza, 26th Fl., New York NY 10017, Tel.: 355-7316, Tlx: 421409, Cable: FIJIREP NEW YORK, Accredited to Canada, Ambassador to the USA.

Fiji Consul-General, Suite 316, Ahmanson Financial Centre, 3701 Wilshire Blvd, Los Angeles, California 90010, Tel.: (213) 389-0292

Fiji Honorary Consul, 6620 Telegraphic Avenue, Oakland, California 94609, Tel.: (415) 654-3970

FOREIGN MISSIONS IN FIJI

American Embassy, GPO 218, Suva, Tel.: 314-466

Australian High Commission, GPO 214, Suva, Tel.: 312-844

Belgium Consulate, GPO 149, Suva, Tel.: 23-091

British High Commission, GPO 1355, Suva, Tel.: 311-033

Embassy of the People's Republic of China, Private Mail Bag GPO, Suva, Tel.: 22-425

Danish Consulate, GPO 200, Suva, Tel.: 315-199

French Embassy, Private Mail Bag GPO, Suva, Tel.: 312-925

Indian High Commission, GPO 405, Suva, Tel.: 312-255

Honorary Israeli Consulate, PO Box 2365 Govt Bldgs, Suva, Tel.: 385-533

Italian Consulate, GPO 686, Suva, Tel.: 24-671

Embassy of Japan, PO Box 2312 Govt Bldgs, Suva, Tel.: 25-631

Korean Embassy, Private Mail Bag GPO, Suva, Tel.: 311-977

Malaysian High Commission, GPO 356, Suva, Tel.: 312-166

Nauruan Consulate, PO Box 2420 Govt Bldgs, Suva, Tel.: 313-566

Netherlands Consulate, GPO 1378, Suva, Tel.: 311-422

Norwegian Consulate, GPO 149, Suva, Tel.: 23-091

Pakistan Consulate, GPO 1470, Suva, Tel.: 361-388

Papua New Guinea High Commissioner, PO Box 2447 Govt Bldgs, Suva, Tel.: 25-420

Philippines Consulate, GPO 1296, Suva, Tel.: 312-344

Swedish Consulate, GPO 1443, Suva, Tel.: 312-644

Taiwan (R.O.C.), GPO Box 53, Suva, Tel.: 315-922

Tuvalu High Commission, GPO 1495, Suva, Tel.: 22-697

West Germany Consulate, PO Box 155, Navua, Tel.: 45-062

INTERNATIONAL AND REGIONAL ORGANISATIONS

European Economic Community, Private Mail Bag, Suva, Tel.: 313-633, Tlx: FJ2311, Cable: DELECOM Suva

Food and Agriculture Org., Private Mail Bag, Suva, Tel.: 22-489

International Labour Org., GPO 1546, Suva, Tel.: 313-866, Tlx: FJ2266

Project on Workers Education, Rm 11, YWCA Bldg, 2nd Fl., Suva, Tel.: 312-783

International Telecomm. Union and Regional Telecoms Project, GPO 1025, Suva, Tel.: 22-841, Tlx: FJ2177

South Pacific Bureau for Economic Co-operation, GPO 856, Suva, Tel.: 312-600, Tlx: FJ2229, Cable: SPECSUVA

South Pacific Board for Education Assessment, PO Box 5082, Suva, Tel.: 383-322, Cable: PACBEA

South Pacific Commission Community Education Training Centre, PO Box 5082, Raiwaqa, Suva, Tel.: 381-733, Cable: SOUTHPACOM

United Nations Development Programme (UNDP); United Nations Fund for Population Activities (UNFPA); United Nations Industrial Development Organisation (UNIDO); World Food Programme (WFP), Private Mail Bag, Suva, Tel.: 312-500

United Nations Educational, Scientific and Cultural Organisation – Population Education (UNESCO), Private Mail Bag, Suva, Tel.: 312-865

United Nations Minerals Prospecting – Geological Survey/UNDP, Pivate Mail Bag, Suva, Tel.: 381-377

United States Agency for International Development (USAID), Loftus St Suva, Tel.: 311-399

United States Peace Corps, Stewart St
Suva, Tel.: 311-344

HISTORY. People first arrived in the Fiji
group more than 3000 years ago. Archaeologists have identified three types of pottery
made by the early inhabitants. These are
called Lapita, paddle-impressed and plain
ware. Lapita pottery, found in the Sigatoka
area of Viti Levu, has been dated back as far
as 1290 BC, and on Yanuca Island, a date of
1030 BC has been established. Paddle-
impressed pottery was also made on Yanuca
Island at least as far back 710 BC. Similar
pottery found at Navatu and Vuda is estimated to have been made from 100 BC
to AD 1100. A subsequent plain pottery-
making phase at Vuda is thought to have
lasted from AD 1250 to European times.
Such pottery is still made in the Sigatoka
valley and elsewhere.

Besides ancient pottery, archaeologists
have found numerous fortified sites in Fiji
that date back to early times. Two types,
'ring ditch' and ridge forts, are extremely
common on Viti Levu, particularly the
windward side, and also on Wakaya Island.
Both types were still in use when the first
Europeans arrived.

European discovery. The European discoverer of Fiji was the Dutch navigator Abel
Janzsoon Tasman, who sailed among some
of the north-eastern reefs in 1643 in his
vessel *Heemskerck*; he named them Prins
Willems Islands. Captain Cook sighted the
small island of Vatoa in the south-eastern
corner of the group in 1774, but it was not
until 1789 that the main islands were seen.
This occurred when William Bligh and some
of his crew were making their celebrated
open boat voyage from Tonga to Timor
following the mutiny on the *Bounty*. A Fijian
canoe chased them near the Yasawas.

Bligh took the opportunity to examine the
islands more thoroughly when he returned
to the Pacific in 1792 in HMS *Providence* to
make a second attempt to obtain breadfruit
from Tahiti. In 1797, some of the northern
islands were reported by Captain James
Wilson of the missionary ship *Duff*.

Sandalwooders began operating in the
area in the early years of the 19th century.
But it was left to the official exploring
expeditions to complete the discovery and

charting of the group. In 1820, two Russian
ships under Thaddeus von Bellingshausen
examined Ono-i-Lau and its two southerly
neighbours, Tuvana-i-Ra and Tavana-i-Colo.
In 1827 and again in 1838, the French explorer J. S. Dumont d'Urville carried out
some extensive surveys; HMS *Victor* did the
same in 1836; and in 1840, the first really
reliable chart of the group was made by
Commodore Charles Wilkes of the United
States Exploring Expedition.

Sandalwood trade. The discovery of Fiji's
sandalwood was made by a survivor of the
schooner *Argo*, wrecked near Lakeba about
1800. Soon there was a scramble to obtain
cargoes of the precious wood from Bua Bay,
Vanua Levu, to be taken to the Far East.
The trade lasted until 1814, by which time
all the accessible sandalwood had been cut
out. It brought the first white settlers to the
group. One of these, a Swede named Charles
Savage, gained considerable influence in
Bau. He was the chief's favourite, had
numerous wives, and was of great service to
the Fijians because of his knowledge of
firearms. Another early beachcomber, Paddy
Connel, was in high favour at Rewa.

After the departure of the last sandalwooders from Fiji, there was a lull in
western contact with the group until the
early 1820s when American and other ships
began calling in search of bêche-de-mer.
Their success depended on the ability of the
captains to maintain good relations with the
chiefs, as it was necessary to have a large
corps of Fijians to work as labourers, as well
as land on which to erect boiling and drying
houses, and a trade store.

The beachcombers. Such beachcombers as
were already in the group became important
as intermediaries and interpreters, and others
soon joined them. Some were deserters from
whalers. The most notable was David
Whippy, a young American from New
Hampshire, who settled at Levuka in 1822.
Like the others, he married a Fijian and
became one of the pioneers of the part-
European community that has existed ever
since. Commodore Wilkes met Whippy in
1840 and had him appointed vice-consul for
the US soon after his return to that country.

The missionaries. Meanwhile, the first
Christian missionaries—two Tahitians—
arrived in the group. They had been sent to

Lakeba from Tahiti in 1826 but were detained in Tonga and did not reach their destination until 1830. Five years later they were joined by two European evangelists, David Cross and William Cargill, of the Wesleyan Church. Although the local chief, Tui Nayau, made the missionaries welcome, he showed little interest in their doctrine and for some time they made few Fijian converts.

The many Tongans who lived in Lakeba, however, were more amenable, and all islanders were eager to learn to read and write. Cross and Cargill tried to simplify things by using a single letter to represent each Fijian sound. Thus it was that the letters b, c, d, g, and eventually q were given the values they have today, namely mb; th (as in that); nd; ng (as in sing); and ngg (as in younger) respectively.

Although the European missionaries had entered Fiji from the east, they soon realised that the most important and populous centre in the group lay in the west—in the SE corner of Viti Levu. Cross tried to obtain a foothold on Bau, a small island off that coast in 1838. Unsuccessful, he went to Rewa where a printing press was set up in 1839. Later, a mission station was also opened on Viwa Island, 3 km from Bau.

Still, the missionaries made few converts. Little by little, however, their pacifism and good example caused the Fijians to question their own customs.

Cakobau. Meanwhile, Cakobau, the chief of Bau, had had considerable success in extending his influence to the coastal villages of Viti Levu, to the islands of Lomaiviti, to Taveuni, and to Lau. By 1850 foreigners were beginning to address him as Tui Viti (King of Fiji), but about this time there was a revolt against him among his conquered subjects because of heavy demands on them that had no sanction in local custom.

Faced with repeated defeats in battle, Cakobau decided on 28 April 1854 to embrace Christianity. A series of events soon afterwards enabled Cakobau to re-establish his fortunes; and by the late 1850s the whole of Fiji had taken sides either with Cakobau or with Ma'afu, a chief of Tongan origin, who had gained considerable power and prestige among the Lau islands. The scene was set for a showdown between Cakobau and Ma'afu when W. T. Pritchard, the first

British consul to be appointed to Fiji, arrived in Levuka in 1858.

International rivalries. Pritchard's appointment followed a period in which several French and American warships had visited Fiji. This had made Britain afraid that one or other of the two powers might try to annex the islands. As it turned out, however, an opportunity soon arose that led Britain to annex the islands herself. Cakobau was being pressed to settle a claim by various American residents for $45,000 and turned to Pritchard for help. Claiming to have 'full and exclusive sovereignty and dominion' in the group, he offered to cede Fiji to Britain provided Britain would pay his debts. Pritchard took a document to this effect to London, but the government was preoccupied with other matters and when he returned to Fiji 12 months later he could only report that the offer of cession was being considered.

In the following year Col. W. T. Smythe, representing the British Government, was sent to Fiji to ascertain whether it would be expedient for Britain to accept the offer of cession. At the same time a botanist, Dr Berthold Seemann, was commissioned to report on Fiji's potential for tropical agriculture. The arrival of Smythe and Seemann caused rumours to spread that Fiji would in fact beome British, and many Britons flocked to the group from Australia and New Zealand to become settlers. When the American Civil War began shortly afterwards, causing a worldwide shortage of raw cotton, the new settlers took to growing cotton on a large scale.

Although Smythe advised Britain not to accept Cakobau's offer of cession, the large influx of British settlers made it inevitable that Britain would eventually be forced to intervene. Meanwhile, various attempts were made (at the instigation of the European residents) to establish a regular form of government. Although some reforms were made, all attempts ended in failure because of the jealousy and hostility of the leading chiefs. Finally, in 1873, the acting British consul, J. B. Thurston, again asked the Foreign Office if Britain would be prepared to annex Fiji.

As the 'blackbirding' of Pacific Islanders to work in Fiji had been causing increasing concern to Britain for several years, the government took the opportunity to appoint a new commission of inquiry. The commission comprised Commodore J. G. Goodenough, commanding the Australian naval station, and E. L. Layard, newly appointed consul in Fiji. On 21 March 1874 these commissioners reported that the offer of cession should be accepted.

Cession. In September 1874 Sir Hercules Robinson, Governor of New South Wales, arrived to determine the terms of cession. A formal Deed of Cession was signed at Levuka on 10 October. Its signatories were Cakobau (Tui Viti and Vunivalu, or war lord), Ma'afu (chief of the Lau confederacy, including Taveuni and much of Vanua Levu), and 11 other principal chiefs. Sir Hercules Robinson, who became provisional Governor, announced that all lands that could be shown to have been fairly and honestly acquired by Europeans would be secured to them; that all lands that were in actual use or occupation by any tribe would be set apart for them; and that all the residue of the land would go to the government for the general good.

Measles epidemic. The first substantive Governor, Sir Arthur Gordon, arrived in the colony in June 1875 and established his headquarters at Levuka. His regime began at an unpropitious time. Earlier that year a measles epidemic had raged through the Fijian villages and had wiped out a third of the native population. Moreover, the cotton market slumped due to the recovery of cotton planting in the United States at the end of the Civil War.

It was soon obvious that one of Gordon's chief problems was to revive the colony's economy. Copra and sugar seemed to offer the best possibilities, but these required large labour forces and Gordon was opposed to Fijians working for Europeans in their own country. It was in these circumstances that Gordon authorised the importation of labourers from India under a five-year indenture system. At the end of five years, the Indians were to be free to return home at their own expense; but if they chose to remain for a second term the Fiji Government was to pay their passages. However, at the end of 10 years they could elect to remain in Fiji.

Indians arrive. The first shipload of 498 labourers reached Fiji on 14 May 1879, and from then until 1916 there were about 2000 such immigrants each year. Although the Indian Government originally insisted that there should be a ratio of 40 women to every 100 men, this ratio was not maintained. As a result there were frequent fights among the male immigrants over women, and other evils and abuses. Yet many of the Indians felt they were in a better situation in Fiji than they would have been at home and they remained in the colony to become independent farmers on land leased from the Fijians.

Sugar industry. Meanwhile, sugar had become by far the most important industry in Fiji. Although there were a number of small companies and individuals with interests in sugar production before the turn of the century, all eventually were swallowed by the Colonial Sugar Refining Company of Australia. CSR moved into Fiji in 1881— the year before the colony's capital was moved to Suva from Levuka (which had severely limited possibilities for development) and established its first mill on the banks of the Rewa River, where the town of Nausori soon sprang up. Its first sugar was exported from there in 1883.

That same year, CSR decided to open another mill at Rarawai on the Ba River on the dry side of Viti Levu, following the success of another company's mill opened at Rakiraki, Ra, in 1881. During the next few years mills were also opened at Labasa, Vanua Levu, and Lautoka.

Although Gordon laid some of the foundations for the development of a highly successful sugar industry during his five years in Fiji, his principal achievement was the introduction of a system of administration whereby Fijian institutions were developed to provide a chain of authority extending from the village headman to the Governor. This system, in its essentials, remained operative throughout Fiji's 96 years as a British colony.

Another area in which there was little change was the system of land ownership. Following its policy of protecting the Fijians' land rights, the British administration insisted that all foreign claims to land dating back to before cession had to be submitted to a Land Commission for adjudication.

Claims to about 162,000 ha were finally substantiated. On the other hand, the sale of Fijian land to foreigners was forbidden; though for four years from 1905 land sales were again permitted, and during that time about 8000 additional hectares were alienated.

Constitutional changes. The depressed economic situation of Gordon's time did not improve until after the turn of the century, by which time both the sugar and copra industries were getting on their feet. Even so, many of the European settlers felt dissatisfied with their lot; and when in 1900 the Premier of New Zealand, R. J. Seddon, visited the colony, they agitated for federation with New Zealand. Although this move failed, it did produce some constitutional concessions. In 1904 the colony's Legislative Council, which had previously been all-European and entirely nominated by the Governor, was made more respresentative, through the election of six Europeans and the nomination of two Fijian members from the Council of Chiefs. In 1916, one Indian member—nominated by the Governor—sat in the council for the first time; but it was not until 1929 that the first elected Indian members took their seats. Some Indians later agitated for a 'common roll' and this led, in 1937, to the introduction of a partly elected, partly nominated council that was somewhat larger than before. It now consisted of the Governor, 16 official members, five European members (three elected, two nominated), five Fijian members nominated from the Council of Chiefs, and five Indian members (three elected, two nominated). Thereafter, the council's composition remained unchanged until 1963 when it was enlarged to a membership of 38—a nominated speaker, 19 official members and 18 unofficial members. The latter were divided equally on racial lines—four elected Fijians, four elected Indians and four elected Europeans, plus two Europeans and two Indians nominated by the Governor, and two Fijians nominated from the Council of Chiefs.

In the 1963 election, women of all races voted for the first time, but each community voted from separate rolls. In 1964, the executive council was enlarged and, in effect, became a cabinet. Its 'Ministers' were called

'Members' but were responsible for specific portfolios.

In 1965, a conference in London led to the adoption of the constitution of 1966, which enlarged the Legislative Council to 40 members. Of these, four were official members and the rest were elected. Fourteen of the elected members were Fijians, 12 were Indians, and 10 (called General members) were Europeans or individuals from other minority racial groups. Nine Fijians, nine Indians and seven General members were elected from separate communal rolls, and the remainder—except two Fijians chosen by the Council of Chiefs—were elected under a system of cross-voting.

The 1966 constitution was not destined to last for long. In April 1970, after the abatement of several years of antagonism between Fiji's two main political parties, another constitutional conference was held in London. It was then agreed that Fiji should become independent on 10 October that year—96 years after the signing of the Deed of Cession. The 1970 conference was attended by the Governor of Fiji, all 40 members of the Legislative Council and senior British officials.

Fiji independence. Prince Charles represented Queen Elizabeth II at ceremonies to mark Fiji's change of status. Ratu Sir Kamisese Mara, who had previously been Chief Minister, became the first Prime Minister; and the former Governor, Sir Robert Foster, became the first Governor-General. Sir Robert Foster was succeeded in January 1973 by Ratu Sir George Cakobau, great-grandson of the Cakobau who had signed the Deed of Cession.

The racial harmony the Alliance Party and the electoral system sought to preserve was given a jolt in 1975 when Sakiasi Butadroka, leader of the newly formed Fijian Nationalist Party, proposed in Parliament that the entire Indian community be repatriated to India, despite the fact that the majority of them had no experience of that country. Despite the defeat of the parliamentary motion, the Nationalists' impact was enough to create a split among Fijian voters, which resulted in the Alliance Party, led by Ratu Sir Kamisese Mara, losing the general election of 1977.

Divisions within the Federation Party

prevented it forming a government and a viceregal decision returned Mara as leader; subsequent elections in September 1977 and July 1982 confirmed the Governor-General's judgment, though the 1982 election was bitterly fought involving accusations and counter-accusations of overseas interference and electoral malpractice.

The formation of the Labour Party in 1986 and its subsequent coalition with the Federation Party set in motion a remarkable series of events, which led to a short-lived victory for the coalition in the elections of April 1987. Barely four weeks later, the first of two military coups resulted in the deposition of the elected government led by Labour Party leader, Dr Timoci Bavadra, and the installation of a military government led by Lieutenant-Colonel (later Brigadier) Sitiveni Rabuka. The constitution of 1970 was suspended and citizens informed that the military regime would exercise power pending the reorganisation of the government and the drafting of a new constitution that would enshrine political power in the hands of ethnic Fijians.

When it appeared that the goals of the coup might be compromised, Rabuka staged a second coup on 25 September, assuming for himself and the army wide-ranging powers, including rigid media censorship and the imposition of a curfew in urban areas. On 7 October 1987 Colonel Rabuka declared Fiji a republic. Withdrawal from the Commonwealth followed, though there was widespread belief that Fiji would seek readmission when its political condition stabilised and its new constitution went into effect.

In November 1987 a form of civilian government was restored when former Governor-General Ratu Sir Penaia Ganilau and former Prime Minister Ratu Sir Kamisese Mara accepted the posts of President and Prime Minister respectively.

The economic consequences of the two coups were far-reaching, affecting especially Fiji's significant tourism business as visitor numbers fell away drastically in the middle of 1987. Two currency devaluations within a few months saw the Fiji dollar fall to its lowest value in years. Political conditions also affected the sugar harvest. By the end of 1987, however, there were indications that a recovery in both sugar and tourism was under way and that trade and aid relations between Fiji and her long-time partners, Australia, New Zealand etc., would return to normal.

In the meantime, the ardently nationalist Taukei movement called for greater assurances that both land and politics would remain forever the preserves of indigenous Fijians and the embattled Fiji Visitors Bureau quietly abandoned its long-standing slogan 'Fiji—the way the world should be'. (See Government section for further political details.)

Further reading. R. A. Derrick's *A History of Fiji*, first published in 1946, takes the story only as far as cession. A proposed second volume was not completed. Other useful books covering aspects of Fiji's history are: Peter France, *The Charter of the Land* (Melbourne, 1969); J. D. Legge, *Britain in Fiji, 1858–1880* (London, 1958); K. L. Gillion, *Fiji's Indian Migrants* (Melbourne, 1962); and Deryck Scarr, *I, The Very Bayonet: A Life of Sir John Bates Thurston* (Canberra, 1973). Asesela Ravuvu, *The Fijian Way of Life* (Suva, 1983) outlines traditional social structures. Other recent and useful works include Jay Narayan, *The Political Economy of Fiji* (Suva, 1984), David Routledge, *Matanitu: the struggle for power in early Fiji* (Suva, 1985) and Norman and Ngaire Douglas, *Fiji Handbook: Travel and Business Guide* (Sydney, 1987). Coup leader Brigadier Sitiveni Rabuka gives his account of the events of 1987 in *Rabuka: No Other Way* (Suva, 1988).

ISLANDS IN DETAIL. As well as more than 300 small islands, Fiji includes the very large islands of Viti Levu and Vanua Levu, and the large islands of Taveuni and Kadavu. As Viti Levu (and Vanua Levu and Taveuni to a lesser degree) contain practically all the population and the developed economic wealth, people look upon those islands as Fiji and forget that hidden behind them there is a great archipelago that equals in beauty, fertility, interest and general attractiveness any other group in the Pacific.

With the exception of a few coral atolls, chiefly in the Lau Group, the islands of Fiji are of volcanic and sedimentary rocks forming two large platforms, the Viti Levu and Vanua Levu platforms. These were once thought to belong to a fragmented continental mass, but it is now known these are platforms of construction rather than remnants of destruction.

The Fiji islands may be divided into seven sub-groups. These sub-groups, working from east to west, are:

Eastern or Lau group of 57 islands, of which 26 are inhabited.

The Moala group, which is included with the Lau group for administration purposes and consists of three volcanic islands.

Vanua Levu (5534 sq. km), **Taveuni** (435 sq. km) and the adjacent islands.

Lomaiviti (or inner Fiji), about 12 islands, scattered about in the Koro Sea (the section of ocean enclosed by the Lau Group on the east, Vanua Levu on the north, and Viti Levu and Kadavu on the west).

Viti Levu (10,389 sq. km) and adjacent islands.

Kadavu group, which lies between 89 and 97 km south of Suva and contains the large island of Kadavu (407 sq. km), the island of Ono (30 sq. km) and numerous small islands lying within the Astrolabe Reefs.

The Yadswa islands, an almost continuous chain of about 20 large and small islands, running generally north and south and forming the western portion of Fiji.

THE LAU ISLANDS AND MOALA GROUP. The islands of Lau can most conveniently be divided into four groups:

Northern Lau — The Exploring Isles (which includes Vanua Balavu, Namalata, Susui, Munia, Cikobia, Sovu Islets, Avea, Qilaqila, Adavaci, and Yanucoloa); Wailagilala; Naitauba; Malima; Kibobo; Kanacea; Mago; Yacata; Kaibu; Nukutolu; Vatu Vara; Katafaga; Vekai; Tuvuca; and Cicia.

Central Lau — Lakeba, Nayau, Oneata; Aiwa; and Vanua Vatu.

Southern Lau — Moce; Karoni; Olorua; Komo; Namuka; Yagasa cluster; Kabara; Marabo; Waqava; Fulaga; Ogea; Ogea Driki; Vatoa; Ono-i-Lau; Tuvana.

Moala Group— Moala; Totoya; and Matuku.

The islands of Lau are scattered over 113,900 sq. km of ocean, but their aggregate land area is only 460 sq. km. The southern

islands are nearer to Tonga than to Suva and the Tongan influence on the group has been great in the past. In 1855, Ma'afu, a Tongan chief, established himself at Lomaloma and encouraged European settlement, particularly on the northern islands, where cotton was grown. In those days Lomaloma was a much more important centre than it is today.

The structure of the islands of the Lau Group is usually a limestone capping on older volcanic rocks. Many of the islands in southern Lau are solely limestone, the underlying volcanic edifice not having been exposed by erosion. Some of the islands, and those of the Moala Group, have no limestone. Several islands show evidence of more than one period of volcanic activity. One island of the Lau Group, Vatu Vara, is more than 300 m high and several others closely approach that height, while Moala reaches 480 m.

Northern Lau

The Exploring Isles. These were named by Wilkes in 1840 after the official title of his expedition (United States Exploring Expedition). They consist of seven islands and numerous islets scattered around the margins of a lagoon about 518 sq. km in area and enclosed by a barrier reef 130 km in circuit. The reef is roughly triangular and has five navigable entrances. The island of Vanua Balavu takes up most of the western end of the lagoon and is the largest island of the group. It is of composite formation (limestone and volcanic) and is 52 sq. km in area. Lomaloma, once an important centre in cotton-growing days, is in the south of the island. It was once a port of entry for Fiji. It was the headquarters of the Hennings Brothers, then the largest trading firm in the Fiji Islands. Its 1986 population was 1323.

The northern part of Vanua Balavu is heavily indented, affording many good anchorages. Munia is about 3 km long and rises to 290 m. Its volcanic soil is very fertile. It is privately owned; local Fijians were removed to Avea in Ma'afu's time.

Naitauba is of composite construction, lies 32 km west of Vanua Balavu, has an area of about 8 sq. km and is roughly circular in shape. From the flat land on the south-west, the island rises steeply to 186 m. The north coast rises straight out of the sea in 34 m high cliffs. It was privately owned by the Hennings family for many years and worked as a copra plantation. It was later owned by Hollywood actor Raymond Burr, who sold it in 1983 to an American religious group.

Wailagilala is a true atoll, 34 km northeast of Naitauba. It is only 1006 m long and 640 m wide and is no more than 4.6 m above sea level. The atoll is about 8 km at its greatest diameter. It has a lighthouse that marks the eastern side of the northern entrance to the Fiji archipelago.

Kanacea is 12 km west of Vanua Balavu, is 244 m high and has an area of 13 sq. km. It is privately owned and worked as a copra plantation.

Mago, height 270 m, is saucer-shaped, 20.7 sq. km and the interior plain is immensely fertile. Cultivation is carried on here and tropical fruits flourish. The 'Sea Island' cotton produced by Mago became world famous. Later sugar was grown there and it is now worked as a copra plantation. Mago in the early days belonged to the Somosomo chiefs, and when they adopted Christianity they agreed to sell the island and remove the population; Mago became the exclusive property of the Ryder family. In November 1985 the island was bought by the Tokyu Corporation of Japan for $6 million.

Vatu Vara, or Hat Island, is 32 km west of Mago and because of its distinctive shape is one of the best known islands of the group. The 'crown' of the hat is a truncated pyramid rising more than 305 m. It is the highest point to which limestone has been elevated in the group. The brim of the hat is a wide belt of gently sloping land not more than 7.5 m above sea level. It is usually uninhabited, though at one time an American seaman named Joe Thompson lived there. He seemed to have a supply of gold coins and the legend grew that treasure was buried there. Thompson died insane and his secret (if any) died with him. Vatu Vara is visible for 56 km and serves as a guide to ships.

Katafaga is a small composite island 40 km south-east of Vanua Balavu. There are no Fijian villages and it is owned privately, and worked as a copra plantation.

Cicia is 27 km south-south-west of Mago and has an area of 34 sq. km. It is of composite formation and has five villages and several privately owned coconut plantations. The 1986 population was 1062.

Central Lau

Lakeba is a rounded, volcanic island of 54 sq. km with several summits in the centre. The highest is Mt Goodenough, a twin peak 220 m high. There is some limestone with several caves. One, near Nasagalau, is quite impressive. Coastal lands are immensely fertile but the interior is poor, covered with grass and screw pines. Yams, kumala, coconuts and all tropical plants grow most profusely on the coastal belt and this is probably the most productive of all the rich islands of the south-east. Lakeba was an important meeting place between Fijians and Tongans, all through their history. The first Wesleyan missionaries settled here in 1835. It was the place most frequently visited by Europeans before they settled in Levuka. It has an airstrip. Lakeba's 1986 population was 2444. Its villages are Tubou, Waciwaci, Waitabu, Nukunuku, Vakano, Yadrana and Nasagalau.

Southern Lau

The islands south of Lakeba have a purely Fijian economy. On the inhabited islands copra and all the Fijian foodstuffs are produced.

The southernmost outliers of the Fiji archipelago are the two Tuvana islands, 32 km south of Ono-i-Lau. They are densely wooded emerged reef material used by Ono people for agriculture.

The Moala Group

Moala, Totoya and Matuku structurally have nothing to do with the Lau group. They are volcano cones of which the main parts are beneath the sea. The people trace their descent from people who came from Viti Levu. Copra and bananas are produced and, as they lie only a night's sail from Suva, foodstuffs are disposed of at that port. They are 97 to 113 km southwest from Lakeba. The 1986 populations were 2035, 1046 and 896 respectively.

The total population of Lau, including the three Moala islands, in the census of 1986 was 14,203.

VANUA LEVU, TAVEUNI AND ADJACENT ISLANDS

Vanua Levu. Vanua Levu, Fiji's second largest island, with an area of 5538 sq. km, has extremely varied terrain, from a rugged and mountainous interior reaching a height of 1032 m at Nasoro Levu, to the arid 'talasiga' or 'sun-burnt' country of the western district around Bua, to the sheltered, palm-fringed coast of Natewa Bay. It contains two towns of significance Labasa, an important sugar-milling centre, and Savusavu, a rapidly growing area with a fine deep-water harbour.

Taveuni. Taveuni (the old name was Somosomo, from its town of that name, being the residence of the ruling chiefs), ranks fourth in size and is one of the finest islands of Fiji.

Lying south-east of Natewa Peninsula, Vanua Levu, it is 42 km long, an average 11 km wide and rises symmetrically on both sides to a backbone ridge, at the highest point of which Mt Uluigalau (1231 m) is notable because it is exactly under the 180th meridian, twelve hours east and west from Greenwich.

In the mountains behind Somosomo there is a lake of considerable size that provides Somosomo with a water supply. Fiji's most beautiful wildflower, the tagimaucia, grows only on the shores of this lake.

Somosomo is on the trunk road that runs from Ura in the south to Qeleni in the north of the island. It also has several good places of accommodation.

The island has a heavy rainfall in the higher ranges and is densely wooded. Virtually all tropical produce will grow and at one time Sea Island cotton was cultivated. Its main product is now copra.

There were two airstrips on the island: Matei, at the northern end of the island, which is government owned; and a privately owned strip at Ura, which is now unused.

Adjacent Islands. Starting in the west and proceeding along the north coast of Vanua Levu, thence down the east coast, the chief offshore islands are:

Yadua.

Yagana, Nukuira, Tevea, Vedrala, Galoa, Nadogo, Vatuka, all close together off the north-west coast.

Macuata, Talailau, Nagano, Nukunuku, Cukini, clustered together off the northern coast.

Vorovoro.

Kia.

Mali.

Mataivai.

Tutu, Kavewa, Druadrua, Namukalau and Bekana, along the northeast coast.

Rabi, 472 m high, and Kioa, two large islands lying between Natewa Peninsula (Vanua Levu) and Taveuni. Rabi, at one time owned by Lever Bros, is now the home of 2860 people, mostly Banabans from Ocean Island, and Gilbertese. Kioa was bought for surplus population from what is now Tuvalu. On Rabi there has been considerable development by the Banabans.

Yabu, Yanuca, Cobia, Nukubasaga, Qelelevu are small islands, lying well out to the north-east of Taveuni and known as the Ring Gold Islands, or islands of Budd Reef.

Vetauua.

Cikobia-i-ra, most northerly of the Fiji Group.

Qamea, Laucala, Matagi are fairly large islands, lying close to Taveuni on the northeast. Matagi is worked as a copra plantation. There is an airstrip on Laucala, which is privately owned.

LOMAIVITI. Lomaiviti, or Central Fiji, consists of seven large islands and a few small ones, situated in or near the Koro Sea. They have an aggregate area of 410 sq. km. The large islands are (from West to East) Ovalau, Makogai, Wakaya, Batiki, Gau, Koro and Nairai. Moturiki (about 10 sq. km) lies close to Ovalau.

The islands are volcanic and Ovalau (nearest the mainland of Viti Levu) is separated from that island by 16 km of shallow sea. Population of the Lomaiviti area was 16,066 in 1986, predominantly Fijian except for a few storekeepers in Levuka.

Communications in Lomaiviti are centred on Levuka. Main population centres in 1986 were Gau, 3253; Koro, 3888; and Ovalau, 7715.

Ovalau ranks first in point of importance, from the fact that its chief town, Levuka, was the capital of Fiji until the seat of government was removed to Suva in 1882. In 1986 the population of Ovalau was 7715.

The island, 13 km by 11 km, is of volcanic formation. It is high and rugged, consisting of very steep hills rising to a height of 626 m, crowned with great crags and by deep gorges, formerly densely wooded.

A tuna fishing enterprise was established

there in 1964–65 and as a result there is now more commercial activity in the town. The fish are caught by Japanese, Korean and Taiwanese fishing boats engaged under contract and are frozen at shore installations and shipped abroad.

The town has a good water supply from the dammed waters of Totoga Creek in the gorge above and a very pleasant swimming pool from the same source. The business section runs along the very narrow coastal flat but the residential area straggles up the steep hills and some of Levuka's streets are, in fact, long flights of steps.

It has a hotel, shops, a club, several schools and some pleasant scenery. A large smooth stone at Nasova, at the edge of the town, marks the spot where the Deed of Cession was signed in 1874 and the Union Jack hoisted.

Levuka is a port of entry for overseas ships. Regular communication with the mainland is by launch to Natovi on Viti Levu and then by bus to Suva, or by light aircraft on a daily service from an airstrip some kilometres out of Levuka.

Nairai, about 23 sq. km in area, was famous in old times for the manufacture of its mats and baskets, and like Batiki, was subject to Bau. Population in 1986 was 692.

Batiki produces all the fruits and roots common in Fiji and sustains a community of four villages. It has no protected anchorage. It is surrounded by reefs extending up to more than a kilometre from shore and through which there are only narrow passages. It is 30 km south-east of Ovalau and about 9 sq. km in area.

Koro is shaped like a shark's tooth, being 8 km wide at the north coast and converging at the south in Muanivanua Point (in Fijian meaning 'end of the land'). There is a lighthouse on the point. Total area is 104 sq. km. The island is rugged, the centre being a plateau of broken country where there are several peaks from 300 to 520 m. The highest peak, 650 m, is in the western range. The island is well-watered by short streams. The plateau has fertile land suitable for planting. The population of 3888 in 1986 was almost all Fijian.

Gau, the most southern of the Lomaiviti islands, is 140 sq. km in extent. Highest peaks are more than 700 m. Population is

about 3253, entirely Fijian in 1986 except for one lone Indian.

Wakaya and Makogai lie to the north-east of Ovalau, and though several kilometres apart are situated within the same reef. There is a remarkable shelf formed near the centre of Wakaya, which goes by the name of the 'Chieftain's Leap', from a tragedy of the distant past.

In September 1917, von Luckner, commander of the German radier *See Adler* that had been wrecked in French Polynesia, landed with a party on Wakaya while trying to escape in a launch. They were captured by a party of police.

Wakaya is currently owned by an American who has spoken of plans to set up an international medical conference centre on the island. Individuals can purchase home sites on Wakaya and the island is also known for its introduced deer.

Makogai has an area of 8 sq. km and with its smaller outlier, Makodroga, was used as a settlement and hospital for the treatment of leprosy patients from Fiji and other parts of the South Pacific until 1969. It is now an agricultural quarantine station.

The highest point on the island is about 275 m and Makogai has fertile soil and a pleasant climate. There is an anchorage in Dalice Bay in the north-west; the old hospital installations are at the southern end of the bay.

Horseshoe Reef is a ring of dangerous reef 1.5 km in diameter 20 km north-east from the lighthouses on Wakaya Reef and Batiki Island. It is in the main seaway, and there have been several wrecks on it.

VITI LEVU AND ADJACENT ISLANDS

Viti Levu. Viti Levu, with an area of 10,390 sq. km, is the largest island in Fiji and contains the largest river (the Rewa) and the highest mountain (Mt Victoria or Tomaniivi) in the country. It is also the most developed island in the group, with several major urban centres; Suva, Lautoka, Lami, Nadi, Ba and Nausori.

Bau's importance as the old native capital, centres in the past. It is built on a tiny island only about 15 m above sealevel, connected with Viti Levu's eastern coast at low water by a narrow causeway of coral formation, about 1.5 km in length. Formerly it was the stronghold and home of the great chief Cakobau and his family, and of the nobles before whom the tribes of other districts owed subjection, and to whom they granted special privileges. Its chief took precedence over all other chiefs; the language of Bau was used when a written form of Fijian was devised.

The island has an area of only 8 ha, but at one time an estimated 3000 or 4000 people lived there. At present there are between 200 and 300. A mission house and school occupy the highest point — a 15 m soapstone rise — and the three villages occupy the flat land, Bau being the home of the high chiefs, Soso that of the craftsmen and Lasakau that of the fishermen. The south end of the village green is occupied by the Cakobau Memorial Church; the north end by the Council House.

Bau is still the home of the highest chiefs in Fiji, many of whom now go to other parts of the country as administrative officers.

Beqa Island, which is separated from the southernmost point of Viti Levu by the Beqa Passage, is 6 km in breadth and has several peaks, the highest being 340 m above the sea. Portions of the island are under cultivation and lemons and shaddocks grow wild in large quantities on the hills. Beqa is beautiful from all points of view; it is clothed in foliage from the summit of the hills to the water line.

The fire-walking ceremony is performed by the people of this island and the Fijian name for it is Vilavilairevo, which means 'Jumping into the Ovens'. The men prepare the ovens by placing large stones in a fire pit. After the fire has been burning for some time and the stones have become white hot, firewalkers jump onto the stones and, stepping from one to another, walk around in the oven in a circle. When they come out no trace of burns can be seen on their feet. Although the ceremony has been closely followed by scientists, no satisfactory explanation of the feat has yet been offered. Beqa's 1986 population was 1262.

Yanuca is a small island on the same encircling reef as Beqa.

Other islands off the Viti Levu coast include:

Viwa, small, inhabited, about 3 km north of Bau.

Qoma, off the mid-eastern coast and the largest of a cluster of small inhabited islands. Nananu Group, off Port Ellington on the north coast; and Malake further east. Both groups have frequently been used for grazing goats and sheep.

Mamanuca Group, 13 small volcanic islands off the west coast and south of the Yasawas. Only two of them are inhabited by Fijians on a permanent basis, but several now have resorts and associated villages for local staff. It is also a popular area for cruising yachts.

Malolo Group, three small islands south of Mamanuca and closer to the Viti Levu coast. There are tourist resorts on each island. Malolo and Malololailai are connected at low tide. Population of the two groups in 1986 was 2013.

Vatulele, a large island of 31 sq. km about 32 km south-east of Sigatoka with several villages and a lighthouse. Population in 1986 was 660. A luxury resort is planned.

Serua, small and close inshore off the most southerly part of the Viti Levu coast, is the seat of the local paramount chief and of considerable Fijian importance. The island consists of a hill at each end and a low saddle in the middle.

Naqara and Namaka are privately owned small islands between Serua and Suva. Right at the entrance to Suva Harbour, and popular picnic spots, are the small sand islands of Nukulau and Makuluva.

KADAVU: The high island of Kadavu is generally the first landmark seen by travellers coming from the south. Next to Taveuni, it is considered one of the finest in the group. It is about 48 km in length and varies in breadth from 400 m to 13 km. At the Namalata isthmus it is nearly divided into two separate islands, the backbone range of hills entirely disappearing, and at Daku isthmus it is only 1 km broad where the range is only 61 m. Total area is 411 sq. km.

Kadavu is of volcanic origin and has some high mountains, of which Mount Washington (Buke Levu, or 'the great yam heap') is most conspicuous, rising to a height of 838 m above the sea. From a high central ridge the land falls away gradually. All the lower parts of the island are well watered, and a white sand beach skirts the coastline. There are numerous sheltered bays and harbours.

The Government Station and hospital are at Vunisea, at the east end of Namalata isthmus. There are mission stations at Richmond and Naidiri. Small amounts of copra, bananas and timber are produced.

The north coast of Kadavu is about 80 km south of Suva; the island and its smaller outliers lie within the Great Astrolabe Reef, the islands being themselves volcanic. The most important of the lesser islands is Ono, with an area of 30 sq. km and a central peak of 35 m. There are several villages. North of Ono are Bulia, Dravuni and Solo (which has a lighthouse and nothing else).

Great Astrolabe is a 50 km loop of coral separated from the North Astrolabe ring by a channel of clear water about 1 km wide. In 1986 the population of the total Kadavu Province was 9805.

YASAWA GROUP. The Western, or Yasawa group (charted on old maps as the Ba or Leeward Islands) extends in a north-north-easterly and south-south-westerly direction, forming a comparatively narrow chain for a distance of 80 km north-west of the north-west coast of Viti Levu. There are 16 definite islands, with numerous islets and rocks.

In 1986 the group's population totalled 2641.

Naviti, 34 sq. km, is the largest of the group, next to which is Yasawa, 28 sq. km. Almost within a stone's throw of Naviti are the four islands of Drawaqa (Eld), Nanuya Balavu (Fox), Naukacuvu (Agate) and Narara (Sinclair).

Thirteen km from Naviti are the three islands and one islet constituting the WAYA group. Waya Island has several singularly sharp peaks, the highest being 570 m above the sea, and it is covered with vegetation from summit to waterline. There is a small dive resort now on Waya.

Other islands include: Alewa Kalou (or Round), Nacula, Tavewa, Yaqeta and Viwa.

ROTUMA. Rotuma is the principal island of a small group that lies about 390 km north-north-west of Fiji. Rotuma is 13 km long and has a maximum width of 4 km. Geographically and ethnically it has little to do with Fiji but is, politically, part of the republic although threats of secession were being made in 1988.

North-north-west of Rotuma is the small inhabited island of Uea (260 m high), and westward of Uea are two islets, Hatana and Hofliua. The latter is otherwise known as Split Island, as it looks as if it has been cleanly split with an axe. Altogether, eight small islands surround Rotuma, the others being Solnahu, Solkope, Afnaha and Hauatiu.

Population at 1986 census was 2688 on Rotuma with 6000 Rotumans living elsewhere in Fiji. It is administered by a District Officer, who is responsible to the Commissioner, Eastern at Ovalau. The Government Station is at Ahau; Motusa, situated on a narrow neck of land at the western end of the island, is also important. Chief industries are copra production and the making of plaited mats, which are much in demand.

Small inter-island vessels from Suva call every few months with passengers and stores and to lift copra, and an airstrip was opened in 1980.

In 1986 the cruise ship *Fairstar* made an inaugural visit to Rotuma despite opposition from many of its inhabitants. It is not a regular port of call, however, with perhaps one or two visits scheduled per year.

There is a wireless station on Rotuma. A medical officer supervises the public health service.

Rotuma's volcanic soil grows yams, tapioca, pawpaw and taro.

An excellent highway circles the main island and there are a number of cars and trucks in use. The Rotuman Sports Club has a large, modern club house, tennis court and golf course.

Chief villages are Motusa, Ahau (Government Station, with the Residency, hospital and Courthouse), Sumi (RC Mission), and Lau. Hilly landmarks on the main island are Suelhof (255 m). Soloroa (220 m), and Satarua (167 m). An unusual feature seen on the 27 km drive around the island is the large number of graveyards, with an array of elaborate tombstones.

The island was discovered in August 1791, by Captain Edwards in the frigate *Pandora*, when searching for the *Bounty* mutineers, and named by him Grenville Island. Captain Wilson visited it in the missionary ship *Duff* in September 1797. French and British navigators wrote accounts of it in 1824 (M. Duperrey), 1827 (Captain Dillon), 1828 (M. Legoarat) and 1841 (Lucet).

Almost from the time of discovery Rotuma was a favourite resort for escaped convicts and runaway sailors. Duperrey in 1824 found there four English sailors who had deserted from the ship *Rochester*.

About 1840 the Roman Catholics and the Wesleyans started missions there. In later years a series of wars commenced between the adherents of the different religious sects, and the distracted chiefs, in 1879, asked that Britain annex the group. This was done on 13 May 1881. The laws are those of Fiji, with some local variations, especially in relation to land. The land belongs to the Rotumans; it may not be sold to non-natives, but may be leased for not more than 21 years.

The Rotumans, unlike the Fijians, are Polynesians and mostly resemble the Tahitians, Hawaiians and Maoris; but in the last few decades, much 'foreign' blood has been mixed with that of Rotuma. The Rotumans speak a language that includes words found in the dialects of almost all the adjacent Pacific groups. They have always been great wanderers and before the European era regularly visited Fiji, Tonga, the Gilbert Islands (Kiribati) and even the New Hebrides (Vanuatu) in their large canoes.

The group is divided into seven districts over each of which there is a chief responsible to the District Officer. Districts are Naotau, Itumutu, Itutiu, Malahaha, Juju, Oonafa and Pepsei. The Rotuman Council, whose members are nominated, meets once a month.

No Rotuman member is sent to the House of Representatives as such, Rotuma being part of a Fijian constituency, but a Rotuman Senator is nominated.

FOR THE TOURIST. The Fiji Visitors Bureau supplies detailed information to visitors, but is not a booking agency. It is financed by the government and donations from local business firms. The Fiji Visitors Bureau has overseas offices in Sydney (including a retail section), Melbourne, Auckland, Tokyo and Los Angeles. Head office in Fiji is Thomson St, Suva; PO Box 92 (Tel. 22 867). There is also an office at Nadi International Airport. The Bureau's infor-

mation is extensive and up-to-date.

Entry formalities. Visitors may be issued with permits to stay for one month. These can be extended to six months on arrival. Visitors must have valid passports, onward or return tickets and adequate funds for their support.

Visas are not needed by nationals or citizens of Commonwealth countries, most West European and South East Asian countries, USA, etc. There is a long list of these countries, but nationals of other countries need a visa unless their stay in Fiji is less than three hours, so if in doubt visitors should enquire before attempting to enter Fiji.

People arriving by air must have a valid international smallpox certificate unless they have been in Australia, New Zealand or specified nearby Pacific islands for at least 14 days before arrival on Fiji. Travellers arriving by sea do not need vaccination certificates unless they came through any country infected by smallpox.

Travellers over one year of age arriving by air must have cholera and yellow fever vaccination certificates if arriving from countries infected by these diseases.

Airport tax. $10 per passenger at departure.

Duty free shopping. Most of the goods sold in Fiji under the 'duty free' label are not completely so, as they bear a 10 per cent fiscal tax, but prices are generally comparable with those in other countries. For many years 'duty free' shopping was a major tourist attraction but changes in price structures in other market countries, devalued currencies and reported cases of improper practices have all affected this form of merchandising.

There are many duty free shops in the major tourist areas of Lautoka, Nadi, Sigatoka and Suva. There is also a very large shop at Nadi International Airport for both departing passengers and those in transit.

Other items that make good 'buys' are silk saris, scarves, woven baskets, mats, tapa cloth and wood ware.

Suva's busy general market is situated near Kings Wharf. It is notable not only for a variety of goods sold but for the opportunity it gives of studying the several races of people who make up Fiji's population.

Popular resorts. Fiji's main holiday areas are the sunny west side of Viti Levu and the cooler but still sunny 'Coral Coast' section along the south Viti Levu coast between Sigatoka and Deuba. The Nadi area has a number of hotels catering for all tastes; it offers interesting tours to the highlands in the interior, through the sugar cane districts, the sugar mills and a number of small outlying islands.

Popular resorts on offshore islands include Castaway, Plantation, Musket Cove, Beachcomber, Matamanoa, Treasure, Mana and Club Naitasi. Cruising for three to seven days through the Yasawa chain of islands is a magnificent experience. Blue Lagoon Cruises operates 'floating' resorts here.

Along the Coral Coast the main resorts are the Fijian at Yanuca, the Reef, the Naiviti and the Hyatt Regency. There are also several smaller resorts here including the Crow's Nest, Casablanca and Tambua Sands.

At Pacific Harbour, Deuba, the Pacific Harbour International Resort and Pacific Harbour Villas are the largest establishments, close to all the facilities and attractions of the Pacific Harbour Cultural Centre.

There are several good hotels in Suva including the Travelodge and the Courtesy Inn. Suva is a vibrant, cosmopolitan city and is the commercial and administrative centre of the country. In Nadi tourists are well catered for with the new 300-room Sheraton Resort, the nearby Regent of Fiji and a number of smaller hotels of varying price range.

The drive around the north of Viti Levu between Lautoka and Suva via Ba, Rakiraki and Tavua is worthwhile, with a stop at Rakiraki, but the Rakiraki-Suva section, while scenically spectacular, is still untouched as a resort area.

Visitors should make the effort to get away from the main island. Vanua Levu, to the north-east of Viti Levu, is easily accessible by plane or roll-on-roll-off ferry. Savusavu, situated on a magnificent harbour and commercial centre for several very large coconut plantations, offers accommodation that includes the large Hot Springs Hotel, the tiny Holiday Home guest house, the Namale Plantation resort, and one of Fiji's newest resorts, Na Koro, which opened in May 1987. The island of Ovalau and it's frontier-like town of Levuka, Fiji's first capital, is also easily accessible by plane or boat. The

Royal Hotel here is the oldest in Fiji. There are at least two guest houses in Levuka but the charm and history of the Royal are irresistible.

The Lau group, though geographically remote, is easy to reach as there are airstrips on Lakeba, Vanua Balavu and Ono-i-Lau with regular flights from Nausori. There are no hotels in the Lau or Lomaiviti groups, but accommodation can usually be found in a Fijian village. There is a small guest house at Lakeba.

Archaeological and historical locations. The Fiji Museum has undertaken limited archaeological exploration. Many areas of Fiji, the Rewa River Delta especially, are pocked with ring forts, relics of the days when villages had to be fortified against attacks by cannibal neighbours. There are large terrace forts on the sides of the Sigatoka Valley and elsewhere. Large earth forts exist on Wakaya Island.

On the north end of Taveuni, at a height of about 300 m, there are mysterious earthworks of a large scale, their origin and purpose a mystery. In several areas of Fiji there are petroglyphs (rock carvings): at Dakuniba in southern Vanua Levu; at Sawailau in the Yasawas; Vola Creek, Savusavu Bay; Taveuni; and Beqa and Yanuca are the best known.

The museum has dated pottery fragments from sand dunes at the mouth of the Sigatoka River as being about 2000 years old.

On Bau Island, home of the great chief Cakobau who ceded Fiji to Britain, the government has restored some of the old chiefly buildings. Serua Island—just off the coast of south Viti Levu—is another interesting example of a fortified islet. A stone monument in Suva marks the site of land auctions after cession. Levuka town on Ovalau Island, once Fiji's capital, has not changed much from how it looked in the 1880s. It contains many charming old wooden buildings. Some Fiji towns have colonial-style wooden houses perhaps 100 or so years old. They are still private homes and not open to the public. The National Trust of Fiji hopes to eventually acquire examples of such buildings.

It has already acquired Burns Philp's old building in Levuka.

Suva — capital, chief port. The city of Suva as we see it today bears little resemblance to the then new capital of the 1880s. The whole foreshore area to the seaward of Victoria Parade, from Nubukalou Creek to the point where the Thurston Gardens run up to Government House, has been reclaimed by draining former mangrove swamps and cutting down the natural soapstone knolls and ridges to make filling. Further reclamation has made way for a broad roadway along the waterfront.

At the eastern end of Victoria Parade most of the buildings on the reclaimed land are set in green lawns and gardens; huge, spreading trees shade the footpath and altogether make up one of the most charming streets in the South Pacific.

Also at the eastern end of Victoria Parade are the Government Offices, Native Land Trust Board building and Broadcasting House, one street back; alongside is Albert Park, where many sporting fixtures are held; opposite Albert Park is the Grand Pacific Hotel and the Travelodge Hotel. East of Albert Park, on the other side of Cakobau Road, the Thurston Gardens with the Fiji Museum in the grounds lead to the brow of the hill and Government House, which is backed by a residential area. The business area of Suva is westward of MacArthur Street in Victoria Parade and in clusters of streets that run on both sides of Nubukalou Creek. The General Post Office, banks, newspaper offices, department stores and streets of Indian tailor and curio shops are all in this area.

Like the tenement area of Toorak, residential Suva is built on rising ground behind the foreshore of the harbour but postwar expansion has resulted in housing development also at Suva Point, and on the slopes looking down on Laucala Bay.

In the opposite direction — westward from the city, beyond Walu Bay — there has been considerable residential development at Lami, which is now a town in its own right. A steep road, a little west of Kings Wharf, runs north through the self-contained suburb of Samabula and turns west again to Tamavau, along the Princes Road, which has excellent views over Suva Harbour, Lami and the mountains beyond.

Suva has the highest concentration of Europeans and Indians in Fiji and Fijians are increasingly attracted to the bright lights of the city. This fact, with a large Chinese community — mostly merchants — Polynesians, other islanders and part-Europeans, makes a walk in Suva's streets an ethnological object lesson and adds considerably to its attraction for tourists.

ACCOMMODATION. There is an enormous range of accommodation in Fiji so visitors of every budgetary persuasion should find something to suit them. With plenty of transport available, Fiji is an easy place to move about in and it is rarely necessary to make bookings in advance, particularly in the low season. This does not apply to the offshore island resorts. Very detailed lists of accommodation are available from the offices of the Fiji Visitors Bureau. This list has been arranged according to price and divided into strategic areas.

SUVA

Capricorn Apartments: 25 apartments, air con, pool, cooking facilities, shop, credit cards: Amex, Visa, Diners, Mastercharge. PO Box 1261, Suva. Tel. 314 799.

Coconut Inn: dormitory 22 beds, communal cooking facilities. 8 Kimberley St, Suva. Tel. 23 902.

Davis Guest House: 2 rooms. 20 Stewart St, Suva. Tel. 24 362.

Grand Pacific Hotel: 72 rooms, air con, pool, coffee-making facilities, restaurant, bar, room service, shop, tour desk, credit cards: Amex, Diners, Visa, Mastercharge. PO Box 2086, Government Buildings, Suva. Tel. 23 011.

Hotel Southern Cross: 31 rooms, air con, pool, coffee-making facilities, shop, tour desk, credit cards: Amex, Diners, Visa. PO Box 1076, Suva. Tel. 314 233.

Hotel Suva: 26 rooms, air con, restaurant, bar. PO Box 578, Suva. Tel. 25 411.

Metropole Hotel: 10 rooms, fans, shared bathroom facilities, breakfast, bar. PO Box 404, Suva. Tel. 24 010.

Miller Private Accommodation: 5 rooms, air con, bed and breakfast or full board, coffee-making facilities. 288 Mead Road, Nabua, Suva. Tel. 383 215.

Motel Crossroad Inn: 12 rooms, coffee-making facilities, fans, communal cooking. 124 Robertson Road, Suva. Tel. 313 820.

New Haven Motel: 12 rooms. Fans, bed and breakfast. 287 Waimanu Road, Suva. Tel. 311 755.

Pacific Grand Apartments: 12 rooms, fans, cooking facilities, dormitory accommodation. PO Box 875, Suva. Tel. 25 583.

South Pacific Inn: 14 rooms, fans, coffee-making facilities. PO Box 1321, Suva. Tel. 311 491.

South Seas Private Hotel: 30 rooms, dormitory, communal kitchen. PO Box 157, Suva. Tel. 22 195.

Sunset Apartment Motel: 12 2-bedroom apartments, air con, cooking facilities. PO Box 485, Suva. Tel. 23 021.

Suva Apartments: 12 rooms, cooking facilities, fans. PO Box 12488, Suva. Tel. 24 281.

Suva Oceanview Hotel: 23 rooms, fans, restaurant, communal kitchen. 270 Waimanu Road, Suva. Tel. 312 129.

Suva Courtesy Inn: 56 rooms, air con, pool, coffee-making facilities, room service, restaurant, credit cards: Amex, Diners, Mastercharge, JCB. PO Box 112, Suva. Tel. 312 300.

Suva Peninsula Hotel: 39 rooms, air con, pool, coffee-making facilities, conference facilities, tour desk, restaurant, bar, credit cards: Amex, Diners, Mastercharge. PO Box 888, Suva. Tel. 313 711.

Suva Travelodge: 134 rooms, air con, pool, coffee-making facilities, restaurant, snack bar, shop, bar, room service, tour desk, convention facilities, credit cards: Amex, Diners, Visa, Mastercharge, JCB. PO Box 1357, Suva. Tel. 314 600.

The President Hotel: 42 rooms, air con, pool, coffee-making facilities, restaurant, bar, room service, convention facilities, credit cards: Amex, Diners, Visa. PO Box 1351, Suva. Tel. 361 033.

The Tanoa House: 12 rooms, fans, pool, restaurant, bar, bed and breakfast. PO Box 704, Suva. Tel. 381 575.

Townhouse Apartments: 28 apartments, air con, cooking facilities, credit cards: Amex, Diners, Visa, Mastercharge. PO Box 485, Suva. Tel. 22 661.

Tropic Towers Apartment Hotel: 29 apartments, air con, pool, cooking facilities, room service, shop, credit cards: Diners. PO Box 1347, Suva. Tel. 25 819.

YWCA Hostel: 27 rooms, fans, coffee-

making facilities, cafeteria. PO Box 534, Suva. Tel. 25 441.

New Garrick Hotel: Share facilities. Renwick St, Suva. Tel. 313 555.

LAUTOKA

Anchorage Beach Resort: 14 rooms, coffee-making facilities, pool, restaurant, bar, water sports, dormitory accommodation, credit cards: Amex, Diners, Visa, Mastercharge. PO Box 9472, Nadi Airport. Tel. 62 099.

Cathay Hotel: 42 rooms, air con, pool, restaurant, room service, bar, credit cards: Amex, Diners, Visa, Mastercharge. PO Box 239, Lautoka. Tel. 60 566.

Lautoka Hotel: 36 rooms, air con, pool, room service, credit cards: Amex, Diners, Visa, Mastercharge. PO Box 51, Lautoka. Tel. 60 388.

Saweni Beach Apartments: 12 rooms, fully self-contained, fans, store, dormitory accommodation, credit cards: Amex, Diners, Visa, Mastercharge. PO Box 293, Lautoka. Tel. 61 777.

Seabreeze Hotel: 27 rooms, air con, coffee-making facilities, breakfast available, bar. PO Box 152, Lautoka. Tel. 60 727.

Sugar City Hotel: 16 rooms, air con, coffee-making facilities, restaurant. PO Box 736, Lautoka. Tel. 61 072.

NADI

Castaway Gateway Hotel: 93 rooms, air con, pool, coffee-making facilities, restaurant, coffee shop, tour desk, conference facilities, room service, bar, spa pool, shop, credit cards: Amex, Diners, Visa, Mastercharge, JCB. PO Box 9246, Nadi Airport. Tel. 72 444.

Dominion International Hotel: 85 rooms, air con, pool, coffee-making facilities, restaurant, tour desk, room service, bar, credit cards: Amex, Diners, Visa, Mastercharge, JCB. PO Box 9178, Nadi Airport. Tel. 72 255.

Fiji Mocambo Hotel: 100 rooms, air con, pool, coffee-making facilities, restaurant, snack bar, tour desk, room service, bar, convention facilities, shops, golf range, tennis, credit cards: Amex, Diners, Visa, Mastercharge, JCB. PO Box 9195, Nadi Airport. Tel. 72 000.

Fong Hing Private Hotel: 17 rooms, air con, restaurant, bar, coffee-making facilities, tour desk, credit cards: Amex, Mastercharge. PO Box 143, Nadi Town. Tel. 71 011.

Johal's Motel: 12 rooms, air con, pool, coffee-making facilities, restaurant, bar, credit cards: Amex. PO Box 213, Nadi Airport. Tel. 72 192.

Melanesian Hotel: 17 rooms, air con, pool, room service, tour desk, restaurant, bar, dormitory accommodation, credit cards: Visa, Amex, Diners, Mastercharge. PO Box 9242, Nadi Airport. Tel. 72 438.

Nadi Airport Travelodge: 114 rooms, air con, pool, coffee-making facilities, restaurant, bar, tour desk, room service, shops, tennis, other sport facilities, credit cards: Amex, Diners, Visa, Mastercharge, JCB. PO Box 9203, Nadi Airport. Tel. 72 277.

Nadi Bay Motel: 12 rooms, restaurant, bar, pool, tour desk, cooking facilities, credit cards: Amex, Diners, Visa, Mastercharge. PO Box 1102, Nadi Town. Tel. 73 319.

Nadi Hotel: 30 rooms, some air con, pool, coffee-making facilities, restaurant, room service, bar, tennis, credit cards: Visa, Diners, Mastercharge. PO Box 91, Nadi Town. Tel. 70 000.

Nadi Motel: 10 rooms, air con, coffee-making facilities. PO Box 653, Nadi Town. Tel. 70 600.

Nadi Sunseekers Hotel: 21 rooms, air con, pool, restaurant, dormitory accommodation, shop, credit cards: Diners, Visa, Mastercharge. PO Box 100, Nadi Town. Tel. 70 400.

Roadway Motel: 8 rooms, air con, cooking facilities. PO Box 9236, Nadi Airport. Tel. 72 570.

Sandalwood Inn: 25 rooms, air con, pool, restaurant, bar, tour desk, coffee-making facilities, room service, credit cards: Amex, Visa, Diners. PO Box 445, Nadi Town. Tel. 72 553.

Sea Shell Cove Resort: 10 self-contained bures, pool, restaurant, bar, cooking facilities, shop, tennis, other sport facilities, dormitory accommodation, credit cards: Amex, Diners, Visa, Mastercharge. PO Box 9530, Nadi Airport. Tel. 50 309.

Sheraton Fiji Resort: 300 rooms, air con, pool, coffee-making facilities, restaurants, bars, convention facilities, tour desks, credit cards: PO Box 9761, Nadi Airport.

Tel. 71 777.

Skylodge Hotel: 48 rooms, air con, pool, coffee-making facilities, restaurant, shop, tour desk, spa pool, other sport facilities, credit cards: Amex, Diners, Visa, Mastercharge. PO Box 9222, Nadi Airport. Tel. 72 200.

Sunny Holiday Motel: 9 rooms, fans, pool, restaurants, dormitory accommodation. PO Box 9335, Nadi Airport. Tel. 72844.

Tanoa Hotel: 102 rooms, air con, pool, spa pool, sauna, restaurant, bar, room service, cooking facilities in villas, snack bar, coffee-making facilities, convention facilities, shop, tennis, other sport facilities, credit cards: Amex, Diners, Visa, Mastercharge, JCB. PO Box 9211, Nadi Airport. Tel. 72 300.

Travellers Beach Resort: Apartments with full kitchen facilities. PO Box 700, Nadi. Tel. 73 322.

The Regent of Fiji: 294 rooms, air con, pool, restaurants, bars, snack bar, coffee-making facilities, room service, convention facilities, shops, tour desk, golf course, tennis, other sport facilities, credit cards: Amex, Diners, Visa, Mastercharge, JCB. PO Box 441, Nadi Town. Tel. 70 700.

NORTHERN VITI LEVU
NAUSORI
Hotel Nausori: 24 rooms, fans, restaurant, bar, bed and breakfast. PO Box 67, Nausori. Tel. 48 833.

BA
Ba Hotel: 14 rooms, air ocn, pool, restaurant, bar, coffee-making facilities. PO Box 29, Ba. Tel. 74 000.

TAVUA
Tavua Hotel: 11 rooms, air con, pool, restaurant. PO Box 4, Tavua. Tel. 91 122.

RAKIRAKI
Rakiraki Hotel: 36 rooms, air con, pool, restaurant, bar, coffee-making facilities, room service, tennis, bowling green, credit cards: Amex, Diners, Visa, Mastercharge. PO Box 31, Rakiraki. Tel. 94 101.

ISLANDS OFF RAKIRAKI
Bethams Beach Cottages: 4 cottages, cooking facilities, snorkelling. PO Box 1244, Suva. Tel. 383 111.

Kon Tiki Island Lodge: PO Box 87, Rakiraki. Tel. 94 275.

Nananu Beach Cottages: 5 bungalows, cooking facilities, snorkelling. c/- Macdonald's Private Mail Bag, Rakiraki. Tel. 22 672.
Nawawa Bay Bungalows: 2 cottages. Sunset Point, c/- Macdonald's Private Mail Bag, Rakiraki. Tel 22 672.

OVALAU ISLAND
Levuka (Ovalau) Holiday Resort: Full board, camping facilities. c/- S. Diston, PO Levuka, Ovalau. Tel. 44 329.
Mavida Guest House: 5 rooms, bed and breakfast. PO Box 91, Levuka. Tel. 44 051.
Old Capital Inn: 10 rooms, bed and breakfast, island tours arranged, dormitory accommodation. PO Box 50, Levuka. Tel. 44 057.
Royal Hotel: 14 rooms, fans, restaurant, bar. PO Box 47, Levuka. Tel. 44 024.
Rukuruku Resort: 6 bures, fans, restaurant, bar, campsites available. PO Box 112, Levuka. Tel. 010. Ask for 100 RP33 311, 491.

NAIGANI ISLAND
Islanders Village: 22 rooms, fans, cooking facilities, restaurant, bar, dormitory accommodation, credit cards: Visa, Diners, Amex, Mastercharge. PO Box 12539, Suva. Tel. 44 364.

GALOA ISLAND VIA KADAVU ISLAND
Reece's Place: Cooking facilities. PO Box 6, Vunisea, Kadavu.

TAILEVU
Tailevu Hotel: 14 rooms, restaurant, bar. PO Korovou, Tailevu. Tel. Tailevu 43; ask operator for 28.

ISLANDS OFF NADI AND LAUTOKA
Beachcomber Island Resort: 27 rooms (tariff includes meals), coffee-making facilities, restaurant, bar, shops, water sports, dormitory accommodation, fans, credit cards: Visa, Diners, Amex, Mastercharge. PO Box 364, Lautoka. Tel. 62 600.
Castaway Island Resort: 66 rooms, fans, pool, restaurant, coffee-making facilities, room service, shop, tennis, other sport facilities, sauna, spa, credit cards: Amex, Diners, Visa, Mastercharge, JCB. PO Box 9246, Nadi Airport. Tel. 61 233.

Club Naitasi: 38 rooms, fans, pool, restaurant, cooking facilities, shops, sporting facilities, credit cards: Amex, Diners, Visa, Mastercharge. PO Box 9147, Nadi Airport. Tel. 72 266.
Mana Island Resort: 132 rooms, fans, pool, coffee-making facilities, snack bar, restaurant, shops, tour desk, bar, sport facilities, credit cards: Amex, Diners, Visa, Mastercharge, JCB. PO Box 610, Lautoka. Tel. 61 455.
Matamanoa Island Resort: 20 bures, restaurant, bar, coffee-making facilities, tennis, other sport activities, shop, credit cards: Diners, Amex, Visa, Mastercharge. PO Box 9729, Nadi Airport. Tel. 60 511.
Musket Cove Resort: 24 rooms, fans, cooking facilities, restaurant, bar, shop, tour desk, pool, sport facilities, credit cards: Amex, Diners, Visa, Mastercharge. Private Bag, Nadi Airport. Tel. 62 215.
Navini Island Resort: 10 rooms, coffee-making facilities, fans, restaurant, water sports, credit cards: Amex, Diners, Visa. PO Box 685, Lautoka. Tel. 62 188.
Plantation Island Resort: 90 rooms, air con, coffee-making facilities, restaurant, bar, pool, spa, sport facilities, dormitory accommodation, credit cards: Amex, Diners, Visa. PO Box 9176, Nadi Airport. Tel. 72 333.
Treasure Island Resort: 69 rooms, coffee-making facilities, restaurant, bar, convention facilities, dormitory accommodation, pool, sport facilities, credit cards: Amex, Diners, Visa, Mastercharge. PO Box 364, Lautoka. Tel. 61 599.
Turtle Island Lagoon Lodge: 12 bures, fans, coffee-making facilities, food and liquor included in rate, shop, tour desk, sport facilities, credit cards: Visa, Diners, Amex. PO Box 9317, Nadi Airport. Tel. 72 921.

CORAL COAST — SIGATOKA
Casablanca Beach Hotel: 8 apartments, air con, pool, cooking facilities, restaurant. PO Box 164, Sigatoka. Tel. 50 766.
Crow's Nest: 18 cottages, fans, pool, cooking facilities, restaurant, bar, shop, sport facilities, credit cards: Amex, Diners, Visa. PO Box 270, Sigatoka. Tel. 50 230.
Hideaway Resort: 15 bures, pool, coffee-making facilities, snack bar, store, sport

facilities, dormitory, credit cards: Amex, Diners, Visa, Mastercharge. PO Box 233, Sigatoka. Tel. 50 177.

Hyatt Regency: 249 rooms, air con, pool, coffee-making facilities, restaurants, snack bar, bars, shops, tour desk, room service, convention facilities, golf, tennis, other sport facilities, credit cards: Amex, Diners, Visa, Mastercharge, JCB. PO Box 100, Korolevu. Tel. 50 555.

Man Friday Resort: 38 bures, fans, pool, restaurant, bar, shop, sport facilities, credit cards: Amex, Diners, Visa, Mastercharge. PO Box 20, Korolevu. Tel. 50 185.

Naviti Beach Resort: 144 rooms, air con, pool, coffee-making facilities, convention facilities, room service, restaurant, snack bar, bar, shop, golf, tennis, other sport facilities, credit cards: Amex, Visa, Diners, Mastercharge. PO Box 29, Korolevu. Tel. 50 444.

Reef Hotel Resort: 72 rooms, air con, pool, coffee-making facilities, restaurant, bar, shop, tour desk, golf, tennis, other sport facilities, credit cards: Amex, Diners, Visa. PO Box 173, Sigatoka. Tel. 50 044.

Sandy Point Beach Cottages: 12 rooms, pool, cooking facilities, bar. PO Box 23, Sigatoka. Tel. 50 125.

Sigatoka Hotel: 6 rooms, restaurant, bar. PO Box 35, Sigatoka. Tel 50 011.

The Fijian Hotel: 364 rooms, air con, pools, coffee-making facilities, room service, restaurants, bars, snack bars, cooking facilities in executive bures, shops, tour desk, convention facilities, tennis, golf, other sport facilities, credit cards: Amex, Diners, Visa, Mastercharge, JCB. Private Mail Bag, Nadi Airport. Tel. 50 155.

Tambua Sands Beach Resort: 19 rooms, fans, restaurant, pool, bar, tour desk, dormitory accommodation, credit cards: Amex, Diners, Visa, Mastercharge. PO Box 177, Sigatoka. Tel 50 399.

Tubakula Beach Cottages: 24 bures, cooking facilities, restaurant, bar, convention facilities, tours, fans, shops, room service, tennis, golf range, credit cards: Amex, Diners, Visa, Mastercharge. PO Box 2086, Gvt Bldgs, Suva. Tel. 50 201.

Vakaviti Units and Cabins: 6 units, fans, pool, cooking facilities, bar, shop, tour desk, dormitory accommodation. PO Box 5, Sigatoka. Tel. 50 526.

Waratah Lodge: 5 bures, pool, fans,

restaurant. PO Box 86, Korotogo. Tel. 50 278.

VANUA LEVU AND TAVEUNI

LABASA

Coral Island Resort: 10 rooms (tariff incl. meals), air con, restaurant, bar. PO Box 7, Labasa. Tel. 81 655.

Grand Eastern Hotel: 18 rooms, air con, restaurant, bar. PO Box 13, Labasa. Tel. 81 022.

Hotel Takia: 34 rooms, air con, pool, restaurant, bar, coffee-making facilities, room service, conference facilities, credit cards: Visa, Diners, Amex, Mastercharge. PO Box 7, Labasa. Tel. 81 655.

SAVUSAVU

Kon Tiki Lodge: 8 bures, fans, cooking facilities, pool, games room. PO Box 244, Savusavu. Tel. 86 262.

Kubulau Plantation House (Buca Bay): 5 rooms, family style dining room. PO Box 219, Savusavu. Tel. 84 010, Diloi 4-k.

Lesiacevu Point, Beach Apartments: Self-contained apartment. c/- G. Mulligan, Lesiacevu Point. Tel. 82 250.

Na Koro Resort: 23 units, fans, coffee-making facilities, bar, restaurant, pool, convention facilities, dive facilities. c/- Post Office, Savusavu. Tel. 188.

Namale Plantation Resort: 10 bures, fans, restaurant, bar, pool, coffee-making facilities, tennis, other sport activities. PO Box 244, Savusavu. Tel. 86 117.

Savusavu Hot Springs Hotel: 48 rooms, air con, restaurant, bar, pool, coffee-making facilities, credit cards: Amex, Visa, Diners, Mastercharge. PO Box 208, Savusavu. Tel. 85 111.

Savusavu Holiday Home: 5 rooms, communal kitchen, fans, bed and breakfast. PO Box 65, Savusavu. Tel. 86 ext. 150.

NAMENA ISLAND

Moody's Namena: 4 bures, restaurant, bar, water sports. Private Mail Bag, Suva. Tel. 81 010.

TAVEUNI

Dive Taveuni: Includes meals, ensuite bedrooms, 1 family bure. PO Matei. Tel. 406M.

Kaba's Guest House: 3 rooms, communal kitchen. PO Box 4, Taveuni. Tel. 87; ask for 58.

Maravu Plantation Resort: 4 bures (tariff

incl. meals), restaurant, bar. Postal Agency, Matei, Taveuni. Tel. 401A.

Taveuni International Holiday Resort: 30 rooms, air con, pool, restaurant, bar, tour desk, room service, credit cards: Visa, Diners, Amex, Mastercharge, JCB. PO Box 1, Taveuni. Tel. 87 286.

QAMEA ISLAND

Qamea Beach Club Resort: 8 bures, fans, restaurant, bar, water sports, credit cards: Amex, Diners. PO Matei, Taveuni. Tel. 87 220.

LAU GROUP

The Homestead: 2 bures, family style dining room, shop, sport activities. Munia Island, Northern Lau Group. Tel. 010; ask for 284 RP7.

Lakeba Guest House: 4 rooms, communal kitchen. c/- Provincial Office, Tubou, Lakeba. Lau. Tel. Lakeba, ext. 35.

Lomaloma Guest House: c/- Mr Poasa Delailomaloma, Lomaloma, Vanua Balavu.

NAVUA-DEUBA

Coral Coast Christian Camps: 6 rooms, 8 cabins, cooking facilities, fans, tour desk.

PO Pacific Harbour, Deuba. Tel. 45 187.

Fiji Palm Beach Club Resort: 14 apartments, fans, cooking facilities, pool, spa, recreation block, bar. PO Pacific Harbour, Deuba. Tel. 45 050.

Navua Hotel: 6 rooms, fans, restaurant, bar, bed and breakfast. PO Navua, Navua. Tel. 46 006.

Pacific Harbour Villas: 20 villas, air con, pool, cooking facilities, use of all hotel facilities, credit cards: Diners, Amex, Visa. Postal Agency, Pacific Harbour. Tel. 45 011.

Pacific Harbour International Hotel: 84 rooms, air con, pool, restaurant, bars, coffee-making facilities, snack bars, tour desk, golf, lawn tennis, other sport facilities, room service, shop, credit cards: Amex, Diners, Visa, Mastercharge, JCB. Postal Agency, Pacific Harbour. Tel. 45 022.

TOBERUA ISLAND

Toberua Island Resort: 14 bures, pool, coffee-making facilities, restaurant, bar, room service, shop, tours helicopter or seaplane arranged, credit cards: Amex, Diners, Visa, Mastercharge. PO Box 567, Suva. Tel. 49 177.

FRENCH POLYNESIA

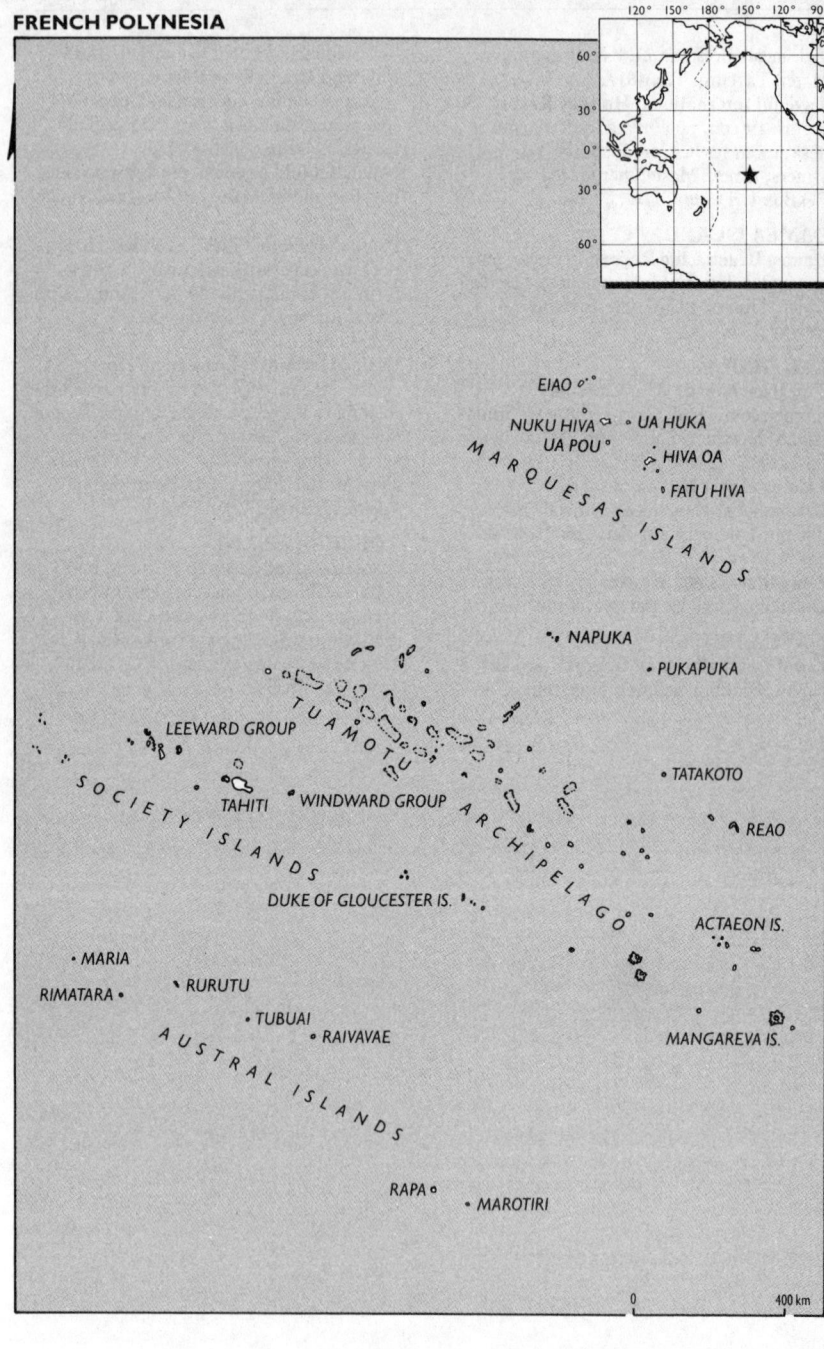

French Polynesia

French Polynesia, an overseas territory of France, consists of five main groups containing some 130 islands. They have a land area of 4000 sq. km in an area of four million square kilometres of ocean. They extend from 7 to 29 deg S latitude and from 131 to 156 deg W longitude. Papeete, the capital, is on the island of Tahiti which is about 5390 km east of Sydney and about 6520 km south-west of California. Local time is 10 hours behind GMT.

The national anthem and flag are those of France. The red and white Tahitian flag is the 'territorial emblem' and is flown on official buildings side by side with the tricolour.

The currency is the French Pacific franc (CFP) with a fixed exchange rate of 18.18 to the French franc.

Public holidays include the traditional French ones: 1 January, Easter Monday, 1 May (Labour Day), Ascension (39 days after Easter Sunday), Monday after Pentecost (about 10 days after Ascension), 14 July (Bastille Day), 15 August (Assumption), 1 November (All Saints), 11 November (Armistice Day) and Christmas Day. Since 1979, 5 March, anniversary day of the bringing of the Gospel to French Polynesia, has also been a public holiday.

THE PEOPLE. The population in 1985 was 172,080, two-thirds of whom lived in Tahiti. Polynesians represent about 70 per cent of the population, Europeans 15, part-Europeans eight and Chinese seven per cent.
Nationality. All Polynesians and most of the Chinese are French citizens.
Languages. The official languages are French and Tahitian.
Religion. More than half of the population is Protestant, with about one-third Catholic, 3 per cent Latter-day Saints, 3 per cent Reorganised Church of Latterday Saints, 3 per cent Seventh-day Adventists and 3 per cent Jehovah's Witnesses.

Practically all Protestants are Polynesians. The Catholics are found among the French and the Polynesians of the Marquesas and Tuamotu Islands.
Lifestyle. It varies considerably from urban Papeete with its large population concentrating on business and administrative activity, tourist facilities and French legionnaires, to the rural life on outer islands.

GOVERNMENT. As an overseas territory of the French Republic, French Polynesia elects the 30 members of its Territorial Assembly by popular vote every five years. The Assembly members in turn elect the seven members of the Government Council (Conseil de Gouvernement).

The French Republic is represented by a High Commissioner who controls all government services — the police, the judicial system, the radio and TV services, and so on.

French Polynesia is represented in Paris by a senator, elected by the local political bodies, and by two deputies — one for a western and one for an eastern constituency — who are elected by direct popular suffrage.

The main political parties are the Tahoeraa Huiraatira party, the French RPR (Gaullist) party, the Pupu Here Aia, which favours the creation of a Polynesian State, associated with France, and the Ia Mana te Nunaa party which favours total independence and a socialist economy. Several independents also sit in the Assembly.

Local government. Since 1972, the territory has been divided into 48 communes or municipalities headed by an elected council which in its turn elects a mayor. The communes have responsibility for school buildings, water supplies, garbage collection, and certain public works. In the annual budget, one-fourth of the revenues is put aside for the use of the communes and distributed on a demographic basis. As a vestige of the colonial system, the communes are supervised by French administrators, one for each of the five island groups.

JUSTICE. There are lower and higher courts (Tribunal de Premiere Instance and Tribunal Superieur d'Appel). There is a President and Vice President (equivalent of judges) of each but, in the lower court, cases are also presided over by magistrates. At the head of the judiciary department is Chief of the Judiciary Service, equivalent to an Attorney-General. Other officers of this department include prosecutors, examining magistrates, etc. Most of the judiciary officials are stationed in Papeete but in Raiatea there is a judge of the lower court.

Law and order is kept by the gendarmerie, which is part of the French National Gendarmerie whose members are recruited in France. They have locally hired assistants. The police corps, on the other hand, are locally recruited and paid by the communes, and act only within their boundaries.

The basic laws in force are those of France, made applicable as occasion may demand by promulgations; plus ordinances, laws, etc., passed by the Assembly, that have a completely local application.

Liquor laws. Liquor is sold in bars, restaurants and cafes from 7 am to 1.00 am seven days a week. In certain bars outside Papeete closing time is not till 2 am. It is illegal to sell liquor to anyone under the age of 18 but there are no other restrictions.

There is little public drunkenness in French Polynesia. The local people usually drink local beer or punch made with rum, lime juice and sugar.

Gambling. There is no official, legalised gambling, but much illegal.

DEFENCE. The elected representatives of the Polynesian people have no say in defence matters which are wholly controlled by the metropolitan French government. For instance, the 30 members of the Territorial Assembly were not even consulted when President de Gaulle in 1962 decided to use some of their islands for nuclear testing, and all their subsequent protests have been disregarded.

A special organisation, the *Centre d'Experimentation du Pacifique*, was created in 1963, and more than 15,000 troops and technicians sent out to French Polynesia. The islands chosen for testing the French nuclear weapons were the two small atolls of Mururoa and Fangataufa in the south-east corner of the Tuamotu group, and a logistic support base was simultaneously established at Hao in the central Tuamotus.

The first atomic blast occurred on 2 July 1966, in the skies above Mururoa, and it was followed by another 40 atmospheric tests, of which five involved hydrogen bombs in the megatonne range. Fangataufa, 40 kilometres south of Mururoa, was used for two of the latter explosions.

As a result of numerous protests from, and trade boycotts in, practically all other Pacific countries, as well as the proceedings instituted in 1973 against France by the governments of Australia and New Zealand in the International Court of Justice at The Hague, the Paris government switched to underground testing. After two trial blasts at Fangataufa in 1975, annual series of between five and 11 explosions have been made at Mururoa.

The installation of the CEP brought considerable changes in the social and economic fields, increasing trade and building activity, as well as bringing an influx of new French settlers. At the same time, thousands of Polynesians gave up farming and came to live in Papeete.

The total expenditure of the defence forces in French Polynesia in 1985 was 39,792 million Pacific francs, of which 28,492 million was spent on salaries and running costs — *frais de fonctionnement*.

It is estimated that about 1300 'locals' — out of a total work force of 58,000 — are employed by the CEP and subsidiary organisations.

EDUCATION. At the primary level, education is financed from the territorial budget while secondary and technical education is conducted with State funds. Private schools are operated by the churches, with the State financing running costs.

There were 285 government primary schools with 33,427 pupils in the school year 1984–85 together with 7376 pupils in 28 private primary schools. There were 9,046 students in 22 government secondary schools, and 3924 students in 10 private secondary schools.

Technical training was being taken by 3204 students in government schools, and 618 in private schools.

State secondary schools include the Lycee Paul Gauguin in Papeete which has annexes in other districts and outer islands; the high school at Uturoa (Raiatea) and the Taaone Technical High School at Pirae in Papeete, which also has a course in Tourism.

Church secondary schools in Tahiti include the College Pomare IV (Protestant) and the College La Mennais (Roman Catholic). These schools have accommodation for boarders and prepare students for the baccalaureat or university entrance.

Other specialised education is available through the Teacher's Training College. The Chamber of Commerce in Papeete conducts courses in business English, shorthand, typing, etc.

Scholarships for higher education and for French universities are made possible by government grants.

Education is compulsory. It is free of charge in the government schools for day pupils; 14 is the legal school leaving age.

LABOUR. Information on the employment situation in French Polynesia is not readily available; 1983 estimates indicate an active labour force of 57,863, including about 6000 self-employed farmers and fishermen. The main employee sectors are:

Agriculture	8032
Industry	10,778
Commerce	39,053
Total	57,863

The installation of the CEP has greatly influenced the territory's employment situation, bringing a shift of workers away from agriculture and fishing into tertiary activities.

Wages. The minimum wage has increased steadily from CFP62 per hour in 1973 to CFP235 per hour in 1982, and CFP402 per hour in 1985.

Workers' accident compensation and other social benefits are financed through a payroll tax paid to the territory's social security fund.

Unions. In 1983 there were at least three 'umbrella' trade union bodies, representing various political tendencies. There were also active trade unions representing dockers, public servants, and teachers in government schools.

HEALTH. Health services are well provided for. More than 60 doctors are available for the civilian population in Tahiti, while military specialists with the CEP may be called in emergencies. The Mamao Hospital in Papeete is well equipped and has over 400 beds. There are also two modern private hospitals in Papeete, the Cardella Hospital and the Paofai Hospital. There is a small hospital staffed by doctors in each group of the outer islands as well as dispensaries attended by travelling doctors.

In Tahiti about 25 dentists serve the needs of the civilian population.

Research. The Insitut de Recherches Medicales Louis Malarde, set up in 1947 with US assistance, but not affiliated with the French Pasteur Institute, conducts research into endemic diseases. The Institut has brought the disfiguring disease of elephantiasis under control and now concentrates more on fish toxicity.

Diseases. Tuberculosis has been the biggest health hazard for the local Polynesians in recent times but vigorous vaccination and X-ray programmes have been undertaken. Filariasis and its end result, elephantiasis, are regarded as now being under control. Diabetes, rheumatic fever, dengue fever and fish poisoning are major problems.

Certain local food habits can cause Tahitian meningitis from eating uncooked prawns, or fish poisoning from eating certain fish.

THE LAND. The five archipelagoes forming French Polynesia are scattered across 4.5 million square kilometres of ocean, although their actual land area is only 4000 sq. km. Tahiti (1042 sq. km) is the largest island.

The Tuamotu archipelago, by contrast, is composed of 76 islands, mostly atolls, with an average surface of 10 sq. km above sea level.

Highest mountain peaks are Mt Orohena (2241 m) and Mt Aorai (2066 m) on Tahiti.

The five archipelagoes, listing the main islands, are as follows:

Society Islands. The Windward Group, comprising Tahiti, Moorea, Mehetia, Tetiaroa and Maiao. And the Leeward Group, comprising Raiatea-Tahaa, Bora Bora, Huahine, and Maupiti.

Tuamotu Archipelago. Anaa, Makemo, Hao, Reao, Napuka, Mururoa, Rangiroa, Apataki and Fakarava.

Gambier Islands. Mangareva, Taravai, Aukena, Akamaru and Temoe.

Austral Islands. Tubuai, Rurutu, Rimatera, Raivavae and Rapa.

Marquesas Islands. Hivaoa, Nukuhiva, Fatuhiva, Eiao, Uapou, Uahuka, Fatuhuku, Tahuata, Motane and Hatutu.

Most of these archipelagoes are composed of now extinct volcanoes, with high mountainous formations and deep well-watered valleys. Such islands are generally surrounded by a coral reef forming sheltered lagoons. Islands like the Tuamotus, however, are coral rings with a central lagoon.

Climate. The climate is tropical, but moderate — average temperature being 27°C, falling to 21°C during July and August. In January and February, hottest months of the year, temperatures reach approximately 32°C. Rain falls through the year but mostly between November and March. Average rainfall in Papeete is 1750 mm annually. Humidity is generally high especially in the wet season. Cyclones have been experienced.

Flora and fauna. The islands of volcanic origin have fertile soil producing prolific vegetation including magnificent flowers, such as the Tahitian tiare. This is a fragrant gardenia, worn in leis or in the hair.

The local fauna on land is mainly introduced with wild animals limited to some pigs and fowls. Thirty-three endemic species of birds are present, most being visible around the shores of Tahiti. The greatest variety and abundance of fauna is found in the sea, with its fish and crustaceans.

Land reclamation. On the Papeete fore-shore land reclamation has provided 14 hectares at Fare Ute for industrial and military purposes. An adjacent 14-ha strip of coral reef was reclaimed to provide extra berthing and shorage facilities in the port of Papeete.

Land tenure. Although French law governs all land tenure, in practice the old Polynesian system of joint land ownership still prevails to a large extent. The absence of accurate land deeds often makes it difficult to apply the French code. Unlike French citizens, foreigners must get special permission to buy land, and it is not easily granted. Nonetheless, since the hotel-building boom, some large parcels of privately owned land have changed hands. In the case of approved businesses wanting to establish themselves, the government will do its best to find suitable land.

Over 85 per cent of the land is in Polynesian hands although a considerable amount of this is leased to the Chinese. It is calculated that 25 per cent of the Chinese population lives by agriculture and only in a minority of cases is the land they work their own.

PRIMARY PRODUCTION. Efforts are continually being made to extend agricultural output in French Polynesia.

Copra. Still the main agricultural product despite fluctuations in world prices, recent output has been:

Copra production (in tonnes)
1982	19,181
1983	11,011
1984	7389
1985	13,443

Coconut oil. The Territory's total copra output is used by the Tahiti Oil Co. (Huilerie de Tahiti) to be processed into coconut oil for export, and into coconut meal for use as cattle feed by the local beef industry, although some is also exported.

Coconut oil exports (in tonnes)
1982	11,006
1983	21,339
1984	16,272
1985	17,823

Copra cake production in 1984 was 18,537

tonnes and in 1985 8765 tonnes.

Vanilla. There has been renewed interest in this crop in recent years. Vanilla exports dropped in 1981 to 0.6 tonnes but picked up again to 10.7 tonnes in 1983 and 14.7 tonnes in 1984.

Coffee. Grown in small plots for the local market. Production has fluctuated and in 1983 142 tonnes were produced but fell again to 63 tonnes in 1984.

Vegetables. Produced mainly on the plains of Tahiti, with about 250 ha devoted to vegetables cultivated by some 300 producers, mostly of Chinese origin. Vegetable production in 1985 was 10,612 tonnes sold on the markets and 5401 tonnes of root crops including taro.

Fruit. Local marketed production in 1985 was 4431 tonnes, the majority being pineapples.

Livestock. While efforts continue to build up the existing cattle herds, imported stock has enabled much of the local demand for milk, chickens and eggs to be satisfied.

Pork production in 1983 was 789 tonnes, and in 1984, 872 tonnes.

In the same years, locally produced beef sales reached 212 tonnes, and 258 tonnes respectively. In 1984 2.04 million litres of milk were produced. Three local companies make yoghurt, butter and cheese, but their output is insufficient to meet all the local demand.

Table poultry production was 426 tonnes in 1984. Egg production reached 1.9 million. In 1948 8 tonnes of rabbit meat was processed.

Fish. Application of the 200-mile economic zone gives French Polynesia over four million square km of sea, and encourages the fishing industry. The 1985 recorded catches were; tuna 1134 tonnes, bonito 2525 tonnes, and other fish, 7945 tonnes.

Shrimp farms. The fisheries office, CNEXO, with territory finance built 5 ha of ponds for farming freshwater shrimps in 1976. Production figures are incorporated into 'other fish'.

Oysters. About 100 oyster growers in the Leeward Islands harvest this sea crop.

Pearl culture. In the Tuamotu and Gambier islands, a number of cooperatives and private companies cultivate pearls, including the 'black' pearl. In 1987 cultivated pearl exports were worth CFP 2251 m. (approx US$ 22 m).

MANUFACTURING AND MINING. There are two breweries and several plants producing soft drinks. Among the few other local products 'monoi' oil, perfumes and handicrafts are the main items.

There are no mineral ventures on land, but seabed surveys seeking deposits of polymetallic nodules are conducted by the National Marine Research Centre (CNEXO).

Phosphate was once the territory's main export, with 368,780 tonnes being shipped out in 1961 from the island of Makatea in the Tuamotus. But the workings were closed in 1966 when the deposits were exhausted.

There is a deposit of about 10 million tonnes of phosphate on Mathiva and in 1988 the Territorial Government announced an economic recovery plan which included the opening of a phosphate mining project in this western corner of the Tuamotus.

TOURISM. The number of tourists visiting French Polynesia and the percentage increase or decrease in relation to the preceding year are shown in the following table.

1984	1985	1986	1987
101,595	122,086	161,238	142,820
− 8.6%	+ 20.2%	+ 32%	− 11.4%

In 1985, 50 per cent of all tourists were from America. The port of Papeete is used by several American cruise lines as a turnaround point for both staff and cruise itineraries in the South Pacific. This accounts for the large percentage of American tourists who normally get several days in Tahiti as part of their cruise package. American Hawaii Cruises operated the *Liberti* out of Papeete on seven day cruises around French Polynesia. However, in 1987 they pulled out of that market, because of financial difficulties. This has left a large gap in the utilisation of tourism plant and facilities that were set up to service the estimated 700 Americans who would fly in weekly for this particular cruise. It is hoped that another cruise operator will fill this gap. In 1988 $US 3.4 m is to be spent on promotion in the US.

The tourist industry is recognised as an important source of employment for the territory. In 1985 over 4000 worked in the hotels and associated tourist facilities. Had the American market remained consistent, it was estimated that by 1989 this figure would have risen to about 9000.

Other markets which are seen as possible replacements in tourist numbers are Australia, Japan and Europe with the promotion budget for tourism being significantly increased in these areas.

The number of hotel rooms at the end of 1986 stood at 2808 rooms acknowledged as of international standard by the Tahiti Tourist Development Board. Half of the rooms were on Tahiti, and one-third on Moorea.

The Tahiti Tourist Development Board is the instrumentality charged with the orderly development of tourism. It is financed by a percentage of some taxes and its functions are widespread. It is not a tourist agency. It has several sections — promotion and planning, visitor facilities, statistics and research, and administration and finance.

HOUSING. The territory's building industry is determined considerably by the level of activity in the two main sectors of the economy — the CEP nuclear test programme and tourism.

In the construction of dwellings, figures from the Territorial Institute of Statistics reflect activity in the Windward group (Tahiti and neighbouring islands).

In 1985 building permits were issued for 1414 dwellings compared with 1361 in 1984. Seventy per cent of permits were for private dwellings, the rest were for reconstruction jobs, particularly of hotels.

The territory's housing industry faced unprecedented problems in 1983 as a consequence of the six cyclones that devastated French Polynesia from December 1982 to April 1983.

In all, it was estimated that 10,000 dwellings throughout the territory — principally in the Leeward, Tuamotu and Windward Islands — were either destroyed or damaged. Something like a third of the territory's population was left homeless.

OVERSEAS TRADE. The rapid growth of French Polynesia's trade over recent years has mainly been due to the needs of the CEP nuclear test centre, as well as the pressures of inflation.

Principal Exports (in CFP millions).

	1984	1985
Coconut oil	2915.0	6189
Vanilla	148.4	224.2
Fresh fruit	49.1	0.4
Mother-of-pearl	149.3	63.3
Pearls	2236.0	9229.1

In 1987 cultured pearls worth CFP 2251 m and coconut oil worth CFP 327 m were the main exports.

Principal Imports (in CFP millions)

	1984	1985
Food & drink	43,539	47,397
Mineral products	72,693	78,711
Timber & timber products	21,909	20,407
Manufactured goods	43,187	46,352
Transport machinery	65,054	76,075

Suppliers. Most imports in 1987 were obtained from France (52 per cent), USA (10.3 per cent), New Zealand (5 per cent), and EEC countries (12.9 per cent).

Customs tariff. Imports are subject to the various port and customs levies, giving preference to goods from France and the EEC. These taxes include customs duty on goods coming from countries outside the EEC (average rate of 10 per cent); import duty imposed on all imports except for certain basic necessities, and various items destined for the CEP (from 1 to 32 per cent).

Sales tax is paid on various products, especially petroleum products, tobacco and alcohol (various fixed charges).

FINANCE. The annual territorial budget for French Polynesia is funded from local (mainly indirect) taxes, certain public service contributions from France and loan monies. Budget expenditure is divided into four sections: the operation of the public service; subsidies and funds given, e.g. to the municipalities; infrastructure, and loan repayments.

In addition to the territorial budget, overseas funds are granted as follows: to account for public service departments maintained by France; French grants for capital works (FIDES); and capital works grants from the European Development Fund.

Expressed in CFP billions	1983 Budget Committed	1984 Budget Authorised
Receipts	**37.6**	**45.3**
− Current revenue	33.0	35.9
+ Direct taxation	6.3	5.9
+ Indirect taxation	21.4	28.0
+ Others	5.3	2.0
− Special revenue	4.6	9.4
Expenditures	**31.0**	**45.3**
− Operations	26.4	35.9
− Equipment & investment	4.6	9.4
French Government expenditures	59.0	75.0

Taxation. Due to the absence of personal income tax in French Polynesia, about 75 per cent of local tax revenue is derived from sales tax and import and export dues. Other taxes include the business licence fee ('patente'), company tax, land tax and transfer fees.

Currency. The overseas note issuing authority or reserve bank (Institut d'Emission d'Outre-Mer), circulates notes in the following denominations: CFP100, 500, 1000 and 5000. Coins are for CFP1, 2, 5, 10, 20, 50 and 100.

Banks. Three banks in the territory operate about 20 branches. They are the Banque de l'Indochine et de Suez (Indo-Suez), the Banque de Tahiti and the Banque de Polynesie.

There are also two finance companies— Credit Caledonien et Tahitien, and Credit du Pacifique. Three additional credit institutions with offices in Papeete are the Caisse Centrale de Co-operation Economique; the Societe de Credit et de Developpement de l'Oceanie (SOCREDO); and the Societe d'Expansion et de Developpement du Pacifique.

Investment incentives. Under investment incentives offered by the territory and the French government, cash premiums may be granted for investment in agriculture, fishing, food production, transport, hotels, health clinics and crafts, provided certain minimum criteria are met concerning jobs created and level of funds invested.

The 'investment code' is overseen by the Bureau for Industrial Development, which is attached to the Planning Office.

TRANSPORT. Public transport on Tahiti is by local bus, called 'le truck', which is cheap and picturesque, leaving from the central market of Papeete. There are over 200 km of roads on Tahiti, mostly following the coastline. On Moorea there are about 100 km of roads, as well as some 60 km on Raiatea and 30 on Bora Bora.

About a dozen firms in Tahiti and several on Moorea and Bora Bora hire out cars, motorbikes and air conditioned buses. There are also local taxis.

Vehicles. There is a relatively high rate of motor vehicle ownership. Figures for registrations of new vehicles and used vehicle sales for the first three months of 1985, and the comparable figures for 1986, were:

	New registrations first four months of 85	New registrations first four months of 86
All vehicles	1173	1315
Including passenger vehicles		
Motorcycles and powered bicycles	560	505
Used vehicle sales	1337	1483

In 1985 there were 33,269 registered vehicles in total.

Overseas airlines. Qantas flies from Sydney three times a week to Papeete, continuing on to Los Angeles. Likewise, it has three flights a week from Los Angeles via Papeete to Sydney.

Air New Zealand flies to Papeete three times a week from Auckland, twice direct to Tahiti, and once via Nadi, Fiji and Rarotonga, Cook Islands. The flight continues on to the US twice a week, and there are two flights a week from Los Angeles to Tahiti then on direct to Auckland.

UTA French Airlines operate flights between Sydney and Tahiti via Noumea and New Zealand once a week, and via Noumea once a week. It also operates a direct flight between Auckland and Papeete once a week, and from Los Angeles to Papeete twice a week.

LAN-Chile has either one or two flights a week from Santiago, Chile, to Papeete via

Easter Island, depending upon the season.
Domestic airlines. In January 1987 Air Polynesie, the domestic airline, changed its name to Air Tahiti. The change was made to avoid further confusion between the domestic airline of French Polynesia and Polynesian Airlines, the international carrier of Western Samoa. Air Tahiti is currently upgrading to ATR 42 turboprops to replace the Fokker 27s. From Papeete there are eight monthly flights to the Australs, four to the Eastern Tuamotus and Gambier Islands and five to the Marquesas.

Air Tahiti also operates over 180 flights per month to Bora Bora, Raiatea, Huahine, Rangiroa, Manihi and other islands in the Leeward group.

Air Moorea operates several daily flights between Tahiti and Moorea. Air Tahiti is partly owned by the territorial government (24 per cent), UTA and private investors.
Port facilities. The port of Papeete is protected by a 1500 m seawall built on a coral reef. The port opens to the sea through a deep water passage. To handle the great increase in traffic caused by the nuclear test base, the berthing and storage facilities were considerably extended over the two years to 1966. This involved the reclamation of about 14 ha of coral reef from the sea. This strip was linked to another reclaimed area of 14 ha at Fare Ute providing industrial and military land.

The harbour installations have separate areas for local small craft, for warships and for cargo vessels. They can accommodate ships up to 35,000 tons and have a depth in parts of 11.5 m alongside at low tide.

Length and depth of the wharves is as follows: Main wharf — 450 m, 11.3 m; inter-island traders — 280 m, 6.6 m; transit wharf — 129 m, 10 m; oil wharf — 105 m, 11 m; passenger liners — 233 m, 9 m; wharf for Moorea — 100 m long; fishing wharf — 90 m; deep sea fishing — 200 m; pleasure craft — 360 m; also naval wharves, and slip-yards.
Overseas shipping. From Australia both Compagnie Generale Maritime and Karlander (Aust.) Pty Ltd maintain regular container services to Tahiti, with Karlander continuing its services to the west coast of US.

Shipping Corporation of New Zealand, Pacifique Polynesie Line, and Compagnie

Tahitienne Maritime, operate between New Zealand and Tahiti on a regular basis. China Navigation provides a service from the Far East via Papua New Guinea and other island ports, and Kyowa Shipping operates between Japan and Pacific Island countries, including French Polynesia.

Services from Europe are provided by Compagnie Generale Maritime, Polish Ocean Lines, and Nedlloyd (Aust.) Pty Ltd, along with Bank Line (A'Asia) Pty Ltd.

The Bank Line & Savill Line, and Polynesia Shipping Services Inc., maintain regular services between the west coast of the US and the Pacific islands, continuing on to Australia, and Marshall Islands Maritime Co. provide a service between Hawaii, Tahiti, and the Samoas.
Inter-island shipping. Copra boats and schooners connect Tahiti with the neighbouring islands and the remote archipelagoes. A number of these boats have either cabin or deck facilities for passengers.
Yachts. Crew and passengers must be in possession of passports, and upon arrival in Papeete must contact the Customs or Gendarmerie. Crew list changes are only permitted in harbours where gendarme approval can be obtained. Prior to departure, yachts must obtain permission to leave from the port captain. Besides Papeete, formalities can be accomplished at other points of entry: Marquesas — Taiohae (Nukuhiva), Uapou, Hivaoa; Austral Islands — Tubuai, Rurutu, Raivavae; Tuamotu/Gambier — Mangareva; Leeward Islands — Raiatea, Huahine, Bora Bora; Windward Islands — Moorea.

It is illegal for owners of visiting yachts to charter them locally or to use them for trading or carrying passengers or freight, without the prior permission of the government.

A number of cruise ships call into Papeete and Bora Bora on itineraries from the US and Australia.

COMMUNICATIONS. There are post offices on Tahiti (Papeete, Pirae, Faaa, Paea, Taravao), Moorea, Huahine, Raiatea-Tahaa, Bora Bora, Maupiti, Rangiroa, Marquesas and Austral islands.

Office hours: Mon to Fri 07.30 to 11.30 and 13.30 to 16.30 (17.00 for cables); Sat. and Sun. 08.00 to 10.00 (cables, mailing letters).

Tahiti has an automatic telephone network, with manual services inter-island.

Telex messages may be sent from the Chamber of Commerce — Mon.–Fri. 07.30 to noon and 13.30 to 17.00; Sat. 8 to 10 am; Táwharaa Hotel — Mon.–Fri. 08.00 to noon and 13.00 to 16.30, Sat. 08.00 to noon; Beachcomber Hotel — Mon. to Sun. 08.00 to 22.00.

Radio and TV. Radio-Tele-Tahiti is government-controlled and operated through RFO (Radio France Outre-Mer).

Press. There are two French-language dailies, *La Depeche de Tahiti* and *Les Nouvelles*.

There is also a number of weekly and monthly publications including a weekly in English, *Tahiti Sun Press*, which is free and directed at English-speaking tourists.

WATER AND ELECTRICITY. Water is abundant on the mountainous islands such as Tahiti, where it is reticulated. The drinking of imported mineral water is also common.

Electricity voltage on Tahiti is 220. In certain other areas it is 110.

A hydro-electric power station on Tahiti's Vaite River was inaugurated in 1981. It has a capacity of 3 million kWh a year. In 1988 funds were allocated to build a tunnel through the mountains linking the Papenoo and Vaihiria Valleys which would carry high tension cables from the hydro electric power station. It is estimated to cost $US1.2 m. By 1991 six hydro-power dams will help to generate electricity for 45 per cent of Tahiti's inhabitants. Solar power is also popular.

MAJOR OFFICE HOLDERS
High Commissioner:
  Pierre Angeli
Secretary of State for the South Pacific:
  Gaston Flosse
President:
  Alexandre Leontieff
Secretary General:
  Roger Moser

GOVERNMENT MINISTRIES AND DEPARTMENTS
Office of the President, PO Box 2551, Papeete; Tel.: 42.44.13
Secretariat General, PO Box 2551, Papeete; Tel.: 42.24.40
Ministre de l'Economie, PO Box 82, Papeete; Tel.: 42.20.20

Ministry of Education, PO Box 104, Papeete; Tel.: 42.24.40
Ministry of Agriculture, PO Box 100, Papeete; Tel.: 42.24.40
Ministry of Financial Affairs, PO Box 97, Papeete; Tel.: 42.46.40
Ministre de l'Equipment, PO Box 84, Papeete; Tel.: 42.46.50
Ministry of Social Affairs, PO Box 1707, Papeete; Tel: 43.80.48
Ministre de la Sante, PO Box 611, Papeete; Tel.: 42.20.30
Ministre de la Jeunesse, PO Box 4249, Papeete; Tel.: 43.97.06
Ministre des Transports, PO Box 2251, Papeete; Tel.: 42.24.40
Ministre de Travail, PO Box 540, Papeete; Tel.: 42.63.75
Assemblee Territoriale, PO Box 28, Papeete; Tel.: 42.76.40
Comite Economique et Social, PO Box 1657, Papeete; Tel.: 42.43.00
Affaires Administrative, PO Box 88, Papeete; Tel.: 42.76.40
Affaires Economiques, PO Box 82, Papeete; Tel.: 42.20.20
Affaires Maritimes, PO Box 495, Papeete; Tel.: 42.02.52
Affaires Sociales, PO Box 1707, Papeete; Tel.: 43.80.48
Cadastre, PO Box 135, Papeete; Tel.: 42.96.00
Caisse Centrale de Cooperation Economique, PO Box 578, Papeete; Tel.: 43.04.86
Caisse de Prevoyance Sociale de la Polynesie Francaise, PO Box 1, Papeete; Tel.: 43.97.71
Centre des Metiers d'Arts de Polynesie Francaise, PO Box 1725, Papeete; Tel.: 43.70.51
Centre Polynesien des Sciences Humaines "Te Anavaharau", PO Box 6272, Papeete; Tel.: 58.34.76
Chambre d'Agriculture et d'Elevage, PO Box 5383, Papeete; Tel.: 42.53.93
Circonscription Territoriale de la Police de l'Air et des Frontiers, PO Box 87, Papeete; Tel.: 42.67.99
Commerce Exterieur, PO Box 82, Papeete; Tel.: 42.98.75
Commissariat a l'Energie Atomique (C.E.A.), PO Box 519, Papeete; Tel.: 42.65.01

Commissariat de Police, PO Box 87, Papeete; Tel.: 42.01.07

Conservatoire Artistique Territorial de la Polynesie Francaise, PO Box 463, Papeete; Tel.: 42.01.07

Direction des Polices Urbaines de Polynesie Francaise, PO Box 87, Papeete; Tel.: 42.01.07

Direction des Renseignements Generaux, PO Box 87, Papeete; Tel.: 42.01.07

Direction Surveillance du Territoire, PO Box 900, Papeete; Tel.: 42.80.91

Domaines, PO Box 114, Papeete; Tel.: 2.03.53

Douanes, PO Box 9006, Papeete; Tel.: 42.01.20

Economie Rurale Agriculture Elevage Eaux et Forets, PO Box 100, Papeete; Tel.: 42.81.44

Education, PO Box 104, Papeete; Tel.: 42.95.20

Energie et Mines, PO Box 3829, Papeete; Tel.: 43.65.96

Enregistrement, PO Box 114, Papeete; Tel.: 42.58.44

Equipement, PO Box 85, Papeete; Tel.: 42.46.50

Establissement Pour la Valorisation des Activities Aquacoles et Maritimes, Papeete; Tel.: 43.92.65

Finances et de la Comptabilite, PO Box 97, Papeete; Tel.: 42.46.50

Forces Armees, Papeete; Tel.: 42.65.01

Hospital, Papeete; Tel.: 42.01.01

Imprimerie Officielle, PO Box 117, Papeete; Tel.: 42.50.67

Institut de Recherches Medicales Louis Malarde, PO Box 30, Papeete; Tel.: 42.76.04

Institut Territorial de la Statistique, PO Box 395, Papeete; Tel.: 43.71.96

Jeunesse et Sports, PO Box 67, Papeete; Tel.: 42.97.67

Justice, PO Box 101, Papeete; Tel.: 42.01.13

Laboratoire de Geophysique, PO Box 640, Papeete; Tel.: 42.80.25

Maison d'Arret, PO Box 127, Papeete; Tel.: 42.00.15

Mer et Aquaculture, Papeete; Tel.: 43.92.65

Musee de Tahiti et des Iles, PO Box 6272, Faaa; Tel.: 58.34.78

Office de Promotion et d'Animation

Touristique de Tahiti et ses Iles, PO Box 65, Papeete; Tel.: 42.96.26

Office de la Main-d'Oeuvre, PO Box 540, Papeete; Tel.: 42.63.76

Office de Recherche Scientifique et Technique Outre-Mer, PO Box 529, Papeete; Tel.: 43.98.87

Office des Anciens Combattants, Papeete; Tel.: 42.03.24

Office des Postes et Telecommunications, Papeete; Tel.: 42.44.68

Office Territorial de l'Habitat Social, PO Box 1705, Papeete; Tel.: 43.68.80

Agence Territoriale Pour la Reconstruction PO Box 552, Papeete; Tel.: 43.88.88

Office Territorial de l'Action Sociale et de la Solidarite, PO Box 3689, Papeete; Tel.: 43.86.03

Office Territorial de l'Equipment Sportif, PO Box 1685, Papeete; Tel.: 43.63.66

Personnel, PO Box 124, Papeete; Tel.:43.89.21

Piscine Municipale, Papeete; Tel.:42.89.24

Plan, PO Box 460, Papeete; Tel.: 42.83.38

Police, PO Box 6362, Papeete; Tel.:42.67.94

Port Autonome, PO Box 164, Papeete; Tel.: 43.60.60

Prison, Papeete; Tel.: 2.00.15

R.F.O. Radio Tele Tahiti, PO Box 125; Tel.: 43.05.51

Reseau General des Radio-communications, PO Box 99, Papeete; Tel.: 42.04.41

Sante Publique, PO Box 611, Papeete; Tel.:42.20.30

Societe d'Equipment de Tahiti & des Iles, PO Box 303, Papeete; Tel.: 42.60.61

Station de Sondages Ionospheriques, PO Box 7009, Papeete; Tel.: 57.11.19

Travail et Lois Sociales, PO Box 308, Papeete; Tel.: 42.27.22

Tresorerie Generale, PO Box 86, Papeete; Tel.: 42.51.40

Vice Rectorat, PO Box 2873, Papeete; Tel.:42.48.18

FOREIGN MISSIONS

Germany, PO Box 452, Papeete; Tel.:42.99.94

Austria, PO Box 78, Papeete; Tel.: 58.01.35

Chile, PO Box 5855, Pirae; Tel.: 43.89.19

Korea, PO Box 2061, Papeete;
Tel.:43.04.47
Denmark, PO Box 10, Papeete;
Tel.:42.03.09
Finland, PO Box 2870, Papeete;
Tel.:42.57.63
Italy, PO Box 420, Papeete; Tel.: 42.82.91
Monaco, PO Box 33, Papeete;
Tel.:42.53.29
Norway, PO Box 306, Papeete;
Tel.:42.97.21
Netherlands, PO Box 2084, Papeete;
Tel.:42.49.37
Sweden, PO Box 2, Papeete; Tel.: 42.53.59

HISTORY. Archaeological evidence indicates that the Marquesas Islands were inhabited at least as far back as AD 300 and that there were people on Maupiti, at the western end of the Society Islands, by 800 AD.

Magellan's visit. The first European to set eyes on any part of the territory was Magellan who discovered Pukapuka in the northeastern corner of the Tuamotus in 1521 during the first voyage round the world. The Spanish navigator Mendana discovered the southern group of the Marquesas in 1595; and other islands of the Tuamotus were seen by Quiros in 1606, Schouten and Le Maire in 1616, Roggeveen in 1772 and Byron in 1765. However, European interest in the area was not aroused until 1767 when Captain Samuel Wallis of HMS *Dolphin* discovered Tahiti and took possession of it in the name of King George III. In the following year, Bougainville, the French navigator, also chanced on Tahiti in the course of a world voyage. He named it La Nouvelle Cythere because it reminder him of Cythera, birthplace of the Greek goddess of love. He later published a glowing account of it.

Cook's visit. Tahiti's third European visitor was Lieut. James Cook, who reached the island in 1769 in HMS *Endeavour*. His visit was inspired by Wallis' discovery and sponsored by Britain's Royal Society. Its purpose was to make accurate observations of the transit of the planet Venus across the sun with the object of simplifying the determination of longitude at sea. Cook anchored at Matavai Bay, eastward of Papeete, and made his observations on the spit since known as Point Venus.

He later took the opportunity to travel round Tahiti and to visit or reconnoitre the neighbouring islands of Huahine, Raiatea, Tahaa and Bora Bora. He named these latter islands the Society Islands because they lay 'contiguous to one another'. (Cook's name has since been extended in meaning to include Tahiti, Moorea and other islands to windward and leeward.)

News of Wallis' discovery had caused considerable alarm in Spain because the Spaniards feared that the British might establish a base on Tahiti from which to attack Spain's South American possessions. An expedition under Domingo Boenechea was therefore fitted out in Peru to go to Tahiti to investigate. It visited in 1772 and returned to report that nothing was amiss.

'Noble savage'. In 1773, Cook visited Tahiti and the other Society Islands in the course of his second voyage to the Pacific in the ships *Resolution* and *Adventure*. He was there again in 1774. One of the consequences of these visits was that an islander called Omai was carried back to England, where he became a celebrity as a 'noble savage'. After much had been written about him, Cook returned him to his home island, Huahine, on his third voyage in 1777. Meanwhile, in 1774, the Spaniards in Peru had sent a second expedition to Tahiti to land two Franciscan friars to work as missionaries. The friars, however, were poorly fitted for their task, and when a ship came with provisions for them in the following year, they begged to be allowed to return to Peru.

After Cook's last visit in 1777, 11 years passed before Tahiti again saw a European ship. This was the *Lady Penrhyn*, which put into the island for provisions after depositing convicts at Botany Bay.

Mutiny on the Bounty. In the following year, 1788, HMS *Bounty* arrived under Lieut. William Bligh to obtain a cargo of breadfruit plants for the West Indies. Bligh anchored in Matavai Bay and stayed five months. Meanwhile, there was loss of discipline on board his ship and some amorous attachments were formed on shore — two factors that led to the famous mutiny in Tonga waters in April 1789. Bligh was subsequently cast adrift in an open boat with 12 companions, and the mutineers under Fletcher Christian sailed back to the eastern

Pacific in the *Bounty*, intent on settling there. After obtaining livestock in Tahiti, the mutineers tried to form a settlement on Tubuai, about 500 km south of that island. When this failed, Christian returned to Tahiti to land 16 men who did not wish to remain with him. Then he sailed off with the remaining eight' mutineers to search for another island to settle on.

Meanwhile, Bligh in the open boat had reached Timor, from where he returned to England. When news of the mutiny reached the Admiralty, Captain Edward Edwards was sent to the Pacific in HMS *Pandora* to find and arrest the mutineers. He headed straight for Tahiti, arrested the mutineers in residence there in March 1791, and continued onwards to a disastrous shipwreck on Australia's Great Barrier Reef. In the following year, Bligh returned to Tahiti in the ships *Providence* and *Assistant* on a second attempt to transplant breadfruit to the West Indies, which he completed without difficulty.

First missionaries. So much had now been written about the South Sea Islands, particularly Tahiti, that the newly-formed London Missionary Society decided to send missionaries there in the ship *Duff*. The evangelists reached Tahiti on 5 March 1797, and 18 of them were landed at Matavai Bay. Although they had the protection of a prominent local chief, they made little progress. Several of them abandoned the mission in 1799 and went to Sydney, and most of the remainder followed in 1809 after a fierce war broke out. However, a number of the latter drifted back a year or two later, and established new headquarters at Papetoai Bay, Moorea. In 1815, their endeavours were finally rewarded when the Tahitian chief Pomare II adopted Christianity and routed a rival heathen clan in battle. From then on Christianity spread rapidly throughout the Society Islands as well as to the Austral group and Tuamotu Archipelago.

French interest. After the death of Pomare II in 1821, the LMS missionaries became increasingly influential in political affairs. Meanwhile, more and more ships visited the islands, as the Pacific whaling industry got into full swing. In 1836, two French priests from a Catholic mission opened on Mangareva in 1834 were sent to Tahiti to try to establish a foothold. The Tahitians, under the influence of the missionaries, drove them away.

In 1838, a French naval officer, Captain Du Petit-Thouars, arrived in Papeete and demanded 'reparations' for the priests' ill-treatment, otherwise he would bombard the island. His demands, which included the payment of 2000 dollars and a gun salute to the French flag, were met. A year later another French commander, La Place, threatened to fire on Papeete unless Tahiti's sovereign, Queen Pomare IV, allowed Frenchmen and others the free exercise of the Catholic religion in Tahiti and her other possessions. The Queen, protestingly, agreed.

Meanwhile, the Queen and principal chiefs of Tahiti had written to Queen Victoria asking that their islands be placed under British protection. Their request was rejected: the British were too busy elsewhere. The French, however, were interested in the islands, as they needed a base in the eastern Pacific for their whalers, gunboats and merchant ships. In 1841, the French consul in Tahiti, J. A. Moerenhout, deceived four of the principal chiefs into signing a document asking for French protection. About the same time, the French government decided to take possession of the Marquesas Islands, and Du Petit-Thouars, now an admiral, was sent to the Pacific again for that purpose. Several months later, in August 1842, he returned to Tahiti where Moerenhout's document provided him with a pretext for seizing that island as well. After a fortnight of threats and bluff, the Queen and principal chiefs signed a protectorate treaty, and Du Petit-Thouars appointed a provisional government to regulate the affairs of foreigners.

A few months later, George Pritchard, the British consul, who had been on leave in England, returned to Tahiti in a British warship. HMS *Vindictive*. Both he and the warship's commander, Toup Nicholas, were astonished at the French proceedings. Nicholas, for his part, told the provisional government that he could not accept the protectorate, and he took it on himself to remain in Tahiti for several months to protect the Queen's interests. He also wrote to the British Admiralty protesting at the 'unprecedented' and 'dishonest' actions of the French.

Protectorate. Nicholas' sentiments had not reached England when the British Foreign Secretary announced that Britain had accepted the protectorate. On the other hand, news of Britain's decision had not reached

Tahiti when, in about November 1843, Du Petit-Thouars arrived there for a third time to inform Queen Pomare that France had ratified his treaty and that it was therefore 'definite and irrevocable'. Inevitably, there was trouble. Pritchard protested that the Queen had never willingly sought French protection and the Queen refused to strike her personal flag.

The upshot was that French troops landed, annexed Tahiti, and replaced the Queen's flag with the French tricolour. Pritchard struck his flag on the grounds that he was not accredited to a French colony, and the Queen fled to the safety of a British warship then in harbour.

Five months later, Pritchard was arrested and deported for provoking Tahitian resistance to the French, and Queen Pomare fled to Raiatea. When news of all this reached Europe, feeling ran high both in England and France and the two countries almost reached the brink of war. Hostilities were averted when the French King Louis-Philippe offered to pay Pritchard an indemnity from his own purse for the treatment he had suffered. In fact, the King was overthrown in 1848 before the amount of the indemnity could be agreed upon, and it was never paid.

Meanwhile, the French had crushed the native resistance in Tahiti, and in February 1847 Queen Pomare finally accepted the protectorate and returned to Papeete from her self-imposed exile on Raiatea. Under a treaty with Great Britain in that year, France agreed that Raiatea and the other leeward islands of the Society Group, which had more successfully fought against French rule, should remain independent. This meant that the French protectorate was confined only to those islands considered to be Queen Pomare's domains, i.e. Tahiti and Moorea.

Cotton plantation. During the next 25 years, the only outstanding event was the establishment of a huge cotton plantation at Atimaono on Tahiti's southern coast. The plantation was run by a British businessman, William Stewart. It sought to cash in on the world-wide shortage of cotton caused by the American Civil War. Because of a shortage of local labour, Stewart persuaded the authorities to allow him to import 1000 Chinese coolies from Hong Kong. These arrived in 1865–66. The plantation went bankrupt in 1873 and the Chinese were never repatriated. They

thus became the nucleus of French Polynesia's large Chinese population of today.

Following the death of Queen Pomare in 1877, the French took steps to convert their protectorate into a colony. Survey work on the proposed Panama Canal had just begun and it seemed likely that Tahiti would become an important refuelling depot for trans-Pacific shipping. In 1880, the Queen's successor, Pomare V, was persuaded to cede Tahiti and its dependencies to France. The Leeward islands of the Society Group remained independent until 1897, when they were forcibly annexed to the new colony, following the abrogation of the 1847 treaty with Great Britain in 1889. France declared a protectorate over Rimatara and Rurutu (Australs), and they were annexed in 1900.

The only noteworthy event from the turn of the century to the beginning of World War I was the bombardment of Papeete by the German raiders *Scharnhorst* and *Gneisenau*.

Tahiti goes 'Free French'. In June 1940, after France capitulated to Germany, Tahiti's governor, J. Chastenet de Gery, remained loyal to the Vichy government of Marshal Petain. However, in a referendum held two months later, only 18 Tahitians opted to remain under Petain while 5564 voted for the Free French government of General de Gaulle. This opened the way for close cooperation between French Oceania and the Allies. Hundreds of islanders enlisted to fight overseas, and Bora Bora was made available to the Americans as an oil depot and refuelling station for US navy ships.

The trauma of the war years and new ideas picked up at Bora Bora and overseas promoted a more aggressive, nationalistic spirit among many islanders after the war. By mid-1947, 26 trade unions had been formed and a committee had been set up under a Huahine-born man, Pouvanaa a Oopa, to 'conduct Tahiti and its archipelagoes towards more political, economic, administrative and cultural freedom'. The Pouvanaa committee showed its strength when it led a huge crowd to oppose the landing of three newly-arrived officials from France. However, Pouvanaa and his associates were arrested and held in custody for five months before being tried on charges of challenging governmental authority. They were acquitted. Pouvanaa's popularity greatly increased after this, and he went on to be elected as French Oceania's representative in the French parliament. He also formed a political party which gained a majority of seats in the local Territorial Assembly in 1953 and 1957.

Becomes French Polynesia. In August 1957, the territory was reconstituted as French Polynesia, the powers of its Territorial Assembly to make laws were considerably extended, and a council of government was created with local people holding ministerial posts. Pouvanaa became vice-president of the new council, with the governor ex-officio president. In April 1958 Pouvanaa announced a plan to secede from France and form an independent Tahitian republic. Soon afterwards, his party introduced an income tax law in the Assembly designed to raise revenue from the (mainly Chinese) traders.

After opponents of the tax law stoned the Assembly building causing the law to be abrogated, the Territory's conservative politicians and others cabled Paris rejecting the proposed republic. At this point, General de Gaulle resumed control of the tottery French government and offered French colonies around the world the chance to become independent by voting for it. In French Polynesia 36 per cent of the people voted for independence.

A few days later, Pouvanaa was arrested and eventually charged with attempted murder, arson and the illegal possession of arms. In October 1959 he was found guilty and sentenced to eight years imprisonment and 15 years exile from Papeete. Fifteen associates received lesser sentences. No one said so publicly at the time, but it was widely felt that Pouvanaa and company had been 'framed'.

After Pouvanaa was spirited out of Tahiti to a French prison, the Tahitian political scene became much quieter, and as the council of government was suspended, the islanders were again without any real power in their own country. Meanwhile, work had begun on an international airport at Faaa, Tahiti, with the aim of developing the tourist industry in French Polynesia. The airport was opened for passenger traffic in October 1960. Among the first to make use of it were actors and film technicians including Marlon Brando, for a new film version of *Mutiny on the Bounty*.

Nuclear tests. In April 1963 the French government announced plans to use Mururoa and several other atolls in the Tuamotu Archipelago for a nuclear testing project. Plans were also announced to modernise and enlarge the port of Papeete to cope with maritime traffic connected with the project. Soon afterwards, French technicians and troops began arriving in Tahiti in large numbers. After Pouvanaa's old party and another protested about this, President de Gaulle outlawed them both. Despite this, the territory's radical politicians continued to oppose the nuclear project at every opportunity, as they have ever since. On the other hand, employment opportunities created by the project, plus a spectacular growth in tourism, brought unprecedented prosperity to Tahiti throughout the 1960s and early 1970s, and many outer islanders flocked to the 'bright lights'.

The first of a series of nuclear devices was exploded in the atmosphere at Mururoa in September 1966. Further tests have been held in most years since then. However, in 1975, world-wide opposition to the atmospheric tests forced the French to begin testing underground at Fangataufa Atoll.

Soon afterwards testing returned to Mururoa, still underground. The tests have continued, to the accompaniment of local and especially regional protests, but the French government is, if anything, more determined to continue testing.

Since 1967, the territory's radical politicians, led for most of the time up to May 1982 by Francis Sanford, have kept up constant pressure on France for internal self-government.

The autonomists had a significant victory in November 1968 when, after considerable pressure from them, Pouvanaa a Oopa was pardoned and allowed to return to Tahiti. He became the territory's representative in the French Senate in 1971. Pouvanaa died in 1977.

Talks in Paris in mid-1983 on a new statute for the territory were snagged on the issue of who would exercise control over the resources in the massive area of ocean covered by French Polynesia's exclusive economic zone.

French Polynesia was ravaged between January and April 1983 by an extraordinary succession of five cyclones, a phenomenon rare in this part of the Pacific.

The human losses must be said to be minimal, considering the force of this succession of cyclones: 17 dead — either crushed by falling walls or trees, or drowned at sea — and about 200 injured.

The gravest consequences of the cyclones were felt in the Tuamotu Islands, where extensive damage was done to the coconut plantations. As a result, many people moved from the outer islands into the already crowded precincts of Papeete.

In 1987 there was speculation that the French Government was considering relocating its nuclear testing to the Kerguelen Islands in the Antarctic. Increased activity between Mururoa and the Kerguelens, the responses union negotiations are receiving in their quest for tenure and the setting up of an official agency to specifically combat rumours and press reports of such a relocation, indicate that such a move is possible.

Further information. In *Tahiti, Island of Love*, Robert Langdon gives a good outline of the fascinating history of this island. For making a circle island tour we recommend Bengt Danielsson's guide *Tahiti*, which is sold in all the territory's bookshops and petrol stations. A searching psychological study of the Tahitian mentality was published by the University of Chicago Press in 1973. Its author is Professor Robert I. Levy. There is a whole series of small booklets, in English and French, on various aspects of Tahitian culture and history, published by the Société des Océanistes, at a very reasonable price. Marie-Thérése and Bengt Danielsson give a highly critical account of more recent events in *Poisoned Reign: French Nuclear Colonialism in the Pacific*. Editions du Pacifique has published guides to the fish, birds and flowers of French Polynesia, which are available throughout the islands. Robert F. Kay's *Tahiti and French Polynesia*, 1985, is a useful general guide.

ISLANDS IN DETAIL
THE SOCIETY ISLANDS. The Society Islands are made up of two groups — the Windward Islands (Iles du Vent, in French) and the Leeward Islands (Iles sous le Vent). The Windward Islands consist of Tahiti (the largest), Moorea, Maiao, Tetiaroa and Mehetia. The Leeward Islands comprise the twin islands of Raiatea and Tahaa, Huahine, Bora Bora, Maupiti and the atolls of Tupai, Mopelia (Maupihaa), Motu One (or Bellingshausen) and Manuae (Fenua Ura or Scilly).

The Windward Islands
Tahiti, the largest of the Windward Islands and commercially the most important in the territory, was formed by two long-extinct volcanoes. The two sections are joined by the narrow isthmus of Taravao. Tahiti thus has the shape of the figure eight. The larger portion, Tahiti-nui, which is almost circular, is about 120 km in circumference. The smaller portion, Tahiti-iti, also called the Taiarapu Peninsula, is more flattened and is about 20 km long by 13 km broad.

The island is encircled by a reef, broken in parts where fresh water streams enter the sea. The breaks or passes allow entrance to the coastal lagoon. The most important pass, commercially, is that into Papeete harbour. The best natural harbour is Port Phaeton on the southern side of the Isthmus of Taravao. However, prevailing moisture-laden winds and high mountains nearby make this part of the island much wetter than Papeete.

The total area of Tahiti is 1042 sq. km and the population is 116,000. Papeete's geographical position is 17 deg 32 min S latitude and 149 deg 34 min W longitude.

The interior of Tahiti is an uninhabited and trackless upland of jagged peaks and steep gorges from which many rivers and streams run to the sea. Between the hills and shore is an alluvial belt of great fertility. The Tahitians are natural coastal dwellers, but they go to the lush river valleys to fish, to gather food and firewood and to bathe in the rivers and under the innumerable waterfalls.

Ever since the exploration of the Society Islands by the early navigators, writers and travellers have vied with each other in giving to tired humanity picturesque and delightful descriptions, and Tahiti has come to be known, as the place above all others which most truly presents the beauty, charm and romance of the South Seas.

The main peaks on Tahiti are Mt Orohena (2241 m), Mt Aorai (2066 m), Mt Maiao, usually called 'Le Diademe' (1310 m), and Mt Roniu (1323 m) on Taiarapu Peninsula. Mt Orohena was climbed for the first time

TAHITI

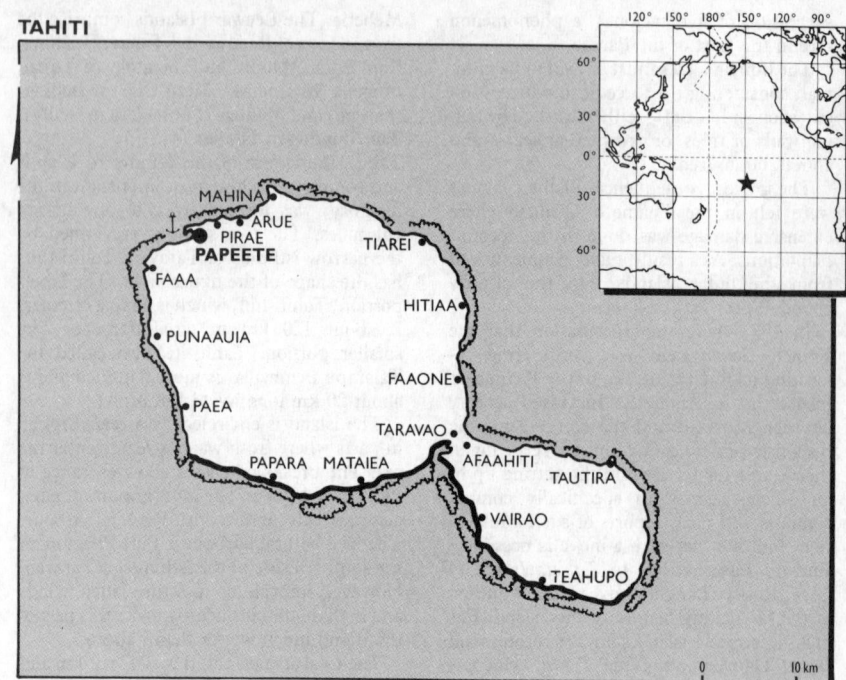

by Europeans in September 1953.

Tahiti has one lake, Lake Vaihiria, imprisoned in an old crater about 458 m above sea level and surrounded by precipitous mountains.

A hydro-electricity station has been established in the Vaihiria River Valley. A motorable road gives access to it. The lake may now be reached after a walk of only half an hour.

At the time of the island's discovery by Europeans there were no villages as such, habitation being strung out right around the coastal belt. This is still more or less the case. The island was traditionally divided into districts rather than villages. The districts are very often natural divisions, being segments of the island, or valleys each separated from the next by the spiny ridges on each side.

Tahiti is divided into 12 communes — 10 for Tahiti-nui and two for Tahiti-iti (the peninsula).

Travelling north then east are the following ancient districts, starting from Papeete:

Pirae, Arue, Mahina, Papenoo, Tiarei, Mahaena, Hitiaa and Faaone. Going south and east, also starting from Papeete, are the following: Faaa, Punaauia, Paea, Papara, Mataiea, Papeari.

In the peninsula are the following districts: Afaahiti, Pueu, Tautira, Teahupoo, Vairao.

A sealed road of about 120 km completely encircles Tahiti-nui and two arms of road go down each side of Taiarapu Peninsula — the north arm ending at Tautira Point and the southern arm at Teahupoo. It was at Tautira that Robert Louis Stevenson lived for some months in 1888. It is now a well-populated centre, with schools, shops, etc. The road has been reconstructed in parts and Tautira is something of a tourist attraction as it is from this point that excursions are made by boat to the islets near the Pari — the steep cliffs that form the coast at the tip of the Peninsula and prevent the construction of an encircling road on Tahiti-iti.

At a point near where the Tautira road joins the main highway at Taravao, a road leads up to a temperate plateau, site of several stock-breeding stations.

The road skirts the coastline, at times on the north coast being only a narrow shelf cut in the cliff. The coastal belt widens in the south-west but nowhere is it very extensive.

The barrier reef-enclosed coastal lagoon provides a waterway for canoes and small craft and safe fishing. Although the Tahitians have forsaken much of the traditional Polynesian way of life, dugout canoes with outriggers are in use everywhere. The beaches of Tahiti are predominantly black sand and are less attractive than some in the other islands for that reason.

Matavai Bay, at the NW corner of Tahiti, was the usual anchorage for the early European visitors to the island. But the bay is exposed to northerly winds for several months of the year, whereas Papeete harbour is safe throughout.

It was for this reason that Papeete developed as Tahiti's capital — from about 1818 when the Rev. William Pascoe Crook established the first mission station here. The town has now spread eastward to Pirae and westward to Faaa, which are communes or municipalities in their own right. Faaa is the site of Tahiti's international airport, while the port of Papeete is the chief shipping and distribution centre in the territory. The port can handle vessels up to 35,000 tonnes.

Between 1962 and 1964 about 14 hectares of land were reclaimed at the northern point of Papeete harbour and this, Fare Ute, is now used as an industrial and military area. In 1963 work commenced on an extension of Fare Ute, a project that has given Papeete a completely new harbour.

Between 1967 and 1970, a waterside boulevard with double carriage-way was constructed. A new ships' passenger terminal was also built and nearby the architecturally striking Fare Manihini, home of the Tahiti Tourist Development Board, on the new Boulevard Pomare.

There are many new buildings facing the boulevard, others have been renovated or painted. The old ramshackle appearance of the waterfront has been completely changed.

The main business area is along the waterfront — just over the street from the cruise ship wharf and the yacht harbour — but commerce is now extending east and west and behind the quays as well, with, in places, some fine new buildings.

The days of division of business between large, European-owned enterprises and small Chinese-owned shops have gone. There are still plenty of the typical 'Chinatown' stores of jumbled merchandise with no attempt at display but Chinese also own modern supermarkets and department stores. Some Europeans, on the other hand, now run small attractive 'boutiques' that would not disgrace the Champs Elysees.

One of the most modern streets is Avenue Bruat, tree-lined, with good buildings and the government offices. Since 1967 the residence of the High Commissioner has been built in the park-like area between Rues General de Gaulle and Dumont d'Urville. Next to it is the Territorial Assembly building which includes a separate convention facility. This building is on the site of the old queen's palace which was demolished in 1967. The Olympic swimming pool is on the harbour side just west of the Tipaerui stream.

Papeete has an attractive post office and radio communications centre on the Boulevard Pomare, one block away from the fashion hub of town, the Vaima Centre. The Bank of Indo-Suez in Rue de General de Gaulle is opposite the cathedral.

Papeete and its Polynesian inhabitants have become much more sophisticated since the end of the war, and life has lost much of its former simplicity. Purists even look back to the pre-1920 days for the 'real' Tahiti — the days when the Tiare Hotel was the centre of social activity.

The town market and bus and taxi station takes up one whole town block, one block behind Boulevard Pomare.

The best time to visit the market is between 5.30 am and 7.30 am, any Sunday. Young people who have obviously been dancing all night meet, mingle and gossip with the older, harder working fraternity who have come in to sell produce or to buy the week's provisions.

Most offices and shops in Papeete open at 7.30 am and close for a long lunch period at 11 am or 11.30 am. In the afternoon they open from 1 or 1.30 pm till 5.30 pm. Some shops open Saturday afternoons, some close.

On boat day, when the overseas passenger ships are in port, tourists throng the streets, cafes and shops and take tours around the island, and at night some tourist hotels put on special floor shows and Tahitian dances. However, most visitors these days arrive by air.

Tahiti's image has been affected recently by its prices, among the highest in the Pacific. Complaints by tourists have led to the Tahiti Tourist Promotion Board and hoteliers offering discounts on drinks. So far little other effect has been obvious. Visitors, however, should bring plenty of money and/or sound credit cards with them.

Moorea (formerly called Eimeo) is situated about 17 km from Tahiti. It has an area of about 13,237 hectares. It is the remains of a huge volcano, of which about half has been eroded away. Spectacular scenery is one of its chief attractions. Two fiord-like bays on the northern side are the remains of the old crater. They are Paopao Bay (or Cook's Bay) and Opunohu (or Papetoai) Bay, which are separated by majestic Mt Rotui, 899 m high. The island's highest peak, Mt Tohivea, is 1207 m. Another remarkable peak, Mt Muaputa, 880 m, overlooking the village of Afareaitu, has a hole through its summit. Population in 1983 was 7249.

The island is a favourite resort for a short stay for discriminating travellers and, increasingly, for day trippers. It may be reached from Tahiti by light aircraft which land at an airstrip at Tamae, at its NE corner. Ferries operating between the two islands take about one hour each way. A road, about 60 km long, has been built round Moorea's narrow coastal strip. Motor vehicles are available for hire at the airport.

Moorea is interesting historically as the centre from which Christianity spread throughout the Society Islands and to the rest of the Pacific. It also has other associations with the early missionaries.

Few of the early explorers visited Moorea because they believed it had no good anchorages. However, Cook discovered otherwise in 1777 and wrote that the 'romantic cast' of Opunohu Bay rendered it 'a prospect superior' to anything in Tahiti.

The village of Papetoai at the western entrance to Opunohu Bay became the headquarters of the LMS missionaries in the Pacific in 1811 and they were there when the Tahitians adopted Christianity in 1815. In 1817, Papetoai was the missionaries' dispersal point for other stations. An octagonal church built there between 1822 and 1829 has the distinction of being the oldest European building still in use in the South Pacific.

At the head of Opunohu Bay is an extensive valley where the LMS tried unsuccessfully to establish a sugar plantation in 1818. The project failed because the islanders feared they would become slaves. A scheme to grow cotton also failed. The property subsequently had a succession of owners, including the German company, Societe Commercial de l'Oceanie, from 1904 to 1914. It is now owned by the territory, which has an agricultural training school there.

As for Cook's Bay, it is interesting to note that Cook himself never anchored there. His name was apparently applied to the bay mistakenly in the early 19th century. Several villages on the island's east coast, namely Temae, Afareaitu and Maatea, figure prominently in Herman Melville's semifactual novel *Omoo* — as Tamai, Afrehitoo and Martair.

Temae, situated on a lake of the same name, is one of the few villages in Polynesia not situated on the sea. Afareaitu was once the site of the famous LMS school, the South Seas Academy, which was opened for the missionaries' children in the early 1820s. It was also at Afareaitu that the pages of the first book to be printed in the South Seas were pulled in 1817.

Pineapples are widely cultivated on Moorea. A pineapple juice factory has been set up, producing juice in cardboard packs.

Maiao, known also as Maiao-iti, Tapuamanu and Tubuai Manu, is a small, little-known island about 105 km due west of Tahiti and 64 km WSW of Moorea. It combines the physical characteristics of a high and low island. There is a weathered mountain ridge of volcanic origin (maximum elevation, 170 m), encircled by low coral flats which contain two shallow lakes. Around all this is a lagoon enclosed by a barrier reef. The total land area is about 9 sq. km. Some of this is barren sand and swamp — breeding grounds for numerous mosquitoes and sandflies.

Small vessels can anchor about 300 m

from the southern reef. But the two passes into the lagoon are navigable only by canoes and very small boats. Communication with the island is therefore difficult. 1983 population was 190.

The only village is on the south-eastern side. The island is unique in the Society group in that no Europeans or Chinese are allowed to live there permanently. Copra is the chief source of income, having ousted yams and manioc for which the island was once noted. Small trading vessels call at Maiao about once every two or three weeks.

Until the French annexation of the Leeward Society Islands in 1888, Maiao was under the sovereignty of Huahine. Wallis, its European discoverer, passed it after leaving Tahiti in 1767 and named it Sir Charles Saunders Island. No European is known to have landed on it until 1809 when two LMS missionaries, sailing from Moorea to Huahine, were forced to put in there.

The Maiao people adopted Christianity without any European missionary being present. During the whaling era, they traded occasionally with passing ships. A Scotsman who lived there in those days may have been chiefly responsible for the occasional occurrence of red hair and light skins among the Maiao people of today.

An Englishman, Eric Trower, tried to obtain sole possession of the island in the late 1920s and early 1930s in the belief that Maiao might be rich in phosphate. His activities led to the present-day ban on non-Polynesian residents.

Further information: Ben Finney, *Polynesian Peasants and Proletarians*, Cambridge, Mass., 1973.

Tetiaroa, 42 km north of Tahiti, is the only atoll in that vicinity. It comprises 13 islets, the largest of which is about 3.25 km long. The total land area is about 640 hectares, most of which has been planted with coconuts. Large colonies of terns, boobies and other sea birds inhabit the atoll, and there is good fishing both inside and outside the lagoon.

In the heyday of the royal Pomare family, Tetiaroa was used as a pleasure resort and as a refuge during political disturbances. The site of the royal residence on Rimatuu islet is still marked by enormous tuu trees, which were apparently planted in very ancient times. The trees cover about 1 hectare with much-appreciated shade. The remains of several ancient 'marae' may still be seen. Female members of chiefly families used to go to Tetiaroa for fattening before marriage, and to live in the shade of the tuu trees so that their skins would become fair.

Until 1790, Tetiaroa was known as Teturoa — recorded as Tethuroa by some of the early European explorers. The only such explorer to visit the atoll was Captain Bligh, who went there in quest of three deserters from the *Bounty* in January 1789.

In 1904, the Pomare family gave Tetiaroa to Dr W. J. Williams, a Canadian dentist, in recompense for his dental services to them. Dr Williams, who was British consul in Tahiti from 1916 to 1935, died at Tetiaroa in 1937. His stepdaughter sold the island to the American film actor Marlon Brando in 1966. Marlon Brando has built the Tetiaroa Village on the atoll with bungalows and A-frame huts for visitors.

Mehetia is an extinct volcanic cone rising steeply from the sea to a height of about 430 m. It is the easternmost of the Society Islands, being about 100 km due east of the south-eastern end of Tahiti. The island is roughly circular, about 20 km in circumference, and 240 hectares in area; its northern side is so steep that only about a third of its total area is suitable for crops and human habitation. There is no anchorage and the only landing place is hazardous.

The name Mehetia, which has become established by usage, is actually an error. The correct name is Me'etia, as is explained below.

In pre-European and early European times, trading canoes proceeding from Tahiti to the Tuamotus (Anaa) used to make for Mehetia to await a favourable wind. The Tuamotuans knew the island as Meketu, whereas to the k-less Tahitians it was Me'etu. However, after Tu (Pomare II) was invested as paramount chief of Tahiti in 1790, the syllable 'tu' in all Tahitian words was changed to 'tia' and Me'etu thus became Me'etia. This is why, in early European times, the island was variously recorded as Maitoo, Maitu and Myetoo as well as Maeatea, Maitea, Myetea, Maitia, etc. Historians have frequently confused Mehetia with the Tuamotuan island of Makatea which, to the Tahitians, is Ma'atea.

The European discoverer of Mehetia was Captain Wallis, who called it Osnaburg Island. It then had about 100 inhabitants. Bougainville, in 1768, called the island Le Boudoir and Pic de la Boudeuse; and it was known as Todos los Santos to the early Spanish explorers. About 1806, the Mehetia people were driven out by Anaa warriors, and it was uninhabited for some years.

In 1835, it was used as a penal settlement. Nowadays the island is privately owned and uninhabited, but visited periodically by copra cutters. A Frenchwoman, Mrs Janine Rouillere, gave the island some notoriety in 1967 when she spent 37 days alone there as a female Robinson Crusoe.

The Leeward Islands. Raiatea and Tahaa. These are two high islands lying about 32 km westward of Huahine. They stand on the same submarine base and are encircled by a single barrier reef. Once inside the reef, it is possible to sail right round the two islands without leaving the lagoon. Tahaa, the more northerly island, is separated from its neighbour by a channel about 3 km wide. The islands have a total length of about 36 km. In general physical characteristics, in productions and in scenic attractions, they conform very closely to the description of Tahiti.

Raiatea is the second largest of the Society Islands. It has the shape of an isosceles triangle and is about 48 km in circumference. A range of mountains runs north and south from which numerous spurs extend to the coast. The highest point is Mt Toomaru, 1032 m. The mountains become lower at the northern end of the island. The extensive Temehani Plateau is in this area.

Uturoa, situated on the NE tip of Raiatea opposite Tahaa, is the principal port for the two islands and administrative centre for the Leeward Islands. It has been a commune (municipality) since 1945 and has all the facilities of a town of its size and importance. An airstrip is situated 2 km northward of Uturoa. Light planes link it with Tahiti. Population in 1983 was 2733.

A road suitable only for four-wheel-drive vehicles provides access to the Tapioi lookout behind Uturoa from which the island's mountains and lagoon, and the surrounding islands may be clearly seen. There is a good road, 32 km long, down Raiatea's eastern coast to Opoa, the religious centre of the Society Islands in pre-European times. Near the Bali Hai Hotel, 2 km south of Uturoa, is the village of Apooiti, the only place on Raiatea where firewalking is still practised.

The next village, about 7 km further on, is Avera, scene of a battle with the French in 1897. There are no other villages until Opoa (population in 1983 was 874) is reached. On a point a little eastward of the village is the celebrated Taputapuatea 'marae', once the most sacred religious site in eastern Polynesia. The 'marae', restored in 1968–69, is made of enormous slabs of coral.

There is no road along the rugged southern coast of Raiatea. But Tautara, the southernmost village of the western side of the island, may be reached by road from Uturoa, a distance of about 43 km. The road takes in the villages of Tevaitoa, Tehurui, Vaiaau and Fetuna. Near Tevaitoa is the Tainuu 'marae', also made of coral slabs.

Tahaa, roughly circular in shape, is about 11 km in diameter. It was once a symmetrical cone, but it is now deeply dissected by broad valleys radiating out from a central mass of peaks. The highest point is Mt Ohiri, 590 m. Vaitoare on the south coast opposite Uturoa is the chief settlement. A launch links the two towns each Wednesday, market day. A road of sorts encircles the island.

Historically, Raiatea and Tahaa are of considerable interest. They have apparently been inhabited for many hundreds of years, but it is not yet clear where the original inhabitants came from. At some stage, however, immigrants appear to have arrived from Samoa. They called Raiatea Havaiki or Havaii after Savaii in their homeland, while Tahaa received the name Kuporu or Uporu after Savaii's sister island, Upolu. The best known figure in the prehistory of the two islands was Hiro. He is said to have been Raiatea's first king and to have been the founder of two dynasties which lasted down to European times.

Australian historian Robert Langdon has postulated in his book *The Lost Caravel* (Sydney, 1975) that Hiro was the leader of a band of Spanish castaways from the caravel *San Lesmes* that had been wrecked on Amanu Atoll, Tuamotu Archipelago, in 1526. Tradition says that Hiro and his associates built a great 'pahi' or canoe on Raiatea in which they eventually sailed away — apparently to Rarotonga and New Zealand. Two of Hiro's sons remained behind. One succeeded him as King of Raiatea; the other assumed sovereignty over Bora Bora.

When Captain Cook visited Raiatea in 1769, the chief of Bora Bora had conquered Raiatea and had driven many of the Raiatean chiefs to other islands. One, who was then living in Tahiti, was the sage Tupaia who accompanied Cook as far as the East Indies, where he died. Cook also called at Raiatea in 1773, 1774 and 1777.

Christianity was adopted in Raiatea and Tahaa soon after the Tahitians accepted it in 1815. The first LMS missionaries to settle on Raiatea were the Revs John Williams and Lancelot Threlkeld who arrived in 1818. The Rev. Robert Bourne went to Tahaa in 1822. It was from Raiatea that Williams and Bourne carried the Gospel to Rarotonga in 1823, and that Williams made his famous voyage to Samoa in 1830. Raiatea thus figures prominently in Williams' book, *A Narrative of Missionary Enterprises*.

After France declared a protectorate over Tahiti in 1842, there was a long struggle for the sovereignty of Raiatea. Tamatoa, a son of Queen Pomare of Tahiti, was crowned king in 1857. France annexed Raiatea and Tahaa in 1888, but a chief called Teraupoo resisted French rule from the Avera valley. Finally, in 1897, the French sent troops to the island to put down the rebellion. After a six-week struggle, Teraupoo and his associates were arrested and deported. Teraupoo was exiled to New Caledonia until 1905; his associates were banished to Eiao in the Marquesas. Raiatea's history has been uneventful since then.

Huahine, lying about 130 km NW of Tahiti, consists of two mountainous masses that form virtually two islands. At one point, the two parts are joined by an isthmus about 100 m long which is exposed at low water. A bridge connects the two parts at this point. The northern, larger portion is called Huahine-nui (great Huahine), and the other Huahine-iti (little Huahine). The highest peaks are Mt Turi, 680 m, on Huahine-nui, and Mt Moufene, 457 m, on Huahine-iti.

The island generally is fertile and rich in all the usual productions of the high volcanic islands of the Society Group. Large areas have been planted with coconuts. The principal village and harbour is Fare-nui-atea, usually known as Fare, on the NW coast. There are two passes into the harbour. Yachtsmen are advised to obtain the services of a pilot before entering them. A road, mainly along the coast, links Fare with the villages of Fitii, Faaua, Haapu (west coast), Parea (south coast), Maeva (NE coast), Faie (east coast) and Maroe (north coast of Huahine-iti).

Maeva, on the corner of a lake of the same name, is built out over the water on stilts. It is reputed to be the only village of its kind in Polynesia. The lake is famed for its fish and crabs. Near the western end of the lake is an airstrip used for regular services to and from Tahiti. About 2 km from the airstrip, just northward of Fare, are the Hotel Bali Hai and the Hotel Huahine.

A whalebone 'patu' (Maori-style hand weapon) found at Huahine in 1972 indicates that the island has been inhabited for at least 1100 years. There are, indeed, many archaeological relics on the island, including more than two dozen 'maraes' near Lake Maeva, some of which have been restored. The lake itself contains fish traps that date back several hundred years.

The first European to give an account of Huahine was Captain Cook who visited it briefly in 1769, 1774 and 1777. Thereafter, the island saw few Europeans until 1808–09 when a party of LMS missionaries, who had fled from Tahiti because of civil war, made it their headquarters for nearly a year. In 1818, after the adoption of Christianity in Tahiti, the LMS reopened a station on the island. One of the missionaries was the Rev. William Ellis, author of the famous *Polynesian Researches* (London, 1829), which describes life on Huahine at length. As a result of early LMS influence, Huahineans are still largely Protestant.

Huahine resisted French rule in 1846, and did not come under French control until 1888. One of the most notable Polynesians of recent times, the political leader Pouvanaa a Oopa, was born on Huahine in 1895. 1983 population was 3877.

Bora Bora (sometimes written Borabora) is one of the most picturesque islands of the Society Group. It lies about 16 km WNW of

Tahaa and 270 km NW of Tahiti. It is primarily of volcanic origin. The main island is nearly 10 km long by 4 km wide. There are two smaller ones, Toopua and Toopua-iti (sometimes written Tupua and Tupua-iti), which are separated from it by a channel on its western side.

All three islands are encircled by a barrier reef on which are a number of low islets. The three volcanic islands are the remains of an ancient crater. The main island is dominated by several peaks, of which the highest are Mt Otemanu, 727 m, and double-peaked Mt Pahia, 658 m. The eastern side of this island has a barren appearance. The western side is fertile. Copra and vanilla are the chief agricultural crops, but tourism is the main industry. Population in 1983 was 3238.

Between the main island and Toopua is a commodious, well-protected harbour called Te Ava Nui (the big harbour). It is about 2 km long by the same distance broad. A pass through the reef into the harbour is north-east of Toopua. Vaitape, the principal settlement and administrative centre, is on the main island opposite the northern part of Toopua.

North of Vaitape, on the NW shore of Faanui Bay, there is a yacht basin. Just off the bay, an area has been set aside for water-skiing, etc. An airstrip on Motu Mute, on the reef north of the main island, is used by small aircraft to link Bora Bora with Tahiti and other islands in the group. However, it is also operational for aircraft up to Electra and DC7 size, and in an emergency a jet can land there and take off again unloaded.

The remains of more than 40 'marae', built by Bora Bora's ancient population, are still to be seen on the island. They are of coral slabs rather than volcanic rocks as in Tahiti. Another relic of ancient times is the 'turtle stone', a petroglyph with representations of several turtles.

Bora Bora was known anciently as Vavau, which suggests that it was once colonised by people arriving from the island of that name in Tonga. Tradition also records the arrival of a 'prince' from Rotuma. Another noted personage in Bora Bora's prehistory was Hiro (see under Raiatea), who is said to have had a hiding place near the southern tip of Toopua, and to have performed various

remarkable feats in that vicinity. Several landmarks still bear his name. A rock in the interior of Toopua which rings like a bell when struck is called the Bell of Hiro. Some rocks between Toopua and Toopua-iti are known as Hiro's canoe; and others that Hiro is reputed to have played with are called the 'timoraa o Hiro'. Hiro's son Ohatatama is said to have been the first king of Bora Bora.

Bora Bora's European discoverer was Captain Cook. He sighted it on his first voyage in 1769, and made a brief visit to the island in 1777.

Cook and his companions rendered the island's name either as Bola Bola or Bora Bora, but it should, in fact, be Pora Pora as the Tahitian language has neither the 'b' nor 'l'.

The first European to live on the island seems to have been James Connor from the British whaler *Matilda*, which was wrecked on Mururoa Atoll in 1792. After the crew sailed back to Tahiti in the ship's boats, Connor married a Huahine woman and went to live on the southernmost point of Bora Bora, which he called Point Matilda, now corrupted to Point Matira. Numerous Society Islanders today, particularly the Bambridge family of Tahiti, are descended from Connor, the earliest known European progenitor in the group.

The Rev. J. M. Orsmond established the first LMS mission station on Bora Bora in 1820 and remained until 1824. He was succeeded by the Rev. George Platt who remained until 1830. The islanders have been largely Protestant ever since.

As with the other Leeward Islands of the Society Group, Bora Bora did not accept French sovereignty when Tahiti became a protectorate in 1842. It remained independent with its own sovereign until France annexed it in 1888. Terii-Maevarua II, the last queen of Bora Bora, died in Tahiti in 1932. She was a grand-daughter of Queen Pomare IV of Tahiti.

In 1928–29, one of the last and most notable silent movies was shot at Bora Bora. This was *Tabu*, the story of the tragic love affair of a Polynesian couple who had broken the ancient 'tabu' laws. The stars and cast were Bora Borans. The noted French yachtsman Alain Gerbault stayed at Bora Bora for long periods during his two voyages round the world in the 1920s and 1930s. In 1948, his remains were transferred to Bora Bora from Timor where he died in 1941, and a monument was later erected to him.

During World War II, Bora Bora was an American air and naval base. The first troops arrived on 23 Feburary 1942, and for the next four years up to 6000 men were stationed on the island. The naval base, built at Faanui Bay, serviced ships on their way to the Solomons. The present-day airstrip on Motu Mutu was completed in April 1943 after less than four months' work. Some Quonset huts and anti-aircraft guns still remain on the island as reminders of the American presence — besides several dozen islanders with American genes. The principal French representative on the island during the war was Francis Sanford, who later became one of Tahiti's leading politicians.

The airstrip on Motu Mutu was restored and put into service again in 1951. Until the international airport at Faaa, Tahiti, was opened in 1961, it was the only commercial airfield in French Polynesia. Until then, Bora Bora was also a base for flying boats. It is now an increasingly popular tourist destination.

Maupiti (formerly Maurua) is situated about 40 km westward of Bora Bora. The island is of volcanic origin and has some remarkable castle-like cliffs. The maximum elevation is about 370 m. A barrier reef encircling a wide lagoon surrounds the island, which is about 10 km in circumference. The reef extends from 3 to 5 km on all sides. Two large reef islands form a semi-circle on the northern part of the reef. A pass on the south side gives access to the sheltered water within the reef. The entrance is intricate and often dangerous. Visiting yachtsmen are advised to secure the services of a pilot.

Vaitea on the northern side of the main island is the only settlement. Population of the entire island in 1983 was 794. Copra and vanilla are the chief sources of income. Production is limited by the lack of cultivable land. Water is obtained from springs, as there are no streams. A visitor to Maupiti in the early 1950s noted that the islanders were more industrious than elsewhere in the

Society Group, and it is said that their dialect differs considerably.

Artifacts unearthed on the island in 1962 were quite different from those of the Polynesians of historical times, and were thought to have much in common with those of the ancient Moa-hunters of the South Island of New Zealand. The artifacts included pendants, adzes and fishhooks. The remains of ancient 'marae' and pig fences are commonplace on the island. Roggeveen in 1722 is thought to have been the first European to sight Maupiti. But Cook in 1769 was the first to record its name. The island was little visited by Europeans until after Christianity was adopted in Tahiti in 1815. The islanders are still Protestants.

Deposits of a black basaltic rock, capable of taking a fine polish, are a feature of Maupiti. An 'umete', or food bowl, made from this rock was taken to Peru in 1775 by Maximo Rodriguez, the interpreter with the Spanish mission at Tautira, Tahiti. The bowl, the only one of its kind known, is now in the Archaeological Museum, Madrid.

Maupiti is well worth a visit to see a local fish drive. About 300 people and a fleet of canoes take part.

Watermelons are now grown on Maupiti, and represent its principal resource: the 1981 harvest was 540 tonnes.

Tupai (otherwise known as Motuiti and Tubai) is a small atoll about 13 km northwest of Bora Bora, of which it was formerly a dependency. There is a narrow passage through the reef at the NW end of the island, and three passages on the eastern side. The atoll is entirely covered with coconut trees — about 150,000 of them. It abounds with sea-birds, and turtles breed there.

In former times, the Bora Bora people used to visit Tupai to fish. In the 1860s the king of Bora Bora leased the atoll to a Nova Scotian called Stackett, who made coconut oil with an ingenious steam engine. It has been privately owned for many years. Legend has it that a Peruvian treasure is buried on Tupai.

Mopelia, Manuae, Motu One. These three islands, all of atoll formation, are the westernmost islands of the Society Group. They are leased until 1999 to the Compagnie

Francaise de Tahiti and have been planted in coconuts. Copra cutters visit them periodically; otherwise they are uninhabited.

Mopelia, also known as Maupihaa or Mopihaa, lies about 160 km WSW of Maupiti. It is roughly circular and about 8 km in diameter. Wallis in 1767 called it Lord Howe Island. Vessels up to 200 tonnes may enter its pass. The atoll is famous as the resting place of Count von Luckner's raider *Seeadler*, which was wrecked there by high seas while being careened during World War I. A few relics of the vessel still remain.

Manuae, otherwise Scilly Island or Fenua Ura, is about 64 km WNW of Mopelia. It was also a discovery of Captain Wallis. It is about 11 km long by 9 km wide. The three-masted vessel *Julie Ann* was wrecked there in 1855. Her complement, which included 24 women and children, remained on the atoll for two months until they built a boat and sailed to Raiatea.

Motu One (meaning 'sandy island') is also known as Bellingshausen, Temiromiro. It consists of four low coral islands, covered with coconut palms and other trees, on a triangular reef. There is no entrance into the lagoon. The Russian explorer Kotzebue discovered the island in 1824.

AUSTRAL ISLANDS. The Austral Islands comprise the five inhabited islands of Rurutu, Tubuai, Rimatara, Raivavae and Rapa as well as the uninhabited Marotiri (or Bass) Rocks and Maria (or Hull) Island. The islands lie to the southward of the Society Islands. The nearest to Tahiti is Rurutu, about 500 km SSW. Geologically, the Australs appear to be a south-easterly extension of the Cook islands, representing all that now remains above water of a vast submerged mountain chain. Following is a detailed description.

Rurutu, an island of volcanic origin, resembles some of the islands of the southern Cook group. Its interior is mountainous. The highest peak, Mt Manureva (Soaring Bird), reaches an elevation of 400 m. A coastal strip of land is protected by a continuous coral reef.

Moerai, in a small bay on the north-east side, is the principal village. The government agent resides there. Other villages are Hauti, south of Moerai, and Avera on the west side. Total population in 1983 was 1971.

If the weather prevents anchorage opposite Moerai, Avera is usually sheltered. The two villages are about 5 km apart, and it is practicable to walk from one to the other across the central uplands. The uplands are clothed in grass and fern, with thick undergrowth in the ravines.

The villages are well laid out, and the people are intelligent and industrious — and mostly prosperous. They build and operate their own schooners, and carry their produce to Papeete. They also call at Tubuai and Raivavae, and sometimes Rapa.

The chief exports are arrowroot, hats, mats, pigs, cattle, copra and vanilla. Tropical fruits are not as plentiful as on some of the other islands. The chief vegetable crop is taro, which the islanders prefer to breadfruit. In recent years, the French Administration has encouraged the islanders to grow European vegetables such as carrots and potatoes. The climate is temperate, especially in the winter months.

Rurutu was discovered by Captain Cook on his first voyage in 1769. He was under the erroneous impression that it was called Ohitiroa. Until the second decade of the 19th century, the island had little contact with Europeans.

A significant event occured in 1821 when a large Rurutuan canoe drifted to Raiatea. LMS missionaries on Raiatea provided its occupants with the means of returning home, and two native teachers. Christianity was adopted on Rurutu soon afterwards. An English visitor to Rurutu in 1828 reported that about 10 years previously a strange disorder had attacked the people, killing about 2500 and reducing the population to about 350. Only two people were then above 25 years of age.

The French established a protectorate over Rurutu in 1889. It was annexed to France in 1900. There is an airstrip near Moerai with scheduled services to Papeete by Air Tahiti.

Tubuai. This is an oval-shaped island about 460 km due south of Tahiti. It is about 10 km long by 5 km wide. Mt Taita (400 m) is its highest point. A barrier reef encircles the island. The only reliable entrance is at Mataura on the north side near a village of the same name where the French gendarme resides. There is an airstrip for light planes linking the island with Tahiti.

The climate is healthy and temperate. Oranges of fine quality, coffee, coconuts, and arrowroot are grown. Population in 1983 was 1741.

Tubuai is thought to have been inhabited for only a few generations when Captain Cook discovered it in 1777. In 1789, the mutineers of the *Bounty* attempted to make a settlement there after obtaining livestock from Tahiti. The mutineers abandoned Tubuai after an affray in which 66 of the islanders were wounded. After returning to Tahiti, some of the mutineers eventually sailed to Pitcairn Island.

Ships sailing between NSW and Tahiti occasionally touched at Tubuai from 1814 onwards. Pomare II of Tahiti visited the island in 1819 when its government was formally delivered to him.

In 1822, the LMS missionaries in Tahiti sent two native teachers to the island at the Tubuaians' request. Many of the islanders were then afflicted by a mysterious disease which had been brought to the island by the survivors of a canoe that had drifted there from Anna Atoll in the Tuamotu Archipelago. A visitor in 1828 reported that the population had dropped in 10 years from about 3000 to 230, of whom about two-thirds were males. By 1831, the number had fallen to 182.

By virtue of the cession of the island to Pomare II in 1819, Tubuai became a French protectorate in 1842 when Tahiti and its dependencies came under French control. It was annexed to France in 1880.

Rimatara, the westernmost of the inhabited islands in the Austral group, lies about 120 km WSW of Rurutu. It is roughly circular in shape and about 4 km across. Its highest point is about 80 m above sea level.

Rimatara is well wooded, well watered and very fertile. It is surrounded by a coral reef which runs close to the shore in most places. Two passages exist near the NE point of the island, and there are four boat landings.

There are three villages, Amaru, Anapoto and Motu Ura, which are connected by road. Total population in 1983 was 9741. Taro is grown extensively, and oranges, bananas, breadfruit and pigs are plentiful. Fish, however, are scarce.

Rimatara remained undiscovered by Europeans until 1821 when Captain Samuel Pinder Henry of Tahiti left two native teachers there the following year; and almost the entire population of about 300 was found to be under religious instruction in 1823. There has been little of note in Rimataran history since then.

The island became a French protectorate in 1889, and was annexed to France in 1900.

Raivavae, described as one of the most beautiful islands in the eastern Pacific, lies about 155˙km ESE of Tubuai. It is about 8 km long and 4 km wide. Its rugged mountains and hills slope gently to the coast. Mt Hiro, the highest point, is about 440 m high.

The island is surrounded by a barrier reef on which are about two dozen wooded islets. There are two passages through the reef on the northern side. Of these, Tetobe, on the NW side, is practicable for small ships. Raiurua Bay at the western end of the island offers an excellent anchorage at all times. There is a jetty at which vessels drawing up to 3 m can lie alongside.

Raivavae has five villages, Matotea, Rairua, Mahanatoa, Anatonu and Vaiuru. Population in 1983 was 1177. Coffee, arrowroot, livestock and a little copra are exported. Oranges and other citrus fruits, bananas and breadfruit grow well. But the island is not commercially important.

Some interesting old 'marae' and hill terraces were investigated in 1956 by members of the Norwegian Archaeological Expedition to Easter Island and the East Pacific. A considerable number of large and small stone statues, reminiscent of those of Easter Island, once existed on the island, but most have now been removed. Two of the largest are now in the grounds of the Gauguin Museum in Tahiti.

The European discoverer of Raivavae was Captain Thomas Gayangos, of the Spanish frigate *Aguila*, who called there briefly in 1775 while sailing southward from Tahiti to pick up a wind for Peru. Captain W. R. Broughton of HMS *Chatham* sighted the island again in 1791 and named it High Island, by which it was known for many years.

In the early 19th century, several European vessels visited Raivavae for sandalwood.

When Pomare II of Tahiti called there in the ship *Arab* in 1819, the island's chiefs formally ceded the government to him. Raivavae thus became a French protectorate in 1842 when Tahiti and its dependencies came under French control. France annexed the island in 1880.

An old name for Raivavae is Vavitao.

Further information: Donald Stanley Marshall, *Island of Passion (Ra'ivavae)*, London, 1962.

Rapa, sometimes known as Rapa-iti (Little Rapa) to distinguish it from Rapanui (Big Rapa), one of the native names for Easter Island, lies some 1130 km SE of the Society Islands. It is roughly horseshoe shaped with a deeply indented coastline. The island is the remains of an ancient volcano, whose crater, now open to the sea, is the present Ahurei Bay. Rapa is roughly 30 km in circumference and ruggedly mountainous. Its highest peak, Perahu, has an elevation of more than 600 m.

Rapa is in approximately the same latitude as Norfolk Island and, being well out of the tropics, it has no barrier or fringing reef, although patches of coral occur. Ahurei Bay, which is on the eastern side, is the best anchorage. It is about 1000 m wide, but the entrance to it is narrow with much foul ground. Yachts wishing to enter should avail themselves of a pilot.

The village of Ahurei, on the shores of the bay, is the main settlement. Most of the houses are of coral blocks, but the villagers sometimes prefer to live in reed houses with thatched roofs, as these are believed to be cosier. A church occupies a cleared space in the centre of the village.

The flora of Rapa is stunted compared with that of the warmer, more northerly islands. Coconuts do not thrive and breadfruit and papaws are lacking. However, oranges, mangoes, bananas, taro, tomatoes and coffee do well, and some produce is exported to Tahiti. 1983 population was 480.

The prehistoric population of Rapa was apparently much larger than at any time since. This is evident from the well-constructed forts on all accessible mountain summits and in the principal passes from one valley to another. The forts are in the form of flat terraces, usually overlooked in each case by a tower. Similar constructions are uncommon in Polynesia. An archaeological expedition under Thor Heyerdahl investigated the forts in 1956.

The European discoverer of Rapa was Captain George Vancouver of HMS *Discovery* in 1791. The island then had no European visitors until 1816. Ten years later, six Tahitians were sent there as missionaries, and within two or three years the entire population of about 2000 had adopted Christianity. Thereafter, as contact with the outside world increased, new diseases caused many deaths. By 1867, about four years after Peruvian slavers had raided the island, the population had dropped to 120.

France declared a protectorate over the island in 1867 when it seemed likely that it would become an important coaling station between Panama and New Zealand. It was annexed to France in 1900.

In the 19th century, the Rapan men were much sought after as seamen and pearlshell divers. As a result, the island usually had a heavy surplus of women. This situation still exists to some extent.

The French administration maintains a school and a weather station on the island, and there is a reticulated water supply to the main village.

Further information: F. Allan Hanson, *Rapan Lifeways*, Boston, 1970.

Maria Island is the westernmost of the Austral group, being about 200 km NW of Rimatara. It is a typical atoll, composed of four islets on a triangular reef. It is uninhabited but is visited occasionally by people from Rimatara on fishing and copra-cutting expeditions.

The island takes its name from the whaler *Maria* (Captain George W. Gardner) from which it was sighted in 1824. Other names that have been applied to it are Hull, Sands and Nororutu. The island was annexed to France in 1901. Lever's Pacific Plantations Ltd are said to have been granted a lease to it in 1902, but the company made no use of the island.

The Marotiri (or Bass) Islands lie about 75 km east by south of Rapa. They are nine in number, of which eight are little more than rock pinnacles rising sheer from the sea. The ninth has two pinnacles with a saddle in between. The saddle contains some stone platforms and towers similar to those on Rapa. The highest pinnacle in the group is just over 100 m.

Why the islands are called Bass is unknown, although there may be a link with George Bass, the discoverer of Bass Strait between Victoria and Tasmania, who visited parts of eastern Polynesia in 1802 in quest of salted pork for the infant colony of NSW. He did not, however, leave any record of sighting the pinnacles.

The islands are seldom visited except by people from Rapa who go in long-boats to fish there. An expedition under Thor Heyerdahl examined the archaeological remains in 1956.

TUAMOTU ARCHIPELAGO. The Tuamotu Archipelago, excluding the high volcanic cluster of Mangareva and its neighbour, Temoe Atoll, consists of 76 islands situated between 14 and 24 deg S latitude and 135 and 149 deg W longitude. It is also called the Paumotu, Low or Dangerous Archipelago. With a few exceptions, all the islands are low-lying coral atolls — rings of coral enclosing salt-water lagoons. The chief exception is the upraised island of Makatea, formerly noted for its phosphate deposits, now exhausted. In the few other islands that are not atolls, the central lagoons that once existed have dried or silted up. The largest atolls are Rangiroa, Fakarava, Makemo and Hao, all about 50 km long. The smallest, such as Pinaki and Taiaro, are barely 1½ km in diameter. The total land area is about 900 sq. km.

The archipelago is remote from all continents and is little known to Europeans. Its low, sometimes badly charted reefs make it hazardous to navigators; and at most atolls only small craft can negotiate the reef passages and find anchorages in the lagoons. Moreover, as coconuts and pearlshell are the only commercial resources, the archipelago is unattractive to all but a few traders. However, since the early 1960s, several atolls, notably Mururoa, Fangataufa and Hao, have figured prominently in the French government's nuclear testing programme in the Pacific.

The climate of the archipelago is hot, with the period from May to October slightly cooler than the rest of the year. The trade winds blow throughout, most rain falls during the warmer period. Hurricanes are sometimes experienced, usually between December and February. The most notable on record were in 1877, 1878, 1903 and 1906 when villages were destroyed; boats, vegetation and soil washed away; and many lives lost. Effects of the 1983 cyclones on the Tuamotus were more severe than anywhere else in the territory. The supply of fresh water is a problem throughout the archipelago, as the porous ground absorbs the rain, and there are no streams or springs. Fresh coconut 'milk' is often used for drinking.

Pisonia, cordia, morinda citrifolia, erythrina, and types of hibiscus are the only native trees in the Tuamotus apart from the coconut palm, which was probably introduced by man. There are also a few bushes and grasses. Lizards and rats are the only indigenous animals. Land birds are also scarce, but there is a variety of seabirds. Fish and shellfish are plentiful, and sharks and turtle common.

The 1983 census showed a total population of the archipelago of 11,793.

Three religious groups are well represented in the Tuamotus — the Roman Catholics, Mormons and 'Kanitos', the local name for adherents to the Reorganised Church of Jesus Christ of Latter Day Saints.

No archaeological information is yet available on how long the archipelago is likely to have been inhabited by man. However, research carried out in 1929–30 and 1934 by expeditions of the Bishop Museum, Honolulu, revealed striking differences in Tuamotuan physical types, language and culture. Some of the stone 'marae' of the eastern part of the archipelago were found to have much in common with the stone remains of Niihau and Necker Islands in the Hawaiian group and with those of the interior of Tahiti and Moorea. This has led some specialists to think that they may be relics of an early wave of migrants who differed substantially from Polynesians of the Tonga/Samoa area who arrived later. Moreover, as the Tuamotuan dialects contain many words that are not found in Tongan and Samoan, it has been suggested that the first Tuamotuans may have been South American Indians.

Pukapuka Atoll, on the north-eastern margin of the archipelago, was the first island in the Tuamotus — and also the first in the Pacific — to be seen by Europeans. Its discoverer was Fernao Magalhaes (Ferdinand Magellan), who crossed the Pacific in 1521 in the Spanish ships *Victoria* and *Trinidad*. About four and a half years later, another Spanish ship, the caravel *San Lesmes*, apparently ran aground on Amanu Atoll in the central part of the archipelago. The caravel became separated from three other vessels in June 1526, shortly after entering the Pacific from the Strait of Magellan en route to the Moluccas. Evidence suggesting that an early European ship had come to grief on Amanu came to light in 1929 when four iron cannon, heavily encrusted with coral, were found near Amanu's north-eastern tip. One was recovered at that time, and two others in 1969. The latter are now at Point Venus, Tahiti. Their recovery followed the publication of an article by an Australian historian, Robert Langdon, in which he speculated that the cannon may have come from the *San Lesmes*. Langdon later published a book, *The Lost Caravel* (Sydney, 1975) in which he expounded the theory that the caravel's crew had survived shipwreck to inter-marry with Polynesian women; that they and their descendants had spread to many Polynesian islands, including New Zealand and Easter Island; and that they had strongly influenced Polynesian culture.

In 1606, 80 years after the disappearance of the *San Lesmes*, the Spanish explorer Quiros passed through the Tuamotu Archipelago and some of his men landed on Hao Atoll. Ten years later, the Schouten and Le Maire expedition (Dutch) landed on Pukapuka and later touched at Takaroa, Takapoto, Manihi and Rangiroa. More than a century then passed before the Roggeveen expedition (also Dutch) got among the Tuamotus. Roggeveen lost one of his three ships, the *African Galley*, on Takapoto in April 1722 and five of his men deserted there. Roggeveen later sailed past Manihi, Apataki, Arutua and Rangiroa before getting some much-needed refreshments at Makatea.

For about 10 years in the third quarter of the 18th century, European ships were in the Tuamotus in a constant succession. In 1765

an Englishman, Commodore John Byron, sailed along the archipelago's northern fringe in HMS *Dolphin*. He discovered Napuka and Tepoto, and later landed on Takaroa, Takapoto's near neighbour, where he found relics of the *African Galley*.

Two years later, the *Dolphin*, on a new voyage under Captain Samuel Wallis, discovered some of the small atolls in the SE corner of the archipelago as well as Paraoa, Manuhangi and Nengonengo. Meanwhile, HMS *Swallow* (Captain Carteret), which had become separated from the *Dolphin* near the Strait of Magellan, became the first European ship to encounter Mururoa, Nukutipipi and Anuanuraro.

In 1768, Bougainville, the French explorer, discovered several of the eastern and central atolls, and coined the name 'Dangerous Archipelago'. Cook passed the same way about a year later, making the important discovery of Anaa, which he called Chain Island.

In 1772, a Spanish explorer, Domingo Boenechea, discovered Tauere and Haraiki, and called at Anaa, in sailing to Tahiti in the ship *Aguila*. A year later, Captain Cook, on his second voyage to the Pacific, discovered three more atolls in the south-central part of the archipelago. On a subsequent visit to the Tuamotus on the same voyage, some of his men landed at Takaroa, and Cook gave the name Palliser's Islands to the four large atolls of Apataki, Toau, Kaukura and Arutua. In 1774, Boenechea made a second voyage to Tahiti from Peru which resulted in the discovery of Tatakoto and Amanu.

For nearly 20 years after this, there were no more European visitors to the Tuamotus. Then several more came in a bunch. In 1791, Captain Edward Edwards in HMS *Pandora* discovered (South) Marutea and Tureia; in 1792, Captain William Bligh discovered Tematangi in HMS *Providence*, and the British whaler *Matilda* was wrecked on Mururoa, and five years later, Captain James Wilson of the missionary ship *Duff* added Pukarua to the charts following his discovery of Mangareva and Temoe.

The first European attempt to exploit the resources of the group was made in 1802 after Captain John Buyers of the British ship *Margaret* saw islanders at previously undiscovered Makemo wearing pearl shells around their necks. He fitted out his ship for a pearling voyage in Tahiti, but was wrecked on Arutua within a few days of returning to the Tuamotus.

Captain William Campbell of the Sydney brig *Hibernia* obtained some bêche-de-mer and pearl shell in some of the north-western atolls in 1809. This encouraged about a dozen other ships to make voyages to the same island for the same purpose during the next five years. However, news of the discovery of sandalwood in the Marquesas in 1814 caused the pearling trade to be abandoned abruptly, and it was not resumed until the early 1820s.

Meanwhile, two Russian exploring expeditions were in the Tuamotus. In 1816, Otto von Kotzebue sailed along the archipelago's northern fringe in the ships *Rurick* and *Nadeshda* and made detailed surveys of some atolls. Four years later, after 300 years of European contact, Thadeus von Bellingshausen in the ships *Vostock* and *Mirnyi* made the first thorough examination of the archipelago. He sighted and often closely examined 20 atolls, of which about half had previously been unknown to Europeans. His charts were published in 1823 by his hydrographer countryman A. J. Krusenstern in an *Atlas de l'Ocean Pacifique* — the first volume of charts devoted solely to the Pacific. This was accompanied by a *Receuil de Memoires Hydrographiques* which critically examined and systematised the hydrographic knowledge acquired in the Pacific over the previous three centuries.

Within a few years of Bellingshausen's Tuamotuan survey, European ships began to appear in the archipelago with much greater frequency than they had ever done before. There were reasons for this. The development of trade between New South Wales and British India on the one hand and Chile on the other opened a new shipping lane through that part of the Pacific in 1819; the pearlshell trade based on Sydney was resumed in 1822; the exploring vessels *Coquille* (French) and *Blossom* (British) arrived to make detailed surveys; and an occasional whaler skirted the archipelago. This increased activity resulted in the discovery of several more atolls and the proliferation of names for both new and old discoveries.

The pearlers who returned to the archipelago in 1822 confined their activities to the north-western atolls, which they described collectively as the Palliser Islands. However, in 1823, an Englishman, Captain Richard Charlton, was tempted to try his luck at Hao Atoll, and from then on the search for pearlshell was chiefly centred on the more easterly atolls. Valparaiso, Chile, became the capital for the pearling industry after adventurers from that port made their first voyage to the archipelago in 1825 and ships from Sydney ceased to participate. In the early years, the pearlers hired islanders from the Society Islands and Anaa to dive for them. But later on the more tractable Rapa Islanders were used.

A survey in 1826 by Captain F. W. Beechey, of HMS *Blossom*, which took in 28 atolls and added three new ones to the charts, completed the primary exploration of the archipelago. Thereafter, only a handful of atolls remained to be discovered. The last of them, Taiaro and Kauehi, were sighted by Captain Robert FitzRoy of HMS *Beagle* in 1835. The first chart depicting all 76 islands of the archipelago was published in 1845 by Commodore Charles Wilkes, of the United States Exploring Expedition, who had made an extensive survey of the Tuamotus in 1839–40. The chart assigned native names to more than 60 of the islands; but for most of those to the north and east of Hao, the names were later found to be inaccurate or assigned to the wrong islands.

Christianity was first taken to the Tuamotus — to Anaa — in 1817 by an Anaan who had been to a school on Moorea run by missionaries of the London Missionary Society. By 1821, Anaa and several neighbouring atolls were all said to have renounced their old gods. However, Christianity did not prosper in those islands. By 1845, Anaa was reportedly in a state of disorder and confusion, with the people frequently quarrelling among themselves. It was at that point that an American Mormon missionary, Benjamin Grouard, settled on Anaa and won 600 islanders to his faith. More than 100 were later baptised on other atolls in the Western Tuamotus.

Meanwhile, in 1842, Tahiti, Moorea and 'dependencies' had become a French protectorate, and in 1849 a French Catholic bishop was installed in Tahiti. News of the progress of Mormonism on Anaa and elsewhere prompted the bishop to send two priests from Mangareva (where a Catholic mission had been established since 1834) to open a mission station in the Tuamotus. The priests began their work on Faaite, but moved to Anaa in 1851. Their arrival provoked violence on the part of the Anaans, which led the French authorities in Tahiti to ban the Mormons from their protectorate. However, Mormon influence persisted and spread through the work of native converts, and it retarded the work of the Catholic missionaries for almost two decades.

The French authorities in Tahiti had first made it known in 1849 that they considered the Tuamotus to be among the dependencies of Tahiti and Moorea, and therefore part of their protectorate. However, it was not until October 1853 that they formally extended their administration to the archipelago. They did this by appointing a leading Anaan chief, Paiore, as regent for Queen Pomare of Tahiti. They also sent a French naval officer, Xavier Caillet, to Anaa as special commissioner. French rule was then gradually extended to other atolls by vesting authority in the local chiefs. By the end of 1858, 46 islands in the western and central part of the archipelago were reported to have 'received and fully accepted the protectorate flag'. The inhabitants of the remaining islands were still looked on as 'cannibals' and 'savages' and navigators were warned to treat them with the 'greatest prudence'.

An abortive attempt to bring some of the eastern atolls under French control was made in 1860. Thereafter, the 'conquest' of the remaining atolls was left to the Catholic missionaries. Pakarua was the first to feel their influence. In 1865, the entire population was persuaded to go to Mangareva to be indoctrinated in the Catholic faith. They were repatriated about a year later.

Most of the remaining islands were evangelised by personal visits from two missionaries stationed on Anaa, Fathers Albert Montiton and Germain Fierens. These priests made several arduous voyages to the eastern islands beginning in 1869. By 1883, all islands in the archipelago were considered Christianised.

After the introduction of Christianity, many atolls that were previously bare or almost bare of coconuts were heavily planted,

often under the guidance of missionaries, and a reasonably prosperous copra industry developed. Meanwhile, the pearlshell industry continued, with ships operating out of Tahiti. In recent years, pearl diving has been strictly controlled to prevent lagoons becoming exhausted. Experiments have also been carried out to try to develop an industry in cultured pearls.

Neither of the two world wars had much impact on life in the Tuamotus, and the islanders largely retained their own distinctive speech habits and ways of doing things. But two developments since the 1950s have tended to obliterate most of the old culture. The first was the introduction of daily radio broadcasts from Tahiti; the second, the inauguration of the French government's nuclear testing programme. The latter, which was first announced in 1963, has brought thousands of foreigners to the atolls, caused some atolls to be evacuated, and has completely altered the islanders' economy. Hao Atoll, in the central part of the archipelago, now has an international airstrip more than 3000 m long. Airstrips have also been built at Rangiroa and Manihi, thus placing the people of those areas within easy reach of Tahiti.

There are few books entirely devoted to the Tuamotus. Two of the most readable and informative are Clifford Gessler's *The Dangerous Islands* (London, 1937), published in New York as *The Road My Body Goes*, and Bengt Danielsson's *The Happy Island* (London, 1952). Scientific studies on the archipelago by Kenneth P. Emory, J. Frank Stimson and Edwin G. Burrows have been published by the Bishop Museum, Honolulu.

Atolls with more than 100 inhabitants at the 1971 census are described below in alphabetical order. Mururoa and Fangataufa, which figure prominently in the nuclear testing project, are also included in this section, although they have no permanent inhabitants. Fangataufa is described under the heading 'Mururoa'.

Ahe is a well-wooded atoll with fine coconut plantations in the north-western corner of the archipelago. It is about 16 km long and about 13 km westward of Manihi. Its lagoon is accessible to small vessels with a draught of less than four metres. The village of Tenukupara is on the south-eastern side.

Population in 1983 was 142.

Schouten and Le Maire in 1616 and Roggeveen in 1722 probably sighted Ahe. But the question of Ahe's European discovery is obscure because of its nearness and similarity to Manihi. The US Exploring Expedition surveyed Ahe in 1839 and named it Peacock Island.

Amanu, an oval-shaped atoll, lies about 800 km due east of Tahiti. It is about 29 km long from SW to NE. A channel about 14.5 km wide separates it from the NE end of the Hao Atoll. There are two small passes through the reef on the western side. The village of ikitake is near the more southerly (and principal) pass. Population in 1983 was 126.

Amanu was first reported by the Spanish explorer Andia y Varela in 1774. Bellingshausen, the Russian explorer, charted it in 1820 and named it Moller Island. The islanders in those days were reputed to be cannibals.

In 1929, the Administrator of the Tuamotus, Captain Francois Herve, found four ancient cannon near the north-eastern tip of Amanu. They were in shallow water and heavily encrusted with coral. One cannon was recovered and later placed in the museum in Papeete, but it has since been lost. The present whereabouts of one of the others is also unknown. However, the remaining two are now in the Museum of the Discoverers at Point Venus, Tahiti, having been recovered from Amanu by a French naval officer in 1969.

Anaa, once the most important and populous atoll in the archipelago, lies about 350 km east of Tahiti and 56 km SW of Faaite. It is composed of 11 islets and is elliptical in shape. It is about 30 km long by 10 wide. The lagoon is shallow and has no entrance, but approach to the atoll is easy on the lee side where the reef is steep-to. There are five villages, of which the chief one is Tuuhora. The population in 1983 was 400, compared with about 2000 in the mid-19th century.

Anaa was formerly inhabited by hardy, warlike, heavily tattooed islanders who roamed over much of the archipelago in huge double-hulled canoes called 'pahi'. They called themselves 'Parata', meaning sharks, and were much feared by the other atoll dwellers. Many of the atolls had been conquered by them.

The first European to sight Anaa was Captain Cook in 1769. He called it Chain Island because of the chain-like appearance of its 11 islets. However, Europeans learned little of the Anaans until 1806 when three of their 'pahi' were blown to Tahiti in a storm. It was then noted that their language differed considerably from that of Tahiti.

Anaa was the first atoll of the Tuamotus to adopt Christianity — in about 1821. It later played an important role in supplying divers for the pearl shell trade; and it was also an important source, first of coconut oil, then of copra. Anaa was the gateway through which Mormonism was introduced to the Tuamotus in the 1840s, and it was there, too, that Roman Catholic missionaries established a base in 1851 from which they evangelised the rest of the archipelago.

In 1853, when France extended its administration to the Tuamotus, Anaa was chosen as the seat of government. However, a devastating hurricane in 1878 resulted in Fakarava usurping Anaa's position. Another hurricane in 1906 further damaged the atoll, and by 1911 its population had dropped to 199. In 1936, the population stood at 371, in 1951 at 481, and in 1956 at 508. The decline since then is attributable to immigration to Tahiti, where the tourist industry and the nuclear testing project offer better employment opportunities.

Anaa's soil is much deeper than that of most atolls and it is heavily planted with coconuts. In certain conditions, its shallow lagoon reflects a clear green image in the sky which may be seen from a great distance.

Apataki Atoll, about 30 km long by 24 km wide, was formerly the headquarters of the administrator of the Tuamotu Archipelago. It is one of a group of four atolls — the others being Toau, Arutua and Kaukuru — which Captain Cook named the Palliser Islands in 1774. The group is roughly 300 km northwest of Tahiti.

Apataki is well-wooded except on its southern side, where the reef is submerged and dangerous. Three passes on the western side give access to the lagoon. Tehere, the northernmost, is the only practicable one for large vessels. Pakaka, the southernmost, is used by local schooners. The village of

Niutahi is on the south side of Pakaka pass. Population in 1983 was 204.

The Dutch explorer Roggeveen sighted Apataki in 1722 and named it Avondstond (Evening). Hagermeister, a Russian navigator, examined it in 1830. It was shown on maps for many years as Hagermeister Island.

Apataki is now equipped with a freezing works for the storage of fish before their dispatch to Tahiti for sale.

Arutua, lying about 14.5 km west of the north end of Apataki, is roughly circular in shape, with a diameter of some 29 km. It is planted with coconuts on its northern side, but much of its reef on the south side is submerged. Porofai pass, near the southern end of the east side, provides an entrance to the lagoon for very small vessels. The nearby village is called Rautini. Population in 1983 was 663.

Roggeveen, the first European to sight Arutua, named it Meerder Zorg (More Trouble) because of its dangerous reefs. To Cook, it was one of the Palliser Islands — (see Apataki above). The British merchant ship *Margaret* (Captain John Buyers) was wrecked there in 1803 on the first pearling voyage to the Tuamotus.

Faaite, oval in shape, lies between Fakarava to the NW and Tahanea to the east. Tahanea, the nearer of the two, is about 11 km away. Faaite is lightly wooded and about 25 km long. Vessels of up to 60 tons may enter the lagoon by a passage at the NW end. Nearby is Hitianau village. Population in 1983 was 185. Bellings hausen, Faaite's European discoverer, named it Admiral Chichagov Island. The first Roman Catholic mission station in the Tuamotus was established there in 1849.

Fakarava, lying about 400 km ENE of Tahiti and 72 km northward of Anaa, is the second largest atoll in the archipelago. It is rectangular in shape, about 65 km long and 24 km broad. The western side is bare reef; but the other three sides, consisting of some long stretches of land and a number of islets, are well wooded, mostly with coconut trees. Ngarue pass, on the northern side, is the best of three entrances into the lagoon. It is nearly 1 km wide, has a depth of nine metres, and is suitable for large vessels. The village of Rotoava, formerly administrative headquarters for the archipelago, stands at the NE extremity of the atoll. It consists of a long avenue bordered by bungalows. Most of the population of 567 (1983) lives there. Another village, Tetamanu, diagonally opposite across the lagoon, was in ruins at last report.

Fakarava is usually said to have been discovered in 1820 by the Russian navigator Bellingshausen, who named it Count Wittgenstein Island. However, seven years before that, eight members of the crew of the British ship *Daphne* were marooned there after the crew mutinied and killed the captain and two other men.

The atoll became the seat of the French Resident in the Tuamotus following a hurricane and tidal wave which devastated Anaa in 1878. Robert Louis Stevenson, who visited Fakarava in 1888, published an account of his sojourn in his book *In the South Seas*. Headquarters for the archipelago were later transferred to Apataki because conditions there were more favourable for experiments on pearl culture.

Fangatau Atoll (also written Fagatau and Angatau) lies about 62 km WNW of Fakahina. It is roughly triangular in shape and only 40 km in circuit. There is no entrance into the lagoon, but landings can be made on the western point where the village of Marupua stands. Fangatau's soil is loose and sandy, and vegetation is more abundant than on most atolls. The local coconuts are renowned for their flavour. 1983 population was 165.

Fangatau was known to the ancient Tahitians as Marupua, but it was not sighted by Europeans until 1820. Its discoverer, Bellingshausen, named it Count Arakcheev Island, usually abbreviated to Arakcheev on 19th-century charts.

In pre-European times, the Fangatauans were skilled canoe builders and navigators. The atoll still contains many well-preserved 'marae'. A Bishop Museum expedition made a study of the Fangatauans and their culture in 1929. The islanders were then found to have 'an extraordinary Caucasian cast of features' and to have philosophical ideas embodied in their chants that seemed to be derived from some 'highly developed ancient civilisation'. Robert Langdon's book *The Lost Caravel* devotes a long chapter to Fangatau.

Hao Atoll, a forward base for the French

nuclear tests at Mururoa and Fangataufa, lies 14.5 km south of Amanu and about 800 km east of Tahiti. It is roughly wedgeshaped and a little more than 50 km long. On the north and eastern sides, there are several long stretches of land; but on the southern and SW sides, the reef is so low in places that the sea washes into the lagoon. Kaki pass, in the middle of the northern end of the atoll, is practicable for vessels with a draught of up to 5.5 m. The fairway, which is about 400 m long, has been swept to a depth of 7 m over a width of about 100 m. There is an anchorage with 22 m depth westward of Otepa, the principal settlement, which is about 8 km from Kaki pass on the NE side of the lagoon. The land at Otepa is somewhat elevated — 'almost a hill', according to one writer. 1983 population was 1167, of whom 249 were non-residents.

The facilities built for the nuclear testing project include a 3300 m airstrip, radio masts, hangars, workshops, port facilities, offices and accommodation for up to 2000 men. Many of the numerous coral heads in the northern part of the lagoon have been marked by buoys and beacons.

Hao was the first atoll in the Tuamotus on which Europeans are recorded to have made a landing. In February 1606, a boat party from the Quiros expedition went ashore there in search of water. Quiros named the atoll La Conversion de San Pablo (St Paul's Conversion). More than 160 years then passed before Bougainville sighted Hao and named it La Harpe. In the following year, 1769, Cook also sighted it from HMS *Endeavour* and named it Bow Island. Bellingshausen made the first chart of it in 1820, and about three years later European pearlers found the passage into its lagoon. From then on, Hao was an important source of pearl shell and also a base for pearlers operating at other atolls in the eastern part of the archipelago.

A visitor to Hao in 1894 reported that the islanders spoke a completely different language from that of Tahiti. If this was so, little is now known of it. In 1903, virtually the whole of Hao's population was wiped out when 261 islanders, who had gone to Hikueru Atoll for the diving season, were carried off by a tidal wave.

In 1986 Hao came to world attention when the two French agents found guilty of

the bombing of the Greenpeace vessel *Rainbow Warrior*, Alain Marfat and Dominique Prieur, had their 10-year New Zealand jail sentence for manslaughter commuted to three years open detention on the atoll. They returned to France before the term was completed.

Katiu, about 24 km long, lies between Raraka and Makemo in the centre of the archipelago. Coconuts cover its NE side, where the village of Toini stands. The southern side is completely bare. Two passes into the lagoon are practicable for small vessels. In 1983 the population was 122.

Bellingshausen discovered Katiu in 1820 and named it General Osten-Saken Island. It is known on some old maps as Saken Island.

Kauehi, a nearly circular atoll about 24 km across, lies about 40 km NE of Fakarava and about 18 km NW of Raraka. It is very low-lying, but is well-planted with coconut trees. A pass on the SW side gives access to the lagoon. The main village is Tearavero. Population in 1983 was 196.

Kauehi, discovered by FitzRoy in 1835 and recorded by him as Cavahi, was one of the last atolls in the archipelago to be seen by Europeans. Wilkes, unaware of Fitz-Roy's discovery, named it Vincennes Island in 1839.

Kaukura Atoll (like Apataki and Arutua, above) was one of the four Palliser Islands of Captain Cook. It is an oval-shaped atoll about 40 km long. It is well planted in coconuts, particularly on its NE side. Only small vessels can enter it shallow lagoon. The 1983 population was 210. Rahitahiti is the only permanently inhabited village.

Europeans had some unhappy experiences with the Kaukurans in the early days. In 1803, a party of Kaukurans attacked the crew of the British ship *Margaret* after she was wrecked on neighbouring Arutua; and in 1831, the master and mate of the British ship *Truro* were murdered after being inveigled ashore at Kaukura.

Kaukura was severely damaged in the hurricane of 1878.

Makemo, a narrow atoll about 64 km long, lies in the central part of the archipelago. It is one of the most productive and populous atolls. The northern side is well wooded, but the southern side is bare and dangerous to approach. There are passes into the lagoon at the NW extremity and about 16 km from the eastern extremity on the northern side. Near the latter is Pukeva village, the only permanent settlement. Many of the inhabitants are expert divers. Total 1983 population was 360.

The sight of islanders wearing pearl shells in 1802 inspired Makemo's European discoverer, John Buyers, to fit out the first pearling expedition to the Tuamotus. He called the atoll Phillips Island. Bellingshausen, who visited it in 1820, saw only two people on shore and concluded that it was not regularly inhabited. He named it Prince Golenitschev-Kutuzov-Smolenski Island.

The atoll has since had its attraction for Europeans. In 1883, an Englishman was reported to have lived there for 40 years; and in 1926, Alain Gerbault met a Dane there who had acted as pilot for Robert Louis Stevenson in 1888.

Manihi, the sister atoll of Ahe, lies in the NW corner of the archipelago. It is about 22 km long by 9.5 km broad, with a pass suitable for small craft at its SW end. Except on the NW side, the whole atoll is thickly planted with coconuts. Pearl shell also abounds. Manihi is one of the most productive atolls in the archipelago. In 1983 the population was 313.

An airstrip at Manihi is used by small planes.

Manihi was probably discovered by the Dutch expedition of Schouten and Le Maire in 1616 (see under Ahe). It was one of the first atolls to be exploited by Europeans for pearl shell. An early pearling vessel, the *Venus*, of Sydney, was wrecked there in 1811. The atoll was later known as Wilson Island.

There is now a small hotel on Manihi. The cultured pearl industry is well developed there.

Matahiva (also written Mataiva) is the westernmost of the Tuamotu atolls. It is circular and about 8 km in diameter. The only pass is a boat entrance on the NW side. Coconuts thrive there.

Before World War II, Matahiva was not permanently inhabited, but was visited periodically from neighbouring Tikehau. In 1983 the population was 183.

Matahiva was known to the anicent Tahitians and was recorded by Europeans as far back as 1774. However, Bellingshausen, in 1820, was the first European to set eyes on it. It was then uninhabited.

Several 18th-century visitors to the Society Islands recorded seeing Matahivans in those islands who had been driven there in storms. In 1806, warriors from Kaukura drove all the Matahivans out. Several canoe-loads of them reached Tahiti.

A phosphate deposit has been discovered on the atoll, under the lagoon, and there are plans to mine it.

Mururoa, one of the most southerly atolls, has become world famous since the French government announced in 1963 that it intended to use it for nuclear tests. The first of a series of nuclear devices was exploded in the atmosphere there in mid-1966; and each year, for the next eight years, there was generally a similar series. Then, following world-wide protests, the tests were conducted underground at Fangataufa, 32 km southward. They returned to Mururoa shortly afterwards.

Mururoa, which is about 27 km long by 13 km wide, is the only atoll in the SE part of the Tuamotus with an entrance for ships into its lagoon. The pass is about 1 km SW of the atoll's northernmost point. It has been dredged to a depth of seven metres. A quay about 45 m long has been constructed on the NE side of the lagoon. Seaplanes can land nearby. There is also an airstrip for land planes. Buildings that have been constructed for the nuclear tests include a group of radio masts near the eastern point, a tall tower on the southern side, and concrete buildings on the northern and western points.

Carteret, the European discoverer of Mururoa, named it Bishop of Osnaburg Island in 1767. It became known as Matilda's Rocks after the British whaler *Matilda* was wrecked there in 1792. Beechey, who visited it in 1826, found no trace of its ever having been inhabited.

Mururoa was planted with coconuts by a Papeete firm to which it was assigned in 1876, and pearl diving was also carried on there. However, no permanent settlement was ever established on the atoll.

Fangataufa is much smaller than Mururoa. It is roughly rectangular in shape, about 8 km long by 5 km wide. There is no entrance into the lagoon. The atoll served as an observation post for the atmospheric tests at Mururoa.

Beechey, Fangataufa's European discoverer, named it Cockburn Island.

French Polynesia's Territorial Assembly ceded both Moruroa and Fangataufa to France in 1964. By 1987 more than 120 nuclear tests had been conducted.

Napuka and its sister island Tepoto are the most northerly of the Tuamotu group. They are separated from their nearest neighbours by more than 160 km, and being away from the main shipping lanes, they have had relatively little contact with outsiders. Byron, in 1765, named them the Disappointment Islands because a heavy surf and the apparent hostility of the islanders prevented him from obtaining badly-needed fresh food.

Napuka, known locally as Te Puka a Maruia, is an atoll shaped roughly like a triangle. It is about 7 km long by 3.5 km wide. The eastern and western sides are well wooded, but the southern side is bare. Population in 1983 was 264.

Copra provides the islanders with a cash income.

Tepoto, which may be seen from Napuka, is an upraised coral island. A lagoon that once existed has dried up. The island is covered with coconut palms. The inhabitants communicate regularly with Napuka by canoe and send urgent messages by smoke signal. The 1983 population was 67.

Until 1870, when a Catholic missionary visited Napuka for the first time, the people of both islands had had virtually no contact with Europeans. Even in 1934, when a Bishop Museum expedition spent several weeks there, they could still claim that no Europeans other than missionaries had ever lived ashore. One of the discoveries of the Bishop Museum team was that the Napukan language contained many words that bore no apparent resemblance to those of other Polynesian languages.

Clifford Gessler's book *The Dangerous Islands* (London, 1937) gives a vivid picture of Napukan life.

Niau, an atoll of elliptical shape, is about 10 km long and 8 km wide. Its nearest neighbours are Kaukura and Toau. Niau is unusually high — about 7.5 m above sea level — and its lagoon is completely enclosed from the sea. The lagoon, which is brackish, contains an excellent fish known as ava, which tastes like salmon.

Deposits of phosphate are found on both the beach and lagoon floor, but they are of poor quality and have not been exploited. However, the land is unusually fertile. Coconuts, oranges, limes, bananas and even breadfruit grow freely. The 1983 population was 140.

Niau was uninhabited when Bellingshausen discovered it in 1820 and named it Greig Island. However, traces of human habitation were seen on shore. The 1878 hurricane severely damaged the atoll.

An old Polynesian name for Niau has been variously recorded as Faau, Fakau and Fakaau.

Nukutavake, Pinaki, Vairaatea. Nukutavake is one of a group of three small islands in the SE corner of the archipelago which are inhabited in turn by the same people. The others are Pinaki and Vairaatea. Nukutavake is unusual for the Tuamotus in that, although it is flat and of coral formation, it has no lagoon, nor evidence of a former one. It is about 8 km from NE to SW, and about 1 km wide. Except near its eastern extremity, it is well wooded. Many of the inhabitants migrate to Vairaatea from May to July, and to Pinaki in August. Vairaatea is about 35 km westward; Pinaki is about 13 km SE. Vairaatea, by far the larger of the two, is about 4.5 km at its greatest width.

Wallis, in 1767, was the first European to see the three islands of the Nukutavake people; but Quiros had discovered Vairaatea in 1606. The Nukutavake people were formerly skilled boatbuilders whose keeled, single-hulled vessels were made of many small pieces of timber sewn together with sinnet. Their ancient culture was little changed until well into the 20th century.

Pukapuka, not to be confused with an island of that name in the Cook group, is situated at the NE corner of the archipelago. It is an atoll with a total land and sea area of about 4 sq. km. Its nearest neighbour is Fakahina, about 160 km SW.

The atoll, seen by Magellan in 1521, was the first island in the Pacific to be discovered by Europeans. It was then uninhabited. But when the Schouten and Le Maire expedition called there in 1616, they found three dogs on shore. For this reason, the atoll was named Honden Eylandt (Dog Island), and it was so known for almost two centuries. When the

US Exploring Expedition called there in 1939, birds as tame as barnyard fowls were seen in 'incredible' numbers.

A visitor in 1904 reported that wild cats were common on some islets. About 100 islanders from other atolls were diving for pearlshell. A few years later, the people of Fakahina — at the suggestion of a French Catholic priest — planted the atoll with more than 35,000 coconut trees. A combination of sun, phosphate, humus and guano brought the trees on remarkably quickly, and the Fakahinans established a permanent settlement. The 1983 population was 166.

Pukarua is an elliptical atoll in the eastern sector of the archipelago, about 48 km WNW of Reao. The lagoon has no entrance, but boats can land on the western side opposite the village of Marautaora, and also north of the NW point.

Captain James Wilson of the *Duff*, who discovered Pukarua in 1797, named it Searle's Island. it was then uninhabited, but traces of former human occupants were seen. Beechey, in 1826, found about 100 people there 'of the same dark swarthy colour' as the islanders of Reao. in 1865, more than 50 Pukaruans were taken to Mangareva to be indoctrinated in the Catholic faith.

A Japanese anthropologist, Sachiko Hatanaka, made a socio-economic study of Pukarua in 1961–64.

Rangiroa, about 70 km long and with an extreme width of 22 km, is the largest atoll in the archipelago. It lies between Tikehau and Arutua, some 320 km NE of Tahiti. The atoll is well wooded all round. Two passes on the northern side lead into the lagoon. Nearby are two villages with the same names as the passes — Tiputa and Avatoru. Total population in 1983 was 181.

The lagoon, once of considerable importance as a pearling centre, is particularly safe. Large vessels can sail between the two villages without difficulty. Air Tahiti runs a daily air service to the atoll from Tahiti.

Rangiroa was well known to the ancient Tahitians as Rairoa. Schouten and Le Maire, who touched there in 1616, called it Vlieghen Eylandt because of its troublesome flies. Roggeveen in 1722 called it Goede Verwaghting (Good Expectations). Another early name for it was Dean's island. Until quite recent

years, it was shown as Nairsa on some maps because of a mistranscription of the name Rairoa in the mid-19th century.

Reao, the easternmost inhabited atoll in the archipelago, lies about 48 km ESE of Pukarua and some 215 km east of Vahitahi. It is about 16 km long and well wooded, but with no entrance into its lagoon.

Reao is remote from regular shipping lanes and remained undiscovered by Europeans until 1822. The first to sight it was Captain John Bell of the British ship *Minerva*. In the same year, the French explorer Duperrey also sighted it and named it Clermont Tonnere. This name remained in use for many years.

Some Reao islanders were taken to Mangareva in 1865 to be taught the Christian faith, and in 1874 a Catholic missionary lived on their island for several months. The Catholic church in Tahiti has taken a close interest in the atoll ever since; otherwise it has had little contact with the outside world.

After cases of leprosy were discovered on Reao in the 1920s, Father Paul Maze (later Archbishop of Tahiti) urged the French administration to establish a leprosarium on the atoll. This was done in 1936, but leprosy cases from all parts of French Polynesia are now treated at Orofara, Tahiti.

The Reao islanders are intimately connected with the inhabitants of Pukarua. They are of particular interest to Polynesian scholars. This is because they are unusually darkskinned and non-Polynesian in appearance; because their language contains many words and forms that are foreign to other Polynesian languages; and because their island is noted for numerous ancient 'marae' which have much in common with some of the stone structures of Easter Island. An expedition organised by a Japanese anthropologist, Miss Sachiko Hatanaka, visited Reao in 1976.

Takapoto and Takaroa, lying about 8 km apart in the NW corner of the archipelago, were named the King George Islands by Byron in 1765. Takapoto, which lies SE of its neighbour, is about 16 km long and well-wooded. The lagoon has no entrance, but boats can land easily near the SW extremity. Total population in 1983 was 309.

Takaroa, about 24 km long and 8 km wide, has an entrance for vessels of up to 3 m draught. Anchorages are good in all parts of the lagoon. The convenience of the lagoon made Takaroa popular with the early pearlers. The 1983 population was 162.

The Dutch explorers Schouten and Le Maire discovered the two atolls in 1615 but, unaware of their duality, they gave them a single name — Zondergrondt Eylandt (Bottomless Island). In 1722, the *African Galley*, one of Roggeveen's three vessels, was wrecked at Takapoto and five of his men deserted there. Iron from the wreck as taken to Tahiti before Europeans reached that island in 1767. Byron found other relices on Takaroa in 1765.

Takapoto and Takaroa came under the influence of the Latter-day Saints in 1851. The village on Takaroa, called Teavaroa, has long attracted favourable comment for its lay-out and pleasant houses. Cultured pearls of excellent quality have been produced at the two atolls in recent years in experiments financed by FIDES.

Tatakoto (also written Takoto), about 145 km NW of Pukarua, is a bean-shaped atoll about 14.5 km long. Its northern side is well-planted with coconut trees. There is no entrance into the lagoon. The 1983 population was 184.

The Spanish explorers Boenechea and Andiay Varela discovered Tatakoto independently of each other on the same day in 1774. Boenechea called it San Narcisco. Duperrey in 1822 called it ile Daugier.

A Frenchman, Albert Javelot, became the atoll's chief about 1900 and held the post until he died in 1927. He planted the island with coconut trees and developed a copra industry.

Dr K. P. Emory of the Bishop Museum reported in 1931 that the people of Tatakoto were 'distinct in language, physical type and culture' and that they deserved a special study.

Tikehau. Tikehau Atoll, about 13 km westward of Rangiroa, is a roughly circular atoll about 26 km across. It consists of a chain of wooded islets. There is a pass into the lagoon for small vessels at the western extremity.

The atoll was discovered by Kotzebue in 1815 and named Krusenstern Island.

The following Tuamotu inhabited atolls and islands had the following populations at the 1983 census: Marokau, 81; Hikueru, 130; Fakahina, 86; Makatea, 43; Tepoto, 67; Vahitahi, 90; Raroia, 66; Vairaatea, 68; Taenga, 83; Raraka, 34; Nihiru, 30; Takume, 22; and Hereheretue, 22. Tepoto and Vairaatea have been described above under Napuka and Nukutavake respectively. Of the others. Marokau Hikueru, Makatea and Raroia merit brief comment.

Marokau and Hikueru, two centrally situated atolls about 25 km apart, have both yielded rich harvests of pearlshell over the years. Both were swamped by tidal waves during a hurricane in 1903. Nearly 100 people perished at Marokau and 379 lost their lives at Hikueru, including 261 islanders from Hao. Jack London, in his *South Sea Tales*, has left a vivid description of the hurricane, based on eye-witness accounts.

Makatea, an upraised coral island which rises to a height of about 100 m, was formerly noted for its phosphate. It lies about 192 km NE of Papeete. In 1962, when its phosphate was still being worked, the population stood at 2273. Only 43 remained in 1983. The phosphate was discovered in the first decade of the 20th century, and was worked until September 1966 by the Compagnie Francaise des Phosphates de l'Oceanie. During World War II, more than 200,000 tons were exported annually.

Raroia is the atoll where the *Kon-Tiki* raft was washed up in 1947 after its voyage from Peru. One of the raftsmen, Bengt Danielsson, later spent 18 months on the atoll and published two books about it.

Uninhabited Atolls. Many of the 37 Tuamotuan atolls that were uninhabited at the 1971 census have been planted with coconuts and are visited periodically by copra cutters. The 37 atolls are: Ahunui, Akiaki, Anuanuraro, Anuanurunga, Fangataufa, Haraiki, Hiti, Manuhangi, Maria, Marutea North, Marutea South, Maturei-Vavao, Morane, Motutunga, Mururoa, Nengonengo, Nukutipipi, Paraoa, Pinaki, Ravahere, Reitoru, Rekareka, Tahanea, Taiaro, Tauere, Tekokoto, Tematangi, Tenararo, Tenarunga, Tepoto, Tikei, Toau, Tuanake, Vahanga, and Vanavana.

Ten of the uninhabited atolls, all very

small, make up three groups — Duke of Gloucester (Anuanuraro, Anuanurunga and Nukutipipi); Raevski (Hiti, Tepoto and Tuanake); and Actaeon (Matuei-Vavao, Tenararo, Tenarunga and Vahanga).

MANGAREVA ISLANDS. The islands of Mangareva (formerly known as the Gambier Islands) are a volcanic cluster within a large lagoon at the SE corner of the Tuamotu Archipelago, some 1450 km SE of Tahiti. A small atoll, Temoe, lies about 40 km SE of the group.

The four largest islands in the group are Mangareva, Taravai, Aukena and Akamaru. There are several others that are little more than rocks. Mangareva, the largest island, is roughly like a reversed L in shape. It is about 6.5 km long with a maximum width of a little over 1.5 km. Mt Duff (440 m) is its highest point. Rikitea, the main settlement in the group and the seat of the local adminsitrator, is at the foot of Mt Duff. The total population in 1983 was 582.

Three passes into Mangareva's lagoon give access to an inner channel to Rikitea. Vessels up to 50 m in length and with a draught of up to 4 m can use the channel.

The reef surrounding the Mangarevan islands is several kilometres distant from them, so the islands are well pretected from the main force of the ocean. On the reef are many coral islets, seldom more than 100 m wide. One of these, Totegegie, is the site of an airstrip built in 1967–68 capable of handling international aircraft.

Mangareva has a mild climate except in mid-summer. Its annual average rainfall is more than 2000 mm, but as there are no permanent streams the islanders must rely on springs or cisterns for their water supplies. A high grass called aeho, which goes brown during the dry seasons, gives the islands a barren appearance at that time. But in the folds in the hills there is rich soil where fruits and vegetables thrive.

The earliest settlers of Mangareva appear to have been castaways from the Tuamotu Archipelago, the Marquesas and Rarotonga. The buccaneer Edward Davis may have been the first European to sight Temoe and Mangareva, in 1687. But the first positive report of them was from Captain James Wilson of the *Duff* in 1797. In 1826, Captain F. W. Beechey of HMS *Blossom* became the first to enter the lagoon and give an account of the inhabitants. In the next few years, pearlers from Valparaiso and Tahiti found their way to Mangareva.

A band of Catholic missionaries who arrived in the group in 1834 soon converted the islanders to Christianity. The most notable of these was Father Honore Laval who remained in the group until 1871. He was responsible for constructing the huge church of St Michel at Rikitea capable of seating 1200 people (which is still in good repair) as well as a convent for Mangarevan girls (now a roofless ruin) and a number of other buildings. The building work was on a scale hitherto unknown in that part of the world. Because the islanders were unaccustomed to the labour demanded, Mangareva's population fell rapidly from more than 2000 in 1840 to a few hundred. Complaints about Laval's activities finally led to him being removed to Tahiti. Ten years later, in 1881, France annexed Mangareva.

The atoll of Temoe, which has some interesting archaeological remains, has not been inhabited since the Catholic missionaries moved its people to Mangareva in 1838.

Peter Buck and K. P. Emory of the Bishop Museum carried out archaeological and ethnological work at Mangareva and Temoe in 1934. In that same year the Tahiti schooner *Pro Patria* was wrecked on Temoe with the American writer James Norman Hall on board. Hall wrote an account of his experiences in *Shipwreck* (London, 1935).

MARQUESAS ISLANDS. The Marquesas Islands, consisting of 10 volcanic islands and a few small islets, are situated between 7 deg 50 min and 10 deg 35 min S latitude and 138 deg 25 min and 140 deg 50 min W longitude. The total land area is estimated at slightly more than 1000 sq. km. The total population in 1983 was 6548.

The six largest islands are Hivaoa, Nukuhiva, Uapou, Uahuka, Tahuata and Fatuhiva. Hivaoa, the greatest in length, is about 40 km long and 16 km at its widest. All the volcanic islands are extremely rugged owing to erosion and faulting. There is generally a central mountain range from which ridges

fall abruptly to the coast, sometimes in pre-
cipices more than 300 m high. Between the
ridges are deep, fertile valleys. Flat land is
scarce, as there are no coastal plains. The
maximum elevation in the six largest islands
ranges from 850 to 1200 m.

The forbidding appearance of the coastline of most islands is redeemed by many
deep bays. On the western sides of the
islands, these are reasonably well sheltered.
A feature of the group is that although it lies
within the tropics, there is very little coral
and no barrier reefs. Even fringing reefs are
rare.

Although there is generally a high degree
of humidity, the climate of the Marquesas is
healthy and fairly pleasant. From April to
October the trade winds prevail from between
east and SE. Less regular winds blow from
between east and NNE during the rest of the
year when there are some hot, calm days.
There is little range in temperature throughout the year. The mean annual temperature
at Atuona, Hivaoa, is about 25°C. The annual rainfall varies greatly and is unevenly
distributed. In wet years, precipitation is
well over 2540 mm; in dry years, it is less
than half that figure. The heaviest rainfall is
on the windward sides of the islands, particularly the larger ones. On Hivaoa and
Nukuhiva, for example, the flora becomes
less luxuriant from east to west.

Lack of labour has retarded the economic
development of the Marquesas. Although
land is plentiful and many crops grow well,
copra is the only significant export. Vanilla,
cotton, sugarcane, taro, coffee, manioc,
oranges and other fruits are other agricultural items that could be developed. There is
also potential for the raising of cattle.

Taiohae on Nukuhiva is the administrative centre and port of entry for the group. It
is about 1200 km NE of Tahiti. The 1983
population was 1157.

The administrator has the title of 'chef
de circonscription' and receives instructions from the high commissioner in Tahiti.
The Marquesas Islands have two elected representatives in the Territorial Assembly of
French Polynesia.

It should be noted that no standardised
form has been adopted for the rendering of
place names in the Marquesas. Thus, the

main island of the group is variously written Nukuhiva, Nuku-Hiva, Nuku-hiva and
Nuku Hiva. In this year book the first form
has been used in all cases.

HISTORY OF MARQUESAS. Archaeologists believe that the Marquesas Islands
were inhabited by man at least as early as
300 AD, and probably several centuries
earlier. However, they are not yet unanimous
as to where the people came from. Pieces of
pottery and adze types have suggested Samoa
to some researchers; others think in terms of
Fiji or Tonga, while Thor Heyerdahl has
insisted that at least some of the ancient
Marquesans originated in South America.

In modern times, the Marquesans had no
migration traditions concerning their ancestors, and their culture seemed to be one of
long development with no recent innovations
from the outside world. Nevertheless, evidence from physical anthropology indicates
that the Marquesas were settled by people of
two distinct racial types and linguists have
established clearcut dialectical differences
between the northern and southern islands.
For example, the word for 'moon' was
'maama' in the north and 'mahina' in the
south — words that crop up elsewhere in
Polynesia, but usually in separate regions.

The Marquesans of the past were skilled
wood carvers and workers in stone. Their
stone work included images in human form,
house platforms, places for ceremonial use
like the 'marae' of eastern and central Polynesia and places of public assembly, with
dance floors. The house platforms, called
'paepae', are still to be found everywhere,
mute memorials of the great population that
once existed in the group. They are built of
large blocks of unhewn stone, cleverly fitted
together and making almost a solid mass.
The places of public assembly ranged down-
wards in size from about 60 m square. One
behind Taiohae is 90 m by 24 m.

The European discoverer of the Marquesas
Islands was the Spanish explorer Alvaro de
Mendana. In July 1595, on a voyage from
Peru in search of the supposed southern
continent, he came upon the islands of Fatu-
hiva, Motane, Tahuata and Hivaoa, which he
named collectively after the Marques de
Mendoza, viceroy of Peru.

No Europeans visited the group again until Captain Cook called there in 1774. Cook added tiny Fatuuku, north of Hivaoa, to the charts. But he missed seeing the seven other islands of the group still further north. Six of the northern islands were discovered by Joseph Ingraham, of the American trading ship *Hope* in April 1791. However, as no account of his discoveries was published until 1810, the credit for discovering them was long given to Etienne Marchand of the French trading ship *Solide*, who passed through the group in June 1791. Motuiti was, in fact, Marchand's only genuine discovery.

William Pascoe Crook, of the London Missionary Society, made a lone but unsuccessful attempt to convert the people of Tahuata after being landed there from the missionary ship *Duff* in 1797. He later went to Nukuhiva; but failing there, too, he returned to England in a whaler in 1799.

Fourteen years later, during the war between Great Britain and the United States, Nukuhiva became the first island in the Pacific to be annexed by the United States — an act that was never ratified. The act was performed by Captain David Porter of the US frigate *Essex*, who had been sent to the Pacific to harass and capture British shipping.

Having captured 12 such ships off the South American coast and in the Galapagos Islands, Porter sailed for the Marquesas. Arriving at Taiohae, Nukuhiva, in October 1813 with several of his prizes, Porter made friends with the local people through a tattooed Englishman, Wilson, who had lived there for several years. He then established a camp on shore to revictual his fleet, but was soon induced to assist the Taiohae tribes in a war against the neighbouring Haapas.

After the Haapas were subjugated, friction developed towards another tribe, the Taipi, and they, too, were conquered. Porter then decided to take possession of Nukuhiva for the United States. On 19 November 1813 he read a formal proclamation, and ran up the American flag to the accompaniment of a 17-gun salute. Then, having buried a copy of his proclamation on what he had renamed Madison's Island, Porter sailed away to continue his war against British shipping. However, Porter's career as a raider was soon terminated, for a few months later he was outmanoeuvred and outgunned by two British warships outside Valparaiso.

Meanwhile, Porter's activities at Nukuhiva had led to a new development in the history of the Marquesas. Soon after his departure a group of British prisoners-of-war, whom he had left in the care of some of his men, escaped from the island and sailed for Sydney in one of Porter's prizes. They reached Sydney in June 1814, bringing news that the Marquesas Islands contained valuable stands of sandalwood.

Within a few weeks, the first of several Sydney ships set out for the Marquesas in quest of this commodity, and for four or five years some profitable cargoes were obtained. Then, as the sandalwood trade petered out, the islands became an increasingly popular calling place for the American whalers which began visiting the Pacific in large numbers. The whalers generally remained in port for three or four weeks, and scenes of drunkenness and licentiousness were commonplace.

The LMS missionaries in Tahiti took a few native teachers to the Marquesas between 1825 and 1831. But these men accomplished little because of internal wars. A second attempt to establish a European mission was made in 1834 when the Revs George Stallworthy and John Rodgerson of the LMS settled on Tahuata. Stallworthy remained there until 1841, while other missionaries came and went. But again little headway was made. Meanwhile, in 1838, two French priests were landed at Tahuata from the French naval vessel *Reine Blanche*, whose commander, Captain Du Petit-Thouars, had been sent to the Pacific to investigate the potential for French commerce.

In 1842 Du Petit-Thouars paid a second visit to the Marquesas and annexed the group to provide a base for French warships, whalers and merchant vessels. After leaving a detachment of troops at Taiohae, Du Petit-Thouars sailed for Tahiti where he found a pretext to establish a French protectorate. This development made the Marquesas unnecessary to France as a base, and twice during the next 17 years the troops were withdrawn. However, France retained jurisdiction over the group and established a civil administration there in 1881.

In 1853, the American Board of Commissioners for Foreign Missions in Honolulu sent some Hawaiian Protestant missionaries to the group. Several such missionaries were still there well into this century. But the French Catholic mission, having the backing of the Administration, made the greatest headway. Meanwhile, the native population was dwindling alarmingly due to the introduction of foreign diseases, drunkenness, prostitution, murder, human sacrifice, cannibalism and warfare.

No reliable figures are available for the 18th century, but it had been estimated that the population stood at approximately 50,000 in Captain Porter's time. By 1842, according to an estimate by Du Petit-Thouars, it had fallen to about 20,000; and 30 years later it was only about 6200. The figures continued to decline in the 20th century and reached a record low of 2225 (including 131 non-natives) in 1926. Since then there has been a slow but steady recovery. In 1946, the figure was 2802; by the census of 1962, it had increased to 4838; and at the 1977 census, it stood at 5419.

During the American Civil War the growing of cotton was instituted in the Marquesas, and about 50 Chinese were taken to the group from Tahiti to work as labourers. The cotton venture was shortlived, but there has been a Chinese community there ever since. The most significant attempt to exploit the economic resources of the group in the past 100 years was made by a German firm, the Societe Commerciale de l'Oceanie, which flourished there from the last quarter of the 19th century until its property was sequestrated during World War I. The German company had several warehouses and maintained a fleet of schooners for the collection of produce, which was taken to Tahiti.

Since World War II, the Marquesas have been popular with yachtsmen sailing between California or Panama and Tahiti. The Marquesas have been accessible by air since 1970 when an airstrip was opened on Uahuka. A good deal of historical information will be found in Louis Rollin's *Les Iles marquises* (Paris, 1929), and Bengt Danielsson's *Forgotten Islands of the South Seas* (London, 1957). Greg Denning's *The Marquesas: Discourses on a Silent Land* (Melbourne, 1983) examines the tragic early period of Marquesan contact.

Details of the islands from south to north are:

Fatuhiva, the southernmost island of the group, is about 13 km long by 6.5 km wide. It is crescent shaped, with a rugged coastline. The highest peak is about 950 m above sea level. The island is the remains of two volcanoes, one of which grew up within the crater of the other. Eventually about half of each slipped into the sea. Most of the remains of the outer side of the larger cone face eastward, falling in serrated, razorbacked sections to the sea. The inner cone is separated from the outer by a moat-like depression. In this are two streams which drain into the sea on the island's western side — at Hanavave Bay in the north and Omoa Bay in the south.

Fatuhiva is the wettest of the Marquesas Islands. Both Hanavave and Omoa Bays have luxuriant vegetation. These two bays, and Uia on the east coast, are the sites of the only settlements. In 1983 the population was 407.

Mendana landed at Omoa Bay in 1595. He named the island Magdalena. The inhabitants were the last in the Marquesas to come completely under French control. They were expert wood carvers and tattoo artists.

The Norwegian ethnologist Thor Heyerdahl lived on Fatuhiva just before World War II. He has described his experiences in a book called *FatuHiva* (London, 1974).

Mohotani (or Motane) is a banana-shaped island, 8 km by 2.5 km, lying about 26 km south of Atuona on Hivaoa. It rises to a height of 520 m in its southern part, becoming gradually lower towards the north. The central part of the island contains a narrow plateau covered by a forest of large trees. The island is uninhabited. In 1971 it was declared a protected site by the French Administration because of the interest to science of its birds and vegetation. However, these are menaced to a considerable extent by sheep and wild cats (originally domesticated) which were introduced to the island last century.

Ancient 'paepae' and stone tools found on the island indicate that it was inhabited in pre-European times. When Mendana discovered it in 1595, he named it San Pedro. The Compagnie Coloniale de l'Oceanie held a lease to the island in 1927 and some of its workers then lived there.

Tahuata Island, formerly known as Santa

Cristina, is located south of Hivaoa and is separated from it by the Bordelais channel. It is about 13 km long, 7 km at its widest part, and 50 km in circumference. It is clearly the remains of a huge volcano. what is left of the crater forms the eastern part. The highest point of the crater rim is about 1000 m above sea level. Towards the south end of the island, the slope from the rim to the coast is very steep, with high cliffs at the ends of buttress-like spurs. In the north, the slope is more gradual. Porous rocks and a low rainfall make it necessary for the inhabitants (555 in 1983) to get their water from the springs near the coast.

Vaitahu Bay, formerly known as Resolution Bay, is the best of three anchorages on the west side. It was the most commonly used haven of the early European visitors to the Marquesas. Mendana, who called it Madre de Dios, anchored there in 1595. Cook, in HMS *Resolution*, was the next visitor in 1774. Both Cook and Mendana's pilot, Quiros, remarked on the light skins and splendid physique of the islanders.

In 1797, William Pascoe Crook, the first Protestant missionary to reside in the Marquesas, was landed at Vaitahu Bay from the *Duff*. Vaitahu was also the first station of the French Catholic preists who arrived in 1838; and it was there that the first French naval garrison was established after French annexation in 1842. The French lost 26 men in a battle with the islanders on 17 September 1842. The garrison was withdrawn in 1847.

A few decaying buildings, a ruined church and refectory are about all that remain of the European activity at Vaitahu in the first half of last century.

Hivaoa, the largest and most fertile of the Marquesas, is about 37 km long with a maximum width of 16 km. It is extremely rugged in its higher parts, with deep gullies alternating between razor-backed ridges. Mt Temetiu, about 1200 m, is the highest point on the island. Another lofty peak is Mt Heani, 1072 m, which towers behind Atuona, the chief settlement at the mouth of the picturesque Atuona Valley on the Bay of Traitors.

Like the other islands, Hivaoa has a forbidding, iron-bound coast. Along the south and south-west coast and along much of the north coast there are many cliffs from 150 to 300 m high. The best anchorages are on the northern side, but because of lack of supplies and the difficulty of communicating with Atuona they are little used.

Taahuku Bay, just eastward of Atuona, provides a sheltered anchorage for vessels up to almost 100 m in length and 6.75 m in draught. In fine weather, landings can be made near Point Feki. Atuona Bay affords an anchorage for local schooners. Cargo and passengers are carried ashore in whaleboats.

Atuona was formerly the seat of the French administration in the Marquesas. It is still the headquarters of the Catholic bishop and Hivaoa's largest populated centre. Among its facilities are a radio station, concrete wharf, hospital and Chinese stores. Other villages on the island are Taaoa (south coast) and Hanaiapa and Puamau (north coast). In 1983 the population of the island was 1522.

Traditions recorded in the 1920s claimed that some valleys on the southern coast of Hivaoa were the first places to be settled by Marquesans. The number and extent of archaeological remains found in all parts of the island indicate that it was once densely inhabited. The Puamau valley at the northeastern end of the island contains the best and largest stone images.

Mendana sighted Hivaoa in 1595 and called it Dominica, which the French converted to Dominique. When more or less continuous European contact with the Marquesas began in the 19th century, Hivaoa was generally avoided because of the islanders' reputation for aggression, and constant wars between two tribes called Pepane and Nuku. Roman Catholic missionaries who were stationed on the island after French annexation in 1842 made few converts for many years, and were constantly robbed and threatened with death.

Despite the internal strife, an American, John Hart, began growing cotton near Atuona in the 1870s, but the project failed within a few years. In 1880, following the murder of a European, the French sent three warships to the island in a determined effort to bring the islanders under control. Peace has reigned there since then.

Atuona became the seat of the Catholic vicariate of the Marquesas under Bishop Joseph Martin in 1893. The church was soon the island's biggest landowner. It was from the bishop that the French painter Paul Gauguin bought a plot of land when he settled on Atuona in 1901. Gauguin died at Atuona two years later and is buried there.

Atuona became the headquarters of the French administration in the Marquesas in 1904 because sandflies had made Taiohae, Nukuhiva, an unpleasant place to live. The headquarters were re-established at Taiohae in the 1940s.

Fatuhuku, called Hood Island by Cook, lies about 25 km north of Hivaoa. It is only about 2 km long and less than 1 km wide. Its highest elevation is about 360 m. The island is bounded on all sides by vertical cliffs or steep slopes and is difficult of access. It seems never to have been permanently inhabited, but fishermen from Hivaoa visited it in ancient times, as their descendants still do. Numerous frigate birds, boobies and terns nest on the island.

Uapou, the third largest and most heavily populated island in the group, lies 37 km south of Nukuhiva and about 88 km WNW of Hivaoa. It is about 14.5 km long from north to south and 13 km wide, with a central ridge running lengthwise which reaches a height of 1232 m. There are a number of secondary ridges. Among the ridges rises a series of spectacular pinnacles like towers and spires. Several small bays on the western side provide anchorages for vessels of schooner size and sometimes larger vessels. The eastern side is exposed to wind and sea.

The main settlements are at Hakahau on a small bay on the NE side and at Hakamai on the west. Hakahau Bay is the only possible anchorage on the eastern side. The total population in 1983 was 1791.

Just over 1000 of the present inhabitants live in the Hakahau district.

The remains of numerous stone fortifications, temples and house platforms are still to be found on Uapou. The European discoverer of the island was Ingraham in 1791. Marchand also sighted it in 1791. Old names for it are Marchand and Adams.

Polynesian missionaries from the Society Islands were taken to Uapou in 1826. But neither they nor later missionaries accomplished much. Even as late as the turn of the present century, the islanders were still said to be practising cannibals. About a quarter of the population was wiped out by smallpox in the 1860s.

Motuoa, a small flat-topped islet off the south coast, is the home of millions of sea birds. It is about 120 m high.

Uahuka, lying 37 km east of Nukuhiva, is the remains of a volcano of which the southern half has disappeared. It is about 14.5 km from east to west and about 8 km at its widest part. A semi-circular ridge, the rim of the old volcano, divides the island in two. Its greatest height is 550 m. This is much lower than in other islands. The rainfall is consequently smaller and the vegetation less luxuriant. The chief settlements, Vaipaee, Hane and Hokatu, are all on the south coast. In 1983 the population was 476.

The island was probably never of great importance in ancient times.

An airstrip was built on Uahuka in 1970. It can only be used by light planes, and is incapable of being lengthened because of mountains at both ends. Communication with Nukuhiva and other islands is by launch.

Uahuka has also been known as Ile Solide and Washington Island. These names date back to Marchand and Ingraham who both discovered the island in 1791.

Nukuhiva, lying about 112 km north of Hivaoa and 37 km west of Uahuka, is the principal island in the northern Marquesas. It is about 32 km long by 19 km wide. Like Fatuhiva it consists of an outer cone within which a later volcano built up. The southern side of both cones have now disappeared. The highest peaks are about 1200 m above sea level.

On the western side of the island is a plateau some 830 to 860 m high. The two principal valleys are Hakaui, narrow and canyon-like, and Taipi, which is much broader. There is a good anchorage in Controleur (Comptroller) Bay at the mouth of the Taipi valley. Another, smaller valley opens into Taiohae Bay, a port of call for overseas ships. On this bay is the village of Taiohae, the principal settlement on the island and seat of the administration for the Marquesas. Other settlements are at Hakaui, Taipivai and Hooumi on the south coast and at Hatiheu and Hakapa in the north. The total population in 1983 was 1797.

Copra is the chief export. Taiohae is the

port of entry for the Marquesas and foreign visitors must obtain permission from the Administration before landing at other islands. An airport was opened on Nukuhiva in December 1979, with an airstrip of 1500 m.

Nukuhiva, once heavily populated, was unknown to Europeans until the French navigator Etienne Marchand sighted it from a distance in 1791 and named it Baux Island. The first European to put into it was Lieut. Hergest of HMS *Daedalus* in 1792. The LMS missionary William Pascoe Crook, who had been landed on Tahuata in 1797, moved to Nukuhiva in 1798. One of the earliest beachcombers, Edward Robarts, was there for eight years from 1800. An account he wrote of the Marquesas was published in Canberra in 1974.

After two Russian explorers, Krusenstern and Langsdorff, visited Nukuhiva in 1804, the island ousted Tahuata as the most common calling place for ships passing through the group. The Porter affair of 1813–14 (see under History) put Nukuhiva firmly on the map. For several years thereafter, the island was visited for its sandalwood. In 1829, the US warship *Vincennes* called at Nukuhiva to try to assure a hospitable reception for all American ships, chiefly whalers, which were visiting the Marquesas in increasing numbers. Missionaries sent from Hawaii arrived in August 1833, but vacated the field to the LMS in the following year.

The French took formal possession of Nukuhiva in 1838 and three French Catholic priests established a mission station there in 1839. In 1842 the French occupied the island. The remains of Fort Collet, built at that time and named after the first French commandant, are still to be seen on a promontory at the eastern end of Taiohae Bay. The American novelist Herman Melville, then a seaman, deserted from the American whaler *Acushnet* in Controleur Bay during the French occupation and spent some time in Taipi valley. His experiences were the basis for his semi-fictional book *Typee*.

The French garrison was withdrawn from Taiohae in 1849, but re-established there soon afterwards. In 1862, two Peruvian slavers called at Nukuhiva and other islands in the group and kidnapped more than 30 men. Some of these were brought back from Peru in the following year afflicted with smallpox.

Although an attempt was made to isolate them in Taiohae, the disease soon spread and within six months a quarter of Nukuhiva's population had been wiped out.

A year or two later, the administration granted William Stewart of Tahiti 4000 hectares of the Taipi valley for the growing of cotton, and 31 Chinese were brought in as labourers. After Stewart's company went bankrupt in the early 1870s the Chinese dispersed and took to growing opium.

After the French annexation of Tahiti in 1881, a civil administration replaced the military regime in Taiohae. However, in 1904 the administration transferred its headquarters to Atuona on Hivaoa because sandflies in plague proportions had made life at Taiohae unbearable. The administration returned to Taiohae in the 1940s.

During World War I the German cruisers *Scharnhorst* and *Gneisenau*, which bombarded Papeete, used Controleur Bay as a base. Czech settlers made a shortlived attempt to form a colony in the interior of Nukuhiva between the wars.

The remains of numerous 'paepae' (stone foundations on which the ancient Marquesans built their houses), 'tohua' (dancing areas), 'akaua' (fortifications) and 'meae' (temples) are to be found on Nukuhiva, testimony to the large population that once flourished there.

Eiao, formerly called Masse Island, is 90 km NW of Nukuhiva and uninhabited. It is about 10 km long by 5 km at its greatest width. The highest point is about 600 m. Most of the eastern side is a precipitous slope. The only anchorage is at Vaituha on the NW side.

The island suffers periodic droughts and was probably not inhabited permanently in pre-European times. However, it was used for making stone adzes from a hard grey phonolite that occurs there. Numerous finished and unfinished adzes and other stone relics of ancient times have been found on the island.

Eiao was used as a convict settlement and place of exile until the turn of the century and was subsequently leased for some years to the Compagnie Navale de l'Oceanie. Sheep, cattle, pigs and donkeys introduced to the island in former times have since multiplied into thousands. In the mid-1960s, they were reported to have eaten almost every growing thing on the island and are dying out themselves from starvation. Their depredations have caused serious soil erosion. In 1972, Eiao was reported to have been investigated as a possible site for underground nuclear tests.

Hatutu, the most northerly of the Marquesas Islands, is separated from Eiao by a channel a few kilometres wide. It is about 6.5 km by 1.5 km. Its highest point is about 330 m above the sea. The island is uninhabited but is visited for its good fishing.

Thousands of ground doves of a species unknown elsewhere in the Pacific are to be found on the island. They are said to have a close resemblance to a South American species.

Motu One is the name of two small islets which are located about 18 km east-north-east of Hatutu, on a shoal on which the sea breaks heavily. The islets, known as Motu One or Ile de Sable, are from 1.8 m to 3 m high. Shoals are common in this vicinity and navigators are advised to give the area a wide berth.

FOR THE TOURIST. The Tahiti Tourist Board (Office de Developpement du Tourisme) is located on the Papeete waterfront, in the Fare Manihini. This office publishes detailed information on French Polynesia, besides facilitating tourist planning and promotion and sponsoring festivals, etc.

There are also various tour agencies, including Tahiti Nui Travel, Tahiti Tours, Tahiti Voyage, Kia Ora Tours, Pacific Travel, Tahiti Poroi, Voyagence Tahiti, Tahiti Holidays, Marama Tours and Manureva Tours.

Bengt Danielsson's *Tahiti — Circle Island Tour Guide* is both charming and vastly informative as an introduction for the visitor.
Entry formalities. All visitors must have a valid passport and a return ticket or a document of outward transportation, failing which they must make a deposit equivalent to the return air fare to their place of origin.

No visa is required by French nationals, citizens of Common Market and certain other countries on visits not exceeding three months, and for citizens of most other countries on visits not exceeding one month (from Australia, Canada, New Zealand, Singapore, US, etc.).

A foreigner may stay up to six months by having his visa renewed in Tahiti. He may be also granted a second six month period. For longer stays a permit must be obtained from the High Commissioner.

Persons entering the territory as tourists are not allowed to take employment, even of a temporary nature. A 'work permit' from the authorities is required for employment.

Smallpox vaccination is required of passengers arriving from infected areas, while those embarked in Fiji and Samoa must have all baggage except hand luggage fumigated at Faaa Airport. This process takes about two hours and is designed to prevent the entry of pests to the coconut industry.

Foreign currency may be taken into the territory and there is no difficulty in changing Australian banknotes, for example, in Tahiti, although the rate is usually slightly below that for travellers cheques. CFP may be reconverted on leaving and CFP notes may also be converted outside the country, e.g., at the French bank in Sydney.

Customs regulations permit a passenger to bring in 400 cigarettes and 1 litre of alcoholic beverages, duty free.
Airport tax. There is no airport tax.
Duty free facilities. There are several duty free shops in the Vaima Centre in Papeete. Luxury imports, including French specialities, are sold at the Faaa international airport and in Papeete boutiques. They include French wines, silks, perfumes and tableware. Many prices reflect high French living costs.

Most interesting local items are the colourful and versatile 'pareu' cloth and dresses, pearl jewellery, Marquesan wood carvings, shell necklaces, woven hats, baskets and mats.
Sightseeing. Tahiti is probably the most famous island in the South Pacific, and it will continue to attract large numbers of tourists who will, as always, be charmed by its spectacular scenery and its atmosphere. They will make 120 km round-island excursions, and short boat and air trips to nearby Moorea, and farther afield to Bora Bora. Some of the more popular sights are listed, but other more detailed information on Tahiti and other islands is to be found under Islands in Detail.
Point Venus. A drive 6.5 km eastward from Papeete brings you, after a short detour, to

the tomb of Pomare V, last king of Tahiti, who was interred there in 1891. Further on the road runs by Matavai Bay, the anchorage of the early explorers. About 10 km from Papeete, there is a side road to Point Venus where Cook observed the transit of Venus in 1769. There are monuments to Wallis, Bougainville and Cook, Tahiti's first three European visitors; and a monument to the pioneer LMS missionaries who arrived in the *Duff* in 1797. Two other points of interest are the lighthouse and the Museum of Discovery. The lighthouse, which is 25 m high, has been in service since 1868. Outside the museum entrance are two 'built-up' iron cannon of the 16th century which were recovered from Amanu Atoll, Tuamotu Archipelago, about the time the museum was opened.

Fautaua Gorge is quite close to Papeete and may be visited on foot or by car. The road leaves the east coast road about 2.5 km from the town and follows the Fautaua river. A short distance up the valley is Pierre Loti's Pool (where there is a monument to this celebrated French author). As the road dwindles in the gorge, it is necessary to go afoot, the distance from the fall being about 10 km. Tracks lead both to the top and the base of the fall, the latter being rough and entailing some walking in the stream, but there are good bathing pools. At the top of the fall is an old fort, a relic of the fighting between French and Tahitians in the 1840s.

Tautira. When making the round-the-island trip many visitors like to take the side trip up Tahiti-iti, the smaller of Tahiti's two parts, to Tautira. It was there that Robert Louis Stevenson lived for about three months in 1888 and wrote part of *The Master of Ballantrae*. Tautira was also the location of the first Catholic mission house in Tahiti — that of some Spanish priests who arrived in 1774. A sign now marks the spot. There is a country-style hotel.

Lake Vaihiria. Up in the mountains in the centre of Tahiti lies deep Lake Vaihiria, surrounded by tremendous peaks. Some wading in Vaihiria River is involved and the ascent to the lake is about 450 m altitude.

Papara is a district on the south coast that is important in Tahitian history. There, in ancient times, stood the great 'marae' (temple) of Mahaiatea, largest and most important

single relic of the pagan religion yet discovered in Polynesia. It has been partly restored.

Gauguin Museum and botanical gardens. The museum is in the Gardens at Papeari, about 50 km from Papeete. As Bengt Danielsson tells the story in his *Circle Guide*: 'The French authorities and settlers in Tahiti treated Gauguin harshly and contemptuously during his lifetime, and redress did not come until 1965, sixty-two years after his death, when this museum was opened. Even then, the idea did not originate in Tahiti but in France while the funds were provided not by the government but by the private Singer-Polignac Foundation whose wealth derives from the English sewing machine family and the princely French cognac dynasty. It would probably have been wiser to designate the resulting constructions as a memorial rather than a museum, since it contains few original pictures or authentic relics. Instead, it tells exactly as intended, with the help of documents, photographs, reproductions, furniture and objects of all sorts, in a visually pleasing manner, the story of Gauguin's life and artistic activities. The buildings, slightly reminiscent of Japanese temples, should be visited in a clockwise fashion, beginning with the one immediately to the left of the entrance.

As explanatory texts accompany all displays, only a few words will be said here about an outdoor exhibit: the seven foot high stone statue on the beach between the pointed tower and the last building to the right. This is a genuine work of primitive art of the sort that Gauguin appreciated so much, and it stood originally on a cult place on Raivavae, one of the six mountainous islands in the Austral group, four hundred miles south of Tahiti, which are part of French Polynesia. Since it weighs more than two tons it was only with the greatest efforts that it was brought on a schooner to Tahiti in 1933 to be conspicuously displayed in a new museum that never materialised.'

Golf course. An 18-hole golf course was opened at Atimaono, 40 km from Papeete on the east coast, in 1970.

In the 1860s, Atimaono was the site of a huge cotton plantation, for which Tahiti's first Chinese residents were imported as labourers.

Other things to do or see. Visit Papeete Municipal Market on a Sunday morning early, when the local people do their shopping; water-skiing; big-game fishing; glass-bottom boat excursions to the reefs; scuba-diving; floor shows in the main hotels; the Olympic swimming pool on the harbour front at Tipaerui; the Ethnographic Museum of Tahiti and its Islands, 15 km from Papeete at Punaauia.

Lookouts. A magnificent view of the coast and town can be seen from Fare Rau Ape, about 550 m above sea level. It is 1.5 km out of Papeete, east bound and 7 km up a steep, narrow road into the mountains. A country style restaurant perches on the side of the mountain.

Other high view points are at Pamatai, reached by a few kilometres of road inland from a point just on the Papeete side of Faaa airport, and from the Taravao Plateau.

Bastille Day fete. Bastille Day (14 July) is extended in Papeete to a week of festivities — and these are sometimes prolonged over the second weekend following.

Dancing and other competitions between district teams are held; side-shows and stalls are erected along the Papeete waterfront and few Tahitians seem to sleep during the entire period of the festival.

Participants test their strength and skills in contests such as canoe-racing in Papeete harbour, races between individuals carrying loads of fruit, javelin-throwing, weaving coconut palm fronds, preparing copra, and canoe-building.

Then there is the big parade on 14 July itself.

Restaurants. Local fruits and seafoods, besides imports, contribute to the interesting variety of French, Chinese and Polynesian cuisine. Prices in restaurants are high and reflect the inflated economy.

Convention facilities. Papeete Cultural Centre is situated on the Papeete waterfront, within walking distance of the centre of the city. The Cultural Centre offers an 865-seat theatre with sound and projection equipment as well as simultaneous translation facilities. An additional auditorium has 120 seats. Accommodation for visiting sports teams or students is provided in 22 rooms.

There is also the Convention Hall of the Territorial Assembly. This is situated in the heart of Papeete, opposite the Post Office. The hall has 463 seats, sound and projection equipment and simultaneous translation facilities. Post Office, telephone and telex installations are available on request.

The Museum of Tahiti and its Islands, 15 km from Papeete at Punaauia, has an airconditioned conference room seating 208 persons with writing table, light and ashtray; podium seats eight people; four lecturer's microphones and 26 mobile ones; two tape recorders in sound cabin; 16 mm movie projector, slide projector.

ACCOMMODATION. Accommodations are listed here alphabetically by island for easy location. Most of those on the outer islands are built along traditional Polynesian lines — small, free standing units, self-contained and sometimes of local materials. Many stand out over the lagoons with the blue waters lapping beneath them. Prices are very high compared to other Pacific countries. A seven per cent government tax is applicable to rates.

The high prices of accommodations, drinks and meals make credit cards ideal travelling companions when holidaying in French Polynesia. In 1987 the tourist industry made some attempts to lower these prices to attract more people. This list includes most of the large hotels and many smaller ones. There are also quite a number of small pensions, which have several rooms with shared facilities. These can be good value and the Tahiti tourist offices in Papeete can supply a list if required.

TAHITI

Climat Punaauia: 40 rooms, some aircon, tennis, pool, restaurant, bar, major credit cards. PO Box 576, Papeete.
Tel.: (689) 43 0881, Telex 339 FP.

Ibis Papeete: 72 rooms, aircon, restaurant, bar, major credit cards. BP 6008, Faaa.
Tel.: (689) 42 8042, Telex 214 FP.

Maeva: 230 rooms, aircon, restaurant, bar, pool, water sports, tennis. PO Box 6008, Papeete. Tel.: (689) 42 8042,
Telex 214 FP.

Matavai: 142 rooms, aircon, restaurant, bar, pool, squash courts, major credit cards. PO Box 32, Papeete. Tel.: 42 6129, Telex 222 FP.

Pacific: 44 rooms, central location.

PO Box 111, Papeete. Tel.: (689) 43 7282.
Princesse Heiata: 36 rooms. PO Box 5003,
Papeete. Tel.: 28 105.
Puunui: 84 units, kitchen facilities, pool,
tennis, water sports. BP 7016, Taravao.
Tel.: (689) 57 1981, Telex 410 FP.
Royal Papeete: 85 rooms, central location,
major credit cards. PO Box 919, Papeete.
Tel.: (689) 42 0129, Telex 348 FP.
Royal Tahitian: 45 rooms, aircon,
restaurant, bar, water sports, major credit
cards. BP 5001, Pirae.
Tel.: (689) 42 8113, Telex 406 FP.
Tahara'a: 200 rooms, aircon, restaurant,
bar, tennis, pool, spectacular cliff
location, shops, major credit cards.
BP 1015, Papeete. Tel.: (689) 48 1122,
Telex 225 FP.
Tahiti: 106 rooms, pool, restaurants, bar,
water sports, major credit cards.
PO Box 416, Papeete. Tel.: (689) 42 9550,
Telex 406 FP.
Tahiti Beachcomber: 200 rooms,
restaurant, bar, shops, tennis, water
sports, major credit cards. BP 6014,
Papeete. Tel.: (689) 42 5110,
Telex 276 FP.
Te Puna Bel Air: 76 rooms, restaurant,
some aircon, bar, pool, tennis, water
sports, major credit cards. BP 6634, Faaa.
Tel.: (689) 42 0900, Telex 354 FP.

MOOREA
Bali Hai: 63 units, restaurant, bar, water
sports, major credit cards. BP 26,
Moorea. Tel.: (689) 56 1359,
Telex 331 FP.
Captain Cook Beach: 43 rooms,
restaurant, bar, water sports, major credit
cards. BP 1006, Papetoai.
Tel.: (689) 56 1060, Telex 211 FP.
Climat Moorea: 80 rooms, some with
kitchen facilities, water sports, some
aircon, restaurant, bar, pool, major credit
cards. PO Box 576, Papeete.
Tel.: (689) 43 0881, Telex 339 FP.
Club Mediterranee: all inclusive tariff,
water sports, restaurant, bar, major credit
cards. Moorea Island. Tel.: (689) 56 1151,
Telex 256 FP.
Hibiscus: 29 rooms, restaurant, supply
own linen. PO Box 31, Moorea.
Tel.: 6 1220.
Ibis Kaveka Village: 100 rooms,

restaurant, bar, pool, water sports, major
credit cards. BP 6008, Faaa.
Tel.: (689) 42 8042, Telex 214 FP.
Kia Ora: 80 units, restaurant, bar, water
sports, major credit cards. PO Box 706,
Papeete. Tel.: (689) 56 1290,
Telex 390 FP.
Moorea Lagoon: 45 units, water sports,
bar, restaurant, some units with kitchen
facilities, major credit cards. BP 11,
Moorea. Tel.: (689) 56 1155,
Telex 327 FP.
Moorea Village: 50 rooms, pool, bar,
restaurant, some units with kitchen
facilities, water sports. BP 1008, Haapiti.
Tel.: (689) 56 1002.
Tipaniers: 28 units, some with kitchen
facilities, restaurant, bar, water sports,
major credit cards. BP 1002, Moorea.
Tel.: (689) 56 1267.
Club Bali Hai: restaurant, bar, water
sports, associated with Bali Hai Hotel,
major credit cards. BP 26, Moorea.
Tel.: (689) 56 1359, Telex 331 FP.
Tiahura: 12 units, some kitchen facilities,
pool. BP 1068, Moorea.
Tel.: (689) 56 1545.

BORA BORA
Bora Bora Hotel: 85 units, restaurant,
watersports, bar, major credit cards.
Nunue, Bora Bora. Tel.: (689) 48 1206,
Telex 225 FP.
Climat Bora Bora: 36 rooms, restaurant,
bar, watersports, major credit cards. PO
Box 576, Papeete. Tel.: (689) 43 0881,
Telex 339 FP.
Club Mediterranee Noa Noa: all inclusive
tariff. PO Box 38, Nunue. Tel.: 2 9699.
Marara: 64 units, restaurant, water sports,
bar, tennis, shop, major credit cards. BP 6,
Bora Bora. Tel.: (689) 67 7046,
Telex 326 FP.
Marina: 30 units, restaurant, bar,
watersports, major credit cards.
PO Box 1366, Papeete.
Tel.: (689) 42 9501, Telex 399 FP.
Matira: 28 units, some with kitchen
facilities, restaurant, bar. PO Box 31,
Viatape. Tel.: 67 051.

TETIAROA
Tetiaroa Village: built by actor Marlon
Brando, tariff all inclusive. PO Box 2418,
Papeete. Tel.: (689) 26 302.

HUAHINE

Bali Hai Huahine: 44 units, water sports, restaurant, bar, major credit cards. BP 26, Moorea. Tel.: (689) 61 359, Telex 331 FP.
Bellevue Huahine: c/-Post Office, Huahine. Tel.: 68 8276.
Huahine Beach: 11 rooms, restaurant, bar. c/- Post Office, Huahine. Tel.: 68 1846.

RAIATEA

Bali Hai Raiatea: 36 rooms, restaurant, bar, water sports, major credit cards. BP 26, Moorea. Tel.: (689) 56 1359, Telex 331 FP.
Raiatea Village: 12 units, kitchen facilities. PO Box 282, Uturoa. Tel.: 66 3162.

RANGIROA

Kia Ora Rangiroa: 30 units, water sports, restaurant, bar, major credit cards. PO Box 706, Papeete. Tel.: (689) 42 8672, Telex 306 FP.
La Bouteille a la Mer: 11 units, restaurant, bar, water sports, c/- Post Office, Rangiroa. Tel.: 1 5334.
Village Sans Souci: 15 units, no electricity, restaurant, bar, water sports. c/- Post Office, Avatoru.
Rangiroa Village: 10 bungalows, restaurant, bar. PO Box 605, Papeete. Tel.: (689) 42 9385.

MANIHI

Kaina Village: 15 units, restaurant, bar, water sports. c/- Post Office, Manihi. Tel.: (689) 42 7553.

RURUTU

Rurutu Village: 16 units, restaurant, bar, water sports. PO Box 718, Papeete. Tel.: (689) 42 6803.

Galapagos

These islands straddle the Equator about 970 km west of the coast of Ecuador. They lie between 1 deg 30 min N and 1 deg S latitude, and at 90 deg 30 min W longitude. The group is of volcanic origin. It takes its name from the Spanish word for the numerous huge tortoises originally found there, but now reduced to comparatively few in the highlands of some of the islands. There are 13 large islands, six smaller ones and 42 rocky outcrops. Most of them have a Spanish and an English name. The land area is about 7700 sq. km.

Tourism provides most of the jobs in the Galapagos. The islands are a province of Ecuador, divided into three cantons, and administered by a civilian governor. The capital is Puerto Baquerizo (formerly Puerto

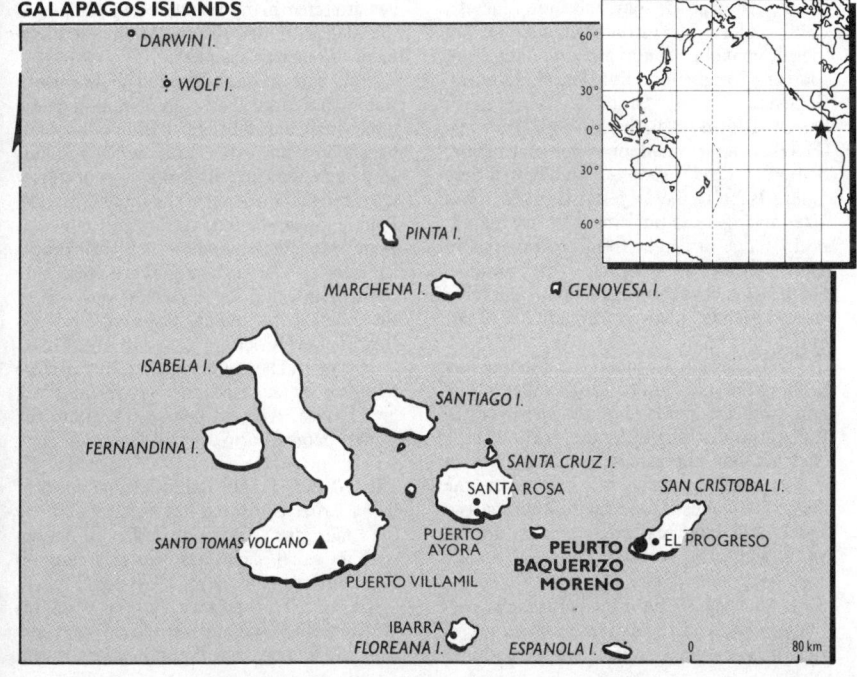

GALAPAGOS ISLANDS

Chico) on San Cristobal (Chatham Island). Ecuadorean currency, the sucre, is used, and other Ecuadorean usages prevail.

POPULATION. The 1986 estimate of the population totalled 6000. The 1982 census had accounted for 7000. The people are mainly Ecuadoreans. Since 1959, Ecuadorean policy has limited the number of permanent non-Ecuadorean residents, but this appears to have been relaxed in the last few years. At the end of 1978 the number of foreign settlers was 300, many of them from the US. There is a closely-knit colony of German settlers on Santa Cruz. They left Germany for Galapagos to escape the hazards of life in wartorn Europe. About half the population lives at Puerto Baquerizo and there are sizeable settlements at Progreso in the hills about five km from Puerto Baquerizo (San Cristobal) and at Puerto Ayora and Bella Vista on Santa Cruz. Spanish is the official language and most of the people are Roman Catholics.

THE LAND. The principal islands from west to east are: Fernandina (Narborough); Isabela (Albemarle); Pinta (Abingdon); Marchena; Santiago or San Salvador (James); Rabida (Jervis); Pinzon (Duncan); Baltra (South Seymour); Santa Cruz (Indefatigable); Floreana, originally Santa Maria (Charles); Genovesa (Tower); Santa Fe (Barrington); San Cristobal (Chatham) and Espanola (Hood). Other small ones are Bartolome, Sombrero Chino, Daphne and North Seymour. Isabela, the largest island, is about 100 km long by 25 km broad. Its five highest peaks range in height from 1690 metres to 1175 metres. Fernandina, San Salvador, Santa Cruz and San Cristobal, the next largest islands, range from eight to 20 sq. km.

The Galapagos are along the dividing line between the cold Peruvian or Humboldt Current from the south, and the warm North Equatorial Current from the north. These currents here curve to flow side by side in a west-north-westerly direction, but the borderline varies. Often the southern coasts and islands have sea-water temperatures of 15°C, while the northern coasts of islands have temperatures of 27°C.

Soil. The soil of the principal islands, particularly of San Cristobal and Santa Cruz, is rich and supports flourishing agricultural and horticultural industries. Production has increased over the years, both in dairy and beef cattle, and there are good yields of fruit, mainly oranges, avocados and pineapples. The Progreso area of San Cristobal has an increasing number of small agricultural holdings, some of which are coffee plantations.

Climate. The climate of the islands is mainly influenced by the prevailing cold, dry, south-east wind which brings drought conditions, sometimes for a year or more. What little rain there is falls mainly on the higher levels of the larger islands where the annual average is estimated at about 1219 mm, with wide variations. Most rainfall is in the form of thundershowers between November and March. At other times some fog and drizzle is experienced at lower levels. Fresh water is very scarce on all islands and absent on many, and fertile land is all at higher levels on the weather or south-east sides of the main islands.

Flora and fauna. Isolation combined with a tropical location in the plankton-rich Humboldt Current have resulted in the evolution of a unique variety of flora and fauna. This has attracted many scientific expeditions to the islands and has resulted in the establishment of research facilities.

Seals and sea-lions abound in the warm waters and large sharks are common as are tuna, crabs and lobsters. Pelicans, boobies, frigate birds and others nest on many islands while penguins and albatrosses occur in isolated colonies on some of the smaller islands. Flamingos can be seen on Santiago, Rabida, Isabella and Floreana where they live in brackish lagoons. Darwin's finches are present on most islands and these species were one of the phenomena which inspired Darwin's theory of evolution.

Marine and land iguanas are found in large numbers on most islands, as are the small lava lizards. And, of course, there are the world's largest tortoises (see History).

TRANSPORT. On Baltra Island, north of Santa Cruz, is a three km airstrip built by the Americans during World War II. An airstrip for small planes has been in service on San Cristobal since early 1974.

TAME (Transporters Aereos Militares Ecuatorianos) operates one flight daily except on Sundays. The flight is expensive and usually heavily booked so it is necessary to confirm and reconfirm any reservation. It is possible to get to Galapagos by sea either on a cruise ship or a navy ship which operates twice monthly around the island group.

HISTORY. The Galapagos islands were uninhabited when Europeans first visited them in the 16th century. However, pieces of pottery found there in 1953 by a team of investigators led by Thor Heyerdahl indicate that American Indian fishermen visited the islands before the Spanish conquest of South America. The fishermen were probably from Ecuador and northern Peru. They probably used rafts of the type in use off the Ecuadorean and Peruvian coasts until the end of the 19th century. The evidence of their visits to the Galapagos has been seen as lending weight to the theory that American Indians reached Polynesia in prehistoric times.

The European discoverer of the Galapagos was Tomas de Berlanga, third bishop of Panama. He landed in the group in 1535 after having been carried there by strong currents while sailing from Panama to Peru. The islands were referred to as the Galapagos on a map published by Ortelius in 1570. But no one visited them much until British buccaneers began using them as hide-outs towards the end of the 17th century. The English names for the islands date from that period.

The buccaneer William Dampier who visited the group in 1684 left one of the earliest accounts of the iguanas and huge tortoises that could then be counted in thousands. The buccaneers made good use of the tortoises as food, as did the whalers and other visitors of the 19th century. Captain David Porter, of the US frigate *Essex*, for example, took on about 500 of the creatures at San Salvador (James Island) in 1813.

In 1832, General Jose Villamil took possession of the Galapagos for Ecuador. He used Floreana (Charles Island) as a colony for political prisoners, military delinquents and criminals sent from Ecuador. The colonists farmed, fished and caught tortoises to supply produce to visiting whalers. When HMS *Beagle* visited the islands in 1835, the naturalist Charles Darwin recorded that there were between 200 and 300 colonists. Darwin's observations on the unique bird and animal life of the Galapagos provided important data in his later studies on evolution.

By 1849 only 25 settlers remained in the group, as the tortoises had been wiped out on Floreana and whalers had stopped calling. However, various other attempts at colonisation were made over the next 80 years. One of the most successful was made on San Cristobal where the Cobos family established extensive sugar cane, fruit and vegetable plantations at Progreso. In 1914, Progreso had a population of 300.

Another successful settlement, first established on Floreana in 1893 and transferred to Isabela four years later, exported sulphur and plantation produce. In 1924 about 200 Norwegians settled on Santa Cruz and Floreana. But their settlement was unsuccessful.

In the 1930s an Austrian baroness, Eloise Bosquet de Wagner Wehrborn, took up residence on Floreana with two German male companions. The baroness set herself up as 'empress' of the island, bullying a few other European settlers already there and making free use of a pistol to keep off new arrivals. She and one of her male companions were apparently murdered in March 1934 by her second companion, Alfred Rudolph Lorenz. Lorenz then fled the island in a launch which was later found wrecked on Marchena (Bindloe) Island. Lorenz and the launch owner apparently died of thirst after reaching shore.

A detailed account of this bizarre affair appeared in a book published in 1983. Written by John Treherne, a Cambridge University zoologist, *The Galapagos Affair*, tells the story not only of the 'baroness', but of the other eccentric settlers, two of whom, Dr Friedrich Ritter and his lover, Dore Strauch, proudly told everyone that they shared the same set of stainless steel dentures.

During World War II, the US Army and Navy had a base on Baltra Island. Water was brought from nearby Santa Cruz (Indefatigable) Island. In 1959, exactly a century after the appearance of Darwin's *The Origin of Species*, plans were laid for the establishment of the Charles Darwin Research Station at Academy Bay on Santa Cruz. The station was built with international help. It was opened officially in 1964, and has quarters and facilities for about 20 to 30 scientists. Among its many projects is one to raise the rarer species of tortoise under control conditions with a view to restocking individual islands. The station is also concerned with controlling and exterminating predatory animals.

Originally there were 15 sub-species of tortoise on the islands of the group; of these, four are now extinct; four are seriously threatened with extinction; four are in reasonable numbers although much reduced from former times; and two are still numerous. The 15th sub-species is regarded as a mystery as only one animal has been seen in modern times. This was in 1906 on Fernandina (Narborough) where tortoises had not been known previously. Many searches have since been made without result although it is considered possible, if not probable, that some may survive on the remote southern slope of the island's volcano. This island is uninhabited by man or animal.

In 1968, the Parque Nacional de Galapagos (Galapagos National Park) was inaugurated with help and advice from the Darwin station. In 1977, the DRS enlarged its facilities and began active marine studies.

A marine national park is being developed and plans are complete for a Marine Science Centre on Santa Cruz. At the beginning of 1979, 80 people were working at the national park and 20 more were permanently employed at the Charles Darwin Station. The Ecuadorean Government continues to assist the work with generous funding, following its grant of nearly $US150,000 in 1977 to the Charles Darwin Station, and donations are being received from the National Park as well as from individuals and organisations all over the world.

Visitors to the park are asked to observe strict rules of behaviour to ensure the survival of the unique flora and fauna which includes giant cacti, masked boobies, seals and giant tortoises. Much of this is seriously threatened by feral pigs, dogs, cats, rats, donkeys, cattle and exotic plants that have been introduced since the 17th century. There is a $US30 entrance fee into the park.

ISLANDS IN DETAIL. The three cantons forming the Province of Galapagos are Isabela, San Cristobal and Santa Cruz. Each includes the islands named and several others. Isabela, whose chief settlement is Villamil, includes the islands of Fernandina. Charles

Darwin and Teodoro Wolf. San Cristobal, site of the capital, Puerto Baquerizo (or, in full, Puerto Baquerizo Moreno), takes in the islands of Santa Maria, Espanola. Genovesa and Santa Fe. Santa Cruz, of which Puerto Ayora is the chief centre, has the islands of Baltra, Marchena, Pita, Pinzon, Rabida and Santiago under its jurisdiction.

Puerto Baquerizo, on San Cristobal, is the residence of the governor. It is the port of entry for the group and the site of naval installations. It has schools, a Catholic Church, cinema, hospital, water supply, electricity and radio services. There is a direct telephone link with Guayaquil and Quito. A wharf is available for small craft. A road links Puerto Baquerizo with Progreso. Originally rough, it has been considerably improved in recent years.

On Santa Cruz there has been considerable development since 1960. The island now has a hospital, schools, telecommunications, post office, restaurants, hotels, cinema and other services on a par with Puerto Baquerizo. The branch office of TAME airlines is located at Puerto Ayora. Aircraft arriving from the South American mainland land at Baltra Island rather than the capital, Puerto Baquerizo on San Cristobal Island. A road, completed in 1975, crosses the island from Academy Bay to Baltra Channel and provides a link with the airfield on Baltra Island. The cross-island trip takes one and a half hours.

Isabela Island has experienced an increase in volcanic activity in recent years with one eruption a year in 1963, 1968, 1973, two in 1979, the last being the August 1982. Fernandina had eruptions in 1968 and 1973.

FOR THE TOURIST. The Galapagos Islands have increased in popularity with the tourist in the last few years and several new hotels have greatly improved tour facilities and now attract increasing numbers of tourists. In 1987 an estimated 20,000 tourists viewed the fantastic fauna of the Galapagos. Of the main islands Santa Cruz is the most frequently visited. The town of Puerto Ayora has a range of accommodations and facilities for tourists but it is advisable to make prior arrangements before making the trip. It is possible to cruise around the islands aboard small, well-appointed vessels which take about 90 passengers. Onboard lectures are given and expert guides escort parties ashore. Enquiries can be made at travel agents or directly to the agents in Ecuador listed under 'Further Information'. Apart from the animal life onshore, the marine life is also excellent and every visitor should be prepared to do some snorkelling. It is advisable to take at least a mask and snorkel in your luggage and not rely on obtaining a set on site.

At Puerto Ayora it is possible for small groups to hire converted fishing boats in which they may cruise around the islands. Costs vary between boats.

The Galapagos are a favourite calling place for American and European cruising yachtspeople, who frequently make it their first call after the Panama Canal and before crossing the Pacific. Tagus Cove, Isabela Island, is considered the best anchorage for yachts, but there are many others. No vessel can visit Galapagos without first obtaining a permit from the Direction De Marina Mercante (Director of Merchant Marine).

Post Office Bay, on the north coast of Floreana (Charles or Santa Maria), was a famous crossroads in the old whaling days. An ancient barrel in which whalers put letters to be picked up later by homeward-bound vessels is still used by cruising yachtsmen. Camping is actively discouraged on each island.

Information on each island is available from the National Park Headquarters at Puerto Ayora. Also provided is a copy of the regulations which visitors are asked to observe so that the unique heritage of the islands may be preserved.

Further information. This may be obtained from: Educadorean Department of Tourism, Direction Nacional de Turismo, Reina Victoria 514 y Roca, Quito, Ecuador. Tel. Quito 239 044. TAME Airlines are at Avenida 10 de Agosto 239, Quito, Eucador. Tel. 510 211.

For information on Galapagos cruises and accommodation: Metropolitan Touring, Avenida Amazonas 239, Quito, Ecuador. Tel. 524 400, Telex 2482 Metour ed., or Adventure Associates, 5925 Maple, Suite 116, Dallas, Texas 75235 USA.

ACCOMMODATION. Accommodations are listed more or less in order of expense, from highest to lowest. This, however, is no indication of quality. Further information can be obtained from Lonely Planet's *Ecuador and the Galapagos Islands — a travel survival kit.*

Hotel Galapagos: 14 rooms with bathroom and most have an ocean view. Restaurant and bar. Puerto Ayora.

Hotel Delfin: 16 rooms with bathroom, beach facilities, restaurant. Puerto Ayora.

Lobo del Mar Hotel: basic accommodations, some rooms with private shower. Puerto Ayora.

Palmeras Hotel: some rooms with private bath. Puerto Ayora.

Salinas Hotel: some rooms with private bath. Puerto Ayora.

Darwin Hotel: some rooms with private bath. Puerto Ayora on outskirts.

Santa Cruz: some rooms with private bath. Puerto Ayora on outskirts.

Elizabeth Hotel: some rooms with private bath. Puerto Ayora.

Colon Hotel: some rooms with private bath. Puerto Ayora.

Hotel Ninfas: all rooms with private baths, restaurant. Puerto Ayora.

Hotel Castro: all rooms with private baths, restaurant. Puerto Ayora.

Hotel Sol y Mar: some rooms with private baths and ocean views, restaurant.

Pension Gloria: 6 rooms, some with private bath. Pelican Bay, Puerto Ayora.

Hotel Angermeyer: some rooms with private bath. Pelican Bay, Puerto Ayora.

Guadalupe

Guadalupe is a mountainous island of volcanic origin lying at 29 deg 11 min N latitude and 118 deg 17 min W longitude 380 km west of the American continent at Baha California. It is a possession of Mexico.

The island is 264 sq. km in area. It rises to 1220 m at its northern end, where there are some fertile valleys, and is 33 km long and 12 km wide.

The southern part of the island is barren, and the cliffs on the western side are almost perpendicular. The eastern side has a more gentle slope. The island is edged with cliffs of lava and is extremely rugged. The best anchorage is at Melpomene Cove at the southern end, where the water is about 18 m deep. There is also a good landing place at the western end of the cove.

The island is uninhabited, except for a small garrison maintained by the Mexican Government.

The island is noted for the Guadalupe seal, which is protected by Mexican law. Guadalupe is treated as a nature reserve, and unauthorised landing is prohibited.

Mean annual precipitation on Guadalupe is 290 mm. Rain falls mainly in the winter. Mean annual temperature range is 14–21°C.

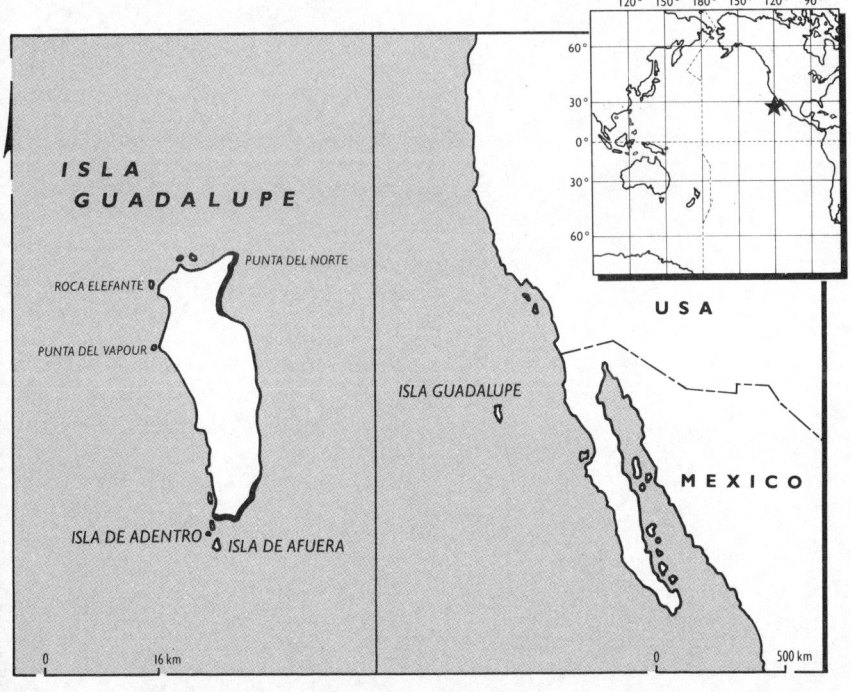

Guam

Guam, a 549 sq. km island at the southern extremity of the Mariana archipelago, is an unincorporated territory of the USA. Its location is 13 deg 26 min N latitude and 144 deg 43 mm E longitude. Local time is 10 hours ahead of GMT.

The capital is Agana which is about 2170 km south of Tokyo and 5300 km west of Honolulu. The population estimate in 1987 was 118,000.

The official flag and national anthem are those of the US. The great seal of Guam depicts a sailboat near a coconut palm on the shore. This seal is the central design of the Guam territorial flag (adopted in 1917). The flag is a deep blue with a red border. Currency is the US dollar.

Official holidays include: New Year's Day, Martin Luther King's Birthday, Guam Discovery Day (first Monday in March) Good

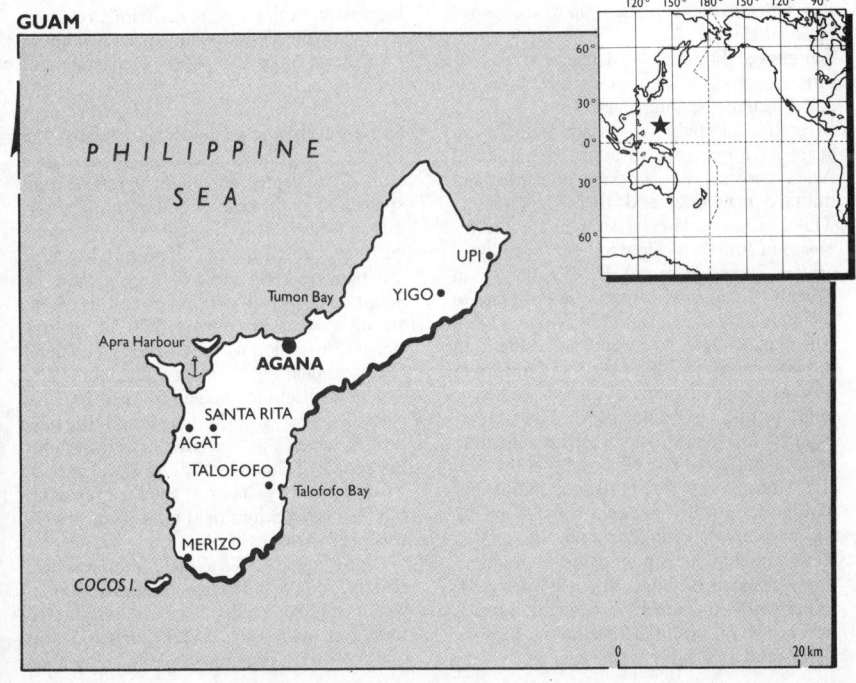

GUAM

PHILIPPINE SEA

UPI

Tumon Bay

YIGO

Apra Harbour

AGANA

SANTA RITA

AGAT

TALOFOFO

Talofofo Bay

MERIZO

COCOS I.

0   20 km

Friday, Memorial Day, 4 July, 21 July (Liberation Day), Thanksgiving, and Christmas Day.

THE PEOPLE. Guam's population has varied over recent years due to influxes of military personnel and dependants, but it was 118,000 in 1987. Of this figure, about 23,355 were military personnel and dependants or US Defence Dept. employees and dependants. Because of the high fertility rate, the population is a young one. About 35 per cent of population is under 15, compared with six per cent over 65. Average family size is five persons. Guam's ethnic composition can best be described as cosmopolitan. Approximately 42 per cent of the people trace their ancestry to the island's natives, the Chamorros, and 21 per cent to the Philippines. The Caucasian population is about 24 per cent. Other areas of cultural influence are Japan, Korea, China, Mexico, Polynesia and Micronesia.

Nationality. Guam has been a territory of the US since 1898. Full US citizenship was granted in 1950 to persons born in Guam. Residents do not have the right to vote in US national elections.

Language. English and Chamorro are the official languages. Many stores have Japanese and Tagalog-speaking clerks.

Migration. Population variations in recent years have occurred through the intake of Asian construction workers and transient military personnel and their dependants. This has particularly accounted for the increase in Filipinos. Slow but continuing migration comes from the US mainland and Hawaii. Chamorros continue to emigrate to the mainland and in the 1980 census 32,000 Guamanians were recorded as resident in the US, nearly 18,000 of them in California. Studies show that many of those classified as migrants may be Chamorros who have retired from mainland occupations and are returning to settle in Guam. It is expected that this will affect the age structure of the population and within the next decade the process of ageing will become increasingly significant.

Religion. The local population is predominantly Roman Catholic, about 93 per cent. Other faiths include Episcopalian, Baptist, Seventh-day Adventist, Mormon, Jewish, Baha'i and Jehovah's Witnesses.

Lifestyle. The Guamanian people developed a lifestyle influenced especially by Spanish Catholic colonialism, giving closer ties to the Filipino or Mexican than the Micronesians further east. Today, however, American customs are predominant. For example, the 'ngingi' or kissing of an elder's hand to show respect is inevitably being replaced with either a handshake or by both the 'ngingi' and a kiss on the cheek.

Islanders live in a variety of European-style houses. Social life centres on the family, the church, weddings, christenings, wakes, and politics, a large extended family being an important factor. Fiestas honouring the patron saint of each village are held at least once each year. The large and permanent proportion of military personnel and dependants on the island has added the atmosphere of mainland US to the local lifestyle.

GOVERNMENT. Guam is an unincorporated territory, administered under the Organic Act of Guam 1950, as amended. The Government consists of an executive, a judicial and a legislative branch, This provides legislative local autonomy. Guam's relationship with the US government comes under the general supervision of the Department of the Interior.

Increased experience at self-government and a developing economy are causing the people to question the role of the US in Guam's affairs. In September 1976, a referendum sponsored by the Guam Political Status Commission was held to 'improve Guam's status with the United States'. A proposal to seek independence was rejected. Steps toward the adoption of a locally-written and ratified Constitution were taken during 1977. A Constitutional Convention was authorised by Federal Congressional legislation on October 1976. A general election was held in April 1977, to elect 32 delegates to the convention, the purpose of which was to draft a constitution for the people of Guam by the end of the year. It was approved by Congress and the President, but in a referendum held on 4 August 1979 was overwhelmingly rejected.

On 31 January 1982 a referendum was held to decide on the following options: Commonwealth status, statehood, incorporated territory, free association, independence, status quo or other. Commonwealth and statehood gained majority of votes, and on 4 September 1982 a runoff vote between commonwealth and statehood resulted in commonwealth status gaining the majority of votes. In 1988 a poll indicated that the majority of voters favoured self-determination rights for Chamorros and limited powers of the US to alter the Commonwealth Act.

Executive. The executive head is the Governor, previously appointed by the US President but in late 1970 elected for the first time by voters at large. The Governor and Lieutenant-Governor are elected for four-year terms. Joe Ada was elected Governor in November 1986.

Legislature. Since 1950, Guam has had a unicameral legislature consisting of 21 senators elected by four legislative districts for two-year terms. Voters must be 18 or over.

Judicial. The District Court of Guam, with a judge appointed for eight years, serves as the Federal Court of Guam. Like a US district court it has jurisdiction over all cases arising under the Constitution, treaties, and laws of the US. The Superior Court of Guam handles all other cases arising under the laws of Guam. Appeals may be made to the Ninth Circuit Court of Appeals or to the US Supreme Court.

Elections. The last election for Governor and Legislature was held in November 1986. There are two parties, Republican and Democratic, both affiliated with their US counterparts. The islands has a non-voting delegate to the US House of Representatives, with an office in Washington (DC). He is elected by popular vote every two years, at the time of the general elections.

At the 1986 general elections (the 18th legislature) the Democrats gained 13 seats to the Republicans' eight. This majority enables a legislature to over-ride any veto by a governor on legislation.

Four currently serving women Senators were re-elected with the addition of two new female Senators. The Guam Senate has the largest percentage (28.6) of women of any island jurisdiction.

Municipal government. The island is divided into 19 municipalities or villages. There is no local government at this level. Elected commissioners, who have no legal authority, carry out varied functions on a village level ranging from ombudsman to social chairman.

Public service. Twenty per cent of all civilian employment is within the federal government and 26 per cent is in the territorial government. In 1986 total employment figures were 40,890, of which 10,520 were employed by the territorial government.

Gambling. Cockfighting is an approved sport, and is held each Saturday, Sunday and public holiday at the Sport-O-Drome in Tamuning. Greyhound racing takes place on a multi-million-dollar track opened in 1976. Bets are taken on the cockfighs and the greyhounds. Bingo is popular. Casino gambling was rejected by a public referendum.

DEFENCE. Units of the US Air Force and Navy are stationed on Guam, and defence installations use one-third of Guam's land. Defence expenditure on Guam dominates the local economy.

As part of the Strategic Air Command's global force for deterrence, the 43rd Strategic Wing is located at Andersen Air Force Base on Guam.

Naval Forces Marianas are under the control of the Commander US Naval Forces Marianas, on Guam, on Nimitz Hill.

Repair and maintenance of the US Seventh Fleet is done by the US Naval Station at Apra Harbour. The Naval Station is also a repair and provisioning base for nuclear Polaris submarines. The Naval Air Station operates the island's commercial airfield and shares its use in a joint-use agreement with the civilian government.

Military personnel totalled 11,800 in January 1986, plus 11,555 dependants. Majority of these were US Navy.

Total military pay for the fiscal year 1984 on Guam totalled $184,568,417, with a further $119.8 million paid to defence service civilians. They paid $35.2 million in taxes. The military spent $29.7 million in construction work, $172.5 million on petroleum products and $28 million on other local purchases on Guam during the year. Guam's major source of revenue is attributed to military spending. In 1987 nine military projects were scheduled for construction, totalling $29.4 million.

EDUCATION. There is a well-organised public school system. Education is compulsory for children from six to 16 years of age. There are 34 public schools, 24 of them elementary, five junior high, two senior high, one trade and technical school and a school for the handicapped. Other schools are operated by religious organisations, particularly by the Catholic Church, which has seven high schools and six elementary schools.

The University of Guam, which opened as the Territorial College of Guam in 1952, has a wide variety of academic and career-oriented programmes being studied by more than 2500 students each semester. The primary objective of the university is to develop managerial and technical resources with a high level of competence for the private and public sectors. It has four colleges: The College of Agriculture and Life Sciences, the College of Business and Public Administration, the College of Education and the College of Arts and Sciences. The university also has three major research components: the Water and Energy Research Institute, the Micronesian Area Research Centre (MARC) and the Marine Laboratory.

The Guam Community College, which is near the university campus, offers high school programmes from grade 10–12, apprenticeship training and adult high school education in addition to job and higher education certificates and associate degrees. In 1985 there were 31,832, students enrolled at schools — 26,568 in public schools and 5264 in private schools. There were 1125 teachers in public schools.

LABOUR. There were 40,890 employees on payrolls in March 1986: 43 per cent were in the public sector, 40 per cent of these in the federal government and 60 per cent in the territorial government. Government employment declined slightly over 1985 figures. About 20% of Guam's civilian force is employed by the military. The distribution of civilian employees in March 1986 was trade (wholesale and retail) 7690, service industries 6630, construction 3960, transport 1850, finance 1690, manufacturing 1320 and agriculture 110.

Wages. Average wage in the private sector was $6.30 per hour in 1986. The Guam Consumer Price Index rose 8.7 per cent in 1984 compared with 4.3 per cent in the US.

HEALTH. Medical care is mainly through the Guam Memorial Hospital and the Naval Regional Medical Center. The naval centre, with a normal bed capacity of 350 and with various dispensaries around the island, is for military personnel and dependants. There is out-patient care at the Catholic Medical Center and the Seventh-day Adventist Clinic. Cases requiring special attention can be evacuated to Honolulu by air.

Heart disease and malignant neoplasm are the major causes of death, although fatal motor vehicle accidents are also significant.

THE LAND. Guam has an area of 549 sq. km. The island is about 51 km long and varies

TABLE 1 GUAM EMPLOYEES BY INDUSTRY BASED ON PAYROLLS

Industry Division	December 1985	June 1986
Agriculture	120	130
Construction	3630	4640
Manufacturing	1220	1360
Transportation	1820	1910
Trade	7720	7870
Finance, Insurance and Real Estate	1600	1740
Services	6540	6660
Total Private	**22,650**	**24,310**
Public Sector		
Federal	7230	7480
Territorial	10,110	8670
Total	**39,990**	**40,460**

from six to 14 km in width. It is the peak of a submerged mountain located in the Marianas Trench. Two other deep areas of the ocean, the Challenger Deep and the Nero Deep, are to the south. The central and northern parts of the island are relatively flat limestone plateaus, 150 m above sea level, with cliffs that drop precipitously into the ocean. The southern part of the island is volcanic in origin with hills and mountains rising to 406 m, which is the highest point, Mt Lamlam. An elongated ridge divides the inland valleys and coastline. The large airstrips of the Andersen Air Force Base are situated on the flat northern plateau of the island, which is the largest single area under military control. The northern half of the island has poor agricultural soils due to the leaching of nutrients.

Climate. The tropical climate is healthy and uniformly warm and humid. The east and east-north-east trade winds prevail for six months of the year, from December to May, during which time it is cooler and there is less rain. The driest month is generally April. From June to November winds become gustier with frequently occurring squalls during the rainy season yielding up to 30 cm of rain per month. Average annual rainfall is 200 to 250 cm. Daily temperatures are usually between 24 and 30°C, with mean annual temperature of 27°C. Night-time temperatures are about 4°C lower.

Tropical cyclones or typhoons form to the south-east of Guam and pass on their way to the Philippines or Japan. Winds of up to 322 km an hour have been recorded inside these storms. Fortunately, storms of this magnitude strike the island only infrequently. Today, the population has access to cyclone-proof shelters, and supplies and communications can be re-established immediately. Tropical typhoon Roy in January 1988 caused millions of dollars worth of damage and Guam was declared a disaster area.

Fauna and flora. Main native animals are fruit bats (fanihi) and lizards. Animals now found on the island include wild deer, doves and other birds, and coconut crabs. Flowers include poinciana (flame tree), *Ixora*, *plumeria* (frangipani), orchids, lilies, allamanda and bougainvillaea creepers. Trees include *Laucaena glauca* (tangantangan), casuarinas, coconuts and pines.

Resources. Various studies have suggested that the resources to be developed should be agriculture and fisheries, tourism, and light industry coupled with financial and commercial development. The great majority of food is imported, and agriculture remains the smallest industry on Guam. Because Guam is near productive fishing grounds, the fishing industry is seen to have great potential. The Overall Economic Development Plan 1986 (OEDP) puts development of all these resources as major priorities.

Land tenure. About one-third of the land in Guam is owned by the federal government, about one-third is privately owned, and one-third is owned by the government of Guam. Most private land holdings are small. Military reservations constitute the bulk of federal land holdings; these installations include an airforce base and several naval bases.

AGRICULTURE. Agriculture is becoming more important due to rising food prices and policies fostering improved marketing and plant variety development. Total employment is only about 130 people, and agriculture contributes less than 1 per cent of gross business receipts. There are two agriculture experiment stations, at Inarajan in the north and at the Ija Agricultural Park in the south.

The College of Agriculture and Life Sciences has several major projects aimed at increasing the agricultural output of Guam and reducing the reliance on imported foodstuffs. One of these programmes is pest control, another is to develop land areas suitable for the promotion of specific crops which are most suited to the type of soil. A soil survey is currently being prepared to assist with future management and planning.

Crops introduced for commerical production include the pineapple, but the market is not expected to go beyond local production because of restrictions on the export markets (mainly Japan).

An animal nutritional programme has been established at the College of Agriculture and Life Sciences to look at the prospect of economically producing animal feeds.

The most important Guam-owned beef producer, the Bar-K ranch, is in fact not on Guam, where commercial beef is thought to be too land-intensive, but on Tinian in the Northern Marianas north of Guam. Most of

TABLE 2 GUAM AGRICULTURAL PRODUCTS

| Fiscal Year | Fruits & Vegetables | | Poultry | | Pork | |
	Value ($)	1000 lb	Value ($)	1000 lb	Value ($)	1000 lb
1980	1,636,288	2976	63,600	91	868,064	964
1981	3,528,653	6280	66,780	196	911,467	1012
1982	3,383,111	4833	70,119	206	957,041	1063
1983	3,438,260	6616	66,613	196	957,137	1116
1984	3,738,615	6631	69,700	205	998,096	1166

Note: The value of livestock is calculated using live weight.

the output of the ranch is shipped to Guam for sale.

Guam has imported most of its food needs since World War II, and agricultural production remains mostly the province of the small-holder growing little more than enough for himself and his neighbours, but US legislation such as the Federal Crop Insurance Act, which extends the crop insurance programme to Guam and widens its coverage, is expected to help stimulate expansion.

FISHERIES. Total island-wide offshore trolling and spearfishing catch during fiscal year 1984 was 264,727 kg. In addition local fishermen inshore were estimated to have caught 121,000 kg, giving a total catch for the year of 385,727 kg. Fish production is easily absorbed by local demand, despite occasional exports of fresh fish to Hawaii.

There is good potential for an increase in local production, and the government has been assisting the Guam Fisherman's Cooperative Association to enlarge its operations. In 1986 the Co-op moved to a newly completed facility adjacent to the Agana Boat Basin, the major port for domestic fisheries. The facility includes a chiller, blast freezer and standard walk-in freezer. The Co-op has continued to export fresh mahi mahi to markets in the US but local demand still exceeds supply and in 1986 Guam continued to import more than 340,909 kg of fish annually. There is some tuna shipment to Japan.

In an effort to remove as many obstacles as possible to the commercial fishing industry, local legislation exempts taxation of fuel used for fishing vessels. Further legislation also relaxes the restriction of fishing vessels by authorising the use of foreign-built vessels up to 200 gross tons for local fishing. Aquaculture development has been increasing rapidly since the completion of the Development Plan for it in 1982. There are currently 100 acres of ponds breeding tilapia, prawns, milkfish, carp and catfish. This represents a 70 per cent increase since 1982. The aquaculture industry is expected to grow significantly over the next five years assisted by foreign investment and the setting up of a research facility.

MANUFACTURING. The manufacturing sector employed approximately five per cent of the total workforce in 1986. There has been a significant drop in business receipts and employment figures for this sector since the petroleum refinery closed in 1984 when it lost the contract to supply fuel for the military. However, in early 1985 several manufacturers established garment and clothing businesses, a concrete pole plant, electronics components plants and several machinery plants. These have helped to replace the losses experienced in 1984. In 1983 the total value of imported manufactured products exceeded $26 million, 60 per cent of which came from the US. Exported manufactured products came to $2.2 million. About 99 per cent of these went to Micronesia. This reflects Guam's role as a transshipment centre rather than as an exporter.

LOCAL COMMERCE. Retail sales in 1984 were $448 million, or 34 per cent of gross business receipts. About 49 per cent of retail sales were generated by the tourist in-

TABLE 2 GUAM AGRICULTURAL PRODUCTS

	Beef Value ($)	1000 lb	Eggs Value ($)	1000 doz	Total Current Dollar Value
1980	49,400	52	2,086,522	1814	4,703,874
1981	51,870	54	2,190,848	1904	6,749,618
1982	54,464	57	1,622,186	1134	6,086,921
1983	57,187	59	811,093	567	5,330,290
1984	55,590	51	902,462	593	5,764,463

dustry, with each tourist spending an average of $600. The military population also contributes substantially to retail sales. There has been a big expansion in the number of shops and outlets, and in their siting, in recent years. More small shops have opened in rural areas. There has been a big increase in the number of restaurants and fast-food shops.

Wholesaling accounted for 6.5 per cent of gross business receipts in 1984, meaning that the wholesale and retail trade together accounted for 40.5 per cent of gross receipts. It employed 2.5 per cent of the labour force. In 1986 the retail sector employed 6410 compared to 6450 in 1985. The retail sector represents approximately 16 per cent of all

TABLE 3 GUAM IMPORTS AND EXPORTS (Dollars)

Country	Trade	1980	1981 (half year)*	1983
Australia	Export	7,911,628	540,774	9,498
	Import	6,199,288	2,007,275	3,606,747
Hong Kong	Export	8,669,038	521,176	768,715
	Import	14,734,033	7,651,183	18,779,940
Japan	Export	7,298,640	14,613,738	1,874,764
	Import	44,983,940	17,573,052	121,720,759
Philippines	Export	459,078	6,956,026	267,638
	Import	7,237,614	3,468,019	7,861,496
Taiwan	Export	958,980	40,604,984	184,794
	Import	5,596,707	3,805,102	11,586,250
USA	Export	5,941,994	4,451,681	9,755,227
	Import	133,818,739	59,005,071	143,167,305
Other countries	Export	12,100,661	1,281,363	1,724,798
	Import	328,564,538	260,847,090	325,383,806
Micronesia	Export	17,682,310	7,529,236	24,620,918
	Import	1,372,742	592,833	1,355,425
Total	Export	61,043,487	76,499,499	39,224,728
	Import	544,183,553	355,406,512	636,081,991

Note: Figures for 1981 are only available for the first six months and 1982 figures are totally unavailable.

employees on the public and private payroll.

In 1982 the construction industry had gross receipts of $64.3 million; transport and communications $44.7 million; finance, insurance and real estate $71.4 million; and service industries $94 million.

OVERSEAS TRADE. Guam is heavily dependent on imports, its exports being only a fraction of imports. In 1983 exports totalled $39.2 million and imports $636 million. Comparative figures in recent years, together with Guam's major trading partners, are shown in the accompanying tables.

Most imports — 49 per cent in 1983 — are crude petroleum and petroleum products, mainly from Saudi Arabia. Another 22.5 per cent of imports are from the US. Other imports come from Japan, Hong Kong, the Philippines, Australia, Taiwan and New Zealand.

The majority of Guam's exports — 62.7 per cent in 1983 — are in fact mainly transhipments to neighbouring island countries. The US got 25 per cent of exports, and Taiwan, Japan and Hong Kong received most of the rest, but these are also largely re-exports. **Customs tariff.** Guam is a free port. However, import duties are levied on alcoholic beverages, tobacco and fuel. Guam is recognised as a developing country by the US and some other nations and is authorised to participate in the Generalised System of Preference, and in the General Headnote 3(a) of the US Tariff Code. Under the Headnote, Guam may export its manufactured goods duty-free into the US provided that at least 50 per cent (30 per cent for watches) of the value has been added in Guam.

TOURISM. The tourist industry is now the most important industry in the private sector, and is the second major revenue earner after federal government expenditure. In economic terms the government considers tourism as an export, since it involves the sale of Guam products or services to non-residents.

The industry has grown rapidly since the inauguration of flights between Tokyo and Guam in 1967. Over the last five years the industry has experienced a consistent growth rate averaging five per cent per annum. In 1987 a total of 483,954 visitors arrived on the island. Tourism's direct contribution to the

TABLE 4 VISITOR ARRIVALS BY ORIGIN, Oct 1985 to Sept 1986

Origin	Number
Japan	299,431
North Am/Hawaii	26,454
Northern Marianas	15,036
Other Micronesia	7574
Philippines	2541
Europe	1416
Taiwan	1554
Other Areas	5598
Unknown	683
Total	374,548

economy amounted to $5.7 million from the 10 per cent hotel occupancy tax, over $230 million in tourism expenditures and provided over 7000 jobs in the private sector. In the eight months to August 1988, 402,266 visitors arrived, maintaining the considerable growth rate. It has been estimated that each visitor spends at least $600.

Guam benefits from tax revenues generated by the tourist. There is a gross business receipts tax (on both wholesale and retail) of 4 per cent to which tourist expenditure greatly contributes. There is also a hotel occupancy tax of 10 per cent of room rental charges, which earned $4.5 million in the first half of 1988. The industry provides about 7000 jobs directly and indirectly, and provides work for about 30 per cent of Guam's total private employment of 23,250.

An analysis of the visitor profile showed that in 1986 Japanese comprised 80 per cent of all visitors with the US accounting for seven per cent and 11 per cent from other countries. The majority of Japanese visitors are young honeymooners or single travellers in group tours.

In 1984 the Federal Government provided the first instalment of $8.7 million to develop the Tumon Bay area with improved water and sewerage and roads.

Most hotels are in the Tumon Bay area

which accommodates 85 per cent of tourist traffic. Of 3600 hotel rooms, nearly 3000 are located near Tumon Bay, with the average occupancy rate about 85 per cent the year around.

It is anticipated that visitor arrivals will continue to increase following the opening of five major hotels in the Tumon Bay area by 1990. There has also been recent development in Southern Guam of both natural attractions and resorts. Other large developments currently being negotiated include a $156 million resort and golf course in the Harmon Cliffline area and two more hotels in Tumon Bay. These would add more than 1000 rooms to tourism resources.

The Port Authority of Guam is planning a passenger ship terminal in Agana. At present only small cruise ships can dock here (in 1984 17 small ships brought 7242 passengers to Guam on short visits), however, many of the world's large luxury ships cruise through Guam's waters and the Visitors Bureau would like them to stop over. The bureau has an annual budget of $2.5 million. The 10 per cent hotel tax is channelled into the Tourist Attraction Fund, established by legislation in 1985. The GVB assesses tourism-related project proposals and directs, with Legislature approval, funds from the TAF to suitable projects. There are detailed master plans for the Tumon Bay and Meriza/Cocos Lagoon area and work has begun on a comprehensive overall master plan for this vital industry.

FINANCE. Guam relies heavily on the US for financial support. Of Guam's employment, 43 per cent is in federal and Guam governments and most of Guam government revenue comes from federal assistance and federal employee income taxes.

Public revenue is raised through local income tax, property tax, a 4 per cent gross business receipt tax, business licence fees, excise duties and various charges for public utilities.

In 1985 Guam Government's revenue totalled $190.8 million, of which taxes accounted for $140.4 million and federal contribution added $40 million to the general fund. All federal taxes collected on Guam can revert to the Guam government, and they usually account for 10 per cent to 15 per cent of government revenue yearly. See accompanying tables for a breakdown of income and expenditure, 1985.

As Table 6 indicates (see also details under Defence) military expenditure is also an important portion of Guam's economy. The military itself is a big spender, and Guam additionally benefits from military and civilian employee wages and expenditure, and taxes.

Currency. Unites States currency is used.

Banks. Guam has a total of 28 financial institutions offering personal, commercial and international banking services. There are 14 banks. Limited loan and loan guarantees for venture capital are also available from the Small Business Administration and the Guam Economic Development Authority.

Among the commercial banks are three foreign bank branches which make loans and accept deposits from off-island only — the result of a 1975 law that prohibits these branches from accepting local deposits.

Guam's only local bank is the Bank of Guam, which started in 1972.

Deposits in the island's financial institutions were $705.1 million at the end of 1984, $187.8 million higher than in December 1983.

Of the total, including the offshore certificates, the banks had deposits of $630.3 million, and they had outstanding loans of $351.5 million (compared with a total of $484.4 million in loans through all financial institutions). In December 1983, financial institutions held over $1 billion in total assets. Since Federal Reserve Board regulations do not apply on Guam there is no restriction on the amount of interest paid on passbook savings and TCDs. Deposits in Guam banks are not required to be covered by reserves in the Federal Reserve Bank, however, banks must be members of the Federal Deposit Insurance Corporation.

Financial centre. The Guam government has been considering the feasibility of establishing Guam as a location for substantial international finance companies or international financial centre. The object is to increase tax revenue for Guam. The Government passed the Offshore Lending Facility Act in March 1979. The US Treasury has since issued temporary regulations to restrict Guam's use as an offshore centre of finance.

TABLE 5 GOVERNMENT OF GUAM
Combined Statement of Revenue, Expenditures and Changes in Fund Balance

Year Ending 30 September 1985	$
Revenues:	
Taxes	140,435,039
Licences, fees and permits	5,353,560
Fines and forfeitures	87,547
Federal contribution	40,068,732
Others	4,883,252
TOTAL	190,828,130
Expenditures:	
General government	46,453,819
Protection of life and property	24,341,330
Public health and community service	21,027,953
Individual and collective rights	3,403,530
Public education	61,824,428
Environmental protection	241,901
Economic development	3,975,262
Others	1,594,830
TOTAL	162,863,053
Revenues over (under) expenditures	27,963,077
Other sources (uses) of funds:	
Amortisation in long term debt	30,242,684
Operating transfer in	41,868,834
Operating transfer out	(47,704,489)
Others	(4,179,097)
TOTAL	20,227,932
Revenues and other sources over (under) expenditures and other uses	48,193,009
Others	630,339
Decrease in reserve for doubtful accounts	4,504,423
Adjustment of prior years revenues and expenditures	(1,857,318)
Adjustment to beginning balance	(7,236,247)
Fund balance 1 Oct. 1984	51,583,735
Fund balance 30 Sept. 1985	$7,596,529

In 1987 this centre had still not been established.

TRANSPORT. Guam has more than 700 km of all-weather roads. Guam in the past relied on private transportation, which caused frequent traffic jams during peak hours, but it has embarked on a plan for highway improvement and encouragement for public bus services — clearly necessary because of the large increase in tourists.

The Mass Transit Authority was established to revitalise the public transport system. However, on 31 July 1984 it ceased operations. Reasons given for the end of the 'I' Bus' system was that the local contract had expired and was not being renewed due to financial difficulties. The government continues to be optimistic about re-establishing a transit system but on a smaller scale. The military runs its own bus services for personnel and dependents and there are numerous taxi and rented car services. Hotels have their own transportation and all the bigger hotels

TABLE 6 MILITARY EXPENDITURES ON GUAM
(in $000)

Fiscal year	1982	1983	1984
Military pay	124,256	169,246	184,568
Civilian pay	90,800	113,070	119,769
Military construction	22,518	48,403	29,674
Purchase of petroleum products	497,854	353,573	172,500
Other purchases	26,317	27,678	28,107
Total spending	761,745	711,971	534,620
Total withholding taxes	32,780	32,630	35,179

meet passengers on arrival at the airport.

In 1984 there were 77,918 licensed vehicles on Guam, the majority, 57,629, being private cars. There were 227 taxis, 15,342 trucks, 3104 motor cycles, 87 buses and 924 military vehicles.

Airlines. Guam is an important Pacific airline crossroad. All Nippon Airways, Continental/Air Micronesia, Japan Air Lines, Air Nauru, Northwest Orient, and Garuda serve international routes, connecting with Hawaii and the US mainland, Japan, the Philippines, Hong Kong and Singapore, among other destinations. Air Micronesia and Air Nauru connect Guam with nearby islands, and Air Nauru operates through Guam to Australia and New Zealand via Nauru. Guam is an important link in the air chain for travellers wanting to move around Micronesia. Air Guam, now flying an interisland cargo service, has been designated the flag carrier for the government.

There are a number of small domestic airlines with regular daily connection flights to Rota and Saipan in the Commonwealth of Northern Marianas, which is an important tourist market — many visitors combine Guam and the Marianas in one package.

Guam International Airport is a modern complex capable of handling the largest commercial jets. The airport operates under a joint use agreement with the US Navy. The Andersen Air Force Base, on the northern corner of Guam, is for military use only. In 1984 there were a total of 7542 aircraft arrivals at GIAT, a slight decrease over the 1983 arrivals of 7643.

The US Naval Air Station is alongside the international airport, and one of its main duties is to provide the support for the Joint Rescue Sub-centre on Guam. JRC handles all search and rescue missions within its three million square kilometre area.

Port facilities. The Port of Guam is the only commercial seaport on Guam and the principal seaport in Micronesia. It is located at the north-east side of Apra Harbour, and shares the harbour with the Navy. Cabras Island and the Glass Breakwater form the harbour's protective northern border, while Orote Peninsula forms the southern boundary.

The Port Authority's terminal facilities are on 13 hectares on Cabras Island. Depth of docks averages 8 to 10 m with 830 m of dock area divided into four berths. Two berths are reserved for container operations. Ships up to 233 m can dock.

Additional wharf space and warehousing is being provided because of the increase in containerisation. But port development is hampered because military interests dominate the harbour area, and there is a safety arc extending from the ammunition wharf located near the commercial port. The navy in 1982 completed a study on moving the ammunition wharf to a new location away from the commercial port.

In 1984 the Port Authority accepted 218 ha of land on Cabras Island, previously federal land. However, the development of these returned Federal lands is restricted under the Brooks Amendment which requires funds generated by sale or lease to revert to the Federal Government. Negotiations are under way to free land from these restrictions so that the development of the commercial port may proceed. The Port Authority reported a record profit in 1984 of $4.8 million, largely due to revenues from new car transshipment.

Among shipping services using Guam are the United States Lines, the Kyowa Shipping Co., Nauru Pacific Line, the NYK Shipping Line, Saipan Shipping Co., American President Lines and EKL Line.

Coastguard. The US Coastguard Service has its Marianas section based on Apra Harbour. Its responsibility extends to the majority of the islands of Micronesia. It enforces laws within the 200-mile zones of Guam and the Northern Marianas, with the use of two vessels, *Cape George* and *Basswood*. *Basswood* is a 55 m buoytender and *Cape George* a 29 m cutter.

COMMUNICATIONS. Guam is included in the US domestic postal service operations, and postal charges and arrangements are the same as in the US. There is no local Guam postage stamp. Full telex, telephone and other communications overseas are available through RCA Global Communications and Island Telecommunications and Engineering Company. Internal telephone services are provided by the Guam Telephone Authority. There were 23,354 telephones in operation in 1985 — of these, 4224 were commercial lines.

Military communications. The Naval Communications Station for the Western Pacific is based on Guam. It provides communication support for the US fleet in the Western Pacific and the Indian Ocean, serving as the master centre for the area (which covers about 40 per cent of the earth's ocean surface).

Radio and television. Guam has three AM and three FM radio stations, two television air stations, one public broadcasting TV station and a cable TV system offering full schedules of major US networks.

Newspapers. The *Pacific Daily News* and *Sunday News* circulate throughout the week; the *Guam Tribune* is published twice weekly. There are military news-sheets and a high quality colour periodical, *Glimpses of Micronesia*.

Water, electricity, energy. Guam generally has an abundant water supply from its heavy rainfall and underground wells, but out-of-date reticulation systems and water storage problems have caused difficulties in recent years, particularly with the expansion of tourism.

The Guam Environmental Protection Agency has implemented a master plan and at the end of 1984 Guam had a total of 102 production wells. Only 45 per cent required chlorination for safety. The Public Utility Agency of Guam is responsible for the overall supply and control of water quality; it works in close co-operation with the GEPA. Total metered consumption in 1984 was four billion gallons.

Electricity rates on Guam are high because of the high cost of fuel oil, and the Guam Power Authority, which is responsible for providing electricity, has been investigating ways of lowering the rates by reviewing alternative sources of energy. A thermal energy conversion plant is one hope for this. The present power generating system is jointly operated by GPA and the Navy. Most electric outlets are 110 and 220 AC.

MAJOR OFFICE HOLDERS
Governor:
Joseph A. Ada
Lieutenant-Governor:
Frank F. Blas
Delegate to Congress:
Ben Blaz
Speaker of Legislature:
Franklin J. A. Quitugua
Judiciary District Court:
Hon. Cristobal C. Duenas
Presiding Judge Superior Court:
Hon. Paul J. Abbate

GOVERNMENT DEPARTMENTS
Governor's Office, PO Box 2950, Agana 96910. Tel.: 472-8931-9
Guam Legislature, PO Box CB-1, Agana 96910. Tel.: 477-9444
Superior Court of Guam, Judiciary Bldg., Agana 96910. Tel.: 472-8961
Administration Department, PO Box 884, Agana 96910. Tel.: 472-8481
Agency for Human Resources Development, PO Box CP, Agana 96910. Tel.: 646-9341/4
Agriculture Department, PO Box 2950, Agana 96910. Tel.: 734-3941

Attorney General, PO Box DA, Agana 96910. Tel.: 472-6841

Budget and Management Research Bureau, PO Box 2950, Agana 96910. Tel.: 472-8312

Civil Defense, PO Box 2877, Agana 96910. Tel.: 477-9841

Commissioners Council, PO Box 786, Agana 96910. Tel.: 472-6940

Commerce Department, GITC Building Suite 601, Tamuning 96911. Tel.: 646-5841/4

Corrections Department, PO Box 3236, Agana 96910. Tel.: 734-2458

Education Department, PO Box DE, Agana 96910. Tel.: 472-8901

Guam Advisory Council on Vocational Education, PO Box CK, Agana 96910. Tel.: 477-7661

Guam Energy Office, PO Box 2950, Agana 96910. Tel.: 734-4452

Guam Environmental Protection Agency, PO Box 2999, Agana 96910. Tel.: 646-8863

Guam Health Planning & Development Agency, 212 W. Aspinall Dr., Agana 96910. Tel.: 472-6831

Guam Occupational Information Coordinating Council, PO Box 2950, Agana 96910. Tel.: 477-8946

Guam Public Library, PO Box 652, Agana 96910. Tel.: 472-6417

Guam Territoral Law Library, 141 San Ramon Road, Agana 96910. Tel.: 477-7623

Guam Veterans Affairs Office, PO Box 3279, Agana 96910. Tel.: 472-6002

Labor Department, PO Box 23548, Guam Main Facility 96921. Tel.: 646-9001

Land Management Department, PO Box 2950, Agana 96910. Tel.: 472-8851-3

Mental Health & Substance Abuse Department, PO Box 8896, Tamuning 96911. Tel.: 646-9261

Parks & Recreation Department, 490 Naval Hospital Road, Agana Heights 96919. Tel.: 477-9620/21/7825

Passport Office, PO Box 2950, Agana 96910 Tel.: 472-6774

Planning Bureau, PO Box 2950, Agana 96910. Tel.: 477-9639

Public Health & Social Services Department, PO Box 2816, Agana 96910. Tel.: 734-2931

Public Safety Department, 287 O'Brien Drive, Agana 96910. Tel.: 472-8911

Public Works Department, PO Box 2950, Agana 96910. Tel.: 646-5831-9

Revenue & Taxation Department, PO Box 2796, Agana 96910. Tel.: 472-8981/9/477-1040

Suruhano Ombudsman, PO Box 2950, Agana 96910. Tel.: 477-9803

Territorial Auditor, W. Soledad Ave., GCIC Bldg., Agana 96910. Tel.: 477-8525

Treasurer of Guam, PO Box 2950, Agana 96910. Tel.: 472-6441

University of Guam, UOG Station, Mangilao 96913. Tel.: 734-2921/9

Vocational Rehabilitation Department, PO Box 2113, Agana 96910. Tel.: 646-1008/9468/9

Youth Affairs Department, PO Box 23672, Guam Main Facility 96921. Tel.: 734-3911/4

INDEPENDENT BODIES

Civil Service Commission, PO Box 3156, Agana 96910. Tel.: 472-8298

Guam Airport Authority, PO Box 8770, Tamuning 96911. Tel.: 646-0300

Guam Contractors Board, PO Box 2033, Guam Main Facility 96921. Tel.: 646-5831

Guam Community College, PO Box 23069, Guam Main Facility 96921. Tel.: 734-4311

Guam Council on the Arts and Humanities, PO Box 2950, Agana 96910. Tel.: 477-7413

Guam Economic Development Authority, PO Box 3280, Agana 96910. Tel.: 472-8821

Guam Educational Telecommunication Corp., PO Box 21449, Guam Main Facility 96921. Tel.: 734-2207

Guam Election Commission, PO Box B6, Agana 96910. Tel.: 477-9791

Guam Gaming Commission, PO Box 3328, Agana 96910. Tel.: 477-2216/19

Guam Housing Corporation, PO Box 3457, Agana 96910. Tel.: 472-4258

Guam Housing and Urban Renewal Authority, PO Box CS, Agana 96910. Tel.: 477-9851/4

Guam Mass Transit Authority, PO Box 2950, Agana 96910. Tel.: 646-7232.

Guam Power Authority, PO Box 2977, Agana 96910. Tel.: 472-6801
Guam Retirement Fund, PO Box 3-C, Agana 96910. Tel.: 477-2173/9290
Guam Telepone Authority, PO Box 9008, Tamuning 96911. Tel.: 646-6971/9221
Guam Visitors Bureau, Bayview Plaza Building, Tumon 96911. Tel.: 646-5278
Port Authority of Guam, 1026 Cabras Highway Suite 201, Piti 96925. Tel.: 477-9931/5
Public Utility Agency of Guam, PO Box 3010, Agana 96910. Tel.: 646-8891

US GOVERNMENT DEPARTMENTS
US AGRICULTURE DEPARTMENT
Animal and Plant Protection and Quarantine, PO Box 8769, Tamuning 96911. Tel.: 646-0388
Farmers Home Administration, PO Box ET, Agana 96910. Tel.: 472-7361
Federal Aviation Administration, Finegayan Rt. 008, Finegayan 96912. Tel.: 366-8159
Plant Protection and Quarantine, 238 O'Hara St., PDN Bldg., Agana 96910. Tel.: 477-9012
Soil Conservation Service, University of Guam Station, Mangilao 96923. Tel.: 734-3496

US COMMERCE DEPARTMENT
Defense Fuel Supply DFQAR Guam, PWD Bldg. No. 104 Upper FPO, San Francisco, CA 96630. Tel.: 339-2109
Defense Property Disposal, PO Box 190, San Francisco, CA 96630. Tel.: 399-5227
US Geological Survey Guam Observatory, PO Box 8001, Agana 96910. Tel.: 355-5259
National Oceanic and Atmospheric Administration, Route 8, Agana 96910. Tel.: 355-5924
National Weather Service, NOCD PO Box 81, FPO San Francisco, CA 96637. Tel.: 344-4175

US DEFENSE DEPARTMENT
Army Corps of Engineers Pacific Ocean Division, Suite 905, PDN Bldg., Agana 96910. Tel.: 344-5203
Defense Communications Agency, PO Box 141 NAVCAMS WESTPAC, FPO San Francisco, CA 96630. Tel.: 355-5865

US HEALTH/HUMAN SERVICES
National Institute of Neurological Diseases and Stroke Center, Room 201 Old GMH, Tamuning 96911. Tel.: 646-8049
US HOUSING URBAN DEVELOPMENT
Federal Housing Administration, 238 O'Hara St. Rm. 304-A, Agana 96910. Tel.: 472-7231
US INTERIOR DEPARTMENT
Fish and Wildlife Service, PO Box 3238, Agana 96910. Tel.: 344-5184
National Park Service, PO Box FA, Agana 96910. Tel.: 477-8528/9362
Office of Inspector General North Pacific Region, 238 O'Hara St., PDN Bldg., Agana 96910. Tel.: 472-7279
Office of Technical Assistance, PO Box BJ, Agana 96910. Tel.: 472-7319
US Geological Survey Guam Observatory, PO Box 8001, MOU#3, Agana 96910. Tel.: 355-5259

US JUSTICE DEPARTMENT
Drug Enforcement Agency, 238 O'Hara St., PDN Bldg., Agana 96910. Tel.: 472-7384
Federal Bureau of Investigation, 238 O'Hara St., PDN Bldg. Rm. 405, Agana 96910. Tel.: 472-7422
Immigration and Naturalisation Services, 238 O'Hara St., PDN Bldg., Agana 96910. Tel.: 472-7484
Land and Natural Resources Division, 238 O'Hara St., PDN Bldg., Agana 96910. Tel.: 472-7311
US Attorney's Office, 238 O'Hara St., PDN Bldg., Agana 96910. Tel.: 472-7283
US Marshall's Office, 238 O'Hara St., PDN Bldg., Agana 96910. Tel.: 472-7351/7394

US TRANSPORT DEPARTMENT
Federal Aviation Administration, Route 8, NCS, Finegayan 96912. Tel.: 355-5026
US Coast Guard, USCG Section Marianas, PO Box 176, FPO San Francisco 96630. Tel.: 399-8181

US TREASURY DEPARTMENT
Internal Revenue Service, Room 404 PDN Bldg., Agana 96910. Tel.: 472-7404
US INDEPENDENT AGENCIES
General Service Administration, Room 1003-C PDN Bldg., Agana 96910. Tel.: 472-7381

Guam Spaceflight Tracking and Data Network Station, Dandan 96916. Tel.: 828-8625

Office of Personnel Management, 238 O'Hara St., PDN Bldg., Agana. Tel.: 472-7451

Selective Service System, PO Box 2194, Agana 96910. Tel.: 477-8216

Small Business Administration, 238 O'Hara St., PDN Bldg., Agana 96910. Tel.: 472-7244

Social Security Administration, 238 O'Hara St., PDN Bldg., Agana 96910. Tel.: 472-7211

US Postal Service, Guam Main Facility 96921. Tel.: 734-3921

Veterans Administration, NRMC, PO Box 7613, FPO San Francisco, CA 96630. Tel.: 344-9200

US CONGRESS
Congressman Ben Blaz, Agana Shopping Center, Agana 96910. Tel.: 472-7251

US JUDICIARY
US District Court of Guam, 238 O'Hara St., PDN Bldg., Agana 96910. Tel.: 472-9411

FOREIGN MISSIONS
Consulate General of Japan, PO Box AG, Agana 96910. Tel.: 646-1290

Korean Consulate General, Suite 305, GCIC Building, Agana 96910. Tel.: 472-6488/472-8076

Nauru Consulate, PO Box AM, Agana 96910. Tel:: 472-8300

Philippine Consulate General, Box CG, Agana. Tel.: 646-4630

Northern Marianas, Box 8366, Tamuning 96911

Federated States of Micronesia, Box 22197, GMF. Tel.: 646-0370

Republic of Palau, PO Box AC, Agana 96910. Tel.: 646-9291

HISTORY. Archaeological excavations on Guam have revealed that the island was inhabited as early as 1320 BC. Two separate prehistoric cultures have been distinguished. One, called pre-Latte, was characterised by redware pottery, a lime-filled impressed ware, shell and stone adzes, shell beads and pendants. The Latte culture is associated with a later people who built their houses ('latte') on large stone pillars called 'halege'. Some of these pillars, arranged in double rows, can still be found.

When the first Europeans reached Guam in the first quarter of the 16th century the people of Guam, called Chamorros, were apparently of mixed origins. Rank and class consciousness were important factors in their lives. There were three classes — the 'matua' (nobles), 'atchaot' (middle class) and 'manachang' (commoners). They were organised in matrilineal clans and lived in villages on the coast, near rivers, or on hilltops for their own protection. They built their houses and canoes with great skill, and were ingenious in making stone axes, chisels, knives, spearheads, hammers, mortars, pestles and slingstones. Their small outrigger canoes could travel at a great speed and were known to the early visitors as 'flying proas'. The Chamorros themselves were tall, well-built and robust, and wore few if any clothes. They are thought to have been of Malaysian origin.

The European discoverer of Guam was Ferdinand Magellan, who reached the island on 6 March 1521 after a hungry voyage of 98 days from the Strait of Magellan. He also sighted Rota and possibly Saipan. Tradition has it that he anchored at Umatac Bay on the south-west side of Guam where he traded with the islanders for food and water. When the islanders stole a skiff, Magellan sent an armed party ashore to recover it and to punish them. Seven Chamorros were killed and 40 or 50 of their houses burned. The thieving propensities of the islanders prompted the Spaniards to call Guam and its neighbours Isles de los Ladrones (Islands of Thieves). Another more flattering name — a tribute to the Chamorro canoes — was Islands of Lateen Sails.

Guam was one of the first islands in the Pacific to have a resident European. In 1526, when the flagship of Garcia Jofre de Losaia called at Guam en route to the East Indies, a Spaniard called Gonzalo de Vigo was found to be living there. He had deserted from Magellan's ship *Trinidad* at an island northward of Guam when the ship, having obtained a cargo of spices in the Moluccas, was trying vainly to pick up a favourable wind for Mexico.

Spain takes possession. In 1565 an expedition under Miguel Lopez de Legaspi, who had been sent from Mexico to colonise the Philippines, called at Guam and took possession of it for the King of Spain. Later, after reaching the Philippines, two of Legaspi's ships became the first to return to Mexico across the Pacific. The route they took was to the north of Hawaii and then down the coast of California. The practicability of return voyages to Mexico was thereby established, and for the next two and a half centuries Spanish galleons plied annually between the two countries, carrying silver ingots from Mexico to pay for the luxuries of the Orient in Manila.

Although the westward-bound galleons passed among the Ladrone Islands (or Marianas, as they were later known), it was not until the latter half of the 17th century that it became customary to call at Guam. In 1668, a group of Jesuit missionaries, led by Diego Luis de Sanvitores, settled on Guam, protected by a garrison of Spanish and Filipino soldiers. In the same year, a royal order required all galleons to put in at Guam; and soon the Spanish military commandant was given the rank of governor.

The Jesuit missionaries were at first well received by the Chamorros, about 13,000 of them being baptised during the first year. However, the islanders soon realised that the Spaniards were a threat to their way of life, and in July 1670 they rose in open rebellion. This was the beginning of 25 years of sporadic warfare. Some of the Spanish governors were particularly repressive, vengeful and brutal, while the Chamorros seized many opportunities to hit back. One early historian claimed that in only two years of fighting, the Chamorros were reduced from 40,000 to 5000. However, it is probable that, as in other parts of the Pacific, unfamiliar diseases were the principal killers among the Chamorros. Smallpox, for example, ravaged the island in 1688. Many lives were also lost in devastating typhoons in 1671 and 1693.

Chamorro resistance to Spanish rule was finally crushed in 1695 after a party of islanders who attacked the Spaniards and then fled to one of the northern islands were hunted down and routed. The islanders then agreed to return peaceably to Guam and become loyal subjects of the Spanish Crown. No Chamorros lived in the northern islands from that time onwards.

During the next 200 years, Guam was a sleepy backwater of the Spanish Empire in which Catholicism permeated most aspects of life. Until 1815, the only events to disturb the island's calm were the annual visits of the galleons, a periodic typhoon, and the occasional appearance of some unexpected foreigner. Among the foreign visitors were two English buccaneers, Woodes Rogers (1710) and John Clipperton (1721). There were also exploring expeditions headed by Crozet (1772) and Malaspina (1792). Crozet, who arrived during the enlightened governorship of Mariano Tobias, described Guam as 'the only island in the vast extent of the South Sea ... which has a European-built town, a church, fortifications, and a civilised population'.

In 1815, some seven years after Spain's defeat at the hands of Napoleon, the galleon trade between Mexico and the Philippines ceased, and Guam fell on hard times. There was little improvement in the remaining eight decades of Spanish rule. However, from that time onwards, foreign vessels put into Guam with much greater frequency, and the islanders derived some benefits from their demands for victuals and repairs. Notable visitors included Kotzebue (1817), Freycinet (1819) and Dumont d'Urville (1828 and 1839).

There were also occasional American vessels trading with the Far East, and for about 30 years from 1823 some 30 whalers called at Guam each year. By 1855, Guam had become sufficiently important to American commerce for the US to establish a consulate there. But there was a serious setback in the following year. A smallpox epidemic wiped out 3644 Guamanians, which so reduced the population that the government permitted many Carolinians and later Japanese to settle on the island to replace them.

American possession. After the Spanish-American War broke out in 1898, four American ships under Captain Henry Glass, USN, were ordered to capture Guam on their way to the Philippines. This order was carried out without bloodshed, and the American flag was raised on the island on 21 June. Two months later when Spain sued for peace, Guam was ceded to the US together with the Philippines for $US20 million. A census two years later revealed that the island's population was 9676, of whom all but 46 were Guamanians.

Captain Richard P. Leary, USN, took over as the first American governor of Guam in August 1899 after President McKinley had decreed that the island should be placed under the control of the US Navy. It became primarily a coaling station and, later, a naval base. Leary and his successors faced many problems bequeathed by the last Spanish governors. Principal among these were illiteracy, disease and unsanitary conditions. By World War I considerable progress had been made in combating these problems as well as in the fields of agriculture, land management and public works.

During the war, the German cruiser *Cormoran* was interned in Apra Harbour and eventually scuttled there by her crew.

In 1971 the First Congress, an advisory council of 34 nominated Guamanian leaders, was convened to give them experience with the problems of government. Fourteen years later an elected congress, consisting of two houses with a total of 43 members, was introduced. Although neither congress could initiate legislation, both were important steps towards Guam's self-government of today.

Pacific War. On 3 November 1940, a severe typhoon caused widespread destruction. Just over a year later, on 8 December 1941, Japanese aircraft attacked the island from neighbouring Saipan. Within two days, thousands of Japanese troops invaded the island, and the Americans, who numbered less than 400, surrendered. For the next 31 months, the Guamanians were subject to stern, often harsh, military rule. An American force of 55,000 men recaptured the island after several weeks of bitter fighting. Nearly 1300 Americans and 11,000 Japanese were killed.

An American military government ruled Guam until the end of May 1946, after which the naval administration was re-established. For the next four years, the Navy had the task of rehabilitating an island that had been almost completely devastated by war. Agana, the capital, was cleared of its ruins and a completely new town was laid out. Other district centres were also re-created.

On 1 June 1950, an Organic Act signed by President Truman made Guam an unincorporated territory of the United States and gave its people American citizenship. The Act also brought an end to naval administration and turned over responsibility for the island to the Department of the Interior. Carlton S. Skinner was appointed the first civilian governor. By June 1960 Guam had its first appointed Guamanian governor, Joseph Flores. Meanwhile, its chief industry was the US defence establishment, which played an important part in the prosecution of the Vietnam War.

In 1962, security measures were rescinded to permit American tourists to visit Guam without formal clearances. This move was designed to facilitate the development of a tourist industry and so reduce the territory's dependence on military expenditure.

The number of visitors grew from 300 in 1964 to 50,000 in 1970 and soon there was a hotel-building boom. In 1986 nearly 400,000 tourists arrived in Guam. In this period, and since, the majority of tourists have come from Japan, together with Japanese capital which has helped build up the tourist infrastructure on the island, as it has in Honolulu.

The Organic Act was amended by Congress to allow for election of a governor, and in 1971 Carlos G. Camacho was inaugurated as Guam's first elected governor. In 1972, Guam elected its first delegate to the US Congress. He has voting power in committee but not on the House floor.

Guamanians defeated a locally-drafted constitution on 4 August 1979, by a 5-to-1 margin. The defeat was generally attributed to a belief among Guamanians that their relationship with the US, not the structure of their government, needed changing.

On 31 January 1982, at a referendum offering different political options, the people voted overwhelmingly to become more closely associated with the US. On a further vote on 4 September 1982 to decide between commonwealth and statehood status, commonwealth status attained the most votes by a 3-to-1 margin. The commonwealth option is being assessed, and in 1988 the voters polled overwhelmingly in favour of self-determination and to limit the powers of the US to alter the Commonwealth Act. A few days before the territorial election of September 1986, Governor Ricardo Bordallo was indicted on various corruption changes. He was subsequently found guilty and imprisoned.

FOR THE TOURIST. Guam has witnessed an enormous boost in tourism since 1970, thanks mainly to the Japanese, who arrive by the Jumbo load on low-cost package tours. The Japanese have widened the cosmopolitan air to be found in this small and attractive island. Although Guam has some of the atmosphere of mainland US, it has a unique flavour of its own due to the mixing of many different cultures.

Guam abounds with relics of Spanish rule and World War II battles. Modern government and commercial buildings, and high-rise hotels along the beaches, are interspersed with colourful reminders of earlier days.

There is some excellent shopping in attractive commercial shopping centres, with a wide range of goods from Europe, the US and the East. Guam is a free port except for liquor and tobacco. Handicrafts from all over Micronesia are available. Excellent woven articles, some highly decorated with shells woven into the design and story boards carved in 'ifil' wood depicting island legends and lore, are highly prized souvenirs.

Restaurants and night entertainment are both to be found in great variety. Bars range from the high class to the strip joint. Dress in Guam is casual.

Scuba diving. Guam is renowned for its scuba diving with superb visibility often up to 65 metres and water that is 27°C all year around. There are over 300 varieties of coral which host a very diverse fish population. Biologists have identified 800 species of fish in the waters around Guam. Near Orote Point the diver can 'free fall' down the Blue Hole to a window 20 metres below. This chasm in the underwater cliff bottoms out at 100 metres. Popular wreck dives include a WWII Japanese Zero, a US tanker and a WWI German cruiser. Many dives can easily be reached from the beach.

Entry formalities. No passport is required for US citizens, although it is recommended in case of emergency stopovers elsewhere. Others require passport and a US visa. The Guam government has been seeking to waive visa requirements for non-US citizens visiting for no more than 15 days, but the decision is a matter for US authorities. Smallpox immunisation is not required, but shots for yellow fever and cholera are required if a visitor arrives from an infected area.

Sightseeing. PUNTAN DOS AMANTES. Puntan Dos Amantes, or Two Lovers' Point, offers a panoramic view of the central coastline and hillsides of Guam. Legend relates that a Chamorro maiden and her Chamorro lover leaped to their death from this cliffline upon receiving word that she was betrothed to a Spanish captain. Located in the northwestern plateaus, this park has excellent varieties of tropical flora found in Guam's limestone forest.

PADRE SAN VITORES. San Vitores Shrine stands behind the beach at the north end of Tumon Bay. The Shrine marks the spot where Padre San Vitores, leader of the first Spanish Jesuit colony, was killed.

IPAO BEACH PARK. A favourite recreational area located within the Tumon tourist resort area, the park was once an ancient Chamorro settlement. It was also used as a penal and leper colony in the early period of the American Administration in 1898.

LATTE PARK. Located beneath the foothill of Kasamata Hill, the latte stones of Latte Park were transferred from Me'pu, an ancient Chamorro settlement in the southern interior valley of Guam. These structures were built around 500 AD and were used as house pillars.

PLAZA DE ESPANA. Guam's most historical site, the Plaza de Espana, is a complex of structures built during the Spanish and early American period. This site was the seat of the Spanish Administration since 1669. The present historical structures include the Kiosko, Azotea, Chocolate House, Tool Shed, Siesta Shed, Spanish Walls, and the Guam Museum.

DULCE NOMBRE DE MARIA CATHEDRAL. The cathedral is located across the street from the Guam Legislature, site of the first Catholic church on Guam, which was constructed with the guidance of Padre San Vitores in 1669.

SANTO PAPA AS JUAN PABLO DOS PARK. Located between the Plaza de Espana and Skinner's Plaza, this park was dedicated in honour of the first Papal visit to the Mariana Islands since the introduction of Christianity three centuries ago.

WAR IN THE PACIFIC NATIONAL HISTORICAL PARK. Created in 1978 to honour those who fought and participated in World War II in the Pacific, the park protects and maintains five battlefield sites located in Asan, Piti, Mount Tenhu', Mount Chauchau and Agat. The park covers approximately 760 hectares of land and water. The Asan Park has a visitors' information centre which houses a mini-museum of war relics and a collection of war photographs.

FORT SANTA AGUEDA. Also known as Fort Apugan or Fort Kasamata, was built in 1800 during the administration of Governor Manuel Muro. The fort, rectangular in shape, was built of burned limestones mixed with coral rocks.

TAILAFAK BRIDGE. During the Spanish era, a coastal road was built between Agana and Umatac known as El Camino Real. Built in 1785, this bridge along the road is an example of Spanish stone construction.

CETTI BAY VISTA POINT. Gives a panoramic view of the coastal areas of the Territorial Seashore park. This site offers an excellent view of Cetti Bay, also once an ancient Chamorro settlement. From here, one has a distant view of the Merizo Barrier Reef and the Cocos Island Lagoon.

FORT NUESTRA SENORA DE LA SOLEDAD. Probably one of the last four forts constructed in Umatac. Built in the early 19th century, it is located on the southwestern bluff of Umatac Bay.

MERIZO PIER PARK. An excellent recreational area for all water related sport. At this park, the annual Merizo Water Festival is held during August. Located in Guam's only barrier reef, this park is the gateway to Cocos Island.

COCOS ISLAND. A 40-hectare island resort surrounded by a crystal clear lagoon. Just a few minutes away by speed boat, or glass bottom boats, Cocos offers numerous water sports activities.

MERIZO CONBENTO. Built in 1856, shortly after the 1856 smallpox epidemic, this is the oldest private residence still in use today on Guam. Built of burned limestone mixed with coral rocks and ifil wood, the original structure was roofed with clay tiles.

INARAJAN VILLAGE. Listed in the National Register of Historic Places in 1977 as an Historic District, Inarajan Village offers a historical insight into architectural development on Guam. There are several houses built during the Spanish era such as the San Nicolas and the Flores houses. The San Jose Church was built in 1941. The Baptist Church was built in 1925.

MT LAMLAM VISTA POINT. A 30-minute hike to this peak reveals the best views of Guam's interior and its dense forests. Towering 444.5 m, Mt Lamlam is Guam's highest point. The underwater base of the mountain is the deepest point in the ocean in the Marianas Trench, making it the highest mountain in the world from base to top.

FORT SOLEDAD VISTA POINT. This historic site offers an excellent view of the village of Umatac. It is assumed that Magellan sailed to this village in 1521, making that event the first contact between the Chamorros and Europeans.

LANCHON ANTIGO. Located in Historic District of Inarajan Village, Lanchon Antigo is a replica of a pre-20th century Chamorro village. The complex represents various dwellings constructed of local materials. An added attraction at the complex are the various traditional cultural exhibits depicting the making of salt and oil, and many artifacts.

TALOFOFO BAY BEACH PARK. One of Guam's most picturesque bays, this park is a surfing spot. The Talofofo, Guam's longest river, empties into this bay.

SOUTH PACIFIC MEMORIAL PARK. In Yigo, where the park is located, the last Japanese garrison under General Obata died after a desperate fight with US forces in August 1944. The memorial park was dedicated in 1970 to symbolise the determination of the two nations for peace. The tower is 15 metres high and symbolically represents a praying figure.

GOVERNMENT HOUSE. The architectural design of the Governor's Palace represents the Chamorro and Spanish heritage and is located on Kasamate Hill, overlooking Agana and Agana Bay.

GUAM TERRITORIAL SEASHORE PARK. This reserve was established in 1978 and encompasses the southern mountains, Fouha Bay and Cocos Lagoon. Historical points include Chamorro village sites, Spanish ruins, an early American school house and a WWII submerged Japanese Zero. Hiking trails, waterfalls, rivers, lakes and beaches are all part of the attractions.

THE MERIZO BELL TOWER or

KAMANAYUN MALESSU. This was built in 1910 under the direction of Father Cristobel de Canals and is included in the National Register of Historic Places. It was restored in 1981.

TO' LAI ACHU. Also known as San Antonio Bridge, it was built in 1800 across the Agana River.

LUJAN HOUSE. Also known as the Guam Institute, it was built in 1915 and was originally a private school.

I MEMORIAS PARA I LALAHITA OVERLOOK. This park, dedicated in 1971, commemorates those men from Guam who died in the Vietnam War. The site offers excellent views of the interior and Umatac Village.

YOKOI'S CAVE. Sergeant Soichi Yokoi hid in this cave from 1944 when the American troops arrived on Guam, until 24 January 1972. The remarkable tools and implements which he used for survival are displayed in the Guam Museum in Agana.

There are also a number of beautiful waterfalls located within the dense interior of Guam but guides are needed to visit them. The local name for people who venture off the beaten track is 'boonie stompers'.

ACCOMMODATION.
Listed alphabetically.

Cliff Hotel: businessmen's hotel in heart of Agana, 50 ac. rooms, room service, restaurants, bars, sports facilities, credit cards. 178 Francisco Javier Drive, Agana Heights, Guam 96910. Tel.: (671) 477 7675, Telex 726451 CLIFF.

Cocos Island Resort: Cocos Island, Merizo, 128 ac. rooms, restaurant, bar, marine sports, credit cards. PO Box 7174, Tamuning, Guam 96911. Tel.: (671) 828 9691, Telex 6519.

Downtown Hotel: Marine Drive, Agana, 46 ac. rooms, restaurants, bar, credit cards. 470 West Soledad Avenue, Agana, Guam 96911. Tel.: (671) 477 7836, Telex 721-6377.

Executive House Motel: Marine Drive Tamuning, 8 ac. rooms. PO Box 1321, Tamuning, Guam 96911. Tel.: (671) 646 5662, Telex 6428 FISI.

Fujita Guam Tumon Beach Hotel: beachfront, Tumon Bay, 283 rooms, restaurants (including Japanese), live

shows, water sports, tennis, pool, credit cards. 153 Fujita Road, San Vitores, Tumon, Guam 96911. Tel.: (671) 646 1811.

Guam Horizon Hotel: overlooking Tumon Bay, furnished 2 bedroom suites with or without cooking facilities, pool, BBQ, credit cards. PO Box 8349, Tamuning, Guam 96911.

Guam Dai-Ichi Hotel: beachfront, Tumon Bay, 538 rooms, restaurants (including Japanese), live shows, pools, bar, water sports, credit cards. PO Box 3310, Agana, Guam 96911. Tel.: (671) 646 5881.

Guam Suehiro Hotel: San Vitores Road, Tumon Bay, 38 rooms, restaurant, bar. PO Box 2767, Agana, Guam 96911. Tel.: (671) 646 6835, Telex none.

Guam Hotel Okura: beachfront, Tumon Bay, 224 rooms, restaurants, bar with live shows, pool, tennis, credit cards. 185 Gun Beach Road, Tumon, Guam 96911. Tel.: (671) 646 6811, Telex 624200KURA GM.

Guam Plaza Hotel: San Vitores Road, Tumon Bay, 119 rooms, restaurants, pool, tennis, shops, credit cards. PO Box 7755, Tamuning, Guam 96911. Tel.: (671) 646 7803, Telex 6274 CITYHILL GM.

Guam Reef Hotel: beachfront, Tumon Bay, 295 rooms, restaurants, bar, live shows, pool, tennis, credit cards. PO Box 8258, Tamuning, Guam 96911. Tel.: (671) 646 6881, Telex 726-6329.

Guam Towers: South Marine Drive, Tamuning, 211 1 or 2 bedroom units. 177B Mall Street, South Marine Drive, Tamuning, Guam 96911. Tel.: (671) 646 7036, Telex none.

Hilton International Guam: beachfront, Tumon Bay, 476 rooms, restaurants (including Japanese), room service, pools, tennis, shops, credit cards. PO Box GPO, Agana, Guam 96911. Tel.: (671) 646 1835, Telex 721-6234.

Hotel Guam American: Harmon area, 50 rooms, restaurant, bar, pool, credit cards. PO Box 7359, Tamuning, Guam 96911. Tel.: (671) 646 9061, Telex 6114.

Hotel Mai'ana: near Guam International Airport, 78 ac. rooms with kitchen, pool, credit cards. PO Box 8957, Tamuning, Guam 96911. Tel.: (671) 646 6961, Telex none.

Hotel Joinus: San Vitores Road, Tumon Bay, 36 rooms, restaurants, bar, pool, shops, credit cards. PO Box 8139, Tamuning, Guam 96911. Tel.: (671) 646 6801, Telex 6319 ASCTSP GM.

Island Garden Guest House: Mogfog area, 3 rooms, bed and breakfast facility. PO Box 2247, Agana, Guam 96911. Tel.: (671) 632 5870, Telex none.

Pacific Islands Club: beachfront, Tumon Bay, 120 ac. rooms, restaurant, bar, live shows, pool, tennis, golf, water sports, credit cards. 162 Pale San Vitores Road, Tumon, Guam 96911. Tel.: (671) 646 9171, Telex 721 6135.

Pacific Islands Hotel: beachfront, Tumon Bay, 194 rooms in garden setting, restaurant, bar, pool, credit cards. 210 Pale San Vitores Road, Tumon, Guam 96911. Tel.: (671) 646 9171, Telex 721-6135.

Pacific Star Hotel: Tumon Bay, 450 rooms, all facilities.

Plumeria Garden Hotel: Maite, 78 rooms, pool. PO Box 7220, Tamuning, Guam 96911. Tel.: (671) 472 8831, Cable: ACMEPLUM.

Inarajan Shores: Near Merizo Village, motel, camping, restaurant, bar, pool, BBQ, credit cards. PO Box 3308, Agana, Guam 96911. Tel.: (671) 828 8343, Telex none.

Terraza Tumon Villa: Tumon Bay, 20 rooms (some with kitchen), bar, credit cards. PO Box 8588, Tamuning, Guam 96911. Tel.: (671) 646 6940, Telex 6286.

Hawaii

Hawaii, a state of the USA, consists of eight major inhabited islands and 124 minor ones (land area 16.641 sq. km) located between 18 deg 50 min and 28 deg 15 min N latitude and 154 deg 40 min and 178 deg 15 min W longitude. The capital is Honolulu on Oahu, which is about 6200 km south-west of San Francisco. Local time is 10 hours behind GMT.

The state anthem is *Hawaii Ponoi*, the state flag consists of eight horizontal stripes (alternatively red, white and blue) representing the eight islands, with the British Union Flag in the upper left corner. The presence of the Union Flag commemorate's the British 'connection' in the late 18th and early 19th centuries when the group was called the Sandwich Islands. The currency is the US dollar.

Public Holidays are: 1 January, third Monday in February (President's Day), 26 March (Kuhio Day), Good Friday, the last Monday in May (Memorial Day), 11 June (Kamehameha Day), 4 July, third Friday in August (Admission Day), 4 July, first Monday in September (Labor Day), second Monday in October (Columbus Day), fourth Monday in October (Veteran's Day), Christmas Day, Thanksgiving Day and all election days except primary election day.

THE PEOPLE. At the last census in 1980 the total population of the state was 964,691. Estimated population in 1986 was 1,062,000.

The population includes 56,400 members of the US armed forces and 64,300 dependants. Most inhabitants are on the main island of Oahu, where the capital, the city of Honolulu, together with the county of Honolulu, has 816,700 people. This excludes visitors — for there are more than 133,000 visitors in the state at any one time, most of them in the Honolulu area.

The population is young (average age in 1980 being 28.3 years) but in recent years there has been a rapid increase in the number of older persons, and the number of children has declined. Persons 65 years and older increased by 72.6 per cent in the 10 years between the censuses of 1970 and 1980, and this continues to be the fastest growing group.

Since 1970, the Neighbor Islands (which is the local term for the islands other than the main one of Oahu) have reversed a long-term decline in population. The growth of tourism is largely responsible for this.

There is a varied racial mixture. Biggest group is Caucasian (or 'white'), with 24.5 per cent, Japanese with 23.2 per cent and Filipino with 11.3 per cent. But 27.3 per cent of the population consists of persons of mixed race, primarily part-Hawaiian (17.9 per cent). These figures include military personnel and departments, who are mostly Caucasian, but if these are excluded the Japanese population ranks first (with 26 per cent), Caucasian second (21.5 per cent), Hawaiian and part-Hawaiian third (20.0 per cent), with Filipinos fourth (11.9 per cent). The average number of persons per household in 1980 was 3.15, the lowest since figures were first compiled in 1940.

Migration. Migration has been a major factor in the growth of the population and official projections indicate that it will continue to affect it. Between 1980 and 1985 there was a net immigration (excluding military personnel and dependants) of 39,000 accounting for 44 per cent of the civilian

HAWAIIAN ISLANDS

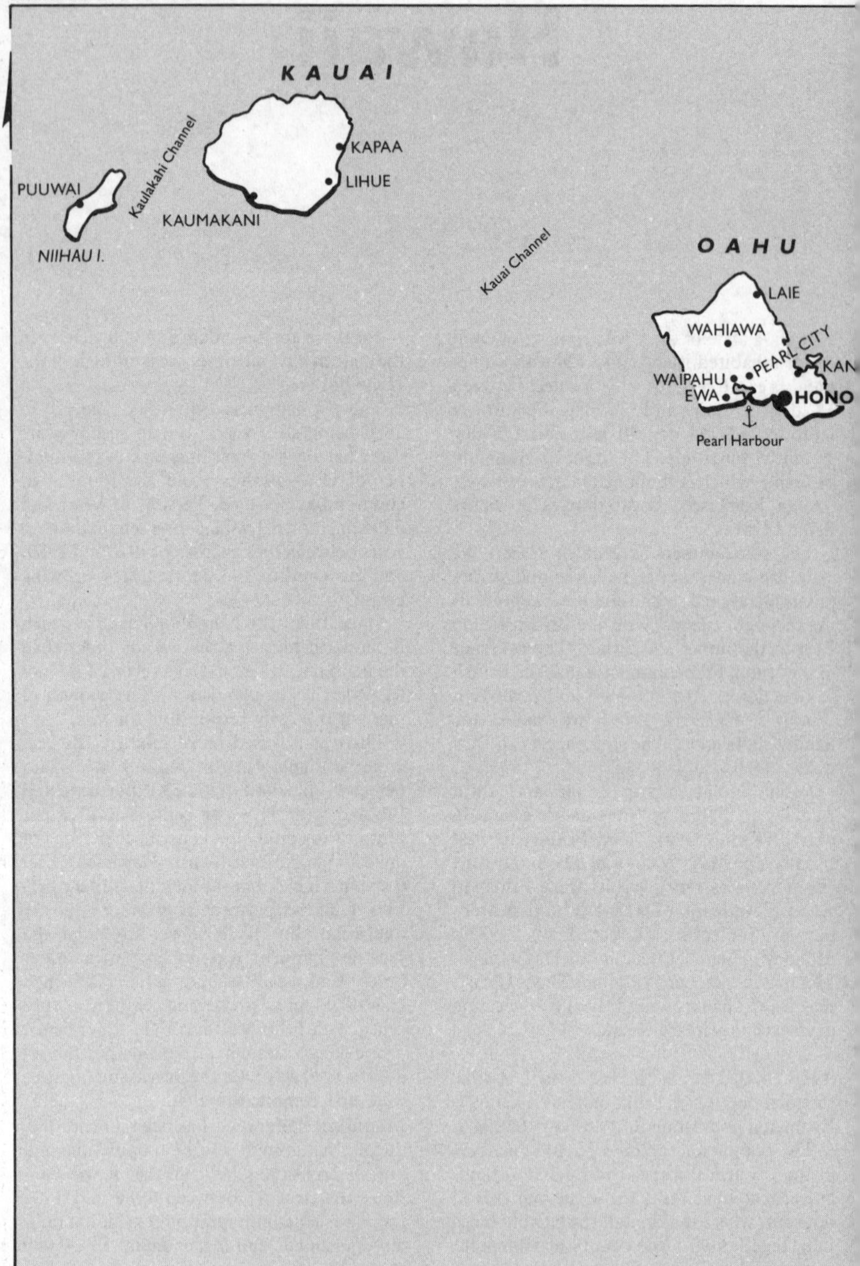

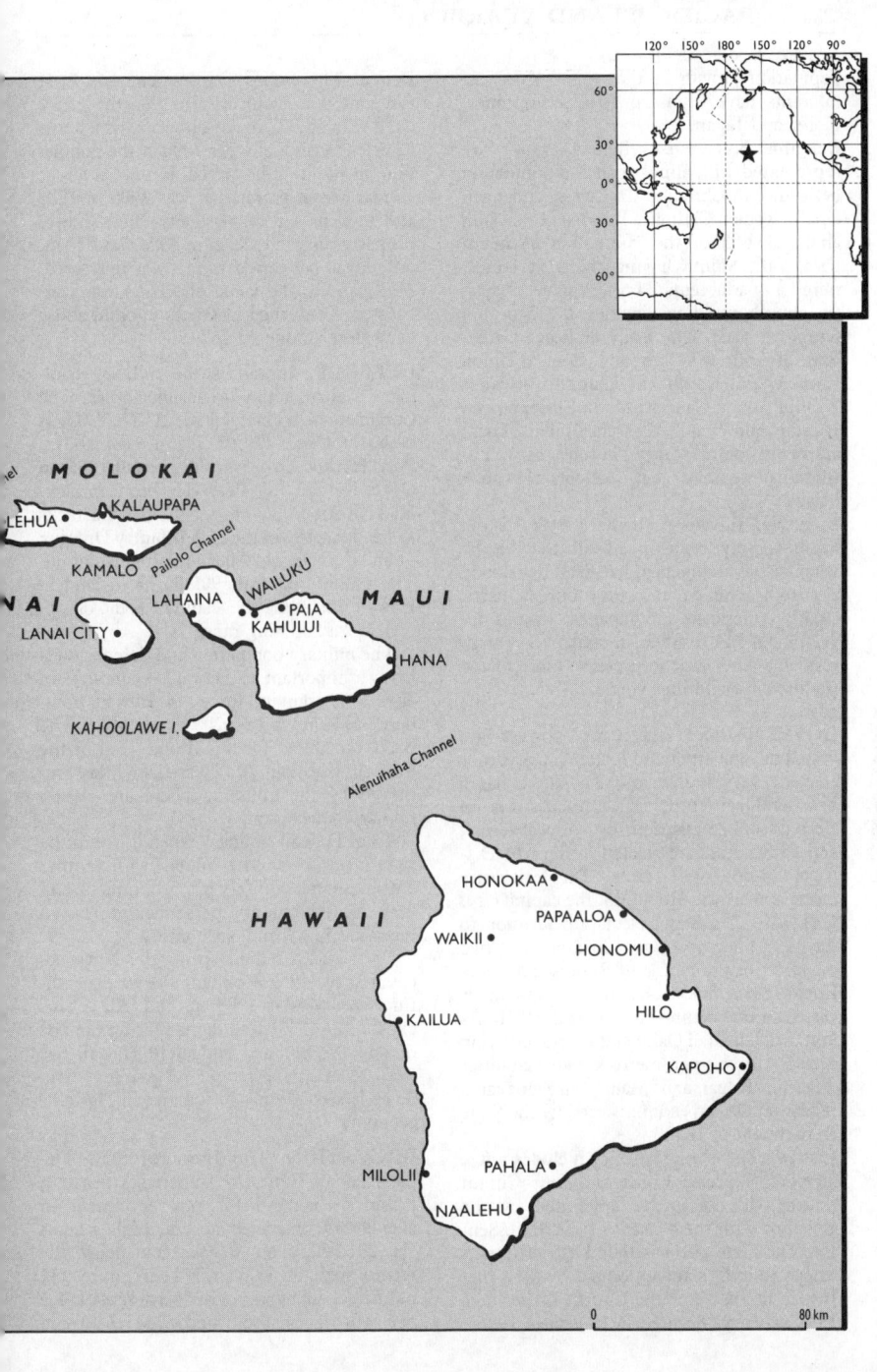

population growth at that time. Most immigrants have been from the Philippines, Korea and Japan.

Religion. Numerous religious groups are represented with almost half the population belonging to Christian Churches, and principally Roman Catholic; Buddist sects claim about a sixth of the population as members, with Shinto having the next largest number of adherents. Hawaii's many beautiful church buildings include the Mormon temple at Laie, Our Lady of Peace Cathedral, St Andrew's Cathedral, Central Union Church, and Kawaiahao Church on Oahu; Kaahumananu Church, Maui; St Benedicts, Hawaii; and Waioli Church, Kauai. There are many contemporary churches as well as Buddhist temples and ancient Hawaiian heiaus.

Lifestyle. Hawaii, particularly Oahu, is the most densely built-up of all the Pacific Islands; the archipelago has been developed as a tropical holiday resort for tourists, particularly Americans and Japanese. Rapid development has resulted in controversy with residents who want to preserve more of the traditional island lifestyles.

GOVERNMENT. Executive powers are vested in a governor and lieutenant governor elected every four years. The State has a bicameral legislature: 51 Representatives are elected from 25 Districts for two-year terms, and 25 Senators are elected from eight Districts for four-year terms. The legislature meets annually in Honolulu, the capital city.

Hawaii, as a State, elects a delegation to the US Congress — two Senators and two members of the House of Representatives.

Local government. Local government is vested in one combined city-county (Honolulu, i.e. Island of Oahu and several outlying islets), three non-metropolitan counties (Hawaii, Kauai and Maui), and one area (Kalawao County) administered by the State Department of Health.

Justice. The State Judiciary includes a five member Supreme Court and four Circuit Courts with 24 judges appointed by the governor with the consent of the State Senate. The State also has four District Courts whose 30 judges are appointed by the Chief Justice of the Supreme Court. There were 3373 attorneys licensed in Hawaii in 1986.

Police. The Police Department has 2831 full time police officers. In 1986 the police dealt with 55,372 major offences, which was 55 offences annually per 1000 of the population including the armed forces. Average annual prison population was 2009 in 1986 and median age of prisoners 30. Value of property reported stolen in 1984 was $27 m, only seven per cent of which was recovered. Marijuana to the value of $47 m was confiscated. Confirmed instances of child abuse or neglect numbered 1670.

DEFENCE. Hawaii is the military command centre of the US Pacific forces. The Commander-in-chief Pacific (CINCPAC) is based at Camp Smith, Oahu, just above, Pearl Harbor. Other military installations on Oahu include the Pearl Harbor complex, Hickam Air Force base, Schofield Barracks — headquarters of the 25th Infantry Division — and the Kaneohe Marine Corps air station. The military controls 90.300 ha of land in Hawaii, including the island of Kaho'olawe, which is a bombing range.

The military population and defence budget are important to Hawaii's economy. In July 1986 military forces in Hawaii numbered 58,600 with 66,200 dependants. The Navy accounted for about one-third of the total. In addition, 20,800 civilians were employed by the military. There are 19,200 military housing units.

Total Federal military expenditure in the state in 1986 was $1.8 billion, with another $563 million in military prime contracts, and with retired military personnel in Hawaii receiving $12.3 million monthly.

Of the $1.8 billion spent, the Navy accounted for $955.3 million. Army expenditure was $780.4 million, and Air Force expenditure $201.0 million. During the last decade the military budget in Hawaii has risen at an annual rate of 7.7 per cent. Defence is second only to tourism in Hawaii's economy.

EDUCATION. The Hawaiian State Department of Education supervises teaching facilities. In 1986–87 total enrolment in elementary, intermediate and high schools was 201,000, about 6.8 per cent below the record high of 1971–72. There were 232 public schools with 165,000 students (81.1 per cent of the total) and 8244 classroom teachers. There were also 145 private schools with 2544 teachers and 37,000 pupils.

Enrolment at colleges and universites in 1986–87 was over 52,000, including 19,666 on the Manoa campus of the University of Hawaii, 443 at West Oahu College, 3200 at UH-Hilo, 20,060 at six community colleges, and 9448 at four private colleges and universities.

East-West Center. This organisation for cultural and technical exchange in the Pacific and South-East Asia is located on the University of Hawaii campus. It provides specialist and advanced academic courses and technical training for more than 1500 students chosen each year from Pacific and Asian countries and mainland USA.

LABOUR. The civilian labour force averages 489,000 people (1986), of which 24,000 were unemployed and seeking work. The unemployment rate averaged 4.9 per cent, but it was down to 3.5 per cent in some islands. Percentage of women in the population aged 16 and older in the labour force in 1983 was 59.1 per cent — the eighth highest ratio in the US.

By occupation, one out of four civilian workers is professional or managerial. The largest numbers of employees are in the service industries (119,000), government (94,000) and retail trade (97,000).

Wages. Average annual earnings of salary and wage workers in 1985 was $17,300 which was almost twice the 1970 average. Average weekly working hours were 31.3 for the retail trade, ranging to 42.4 for communications and utilities. Average weekly wages for representative groups were: construction, $570.57; manufacturing, $327.94; communication and utilities, $601.25; hotels and lodgings, $269.27; wholesale and retail trades, $238.60.

The legal minimum wage as at January 1988 was $3.85 per hour. While wage and salary levels are above the national average they do not compensate for the Islands' higher cost of living. Labour union membership was estimated at 157,000 in 1985. There are 79 trade unions and associations.

HEALTH. Hawaii has high health standards. Expectation of life at birth in 1985 was 75.04 years for males, and 81.45 years for females, the highest in the US. There were 5788 resident deaths in 1985, or 5.4 per 1000 resident population. The State had 23 acute care hospitals (with 2870 beds) and 33 long-term care facilities, and nine special treatment facilities in 1986. It had 288 care homes (with 1631 beds) in 1983. There were 2150 physicians and surgeons, 847 dentists, 7088 registered nurses, and 469 pharmacists licensed and living in Hawaii as of November 1986. Health services available include those of chiropractors, osteopaths, veterinarians,

TABLE 1 EMPLOYMENT, HAWAII, 1980 TO 1986

Year	Total jobs	Non-agriculture			Agriculture			Labour disputes
		Total	Wage & salary	Self-employed	Total	Wage & salary	Self-employed	
1980	448,150	432,400	404,100	28,300	15,250	10,650	4600	500
1981	449,900	433,950	404,800	29,150	15,900	11,550	4350	50
1982	446,050	430,700	399,400	31,300	15,250	11,300	3950	100
1983	453,750	438,500	406,200	32,300	15,100	11,200	3900	150
1984	461,000	446,100	412,650	33,450	14,450	10,800	3650	450
1985	470,000	456,100	423,100	32,900	13,900	10,400	3500	100
1986 (p):								
1st Q	473,150	459,850	427,650	32,200	13,250	10,150	3050	50
2nd Q	477,450	463,200	429,450	33,750	14,200	11,300	2900	50

optometrists and others.

The Family Health Services Division administers programmes concerned with the provision of health services to women of childbearing age, infants, children and youth, and of community services for the developmentally disabled. These include family planning services, which were provided to 12,405 in fiscal year 1984 and school health services which focus on the co-ordination of health resources for more than 200,000 school-aged children in Hawaii.

Budget allocation for public health services for fiscal year 1986–87 was $197.2 m. The State Health Department employs 5205 people.

THE LAND. The State consists of eight major islands and 124 minor ones with a total land area of 16,641 square kilometres.

Honolulu, on the island of Oahu, is 342 km from the second largest city, Hilo, on the largest island, Hawaii. Triangular in shape, Hawaii is 150 km long by 120 km wide. The archipelago extends 2560 km. Highest mountains are Mauna Kea (4206 m) and Mauna Loa (4170 m), both on the island of Hawaii.

The Hawaii islands are mountainous, of volcanic origin, with extensive coastal plains and cool plateaus, as on Hawaii itself.

Natural features. The longest stream is Kaukonahua Stream (Oahu), 53 km in length; the biggest lake is Halaii, 336 hectares, on Niihau Is; and the biggest named waterfall is Kahiwa, a 574-metre cascade, on Molokai. Daily information for best volcanic viewing areas and any earthquake activity is provided by the Hawaii Volcanoes National Park telephone service. Further detailed geographical data are given in *Hawaii, the Natural Environment*, published by the State Department of Planning and Economic Development.

Climate. The islands have balmy temperatures and wide variations in rainfall. The all-time temperature range in down-town Honolulu, for example, is from 14–31°C. Normal precipitation, however, ranges from 140 mm near Kawaihae to 13.28 m atop Waialeale. The islands are not normally subject to typhoons.

National parks. Hawaii has seven national parks and similar areas, 74 state parks, 57 golf courses, 259 public tennis courts, 2033 small boat moorages, 1600 recognised surfing sites and 39 km of safe, sandy and accessible beaches.

Recreational and cultural facilities reporting more than one million visitors annually include four national or state parks, the National Memorial Cemetery of the Pacific, the USS *Arizona* Memorial in Pearl Harbor, Castle Park and the Honolulu Zoo.

Forestry. There are 500,000 ha of forests and water reserves, and 382,000 ha of commercial forests, most of it on the island of Hawaii. About 18,000 ha are planted with eucalyptus.

Land ownership. The total acreage in Hawaii, including inland water, is 1,664,283 ha. The state Land Use Commission has classified 796,996 ha as conservation land, 798,973 ha as agricultural land, 64,194 ha for urban use, and 4,120 ha as rural land.

Federal, state, and county governments own 622,155 ha, or about 39 per cent of the 1,593,255 ha available for ownership. The remaining 971,098 ha, or about 61 per cent, are privately owned, with six large landowners owning 381,060 ha, or 23.9 per cent, of the 1,593,255 ha available for ownership, or 39.2 per cent of all privately owned land.

The six largest private landowners are:

Bernice P. Bishop Estate	138,059 ha
Castle & Cooke, Inc	60,705 ha
Richard P. Smart (Parker Ranch) (incl. leased land)	89,034 ha
Samuel M. Damon Estate	49,235 ha
C. Brewer & Co., Ltd	38,288 ha
Alexander & Baldwin, Inc	38,366 ha

Other major landowners are:

James Campbell Estate	31,987 ha
Amfac, Inc	26,321 ha
Molokai Ranch	24,282 ha

Housing. Housing is expensive in Hawaii due, in part, to the limited availability and resulting high price of land. The number of housing units in the State increased from 284,000 in 1975 to 371,000 in 1986. Owner-occupied units numbered 116,000 in 1975 and 153,000 in 1986; the latter total included 36,000 on leased land. Condominium units, first authorised in 1961, numbered 98,000 at the end of 1982. Military and public housing accounted for 26,000 units as of 1986. Housing was in short supply throughout most of the past decade: on Oahu, the vacancy rate in May 1986, according to the Federal Home Loan Bank of Seattle, was only 2.3 per cent. The average selling price of single family homes on Oahu during 1986, based on Multiple Listing Service data, was $209,000; for condominium units it was $108,000. The median gross monthly rent for Oahu rose from $141 in 1970 to $413 in 1983, and the median value of owner-occupied single-family units increased from $38,400 to $163,400.

Construction. There were over 20,000 building permits issued in 1986, with an estimated value of $1024 million. The total included $549 million for private residential construction and $474 million in private non-residential structures.

Construction put in place, as indicated by the contracting tax base, totalled $1.4 billion in 1985 and $1.8 billion in 1986. The value of land transfers in 1987 was $7.2 billion. Mortgage loans outstanding at the end of 1984 amounted to $7.6 billion. The July 1985 construction cost index for Honolulu

(1967 = 100) was 357 for single-family residences and 373 for high-rise buildings.

PRIMARY INDUSTRY. Agriculture is an important industry particularly in the Neighbor Islands. There were 4600 farms in Hawaii as of 1985, with a total area of 1.96 million acres. The value of crop sales in 1985 was $445 million, or 10 per cent lower than the total for 1974.

Major crops were sugar ($256 million in sales, down 42 per cent over the decade), pineapple ($90 million, or 123 per cent over the 1974 total), flower and nursery products ($43 million, or 423 per cent more than in 1974), vegetables and melons ($26 million, up 164 per cent), and macadamia nuts ($26 million, up 398 per cent).

Diversified crops, defined as all crops other than sugar and pineapple, rose from $41 million in 1975 to $132 million in 1985, or approximately 225 per cent. Important products of livestock farms as of 1985 included cattle ($27 million in sales), milk ($29 million), and eggs ($14 million). In 1985,

TABLE 2 AGRICULTURAL STATISTICS 1984

Crop	Hectares	No. of farms
Sugar	85,636	185
Pineapple	15,909	18
Vegetables, melons	2409	677
Fruits	2955	800
Coffee	909	615
Macadamia nuts	7682	605
Taro, flowers, feed and nursery products	1330	813

MANUFACTURING ($ MILLIONS)

Categories	Employees	1979	1983	1984
Petroleum refining	985	770.4	1115.4	1175.6
Sugar processing	3700	345.7	409.6	397.6
Pineapple processing	2150	222.8	219.0	249.5
Diversified manufacturing	15,465	552.0	517.3	525.1

Hawaii produced 41 per cent of the fresh market vegetables consumed locally, 28 per cent of the fresh market fruits, 31 per cent of the beef and veal, 21 per cent of the chickens, none of the rice, and 83 per cent of the eggs.

Aquaculture has been growing in importance in recent years. Freshwater prawn production amounted to 318,000 pounds in 1984, with a value of more than $1.7 million. Ten years earlier the corresponding figures had been only 11,000 pounds and $38,000.

MANUFACTURING.   Manufacturing contributed about $2.35 billion to the economy in 1984 — up slightly from the $2.26 billion recorded in 1983 but below the record $2.6 billion logged for 1980. Manufacturing falls into three general categories: petroleum refining; sugar and pineapple processing (considered as a single entity); and diversified manufacturing, which consists of food processing (exclusive of sugar and pineapple); printing and publishing; the garment and apparel industry; processing and fabrication of construction materials; machinery/transportation equipment; furniture/fixtures; and miscellaneous, including the fabrication and application of high technology.

The value of petroleum refining amounted to $1.176 billion in 1984, up 5.4 per cent; and representing 50.3 per cent of all manufacturing sales. The state's two oil refineries — Hawaiian Independent Refinery, Inc., a subsidiary of Pacific Resources, Inc. (PRI), and Chevron USA, Inc. — have a combined daily capacity of 115,000 barrels at Barbers Point on Oahu. Petroleum refining provided 985 jobs in 1984.

The value of refined sugar and canned pineapple was $647.4 million, about 27.6 per cent of the manufacturing total, with sugar accounting for $397.9 million. The other 22.1 per cent of manufacturing sales came from diversified manufacturing.

In diversified manufacturing, food processing has grown consistently since statehood and is the largest segment in terms of jobs and business entities. The number of jobs has increased by 50 per cent and stood at 5250 in 1984. Since statehood, total wages paid in the food processing industry have increased by more than 425 per cent.

In terms of employment, printing and publishing constitutes the second largest segment of diversified manufacturing. Jobs in printing and publishing have grown by 45 per cent since statehood and numbered 3435 in 1984. Total wages paid have increased by almost 475 per cent. In 1982, there were 177 printing and publishing companies in Hawaii.

The garment and apparel industry, with 145 business units, is the third largest segment of diversified manufacturing in terms of employment. The number of jobs in this field reached its peak 10 years ago but by 1984 had dropped to 2900. Total wages paid in 1984 came to $28 million; annual wages averaged $9500, lowest in the manufacturing segment.

The fourth largest segment of manufactur-

TABLE 3 DIVERSIFIED MANUFACTURING GROUPS

	Employees	Companies
Food processing (excl. sugar, pineapple)	5250	221
Printing and publishing	3435	177
Garment and apparel	2900	145
Construction products	1900	
Machinery and equipment	580	424
Furniture and fixtures	400	
Miscellaneous	1000	
Totals	15,465	967

ing involves the processing and fabrication of construction materials. Like the apparel industry, this area has experienced a notable drop in the total job count. Numbers declined 40 per cent from a peak of 3245 in 1971 to 1900 in 1984. The cutback in construction activity is largely responsible. With the reduction in construction, Hawaii now has only one cement producer: Hawaiian Cement, which has an annual capacity of 600,000 short tons.

Manufacturing and transportation equipment employed 580 workers in 1984, more than double the 280 employees in 1959. Prospects for continued growth appear good.

On the other hand, furniture and fixture manufacturing declined dramatically to half its previous levels, employing fewer than 400 workers at the end of 1984.

The miscellaneous category, with a thousand jobs, includes the high technology field.

LOCAL COMMERCE. Hawaii has increasingly become a marketplace in which trade and services are the dominant activities. One of every three jobs in private industry is in trade. These activities have undergone rapid growth in recent decades, in part because of higher price levels. Retail sales increased from $751 million in 1963 to $1.9 billion in 1972 and $5.2 billion in 1982. Wholesale sales rose from $1.6 billion in 1972 to $4.1 billion in 1982. Hotels, amusements, and other services reported receipts exceeding $2.6 billion in 1982, compared with $665 million in 1972.

General excise and use tax base data for more recent years indicate continued increases; between 1982 and 1985, the retailing tax base rose 24 per cent, the wholesaling base by 28 per cent, and the base for services by 30 per cent.

Major retail concentrations include Waikiki, Ala Moana Center, Pearlridge Center, and downtown Honolulu. In addition to civilian retail outlets, there are many commissaries, exchanges, clubs, gasoline stations and food services maintained by the armed forces; these facilities had sales of $470 million in 1984.

Eighty-one feature motion pictures and television specials and series were filmed in Hawaii in 1986, accounting for local expenditures of $35 million.

TOURISM. Tourism represents the major source of income for the Hawaiian economy. Approximately 5,600,000 visitors stayed overnight or longer in Hawaii during 1986, compared with 2,829,000 in 1975 and only 687,000 in 1965. The average number present daily was 133,000. Total visitor expenditures (exclusive of trans-Pacific fares) in 1986 amounted to $5.5 billion, compared with $1.2 billion a decade earlier.

The 1986 visitor total included 3.7 million from other States, 282,000 from Canada, and 944,000 from Japan. Expenditures per visitor day in 1986 averaged $95 for westbound visitors and $257 for the Japanese.

Hotel units in the State rose from 33,000 in 1971 to 66,000 in 1986 when there were 501 hotels, motels and apartment-hotels including 309 on the Neighbor Islands. Occupancy rates averaged 85.7 per cent in Waikiki and 75.3 per cent on the Neighbor Islands during 1986.

TABLE 4 VISITOR STATISTICS

Year	Number of visitors	Westbound	Eastbound and northbound	Number of hotel rooms
1980	3,934,504	3,046,132	888,372	54,769
1981	3,934,623	2,974,791	959,832	56,769
1982	4,242,925	3,278,525	964,400	57,968
1983	4,367,880	3,396,115	971,965	58,765
1984	4,855,580	3,721,385	1,134,200	62,448
1985 (est.)	4,905,000	3,710,000	1,195,000	65,919

PUBLIC FINANCE. Government at all levels — Federal (both defence and non-defence), state and local government — is a major contributor to Hawaii's economy.

Total Federal government expenditure in 1984 was $4.23 billion. Military expenditure accounted for $1.87 billion of the total.

Total Federal tax receipts were $2.10 billion, an increase of 6.7 per cent on the previous year.

The 33,270 Federal government employees were paid a total of $855.4 million.

The state maintains an average staff of 43,000, paying $785.5 million in wages in 1984.

State operating revenues in 1984 were $2.163 billion, $1.32 billion being received from taxes. Federal grants-in-aid were $365 million, with local departmental revenues of $165.9 million. Royalties and land income brought in a further $62.4 million.

Total state operating expenditure amounted to $2.07 billion — the largest expenditure being on education ($696.2 million), followed by public welfare ($328.4 million), with debt service of $213.3 million and health services $187.1 million.

Combined revenue for the state's four counties in 1984 was $559.0 million. Operating expenditure for the counties was $555.4 million. County governments employed 13,201 persons, with a total wage bill in 1984 of $259.2 million.

Taxes ($342.7 million) accounted for more than half the revenue of the counties, with Federal grants accounting for $87.6 million. Property taxes were transferred from the state to the counties in July 1981.

Taxation. The State's four counties establish real property tax rates, and assess and collect real property taxes, but except for licences, permits and fees, other tax collections are the responsibility of the State which operates a centralised tax system.

Tax collections by Federal, state and county governments in fiscal 1984 reached $3.66 billion. The 1984 total included $1.98 billion in Federal taxes, $1.33 billion in State taxes and $343 million in county taxes, licences and fees.

Individual income taxes accounted for 87 per cent of Federal collections and 30 per cent of the state collections in Hawaii in 1984. Hawaii has no personal property or inventory taxes.

Banking. Hawaii has 10 banks, eight savings and loan societies, 66 industrial loan licensees, three trust companies and 139 credit unions. Total bank assets in 1985 were $8.8 billion, with total deposits of $7.8 billion.

Financial services in the state are concentrated in the two biggest banks, Bank of Hawaii and the First Hawaiian, which together account for 74.4 per cent of total bank deposits. For all 730 insurance companies doing business in the Islands, Hawaii premiums amounted to $967 million in 1984 and losses, claims, and benefits paid came to $530 million.

Gross State Product. Hawaii's GSP, which is the combined sales of all its businesses and services, was an estimated $16.2 billion in 1985, an increase of 22 per cent over that of 1981.

OVERSEAS TRADE. Honolulu is the only port equally accessible to all major markets of the Pacific Basin. It serves as a natural commerce crossing point.

Imports to Hawaii from foreign nations rose from $645 million in 1974 to $1.6 billion in 1986. Exports to foreign countries amounted to only $115 million in 1974, but by 1986 reached $231 million. (These figures, it should be noted, refer to merchandise imports and exports through the Honolulu Customs District. They do not necessarily represent exports of commodities originating in Hawaii, nor imports for direct consumption within the State.)

Merchandise received from the Mainland United States increased from $1.3 billion in 1970 to $5.6 billion in 1985. Estimates of the value of merchandise exported to the Mainland are no longer available.

Among the foreign nations, Hawaii's leading trading partners in 1984 were Indonesia for imports and Taiwan for exports. Imports from Indonesia amounted to $373 million, or 2.3 per cent of the total, while exports to Taiwan reached $64 million, or 20 per cent of all foreign exports. About 57 per cent of all imports for consumption were petroleum and natural gas products and monolithic integrated circuits.

Honolulu Foreign-Trade Zone No. 9 at Pier 2, Honolulu Harbor, handled merchandise valued at $54 million in fiscal year

TABLE 5 HAWAII'S FOREIGN TRADE PARTNERS ($ MILLIONS)
Imports[1].

Country & Rank[3]	1983	1984	Per cent change
1. Japan (2)[3]	$305.0	$364.0	19.3
2. Indonesia (1)	629.0	373.1	(40.7)
3. Singapore (3)	218.6	203.0	(7.1)
4. Taiwan (5)	116.1	145.2	25.1
5. Australia (7)	44.6	127.6	186.1
6. Philippines (6)	69.2	76.1	10.0
7. Malaysia (4)	163.1	61.0	(62.6)
8. China (11)	25.7	41.2	60.3
9. France (9)	31.7	36.7	15.8
10. Hong Kong (12)	22.8	30.7	34.6
Total (Top 10)	$1625.8	$1458.6	(10.3)
Total (All Countries)	1828.1	1614.2	(11.7)

Exports[2]

Country & Rank[3]	1983	1984	Per cent change
1. Taiwan (3)[3]	$16.5	$64.1	288.5
2. Japan (1)	72.1	54.7	(24.1)
3. Australia (2)	19.1	54.4	184.8
4. China (20)	0.05	45.5	889.1
5. Micronesia (4)	14.1	17.3	22.7
6. Korea, Republic of	8.9	16.8	88.8
7. Indonesia (8)	8.9	13.4	50.6
8. New Zealand (6)	9.7	13.3	37.1
9. Canada (5)	10.9	13.1	20.2
10. Pap. New Guinea (10)	6.0	7.2	20.0
Total (Top 10)	$166.3	$299.8	80.3
Total (All Countries)	203.4	316.9	55.8

1. Imports for consumption.
2. Exports of domestic merchandise.
3. Countries ranked by 1984 volume; 1983 ranking is in parentheses.

1986. Merchandise handled by Subzone No. 9A, the PRI refinery in Campbell Industrial Park, was valued at $922 million, almost all of it in petroleum and petroleum products. Subzone No. 9-B at Pier 23 in Honolulu Harbor is occupied by Hawaiian Flour Mills, and the Dole Processed Foods Company, a Castle and Cooke subsidiary, occupies Subzone No. 9-C at Iwilei in Honolulu.

During the year ended 30 June 1985 some 2969 new domestic (Hawaii) corporations were formed. Another 581 out-of-state (foreign) corporations were registered to do business in the Islands. The total number of domestic profit corporations was 26,362 as of 30 June 1985, and the total of foreign corporations was 4320.

ENERGY. Hawaii is dependent upon imported petroleum, which it uses for 90 per cent of its energy needs. Most of it originates in Indonesia. Petroleum cost in 1984 was $1.3 billion, with its price increasing dramatically in recent years. More than 82 per cent of the state's energy is used on Oahu.

Hawaii has done a great deal of work towards developing alternate sources of energy, and five major resources are seen to have potential. Geothermal energy, heat released from the earth, is one important source, and the state's first commerical operation in geothermal energy began on the island of Hawaii in 1982 and a 3 megawatt geothermal generator produced 20 million kW hours of electricity in 1984.

More than 500 wind machines, many supplying electricity to local utilities, have been installed and a 3.2-megawatt wind machine has been proposed for Kahuku, Oahu. Biomass, especially sugarcane waste, is Hawaii's primary source of renewable energy. Fast-growing tree farms and refuse-burning plants are being studied as added sources of energy. Comparatively small amounts of electricity now produced by hydroelectric power may be increased. More than 600 Island homes have installed photovoltaic systems to furnish all or part of their electric power. Hawaii has an estimated 39,000 households with solar water heaters. On Oahu, a municipal refuse-burning plant is being developed. State and Federal energy conservation programmes have achieved savings of millions of dollars in reduced oil imports.

Hawaii continues to pioneer in ocean thermal energy conversion (OTEC) using sun-heated ocean waters and deep cold waters to produce electricity. A 50-megawatt OTEC plant is being considered for Kahe Point, Oahu. The Natural Energy Laboratory of Hawaii (NELH) at Keahole Point on the Island of Hawaii is the world's foremost test facility for both OTEC and cold-water aquaculture. In 1985, 14 projects were conducted and two which produced cultured abalone and microalgae began successful production and sale of their products.

TRANSPORT. Most local travel in Hawaii is by private car, although there is an excellent bus service on the main island. Motor vehicle registration in 1986 was 772,000. Hawaii residents bought 58,700 new passenger cars in 1986, and 10,000 trucks. By the end of 1986, 612,000 licensed drivers had access to 6500 km of road.

Bus passengers carried by the Honolulu Mass Transit Lines totalled 74 million in 1986. There were 94,000 registered bicycles. **Aviation.** Most inter-island travel is by air. In 1985, the major airlines and a number of air taxis carried 7.9 million inter-island passengers, and 51,000 tons of cargo. The major airlines are Hawaiian, Aloha and Mid Pacific Airlines.

Hawaii has 8 commercial airports, 13 general aviation, military or semi-private airports, 10 civilian heliports, 3187 active pilots and about 463 aircraft in general aviation.

Trans-Pacific air travellers to Hawaii increased from 224,000 in 1959 to 5.3 million in 1985, 3.8 million of them arriving from North America and 1.5 million eastbound (from Asia or Oceania). At June 1985, 13 foreign airlines served Hawaii.

Honolulu airport, the 17th busiest in the world in 1984, served 16.2 million passengers and recorded 343,818 aircraft movements. **Shipping.** Passengers arriving by ship have dropped considerably in numbers over the years as air transport figures have risen, but more than 98 per cent of cargo in and out of Hawaii is still carried by ship. In 1984, 1686 overseas and 2660 inter-island vessels docked at the port of Honolulu. 11.8 m tonnes of overseas and 8.3 m tonnes of inter-island cargo were carried in 1983. During that year 688,689 passengers used the port of Honolulu. Main cargo carriers are Matson Navigation Co. and United States Lines.

Ports and harbours. There are eight commercial ports in Hawaii. These are, together with the length of their piers in linear feet: On Hawaii, Hilo (2787 ft) and Kawaihae (1012); on Maui, Kahului (2749); on Molokai, Kaunakakai (691); on Oahu, Honolulu main wharf 1520 ft, Kapalama 1000 ft; on Kauai, Nawiliwili (1216), Port Allen (1200).

There were 1306 vessels documented in Hawaii in 1985, and 13,122 numbered. All commercial vessels over five net tons, and all yachts over that tonnage, must be documented with the Coast Guard; any mechanically-propelled boat or sailboat over eight feet must be numbered and registered.

Ports of entry. Honolulu, Hilo (on Hawaii), and Kahului (on Maui). There are two yacht harbours in Honolulu — one in the harbour proper and the other, Ala Wai yacht harbour, at Waikiki. Most berths at Waikiki are permanently occupied by local yachts. There are numbers of yacht anchorages, and cruising yachts will be told where to tie up after the usual quarantine and migration formalities are completed.

COMMUNICATION. Hawaii is served by all major communications media. In 1985 it had 140 post offices and stations handling 339 million pieces of mail and accounting for postal receipts of $95 million. There were 472,000 telephone access lines in service, 339,000 telephone homes, about 2.1 billion local calls originated, 12 million completed inter-island calls (in 1981), and 32 million incoming and outgoing transpacific calls (in 1980). Telegraph messages to and from Hawaii in 1984 totaled 112,000.

Hawaii is currently the site of ground relay stations for worldwide satellite communications systems.

Two undersea cables link Hawaii with the West Coast of the US; other cables link Hawaii with Japan, and the Commonwealth COMPAC cable passes through Hawaii. The Hawaiian Telephone Co. participates in the Communications Satellite Corporation (COMSAT), and the University of Hawaii uses PEACESAT for scientific and educational communication with institutions and groups in other Pacific nations.

Radio and television. The 45 commercial, public and educational radio stations in the Islands in 1985 included 26 on the regular broadcast band and 19 FM stations. The State also had 15 television stations (13 commercial and 2 public), including satellites but excluding translators. Nine cable TV companies served 211,000 subscribers in 1984. An estimated 97 per cent of all households had television sets.

Newspapers. Island publishers printed nine daily newspapers, numerous magazines and other periodicals, and a wide diversity of books. Hawaii's two major daily newspapers are the afternoon *Honolulu Star-Bulletin* and the morning *Honolulu Advertiser* with daily circulations in 1984–85 of 110,045 and 86,998 respectively.

PUBLIC UTILITIES. Electricity sales exceeded 7.0 billion kilowatt-hours in 1986, a total that has increased 29 per cent since 1974. Electric power for residential and industrial use is supplied by five power companies — Hawaiian Electric Co., Inc. (Oahu); Hawaii Electric Light Co., Ltd. (Hawaii); Kauai Electric (Kauai); Maui Electric Co., Inc. (Maui); and Molokai Electric Co., Ltd. The Hawaiian Electric Company owns the Hawaii and Maui companies and furnishes power on the Island of Lanai. In addition, some plantations and military installations, especially the Pearl Harbor Naval Base and Shipyard, generate and distribute their own power.

The Gas Company (Gasco, Inc.), a subsidiary of Pacific Resources, Inc., provides the State's pipeline (utility) gas and also supplies tank and bottled propane gas service. Utility gas sales reached 31.0 million therms in 1986. Average residential use of both gas and electricity (194 therms and 6714 kW hours in 1984) has declined significantly in recent years.

MAJOR OFFICE HOLDERS
Congressional Members
US Senators:
   Daniel K. Inouye, Spark M. Matsunaga
US Representatives:
   Daniel K. Akaka, Patricia Saiki
State Officers
Governor:
   John D. Waihee III
Lieutenant Governor:

Benjamin J. Cayetano
Attorney-General:
Warren Price III
Chief Justice:
Herman T. F. Lum

HAWAII — STATE GOVERNMENT OFFICES

Governor of Hawaii, Hon. John D. Waihee 3rd, State Capitol, Honolulu, HI 96813. Tel.: (808) 548 5420

Lieutenant Governor, Benjamin J. Cayetano, 5th Floor, State Capitol, Honolulu, HI 96813. Tel.: (808) 548 2544

Hawaii Department of Defense, Adjutant General, 3949 Diamond Head Road, Honolulu, HI 96816. Tel.: (808) 734 2195 (note: above office is National Guard)

Airports Division, Hawaii Dept of Transportation, Honolulu International Airport, Honolulu, HI 96819. Tel.: (808) 863 6432

Hawaii Department of Agriculture, 1428 S. King Street, Honolulu, HI 96814. Tel.: (808) 548 7101

State Archivist, Division of Archives, Dept of Accounting and General Services, Iolani Palace Grounds, Honolulu, HI 96813. Tel.: (808) 548 2355

Foundation on Culture and Arts, Dept of Accounting & General Services, 333 Merchant St, Room 202, Honolulu, HI 96813. Tel.: (808) 548 4145

Attorney General, Warren Price 3rd, State Capitol, Honolulu, HI 96813. Tel.: (808) 548 4740

Division of Financial Institutions, Commissioner, Hawaii Dept of Commerce and Consumer Affairs, 1010 Richards St, Honolulu, HI 96813. Tel.: (808) 548 5855 (note: above office administers Hawaii banking laws)

Hawaii Dept of Budget and Finance, State Capitol, PO Box 150, Honolulu, HI 96810. Tel.: (808) 548 2325

Chief Justice of Hawaii, Hon. Herman T. F. Lum, Supreme Court, The Judiciary, 417 S. King St, Honolulu, HI 96813. Tel.: (808) 548 5930

Hawaii Dept of Commerce and Consumer Affairs, Director, 1010 Richards Street, Honolulu, HI 96813. Tel.: (808) 548 7505

Hawaii Dept of Accounting and General Services, Director, 1151 Punchbowl St, Honolulu, HI 96813. Tel.: (808) 548 3050

(note: above is the principal accounting & disbursing office of the state government)

Office of Consumer Protection, 250 S. King St, Room 520, Honolulu, HI 96813. Tel.: (808) 548 2560

Administrative Office of the Courts, The Judiciary, 417 S. King St, Honolulu, HI 96813. Tel.: (808) 548 4605

Criminal Justice Data Center, Hawaii Dept of Attorney General, 465 S. King St, Room 101, Honolulu, HI 96813. Tel.: (808) 548 2090

Hawaii Dept of Business and Economic Development, 250 S. King St, Honolulu, HI 96813. Tel.: (808) 548 6914

Hawaii Dept of Education, Superintendent, 1390 Miller St, Honolulu, HI 96813. Tel.: (808) 548 6583

Employment Service Division, Dept of Labor and Industrial Relations, 830 Punchbowl St, Room 329, Honolulu, HI 96814. Tel.: (808) 548 6468

Environmental Protection & Health Services, Director, Hawaii Dept of Health, 1250 Punchbowl St, Honolulu, HI 96813. Tel.: (808) 548 4139

Hawaii Dept of Health, Director, 1250 Punchbowl St, Honolulu, HI 96813. Tel.: (808) 548 6505

Insurance Commissioner, Division of Insurance, Hawaii Dept of Commerce and Consumer Affairs, 1010 Richards St, Honolulu, HI 96813. Tel.: (808) 548 6522

Hawaii Dept of Labor and Industrial Relations, 830 Punchbowl St, Honolulu, HI 96813. Tel.: (808) 548 3150

Hawaii Criminal Justice Commission, Director, 222 S. Vineyard St, Room 703, Honolulu, HI 96813. Tel.: (808) 548 6714

State Librarian, State Public Library System, Dept of Education, 465 S. King St, Room B-1, Honolulu, HI 96813. Tel.: (808) 548 5596

Hawaii Dept of Transportation, 869 Punchbowl St, Honolulu, HI 96813. Tel.: (808) 548 3205

Dept of Land and Natural Resources, 1151 Punchbowl St, Honolulu, HI 96813. Tel.: (808) 548 6550

State Ombudsman, Office of the Ombudsman, 465 S. King St, Honolulu, HI 96813. Tel.: (808) 548 7811

State Parks, Outdoor Recreation and Historic Sites Divn, 1151 Punchbowl St, Honolulu, HI 96813. Tel.: (808) 548 7455

Office for State Planning, Director, PO Box 2359, Honolulu, HI 96804.
Tel.: (808) 548 6222
Public Utilities Commission, Dept of Budget and Finance, 465 S. King St, Room 103, Honolulu, HI 96813.
Tel.: (808) 548 3990
Purchasing & Supply Division, Dept of Accounting and General Services, 1151 Punchbowl St, Honolulu, HI 96813.
Tel.: (808) 548 4057
Hawaii Dept of Taxation, 425 S. Queen Street, Honolulu, HI 96813.
Tel.: (808) 548 7650
Hawaii Dept of Social Services, 1390 Miller St, Honolulu, HI 96813.
Tel.: (808) 548 6260
Tourism Divn, Hawaii Dept of Business & Economic Development, 250 S. King St, Honolulu, HI 96813. Tel.: (808) 548 6914
Research and Statistics Office, Dept of Health, 1250 Punchbowl St, Honolulu, HI 96813. Tel.: (808) 548 6454
(note: above office is responsible for records of births, deaths & marriages in Hawaii)

FEDERAL GOVERNMENT OFFICES
United States Department of Agriculture, Hawaii District Office, Prince Kuhio Federal Building, Honolulu, HI 96850.
Tel.: (808) 546 5527 (Statistical Reporting Service)
United States Air Force, Hickam Air Force Base, Honolulu, HI 96853.
Tel.: (808) 471 7411
United States Army, Fort Shafter, Honolulu, HI 96858. Tel.: (808) 471 7411
United States Navy, Pearl Harbor Naval Base, Honolulu, HI 96860.
Tel.: (808) 471 7411
International Trade Administration, US Department of Commerce, Prince Kuhio Federal Building, Honolulu, HI 96850.
Tel.: (808) 546 8694
National Weather Service, National Oceanic & Atmospheric Administration, Prince Kuhio Federal Building, Honolulu, HI 96850. Tel.: (808) 546 5690
Clerk of the Court, US District Court, Prince Kuhio Federal Building, Honolulu, HI 96820. Tel.: (808) 546 3737
District Director of Customs, Hawaii, US Customs Service, Room 228, Federal Building, Honolulu, HI 96850.
Tel.: (808) 546 3116

US Department of Defense, Prince Kuhio Federal Building, 300 Ala Moana Blvd, Honolulu, HI 96850.
Tel.: (808) 546 3168
(Army Liaison Office)
East-West Center, 1777 East-West Road, Honolulu, HI 96848.
Tel.: (808) 944 7111
US Department of Energy, Prince Kuhio Federal Office Building, 300 Ala Moana Blvd, Honolulu, HI 96850.
Tel.: (808) 546 2184
Federal Bureau of Investigation, US Department of Justice, Prince Kuhio Federal Office Building, 300 Ala Moana Bldg, Honolulu, HI 96850.
Tel.: (808) 546 521 1411
Federal Communications Commission, Prince Kuhio Federal Building, 300 Ala Moana Blvd, Honolulu, HI 96850.
Tel.: (808) 546 5640
Federal Trade Commission, Prince Kuhio Federal Building, 300 Ala Moana Blvd, Honolulu, HI 96850. Tel.: (808) 546 5685
General Services Administration, Prince Kuhio Federal Office Bldg, 300 Ala Moana Blvd, Honolulu, HI 96850.
Tel.: (808) 546 7516
US Dept of Health & Human Services, Prince Kuhio Federal Bldg, 300 Ala Moana Blvd, Honolulu, HI 96850.
Tel.: (808) 546 8379 (Food & Drug Admin), (808) 546 2110 (Social Security)
US Dept of Housing & Urban Development, Prince Kuhio Federal Building, 300 Ala Moana Blvd, Honolulu, HI 96850. Tel.: (808) 546 5554
US Dept of the Interior, 300 Ala Moana Boulevard, Honolulu, HI 96850.
Tel.: (808) 546 5608 (Fish & Wildlife)
Immigration & Naturalization Service, US Dept of Justice, 595 Ala Moana Boulevard, Honolulu, HI 96813.
Tel.: (808) 546 8920
Internal Revenue Service, US Dept of the Treasury, Prince Kuhio Federal Building, 300 Ala Moana Blvd, Honolulu, HI 96850. Tel.: (808) 546 8660
US Attorney's Office, US Dept of Justice, Prince Kuhio Federal Building, 300 Ala Moana Blvd, Honolulu, HI 96850.
Tel.: (808) 546 7170
US Dept of Labor, Prince Kuhio Federal Building, 300 Ala Moana Blvd, Honolulu, HI 96850. Tel.: (808) 546 7500 (labor stats.)

Passport Agency, US Dept of State, Prince Kuhio Federal Bldg, Honolulu, HI 96850. Tel.: (808) 546 2131

Federal Aviation Administration, US Dept of Transportation, Prince Kuhio Federal Bldg, 300 Ala Moana Blvd, Honolulu, HI 96850. Tel.: (808) 546 8641

HISTORY. The Hawaiian Islands are believed to have first been settled from the Marquesas Islands about 650 AD. Artefacts found at several sites on the island of Hawaii and also at Bellows Beach, Oahu, are similar to artefacts found in the Marquesas. A second migration probably reached the islands from Tahiti some centuries later and overcame the original inhabitants, known in tradition as dwarfs called 'menehune'. Close resemblances between the languages of Hawaii and Tahiti, and Hawaiian traditions of an island called Kahiki (i.e. Tahiti) lend weight to the theories of a migration from Tahiti. Whatever the truth, Hawaii's migrants brought with them breadfruit, bananas, yams, sugar cane, taro, the sweet potato, dogs, pigs and chickens. The presence of the sweet potato suggests contact with South America at some period.

Spanish visits. Historical research has refuted old claims that the Hawaiian Islands were discovered in 1555 by a Spaniard named Juan Gaetan or Gaetano. However, survivors from one or more of the Spanish galleons that disappeared in the 16th and 17th centuries on voyages between the Philippines and Mexico may have reached the islands. Evidence suggesting this came to light in the early sixties when scientists at the Bishop Museum, Honolulu, found a piece of iron and a length of woven cloth (probably sail cloth) in the burial casket of a deified Hawaiian chief. The chief is reputed to have lived on the island of Hawaii in about the 16th century. Moreover, tradition has it that a number of white men once came ashore at Kealakekua Bay, Hawaii, that they were given wives, became chiefs and left light-skinned descendants. The elaborate helmets and feather capes that were worn by chiefly Hawaiians in the latter part of the 18th century may be further evidence of the arrival of castaway Spaniards. A few pieces of iron were also found in their possession at that time.

Cook's Discovery. The Hawaiian Islands remained unknown to Europe until Captain James Cook discovered them on 18 January 1778, naming them the Sandwich Islands after his patron, the Earl of Sandwich. Cook was then on his third voyage to the Pacific, and was sailing northwards in search of the North-West Passage. At that time he touched only at the north-westerly islands of Kauai and Niihau. But about 12 months later, in returning from the north-west coast of America, he also called at Maui and Hawaii. He was killed at Kealakekua Bay on 14 February 1779, after the Hawaiians had apparently mistaken him for the god Lono. Cook's visit to the American coast resulted in the discovery of the sea otter whose fur was much in demand in China. This soon brought adventurers from Europe and the United States to the same area, and in crossing the Pacific to China to sell their furs, they generally put in to Hawaii. The first ships to call were the British vessels *King George* and *Queen Charlotte* in 1786. Their commanders had both been on Cook's last voyage. The first American ship, *Columbia*, arrived in 1789.

Kamehameha I. The coming of the fur traders coincided with the rise of Kamehameha I, a member of a chiefly family of the island of Hawaii. After a series of wars, Kamehameha unified all the Hawaiian islands under him and created a kingdom which lasted until 1893. He won a great naval victory in 1793 with cannon supplied by Europeans. Three years later, he sought help in his wars from the British explorer Captain George Vancouver, who misinterpreted his request, raised the British flag and took possession of the islands for the British Crown. Vancouver's proceedings were never ratified.

But Kamehameha's conquests continued. By 1795 Maui, Molokai, Oahu and Hawaii were under his control. Kauai submitted in 1810.

Disease strikes. Meanwhile, visiting European and American ships, including numerous whalers from 1819 onwards, brought in new diseases that caused a rapid decline in the islands' native population. From perhaps as many as 300,000 in Cook's time, the numbers fell to about 135,000 in 1820, about 85,000 in 1850, and 40,000 in 1890. The heavy mortality was accompanied by orgies of drunkenness, prostitution, gambling and other excesses. In 1819 there was a climax to this when the newly-installed Kamehameha II abolished the 'kapu' (tabu) system that had previously ruled the lives of the commoners. He also ordered the destruction of the ancient idols and places of worhsip.

First missionaries. When the first missionaries reached Hawaii in 1820, they were appalled by the disorder and demoralisation among the islanders. The missionaries, Calvinists from New England sponsored by the American Board of Commissioners for Foreign Missions, quickly learned Hawaiian and concentrated their attention on the chiefs. While the women taught needlework, the male missionaries won friends by treating the sick. They produced their first printed work in Hawaiian in 1822 and conducted their first baptism the following year. Meanwhile, the Hawaiian chiefess Kaahumanu, who acted as regent following the death of Kamehameha II in 1824, did much to bring about the formal conversion of the islands to Christianity. First, she ordered strict obervance of the Sabbath; and later, in co-operation with the other chiefs, she decreed a code of laws against murder, theft, fighting and the breaking of the Sabbath. She also ordered the establishment of schools. The number of schools grew rapidly. By 1831 they had 50,000 students.

Christianity suffered a temporary setback after Kaahumanu's death in 1832. The young king Kamehameha III was a lukewarm convert. However, by 1835 another woman, the king's half-sister Kinau, had gained control of political affairs and, through her, as one observer put it, the American missionaries could 'govern the islands with an unlimited sway'. In 1838, under their influence, strict liquor laws were introduced, and four years later there were temperance laws. Increasingly, the missionaries, particularly those in Honolulu, became involved in the government. Some actually resigned from the mission and joined the government. Among those who exerted considerable influence were William Richards, Hiram Bingham, and Gerrit P. Judd. Judd was virtual dictator of Hawaii during a series of events that led Captain Lord George Paulet, of HMS *Carysfort*, to annex the islands for

Great Britain on 25 February 1843. However, Hawaiian independence was restored by Paulet's commanding officer, Rear-Admiral Richard Thomas, five months later.

Annexation efforts. In 1854 Judd, who had then been dismissed from office, pressed the United States to annex Hawaii. The proposal was strongly supported by American residents. But with the accession of Kamehameha IV, who had once been mistaken for and was victimised as, a Negro in the United States, all hope of annexation vanished for the time being. It was during the reign of Kamehameha IV (1854–63) that the first successful oil well was drilled in the United States — at Philadelphia in 1859. This event, and the outbreak of the American Civil War, caused a rapid decline in the Pacific whaling industry that had been the basis of Hawaii's economy for many years. (By 1830, 150 ships had been visiting Hawaii annually; in 1846 there was a peak of 596; and even in 1859, the annual average was still over 500.)

With the loss of revenue from the sale of provisions and other goods to the whalers, Hawaii experienced hard times for several years. Then a new industry developed: sugar. This required plenty of labour, a commodity that Hawaii could not supply. As a result, thousands of Islanders, Chinese, Japanese and Portuguese were imported — the basis for today's multi-racial population.

With the development of the sugar industry and the decline in numbers of the Hawaiian population, the American Calvinist missionaries lost their predominance, and newer American settlers began to exert influence. Among these was the unscrupulous Walter Murray Gibson, originally a Mormon missionary. Other settlers married into the Hawaiian royal family and thus gained an interest in large tracts of land. A well-known example of this was Charles Reed Bishop, a banker and statesman in the Hawaiian Government, who married the chiefess Bernice Pauahi, the last direct descendant of Kamehameha I. (In 1889, after her death, Bishop founded the Bernice Pauahi Bishop Museum as a memorial to her.)

Hawaii becomes republic. The last four monarchs of the Hawaiian kingdom were Kamehameha V (1863–72), Lunalilo (1873–

74), Kalakaua (1874–91) and Queen Liliuo-kalani (1891–93). During Kalakaua's reign, Hawaii signed a reciprocity treaty with the United States that laid the foundation for the eventual annexation of the islands. The treaty was precipitated by political insta-bility and corruption, and was followed by a revolution that broke out in 1893. An American move for annexation failed at that time because President Cleveland opposed it. The result was that Hawaii became a republic with Sanford B. Dole as president. However, agitation for annexation con-tinued, and a resolution approving this was passed by the US Congress in June and July 1898.

US flag raised. On 12 August of that year, the American flag was raised in Hawaii and President Dole transferred jurisdiction to the US. The islands were formally constituted as the Territory of Hawaii on 14 June 1900. Dole was appointed first governor.

The years 1900 to 1940 were chiefly remarkable for the growth of the sugar industry and the islands' multi-racial popu-lation. The area devoted to sugar increased from about 51,000 to 95,000 ha, while production increased from around 153,000 tonnes to well over one million tonnes annually. Pineapple-growing also thrived. At the same time, the total population increased from 154,000 to more than 423,000. The Japanese, with 61,116 in 1900 and 157,905 in 1940, were by far the largest ethnic group. Their percentage of the popu-lation remained more or less constant at about 40. Caucasians, with 26,252 in 1900 and 103,791 in 1940, became an increasingly larger percentage of the total — 17 per cent in 1900 and 24.5 per cent in 1940. Hawaiians and part-Hawaiians, on the other hand, declined from nearly 25 to 15, although their numbers increased from 38,254 to 64,310. The fourth largest ethnic group in 1940 were the Filipinos. Their numbers then stood at 52,569, or 12.4 per cent of the whole population, compared with nil at the turn of the century.

Pacific War. World War II came to Hawaii on 7 December 1941, when the Japanese bombed the naval base at Pearl Harbor on Oahu. Eighteen of the 96 ships in the har-bour were either sunk of severely damaged. There were 2403 Americans killed, and 1178

wounded. The attack brought the US into the war. Soon Oahu had become a staging centre for fighting the Japanese both in Asia and the Pacific islands. Camps for basic and special training were set up, as well as hospitals, intelligence and operations centres. More than a million men passed through the Schofield Barracks during the war, and at its end there were 253,000 troops on Oahu, compared with only 43,000 when Pearl Harbor was bombed. Martial law prevailed until October 1944.

Postwar development. After the war, Hawaii's two largest industries, sugar and pineapple-growing, grew apace while beef, dairy milk, vegetables, eggs, coffee, poul-try, tropical fruits and nuts became increas-ingly important money-earners. However, the most spectacular growth was experi-enced in the tourist industry. Large hotels sprang up throughout the group, especially on the outer islands. Tourist numbers grew from 46,000 in 1950 to 243,000 in 1959, and then the figures began to soar to spectacular heights. The reason for this was Hawaii's emergence as the 50th state of the United States. The news coverage of this develop-ment had the effect of a multi-million-dollar advertising campaign for the tourist industry.

Statehood. An official proclamation de-claring Hawaii a state was issued by Presid-ent Eisenhower on 21 August 1959. It ended a long struggle in Hawaii to attain first-class American citizenship. Significantly, Hawaii's first representatives in the US Con-gress were drawn from three different ethnic groups — Caucasian, Japanese and Chinese. At that time, the number of Caucasians in Hawaii (202,000) almost matched the num-ber of Japanese (203,000), due to heavy post-war migration. Each represented about a third of the total population. Since then, the number of Caucasians has surged well ahead. By 1967, for example, they repre-sented 37 per cent of the total while the Japanese had dropped to 28 per cent.

During Hawaii's first decade of statehood, sugar and pineapples declined in economic importance while the tourist industry grew phenomenally. In 1966, for the first time, income from tourism passed the combined value of sugar and pineapples shipped to the mainland. That same year, almost a million tourists visited Hawaii, among whom were tens of thousands of GIs from Vietnam. During the next year or two, government spending associated with the Vietnam War was the state's biggest source of income. Now tourism has resumed first place.

Further information. Gerrit P. Judd, *Hawaii: An Informal History*, New York, 1961; Gavan Daws, *Shoal of Time: a History of the Hawaiian Islands*, Honolulu, 1968; Bryan H. Farrell, *Hawaii: The Legend That Sells*, Honolulu, 1982.

ISLANDS IN DETAIL. The eight major Hawaiian Islands are of volcanic origin, with coral reefs partly encircling most of them, but fully encircling none.

From south-east to north-west they are Hawaii, Maui and Kahoolawe, Lanai and Molokai, Oahu, Kauai, Niihau, plus the North-West Islets that in all, amount to 13 sq. km. The archipelago is 2560 km long and is situated between 18 deg 50 min and 28 deg 15 min N latitude and 154 deg 40 min 178 deg 15 min W longitude. Total land area is 16,641 sq. km and includes 130 atolls, islets, reefs and pinnacles.

The best harbours are at Honolulu and Pearl on Oahu; but there are deep water ports at Hilo and Kawaihae, on Hawaii (with container service available at Hilo); and at Kahului, Maui: barge facilities are available on Molokai, Lanai and at Hana on Maui. Ocean freighters can be berthed at all but Molokai; and Hilo and Honolulu can take large passenger liners.

Hawaii. With an area of 10,456 sq. km, Hawaii is the largest island and also has the two highest mountains — Mauna Kea (4206 m) and Mauna Loa (4169 m) which are snow-capped in winter. There is also Kilauea, an active volcano and others which are dormant. The island is traversed by other mountains. In places, cliffs rise up to 900 m above the sea. Hawaii, triangular in shape, is 150 km long by 170 km wide, and is known as the 'Big Island'. There are cool plateaus on Hawaii, and thousands of sheep are grazed on Mauna Kea foothills. Several small rivers (the biggest being the Wailuku, which flows into Hilo Bay, through the city of Hilo) run off the slopes of Mauna Kea on to the eastern coast.

Principal industries are sugar-growing and milling, coffee production, beef cattle raising (Hawaii is responsible for 65 per cent of the beef produced in the state), and the growing and processing of macadamia nuts and fruit and vegetables. Hawaii grows 75 per cent of the fruit (other than pineapples) in the state. Orchids are produced for export to the mainland and there is a growing tourist industry. Hilo airport will take large commercial jets but Honolulu on Oahu is the international terminal. Hawaii island had 695,000 visitors in 1985. Its resident population in 1986 was 111,800.

Maui, the second largest island with an area of 1887 sq. km, is 89 km long and 40 km wide. It is divided into two masses by a low sandy isthmus. The eastern part consists of Haleakala ('House of the Sun'), a volcanic dome 3055 m high with a crater-like depression in its summit, measuring 6.4 km by 11.2 km with walls up to 900 m deep, and cinder cones up to 300 m high on its 65 sq. km floor.

West Maui mountains result from an older, much eroded volcanic dome (1764 m high), cut by great valleys. Rainfall here approaches 10,200 mm a year. Maui's resident population was 78,700 in 1986. Chief population centres are Kahului, Wailuku, Lahaina and Kihei.

The low isthmus is dry, but the soil is fertile and is suitable for sugar cane when irrigated. Water is brought from the wet windward slopes of Haleakala in ditches which run through tunnels. On slopes above, pineapples and a variety of truck crops are grown on homesteads. Cattle graze on lush grasslands.

Pineapple and sugar cultivation are the main industries on Maui but there is also a rum distillery, food processing and garment manufacture. Tourism and scientific research are also important sources of revenue. Maui had 1,827,000 visitors in 1985.

Scientific laboratories are located on the rim of the Haleakala Crater where an infrared tracking station and astro-physical observatory is used by the Defence Department. The observatory houses a 152.4 mm reflector telescope and two 122 mm infra-red telescopes. There is also a deep-space surveillance system.

The University of Hawaii also has observatories on Haleakala — a solar laboratory and an air-glow zodiacal light observatory.

The US Air Force and the Federal Aviation Agency also have facilities there. Haleakala is part of the Hawaii Volcanoes National Park. There are state airports at Kahului and Hana and private airstrips at other places.

Molokai (676 sq. km) is the main pineapple-growing area and it is also a cattle raising location. There is a leprosy hospital on an isolated peninsula off the north coast and there is also an airport. From the Sheraton-Molokai Hotel at the western end of the island, visitors can see African and other exotic animals on Molokai Ranch where they are bred and raised for sale to zoos. There is a population of 6700.

Kahoolawe (116.5 sq. km), just south of Maui, is barren and uninhabited. It is used as a target island for gunnery and other practice by the US armed forces.

Lanai (364 sq. km), a hilly island with a peak of 1027 m, is south of the passage between Molokai and Maui. Its people are mostly pineapple growers. This island has an airport and a population of 2200.

Oahu with the city of Honolulu ('Fair Haven', originally known as Brown's Harbour), is intensively developed and has a very large population. It is the third largest island (64 km long and 42 km across) and the two mountain ranges have altitudes up to 1500 metres, but are eroded into ridges and valleys. Pearl Harbor, a naval base, is situated on the southern coast.

The City of Honolulu and, in effect, the whole island of Oahu is the centre of business, government and tourism for the State of Hawaii. Although it is the smallest area of the four counties into which the state is divided, it has the biggest population. Total area is 1537 sq. km.

Pineapples, sugar and diversified crops are grown in the rural areas but there are also heavy and light manufacturing industries and rapidly expanding research and developmental activities, especially in the fields of oceanography, astrophysics, geophysics and biomedicine. In addition to governmental organisations engaged in research, the Oceanic Institute, the Bishop Museum, the Pineapple Research Institute and the Hawaiian Sugar Planters' Experiment Station are among the private research organisations.

Waikiki is the primary destination of the millions of tourists who visit each year. Apart from the beaches, hotels, restaurants and night-life, tourists find much to interest them in Honolulu and its environs. It is the academic centre of the state, has the State Library, the Academy of Arts and historical buildings like the Iolani Palace (once the residence of Hawaiian royalty) and the State Capitol built in 1969. The National Memorial Cemetery is located in Punchbowl, an extinct volcano crater, and there lie thousands of the dead of the Pacific War.

The island has a first-class highway system (exceeding 2200 km of high quality roads) and spectacular scenery. At Makaha on the west coast, a spectacular surf provides the venue for international surfing competitions. At Laie, on the north-east coast corner of Oahu is the Brigham Young University's Polynesian Cultural Center where the cultures of Hawaii, Tahiti, Tonga, Samoa, Fiji and the New Zealand Maori are displayed in recreated surroundings.

The rainfall varies with location in relation to the prevailing winds and the mountains. Honolulu City itself receives about 700 mm a year but the rainfall a few kilometres away in the hills can be many times this.

Average annual temperature in Honolulu is 24°C, with little seasonal variation.

In 1986 Oahu's population was 816,700.

Kauai (1423 sq. km) is fourth in size and has an oval shape roughly 48 km by 41.5 km. It is considered by many to be the most beautiful island of the group. Its high interior (up to 1598 m) has heavy rainfall, up to 11.5 metres a year, which forms numerous rivers that rush down fertile valleys. The slopes are well forested and plantations of sugar cane and pineapples are established on the coastal plains. The largest town is Lihue; most people live on the south-east and north coastal plains.

Growing and processing sugar cane is the main industry but tourism has now become a significant influence on the economy. Hotel building has boomed and as the island is only 166 km from Honolulu, day trips by air are popular.

There is excellent swimming at beaches and freshwater pools, good hunting and fishing. There are many camping grounds, picnic facilities and playgrounds. The airport at Lihue is capable of taking short range jets. There are 545 km of roads. Kauai's resident population in 1986 was 46,100. Visitors in 1986 numbered 1,015,000.

Kauai is the main island in Kauai County which also includes 181 sq. km of Niihau and the two small uninhabited islands of Kaula and Lehua (less than 1.5 sq. km each). Niihau is privately owned by the Sinclair family and not accessible to the public, though almost 200 people live there, most of them Hawaiian.

FOR THE TOURIST. Hawaii's fame as an international pleasure destination hardly needs describing. There are volcanoes, luxuriant flowers and fruits and the surf. Lessons in human communications flow from its East-West Center, the Bishop Museum, Polynesian Cultural Center, or even Sea Life Park, but mostly from Hawaii's unique cultural mixture. Detailed, descriptive brochures may be obtained from the Hawaii Visitors Bureau or the Department of Planning and Economic Development, PO Box 2359, Honolulu, Hawaii, 96804.

Duty free. These facilities are available at Honolulu international airport.

Airport tax. There is an airport departure tax of $13.

Sightseeing. The two remaining centres of volcanic activity in the Hawaiian Islands, Mauna Loa and Kilauea, lie within the Hawaii Volcanoes National Park, covering 92,000 hectares on the island of Hawaii. Each has a caldera (or super-crater), within which there are periodic outbreaks of molten lava. The park's craters, active and dormant, are among the most important in the entire world and even the active ones may be visited with reasonable safety.

State monuments. On Oahu Is: Diamond Head State Monument: Iolani Palace; Puu O Mahuka; Royal Mausoleum; Ulu Po Heiau, Washington Place; USS Arizona Memorial.

Hawaii: Hikiau Heiau State Monument, Lava Tree.

Maui: Hale Kii-Pihana State Monument

Kauai: Russian Fort State Monument

Bernice P. Bishop Museum. One of the most important scientific and cultural institutions in the Pacific is the Bernice P. Bishop Museum. Its field workers have carried out exacting ethnological and natural history research in almost every group of South Pacific islands and its ancient Polynesia collections and present-day specimens are world famous. The Museum is a memorial to the Princess Bernice Pauahi, last of the Kamehameha family of Hawaii chiefs, and was founded in 1889 by her husband, Charles Reed Bishop, who was prominent for 50 years in the public and business affairs of Hawaii.

ACCOMMODATION. Limitations of space preclude even a representative listing of Hawaii's hundreds of hotels, which cater for a variety of accommodation needs, from self-catering apartments to luxury resorts and for almost every budget. Waikiki is, of course, the tourist and accommodation centre, but some of the outer islands have grown in popularity as destinations with a consequent growth in tourist facilities. A comprehensive accommodation guide — revised annually — may be obtained from the Hawaii Visitors Bureau, 2270 Kalakaua Ave, Honolulu, Hawaii, 96815.

Howland, Baker and Jarvis Islands

These three island, all American possessions, are almost on the Equator; Howland and Baker are 1100 km due east of Kiribati and about 600 km NW of Kanton and Enderbury Islands in the Phoenix group. They are about 56 km apart. With Jarvis Island, which lies approximately 1900 km due east cf these two, the islands were declared American possessions by Presidential order in 1936 when various islands in the Central Pacific

seemed potentially valuable to trans-Pacific aviation. The US claim to the three islands was based on the Guano Act of 1856 which had listed them as American possessions. Earlier, in May 1935, several American colonists were landed on each island. They were evacuated after Japan entered World War II.

HOWLAND ISLAND is about 2.5 km long by a little less than 1 km wide. It is low

HOWLAND & BAKER ISLANDS

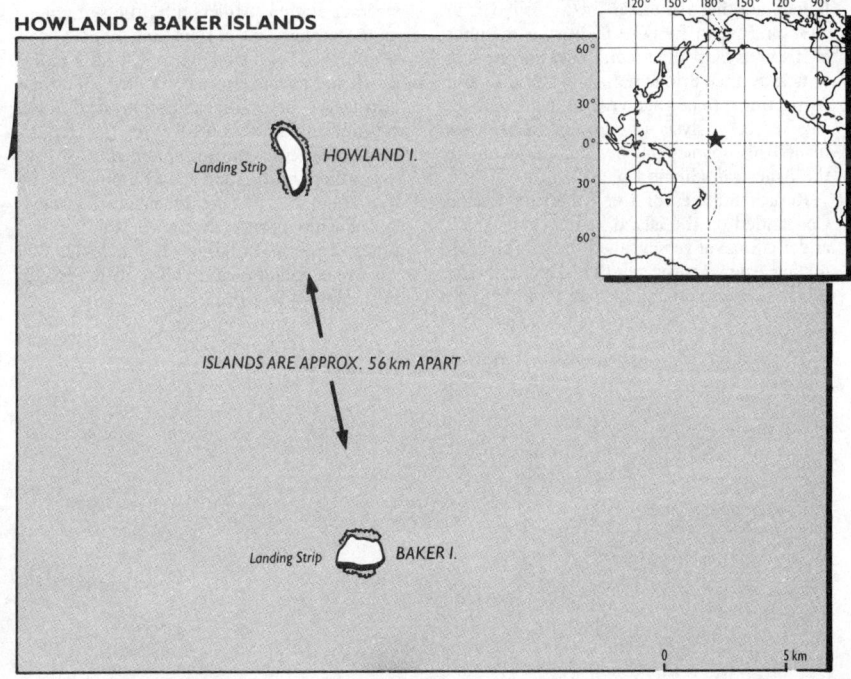

and sandy, with one patch of trees about three metres high. A fringing reef surrounds it. Vegetation is sparse but there is a large bird population, of which the most common species is the blue-faced booby.

Captain Daniel Smith of the New Bedford whaler *Minerva* discovered the island in 1828 and named it after his ship's owner. American then British interests worked the island's guano between 1858 and 1890. Thereafter, the island was deserted until American colonists were landed there in 1935. Two years later, an airfield was hurriedly constructed for the US fliers Amelia Earhart and Fred J. Noonan who were attempting to fly around the world. However, the pair disappeared after leaving Lae, PNG, on 2 July 1937. A beacon there is now called the Amelia Earhart Light. The island is unoccupied.

BAKER ISLAND is about 1.5 km long and a little less wide. It is about eight metres above sea level, and treeless. Captain Orbed Starbuck of the whaler *Loper* discovered the island in 1825 and named it New Nantucket. It takes its present name from Captain Michael Baker, another American, who visited it in 1832 and again in 1839 to bury a member of his crew. On the second occasion he was struck by the curious nature of the soil, and suspecting it to be guano raised the American flag. After analysis of samples taken confirmed his suspicions, he sold his claim to the American Guano Co.

Representatives of the American Guano Co. landed on the island in February 1857, and a US naval vessel called there in the following August to survey the island and take official possession in the name of the US.

The company worked the deposits from 1859 to 1878. John T. Arundel & Co., of London, did the same from 1886 to 1891.

American colonists landed on the island in April 1935 and built a lighthouse and several substantial dwellings. Today it is uninhabited.

JARVIS ISLAND is a small, bleak, bowl-shaped place, about 3 by 1.5 km lying just south of the equator, 0 deg 23 min and 160 deg 0.2 min W longitude. It was first reported by Captain Browne of the British ship *Eliza Francis* in 1821, and has been called Bunker, Volunteer, Jervis and Brook. The American Guano Co. claimed it in 1857, it was annexed by the US *St Mary* for the US in 1858 after earlier 'protective' visits by US ships, and from then until 1879, when it was abandoned, large quantities of guano were removed. It was annexed by Britain in 1889 and in 1906 leased to the Pacific Phosphate Co., but apparently never worked. When US officials occupied and claimed the island in 1935, Britain offered no objection; and at various times since that date it has been used as a weather station. Millersville, the settlement on the western side of the island, consisted of several wood and stone houses, with a radio-shack and towers. It was occupied for a time during the International Geophysical Year. It is now under the control of the US Department of Interior and uninhabited.

Further information may be obtained by writing to the Refuge Manager, Hawaiian and Pacific Islands National Wildlife Refuges, Federal Building, Room 5302, 300 Ala Moana Boulevard, PO Box 50167, Honolulu, Hawaii 96850.

Irian Jaya

Editors' Note: The last edition of Pacific Islands Yearbook carried in this space an explanation for the fact that some of the information in this entry was deficient and that other parts were out of date. This situation was caused by Indonesia's lack of co-operation in providing more recent details. The present editors had hoped to overcome this problem by appropriately diplomatic methods. They were unreasonably optimistic. No information was received from Jakarta or Jayapura, despite numerous requests. Officials in the Embassy of the Republic of Indonesia in Canberra, Australia, offered to assist the project at first but subsequently changed their minds. The last letter received from that source is illustrative of Indonesian attitudes towards Irian Jaya and the Pacific, and it is quoted in part: '[We] have not seen your Yearbook so far, but the impression I have from the materials you are trying to gather is that you put Irian Jaya in your Pacific Profiles. In this case you are deforcing[sic] Irian Jaya from Indonesia which is against our constitution.'

The entry that follows, therefore, is based on a minimum of recent assistance from official sources. We doubt that its validity has been impaired.

Irian Jaya, the easternmost province of the Republic of Indonesia, consists of that half of New Guinea west of the 141 deg E longitude, and certain offshore islands. The capital of the province is Jayapura and local time is nine hours ahead of GMT. Population was estimated at 1,424,800 in 1983.

The national anthem and flag are those of Indonesia, as are the public holidays. The currency is the rupiah.

THE PEOPLE. The inhabitants of Irian Jaya are composed of various tribes, such as the Mukoko of Baliem Valley, the Ekari of the Wissel Lakes region, the Arfak at Kepala Burung, the Muju of Merauke District, and so forth. Each tribe is broken down again into still smaller units. Because of the harshness of the terrain, they are spread over a large area in small groups, kept apart by such other factors as dialect and cutoms. The various races evident in West Irian are Australoid, Melanesoid, Pygmoid, Weddoid and Paleo-Mongoloid according to anthropologist Professor Kleiweg de Zwaan.

The people inhabiting the coastal areas consist mostly of overseas aliens and emigrant families from the interior living in mixed villages.

The Papuan population is estimated at approximately 1,200,000.

Irian Jaya's largest town is the provincial capital, Jayapura, with some 80,000 inhabitants.

Nationality. All original inhabitants of Irian Jaya are 'Indonesians' and 'Indonesian citizens' ('warga negara') by law. Terminologies used by the Indonesians with reference to Irian Jayan people include 'penduduk asli' (autochthones). Now the politer term 'putra daerah' (son of the region) is more commonly used to contrast with the immigrant group referred to as 'pendatang (newcomers).

Although the younger generation call themselves 'orang Irian' (Irianese), the older generation refer to themselves as 'orang Papua' (Papuans).

Irian Jaya has its representation in Jakarta, the SEKUIB ('Sekretariat Urusan Irian Barat' — Secretariat for West Irian Affairs) which until 1969, the year of the Act of Free Choice, was part of the Ministry of Internal Affairs but was later transferred to the Ministry of Foreign Affairs.

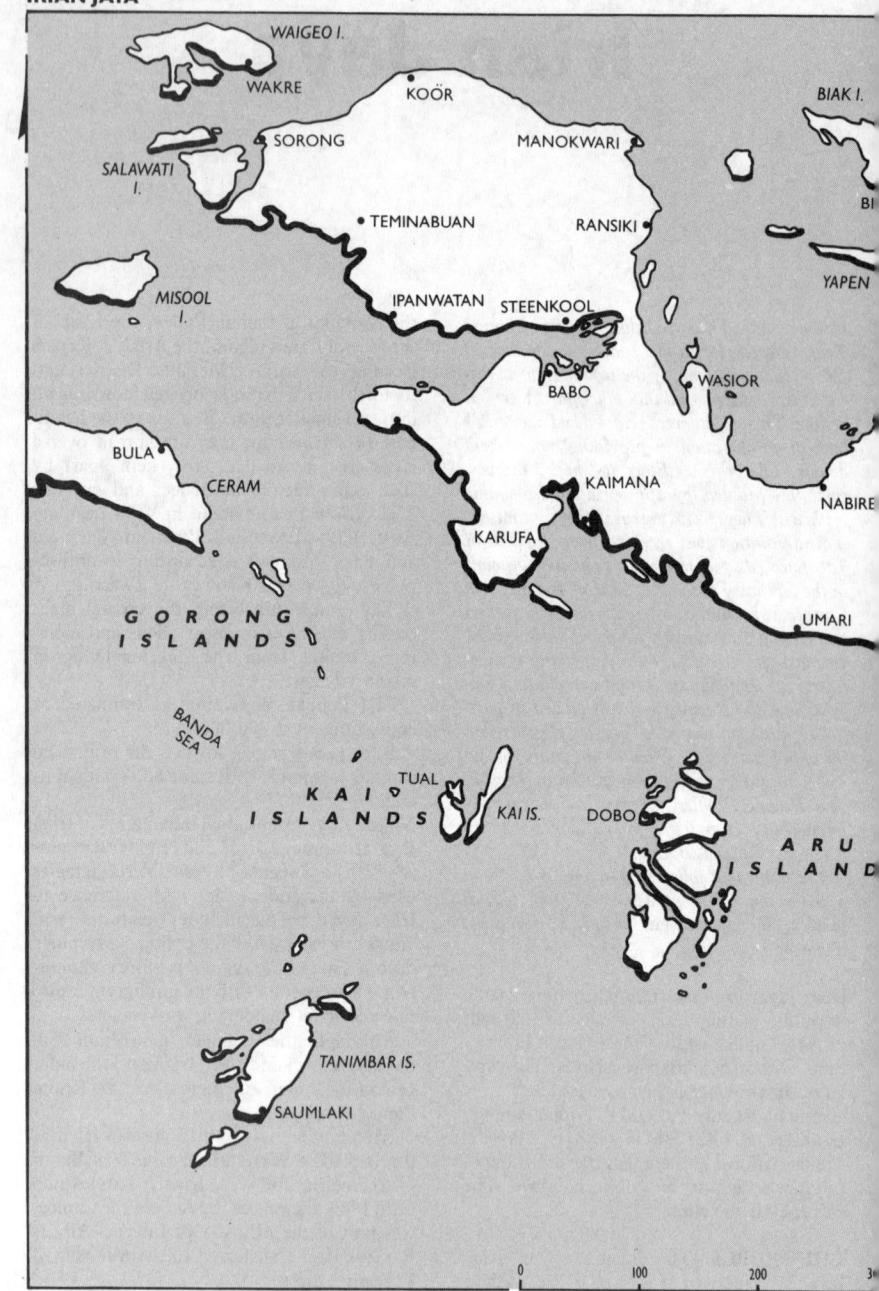

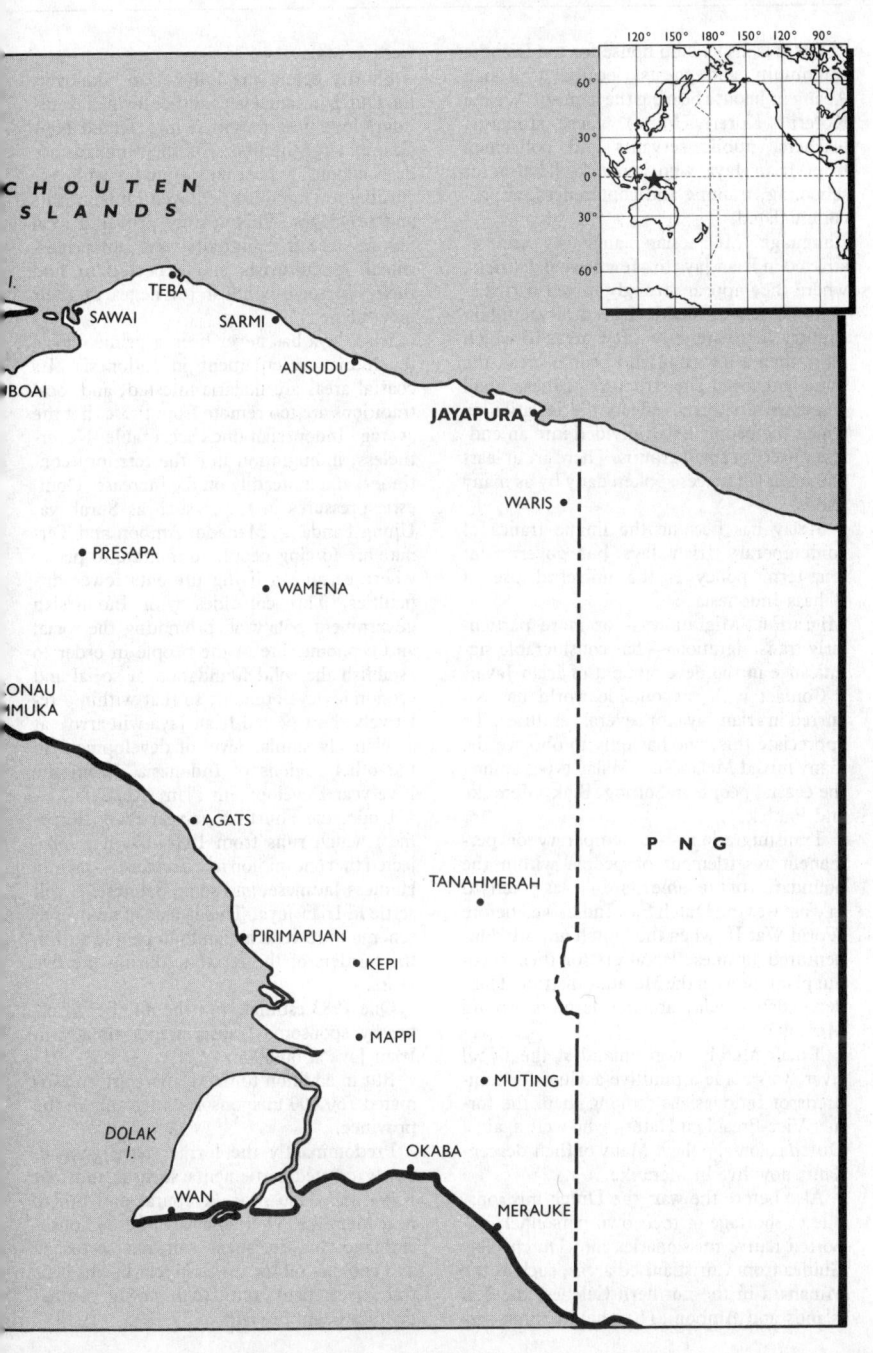

There is also a club house for the Irianese community and guests, located at Tanah Abang in Jakarta bearing the name of 'Wisma Koreri' (Koreri House) where students, teachers, public servants and policemen from Irian Jaya who come to Jakarta for schooling, training and conferences, are accommodated.

Language. Melanesian languages are restricted in Irian Jaya to a few coastal districts, where they appear strongly mixed with Papuan elements. Outside the central mountain country there are only a few areas in which more than a few thousand people speak the same language. The structure of these small language territories reflects the isolation in which the people lived, divided into an endless variety of small groups. There are at least 250 main languages spoken daily by as many tribes.

Malay has become the lingua franca of contemporary Irian Jaya but government long-term policy is the universal use of Bahasa-Indonesia.

Migration. Migration — or more particularly transmigration — has considerable significance in the development of Irian Jaya.

Contact with the outside world has occurred in Irian Jaya for several centuries. To appreciate this, one has only to observe the many mixed Melanesian-Malay types among the coastal people in Sorong, Biak, Merauke and Fakfak.

Transmigration — a temporary or permanent resettlement of people within the boundaries of the same State — was practised in what was the Dutch East Indies well before World War II, when the Dutch imported indentured Javanese labourers for their coconut plantations in the Merauke district. Their descendants today are rice farmers around Merauke.

Tanah Merah, more inland at the Digul river, was made a punitive asylum for hundreds of Indonesians (among them the former Vice-President Hatta), who were against Dutch colonial policy. Many of their descendants now live in Merauke.

Also before the war, the Dutch missions, due to shortage of their own personnel, imported native missionaries into Dutch New Guinea from Christianised areas, such as the Minahasa in the northern Celebes, the Kai islands and Ambon. They held church services in Malay.

Shortly before the Indonesian take-over, the Dutch initiated yet another form of transmigration: they imported into Dutch New Guinea large numbers of their mixed-race descendants in Java and Sumatra who, according to Dutch law, enjoyed Dutch rights and privileges. This venture proved a total failure since the migrants were not professional agriculturists and expected to find their old socio-political privileges in their new 'home'.

Irian Jaya has never been a prime choice for human resettlement in Indonesia. Its coastal areas are malaria-infested, and local traditions are too remote from those that the average Indonesian finds acceptable. Nevertheless, immigration into the territory continues, and is steadily on the increase. Domestic pressures in towns such as Surabaya, Ujung Pandang, Manado, Ambon and Ternate are forcing people to migrate to places where earning a living presents fewer difficulties. This coincides with Indonesian government policy of 'promoting the social and economic life of the people in order to establish the solid foundation of social and economic development, so that within a relatively short period Irian Jaya will arrive at a relatively similar level of development to the other regions of Indonesia' (from the Five-year Development Plan, 'Repelita').

Under the Fourth Five-year Plan ('Repelita') which runs from 1984–89, it is projected that one million non-Irianese — mainly landless Javanese, and some Balinese — will settle in Irian Jaya. This is part of an overall scheme to resettle five million people within the borders of the republic during the five years.

One 1983 estimate put the number of officially sponsored transmigrants already in Irian Jaya at 60,000.

But in addition to them, there are an estimated 160,000 unsponsored migrants in the province.

Predominantly the former have gone to newly created settlements such as those at Koya and Arso near Jayapura, and others near Merauke. There they are offered houses and land, and free sugar, salt, rice, kerosene and cooking oil for the first year by the central government, until their newly planted paddies begin to yield.

In 1983 there were 21 transmigration centres, with the number planned to increase to 40 during Repelita IV.

The latter — and much more numerous — group tend to gravitate to the big towns, where their Southeast Asian-style entrepreneurial spirit causes big problems for the local Irianese, who can't compete.

Some observers, especially longtime missionaries, see the seeds of trouble in the activities of these unsponsored transmigrants, and call for action to stop them coming. But others point out that, as Indonesian citizens, they are free to come and go as they please within the national borders.

The transmigration policy in Irian Jaya is only part of the government's internal policies of bringing the big province, which makes up 21.6 per cent of Indonesia's total land area, into the mainstream of an 'Indonesia Raya (Greater Indonesia), stretching from Sabang at Sumatra's northern tip, to Merauke in the south-east corner of Irian Jaya'.

A reverse flow — although negligible in numbers, and designed only for short periods — of Irianese visiting other parts of Indonesia, mainly Java, is also subsidised by the Indonesian government. Irianese public servants, members of the local House of Representatives, students, sports teams, village chiefs and action group leaders, including women, are regularly sent to Jakarta and other big towns to give them a first-hand impression of Indonesia's technical advancements, and to imbue them with 'the feeling of pride to belong to the Indonesian nation'. Marriages of Irianese with Indonesians are encouraged.

Religion. Statistics published by Christian religions in Irian Jaya claim that 93 per cent of the indigenous people profess the Christian faith. Of these people, the Catholics claim 30 per cent and the rest are split between two Protestant groups: the GKI (Gereja Kristen Injili), and the TMF (The Mission Fellowship). TMF members are APCM (Asian Pacific Christian Mission), ABMS (Australian Baptist Missionary Society), NRC (Netherlands Reformed Congregation), RBMU (Region Beyond Missionary Union), TEAM (The Evangelical Alliance Mission) and ZGK (Zending Gereformeerde Kerk). The GKI, TMF and Catholic missions have their main headquarters in Jayapura.

Official figures, however, claim that Moslems account for almost 25 per cent of the population, a figure probably influenced by the vigorous transmigration programme. The affairs of the Moslem community are managed by the Department of Religious Affairs in Jayapura.

The Christian missions in Irian Jaya run their own schools, hospitals, transport and agricultural projects. They receive some subsidies from the Indonesian government and from supporters overseas. Especially in the interior, they also assist the government and the general public by providing air transport: the Mission Fellowship with its MAF (Missionary Aviation Fellowship): and the Catholic Mission with its AMA (Associated Mission Aviation) aircraft. Both MAF and AMA have ticket offices at Sentani airport, Jayapura.

One Protestant missionary told a 1983 visitor to the province: 'The government (in Jakarta) knows that without the missionaries, the MAF, this country would virtually stop — schools, hospitals, communications, everything.'

However, many people still adhere to the traditional New Guinea religious belief, which may be termed dynamic-animism.

GOVERNMENT. Following the pattern of Indonesian administration, the province ('propinsi') of Irian Jaya, is divided into nine administrative districts ('kabupaten'). These are the border districts of Jayapura and Merauke, the highland districts of Jayawijaya and Paniai, the island district of Teluk Cenderawasih (Bird of Paradise Bay), and the coastal districts of Yapen-Waropen, Manokwari, Sorong and Fakfak, with their capitals respectively Jayapura, Merauke, Wamena, Nabire, Biak, Serui, Manokwari, Sorong and Fakfak, Jayapura is also the provincial capital of Irian Jaya.

Five of the nine district commissioners in 1983 were Irianese.

The chief administrator of the province is the governor ('gubernur'), who is appointed by Jakarta. The post is at present held by Barnabas Suebu, an Irianese. Most of the bureau chiefs in his office are also Irianese.

The nine districts are further divided into 116 sub-districts ('kecamatan'), each administered by a 'camat'. Each sub-district is made up of a number of administrative villages ('desa') headed by a village chief ('kepala desa'). While both Irianese and non-Irianese are represented in the ranks of 'camat', the post of village chief appears to be exclusively reserved for Irianese.

In the interior, however, many tribes still live in a neolithic state as nomadic hunters and practising agriculture mainly as slash-and-burn cultivation of their foods. There are tribes — living deep in the jungle — who may not have heard of the Indonesian Government and never seen the world beyond their villages. These nomads are commonly called 'suku terasing' (an Indonesian term meaning isolated tribes). Exercising administration over them cannot be effective unless they can be persuaded to change their transient hunter's life into that of settled farmers. The Indonesians believe that rural development can be achieved only by resettling these 'isolated tribes' along roads which link their new villages with towns. It is hoped that the tribes will have more frequent contact with the other tribes and townspeople, and thus accelerate their social, economic and cultural assimilation with other tribes and people. Also, in time it is intended that the villages will serve as food production areas for the towns, and thus reduce the quantity of imported food.

It is intended that in this process the tribes would increasingly participate in the cash economy which should stimulate them to produce surplus crops to earn cash. In turn, this should enable them to abandon their present subsistence economy. It is anticipated that with these expectations of development, the economic life of the villagers can be improved, and their villages can be better administered.

The creation of the 'desa' — the new administrative village — will bring drastic changes in village authority as the requirements for becoming a new style village 'chief' include possession of a primary school certificate, or knowledge of reading and writing, and the ability to speak Bahasa Indonesia, Indonesia's national language. Previously, in villages of Irian Jaya, the traditional leaders gained authority through superior performance in fighting (or as strategists and negotiators) in tribal wars. Now the village head

has to be elected from several eligible candidates who, in the final choice, need to be sanctioned by the 'bupati' (district administrator). This is necessary to comply with legal provisions and regulations which are also applicable elsewhere in Indonesia.

Since West Irian — now Irian Jaya — was declared autonomous by President Suharto on 16 September 1969, the province gained the status of 'daerah' (autonomous region). The province is further referred to as a First Level — and the district as a Second Level — autonomous region, with the governor and the 'bupati' as their respective heads. Regional autonomy in Indonesia does not extend to the sub-districts, hence the 'camat' (sub-district administrator) functions mainly as a liaison between the 'bupati' and the villages.

Legislature. The governor as chief executive of the autonomous province makes legislation together with his House of Representatives. While legislative initiatives may emanate from the House of Representatives, final legislative authority nevertheless resides with the governor at the provincial level, and the 'bupati' at the district level.

The dual function of the governor of Irian Jaya as the Chief Executive in the province and, at the same time, the most senior public servant in Irian Jaya, responsible to the President and Minister of Home Affairs, indicates that Indonesia's policy toward Irian Jaya is one of increasingly strengthening its ties with Jakarta rather then lessening them.

Although Jayapura is the provincial capital and the seat of the provincial government, the offices of the governor and his staff, together with the various departments, were moved in 1974 to Kotaraja, 10 km from Jayapura on the Sentani highway.

Liquor laws. Before 1963, the Dutch Liquor Ordinance allowed a maximum of five bottles of beer to be sold to adults (over 21 years) while restaurants could serve beer only with a meal.

During a ban on beer imports from 1963–66. People drank 'saguwer' brewed locally from fermented palm wine; and 'sopi', a wine imported from Manado (Northern Celebes); and whisky from Ujung Pandang.

The ordinance was finally abolished and beer is now freely available. It is supplied by breweries in Java and augmented by imports from Holland, Australia and Singapore. Bars, restaurants and hotels in Jayapura, Biak and Sorong serve most types of liquor.

The 'Rukum Kampung' and 'Rukun Tetangga' (neighbourhood organisations) deal with drunkards in their respective regions. Habitual drunkards can face disciplinary measures and discharge from employment, or resettlement in a 'dry' area where liquor is not available.

Sport. Western sports have only recently been introduced into Irian Jaya, particularly soccer and boxing, designed to serve as a means of neutralising tribal conflict, especially in the highlands and the interior. The idea has been to channel the warrior spirit into the peaceful pursuits of contact games. Other popular recreations are water skiing, spear fishing, yachting and tennis but these are mainly confined to the expatriates and upper classes.

Gambling. Games played with cards and dominoes — indeed all forms of gambling — are strictly forbidden in Irian Jaya. People found guilty of gambling by the police face a trial and their names may be published in the Jayapura newspaper.

Night life. Little regular entertainment is available in the hotels, even in Jayapura. However, although the term 'night club' is prohibited, 'Bars' and 'Discotheques' employ 'hostesses' and conduct a thriving business in the commercial and administrative centres. The hostesses are imported from Java, Ujung Pandang (South Sulawesi) and Manado (North Sulawesi).

DEFENCE. The province of Irian Jaya is grouped with Maluku to form the Seventh Military Region of Indonesia.

Three battalions of Indonesian army troops totalling about 2400 men are stationed in Irian Jaya, one each at Jayapura, Manokwari and Sorong. There are about the same number of police.

The military force was commanded in 1983 by Brigadier-General Sembiring, who is a Christian from North Sumatra.

EDUCATION. Irian Jaya has an education system embracing kindergarten, primary, junior high school and senior high school systems.

There are also a teacher-training school

system and two tertiary institutions.

The first university in the history of the area, Cenderawasih University, was established in 1962.

The public education policy of the government is to harmonise the school system and curricula in Irian Jaya with the rest of Indonesia. One difference is that the medium of instruction, 'Bahasa Indonesia', the national language of Indonesia, is taught from Grade 1 onwards, whereas in the other provinces of Indonesia the first three years of instruction at primary school level are given in the local vernaculars.

Statistics available in 1977 indicated that, due to lack of available finance, 16 per cent of youngsters entitled to receive primary education would be unable to receive any. A year earlier, the number of primary pupils in Irian Jaya was 132,772 and there were 18,633 pupils in secondary school.

Nevertheless, the Indonesian government claimed that most villages possessed a primary school and in several sub-districts, there were junior high schools.

By 1977, the Indonesian government had established vocational training centres in several district capitals in Irian Jaya. Their instruction included automobile and machinery techniques, building construction, radio techniques, etc.

The premier institution of tertiary education, the Universitas Cenderawasih, now provide courses for the Master of Arts degree. Other tertiary studies may be pursued through the Academy of Administration and Accountancy in Jayapura. There was also the College for Local Administration where some sub-district administrators for Irian Jaya have been trained.

Recently Roman Catholic and Protestant Academies of Theology were opened in Abepura and there is a branch of the California-based Summer Institute of Linguistics (SIL) in Jayapura. Activities of the SIL include Bible translation into Irian Jaya languages and English classes at Cenderawasih University. It also organises evening classes in English for government officials in Jayapura.

In early 1988, 130 Irianese students had been provided with scholarships by the Irian Jaya Joint Development Foundation (IJJDI). Although the scholarships enable the students to study at universities in Java as well

TABLE 1 IRIAN JAYA — SCHOOLS

1983	Number	Enrolment
	Privately operated	
Primary schools	940	106,746
Junior high schools	74	14,142
Senior high schools	35	7671

1984	Number	Enrolment
	Government operated	
Primary schools	1587	193,659
Junior high schools	171	33,247
Senior high schools	43	11,836
Senior technical high schools	n/a	1102

CENDERAWASIH UNIVERSITY — ENROLMENTS AND LECTURERS, 1984

Faculty	Students	Lecturers
Law	370	8
Social and Political Science	886	14
Education	1001	66
Agriculture	434	21

as Jayapura, they are expected to return to their own districts on completion.

LABOUR. Of Irian Jaya's population, 80 per cent, or 820,000 people, live in the interior, and of them, about 534,000 are aged between 10 and 69 years and live by subsistence farming. It is estimated that of about 50,000 students who attended secondary schools, 60 per cent attended non-vocational establishments. This results in a difficulty for Irian Jayan students to get jobs either through lack of experience, or through lack of job vacancies.

In 1975–76, it was estimated that the highest percentage of job seekers (who had attended primary and/or secondary schools), 86 per cent in 1975 and 97.6 per cent in 1976 were aged between 20 and 29.

One problem faced by the Government is the disproportionate number of jobs held by non-Irianese. For every three non-Irianese holding technical positions, only one Irianese is employed in a similar capacity.

The situation is worse in administration where Irianese hold only 20 per cent of the jobs; only in unskilled work such as manual labourers do Irianese hold four jobs to each held by an outside Indonesian.

Although no exact figures are available, an Australian visitor in 1983 recorded the view of a longtime missionary in the province that there had been 'a dramatic increase' in the employment of Irianese in government, banks and shops since 1979.

The number of unskilled vacancies on multi-million dollar enterprises (such as oil drilling and copper mining) is high only in the initial stages of construction when roads and buildings must be established. Once the base facilities are provided, local workers are dismissed and more sophisticated outsiders are employed to handle the machinery.

Another problem is that of Indonesian transmigrants. Most have equal or superior technical or nontechnical training to that of the Irianese. In coastal areas, where most development projects have been conducted, local Irianese have found it hard to compete for jobs against transmigrants, even when the local people possess competitive diplomas or other qualifications.

In 1975, 763 business enterprises and corporations in Irian Jaya employed 38,452 labourers — an increase of 2926 over requirements in 1971. No more recent figures are available.

HEALTH. In 1978, each of the nine 'kabupaten' (districts) of Irian Jaya had its own government health office and its own district hospital. Total beds in these establishments were 823. There were also five hospitals for special diseases, a psychiatric institution (75 beds) at Abepura, and leprosy rehabilitation centres (235 beds) at Sorong, Kaimana, Merauke and Yapen.

The 116 'kecamaten' (sub-districts) had 110 community health centres and of these, four had hospital facilities (68 beds). There were also 61 mother-and-child care centres, mostly located in the interior. There were also two hospitals for the armed forces (154 beds), 7 health care centres (85 beds), 23 polyclinics and 17 mother-and-child care centres in the district capitals or other urban centres. For the most recent available figures see table below.

Christian missions and the Muslim Muhamadiah were responsible for a further six hospitals, a 16-bed leprosy hospital, 70 polyclinics and 11 mother-and-child care centres.

In 1978, the Government health department staff in Irian Jaya was 2430 including 64 general practitioners, 4 medical specialists, 9 dentists, 11 health inspectors, 95 midwives, 346 nurses, 3 chemists, 33 malaria controllers and 1 nutritionist.

Health care was included as one of the priorities in the Repelita II (1974–79) programme for developing the source of human labour, but in 1978–79, only 8.4 per cent of the provincial budget (3.18 per cent in 1976–77) was devoted to health care, and of this, 47.8 per cent (58 per cent 1976–77) was allocated for salaries.

However, INPRES (presidential decrees) provided further sums for medicines, equipment, construction of houses for professional staff and other matters. INPRES grants enabled 40 health centres to be built in 1976–77. It has been estimated that between 1976 and 1978 203,161 residents were protected from malaria by DDT spraying; 522,581 received BCG vaccination; 750,109 received primary smallpox vaccination and 5711 received medical help for leprosy.

Foreign enterprises in Irian Jaya which

IRIAN JAYA — HOSPITALS AND BEDS 1978

	Hospitals No.	Beds No.
Jayapura	3	451
Teluk Cenderawasih	2	165
Yapen Waropen	1	75
Manokwari	1	104
Sorong	4	220
Fak-Fak	1 — 1 (M)	44 — 12
Merauke	1	106
Paniai	1 — 1 (M)	40 — 12
Jayawijaya	1 — 1 (M)	25 — 25

Note: (M) indicates Mission hospitals.

run their own hospitals, mainly for their own workers, are Freeport Sulphur and Pacific Nickel; and the domestic Pertamina national oil company, the state electricity company, the Irian Bhakti enterprise and the Bank of Indonesia.

Diseases. It has been estimated that 14.69 per cent of the people are affected by skin and subcutaneous tissue diseases (including scabies): 14.59 per cent are suffering from malaria and the yearly average for influenza is 11.04 per cent.

Since 1971, aid from a UN Development Programme and the WHO has enabled a systematic malaria eradication scheme to be initiated in the larger towns by spraying twice a year. Only at Biak and Merauke are the results considered satisfactory. In 1978 there were 754 patients with tuberculosis but only 524 were in hospitals.

Yaws (framboesia) which is still present in the interior and in isolated coastal areas claimed 78,741 victims in 1978 but only 993 were in hospitals, and 1285 people were vaccinated against the disease. A cholera epidemic occurred in 1979 from 14 to 23 October. There were 85 cases reported in Jayapura.

Mortality rates from influenza and pertussis (whooping cough) were high in 1978. Venereal disease is mainly confined to towns where there is prostitution. Jayawijaya reported 219 cases of gonorrhoea in 1977.

THE LAND. Irian Jaya has an area of 410,660 sq. km including 54,668 sq. km of rivers and lakes. Mainland Irian Jaya is approximately 1130 km in length and 724 km at its broadest.

The highest peak, which is also the highest in the whole island of New Guinea, is Puncak Jaya in the Sudirman Range, which rises to 5093 m. Ten other peaks in this range exceed 4880 m. Although Irian Jaya lies close to the equator, some mountain tops are perpetually snow-capped.

The interior is mostly a heavy rainforest rising in great, ragged ridges, pock-marked by villages and patches of cultivation. The rest of the land is coastal, holding vast sago and mangrove swamps. The configuration of the country is thus one of extremes: endless swamps and gigantic massifs. The swamps are among the most extensive in the world, and the mountains are so high they make

possible the existence of glaciers.

The climate is equatorial, except in the highlands where the temperature can fall to freezing.

Rainfall varies between an average of 2000 to 3000 mm per annum in most coastal areas to between 3000 and 4000 mm in the uplands.

Irian Jaya's largest rivers are the Mamberamo and Digul. Only the Mamberamo is navigable as far as Marine Falls by ships with a draught of 2 m.

Irian Jaya's interior is characterised by huge lake systems, among the largest of which is the Wissel Lakes area. Other mountain lakes are found near Baliem (Archbold and Habbema), between Habbema and Wissel (Hagers), and in the Vogelkop (Bird's Head) area (Ajamaroe and Anggi).

Islands close to the coast of Irian Jaya are included therein; but the small groups of Aru, Kai and Tanimbar, in the Arafura Sea, just north of Australia, have always been part of Indonesia.

Islands of Irian Jaya. There are several groups of islands of which the island groups in Teluk Cenderawasih or Bird of Paradise Bay (formerly the Schouten Islands), and Yapen are the most significant. Each of these groups represents an administrative district ('kabupaten'). The first group consists of two main islands. Supiori and Biak, and the Padaido islands. As these islands have been in contact with the outside world for several centuries, one can see Melanesian and Malay mixtures among their people.

During World War II Biak was of strategic importance and both Japanese and the Allies used the coral island as a springboard for further operations in the south-west Pacific.

Biak is now an important transit station for ships and aircraft. The runway of Mokmer airport at Biak was built by the Americans during the War and has remained the best in Irian Jaya. Biak is now also the headquarters of the Supreme Commander of all Indonesian military forces in Irian Jaya. Travel between Indonesia and Irian Jaya has substantially increased and the development of Biak is geared to provide this transit traffic with facilities such as offices, hotels, stores, restaurants and entertainment.

The Biak district administration has also established an agricultural experimental station at Wirmaker — 40 kilometres north of Biak town, where new fruits imported from other parts of Indonesia are tested and established. Biak people are considered to be the most advanced of those in Irian Jaya and some occupy top positions in politics, education, the public service and administration in Irian Jaya. There has always been a regular flow of Biak people leaving their island to work elsewhere.

Yapen islands are rather isolated, and rely heavily on trade from Biak. Now that Nabire has developed into an agricultural hinterland, Yapen island (with Serui as its capital) serves as transit station for the export of soya beans and cassava (manioc) from Nabire to Biak. Imports include construction materials and household goods from Biak for distribution to Yapen, Waropen, Manokwari and Paniai.

Serui is where Indonesian nationalists including Dr Sam Ratulangi were exiled by the Dutch. The exiles lived among the local people and some pro-Indonesian Irianese leaders including Silas Papare, came from Serui.

Were it not for the discovery of oil and minerals in the Bird Head area (Vogelkop) around Sorong, such islands as Gag (where nickel has been found) would remain undeveloped, like the groups in the South — Kai and Aru. During the past decades, there was a tendency among job-seeking islanders to migrate to the mainland and a large contingent of Kai islanders now live in Merauke. The people on the many tiny islands in Yos Sudarso (formerly Humboldt) Bay are mainly fishermen. Close to Jayapura, these people were strongly influenced by Dutch politics and education, especially from 1945 to 1962. The people near Jayapura have always been noted for accelerated social and economic transition, and it has been the breeding place for West Irianese regionalism. It was mainly from this area — including bay islands such as Tobati — that discontented elements among the West Irianese crossed the border into PNG as political refugees.

Flora and fauna. The flora are a mixture of Indo-Malayan and Australian types. For centuries the highland peoples burnt forests to flush game and make room for agriculture. This has created the great highland grass plains of the Baliem Valley and Wissel Lakes

country, both large centres of populations.

The native plant with the widest variety of uses is the coconut, which provides food, drink, oil, wood, leaves for thatching, fibre for matting, and shells for water vessels. Nipa and areca palm leaves are also used for thatching. Other plants mainly used for food are: sugar cane, banana, sweet potato, sago palm, taro, papaw, yam and the breadfruit. Other varieties of trees of high economic value are also found, such as copal and rattan.

There are many known species of birds, mostly related to Australian types, though a few, such as the hornbill, are exclusively Asian. However, the high mountains limit the range of birds. Important groups are the birds of paradise, of which there are many varieties; kingfishers, flycatchers, parrots and honeyeaters; pigeons and doves including goura, the largest pigeon in the world; the flightless cassowary which provides the natives with food, plumes for head-dresses and sharp bones for daggers; and many water birds, including pelicans, cranes, cormorants, ducks, herons, storks and ibises.

Irian Jaya is the home of many marsupials, including several species of wallaby and the tree kangaroo, a native cat and various bandicoots, pouched mice and possums. Possums vary in size from mouse-like gliding possums to the cuscus, the largest of the possum family. Also found are wild pigs, wild dogs, several species of fruit bats or flying foxes, and the world's largest tree-climbing water rats. Large mammals are not found on the island except for those imported from other regions, such as livestock (oxen, horses, etc.). Marine mammals include the dugong and dolphin.

The reptiles are generally related to Australian species. Of the venomous type are death adders, whip snakes and banded sea snakes. Also found are big monitor lizards, the oceanic gecko, the giant skink, crocodiles, turtles, the Pacific boa and the scrub python.

Land use. It was estimated in 1977 that only 200,000 ha (0.5 per cent) of the land in Irian Jaya is considered favourable for agricultural development. A further million hectares (2.5 per cent) could be available if the primary forest was cleared. There is also 265,000 ha of sago palm growing in swampy coastal regions which provides staple food for people in those areas.

Many observers fear that the alienation of land by Indonesian authorities in favour of transmigrants — two hectares per family, as a rule — could lead to conflicts with the Irianese, to whom the concept of private ownership of land is quite foreign. In their view, land may certainly be used by others, but compensation must be paid to the clan or group who have traditionally used it. The Indonesian authorities appear unconcerned about this problem.

PRIMARY PRODUCTION. Irian Jaya's main food crops are sweet potatoes, taros, yams, cassava (tapioca) and vegetables. These have long been the staples for the local people.

Cash crops. Cultivation of cash crops for export is still limited to specific areas. The main export crops and their areas of cultivation are:

Copra: Merauke, Raja Ampat Is. (Sorong), Sarmi, Kaimana, Numfor and Biak

Nutmeg: Fakfak and Kaimana

Cocoa: Serui-Yapen, Waropen, Manokwari, Genyem, Sentani, Sarmi

Rubber: Merauke district (Digul, Mindiptana, Bada, Kepi, Muting), Ransiki, Timika, Kokonau

Coffee: Enarotali, Serui, Bokondini

Feasibility studies are being pursued by the horticulture department to cultivate cloves, tobacco, cashew nuts, kapok, sugar cane and pepper. However, during 1976–77, total exports of cash crops from Irian Jaya were worth $US 1.9 million or 0.5 per cent of total export earnings.

Livestock. As a potential source of income for the people, most types of livestock have been introduced experimentally to Irian Jaya. Except for the ubiquitous pigs, the areas most suitable are considered to be:

Grime (1200 ha) and Sekoli plains (3500 ha) Nabire plain (1200 ha)

TABLE 2 MAIN FOOD CROP PRODUCTION IRIAN JAYA, 1985–86 SEASON

	Acreage (hectares)	Tonnes
Cassava	3664	38,336
Sweet potato	47,708	349,808
Taro and other tubers	52,621	368,863

TABLE 3 IRIAN JAYA — LIVESTOCK POPULATION

	1976	1977
Cattle	8512	9226
Water buffalo	21	27
Horses	1642	1684
Sheep	9226	10,162
Goats	763	1090
Pigs	189,715	196,617
Poultry	330,454	391,254
Ducks	24,819	26,416
Rabbits	6422	n.a.

Near Manokwari (300 ha) and Ransiki (2000 ha)
Digul and near Merauke (5000 ha)
Plains in the Balim highlands, Enarotali, Kebar and other areas (14,000 ha).

Fisheries. Around Sorong, Merauke, Jayapura and elsewhere along the coast of Irian Jaya, fishing represents the main source of income for the local population. Freshwater fisheries in ponds, rivers and lakes cover 800,000 ha.

The production of fish, both freshwater and sea, increased from 14,341 tonnes in 1976 to 17,028 tonnes in 1977, an increase of 17.1 per cent. Exports of all sea products in 1977 increased by 933.5 tonnes (26.8 per cent) over the previous year's total representing a price increase of $US5,065,767. Total value of exports in 1977 was $US18,849,219.60. At Sorong, cold storage rooms with 250 tonnes capacity have been built by the West Irian Fishing Industry and Maviva Product Development. Surveys for upgrading the fisheries industry have been carried out by the Fund for West Irian/United Nations Development Programme (FUNDI/UNDP).

Exports of marine products in 1986 amounted to more than 19,000 tonnes, a value of $US29.25 million. In 1985 the figures were nearly 14,500 tonnes and $US23.9 million respectively.

The greatest Government investment in a fishing enterprise is the Usaha Mina Ltd Co. which has 30 fishing boats, each of 30 tonnes and cold storage facilities with a capacity of 1300 tonnes. Its base equipment includes a 300 tonne capacity dockyard, instrument workshop, radio station and housing for its administrative personnel. Total staff is about 700.

There are five other private fishing companies operating in Irian Jaya waters and their catch includes prawns and other fish. There are ice factories at Jayapura (two), Biak (one) and Sorong (two). Their main task is to supply ice to fishing vessels but they also sell it to the general public.

Indonesian Government policy for Irian Jaya's agriculture was, in the first instance, to introduce new food crops in order to improve the nutritional value of the local staple foods — which consist mainly of carbohydrates such as sweet potatoes, taro, yam and sago — and, secondly, to encourage production for the cash market in order to raise per capita income.

But the achievement of these aims faces formidable obstacles, not the least of which is the reluctance of the Irianese to change their methods of farming which have been practised on their land from time immemorial. In the 1980s therefore, agriculture in Irian Jaya still presents a picture of predominantly subsistence farming.

The development of food resources for domestic consumption has thus been slow, occurring mainly in the transmigration centres where the migrants from other provinces have started rice and vegetable cultivation.

The Government has succeeded in developing some fish-breeding, and in introducing some new plant foods in the highlands. However, the bulk of food, if it is not grown locally (sweet potatoes, yam, etc.), must still be imported.

Forestry. Although 75 per cent of the entire surface of Irian Jaya is covered with forest, only 100,000 ha of productive forests are at present being exploited.

Current estimates are that there could be a further 650,000 ha of accessible productive forests not yet in use; and in those areas still inaccessible to transport, there may be a further 3.75 million ha of productive forests.

At present, the main export commodities are logs ($US118,958 in 1985–86). Another important forestry byproduct is copal, a resin used in varnish manufacture. Exports of copal in 1976 were worth $US41,120.

MINING AND OIL. Although some initial assays have indicated that Irian Jaya may possess substantial deposits of minerals, the main income producers to date are oil and copper.

Export income from minerals (in $US million) is as follows:

	1975–76	1985–86
Oil	257.8	286.6
Copper	77.9	103.4

The main mining operations are the following:

Tembagapura (Ertsberg) Copper Project. Discovered in 1936, Ertsberg (Ore Mountain) represents possibly the largest base metal outcrop in the world, and was developed in the 70s by Freeport Indonesia Inc., a subsidiary of Freeport Minerals Company. It rises 2800 m above sea level in Irian Jaya's primitive interior. A three-unit tramway claimed to be the world's largest, and a 104 km long pipeline said to be the longest copper concentrate pipe in the world, developed by Bechtel-Pomeroy of San Francisco, delivers the copper concentrate slurry through 38 km of rugged mountain terrain and 62 km of mangrove swamp and tropical rainforest to the port of Kokonau on the Arafura Sea. The $US163 million project, completed and in service in 1973, handles 250,000 tonnes annually, opening the 35-million-tonne Ertsberg deposit to international markets.

Damage assessed at $US1 million was caused to this project in July 1977 when sabotage was directed at the pipeline carrying copper concentrate from the mine to the coast, and at a parallel fuel pipeline which supplies the mine machinery. The damage was the result of raids by the Irian Jaya liberation movement, the so-called Provisional Revolutionary Government of West Papua New Guinea, which was fighting against Indonesian control.

In early 1988 a joint venture between an Indonesian and an Australian company won a $US1.5 million tender from Freeport International to expand the mine and increase production of copper concentrate from 16,000 to 20,000 tons per day.

P. T. Pacific Nickel Indonesia. Since 17 February 1969 this consortium of American, Canadian and Dutch companies has been working under contract with the Indonesian government. In 1971, the company discovered nickel laterite layers on the island of Gag in the Waigeo area of the Sorong district.

In 1972 a feasibility study by Bechtel Corporation was aimed at establishing development facilities on Gag Island for producing 52,000 tonnes of nickel annually, and the Indonesian government assigned the company to build the mining and processing facilities. $US550 million was invested in the project while another $US15 million was spent on survey and research.

With worldwide over-production of nickel, work on Gag Island was deferred temporarily. However, mineral prospecting by the consortium was continued elsewhere in Indonesia. The plan to erect a smelter costing $US1,000 million was still 'active' with a completion

date set for the mid-1980s. In 1974 the Indonesian Government decided to provide 20 per cent of the capital needed.

Petroleum industry. After oil exploration in the Bird's Head area of Sorong by the Netherlands New Guinea Petroleum Company ceased in 1959, a 10-year period of inactivity ensued. Oil production by Pertamina, Indonesia's state-owned oil company, was limited to the Klamono area. After 1966 there was some rehabilitation of the Sele oilfields.

Offshore exploration was renewed by AGIP and Phillips Petroleum, both functioning as contractors of Pertamina, in mid-1969, and there was more inland in the Bomberei and Kasim areas at the end of 1971 by Gulf and Petromer Trend.

Further exploration was conducted in the Mogoi and Wasian locations in 1972, and in the Klamono and Bintuni areas in August 1973, by the *Compagnie Générale de Géophysique*, another contractor of Pertamina. Using the seismic method, oil was found in substantial production quantities in the Kasim area by Petromer Trend in the first quarter of 1973.

By 1977, three companies were conducting active drilling programmes and in 1976, 28 holes were drilled. Of these, eight revealed oil and/or gas. Two other companies were conducting geophysical exploration.

At Sele and Kasim about 175–200 foreigners, mostly Americans, are working on contracts, earning net salaries of about $US2,000 a month with free food and accommodation. After every four weeks, they are entitled to two weeks' leave with return air transport free to the places of their recruitment (Singapore and Bangkok).

The Indonesian labourers earn above-local salaries and are entitled to a week's holiday after every four weeks of work. This is mostly spent in Sorong. This situation has sent local food prices skyrocketing and makes Sorong the most expensive place to live in the province.

With the oil boom, the district capital of Sorong was transformed into a busy town with an increasing immigrant population coming from outside Irian Jaya, mainly from the Moluccas and Sulawesi, to work as labourers on the oilfields.

Because of the difficulty of transporting fuel oil overland in Irian Jaya, a seventh seaport depot was completed in early 1987 at Manokwari, a town of some 110,000 people on the north coast. Others are at Jayapura, Merauke, Biak, Serui, Nabire and Sorong.

TOURISM. With a need for accommodation for visitors to the administrative centre of Jayapura, the business centre of Biak and the oil industry at Sorong, there has been a rapid increase in numbers of hotels, guest houses, travel agencies and restaurants in Irian Jaya. In 1972 BAPPARDA (Body for Developing Local Tourism) was established, but in most places, the standards of accommodation are below international levels and prices are high.

Indonesian sources report that in the first 11 months of 1986 only 2291 foreign tourists visited Irian Jaya, and in the corresponding period for 1985 only 1858, figures which make nonsense of previously published tables giving numbers such as 20,000–24,000 overseas tourists annually. In 1976 it was claimed that the combined spending of domestic and foreign tourists was $US11.1 million. No more recent figures are available.

Foreign tourists to Irian Jaya came from the USA, Japan, Holland, Germany, France, Switzerland, Italy and other west-European countries.

According to an official announcement in October 1983, authorities have identified 37 tourist destinations in seven of the nine administrative districts of Irian Jaya.

The official in charge of tourist development in the province, said that nine were located in Jayapura, and three in Baliem Wamena. Seven were located in Cenderawasih Bay Region, four in Manokwari, six in Sorong, five in Merauke, and three in Pantai Regency, he said. The tourist destinations had characteristics of their own, but had not been properly developed or promoted for lack of funds.

The official said tourism was practically a new thing for the vast majority of the people of Irian Jaya, and they associated tourists with foreigners on a visit to the region. In connection with this, he called on the appropriate authorities to give the people of Irian Jaya more information on tourism.

In 1986 most overseas tourists visited only three regions in Irian Jaya: Jayapura, the capital, Biak Numfor and Jayawijaya. The majority of visitors to Jayapura were Americans interested in World War II relics, those going to Biak Numfor were said to be attracted there by the caves used as hiding places by Japanese soldiers in that war, and those going to Jayawijaya went primarily to view the two-century-old mummies kept by villagers.

LOCAL COMMERCE. The local Irianese mostly lack any tradition of commercial activity. This fact coupled with the presence of commercially active migrant elements from other provinces and of Chinese, makes it extremely difficult for them to develop business talents and initiatives.

Only a small number of Irianese are to be seen selling inside the 'Pasar Sentral' (Central Market) in Jayapura's Hamada district. Mostly, they are still in their traditional places, squatting outside the building to sell their simple produce.

Retail stores, repair shops, eating stalls, restaurants, bars, nightclubs, minibus transport, small hotels and inns are all owned either by Indonesians from outside the province or by Chinese.

In an effort to cope with this situation the West Irian Joint Development Foundation lends money with preference to Irianese, to finance small-scale enterprises such as crop-growing and cattle breeding. Loans are also made to Irianese fishermen for the purchase of outboard motors to be attached to their outrigger canoes to help them increase their catches.

Industry and labour. At the close of the fiscal year 1978/79 there were listed 453 licensed industries employing 13,318 workers. It was estimated that these industries represented an investment of Rp 3,450,098,000 compared with an investment in 1977/78 of Rp 3,089, 912,000 in 423 industries employing 3220 workers, an increase of 7.8 per cent in the number of industries, 3.4 per cent in the workforce and 11.6 per cent in investment value.

OVERSEAS TRADE. The value of Irian Jaya's exports and imports for the fiscal years 1976–77 and 1985–86 are shown in the accompanying tables.

FINANCE. No recent figures are available showing the budgetary situation in Irian

TABLE 4 IRIAN JAYA — EXPORTS AND IMPORTS (in $US000)

	Exports	Imports	Balance of trade
1976–77	452,134	1014	+451,120
1985–86	410,971	3007	+407,964

TABLE 5 IRIAN JAYA — EXPORTS (in $US000)

	1976–77	1985–86
Oil and gas	335,924	286,622*
Copper	101,151	103,403
Prawns	16,834	15,478
Spices	1211	450
Fresh and frozen fish	806	4276
Copra	603	n/a
Crocodile skins	601	73
Trepang	492	n/a
Timber, logs	442	119
Crabs, frozen	132	n/a
Rubber	84	n/a
Copal	41	n/a
Cocoa	21	13

* *Barrels of oil only*

Jaya. The first five year development programme from 1969–74 ('Repelita I') was followed by other five-year plans, current of which is Repelita IV (1984–89).

Taxes. Neither Government personnel nor members of the Indonesian armed forces have to pay taxes; the only deduction from their monthly wages is 7 to 12 per cent as a contribution to pension funds. Revenues are derived from imports and exports. The Indonesian State Navigation 'Pelni' in Jayapura handles all foreign imports which come mostly from Singapore and Hong Kong. All exports from Irian Jaya also pass through this department and they include oil, copper, crocodile skins, timber, mace, etc.

All revenues from exports and imports are sent to Jakarta where the central government then allocates funds for the provincial budget. The provincial government then distributes such funds to the districts.

For the autonomous province of Irian Jaya, the only internal taxes levied are automobile registration fees. Eventually, for the administrative districts ('kabupaten'), sales tax will represent their main source of revenue.

Currency. The same notes and coins are circulated in Irian Jaya as in other parts of Indonesia. The denominations of the notes in rupiah (Rp) are Rp 25, Rp 50, Rp 100, Rp 500, Rp 1000, Rp 5000 and Rp 10,000. For coins the denominations are Rp 1, Rp 5, Rp 10, Rp 25, and Rp 100. Since the 'Act of Free Choice' in 1969 the rupiah has been the only currency permitted in Irian Jaya.

After 15 November 1978, the Indonesian rupiah was allowed to float but was linked to the US dollar with an exchange value of $US1.00 eq. Rp 625. Before the change the rate was $US1.00 eq. 425. A series of devaluations in recent years has seen the rupiah descend in value to $US1 = Rp 1600 and $A1 = Rp 1130 in early 1988. The instability has made the rupiah difficult to change outside of Indonesia and nearby South-east Asian countries.

TRANSPORT. Road-building work of recent years has included construction of roads connecting food-producing hinterlands with provincial capitals, such as the Genyem-Jayapura and Wirmaker-Biak roads, and roads linking towns with transmigration centres such as the Sobron-Dorsai-Jayapura and Kuprik-Merauke roads. Work has been in progress for several years to build a 150 km highway from Nabire to Enaratoli in the Paniai highlands. The longest overland route passable to cars in Irian Jaya is less than 200 km, but over the years to mid-1979 seven overland roads had been constructed. These are: Sentani-Boroway-Genyem (Jayapura district): Sentani-Doyo-Depapre (Jayapura district); Biak-Korem (Teluk Cenderawasih district); Manokwari-Warmare (Manokwari district); Sorong-Klamono (Sorong district); Tanah Merah-Mindiptana (Merauke district); Teminabuan-Ayamaru (Sorong district).

The most ambitious of all road-building projects in the province is the north-south road, planned to link Jayapura in the north with Merauke in the south. Estimates of the time needed for completion of the road, some sectors of which are already in use, vary from five to 10 years. The road is planned to serve as the axis for a large-scale Javanese resettlement project.

The trans-Irian Jaya highway has been under construction since 1981 and is now divided into eight construction sections. By February 1987 465.8 kilometres of the highway had been completed.

Hugging the PNG border as it does, the road has some potential for creating problems between the Indonesians and PNG. This was dramatically illustrated in 1983 when it was discovered that, due to errors on the part of a Japanese surveyor employed by a Jakarta construction company, the road crossed into PNG territory at three points near Erambu,

north of Merauke. The Indonesian Government apologised, but the affair caused a brief period of strain in relations between the two countries.

Some short-distance roads have been made to give access to natural resources such as oil, copper, nickel and timber, but these are not considered to be public roads.

Airlines. Ten airlines, the majority belonging to religious missions, were operating inside Irian Jaya in 1979. Air Niugini, Papua New Guinea's flag carrier, flies between PNG and Irian Jaya. The two national airlines are Garuda Indonesian Airways (GIA) which operates daily and Merpati Nasantara Airlines (MNA) three times a week. The routes are — GIA: Jakarta-Ujung Pandang-Sorong-Biak-Jayapura and return and also Jakarta direct to Ujung Pandang. MNA: Jayapura-Biak-Ujung Pandang-Surubaya-Jakarta.

Airlines are: Merpati Nasantara Airlines, 13 aircraft; Garuda Indonesian Airways, 2 aircraft; Missionary Aviation Fellowship 16; Associated Mission Aviation, 4; Seventh-day Adventist, 2; Region Beyond Missionary Union, 2; Summer Institute of Linguistics, 2; Air Niugini, 1; Pelita Air Service (Pertamina), 10; Nation Utility Helicopters, 7.

The two mission airlines, Missionary Aviation Fellowship (Protestant) and Associated Mission Aviation (Roman Catholic), operate charter and passenger and cargo flights inside Irian Jaya at fares similar to those of MNA.

The Indonesian Air Force (AURI) is based at Biak, and besides providing regular military transport, it also provides Dakotas for air-drops of food in remote locations, or in disaster areas.

The only Indonesian airline maintaining regular flights to South-East Asia, i.e. Singapore and Bangkok, is Pelita Air Service — owned by the Indonesian State Oil Industry (Pertamina) — to fly expatriate personnel from the oilfields to places of recruitment and recreation.

The only foreign airline operating in Irian Jaya is Air Niugini, Papua New Guinea's state airline, which has weekly flights from Vanimo to Jayapura with Trislanders. These aircraft land only at Sentani airport (35 km from Jayapura), refuel and return immediated to PNG. In late 1986 Garuda organised DC-10 flights from Los Angeles to Jakarta

TABLE 6 AIRPORTS/AIRSTRIPS

District	Govt.	MAF	AMA	Private	Total
		Owned and managed by			
Jayapura	13	29	5	1	48
Jayawijaya	3	71	6	2	82
Teluk Cenderawasih	3	—	—	—	3
Manokwari	7	19	4	—	30
Sorong	3	3	—	1	7
Piniai	5	23	11	—	39
Merauke	7	12	7	—	26
Yapen Waropen	2	—	—	—	2
Fakfak	4	3	3	2	12
Total	47	160	36	6	249

via Biak. The service has had reasonable success.

To reach Tembagapura (Ertsberg copper mine), Merpati have flights to Kokonau where passengers transfer to helicopters for Tembagapura. With the exception of Biak, built during World War II by the USAF and capable of taking DC-10 aircraft, the largest airfields in Irian Jaya are Jayapura (F-28 jet) and Sorong (F-28 jet). Airfields capable of accommodating the Fokker F-27 'Friendship' are Merauke, Piniai, Manokwari and Wamena. There are only Twin Otter facilities at Fakfak and Yapen.

All these strips (excepting Yapen) have an asphalt landing area. Other asphalt strips include Boruku (Indonesian Air Force) suitable for Hercules; Numfor and Kemiri are capable of taking DC-3s. These latter airfields are all in the Cenderawasih Bay area.
Port facilities. Much of the rehabilitation work done on harbours and docks in recent years has been directly related to economic development projects such as the oil and prawn-freezing industries in Sorong, and the timber export industry in Jayapura and Manokwari.

Under the auspices of the United Nations Joint Development Foundation — which has its headquarters at Jayapura (Jalan Percetakan Negara 4-6) — the building of 20-tonne ferrocement workboats was started in 1977

in the Waena area near Abepura. The boats are engaged in picking up copra and other produce from harbours such as Sarmi and taking the cargo along the coast or, even, outside Irian Jaya (e.g. to Halmahera).

COMMUNICATIONS. Since the launching of the 'Palapa' satellite in July 1976, Indonesia has had domestic satellite communication linking all parts of the nation with direct telephone, telegraph and telex systems. The satellite is also used to transmit television programmes and it is planned to include television for educational purposes. All transmissions are in 'Bahasa Indonesia', the national language.

Eight of the 40 earth stations in Indonesia are located in Irian Jaya. They are at Jayapura, Biak, Manokwari, Fakfak, Sorong, Merauke, Tembagapura (for the Ertsberg copper mine) and Gag Island (for the nickel project). Television reception in Irian Jaya is limited to Jayapura and Biak and only between 6.30 pm and 12.30 am.
Internal radio network. When Irian Jaya was transferred to Indonesia in 1963, there were radio stations at Jayapura and Biak. Others have since been opened at Sorong, Manokwari, Fakfak, Merauke, Serui, Nabire and Wamena with the R.R.I. Jayapura being the central transmitter.
Public information. 'Kantor Wilayah' or

'Kanwil', the Regional Office of Information, is directly controlled by the Department of Information in Jakarta and has been established to disseminate policies of the central government. Its information programmes include election campaigns and the 'Repelita' (five-year national development programmes).

All forms of media are used for public information including press, pamphlets, photo exhibits, public lectures, radio, film and television. Lack of transport and shortage of funds prevents information projects from being sent to many villages in the interior where illiteracy is also a problem.

Films exhibited in Irian Jaya are censored. They are imported from Jakarta, Hong Kong and the USA.

WATER. Jayapura has a reticulated water supply, originally constructed by the Dutch, and supplied from a rain-filled reservoir at Angkasa. The water is not treated with caporite. Sentani, 35 km from Jayapura, obtains its supplies from the Kemiri reservoir which is also used for swimming and other recreational pursuits by Jayapura residents. Similar supplies are provided at Manokwari, Sorong, Fakfak, Nabire and Wamena. Biak, an arid coral island, obtains its water from Sorido dam. This water is scarce, and brackish. At Merauke, water is obtained from neighbouring swamps. With the possible exception of Wamena, *all* water in Irian Jaya should be boiled before drinking in any form.

ELECTRICITY. Generation of electricity in Irian Jaya is powered entirely by diesel engines, some installed as early as 1953. Under Indonesian administration, there has been rehabilitation or replacement of some generators and installation of new ones, mostly at airports.

Electric power stations in Irian Jaya are located at Jayapura, Sentani, Ifar, Sarmi, Biak, Serui, Manokwari, Sorong, Jefman Is (Sorong airport), Doom Is (near Sorong), Fakfak, Tanah Merah and Merauke. A scheme has been proposed to utilise the waters of Lake Sentani for generation of hydroelectricity.

HISTORY. Writing in the Indonesian archipelago developed only after considerable contact had been enjoyed with Indian traders,

and then only in the courts. Therefore, although the coasts of Irian Jaya were known from early times, at least within the archipelago, there is no written proof of it. We must look to foreign sources for records referring to the existence of the island and its relationship with other peoples of the area in which it was located, during the early period.

Because of the spices which grow abundantly in the easten islands of the Indonesian archipelago — the Moluccas, Irian Jaya and adjacent islands — they could not long remain isolated from the rest of the world. Early Indian traders at the beginning of the Christian era gave the area the name of Samudranta or the Sea's Edge. It was written that at one end of Samudranta was located the island of Dwipanta or Islands' End since it was situated farthest east of the islands in the archipelago. The Indian poet Walmiki, in his epic Ramayana, wrote that in eastern Yawadwipa were located the Sjisjira Hills (Snowy Hills). Prof. H. Kern, Sanskrit scholar, and later Prof. N. J. Krom, historian, found evidence that Yawadwipa designated the Indonesian archipelago and that the Sjisjira Hills were the snowy peaks of Irian Jaya.

The great Sriwijaya empire of South Sumatra was a centre of Buddhistic learning during the first millennium of the Christian era. It was also the centre of a bustling sea trade in goods from China and India and indigenous produce including spices, aromatics, pearls, coral and jet, mother-of-pearl, and bird-of-paradise plumes.

In the 7th century, enterprising merchants from Sriwijaya arrived at the island of Irian, which they called Janggi and claimed it as part of the empire.

In the 8th century a Chinese traveller in his annals referred to Irian as Tung Ki and stated that it was part of the Moluccas.

The Javanese poet Prapantja in his work Nagarakertagama (AD 1365) mentioned that Irian formed a part of the Majapahit empire of East Java.

The Batjan chronicles relate that in 1512 a younger brother of the sultan, one Kaitjil Jelman, became ruler of the sub-kingdom of Misool and the first Islamic ruler in the region.

In the 16th century the islands of Irian, more popularly known as the Four Kings Island Group (Waigamo, Misool, Waigeo,

Salawati), were brought under the authority of the Moluccan sultans. The Kingdoms of the Waigama and Misool became part of the Batjan sultanate while the sultans of Ternate and Tidore fought over the Kingdoms of Waigeo and Salawati. The wars which often erupted in this area due to the territorial expansionist ambitions of the two sultans resulted in a re-arrangement of their authority: Ternate extended its power over the Celebes and those islands west of Halmahera, Tidore gained the area south to East Ceram and east to and including West Irian. Early in the 17th century, Tidore subjugated the Batjan subkingdom of Misool, thereby gaining control of the islands of the Four Kings Island Group, including East Ceram and West Irian.

The coming of the Europeans. By the 16th century, spices had become a necessity to Europeans, Asians and Africans alike, not only for food but also for medicinal purposes. The return of Magellan's ship *Victoria* in a Spanish port on Sunday, 6 September 1522, the first ship to have circumnavigated the world, brought a shipload of spices and a diary describing the area from which the spices came. This diary, belonging to an Italian passenger, is the first known European reference to the islands of Irian, making mention of a pagan King of Papua. However, he mislocated Papua.

Energetic Europeans saw a way of making a goodly profit, by transporting spices and other valuable produce — pearls, sandalwood, bird-of-paradise plumes — themselves, instead of depending on others. Such things, being light, took little space and brought in rich rewards. And so began the race to the Spice Islands.

The Spanish. After the first Spanish ship touched at Tidore in the year 1521 (the *Victoria*), many Spanish ships visited it, travelling to and from Mexico. Some had to lay over in the islands, awaiting favourable winds, and so discovered new islands, for example Alvaro de Saavedra in 1528 on his way to Tidore from Mexico. On 20 June 1545, the Spaniard Ortiz Retez, on his way to Panama, landed and, finding no hindrance, took the islands of Irian in the name of the Spanish King, calling it 'Nueva Guinea'. However, the Spanish never again returned to take actual possession and with the Utrecht Agreement in 1714 Spain lost any rights it may

have had to the island.

Of the Spanish sailors who travelled this area, it is necessary to mention Luis Baez de Torres, who in 1606 had completely navigated the south coast of Irian and found a passage for ships in between the islands and coral reefs, that is the Torres Strait which separates the island of New Guinea from the Australian continent. This adventure remained unknown to many other European sailors for some time. In the 18th century, one-and-a-half centuries later, a map of 'Nova Guinea' pictured it as an extension of 'Nova Hollandia' (Australia).

Torres also visited 'Onin' peninsula where he met with merchants professing the Islamic faith. They divided their time between trading and propagating Islam among the natives.

The Dutch. The first Dutchman to visit Irian, Willem Jansz in his ship the *Duyfken* in 1606, also touched at Kai and Aru islands in the south-western coast of Irian where he found the land covered with dense forestation and scattered settlements of people 'wild, savage, black and uncivilised', who had 'murdered several of the ship's hands'. Jansz was searching for new areas of trade for the Netherlands' Indies Company. However what he found was far from encouraging. The Dutch thereafter evidenced little interest in the island until it seemed that another European power had plans for opening trade stations and building a fort on the island. Dutch knowledge of Irian and adjacent islands remained slim until the beginning of the 20th century.

The British. In 1761 news reached Europe that English ships had entered the Moluccas and built a fort at Salawati. The Netherlands' Indies Company, having no idea as to whether the Company had any legal title to the area, whether spices coming under the Dutch monopoly were to be found there, or even where Salawati was exactly, established a committee, comprising two extraordinary members of the Netherlands' Indies Council and Council secretary to look into the matter. After several months of studying all available material, on 23 November 1761 a thick report of findings was submitted, containing all evidence relating to the Company's 'legal title' over the entire Great East (Groote Oos) which included West Irian.

In 1774 another Englishman succeeded in

breaking the Dutch monopoly in the Moluccas. On 9 November, Captain Forrest sailed out of Balambangan, an island north of British North Borneo, heading for the northern Moluccas and Irian on British East-Indies Company business. For five months he explored the north-eastern seas in his ship *La Tartare*. From 27 January to 18 February 1775 he anchored at Dore Bay (Manokwari) where he took 100 nutmeg seedlings for planting in North Borneo.

Fifteen years later the British East-Indies Company ordered Captain MacCluer to explore and map carefully the coastline of any islands around Irian Jaya. Based on MacCluer's findings, the British built a fort at Dore Bay (Manokwari) with the permission and guidance of Nuku, a prince of Tidore governing West Irian and adjacent islands who had no love for the Dutch.

At the insistence of the Dutch Governor at Ternate, Sultan Kamaludin Sjah of Tidore registered a strong protest at this unlawful occupation of his sovereign territory. In his letter of protest dated 15 September 1794, the Sultan stated that Irian and adjacent islands had always been part of the Tidore Sultanate and demanded the immediate and absolute withdrawal of the British from the area. The English did relinquish their post by early 1795, but more probably from lack of food and resulting incidences of beriberi than as a result of Sultan Kamaludin's protest.

Twice during the early part of the 19th century the English wrested the Moluccas from the Dutch and twice they were returned with the signing of peace treaties, the last in 1814 in London. However, the return of the Moluccas as well as Irian was not de facto until 1817.

The Dutch take permanent possession. Regaining possession, the Dutch guarded their monopoly more closely than ever; the Government worried very much lest a foreigner come to occupy any part of the islands in order to break the monopoly. They would have enlarged their possessions on more than one occasion, but had not the military strength to do so. So weak were they, in fact, that when the Sultan of Sarawak requested assistance in his struggle with Brunei in 1838, the Batavian Government had to refuse, thereby losing all the North Borneo colonies (British North Borneo, Sarawak and Brunei).

During the 19th century Irian was frequently visited by European sailors and natural scientists. Among others Dumont d'Urville, the Frenchman who circumnavigated the globe in 1826–28, searching for places yet unknown to Europeans, put in at Irian at the Mamberamo estuary. There were so many visitors, some claiming parts of the island for their country, that the Dutch Government felt the need to build a fort as a sign of their legal title to Irian and to place markers on those parts of the coast which came under its law.

The first Dutch fort to be built in Irian Jaya was Fort Du Bus, erected near the Lobo settlement on Lobo Bay (Triton Bay) in 1828. Fort Du Bus suffered an unhappy history over the next eight years. Many of its residents succumbed to malaria and beriberi. The Irianese living in its vicinity persisted in their unfriendliness. Several times the fort was attacked by land and by sea by armadas from Seramlaut and Gorong in league with warriors from the local tribes. For as long as the fort remained standing with its complement of Dutch soldiers, they were not free to trade as they wished. (Note that from the 16th century the south-western coast had been monopolised at various times by rulers of Seramlaut, Geser, Gorong and Keffing.) After obtaining the authority and permission of the Dutch King, the fort was torn down and left behind forever on 22 February 1836.

Meanwhile, on 24 August 1828 it was proclaimed with ceremony that 'West Irian from 141 degrees East longitude on the south coast to the west, north-west and north up to Jamurseba, excepting that part already under the suzerainty of the Sultan of Tidore' was taken as a possession in the name of the Dutch King. It is noteworthy that from Jamurseba Point eastwards to Humboldt Bay, the region including Amberbaken, Dore, Wandamen, Great Irian Bay, Waropen, Tanah Merah, did not have to be claimed since it was part of Tidore which was already under Dutch rule.

The boundary is defined. In 1836 an extremely difficult question was put to the Dutch Government by the British Government. Exactly which areas came under Dutch authority; a question which was raised after the Dutch protested that the English had illegally entered Dutch territory, when British ships attacked a nest of pirates on Galang Island, a Dutch holding in the Riau group north-east of Bintan Island. An article in the 'Singapore Free Press' a few years later to the effect that Lt. Yule of the British Navy had hoisted the Union Jack on the south coast of Irian added to the pressure on the Dutch to formulate a list of possessions.

The Colonial Government at The Hague found itself unable to come up with a satisfactory reply and in 1843 it instructed the Governor-General to prepare a detailed list of all areas considered to be directly or indirectly under the sovereignty or the influence of the Netherlands' Indies Administration. Should he come up with any 'vacancy', he was to fill in said 'vacancy' immediately by 'conducting some act of sovereignty or by making some agreement (with the princes) which would include articles confirming sovereignty'. It was necessary to conduct an accurate examination of all factors, which duty was allocated to the Governor in Borneo, A. L. Weddik.

In a note concerning the administrative connection of the Moluccas, Weddik reported, after his study had been completed, that in the year 1678 the west coast, the southwest coast and a large part of the northern coast of Irian were already under the suzerainty of Tidore. Based on this, the Netherlands' Indies Government issued a classified decree dated 30 July 1848 in which it was noted that the authority of the Sultan of Tidore over Irian covered the area 'beginning from the tip Saprop Maneh 140 degrees 47' meridian on the northern coast, along the coastline, from Wandamen Bay to Kainkain Beba (Jamurseba) and further west, south and south-east as far as the border line stipulated ad interim in the proclamation dated 24 August 1828, that is the 141st meridian on the south coast; including also the interior as far as it seemed this region was considered a part of the Netherlands' Indies after further exploration which would be held concerning the condition of nature of the area and the arrangement of administration of its inhabitants'. Further, it was stipulated that included in the referenced area were all adjacent islands. In brief, the whole of Irian Jaya which formed an area of dispute or which the Dutch had disputed was recognised as part of the Tidore Sultanate.

Britain and Germany set up colonies. The interest of other nations in Irian was aroused. Natural scientists, sailors and travellers visited the island in considerable numbers. Warships from Italy, Russia, Britain and Germany often put in, especially at the eastern end (Papua New Guinea) whose status had not yet been defined, all contending for its ownership.

On 27 November, 1882, a German reporter, Emil Deckert, outlined in the 'Augsburger Allgemeine Zeitung' deliberately and with feeling the case for Germany's occupation of the eastern half of the island. The Germans reacted by collecting funds and setting up a trading company, the 'Neu-Guinea Compagnie'. The Australians reacted by registering a strong protest at the German plans. 'The peace and security of Australia and its national importance will be threatened should a foreign nation, strong and powerful, occupy an area so close to Australia. Therefore, it is of the utmost importance that the entire east end should be immediately annexed.' Not waiting for the go-ahead from the British Government in London, the Colonial Administration in Queensland proclaimed that East Irian was a possession of the Crown of England. The proclamation was dated 4 April 1883. It was not ratified by the British Government and was therefore declared null and void on 11 June 1883.

The Germans were so active in Papua New Guinea that on 7 July 1884 the British Government proclaimed its intention to occupy that part of Irian running from the 141st meridian on the south coast, eastwards to the farthest point and from there westwards to the 145th meridian East longitude. On 18 September 1884 official notification was made to the German Government with the implication that the north coast between the 141st and 145th meridians East longitude was available should somebody wish to avail themselves of the opportunity. The Kaiser needed colonies for economic reasons and did not therefore look well upon the statement from Great Britain. He took possession of the entire northern coast of New Guinea from the 141st meridian East longitude to the most eastern tip. Fortunately, the two countries were able to come to an agreement in 1885 on the boundaries of their respective colonies: a broken line beginning from the point cutting through 141 degrees East longitude and 5 degrees South latitude to 8 degrees South latitude at Mitrarock near Hercules Bay, the north-east coast at Mitra-rock being dissected by the 8 degrees South latitude, which parallel also served as the borderline between the islands located on the east side of Irian.

By this agreement a strip of the north coast with a width of 0 degrees 13' without protest by the parties involved (Germany and Great Britain) was considered to be a part of the Tidore Sultanate, at that time itself being a part of the Netherlands' Indies Colonies. The boundary with West Irian, although never stipulated in any agreement was respected by Germany and later also by Australia to whom the German colony was passed as a mandate territory at the end of World War I.

In 1901 the south coast of Irian was brought under the direct authority of the Netherlands as an assistant residency with its capital at Merauke. The rights of Tidore were exchanged with a reparations payment. Then Irian Jaya was made respectively a part of the Ternate Residency, a separate residency (1920–1924), and finally an assistant residency to the Ternate Residency which was, in turn, a part of the Great East Province (Gouvernement Groote Oost). With the division of West Irian regions within the Province of the Great East, the Netherlands' Indies authories thereby did not treat Irian Jaya as anything other than an integral part of the Tidore Sultanate.

After the capitulation of Japan at the end of the Pacific War, Irian Jaya was given the status of a full residency.

During the Japanese occupation several underground movements had sprouted up, including the Jajabaya movement under the leadership of Martin Indey, the Manseri Mangundi movement at Biak, the Simson movement at Jayapura and various others. At the end of the Pacific War, Silas Papare, a guerrilla leader against the Japanese, was awarded the Bronze Cross by the Allied Forces, who were in Irian at the time. The Allies then turned the island over to the Dutch colonial administration, irrespective of the Proclamation of Indonesian Independence of 17 August 1945.

The Proclamation of Indonesian Indepen-

dence encouraged the continued opposition of the West Irianese against the Dutch Administration. Guerrilla headquarters were found, among other places, in Sorong, Jayapura, Merauke and Manokwari. The Independent Indonesia Party, led by Silas Papare, was established on 30 November 1945 at Serui.

Round Table Agreement. The Round Table Agreement of 1950 stipulated that the Residency of Irian Jaya would be handed over to the United States of Indonesia within one year.

On 17 August 1950, the United States of Indonesia became the Unitary Republic of Indonesia. Immediately the leaders of the West Irianese declared their loyalty to the Republic. Meanwhile the continuation of Dutch colonialism in West Irian Jaya ran unchecked. So as not to lose hold of their last colony in the area, the Dutch claimed that they wished only to bring advancement and betterment to the people.

One year passed and no settlement had been reached which accorded to the wishes of the West Irianese and the Republic. Opposition in the form of guerrilla warfare increased in intensity. Efforts to settle the question through diplomatic channels on the part of the Republic also failed. In 1956 the Republic of Indonesia therefore announced that the Round Table Agreement had been unilaterally voided.

On 16 August 1956 the Republic of Indonesia formed the autonomous province of West Irian with the interim capital of Soa Siu on Tidore Island. Simultaneously, the Dutch formulated the plan to set up a separate state of Papua.

The President of the Republic of Indonesia delivered the Trikora Command on 19 December 1961, a three-pointed order to: (1) Fly the Indonesian flag in West Irian; (2) Defeat the formation of the Papuan state by the Dutch, and (3) Have the Indonesian armed forces ready to 'liberate' West Irian. The first clash took place on 15 January 1962, in what is now known as the Aru Bay Incident. One by one the Dutch strongholds fell into the hands of the Volunteers for the Freedom of West Irian.

As a result, the Dutch took the question to the United Nations. With Ellsworth Bunker acting as intermediary, the New

York Agreement of August 1962 was reached, in which it was prescribed that the Dutch surrender West Irian into the hands of United Nations Temporary Executive Authority, which action was finalised on 6 October 1962.

On 10 November 1962, with the knowledge of UNTEA, the University of Cenderawasih was established at the capital city of Jayapura with two faculties, covering the fields of Education and Law.

Indonesian control. The Indonesians made certain that relations with the UNTEA were carefully nurtured right up to the handing over of West Irian to the Republic on 15 May 1963.

In 1969 the process known as 'PePeRa', an Indonesian acroym for 'Penentuan Pendapat Rakya' or 'Determination of People's Opinion', but commonly referred to as the 'Act of Free Choice', took place. Indonesia then took full control over West Irian.

The 'Act of Free Choice' was not without its opponents and critics, many of whom were observers from other countries. 'My vivid recollection of the Act', wrote journalist Bob Hawkins in the Melbourne *Age* some time later, 'is of an Indonesian officer prodding, with a thin cane stick, Papuans into position in a meeting hall in Wamena ... so that, on command, they would vote "unanimously" for ties with Indonesia.' Many indigenous people were reported to have felt cheated at being let down by the world community, especially by Australia.

The incorporation of West Irian into the republic was virtually a *fait accompli*, however. In September 1969 President Sukarno proclaimed it to be an autonomous province of Indonesia. It was renamed Irian Jaya in 1973.

Rebel movements based on the idea of Melanesian identity and opposition to Indonesian control have troubled the Indonesian authorities in Irian Jaya in the intervening years. One of them, the so-called Provisional Revolutionary Government of West Papua, claimed responsibility some years ago for the sabotage of the Ertsberg copper project. Leaders of the Movement for a Free West Papau (or OPM, after the Indonesian words 'Operasi Papua Merdeka'), are elusive, and various individuals have, at times and simultaneously, claimed leadership.

The opposition of the OPM to Indonesian control was strengthened in the early 1980s when various development schemes, especially Repelita IV, made evident the full extent of the Indonesian government's transmigration plans — the resettling of hundreds of thousands of Indonesian peasant farmers from the overcrowded islands of Java, Sumatra and Bali in less populated regions such as Irian Jaya. According to Repelita IV, Irian Jaya was to receive around one million migrants, people whose concept of land tenure — like that of their Government — was, and is, entirely different to that of the indigenous Irianese.

As a result of increasing friction between Melanesians and Asian Indonesians in the province — not all of it concerned with OPM activities — an estimated 10,000 people fled the province in early 1984 seeking sanctuary in Papua New Guinea. 'The land issue has been the greatest source of conflict', writes Robin Osborne, one of the few to have studied this troubled area closely.

Papua New Guinea criticism of the transmigration scheme as 'inhumane' drew the response that the programme was 'the government's project so that is Indonesia's business.'

Despite the aims of Repelita IV, by late 1987 the transmigration scheme in Irian Jaya had not been meeting its human quotas. Official announcements from Jakarta claimed that only 23,723 families, comprising 97,503 people, had been resettled in the province since 1970. A spokesman for the Transmigration Ministry said that the programme would continue, and he expressed the hope that the private sector would come to the assistance of the goverment in seeing it succeed. The government was said to be implementing the 'Swakarsa' or self-initiated trans-migration system to resettle people in the vast but sparsely populated eastern region of Irian Jaya — the area closest to Papua New Guinea and territorially and politically the most volatile part of the province.

Further reading. Literature in English concerning Irian Jaya is almost always critical, either of the Indonesians or their predecessors, the Dutch. If a 'balanced' view exists it is difficult to locate, with the possible exception of the 'impartial' anthropological writings on the area. Some useful and accessible works are: Kees Lagerberg, *West Irian and Jakarta Imperialism* (London, 1979); Nonie Sharp, *The Rule of the Sword: The Story of West Irian* (Malmsbury, 1977); Ron Crocombe and Ahmed Ali (eds), *Politics in Melanesia* (Chap. One) (Suva, 1982); Robert Mitton, *The Lost World of Irian Jaya* (Melbourne, 1983); Robin Osborne, *Indonesia's Secret War* (Sydney, 1985).

FOR THE TOURIST. Entry formalities for Irian Jaya are now slightly less onerous than they were, so reflecting the increasing Indonesian confidence in its policies concerning the province. If the traveller is already in Indonesia, no additional visa or permit is necessary to go to Irian Jaya. However, if entry is being made from Papua New Guinea a visa, obtainable from the Indonesian Embassy in Port Moresby, is essential. The ease with which one may be obtained varies according to time and circumstance: intending travellers should check these details in advance.

Limited money exchange facilities are available in Jayapura and some other towns in Irian Jaya, but exchange rates are less favourable than in other parts of Indonesia. The PNG kina is not always easy to change in Indonesia. Neither for that matter is the Indonesian rupiah easy to exchange outside of its home country, except perhaps in Singapore. Travellers would be well advised to change surplus rupiah before departing Indonesia.

For the traveller dedicated to discomfort in the interests of authentic experience boat travel is possible between Jakarta and ports in Irian Jaya via the vessels of the Pelni shipping service. This is very time-consuming and not outstandingly cheap.

Sightseeing. Although tourism authorities in Irian Jaya have identified a number of tourist interest areas, getting to them is not particularly easy. There are relatively few organised tours, although guides can be obtained for a fee from the Cenderawasih University in Jayapura. For a reasonable understanding of the indigenous people and cultures of Irian Jaya, a guide or some study in advance is recommended. Travellers should note that several parts of the interior are regarded as out-of-bounds to foreign tourists.

Jayapura (once Hollandia, later Kota Baru and still later Sukarnopura) is an Asian rather than a Melanesian-Pacific town and does not offer a great deal of interest. Apart from the fact that the Dutch established it, the town's main claim to historic significance is its association with General Douglas MacArthur's invasion of the Philippines. World War II relics may be seen in various places. The university's museum is of some importance and accessible by bus from town. The distinctive handicrafts of the Asmat region may be purchased in Jayapura at a few locations. Overseas demand for them has made them increasingly expensive in recent years.

Outside Jayapura the most interesting accessible area to visitors is the Baliem valley, home of the Dani people, much pictured and written about, though they became known to the West only as recently as 1938. As a result both Westernisation and Indonesianisation are in their infancy here, and both have been violently resisted at times. The latter process, however, is gaining ground. Guides may be obtained in Wamena (the chief town in the valley) and are advisable if one wants to make the most of one's experience. Dani women and men are excellent craftspeople. Wamena is not a particularly attractive town although its market is of considerable interest, particularly on weekends.

Additional information on tourist facilities may be obtained from: The Tourist Development Board of Irian Jaya, Bapparda, Governor's Office of Irian Jaya, PO Box 499, Jayapura, Irian Jaya, Indonesia.

ACCOMMODATION
JAYAPURA

Hotel Dafonsoro: on Jalan Percetakan, some a/c rooms, others with fan, television, bathrooms attached, tariff includes light breakfast. Tel.: 21870, 22285.
Hotel Triton: on Jalan Ahmad Yani, a/c rooms, bathrooms attached, television.
Mess Gki: on Jalan Sam Ratulangi, rooms with fan and attached bathrooms, meals included in tariff. Tel.: 503.
Losmen Sederhana: on Jalan Halmahera, some a/c rooms, others with fan,

bathrooms attached, meals available.
Tel.: 21291.

WAMENA

Nayak Hotel: on Jalan Angkasa, rooms with
bathroom attached, meals available.
Hotel Baliem Cottage: on Jalan Thamrin,
bungalow-style units with bathroom
attached, meals available.

BIAK

Hotel Irian: near airport, rooms with
bathroom attached, meals available.
Tel.. 21139.
Hotel Mapia: on Jalan Ahmad Yani, some
rooms a/c, others with fan, bathroom
attached, meals available. Tel.: 21383,
21961.
Hotel Titawaka: on Jalan Selet Makassar,
rooms with a/c or fan, bathrooms
attached, meals and airport transfers
included in tariff. Tel.: 21835, 21885.

Johnston Island

This is a coral atoll 25 km in circumference, about 1130 km WSW of Honolulu. It lies in 16 deg 44 min N latitude and 169 deg 17 min W longitude. Its height varies from about 4 metres in the west to 13 metres at Summit Peak at the eastern end. It is one of the most isolated atolls in the world. It rests on a core of an ancient volcanic island now buried under a limestone cap thousands of feet thick which resulted from 70 million years of reef growth on the slowly sinking island. Johnston Island is now a broad shallow platform with a marginal reef emergent only on the north-west. Two of the small islands in the lagoon are entirely man-made (North Island and East Island). A fourth island, Sand Island, is half man-made and half natural, the two parts now connected by a causeway approximately 400 metres long. Only low-growing vegetation is found here.

JOHNSTON ISLAND

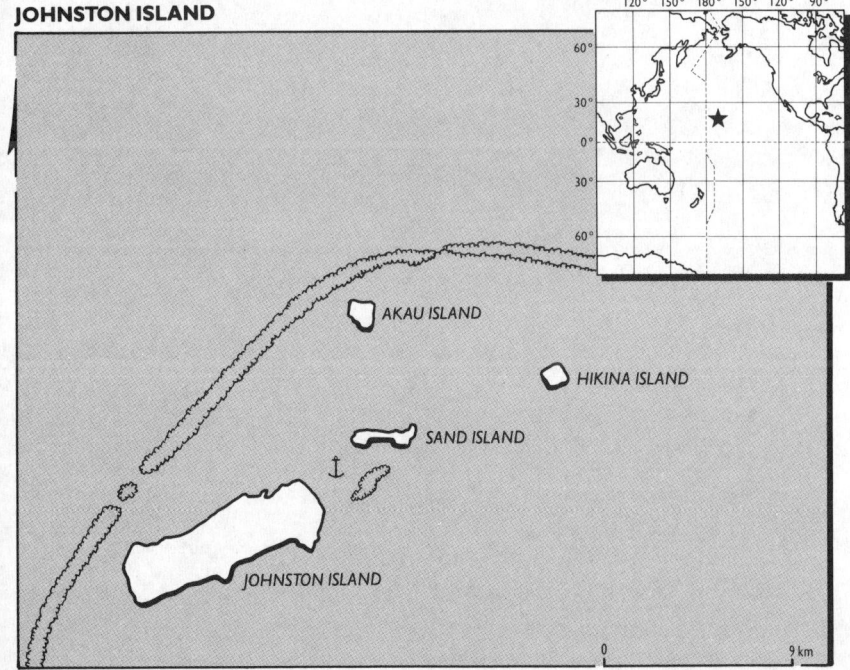

The island was first discovered by Captain Joseph Pierpoint of the brig *Sally* in 1796. Landing was first accomplished by Captain J. Johnston of HMS *Cornwallis* in 1807.

Both the US and the Kingdom of Hawaii annexed the atoll in 1858 although the Guano Act of 1856 had already granted the Americans the rights to mine the extensive deposits of this mineral. The operation was abandoned in the late 1880s. In 1923 the Biological Survey of the US Department of Agriculture and the Bishop Museum of Hawaii visited the island to research the bird and marine life. The visit led to its being designated a bird refuge.

In 1934 the US Navy took over the island and a seaplane base was built. It was fortified during World War II and used as a submarine base. In 1941 the atoll was shelled by the Japanese as they returned to Japan after bombing Pearl Harbor.

Jurisdiction was handed to the US Air Force in 1948. It was used as a testing site for high-altitude nuclear devices in the 50s and 60s and facilities were expanded and upgraded, including the construction of an airstrip which runs almost the full length of Johnston islet.

The island is serviced by Air Micronesia although passengers may only disembark with prior permission.

Today Johnston Island remains an unincorporated territory of the United States with operational control held by the Defense Nuclear Agency (since 1958). It is maintained as a storage site for chemical munitions and as a standby test site should the United States ever decide to resume atmospheric testing of nuclear weapons. The civilian and military personnel stands at about 300.

Johnston Island is also classified as an overlay refuge and is included in the Pacific Islands National Wildlife Refuge listings. Twelve species of seabirds breed here, including shearwaters and petrels, terns and noddies, tropicbirds, frigatebirds and boobies, and the lagoon shelters diverse marine life including the green turtle.

Further information may be obtained from the Fish and Wildlife Service, PO Box 50167, Honolulu, Hawaii 96850.

Juan Fernandez Islands

The Juan Fernandez Islands, three small islands of volcanic origin, lie at a distance of 667 km and more west of Valparaiso. They are Chilean possessions. The largest, most important and nearest to Chile was formerly known as Mas-a-Tierra (Nearer to Land) and is now officially designated Robinson Crusoe's Island. It has an area of 93 sq. km. Just off the south-west tip of this is Santa Clara Island, otherwise known as Goat Island

because it is inhabited only by wild goats. This island has a maximum height of 375 m above sea level. Heavy seas make access to the coast difficult. About 170 km further west is Mas-Afuera (Further Away), which the Chilean Government has called Alexander Selkirk's Island since 1966. It has an area of 85 sq. km and the highest point is 1836 m.

The climate is mild with an annual average temperature of 18°C. Regular year-round air

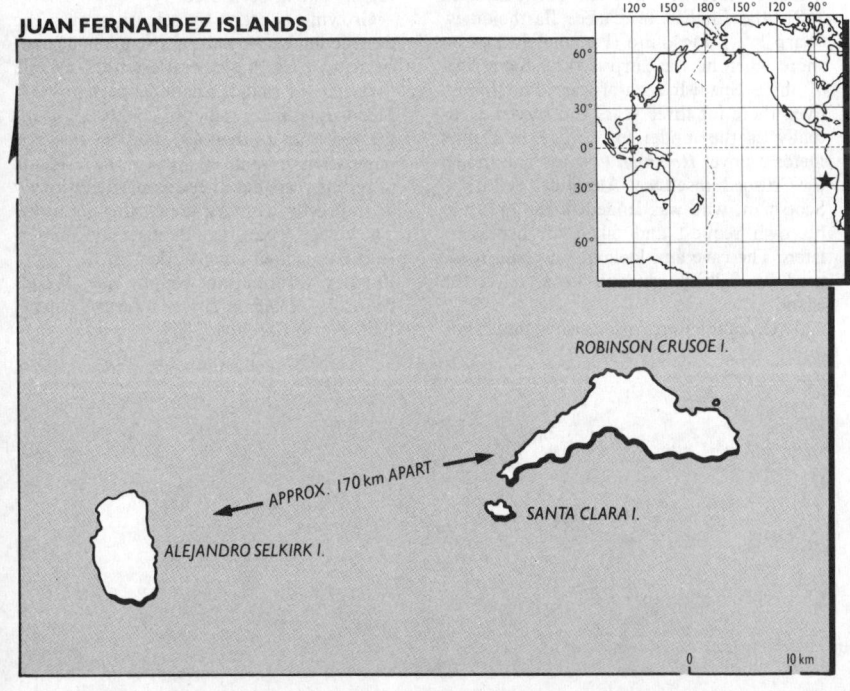

JUAN FERNANDEZ ISLANDS

ROBINSON CRUSOE I.

APPROX. 170 km APART

SANTA CLARA I.

ALEJANDRO SELKIRK I.

0   10 km

services link Robinson Crusoe Island with Santiago and Valparaiso, and in the summer a monthly boat service operates between the islands and Valparaiso. There are many sporting activities to be enjoyed with skin-diving in the clear warm waters (constant at 22°C) a popular pursuit for visitors. The lobsters, which are plentiful in the surrounding waters, are said to be the largest in the world.

Hotels on Robinson Crusoe are the Hosteria Robinson Crusoe, Cabanas Daniel Defoe, El Pangal, Renaldo Green Pension, and many islanders rent low-cost accommodation to visitors.

The islands were uninhabited in pre-European times. Their European discoverer, Juan Fernandez, came upon them in 1574 on a voyage to Valparaiso from Callao, Peru. Spanish fishermen first settled them in 1591 and introduced the first goats. This and subsequent settlements, such as one by Jesuits from Chile in the 1660s, were short-lived. However, passing ships, particularly those of English buccaneers, found the islands useful sources for water and provisions. In 1681, the English buccaneer Bartholomew Sharp left a Mosquito (Panama) Indian on shore when he was surprised by the arrival of three Spanish men-of-war. The Indian lived there for three years and served eventually as the model for Friday in Daniel Defoe's novel *Robinson Crusoe*. The model for Crusoe himself was Alexander Selkirk, a Scotsman, who was landed in the group at his own request and taken off five years later. The cave and lookout post said to be used by Selkirk can still be seen on the island.

After Commodore Anson visited the islands in 1740 and went on to capture a Spanish galleon, the Spaniards in Chile sent several hundred men and women to occupy Juan Fernandez and build a fort. Their settlement eventually became a penal settlement, but was abandoned in 1814. Between 1797 and 1808 a number of American and British sealing vessels made profitable visits to Mas-Afuera; and for much of the rest of the century numerous whalers, particularly from the US, fished in the vicinity and called at Mas-a-Tierra for provisions.

Juan Fernandez came under Chilean control after Chile achieved independence in 1819. From then onwards the islands were occupied almost coninually either as a penal settlement, place of exile for political prisoners or for fishing and agriculture. The development of steam navigation and the opening of the Panama Canal in 1914 reduced the group's importance to shipping. In 1915, Cumberland Bay on Mas-a-Tierra was the scene of an engagement between the German warship *Dresden* and HMS *Glasgow* in which the Germans blew their own vessel up after a few shots had been fired.

Growing concern by scientists over the destruction of the natural resources of Juan Fernandez led President Alessandri of Chile to decree the islands a national park in 1935. Meanwhile, the number of colonists had increased to more than 400, and by 1983 the population stood at 800. Most of the residents of recent years have been associated directly or indirectly with the crayfishing industry. The village of San Juan Bautista on Cumberland Bay is their chief settlement.

Further information. Ralph Lee Woodward, Jr, *Robinson Crusoe's Island*, Chapel Hill, North Carolina, 1969.

Kermadec
Islands

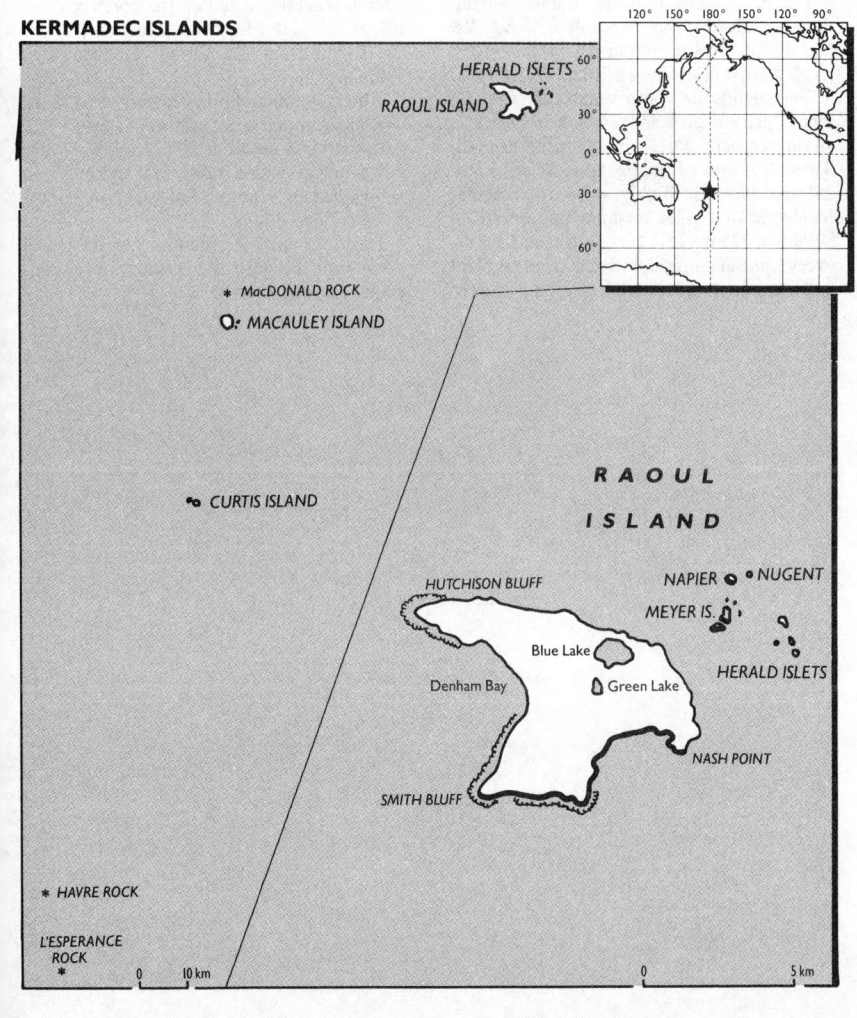

KERMADEC ISLANDS

HERALD ISLETS

RAOUL ISLAND

* MacDONALD ROCK

O: MACAULEY ISLAND

•o CURTIS ISLAND

R A O U L

I S L A N D

HUTCHISON BLUFF

NAPIER O • NUGENT

MEYER IS.

Blue Lake

HERALD ISLETS

Denham Bay

Green Lake

NASH POINT

SMITH BLUFF

* HAVRE ROCK

L'ESPERANCE
ROCK
*

0   10 km

0   5 km

The Kermadec Islands are a rocky group lying 965 km northwards of Auckland, between S latitudes 29 deg 10 min and 31 deg 30 min. They are a New Zealand dependency administered by the New Zealand Land and Survey Department for the preservation of indigenous flora and fauna. The only inhabitants are a few New Zealanders on Raoul Island, who man the meteorological station which is maintained there by the NZ Ministry of Transport but the islands may have had a prehistoric Polynesian population.

The principal islands are: Raoul (or Sunday) Island, 2916 ha; Macauley Island, 309 ha; Herald Group, 34 ha; Curtis Island, 59 ha; L'Esperance (French Rock), 5 ha.

The islands are volcanic and thermal activity is present on Raoul, which is 32 km in circumference. There is plentiful rainfall. Total land area of the group is 33 sq. km.

Raoul Island is thickly wooded, triangular in shape, and rises towards one end to a height of 525 m. It is very fertile and almost every kind of tropical and sub-tropical plant will grow on it. There are four crater lakes or swamps, and at least two of them fresh water, which is not potable.

Raoul is the island regarded as most habitable. Communication is difficult — there is no sheltered anchorage, and ships cannot land a boat in rough weather. There is no public passenger service to the islands. In 1936, as trans-Pacific aviation developed, the group attained a new significance, because it is about halfway between Tonga and New Zealand.

In July 1937, a meteorological reporting station was established on the north coast of Raoul, just off Fleetwood Bluff and across the island from the former Denham Bay settlement.

The prevailing wind is easterly and light. The mean annual temperature is about 19°C, with extremes of about 28°C and 9°C. Rainfall averages about 1450 mm annually. In good weather there is a fair yacht anchorage at Boat Cove.

Landings are permitted only with special permission because the islands are an important nature reserve.

Kiribati

This group of 33 islands, lying astride of the equator over an area of five million sq. km of ocean, was named the Gilbert Islands in the 1820s and was administered by Britain from 1892 until 12 July, 1979, when it became an independent republic with the name of Kiribati (pron. Kiribas, the nearest pronunciation in the indigenous tongue to the word 'Gilberts').

The country, a member of the Commonwealth of Nations, consists of three main groups — the Gilberts proper, Phoenix, Northern and Southern Line Islands with Ocean Island. They are situated between 4 deg 43 min N and 11 deg 25 min S latitude and 169 deg 32 min E to 150 deg 14 min W longitude. The most populous island, Tarawa, is about 1800 km north of Suva, Fiji. The administrative centre, Bairiki, is on Tarawa. Local time is 12 hours ahead of GMT. The population shown in the 1978 census report published in 1980 was 58,512. The population shown in the 1985 census was 63,883.

Kiribati has retained the original design of the flag of the former British Colony of the Gilbert and Ellice Islands. It depicts a frigate bird poised in flight over a sun on the horizon. Three wavy lines underneath the sun represent the three island groups, the Gilberts, the Line Islands and the Phoenix Islands. The country's motto under the Coat of Arms is 'Te Mauri, Te Raoi, Te Tabomoa' (Health, Peace and Honour), a traditional phrase formerly used for toasts, good wishes and for ending speeches. The National Anthem is *Teirake Kain Kiribati* (Stand Kiribati).

The Gilbert group of islands was formerly known as Tungaru in the Micronesian language but, as other islands now forming part of Kiribati were not known by that name and were not a part of the original group, it was decided, in the interests of unity, to adhere to the name Gilberts bestowed on the whole group by the Russian hydrographer A. I. Krusenstern in the 1820s and retained by Britain.

The people are now known as I-Kiribati. As there are only 13 letters in the language, and 's' is not one of them, Kiribati is the nearest one can get to the phonetic sound of Gilberts. A 't' followed by 'i' becomes an 's', hence Kiribas. The final 'i' is not sounded unless followed by another word beginning with a consonant. In any event a 't' cannot end a word.

Australian currency is legal tender but it is expected that Kiribati will, eventually, have its own currency.

Local public holidays are: 1 January; Good Friday; Easter Monday; 12 July (Independence Day); Youth Day (first Monday in August); Christmas Day; Boxing Day.

THE PEOPLE. Until 1 October 1975 the Gilbert Islands were joined with the Ellice Islands in a single British colony. On that date the Polynesian inhabitants of the Ellice Islands seceded to form Tuvalu (see entry under that name). The Gilbert Islanders (I-Kiribati) are Micronesians. The last census was held in May 1985, at which time the local population was 63,883, of which 61,419 were I-Kiribati. The remainder included 264 Europeans.

Population distribution. In 1985 there were 21,393 people in urban Tarawa, forming 33.5 per cent of the total for the republic. Kiritimati (Christmas Island) on which sev-

KIRIBATI

KINGMAN R.
PALMYRA

GILBERT ISLANDS

NORTHER

ISLAN[

MAKIN
BUTARITARI
ABAIANG • *MARAKEI*
TARAWA
MAIANA •
KURIA • *ABEMAMA*
• *ARANUKA*
NONOUTI • *BERU*
• *BANABA*
TABITEUEA • *ONOTOA* • *NIKUNAU*
TAMANA • *ARORAE*

• *HOWLAND (US)*
• *BAKER (US)*

KANTON
? • *ENDERBURY*
McKEAN • *BIRNIE* • • *PHOENIX (RAWAKI)*
• *MANRA*
NIKUMARORO • *ORONA*

PHOENIX ISLANDS

eral development projects have started or are planned, had the most rapid population growth. In 1976 there were 674 people on the island and, according to the 1985 census this total had grown to 1737.

Demographic projections indicate that, with a growth rate of 4.3 per cent per year for the years to 1993, the Tarawa urban population would increase by 15,950 to a total of 34,066 at which level the density would be 4705 persons per sq. km against the existing density figure of 2502.

The population of the rural islands was virtually static from 1968 to 1973, but returns from the 1978 census suggested an increase from 1973 to 1978 of about 1500, or

0.8 per cent per year. Between 1978 and 1985 the increase was 1960, an increase of 5 per cent. With the end of phosphate mining on Ocean Island (Banaba) at the close of 1979, about 1270 I-Kiribati left the island for their home islands.

The population in the outer islands in 1985 was: Makin 1777; Butaritari 3622; Marakei 2693; Abaiang 4386; Tarawa North 3205; Maiana 2141; Abemana 2966; Kuria 1052; Aranuka 984; Nonouti 2930; Tabiteuea North 3171; Tabiteuea South 1322; Beru 2702; Nikunau 2061; Onotoa 1927; Tamana 1378; Arorae 1470; Banaba 46; Kiritimati 1737; Tabuaeran 445; Teraina 451.

Nationality. On independence (12 July,

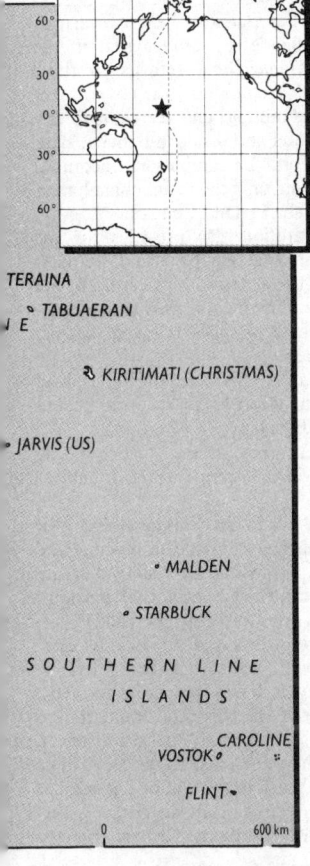

TERAINA

↘ TABUAERAN

↲ E

↘ KIRITIMATI (CHRISTMAS)

↗ JARVIS (US)

• MALDEN

◦ STARBUCK

S O U T H E R N   L I N E
        I S L A N D S

                    CAROLINE
VOSTOK ◦   ◌

FLINT ▾

0   600 km

crewing overseas ships and have acquired an excellent reputation. Their earnings, sent home for support of their families, play an important part in the country's economy. Others are working in other South Pacific countries but the end of phosphate mining on Banaba has forced more than 1000 to return to their home islands. More than 1000 are still employed in the phosphate workings in Nauru.

Religion. The main Christian denominations are Roman Catholic and the Gilbert Islands Protestant Church (Congregational). There are small numbers of Seventh-day Adventists, Baha'i, Church of God and the Church of Jesus Christ of Latter Day Saints (Mormons).

Lifestyle. The Gilbertese are very much men of the sea. Traditional skills include cultivating babai (taro), fishing, making and sailing canoes. Outer island life is essentially affluent-subsistence with cash income from copra and some remittances. In urban Tarawa the cash economy prevails and population pressure has resulted in a dependence on imported foods.

Recreation. Islanders' main interests are dancing, canoe-racing, volleyball, soccer and traditional games.

GOVERNMENT. From November 1976 to 12 July 1979 Kiribati had internal self-government. It was originally decided that the country would gain its independence in June 1978, but the protracted bid by the Banabans to secede and to have their island placed under the protection of Fiji as their 'other' island of Rabi is in Fiji, caused a postponement. The date was eventually set after the British Government had ruled against the Banabans' claim.

The government consists of the President (Beretitenti), who is Head of State and Head of Government, a Cabinet composed of the President, the Vice-President (Kauoman-ni-Beretitenti), not more than eight other ministers from among the elected members of the legislature, formerly called the House of Assembly and, now the *Maneaba-ni-Maungatabu* and the Attorney-General. The President appoints his own Cabinet.

The President is elected nationally from among members of the House of Assembly (*Maneaba-ni-Maungatabu*) which nominates

1979), all persons of Kiribati descent automatically became citizens of Kiribati. Those born in Kiribati but not of Kiribati descent also became citizens at independence. Wives of I-Kiribati are also eligible for citizenship. Dual nationality is prohibited. Banabans automatically became citizens and the Constitution also safeguards other rights with regard to representation in the House of Assembly, Banaba land and entry into Banaba.

Language. The people speak a Micronesian dialect and English, which is used in official communications.

Migration. As a marine training school has operated successfully for several years in Tarawa, several hundred Kiribati men are not less than three or not more than four as candidates. No one other than an elected member of the Assembly can be a presidential candidate. In the event of parliament's dissolution as a result of the President ceasing to hold office following a vote of no confidence, the Constitution provides for a Council of State, composed of the Chairman of the Public Service Commission, the Chief Justice and Speaker of the *Maneaba-ni-Maungatabu*, which carries out the functions of president and government until an election has been held.

The term of office for both the president (Beretitenti) and the *Maneaba-ni-Maungatabu* is four years. A president can be re-elected for two more terms. A vice-president who assumes the office of president before the president's full term has expired, can serve only two further terms in the office of president.

Presidential powers include the granting of pardons, on the advice of Cabinet, to persons convicted of offences in law, or remit or substitute punishment ordered by the courts.

With regard to the *Maneaba-ni-Maungatabu*, the president can withhold assent to a Bill if he is of the opinion that the Bill would be inconsistent with the Constitution. In such a case, the Bill is returned to parliament. If parliament again presents the same Bill to the president and he is still of his original opinion, he then refers it to the High Court. If the High Court declares that the Bill is not inconsistent with the Constitution, it is returned to the president who must then assent to it. A contrary decision by the High Court means that the Bill must go back to parliament. Parliament can alter provisions of the Constitution by an Act of Parliament subject to certain limitations with one exception — the provisions protecting the fundamental rights and freedoms of the individual. An act to alter any of these provisions must have the consent of not less than two-thirds of the electorate voting in a referendum.

The single-chamber legislature consists of 36 elected members, including a representative of the Banabans and the Attorney-General as an ex officio member. If the president is the elected representative of a constituency entitled to only one member of the assembly, a by-election is held in that constituency for the election of an additional member.

So far as the Banabans are concerned, the Constitution gives them a seat in the *Maneaba-ni-Maungatabu*, returns to them land on Banaba acquired by the government for phosphate mining, and the right of any Banaban to enter and reside in Banaba. Banaba land can only be compulsorily acquired by leasehold and only then after consultation with the Banaban Island Council.

The Constitution also provides for the establishment of a Banaba Island Council. Any constitutional provision relating to the Banabans can only be amended if the Banabans' representative does not vote against any amendment.

Residence of any Banaban on Rabi Island in Fiji does not affect his rights or interest in any land on Banaba.

Local government. Island Councils are established on all permanently inhabited islands.

Since 1958 Island Councils have been able to make their own estimates of revenue and expenditure. Because of the scattered nature of the territory, the councils have considerable freedom from direct supervision.

By 1970 councils on all the islands were functioning with elected members only.

Legislation is being prepared to make slight changes in the District Administration policy. If it is approved, the six districts, each in the charge of a district officer, will be abolished and each island will be regarded as one district. At present the districts are Tarawa, Northern, Southern, Central, Banaba and Line Islands.

Justice. The constitutional provisions governing justice are similar to those in force in other former British possessions. There is a High Court, which is a superior court of record with a chief justice and such number of other judges, if any, which might be prescribed. The chief justice is appointed by the president acting on the advice of the Cabinet tendered after consultation with the Public Service Commission. Other judges are appointed by the president on the advice of the chief justice sitting with the Public Service Commission. To qualify as a judge, a person must have held office as a judge in any country or have been qualified for not less than five years to practise as a barrister or solicitor.

Judges can only be removed from office by the president and such removal must be by parliamentary resolution with parliament acting on the advice of a tribunal.

The High Court has original jurisdiction to hear and decide questions relating to interpretation of the Constitution and to hear and decide on any civil or criminal proceedings including those in any subordinate court.

There is a Court of Appeal for Kiribati which has jurisdiction and powers to hear and determine appeals as may be conferred on it by any law in force in Kiribati. The judges of the Court of Appeal are the chief justice and other high court judges and any other qualified persons who may be appointed by the president on the advice of the chief justice and the Public Service Commission. In mid-1983 two Fiji judges, Judge R. Q. Kermode CBE and Judge G. Mishra, were sworn in as judges of the Kiribati Court of Appeal. There is also the right of appeal to the Judicial Committee of the British Privy Council.

There are magistrates' courts as main courts of first instance on each inhabited island with five on Tarawa. Three magistrates sit together to try criminal and civil cases and five to hear lands cases. Their jurisdiction in land matters is unlimited but their criminal jurisdiction is limited to cases carrying a punishment of up to five years imprisonment and a fine of up to $500. Their maximum civil jurisdiction is $3000.

Police. As well as having the responsibility for the maintenance of law and order, the Kiribati Police Force has responsibility for fire fighting services at airports and for domestic fire services in the urban area of South Tarawa. For police purposes, the country is divided into seven districts: Northern, Tarawa, Central, Southern, South Eastern, Banaba and the Line Group. Each district is commanded by an assistant inspector with the exception of Tarawa district, which is commanded by an assistant superintendent.

In January, 1986 the force consisted of over 250 men. Police stations linked by radio are Betio, Bairiki, Bikenibeu, Abaokoro, Banaba, Police HQ (Betio) and the airport (Bonriki) fire tender. The rest are in contact through the normal radio telephone service.

Prisons. There are several prisons and lockups, the main ones being at Betio and Bairiki on Tarawa, Tabiteuea North and on Kiritimati (Christmas Island). The prison population over the past few years has averaged nearly 60. The Community Affairs Division of the Ministry of Health and community Affairs concentrates on employing prison labour for public benefit and as part of a rehabilitation programme.

Liquor. The islanders may drink beer, liquor or sour toddy (made from the coconut palm) but may not sell any without a licence. At least seven islands have banned the sale of alcohol.

EDUCATION. There was no basic change in educational policy with the coming of independence. The policies framed in 1975 are still valid. These were basically: To provide free and compulsory primary education for classes 1 to 7; integrate as far as possible all primary schools into a unified system; establish post-primary 'Community High Schools' with a curriculum in accord with the rural environment; and provide, in association with the missions and churches, sufficient places in academic secondary schools to produce the students needed to meet requirements for skilled technical, professional and administrative manpower.

Primary education. So far as primary education is concerned, there has been a considerable improvement in the number of qualified teachers. In 1986 all of the 447 teachers in the government primary schools were trained. In 1986 there were 13,196 primary pupils at government schools giving a ratio of 1:29 pupils to one teacher, a lower ratio than the 1983 figures of 1:31. There are 110 government primary schools, and two private primary schools. School fees were abolished in January, 1983, for all pupils in the Government primary schools except those on South Tarawa and in the Line Group. In 1977, most former mission schools, together with the mission teachers, were absorbed into the government primary school system. The Government indicated its willingness to absorb all private schools if they sought it.

The private primary schools are run by the Seventh-day Adventist Church and the Church of God.

As a result of the absorption of four community high schools into the primary school system in 1981, new policies evolved for classes 7, 8 and 9. Consequently children aged 6 to 12 are classified in the lower primary classes and aged 13 and 14 are in the upper primary classes. In 1986 there were 2091 students in this category.

Primary school enrolment and staffing in 1986 was:

	Number of Schools	Pupils	Teachers
Govt. Schools	110	13,196	447
Pte. Schools	2	150	10
All Schools	112	13,346	457

Community high schools. There were only two community high schools in Kiribati in 1986, several others having been reclassified as academic secondary schools. The St Louis CHS is likely to become a junior academic secondary high school in the near future. The CHS had an enrolment of 600 in 1986.

Academic secondary schools. These schools are intended to provide manpower in the technical, professional and administrative fields. There were six secondary schools with a total of 1567 students and 71 teachers in 1986 — the Government's King George V and Elaine Bernacchi School on Tarawa with 481 students; the Catholic Senior College, North Tarawa, with 114 students; the Catholic Junior College, Abaiang, with 226 students; the Hiram Bingham High School, Beru, with 193 students; the Seventh-day Adventist School, Abemama, with 158, and the Moroni High School with 395. All schools are coeducational and take boarders.

Students aim for the Kiribati Junior School Certificate and at the KGV and CSC, students may sit the New Zealand School Certificate. Form 7 was established in 1986.

Overseas studies. In 1986 there were 85 students pursuing pre-service courses overseas, the majority studying for BA or science degrees or diplomas. Fiji and New Zealand have the highest proportion of students.

Technical training. The Tarawa Technical Institute on Betio provides all 'short' full-time, part-time and evening courses. It is heavily committed to training outer-islands people in skills associated with technical projects. It also offers secretarial studies, accountancy and clerical classes in both full-time and part-time courses. In 1985 there were 362 students, a considerable decline in enrolments being evident over the last two years. In 1983 enrolments were 659, falling to 461 in 1984 and declining still further in 1985.

Teacher training. The Tarawa Teachers College is responsible for all basic primary teacher training in Kiribati. The total roll in 1985 was 510 including 97 on a one-year upgrading course. Enrolments have increased steadily in recent years; 398 in 1983, 436 in 1984 and up by 17 per cent again in 1985.

Marine training. The Marine Training School, which was started by the Government of the Gilbert and Ellice Islands with assistance from the United Nations and a British and a German shipping company, in 1967, conducts training courses in basic seamanship which last 18 months.

The enrolment in 1985 was 385 with about 77 per cent completing their course as OS-Deck, OS-Engine or OS-Catering. The school also conducts an upgrading course, including fire-fighting and lifeboat courses for seamen returning from service on overseas vessels and wanting to become able seamen, qualified stewards or qualified motormen. The length of these courses is four weeks with a success rate of about 90 per cent. The school is supported by the New Zealand Government.

The school has been a great success and of great benefit to Kiribati with nearly 1000 qualified I-Kiribati employed on overseas ships, mainly those of China Navigation, Columbus Lines and South Pacific Marine Service, a consortium of German shipping lines. Many Kiribati seamen, by sending a large share of their wages to their families, provide the country with valuable foreign exchange. In 1986 this income was estimated at A$2 million annually. Overseas maritime unions have frequently frustrated the I-Kiribati in their search for jobs at sea by imposing wages and service conditions without reference to Kiribati. However, the formation of the Kiribati Trade Union Congress with the help of the Australian Council of Trade Unions and recent contact with the

Australian Waterside Workers' Federation have eased conditions for Kiribati seamen.

LABOUR. Because the concept of formal employment is unfamiliar to many I-Kiribati, information concerning the strength of the labour force is sparse, the only reliable figures available being from the 1978 Census. At that time (midnight, 12/13 December), the total workforce was 28,859 (13,769 males, 15,090 females), composed of 21,484 active in the villages, 6 employers of labour, 6296 wage employees, 184 in own business, 394 seeking work and 441 not active. In addition, there were 1805 students. The principal occupations are provided by the copra plantations, particularly in the Line Islands, central and local government, the co-operatives, missions and private companies. In 1985 distribution of wage employees according to occupation showed 3669 in the public service, 1011 in transport and communication, 902 in commerce and 231 in utilities.

Christmas Island, planned as an alternative economic centre and undergoing development in several areas, is attracting more workers and their families. The 1985 Census counted 1737 persons, comprised of 1561 I-Kiribati, 147 I-Kiribati Mixed, 13 Tuvaluan, nine European and seven other.

Wages. The minimum wage level early in 1976 was 39 cents an hour with persons under 18 years of age on 30 cents an hour. Some government wage earners were getting 67 cents an hour. Seamen overseas are on considerably more, but figures are not available to give a clear picture of the more up-to-date earning capacity of the people. However, National Income figures suggest an increase in personal incomes of about 6 per cent a year.

Trade unions. Trade unions have developed in association with particular companies or the government service and just before and after independence some unions became more militant, particularly the Public Employees' Union and the BKATM, and there have been some strikes. The latter union, which was formed by the employees of the now defunct Gilbert Islands Development Association (GIDA), amalgamated in 1979 with the Banaba Phosphate General Workers' Union and the Line Islands International Union. Another union, the Kiribati General

Workers' Union, appeared on the scene in 1979. Government plans are to promote increased understanding and co-operation between the unions, employers and the Government. The unions, with help from the Australian Council of Trade Unions, formed the Kiribati Trade Union Congress (KTUC) in June, 1982 and the KTUC joined the International Confederation of Free Trade Unions late in 1982.

HEALTH. The Ministry of Health and Family Planning (formerly the Ministry of Health and Community Affairs) is responsible for health services, which include village work in sanitation and water supplies, disease control and family planning.

Hospitals. There are two major hospitals on Tarawa, the Tungaru Central Hospital at Bikenibeu, with 147 beds, and the Betio General Hospital with 10 beds. Both include dental clinics and the Tungaru Hospital has a mental health department and leprosarium. They are supported by 22 dispensaries and 39 medical clinics distributed throughout the islands. Valuable assistance is received from organisations such as UNICEF, WHO, SPC, New Zealand foundations and the Red Cross, as well as from the medical profession in overseas countries.

At 12 December 1981 there were 16 medical officers, one dental officer, eight principal nursing officers and 17 senior nursing officers.

Diseases. Diarrhoeal disease is very common and can only be reduced as safe water supplies and better waste disposal are provided. Programmes under way for the control of tuberculosis and leprosy resulted in a fall in the registration of new TB cases from 433 in 1961 to 158 in 1974. However in recent years there has been an increase in reported cases; in 1985 there were 285 cases of TB. The number of cases of leprosy has fallen steadily over the years, from 120 still under treatment in 1974 to 49 under treatment in 1985.

An environmental health programme has provided protected water supplies and sanitary latrines and the effect of these has been to lower the rate of child morbidity. Child health is one of the areas in which the health officers are concentrating their efforts, particularly in the areas of nutrition and hygiene.

Family planning. This policy is being

actively pursued, but there are few statistics available to indicate that it is succeeding to any great extent.

Eye diseases. There is a continued agreement between the Kiribati and Australian Governments for medical teams to treat eye diseases in the country. They also train local staff and provide equipment.

THE LAND. The land area of Kiribati is 810.68 sq. km with sea limits enclosing 3,000,000 sq. km, although with Kiribati's declaration of a 200-mile economic and fisheries zone the area is much greater. The country consists of the Gilberts Group (285.52 sq. km); the Line Group and the Phoenix Group. Several islands in the Phoenix and Southern Line Groups are uninhabited.

There are 17 islands in the Gilberts Group, Banaba (Ocean Island) now being officially claimed as part of the group, which consists of: Makin, Butaritari, Marakei, Abaiang, Tarawa, Maiana, Abemama, Kuria, Aranuka, Nonouti, Tabiteuea (North and South), Beru, Nikunau, Onotoa, Tamana, Arorae, Banaba.

The Line Group. Tabuaeran (Fanning), Teraina (Washington), Kirimati (Christmas or Abakiroro, the Northern Line Group); Malden, Starbuck (the Central Line Group); Vostok, Caroline, Flint (Southern Line Group).

The Phoenix Group. Kanton (Canton or Abariringa), Orona (Hull), Nikumaroro (Gardner), Manra (Sydney), Rawaki (Phoenix), Birnie, McKean, Enderbury.

Christmas Island — locally Kiritimati (Kirisimas) is the largest island with an area of 388.39 sq. km. The largest in the Gilberts Group is Tabiteuea (36.63 sq. km) and the smallest Tamana (only 4.73 sq. km). Kiribati extends about 3870 km from Banaba in the west to Christmas Island in the east, and 2050 km from Washington Island in the north to Flint Island in the south. The country stretches from 4 deg 43 min N to 11 deg 25 min S and from 169 deg 32 min E to 150 deg 14 min W. The islands are all low-lying atolls except for Banaba which is 87 m above sea level.

Natural features. With the atoll terrain, the coral rock is covered with only about 2.5 m of hard sand and scanty soil. There are no rivers but most islands enclose a lagoon.

Resources. Only Banaba was endowed with natural resources, in the form of once enormous and rich deposits of phosphatic rock which have been almost worked out.

Climate. The climate of the groups is not unduly trying, particularly during the season of the north-easterly trade winds (March–October). But it becomes enervating during the season of rains and westerly gales (October–March). The thermometer varies little, the lowest reading being 22°C and the highest 37°C in the shade — but usually it is between 26 and 32°C.

Rainfall varies considerably, not only between the islands, but also from year to year. In an average year annual rainfall in the Gilberts ranges from 1000 mm in the vicinity of the equator, including over 1500 mm at Tarawa, to 3000 mm in those islands furthest to the north. In the Phoenix Islands between 1000 and 1500 mm in one year is a good figure, whilst the Line Islands' average varies from about 700 mm at Christmas Island to more than 4000 mm at Washington Island 400 km away. Ocean Island, the central and southern Gilberts, the Phoenix Islands and Christmas Island are subject to severe droughts lasting many months. At such times as little as 200 mm of rain may fall in a year.

Flora and fauna. The thin layer of soil on the atolls supports little growth, apart from seaside scrub, pandanus and coconuts. Native land fauna is limited to the Polynesian rat and two species of lizard. Sea life is considerably richer, with its birds, fish and coral.

Land reclamation. On urban Tarawa the Temaiku Reclamation Scheme in 1970 retrieved almost three sq. km of land from the lagoon adjacent to the airport runway. There is often a need for sea walls to protect land from further invasion by the sea.

Land tenure. Most of the land in the Gilberts is owned by islanders in small holdings. The sale of land by locals to non-nationals has been prohibited since 1917. Only an insignificant area remains alienated, mostly owned by missions. Land affairs are supervised by the Ministry of Home Affairs and Decentralisation.

For many years, until 1983, Teraina and most of Tabuaeran in the Line Group were the freehold property of a subsidiary of Burns, Philp and Co. Ltd., but, after negotiations spread over several years, the Government acquired Teraina and the company's holding on Tabuaeran for $A1.5 million. Christmas Island is owned and worked as a plantation by the Government, which has plans to develop the island in several ways including the creation of a tourist centre.

Land ownership in customary law, which has been codified, does not include unrestricted right of disposal. Tenure is a form of limited entail and generally speaking, the owner is regarded as having no more than a life interest and is required to pass-on the land to his next-of-kin at his death.

There are a few circumstances, however, under which an owner may dispose of land to other than his next-of-kin and these circumstances account for most of the incessant land litigation which is so marked a feature of life in Kiribati.

The customary inheritance law whereby each child receives a share of the parents' land has led to continuous subdivision so that some holdings now consist of only three or four coconut trees.

As is to be expected, this form of subdivision is accompanied by widespread fragmentation of the holdings of individuals, both on one island and between several islands. The result is the anomaly that despite such land-hunger, the general standard of cultivation and development is low.

The Administration has tried to contend with these twin problems by encouraging owners to consolidate their holdings by exchange or leasing, and by advising Lands Courts when distributing estates to avoid the customary practice of subdividing every plot of land and instead to share the plots between the next-of-kin. In addition, following the Neglected Lands Ordinance of 1959, the government redistributed considerable holdings.

Main problems in recent times, apart from land ownership, have centred on the adequate supply of development land in urban Tarawa, which the Government is seeking to provide under leasing arrangements.

The Government began in 1983 a land-leasing system on Christmas Island.

PRIMARY PRODUCTION. Copra is the only exported agricultural product, earning the country more than $A4.7 million in 1985. However, experiments have been carried out privately on the coconut to extract the oil without using copra driers or an oil mill, but the process is restricted to small amounts. Copra production was low in the 1970s, averaging about 7400 tonnes a year, but little incentive was provided to improve production and there was almost no replanting. The Government is now encouraging new planting and improvement of existing groves, particularly on the Line Islands and especially on Christmas, Tabuaeran and Teraina islands. Production fluctuates, however, as do world prices which peaked at $950 per tonne in 1984 and fell again to $200 per tonne in 1986.

TABLE 1 COPRA PRODUCTION AND EXPORT EARNINGS

	Tonnes	*$A000*
1980	7527	2171.1
1981	11,270	2637.9
1982	9889	1453.7
1983	6948	2157.9
1984	13,388	6987.3
1985	8483	4718.4
1986	4611	459.0

Fruit and vegetables. Food crops for local consumption are mainly babai (taro), coconuts, bananas, pandanus, breadfruit and pawpaw. Tomato growing is also encouraged. The range will widen considerably if the growing of crops by the hydroponic process, a pilot project showing success on Christmas Island, is developed throughout the country.

Livestock. Efforts are being made to establish strains of pigs, poultry and goats suitable for local breeding.

Fisheries. Locally caught fish form the staple of the islanders' diet. Kingfish, snapper and tuna are the main varieties caught by netting, trolling on lines and in fish traps. The creation of the 200-mile economic and fisheries zone has given the: I-Kiribati great hopes of developing their marine resources to a point where fish could be the country's main source of revenue, in export earnings and licensing fees paid by fishing nations like Japan and the US. A survey by the South Pacific Commission of fish resources in the Pacific has revealed large stocks of tuna but in some waters, Kiribati waters among them, stocks of bait-fish are comparatively low. Kiribati began in the 1970s to raise bait-fish in ponds. These are proving to be a success. Fishing trials by Japanese experts using the cultured bait-fish have been successful for both skipjack and yellowfin tuna and sufficient quantities of bait-fish are being produced in 40 ha of ponds at Temaiku, South Tarawa, yielding about 2820 kg per hectare a year. It is expected to produce more bait-fish on Christmas Island.

Fisheries zone. Kiribati declared a 200-mile economic and fisheries zone in April 1978, giving the country potential control of a sea area of about 1,061,300 sq. km, but this was confined to the Gilberts Group as a long-standing claim by the United States under its Guano Act to ownership of 14 islands in the Line and Phoenix Groups made future control of those waters uncertain. But, on 21 June 1983 the US announced that it had abandoned its claims and Kiribati added many more square kilometres to its economic and fisheries zone.

Licensing. At the beginning of the 1980s, there was considerable optimism over the money-making potential of the zone so far as licence fees were concerned. Kiribati concluded an agreement with Japan for licensing Japanese ships to fish in its 200-mile zone, the Japanese agreeing to pay Kiribati $A520,000 a year in 1980 and 1981 and to provide a further $300,000 'in kind' for development projects.

The fee had risen in 1982 to about $1 million but in October 1982, negotiation between Kiribati and the Japanese Tuna Fishing Association for a new agreement broke down, the latter rejecting Kiribati's request for an increase in the fee. Difficulties were also being experienced with Taiwan and South Korea over licence fees. However, by 1984 treaties had been renegotiated. There are indications that the member countries of the South Pacific Forum, including Kiribati, will work collectively through the Forum's Regional Fisheries Agency in negotiations with the fishing nations. Late in 1983, Kiribati, along with other countries in the region,

signed an agreement with the American Tuna Boat Association. Kiribati was also party to the signing of the South Pacific Regional Fisheries Treaty in PNG in April 1987. This treaty allows the US to buy fishing licences at $US50,000 per vessel annually as well as supplying technical assistance to island countries to help them develop their own fishing industries.

In 1985 Kiribati became the first South Pacific country to sign a fishing agreement with the Soviet Union. Both parties settled on a fee of $A1.5 million. The Russians were not allowed to land at any of the islands in Kiribati, except in an emergency, nor were they allowed within the 12 mile zone. However, in October 1986 the agreement was not renewed. The Russians claimed that catches had not been up to expectations and they wanted to reduce the size of the fleet and halve the annual licence fee.

In early 1988 Kiribati and South Korea signed a fisheries agreement which gave the host country a fee of $A42,000 for a one-year licence.

Fish farming. Kiribati placed great hopes on development of marine resources on Christmas Island, particularly in brine shrimp and milkfish projects, but the brine shrimp project, which was expected to add up to $4 million a year to Kiribati's income, was abandoned in 1980, due to slow progress, but more particularly, to a slump in world prices. Milkfish and lobster farming offered more promise and was expected to earn $350,000 in 1980 in exports, milkfish to Nauru and lobsters to Honolulu. However, fish exports have been much slower in realising their potential. In 1983 and 1984 exports were worth $A1.5 million and $A2.2 million respectively.

Training. A fisheries training section has been formed by the Fisheries Division to train technicians and some fisheries staff have attended courses in Japan, Israel and the Solomons. Others are receiving training on ships working in Kiribati waters.

Local fishing industry. Plans to establish a tuna fishing industry in partnership with an established company with Butaritari as the base and to establish a long-line fishing fleet in the Line and Phoenix groups have been partly carried out with the establishment of a fishing company, Te Mautari Ltd, in 1981.

The company provides fish for the local market and for export.

In 1987 the Fiji Government Shipyard in Suva signed a contract worth $3 million to build two pole and line tuna boats for Te Mautari Ltd. The contract was to be funded by a grant from the EEC. Provisional 1984 figures for the company showed an annual catch of 2353 tonnes with a total sales value of $2.1 million.

In 1986 Japan donated a new vessel, *Moamoa*, to the national fishing company, enabling a ship being leased from the Starkist company to be returned. *Moamoa*, worth $3 million, has a 400 tonne capacity and will be used as a mothership for the fleet.

Forestry. Trial plantings of local and imported trees being conducted in collaboration with CSIRO, Melbourne, had achieved little success. The aim is to encourage local production and reduce timber imports which have been costing some $150,000 annually. Research is proceeding on growing types of timber in an atoll environment. It is intended to concentrate trials on Christmas Island where there is adequate land. Attention is also being paid to the opportunities for producing workable timber from old coconut trees felled and left to rot as a result of the coconut replanting programme.

Salt. The Christmas Island Solar Salt project was producing 500 tonnes annually by 1987. Currently the salt is bought by the Te Mautari Fishing Company but it is hoped that other markets, preferably fishing canneries in neighbouring Pacific countries, will enable the output to be trebled and become a viable earner of foreign exchange. The project is being sponsored by New Zealand and the US.

MANUFACTURING AND MINING.
Local industry is confined to small operations such as handicrafts, the salting of fish and kamaimai and small boat building. The handicrafts (fans, mats, bags) are made principally from the pandanus leaf and have particularly intricate and colourful designs.

Most private businesses are centred on South Tarawa, but the government, using the National Loans Board, is assisting private enterprise to increase the number of small business opportunities.

The Commonwealth Fund for Technical Co-operation also assists with the establishment of small industries and in 1986 it helped such businesses as ice-cream manufacturing, a photographic studio and a snack bar.

Minerals. The phosphate mining industry based on Banaba disappeared from the records in 1980, the mining operations on Banaba closing down at the end of 1979. It had a drastic effect on the country's income, cutting export earnings by 88.6 per cent compared to the 1979 total, when phosphate exports of 445,700 tonnes earned $17,952,995, the government taking an estimated $6.6 million. The Banabans, most of whom are now on Rabi Island in Fiji, were paid $14.6 million ($10 million ex gratia payment plus interest) by Britain in April 1981 as compensation for 50 years exploitation of the island.

The Banabans accepted the payment in return for indemnifying the British, Australian and New Zealand Governments from further legal action. In late 1988, however, the possibility of recommencing phosphate mining was being considered.

TOURISM. In recent years tourism has been given increased priority in development plans. In 1985 a tourism officer was appointed to co-ordinate development. Links have been established with Micronesia via Airlines of the Marshall Islands with a weekly flight through Fiji. The American market is seen as having potential and air connections are possible through Honolulu. The New Zealand Government is supplying funds to build a new tourist office in Bikenbeu Village, South Tarawa. There are plans to promote Christmas Island as a resort area but its isolation may disenchant possible developers. In 1986 1170 visitors arrived at Christmas Island by air, the majority having a specific purpose other than vacation.

Tarawa had 2031 visitors by air and 149 by sea; again most had business intentions.

LOCAL COMMERCE. Local retail trade is dominated by co-operative societies. The movement has the major share of trading in Tarawa and a virtual monopoly outside the capital, except for Banaba and Christmas Island. In addition, several private trading firms based on Betio operate retail stores there and elsewhere.

OVERSEAS TRADE. Kiribati was prepared for the big drop in export earnings in

1980 with the end of phosphate mining in 1979, but had no substitute with which to close the 88.6 per cent gap. The trade deficit grew from $5,663,425 in 1979 to $14,422,834 in 1980 and in 1981 (provisional) to $16,378,000 though the 1981 figure is somewhat misleading as imports include a Boeing

TABLE 2 EXPORTS $000

	1982	1984	1986
Fish — fresh and frozen	515	1718	1751
Copra	1454	6987	459
Shark fin	30	49	22
Handicrafts	2	4	3
Other n.e.s.	17	10*	35*
Total Domestic	2017	8768	2270
Re-exports	335	3687	202*
Total exports	2353	12,455	2472

Note: Boeing 727 included in re-exports of 1984.
* Estimated

727-100C aircraft bought by the local airline, Air Tungaru, and valued at an import price of $3,300,000. Deduct that figure and the trade deficit shows a drop on the 1980 figure of $1,344,834. Although world copra prices were low in 1981, copra exports for that year, for 11,957 tonnes, totalled $2,630,000, $459,000 higher than the 1980 figure. By 1984 world copra prices had escalated to $950 per tonne and earned Kiribati nearly $7 million dollars. As a result Kiribati has been able to balance its budget quite successfully since then.

Imports. Imports consist mainly of food, fuel and manufactured goods. After phosphate mining on Banaba finished in 1979, Kiribati carried substantial debit balances for several years in the early 1980s. However with record copra prices in 1984, the balance of trade became briefly more favourable.

Suppliers. Australia continues to be the major supplier of imports to Kiribati. In 1986 it had 40 per cent of the market, its nearest competitor being Japan with 19 per cent. Fiji follows with 11.8 per cent. This trade balance has remained fairly constant throughout the eighties.

TABLE 3 IMPORTS ($000)

	1982	1983*	1984*
Food	5213	5468	5424
Beverages & tobacco	1174	1196	1162
Crude materials	375	526	302
Mineral fuels, lubricants etc	3441	2291	2214
Animal & vegetable oils, fats	30	14	37
Chemicals	917	801	1118
Manufactured goods, class. chiefly by material	2843	3463	3133
Machinery & transport equipment	6276	4577	8564
Miscellaneous manufactured articles	2356	1466	1332
Miscellaneous commodities	146	106	100
Totals	22,771	19,907	23,387

* 1983/84 figures provisional.

TRADE BALANCE ($000)

	Export	Import	Balance
1982	2353	22,771	−20,418
1983	3999	19,907	−16,008
1984	13,006	23,387	−10,381
1986 (est)	2472	21,554	−19,082

Customs tariff. A single-line metricated tariff structure was introduced in 1975 but this was replaced in February, 1981, with the international system of tariff classification based on the Customs Co-operation Council's Nomenclature (CCCN). Tariff matters are handled by the Division of Customs and Excise within the Ministry of Finance.

FINANCE. A government tax on phosphate mined on Banaba (Ocean Island) for some years provided more than half of the total revenue derived by the Gilbert Islands but this source of income ceased with the end of mining in 1979.

Through a Revenue Equalisation Reserve Fund (RERF) government savings, notably from phosphate tax income, have been used to acquire an investment portfolio to help overcome the budget deficit expected when phosphate revenue ended. RERF's value at the end of 1986 was $168.9 million, invested in bonds in the currencies of the US, Germany, Japan, Australia and United Kingdom. The fund is managed by a London stockbroking firm.

The EEC's STABEX Fund, which compensates developing countries for losses on the export earnings of certain primary products, such as copra or coconut oil, exported to Europe, has benefited Kiribati in certain lean years — $3 million in 1975/76, but this was regarded as a loan to be repaid. However, the EEC agreed in 1979 that any future STABEX payments would be in the form of grants and not loans. In 1981 and 1982 STABEX contributed $1.1 million and $114,000 respectively.

In 1987 Kiribati, along with Tuvalu, was added to the United Nations' list of least developed countries. This will give the country access to concessional loans from the World Bank and the International Monetary Fund while exports will qualify for special tariff concessions under the General Agreement on Tariffs and Trade. Kiribati also became the 150th member of the IMF.

External aid. Most aid comes from the United Kingdom as part of the settlement made when Kiribati, as the Gilbert Islands, became independent on 12 July 1979 having, with Tuvalu (the Ellice Islands), formed the

TABLE 4 CENTRAL GOVERNMENT FINANCE ($000)

	1982	1983*	1984*
Recurrent revenue	16,576	16,054	15,368
Capital revenue	3878	4757	3423
Total revenue	20,454	20,811	18,791
Recurrent expenditure	15,889	15,922	15,595
Capital expenditure	5050	5601	3142
Total expenditure	20,939	21,523	18,737
Balance	−485	−712	+54

* *Provisional*

TABLE 5

RECURRENT REVENUE ($000)

	1982	1983	1984
Direct taxation	1020	1303	1037
Indirect taxation	3447	4311	5357
Externally funded	9424	8223	7788
Other revenue	2685	2217	1186

CAPITAL REVENUE (CASH AID ONLY) ($000)

	1982	1983	1984
United Kingdom	3140	2817	2117
Australia	79	169	496
New Zealand	256	145	188
Japan	33	—	—
Australian Food Aid	9	—	—
UNFPA	21	38	9
European Dev. Fund	152	867	236
Asian Dev. Bank loan	—	—	—
Other overseas aid	169	721	224
Japanese Rice Aid	19	—	153
Total	3878	4757	3423

Note: This table covers cash aid received and disbursed by the Kiribati Government only. No account is taken of 'in kind' aid or other aid which does not go through the Government accounting system.

British Colony of the Gilbert and Ellice Islands. Other donors include Australia, New Zealand, the EEC and the various United Nations agencies. Aid is in three kinds — capital aid in actual finance for construction or engineering projects; aid in kind, equipment, materials; technical aid, the provision of personnel for particular positions and provision of finance and facilities for training and higher education.

Since fishing agreements began with Japan, the Japanese Government has also given considerable aid to Kiribati, particularly towards the national fishing industry. Various international organisations such as the European Development Fund and the Asian Devel-

opment Bank support programmes within Kiribati.

Recent projects include the construction of a causeway between Betio and Bairiki islets at a cost of A$7 million, financed partly by grant aid from Japan; new fisheries jetty at Betio worth $2 million financed by Britain; the upgrading of the Bonriki Airport, Tarawa, to be financed by the EEC at a cost of A$800,000; installation of a sewage treatment system on Tarawa, funded by ADAB for A$6.4 million. The estimate of ADAB grants for 1985/86 financial year was $2.6 million.

Tax system. Past reliance on phosphate earning resulted in the phosphate tax providing more than half of locally-derived revenue. Import duty accounts for more than one tenth of local revenue while less than 10 per cent comes from personal and company tax.

Banks. The Bank of Kiribati (partners are the Westpac Corporation 51 per cent and the Kiribati Government 49 per cent) announced in 1986 that it would like to divert some of its international investments into local development projects. It operates agencies on most islands and undertakes various central bank functions.

Currency. Australian currency is legal tender. Sterling coins are accepted but circulate at par with Australian coins.

Overseas investment. The government welcomes investment from overseas sources as in the case of shipping companies supporting the Marine Training School, and fish farming projects at Christmas Island.

Development plan. Planning since 1973 has concentrated on creating a new economic foundation needed with the end of phosphate mining on Banaba. Development plans have been formulated with external aid in mind as Kiribati cannot hope to continue as a viable country without a certain amount of external aid. Many projects aim to bridge the gap created by the loss of income from phosphate, raise living standards in the outer islands and, at the same time, preserve the 'distinctive culture' of I-Kiribati. The tuna fishing industry is seen as the major national asset for economic development, but efforts will also concentrate on tourism, fish farming, the copra industry and growth in air transport to strengthen links with the outside world. Christmas Island, which is over half the area of Kiribati, is planned as an alternative growth centre to Tarawa. External aid will play a big part in the plan.

Christmas Island represents a very promising asset as it is wholly owned by the government. A survey carried out in 1983 confirmed the presence of plentiful supplies of fresh water to support produce growing by hydroponics and an expansion of the tourist industry. A second tourist resort is planned and an air link is established with Honolulu but the relative isolation and slow development is hampering hopes for increased tourism in the immediate future.

Postage stamps. Income from philatelic sales was high in the 1970s and in 1979 the government joined forces with an important philatelic firm in Bristol, England, in a joint commercial venture with the UK firm directing sales. Philatelic sales in 1982 totalled nearly $1 million but fell dramatically until in 1984 barely $2000 of income was generated this way.

TRANSPORT. The high cost of transport and Kiribati's remoteness are significant factors in the high price of imports. Local transport is mainly via the lagoons and by air.

Roads. There is a reasonably good road running the length of South Tarawa from Bonriki through to Bairiki and work on sealing this road on its entire length was carried out in 1979. There are high hopes that communications will improve with the building of a four-kilometre causeway between Bairiki and Betio which are linked by launch service. The project was started in the early 1980s with a loan of $1.15 million from the Asian Development Bank, however the work was abandoned because of engineering problems. Work began again in 1986 when a team of Japanese engineers, funded by Japanese aid of $6 million, arrived in Tarawa to restart the project. It is expected to be completed in 1988.

Each island has roads suitable for bicycles and motor cycles and, usually, there is a road running alongside the lagoon.

Vehicles. There are several thousand vehicles in Kiribati, the majority being motor cycles, the most popular form of transport. There are also several bus companies.

Overseas airlines. Air Nauru has regular services connecting Tarawa with Nauru and Suva, where other connections can be made. Airline of the Marshall Islands began a service between Majuro, Suva, Tarawa and Funafuti in 1983.

Domestic airline. The internal Air Tungaru Corporation operates from Tarawa to Abemama, Tabiteuea, Butaritari, Nonouti, Marakei, Maiana, Nikunau, Onotoa and Beru, at least twice a week. There is also a service to Christmas Island.

Kiribati has obtained from the US a permit to operate a service by Air Tungaru from Tarawa to Honolulu via Christmas Island.

Local airfields. International flights operate through Tarawa at Bonriki Airport. In 1987 the EEC began funding improvements to the runway to the value of $800,000 to allow 737s to land.

Domestic airfields are Makin, Butaritari, Marakei, Abaiang, Maiana, Abemama, Kuria, Aranuka, Nonouti, North Tabiteuea, South Tabiteuea, Onotoa, Beru, Nikunau, Tamana, Arorae, and Kiritimati. There are also airstrips on Tabuaeran and Teraina.

Port facilities. The main overseas port in the country is on Betio, Tarawa. The wharf has a frontage of 92 m. There are three cranes in operation. There are three warehouses with a total floor space of 1205 sq. m. Night operations are hampered by inadequate lighting.

All overseas vessels are worked by tugs and barges from anchorages off shore, since neither the length of the wharf nor the depth of the harbour are adequate to accommodate overseas vessels. Three tugs and five barges are in operation. The port is equipped to handle container vessels.

The construction of wharves and ports elsewhere in the country is made difficult by the extensive reef areas, nearly dry at low tide, which surround most of the islands. The lagoons, however, offer safe anchorages. The lagoon at Butaritari is of a depth and size which make it a natural harbour and it is proposed as the location for a shore-based tuna fishing operation.

Shipping services. Kiribati is away from the regular shipping routes and has had difficulty in attracting shipping lines, but was assured in 1983 by the Pacific Forum Line that it would service Tarawa through Suva. The Kiribati Government, in an effort to make the Forum Line's special service to Tarawa profitable, announced that it would refuse to accept cargo through Suva unless it was carried by the Forum Line.

Nauru Pacific Line operates a regular cargo/passenger service from Melbourne to Tarawa via Nauru and Majuro; the Philippines, Micronesia and Orient Navigation Co. operates a regular container service from Honolulu to Tarawa; Asia Pacific operates a direct service from Melbourne; KAP New Guinea Line from PNG and China Navigation's New Guinea Pacific Line has a regular container service to Tarawa via Apia and Rarotonga. Star Shipping's service originates in Honolulu.

Internal shipping services are operated by

the Kiribati Shipping Corporation (KSC) and two small private operators. The corporation was established following the liquidation of the Gilbert Islands Development Authority, which was previously responsible for the operation of shipping services. The corporation operates inter-island services and various ferry services, including the service between Betio and Bairiki. About 9100 passengers are carried from Tarawa to outer islands and back each year. Carriage of cargo and passengers between outer islands is very small.

The inter-island fleet operated by the KSC consists of three motor vessels and two landing craft and two private vessels, of 12 and 8 tonnes are operated by Compass Rose Enterprises and Teikaraoi Co. respectively.

COMMUNICATIONS. The Telecommunications Division of the Ministry of Communications is responsible for telecommunications throughout Kiribati and maintains the following services: high frequency radio links to all except the Line Islands; Tarawa and international telephone services; internal and external telegraphic services; internal teleprinter circuits; ship-to-shore communications and marine safety network; ground-to-air and air-navigation systems and specialist communications for ministries and statutory authorities.

Improvements to all these services were foreshadowed in the Development Plan. These include the provision of a Standard B earth station at Bairiki on Tarawa at a cost of more than $A2.2 million funded by the European Economic Community as an outright grant, and a new digital automatic telephone exchange built on Betio, Bikenibeu and Bairiki, all on Tarawa Atoll, under a separate $2.2 million contract. A telex service links Kiribati with Sydney. Upgrading of telecommunication links with the outer islands is also planned. In mid-1983 commercial radio-telegraph services were provided to Suva and Nauru, and there is an international radio telephone through Suva.

Radio. The Broadcasting and Publications Authority (BPA) was established by law and began operating in January 1979, replacing the Broadcasting and Publications Division of the then Chief Minister's Office. The authority has a chairman and not less than five members appointed by the Minister of Home Affairs, and has a monopoly of broadcasting in Kiribati. It is financed by government grant and advertising revenue. Radio Kiribati broadcasts on 846 kHz on a medium wave band using a 10 kW transmitter and is heard throughout Kiribati and Tuvalu. Another transmitter on Betio, belonging to Telecommunications, relays off-air signals to Christmas Island. Radio Kiribati is on the air from 0600 to 2200 Monday to Friday, from 1200 to 2200 on Saturdays and from 1100 to 2200 on Sundays.

Newspapers. BPA also produces a weekly newspaper *Te Uekera* with articles and items in both Kiribatese and English. There are also monthly newspapers in the vernacular published by the churches. Tarawa is on the Peacesat network which is used for educational transmissions through the University of the Pacific centre at Suva.

WATER AND ELECTRICITY. Water supplies come from wells, roof catchments and galleries on urban Tarawa and from wells and some roof catchments in the rural areas. Drinking water from the galleries is piped along South Tarawa to fill communal tanks and storage tanks, the latter being filled by tanker delivery in times of drought. Roof catchments are mainly on private houses. No charges are made for water supplies except for bulk delivery by tankers when the rate is $3.25 per 1273 litres. Following the cholera outbreak in 1977, it is planned to provide all households with access to protected supplies of drinking water and upgrade the water supply system on Tarawa. Australia, through the Australian Development Assistance Bureau (ADAB) is funding the installation of water supply and sewerage systems, spending $3.21 million to upgrade and extend Tarawa's water supply. Salt water sewerage systems have already been installed at Betio, Bairiki and Bikenibeu. A power house on Betio supplies electricity to the whole of South Tarawa and there are a number of small private and local government-owned generators in the outer islands. In 1986 the Utilities Board on Tarawa announced that four of the seven generators were reaching the end of their operational life. The Government was looking into purchasing a 1000 kW power plant to replace the old units.

MAJOR OFFICE HOLDERS
President (Beretitenti):
  Hon. Ieremia Tabai
Minister for Trade, Industry and Labour:
  Raion Bataroma
Minister for Home Affairs:
  Babera Kirata
Minister for Works and Energy:
  Ieruru Karotu

GOVERNMENT MINISTRIES AND DEPARTMENTS
Office of the President, PO Box 68, Tarawa, Kiribati; Tel: 21183 Tlx: 77054
Public Service Commission, PO Box 65, Tarawa, Kiribati; Tel: 21354
Commissioner of Police, PO Box Betio, Tarawa, Kiribati; Tel: 26061 Tlx: 77025
Ministry of Foreign Affairs, PO Box 68, Tarawa, Kiribati; Tel: 21177 Tlx: 77054
Immigration Division, PO Box 68, Tarawa, Kiribati; Tel: 21228 Tlx: (761)77054
Ministry of Finance, PO Box 67, Tarawa, Kiribati; Tel: 21216 Tlx: (761)77065
Office of Audit, PO Box 63, Tarawa, Kiribati; Tel: 21250
Ministry of Natural Resource Development, PO Box 64, Tarawa, Kiribati; Tel: 21074 Tlx: 77039
Fisheries Division, PO Box 241, Tarawa, Kiribati; Tel: 28061 Tlx: 77039
Agriculture Division, PO Box 267, Tarawa, Kiribati; Tel: 28108 Tlx: (761)77039
Ministry of Trade, Industry & Labour, PO Box 69, Tarawa, Kiribati; Tel: 21097 Tlx: (761)77024
Cooperative Division, PO Box 510, Tarawa, Kiribati; Tel: 26155 Tlx: 77053
Marine Training School, PO Box 511, Tarawa, Kiribati; Tel: 26022 Tlx: 77627
Ministry of Line & Phoenix Groups, Kiritimati Island, Kiribati; Cable: LINNIX KIRITIMATI
Ministry of Communications, PO Box 487, Tarawa, Kiribati; Tel: 26121 Tlx: 77022
Postal Division, PO Box 487, Tarawa, Kiribati; Tel: 26510 Tlx: 77022
Marine Division, PO Box 506, Tarawa, Kiribati; Tel: 26465 Tlx: 77022

Meteorological Services, PO Box 486, Tarawa, Kiribati; Tel: 26511 Tlx: 77033
Civil Aviation Division, PO Box 487, Tarawa, Kiribati; Tel: 21287 Tlx: 77022
Ministry of Health & Family Planning, Bikenibeu, Tarawa, Kiribati; Tel: 28151 Tlx: 77063
Ministry of Education, PO Box 263, Tarawa, Kiribati; Tel: 28091 Cable: EDUCATION TARAWA
Tarawa Teachers College, PO Box 266, Tarawa, Kiribati; Tel: 28062 Cable: TTC TARAWA
Ministry of Works & Energy, PO Box 498, Tarawa, Kiribati; Tel: 26142 Tlx: 761-77053 KITELECBET
Lands & Survey Division, PO Box 7, Tarawa, Kiribati; Tel: 21302 Cable: LANDS TARAWA
Office of the Attorney General, PO Box 62, Tarawa, Kiribati; Tel: 21242 Cable: PRINTERY TARAWA
Office of the Chief Justice, PO Box 501, Tarawa, Kiribati; Tel: 26451 Cable: JUSTICE TARAWA

STATUTORY BODIES
Air Tungaru Corporation, PO Box 271, Tarawa, Kiribati; Tel: 28025 Tlx: 761-277023
Broadcasting & Publication Authority, PO Box 78, Tarawa, Kiribati; Tel: 21187 Cable: BPA TARAWA
Kiribati Housing Corporation, PO Box 491, Tarawa, Kiribati; Tel: 26116 Cable: HOUSING TARAWA
Kiribati Insurance Corporation, PO Box 38, Tarawa, Kiribati; Tel: 21260 Tlx:761-77042
National Loan Board, PO Box 33, Tarawa, Kiribati; Tel: 21297 Tlx: 761-77041
Kiribati Provident Fund, PO Box 76, Tarawa, Kiribati; Tel: 21300 Cable: NPF TARAWA
Public Utilities Board, PO Box 433, Tarawa, Kiribati; Tel: 26106 Tlx: 761-77021
Kiribati Shipping Corporation, PO Box 495, Tarawa, Kiribati; Tel: 26521 Tlx: 761-77080
Te Mautari Ltd., PO Box 508, Tarawa, Kiribati; Tel: 26302 Tlx: 761-77034
Kiribati Shipyard Ltd., PO Box 483, Tarawa, Kiribati; Tel: 26282 Cable:

SHIPYARD TARAWA
Public Sector Companies, PO Box 492, Tarawa, Kiribati; Tel: 26263 Tlx: 761-77031
Atoll Motors & Marine Services Ltd., PO Box 49, Tarawa, Kiribati; Tel: 21113 Tlx: 761-77041
Otintai Hotel Ltd., PO Box 270, Tarawa, Kiribati; Tel: 28045 Tlx: 761-77032
Kiribati Copra Cooperative Society Ltd., PO Box 489, Tarawsa, Kiribati; Tel: 26534 Tlx: 761-77020
Kiribati Cooperative Wholesalers Society Ltd., PO Box 485, Tarawa, Kiribati; Tel: 26342 Tlx: 761-77028
Bank of Kiribati, PO Box 66, Tarawa, Kiribati; Tel: 21095 Tlx: 761-77052
Kiribati Visitors Bureau, PO Box 64, Tarawa, Kiribati; Tel: 21075

OTHER ORGANISATIONS
AIA Maea Ainen Kiribati, PO Box 240, Tarawa, Kiribati; Tel: 28067 Cable: AMAK
South Pacific Marine Services, PO Box 500, Tarawa, Kiribati; Tel: 26310 Tlx: 761-77026
Kiribati Red Cross, PO Box 213, Tarawa, Kiribati; Tel: 28128 Cable: Kiriros
Atoll Research Unit, PO Box 806, Tarawa, Kiribati; Tel: 21085 Cable: USP
University of the South Pacific, PO Box 59, Tarawa, Kiribati; Tel: 21085 Cable: USP
Foundation for the People of the South Pacific, PO Box 43 Tarawa, Kiribati; Tel: 28101 Cable: FSP
Save The Children Foundation, PO Box 203, Tarawa, Kiribati; Tel: 28068 Tlx: 761-77042

FOREIGN MISSIONS
Australian High Commission, PO Box 77, Tarawa; Kiribati; Tel: 21184/85 Tlx: 761-77060
British High Commission, PO Box 61, Tarawa, Kiribati; Tel: 21327 Tlx: 77050 UKREPKI

HISTORY. The I-Kiribati (Gilbert Islanders) are of Micronesian stock but recent archaeological discoveries suggest that the islands were first settled by Austronesian-speaking people long before the birth of Christ. A subsequent invasion of Fijians and

Tongans about the 14th century AD, resulted in a merging of the older and newer groups through inter-marriage. The result, by the time Europeans first began describing the islanders in detail in the early 19th century, was that the population was reasonably homogeneous in appearance and in traditions.

Although the Gilbertese people have many common traditions, social organisation was not uniform throughout the group. Social units in the north tended to be larger than those in the south and on most islands, there were at any time, several leaders competing for dominance. In some instances (for example Butaritari-Makin and Abemama-Kuria-Aranuka), paramount chiefs emerged. With European contact, firearms and sometimes trading monopolies, these men were able to consolidate their position.

In contrast, authority in the southern islands was vested in 'maneaba' (meeting house) councils of old men and each was the leader of his own 'kainga' or clan hamlet. Most of the islands were divided into several competing 'maneaba' districts and throughout the group, 'maneaba' has remained the focal point of all social and political activity.

European discovery. The Gilbert Islands may have been sighted by the crew of a ship originally commanded by Hernando de Grijalva which crossed the Pacific from Mexico in 1537. However, details of that voyage are too vague for any positive identifications to be made. The first undoubted European discovery in the Gilberts was that of the Spanish explorer Quiros who sighted Butaritari in 1606 and named it Buen Viaje (Good Voyage).

A local tradition that appears to date from about that time tells of a white-skinned, red-haired, red-bearded man who drifted ashore at Beru in a boat shaped like a box, who took eight sisters as wives, and who had 23 children. The descendants of that stranger are now supposed to be scattered throughout the group. The tradition has never been thoroughly investigated. But it has been suggested that the red-bearded man may have been a survivor of one of the lost ships of the Mendana expedition to the Pacific of 1595.

The modern discovery and exploration of the Gilbert Islands began in 1765 when Commodore John Byron discovered Nikunau in HMS *Dolphin*. In 1788, Captain Thomas Gilbert of the *Charlotte* and Captain John Marshall of the *Scarborough* discovered several more islands when sailing from Sydney to China. The remaining islands were discovered by Europeans between 1799 and 1826.

Gilberts named. The name Gilbert Islands was given to the group by the Russian hydrographer A. I. Krusenstern in the 1820s. From that time until about 1870, many British and American whaling vessels sought sperm whales in Gilbertese waters. Seamen from some of these vessels occasionally deserted in the islands and became beachcombers, while adventurous Gilbertese were taken on as crewmen. The first European to live in the group landed there in 1837. After trading vessels began visiting the group from about 1850, some of the beachcombers became traders and agents for firms in Australia, Germany and the US. Other traders were sent there by their firms. Coconut oil was the chief commodity of trade until copra completely replaced it about 1870–1880.

Labour recruiting. In the second half of the 19th century about 9000 Gilbertese worked overseas, especially on plantations. In the 1860s the Peruvian recruiters were virtually slave-traders and islanders later learned to fear the 'men-stealing ships' from Tahiti. Nevertheless, many Gilbertese were willing, even eager, recruits, especially in times of drought.

The main destinations of these labourers were Fiji, Samoa, Tahiti, Hawaii and, towards the end of the century, Central America. The recruiting at this time established a pattern of 'family' migration which was most unusual for the labour trade in the 19th century. It also established patterns for 20th-century migration to Ocean Island and Nauru.

The first European missionary to live and work in the Gilberts was the Rev. Hiram Bingham, a Protestant, of the American Board of Commissioners for Foreign Missions. He established a mission on Abaiang in 1857, and with the help of Hawaiian pastors spread Christianity throughout the northern islands. In 1870, after Polynesian teachers of the London Missionary Society had established missions in the Ellice Islands (now Tuvalu), the Rev. S. J. Whitmee of the LMS brought Samoan pastors to Arorae, Tamana, Onotoa and Beru. From those islands, the LMS continued to spread northwards until, in 1917, the American Board agreed to withdraw from the group. In the islands north of the equator, however, the LMS never enjoyed the same success that it had in the south, and Roman Catholicism tended to become the dominant religion in those islands. Catholic priests of the Sacred Heart order began work in the Gilberts in 1888, using Nonouti as their first base. Missionaries from the Seventh-day Adventist Church, the Baha'i faith, Church of God and Mormons have also gained adherents since World War II.

British interest. The first attempt by Europeans to exert formal authority in the group followed the appointment in 1877 of the Governor of Fiji as High Commissioner for the Western Pacific. This gave the Governor jurisdiction over British subjects, and his authority was exercised through British naval commanders who were made deputy commissioners. In 1892, Captain E. H. M. Davis of HMS *Royalist* visited the group and proclaimed it a British protectorate in a ceremony at Abemama. After the British flag was also raised over the Ellice Islands, headquarters for the new protectorates were established at Butaritari and in 1896 at Tarawa. At first the administration consisted only of the British Resident; later, district magistrates were appointed. Councils of island elders, known as native governments, were set up to administer a simple code of laws based as far as possible on traditional forms of government and laws, often modified by mission and other foreign influences.

In 1900, following the discovery of phosphate there, Ocean Island was annexed by Great Britain and placed under the Resident Commissioner's jurisdiction. Seven years later, the exploitation of Ocean Island phosphate had become so important that the protectorate's headquarters were transferred to that island.

British annexation. In 1915, after obtaining the formal approval of the native governments, Britain annexed the Gilbert and Ellice Islands by an Order-in-Council. The order came into effect on 12 January 1916,

from which date the two groups became the Gilbert and Ellice Islands Colony.

In that same year, Ocean Island and also Fanning and Washington Islands (which Britain had annexed in 1888 and 1889 respectively) were incorporated within the colony, as were the three Tokelau Islands (then known as the Union Group), which had been a British protectorate since 1889. Christmas Island (which had been annexed in 1888) was added to the colony in 1919. But the Tokelau Islands were transferred to New Zealand administration in 1925 because of the difficulty of communicating with them from Ocean Island. The uninhabited Phoenix Islands became part of the colony by an Order-in-Council of 18 March 1937. Three of the Phoenix Islands, Gardner, Hull and Sydney, were colonised in 1938 by land-hungry islanders from the southern Gilberts.

By 1940, 600 Gilbertese had settled there, Meanwhile, in 1939, the British Government had agreed that two of the Phoenix Islands, Canton and Enderbury, should be administered jointly with the US. The two islands were of interest to the Americans because of their value in trans-Pacific aviation.

Pacific War. In December 1941, within two days of the Japanese raid on Pearl Harbor, Japanese aircraft bombed Ocean Island and reconnaissance parties landed briefly on Tarawa and Butaritari. A few months later, most Europeans on Tarawa and Ocean Island were evacuated. Some government officials and missionaries elected to stay and were joined by coastwatchers sent from New Zealand, Twenty-two Europeans, most of them coastwatchers, were subsequently killed by the Japanese.

Meanwhile, temporary headquarters for the administration of those parts of the colony not in enemy hands were established in Sydney. It remained there until November 1943 when American forces drove the Japanese from the Gilberts. New headquarters were then set up on Tarawa, where they have remained.

When Ocean Island was reoccupied in 1945, it was found that the Japanese had recently massacred all but one man (who had miraculously escaped) of the Gilbertese labour force, and that the native inhabitants, the Banabans, had been deported to Nauru and Kusaie in the Caroline Islands. On being rescued, the Banabans elected to live on Rabi Island, Fiji, which had earlier been bought for them.

Resettlement. Within a few years of the war, the authorities concluded that Sydney Island in the Phoenix Group could not support a permanent population, and arrangements were made to resettle that island's colonists at Gizo in the Solomon Islands. Later, to suit administrative convenience and overcome the difficulties of communication with the Phoenix group (reinforced by a prolonged drought on Hull and Gardner Islands), it was decided to transfer the remaining Phoenix Islands settlers to Wagina in the Solomon Islands. The transfer was made in 1963–64.

One of the most important post-war moves in the main islands was the strengthening of the co-operatives that had been established before the war. This made it unprofitable for any overseas trading firm to return to the group. There were also moves to give the islanders a more active role in their own government. In 1951, the first of three biennial conferences for magistrates was held. These meetings led to the inauguration of annual Colony Conferences (from 1956 to 1962) at which nominated representatives met to discuss the colony's affairs.

In 1963, an Executive Council and an Advisory Council were created to give the islanders an advisory role in government. Membership of both bodies was by nomination of the Resident Commissioner. In 1967, the Advisory Council was replaced by a House of Representatives that had no legislative powers, but could make recommendations to the Governing Council.

Legislative Council. In 1971, further constitutional developments took place. The House of Representatives was replaced by a Legislative Council of 23 elected members, three ex-officio members and two public service members; and the Government Council was superseded by an Executive Council. The elected members of the Legislative Council had the right to elect a Leader of Government Business to act as their chief spokesman, but the Council's legislative functions were limited. As for the Executive Council, its powers were advisory, but the Resident Commissioner could assign members to formulate policy on various subjects.

On 1 January 1972, the colony ceased to come under the jurisdiction of the Western Pacific High Commission, as it had done for the previous 80 years, and the Resident Commissioner, Sir John Field, was sworn in as Governor.

At the end of 1972 the colony became responsible for the Southern Line Islands. In 1974, the colony moved forward to a ministerial form of government. The Legislative Council was replaced by an elected House of Assembly, and a Chief Minister. Later that year, the Ellice Islanders, by an overwhelming majority, voted in a referendum to secede from the colony. The separation took place on 1 October 1975, although joint administration from Tarawa continued until 1 January 1976.

On 1 November 1976, another stage in the progression to independence came with the appointment of a Minister of Finance and full internal self-government was attained on 1 January 1977, when the Council of Ministers became entirely 'localised' with the exception of the position of the Attorney-General. In April/May 1977, more than 200 representatives of local government councils, churches, traditional leaders, women's clubs and co-operative societies met on Tarawa and made recommendations for a new Constitution. Independence came on 12 July 1979, when Princess Anne, daughter of Queen Elizabeth II, who was accompanied by her husband, Captain Mark Phillips, presented the Letters Patent formally declaring the country's independence from Britain. With independence, the name Kiribati was adopted.

In September 1979, a treaty of friendship was signed between the Republic of Kiribati and the United States. Under the treaty, the US relinquished all claims, made under the Guano Act of 1856, to 14 islands in the Line and Phoenix groups. For practical purposes, however, Kiribati agreed to joint administration of Canton Island (now Kanton Island).

However, late in 1982, US senators opposed ratification of the treaty of friendship, but on 21 June 1983 the US Senate approved recognition of Kiribati's sovereignty of the Line and Phoenix groups.

Banaban case. In February 1975, the

Banabans initiated a suit in the High Court, London, against the British Government and British Phosphate Commissioners, claiming more than seven million pounds for back royalties on phosphate mined from Ocean Island and unspecified recompense for damages to that island. Later a party of 36 Banabans landed on Ocean Island from Rabi in support of their claim that Ocean Island should be granted independence from the Gilbert and Ellice Islands Colony. Towards the end of the year, talks on the subject were held in Tarawa between the Banabans and the Gilbert Islanders, but nothing was resolved.

Late in 1977, the Gilbert Islands Council of Ministers and the Rabi Council of Leaders signed eleven Resolutions to be known as the Bairiki Resolution concerning the relationship between the Banabans and the Gilbert Islands Government and the future of Ocean Island, which would henceforth be called only by its Gilbertese name 'Banaba'.

Three of the Resolutions agreed that a referendum be held to determine the future of Banaba and what would be the status of phosphate revenue, employment, access, etc., whether the outcome be in favour of the status quo or in favour of separation.

Both parties agreed that the British Government should be bound to honour the outcome of the referendum, when deciding on the future of Banaba at the Gilbert Islands Independence Constitutional Conference.

Other Resolutions concerned financial arrangements, the rehabilitation of Banaba and the management of the phosphate industry.

The parties also resolved to continue discussions on matters of common interest and to be united in their submissions to the British or other governments.

Meanwhile, the case in the High Court continued until June 1976 — the longest in British history.

In his judgment Justice Megarry found against the Banabans on the Royalties case but found that under a 1913 agreement, the BPC was obliged to replace certain portions of Ocean Island. Damages for this breach were to be negotiated by the parties. He also found that the British Government had, in some ways, failed to fulfil its colonial

trust but pointed out that in such matters the Court had no power. Subsequently the British, Australian and New Zealand Governments offered the Banabans an *ex gratia* payment of $10 million in addition to any damages decided upon. $14.5 million was paid in 1981.

Banaban rights. Mining on Banaba finished at the end of 1979. The Banabans, however, failed to persuade Britain or I-Kiribati to allow them to secede with their island, and the island continues to be part of Kiribati. The Kiribati Constitution makes special provision for the Banabans, ensuring them a seat in the House of Assembly, the return of the land on Banaba acquired by the government for phosphate mining and the right of every Banaban to enter and live in Banaba. Banaban land can only be compulsorily acquired by leasehold and only after consultation with the Banaban Island Council. The constitution also provides for a Commission of Inquiry which, three years after independence, will review the special arrangements made for the Banabans in the constitution.

Any amendment to the provisions of the constitution relating to the Banabans can only be effected if their elected representative in the House of Assembly does not vote against such amendment. In all other respects, Banaba is treated as any other outer island of Kiribati. British aid to Kiribati includes an allocation for the redevelopment of Banaba.

COMMISSIONERS. Only 14 men held the office of Resident Commissioner or Governor of the Gilbert and Ellice Islands colony in the 84 years from 1892 to 1976 when the Ellice Islands, as Tuvalu, became a separate dependency. They were:

1893: C. R. Swayne
1895: W. Telfer Campbell
1909: Captain J. Quayle Dickson
1913: E. C. Eliot (later CBE)
1922: H. R. McClure
1926: A. F. Grimble MA (later Sir Arthur Grimble, KCMG)
1933: J. C. Barley
1942: V. Fox-Strangways
1946: H. E. Maude, MA, MBE (later OBE)
1949: W. J. Peel, BA

1952: M. L. Bernacchi, CMG
1962: V. J. Andersen, OBE, VRD
1970: Sir John Field, KBE, CMG (Governor from 1972)
1973: J. H. Smith, CBE
1978: R. O. Wallace

Mr Wallace continued as Governor until Independence.

Further information. Some of the early history is covered in H. E. Maude's *Of Islands and Men* (Melbourne, 1968). This also gives an account of the Phoenix Islands Settlement Scheme. Sir Arthur Grimble's *A Pattern of Islands* (John Murray, London, 1952) is based on his period as governor and his early writings on the group were collated by his daughter Rosemary Grimble in *Migrations Myth and Magic from the Gilbert Islands* (Routledge and Kegan Paul, London 1972). This contains descriptions of the prehistoric astronomy and navigation of the people.

Dr Barrie Macdonald's *Cinderellas of the Empire* (Australian National University Press, 1982) covers the period of colonial history in some detail. A history of the Roman Catholic Mission in the Gilberts is to be found in Ernest Sabatier's *Sous l'equator du Pacifique* (Editions Dillon, Paris 1939). Austin Coates' *Islands in the South* offers an interesting hypothesis on prehistoric migration by Austronesians which is contrary to most accepted theories, and which makes many references to the Gilbertese as navigators. Edwin H. Bryan Jnr.'s *American Polynesia and the Hawaiian Chain* (Honolulu, 1942), gives histories of the Line and Phoenix Islands. Details of Ocean Island history are to be found in Albert F. Ellis' *Ocean Island and Nauru* (Sydney, 1936). In 1979, to mark Independence Year, the Kiribati Ministry of Education, Training and Culture with the Institute of Pacific Studies and Extension Services of the University of the South Pacific published *Kiribati — Aspects of History* (Fiji Times & Herald Ltd, Suva) both in English and the Kiribati language. This was followed in 1985 by *Kiribati: A Changing Atoll Culture*. Both books were written by I-Kiribati.

ISLANDS IN DETAIL

Banaba. Banaba, which is now the name of Ocean Island on official lists, is situated just south of the Equator some 260 km east of Nauru and 400 km west of the Gilbert Islands. It has the shape of a pearl oyster shell, and is about 10 km in circumference with a maximum elevation of about 78 m. The island may have been first settled, like the Gilbert Islands, by migrants coming via Micronesia. It later had continuing contact with the islands of the Gilbert group. The Banaban language is a variant of Gilbertese. Ocean Island's modern history is completely intertwined with the exploitation of its phosphate deposits. The industry closed down at the end of 1979.

The phosphate deposits were worked on behalf of the British, Australian and New Zealand Governments by British Phosphate Commissioners (BPC). The key personnel were Europeans. The labouring work was done by Gilbertese, Tuvaluans and Chinese.

Ocean Island was first reported to the western world by Captain Jered Gardner of the American ship *Diana*, who sighted it on 3 January 1801 and named it Rodman's Island. The name Ocean Island is due to Captain John Mertho of the ship *Ocean* who came upon the island in 1804 and thought he was the first European to sight the island.

Except for occasional visits by whalers and traders from the 1820s onwards, Ocean Island had little contact with the outside world until phosphate was discovered there in 1900. Although it came within the British sphere of influence when Britain signed an agreement with Germany in 1886 partitioning the Western Pacific, Britain did not annex it or make it part of the Gilbert and Ellice Islands Protectorates when those governments were proclaimed in 1892.

The phosphate was discovered by Albert F. Ellis, an employee in the Sydney office of the Pacific Islands Company, of London. The discovery was made after Ellis analysed a strange piece of stone, thought to be fossilised wood, that had been brought to Sydney from Nauru. In May 1900, he negotiated an agreement with the Banabans which gave his company the sole right to work the phosphate deposits for 999 years for an annual payment of £50.

Meanwhile, the company obtained a licence from the British Colonial Office which stated, among other things, that Ocean Island was a British possession and that the licensees had exclusive right to occupy the island from 1 January 1901 and to display the British flag in token of occupation. The British High Commissioner for the West Pacific in Fiji was later instructed to issue a proclamation to make Ocean Island part of the Gilbert and Ellice Islands Protectorate. The High Commissioner, however, declared that the island had been annexed because the licence issued by the British Government had referred to the island as a 'possession' of Her Majesty. The matter was further confused when the commander of the HMS *Pylades* hoisted the British flag at Ocean Island on 28 September 1901.

Meanwhile, the Pacific Islands Company (reconstituted as the Pacific Phosphate Company) had organised the exploitation of the phosphate, and by about 1909 about two million tonnes had been exported. Apart from their annual fee of £50, the only financial benefit that accrued to the Banabans was about £20 an acre for mining land bought from them, plus compensation for fruit trees destroyed.

These ungenerous terms eventually provoked numerous questions in the House of Commons and made the Banabans so bitter that they refused to sell any more land to the phosphate company. The impasse was resolved in 1913 when the company agreed to pay the Banabans a royalty of 6d a ton on all phosphate mined. The activities of the company continued to attract unfavourable press and parliamentary comment and partly to ensure against future embarrassment, and partly to tidy up the various legal entities all administered by the Resident Commissioner, steps were taken to establish the Gilbert and Ellice Islands Colony.

After World War I, when Britain, Australia and New Zealand were given a League of Nations mandate over nearby phosphate-producing Nauru, the governments of those three countries bought out the Pacific Phosphate Company for £3½ million. The British Phosphate Commissioners (BPC) were then appointed to exploit the phosphate deposits of the two islands on behalf of the three governments.

When the Banabans refused to sell more land in the late 1920s, the government compulsorily acquired what it wanted, but paid for it a price that it considered reason-able. At the same time, the royalty rate was increased to 10½d per ton but this remained unchanged until 1942. Further land was compulsorily acquired in 1931, but the royalty remained unchanged until 1942. However, since 1913 the government had also been putting money away on the Banabans' behalf against the day when Ocean Island was mined out. In 1942, after the Japanese had occupied Ocean Island, some of this money was used to buy Rabi Island for them.

The Japanese occupation began in August 1942. Most Europeans had then been evacuated, but there were about 700 Banabans on the island, plus 800 Gilbertese labourers and their wives and children. The Banabans and some of the Gilbertese were deported to Kusaie (Kosrae), in the Carolines. Other Gilbertese were sent to Nauru and Tarawa, but 200 were retained on Ocean Island to work as fishermen. All were treated badly and some died.

After news of the Japanese capitulation reached Ocean Island in August 1945, the Japanese massacred all the remaining Gilbertese except one who escaped miraculously. This sole survivor later gave evidence at a war crimes trial at which the garrison commander and the quartermaster were sentenced to death.

In September 1945 the Banabans and Gilbertese on Kusaie (Kosrae), then numbering 1003, were brought to Tarawa. As Ocean Island was still a shambles, they elected to live on Rabi Island where they have since remained. They are Fiji citizens. Meanwhile, the BPC re-established itself on Ocean Island, and in 1947 exported 120,360 tonnes of phosphate. The tonnage had more than doubled by 1950. In 1965, the export figure was 350,000, and in 1969 it was well over 500,000 tonnes. The royalty paid to the Banabans was 1/3d a ton from 1947 to 1958; 1/9d a ton from 1958 to 1964; then 2/8 a ton. When the last named figure was adopted, the BPC was also paying a royalty on Ocean Island phosphate of 23/- to the Gilbert and Ellice Islands Colony. Meanwhile, the Nauruans were receiving 13/6d a ton for their phosphate.

Banaban resentment, anger and bitterness over the comparatively poor deal they were getting almost led to violence on Rabi in

April 1965. Thereafter, the British Government treated them with much more consideration and their share in the phosphate revenue was increased from time to time. In 1968, the government also made an ex-gratia payment to them 'in consideration of the effects of phosphate mining upon Ocean Island since 1900', but the Banabans were not satisfied. They employed public relations advisers to publicise their cause, and economic and legal advisers to help them take their case to the United Nations. Finally, in February 1975, the Banabans sued the British Governmet in the High Court of Great Britain, claiming £7 million for back royalties and an unspecified amount as recompense for damage to Ocean Island. Meanwhile, with the Gilbert and Ellice Islanders moving towards separation and independence, and Ocean Island's phosphate due to run out in 1979, the Banabans sought independence for their original homeland.

Despite protests, demonstrations and a petrol bomb attack on mining plant on Banaba early in 1979, the Banabans were unable to obtain separation from Kiribati, but certain rights with regard to land ownership and representation in the Kiribati House of Assembly were reserved for the Banabans in the Kiribati Constitution. In 1988 studies were being conducted to assess the possibility of recommencing the extraction of phosphate.

Makin. This, the northernmost of the Gilbert Islands, is only about 4.5 km long and 1.5 km wide. When the wind is NNE to ESE, there is a sheltered anchorage for small craft. The government station is at the village of Makin on the main islet. Rainfall is heavy. In pre-colonial times this island was ruled, with Butaritari, by a single paramount chief.

Butaritari. This is a roughly triangular atoll measuring about 17 km from east to west. Its fine deep lagoon has three entrances for ships and provides good anchorage. From the mid-19th century until World War II it was the main trading centre within the Gilbert group. Robert Louis Stevenson lived there for a short time in the 1880s.

Most of the land is on the south side of the lagoon, and the principal villages are on the two main islets. Butaritari and Kuma. Other islets are: Ubantakoto, Namoka, Natata, Kotabu, Tukerere, Nabuni, Oteariki and Bikati. The south side of the atoll is a continuous grove of coconuts and pandanus.

The principal settlement is also called Butaritari, near the SW corner of the westernmost islet, which is nearly 13 km long.

Butaritari was occupied by Japanese forces in 1942 and, shortly afterwards, was attacked by allied forces in the 'Carlson Raid'. Partly as a consequence of this raid Betio islet on Tarawa was fortified.

The American Army landed on Butaritari and the Marines on Betio (Tarawa) simultaneously. Butaritari was secured first, after which the Americans concentrated on Betio, having established a naval and air base on Butaritari. The airstrip has now been restored for regular air services with Tarawa.

The European discoverer of Butaritari was the Spaniard Quiros who sighted it in 1606 and named it Buen Viaje. It was rediscovered in 1788 when Captain Thomas Gilbert in the *Charlotte* and Captain John Marshall in the *Scarborough* were sailing to Canton from Botany Bay. Marshall gave the names Allen's, Gillespie's, Touching's, Clarke's, Smith's and Scarborough to the principal islets.

Marakei. Marakei is about 8 km by 5 km. The government station is at the village of Rawannawi. Marakei is a 'classical' atoll; two islets, north and south, almost completely enclose a small lagoon, leaving only a boat entrance. Sponges are plentiful in the surrounding waters.

Captain L. I. Duperrey of the French exploring vessel *Coquille* is credited with the European discovery of Marakei in 1824. However, he was under the impression it was Abaiang — the Matthew's Island of Captain Gilbert.

Abaiang. This atoll is about 25 km long by 8 km wide. Six islets ring the lagoon — Teirio, Nuotaea, Nanikirata, Twin Tree, Ribono and Iku. The land is continuous on the eastern side. Vessels drawing up to 4.8 metres can enter the lagoon, which provides a sheltered anchorage.

Captain Thomas Gilbert, its European discoverer in 1788, named it Matthew's Island, after the owner of his ship, the *Charlotte*. He called the lagoon Charlotte Bay and the main island Point Charlotte. Subsequent errors in identification led to the island being known as Charlotte Island. Its local name is sometimes written Apaiang.

The first Protestant missionaries to the Gilberts, led by the Rev. Hiram Bingham, settled on Abaiang in 1857.

Tarawa. This atoll is shaped like an isosceles triangle. It has islets on its southern and eastern reefs, but not on its western reef. The islets, in total, extend over 64 km and have an area of 920 hectares. The principal ones are: Betio, Bairiki, Eita, Buota, Taritai, Abaokoro, Noto, Buariki, Teaoraereke, Nabeina, and Bikenibeu.

Tarawa is a port of entry and the main centre of the group. The lagoon has one navigable entrance. At Tarawa are the government headquarters, central hospital, government secondary schools, teacher training college, etc. All are situated on the islets of Bairiki, Betio and Bikenibeu.

Betio, in the south-west corner, was the scene of one of the fiercest American landing-assaults during the Pacific War, when on 24 November 1943 US Marines captured it from a strongly-entrenched Japanese garrison after a grim five days' battle.

Until 1942, the Administration office was in Betio. After the recapture, the settlement and Administration offices were established in Bairiki which, in turn, became head-quarters for the Gilbert and Ellice Islands Colony. In 1954 new permanent buildings for the District Office and station establishments were constructed on Betio, where the Wholesale Society installations are also situated. Betio harbour has been reconstructed and developed as the main Tarawa port. Also on Betio are a club, a public bar and cafe, cinemas, a small slipway, workshops and a fuel depot. Government House, the official residence of the Beretitenti, is situated on nearby Bairiki, as is Tarawa's main 'maneaba' (community centre and meeting-place). About 18 km to the NE is Bikenibeu, where the Central Hospital, secondary schools, teachers' training college and hotel are situated.

Bonriki, in the SE corner of the atoll, is the site of the atoll's airstrip. In 1963 two causeways were completed, linking the

TARAWA

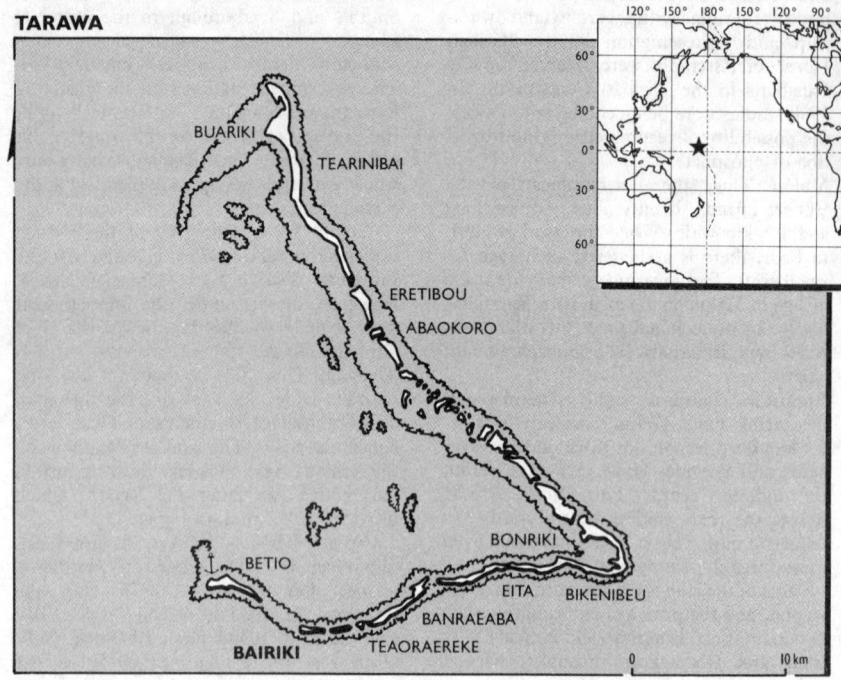

southern islets and a motor road now extends some 32 km from Bonriki to Bairiki.

The headquarters of the Roman Catholic Church in the colony is at Teaoraereke and that of the Protestant Church at Antebuka.

In 1788, Captain Thomas Gilbert of the *Charlotte* became the first European to sight any part of Tarawa. He called three of the northernmost islets Gilbert's, Marshall's and Knox's Islands. A later navigator called it Cook's Isle.

Maiana. Maiana is roughly oblong, measuring about 14 km by 9 km. Its eastern side is a single long island. There are a few smaller islets on the north-west and south-west. The lagoon is studded with coral heads and ships cannot enter it. The principal villages are: Tebangetua (government station), Bubutei, Temangaua, Tebiauea, Tebanga and Temantongo. Although near Tarawa, inaccessibility of the lagoon resulted in Maiana being visited infrequently until an airstrip was completed in 1976.

The atoll's European discoverer was Captain Patterson of the brig *Elizabeth* in 1809. He called it Hall's Island.

Abemama. Abemama is 19 km by 8 km. Its chief villages are Kariatebike (government station), Tebanga, Tabiang and Baretoa. Vessels up to 500 tonnes can enter its lagoon where there is good anchorage. Tabiang-Binoinano Islet occupies the northern and NE sides of the atoll. In the SE and SW are Tabonua, Kabaungaki, Bike and Abatiku.

Abemama's European discoverer was Captain Charles Bishop of the brig *Nautilus*. He came upon it in 1799 and named it Roger Simpson's Island after an associate who was on board. The native name is also written Apemama and Apamama.

During the 19th century, Abemama, Kuria and Aranuka were united by a line of paramount chiefs. Of these, Tem Binoka (described by Stevenson in *In the South Seas*) became the best known and probably the most despotic. It was here that commander H. M. Davis, of HMS *Royalist* proclaimed the Gilbert Islands a British protectorate on 2 May 1892.

Abemama was occupied by the Japanese during the whole of 1942, but was retaken by the Americans and used as a supply and air base until the end of the Pacific War. The wartime airstrip has been restored for services connecting it with Tarawa and other islands.

Towards the end of the war, it was proposed that Abemama should be the post-war capital for the Gilbert and Ellice Islands Colony. This proposal was abandoned in 1947 because of the better passage into Tarawa's lagoon.

Abemama is the headquarters for the SDA church.

Kuria. Kuria, some 6 km by 3 km, has only one important village — Buariki — which is the site of the government station. It has no lagoon. To the north of it, separated by a narrow passage, is the islet of Oneke. Kuria was another of the discoveries of Captains Gilbert and Marshall in 1788. They named it Woodle's Island. In pre-colonial times Kuria was 'ruled' by the chiefs of Abemama.

Aranuka. Aranuka consists of two islets on a triangular reef about 9 km long. The islets are at the eastern and western ends, with some very small islets in between, in the north. The government station is at Buariki village. The land area is about 1500 hectares. The small lagoon has no ship passage.

In 1788, Captain Marshall of the *Scarborough* called the eastern and western portions of Aranuka Hopper's and Henderville's Islands respectively. This later led to the belief that Marshall had discovered Abemama and that his name for it was Hopper's Island. In pre-colonial times Aranuka was included within the domain of the chief of Abemama.

Tabiteuea. After Tarawa, this atoll is the most populous in the group. The government stations are at Utiroa in North Tabiteuea and Buariki, South Tabiteuea. Other villages are Eita, Tanaeang and Teuabu.

The two largest islands are Buariki-Taku in the SE and Eanikai-Utiroa on the NE side of the reef's northern end. A string of small islets separates them. A long, tortuous ship channel gives access to the southern part of the lagoon.

This is the largest island and once had the largest population. For administration and elections it is divided into north and south; the government station in the north is at Utiroa (a location shelled by the Wilkes expedition in 1841 after a seaman was killed); and the station in the south is at Buariki.

In the early 1880s the northern 'Christian armies' led by Hawaiian pastors massacred the 'Pagans' of the south (in the name of 'The Book' and in pursuit of land) and killed about 1000.

The name Tabiteuea (Tapu-te-uea) means 'chiefs are forbidden'. The society is egalitarian and there are no 'noble' families. Elders met in maneaba (meeting houses) and controlled district affairs. These traditions are still strong.

Captain Charles Bishop of the *Nautilus* was its discoverer in 1799. He named it after himself, while he called Eanikai, the main islet, Drummond's Island.

Nearby Bishop charted a shoal which he called Nautilus Shoal. The whaler *Corsair* is reputed to have been wrecked on it in 1835, but in 1966, Captain E. V. Ward, an experienced local mariner, cast doubt on its existence.

Beru. Beru, which is about 18 km long, was the headquarters in the GEIC of the London Missionary Society for 60 years until they were moved to Antebuka Tarawa, in 1960. The mission's printing press followed shortly afterwards, but a post-primary school for girls and boys has remained on Beru.

The government station on the atoll is at the village of Tanukinberu. Other villages are Tabiany and Taboiaki.

Captain J. Clerk of the whaler *John Palmer* was the European discoverer of the atoll in 1826. He named it Maria Island. Peru, Francis, Sunday, Eliza and Peroat are other names that have been applied to it.

Nikunau is an island about 13 km long and 2.5 km broad. Its chief villages are Rungata (government station), Muribenua, and Nukumanau. There is a small landlocked lagoon in the north. Small vessels anchor just off Rungata and larger vessels about 1 km to the north. The island was once known as Byron Island because Commodore John Byron of HMS *Dolphin* discovered it in 1765.

Onotoa. Onotoa is about 19 km long and has no sheltered anchorage. The villages are Buariki (government station), Tabuaroarae and Aiaki. The lagoon is bordered by a reef on the western side, with a good boat channel near the centre. Its islets are: Tanaeang, Bowerick, Sand, Otoeie, Hack, Tabuaroarae, Onutu, and Temuah. The first European to sight Onotoa was Captain J. Clerk of the *John Palmer* in 1826. He called it Eliza Island, but it also came to be known as Clerk Island.

Tamana. This is a small island about 5 km long by 1.25 km wide. The government station is at the village of Bakaka. Tamana was once known as Rotch's Island, the name given it by its European discoverer, Captain J. Clerk in 1826.

Arorae. This island, the southernmost of the Gilbert group, is about 6.5 km by 3.25 km. Its villages are Tamaroa and Roreti. The government station of Taribo divides them. Captain Patterson of the brig *Elizabeth* named it Hope Island in 1809. This was later changed to Hurd Island by the hydrographer John Purdy.

Phoenix Islands. The Phoenix group consists of eight scattered islands located between 2 deg 30 min and 4 deg 30 min S latitude and between 170 deg 30 min and 174 deg 30 min W longitude. The islands are Kanton (now with a 'k' as there is no 'c' in the Kiribati language), Enderbury, McKean, Birnie, Phoenix, Nikumaroro (Gardner), Orona (Hull) and Manra (Sydney). Kanton and Enderbury have been jointly administered by Britain and the US until Kiribati independence when they became part of Kiribati, the United States relinquishing all claim to them and other islands in Kiribati and Tuvalu. Total land area of the Phoenix Group is 28.70 sq. km. All the islands are low atolls enclosing lagoons. Only Kanton is inhabited.

Archaeological evidence indicates that Manra, Orona and Nikumaroro were inhabited by man in pre-European times. However, all were without people when the first European whalers visited the group, probably in the early 1820s. Between 1859 and 1877, Enderbury, McKean and Phoenix Islands were worked for their guano by an American firm, the Phoenix Guano Company.

A British subject, John T. Arundel, acquired rights to all the islands in 1881 and obtained leases to them from the British Government. He worked the guano on some and planted them and others with coconut trees. In 1889, most of the islands were annexed to Great Britain by Commander Oldham of HMS *Egeria* Captain H. W. S. Gibson of HMS *Curacao* annexed Nikumaroro Island in 1892.

After the guano deposits were exhausted, Orona and Manra developed into successful coconut plantations and the other islands were neglected. Nevertheless, during the years leases to all the islands, except Enderbury and McKean, passed from one company to another — from J. T. Arundel & Co. to the Pacific Islands Company Ltd, to Lever's Pacific Plantations Ltd, to the Samoa Shipping and Trading Co. Ltd. In 1937, the eight islands were included within the boundaries of the Gilbert and Ellice Islands Colony, and administration officials were stationed on Kanton and Hull. A little later, the GEIC Government bought the islands from Burns Philp to resettle land-hungry Gilbertese. Settlement began on Hull, Sydney and Gardner that same year, and within a few years more than 1000 islanders were living there.

Meanwhile, in 1938, the US sent small parties of men to occupy Kanton and Enderbury Islands because of their potential value in trans-Pacific aviation. In the following year, the British and United States governments signed a 50-year agreement for the joint administration of Kanton and Enderbury. The Americans immediately began to build aviation facilities on Kanton. These remained in use until 1967. As for the colonisation scheme, this was abandonded in 1963 following a prolonged drought and difficulties in maintaining communication. All Gilbertese residents were resettled in the Solomons.

Details of the six islands administered solely from Tarawa are:

McKean Island. This is an almost circular island with a diameter of little more than 1 km and with an area of 56 ha is the smallest of the group. It has a shallow lagoon. Captain Henry Barber of the *Arthur* discovered it in 1794 and named it Drummond's Island. Its present name is that of a member of the United States Exploring Expedition who was first to sight it during a survey in 1840. The island has not been occupied since American guano interests ceased operations there some time between 1859 and 1871.

Birnie Island. Birnie is about 1.25 km long and about 500 metres wide, enclosing a salt water lagoon. A whaler, Captain Emment, discovered it about 1820. Its name is that of a well known British shipowner of that time. The commander of HMS *Egeria* annexed the island for Great Britian in 1889, but no use was ever made of it.

Phoenix Island. Phoenix, which has the native name of Rawaki, is a pear-shaped island less than 1.25 km long and 1 km wide. A plateau at one end of the island, about six metres above sea level, slopes away to a shallow lagoon. The island is uninhabited and was reported to be overrun with rabbits. There are also many thousands of sea birds.

The European discoverer of Phoenix Island is unknown. It was probably the captain of a whaler of that name who came upon it some time before 1828. Between 1862 and 1872, the island was worked by the Phoenix Guano Company. It has not been used since. The commander of HMS *Egeria* took possession of it for Great Britain in 1889.

Nikumaroro (Gardner Island). This is an atoll about 6.5 km by 2 km, enclosing an ample lagoon. The width of the land varies from about 100 metres on the east and northeast side to about 1 km on the west. There are two narrow passages into the lagoon. The island has a brown, peat-like soil that is very fertile. Puka trees (*Pisonia grandis*) and *Cordia subcordata* grew prolifically in the 1930s.

The island's European discoverer was Captain Kemin in 1824. But the atoll is said to take its name from Gideon Gardner, owner of the ship *Ganges* from which a Captain Coffin sighted it in 1828. J. T. Arundel planted part of the island with coconuts in 1892, the year in which Captain H. W. S. Gibson of HMS *Curacao* annexed it for the British Crown.

Because of a drought in the 1890s, Arundel's coconuts did not thrive, and the island was not further utilised until Gilbertese colonists went there in 1938–39. The Gilbertese called the island Nikumaroro. All the settlers were removed to Wagina Island, Solomons, in 1963.

Orona (Hull Island). This atoll, which lies eastward of Nikumaroro, is about 11 km long by 5 km wide. There are numerous small islets on the reef and many entrances into the big lagoon.

Stone structures found on the island in 1933 indicate that it was inhabited long before it became known to Europeans in the 1820s. The island was named and first charted by Commodore Charles Wilkes of the United States Exploring Expedition in 1840, but a Frenchman and 10 Tahitians were then living ashore.

J. T. Arundel & Co. started planting the island with coconuts in 1887, two years before the commander of the HMS *Egeria* proclaimed it a British possession. The British companies that subsequently leased the island shipped some copra from it. The Burns Philp ship *Makoa* was wrecked there in 1937.

After Gilbertese settlers went there in 1938, the island's population grew to 610. The Gilbertese were resettled at Wagina, Solomon Islands, in 1963. Since then the US has built a radar station on the island.

Manra (Sydney Island). Manra is roughly circular, and encloses a land-locked lagoon. It measures about 3.25 km from west to east and 2.5 km from north to south. Fish traps in the lagoon indicate that this was once open to the sea and that the island supported a pre-European population. Numerous ancient stone structures have also been found there.

Like Birnie Island, Sydney was discovered by Captain Emment about 1820. J. T. Arundel & Co. shipped guano from the island between 1882 and 1885, and planted it with coconuts. The British companies that subsequently leased the island exported copra.

The island was annexed for Great Britain by the commander of HMS *Egeria* in 1889, Gillbertese colonists went there in 1938 and within two years they numbered 260. However, by 1950 the authorities had decided that the island could not properly support a permanent population. In 1958, the entire population was evacuated and most of them resettled at Gizo, Solomon Islands. Since then the island's coconut plantations have been worked by the Phoenix Islands Co-operative Society.

Kanton Island (Canton). As there is no letter C in Gilbertese, the letter K has been substituted for the initial capital letter C — Kanton — in official lists. Canton Island is about halfway between Honolulu and Noumea, a distance of 5400 km. It is an atoll enclosing a chop-shaped lagoon about 11 km long and about five km broad. There are

several entrances into the lagoon, and the atoll offers the best anchorage in the Phoenix group. The land is merely a coral sandbank about 14½ km long and seldom more than 600 metres wide. Except where trees have been planted in recent times, the vegetation is low and stunted.

Canton was named after a New Bedford whaler that was wrecked there in 1854. It was known previously as Mary and Mary Balcout Island, but its discoverer is unknown. The island was worked for its guano between 1881 and 1891 by J. T. Arundel & Co., of London, who obtained a lease to the island from the British Government. The lease was subsequently transferred to other British companies. A party from HMS *Leith* erected a sign asserting British sovereignty over the island in August 1936. In the following year, the boundaries of the Gilbert and Ellice Islands Colony were extended to include all the Phoenix Islands and the rights to those islands were bought by the colony from Burns, Philp (South Sea) Co. Ltd. Two British officials were stationed on Canton in August 1937, and some Americans arrived in the following March. Just over a year later, the UK and US Governments signed the treaty providing for the joint administration of both Canton and Enderbury.

During 1938–39, Pan American Airways developed an airport and cleared the lagoon of coral heads. When war came to the Pacific in December 1941, the airport came under military control and the US Air Force built an airfield for land planes on the northwestern rim. From 1945 to 1958, the airfield was regularly used by the trans-Pacific airlines, Qantas and PAA. The development of long-range aircraft then made the airfield superfluous except in emergencies.

In the early 1960s, a satellite tracking station was established on Canton for the Project Mercury space research programme. Meanwhile, the United States Federal Aviation Agency continued to maintain landing facilities and navigational aids. More than 60 Gilbert and Ellice (Tuvalu) Islanders were employed on the island on various installations and both the US and Britain continued to maintain administrative officers there until 1968. They were then withdrawn, and in October 1970 it was officially stated that the island was uninhabited. However, early in 1971 it was revealed that in 1970 Canton had become a US tracking station for anti-ballistic missiles and that it was serviced by US and American Samoan personnel. There is now no tracking station on the island which, in November 1980, was peopled by seven I-Kiribati and one Samoan.

Enderbury Island. Enderbury Island lies about 60 km ESE of Canton Island. It is about 4½ km long by 1½ km wide. The lagoon that once existed is now only a shallow puddle. Slabs of compact coral rock make up much of the land area. Grasses, low bushes and a few small trees are the only vegetation.

The island is said to have been discovered by Captain James J. Coffin of the British whaler *Transit* in 1823. The name is thought to be a corruption of Enderby, the British whaling house. The island was surveyed by vessels of the United States Exploring Expedition in 1840 and 1841. The Phoenix Guano Company, an American concern, worked the island's guano deposits between 1859 and 1877. J. T. Arundel & Co., of London, did likewise for several years after 1881. Thereafter no one troubled about Enderbury until 1937 when, with other islands in the Phoenix group, it was investigated as a place of settlement for land-hungry Gilbertese.

Although the island came under Anglo-American administration in 1939, it has been little utilised since then. In the 1960s, scientists of the Smithsonian Institution set up camps there during bird-tagging expeditions connected with their study of migratory birds in the Pacific. More recently, it has had a part in the US anti-ballistic missile programme.

Line Islands. The Line Islands group in Kiribati is made up of three northern islands, Teraina (Washington), Tabuaeran (Fanning) and Kiritimati (Christmas) and five southern islands, Malden, Starbuck, Vostok, Caroline and Flint. The northern, inhabited islands, lie a few degrees north of the Equator some 15 to 20 degrees south of the Hawaiian chain and nearly 30 degrees eastward of the Gilberts. With Kingman Reef and Palmyra Island (two United States possessions), all the islands form a chain running in a NW to SE direction. Washington is about 190 km SE of Palmyra and about 120 km NW of Fanning. Christmas Island is about 245 km SE of Fanning.

Teraina (Washington Island), which has

also been called Prospect Island and New York Island, is about 4 km long by 2 km wide. It is about 3 m above sea level and has a large fresh water lake at its eastern end. A fast-multiplying fish, tilapia, has been introduced to the lake in recent years. The island has been described as 'the most difficult and dangerous loading port in the Pacific'. An anchorage at the west point may be used only in calm weather.

The island was owned by Fanning Island Plantations Ltd, a subsidiary of Burns, Philp & Co. Ltd of Sydney until 1983. It is completely covered with coconut palms — some 200,000 of them. I-Kiribati are employed in copra-making. There were no indigenous inhabitants in historical times; but archaeological discoveries on the island suggest that it was reached or visited in the past by mariners from Tonga.

Captain Edmund Fanning who discovered the island in 1798 named it after the US President. The United States Exploring Expedition visited it in 1840. Its history, since then, has been closely linked with Fanning Island's. Britain annexed it in 1889.

Tabuaeran (Fanning Island) is an atoll about 50 km in circumference. The land area is 34.54 sq. km; that of the lagoon about 110 sq. km. The land is never more than 1 km wide.

Most of the land was owned by Fanning Island Plantations Ltd, a subsidiary of Burns, Philp & Co. Ltd, Sydney. Somewhat more than a third of its holdings is under coconuts.

English Harbour provides a sheltered anchorage for vessels up to about 1000 tonnes. There is also a calm weather port known as Whaler's Anchorage, but as this is too far from the lagoon entrance for easy cargo handling, vessels usually drift off the entrance.

Provisions for Fanning Island and the other islands in the administrative district are carried by copra and colony vessels, and by vessels used for the recruitment and repatriation of plantation labour.

The island was discovered by Captain Edmund Fanning of the American ship *Betsey* in 1798. By 1850, a Captain Henry English was conducting valuable trade in coconut oil from the island. He was followed by William Greig (British) and George Bicknell of Hawaii. These men also planted Washington Island. About the turn of the century, their interests were acquired by Father Emmanuel Rougier of Fiji, later Tahiti. Three years after Rougier's death in 1932, the island was bought by Fanning Island Plantations Ltd.

Captain Sir William Wiseman of HMS *Caroline* annexed the island to Great Britain in 1888 after it was found that it lay in the line of the proposed trans-Pacific cable. From 1902 to 1963, the island was the connecting link for the cable between Bamfield, Canada, and Suva, Fiji. Then the new British Commonwealth coaxial cable was opened, and the cable station on Fanning, operated by Cable and Wireless Ltd, was closed.

Kiritimati (Christmas Island). Kiritimati, in about 1 deg 59 min N latitude and 157 deg 30 min W longitude, is about 160 km in circumference. It is the largest island of purely coral formation in the world. In shape, it resembles a chop. It stretches from NW to SE. The larger portion is the NW and encloses a spacious lagoon. The interior of the land area is remarkable in being dotted with more than 100 sheets of water. Some of these are lakes several kilometres in diameter. A large bay exposed to winds and currents from the east is known as the Bay of Wrecks because of the large number of ships that have come to grief there.

Coconuts have been planted north and south of the lagoon. There is a good anchorage off Cook Island near the entrance. Only fairly small craft can enter the lagoon safely, as there are many coral patches and not much depth. The main settlements are London, to the north of Cook Island, Poland and Banana.

Pre-European artifacts of different periods and a number of stone structures have been found on the island, but it was uninhabited when Captain Cook discovered it on 24 December 1777, and spent Christmas Day there. However, the Spaniards might have been there before Cook's voyage. The first ship known to have been wrecked there was the *Briton* in 1836.

The island was examined for guano in the 1850s, and an American, Captain J. L. Pendleton, of the ship *John Marshall*, took possession of it in 1857. The US Guano Company worked the island for several years after November 1858. Subsequently, the British Government leased the island to the Anglo-Australian Guano Co. and Alfred Houlder, but when a representative of the

latter visited in 1872, he found it occupied by three men working for a Honolulu man. Moreover, the USS *Narragansett* had just been there and had taken formal possession for the United States. Despite this and an American protest, Captain William Wiseman of HMS *Caroline* annexed the island to Great Britain in 1888.

Lever's Pacific Plantations Ltd leased the island from the British Government in 1902 for 99 years and planted it with nearly 73,000 coconuts. The lease was taken over by Father Emmanuel Rougier in 1913 and worked in the name of Central Pacific Coconut Plantations Ltd, from 1914. After Rougier died in 1932, his nephew took charge of the plantation, but abandoned it during the depression.

With the development of aviation in the mid-1930s, Christmas Island began to attract attention as a possible refuelling base for trans-Pacific aircraft. The British Government forestalled any new American claim to the island by sending representatives there in 1937. However, during World War II both American and New Zealand troops garrisoned it and it was used as an air base to link Honolulu with the US base at Bora Bora. The Americans did not leave until 1948. Meanwhile, the Rougier lease was deemed to have terminated, and the Gilbert and Ellice Islands Colony took over the running of the coconut plantation.

In 1956–58, Britain used Christmas Island as a base for nuclear experiments. The US did the same in 1962. As a result, more than 100 km of sealed roads were made, but they have not been maintained.

As the island, wholly owned by the Government, has more than half the total land area of Kiribati, the Government plans to develop it into an alternative economic centre to South Tarawa. Already fish farms have been established, the island is linked by air with Tarawa and Honolulu, and there is a hotel, the Captain Cook, with 24 rooms. Another hotel is planned and the copra industry will be developed. By 1986 the population had grown to 1737.

A solar salt-producing plant is proving quite successful with the potential of producing 2000 tonnes annually. In late 1987 proposals were being considered for the building of a Japanese space centre at a cost of $US8 billion.

Malden Island. This island lies about 386

km south of the equator in 155 deg W longitude. It is flat and triangular, on a reef measuring about 6.5 km by 8 km and enclosing a large lagoon. Only stunted vegetation grows there.

Stone-faced platforms and graves found on Malden indicate that Polynesians lived there for several generations before Europeans discovered it. It was uninhabited. K. P. Emory, of the Bishop Museum of Honolulu, estimated in 1924 that the pre-European population must have reached from 100 to 200. The occupation of the island was known in tradition to the people of Manihiki, Northern Cook Island.

The European discover of Malden was Lord Byron of HMS *Blonde*, who came upon it in 1825 after conveying the remains of the King and Queen of Hawaii from England to Honolulu. Byron named it after his surveying officer.

Guano deposits were discovered on the island about 1849, and a series of Australian guano enterprises worked them profitably for about 70 years. About 1889, Grice, Sumner & Co., of Melbourne, had about eight Europeans working there with 150 Polynesians from Niue and Aitutaki. In 1922, the island was leased to Malden Island Pty Ltd, of Melbourne, a successor of Grice, Sumner. But this firm did not exercise its lease after 1929. From 1956 to 1964, the island was used as a base for members of the British armed services during nuclear tests at Christmas Island.

Starbuck Island. Starbuck Island lies about 540 km south of the equator and 174 km SSW of Malden Island in 155 deg W longitude. It is barely 4.5 metres at its highest point, 10 km long and about 3 km wide. It is barren and treeless, with a shallow lagoon.

Captain Obed Starbuck of the US whaler *Hero* discovered it in 1823, but it was named after his namesake, Captain Valentine Starbuck, who sighted it three months after its discoverer. Captain William Swinburne of HMS *Mutine* annexed it for Great Britain in 1866.

Houlder Bros and Co. of London began digging guano from the island about 1870 and, during this period, an opening for small boats was made in the reef on the northwest. The island was worked for some years by J. T. Arundel & Co. and later by the Malden Island guano-seekers. It has been unoccupied and unworked since 1920. Attempts to plant coconuts on the island failed.

The British built a beacon on the western end as a warning to shipping. Starbuck has been called also Low, Starve, Hero, Barren, Coral Queen and Volunteer.

Caroline Island. This island measures about 10 km north and south, by about 1 km wide. There are over 20 islets strung along the reef enclosing a shallow lagoon, which is closed against anything larger than a ship's boat. Some of the islets are 4.5 to 6 metres high, and most are covered with coconut palms, pandanus and similar growth. There is no anchorage, and approach to the wooded shores is difficult. Water can be had by digging.

Graves containing adzes and 'marae' platforms have been found on the island, indicating that Polynesians once inhabited it. Its European discoverer was Captain W. R. Broughton, of HMS *Providence* in 1795. Several British and American captains subsequently gave it different names.

The British firm of Collie and Lucett, of Tahiti, formed a small stock-raising settlement there in 1846. In 1868, Captain Edward Nares of HMS *Reindeer* took possession of it and reported that 27 people were living there, raising pigs and poultry, salting fish, and planting coconuts. In 1872, the island was leased to Houlder Bros and Company, of London. Some guano was extracted.

J. T. Arundel & Co. took over the Houlder Bros lease in 1881 and planted numerous coconuts. A total eclipse of the sun was observed there in 1883. In 1910, the island was leased to S. R. Maxwell & Co., of Auckland, for coconut growing. After World War II, leases to it were held by Mr M. P. A. Bambridge and, later, Captain Omer Darr, both of Tahiti.

The island has also been called Thornton, Hirst, Clark, Independence and Carolina.

Vostok Island. This is a low, uninhabited, triangular coral lump less than 2 km square. A central clump of puka trees, about 25 metres high, is its principal feature. At the south-west corner is a boat passage through the reef, but there is no anchorage.

The Russian explorer Bellingshausen discovered it in 1820 and named it after his ship. It later acquired the names Stavers, Reaper, Leavitts and Anne. The United

States claimed it under the Guano Act of 1856, but the claim was never pressed. In 1873, Mr J. T. Arundel of Houlder Bros and Co., London, took possession of it for the British Crown. It is not known whether it was worked for guano. Although subsequently leased to various companies none of them made use of it. Captain Omer Darr, of Tahiti, acquired the lease in 1964.

Flint Island. Flint Island is situated in 11 deg 25 min S latitude and 151 deg 48 min W longitude. It is about 5 km long by one km broad, flat, and with a maximum height of about 7.5 metres. It is well-wooded and entirely surrounded by a coral reef, through which a boat passage has been blasted. The passage leads to a landing place on the western side.

The European discovery of the island is said to date back to 1801, but the name of its discoverer is unknown. A vessel of the US Exploring Expedition surveyed it in 1841, and it was claimed as an American possession under the US Guano Act of 1856. However, the island was occupied by Mr J. T. Arundel of Houlder Bros and Co., London, in 1872, for the purpose of exporting guano. Coconuts were planted there from 1875, and the island was solely used as a coconut plantation after the export of guano ceased in 1893. A lease that J. T. Arundel & Co. had had from 1885 was acquired by the Pacific Islands Co. Ltd in 1897, and later by Lever's Pacific Plantations Ltd. S. R. Maxwell & Co. Ltd of Tahiti and Auckland held the lease from 1910 to 1934. In 1922, 30,000 palms were growing on the island. From 1951 to 1964, the island was leased to Mr M. P. A. Bambridge of Tahiti and subsequently to Captain Omer Darr of Tahiti.

FOR THE TOURIST. The very remoteness of the islanders and their adaptation to atoll existence can tempt the traveller seeking a really new experience. The remaining scars of the Battle of Tarawa in the Pacific War are of interest to those who study war relics. While there are no regularly scheduled excursions for tourists, visitors can organise fishing trips, swimming, picnicking and shelling excursions by launch from Tarawa. Boat trips can also be made to other islands. Air flights operate to Butaritari, one of the first islands to be colonised, Christmas Island,

North Tabiteuea, Abemama, Marakei, Nonouti, Beru, Maiana, Nikunau, Onotoa, Tamana, Arorae, Makin and Banaba. Abemama was the home of Robert Louis Stevenson in 1889, and Tabiteuea is well known for its dances. Christmas Island is well known for its distinctive bird life and there are facilities for game fishing.

Visas are not required for entry up to four months by citizens of a large number of countries which have diplomatic relations with Kiribati. Other travellers may apply to any British Consulate or directly to the Principal Immigration Officer, Ministry of Foreign Affairs, PO Box 68, Bairiki, Tarawa, Republic of Kiribati.

Vaccinations are only required for travellers coming from areas infected with yellow fever.

Access to Kiribati is through Suva, Fiji and Funafuti, Tuvalu, either by Air Nauru or Airline of the Marshall Islands. It is also possible to fly from Honolulu via Christmas Island. There is a $5 departure tax.

A new tourist office is being built and information is available from the Kiribati Visitors Bureau, PO Box 64, Bairiki, Tarawa, Republic of Kiribati, Tel.: 21075.

ACCOMMODATION. This list is alphabetical. Accommodation on outer islands is in guest houses, usually built of local materials and of basic standards. Cooking facilities are available and it is possible to hire someone to do the cooking if required.

Captain Cook Hotel: 24 rooms, some aircon, restaurant, bar. C/- Post Office, Christmas Island.

Hotel Kiribati: 10 rooms, aircon, restaurant, bar, water sports arranged. PO Box 504, Betio, Tarawa. Cables JKKBS Betio.

Kiribati Seamen's Hostel: 12 rooms, share facilities, restaurant, bar, water sports arranged, situated on Battle of Tarawa invasion beach. PO Box 478, Betio, Tarawa. Tel.: 26133.

Otintai Hotel: 28 rooms, aircon, restaurant, bar, shop, rental cars and motorcycles, situated on lagoon, traditional entertainment. PO Box 270, Bikenibeu, Tarawa. Tel: 28020.

Robert Louis Stevenson Hotel: Abemama Island, 11 rooms, share facilities, tariff includes breakfast. PO Box 462, Betio, Tarawa. Tel.: 26305.

Line Islands

Beginning about 1500 kilometres south of the Hawaiian group is a string of small, low, semi-barren islands known as the Line Islands. They run in a SSE direction towards French Polynesia. From north to south they are Kingman Reef and Palmyra, Teraina, Tabuaeran, Christmas, Jarvis, Malden, Starbuck, Caroline, Vostok and Flint Islands. Kingman, Palmyra and Jarvis (see entry Howland, Baker and Jarvis Islands) are US possessions; the rest are in Kiribati. Details are in the Kiribati section.

Guano was extracted from some of the islands late last century and early this century; some have been planted with coconuts. All the islands are of coral formation, but only six — Caroline, Malden, Christmas, Teraina, Palmyra and Kingman — have interior lagoons and so qualify to be called atolls. Most of the lagoons are shallow. Tabuaeran is unusual in having a large fresh water lake.

Accounts of each island to 1942 can be found in Edwin H. Bryan Jr, *American Polynesia and the Hawaiian Chain*, Honolulu, 1942.

Kingman Reef. Kingman Reef is 1480 km south of Honolulu in 6 deg 23 min N latitude and 162 deg 25 min W longitude It is a bare, triangular reef, about 15 km long by 8 km wide, sheltering a deep lagoon. In times of high seas the whole island goes under water, thus rendering it almost useless for development. It is wet or awash most of the time. Height above sea level is about one metre, which makes it a navigational hazard. Captain Edmund Fanning, of the American trading ship *Betsey*, discovered it in 1798. Captain W. E. Kingman described it in 1853. It was annexed to the United States on 10 May 1922; and in 1934 when trans-Pacific aviation was under discussion, the reef was placed under the control of the US Navy.

In 1937, Pan American Airways, pioneering the new airmail service with flying-boats between Hawaii and New Zealand, used its sheltered lagoon as a half-way station between Honolulu and Pago Pago. The route was abandoned after a flying-boat was lost off Pago Pago in January 1938. Kingman is still under the control of the US Navy and is the ultimate responsibility of the US Department of Defence.

Palmyra Island. Palmyra Island is located at 5 deg 53 min N latitude and 162 deg 5 min W longitude. It consists of 39 islets totalling some 565 ha of dry land. The island was discovered by Captain Sawle, of the American ship *Palmyra*, in 1892. It has also been known as Samarang.

The Kingdom of Hawaii annexed it in 1862; Britain did the same in 1889; and the United States included it among the Hawaiian Islands by Congressional Act of 1898. The US cruiser *West Virginia* took formal possession in 1912. It was excluded from the boundaries of Hawaii by the Hawaii Statehood Act, and is now the responsibility of the US Department of the Interior. Judge Cooper, of Honolulu, acquired title to the island in 1911, and used it for growing coconuts. He sold all but two islets to Leslie and Ellen Fullard-Leo. When Cooper died in 1929 the other two islets (Home Islands) passed to his heirs. These became one island as a result of dredging in World War II.

Palmyra's central lagoon was originally divided into three by coral reefs. During World War II the US Navy had 6000 men on the island, and they dredged a seaplane runway that merged the two western lagoons into one. A causeway was built on the remaining reef. At the same time the Navy made a total of 52 islands into 39. They built a landplane runway of about 1800 metres which was used by the US Air Force until 1961. It is now unserviceable.

The main harbour is West Lagoon, which is entered by a channel on the SW side of the atoll. Both the channel and harbour will accommodate vessels drawing six metres of water. The atoll is only about two metres above sea level, but as it has a high annual rainfall — about 4400 millimetres — the islets are covered in dense vegetation. Many of the roads and causeways built during the war have become unserviceable and overgrown.

In 1962, a Californian firm tried to promote Palmyra as a resort and tourist area, but it did not eventuate.

Palmyra was the setting, in 1974, for a murder and theft. An American couple sailed into the lagoon on board their luxury yacht *Sea Wind*. Another arrival in the lagoon was *Iola*, a vessel in a state of ill repair, her American crew with no provisions. Several months later the *Sea Wind* sailed into Honolulu, and although she had been repainted several local yachtsmen recognised her. When questioned, the couple on board claimed that the previous owners had been lost on a fishing trip and that they had taken *Sea Wind* over. The second couple were the previous owners of the *Iola*. Subsequent police investigations and the washing up on Palmyra of a metal box containing bones identified as those of the original female owner all revealed that Palmyra had been the setting of an act of piracy. The skipper of *Iola* had made the skipper of the *Sea Wind* walk the plank into a shark-infested lagoon, had killed the man's wife and attempted to destroy the evidence by burning the metal box with her remains inside. He had commandeered the *Sea Wind* to return to Hawaii. He was convicted of murder but his partner was released.

Main ownership of Palmyra is shared by Fullard-Leo's three sons, Leslie, Dudley and Ainslie who live in Hawaii. The US Government announced in 1979 that it was considering buying Palmyra to use as a nuclear waste dump, but nothing came of the plan following strong opposition from the South Pacific Forum and the Fullard-Leo brothers.

Palmyra is uninhabited, and in 1986 there were no plans for its development.

Teraina, Tabuaeran, Christmas, Malden, Starbuck, Vostok, Caroline and **Flint**. See under Kiribati.

Lord Howe Island

Lord Howe Island is a dependency of New South Wales, lying 702 km north-east of Sydney. Its position is 30 deg 30 min S latitude 159 deg 50 min W longitude. The population (1987) is about 270 permanent residents.

The island is volcanic in origin and covers about 1455 ha. It is covered with luxuriant vegetation, dominated by two mountain peaks. The island is included in the Elizabeth electorate for the New South Wales State Parliament and is managed by the Lord Howe Island Board, located on Lord Howe Island.

Island time is 10½ hours ahead of GMT.

THE PEOPLE. Today's islanders generally were born on Lord Howe, although mostly their families originally came from Australia. There has been a gradual increase in population over the last 33 years from 228 in 1954 to 270 in 1987 owing to higher growth

LORD HOWE ISLAND

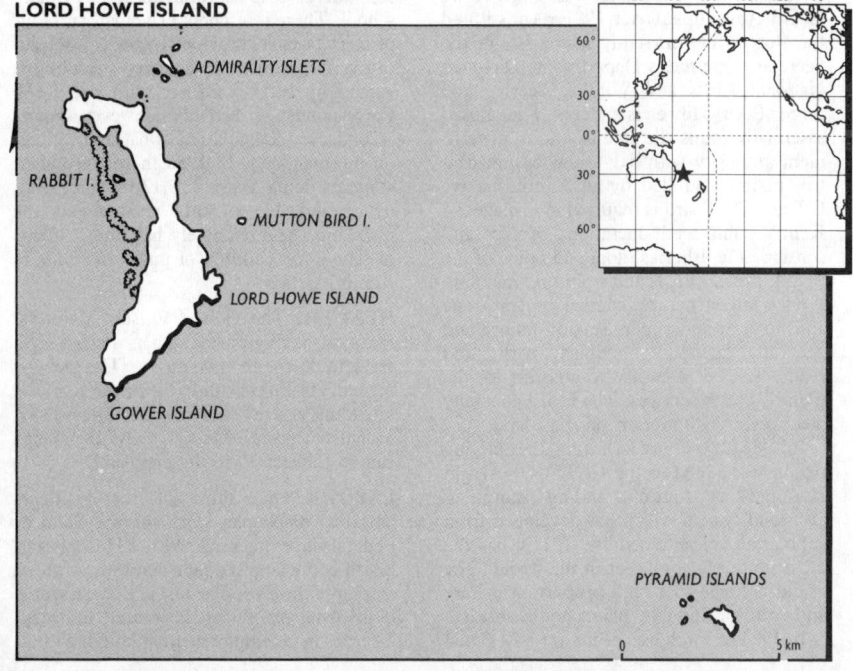

in semi-permanent residents employed in administration and in a developing tourist industry. Except for government employees, settlement on Lord Howe by non-islanders has been negligible. Rental accommodation is scarce and the opportunities for a non-islander to buy a house are very limited. It is likely that population growth will be limited in the future owing to the land tenure system, absence of suitable building blocks and a stabilisation in the growth of tourism. The population is an ageing one as many young people seek education and employment opportunities on the mainland.

GOVERNMENT. By the Lord Howe Act of 1953, the island was vested in the Crown. The act provides for leases in perpetuity for 'Islanders' (as defined by the Act) but there is provision for transfer of a lease to a non-islander where it is established that there is no islander willing or able to take it on.

In 1954 the former Board of Control was reconstituted as the Lord Howe Island Board. This board, with offices on the island, is charged with the care, control and management of the island. The Lord Howe Island (Amendment) Act, 1981, reconstituted the Board, and currently it consists of the Secretary, Premier's Department, Director, National Parks and Wildlife Service and three Lord Howe Islanders. The Board essentially fulfils the role of a local government authority with day-to-day administrative matters handled by an Administrative Officer. The board is required to manage the Kentia palm seed operation; protect and conserve the fisheries, flora and fauna of the island; protect the island from fire; maintain service infrastructure; control general trade and finance; and supervise land tenure and generally maintain buildings, parks and roads. The board is also responsible for the island's health services. The board generally meets every two months on the island.

In 1982 Lord Howe Island and the outlying region was added to the UNESCO's World Heritage List as an outstanding example of an island system which has developed from submarine volcanic activity. It also has the most southerly coral reef in the world. The island is home to a high proportion of rare and endemic animals, plants and seabirds.

In 1984 research was begun for a Regional

Environmental Plan (published in 1986). The plan sets the framework for the Lord Howe Island Board to make decisions on any future developments, ensuring that the regional environment will be protected as well as the lifestyle of the residents. It replaces the Lord Howe Island Management Scheme which was the planning control since 1976.

A copy of the plan may be obtained from the Administration Office, Lord Howe Island Board, Lord Howe Island, or The Chairman, Lord Howe Island Board, State Office Block, Phillip Street, Sydney 2000.

Police. There are three special constables on the island, but there is little crime.

Liquor. The board conducts a public liquor store, where liquor is retailed at Sydney prices plus freight. The board issues licences for retailing liquor. Applicants state their requirements, which are considered by the board, which then fixes the conditions for the licences.

EDUCATION. The island school offers schooling from kindergarten to Year 6. In 1986 there were 34 enrolments in the primary school. There is a school principal, and four primary teachers provided by the NSW Education Department. Secondary schooling is gained by correspondence with the NSW Correspondence School. However, many secondary students attend boarding schools on the mainland. In 1986 there were eight students doing Years 7 to 12 by correspondence and 13 students resident on the mainland. Approximately half the students in school are children of public servants in Administration.

HEALTH. The Gower Wilson Memorial Hospital has four beds and is staffed by a resident doctor and two nurses. The Department of Health subsidises the health services, including visits at four-monthly intervals by a dentist from NSW. Seriously ill patients can be transferred to the mainland.

LABOUR. One third of the residents (approx. 90 people) work for the State or Federal Government. The Lord Howe Island Board is the largest single employer with 20 employees in 1984. The rest of the workforce is involved mainly in the tourist industry. There is no unemployment although a number of people work only on a part-time basis because of the fluctuating demands of tourism and the Kentia palm industry.

THE LAND. The island is crescent-shaped, about 11 km long and from one to three km in width, with an area of 1455 ha. The two peaks covering about two-thirds of the island are Mt Gower, 875 m, and Mt Lidgbird, 777 m. Mt Gower is usually capped with cloud. Mt Lidgbird rises in a succession of steep terraces and is pyramidal in shape.

Because of the peculiar boulder formation, the island has scarcely more than 120 ha suitable for agriculture. However, this land is extremely rich, and will produce almost any type of sub-tropical vegetation. A Permanent Park Preserve for the protection of flora and fauna is controlled by the board and covers about 75 per cent of the island.

A coral reef on the western side of Lord Howe Island is the most southerly in the world. It encloses a broad lagoon, about six km long by two km wide.

Only islanders are granted perpetual leases of land. Islander residents have first preference for purchase of any houses for sale.

Climate. The average rainfall is 1686 mm with July being the wettest month. Cloud cover causes a much higher rainfall in the mountains than elsewhere on the island. February has a monthly average temperature of 25.1°C, while July and August have the lowest monthly average of 13.5°C. Moderate to high relative humidity is maintained thoughout the year. Winds are predominantly easterly in the summer and south-westerly in the winter.

Flora and fauna. There are many rare unique Howea (Kentia) palms and huge banyans.

At first settlement there were neither mammals nor snakes on the island, but cats, pigs, goats and rats have been subsequently introduced.

The slopes of the mountain are honeycombed with the burrows of the rare Bighill muttonbirds that make this island their home. The commoner species of muttonbirds occupy the dense palm forest on the eastern side of the island — it is virtually one huge muttonbird rookery.

Other birds include the strong-billed magpie, the kingfisher, and the rare woodhen which lives at the top of the mountains. The woodhen is one of the rarest birds in the world. A successful woodhen breeding project has increased the woodhen population to more than 100. The sea birds are protected, as are certain fish which must not be taken from the lagoon or Ned's Beach, where tame fish are fed by hand.

PRIMARY PRODUCTION. The island's only export is the seeds and seedlings of the Kentia palm (Howea). For over 100 years this export has been the major economic contributor to the economy of the island, however in recent years this income has been far outreached by the turnover of tourism. In 1981 the Lord Howe Island Board, which manages the palm industry, decided to sell only seedlings but a study commissioned in 1984 recommended that a joint seeds/seedlings programme be implemented and that coupled with a more vigorous marketing strategy the revenue generated would increase. A nursery manager has been appointed who is currently training islanders to take over the management of the programme. A further study by the staff of the Royal Botanic Gardens in Sydney (1984) has also suggested guidelines which are followed to ensure the viability of the industry. The industry provides local employment for four full-time employees and casual employment for up to 12 people during the collection season. As well as being the only export, Kentia palms are the main souvenirs taken home by tourists.

AGRICULTURE. The island at one time was self-sufficient in agricultural production, however increased population and the development of tourism has meant that most requirements are now imported. Locally produced milk, meat and vegetables make a considerable contribution to supplies. Local fish is also available in stores and restaurants.

TOURISM. Tourism is the major source of revenue and employment. During the peak season of December/January more than 50 per cent of the workforce is involved directly or indirectly in this industry. In the summer a number of workers are recruited for a short season from the mainland. A tourism study in 1984 recommended that future development of tourism should concentrate on capitalising on the island's unique features. Promotion should be directed at special interest groups. Accommodation tends to be in self-contained units and in 1985 the number of beds available was 387. In 1983, 7950 tourists visited the island and a steady four per cent growth is expected. The majority of tourists come from New South Wales.

LOCAL COMMERCE. There are several general trading stores carrying a variety of grocery lines, fruit and vegetables, frozen meat, chemist lines, souvenirs and clothing. There are also several art and craft gift shops. Trading hours are basically 9 to 5. Westpac Banking Corporation and the Commonwealth Bank have agencies in Thompson's Store and the Lagoon Store respectively, and the State Bank of NSW has an agency at the rear of the liquor store. The post office operates on mainland regulations. The liquor store has trading hours from 9 am to 12 noon Monday to Friday and 2.30 pm to 4 pm Tuesday to Friday. Films are shown in the public hall as advertised.

TABLE 1 LORD HOWE ISLAND BOARD BUDGET (Gain/Loss) 1985–86

Revenue producing operations

Seedling industry	$251,700
Investment income	30,000
Sundry income	72,600
Liquor trading	87,970
Total	$442,270

Service operations

Airport	8400
Local authority	−220,195
Tourist industry	28,130
Lighterage	26,000
Total	−139,665

Expenses

Administration	−224,420
Sundry expenses	−61,400
Total	−285,820
Surplus on operations	$16,785

FINANCE. Lord Howe Island derives its income from the sale of palm seedlings, liquor sales, a tourist charge and other charges for services. The NSW Government provides a subsidy to run the hospital, electricity department and administration. The Federal Government gives assistance to maintain the airport and telephone exchange.

TRANSPORT. There are about 16 km of road, the major sections of which are sealed and lit at night. There are about 200 vehicles on the island, including motor cycles. The most popular and convenient form of transport is bicycle, but Mini Mokes and small sedans can be hired locally.

Airlines. A 1000 m airstrip came into use in November 1974. Previously the island had been served by Sandringham flying-boats from Sydney, landing in the lagoon only when tides were suitable.

Lord Howe Island is currently serviced by two airlines, Norfolk Island Airlines operating out of Sydney and Brisbane and Oxley Airlines operating out of Port Macquarie and Coolangatta. The small aircraft take from eight to 10 passengers. During the peak summer season each airline operates several flights a day according to demand but during the low season the number drops to several flights per week.

Shipping. Regular visits are made to the island by cargo ships; the *Sitka* sails from the Port of Yamba on the north coast of New South Wales, and in May 1987 the *Seini* and the *Norfolk Trader* were running trial services out of Sydney. Offloading is done by lighters. No passenger services call at the island. Hetherington Wesfarmers Shipping in Sydney are also agents.

COMMUNICATIONS. The board publishes a regular newsletter, and mainland newspapers arrive on a regular basis. There is an internal telephone network and the island was linked with Australia by radio telephone until 1986. Since then, the establishment of an Aussat satellite station has provided overseas telephone services. A receiving station for television transmissions was also established in 1986 and ABC TV is broadcasted. Most homes also have video recorders.

Radio. A local radio station broadcasts with a staff of volunteers and with contributions from the island board. Programmes include music and discussions. The broadcasts are daily during daylight as volunteers are available. Islanders can also listen to radio programmes from Sydney.

A radio beacon on the island is an important navigational aid to trans-Pacific aircraft.

Weather station. The Lord Howe Island meteorological station is an important link in Pacific sea and air navigation. The station is operated by the Department of Science and Technology.

WATER AND ELECTRICITY. The Department of Aviation runs a diesel-operated generator producing 240 volts for all island needs. Rainwater is collected in tanks; other supplies are sold from chemically treated wells.

MAJOR OFFICE HOLDERS

Members were appointed to the Lord Howe Island Board for a three-year term following elections in February 1988.

Director, National Parks and Wildlife Service, Government appointed member:
 J. Whitehouse
Government appointed member:
 Vivienne K. Ingram
Vice Chairman, elected:
 Bruce McFadyen
Island member, elected:
 Allan Williams
Island member, elected:
 Gower Wilson
Administrative Officer:
 Judith Mortlock
Secretary:
 James Lonergan
Board Head Office:
 Administrative Office,
 Lord Howe Island, NSW 2898. Tel. 2066.

HISTORY. Lord Howe Island was uninhabited when it was first seen by a European, Lieut. H. Lidgbird Ball, of HMS *Supply* on 17 February 1788. Lieut. Ball was en route to Norfolk Island with Lieut. P. G. King to found a settlement there, and named the island Lord Howe's Island after the First Sea Lord of the Admiralty. Lieut. Ball named the nearby rock tower Ball's Pyramid, after himself. The ship did not put in to Lord Howe Island on this sighting, but a boat was sent ashore to investigate on the return journey from Norfolk Island on 13 March when

Ball formally took possession of the island for Britain.

It was visited regularly by ships during the next two years or so, but after the novelty wore off and the infant colony at Port Jackson became more involved in its own affairs, the island was neglected again.

It was not until 1834 that it got its first settlers when three men, their Maori wives and two Maori boys arrived in the whaler *Caroline*, and were put ashore probably at what is now known as Blinky's Beach. Master of the whaler was captain John Blenkinthorpe.

These settlers left after about seven years, and over the next 40 or 50 years other settlers drifted in and established themselves. Some were families from Sydney who grew produce and raised pigs. Some were stranded by shipwreck, or else were ships' deserters. Some made a good living by selling provisions to whaling vessels. The settlers had no legal right of occupancy, but they were not interfered with. Several proposals to make the island a penal colony, like Norfolk Island, came to nothing.

The NSW Government placed Captain Richard Armstrong as Resident magistrate on the island in 1879, and he virtually became island leader, helping to develop among other things an export business in Howea palm seeds. He was also responsible for attracting a schoolteacher to the island, Thomas Wilson, who remained there for many years, although after he left the school remained closed until 1922.

Captain Armstrong's administration resulted, in 1882, in a Commission of Inquiry which was critical of him, but the captain fought the commissioner's findings on appeal and won. He afterwards left the island.

There were further royal commissions in 1911 and 1912, mainly to inquire into complications surrounding the palm seed industry, which was out of control, and the land situation, which was equally unsatisfactory. Settlers had 'permissive occupancy', but no real title to land.

The findings of the commissions resulted in establishment in 1913 of the Lord Howe Island Board of Control, which not only controlled the then declining seed industry but also involved itself with most other aspects of island life. It was not until April 1953 that the land situation was put into some sort of order. This was when NSW brought into force the Lord Howe Island Act, which put the NSW Government in firm control of the island's affairs.

In the intervening years, life on Lord Howe Island went on quietly, broken only occasionally by an unusual event such as the unexpected landing in 1931 of a tiny seaplane flown solo from New Zealand via Norfolk Island by Captain Francis Chichester, who many years later was to be knighted for his equally courageous solo sailing exploits.

Chichester's plane was severely damaged after his landing — the first aircraft to reach Lord Howe — and he remained on the island for nine weeks while he and the islanders repaired the aircraft for its final successful flight to Australia.

In September 1948 a RAAF crew were not so lucky when their Catalina crashed into the bush while attempting to land at Lord Howe and seven crewmen were killed.

An important change in Lord Howe's lifestyle followed the advent of the flying-boat service in 1947, making the island more accessible. The service finished after the opening of the airport in 1974. Another significant development was the reconstitution of the Lord Howe Island Board in 1981.

In 1982 Lord Howe Island was added to UNESCO's World Heritage List in recognition of the region's unique character. In 1984 a Regional Environmental Study was commissioned incorporating policy on tourism, heritage, social and economic environment, marine environment, land resources, bushfire hazard, vegetation and visual assessment. This was published in 1986 and is used as the framework for all future development decisions.

OTHER ISLANDS. A group of rocky islets, called the Admiralties, lie on the northeast side of Lord Howe and are difficult to approach, except in calm weather. They are the nesting-place of myriads of sea-birds. Ball's Pyramid, about 20 km SE of Lord Howe, was named after Lieut. Ball of *Supply*. It is a spectacular, 560 m pinnacle of rock, rising out of the sea. All these islands are part of the Permanent Park Preserve.

FOR THE TOURIST. Virtually all tourists visiting Lord Howe are Australians.

They number about 9000 each year. Guest houses and flats have sufficient facilities to accommodate a total of up to 400 people at a time. Bookings can be made through the NSW Government Travel Centre, 16 Spring St., Sydney, the Lord Howe Island Tourist Centre, 20 Loftus St, Sydney, or travel agents. A number of lodges keep booking offices in Sydney.

Recreation available on the island includes fishing, swimming, scuba diving, bush walking and bicycle riding. A golf course and tennis courts may be used by visitors. Swimming is possible throughout the year and there are some excellent beaches. There are organised island tours available, and round-island boat trips.

Dress on the island is informal and light clothing is advised, although at some times of the year, June, July and August especially, it can be cold at night and cardigans are required. For reef walking sneakers need to be worn.

There are clubs for bowls, and a 9-hole golf course, overlooking mountains and lagoon, all clubs with liquor licences.

The Seventh-day Adventists and Anglicans have churches on the island.

Visitors to the island are fascinated at being able to hand-feed tame fish in the sea at Ned's Beach. Schools of mullet, parrotfish and silver drummer are fed by people who go into the water to knee depth.

Parties who go fishing in boats may be assured of a catch, mostly kingfish. Lodges have packs of locally frozen fish available to take back to Australia.

ACCOMMODATION. All accommodation is listed in alphabetical order. Prices should be obtained directly from manager or agent. The quality is excellent in all establishments listed with all having lovely garden surroundings and being very accessible to beaches.

SELF-CONTAINED APARTMENTS
Broken Banyan, 6 units, BBQ, kitchen, all linen. Pacific Unlimited, 50 York St, Sydney. Tel.: 290 2266.
Coral Court: 3 units, BBQ, bus tours, fishing boat, community kitchen. c/- Lois and Jim Whistler, Lord Howe Island.
Ebbtide: 3 units, BBQ, hire car, bikes, fruit and vegetables supplied. c/- Pacific Un-

limited, 50 York St, Sydney. Tel.: 290 2266.

Hideaway Apartments: 6 units, BBQ, fishing gear. Middle Beach Road, LHI. Tel.: 2054.

Leanda Lei: 14 units, BBQ, hire cars, bikes, cruise boat. c/- Roy Wilson, LHI. Tel.: 2015.

Mary Challis Cottages: 2 units, BBQ. c/- Ginny and Bill Retmock, Post Office, Lord Howe Island. Tel.: 2076.

Milky Way Apartments: 6 units, licensed restaurant, push bikes, milk supplied. Old Settlement Beach, Lord Howe Island Tel.: 2012.

Polynesian Apartments: 4 units, half day bus tour provided. c/- R. and I. Giles, Post Office, Lord Howe Island.

Somerset Holiday Apartments: 14 units, BBQ. c/- C. Williams, Post Office, Lord Howe Island. Tel.: 2061.

Trader Nick's Apartments: 6 units. c/- Lord Howe Island Tourist Centre, Loftus St, Sydney. Tel.: 27 2867.

Waimarie: 2 units, BBQ. J. and M. Fitzgerald, Lagoon Road, Lord Howe Island Tel.: 2057.

GUEST LODGES

Beachcomber: 5 rooms, ensuite bathroom, licensed restaurant, tariff all inclusive. c/- D and U. Payten, Post Office, Lord Howe Island Tel.: 2032.

Blue Lagoon: 15 rooms, ensuite bathroom, bar, restaurant, fishing, boat, bikes, tariff all inclusive or bed and breakfast Lord Howe Island Tourist Centre, 20 Loftus St, Sydney. Tel.: 27 2867.

Lorhiti: 6 rooms, ensuite bathroom, BBQ, bar, tariff all inclusive. c/- D. and G. Owens, Post Office, Lord Howe Island Tel.: 2081.

Ocean View: 18 rooms, ensuite bathroom, bar, restaurant, tennis court, pool, fishing boat, tariff all inclusive. c/- Lord Howe Island Tourist Centre, 20 Loftus St, Sydney. Tel.: 27 2867.

Pinetrees: 85 guests, ensuite bathroom, bar, tennis court, restaurant, tariff all inclusive. c/- Pinetrees, Lord Howe Island. Tel.: 2898.

Seabreeze: 10 rooms, ensuite bathroom, bar, restaurant, dinner, bed and breakfast in tariff. c/- Norfolk Island Airlines, 229 Elizabeth St, Brisbane. Tel.: 229 5872.

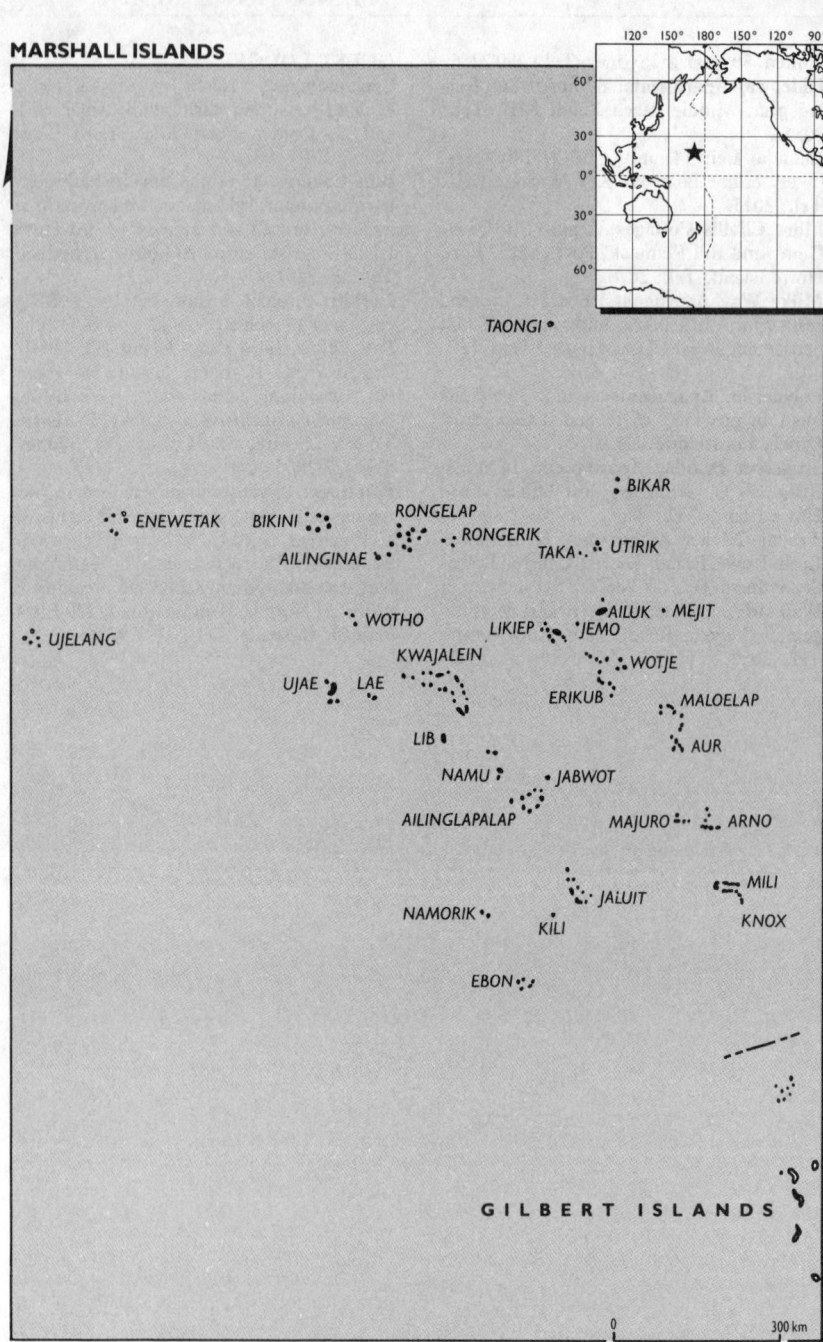

TAONGI •

BIKAR

ENEWETAK   BIKINI
RONGELAP
AILINGINAE   RONGERIK
TAKA   UTIRIK

WOTHO
AILUK   • MEJIT
LIKIEP   •JEMO
UJELANG
KWAJALEIN   WOTJE
UJAE   LAE   ERIKUB   MALOELAP
LIB   AUR
NAMU   JABWOT
AILINGLAPALAP   MAJURO   ARNO

JALUIT   MILI
NAMORIK   KNOX
KILI

EBON

GILBERT ISLANDS

0   300 km

Marshall Islands

Marshall Islands, a republic associated with the US in a compact of free association, consists of a double chain of coral islands, comprising 34 islands and 870 reefs which lie between 5 deg and 15 deg N latitude and 162 deg and 173 deg E longitude The two chains are approximately 208 km apart and lie north-west to south-east. The eastern group is the Ratak (Sunrise) Chain and the western is the Ralik (Sunset) Chain. No island is more than a few metres above sea level.

Total land area of the group is only 171 sq. km and there are several islands of similar dimensions. Some of the atolls enclose lagoons of enormous proportions, although their land areas are quite small. Kwajalein, for instance, the largest in the group, has a total surface area of 2335 sq. km. The administrative centre is Majuro, which had a population of 11,971 in 1980. Estimated population of the entire group in 1986 was 39,060. Local time is 12 hours ahead of GMT, but for the sake of military convenience Kwajalein Missile Range keeps the same time as Western California.

The flag comprises a 24-pointed star and two diagonal rays on a blue field. The 24 points represent the 24 municipalities of the Marshall Islands, while the four longest points also represent the capital Majuro and the sub-centres of Ebeye, Jaluit and Wotje, In addition, the long points also form a cross, signifying the importance of Christianity in these islands. The rays represent the parallel chains of islands which make up the group: the white ray standing for the Ratak (Sunrise) Chain and the orange for the Ralik (Sunset) Chain.

Public holidays include New Year's Eve, New Year's Day, Good Friday, Constitution Day (1 May), Memorial Day (last Monday in May), Labour Day (first Monday in September), United Nations Day (24 October), Thanksgiving Day (last Thursday in November), and Christmas Day.

THE PEOPLE. Marshall Islanders are categorised as Micronesian in the wide sense and as Marshallese more specifically. Relatively little is known about the pre-contact history of the people. They are thought, like other Pacific islanders, to have originated in South-East Asia and to have established themselves on their scattered islands centuries before European voyagers reached this area. Early accounts depict Marshallese society as having much in common with other Micronesian islands, such as the Carolines. Chieftainship was strong and material culture — given the paucity of natural resources — was relatively advanced. Early Marshallese were regarded as superb canoe builders, for example. Society is organised along matrilineal lines: chiefly titles and rights to property descend through the line of the mother. A rather complex class structure still exists. At the lower levels are the *alap* (headmen) of clans of common status, directing their affairs and speaking for them in larger councils. At the higher levels are the chiefs, *iroij*, of families of elevated status, of whom the highest are the paramount chiefs. Between these extremes are chiefs and families of varying status.

Like other parts of Micronesia, however, the Marshall Islands have been subjected to a number of colonial influences, and these have left obvious effects on the native society.

The population of the group has increased quite rapidly in recent years, from 14,163 in 1958 to 30,873 in 1980, then from 39,060 in

1986 to 43,355 in 1989, and is expected to be 45,569 by 1990. Majuro has a population density of 3142 per square mile. About 66 per cent of the total population lives on Majuro and Ebeye Island, Kwajalein.

Nationality. As members of a now 'sovereign and self-governing nation', Marshallese people are citizens of their own country, having finally shed the ambiguous status which existed during the many years of the US Trusteeship.

Language. The languages spoken in the Marshall Islands are branches of the great Malayo-Polynesian language family. Dialects vary from island to island. The Marshalls as a whole are said to have closer affinities with Polynesia than other Micronesian islands have. Marshallese is the official language but English, encouraged by early missionaries and further encouraged by US administrators, is widely spoken. There are still some older people who can speak Japanese, but very few who can speak German.

Religion. In common with other Micronesians, the Marshallese are overwhelmingly Christian, having been missionised by both Germans and Americans. Protestants are in the majority but Catholicism is also represented, as are a number of lesser Christian denominations: Mormons, Seventh-Day Adventists, Assembly of God, etc. No recent figures on religious affiliation are available, but a de facto census in 1973 listed the population as 90.1 per cent Protestant, 8.5 per cent Roman Catholic and 0.5 per cent other religions.

Lifestyle. The influence of the US, especially on Majuro and Kwajalein, has been vast, affecting almost everything from diet to social behaviour. In the more remote atolls this is still present though far less pronounced. Despite this, traditional chiefs still command a good deal of respect, and their importance has been acknowledged by the constitution of the republic.

Recreation. Sports are mainly those introduced from the US. Traditional crafts such as weaving and carving are still practised, but the products are for sale rather than purely recreational. Stick charts, once used to train navigators, are still produced.

GOVERNMENT. An elected President is both head of state and in charge of a cabinet of ministers, whom he appoints. There is a legislature of 33 members known as the *Nitijela*, elected every four years, in which all legislative power is centralised, there being neither provinces nor states in the Marshalls. A 12-member Council of Chiefs (Iroij) has a consultative function on matters relating to land and custom. Each of the 24 inhabited atolls has a local government.

JUSTICE. The Marshalls have a Supreme Court, a High Court, a district court and community courts.

The Supreme Court consists of three judges. The district court is composed of one Presiding Judge and one Associate Judge who have been appointed for 10-year terms. The district court's area of jurisdiction comprises the entire nation, but in criminal matters it is limited to offences for which the maximum penalty is less than three years' confinement and fines of $2000. It may hear appeals from the community courts.

There are about 20 community courts throughout the republic whose jurisdiction is limited to their respective communities. Criminal jurisdiction is limited to those offences which involve a possible sentence of not more than six months and a fine of not more than $200. A judge of a community court is not required to have proper legal training or experience. Appointments, made on the basis of local government recommendations, are for not more than four years. Kwajalein Community Court Judges are appointed for only one year terms.

A special court, the Traditional Rights Court, holds hearings and determines opinions on substantial questions relating to titles, land rights or other items of traditional practice or customary law referred to it by trial judges from all courts except the Supreme Court.

Attorney General. The functions of this office include: providing legal advice to the Cabinet; litigation, criminal and civil prosecution and defence work on behalf of the government; maintaining responsibility for the republic's police department.

Legal services. Legal services in the Republic are provided by the Public Defender and the Micronesian Legal Services Corporation. The latter is a Micronesia-wide organisation, with a central administrative office in

Saipan. During 1985 the MLSC handled 142 cases, ranging from war claims to divorce and from employment disputes to nuclear damage claims.

Department of Public Safety. This is a department of the Ministry of Justice and is charged with the responsibilities of both a police department and a fire department. During 1985, 854 criminal cases were reported to the department for investigation, including 161 felonies. Some 560 cases were closed. Some 16 persons were sentenced and committed to jail between January 1984 and September 1985.

DEFENCE. Defence in the Marshall Islands, as in the other Micronesian countries which were once part of the US Trust Territory, is the prerogative of the USA. The Statement of Agreed Principles for Free Association (Hilo, Hawaii, 1978) declares that 'the United States will have full authority and responsibility for security and defense matters in or relating to Micronesia, including the establishment of necessary military facilities and the exercise of appropriate operating rights ... The authority and responsibility will be assured for 15 years, and thereafter as mutually agreed.' In the case of the Republic of Palau (Belau), however, the period of responsibility is 50 years. The Kwajalein Missile Range in the Marshall Islands is to be operated for a period of up to 30 years.

EDUCATION. Primary executive authority for education is vested in the Education Minister. Since 1979 the Minister of Education has been the Hon. Tom D. Kijiner. General direction, supervision and operation of the department is carried out by the Secretary of Education, appointed by the Public Service. The Department of Education is organised in four programme divisions: Elementary and Secondary; Post-Secondary and Higher Education; Programmes and Development; and Administrative Services.

Schools and enrolments. During the 1984–85 school year the Department of Education operated 70 public elementary schools and two public secondary schools, providing cost-free instruction to a total of 8372 students, of whom 7517 were elementary. Some 354 teachers were employed in the public schools. In addition a number of private schools operate in the Marshall Islands under charters granted by the Minister of Education. During 1984–85, 16 private elementary schools and five private secondary schools enrolled 3008 students, 2260 of whom were elementary. There were 163 teachers in private schools. Most private schools are church-affiliated.

Instructional programmes. The elementary school system provides a basic education to all children from ages six to 14. Instruction in both Marshallese language (Kajin-Majol) and English is provided, in addition to mathematics, science, social science, art and health. Students may then progress to four years of high school, although secondary education is not universal in the Marshall Islands. Admission to public high schools is selective. Most students admitted require extensive remedial studies in English before they are considered capable of secondary school studies.

The Department of Education also operates the public library at Majuro. This contains a collection of 7600 titles, including an extensive collection of material related to the Pacific region. An average of 800 readers per month use the library.

LABOUR. The Government is a significant employer of labour in the Marshall Islands, though most of the labour force is located in two areas, Majuro and Ebeye on Kwajalein. The subsistence sector is relatively large, especially on the outer islands. At the 1980 Census, 3560 workers were regarded as taking part in the 'money economy', while 3002 were classified as participating in the 'subsistence economy'.

In 1982 there were 4753 Micronesians and 2414 non-Micronesians in employment. Mean income for public sector employees was $4141 and for private sector employees, $2080. The annual income for approximately half of all employees was in the range $1001–5000. During Census week in 1980, 2646 people were in employment on Majuro atoll and 1101 in employment on Kwajalein.

Most recent analysis of employment structure is based on the 1980 census when, of a total of 6598 workers, 3044 or 46.1 per cent were in agriculture; 926 or 14.1 per cent in professional or related services; 591 or nine per cent in public administration; 606 or 9.2 per cent in business or repair services; and

543 or 8.2 per cent in wholesale and retail trades, restaurants and hotels.

Peace Corps. Since October 1985 the Peace Corps serving in Micronesia has been reduced in size. At the end of 1985 there were 15 volunteers serving in the Marshall Islands, most of whom were engaged in health projects. The Peace Corps is negotiating separate agreements with the governments of the Marshall Islands, the Federated States of Micronesia and Palau.

HEALTH. Health care services in the Marshall Islands are provided by two hospitals and 69 dispensaries. The hospitals, one each on Majuro and Ebeye, provide primary and secondary care on an inpatient and outpatient basis, including surgery, dentistry, maternity, physical therapy and mental health services. The 69 dispensaries provide only rudimentary medical care.

Public health services including immunisation and family planning are provided in the Public Health Clinics of the two hospitals. The outer islands are visited by health teams from Majuro.

Diseases. Reported cases of notifiable diseases are led by gastroenteritis, 1476 cases in 1985, followed by influenza with 825 cases and conjunctivitis with 394. Sexually transmitted diseases accounted for 240 cases. The incidence of diabetes in the Marshall Islands is high and shows cause for great concern. Three out of every four inpatients at hospitals are diabetics. The 1982 statistics show that nearly 18 per cent of the population over 40 years of age is a diabetic.

Causes of death are led by respiratory diseases, with 55 in 1985. There were 37 deaths from heart disease and 18 from cancer in that year. The infant mortality rate was 33 per 1000 live births.

The crude birth rate in 1984 was 35.9 per 1000 of population and the death rate 3.6 per 1000.

Protected water supply and excreta disposal systems are limited to housing areas for Government employees, hospitals and to a few Government and mission schools. In the Marshall Islands population served by both protected water supply and excreta disposal numbered 10,050 in 1985, 9150 of whom were on Ebeye, the dormitory area for the Kwajalein Missile Range. Without chlorination, no water supplies except those on the missile range can be considered safe for consumption.

THE LAND. The total land area of the Marshall Islands is 171 sq. km scattered over about two million sq. km of ocean. Largest of its many atolls is Kwajalein, made up of about 90 islets around a lagoon 120 km long and 24 km wide. Other significant atolls include Rongelap (land area 4.9 sq. km, lagoon area 623.9 sq. km), Enewetak (land area 3.6 sq. km, lagoon area 624.3 sq. km) and Maloelap (land area 6.1 sq. km, lagoon area 604.3 sq. km). Lib, Jabwot, Kili, Mejit and Jemo are low coral islands without lagoons. Most of them are less than one sq. km in area but Kili has a population of 489 (1980). The distance from Taongi in the north of the group to Ebon in the south is about 1300 km.

Since they are all either atolls or raised coral islands, elevation is slight. Highest point in the entire group is on Likiep, 10 metres above sea level.

Soils on coral islands or atolls are generally poor, requiring much persistence for the production of even basic crops, but coconut, pandanus and breadfruit grow easily.

Climate. The predominant influence is that of the north-east trade winds and temperature variations are slight, although the northern islands are slightly cooler than the southern. Rainfall also varies somewhat from north to south; Ujelang has an average of 2030 mm annually while Jaluit, further south, has twice that amount. Mean monthly temperature in the southern islands is 27°C and mean humidity 85 per cent.

Flora and fauna. Poor atoll soils support only a limited range of plants and the growth of vegetation is hampered also by saltwater spray which sweeps over the islands during the season of the north-east trades, killing or seriously inhibiting plant growth. Even by atoll standards the vegetation of the Marshall Islands is poor.

Indigenous fauna on most atolls is scant, although rats, pigs and fowls have been around almost long enough to qualify for indigenous status. Land birds are not common although sea birds will sometimes nest on the more remote atolls. Land reptiles in the Marshalls are limited to geckoes and skinks. Marine fauna is more plentiful and the diver or snorkeller will probably be well rewarded, even in some of the more contaminated lagoons. There are still many sharks in the lagoon at Kwajalein despite the frequency of the missiles.

Land tenure. In this matrilineal society, each individual belongs to the *bwij* (clan) of her or his mother, and has certain rights to the land and other property of the *bwij*. Land tenure, therefore, is based on customary forms and ownership is limited to Marshallese, but it may be leased to noncitizens.

PRIMARY PRODUCTION. Lack of fertile soil is one factor which keeps agricultural production in the Marshall Islands at a low level; others are a concentration of much of the labour force in the 'high-paying' areas of Majuro and Kwajalein and an excessive reliance on food aid from the US.

The country produces only one agricultural crop of any economic importance, copra, which in 1985 amounted to 4553 tonnes to a total value of $905,000. This is the lowest annual production since 1973, and the Department of Agriculture admits that present levels of production are running about 24 per cent below normal. The atoll of Arno in the Ratak chain produces the most, averaging 901 short tons per year. Per capita income from copra in 1985 was $49.90. An estimated $33,000 worth of cash crops, including banana, papaya, pandanus and breadfruit was sold in markets in Majuro and Ebeye. A farm operated by the Taiwanese Agriculture and Trade Mission at Laura on Majuro atoll produced 6000 kilos of assorted vegetables in 1985.

Livestock. Figures received from the Department of Agriculture — which should be treated cautiously — show the livestock count to be 25,000 chickens, 18,000 pigs, 10,000 ducks and 40 goats. The department maintains pigs, goats, ducks and geese for breeding purposes.

Fisheries. The vast marine resources of the group are as yet largely unexploited, although Japanese fishing fleets are active, landing 22,661.5 tonnes of tuna, mostly skipjack, in 1983. The previous year fishermen of the Majuro co-operative landed 38,389 kilos of all species. As the amount of fish taken by overseas fleets increases, the catch by local fishermen decreases. Like many Pacific islands, the Marshalls continues to rely on imports of canned fish for most of its needs. A number of private companies have begun joint venture projects in fishing. Trochus shell processing and black pearl culture are being attempted, as are oyster and clam farming. The development and protection of the country's marine resources is a major concern.

TOURISM. If tourism in the Federated States of Micronesia is in its infancy, tourism in the Marshall Islands has barely been conceived. There are indications, however, that the Government is seriously considering the economic advantages to be gained from tourism development and promotion since at present they cannot be gained from much else. This new seriousness can be inferred from the following details. In 1984, 1882 tourists came to the Marshalls. In 1985, 1791 came. While these are hardly record-breaking statistics, the tourism division takes heart from the fact that Europeans are beginning to make up a significant percentage of tourists and sees this as a direct result of the division's good record in answering its correspondence. In 1985 the tourism division received and answered 120 letters.

A report on tourism has been prepared for the Marshalls by the United Nations Development Programme and the World Tourism Organisation, and in the light of its recommendations 'a tough new anti-litter law is being enforced in the Republic'. One of the penalties for offenders is 'bringing to the court several sacks of trash'. The subsequent fate of the sacks of trash is not recorded. The agriculture division is said to be involved with beautification projects in Majuro and Ebeye.

New restaurants and at least one new hotel are being constructed in Majuro, but the prospects for tourism were not aided by the withdrawal in 1985 of both South Pacific Airways and Air Nauru from service to the Marshalls. There are 25 airstrips in the islands, serving 22 inhabited atolls. Some atolls have two.

OVERSEAS TRADE. Given the country's limited resources it is not surprising that the Marshall Islands suffers from a severe trade imbalance. This deficit was at its worst in

TABLE 1 COMMERCIAL IMPORTS BY COMMODITY GROUP, 1979–1982 ($000s)

	1979	1980	1981	1982
Food and live animals	4221	4678	5183	5215
Beverages and tobacco	1475	1792	2234	1884
Crude materials	235	342	407	192
Mineral fuels and lubricants[a]	2086	2718	3317	3684
Animal and vegetable oils	19	22	23	33
Chemical products	611	657	703	681
Manufactured goods	2252	2976	3548	1525
Machinery and transport equipment	1676	2013	4274	1966
Other manufactures	1663	1957	2519	1031
Total	14,238	17,155	22,208	16,211

[a] *Excluding re-exports.*

1981, when imports amounted to $22.2 m and exports to only $2.9 m, a trade deficit of $19.24 m. In 1983 imports amounted to $20.2 m and exports to $2.2 m and in 1984 the respective figures were $17.5 m and $3.1 m.

In 1982 exports went to only four recipients, all with a US connection: Guam, Hawaii, mainland US and other Trust Territory countries. Major sources of imports were: Guam, mainland US, Japan, Hawaii and Australia. In 1983 coconuts accounted for about 99 per cent of exports. Handicrafts accounted for the remainder. Table 1 shows the country's main imports.

In 1987 the Marshall Islands began to consolidate economic agreements with the People's Republic of China in an attempt to slightly alleviate its excessive dependence on aid from the US.

FINANCE. Funding for government operational support and capital improvement programmes in the Marshall Islands (and other Trust Territory countries) was derived from three major sources: (1) an annual grant provided from funding appropriated to the Secretary of the Interior of the United States; (2) Federal categorical grants provided on a matching or outright basis. In effect the Trust Territorty was treated as a state for

participation in federal programmes; (3) tax revenues levied by the governments of the Marshall Islands.

Revenues for 1984 included: Department of Interior funds, $13.34 m; Federal grant funds, $5.58 m; CIP funds $3.88 m; and local revenues and reimbursements, $16.69 m. Local revenues are raised from taxes on income, imports, gross business revenues, fees and utilities. Expenditures in 1984 amounted to $22.23 m. Tables 2 and 3 shows revenues and expenditures for the years 1981–84.

In 1986 the Department of the Interior annual grant was $10.94 m, $0.46 m less than the previous year. An additional grant of $857,000 was made for Enewetak support and one of $1.66 m for the Bikini resettlement study.

Under an agreement in October 1986 the Marshall Islands had been promised funding for the Compact of Free Association retrospective to 1985. A week later, however, the US Congress vetoed the arrangement, removing a potential $16 m from the Marshalls' treasury. With the dismantling of the Trust Territory, the nuclear compensation fund of $150 m has been turned over to the Marshalls Government, and invested with several large US finance companies. A $10 m development

TABLE 2 RECURRENT EXPENDITURES BY PROGRAM AREA, 1981–84 ($000s)

	FY 1981	FY 1982	FY 1983	FY 1984
General fund				
Health services	3220	3275	3880	4342
Education	2874	2974	2589	2774
Transportation and communications	2228	1795	1348	1678
Interior and outer island affairs	164	236	213	138
Resources and development	1453	1119	702	633
Internal security	653	766	743	742
Administration /chief secretary office	190	208	265	266
Finance	399	709	1920	773
Public works	4135	4390	3589	2578
Social services	234	253	170	156
Foreign affairs	536	411	362	418
Cabinet	355	439	429	564
Nitijela	614	648	557	741
Council of Iroij	102	104	105	139
Auditor General	38	75	42	73
Public Service Commission	181	135	288	233
Public Defender	51	57	49	57
Judiciary	54	107	196	274
Electoral Commission(a)	—	—	—	90
Total	17,463	17,701	17,447	16,651
US federal grants(b)	6166	6252	5444	5582
Other	1030	1267	730	—
Total	24,659	25,220	23,621	22,233

(a) The expenditures of the Electoral Commission were included in those of Internal Affairs until 1983.
(b) These are authorisations, which do not equal expenditures.

fund has also been created to offset the cut in federal programmes.

Income tax. The Government is attempting to generate additional domestic revenues. During 1985 the *Nitijela* passed legislation to increase the income tax rate from six to eight per cent on the first $11,000 earned and from 10 to 12 per cent on earnings above $11,000. This measure yielded an additional $500,000 in revenue in fiscal year 1985.

Currency. Official currency is the US dollar. Credit cards are not yet accepted in the Marshall Islands.

Banking. Residents have access to banking institutions in Guam, Hawaii and the US mainland as well as branch banks in the Marshall Islands. There is a Bank of the Marshall Islands as well as a branch of the Bank of

TABLE 3 RECURRENT REVENUES, 1981–84 ($000s)

	FY 1981	FY 1982	FY 1983	FY 1984
Local revenue				
Income tax	2011	2448	2747	3050
Business gross revenue tax	1928	1808	2190	1670
Import tax	1009	1270	1912	2612
Sales tax	281	261	231	197
Fuel tax	39	91	—	694
Business license fees	—	—	144	146
Total indirect tax	3257	3430	4447	5319
Fishing rights income	1000	1275	763	842
Interest income	—	—	22	7
Loan repayments	—	—	54	—
Non-tax revenues (fees and sales)	881	1084	993	1223
Seaport, shipping & telecom receipts	—	—	—	930
Total	7149	8237	9056	11,371
US grants				
Basic grant	7831	9769	10,484	11,277
Fuel supplement	828	343	—	—
Transition funds and other	600	537	510	241
Special maintenance	430	730	712(a)	1821
Federal grants	6166	6252	5444(a)	5582
Total US revenues	15,855	17,631	17,150	18,921
Total revenue	23,004	25,631	26,206	30,292

(a) Pro-rata for 12 months.

Guam in downtown Majuro. Banking hours are: Monday–Thursday 10 am–3 pm, Friday 10 am–5 pm.

TRANSPORT. There are 152 km of primary (paved) roads in the islands, mostly on Majuro and Ebeye. In 1985, 967 registered private motor vehicles were using these roads, including 447 sedans, 261 pick-up trucks and 45 buses. Motor cyclists are a minority in the Marshalls — only 37 scooters were registered. There are generous numbers of taxis on both Majuro and Ebeye. There is a regular bus service to and from Laura community, at the western end of the atoll, along what is said to be the longest paved road in Micronesia.

Airlines. The national flag carrier, Airline of the Marshall Islands, flies to the Federated States of Micronesia and to Nadi, Fiji via Kiribati and Tuvalu, using a British built HS748. Continental Airlines flies Honolulu–Majuro and on to Guam via the FSM. Air Tungaru flies weekly between Majuro and Tarawa in Kiribati. Two other carriers, Air Nauru and South Pacific Island Airways, discontinued services to the Marshalls in 1985. The outer islands of the group are well served by air services and airstrips. In 1985 there were 25 airstrips and another five about to be constructed.

Port facilities. Majuro's harbour and port are host to a variety of international and inter-island craft, including bulk cargo vessels, international fishing fleets, passenger-carrying copra boats, small local fishing boats, which can be launched from a number of ramps in the lagoon, and a growing number of cruising yachts which have to clear customs here. Majuro's old dock is about half-way down the western side of the commercial and business area, while its new dock is at the southern tip, just beyond the government buildings.

Shipping services. Nauru Pacific Line operates regular cargo services from Melbourne to Nauru, Majuro and Tarawa (Kiribati). NYK (Japan) Shipping line operates monthly between Japanese and Micronesian ports, including Majuro and the FSM. PM&O lines operate monthly between US west coast and Pacific island ports, including Majuro, Ebeye and the FSM.

COMMUNICATIONS. A recently installed satellite communications station permits telephone calls to be made to and received from most international numbers. In 1984, 19,983 international calls passed through the country's telephone system, accounting for $600,839 of the total communications revenue of $681,744. Telegraphic and telex services are available seven days a week. The telephone exchange is open Monday–Friday only. The Marshall Islands uses the US postal service and domestic mail rates apply for letters between the Marshalls and the US and Guam. However, the country also issues its own well-designed stamps and philatelic issues are seen as a potentially useful source of revenue. The main post office is open on weekdays and Saturday mornings. Majuro's US zipcode is 96960.

Radio, TV. The Government-owned radio station WSZO broadcasts in both Marshallese and English, including news services from Radio Australia and the Voice of America. There is also a small privately-owned FM station, Radio KUP 65. The Marshalls Broadcasting Co. (private) operates a subscriber-funded TV station.

Newspapers. The *Marshall Islands Journal*, containing items in both Marshallese and English, is published every Friday.

WATER AND ELECTRICITY. A public water supply, treated and safe for drinking, is available throughout downtown Majuro (the DUD area) only. Elsewhere, except for the missile range at Kwajalein, water is unfit for consumption. Electricity depends entirely upon imported petroleum for its generation. In 1984 total power demand from the Majuro power plant was 7.57 m kW hours, fuelled by 1.5 m gallons of petroleum products at an estimated cost of $1.17 m.

MAJOR OFFICE HOLDERS
President:
  Amata Kabua
Minister of Foreign Affairs:
  Anton deBrum
Minister of Finance:

Henchi Balos
Chief Justice, Supreme Court:
  Harold W. Burnett
Chairman of the Council of Iroij:
  Michael Kabua

GOVERNMENT MINISTRIES AND DEPARTMENTS
Office of the President, Majuro, Republic of the Marshall Islands 96960 Tel.: 3445
Minister of Education, Majuro, Republic of the Marshall Islands 96960 Tel.: 3445
Minister of Public Health, Majuro, Republic of the Marshall Islands 96960 Tel.: 3445
Minister of Foreign Affairs, Majuro, Republic of the Marshall Islands 96960 Tel.: 3445
Minister of Justice, Majuro, Republic of the Marshall Islands 96960 Tel.: 3445
Minister of Transportation & Communication, Majuro, Republic of the Marshall Islands 96960 Tel.: 3445
Minister of Resources & Development, Majuro, Republic of the Marshall Islands 96960 Tel.: 3445
Minister of Social Services, Majuro, Republic of the Marshall Islands 96960 Tel.: 3445
Minister of Interior and Outer Islands, Majuro, Republic of the Marshall Islands 96960 Tel.: 3445
Minister of Public Works, Majuro, Republic of the Marshall Islands 96960 Tel.: 3445
Minister of Finance, Majuro, Republic of the Marshall Islands 96960 Tel.: 3445
Chief Secretary, Cabinet, Majuro, Republic of the Marshall Islands 96960 Tel.: 3769
Secretary, Transportation & Communication, Majuro, Republic of the Marshall Islands 96960 Tel.: 3621
Secretary, Resources & Development, Majuro, Republic of the Marshall Islands 96960 Tel.: 3206
Secretary, Health Services, Majuro, Republic of the Marshall Islands 96960 Tel.: 3230
Secretary, Education, Majuro, Republic of the Marshall Islands 96960 Tel.: 3202
Secretary, Finance, Majuro, Republic of the Marshall Islands 96960 Tel.: 3320
Secretary, Public Works, Majuro, Republic of the Marshall Islands 96960 Tel.: 3431

Secretary, Foreign Affairs, Majuro, Republic of the Marshall Islands 96960 Tel.: 3181

Secretary, Interior and Outer Islands, Majuro, Republic of the Marshall Islands 96960 Tel.: 3264

Secretary, Social Services, Majuro, Republic of the Marshall Islands 96960 Tel.: 3351

Secretary, Justice, Majuro, Republic of the Marshall Islands 96960 Tel.: 3445

Judiciary, Chief Justice, Majuro, Republic of the Marshall Islands 96960 Tel.: 3652

Nitijela (Parliament), Speaker, Majuro, Republic of the Marshall Islands 96960 Tel.: 3621

Nitijela (Parliament), Vice Speaker, Majuro, Republic of the Marshall Islands 96960 Tel.: 3621

MARSHALL ISLANDS HISTORY.

Little is known about the pre-history of the group. European contact with the islands began when the first Spanish ships were groping their way across the Pacific in the early 16th century, but there was no continuous contact until the third decade of the 19th century.

Taongi, the northernmost atoll, was the first island to be discovered by Europeans. This was a landfall of the Loaisa expeditions in 1526. In the following year, three ships under Alvaro de Saavedra, sent from Mexico to seek news in the Moluccas of the Magellan and Loaisa expeditions were also among the Marshalls. Two of them were subsequently lost. The next visitors were the four ships of the Legaspi expedition, proceeding to the Philippines in 1565. One of them was almost wrecked in the group. A year later, some of the crew of the ship *San Jeronimo*, which was taking supplies to Legaspi, staged a mutiny while among the Marshall Islands. The pilot, Lope Martin, and two dozen fellow conspirators were marooned on an atoll that has since been identified as Ujelang. They were never seen again, although the Spanish explorer Mendana touched at a nearby atoll in 1568 following the discovery of the Solomons.

Two centuries then passed before the next Europeans were among the Marshalls, as the Spanish galleons sailing from Mexico to the Philippines were instructed to proceed to the northward of the dangerous low-lying islands. In 1767, Captain Samuel Wallis, the discoverer of Tahiti, chanced on Rongerik and Rongelap in sailing northward to reach Tinian in the Marianas. Twenty-one years later, the *Scarborough* (Captain John Marshall) and *Charlotte* (Captain Thomas Gilbert) sighted Mili, Arno, Majuro, Aur, Maloelap, Erikub and Wotje Atolls in proceeding to China from Botany Bay. The name Marshall Islands was later applied to the group as a whole by the Russian hydrographer A. J. Krusenstern. In 1792, Captain E. H. Bond sighted Namorik in the British ship *Royal Admiral*. The Russian explorer Otto von Kotzebue made an extensive examination of the group in 1817 and gave the names Ralik and Ratak to the western and eastern chains respectively. He revisited the Ratak chain on his second voyage to the Pacific in 1824. His accounts of the Marshalls are easily the most comprehensive of the early 19th century.

From the 1820s onwards, the Marshalls were visited by American whalers seeking food and water. Some of these occasionally left men ashore to become beachcombers and, later, traders. American and Hawaiian Protestant missionaries arrived in the group in the 1860s, sent by the Hawaiian Evangelical Association, an auxiliary of the American Board of Commissioners for Foreign Missions. About this time, J. C. Godeffroy und Sohn, of Samoa, established trading stations on Mili, Aur, Jaluit, Ebon and Namorik. A few years later, two other German companies, Hernsheim & Co. and A. Capelle & Co., were also in business there. Copra was their principal interest.

German protectorate. In 1878, Germany secured a coaling station on Jaluit by a treaty negotiated with the island chiefs during a visit by a German warship. A German consul was appointed to Jaluit in the same year. In 1886, by agreement with Great Britain, the Marshall Islands became a German protectorate. Later, the Germans formed the Jaluit Gesellschaft which bought out two foreign competitors based in San Francisco and Auckland. However, Burns, Philp & Co. of Sydney, which had been trading in the group for some years, continued to do so, sending a ship there once every two months. This prompted the Germans to charge discriminatory port dues, but the Sydney company remained in the group until World War I.

In 1906, the German Government took over the rights of the Jaluit Gesellschaft (which had expanded into the Carolines) to strengthen its position in the South Seas. From that year, the Marshalls were administered from Rabaul, capital of Germany's colony in New Guinea. This situation continued until the outbreak of World War I when the Marshalls, like the Marianas (except Guam) and the Carolines, were occupied by the Japanese.

Japanese administration. After the war, the Marshall Islands were mandated to Japan by the League of Nations, together with the other occupied islands. The group was administered as a separate district. The Marshallese were given little voice in their own government; but the copra industry was left in their hands. However, the copra had to be exported to Japan at a price fixed by the Japanese.

From 1935, when Japan withdrew from the League of Nations, the Marshalls, like the other mandated archipelagos, were fortified and provided with facilites for Japan's adventure in the Pacific in World War II. It was from there that the Japanese attacked and invaded Nauru, Ocean Island and Kiribati (Gilbert Islands). The Allies were unable to launch a counter-attack on the area until strategic islands in Kiribati had been occupied in late 1943. Kwajalein Atoll was the first island to be captured — in February 1944. The concentration of fire directed at Kwajalein exceeded any artillery barrage in the two World Wars.

US Trusteeship. The Marshall Islands became part of the United States Trust Territory of the Pacific Islands in July 1947, following three years of American military administration. In 1946, the Americans had used Bikini Atoll for atomic bomb tests, having resettled its inhabitants on Rongerik. Isolated Enewetak Atoll was chosen for further tests in December 1947, and its 146 people were provided with new homes on Ujelang. The first US hydrogen bomb was exploded at Enewetak on 1 March, 1954; two others were detonated in the following few weeks. Further tests were carried out in 1956, 1958 and 1962. Meanwhile, the US spent billions of dollars developing Kwajalein as an anti-missile base, and many Marshallese were attracted to work there by the high wages. Bikini Atoll was announced to be fit again for human habitation in August 1968, and by 1971 two of its islets had been cleared of debris and preparations were under way for the Bikinians (who had latterly been living on Kili) to be resettled there. About 140 were allowed to return.

Enewetak Atoll was formally handed back to its original inhabitants in September 1976, and the US authorities undertook to carry out a $20 million clean-up and rehabilitation programme over the ensuing three or four years. In 1980 about 550 people returned from Ujelang.

Bikini aftermath. Tests conducted at Bikini in 1977 revealed that despite a $3 million decontamination project, Bikini groundwater was still too radioactive for human consumption, as were the coconuts, fruit and vegetables grown in Bikini soil. As a result, early in 1978, the US Department of the Interior asked Congress for $15 million to resettle the Bikinians once again. In 1983 the majority were still at Kili, but others were scattered in small communities about the Marshall Islands, including Majuro, Ebeye and Jaluit atoll. Bikini cannot be resettled for at least 20 years, but other estimates range from 30 to 90 years. Enui Island in Bikini atoll could be resettled in the near future, but all the risks have not yet been determined.

In an attempt to dispose of radioactive debris, the Americans dug a huge pit on the islet of Runit on Enewetak in 1980. They buried 84,150 cubic metres of radioactive sand and debris mixed with cement and over the crater built a concrete dome 113 m in diameter, 7.6 m high and nearly 0.5 m thick. Nuclear scientists say the contents of the pit will remain radioactive for 25,000 years.

It was also revealed at the same time that inhabitants of Rongelap and Utirik, more than 160 km from Bikini, were developing thyroid problems as a result of the 1954 explosion.

Settlement of compensation claims as a result of the US nuclear testing in the Marshalls is still proceeding, and is associated with the various agreements being made as part of the Compact of Free Association package. There are also outstanding court cases.

Compact of Free Association. Following a lengthy period of negotiation with the US on the matter of self-government, an issue protracted by problems peculiar to these islands, the Marshalls and the US signed the Compact of Free Association, under which the US retained responsibility for defence and especially the use of the missile-testing range at Kwajalein. In return for this, the Marshalls will receive some $700 million in economic aid over 15 years. The Compact, signed in 1982, did not come into full effect until late 1986, when the UN Trusteeship was finally terminated. (See also Caroline Islands history in Palau and Federated States of Micronesia sections.)

Further information. Works devoted exclusively to the Marshall Islands are not numerous. These are among the most useful. Francis X. Hezel, *The First Taint of Civilization: A History of the Caroline and Marshall Islands in Pre-Colonial Days, 1521–1885*, (Honolulu, 1983). Gerald Knight, *Man This Reef*, (Majuro, 1983). Ann Nakano, *Broken Canoe: Conversations and Observations in Micronesia* (New York, 1983). Robert C. Kiste, *The Bikinians: A Study in Forced Migration*, (Minneapolis, 1974). Micronitor News and Printing Co., *The Marshall Islands Guidebook*, (Majuro, 1984).

MAJOR ISLANDS IN DETAIL

Majuro Atoll has the largest population in the Marshalls and is the republic's administrative centre. It also has one of the highest population densities of any municipal area in the Pacific islands. The administrative area is frequently referred to as DUD, initials which stand for Dalap, Uliga and Darrit, three small islands which were joined by landfill creating the impression of one long, narrow island. Most of DUD is only about 200 metres wide. The atoll as a whole consists of 64 islets around a lagoon of 113.9 sq. km. Virtually all of the Marshall Islands hotels and other tourist facilities are located on Majuro, as are most of the restaurants and other necessary services.

A good sealed road links most of the former islets so that it is possible to drive for many kilometres from the expanding business and commercial centre, where the modern port is, out past the modern airport to Laura, where there is a lengthy break in the reef.

The airport was formerly on Dalap, near the business centre, but this area is now the site of a new hospital and a new administrative capital for the Marshalls.

Majuro has a bustle about it, with a lot of traffic along the main island road — much of it little more than young people joy-riding. **Kwajalein** is an atoll consisting of some 90 islets around a lagoon with a total surface area of 2335 sq. km. It is 120 km long and on average 24 km wide. A large part of the atoll is under the control of the US Defence Department on a lease agreement with the government of the Marshalls.

Kwajalein was the first of Japan's pre-war territories to fall to American forces in the Pacific War, and was in American hands in February 1944. It was retained by the US Navy as a base after the war, and the period 1951–56 saw increased activity there because of its position on supply routes for US operations in Korea and nuclear testing in the Enewetak/Bikini area. Many improvements were made, particularly to the main island of Kwajalein.

But it was regarded as surplus to US defence requirements in 1959, and the Navy intended abondoning it. It was then decided to use it as a testing site for the NIKE ZEUS anti-missile programme of the then US Army Rocket and Guided Missile Agency, and for missile re-entry studies by the Advanced Research Projects Agency of the Defense Department.

Naval Station Kwajalein became the Pacific Missile Range Facility, Kwajalein, under the command of the Navy's Pacific Missile Range command, California, with the Army and the research agency as tenants, carrying on their own activities.

All this activity led to further extensive development of the atoll, which had already been changed by landfill and reclamation projects. On the main island of Kwajalein a complex of highly technical buildings, radars, missile assembly and missile launching facilities was constructed at the western end, and some other islands particularly Roi and Namur, on the northern end of the lagoon, were developed.

These last two named islets were eventually joined, and today Roi-Namur is one island.

Roi-Namur's present total area of 161 ha includes more than 16 ha landfill. Kwajalein island, now 302 ha, includes no less than 83 ha of postwar landfill.

New and longer runways were built on Roi-Namur and Kwajalein, with underground water and fuel storage, sealed roads, and on Kwajalein, clubs, schools, shops and other facilities for contract workers and their families who had largely replaced military personnel.

In July 1964 command of Kwajalein was transferred from the Navy to the Army and it became the Kwajalein Test Site. History had been made in July 1962 with the announcement that a ZEUS fired from Kwajalein had intercepted an ICBM launched from Vandenberg Air Force Base, California.

There was a further change in name in April 1968 when Kwajalein became the Kwajalein Missile Range, which it still is. It is under the control of the Ballistic Missile Defense Systems Command at Huntsville, Alabama. There is a military commander based on Kwajalein responsible to Huntsville.

Today the range is a national range involved with missile and space test programs for a dozen users, not all of them American.

Only 11 of the islands on the atoll are reserved for range activities, together with what is called the 'mid-atoll corridor' section of the lagoon, where splashdowns occur. The islands in use face this corridor.

Many of the islands in the mid-atoll corridor section are developed with all sorts of sophisticated monitoring and measuring equipment, and several have airstrips, serviced by regular routine fixed wing and helicopter flights from Kwajalein — like an aerial bus service.

The non-military operations for service and support on the atoll are handled under contract by Global Associates of California. Global operates Kwajalein's power, light, water, transport, housing, fire services, schools, theatres, clubs, restaurants, shopping facilities, library, golf course, etc. There is television and a newspaper.

Population on the range (1983) was 3481, of whom 2250 were contract workers, with 1164 dependents. There were only 23 US Army personnel and 44 civil servants.

Total Marshallese population of the atoll is about 8000, but the greater part of these — 7000 — are on small 30 ha Ebeye island, within sight of Kwajalein and less than an hour across the lagoon by regular ferry. The remainder normally occupy the outer islands of the lagoon, particularly to the north-west and away from the corridor area.

With its big population plus about 250 cars, Ebeye is the most densely populated island in the Pacific. Many of these are not Kwajalein people, but other Marshall Islanders, and people from other parts of the Micronesian States attracted to Kwajalein by higher rates of pay at the missile range.

Fewer than 1000 have jobs on Kwajalein (commuting daily by ferry) or work for the government or commerce on Ebeye. The rest are mostly dependants or members of the extended family.

Under an Interim Use Agreement with the US, atoll landowners received something like $US9 million annually. The agreement went to 1986 but when the Compact of Free Association came into force, the provisions of the Compact and various subsidiary agreements began to apply. The Compact gives the US the right to lease the atoll for a further period, a minimum of 15 years.

In late 1986 the Pentagon announced plans to build a new launching facility at the Kwajalein Missile Range for the testing of weapons in the US's Strategic Defence Initiative (or Star Wars) programme. The complex, to cost $1.3 m, will be used to launch interceptors for missiles. The project was seen by American observers as one of several indications that the 'Star Wars' plans were beginning to take actual shape.

The Compact agreement allows islanders to visit the islands of the mid-atoll corridor for several periods during each year, except for the islands of Meck, Illeginni, Gagan and Legan.

The 11 islands under US defence control are (within the mid-atoll corridor): Meck, Enewetak, Omelek, Gallinam, Gagan, Illeginni and Legan. Outside the corridor they are: Kwajalein, Roi-Namur, Ennugarret and Ennylabegan. Only portions of these two last-named islands are for exclusive use by the US.

Visitors may disembark at Kwajalein airport only if they have authority from the Marshalls government to visit Ebeye or other islands in the atoll, but separate authority from the Defense Department is needed if they want to stay on Kwajalein and is most unlikely to be given. Continental/Air

Micronesia has regular services from the US West Coast and Guam.

Bikini and Enewetak. Details of these atolls, the post-war history of which has been dominated by the nuclear tests carried out by the US in the late 1940s and 1950s, may be found in the history section of this entry. Bikini (east of Enewetak) is large with 36 islets and wide ship-passages to the south, and was uninhabited until 1968. Its people were transferred to Rongerik to the north of the Ralik Chain before the first nuclear explosions in 1946. Later they were moved to Kili in the extreme south of the chain.

Jaluit Lagoon is triangular in shape, about 48 km long by 19 km wide. There are three deep passages through which vessels of any size can pass to a safe anchorage of 45–55 m depth. It has more than 80 islets.

Vessels of considerable size may anchor safely in the Jaluit Lagoon, a fact which made the atoll of some importance to both German traders and administrators, and later to the Japanese, who established a town at Jabor (Jabwor) and encouraged the growing of copra and other crops.

Ebon (or Boston) Atoll. This is the most southerly of the group and also contains a large and safe anchorage. Ebon was the best-known port of the Marshalls in the early part of the 19th century, when these islands were freely used as a wintering ground by whalers, etc., who roved the south Pacific from the 1820s to 1870s.

The islets of importance are called Jurijer, Enijarmek, Ebon, Dereg, Enijadok, Guamagumlap, Euer, Munjak, Taka, Enlio, Jio, and Met. Ebon forms the south and south-east side of the atoll. It is 8 km long and is the largest and most important of the atoll islets.

Ujelang is the westernmost island of the Marshalls; narrow, with 27 scattered islets, it became home for the population of Enewetak (to the north) when that island was used for nuclear bomb tests.

Allinglapalap, and nearby **Namu** (each with 50 islets) are inhabited. **Namorik** is small with an enclosed angular reef, and has a land area of 2.5 sq. km.

Best known of the other Ratak atolls are: Likiep, which has the highest point in the group, only 10 m above sea level, and 72 islets mostly on the straight north-east side; Arno (large, bib-shaped, with reef openings near the middle: land area of 8 sq. km); and Mili (south of Arno, has 90 islets extending for 51 km).

FOR THE TOURIST. Tourism and, hence, tourist services are still in their infancy in the Marshall Islands, but the Government is anxious to encourage visitors, although the accommodation infrastructure is as yet limited. A variety of historical sites dating from World War II and earlier can be seen, although the most spectacular of them lie beneath the surface of the lagoons of such atolls as Kwajalein, Wotje, Maloelap and Jaluit, where the detritus of the war may still be seen by experienced divers. The outer islands, most of which are accessible by aircraft, offer the sort of scenery and life-styles still described, misleadingly, as 'unspoiled', and provide a welcome relief from the downtown area of Majuro. There are no recognised visitor accommodations on them, however. Something of the quality of outer island life may be glimpsed at the community of Laura, some 48 km by bus from downtown Majuro.

Tour operators can suggest a number of ways to diversify the visitor's time in the Marshalls: fishing, diving and scenic flights can be arranged, and there are a number of rental car outlets, although the cheap taxi service tends to make renting unnecessary.

Shopping. The Marshall Islands is not a duty free area, and most consumer goods are not cheap. But they do have a fixed price. Bargaining for any commodity is not customary. Local handicrafts are considered to be of reasonable quality, especially the woven pandanus ware.

Entry formalities. Valid passports are required from all travellers, including US citizens, though the latter do not require a visa for a stay of 30 days or less. Citizens of other countries require a US visa or a Marshall Islands entry permit. Certificates of vaccination against such diseases as smallpox, cholera and yellow fever are only required of travellers coming from an infected area. Various quarantine regulations apply to the entry of agricultural produce from nearby countries, depending on the point of origin.

Airport tax. A passenger departure tax of $5 is payable at Majuro airport for international flights only.

ACCOMMODATION. (Details provided by Tourism office, Majuro.) A three per cent government room tax and a $2 per day local government tax are added to hotel bills.

Marshall Sun Hotel: between airport and downtown area, 35 rooms, a/c, private facilities, bar, restaurant, beach frontage, laundry service, boat charters. PO Box 1215, Majuro, MI, 96960. Tel. 3118.

Tre Hotel: in downtown area, 18 rooms, a/c, private facilities, mini-bar, colour TV, laundry service, boat charters. PO Box 1, Majuro, MI, 96960. Tel. 3250.

Ajidrik Hotel: in downtown area, 15 rooms, a/c, private facilities, some rooms with re-frig. PO Box E, Majuro, MI, 96960. Tel. 3171.

Majuro Hotel: in downtown area, 18 rooms, most a/c, private facilities, laundry service. PO Box 185, Majuro, MI, 96960. Tel. 3324.

Eastern Gateway Hotel: in Delap area on lagoon, 21 rooms, a/c, private facilities, restaurant, laundry service. PO Box 106, Majuro, MI, 96960. Tel. 3337.

Midway Island

Midway is about 1900 km from Honolulu at the end of the chain of rocks and atolls extending to the north-west of Hawaii. It is an atoll about 25 km in circumference and an American possession. The entrance to the lagoon is on the south side, between the two islets of Eastern and Sand.

Midway was first reported in 1859 by Captain N. C. Brooks of the Hawaiian barque *Gambia*. For some time it was referred to as Brooks Island. Captain William Reynolds of the USS. *Lackawanna* took possession of it for the US on 28 August 1867. It had no indigenous population. The atoll was placed under the jurisdiction of the US Navy in 1903, and is still under naval jurisdiction, with the Department of Defence having final responsibility. In the thirties a hostel was built on Sand Island for overnighting plane passengers. Later, in 1939, hundreds of men were camped on Eastern Island to convert it into a submarine and air base. The air

MIDWAY ISLAND

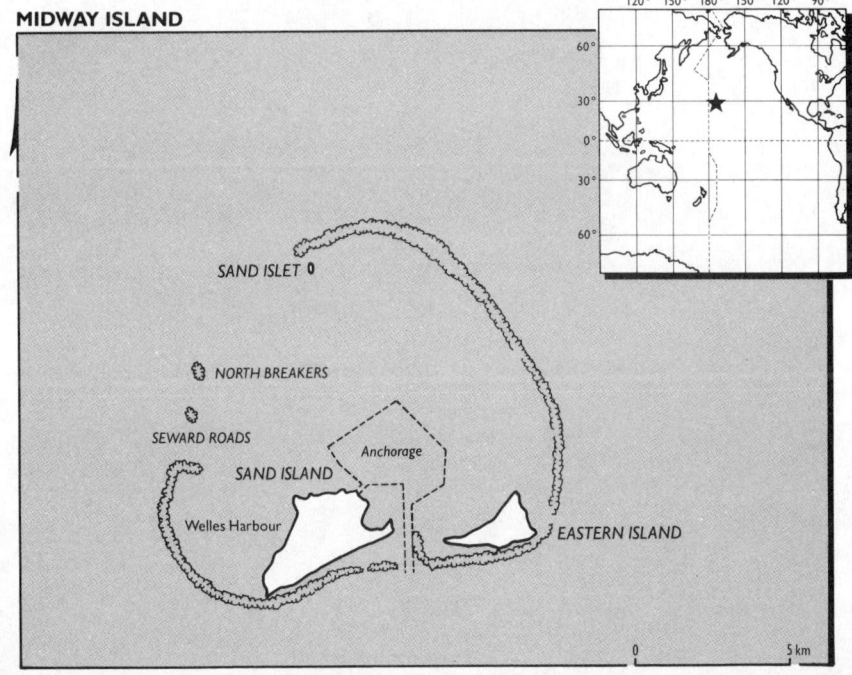

station was completed in August 1941, and attacked on 7 December 1941 by the Japanese on their return from bombing Pearl Harbor. The Japanese tried hard to capture Midway, but failed. The sea battle off Midway against US naval forces, June 3–5 1942, was one of the turning points of the Pacific war. The defeat of the Japanese forces gave the US Navy control of the Pacific.

Eastern and Sand Islands still serve as a naval station and air facility for the Navy. Supply flights but otherwise no regular services use the 2400 m sealed airstrip on Sand Island, where there are refuelling facilities. Midway is also a World Meteorological Organisation Upper-Air Observatory Station, which is operated by the Naval Weather Service. This service provides data on upper level winds and temperatures to worldwide users who utilise the data in current analysis, as well as for research purposes.

The islands are also classified as a National Wildlife Reserve to protect the bird life. This includes the laysan albatross (gooney bird), the frigate bird, the fairy tern and the bosun bird. This facet of the islands falls under federal statutes as set forth by the US Department of Interior.

Further information may be obtained from the Fish and Wildlife Service, PO Box 50167, Honolulu, 96850 or from the Public Affairs Officer, US Naval Air Facility, FPO San Francisco, CA. 96614-1200.

Nauru

Nauru, a single raised coral island of 21 sq. km with a circumference of 19 km, is an independent republic and an associate member of the Commonwealth. It is located 41 km south of the equator at 166 deg 56 min E longitude; it is about 4000 km north of Sydney and 4457 km west of Honolulu. Local time is 12 hours ahead of GMT. Its closest neighbour is Banaba (Ocean Island) 300 km to the east. The administrative centre is in the Yaren district.

The national anthem is *Nauru Ubwema*

(Nauru, Our Homeland) and the flag is royal blue, divided by a narrow horizontal gold band with a 12-pointed star in the lower left quarter. Australian currency is used.

Public holidays include New Year's Day, Easter, Christmas Day, and three specifically national holidays; Independence Day, 31 January, Constitution Day, 17 May and Angam (Homecoming) Day, 26 October.

THE PEOPLE. Of a toal 8042 population on Nauru in May 1983, 4964 were Nauruan.

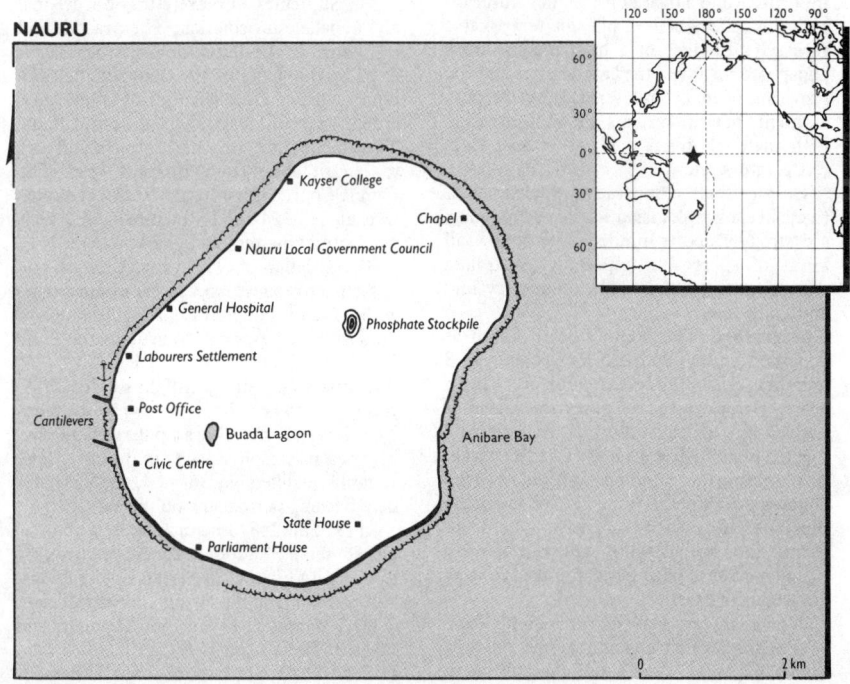

NAURU

The other 3078 were mostly phosphate workers from Kiribati and Tuvalu and other Pacific Islanders, Chinese, Filipinos and Europeans also working for the Nauru Phosphate Corporation or the government.

The Nauruan population is widely scattered along the coastal fringe of the island with one village, Buada, inland; the migrant workers are concentrated in dormitory apartment blocks in the NPC area on the waterfront near the loading cantilevers.

The 'town centre' of the island is situated between the airport and the cantilevers, where the post office and the civic or conference centre are situated. The main government offices are near the airport.

Citizenship. Nauruans are citizens of Nauru.

Language. The national language is Nauruan but English is widely understood and spoken.

Religion. The Nauruans are Christian and adhere either to the Nauru Congregational Church or the Catholic Church. About 60 per cent of Nauru's population is Protestant. There are also pastors of the Kiribati Protestant Church and Tuvalu Protestant Church on Nauru for the benefit of phosphate workers.

Lifestyle. Because of a high income from phosphate royalties, the lack of taxes and the provision of many free services by the government, most Nauruans are well provided with material things such as radios, cars, refrigerators, etc.

Despite their comparative wealth, Nauruans live a simple, island-style life. They are strongly sports-minded, and follow all kinds of sports but especially Australian Rules football, tennis, golf, cricket, cycling and volley ball.

Government. The Republic of Nauru is governed by the Nauruan Parliament of 18 members elected by common roll every three years. For electoral purposes the island is divided into districts, most districts electing two members. After each election the parliament elects the republic's president, who chooses a Cabinet of four or five members plus himself, to act as executive. The president is thus both head of state and de facto prime minister. Voting is compulsory for all Nauruans over 20.

Nauru is an associate member of the Commonwealth, which means that the republic has all the benefits of Commonwealth status

except the right to attend meetings of the Commonwealth Heads of Government.

Local government. The Nauru Local Government Council has both important responsibilities and a large income (mainly through phosphate royalties). This development has resulted in a two-tier system of government, with responsibilities for some Nauru affairs being divided between the council and the government. As an example, Nauru's shipping line is operated by the Nauru Local Government Council, but Nauru's airline is operated by the Nauru Government, although both can be important instruments of national policy.

The council is an elected body of nine members, and it elects one of its members to be Head Chief. Since 1955, the Head Chief has been Hammer DeRoburt.

Justice. The judicial arm of government is composed of the Supreme Court of Nauru, presided over by a Chief Justice, the District Court, presided over by a Resident Magistrate, and the Family Court. All are courts of record.

The Supreme Court exercises both original and appellate jurisdiction. The practice and procedure of the Supreme Court was regulated by the Rules of the Court of the Supreme Court of Queensland, but is now governed by several local statutes and regulations. The Chief Justice lives in Melbourne and goes to Nauru about four times a year. The Family Court consists of the Resident Magistrate and at least two lay members, and deals with family matters and child welfare.

By legislation of Nauru and Australia and at Nauru's request, appeals lie in most cases with leave of the High Court of Australia or the Supreme Court of Nauru, to the High Court of Australia.

Public service. Strength of the service (1986) was 1165, of whom 70 per cent were Nauruan. The Government follows a policy of employing specialists from outside in the absence of suitably-qualified Nauruans. Only Nauruans may become permanent public servants.

In 1986 the 348 'other nationals' within the public service included 25 Australians, 28 Chinese, 14 Fijians, 26 Filipinos, 54 Indians, 84 I-Kiribati and Tuvaluans, 6 New Zealanders, 5 Samoans, 49 Solomon Islanders and 11 other Pacific Islanders.

Police. The police force of about 57 is under

a local director. All members of the force are Nauruan.

Liquor laws. The legal age for drinking liquor is 21. Hotel bar trading hours are 5.00 pm to 10.00 pm, Monday to Friday, 10 am to 10.00 pm Saturday.

DEFENCE. Nauru does not have any defence pacts or treaties or defence force. Her defence is assured by Australia but no formal agreement exists.

EDUCATION. Education is free and compulsory for Nauruan children from six to 16 years. In 1986 the government had five infant schools, two primary schools and one secondary school. The Sacred Heart of Jesus Mission had one infants' school, a primary school and a secondary school, all in the same establishment.

In the government primary school, Aiwo District, European and Nauruan children are taught together in English. The second government primary school is the Location School, which caters for children of phosphate workers — mainly Gilbertese, Chinese, Tuvaluans and a number of Nauruan scholarship children.

There is also a trade school.

Overseas study. Most European children go to boarding school in Australia or New Zealand for education at secondary level. The government makes a grant towards the cost. Nauruans also study at tertiary level overseas. Most of them go to Australia. Some go to Papua New Guinea, Fiji and New Zealand.

The teaching staff in all schools totals about 130. For teacher-training, cadetships are offered in Australia. This is supplementary to local teacher-training. Some teachers are recruited from Australia and New Zealand.

LABOUR. As the local labour force is insufficient to meet requirements of the phosphate industry the Nauru Phosphate Corporation (NPC) recruits workers from Kiribati (15 per cent), Tuvalu (9 per cent), Hong Kong, Niue and the Philippines. Labour contracts vary from one to two years. Migrant workers receive board and lodgings as part of their remuneration.

While there are no trade unions as such in the industry each of the ethnic groups has its own Workers' Committee who have regular meetings with management.

HEALTH. Nauru's health services include two well equipped hospitals, but sophisticated services are restricted. If specialist treatment is necessary, the patient is sent to Australia. The government bears the cost in the case of Nauruans. There are no fees for medical or dental services in the government hospital, or in the NPC hospital which is for NPC employees and their families. Others can attend the NPC hospital if they pay a fee. Cost of government health services for 1985/86 was $1,932,500.

The fight against disease has been largely successful. With the exception of filaria, other tropical diseases of the Pacific are either rare or have been completely eliminated. Typical examples are tropical ulcers and yaws, which are now non-existent. Tuberculosis is also well under control. All new arrivals on the island must be X-rayed before entry, or within 24 hours of arrival. Diabetes is very common in Nauru.

Both hospitals are staffed by trained doctors and nurses and have schools of nursing for local trainees. The government maintains 11 maternity and child welfare clinics. TB, dental and diabetes clinics are maintained at the government hospital.

THE LAND. The ground rises from a sandy beach to form a fairly fertile belt, 50 to 300 m wide, encircling the island. Further inland the coral cliffs rise to a central plateau about 30 m above sea level. The plateau is composed largely of phosphate-bearing rock, which covers about three-fifths of the entire area. Highest point is 70 m.

Because of the generally poor, highly porous soil and irregular rainfall, cultivation is restricted to the coastal belt, where coconut palms and pandanus grow, and to the fringe of the land surrounding the shallow Buada Lagoon, where bananas, pineapples and some vegetables are grown.

There are 179 varieties of plants and trees and many species of moths, butterflies and dragonflies.

Many migrating species of birds 'rest' on Nauru, swelling the local bird population by thousands several times a year. Common birds are the black and the white noddy tern and the frigate bird, often a household pet in

Nauruan homes. There is also a small nightingale reed warbler, known locally as the Nauruan canary.

Nauru has no indigenous mammals. Mice, rats and feral cats have all arrived as new settlers. Sea snakes are found around the island.

There are no rivers on Nauru and after periods of prolonged drought, the landscape appears quite dry, dusty and barren. However, after heavy rain, the vegetation rapidly becomes quite lush. Coconut, banyan, frangipani and pandanus trees are the most common.

With the exception of small allotments held by the government, the NPC and missions, the island is owned by individual Nauruans.

Climate. The climate is tropical, and tempered by sea breezes with a day temperature of 30°C. The average annual rainfall is 1500 mm, but actual rainfall is extremely variable — it has been as low as 300 mm, and as high as 4572 mm in a year. The wettest period is during the westerly monsoon season, from November to February. For the rest of the year easterly trade winds prevail.

Reclamation. At various times the Nauru Government has investigated the possibility of reclaiming or otherwise making use of the worked-out phosphate land in the centre of the island. One possibility, not yet abandoned, is that an international airstrip be built across the coral pinnacles with the dual purpose of it serving as a rain catchment area. Rainwater would be run off into underground reservoirs to eliminate the island's regular water shortages. Because of a reclamation programme using garbage and other waste as filling, large areas of worked-out land have reverted to bush.

PRIMARY PRODUCTION. Primary production is confined to fruit and vegetables, livestock and fish. Coconuts are the main crop. The seas around the island teem with fish, but the people catch only enough for their own use. Any surplus is stored in the Co-operative cool store. The people keep pigs and chickens, which provide some fresh meat. Otherwise all food requirements come from overseas.

MINING. The economy of Nauru is based on phosphate, which is mined and marketed by the Nauru Phosphate Corporation, incorporated in June 1969, and which assumed full control of the industry from the British Phosphate Commissioners on 1 July 1970. The corporation is an instrumentality of the Government of Nauru.

Nauruan phosphate is the highest grade in the world, 84 per cent BPL guaranteed, with rock treated in Nauru's modern calcination plant as high as 91 BPL and averaging 89 per cent, the highest grade phosphate available to the chemical and fertiliser industries.

After the scrub and overburden are removed by bulldozers, the alluvial phosphate and the large lumps of rock phosphate are removed from around the coral pinnacles by mechanical extractors with clam-shell buckets.

The phosphate is trucked to the raihead for primary crushing and reduced to less than 50 mm. A narrow gauge railway system using diesel locomotives transports the crushed material to the treatment plant where it is dried to 3.0 per cent water before further crushing to less than 12 mm (run of mine).

A proportion of the fine material is further upgraded by high temperature calcination to remove organic carbon and cadmium. This product is marketed as Nauru Calcined Rock (NCR). Ships up to 30,000 tonnes capacity are loaded by cantilever loading systems while moored to buoys in an open water port. The moorings are the deepest in the world.

	Run of Mine (tonnes)	NCR (tonnes)
1977/78	1,486,956	8,500
1978/79	2,200,000	30,000
1980/81	1,534,619	55,435
1981/82	1,709,435	26,401

Maximum production was 2,394,000 tonnes in 1973/74.

In June 1981 it was estimated there were 505 ha of phosphate land left to be mined, with a total ore reserve of 24 million tonnes. At an average extraction rate of 1.75 million tonnes annually, about 13.7 years still remained for the industry.

TOURISM. Nauru has not been developed as a destination point but it possesses two hotels, the council-owned Menen, which has all facilities, and the Od-n-Aiwo, near the boat harbour, which serves breakfast only. Most guests are transit passengers but in recent years there has been an increase in Japanese visitors touring the Pacific War battlegrounds.

LOCAL COMMERCE. The Nauru Corporation, operated by the Nauru Local Government Council, runs two general stores and a liquor store. The Local Government Council also operates the hotel and hotel hire car service, the Nauru Pacific Line, the Nauru Insurance Corporation and the Nauru Fishing Corporation. There is a large number of small Chinese-operated food and general stores, together with cinemas and small cafes.

OVERSEAS TRADE. Nauru does not publish import and trade statistics. The sole export is phosphate. However, trade figures published by the South Pacific Commission show that in 1982–83 (the most recent figures available) Nauru's exports totalled $121.6 million in value. The country's imports in that period were valued at $14.4 million, giving a favourable balance of $107.1 million, one of the few favourable trade balances in the region. Main supplier was Australia, providing $13.7 million worth. The remainder came from New Zealand.

Customs tariff. There are no import duties except on tobacco and alcoholic beverages, which are almost nominal rates. The import of firearms, ammunition, and animals, including domestic pets, requires a licence.

FINANCE. For the financial year 1985/86 government expenditure was estimated at $76,205,700 and revenue at $77,298,700. Main revenue comes from phosphate sales, with the government taking about half the profits per tonne, but the amount varies from year to year. The rest is paid out to Nauruan landowners, long-term trust funds to provide an income for the Nauruan people when the phosphate runs out, and the Nauru Local Government Council. The government also has income from overseas investments, such as the 52-storey Nauru House in Melbourne, and real estate including hotels, in other island groups, New Zealand, Hong Kong and the US, and from financial dealings. Some of this real estate is owned by the Nauru Local Government Council.

The main areas of revenue for 1985/86 are shown in Table 1.

The revenue from the Secretariat of the Department of Island Development and Industry was contributed largely by the Nauru Phosphate Corporation ($37 million). The Civil Aviation sector raised revenue from passenger sales ($9 million), charters ($3.5 million) and the balance from aircraft sales. The Department of Finance had revenue from corporation fees and licences ($185,600), philatelic sales $250,000 and interests on loans and investments $216,600.

Estimated Government expenditure for 1985/86 is shown in Table 2.

Philatelic Bureau. The Nauru Philatelic Bureau, attached to the Treasury, produces usually four commemorative stamp issues and related philatelic material each year, and puts out a bulletin. Nauru's stamps are recognised as being of high standard. The bureau accepts standing orders. Philatelic Bureau sales for 1985/86 were expected to be $250,000.

Taxation. There is no income tax or direct tax in Nauru.

TABLE 1

Department

Chief Secretary	40,100
Island development & industry	
Secretariat	56,043,000
Civil aviation	18,647,600
Telecommunications	581,400
Govt. printer	90,500
Finance	
Secretariat	874,500
Computer bureau	175,600
Justice and judiciary	81,000
Works	
Secretariat	56,900
Nauruan housing	612,300
Health and education	44,700
External affairs	91,200
Total	· $77,298,700

TABLE 2

Department

Chief Secretary	2,665,400
Island development & industry	
Secretariat	1,718,500
Civil aviation	29,919,900
Telecommunications	822,200
Govt. printer	413,300
Lands & survey	337,500
Audit	133,800
Finance	
Secretariat	4,139,900
Public debt	23,522,500
Computer bureau	351,100
Justice & judiciary	1,236,800
Works and community service	4,042,700
Education	2,511,600
Health	1,932,500
External affairs	2,458,000
Total	$76,205,700

Banking. The Bank of Nauru was established in October 1976, taking over the operations of the Bank of NSW. Since March 1977, the Bank of Nauru has been wholly owned and guaranteed by the government. By special arrangement Nauru has remained within the Australian monetary system and Australian banknotes and coins are legal tender.

Financial centre. The Nauru government receives registration fees for the registration in Nauru of overseas corporations which use the island for tax planning purposes. Nauru's modern corporate and trust laws were specifically designed to promote development of Nauru as a financial centre.

TRANSPORT. There is an excellent wide, sealed coastal road right around the island, linking all villages. The Buada district inland is also linked by sealed road with the coast, and other sealed roads connect residential areas of the NPC and government. Vehicular traffic is heavy on Nauru, as a high proportion of Nauruans own cars or motor cycles and there are also drive-yourself facilities.

The NPC operates about 6 km of 30 gauge railway line in connection with phosphate recovery.

Aviation. The republic has its own airline, Air Nauru, begun in 1970, which has scheduled services to Pacific rim countries including Hong Kong, Japan, the Philippines, Australia and New Zealand, as well as many island states. The airline uses modern Boeing jets. Servicing is done in New Zealand.

Nauru international airport has a single sealed 1708 m runway, and a modern terminal building. Preliminary work began in 1983 to extend the runway south-east over the coral reef.

Shipping. The Nauru Pacific Line operates vessels servicing the island, and also offers regular commercial cargo services to other users. Services include regular cargo-passenger service from Melbourne to Nauru and Tarawa (Kiribati), a container service from Melbourne to Micronesia including Guam and a conventional/container and passenger service from San Francisco and Honolulu to Majuro, Pohnpei, Truk and Saipan. The line is wholly owned by the Nauru Local Government Council. The Nauru Phosphate Corporation also charters vessels for its special needs.

Nauru has no wharves. Passenger and cargo handling is by barge, operating between a small artificial boat harbour and the vessels are usually tied to deep-sea moorings near the phosphate loading cantilevers.

COMMUNICATIONS. A satellite/earth receiving station was installed in 1975, giving Nauru worldwide telephone communication. There is also a telex system with the number 775. There is a modern internal telephone service on Nauru. ISD country code is 674.

A medium-frequency shipping watch is maintained in the international distress frequency; two high-frequency schedules are observed at 0015 and 0830 GMT.

Radio Nauru broadcasts daily from 0630 to 2300. Local news is covered as well as international news from Radio Australia. Newspapers include *The Bulletin*, a news sheet published weekly by the government, the *Government Gazette*, a weekly news sheet of official government notifications, the *Young Post*, a privately owned weekly paper which often takes an anti-government stance and the weekly *Observer*, also privately owned.

WATER AND ELECTRICITY. Nauru has full electricity services, supplied by engines of the Nauru Phosphate Corporation. Voltage is 240v 50 cycle AC. Water supplies are mainly from roof storage tanks. And in prolonged dry periods water is imported as ballast in the regular shipping which calls at the island, pumped ashore into cement storage tanks, and distributed to houses by tanker. This operation is handled by the NPC.

MAJOR OFFICE HOLDERS.
President:
    Hammer DeRoburt GCMG,OBE
Speaker:
    Pres Nimes Ekwona
Chief Justice:
    Gaven Donne KBE

GOVERNMENT DEPARTMENTS
Parliament, Republic of Nauru, Central Pacific; Tel.: 3387
Office of the President, Republic of Nauru, Central Pacific; Tel.: 3100
Department of Audit, Republic of Nauru, Central Pacific; Tel.: 5235
Cabinet, Republic of Nauru, Central Pacific; Tel.: 3140
Chief Secretary's Department, Republic of Nauru, Central Pacific; Tel.: 5236
External Affairs Department, Republic of Nauru, Central Pacific; Tel.: 3330
Finance Department, Republic of Nauru, Central Pacific; Tel.: 5225
Health and Education, Republic of Nauru, Central Pacific; Tel.: 3350
Island Development and Industry Department, Republic of Nauru, Central Pacific; Tel.: 3320
Judiciary, Republic of Nauru, Central Pacific; Tel.: 3365
Justice Department, Republic of Nauru, Central Pacific; Tel.: 3360
Works and Community Department, Republic of Nauru, Central Pacific; Tel.: 3165
STATUTORY BODIES
Nauru Local Government Council, Republic of Nauru, Central Pacific; Tel.: 5215
Nauru Phosphate Corporation, Republic of Nauru, Central Pacific; Tel.: 4180/4198

Air Nauru, Republic of Nauru, Central Pacific; Tel.: 3418
Menen Hotel, Republic of Nauru, Central Pacific; Tel.: 3210
NLGC Cool Store, Republic of Nauru, Central Pacific; Tel.: 4048
Nauru Insurance Corporation, Republic of Nauru, Central Pacific; Tel.: 3346
Nauru Pacific Lines, Republic of Nauru, Central Pacific; Tel.: 4581
Nauru Fishing Corporation, Republic of Nauru, Central Pacific; Tel.: 4582

OVERSEAS REPRESENTATIVES
Consulate-General of Nauru, Nauru House, Level 50, 80 Collins St., Melbourne, Vic. 3000, Australia; Tel.: 635-5709
Consulate for Nauru, 6th Floor, 70 Pitt St., Sydney, N.S.W. 2000, Australia; Tel.: 233-8044
Consulate of Nauru, Clarke & Ingram Builing, PO Box 146, Avarua, Rarotonga, Cook Islands; Tel.: 22-223
Consulate of Nauru, 7th Floor, Ratu Sukuna House, MacArthur St., Suva, Fiji; Tel.: 312377
Consulate of Nauru, PO Box AM, Agana, Guam 96910; Tel.: 472-3300
Consulate of Nauru, Davies Pacific Centre, 841 Bishop St. Ste. 1818, Honolulu, HI 96813; Tel.: 808-523-7821
Consulate of Nauru, Pacific Star Bldg. 1/Fl, No. 2 Canton R., Tsim Sha Tsui, Kowloon, Hong Kong; Tel.: 3-7233525-Kowloon
Consulate-General of Nauru, C/5/4 Safdarjung Development Area, New Delhi, India 110016; Tel.: 667-977/651-274
Consulate of Nauru, First Floor, Room No. 0122, Tokyo Club Building, 2–6 Kasumigaseki 3-Chome, Chiyoda-Ku, Tokyo 100, Japan; Tel.: 03-581-9277/ 03-581-9278
Consulate-General of Nauru, Samoa House, 283 Karangahape Rd, PO Box 68536, Newton 1, New Zealand; Tel.: 799-348
Nauru Representative, PO Box 590, Nauru Building, Saipan Island, CM/USA; Tel.: 234-6924/6941/6840
Consulate of Nauru, Chung Shan Building, Ground Floor Room IB, 2 Min-Tsu East Rd, Taipei, Taiwan, Republic of China; Tel.: 598-1975/594-8115

Consulate of Nauru, Tungi Arcade, Nuku'
Alofa, Tonga; Tel.: 22109
Republic of Nauru London Office,
Livingston House, 11 Carteret St., London
SWIH 9DJ, England; Tel.: 01-222-3373
Consulate of Nauru, 2333 Harrison St.,
Oakland, CA 94612 USA; Tel.:
415-832-5249
Consulate of Nauru, PO Box 1429, Apia,
Western Samoa; Tel.: 23-320

HISTORY. Nauru has been inhabited for
an unknown number of centuries. The original inhabitants were probably castaways
who drifted there from some other island.
The Nauruan language is said to be 'absol-
utely distinct' from all other Pacific languages, being a fusion of elements from the
Gilberts, Carolines, Marshalls, and Solomons. Early this century, people of distinct
ethnic types were to be seen on the island.
Those of the south had curly hair, those on
the western side had very straight hair,
suggesting Gilbertese descent, and elsewhere
they appeared to be of mixed origins. The
islanders were divided into clans and spoke
different dialects. But after European missionaries fixed on the principal dialect for
Bible translation work early this century, the
others gradually became obsolete.

The European discoverer of Nauru was
Captain John Fearn of the British ship
Hunter in 1798. He named it Pleasant Island
because of its attractive appearance, and it
was thus known to Europeans for the next
90 years. However, there was little contact
with Europeans until the 1830s when whalers
operating in the Line whaling grounds called
there for food and water. It was then that
Nauru received the first of its beachcombers.
Beachcombers. One of these, John Jones,
an Irish convict, poisoned seven and shot
four of his fellow beachcombers in October
1841 because he feared they would usurp his
influence over the Nauruans. The evil influence of such men spread to the Nauruans,
who then numbered about 1400. In 1852,
some of them were involved in the massacre
of part of the crew of the American brig
Inga.

Most beachcombers, of course, were not
as bad as Jones and conformed to the social
patterns of the island. Two whose descendants still live in Nauru were William

Harris, who settled there in 1842, and
Ernest M. H. Stephen, who was left there by
a ship's captain in 1881 when only 13 years
old. The beachcombers were useful to the
Nauruans in acting as intermediaries with
visiting ships. They helped them to obtain
steel tools, firearms, alcohol and other white
men's goods. They were also useful in
repairing weapons and as allies in clan
warfare, always an essential part of Nauruan
life. This became deadlier and more frequent
as the Nauruans' stock of firearms increased,
and for 10 years, from 1878, it was virtually
incessant. Meanwhile, some German traders
who had settled on the island requested that
it be incorporated within Germany's Marshall Islands Protectorate. This was done
formally in October 1888 when the German
gunboat *Eber* landed an imperial commissioner on the island who arrested all 12
chiefs and threatened to deport them to
Jaluit unless all firearms on the islands were
surrendered. During the next two days, 765
weapons were handed in. This represented
almost one firearm for every adult, as the
population then stood at about 1300, of
whom about 300 were children. Because of
the recent carnage, women outnumbered
men by 30 per cent.

German administration. After the German
flag had been raised on 2 October, a German
trader was placed in provisional charge of
the island's administration and the gunboat
left. Traders generally doubled as administrators until 1905. Meanwhile, in 1899, the
first Western missionary arrived — the Rev.
P. A. Delaporte, German-born American
Protestant. He took up the work of several
earlier Gilbertese pastors, soon had a large
following, and was exerting considerable
influence. A German Roman Catholic missionary. Father Grundl, settled on the island
in 1902. Although conflict ensued between
the two missionaries, they both did valuable
work in reducing the Nauruan language to
writing.

A development of a different kind was
then in the making. In 1898, H. E. Denson,
manager of the Pacific Islands Company,
Sydney, which had planting, trading and
guano interests, had called at Nauru and had
become fascinated by what he thought was a
fossilised tree. He took two specimens of the
'tree' back to Sydney. A year or so later, one

of these attracted the attention of Albert F. Ellis, a company employee with wide experience on the guano islands of the Central Pacific. Thinking that it resembled rock guano, Ellis analysed it and found it to contain 78 per cent phosphate of lime. This led to the realisation that the phosphate deposits on Nauru were 'simply enormous' because, as Denson put it, the whole island was 'one mass of rock' of the same nature. **Phosphate.** As the Jaluit Gesellschaft had the sole right to work any guano deposits in the Marshall Islands Protectorate, the London board of the Pacific Islands Company began delicate negotiations with it in the hope of exploiting the new discovery. Meanwhile, Ellis was sent to Ocean Island, Nauru's nearest neighbour, to see if it, too, contained high quality phosphatic rock, as its geological formation was known to be the same. He reached that island in May 1900 and found that it did indeed contain vast deposits. He then got two local chiefs to put their marks to a document granting his company the right to mine the deposits for 999 years for an annual royalty of £50.

Ellis' company was able to start exploiting the Ocean Island phosphate almost immediately because, according to an agreement between Great Britain and Germany of 1886, which had divided the Western Pacific between them, Ocean Island was in the British sphere of influence. By 1906, there was a thriving industry on Ocean Island. That same year, the Pacific Phosphate Company (which had grown out of the Pacific Islands Company) concluded an agreement with the German Government and the Jaluit Gesellschaft. This enabled it to begin operating on Nauru with a part-British, part-German staff. The Gesellschaft was given a share in the company plus a royalty for every ton of phosphate it mined on Nauru, Ocean Island, or elsewhere. On the other hand, there were no direct benefits for the Nauruans. At the time it was not even thought necessary to negotiate for rights to mine their land.

By the end of 1907, 11,630 tons of Nauruan phosphate had been exported to Australia. Over the next six years, a total of about 630,000 tons were shipped. Caroline Islanders and Chinese were imported to work the deposits. Some brought dysentery, infantile paralysis and tuberculosis which caused many Nauruan deaths.

World War I. When World War I broke out in Europe on 4 August 1914, the Germans placed Nauru under martial law. A month later, the many British subjects on the island were shipped to Ocean Island. However, in November, an Australian force of 60 men, under Major-General W. Holmes, was sent from Rabaul in the phosphate company's ship *Messina* to take possession of Nauru. Holmes' orders were to embark the deported Britons at Ocean Island and take them back to Nauru, establishing them there through the use of force if necessary. However, as the Germans on Nauru offered no resistance, the orders were carried out without difficulty. The Germans were then deported to Australia, and the phosphate industry carried on under the protection of an Australian garrison.

For a number of years it was believed that shortly after the establishment of Australian control on Nauru, a Japanese warship arrived to take possession of the island in the manner in which Micronesian islands north of the equator had been taken over. This is the view expressed in previous editions of this yearbook. Recently, however, Japanese scholar, Hiroshi Nakajima, has cast doubt on this version of events. Arguing from his examination of Japanese Government records that 'it is inconceivable' that Japan should have dispatched a warship to Nauru for this purpose, Nakajima points out that the ship in question, the *Nitsshin*, was at Nauru for another purpose entirely — to obtain coal and water from the transport, *Nankai Maru*.

For the next five years Nauru continued to be garrisoned by Australian troops and phosphate mining went on. In 1919, a mandate for the island's administration was conferred jointly on Great Britain, Australia and New Zealand by the League of Nations. But, for convenience, Australia continued in sole administrative control. At the same time, the Pacific Phosphate Company was bought out on both Ocean Island and Nauru at a cost of £3,500,000, and all titles to the phosphate deposits, etc., were vested in a board representing the three powers, known as the British Phosphate Commissioners. By agreement, the phosphate was to be distributed for home consumption in the proportion that the three Governments had compensated the phosphate company. This was 42 per cent each to both Great Britain and Australia, and 16 per cent to New Zealand. An agreement of the three powers made it clear that Nauru's phosphate was a government-owned monopoly.

Royalties. The company paid a royalty of a half-penny per ton of phosphate shipped to those Nauruans holding land claims in areas mined but there was no written agreement. Through the intervention of the first Australian Administrator, General T. Griffiths, the Nauruans were paid a royalty of 2d per ton and another 1d per ton was set aside 'for the benefit of the natives as a whole'. In addition, £20 per acre was paid in advance to Nauruan land-owners when their phosphate land was taken over. The royalty rate remained in force until 1927. By 1939, the Nauruans were getting 8d per ton. Meanwhile, phosphate exports rose from 182,170 tons in 1922 to 932,100 tons in 1939. In 1940 there was a drop to 808,400 tons when war again came to Nauru.

Early in December 1940, a westerly gale lashed the island, and seven ships which arrived to load phosphate could not get alongside the cantilever. Two German raiders arrived, the *Komet* and *Orion*, disguised as *Nanyo Maru* and *Narvik*. The phosphate ships were 'sitting shots' for the raiders. Five of them — *Triona* (4413 tons), *Vinni* (5181), *Komata* (3900), *Triadic* (6378) and *Triaster* (6032) — were sunk.

The Germans took the survivors from these and from other ships they had sunk south to Emirau Island, near Kavieng, New Ireland, and put them ashore on 21 December 1940. Then the *Komet* went back to Nauru and shelled the cantilever loading gear and some other phosphate installations. However, the damage was not enough to dislocate the phosphate workings, and no one was killed.

A year later, Nauru was attacked again. On 9 December 1941, two days after Pearl Harbor, Japanese planes bombed the island. Further bombing attacks occurred later. Meanwhile, all Europeans on the island were evacuated except seven who insisted on remaining to care for the Nauruans. They included the Australian Administrator, Lieut.-Colonel F. R. Chalmers, and two missionaries.

Japanese occupation. The Japanese occupied Nauru in August 1942. In the following year, 1200 Nauruans and the two missionaries were deported to Truk, Caroline Islands, to work as labourers. Meanwhile, the Japanese had built an airstrip on Nauru. By January 1943, their bombers could make use of it. This provoked an American bombing raid on 25 March 1943, in which eight Japanese bombers and seven fighters were caught on the airstrip and destroyed. Te Japanese retaliated by executing the five Europeans still on the island.

American bombing attacks continued throughout 1943 and became more frequent after the Americans recaptured the Gilbert Islands in November that year and occupied the Marshalls in February 1944. The attacks foiled Japanese plans to export phosphate. Australian forces re-occupied Nauru on 13 September 1945. Four and a half months later, on 31 January 1946, 737 Nauruans were returned to their home in the BPC ship *Trienza*. Five hundred others had died of starvation, disease and Japanese brutality.

Trust territory. At the end of World War II Nauru was made a United Nations trust territory, in November 1947, with Australia, Great Britain and New Zealand as the trust powers. Australia again provided the administration. Meanwhile, the BPC moved quickly to reorganise the phosphate industry. In 1950, exports exceeded one million tons for the first time. Except in the following year, the annual figure was well above the million mark — generally from 1½ million to 2 million tons — until the Nauruans became independent in 1968. Two and a half years later, they gained full control of the phosphate industry.

The political advancement of the Nauruans began in December 1951 when the Nauru Local Government Council replaced a Council of Chiefs, a largely hereditary body with no powers. The formation of the council and the emergence of strong leaders, particularly Timothy Detudamo and Hammer DeRoburt, accelerated the Nauruans' desire to control their own affairs. Visits to the island by United Nations missions gave them opportunities to voice their views. The leaders also addressed the United Nations in New York and employed economic advisers to help them negotiate with the partner governments.

The Nauruans rejected proposals for re-settlement on other islands because they did not want to lose their identity.

The Nauruans made a significant step forward in 1965 when they obtained an increase in their phosphate royalties from 37 cents to $1.75 per tonne. In 1966, this was increased to $4.50; and that year a Legislative Council was established and a large measure of self-government was granted. In 1967 the Nauruans extracted an agreement that the phosphate would be purchased at $11 per tonne for the next three years, subject to world price adjustments. Much more importantly, the partner governments agreed to hand over control of the phosphate industry from 1970. In return, the Nauruans were to pay the BPC $21 million for its capital assets. An agreement granting the Nauruans independence was signed on 24 October 1967.

Republic of Nauru. The date chosen for the inauguration of the Republic of Nauru — 31 January 1968 — was the 22nd anniversary of the return from Truk of the islanders deported by the Japanese. Head Chief Hammer DeRoburt was elected first president in May 1968.

In December 1976 Bernard Dowiyogo was elected President but on 19 April 1978 Chief Hammer DeRoburt's supporters forced the resignation of Dowiyogo by defeating a bill in Parliament dealing with phosphate royalties.

Mr Lagumot Harris succeeded Mr Dowiyogo but he resigned after only a week or two in office when Parliament rejected an appropriations bill designed to finance the republic until the end of the year.

In the ballot that followed, Chief Hammer DeRoburt was again elected President and was still in office in 1988, having survived an increasingly depressed economy and a number of challenges to his leadership. In early 1987 the Democratic Party was formed under the leadership of Kennan Adeang. The party's chief aim was to overthrow President DeRoburt and 'restore democracy'.

The long-standing issue of the rehabilitation of mined land on Nauru was the subject of protracted discussion during 1987, most of which took place in Australia, one of the countries from which Nauru seeks compensation. Lawyers representing Nauru were confident of a successful outcome for the island nation. The Australian Department of Foreign Affairs was less certain.

Further information. Nancy Viviani, *Nauru: Phosphate and Political Progress*, Canberra, 1970; Maslyn Williams, *Three Islands*, Melbourne, 1971 (gives a history of the phosphate mining on Nauru, Ocean Island and Christmas Island).

FOR THE TOURIST. Nauru has not developed a tourist industry and there is a general attitude of indifference to visitors. This is not to say that Nauruans are un-friendly — they are just indifferent to a tourist industry. The only airline connecting Nauru with the rest of the world is Air Nauru which has flights scheduled to and from other Pacific Island countries, Australia, New Zealand, Hong Kong and the Philippines. There is a $10 departure tax.

Sightseeing includes Japanese war relics and the incredible landscape.

Entry formalities. Visitors planning to stay need to apply for visas before arrival, either through Nauru or one of several overseas offices. Nothing is required by transit passengers catching the next available flight.

Outsiders cannot obtain residential status.

Visas permit a stay of no more than one month, even for non-Nauruan husbands or wives of Nauruans, who have to apply each subsequent month for a new visa, if wishing to stay in Nauru. Visitor visas are usually issued for seven days, and business visas are issued to businessmen who have sponsors on the island.

ACCOMMODATION

Meneng Hotel: 60 rooms, some air con, restaurant, bar. PO Box 298, Nauru. Tel.: 3210, Telex: ZV33092.

Od-N-Aiwo Hotel: bed and breakfast in tariff. PO Box 299, Nauru. Tel.: 3591, Telex: ZV33093.

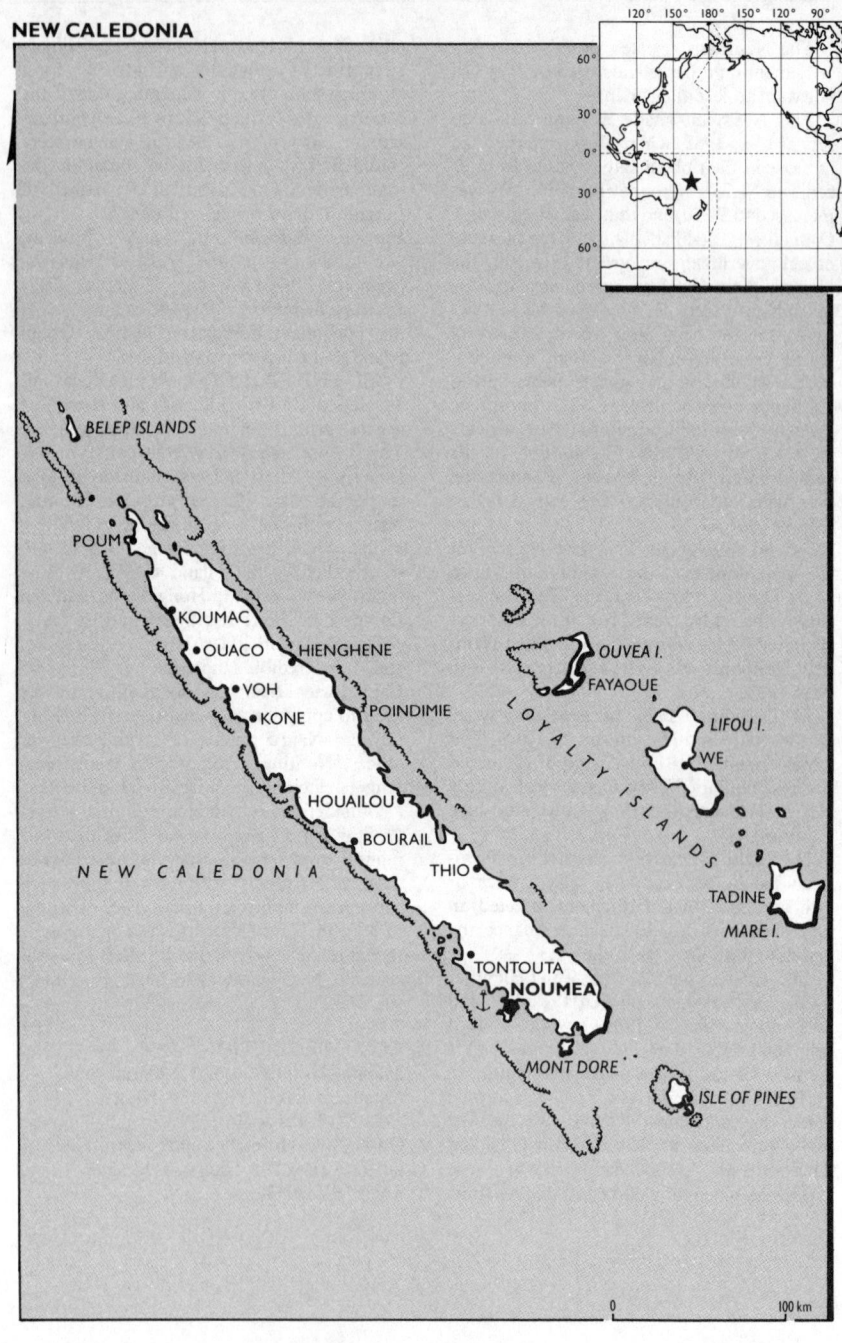

NEW CALEDONIA

BELEP ISLANDS

POUM

KOUMAC
OUACO HIENGHENE
VOH
KONE POINDIMIE

HOUAILOU

BOURAIL

NEW CALEDONIA THIO

TONTOUTA
NOUMEA

MONT DORE

OUVEA I.
FAYAOUE

LIFOU I.
WE

TADINE
MARE I.

ISLE OF PINES

L O Y A L T Y   I S L A N D S

0   100 km

New Caledonia

New Caledonia consists of one large and one small island, and the Loyalty and Huon groups. The largest island has an area of 16,750 sq. km and is one of the largest in the Pacific. The group is located between 19 and 23 deg S latitude and 163 and 168 deg E longitude. The main island, New Caledonia, known in French as La Grande Terre, and the other groups form a French overseas territory.

The capital is Noumea, on New Caledonia, and is about 1850 km north-east of Sydney. Local time is 11 hours ahead of GMT.

In April 1983, the population of the group was 145,368.

The national anthem and flag are those of France. Currency is the French Pacific franc (Comptoirs Francais du Pacifique — CFP).

Public holidays are: 1 January, Easter Monday; 1 May (Labour Day); Ascension (39 days after Easter Sunday); Monday after Pentecost (about 10 days after Ascension); 14 July (Bastille day); 15 August (Assumption); 24 September (Anniversary of French Possession); 1 November (All Saints); 11 November (Armistice Day); Christmas Day.

THE PEOPLE. The indigenous people of New Caledonia are Melanesians. Before European annexation they are estimated to have numbered between 50,000 and 70,000. They lived a fairly typical Melanesian existence of subsistence agriculture. The political unit was the village or a loosely knit group of villages; a multiplicity of dialects was spoken and intertribal wars and family feuds were common. Some groups practised cannibalism.

Evidence of the former large populations is seen throughout New Caledonia even today in the evenly terraced mountainsides which are all that remain of irrigation systems for the cultivation of taro. (Some examples can be observed from the road between Noumea and Tontouta international airport.)

For many years after annexation the Melanesians bitterly resisted the French but gradually they were forced to submit, with the usual result — the population began to decline, probably as a result of disruption of cultural patterns and introduced diseases. The Melanesian population reached its lowest point shortly after World War I and has since increased fairly steadily. The census of 1963 showed approx. 42,000 Melanesians; that of 1976, 55,598, and the most recent, April 1983, counted 61,870 Melanesians in the population.

Census. At the 1983 census, Noumea's population totalled 60,112 and the other smaller urban localities (Thio, Bourail, Kone, etc.) 27,281. Rural areas contained 57,975 people, including 15,510 on the Loyalty Islands.

Ethnic divisions of the population may be seen from the figures in Table 1.

Of the population of 145,368 in 1983, 53 per cent of Melanesians and 40 per cent of Europeans were under 20 years.

Nationality. The territory's Melanesian population has full French citizenship. Members of foreign communities, such as the Vietnamese and Indonesians who were originally brought to the island for labour purposes, may acquire French citizenship; many have done so and have also gallicised their names.

Language. Many languages are spoken in New Caledonia, reflecting different ethnic origins, but the official language is French. These are about 30 Kanak dialects.

Migration. The rapid development around

TABLE 1

	Census 1969	Census 1976	Census 1983
Melanesians	47,300	55,598	61,870
Europeans	36,900	50,757	53,974
Wallisians	6200	9571	12,212
Tahitians	3370	6391	5524
Others	6790	10,916	11,788*
Total	100,580	133,233	145,368

* Includes about 5300 Indonesians and 2300 Vietnamese.

Noumea since the late sixties has been through a shift of population from rural areas as well as immigration from France, North Africa, Vanuatu, Wallis Is., French Caribbean and Tahiti. This was prompted by the planned massive expansion of the nickel industry.

Religion. The population is divided between the Roman Catholic and Protestant churches. Protestant teachers of the LMS particularly influenced the Loyalty Islands and east coast of the mainland. Noumea also has small communities of Mormons, Baha'i and Seventh-day Adventists.

Lifestyle. Noumea, with its nickel works, is the most industrialised city in the South Pacific and life in this urban centre with the numerous services and social activities offered is markedly different from the rural lifestyle. Many Melanesian communities still remain relatively isolated, living by fishing and subsistence agriculture, although health and education facilities are available to all.

Recreation. Among favourite recreations are water sports and hunting (deer, bird, game), petanque (bowls), cycling, football and tennis.

GOVERNMENT. New Caledonia is an overseas territory of France, with executive control vested in the High Commissioner, who is at present a political appointee of the French Government.

Legislature. There is a 36-member Territorial Assembly, elected by universal suffrage to debate and approve the territorial budget submitted by the administration. In addition, the assembly may express its 'desires' on

policy matters outside its jurisdiction and controlled from Paris.

Executive. In his capacity as head of the territory, the High Commissioner meets weekly with his seven-member Government Council (Counseil de Gouvernement) of which he is the president, the other members being elected by the Territorial Assembly.

Autonomy. Previous conservative French Governments have continually resisted the agitation for internal self-government. Instead they have offered decentralisation. Under statutory changes effected in 1977, the Government Council was enlarged from five to seven elected members. The High Commissioner retained executive control.

The Socialist government of President Mitterrand, elected in May 1981, took the power to rule New Caledonia by decree during 1982 in order to institute land, economic, social and judicial reforms. Under these reforms, provision was made for the return of much tribal land to its Kanak owners, for the economic development of the interior and the islands, for the incorporation of Kanak assessors into the judicial system, and for the establishment of a Kanak cultural office.

Electoral system. Two deputies represent New Caledonia in the French National Assembly, and are elected by universal suffrage. A senator represents the territory in the French Senate. The senator is elected by an electoral college of representatives from the municipal councils, and all members of the Territorial Assembly.

The 36 members of the Territorial Assembly are elected for a five-year term.

The elections of July 1979, saw a reduction in the number of splinter parties. Representatives of three political parties were elected.

Two were pro-French administration: the Lafleur–Laroque group's Rassemblement Pour la Caledonie dans la Republique (RPCR) with 15 seats, and Lionel Cherrier's Federation pour une Nouvelle Societe Caledonienne (FNSC) with seven. The third party was the independence-seeking Pidjot-Lenormand-Uregei group, Front Independantiste (FI), which won 14 seats. The FI linked the Union Caledonienne with the other pro-independence groups Palika, Fulk, UPM and PSC. Since the election, the LKS group has broken away from Palika, with the two former Palika members of the assembly joining LKS.

Later shifts and alliances between parties saw the emergence of the FLNKS (Kanak Socialist National Liberation Front), a coalition of most pro-independence parties under the leadership of Jean-Marie Tjibaou. The appearance of the FLNKS served to further harden the already obvious distinctions between Gaullist and opposition parties in New Caledonia.

For general electoral purposes the territory is divided into four electorates — South (including Noumea), Centre, North and Loyalty Islands.

Local government. The above names, but with different boundaries, are used to describe the four administrative subdivisions in the territory. Each subdivision is headed by a 'Chef de Subdivision', a public servant from France.

The municipality of Noumea is administered separately, under the territory's secretary-general, who is second in command to the High Commissioner.

The administrative subdivisions are further divided into 32 'communes', or municipalities, each with an elected municipal council and mayor. Final authority rests with the public servant at the head of the sub-division, who must approve all mayoral decisions.

Pons plan. Under the plan for New Caledonian autonomy announced by the French Minister for Overseas Territories, Bernard Pons, in October 1987, following the referendum of 13 September which

endorsed continuing association with France, electoral boundaries will be redrawn and the office of the High Commissioner will diminish in importance. In addition, an expanded Executive Council will replace the popularly elected Territorial Congress. Regional councils will continue to operate although their functions will be reduced. The plan, adopted by the Government of Prime Minister Jacques Chirac in November 1987, quickly attracted a number of critics including the President of France, Francois Mitterand. (See History section for recent political developments.)

Public service. The top echelon of most government departments in New Caledonia consists of metropolitan French public servants, many of them trained in leading French schools for administrators and engineers. Since France is governed by its bureaucracy rather than political parties which are constantly splitting and regrouping, the public service is regarded as a highly-trained elite. Very few Caledonians have been appointed as departmental heads.

In 1983–84 the Territory's public service comprised 9904 persons, including 4275 involved in territorial administration, 1757 in state administration, 3232 in the army (a figure significantly increased since then) and 640 in the CHT (Haut de le Territoire).

Justice. The laws generally are the laws of France plus such subsidiary legislation and decrees by the High Commissioner that pertain specifically to New Caledonia.

The principal officers of the courts are appointed by the Minister of Justice in France and include the President of the Court of Appeal, the President of the Civil Court, the President of the Court of First Instance, Attorney-General, Magistrates, etc.

A division of the National Gendarmerie is stationed in the territory. Officers of this force are recruited in France although there is an auxiliary gendarmerie of Melanesians. The service includes a Maritime Gendarmerie and a Riot Squad (Gardes Mobiles). The police force, as distinct from the gendarmerie, is locally recruited and operates in the city of Noumea, under a French officer.

In 1985 there were 23 magistrates in New Caledonia, including 16 empowered to serve on the bench. Some 22 solicitors were recognised by the bar in Noumea.

About 31 per cent of offences before the courts involve theft, fraud and similar crimes. Slightly less than 30 per cent involve traffic offences.

The territory's prison, Camp Est, is at Nouville, opposite the harbour from Noumea, and dates from times of the penal settlement.

Liquor laws. Liquor is obtained from bars, cafes, restaurants or from liquor stores and supermarkets, except between midday on Saturday and Monday morning. Bars are open from early morning to 11 pm. Although it was previously forbidden, the French aperitif pastis has been allowed in the territory since 1975.

Gambling. The Casino Royal opened at the Chateau Royal Hotel in December 1974 and offered games such as roulette, baccarat and chemin de fer. Visitors were required to be adequately dressed and to show their passports. A more casual atmosphere prevailed in a poker machine saloon. Changed ownership of the hotel in 1979 was long expected to cause a re-location of the casino, and in fact it was moved to the new Surf Hotel on Noumea's Anse Vata beach in 1983.

DEFENCE. Since Noumea was an important base for US and Allied forces in the Pacific War, France has emphasised the strategic necessity of maintaining troops in New Caledonia. Their role is to help assure the defence of French territories in the Pacific and to render service locally in case of natural disaster or possible disorders.

Under the French national budget, military expenditure in New Caledonia in 1981 for running expenses was CFP1,974,762,736 together with CFP486,132,433 for capital expenditure.

Various bases for marines, paratroopers, etc., are located in Noumea, Plum and Bourail. The naval installations are at Pointe Chaleix, Noumea.

In 1976 an air force base was built at Tontouta, and an army helicopter landing site in Noumea.

Since the political troubles of the mid-1980s, several other improvements in army/air force facilities have taken place, including further extensions to Tontouta Airport.

Military personnel stationed in New Caledonia were estimated to number 8000–8500 in late 1987. They included regular army, paratroopers and gendarmerie, navy and air force. About 200 of the young Caledonians undergoing compulsory military service were then training in France.

Growth in the numbers of locally-stationed military personnel in the last few years has also been a consequence of the territory's political difficulties.

EDUCATION. Schools are operated by both the state and churches under the supervision of the Department of Education. France finances the state secondary system and in 1975 offered to take over the primary sector also from the territorial budget: the change-over applied from 1978.

At the primary level in 1984 there were 278 schools; 185 of them public schools and 93 private. At the secondary level, there were 41 schools, 18 public, 23 private. (Nine years before, in 1975, there were only 12 private schools.)

There were four higher-education institutions, one of them private, offering training in teaching, technology, and various trades, and preliminary courses in law and economics towards a French university degree.

The 1984 student population is summarised below.

TABLE 2 SCHOOL ENROLMENTS

	State	Private	Total
Primary	22,432	11,452	33,884
Secondary (general)	7604	4877	12,481
Secondary (technical)	3610	1654	5264
Higher education	615	45	660
Totals	34,261	18,028	52,289

Overseas studies. About 150 higher-education students benefit from a system of territorial and state bursaries, and are studying either in metropolitan France or in the territory. A number of New Caledonian students are enrolled in Australian private schools.

In 1986 there were about a dozen Melanesian students doing courses at the University of the South Pacific, Suva, and the University of Papua New Guinea, Port Moresby.

Ever since 1966 when de Gaulle promised New Caledonia a university, plans have been discussed. It has been intended to encourage foreign students to come to Noumea as a centre of French culture in the Pacific. At the same time the local population would be served by courses of a technological nature. The embryo of such an institution could be seen in courses started in 1977 in association with the National Institute of Technology (Centre National des Arts et Metiers — CNAM). The notion of a university was more energetically promoted in 1986–87 by France's new Minister of State for the South Pacific, Gaston Flosse of French Polynesia.

In the meantime, each January the French Government organises a Summer School in Noumea for teachers of the French language from New Zealand, Fiji, and Australia. This is accompanied by a Summer Festival presenting French art, music and drama. Numerous French language student groups visit Noumea each year to improve their knowledge of living French.

The language laboratories at the Chamber of Commerce in Noumea are used by visiting students in addition to providing English instruction for young Caledonians. The Chamber of Commerce also conducts business courses in shorthand, typing, etc.

New Caledonia's total expenditure on public education in 1983 was CFP14.54 million, CFP11.4 million of which came from France. Salaries of teachers and other personnel accounted for 81 per cent of the total.

LABOUR. The chief source of labour statistics is the social service organisation, CAFAT, which records the number of employers paying payroll tax and the number of employees thus covered for social service benefits.

The total number of wage-earners covered in this way in the last quarter of 1984 was 31,250 according to CAFAT figures.

Wages. Wage levels, as recorded by the territory's Labour Department, rose from a guaranteed minimum hourly rate of CFP201 at the end of 1980 to CFP330 in December 1984.

Total wage and salary earnings in 1984 were CFP39,685 million.

The territory's Department of Statistics, however, classifies the economically active population into five somewhat broad categories, excluding agriculture. By this count there were 36,234 in various wage or salary-earning occupations. There were, in addition, 29,000 people engaged in agricultural pursuits throughout the territory's 32 communes. The greatest concentration of these was in the Loyalty Islands.

Social security. Through the CAFAT social service organisation employees receive benefits derived from a payroll tax of about 25 per cent paid by employers. Among benefits are ante-natal and maternity leave for working mothers, and child endowment.

According to the locally calculated cost of living index living costs rose by 12 per cent in 1980, by a record 15.7 per cent in 1981 but by only 7 per cent by 1984.

HEALTH. Government health services in New Caledonia are administered by military personnel. This ensures that medical facilities are available throughout the territory, including areas where private doctors may not choose to live.

New Caledonia had 194 doctors at the end of 1983 compared with 185 in 1981. There were also 48 pharmacists (42 worked in private pharmacies), and 37 dentists, compared with 53 the previous year. Most were in private practice.

Noumea's main hospital is the Hopital Gaston Bourret, which dates from early colonial days. It has 530 beds. After many years of public discussion, on 1 July 1983 the more modern Clinique de Noumea (Magenta), which opened in 1976 and has 176 beds, was officially integrated with the Hopital Gaston Bourret. It has previously been privately operated. The move was designed to meet the demand for more modern public hospital facilities.

There are several private hospitals in Noumea, including the Clinique Magnin (in Vallee des Colons), and the Polyclinique (Anse Vata), with 112 beds between them.

There are constant efforts to expand the system of medical centres, nursing centres, and dispensaries in the interior where most of the Melanesian population lives.

Many cases requiring emergency or highly specialised treatment are flown for hospitalisation to Australia. Psychiatric patients are treated at the Nouville Centre, which has 287 beds.

For TB patients, La Pirogue Sanatorium just outside Noumea has 46 beds.

Leprosy patients are treated at the Raoul Follereau centre at Ducos, in Noumea, which receives assistance from the New Zealand Lepers Board. On 1 January 1983, there were 491 cases of leprosy under treatment, and on 31 December 487.

There is one home for the aged, Ma Maison, operated by Roman Catholic mission sisters including Australians and other foreigners.

Research Institute. Medical research into local health problems is carried out by the Institut Pasteur, adjacent to the Gaston Bourret hospital.

Diseases. Intestinal parasites and enteric-type diseases are fairly common. There is no malaria. With two widespread epidemics of dengue fever in the Pacific Islands in recent years, strict measures are taken to combat the mosquito vector of this disease. Fish poisoning, from the eating of certain fish, is another local health hazard. Respiratory infections and VD are significant problems, and cancer, alcoholism and traffic accidents are increasing. Diseases of the circulatory system made up the most significant single cause of death. The expenditure on public health in 1984 was CFP2.3 million.

THE LAND. The territory of New Caledonia and dependencies has a total land area of 19,103 sq. km. The New Caledonian mainland is extended cigar-shape, about 400 km long and 50 km across giving a total area of 16,750 sq. km. Lying in the same axis as the mainland are the Isle of Pines and Walpole Is, in the south, together with the Belep, Surprise and Huon islands in the north.

The Loyalty Islands, about 100 km to the east, consist of Lifou, Mare and Ouvea in addition to several small islands, the only inhabited one being Tiga. The Loyalties have a land area of 1970 sq. km.

The third group of islands in the territory is the Chesterfields, which lie 400 km north-west of the mainland and are uninhabited.

From the Huon group in the north to Walpole in the south, the territory extends 900 km. From the Chesterfields in the west to Mare in the east is a distance of 1000 km.

The chain of mountains extending along the centre of the mainland divides the island into two distinctly different areas — the lush east coast, and the broad cattle plains of the west coast.

The highest mountain peak is Mount Panie of 1628 metres, in the north of the mainland.

Natural features. The Diahot river, in the north of the mainland, is the longest in the territory, extending for 90 km. In addition, 10 rivers flow to the east coast and 13 to the west coast, but there are no rivers on the other islands.

There are thermal springs in the central mountains at La Crouen, where a health centre and guest house are located.

The islands are surrounded by coral reefs, enclosing calm lagoon waters.

Soil resources. The main richness of the Caledonian soil lies in its mineral wealth — iron, chrome, cobalt and, especially, nickel. The open-cut mining of this wealth has very much over-shadowed agricultural development.

Climate. New Caledonia's tropical climate produces an average annual temperature of 23°C with little variation — only 6° or 7°C — in monthly averages throughout the year. The island is cooled by the south-east trade winds.

During the wet season, December to March, cyclones can occur, sometimes bringing heavy rains. The east coast receives about twice the rainfall of the west coast, an average of 2000 mm in the east, compared with 1000 mm in the west, including Noumea.

Fauna and flora. Local flora are of considerable interest to botanists because of the many endemic varieties. One local specimen which can be noted by casual observers is the sentinel-style pine, the *Araucaria cookii* sighted by Captain Cook. On the west coast, the sparsely-wooded plains with *Melaleuca leucadendron* paper bark trees remind Australian visitors of inland Australian landscapes.

The most interesting of local fauna is the cagou bird, with a prominent white crest. This bird does not fly but runs along the ground and makes a sound like the barking of a dog. It can be domesticated.

Land reclamation. There has been considerable land reclamation around Noumea. The city was actually built on a marshy harbourside, which necessitated the filling of large areas, especially around the Quartier Latin. Extensions have included the car park built on the shores of the Baie de la Moselle, as well as the massive port extensions built across the main harbour, and linking of Ile Nou to the mainland by way of reclamation and a bridge.

Land tenure. When France took possession of the islands, all land was taken over by the state which subsequently made grants to individual settlers besides allocating areas for Melanesian reserves.

The Loyalty Islands, Belep group and Isle of Pines are almost exclusively Melanesian reserves. Missions throughout the territory own about 2000 ha and Melanesian reserves 389,409 ha.

There is a high degree of privately owned land on the mainland.

The law forbids the alienation of Melanesian reserves other than to the state. Foreigners may acquire land with the approval of the High Commissioner.

Since 1978 the state has been purchasing private land for re-allocation to Melanesian reserves on the east and west coasts.

Largely as a result of this process, Melanesian reserves have grown in area from 142,000 ha in 1960 to 389,409 ha at the end of 1985. This area constitutes 21 per cent of the total land area of the territory. Land reforms are expected to continue.

PRIMARY PRODUCTION. In an economy very much pivoted around nickel production, labour costs and the poor organisation of distribution circuits have kept agricultural production at a relatively low level.

Coffee and copra. New Caledonia's only agricultural exports are coffee and copra. However, quantities remain small.

Total coffee production from the 1984–85 crop was 312 tonnes — 285.5 of robusta, and 26.8 of arabica. Robusta grows best in moist conditions, without great temperature changes. It therefore does best on New Caledonia's east coast. Arabica, on the other hand, is more resistant, and does well in the south of the main island, and on the dry west coast. Robusta is richer in caffeine than arabica, but connoisseurs prefer the latter because of its finer aroma.

Copra production in 1984 was 680 tonnes, most of it from the Loyalty Islands.

The 1984 export figures show 80 tonnes of copra exported (worth CFP7,300,000), and 39 tonnes of coffee (worth CFP10,000,000).

Livestock. In 1984 there were an estimated 120,790 head of cattle in New Caledonia — bullocks, cows, calves, steers. Horses, donkeys, etc. numbered 8789, pigs 35,086, goats 17,649, sheep 2971 and poultry 463,716. There were also 2088 beehives.

Local production of all meats (except poultry meat) was 3224 tonnes in 1984. Meat imports (again excluding poultry) in the same year were 1146 tonnes. Poultry meat imports in 1984 were 3008 tonnes (2860 tonnes in 1980).

Fisheries. At the end of 1984 New Caledonia had 261 registered fishing vessels, with 256 of them motorised — 194 with engines using motor spirit, and 62 equipped with diesel engines.

The 1985 catch, according to official reports, amounted to 2932 tonnes, covering a great variety of fish and crustaceans. There were 502.8 tonnes exported.

In addition, an estimated 2100 tonnes of fish were caught in traditional subsistence fishing activity, and in sports fishing.

Forestry. The area of forest land (Grande Terre only) is estimated at 374,000 ha of dense forest, or 22 per cent of the total land area; 226,000 ha of niaoulis-covered land (13.8 per cent); 21,000 ha of land covered with trees of other types (1.3 per cent); and 412,000 ha of scrubland (25.1 per cent).

In 1984 the territory produced 4980 tonnes of usable timber of all types to a value of CFP196,000,000, compared with 9762 tonnes in 1981. Local production in 1984 accounted for only 37.2 per cent of timber requirements.

MINING. New Caledonia has immense mineral resources. Apart from nickel and chrome, there are large deposits of iron, manganese and cobalt. Antimony, mercury, copper, silver, lead and gold have also been found.

Nickel. The nickel mines are generally worked by bulldozers from the mountain tops with the ore being carried down to the coast by various mechanised systems or by truck. From the coast it is shipped to the smelters in Noumea or exported.

New Caledonia is the world's fourth largest producer of nickel ore, after Canada, the USSR and Australia.

The traditional chief mining towns, operated by the island's sole smelting company (SLN), are at Thio, Kouaoua and Poro on the east coast and at Nepoui on the west coast.

What has characterised the territory's nickel industry in recent years is a series of desperate measures to cushion the crisis caused by falling demand for nickel, and world recession — desperate measures by metropolitan French sources, government and private, in injecting funds into the industry to keep it afloat; desperate measures by SLN management to reduce production capacity, staff, and hence costs; and desperate measures by the trade unions representing SLN's workers to ensure that the inevitable blows do not fall too heavily on them.

Although SLN has not been nationalised by the Socialist Government of President Mitterrand, various moves undertaken by it have resulted in the French Government now having a majority shareholding in the company.

New Caledonia's production of nickel metals in 1981 and 1984 is shown in Table 3.

In the nickel boom year of 1970, the comparable figure was 74,797 tonnes, and in 1971 68,332 tonnes.

Exports of nickel ore in 1984 had an FOB value of CFP4262 million, and refined nickel CFP24,413 million. Chrome ore brought CFP1144 million.

Other industries. The chief industrial area

TABLE 3 NEW CALEDONIA NICKEL METAL PRODUCTION
(In tonnes of nickel content)

	1981	1984
Ferro-nickel	27,989	29,158
Mattes	15,380	5642
Total	43,369	34,800

of Noumea is at Ducos, which has many warehouses and workshops.

Local products include soft drinks and foods of various kinds, handicrafts, automobile accessories, boats and their accessories, building materials, detergents, plastic packaging, house furniture, printed materials, industrial chemicals, animal fodder, clothing, and cassette tapes.

New Caledonia's brewery, the Grande Brasserie de Nouvelle Caledonie, at Magenta, produced 42,406 hectolitres of beer in 1981, double its 1978 production.

The Numbo Cement Works produced 50,154 tonnes of cement; 3147 tonnes of sheet iron was produced for the building and other industries. There is a local paper goods industry which in 1979, the last year for which figures are available, turned out 3,600,000 rolls of toilet paper, and 100,000 boxes of paper tissues, among other paper products.

TOURISM. Tourism has long been regarded as New Caledonia's second most important industry, after nickel. High local living costs, and pre-occupation with the nickel industry, have often made things difficult for any development of the tourist industry. In periods of nickel slump, however, local authorities have tended to look with more interest at tourism.

The argument swayed back and forth for years, with circles closely associated with nickel undoubtedly encouraging the public resistance expressed to large-scale investment in tourism.

But, in view of the protracted, intractable crisis in the nickel industry, the air was finally cleared in 1981: the local Government Council finally announced a plan of development which placed tourism not in second but in first place among the territory's economic priorities.

It seems that the decision was soundly based. Visitors in that year totalled 78,892, leaving aside 43,573 cruise-ship passengers who made day visits.

By 1982 the visitor numbers had risen to 84,100 and by 1984 to 92,900, though they declined sharply the following year because of the country's political troubles. In 1984 Australia provided the most visitors, followed by Japan, France, and New Zealand. There are no specific figures for tourist-derived revenues.

LOCAL COMMERCE. The three largest importing firms with retail stores are Ets. Ballande, Maison Barrau and Prisunic.

Local agricultural produce is marketed partly through the wholesale market opened at Ducos in Noumea in late 1974. Municipal markets operate near the Noumea central square.

Of the territory's 1384 registered commercial establishments in 1985, 957 were in Noumea, accounting for 3276 of the total of 3618 paid employees.

OVERSEAS TRADE. New Caledonia's exports are almost entirely restricted to nickel in various forms. Thus in 1984 exports of smelted nickel — ferro-nickels and mattes — were valued at CFP 24,413 million, and nickel ore exports at CFP 4262 million, giving total nickel exports a weight of CFP 28,675 million in the territory's total exports, which were valued at CFP 33,452 million.

Imports for the same year were CFP 49,605 million.

Of all exports, 71.9 per cent went to metropolitan France. There was somewhat greater diversity in the sources of the territory's imports, although imports from France in 1984 still exceeded those from all other major suppliers combined by a value of CFP 2.5 million. Imports from France totalled CFP 19.8 million. Other suppliers were Australia, EEC (without France), Japan, New Zealand and the US.

Customs tariff. Import taxes are imposed at several levels and include: customs duty levied on goods from foreign countries (excluding the EEC) — the average rate is 10 per cent; taxes imposed on all imports — the general import tax is 17 per cent; and a consumption tax on various items, particularly

petroleum products, sugar, tobacco and alcohol.

FINANCE. Locally derived income finances the so-called territorial budget, which is spent on maintaining public service departments such as social services, public works, and municipal activities.

Such government activities as education, civil aviation and the armed forces are financed by the French national budget.

Some relationship between territoral contributions and contributions from metropolitan French sources is shown in Table 4 outlining the budget for 1985.

Local tax system. The first stages of personal income tax were introduced to the territory at the beginning of 1980, and were extended in 1982.

Other, more traditional, sources of government revenue are import and export duties, and indirect taxes. The latter indeed represent the most important source of revenue for territorial finances, and in 1985 accounted for CFP 9993 million.

Banks. There are five banks installed in New Caledonia, four of which have opened since 1967.

The oldest bank in the territory, the Bank of Indochina, amalgamated in 1975 with the Bank of Suez to be renamed Banque de l'Indochine et Suez or, more commonly, Indo-Suez.

Other banks are the Banque Nationale de Paris (BNP), the Societe Generale, the Banque de Paris et des Pays-Bas (PARIBAS). The fifth bank, Banque de Nouvelle-Caledonie, opened in September 1974.

Overseas investment. The investment of foreign funds in New Caledonia is strictly controlled by the French Government, which insists that 50 per cent of any such enterprise should be French-owned. The only area of active encouragement is the tourist field. Funds from EEC countries have greater facility of entry.

Certain tax benefits are granted to approved companies planning investment which would promote local agricultural, industrial or hotel sectors. Upon approval from Paris or the High Commissioner, such companies avoid certain import duties, business licence fees and land tax.

Development plans. Superseding all earlier

**TABLE 4 BUDGET
OF THE TERRITORY 1985
(CFP millions)**

Revenue

Direct taxation	5540
Indirect taxation	9993
Registration fees and stamp duty	1139
Taxes for services and miscellaneous	352
Revenue from public property	162
Revenue from tobacco board	2700
Revenue from various services	807
Miscell. and casual revenue	170
Contributions and grants from French budget	8631
Grants and reimbursements	131
Deduction from reserve fund	140
Total current revenue	29,765

Expenditure

Public debt	3291
Local and national parliamentary allowances	302
Government of the territory	252
General services	949
Financial services	1318
Economic services	1524
Dept of works and infrastructure	2249
Social and cultural services	9578
Joint expenses and miscell.	506
Contributions imposed by legal, statutory or contract provisions or international agreements	3587
Refunds and rebates	112
Grants, assistance funds, bursaries etc.	6097
Total running costs	29,765

plans was the so-called States-General of Development, which in June–July 1983 brought together in Noumea well over 400 people from every field of political and economic activity in the territory to establish a territorial development plan.

Running from 20 June to 1 July, the meeting perhaps owed something in inspiration to the National Economic Summit called by the Australian Labor Government soon after its election in March 1983. But whether this was so or not, its happening in the New Caledonia context at all was nothing short of historic.

The fact that employers, trade unionists, and political and Custom leaders could spend 11 days together attempting to thrash out a development strategy for the territory speaks volumes for the new sense of responsibility for the territory's own affairs which appeared to be pervading many leaders on the New Caledonian scene.

In a message to the closing session of the States-General, Secretary of State for Overseas Departments and Territories, Georges Lemoine, said the States-General will certainly 'leave a great mark on the history' of the territory.

Subsequent political events, and the degree of economic dislocation caused by them, however, have made the implementation of any concerted development strategy difficult.

Transport. Regular air services and the steadily lengthening seal on the road around New Caledonia are reducing the isolation of the island's picturesque east coast. Coastal roads permit a complete driving circuit of the 'Grande Terre'. In addition there are several cross roads into the interior of the island. But some of the side roads running off these are suitable only for heavy mining trucks, or adventurous drivers in the territory's various motor rallies.

Noumea itself boasts various scenic promenades as well as an expressway leading out of town. From 7.5 km of sealed expressway at the end of 1979, the 'steadily lengthening seal' on New Caledonia's roads had reached 25.5 km of sealed expressway at the end of 1980, and 26.2 km at the end of 1981. By 1985 there were 1208 km of major roads and 4772 km of minor roads in the territory.

Vehicles. Local statistical authorities estimate that there were 44,980 motorised vehicles in the territory at the end of 1984, 1650 of which were in administrative use. Noumea has one motorised vehicle for every two inhabitants.

Overseas airlines. New Caledonia is served by UTA French Airlines which includes the island on its flights across the Pacific to Los Angeles and via Asia to Paris, using B747 and DC10 aircraft.

Air New Zealand operates to the territory from Auckland using B737s and B767s.

Qantas flies from Sydney using B747s.

Domestic airlines. The territory's internal airline, Air Caledonie, which was originally known as TRANSPAC, underwent a second transformation in November–December 1983. At that time it became Air Caledonie International, assuming a regional role for the first time. Agreements were signed in mid-1983 between French and Australian civil aviation authorities authorising the new regional airline to operate flights from the Australian ports of Melbourne and Brisbane to Noumea.

Formation of Air Caledonie International, and the introduction of the new services, followed years of supporting agitation in the territory, spearheaded by tourist industry interests.

During 1984 Air Caledonie carried 128,776 passengers on domestic routes, with services to and from the Loyalty Islands accounting for 56 per cent of them.

Local airfields. New Caledonia has 18 commercial airfields as well as a number of private airstrips. The international airport at Tontouta is 53 km from Noumea and had an international passenger terminal opened in 1972. The runway measures 3250 m by 45 m.

Apart from Tontouta international airport and various private airstrips. New Caledonia has the following airfields:

Magenta (Noumea) sealed airstrip, 1100 metres long;
Houailou, east coast, 1000 m, sealed;
Touho, east coast, 1100 m, sealed;
Kone, west coast, 1000 m, sealed;
Koumac, west coast, 1450 m, compacted soil;
Ile des Pins (Isle of Pines), 1100 m, sealed;
Art (Belep Is.), 500 m, compacted soil;

Lifou Is., 1100 m, sealed;
Ouvea Is. (at Ouloup), 1100 m, sealed;
Mare Is. (at La Roche), 1100 m, compacted coral;
Tiga Is., 1100 m, compacted coral and soil;
Hienghene, east coast, 800 m, grass;
Ile Ouen, 460 m, compacted soil;
Mueo, west coast, 700 m, sealed;
Voh, west coast, 600 m, compacted schist;
Poindimie, east coast, 500 m, sand and grass;
Poum, west coast, 650 m, schist and grass.

Ports. Most traffic is through the Port of Noumea and nearby wharves of the nickel company. Completely new installations were built across the harbour in the early seventies, including a causeway which linked Noumea to what was formerly Nou island.

Shipping has thus been taken away from the old wharves along rue Jules Ferry instead uses the following new facilities:
Deep sea wharves, 1120 m long with depths of 6 to 10 m;
Island traders' wharf, 340 m long with depths of 3 to 5 m;
SLN nickel company wharves, 530 m long with depths of 8 to 9 m;
Floating pontoon with 10 m depth at Baie de Numbo cement works.

Elsewhere on the mainland, ore carriers load nickel at harbour installations such as those at Nepoui and Thio, while using barges at Houailou, Kouaoua and elsewhere.

Small coastal vessels ship supplies through wharves at the following points: Isle of Pines, and the Loyalty Islands of Lifou, Ouvea, Mare and Tiga, also Belep Is.

Shipping services. Shipping companies serving New Caledonia from Australia and New Zealand include Pacific Forum Line and Sofrana Unilines, with cruise ship companies also operating, including P&O, Royal Viking, Sitmar and CTC.

From the Far East operate China Navigation Company and Kyowa Shipping, and McKay Shipping operates out of New Zealand. Sofrana Unilines SA operate routes between New Caledonia and the US and from Europe operate Polish Ocean Lines, Nedlloyd, and Bank Line & Columbus Overseas Shipping.

Local maritime transport carried a total of 1.8 million tonnes of cargo in 1984, 1.77 of which consisted of minerals.

COMMUNICATIONS. Telephone services connect Noumea with most centres on the mainland and outer islands. The automatic service extends from Noumea as far as Koumac on the west coast and Hienghene on the east coast. At the end of 1984 there were 18,843 principal lines throughout the territory of which 13,908 were in Noumea.

For overseas calls, most radio-telephone communications are with Paris, Sydney and Auckland for which there is a 24-hour continuous service.

A 'Telspace' antenna installed at Nouville in December 1975 considerably improved telephone, telex, radio and TV links with New Caledonia, allowing satellite transmission.

Telex. Noumea is served by telex and businessmen may put messages through the Chamber of Commerce.

Radio and television. Local radio and Tele-Noumea are French Government-controlled and operated through RFO (Radio-telediffusion France d'Outremer), the overseas arm of the French broadcasting service, formerly known as FR3.

Tele-Noumea has been operating since 1965 and extends through most of the mainland and, since late 1975, to the Loyalty Islands. It transmits in colour. A second TV channel commenced operation in early 1984.

Many of the programmes for radio and most of those for television are dispatched from metropolitan France. All programmes are in French.

Following recent changes in French regulations, a private, non-commercial radio station, Radio Rythmes Bleus, is broadcasting from Noumea.

Printed media. New Caledonia has one daily newspaper, *Les Nouvelles Caledoniennes* and a weekly political magazine, *Corail*. A reasonable selection of English language publications is available in Noumea.

In addition, many of the political formations in the territory publish party-political periodicals.

WATER AND ELECTRICITY. Noumea has a good water supply provided by the Dumbea Dam outside the capital.

The local electricity authority UNELCO supplies power for Noumea and its surrounding area from the hydro-electric installation

at Yate Dam as well as from diesel-operated generators shared with the SLN at its nickel factory in Noumea. Inland electricity supplies come from municipal and private generators. In Noumea, the voltage is 220.

MAJOR OFFICE HOLDERS
High Commissioner:
    Bernard Grasset
President of Territorial Congress
(Executive Council):
    Dick Ukeiwe
Deputies to the National Assembly in Paris:
    Jacques Lafleur, Maurice Nenou
Senator:
    Dick Ukeiwe
Secretary-General of the Territory:
    Jacques Augustin

GOVERNMENT DEPARTMENTS
High Commissioner's Office, PO Box M2, Noumea Tel.: 272822
Government Council, PO Box C5, Noumea Tel.: 281977
Administrative of Finances and State Personnel, PO Box 2506, Noumea Tel.: 272822
Administrative Methods and Computer Services, PO Box C5, Noumea Tel.: 275888.
Air and Border Police, PO Box 232, Noumea Tel.: 275070
Armed Forces of New Caledonia, PO Box 28, Noumea Tel.: 274772
Civil Aviation, PO Box H1, Noumea Tel.: 272508
Customs, PO Box 699, Noumea Tel.: 275196
Economical Action and Development, PO Box C5, Noumea Tel.: 273211
Foreign Trade Delegation, PO Box 367, Noumea Tel.: 273995
Gendarmerie, PO Box 12, Noumea Tel.: 282142
General Radio Communications Network, PO Box A1, Noumea Tel.: 273229
General Treasury, PO Box E4, Noumea Tel.: 272903
Government Police, PO Box 232, Noumea Tel.: 272822
Justice, PO Box F4, Noumea Tel.: 272061
Labour Regulations and Arbitration Bureau, PO Box 141, Noumea Tel.: 275572
Legislative Inquiries and Disputes Claims, PO Box C5, Noumea Tel.: 273211

Maritime, Mercantile Shipping and Fishing Affairs, PO Box 36, Noumea Tel.: 272622

Mines and Energy, PO Box 465, Noumea Tel.: 273944

Museums and Heritage, PO Box 2393, Noumea Tel.: 272342

New Caledonia's Delegation at Paris, 27 rue Oudinot 75007, Paris, France Tel.: 7830510

Penal Administration, PO Box 491, Noumea Tel.: 272527

Planning, PO Box 431, Noumea Tel.: 273210

Police, PO Box 289, Noumea Tel.: 272253

Police Administrative and Technical Services, PO Box M1, Noumea Tel.: 272822

Public Service Department, PO Box C5, Noumea Tel.: 276038

Public Works, PO Box H4, Noumea Tel.: 273339

Rural Economy and Development, PO Box 699, Noumea Tel.: 272674

Sanitary and Social Affairs, PO Box 3278, Noumea Tel.: 273992

Statistics and Economic Surveys, PO Box 823, Noumea Tel.: 275481

Taxation, PO Box D2, Noumea Tel.: 273211

Territorial Finances, PO Box C5, Noumea Tel.: 273211

Territorial Surveillance Bureau, PO Box MI, Noumea Tel.: 272822

Topographical Surveys, PO Box C5, Noumea Tel.: 273210

Trade, Prices and Consumption, PO Box C5, Noumea Tel.: 273211

Youth and Sports, PO Box 810, Noumea Tel.: 272384

STATUTORY BODIES

Coffee Price Stabilization Fund, PO Box 2592, Noumea Tel.: 285701

Employment Bureau, PO Box 141, Noumea Tel.: 281082

French Government Radio and Television (Overseas), PO Box G3, Noumea Tel.: 274327

Interior and Islands Development Bureau, PO Box 4166, Noumea Tel.: 274215

Land Redistribution Bureau, PO Box 4228, Noumea Tel.: 284131

Meat and Potato Marketing and Cold

Storage Board, PO Box 258, Noumea Tel.: 272484

Medical Care Centre, PO Box L5, Noumea Tel.: 284820

Melanesians Cultural, Scientific and Technical Bureau, PO Box 378, Noumea Tel.: 283290

Noumea Harbour Management Board, PO Box 14, Noumea Tel.: 275966

Overseas Scientific and Technical Oceanographic Research Bureau, PO Box A5, Noumea Tel.: 261000

Social Medical Centre, PO Box L5, Noumea Tel.: 282030

Territorial Postal Services Department, 14, rue Edouard Glasser, Noumea Tel.: 261642

Territorial Public Hospital Management, PO Box J5, Noumea Tel.: 272121

Territorial Tourist Bureau, PO Box 688, Noumea Tel.: 272632

Workers Compensation, Pension and Child Endowment Fund, PO Box L5, Noumea Tel.: 285033

FOREIGN MISSIONS

Consular Correspondance with Switzerland, PO Box 2352, Noumea Tel.: 273809

Consulate General of Australia, PO Box 22, Noumea Tel.: 272414

Honorary Consulate of Belgium, PO Box 2683, Noumea Tel.: 284646

Honorary Consulate of Italy, PO Box 165, Noumea Tel.: 273347

Honorary Consulate of Japan, 45 rue du 5 mai Haut-Magenta, Noumea Tel.: 281775

Honorary Consulate of the Netherlands, PO Box L2, Noumea Tel.: 285720

Indonesian Consulate, PO Box 26, Noumea Tel.: 282574

New Zealand Consulate, PO Box 2219, Noumea Tel.: 272543

South Pacific Commission, PO Box D5, Noumea Tel.: 262000

NON-GOVERNMENTAL BODIES

Chamber of Agriculture, PO Box 111, Noumea Tel.: 272056

Chamber of Commerce and Industry, PO Box 10, Noumea Tel.: 272551

Chamber of Manual Trades, PO Box 4186, Noumea Tel.: 282337

HISTORY. New Caledonia was evidently populated many hundreds of years before being discovered by Europeans, with probable migrations from Papua and certainly Polynesian settlers who landed in the Loyalty Islands.

Bougainville, sailing south from the New Hebrides in 1768, noted signs of nearby land; and when Captain James Cook came into these seas six years later, he made a search and discovered an island which he named New Caledonia because the pineclad ridges suggested a resemblance to Scotland. He landed at Balade, on the north-east coast, on 4 September 1774, remained several days and, before leaving, marked on a tree the name of his ship, date, etc., to show that the British were the first to arrive.

Cook tried to sail round to the west, but could not get outside the encircling coral reef on the west coast, so he doubled back along the east coast and, coming south, discovered and named the Isle of Pines on 20 September 1774.

Searching for the lost La Perouse, a French expedition, under d'Entrecasteaux and de Kermadec, arrived at Isle of Pines on 16 June 1792, and sailed along the east coast of New Caledonia very thoroughly exploring it.

During the next 50 years, the great island was visited by various navigators, explorers, sandalwood traders and runaway seamen, and convicts from New South Wales. Among them, English trader James Paddon settled on the Isle of Nou, in Noumea harbour. Missionaries from the London Missionary Society, then the Marist Brothers, arrived from 1840.

Penal settlement. Both Britain and France coveted the big island and its smaller outliers of the three Loyalty Islands and the Isle of Pines but were reluctant to come to the point of upsetting the existing status quo. Towards the mid-19th century, however, the French began to see the island as a penal settlement and also as a naval and mercantile base close to Australia, from which there was already beginning a promising trade with Europe. At the same time there was agitation from within France for annexation in order to protect French missionaries who were occasionally attacked by the natives, killed and eaten.

The final decision was probably taken in 1850, following a native attack on a French survey ship *Alcmene* when the entire crew was eaten at Paaba, but it was not until 1853 that Admiral Febvrier-Despointes raised the French flag — at Balade on 24 September, and on the Isle of Pines on 29 September.

At the time, Captain Denham of the *Herald* was there from the Sydney station, surveying the coastline. The British were incensed at the French annexation but not sufficiently so to do anything about it.

In 1854 Captain Tardy de Montravel selected the site for a capital and construction began — it was called Port-de-France — known since 1866 as Noumea.

The use of New Caledonia as a penal settlement was commenced in 1864, and the history of the place, for forty years thereafter, is associated with the stories of penal island horrors, common to such establishments. About 40,000 prisoners were transported there, the headquarters being the notorious Ile Nou.

Most of France's long-term political prisoners were sent to New Caledonia, particularly socialists, in the round-up which followed the Franco-German War.

These political deportees were imprisoned at Ducos, near Noumea, and on the Isle of Pines.

Transportation ceased in 1897, but a large section of the European population for years afterwards were long-term prisoners and their descendants.

From 1853 until 1884 New Caledonia was administered by military governors; in 1885, a civilian governor was placed in charge, assisted by a Conseil-General (elected advisory council).

Other than turn it into a penal settlement, the French were able to do little with their new colony initially. They tried to encourage colonists to take up land but in the face of native hostility, few newcomers were prepared to try it, although a number of individualists, English, Irish, Scandinavian, had dug themselves in long before annexation. In their early years, the French were continually suppressing native risings, the bloodiest of them in 1878 and the last skirmish in 1917.

The colony's economic development was marked by the discovery of nickel by Jules Garnier in 1863, and the 'gold rush' beginning in 1870. John Higginson spearheaded the development of the Caledonian nickel industry.

In the first half of the 20th century, the Caledonians proved their valour fighting for France in two world wars. In World War I the islanders joined the Tahitians to form the Bataillon du Pacifique (Pacific Battalion) and fought in France. In World War II, the Caledonians were among the first overseas French to respond to General de Gaulle's appeal to fight as 'Free French' after Paris fell to the Germans. The islanders served mainly in North Africa.

In the Pacific War. US General Patch arrived in New Caledonia in March 1942 with the first contingent of men, to turn the island into a great US military base for operations against the Japanese.

The Americans built four airfields, impressive roads and launched the territory into the modern era.

Postwar developments. The years after World War II saw some advance in social and political conditions for the territory's indigenous inhabitants, Melanesians were permitted to leave their reserves in 1946 and were granted the right to vote in elections concerned with their country's politics in 1951. A movement towards independence for the territory was evident as early as the 1950s, although a referendum on the subject of independence for French territories returned a 'No' vote from New Caledonia in 1958.

The problem of independence for New Caledonia is vastly complicated by the historically evolved population balance which has left the original Melanesian inhabitants a minority in their own country, even though they remain the largest single group. Balancing the 'legitimacies' claimed by the various communities — especially the Melanesians and the locally-born French — would test the proverbial wisdom of Solomon. It is, as a French journalist wrote after a visit to the territory in early 1983, 'an extraordinary challenge to human intelligence'.

It was this challenge which faced the Round Table conference of New Caledonian political leaders held at Nainville-les-Roches, near Paris, on 8–12 July 1983.

A final declaration by the conference re-

cognised the rights of the Melanesian community as the original inhabitants of the territory, and the legitimacy of their 'innate and active right to independence.' The declaration was signed by representatives of the coalition partners in the Government Council — the Independence Front and the Centrist FNSC — but not by the anti-independence RPCR party. However, the RPCR did not speak *against* the declaration, and it was generally felt that the cordial atmosphere prevailing in relations between erstwhile political adversaries present at the conference augured well for the future.

What cordiality may have been achieved at the conference was shattered by subsequent events. In an atmosphere, described by a French anthropologist as being 'very South African', more and more Europeans in New Caledonia began to arm themselves. 'All this,' wrote anthropologist Jean Guiart early in 1984 'points to a tense situation in New Caledonia, where murders and death threats have been coming from the European side for years. Melanesians are losing patience and could start answering in kind — death for death.' Regional Prime Ministers David Lange of New Zealand and Walter Lini of Vanuatu expressed similar views later that year.

The violence which had been building up for some time came to a head at the Territorial Assembly elections in November 1984. Barricades were erected and firebombs thrown in Noumea. Ballot boxes and ballot papers were destroyed by Kanak activists, and a widespread boycott of the elections by supporters of independence resulted in an estimated 50 per cent of registered voters abstaining. Additional police and soldiers were flown in from France. Their numbers in New Caledonia have been increasing ever since.

The following month saw both pro-France and pro-independence parties take a more hard-line stance towards each other and to the possibility of any compromise solution. It also saw the appointment of Edgard Pisani as High Commissioner with special powers and a major task — to find a solution acceptable to all parties in New Caledonia within two months.

The Pisani Plan, as it came to be called, was formulated in an atmosphere of increasing tension. In December 1984 10 Kanaks, including brothers of FLNKS leader Jean-Marie Tjibaou, were ambushed and murdered. The following month Eloi Machoro and Marcel Nonaro, significant figures in the FLNKS, were shot by police. Violence grew in areas such as Thio on the east coast. The territory's two most important industries, mineral extraction and tourism, were severely disrupted, the latter falling away almost completely.

By August 1985, as a result of implementation of a modified version of Pisani's recommendations, New Caledonia was divided into four regions, each with a certain measure of autonomy. A referendum on the subject of independence was scheduled for late 1987.

Following elections based on the newly drawn regions, the FLNKS gained a majority in three of them. Noumea was taken convincingly by the Gaullist RPCR. For a short while it appeared as though a Kanak dominated independence for New Caledonia might become a reality.

But political events in France itself began to affect political change in the territory. The decline in domestic popularity of President Francois Mitterrand and the accession to the Prime Ministership of his political opponent, the conservative ex-mayor of Paris, Jacques Chirac, resulted in a setback for the independence movement in New Caledonia, notwithstanding the territory had been relisted for decolonisation by the United Nations committee on the subject.

As a consequence of the scaling down in importance of the regional councils by the Chirac government and an apparent loss of ardour by a number of erstwhile supporters of independence, the referendum of September 1987 resulted, despite large-scale abstentions by FLNKS supporters, in an apparent victory for those who favoured continuing ties with France.

The now redundant Pisani Plan was replaced by the Pons Plan (after the French Minister for Overseas Territories) which anticipated another redrawing of electoral boundaries and a scaling down of the role of the France-appointed High Commissioner. But few observers of any political persuasion were convinced that this represented the end of New Caledonia's troubles.

In late April 1988, shortly before the

French national elections, a band of Kanaks attacked police quarters on Ouvea in the Loyalty Islands, killing four gendarmes and taking another 27 hostage, later releasing 11 of these. During the subsequent recapture of the hostages by French security forces, another 21 people were killed, two soldiers and 19 Kanaks. In France President Mitterrand accused Conservative leader Jacques Chirac of over-reaction to the crisis, and later of using it for political ends. The results of the elections — boycotted by most Kanaks — saw the return to office of M. Mitterrand. In mid-1988 the prospects of a temporary partition of New Caledonia were discussed, as was a period of direct rule by France, followed by yet another referendum on the subject of independence. This scheme, known as the Rocard Plan, was put to a national poll in November 1988. Results were favourable to the plan.

Further information. Wilfred Burchett, *Pacific Treasure Island* (Melbourne, 1941) is an early but incisive account of French social and commercial policies in the territory. More recent works include: John Lawrey, *The Cross of Lorraine in the South Pacific*, Alan Ward, *Land and Politics in New Caledonia* (Canberra, 1983), Jean-Marie Tjibaou, *Kanake: The Melanesian Way* (Noumea, 1982), Myriam Dornoy-Vurombaravu, *The Politics of New Caledonia* (Sydney, 1983) and Martyn Lyons, *The Totem and the Tricolour* (Sydney, 1986).

NEW CALEDONIA'S ISLANDS IN DETAIL

New Caledonia. Known as 'la grande terre', the Caledonian mainland is about 400 km long by 50 km wide. With an area of 16,750 sq. km it is the next largest island in the South Pacific after New Zealand. It is surrounded about 10 km offshore by a barrier reef measuring 1600 km in length.

The mainland is cigar-shaped and divided by a central mountain chain from which numerous rivers make their way to the sea, particularly on the east coast. They cause sudden dangerous floods in the wet season. The island's capital, Noumea, is situated at the south-west tip, Other centres are Bourail, Kone and Koumac, travelling north along the west coast, and Thio, Houailou and Poindimie along the east coast.

Isle of Pines. Known in French as Ile des Pins and in Melanesian as Kunie, it is situated at 22 deg S latitude and 165 deg E longitude, about 50 km SE of Cape Queen Charlotte on the mainland. Navigation through the reefs is via the Havannah and Sarcelle passes.

The island has an area of 134 sq. km and extends about 17 km north–south and 15 km east–west. It was named in 1774 by its discoverer, Captain Cook, who noted its tall, narrow pine trees which now bear his name — *Araucaria cookii*. The first Protestant missionaries arrived there in 1841, followed in 1848 by the Roman Catholic mission which continues today at Vao, in the south-east. Seven kilometres west is the harbour of Kuto, the administrative centre. Five kilometres inland towards the aerodrome are the remains of the prison and graveyard for French political deportees who were kept on the island from 1872 to 1900. The chief settlement in the north is around the anchorage at Gadji. Population (1983) was 1287.

Belep Islands. This archipelago is situated about 50 km north-west of the northern tip of the mainland, in 19 deg 41 S latitude and 163 deg 19 E longitude. It comprises Art Is. (5560 ha), Pott Is. (1184 ha), Nienane Is. (245 ha) and the northern and southern Daos (55 ha).

According to tradition, Belep was the name of a mainland chief who settled there ten generations before the missionaries arrived in 1856. The chief centre is Uala, on Art Is. The islands are a Melanesian reserve, with a Catholic mission established there. There are 686 people living in the Beleps.

Huon and Surprise Islands. These are among a cluster of small sandy phosphate formations which surround the d'Entrecasteaux Reef, north of the Belep group. Huon is 260 km northwest of the northern tip of the mainland. Surprise, to the south-west, has a good anchorage on the leeward side and is 60 ha in area.

Loyalty Islands. These lie parallel to the east coast of the mainland, about 100 km offshore. From south to north, the three main islands of Mare, Lifou and Ouvea are about 50 km one from the next. They are formed of upraised coral forming low plateaux never reaching 100 m above sea level, often falling straight into the sea or bordered by a narrow,

flat coastal plain. In early times, Polynesian migrations mingled with the Loyalties' Melanesians. The islands are treated largely as Melanesian reserves, with both Roman Catholic and Protestant missions present. There are no rivers in the Loyalty Islands.

Mare Is. is located on 21 deg 30 S latitude and 168 deg E longitude. It has a maximum length of 40 km and an area of 650 sq. km. It is shaped like an irregular hexagon, with its rocky cliffs surrounding the island like a fortress. Inland are the two small volcanic hills of Rava and Peorawa, rising 10 to 15 m above the coral plateau. The chief centre is Tadine on the west coast. Other centres are La Roche, on the north coast, Netche on the west, and Penelo on the east coast. Population in 1983 was 4610.

Lifou Is., like Mare, is a plateau bordered by high cliffs along a coastline indented with deep bays, such as Sandal Bay, bordered by the town of Chepenehe in the west, and Chateaubriand Bay in the east with the town of We. We is the administrative headquarters of the Loyalty Islands subdivision. Limestone rocks on Lifou have numerous caves, the most beautiful being perhaps Tingeting, about 6 km north of Nathalo, in the northeast. Lifou Is. is situated in 21 deg S latitude and 167 deg E longitude. It is the largest of the Loyalty Islands, with an area of 1150 sq. km. It extends about 60 km in length and 50 km wide. Population in 1983 was 8128.

Ouvea Is. is an atoll situated at 20 deg 30 S latitude and 166 deg 30 E longitude and has an area of 160 sq. km. The main island, to the east, is composed of two segments connected by a band of coral barely 40 m wide in places. The lagoon is enclosed on the western side by a string of islets. The chief centre, with holiday resort, is Fayaoue, on the south-west of the main island. Ouvea has a population of 2773.

Tiga Is. lies between Lifou and Mare, about 30 km north of Mare. It is about 6 km long and 2 km wide.

Walpole Island is in line with the Loyalty Islands at their southern tip, about 150 km east of the Isle of Pines and the same distance SE of Mare, i.e. about 22 deg 30 S latitude and 168 deg 40 E longitude. Walpole is about 1 sq. km in area formed of limestone strata up to 70 m high. The island is surrounded by steep cliffs with very difficult access, as it has no protective barrier reef. Durand Reef lies to its northwest. The exploitation of phosphate from 1910 to 1936 has left the island barren of trees. It is believed to have been discovered in 1800 by Captain Butler who named it after his ship, the *Walpole*.

Matthew Island, Hunter Island. Situated about 450 km due east of the southern tip of the New Caledonian mainland, and about 350 km SE of Aneityum in Vanuatu, Matthew Island is conical in shape, and of volcanic origin. (It is reported to have tripled in size during an eruption in the 1950s). It is 500 m in diameter and up to 177 m high. It is uninhabited. Together with Hunter Island, an uninhabited volcanic rock outcrop to the SE of it, Matthew Island has become the centre of a dispute between the governments of France and Vanuatu.

Pacific Islands Monthly in April 1963 described Matthew Island as 'one of the most useless parcels of land in the South Pacific ... It is miles from anywhere. There is no water on it. It has no vegetation except grass, and no animal life apart from crabs and seabirds.'

But with the advent of the United Nations Law of the Sea the two tiny islands suddenly assumed the greatness of their surrounding 200 miles of ocean, as an exclusive economic zone.

French authorities in New Caledonia in December 1975 dispatched a warship, *La Bayonnaise*, to take official possession of the islands in the name of France. Plaques were affixed to each island to commemorate the occasion. A year later, for the first time, the French Government adopted a law saying that the two islands were part of the territory of New Caledonia and dependencies.

But the problem is, as pointed out by the now independent government of Vanuatu, that the French — with the assent of the British — had already declared the islands to be part of the old New Hebrides Condominium, to which the Vanuatu Government is the successor.

For most of the life of the condominium, France had responsibility for its mapping programme. These French-made maps clearly showed the islands as part of the New Hebrides, within the administrative jurisdiction of the Tanna district agent.

On 9 March 1983, an official Vanuatu Government party landed on Hunter Island and hoisted the country's flag. They also removed the plaque proclaiming French sovereignty. French helicopters were reported on Hunter late in March, amid speculation that they were preparing a landing pad on the island, and replacing the missing plaque.

As matters stand at present the French Government declares that its claim to the islands is 'incontestable'.

The Vanuatu Government, for its part, refuses to accept that any French claim to the islands existed.

On the basis that there are claimed to be strong customary links between Matthew and Hunter and the Vanuatu islands of Tanna, Futuna and Aneityum, New Caledonia's Independence Front in 1982 recognised the sovereignty of Vanuatu over the two islands.

Chesterfield Archipelago. This lies about 600 km west of the northern tip of the Caledonian mainland and extends about 500 km north–south. The group includes several small atolls of 15 to 20 ha. They are inhabited by numerous seabirds, and guano was worked there around 1879 by Austral Guano. The main atolls are Long, Brampton Passage, Mouillage (Anchorage). Reynard, Loop and Avon.

The archipelago was discovered in 1793 by the ship *Chesterfield*. The French took possession officially in 1877, although an Englishman, Captain North, had previously occupied these islands. Their main interest now lies in resources of the seabed with oil leases taken out in the area.

FOR THE TOURIST. New Caledonia has something for everyone — lush tropical landscapes and harsh mining terrain, from rugged mountain to soothing lagoon. Noumea, the capital, has developed as a showcase of the French way of life, with lavish restaurants or delicious take-away food from the supermarkets; sophisticated dressing in the Paris-style boutiques or chic Tahitian pareos worn on the beach. There are multi-storeyed hotels and seaside thatch bungalows or camping areas throughout the mainland, for anyone who really likes to rough it. Those who get upset by misunderstandings with the French, may be advised to take a dose of good humour with their cognac.

Noumea transport ranges from taxis and rental cars to the 'baby-car' small buses which run through all the suburbs from a new bus station between the central square and the Baie de la Moselle.

Duty free shopping. Under a system introduced in 1975, certain stores displaying the 'DUTY FREE from NOUMEA' sign will allow a 20 to 30 per cent discount on certain items on a minimum bill of CFP 2000 when visitors produce their passport and ticket. The purchases involved must be handy for Customs inspection in hand luggage on departure at the airport, bottles sealed, etc. Relevant receipts must be handed to Customs so the storekeeper may be officially reimbursed. Failure to surrender receipts means a loss for the storekeepers.

There is also a duty free shop in the departure lounge of Tontouta airport. Cruise ship passengers have duty-free purchases in town delivered to their ship. There is also a boutique in the shipping passenger lounge where black coral jewellery, local handicrafts and styles of clothing can be bought.

Entry formalities. All visitors must hold a valid passport and have an onward or return ticket.

Citizens of the following countries may stay in New Caledonia for three months without a visa: member countries of the European Economic Community; countries of former sub-Saharan French Africa with the exception of Guinea, Chad, Cameroon and Madagascar; Monaco, Spain, Portugal, Switzerland, Austria, Sweden, Norway, Iceland, Australia and New Zealand.

Citizens of the following countries may stay one month without a visa: Western European countries not mentioned above; the United States, Canada: Israel, Japan, South Korea, Morocco, Tunisia, Djibouti.

Citizens of all other countries require visas to visit New Caledonia.

Visiting yachts must report to the Port Captain in Noumea who will also call upon yachts at the Cercle Nautique yacht club in the Baie des Pecheurs to complete formalities.

Airport tax. This is not levied in New Caledonia. Tipping is not encouraged.

Sightseeing. City tours of Noumea include hilltop lookouts, the excellent museum and the world-famed aquarium with its fluorescent corals.

Nouville, the former island now linked by causeway across Noumea harbour, retains many old buildings from early convict days, including a disused chapel which has been converted into a theatre 'le Theatre de l'Ile'.

The small zoo and botanical gardens near Mont Te on the outskirts of Noumea contain local wildlife. They are open to the public at specified hours.

Visitors travelling inland may see the New Zealand War Cemetery at Bourail. By proceeding further across the central mountains, one may drive along the lush East Coast with numerous Melanesian villages.

An interesting circuit closer to Noumea takes one from Boulouparis across the central mountains to the nickel centre of Thio on the East Coast then through rural Canala to La Crouen spa and on to Melanesian villages at Couli before returning via the Relais Melanesian restaurant at La Foa and back to Noumea.

After sampling the feasts for the eye, one finds eating is a major pleasure in Noumea where the diversity of the local population offers all manner of cuisine from Indonesian and Vietnamese specialties to dishes from North Africa and all the regions of France, as well as local mangrove oysters, heart of coconut palm and Tahitian fish salad.

Tourist representatives abroad. Japan: French Government Tourist Office, Akasaka Park Building No. 2, 10–9 Akasaka 2, Chome, Minato-Ku, Tokyo; France: Direction du Tourisme, rue de l'Ingenieur Keller, 75015, Paris; Australia: New Caledonia Government Tourist Office, 13th Floor, Erskine House, 39 York Street, Sydney 2000; New Zealand: UTA French Airlines, 11 Commerce Street, Auckland.

ACCOMMODATION
Noumea hotels

Hotels known as 'Tourism Hotels' are classified from 1 to 4 stars, according to various norms of comfort and service. The revision of the classification of a 'Tourism Hotel' is brought up to date each year.

Inland and Islands hotels

The hotels, also known as 'Relais' are classified in three categories: Comfort 'Relais' 3 stars, Tourist 'Relais' 2 stars, Halting-place

'Relais' (or halting place lodging) one star. Generally of a small or medium capacity (10 to 40 rooms or bungalows) these 'Relais' offer personalised service in conditions of comfort which vary according to their classification.

Rural lodgings — tribal lodgings

The 'rural lodging' or 'tribal lodging' is situated in a Melanesian village or property, offers individual accommodation in close touch with the natural and human context of the region. The bungalows are Melanesian-style huts.

NOUMEA

Caledonia*: City (Quartier Latin). Tel.: 27.38.21. 25 rooms, 6 with kitchen, bar, restaurant, air cond.

Club Mediterranee***: Anse Vata Beach, Tel.: 26.12.00. 280 rooms, village club, conv. facilities.

Escapade Resort***: Ilot Maître Island. Tel.: 28.53.20. 44 rooms, 2 suites, bar, restaurant, air cond., lounge, TV, water activities.

Isle de France Travelodge***: Anse Vata. Tel.: 26.24.22. 92 rooms, 8 suites, bar, restaurant, lounge, conference room, air cond., TV, swimming pool, lounge.

Le Lagon**: Anse Vata. Tel.: 26.22.12. 60 rooms, bar, restaurant, lounge, conference room, air cond., TV, boutique. Sport/water activities (Noumea Club).

La Perouse*: City (Sebastopol Street). Tel.: 27.22.51. 29 rooms, bar, lounge, snack.

Mocambo**: Baie des Citrons. Tel.: 26.27.01. 28 rooms, 2 suites, bar, lounge, air cond., TV, conference room.

Motel Anse Vata**: Anse Vata. Tel.: 26.26.12. 22 rooms, lounge, air cond. (sup.), full equip. units, TV.

Motel Le Bambou*: Val Plaisance. Tel.: 26.12.90. 16 rooms, TV, lounge, air fans, fully equip. units.

Noumea Village**: City (Sebastopol Street). Tel.: 28.30.06/27.32.99. 36 rooms, 12 flats, TV, lounge, air cond., swim. pool, pool bar, restaurant, boutiques (12 flats fully equipped).

Lantana Beach**: Anse Vata. Tel.: 26.18.39. 37 rooms, bar, lounge, TV, air cond., boutiques, UTA desk, snack, bank.

Noumea Beach**: Baie des Citrons, Tel.: 26.20.55. 60 rooms, bar, lounge, TV, restaurant, boutique, Japanese restaurant, swim. pool.

Nouvata***: Anse Vata. Tel.: 26.22.00. 50 rooms, bar, lounge, TV, restaurant, pizzeria, Chinese restaurant, snack, boutiques, night club, gardens, swim. pool, Air cond. (10 motel type fully equip. units: sup. 850 CFP).

Paradise Park Motel***: City suburb (Vallée des Colons). Tel.: 27.25.41. 62 units, fully equipped units and flats, swim. pools, air cond., TV, restaurant, snack bar.

Le Paris**: City (Sébastopol Street). Tel.: 28.17.00. 44 rooms, 4 suites, bar, snack, restaurant, TV, air cond., 24 hr. coffee shop, night club, lounge, conf. room.

Residence*: Baie des Citrons. Tel.: 26.18.66. bar, lounge, restaurant, air cond.

Novotel Le Surf***: Anse Vata. Tel.: 28.66.88. 135 rooms, 2 suites, bars, restaurants, lounge, air cond., TV, swim. pool, boutiques, conf. room, casino.

Trianon Hotel: City suburb. Tel.: 26.24.92. 38 rooms, fully equip. units, Vietnamese restaurant, air cond. (sup.).

Youth Hostel. City. Tel.: 27.58.79. 60 beds.

Tontoutel***: Tontouta International Airport (45 km from Noumea). Tel.: 35.11.11. 43 rooms, restaurant, bar, swim. pool, air cond., TV.

WEST COAST

Tontoutel — (see Noumea). Tontouta.

Les Paillotes de la Ouenghi***: Bouloupari. Tel.: 35.17.35. 15 rooms, restaurant, bar, air cond., swim. pool, tennis, river activities.

Relais Melanesien**: La Foa. Tel.: 42.12.11. 11 rooms, restaurant, bar.

Hotel Banu: La Foa. Tel.: 42.11.19 restaurant, bar.

Evasion 130***: Sarramea. Tel.: 42.12.35. 23 rooms, restaurant, bar, swim. pool, disco.

Hotel le Niaouli*: Bourail. Tel.: 44.12.02. 22 rooms, restaurant, bar, air cond. (sup.).

Hotel Douyere*: Bourail. Tel.: 44.11.50. 10 rooms, restaurant, bar, air cond. (sup.).

El Kantara***: Bourail. Tel.: 44.13.22. 20

rooms, restaurant, bar, swim. pool, tennis, boat.
Le Bougainville**: Pouembout.
Tel.: 35.51.32. 8 rooms, restaurant, bar, air cond.
Koniambo***: Koné. Tel.: 35.51.56.
8 rooms, restaurant, bar, swim. pool, tennis, boutique, horse riding.
Koniambo Motel***: Koné.
Tel.: 35.53.02. 15 rooms, air cond., TV, boat trip (fully equip. units).
Tropical**: Koné. Tel.: 35.52.61. 9 rooms, restaurant, bar, air cond. (sup.).
Coppelia**: Koumac. Tel.: 35.62.66.
10 rooms, restaurant, bar, air cond. (sup.).
Madona**: Koumac. Tel.: 35.61.05.
13 rooms, restaurant, bar, air cond. (sup.).
Passiflore*: Koumac. Tel.: 35.62.10.
8 rooms, restaurant, bar, air cond. (sup.).
Le Grand Cerf*: Koumac. Tel.: 35.61.31.
8 rooms, restaurant, bar.
Le Caillou*: Ouégoa. Tel.: 35.64.03.
5 rooms, restaurant, bar.

EAST COAST
Nounous**: Thio. Tel.: 43.11.11.
10 rooms, restaurant, bar, air cond. (sup.).
Relais de la Moara*: Thio. Tel.: 43.11.33.
10 rooms, restaurant, bar.
Bel Air*: Houailou. Tel.: 42.51.11.
11 rooms, restaurant, bar.
Hotel de la Plage**: Poindimié.
Tel.: 42.71.28. 9 rooms, restaurant, bar, air cond. (sup.).
Relais d'Amoa***: Poindimié.
Tel.: 42.71.61. 9 rooms, restaurant, bar, pool, boat, air cond.
Tapoundari: Poindimié. Tel.: 42.71.11.
20 rooms, restaurant, bar, some air cond. rooms, some kitchenettes.
Relais Alison: Touho. Tel.: 42.88.12.
5 rooms, restaurant, bar, air cond. (sup.).
Hotel de la Baie*: Touho. Tel.: 42.88.37.
6 rooms, restaurant, bar.

SOUTH
Vallon Dore*: Mont Dore. Tel.: 43.32.08.

5 rooms, restaurant, bar, swim. pool.
La Siesta**: Plum. Tel.: 43.35.77.
20 rooms, restaurant, bar, swim. pool.

Islands
Relais des Cocotiers*: Lifou.
Tel.: 45.11.36. We. 10 rooms, restaurant, bar.

RURAL — MELANESIAN LODGINGS
(Gites Ruraux Melanesiens)
Gite Guei (Tel.: 45.71.27), Ouvea, 4 bungalows.
Gite Fleury (Tel.: 45.71.36), Ouvea, 2 bungalows.
Gite Watau (Tel.: 45.71.25), Ouvea, 5 bungalows.
Gite Loka (*), Ouvea, 4 bungalows.
Gite Beautemp-Beaupre (*), (Tel.: 45.71.32), Ouvea, 3 bungalows.
Gite Luecilla (Tel.: 45.12.43), Lifou, 6 bungalows.
Gite Wilfried, Isle of Pines, 5 bungalows.
Gite La Reine Hortense (Tel.: 46.11.19), Isle of Pines, 3 bungalows.
Gite Manamaky (Tel.: 46.11.31), Isle of Pines, 4 bungalows.
Gite Nataiwatch (Tel.: 46.11.13), Isle of Pines, 4 bungalows.
Gite Oure (Tel.: 46.11.20), Isle of Pines, 8 bungalows.
Gite Kodjeue (Tel.: 46.11.42), Isle of Pines, 9 bungalows.
Gite Si Med, Mare, 4 bungalows.
Gite Wadiana (Tel.: 46.41.12), Goro (South), 5 bungalows.
Gite St. Gabriel, Touaourou (South), 3 bungalows.
Gite Ouroue (Tel.: 43.12.52), Thio, 4 bungalows.
Gite Poingam (Tel.: 35.63.40) Poum, 4 bungalows.
For further information phone Melanesian Holiday Services 28.21.86. Air Caledonie 25.20.20.

Niue

Niue, an uplifted coral island of 258 sq. km and located at 19 deg S latitude and 169 deg W longitude, is about 480 km east of Tonga and about 560 km south-east of Samoa. It is a self-governing Commonwealth country in free association with New Zealand. The administration centre is Alofi, on the west coast. Local time is 11 hr 20 min behind GMT.

The flag is yellow with the Union Flag in the top left quarter. New Zealand currency is used.

Public holidays are those observed in New Zealand plus: Peniamina Day (a religious celebration of the anniversary when the first missionaries arrived); Annexation Day which celebrates the day that the island was annexed by New Zealand; Constitution Day, which marks the introduction of self-government; and Takai, during the first week of the year.

NIUE

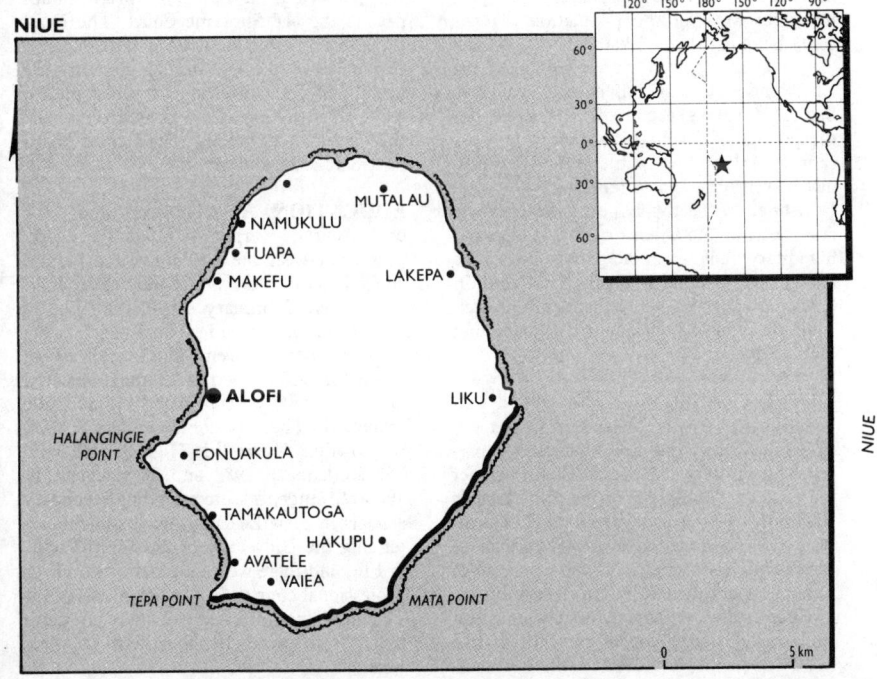

THE PEOPLE. The Niueans are Polynesians. The 1986 estimates based on 1984 census figures gave the provisional population total of 2532 comprising 1310 males and 1222 females. This was approximately 12 per cent below the 1984 census and the drop is attributed, once again, to outgoing migration, mainly to New Zealand, where the numbers of Niueans are about treble those resident on the island. The population of Alofi, the administration centre, was estimated to be about 900.

Citizenship. Under the 1974 Constitution the Niueans remain British subjects and New Zealand citizens.

Language. While the indigenous language is a Polynesian tongue closely related to Tongan and Samoan, the islanders also use English because of their long attachment to New Zealand.

Migration. The restricted nature of local resources has led many Niueans to migrate to New Zealand, regarded as their second home as they enjoy dual citizenship. Nearly 100 people annually leave Niue to make permanent homes in New Zealand.

Religion. Most of the population (75 per cent) belongs to the Ekalesia Niue, which has evolved from initial contact with the LMS under Samoan influence. Latter-Day Saints (Mormons) account for 10 per cent of the population, Roman Catholics for 5 per cent, while Jehovah's Witnesses and Seventh-day Adventists are also represented.

Lifestyle. While the Niueans are Polynesians, there are no chiefs or tribal system and hereditary rank is of no importance. The head of each extended-family has a voice in land matters only, while the elders of each community have a voice in matters affecting each village.

GOVERNMENT. Niue was granted self-government by New Zealand on 19 October 1974. Previously the island had been represented in Alofi by a Resident Commissioner who acted as President of the Niue Islands Assembly of 14 elected members. The Resident Commissioner was also Chairman of the executive Committee which consisted of four members elected by the Assembly.

Under self-government the new constitution provides for Niue to continue in free association with New Zealand which remains responsible for defence and foreign affairs and ready to provide necessary economic and administrative assistance.

Legislature. The constitution provides for a Legislative Assembly consisting of 20 members, 14 to be elected from village constituencies and six from a common roll.

Executive. The constitution provides for the general direction and control of the island to be in the hands of a Cabinet of four members — the Premier, elected by the Assembly, and three other ministers, chosen by the Premier from among Assembly members.

Local government. This takes the form of Village Councils, first set up in 1967. There are 14 councils and councillors are elected for a 3-year term.

Justice. Serious crime is rare. The court has to deal mainly with cases of disturbing the peace, making and consuming liquor, petty theft, etc. Approximately one-third of cases are traffic offences.

Courts. There is a High Court under the control of a Chief Justice and, a puisne judge, and, in their absence a Commissioner and Justices of the Peace, with right of appeal to the NZ Supreme Court. The Land Court has jurisdiction over land disputes.

Liquor laws. Persons under 20 years are prohibited from drinking in public places, while all drinking is prohibited on roads, thoroughfares or greens. The Liquor Board controls licensed premises.

EDUCATION. All schools are under the control of the government. Education is compulsory between the ages of five and 14, and educational facilities are rapidly expanding. There were 7 primary schools on Niue in 1983 including one side school which caters for expatriate children. The overall school intake for 1983 totalled 847. Pupils registered on school rolls were primary 451 and side school 39. There is one secondary school, the co-educational Niue High School, with 357 students in 1983 and 28 teachers. In 1983, 22 students were attending secondary schools in New Zealand and 9 students attending the University of the South Pacific in Fiji, and there were 21 others on trade or professional courses in the Solomon Islands Technical Institute and elsewhere. In addition, there were 19 short-term trainees overseas.

Teaching staff on Niue is predominantly local but in any year there are from 15 to 20 teachers seconded from New Zealand and elsewhere. Education cost the Niue Government $762,079 in the 1983 financial year.

LABOUR. Opportunities for paid work exist only within the government services, small industries and the Niue Development Board. With approximately 31 per cent of the population aged under 15 years, in 1986, about 60 per cent of residents were of working age, between 15 and 59 years. Most islanders, who do not work for wages, are engaged in their family plantations.

Wages. Maximum basic wage rates, at September 1981, were $1.16 per hour for unskilled labour, $1.43 for semi-skilled and $1.75 per hour for skilled workers. Beyond skilled workers level, a special rate of from $1.82 to $2.67 is applicable for those workers regarded as highly-skilled and experienced. Apart from the local Public Service Association, there are no industrial unions.

Social security. Persons 60 years of age and over are entitled to a pension at the rate of $4 a week.

HEALTH. All medical and dental treatment, including hospital services, is provided free of charge, subsidised by New Zealand government grants. Visitors unattached to the local public service pay medical and dental charges at the rate fixed by the government. There are no private practitioners. There is a 30 bed hospital at Alofi called the Lord Liverpool Hospital. It has a maternity section. Attached to the hospital are outpatients' departments, X-ray unit, laboratory and dispensary. Clinics operate in three large villages.

Other public services include public health education, routine refuse collection and disposal service, mother and child care services, visits by medical doctors twice weekly to villages without clinics, and dental clinic services. Transportation is provided by the Health Department for all cases requiring hospital treatment.

All school children receive free fluoride tablets when the dental section visits as well as visits from the child welfare section and routine health inspections.

Family planning services include the dispensing of birth control pills, health education

and education in the use of other methods of birth control.

The amount spent on public health has increased from $448,800 in 1981/2 to over $600,000 in 1985. The total number of employees in the Health Department in 1985 was 81. There were four qualified doctors, two Niueans and two United Nations volunteers from the Philippines. Nursing staff are trained by Medical Officers, the hospital matron and public health staff. In 1985 there were 30 nurses on Niue.

Statistics show that the birth rate in 1985 was 30.34 per 1000 population while the death rate was 7.9 per 1000 population, mainly elderly people with respiratory infections. In the mid-1980s life expectancy for females is 80 and for males 75 years.

Disease. The Niuean standard of general hygiene is high, and although situated in the tropics Niue is largely free from tropical diseases. However, there have been outbreaks of dengue fever over the years, the worst occurring in 1980. At its peak in March 1980 a third of the population was reported to be suffering from the disease, which caused four deaths. In 1987 respiratory diseases were the main causes of illness and death.

THE LAND. The island has an area of 258 square kilometres, with a circumference of over 60 km by road. The island extends 19 km from north to sourth. In general formation it takes the shape of two terraces, the lower being 27 metres above sea level and the upper saucer-shaped plateau rising to 65 metres.

Natural features. Niue is a raised coral outcrop and is probably the result of a series of tectonic upheavals, indicated by many deep chasms, especially those of Vailoa and Matapa. A coral reef encircles a precipitous and broken coastline. The soil composed of worn-down coral, is fertile but not abundant and this factor, combined with the rocky and broken terrain, makes cultivation difficult. Early in 1983, a New Zealand horticultural expert warned that Niue was in danger of losing most of its soil unless farmers abandoned traditional burning methods to clear land. Crops should be grown through weeds to conserve soil moisture and organic matter. Most people live in villages on the western side of the island.

Climate. Niue has a pleasant climate, fanned by the south-east trade winds. The island is on the edge of the hurricane belt and the last major disturbance was in 1979. The mean annual temperature is 24.7°C and the average rainfall is 2177 mm.

Land tenure. As the Niuean's livelihood depends on his family lands, alienation is forbidden, so that there are no landowners apart from the Niueans and the Government. However, under the 1969 Land Ordinance, it is possible for the Government to grant a lease of land for up to 60 years.

PRIMARY PRODUCTION. Productive ventures in agriculture and livestock are carried out by the Niue Development Board, under the guidance of the Agricultural Department. The board which is responsible for planning and financing schemes, produces lime juice, passionfruit pulp and juice, honey, copra and reconstituted milk.

Crops. Of the total area of about 26,000 hectares, about 20,400 ha are available for agriculture. The Development Board has encouraged increased planting of lime trees and passionfruit vines. At the same time the agricultural authorities have a programme for soil study and improvement of stock, including coconuts and pasture grasses.

Honey. Beekeeping has been a minor industry for some years and the honey produced is of high quality. It is exported.

Livestock. The main livestock owned by islanders are pigs and poultry. In addition, progress has been made in grazing cattle under coconut trees, thereby serving the dual process of keeping the plantations clear of undergrowth. This programme has been assisted by the provision of deep bores to

help overcome the water problem. These cattle, many of them Friesians, are used for beef.

TIMBER. About 5400 ha of land is forest containing some good millable timber. The government sawmill produces several hundred cu. metres of sawn timber each year for local building.

MANUFACTURING. Main activity centres on food processing for export, with lime juice extraction, preparation of passionfruit juice and pulp and honey. The Development Board has also assisted in establishing other small industries such as building and joinery, garage, local fishery, etc.

TOURISM. The island's first hotel was completed in 1975. The first wing, of 20 beds, was completed in time to accommodate guests at the island's self-government celebrations in October 1974. Since then a second wing has raised capacity to 40 beds. There is also a swimming pool. All guests' rooms have panoramic views of Alofi Bay. There is also another accommodation called the Hinemata Motel. It has three bedrooms whose occupants share a bathroom and kitchen. In addition there are two guest houses.

In 1985 there were 1495 visitors, 1092 from New Zealand, 25 from Fiji, 59 from the US, 8 from Canada, 28 from Europe, 81 from Australia and the balance from other Pacific countries. More than a third were there for business reasons. The figures for the first 9 months of 1986 were 1155, with 839 coming from New Zealand, 24 from Fiji, 42 from the United States, 9 from Canada, 40 from Europe, 47 from Australia and the balance from other Pacific countries.

TABLE 1 NIUE LOCAL MEAT PRODUCTION

	Beef		Pork	
Year	Quantity kg	Value $	Quantity kg	Value $
1979	9146	13,720	837	1761
1980	25,909	28,499	268	563
1981	31,028	52,570	115	241
1982	8917	21,656	—	—
1983	24,648	39,686	—	—

CO-OPERATIVES. There are several registered co-operative societies — Niue Handicrafts, the Women's Handicrafts Co-operative, the Public Service Savings and Loan Society and the Hospital Aid Society. Niue Handicrafts was financed by the Niue Development Board to handle the production and marketing of the very fine ware plaited from pandanus and coconut palm leaf. Exports of handicrafts earned $22,544 in 1985. Several other organisations operate privately.

OVERSEAS TRADE. Most of Niue's trade, exports and imports, is with New Zealand. The value of exports and imports has been as follows in recent years.

	Exports	Imports
1983	$632,976	$3,158,778
1984	$247,235	$4,209,791
1985	$175,274	$3,753,384

Imports. Most items come from New Zealand which supplied about 60 per cent of the $3,753,348 worth of imports in 1985. Other imports come from Fiji, Japan, Western Samoa and Australia.

Exports. Exports go mainly to New Zealand, then to Fiji and Australia and the Cook Islands. See Table 4 for details of the value of various export commodities.

Customs tariff. By an act of 1982 legislation for a single line tariff came into force on 1 January 1983. A port and service charge of $50 a tonne overall replaces the 5 per cent value Port and Service Tax which previously applied. Tax relief is given for specific items regarded as a necessity. Children's clothing, for example, is admitted free of duty. Luxury items attract a higher tariff with duty on cigarettes and tobacco rising to 100 per cent. Items free of duty include new and used commercial utility vehicles and vans under 1½ tonnes, all milk and milk products, video, television and stereo equipment under $100 value, pot plants with bulbs/roots, etc. for gardeners and chicken meat. Passenger cars of 1500 cc and under, previously taxed at 65 per cent, are now 35 per cent. There is free trade between Niue and New Zealand.

Budget. A comparative statement of receipts and expenditure in recent years appears in Table 6.

Taxes. Local revenue is raised mainly from income tax, (including 'aid to revenue' tax), customs duty and manufactured goods tax.

External aid. Under the Constitution Bill 1974, New Zealand undertook to supply

TABLE 2 IMPORTS — VALUES AND PERCENTAGES

	1983	%	1984	%	1985	%
Foodstuffs	$848,382	26.9	$1,171,600	27.8	$1,143,893	30.5
Beverages & tobacco	457,003	14.5	343,033	8.1	351,822	9.4
Crude materials	19,770	0.6	26,199	0.5	19,431	0.5
Mineral fuels & related products	647,682	21.4	1,435,206	34.1	748,230	19.9
Animals & vegetable oils	5415	0.2	6713	0.2	7313	0.2
Chemicals	176,314	5.6	150,024	3.6	139,213	3.7
Manufactured goods chiefly classified by materials	288,956	9.1	319,205	7.6	338,381	9.0
Machinery and transport equipment	402,983	12.8	514,066	12.2	736,353	19.6
Miscellaneous manufactured articles	285,273	9.0	243,648	5.8	268,748	7.2
Total	3,158,778		4,209,791		3,753,384	

TABLE 3 IMPORTS — COUNTRIES OF ORIGIN

	1981	1983	1985
New Zealand	$2,754,403	$2,046,822	$2,232,708
Fiji	699,960	672,223	753,159
Japan	114,307	136,576	499,092
Western Samoa	68,526	136,110	90,189
Australia	63,604	64,552	59,820
United States	43,680	39,320	2247
China	22,747	30,341	8978
Hong Kong	13,384	7592	9596
Taiwan	11,881	339	16,900
Cook Islands	7797	8528	31,214
Singapore	7313	2440	6784
Korea	3371	—	—
United Kingdom	2510	8410	—
Others	7151	5525	42,715
	$3,837,575	$3,158,778	$3,753,384

necessary economic and administrative assistance.

Currency. Niue uses New Zealand currency. The Post Office operates a savings bank and the Westpac Corporation opened a branch in April 1987. The Treasury Department handles foreign exchange, travellers cheques and other banking.

Development Plans and Guides. Niue produced its first Five Year National Development Plan for the period 1980 to 1985. Its goal was to increase the degree of Niue's self-reliance materially and to create self-confidence in the country's ability to meet a substantial share of its annual budget, The South Pacific Bureau for Economic Co-operation, in association with the Government, produced in 1982 *Niue, A Trade and Investment Guide* to encourage possible foreign investment in agriculture and tourism projects which would involve Niue's small work-force, thus hopefully stopping the population decline caused by migration to New Zealand. Niue also has a Tourism Development Strategy 1985–1990, prepared by a consultant under the auspices of the United Nations Development Programme and the World Tourism Organisation.

Postage stamps. The sale of postage stamps to collectors makes a significant contribution to local revenue and amounted to $470,000 in the year ended 31 March 1981, $500,000 in 1982 and $440,000 in 1983. From March 1984 to March 1986 average annual sales amounted to $516,686. Numismatic coins are also being struck.

TRANSPORT. There are approximately 128 km of all-weather roads plus 96 km of bush tracks negotiable by heavy trucks and four-wheel-drive vehicles. The main 60 km road circles the island but cross-island roads exist between Alofi and Lakepa. Alofi and Liku and Alofi and Hakupu.

Vehicles. There were 1438 registered motor vehicles at 31 March 1982, compared to 1022

TABLE 4 CHIEF EXPORT COMMODITIES

Year	Passionfruit products	Lime products	Root crops	Honey products	Handicrafts	Coconut cream	Footballs
1983	$24,747	$12,384	$3,235	$6,600	$16,728	$433,544	$119,553
1984	45,376	33,629	407	10,607	23,482	20,748	61,387
1985	14,142	18,895	55,727	19,567	22,544	—	22,559

TABLE 5 EXPORT DESTINATIONS

	1983	1984	1985
New Zealand	$611,911	$196,303	$154,881
Cook Islands	3617	42,750	12,209
Fiji	4628	5132	2810
Australia	3170	1752	2436
Western Samoa	7438	—	—
Tonga	1612	—	89
American Samoa	—	—	600
Others	600	1298	2248
	$632,976	$247,235	$174,274

TABLE 6 NIUE BUDGET FIGURES ($'000)

Year	Internal Revenue	External aid New Zealand	Australia	Expenditure
1980	1996	2462	—	4702
1981	1647	3142	56	5881
1982	1842	3847	300	7453
1983	2107	4600	526	6661

vehicles in 1980 and 921 in 1978. Of the 1438 total of 1982, 321 were cars, 989 motor cycles, 100 trucks 6 buses and 24 tractors.
Overseas airlines. Niue is serviced only by Air Nauru on a weekly flight from Auckland. Hanan International Airport has a runway of 1176 m which was resealed in 1981 to take jet aircraft. It can be extended to 1973 m.
Port facilities. The port of Alofi is an open roadstead. Vessels anchor offshore and cargo is brought ashore by launches towing lighters through a natural passage in the reef that has been widened from time to time but on which coral is still encroaching. There are landings, of a sort, at Tuapa and Avatele.

Plans to widen the access channel of Alofi are still being considered. However, a harbour development project was carried out in 1980–81 with funds provided by Australia.
Shipping services. A shipping service is

operated by the New Zealand Shipping Corporation, from New Zealand to Niue, the Cook Islands and Tahiti.

COMMUNICATIONS. All communication services on Niue are provided by the Government. Services provided include telegraphic communication, international calling and internal telephones. Telex and teleprinter services are also available. Niue is a participant in the UNDP/ITU Regional Communication Network whose object is to improve and rationalise communications in the South Pacific.

Radio. Broadcasts from Radio Niue, 'Radio Sunshine', are made on a part-time basis, providing local and overseas news, notices, advertisements and light entertainment. Programmes are broadcast six mornings, afternoons and evenings a week. Cable television is available and videos are in general use.

Newspaper. The island's weekly newspaper is *Tohi Tala Niue*, which is published in English and Niuean by the Information Office of the Central Office, Government of Niue.

WATER AND ELECTRICITY. There is no surface water, but pure drinking water is drawn from deep wells in the coral. A power reticulation project was completed in 1978 and nearly all homes are supplied with electricity. 340 kW can be produced from two generators. In 1983 2.4 million kW of power were produced, a decline from the 1981 production of 2.5 million kW. Most of the energy utilised on Niue comes from diesel generators. In 1983 744,000 litres of fuel were used.

MAJOR OFFICE HOLDERS
Premier, Minister for Economic Affairs, Public Service, Police:
  Hon. Sir Robert Rex
Minister for Finance and Agriculture:
  Hon. Dr. Enetama
Minister for Community Affairs, Health, Education:
  Hon. Frank Lui
Minister for Works, Administrative Services, Telecommunications:
  Hon. Robert Rex Jr.
Secretary to the Government:
  Terry M. Chapman

Chief Justice of the High Court:
  J. D. Dillon

GOVERNMENT MINISTRIES AND DEPARTMENTS
Economic Affairs (includes Civil Aviation, Shipping, Trade and Marketing, Tourism and Development), Government Buildings, Niue.
Community Affairs (includes Housing, Village Affairs, Information Services, Cultural Affairs, Sport and Recreation, Social Welfare, Religious Affairs, Women's Affairs), Government Buildings, Niue.
Administrative Services (includes Lands, Survey, Justice, Immigration, Statistics, Personnel Management, Secretarial Services, Government Houses), Government Buildings, Niue.

HISTORY. The island is believed to have been inhabited for more than 1000 years. The origin of the first migrants was probably Samoa or one of the islands of eastern Polynesia. A second migration, according to tradition, was a war expedition from Tonga about the beginning of the 16th century. A third, led by a Tongan chief of part-Niuean descent, resulted in the chief's assuming power over the whole island. Other contacts with Tonga seem to have been frequent, and usually hostile.

Two distinct dialects are still spoken on Niue. One called Motu, meaning 'the people of the island', is used in the north. The other, Tafiti, meaning 'the strangers' or 'people from a distance' is used in the south. Tradition has it that the Tafiti district was more affected by Tongan immigrants than the other. The Niuean vocabulary generally resembles Tongan. However, it contains many words that are absent in Tongan but are common to Samoan, the eastern Polynesian languages, or both.

European discovery. The European discoverer of Niue was Captain James Cook who made three landings on the west coast on 20 June 1774. Because of the fierce appearance and hostile conduct of the islanders, he called it Savage Island. This name persisted for more than a century, but has fallen into disuse.

In 1830, two LMS missionaries, the Revs

John Williams and Charles Barff, called at the island in the *Messenger of Peace* and tried to land two Polynesian teachers. They were repulsed. A similar thing happened in 1842. However, in 1846, the Revs W. Gill and H. Nisbet landed a Niuean on the island who had lived in Samoa for some years and had been trained at the LMS seminary at Malua. This man, Peniamina, was eventually accepted by his people, and he persuaded them to allow a Samoan missionary, Paulo, to settle on the island in 1849. By 1852, between 200 and 300 Niueans had accepted Christianity; and by 1854, when the first books in Niuean were brought to the island from Samoa, heathenism had been virtually abandoned.

In 1861, the Rev. W. G. Lawes became the first resident English missionary. He was joined in 1868 by his brother, the Rev. F. E. Lawes, who remained on the island until his retirement in 1910. W. G. Lawes left in 1872. A census in 1861 revealed a population of 4700 compared with the largest known figure of 5070 in 1884 and a record low of 2532 in 1986. However, during the second half of the 19th century, large numbers of men were frequently absent. Some never returned. In 1863, a Peruvian slaving vessel carried off about 130 men, most of whom died of disease in the Kermadecs. In 1868, the notorious 'Bully' Hayes kidnapped about 60 men and 30 women, and took them to Tahiti. Many others later went voluntarily to work on phosphate islands in the eastern Pacific. In 1899, for example, 561 Niueans were away.

The absence of so many men retarded economic development, but there were some advances. In 1872, for example, 85,000 lb of hand-picked cotton was exported as well as large quantities of arrowroot, coconut fibre and fungus. Trade was fostered by several Europeans who settled on the island. Among these was an Englishman, Henry Head, who was shipwrecked there in 1867. He married the high chief's daughter, had 15 children, and became the most influential person on the island, apart from the resident missionary.

A king elected. In 1876, the Niueans elected a king, Mataio Tuitoga. Under Head's influence, his successor, Fataaiki, petitioned Queen Victoria to take Niue under her protection. This, and similar requests in 1898 and 1899 were refused. But in April 1900,

the Union Flag was hoisted over the island and a British official, Basil Thomson. declared it a British protectorate. (Thomson, later Sir Basil Thomson, was in 1890 Assistant Premier of Tonga, later a magistrate in Fiji, head of the British Secret Service in World War I and after the war Governor of Dartmoor Prison in Devon.) British sovereignty was proclaimed on 10 October 1900, when the Earl of Ranfurly, Governor of New Zealand, visited the island.

Annexation. Niue was formally annexed to New Zealand as part of the Cook Islands in September 1901, and S. Percy Smith became the first government resident. The island was made a separate administration with its own resident commissioner and island council in 1904.

There was no constitutional change until 1960 when the first Niue Assembly was established with an elected representative from each of the island's 13 villages, under the presidency of the resident commissioner. In 1966, some of the resident commissioner's powers were delegated to the Assembly following the introduction of the member system of government and the designation of Mr R. R. Rex as leader of government business. Further constitutional advances were made in 1968 and 1972.

Self-government. Then, on 19 October 1974, Niue attained the status of 'self-government in free association with New Zealand' when the Niue Constitution Act 1974 came into force. Celebrations to mark the occasion were attended by distinguished visitors from several Pacific Island countries as well as New Zealand, Australia and Britain. Mr R. R. Rex headed the first government as Premier, with a cabinet of three.

In October 1984 Niue celebrated 10 years of self-government with the proceedings presided over by the now Sir Robert Rex. Government leaders from various South Pacific countries as well as representatives of governments from Australia, New Zealand and the United States all attended the week-long celebrations.

Further information. S. Percy Smith, *Niue, the Island and its People*, Suva, 1983, is a reprint of a classic study; Solomona Kalauni et al, *Land Tenure in Niue*, Suva, 1977, examines land issues from a number of viewpoints.

FOR THE TOURIST. Niue is the world's biggest raised coral island and as such it offers excellent scuba diving and snorkelling. Its remarkable uplifted limestone formations house huge caves, many containing deep pools. Great clefts in the cliffs lead to little white sand beaches. Offshore fishing is excellent. On the south-western side of the island on the coastline great fingers of makatea thrust themselves high above the water line, completely devoid of any vegetation. It is possible to walk across this surface on a precarious track down to the sea. Stout shoes and gloves are advisable to protect feet and hands from the razor sharp stone. Tongo Chasm at the end of this trail is a scenic marvel. At the bottom of the chasm is a white sand valley with a few palm trees growing in it. There are pools at either end which are fed by underground caves connecting with the ocean. Close by is the Vaikono Chasm with an equally spectacular, if somewhat difficult, access walk but an even more challenging entry point. A stout rope drops into the depths of a cleft in the rocks to the grotto below. There are two swimming pools, surrounded by the soaring cliffs. Most of the other gorges, chasms and grottoes are more accessible than these but all are equally beautiful. Niue has a great deal to offer the visitor who is seeking spectacular scenery and some great hiking.

There is very little evening entertainment. Occasionally a dance will be held in Alofi or in association with one of the church groups in a village. The Niue Hotel has a restaurant and provides a takeaway service as well. The general stores in Alofi have snack counters which are open during business hours. There is a Visitors Information Office in central Alofi.

Archaeological sites. Research excavations of ancient burial caves have been carried out by a New Zealand university, investigating bones found in limestone caves. For information on this survey see a publication entitled *Niue Island Archaeological Survey*: Canterbury Museum (NZ) Bulletin Number 7, 1979, by Micheal M. Trotter.

Further details of the island are available from the Niue Tourist Board.

Shopping. Niue Handicrafts offers an excellent selection of locally produced artifacts. The Niueans make finely woven hats, as well as tightly woven baskets of narrow design, featuring intricate black and white pandanus patterns. There is a weekly early morning market near the post office where it is also possible to buy some handicrafts. The women from the outlying villages bring their work in to sell to the co-op. Visit before 7 am!

Tours: Niue Adventures, specialising in scuba diving and other water sports.

ACCOMMODATION

Niue Hotel: 20 rooms, swimming pool, restaurant, bar, hire cars and motorscooters. PO Box 80, Alofi. Tel.: 91.

Hinemata Motel: three rooms, share kitchen and bathroom facilities, hire cars and bikes. PO Box 81, Alofi. Tel.: 167.

Esthers Village Motel: at Avatele village, two self-contained units.

Pelenis Guest House: three bedrooms, share all other facilities, meals available. Alofi.

Niue Island Lodge: Near Niue Hotel, three bedrooms, share lounge and bathroom, guests may use facilities of Niue Hotel. Alofi.

Norfolk Island

Norfolk Island, a territory under the authority of Australia, is located at 29 deg 02 min S latitude and 167 deg 57 min E longitude. Its area is 34.5 sq. km and it is 1676 km east-north-east of Sydney and 1065 km north of Auckland. The population in the 1985 census was 1880 including several hundred persons holding temporary entry permits allowing them to reside on the island for six months.

Kingston, on the south coast, is the administrative centre and Burnt Pine, in the centre of the island, is the commercial and shopping centre. Local time is 11 hours 30 minutes ahead of GMT.

The Australian flag and the Norfolk Island flag are flown side-by-side. The flag is a stylised Norfolk pine free between two green bars. There is a traditional choral work, the *Pitcairn Anthem*.

In addition to major Australian holidays

NORFOLK ISLAND

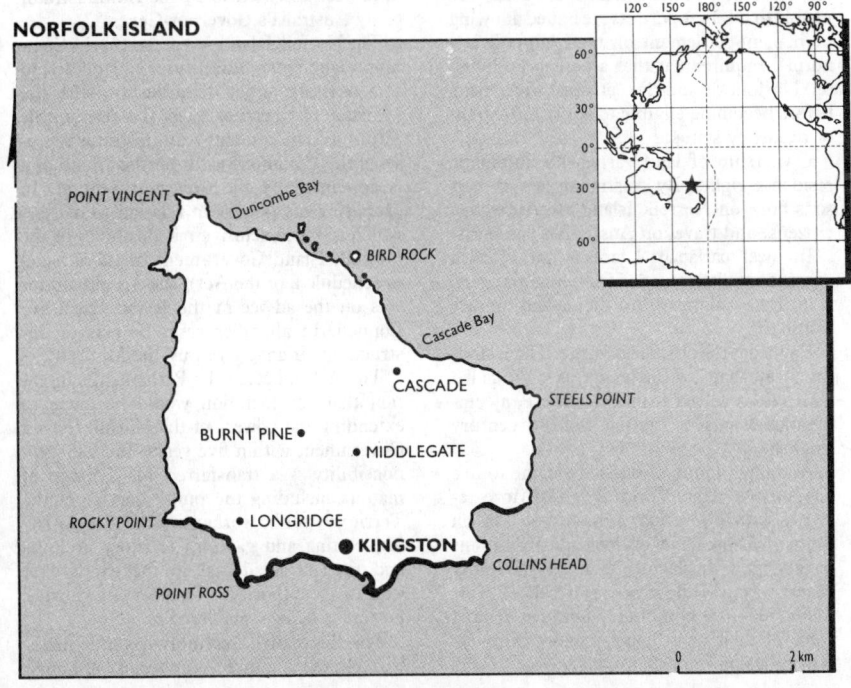

which are observed on the island, Norfolk celebrates Bounty, or Anniversary Day, which commemorates the arrival of the Pitcairners on 8 June 1856; Foundation Day, the anniversary of the establishment of the first settlement (from Australian mainland) on 6 March 1788; and Thanksgiving Day, usually on the last Wednesday in November.

THE PEOPLE. Norfolk Island is populated partly by the descendants of the *Bounty* mutiny families, who moved there from Pitcairn Island in 1856, and partly by more recent settlers, mainly from Australia and New Zealand.

Migration is carefully controlled. Visitors may stay for 30 days without a written permit and may apply for a written permit to stay an additional 30 days. Extension of a written permit may be granted up to a maximum of 120 days from the date of entry. For longer stays temporary entry permits may be granted, subject to conditions, for up to a year and may be extended. Such permits are normally granted for employment purposes only, to fill positions which residents are unable to fill. Few permits are issued allowing permanent settlement on the island. It is a normal requirement that a person be living on Norfolk Island for at least five years before becoming eligible to apply for a grant of residency status.

Ownership of land carries no automatic residence rights. By Australian law all persons born on Norfolk Island are Australian citizens, and travel on Australian passports.

In local parlance 'Islanders' of Pitcairn descent are distinguished from 'mainlanders' who have migrated to the island or are visiting.

English is the official language. The Islanders speak their own language as well, called 'Norfolk', evolved from Pitcairnese, a combination of ancient Tahitian and 18th century English.

A gradual influx of outsiders came to live on Norfolk after World War II. More recently with increasing prosperity based on tourism, a 'mainland' outlook and aspirations have begun displacing some of the older island ways. While more than half of Norfolk's 600–700 households produce at least some of their own food, virtually everyone now relies on imported foods.

Religion. Resident clergymen conduct regular services in four Norfolk churches, the Church of England, Roman Catholic Church, Uniting Church in Australia, and the Seventh-day Adventist Church. Services are occasionally held in St Barnabas Chapel, built when the Melanesian Mission was headquartered on Norfolk.

GOVERNMENT. The island has an Australian-appointed Administrator and locally-elected Legislative Assembly. The laws include certain Australian laws, which apply at the discretion of the Australian Parliament, and a range of local ordinances and acts governing essentially local matters. In any matters of law not covered either by Commonwealth or Norfolk laws, the English common law, as it existed in 1828, applies.

Under the Norfolk Island Act 1979, Australia established the Norfolk Island Legislative Assembly and gave it executive and legislative authority in certain Island matters, mostly of a municipal nature. Enactments of the Assembly become law only when they have been assented to by the Administrator or by Australia's Governor-General.

The Norfolk Island Act preserves the Commonwealth's responsibility for Norfolk Island as a territory under its authority, with the Minister for Territories as the responsible Minister. The resident Administrator represents the Commonwealth on the Island and is appointed by the Governor-General. In exercising his powers in relation to matters which are the exclusive responsibility of the Norfolk Island Government (matters listed in schedule 2 of the Act), the Administrator acts on the advice of the Island Executive Council. In all other cases he acts on instructions, if any, given by the Minister.

The Act indicated the Parliament's intention that consideration would be given to extending the powers of the Norfolk Island Government within five years. In 1985, responsibility was transferred for a range of matters including the public service of the Territory; public works; civil defence; lotteries; betting and gaming; territory archives and matters incidental to the exercise of executive authority. Transfer of further powers is being considered.

The Legislative Assembly has nine members elected for three-year terms, although the Administrator may direct that a new election be held at any time. The Assembly elects from its members a president and deputy president, and such executive ministers as it chooses to.

Day-to-day administration of the island's government is carried out by the Norfolk Island public service, which numbers about 172 persons. It is headed by a Chief Administrative Officer nominated by the Assembly.

Justice. The judicial system consists of a Supreme Court and a Court of Petty Sessions. The Supreme Court is the highest judicial authority on the island and is a superior court of record with original, civil and criminal jurisdiction. Its judges are not resident on the island.

Mr Justice Russell Fox, a Judge of the Supreme Court of Australia, was appointed Chief Justice of Norfolk Island in 1982 and there are three other judges appointed to the court. The court, other than in its criminal jurisdiction, may sit in NSW, Victoria or the Australian Capital Territory. Criminal cases are heard with juries.

The High Court of Australia has jurisdiction, with some exceptions, to hear and decide appeals from all judgments, decrees, orders and sentences of the Norfolk Island Supreme Court.

The jurisdiction of the court of petty sessions is exercised by the Chief Magistrate, or any three magistrates. It deals with summary matters, civil and criminal. Appeals may be made to the Supreme Court against petty sessions decisions. The Chief Magistrate is stationed in Canberra and goes to the island when required.

The courts of Norfolk Island have jurisdiction in, and relation to, the Coral Sea Islands Territory by virtue of the Coral Sea Islands Act 1969. In exercise of its jurisdiction a court of Norfolk Island may sit in the Territory, in Norfolk Island or in Australia. The Sydney Registry of the Family Court of Australia is the principal registry for Family Law matters other than those which may be dealt with by the Court of Petty Sessions.

Police. The full-time police establishment is one sergeant and two constables, seconded from Australia, with assistance from part-time local special constables when required.

Norfolk Island Airport is designated a security airport and requires an officer to be present during the screening of departing passengers. Since 1984 there has been a marked increase in reported crimes, especially shopbreaking. However, traffic offences still account for the majority of matters dealt with by the court. The island has no real gaol.

Liquor. A three-man Liquor Licensing Board hears applications for licences to serve liquor in hotels, guest houses or restaurants. Bars normally trade until 10 pm, but may get licences for later closing on special occasions. All liquor is imported by the Administration, which supplies it to individual purchasers or licence holders through the island's bond store. The Administration applies import duty, and other charges, to liquor sales, and also levies licence fees.

EDUCATION. Education is free and compulsory for all children between six and 15. The Norfolk Island Central School follows the NSW system of education, and teaches to Form IV, or 10th year level. The New South Wales State Education Department seconds the teaching staff at Norfolk Island's expense. The Administration is responsible for maintenance and construction of buildings.

School enrolments in 1986 totalled 306 — infants 83, primary 112, secondary 111. There is a school principal and 17 teachers.

Administration bursaries are available for pupils wanting higher school or tertiary education on the mainland, and trainee scholarships are available for school leavers.

A Seventh-day Adventist primary school, established in January 1981, operates in accordance with the Education Ordinance 1931 under the authority of the NSW Seventh-day Adventist school system. The school is staffed by a qualified teacher and has an enrolment of nine children. Some sports and cultural activities are shared with the Norfolk Island Central School.

LABOUR AND SOCIAL SERVICE. For many years a system of 'public work' required male residents to offer their labour free for work on the roads, or for other public work, for a certain number of days per year, or pay a set sum in lieu. The system developed from the early Pitcairn origins of the island people. In 1976 this option was replaced, and residents who are in employment and over the age of 18 now pay a twice yearly 'public works levy', which in fact is a personal tax.

The island has its own Social Services Act providing aged, widows, disability and certain other benefits at about 78 per cent of Australian levels. Burials and funeral services are free for everyone. There is virtually no unemployment.

HEALTH. The Public Hospital is under the control of a medical superintendent who is also the island's Government Medical Officer. The hospital is administered by a local board, which sets fees for medical and hospital services. The hospital is also supported by a subsidy from the island's revenues. Hospital and medical services are free to the old or invalid.

There are 21 beds in the hospital, which handles both minor and major operations. Specialists from Australia and New Zealand visit the hospital. Both the RAAF and the RNZAF carry out emergency evacuations when required.

A District Nursing Service funded by the Emilie Channer Trust and supervised by the Medical Superintendent provides for the requirements of older residents in their homes. A baby clinic is staffed by a qualified Sister who also conducts ante-natal and post-natal classes and assists with the school health programme of examination, immunisation and education. A government dental officer provides a free service for eligible children, pensioners and expectant mothers, and at prescribed fees for other patients.

THE LAND. Norfolk Island is of volcanic origin, about 8 km by 5 km with an area of 3455 ha. The coastline of 32 km consists chiefly of high cliffs, but the land slopes down to the sea in one small area on the south side, where Kingston is situated, on Sydney Bay. Average elevation of the island is 110 m. Two peaks, Mt Pitt and Mt Bates, rise to about 305 metres on the north-west corner. There is a large number of small streams.

Within sight of the southern shore are two small uninhabited islands. Nepean, the smallest and closest, is about 0.8 km to the south, and is of coral sandstone approximately 4 ha in extent and rising to 32 m. Philip is a volcanic island of 258 ha, and 280

m high. It is about 5.6 km south of Norfolk. Both islands lack water.

Climate. The climate is mild and subtropical. The average daily maximum temperature during the year varies from 16°C to 26.5°C and the average daily minimum from 11.2°C to 17.6°C. The annual rainfall is about 1326 mm, fairly well distributed.

The climate is suitable for cultivating a variety of crops, and for grazing. The volcanic soil is friable and chemically rich. Restrictions are imposed by the limited land area, the steep terrain, the porosity of the soil and the depth of any basic water table. The top soil, too, is well drained. Water for irrigation and for stock is drawn from streams and subterranean sources.

Flora and fauna. The Norfolk Island pine (*Araucaria heterophylla*), which is endemic to the island, grows to a height of 55 m and has been exported to many countries. A flowering white oak is prevalent. The seed of Kentia palms form a small commercial crop. A subtropical rainforest on Mt Pitt includes palms and giant ferns. Introduced kikuyu grass covers many slopes, while various ornamental shrubs and trees have been introduced, including hibiscus, wild lemon, macadamia nut, red and yellow guava and avocado trees.

The island has no reptiles and no spiders dangerous to man but its insect population includes many varieties of butterflies and moths. There are 55 species of birds including white terns, vivid parrots and the endemic and rare green parrot.

Philip Island, a major nesting site for a number of species of birds, was almost completely denuded of vegetation because of rabbit infestation. However, a programme to eradicate the rabbits and restore the habitat is nearing successful completion. On 21 February 1985 the Norfolk Island National Park and Norfolk Island Botanic Garden were gazetted under local legislation. On 31 January 1986 the Park and Botanic Garden were gazetted under the Commonwealth's National Park and Wildlife Conservation Act 1975, following an agreement signed by the Commonwealth and Norfolk Island Governments in May 1985. The area covered is approximately 480 ha.

Land tenure. Of the total area of 3455 ha, about 1700 are held on freehold, 1010 ha are Crown leasehold and 745 ha are designated roads, commons and public reserves.

The present system of land tenure was developed directly from the system established when the Pitcairn Islanders were settled on Norfolk Island in 1856, when the head of each family was granted a 20 ha block, or a 10 ha block was granted to males on marriage after settlement. The descendants of the original grantees sub-divided the freeholds many times, and thus many of the present small holdings are suitable only for residential or commercial non-agricultural uses.

Freehold land may still be purchased, but there are controls over sub-division. Lands not granted to the original Pitcairn Island settlers and their descendants were at the time set aside as public reserves and commons. Most commons are now used for grazing and afforestation. Crown leases are used for grazing, agriculture and housing.

Under the Norfolk Island Act 1979, Australia retains full control over land policies and Crown land usage. Crown leases may be granted for 99 years for non-business purposes and for 50 years for business purposes; however, present policy is for the grant of leases for not more than 28 years, usually available only to residents.

Development plan. In 1984 the Norfolk Island Government retained Harrison, Grierson Consultants Limited, of New Zealand, to assist in the preparation of the first development plan for the island. The document, entitled *Norfolk Island Development Plan (A Conservation Strategy)* was released in July 1985 (parts 1–3). The Australian Department of Territories considers the plan provides an appropriate framework for the establishment of the controls necessary to provide for the responsible development of the island, conservation of its natural resources and heritage features.

PRIMARY PRODUCTION. Fragmentary subdivision of land hampers its use for commercially viable agriculture. Porous soils prevent water storage in earth dams and the development costs are high for irrigation from streams and subterranean sources. Market gardeners have improved the supply of fresh vegetables by hydroponic cultivation and by the use of glass-houses. Hotels and restaurants provide a ready market for their produce.

A primary production Development and Marketing Committee was formed in 1984 to organise the growing and marketing of local produce and a feasibility study is being carried out into the cost and effectiveness of establishing a cool store and processing factory to be powered from produce on its own property.

The island has four piggeries which carry more than 300 pigs and supply the local market in bacon, ham and other pork products. Methane gas is produced at one of the piggeries and is used for processing cooked meats. Cattle are slaughtered for local consumption but demand exceeds supply and meat is imported from Australia and New Zealand. Subsidies on imported stock and fertiliser are available for the encouragement of stock and pasture improvement.

For export the island produces seed from Norfolk pines (which drop in large quantities about once every four years) and Kentia palm seeds.

Although big catches of fish may be made in the surrounding sea, the establishment of a large-scale fishing industry is inhibited by the vagaries of the weather and the lack of a harbour. Fishing boats are limited to a size which can be lifted by crane and moved by trailer. Trumpeter, kingfish, trevally, snapper and hapuku are most commonly caught, and sold locally.

There are jetties at Cascades, on the northern side, and Kingston, on the southern side. Operations of foreign fishing vessels in the Australian 200-mile fishing zone surrounding Norfolk Island are quite small. The main catch is tuna, shark and billfish. The area is patrolled by the Australian Navy.

Hardwoods from natural forests are negligible. Softwood from the Norfolk Island pine, the only local timber used for building, is now limited. A programme for the regeneration of Norfolk Island pine on government reserves is being pursued.

TOURISM. During 1985/86 28,927 tourists visited the island, more than half from Australia and the rest mainly from New Zealand. Their average stay was just under 10 days. Visitors are attracted to the island's historical buildings and ruins, the beautiful scenery, peaceful atomosphere and (particularly for New Zealanders) low-duty shopping.

LOCAL COMMERCE. Because of its remoteness, small size and lack of a harbour,

Norfolk Island was for generations unable to develop any significant, steady local industry until increased tourism was made possible by the construction of an airstrip during World War II. Various small industries have flourished for a time and then waned, including whaling, bananas, bean seeds and passionfruit.

Tourism figures have increased steadily since 1983 with April and October being the peak months. Air services operate regularly from Sydney, Brisbane, Coffs Harbour and Auckland with occasional charter flights from Noumea. More than half the population is directly employed in the tourist industry. A large part of the remaining income and employment is indirectly dependent on tourism. The Norfolk Island Government Tourist Bureau was established in 1980 to handle accommodation, transport, tours and information distribution.

Tourism policies adopted in 1983 do not encourage overseas investment in the island's tourist industry.

For several years starting in the late 1960s the island attracted some notoriety as a tax haven for Australians, and there was a boom in the registration of newly-formed companies. Changes in Australian law and closer attention from the Australian tax authorities brought the boom to an end in 1973.

OVERSEAS TRADE. A special aspect of Norfolk's economy is that a large quantity of the island's imports are 'invisible exports' comprising cameras, radios, watches, jewellery, musical instruments and liquor, etc., which enter the island at a low rate of customs duty and are sold to tourists returning to higher duty areas, mainly Australia and New Zealand. Other exports included pine and palm seeds (valued at $334,800 in 1984/85) and motor vehicles (which were re-exports).

The value of imports and exports in recent years has been:

Year	Imports	Exports
1979–80	10,826,352	1,627,255
1980–81	13,354,676	1,767,513
1981–82	12,101,879	1,246,153
1982–83	15,091,219	1,387,372
1983–84	15,972,054	2,288,517
1984–85	17,243,240	2,012,842

GRAPH 1 NUMBER OF VISITOR ARRIVALS BY MONTH
1 January 1982 to 31 December 1985

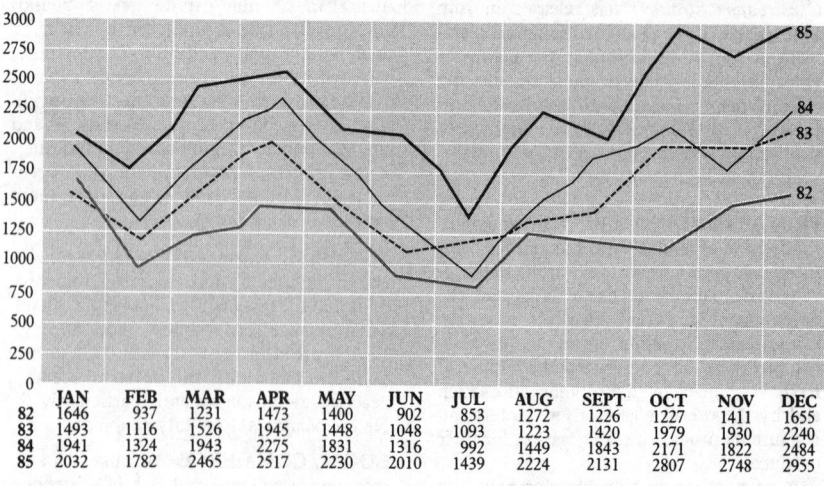

	JAN	FEB	MAR	APR	MAY	JUN	JUL	AUG	SEPT	OCT	NOV	DEC
82	1646	937	1231	1473	1400	902	853	1272	1226	1227	1411	1655
83	1493	1116	1526	1945	1448	1048	1093	1223	1420	1979	1930	2240
84	1941	1324	1943	2275	1831	1316	992	1449	1843	2171	1822	2484
85	2032	1782	2465	2517	2230	2010	1439	2224	2131	2807	2748	2955

Sources of imports in 1984–85 were:

Australia & Pacific Islands 8,933,038
New Zealand 3,664,067
Asia 2,728,734
Europe 1,917,401

Exports in 1984–85 went to:

Australia & Pacific Islands 1,262,840
New Zealand 399,061
Asia 35,664
Europe 315,277

Customs. Norfolk Island has its own customs law, the island being outside Australian customs. Duties are levied on a wide range of goods, mostly at 8 per cent, though motor vehicles attract 15 per cent duty. Customs officials attend the arrival of ships and aircraft. The import of fruit is prohibited because the island is free of fruit-fly. Passengers' effects of a normal nature are duty free.

Import duties are levied on liquor, sale of which is a government monopoly. In July 1983, a Bill was introduced into the Norfolk Legislative Assembly seeking to increase customs duties on existing items and applying them to a new range of goods including liquor.

FINANCE. Norfolk Island is a separate and distinct financial entity, expected to support itself without any grants or aid from Australia. The Commonwealth pays for its own direct operations on the island, including the salaries of the Administrator and his staff of four, the cost of operating the Australian-owned airport on the island, and the expense of a programme of restoring and maintaining historic Crown buildings in Kingston. In recent years Australia has also provided Norfolk with an increasing range of technical assistance and expert advice in conservation, quarantine and health.

The Norfolk Island Legislative Assembly has responsibility for the island's budget. The island's own public revenues and its expenditures in the financial year ended 30 June 1985 were: $4,448,392, with principal sources being customs duty and port fees $1,373,529; postal operations $800,981; liquor sales $439,336; public works levy $239,299; electricity service $256,654 and departure fees $223,207.

Expenditure. These were $4,188,400, with principal items being administrative expenses $1,669,288; education $626,807; repairs and maintenance $570,657; welfare services $264,255; health $249,864; and Norfolk Island Legislative Assembly $229,981.

In 1986 public revenue totalled $4,239,918 and expenditure $4,246,423, leaving a debit of $6505. Levies and taxes yielded $2,617,753, services, including liquor service, $577,281 and net profit of $123,992 from philatelic and postal services. In 1986, expenditure on health and education accounted for $1,201,308 and other community services $768,921.

Taxes. Norfolk Island has no income tax, death duties, property tax or stamp duties. There is a 'public works levy' on residents, in reality a personal tax (see Labour and social service), a $10 departure fee, and an absentee landowner's tax.

Currency. The legal currency is Australian bank notes and coins.

Banks. Westpac and the Commonwealth Bank of Australia have branches on the island. Major international credit cards are honoured by many shops and restaurants, many of which also accept Australian or New Zealand cheques.

TRANSPORT. The island has about 80 km of roads, all of which except for about 8 km may be used by motor vehicles. About 18 km of roads are sealed. The rest are either earth-formed or coral surfaced. There were 2425 vehicles registered at 30 June 1985.

Revenue from vehicle registration and licences was $117,035 in 1984–85. Speed limits are 50 km/h in the country and 40 km/h in the built up area.

A private bus service operates between some hotels, the shopping centre and the beach at Kingston. There are inexpensive hire services for motor cars, bikes and scooters. Bus tours of the island are provided.

Aviation. The airport is controlled by the Australian Department of Aviation. There are two hard-surfaced runways, one about 2020 m and the other about 1550 m. East West Airlines, with Fokker Fellowship F-28 jets, provides services from Sydney. Air New Zealand, with a B-737, operates from Auckland. Air New South Wales flies an F-28 from Brisbane, Norfolk Island Airlines flies from Brisbane and Sydney in a BE-200 and

Qantas flies from Auckland in a B-737. Airlines provide extra services in peak summer holiday season.

Upgrading of the airport to accommodate medium-sized jets such as the Fokker F-28 or the BA 146 was completed in 1983.

Shipping. Regular shipping services are provided from Australia and New Zealand by Compagnie des Chargeurs Caledoniens. Because there is no harbour all cargo and passengers are carried between ship and shore by lighter, operated by the Administration. The minimum cargo that can be handled economically is 200 tonnes and ships discharging less than the minimum are required to pay the difference between the minimum tonnage and the tonnage discharged. Larger cargoes requiring transport on two lighters lashed together are charged at double rates. Any one lift exceeding four tonnes in weight requires the importer to arrange, through the Administration, insurance cover of $15,000 to cover the possible loss or damage of a lighter.

Loading jetties are at Kingston in the south and Cascade in the north. The weather and state of the sea determine which jetty is used.

COMMUNICATIONS. The automatic telephone exchange has a capacity of 1000 lines. There is an international telephone service, connected to Sydney via the ANZ-CAN cable; telephone calls may be made to most overseas countries and to ships at sea.

Norfolk is a major link-point in the ANZ-CAN trans-Pacific cable. Full International Subscriber Dialling (ISD) facilities have been available since December 1984. Overseas Telecommunications Commission (Australia) provides an overseas telegram, telex and facsimile service. OTC also provides an 'on demand' coast radio station for shipping by radio telephone.

The Department of Aviation and the local meteorological office of the Department of Science have radio communication with Australia. The Department of Aviation also operates a medium frequency non-directional beacon service, call sign NF with a range of 725 km, a high-frequency point-to-point communication service, and a very high-frequency air-ground-air service.

The Administration operates radio station VL2NI for local broadcasts, providing about 106 hours a week of regular programmes of news, announcements and music. Most residents have radios capable of receiving broadcasts from stations in Australia and New Zealand.

There are two weekly news publications, *The Norfolk Islander*, and *Dem Tull*, named after the Pitcairn expression meaning 'they say'. The official *Norfolk Island Government Gazette* is produced weekly, or as the occasion demands.

WATER AND ELECTRICITY. There is currently no public water supply or sewerage scheme. Water is available from roof catchments, wells and bores. However, the Commonwealth and Norfolk Island Governments have agreed to joint funding of a water and sewerage scheme estimated to cost $4.6 million (at February 1986 prices). Survey and design work is under way.

The Administration Electricity Undertaking supplies electricity throughout the island from the power station near the airport. Electricity is generated at 240 V, is charged at 24 cents per unit and the output for 1984–85 was 5,106,688 kWh. The Commonwealth Department of Housing and Construction has recently carried out a feasibility study for additional generating equipment.

MAJOR OFFICE HOLDERS
Administrator:
   Commodore J. A. Matthew, CVO, MBE, RANEM, appointed 29 April 1985
Official Secretary:
   Peter Ilyk
President of the Legislative Assembly:
   John T. Brown
Executive Members:
   Geoff J. Bennett — Commerce and Health
   Ed D. Howard — Finance
   Bill W. Sanders — Planning
Members of the Legislative Assembly
(elected May 1986 for 3 years):
   John Brown, Geoff Bennett, Gerry Aafjes, Ed Howard, Bill Sanders, David Buffett, Gaye Evans, Helen Sampson, David Rodgers.
Chief Administrative Officer:
   Ron Malcolm

HISTORY. Norfolk Island is the second oldest British settlement in the South Seas, having been occupied within a few weeks of the first British settlement at Sydney in 1788. It is the oldest of Australia's external territories.

Its European discoverer was Captain James Cook, on 10 October 1774, who landed at Duncombe Bay, where today a monument stands. He found the island uninhabited. He took possession of it for Britain and named it Norfolk Isle, 'after the noble family of Howard', to which the Duke of Norfolk belonged. Little is known of the island's previous history, although there is evidence that it may have been inhabited in earlier times.

Cook was impressed by the Norfolk Island pines and the wild flax plant, and felt the British Navy could use them for spars and masts, and for sail-making. As a result Captain Arthur Phillip, some years later, was instructed to send a detachment to occupy the island after having established a British colony in New South Wales. The Sydney colony was established on 26 January 1788 and on 14 February the armed tender *Supply* carrying Lieut. Philip Gidley King and commanded by Lieut. Henry Lidgbird Ball and with a party of convicts set sail from Sydney for Norfolk. They came ashore in what is now the Kingston area on 6 March 1788. King had been appointed Superintendent and Commandant of Norfolk.

First Settlement. As it happened, the timber and the flax were unsuited to the navy's needs, and the early days of settlement were difficult, especially because of the heavy clearing that had to be done before crops could be planted. The settlement almost starved following the wreck of HMS *Sirius*, bringing supplies, on the reef in front of Kingston on 19 March 1790, for it meant that another 80 people also had to be fed. This period has become known as the First Settlement.

Lieut. King spent two terms on the island, and when he left in 1796 the settlement was still a developing community of nearly 900 people with many public buildings. By 1804 the population, both settlers and convicts, had reached 1100 and by 1810 more than a quarter of the island had been cleared.

But the long sea connection to Sydney, and the general difficulties and expense of keeping the Norfolk Island settlement going (it was never self-supporting) resulted in the settlement gradually being run down and abandoned. Some of the people were moved to Van Diemen's Land (Tasmania). The last inhabitants left in 1814, and the island was deserted for the next 11 years.

Second Settlement. On 6 June 1825, Captain Turton, of the 40th Regiment, with a detachment of soldiers and convicts, landed at Kingston to begin the Second Settlement. This was a penal settlement, and the prisoners were the worst of those from the gaols of New South Wales and Tasmania. The island prison was officially described as being meant as 'a place of the extremest punishment, short of death'. No private settlers were allowed. Many stories of brutality and sometimes rebellion date from this period. 'I wish it to be understood that the felon who is sent there is for ever excluded from all hope of return,' wrote Governor Brisbane of NSW.

During this time Norfolk Island deservedly earned itself the name of 'Hell on Earth'. Rumours of brutality and inhumane treatment continually reached the mainland, and there was growing agitation in some quarters to have the penal settlement closed. But the decision to cease using Norfolk Island as a penal colony was not made until 1852, and the last of the convicts did not leave until 1856.

The colonial stone buildings standing today date from this period. They were convict-built in local stone and consist of houses, gaols (these are mostly razed), stores, military barracks, a mill, grain silos, bridges and the fine old Government House. Settlements were made at Kingston, Cascade and Longridge, and joined by an extensive road system.

Pitcairners arrive. Meanwhile, the people of Pitcairn Island had been looking for a new home. Most of the population in this small island east of Tahiti were descendants of the mutineers of the *Bounty*, who had scuttled their ship and hidden on the island in 1790. Their population was increasing on Pitcairn, and it was feared they would become short of land. One attempt at immigration, to Tahiti in 1831, had proved a failure, and they felt that if they were compelled to immigrate a second time it should be to an uninhabited island.

The entire population of Pitcairn, 194

persons, landed on Norfolk from the *Morayshire* on 8 June 1856 (now observed as Bounty Day or Anniversary Day). Those few prisoners remining on Norfolk Island had gone by the end of the month.

For the benefit of the Pitcairners, the island was created a 'distinct and separate settlement' on 24 June 1856. The Governor of New South Wales was appointed Governor of Norfolk Island as well, but his powers were limited to acting as a link between the island and the British Crown. The Pitcairners established the same kind of land tenure and community disciplines they had had at home, an indelible mark that can still be observed on Norfolk.

Some of the island's governors, notably Sir William Denison (1856–61), Sir John Young (1861–67) and Viscount Hampden (1895–97) exceeded the limitations that Britain had placed on their powers concerning Norfolk Island. This was resented by many islanders and two small groups of families (possibly motivated by homesickness) returned to Pitcairn in 1858 and 1863, leaving the majority of the Pitcairners to settle on Norfolk, where old *Bounty* names like Quintal, Young, Adams, Christian and McCoy are still prominent.

Melanesian Mission. The Melanesian Mission established a missionary training school, and headquarters for the Bishop of Melanesia, in October 1866, after having been granted, free, by the British Government 99 acres of land and purchasing a further 933 acres. The station was named St Barnabas, on whose feast day the site was selected. The beautiful St Barnabas Chapel was completed in 1880. From this base the mission did important work in taking Christianity to the islands in the Western Pacific until 1920, when mission headquarters was moved to the Solomon Islands.

Further political developments. During the 1880s Sydney-based governors became concerned at the island's resistance to outside authority, its inability to develop commercial trade, and its unwillingness to enforce strict standards of law and propriety. In 1896, Governor Viscount Hampden proclaimed the end of the islanders' right to govern themselves, and sent a Chief Magistrate to the island.

Although the islanders protested, the British Government upheld the Governor's action, and in 1897 Norfolk became a dependency of New South Wales, although legally remaining a separate colony. In 1914, again over protests, a British Order in Council placed Norfolk under the authority of the Commonwealth of Australia. Annexation to Australia has never been carried out.

From 1897 until 1979, various forms of locally-elected representative bodies were established by Australia, but were given little more than advisory powers. During those eight decades the island developed 'a rich history of disputation' with Australian authorities. This had included Royal Commissions, delegations of protest, petitions to English monarchs, numerous inquiries, and approaches to the United Nations.

The most exhaustive inquiry was conducted in 1975–76 by Sir John Nimmo, a judge of the Australian Industrial Court, and former Chief Justice of Fiji. His report was tabled in the Australian Parliament in November 1976.

The report made 74 recommendations, essentially that Norfolk Island should be integrated into the Australian political system of laws, social benefits and taxes, with the island becoming part of the electorate of Canberra. It recommended against holding a local referendum on the island's future status, saying that if Australia is to be responsible for Norfolk Island's financial affairs, Australia should determine its form of government.

The report precipitated controversy. The eight elected members of the Norfolk Island Council unanimously opposed the proposal that the island should lose its separate political status and, in February 1977, acting as private citizens, appealed to the United Nations to protect Norfolk Island from being integrated into Australia without the consent of the electors. A petition signed by 158 residents favouring the Nimmo Report was cited by the Australian Minister for Administrative Services as an indication of feelings on the island. The petition was countered by more than 600 signed 'solemn declarations' from electors who supported the local council and wanted separate status to continue.

In May 1978, the Australian Minister for Home Affairs, Mr R. J. Ellicott, announced that the government had decided that Norfolk

Island did not have to be governed by the same laws that apply in the rest of Australia. While insisting that the island was part of Australia, he said the government was prepared to see whether a form of self-government could be developed, with Norfolk taking responsibility for its own finances and controlling a range of municipal matters. In discussion with the council he said that the proposed new arrangements would operate on a basis of consensus between the island and the Commonwealth, but that self-determination for the island was out of the question.

The new administrative arrangements were embodied in the Norfolk Island Act 1979, which was passed by the Australian Parliament in May of that year. It created the Legislative Assembly, which has the right to introduce legislation on almost any subject related to Norfolk. Its legislation does not become law unless approved by Australian authorities. The Assembly's powers were to be reviewed, and possibly increased.

In 1985 the legislative and executive responsibility for a range of matters was transferred to the island Government including the public service of the Territory, public works, civil defence, lotteries, betting and gaming, Territory archives and matters incidental to the exercise of executive authority. Further extension of powers is a continuing exercise.

The election of the first Assembly was affected by Australia's requirement that Norfolk's traditional first-past-the-post voting system be changed to one of proportional representation. The election was based on the new system despite bitter objections from the council.

Following a study by the Australian Electoral Office in 1982, a new cumulative voting system was approved at referendum and was used for the first time in a general election in May, 1983.

Norfolk and the Pacific. In 1979, the island sent its first team to participate in the South Pacific Games at Suva, where it won several medals. Later that year Norfolk's Chief Minister attended the South Pacific Conference at Tahiti, as the island's first representative. Subsequently Australia introduced changes to the South Pacific Commission's membership which, in effect, removed Norfolk's right to participate.

Further reading. Merval Hoare, *Norfolk Island: An Outline of Its History 1774–1968*, Brisbane, 1969 and reprinted since; Merval Hoare, *Rambler's Guide to Norfolk Island*, Sydney, 1965 and subsequent revised editions (this booklet, containing many maps, describes in detail the various places of historic interest on the island); R. Nixon Dalkin, *Colonial Era Cemetery of Norfolk Island*, Sydney, 1974 (contains chart, inscriptions and notes on the burials in Kingston cemetery); Philip Cox and Wesley Stacey, *Building Norfolk Island*, Sydney, 1971 (photographs, plans and charts, showing the architectural development of the island during its various periods); Merval Hoare's *The Winds of Change: Norfolk Island 1950–1982*, Suva, 1983, deals with the island's more recent, particularly political, development; and *Which Future for Norfolk Island?*, Christopher Nobb, Norfolk Island, 1983, is an economic survey.

FOR THE TOURIST. Casual clothing is the general rule. Warmer but not heavy clothing is needed for June–August. Comfortable walking shoes will assist in the exploration of the island's many ruins and byways. There is a variety of activity on the island, including swimming, scuba-diving, fishing, horse riding and sports.

There are several excellent restaurants on the island, many featuring local produce and fish. Restaurants are BYO (bring your own) or licensed and it is advisable to make early reservations, particularly during peak seasons. The Tourist Bureau offers a reservation service for all restaurants. Some of the guest houses will also accept casual dinner bookings.

Entry requirements. Australian and New Zealand citizens require onward or return tickets, and Australians require a passport for their re-entry into Australia (or less expensive certificate of identity). Visitors from elsewhere must have any necessary visas. There are no special health requirements. There is a $10 departure tax.

Sightseeing. Things of interest on the island include: a tour of Kingston, where most of the prisons and administrative buildings of the penal days stood. Some of these buildings have been restored and all are of great historic interest. Nearby is the old cemetery, with its early tombstones, many marking the graves of convicts.

The Melanesian Mission area, on the Uplands, was once a thriving settlement, but little remains now but the attractive vicarage and the beautiful old St Barnabas chapel. Nearby is the old mission cemetery, not now in use.

Near the airport can be found the remnants of beautiful old Pine Avenue, and remnants of a small convict settlement identified by nothing more than stone arches.

There are superb views of the island after an easy climb of Mt Pitt and Mt Bates. Both Nepean and Philip Islands may be visited, but this should be undertaken only with experienced local people in good weather. Both islands have difficult access and are waterless.

ACCOMMODATION. Accommodation is available in licensed hotels, motels, guest houses and self-contained flats. The majority are sold through various packaged holidays available from travel agents or direct arrangements with the Norfolk Island Tourist Bureau, PO Box 211, Norfolk Island or from the New South Wales Tourist Office, Spring Street, Sydney. Informality is the key to Norfolk accommodations. Most enterprises are small and try to maintain personal service. Some of the guest houses have an all inclusive tariff or just bed and breakfast while all the apartments are fully self-contained with kitchen facilities. All accommodations have garden surrounds and many are very close to beaches. Facilities are listed here alphabetically.

HOTELS

Castaway Hotel: 23 rooms, restaurant, bar, major credit cards. PO Box 34, NI 2899. Tel.: 2625, telex NV 766 32006.

Hillcrest Hotel: 24 rooms, restaurant, bar, tennis court, pool, major credit cards. PO Box 64, NI 2899. Tel.: 2255, telex NV 766 32026.

Hotel Norfolk: 51 units, restaurant, bar, pool, some with kitchen facilities, major credit cards. PO Box 70, NI 2899. Tel.: 2177, telex NV 766 32005.

Polynesian Motor Hotel: 11 rooms, restaurant, pool, some with kitchen facilities. PO Box 217, NI 2899. Tel.: 2309.

South Pacific Hotel: 68 rooms, restaurant,

bar, shop, pool, major credit cards. PO Box 215, NI 2899. Tel.: 2166, telex NV 766 32016.

GUEST HOUSES

Aunt Em's: 8 rooms, bed and breakfast. PO Box 121, NI 2899. Tel.: 2373.

Bounty Lodge: 4 rooms, dinner, bed and breakfast. PO Box 231, NI 2899. Tel.: 2019.

Highlands: 12 rooms, dinner, bed and breakfast, tennis court, pool. PO Box 236, NI 2899. Tel.: 2741, telex NV 766 32010.

Norfolk White Heron Lodge: 7 rooms, dinner, bed and breakfast. Douglas Drive, NI 2899. Tel.: 2377.

Saint's Pine Tree Inn: 4 rooms, dinner, bed and breakfast, bar. PO Box 381 NI 2899. Tel.: 2617, telex NV 766 32010.

Tavener's Farm: 6 rooms, bed and breakfast. PO Box 190 NI 2899. Tel.: 2693, telex NV 766 32010.

APARTMENTS

Most of these have barbecue facilities set in lovely grounds for outside dining. All have fully equipped kitchens and are serviced daily.

Ainsley Lodge: 2 units. PO Box 296, NI 2899. Tel.: 2312.

Anson Bay Lodge: 2 units. c/- Post Office NI 2899. Tel.: 2357.

Bergagnin's Cottage: 1 unit. c/- Post Office NI 2899. Tel.: 2653.

Bligh Court: 7 units. PO Box 451, NI 2899. Tel.: 2216, telex NV 766 32010.

Bumbora's Apartments: 2 units. PO Box 48, NI 2899. Tel.: 2218, telex NV 766 32010.

Callam Court: 4 units. PO Box 246, NI 2899. Tel.: 2770, telex 766 32006.

Cascade Gardens: 5 units. PO Box 236, NI 2899. Tel.: 2741, telex NV 766 32010.

Channer's Corner: 6 units. PO Box 235, NI 2899. Tel.: 2645, telex NV 766 32010.

Colony Lodge: 4 units. PO Box 308, NI 2899. Tel.: 2174, telex AA1193.

Crest Apartments: 12 units. PO Box 88, NI 2899. Tel.: 2280, telex NV 766 32003.

Cumberland Close: 6 units. c/- Post Office, NI 2899. Tel.: 2721, telex NV 766 32006.

Fletcher Christian Apartments: 12 units. PO Box 144, NI 2899. Tel.: 2169, telex NV 766 32006.

Hibiscus Apartments: 50 units. PO Box 34, NI 2899. Tel.: 2325, telex NV 766 32027.
Hillsdene: 4 units. c/- Post Office, NI 2899. Tel.: 2432.
Islander Lodge: 5 units. PO Box 169, NI 2899, Tel.: 2114, telex NV 766 32008.
Nobbs Apartments: 7 units PO Box 47, NI 2899. telex NV 766 32010.
Nuffka Apartments: 4 units. PO Box 144, NI 2899. Tel.: 2169, telex NV 766 32006.
Pacific Palms: 2 units. c/- Post Office, NI 2899. Tel.: 2617.
Pam's Place: 2 units. c/- Post Office, NI 2899. Tel.: 2778.
Panorama Court: 12 units. PO Box 266, NI 2899. Tel.: 2364.
Pine Valley: 13 units. PO Box 249, NI 2899. Tel.: 2202, telex NV 766 32012.

Ponderosa: 8 units. PO Box 76, NI 2899. Tel.: 2466.
Ross-haven House: Executive house. c/- Post Office, NI 2899. Telex NV 766 32010.
Seaview Cottage: 5 units. PO Box 240, NI 2899. Tel.: 2256.
Shiralee Executive Cottage: 4 units. PO Box 48, NI 2899, Tel.: 2118, telex NV 766 32010.
Sundowner: 4 units. PO Box 70, NI 2899. Tel.: 2785, telex NV 766 32005.
Sunhaven: 4 units. PO Box 60, NI 2899. Tel.: 2709, telex NV 766 32010.
Town Villas: 2 units. PO Box 144, NI 2899. Tel.: 2169, telex NV 766 32006.
Wynhaven: 1 unit. c/- Post Office, NI 2899. Tel.: 2219.

Northern Marianas

The Northern Mariana Islands are a chain of 17 islands in the north Pacific which together constitute the self-governing Commonwealth of the Northern Marianas, in union with the United States under a Covenant signed in 1975.

The chain runs approximately north to south for a distance of some 543 km, from Farallon de Pajaros (20 deg 33 min N latitude) to Rota (14 deg 08 min N latitude), all within the longitude of 145 deg and 146 deg E. The main island of Saipan is at 15 deg 12 min N latitude and 145 deg 43 min E longitude.

The 17 islands include one group of three tiny islands known collectively as Maug, and thus the chain is sometimes recorded as consisting of 15 islands. From north to south the islands are Farallon de Pajaros, Maug, Asuncion, Agrihan, Pagan, Alamagan, Guguan, Sarigan, Anatahan, Farallon de Medinilla, Saipan, Managaha, Tinian, Aguijan and Rota.

Only six of these islands are regularly inhabited — Saipan, Rota, Tinian, Alamagan, Anatahan and Agrihan. The population of Pagan (then about 54) was evacuated in 1981 when Mt Pagan erupted and the people were moved to Saipan.

Total land area of the chain is approximately 475 sq. km, and the northernmost inhabited island, Agrihan, is located about 330 km north of Saipan, where most of the total population of 20,350 (1985 est.) is concentrated.

The major islands are Saipan (116.5 sq. km, population 17,840); Rota (83 sq. km, population 1444); Tinian (101 sq. km, population 944); Alamagan (11 sq. km, population 48); Pagan (48 sq. km, sporadically popu-lated); Anatahan (33 sq. km, sporadically populated); and Agrihan (47 sq. km, population about 25).

Public holidays include New Year's Day; Martin Luther King's birthday (20 January); President's Day, honouring the birthdays of George Washington and Abraham Lincoln, (17 February); Marianas Covenant Day (24 March); Memorial Day (27 May); Labour Day (1 September); Columbus Day (14 October); Veterans' Day (11 November); Thanksgiving Day (4th Thursday of November); Constitution Day (9 December); Christmas Day. There are also numerous festivals and fiestas.

THE PEOPLE. Because at one time the population of the Northern Marianas was moved by the Spanish to Guam and to the Caroline Islands, the present inhabitants have great cultural and social diversity. There is a Chamorro majority with an important minority group with a Carolinian background, but there is also mixture of many nationalities in the Marianas, including Spanish, German and Japanese. The Western family structure has been adopted, with the traditional social class structure of nobles and commoners of Chamorro society completely gone. But within the Saipan area the central Carolinian communities still retain a more typically Micronesian matrilineal social organisation.

The Micronesian population is equally divided between male and female and relatively young, with over 40 per cent of all Micronesians under the age of 15 at census time.

This age structure results from a high birthrate, estimated at 30.1 live births per 1000 of the population, a relatively low

NORTHERN MARIANAS

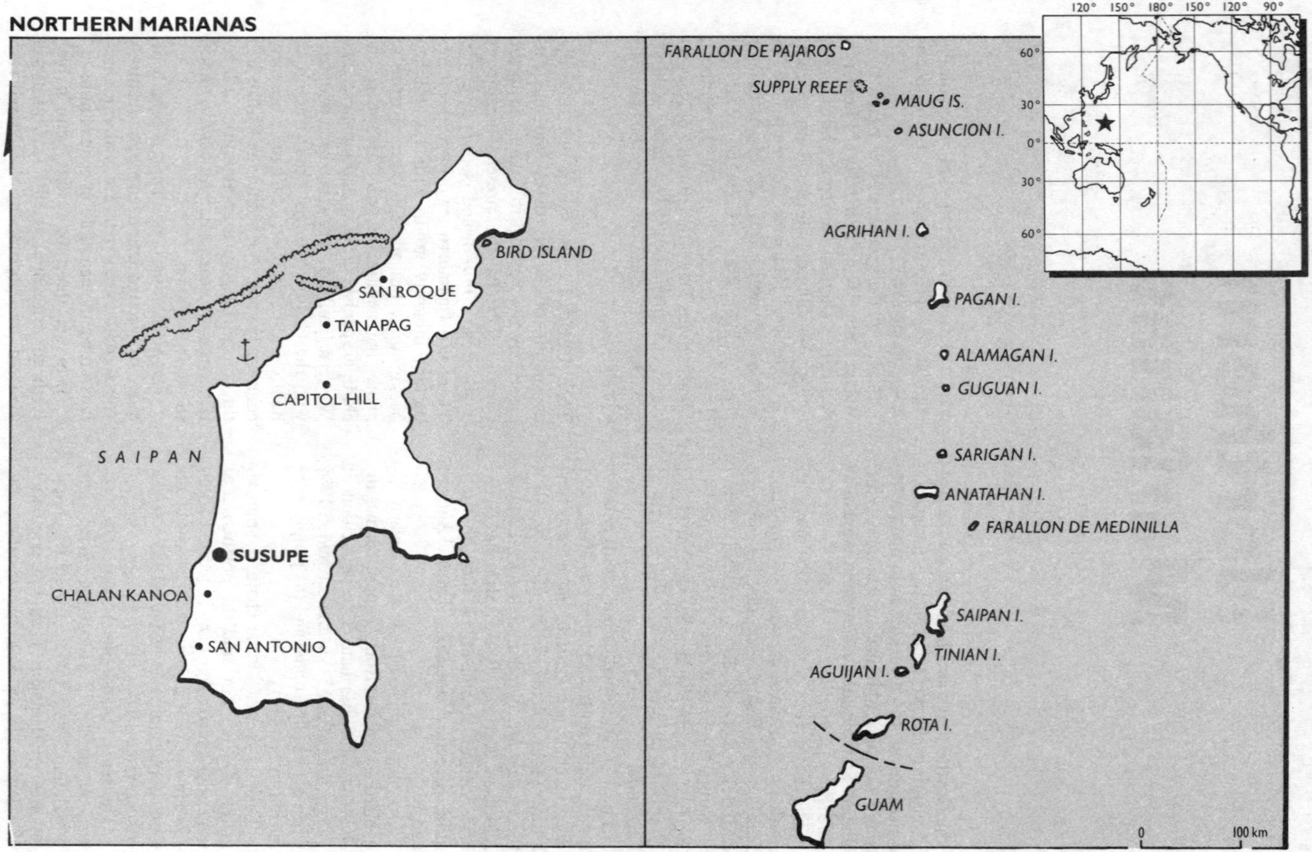

Inset map labels: 120° 150° 180° 150° 120° 90°, 60° 30° 0° 30° 60°

FARALLON DE PAJAROS
SUPPLY REEF
MAUG IS.
ASUNCION I.

AGRIHAN I.

PAGAN I.

ALAMAGAN I.

GUGUAN I.

SARIGAN I.

ANATAHAN I.

FARALLON DE MEDINILLA

SAIPAN I.

TINIAN I.

AGUIJAN I.

ROTA I.

GUAM

0   100 km

SAIPAN

BIRD ISLAND

SAN ROQUE

TANAPAG

CAPITOL HILL

SUSUPE

CHALAN KANOA

SAN ANTONIO

infant mortality at 23.8 per 1000, and a death rate of 5.4 per 1000, but probably underestimated.

Citizenship. The people, once regarded as 'temporary citizens' of the US, have become full citizens, following the discharge of the United Nations Trusteeship.

Language. Chamorro and Carolinian are spoken in the family, but English is widely spoken, particularly among the younger generation. English is the main language of instruction, but Chamorro and Carolinian are also taught. Conversational Japanese is also spoken by many older people as a result of the former Japanese association with the islands, and the big proportion of Japanese tourists.

Religion. The people are Christian, although traditional beliefs and taboos may still be found. The majority follow the Roman Catholic faith.

GOVERNMENT. The government has three branches — Executive, Legislative and Judiciary. An elected Governor and Lieutenant Governor head the executive branch. The legislative branch consists of the Senate and House of Representatives. The Senate has nine popularly elected members, three from each Senatorial District — Rota, Tinian and Aguijan; Saipan and the islands north of Saipan. The House of Representatives has 14 popularly elected members. The four areas of Rota, Tinian, Saipan and the northern islands, each have a popularly elected mayor.

The Judiciary Branch is made up of a US District Court headed by a Federal Judge and a Commonwealth Trial Court. There is a system of trial by jury.

Government power comes from the Constitution of 9 January 1978, Secretarial Order 3989 of 24 March 1976, providing for the separate administration of the Northern Marianas, and the Covenant of the same date 'establishing a Commonwealth of the Northern Mariana Islands in Political Union with the United States of America'.

EDUCATION. There were 6050 children in Commonwealth schools in the 1986–87 school year, 5113, or 84 per cent, attending public schools. Of the 30 schools, 16 were public and 14 private institutions. Since 1982–83 public school enrolments have increased by 10 per cent and private schools

by 30 per cent. About 220 students are enrolled in post-secondary courses in schools and universities in Guam, Hawaii or the US mainland. About half of all students who enter the Commonwealth school system fail to complete high school.

The Northern Marianas College is the only institution of higher education located within the CNMI. In 1985 it was granted full accreditation by the Western Association of Schools and Colleges. The college offers Associate degrees in Arts and Science, and had an enrolment of 1309 students in 1985.

HEALTH. The Department of Public Health and Environmental Services provides health care services in the Commonwealth. There are no private doctors in practice, although there are 2 private dentists and 2 optometrists.

Dr Torres Hospital, a 62-bed former US Army field hospital, is the major Commonwealth hospital, sited on Saipan. There are what are described as 'sub-hospital facilities' with full time doctors and nurses, on Tinian and Rota, and eight dispensaries throughout the islands.

The Dr Torres Hospital is inadequate for the demands put on it (in 1981 outpatient visits totalled twice the population of Saipan) and a new 74-bed hospital is being completed.

Diseases. Infectious diseases typical of a tropical climate or underdeveloped societies are not generally present. Highest number of reported diseases are those of the respiratory system, while the two outstanding causes of death are heart disease and cancer. Diseases transmitted by consumption of non-potable water occur frequently on Saipan, a fact attributable to the contamination of groundwater by overflowing cesspools and pit privies.

LABOUR. There are 5976 members of the labour force in the Commonwealth (1985), of whom 3072 are adult males and 1944 adult females. There are 2752 government employees and 2632 are in private employment. The number of unemployed was 592, 9.9 per cent of the total.

A feature of recent labour trends has been the drop in the number of TTPI employees — the total employees being 156 in 1985 compared to 533 in 1982. GCNMI employees

TABLE 1 NUMBER IN EMPLOYMENT BY INDUSTRY, 1985 (CNMI LABOUR FORCE)

Industry	Employed
Agriculture/fishing	108
Mining	104
Construction	80
Manufacturing	4
Transportation/utilities	468
Wholesale trade	968
Retail trade	120
Finance, insurance & real estate	696
Public administration	876
Non-classifiable establishments	1960
Total	5384

TABLE 2 NUMBER OF NON-RESIDENT WORKERS BY OCCUPATIONAL GROUP CNMI, 1985

Industry	Employed
Professional, technical & managerial	839
Clerical & sales	336
Service	1849
Agricultural, fishery, forestry & related	314
Processing	38
Machine trades	596
Benchwork	441
Structural work	2100
Miscellaneous	166
Total	6679

totalled 2596 in 1985 compared to 1849 in 1982.

The majority of workers are CNMI citizens (5152), with most of those being of Chamorro descent (3880). The number of Micronesian women, especially younger women, in the labour force has risen considerably and is now estimated to be about 40 per cent. There are comparatively large numbers of non-resident workers in the CNMI, who are classified separately by the Department of Commerce and Labour. In 1985 these included 5125 Filipinos, 575 Koreans, 562 Chinese, 349 Japanese and 68 others. The majority are in construction or service industries (see below).

Income. The mean average income of a household is $9000–$10,000 annually. This figure, however, does not give an indication of the differences between government and private sector wage scales or between wages earned by Micronesian and non-Micronesian workers. These differences remain considerable.

THE LAND. The Northern Marianas, together with Guam, which is a separate US territory to the south, comprise the highest slope of a massive mountain range rising more than 9.5 km off the floor of the Marianas Trench in the ocean bed, and forms a boundary between the Philippine Sea (to the west) and the Pacific Ocean.

Geologically the Marianas are mountainous 'high islands' of either limestone formation (the southern islands) or of volcanic rock. They generally rise out of the sea in successive level terraces, with tables of fringing reefs.

Saipan is the only island having a sizeable lagoon, extending almost the entire length of the western side of the island.

At least seven of the northern islands are still regarded as volcanic — Pagan (which last erupted in May 1981), Agrihan, Alamagan, Guguan, Sarigan, Anatahan and Farallon de Pajaros.

Climate. The climate is tropical with very little temprature variation year round. Average temperature is 27°C and average annual rainfall 2032 mm. The highest rainfall is between July and October, with the dry season from February to April (with less than 250 mm).

Land tenure. Of the total of 47,445 ha of land, 38,905 ha are public land and about 8540 ha, or about 18 per cent of the total, private land. The large proportion of public land results from the policies of the German and Japanese administrations of acquiring land not enclosed or cultivated.

Title to CNMI public lands vests in the Marianas Public Lands Corporation (MPLC), which is responsible for management and disposition of all public lands. The MPLC may grant private leases of public land and make land available for both village and agricultural homesteads.

Ownership of land is limited by the constitution to persons of Northern Marianas descent — defined as individuals of at least one quarter Northern Marianas Chamorro or Carolinian blood, or corporations whose directorships and voting are held 51 per cent by such individuals.

Defence land. The US Department of Defense has entered into a lease agreement for 7190 ha of land on Tinian, or more than two thirds of the island, for military use. Its agreement provides for the lease back of about 2600 ha, including portions of the Micronesian Development Corporation's ranch which is within the area, if not required for direct use. The military land has so far been used for occasional exercises and there are no plans for permanent military installations.

PRIMARY PRODUCTION. Only about 240 ha of land is under cultivation and about 9000 ha in grazing, and there are probably only 64 full-time commercial farmers or ranchers. Most production is of vegetables, with some fruits and staples, but production has been dropping in recent years. Total domestic sale of vegetables, fruits and staple crops in 1985 was about $682,510 worth. Fifty per cent of vegetable needs are imported.

Livestock consists of about 3098 pigs and 9420 cattle, most of them accounted for by the 2800 ha Bar-K ranch on Tinian, owned by the Micronesian Development Corporation of Guam. All milk and almost all meat sales are generated by the Bar-K ranch, and

TABLE 3 TOTAL SALES OF AGRICULTURAL COMMODITIES COMMONWEALTH OF THE NORTHERN MARIANA ISLANDS
Financial year 1985 (in lb)

Categories	Domestic	Export	Total
Vegetables	1,046,628 $522,189.71	68,213 $18,411.65	1,114,841 lb $540,601.36
Fruits	203,052 $88,240.80	6742 $3753.80	209,794 lb $91,994.60
Staples	132,091 $72,079.64	2669 $1489.50	134,760 lb $73,569.14
Meat	93,774 $123,596.14	264,534 $335,524.64	358,308 lb $459,120.78
Pork	1991 $2912.90	751 $976.30	2742 lb $3889.20
Fish	400,847 $538,795.96	—	400,847 lb $538,795.96
Eggs	89,510 $114,949.01	—	89,510 lb $114,949.10
Milk	1,323,705 $237,640.20	—	1,323,705 lb $237,640.20
Grand total			3,634,507 lb $2,060,560.34

most of the production is exported to Guam. In 1985 sale of all agricultural produce totalled $2,060,560 — with meat and milk accounting for 30 per cent of the total.

Fisheries. Fishing consists largely of semi-subsistence activity, with three to four small scale commercial operations. The commercial operations have about seven boats of 9 to 12 m in length. About 40 full-time fishermen are employed, catching only about 182.2 tonnes annually, a value of $538,796.

Japanese and Korean fishing vessels are reported to take about 8000 tonnes of fish annually in waters within the 200-mile limit of the Commonwealth.

COMMERCE. Construction, retailing and a range of service industries account for most commercial business. There are about 1599 different business activities (1985 statistics), with general business making up about 1402 of the enterprises. Manufacturers account for 76 of the total and wholesalers for 67. Thirty businesses deal with insurance and there are 16 registered roadside vendors. A total of seven banks are now registered compared with 56 in 1983.

Gross business revenue recorded by the government in 1982 was $165 million, which was nearly 500 per cent greater than estimated gross business revenue in 1974, and indicative of the development of commerce since the Commonwealth's change in constitutional status.

The rate of economic growth has increased dramatically during the past five years due to the growth of tourism and expanded Commonwealth and Federal expenditures following the new political status. Wage and salary incomes have been steadily increasing, as has the number of wage-earners.

Private business entrepreneurs continue to increase as the economic base develops. Estimated gross island product has shown an increase of 250 per cent over a six year period.

In May 1988 a Bill was passed banning foreign investments of less than $1 million, and prohibiting foreigners from entering businesses which can be run by locals.

Economic Development Loan Fund. The EDLF is wholly funded by the US, and is available to provide loans for narrowly-defined enterprises that appear 'economically feasible with a substantial degree of success', but that are not bankable. All loans are secured by real and/or personal property.

Funds appropriated for the fund are deposited with the Northern Marianas Development Bank, which is responsible for carrying out the provisions of the fund. Lending is made to citizens of the Northern Marianas for starting or expanding business ventures that are held to contribute to the local economy.

Under the terms of the fund, $500,000 each year is reserved for small loans for farmers and fishermen and to agricultural and marine co-operatives. Another $250,000 a year is reserved for low interest housing loans for low income families. These sums are in addition to the funds available for business loans and are adjusted for inflation.

In fiscal years 1984 and 1985 EDLF invested in 164 enterprises for a total expenditure of $15.2 million. It was also encouraging applications for EDLF investment as an equity partner in new business, offering to help to bear start-up costs or share the establishment risk.

TOURISM. The tourist industry represents the major economy industry, and it has been identified by the government as the most promising sector for development.

There were 186,203 visitors in 1987, an increase of 16 per cent over the 1986 figures. About 76 per cent of all visitors come from Japan, and about 18 per cent from the US. Tourism contributed $141 m to the economy in 1987.

There were 983 hotel rooms available in all areas in 1985 and these were being added to by 442 in 1986.

FINANCES. The Commonwealth gets its finance from three sources—Covenant funds, internal resources and Federal programme funds. The Covenant funds are committed under the Covenant which established the Commonwealth, and are meant to assist the CNMI to become more self-supporting and achieve progressively higher standards of living. These payments are earmarked for government operations, capital improvements and economic development loans.

Covenant funds. The Covenant grants are set at $14 million annually, in 1975 dollars and adjusted for inflation. In FY 1986 Coven-

TABLE 4 CNMI CONSUMER PRICE INDEX 1983–1985

	Food item at home	Housing	Transportation	Apparel & upkeep	Health & recreation	All items
CY 1983						
1st Quarter	150.7	211.4	162.7	195.5	209.5	185.9
2nd Quarter	153.2	221.7	164.5	208.1	213.4	192.2
3rd Quarter	152.5	237.1	151.4	211.5	214.9	193.5
4th Quarter	154.1	242.8	152.5	204.5	214.9	193.8
CY 1984						
1st Quarter	154.7	245.6	160.4	200.4	215.5	195.3
2nd Quarter	152.6	251.8	173.8	197.5	208.7	196.9
3rd Quarter	155.8	252.8	173.9	198.6	214.6	199.1
4th Quarter	157.9	253.4	175.0	198.9	214.8	200.0
CY 1985						
1st Quarter	159.5	253.8	178.1	204.9	217.1	202.68
2nd Quarter	160.6	254.2	178.9	205.4	217.5	203.32
3rd Quarter	163.0	254.5	180.0	205.7	218.0	204.24
4th Quarter	165.1	254.6	179.2	204.8	217.9	204.32

ant direct grants totalled an estimated $27.726 million in 1986 dollars, including $17.760 million for Government operations, $8.466 million for capital improvements, and $1.5 million for special programmes.

The Covenant stipulates that these direct grants will be provided for seven full fiscal years from the establishment of the Commonwealth (1978), which took them to the end of the 1985 fiscal year. After that date the Commonwealth will continue to receive the grants under a new agreement lasting until 1992 for a total appropriation of $228.0 million.

Covenant grants represented about 60 per cent of the CNMI financial resources in FY 1984.

Internal revenue. Total GCNMI internal revenue was estimated at about $15.64 million for 1984. Major income was from utilities, income taxes and gross receipts tax on businesses. For the details see accompanying table.

Federal programmes. Under the provisions of the Covenant the Commonwealth is eligible for all the programmes that are provided to the 50 states and to the other US territories. The Commonwealth can also use the direct US grants as matching funds to obtain categorical Federal programme awards.

CNMI departments and agencies were awarded Federal programme grants in FY 1985 totalling about $14.86 million. They were made by about 15 different Federal government departments.

In addition to the current array of Federal grants, major capital improvement projects for hospital, housing, port and road construction, are planned over the next five to ten years. Medicaid was introduced in 1983 and a USDA Food Stamp programme, to replace a direct food distribution under the Needy Families Food Programme, has begun.

Currency and banking. Currency is the United States dollar. There are the government's Northern Marianas Development Bank and three commercial banks: the Bank of Hawaii, Bank of Guam and the California First Bank. There are two savings and loan institutions, and the Saipan Credit Union.

A decline in recent years in the number of commercial and offshore banks has been due to a new banking code which establishes additional operating requirements.

Taxation. Major taxes are the business gross revenue tax, applied on a graduating scale on business revenue; duties and excise; and local income tax. The US Internal Revenue Tax applies, but has been deferred on income earned entirely in the Northern Marianas,

TABLE 5 COMMONWEALTH OF THE NORTHERN MARIANA ISLANDS COLLECTIONS FOR CALENDAR YEAR 1984

Account	Amount Collected
Business gross revenue tax	$8,100,000
Wage and salary tax	2,031,000
Territorial income tax	155,000
Corporate tax	15,000
Bar tax	138,000
Room occupancy tax	922,000
Amusement license fees	403,000
Business privilege fee	97,000
Admiralty and maritime fee	2000
Vehicle registration fee	190,000
Driver's license	55,000
Corporation fees	22,000
Weapon license fee	7000
Penalty and interest charges (on taxes)	267,000
Utilities	3,185,000
Miscellaneous collections	4000
Collections from Department of Commerce and Labour	46,886
TOTAL	$15,639,886

TABLE 6 CNMI COMMERCIAL IMPORTS, BY COMMODITY GROUP

Commodity group	Value $
Meat and meat preparations	6,911,470
Dairy products and eggs	668,016
Fish and fish preparations	468,584
Fruit and vegetables	305,348
Coffee, tea, cocoa, etc.	32,606
Animal feed	145,521
Misc. food preparations	2,792,446
Beverages	1,316,120
Tobacco and tobacco products	1,365,747
Beer	1,410,895
Wood, lumber and cork	8,678,565
Petroleum and petroleum products	6,173,397
Perfumes and toiletries	1,432,223
Plastic and cellulose materials	44,948
Paper and paper products	205,953
Electrical machinery and appliances	1,125,949
Transport equipment	4,319,320
Plumbing, heating and lighting	295,442
Furniture	184,519
Clothing	1,894,045
Footwear	869,081
Professional and scientific equipment, photographic, etc.	963,149
Jewellery	576,228
Total imports	45,284,960

TABLE 7 MAIN SOURCES OF IMPORTS

United States	28,013,905
Japan	10,664,139
Australia	1,316,146
All other countries	5,310,769

but not outside it. In 1983 the Northern Marianas government sought to obtain a permanent deferral of the US tax code, and for the Marianas to have authority to develop and administer its own tax system.

Income. Mean household income in 1985 was estimated at about $9000–$10,999.

TRANSPORTATION. There are regular air and sea links between the Northern Marianas and the US mainland and nations throughout the Pacific Basin, and services linking the main islands of the Commonwealth.

Shipping. Two shipping services from the Far East to Saipan service the Commonwealth at about monthly intervals with vessels of about 5000 tons gross. There is also a quarterly service which transships at Rota. Other services connect the West Coast of the US at about 21 day intervals. Two local shipping companies operate weekly barge services (about 1000 tons gross capacity) from Guam to Saipan, with calls at Tinian and Rota.

The number of vessel entries to Saipan in 1985 was 265 with total cargo of 49,939 tons and passengers numbering 6323.

Ports. Ports are at Saipan, Rota and Tinian. The Government plans to upgrade Saipan's port with the construction of two large new docks and warehouse and container facilities. Rota's West Harbor has undergone substantial reconstruction and is capable of handling small freighters. Tinian harbour provides port capacity that exceeds the needs of the harbour and averages 15 tuna ship operations per month.

Aviation. The Commonwealth is served by two major airlines — Continental Air Micronesia and Japan Airlines — giving it trunk routes with Japan and the US respectively. Air Micronesia and Air Nauru also connect Saipan with other islands of Micronesia (and

Air Nauru has further links with Australia and New Zealand).

There are frequent daily connections to Guam by the smaller airlines and air taxis, some of them calling at Rota and Tinian. Charter services are operated to Saipan by Japan Airlines and All Nippon Airways.

During 1985 there were 4168 aircraft entries at Saipan, over 5000 air taxi entries at Rota and over 6000 air taxi entries at Tinian. Air charter services are available to the northern islands. There are modern air terminals at both Saipan and Rota.

Road transport. Commonwealth road transport is highly developed, with an estimated 7000 vehicles on Saipan and about 6500 regularly on the road, giving a density of about one vehicle for every three poeple, or about 1¾ vehicles per household.

The road system is primarily a legacy of World War II, but major reconstruction work is now going on with the aid of special Federal funds. The road network consists of about 473 km of roads, about 98 km of them primary roads and 111 km secondary roads — the remainder being village and scenic roads.

COMMUNICATIONS. A Comsat earth station on Saipan, which began operating at the end of 1980, handles tele-communications in the islands. Internal phone links on Saipan and Tinian are served by MTC, a commercial company.

The government maintains and operates a short-wave radio for communications with the northern islands and ships within territorial waters.

There are two commercial AM/FM radio stations on Saipan which effectively serve Saipan and Tinian. Several stations on Guam can also be received. There is a commercial cable TV station on Saipan.

Newspapers. There are two weekly newspapers, the *Commonwealth Examiner* and the *Marianas Variety*. The Guam-based *Pacific Daily News* also circulates in the main islands.

Water. Water supply on Saipan, Rota and Tinian is from ground sources, tapped by wells. Distribution is handled by the CNMI Public Works Department but the pipes and equipment are old. The Government has water and sewerage improvement plans

for Saipan, Rota and Tinian, and Rota already has adequate storage of water.
Power. Power is operated by the Public Works Department. On Saipan the primary source is a new plant with a 21 MW capacity. Existing plant, even with recent upgrading, is regarded as inadequate to meet the greater-than-forecast demand for electric power. Power failures occur on Saipan, Rota and Tinian. Electricity is 120 volts.

MAJOR OFFICE HOLDERS
Governor:
  Pedro P. Tenorio
Lt. Governor:
  Pedro A. Tenorio
Attorney-General:
  Alexandro Castro
Chief Justice:
  Robert A. Hefner
Speaker of House of Representatives:
  Jose R. Lifoifoi

GOVERNMENT DEPARTMENTS
Governor's Office, Saipan; Tel.: 234-6407 Divisions: Governor's Office, and Lt. Governor's Office
Attorney General, Saipan; Tel.: 234-6207 Divisions: Attorney General, Prosecutor, Investigation, Registrar of Corporation, and Immigration
Commerce and Labor Department; Tel.: 234-7261 Divisions: Dicrector's Office, Economic Development, Business License, Labor and Statistical Research
Community and Cultural Affairs Department, Saipan; Tel.: 322-9048 Divisions: Director's Office, Nutrition Assistance Program, Historic Preservation, Youth Services, Aging, Arts and Culture and Veterans Affairs
Finance Department, Saipan; Tel.: 322-98189 Divisions: Director's Office, Customs, Finance and Accounting, Procurement and Supply, Revenues and Taxation, and Treasury
Heath & Environmental Services Department, Saipan; Tel.: 234-6112 Divisions: Director's Office, Hospital Administration, Dental Health, Public Health, Vocational Rehabilitation, Environmental Quality, and Medicaid
Office of Planning and Budget, Saipan; Tel.: 234-7172 Divisons: Budget, Federal Programs, and CIP Advisor

Natural Resources Department, Saipan; Tel.: 322-9830 Divisons: Director's Office, Animal Health and Industry, Fish and Wildlife, Parks and Recreation, Plant Industry and Land & Surveys
Public Safety Department, Saipan; Tel.: 234-6505 Divisions: Public Safety, Corrections and Fire
Public Works Department, Saipan; Tel.: 322-9482 Divisions: Director's Office, Administrative Services, Automotive/Equipment Maintenance, Building Maintenance, Road Maintenance, Technical Services, Power Plant, Power Distribution, Transportation/Equipment, Water and Sewer
Commonwealth Legislature, PO Box 586, Saipan; Tel.: 234-6588 Divisions: House of Representatives, Senate and and Legislative Affairs Bureau
Judiciary, PO Box 307, Saipan, CM 96950; Tel.: 234-6401
Mayor of Saipan, Saipan; Tel.: 234-6208
Mayor of Tinian, Tinian; Tel.: 433-9250
Mayor of Rota, Rota; Tel.: 532-9451
Mayor of the Northern Islands, Saipan; Tel.: 234-6407

INDEPENDENT BODIES
Board of Elections, PO Box 470, Saipan, CM 96950; Tel.: 234-6880
Commonwealth Development Authority, PO Box 2149, Saipan, CM 96950; Tel.: 234-7145
Commonwealth Ports Authority, PO Box 1055, Saipan, CM 96950; Tel.: 234-8319
Commonwealth Utilities Commission, Saipan, CM 96950; Tel.: 322-9229
Marianas Islands Housing Authority, PO Box 514, Saipan, CM 96950; Tel.: 234-6866
Marianas Land Commission, PO Box 2643, Saipan, CM 96950; Tel.: 322-9420
Marianas Public Land Corporation, PO Box 380, Saipan, CM 96950; Tel.: 234-9614
Marianas Visitors Bureau, PO Box 861, Saipan, CM 96950; Tel.: 234-8327
NMI Retirement Fund, PO Box 1247, Saipan, CM 96950; Tel.: 234-7228
Northern Marianas College, Saipan, CM 96950; Tel.: 234-7542

REPRESENTATIVES OVERSEAS

Marianas Guam Office, Asia Plaza Building, PO Box 8366, Tamuning, Guam 96911; Tel.: 646-9181/646-9182; Tlx: 721 6664 CM LNO

Marianas Hawaii Office, 1221 Kapiolani Blvd, Room 348, Honolulu, HI 96814; Tel.: (808) 523-8156/523-8434; Tlx: 723 8400 CM LNO HR

Northern Marianas Washington Office, 2121 R Street, Ave, N. W. Washington, DC 20008; Tel.: (202) 328-3847; Tlx: 650 2616638 MCI

HISTORY. Archaeological excavations in the Mariana Islands have revealed that man inhabited the archipelago at least 3500 years ago. The earliest radiocarbon date so far obtained is from Saipan — 1527 BC. Two separate culture periods have been identified and named pre-Latte and Latte. The Latte period was characterised by the erection of double rows of capped, short, stone pillars as foundations for important houses. The making of redware pottery was a feature of the pre-Latte period. Impressions of rice husks on potsherds dating back to AD 1335 indicate that rice was cultivated before the arrival of Europeans.

Three of the Mariana Islands, Saipan, Rota and Guam, were discovered by Magellan in 1521 and named the Ladrones Islands. A year or so later, three men from one of Magellan's ships, the *Trinidad*, deserted in the Northern Marianas when that ship was attempting to sail from the Moluccas to Mexico with a cargo of spices. Two of the men were killed, but a third, Gonzalo de Vigo, was found at Guam in 1526 when the flagship of the Loaisa expedition called there.

Spanish rule. In 1565, the Spanish explorer Miguel Lopez de Legaspi took possession of the Ladrones Islands for the Spanish Crown on his way to colonise the Philippines. Subsequently, when the galleon trade between Mexico and the Philippines was inaugurated the captains of the galleons were instructed to sail in the latitude of the Ladrones on their westward voyages to avoid the low and troublesome Marshall and Caroline Islands. But for over a century there was no permanent Spanish settlement in the group and it was not until a Jesuit mission was established on Guam in 1668 that the galleons began

putting into those islands. The name Mariana Islands was adopted at that time — in honour of Queen Mariana of Austria (mother of the Spanish king, Charles II). Several British explorers — Anson (1742), Byron (1765) and Wallis (1767) — called at Tinian for supplies during their voyages.

The early period of the Spanish rule was a period of continuous revolt by the local inhabitants, the Chamorros; the result was that the whole population was removed to Guam — only a small number escaping by hiding in caves. Some of the exiled Chamorros later settled in Yap and Palau.

In about 1815 some of the people from Truk and Yap were allowed to settle in Saipan when their islands were devastated by typhoon, and descendants of these Carolinian migrants today comprise an important minority in the Northern Marianas. Other Chamorros were allowed to return later in the 19th century.

In 1898, at the end of the Spanish-American War, the US, by virtue of the Treaty of Paris, took possession of Guam and in June 1899 Spain sold all the northern islands of the Marianas, exclusive of Guam, to Germany.

German rule. Germany expanded copra production and improved health, education and roads. A poll tax was introduced, and a system of compulsory government labour established. About 700 people from the Pohnpei area of the Carolines were resettled in the Marianas after a typhoon in Pohnpei.

The Germany period was short and only a few government officers were stationed in the district at any one time. There was not the opportunity for the Germans to make any great impact before World War I and they departed, their place being taken immediately by the Japanese.

Japanese period. The Japanese occupation, which also included the Caroline and Marshall groups, was formalised in 1920 when all the Micronesian islands, with Guam's exception, were made a League of Nations mandate under the administration of Japan.

This period saw the extensive development of the Northern Marianas. Much of the roads, docks, even water systems in the islands date from this period, which lasted until 1944. Meanwhile, Japan had left the League of Nations.

The Japanese civil population rose from 1758 in 1920 to 44,991 in 1938, mostly on Saipan, but Rota and Tinian were also developed extensively as centres of sugar production. Local population was about 4000, and lived on Saipan and Rota. There was no significant local population on Tinian. Agricultural products, particularly sugar and alcoholic drinks made from molasses, were the main exports and nearly all production went to Japan. There were 13 distilleries on Saipan in 1938. Japanese tenant farmers and labourers and not Chamorros were employed in the sugar industry.

With the outbreak of the Pacific War in 1941 roads and ports improved and fortifications made. There were about 80,000 Japanese troops in the Northern Marianas when the US forces invaded Saipan on 15 June 1944. During the heavy fighting that followed there was so much devastation that, later, the seeds of quick-growing tropical scrub had to be sown from the air to prevent erosion. The Americans lost 3426 dead and 13,099 wounded in the fighting, and the Japanese garrisons were virtually exterminated — probably as many as 30,000.

Many of the Japanese survivors jumped to their deaths from Mt Marpi or from the cliffs on the north of Saipan into the sea. On Tinian 5000 Japanese were killed, 380 surrendered and another 3000 either died in caves or committed suicide.

After their occupation, the Americans built Saipan and Tinian into military bases for the attack on Japan. There were 200,000 invasion troops on Saipan in 1945. Five kilometres away, on Tinian, the Americans built what were then the longest runways in the world. It was from one of them that a B29 bomber took off on 6 August 1945, with the atomic bomb that was dropped on Hiroshima. Three days later a second nuclear bomb was flown from Tinian to be dropped on Nagasaki.

US Trust Territory. The Marianas, other than Guam, became part of the United States Trust Territory of the Pacific Islands in 1947. However, from 1953 to mid-1962 all islands except Rota were controlled by the US Navy Department for special security purposes. Saipan was used by the CIA to train Nationalist Chinese (Taiwanese) guerrillas to infiltrate the People's Republic of China.

In July 1962 the administration of the Northern Marianas was returned to the US Department of Interior, and Rota, which had remained with the Interior Department, was re-integrated.

The District Centre for the Northern Marianas under the Trusteeship government was established on Saipan, and Trust Territory headquarters was also moved there from Guam, in separate buildings on what was known as Capitol Hill.

But there were growing pressures within the Northern Marianas for separate political status for the Marianas, which did not want to proceed in constitutional tandem with the rest of the Micronesian districts in the Trust Territory. The US permitted the Northern Marianas in 1972 to negotiate for separate status.

On 17 June 1975 78 per cent of the people of the Northern Marianas voted for the islands to become a Commonwealth of the United States rather than continuing with the Carolines and Marshalls in the Trusteeship, and on 24 March 1976 US President Ford signed the Commonwealth covenant giving the Marianas internal self government, with the US controlling defence and foreign relations with the right to maintain military bases in the territory.

The new Constitution came into effect on 9 January 1978, the voters having, in December 1977, elected a governor, lieutenant-governor and members of a bicameral legislature of the new government.

Although technically the Commonwealth did not become a fully legal entity until the US was granted a discharge of its UN trusteeship obligations (the people meanwhile were 'temporary' citizens of the US), for most practical purposes the Commonwealth has been a reality since 1978, and its status is now rather like that of a state of the US.

Further information. Glynn Barrat (ed.), *Russian exploration in the Mariana Islands 1817–1828*, Saipan, 1984, is an examination of a usually neglected topic. *Politics in Micronesia*, Suva, 1983, contains articles by a number of contributors and discusses recent changes and present political statuses. There are a number of books written in the 1970s on various aspects of the US policy in Micronesia, Most are critical.

ISLANDS IN DETAIL

Saipan. The area of the island is 116.5 sq.

km which is the largest in the group. There is a lagoon along its west coast and a range of hills extends from north to south for about two-thirds of its length. Mt Tagpochau (474 m) is the highest point. Nothing now remains of the Japanese sugar plantations on the flat land below Mt Marpi.

The Germans had their district administrator's residence at Garapan, on Tanapag harbour on the west coast where the present port and wharf are situated. The Japanese extended Garapan into a town of 10,000–20,000 people overflowing around Mutcho Point.

The town was completely obliterated in the fighting of 1944, but it is now flourishing again with a population of nearly 4000 people (the largest concentration on Saipan), and with some first-class resort hotels among other businesses.

The village of Chalan Kanoa is now the second largest population centre, with a shopping complex and resort hotels there and on adjoining Susupe. Government offices, including the Governor's office and the legislature, are in Susupe. Another landmark is the seven storey Nauru building, topped with a revolving restaurant.

The tourist industry and Commonwealth status have helped to change the lifestyle of the Saipanese dramatically. Where only a few years ago the island's economy was mainly a subsistence one, or dependent on wages paid to local employees by Trust Territory headquarters, today the Saipanese benefit from their own businesses, or from work in the tourist industry.

Trust Territory headquarters on Capitol Hill with its green lawns, offices and bungalows, has lost its significance to the island's economy, and the buildings have been handed over to the Commonwealth, which has not yet decided how best to make use of them.

Saipan is busy and bustling, especially on the west coast, where most of the commercial activities are. There are good restaurants, nightspots and bars, with multilingual signs everywhere (in English and Japanese). The beaches alongside the hotels are broad, of white sand, and despite Saipan's superb climate, uncrowded. A strong government-sponsored beautification programme, with tree and shrub plantings, and regular junk collections, has made the island very attractive. Good roads link all the villages, airport, and tourist spots.

After the Americans had occupied Saipan in 1944 several airfields were built, and the remains of some of these are to be seen; one, the former Isley Field in the south not far from the main business and government centre, has been developed as Saipan's modern international airport with an award-winning terminal building.

Managaha Island, off Saipan's west coast, is a popular picnic island, ideal for water sports and reef diving. There are regular day trips organised by tour companies.

Tinian is separated from Saipan by a strait about 4.8 km wide. The total area of the island is 101 sq. km, and it is the second largest island in the Northern Marianas chain.

Tinian's most noted historical monuments are the huge runways built by the Americans after 1944 and from which the bombers took off on 6 and 9 August 1945, to drop the first atomic bombs on Hiroshima and Nagasaki. Plaques mark the place where the bombs were loaded. Some of these runways are still in excellent order, and are used by military aircraft on manoeuvres from Guam. Local commuter aircraft make regular flights between Saipan and Tinian. The US military has leased a large part of Tinian for possible use in the future, but there is no real military presence there.

Tinian has no lagoon and most of its shores are steep. The Japanese utilised the interior plateau to grow sugar cane and pineapples and vegetables for home consumption. Vegetable growing is still an important occupation, and there is also a large ratch, the Bar K, which supplies Guam and Saipan with fresh milk and other produce, including meat. It is owned by the Micronesian Development Corporation.

There is a modern airport building on the airstrip near the port which is used by the commuter airline. Both the airstrip and port have been upgraded in recent years. Tourism is a growing industry on Tinian, because of sun and sand, excellent deep sea fishing, and interest in Micronesian history. On Tinian there are notable Chamorro Latte stone ruins, including the House of Taga ruins, located in the main village of San Jose.

Rota. (Luta or Zarpane) has an area of 83 sq. km. Vegetable raising and tourism are the main occupation of the people. Just north of Rota village, a peak 491 metres high is said to be an extinct volcano. The people of Rota speak purer Chamorro than those elsewhere in the Northern Marianas and are believed to be of purer stock. Throughout the Spanish purges during the late 18th century many Rota people hid in caves and escaped death or deportation to Guam.

Rota has an excellent new airstrip and terminal building and it is a growing tourist destination. Among the attractions are good beaches, archaeological sights such as the Latte stone quarry and many fine examples of Latte stones, and ruins of the Japanese period of occupation — including sugar mills, phosphate mines, a cemetery and various buildings. In 1985 Rota had 6358 visitors.

Among natural wonders is Tonga Cave, near the island's main village of Songsong. An ancient Chamorro village is at Mochon Beach, on the northern tip of the island.

Anatahan has an area of 33 sq. km. It is an extinct crater, elongated into two peaks, 714 m and 782 m high.

Pagan (San Ignacio), largest of the purely volcanic islands, is 13.6 km long by 5.6 km wide. Mt Pagan (574 metres) in the northeast, last erupted in 1981; the volcanic peaks in the south-west corner periodically emit steam. The population was evacuated to Saipan during the eruption and has not yet returned to the island.

Agrihan is a volcanic island 9.6 km long by 5.6 km wide and 965 metres high. In 1810, Captain Brown and other Americans, with several families of Hawaiians, formed a colony on this island, but it was dispersed by the Spaniards, who destroyed the plantations. The Chamorros made their last stand against the Spaniards on the terraces of Agrihan, above the vertical cliffs.

Farallon de Pajaros, northernmost of the Marianas, is known also as Uracas. It is an active volcano 318 metres high.

Maug Islands are a group of three steep peaks surrounding a lagoon, which is a sunken crater. There was once a Japanese weather station on this uninhabited island.

FOR THE TOURIST. Sun, good climate, extensive white sand beaches, diving, and tours of wartime sites are the main attractions.

There is a wide choice of hotels on Saipan, and other hotels on Tinian and Rota, with a total of 983 rooms. There is also a wide range of tour operators and travel agencies, and six car rental firms.

Most tourists are Japanese tour parties who have a special interest in wartime relics in the islands..

Entry formalities. All citizens must show proof of citizenship and a round-trip or onward ticket to the next destination if other than their home country. US citizens need have no passport provided they have other proof of citizenship. Non-US citizens must have a valid passport and a US visa, but Japanese citizens travelling in a group need only a valid passport. Non-US citizens may also be required to have an entry permit, which can be issued on entry for a fee.

Sightseeing. Much intensive fighting took place in the Northern Marianas during World War II and many visitors go there to see the former battlegrounds. The area is also renowned for its reefs and lagoons. Particular attractions include:

Saipan: Suicide Cliff, the old Japanese jail, the last Japanese command post, old Japanese hospital, Peace Memorial, Sugar King monument, blue grotto, Bird Island.

Tinian: Atomic bomb loading sites; Japanese command post, House of Taga.

Rota: Latte stones, swimming hole, Wedding Cake Mountain, Japanese cannon site.

ACCOMMODATION
SAIPAN
Chalan Kanoa Beach Club: 20 ac units, laundry service, coffee terrace, restaurant, tennis court, swimming pool, credit cards. PO Box 356, Saipan, CM 96950. Tel.: 234 789, telex 717 CKBCLUB.

Hafadai Beach Hotel: 162 ac rooms, restaurants, teppan yaki, cocktail lounge, coffee shop, laundry service, swimming pool, gift shop, car rental desk, glass-bottom boats, sightseeing and fishing by arrangement, credit cards. PO Box 338, Saipan, CM 96950. Tel.: 234 6495/8, telex HAFADAI MN 616.

Hyatt Regency Saipan: 183 ac rooms, laundry service, restaurants and snack bar, bar and disco, beauty salon and barber, gift shop, baby sitter, tennis court, swimming pool, windsurfing, golf putting and driving range, cable and telex facilities, car desk, tours and sightseeing, credit cards. PO Box 87 CHRB, Saipan, CM 96950. Tel.: 234 6811/15 and 234 6426/28, telex HYATT SPN 659.

Islanders Inn: 19 ac rooms, some with kitchen, restaurants, laundry facilities, credit cards. PO Box 95, Saipan, CM 96950. Tel.: 234 7230, 234 6071, telex REALTY SPN 648.

Marianas Hotel (at two locations, Navy Hill and Marpi): 31 ac rooms and three cottages, restaurant, club house, swimming pool, 18 hole golf course, credit cards. PO Box 527, Saipan, CM 96950. Tel.: 322 9708, 322 9968, 322 9903, telex 608 KANPAC SPN.

Pacific Gardenia Hotel: 14 ac rooms, beauty salon and barber, coffee house, laundry service, secretarial services, conference room, car rental desk, credit cards. PO Box 144, Saipan, CM 96950. Tel.: 234 3455 66 77, telex 783 747.

Saipan Beach Hotel: 180 ac rooms, restaurant, coffee shop, laundry service, cocktail lounge, gift shop, tennis court, swimming pool, volley-ball, games room, beauty salon and barber, water sports, car rental desk, travel agency, conference rooms, credit cards. PO Box 1029, Saipan, CM 96950. Tel.: 234 6412/4, telex SBH SPN 694.

Saipan Grand Hotel: 139 ac rooms, restaurant and snack bar, laundry service, gift shop, tennis court, swimming pool, games, water sports, tours by arrangement, credit cards. PO Box 369, Saipan, CM 96950. Tel.: 234 6601/3, telex 628.

Sugar King Hotel: 20 ac rooms and 10 cottages, cocktail lounge, laundry service, meeting room. PO Box 1939, Saipan, CM 96950. Tel.: 234 6164, 234 6154.

Sun Inn: 20 ac rooms, some with kitchenette, snack bar, cocktail lounge, laundry service. PO Box 920, Saipan, CM 96950. Tel.: 234 6639.

Surf Hotel: 38 ac rooms and ten lodges,

restaurant, coffee shop, garden bar, barbecue, meeting rooms, gift shop, swimming pool, water sports, bicycles, car rental desk, entertainment, credit cards. PO Box 2370, Saipan, CM 96950. Tel.: 234 7976, 234 7986, telex SURF 715.

Beach Motel: 20 ac rooms, cocktail lounge, restaurant, coffee shop, laundry service, car rental desk. PO Box 1729, Saipan, CM 96950. Tel.: 234 7992, 234 6890.

Casa de Felipe: 8 ac units kitchenettes, cocktail lounge, laundry facilities, barbecue. PO Box 777, Saipan, CM 96950. Tel.: 234 7953.

Flametree Terrace Apartments: 34 ac units and three cottages, full kitchens, laundromat, store. PO Box 859, Saipan, CM 96950. Tel.: 322 3366.

Captain's Lodge: 7 ac rooms (no private baths), scuba diving and fishing by arrangement. PO Box 353 CHRB, Saipan, CM 96950. Tel.: 234 6670.

TINIAN

Meitetsu Fleming Hotel: 15 ac rooms, restaurant, laundromat, barbecue, supermarket, tours and fishing by arrangement. PO Box 68, Tinian, CM 96952, Tel.: 433 3232.

ROTA

Blue Peninsula Hotel: 22 ac rooms, some without private bath, bar, restaurant, laundry service, supermarket, coral viewing and scuba diving by arrangement. PO Box 539, Rota, CM 96951.

Rota Coconut Village: 20 ac rooms, restaurant, bar, gift shop, laundry facilities, swimming pool, car rental, sightseeing, fishing, scuba available. PO Box 855, Rota, CM 96951. Tel.: 532 3448.

Rota Pau Pau Hotel: 50 ac rooms, restaurant, bar, gift shop, laundry service, swimming pool, conference room, tours and water sports available. PO Box 503, Rota, CM 96951. Tel.: Air Call Guam 472 0724.

OGASAWARA (BONIN) ISLANDS

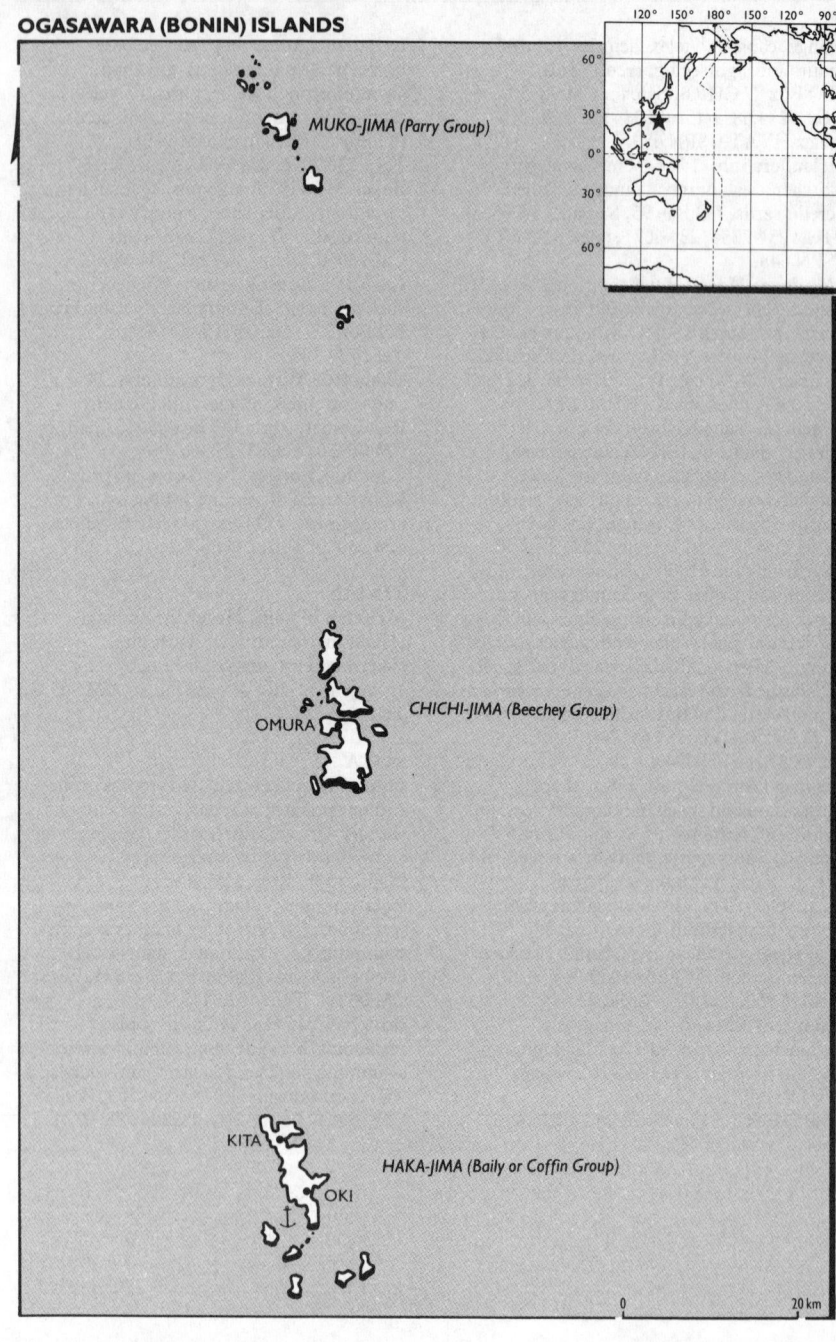

MUKO-JIMA (Parry Group)

CHICHI-JIMA (Beechey Group)

OMURA

KITA

OKI

HAKA-JIMA (Baily or Coffin Group)

0   20 km

Ogasawara Islands

These islands, almost 30 of them, are 1080 km south of Tokyo. They are also known as the Bonin Islands. They are named after the Japanese Ogasawara who was reported to have discovered them in 1593. In 1876 they were internationally admitted as part of Japanese territory. They came under the control of the US Navy in 1946, and reverted to Japan in 1968.

The main islands, Chichi-jima and Haha-jima mean Papa Island, Mama Island, etc., including Elder Brother, Little Brother, Bride, Matchmaker, etc.

The islands may be classified into five groups, and those having an area above 1 sq. km are indicated:

Muko-jima (3 sq. km), Nakodo-jima (1.58), Yome-jima, Kitano-shima.

Immediately to their south are the Chichijima or Beechey Islands — Chichi-jima (23.95), Ani-jima, (7.85), Ototo-jima (5.3), Mago-jima, Nishi-jima, Hyotan-jima, Hitomaru-jima, Higashi-jima, Minami-jima.

The third group comprises the Haha-jima or Bailey Islands — Haha-jima, (20.8), Mukou-jima (1.45), Katsuotori-shima, Hira-jima, Futago-jima, Maru-jima, Ane-jima, (1.67), Imoto-jima (1.36), Mei-jima (1.13).

Further south again are the Volcano Islands of Iwo-jima (22.36), Kitaiwo-jima (5.52), Minamiiwo-shima (3.67).

The other three islands, located at the north-west, eastern and south-west extremities respectively are Nishino-shima, Okinotori-shima and Minamitori-shima (1.1). Okinotori-shima is the newest of the islands, formed by the explosion of a submarine volcano. All the Ogasawara islands are protrusions caused by submarine volcanic activity.

The islands are mountainous with many cliffs and there are no beaches except on Iwo-jima, Chichi-jima and Hira-jima. The highest mountains are Minamiiwo-jima (918 m), Chibusayama (462 m) on Haha-jima and Chuouzan (321 m) on Chichi jima.

The islands have a total registered population of 1804 including 1436 on Chichi-jima and 368 on Haha-jima, as at April 1986. They are a municipal unit of Tokyo with a mayor elected by direct popular vote.

Schools on the two main islands had 155 primary level students on Chichi-jima and 27 on Haha-jima, while in Junior High School there were 36 and 16 students on the two islands respectively in 1986. There is a senior high school on Chichi-jima with 18 students. Doctors from Tokyo serve in medical centres on Chichi and Haha.

The islands are served by a regular weekly ship from Tokyo to Chichi-jima, taking 29 hours for the trip. There are three regular services a week between Chichi-jima and Haha-jima.

The main harbour is Futami at Chichi-jima. Both islands have a general port and Chichi-jima also has a fishing wharf. A feasibility study is under way to construct an airport at Ani-jima.

Telecommunications are established between the main islands of Japan and Chichi-jima, where in 1986 there were 757 local telephones, and Haha-jima, where there were 178 telephones.

The main production in the group centres on vegetables for local consumption and foliage plants, such as Alekayashi as well as fishing for tuna, crayfish, prawns and turtles.

The natural beauty of the islands is expected to encourage their development for tourism. The subtropical climate produces an average temperature of 17° C in winter and 27° C in summer. Annual rainfall is 1200 mm. Typhoons occur in the area.

Wildlife includes the Ogasawara big bat, Ogasawara dragonfly, scorpion, big centipede, wild goats and cattle besides marine animals, coral and tropical fish. Local fruits include banana, orange, pawpaw and mango.

The Ogasawara Islands were designated as a National Park in 1972. There are 37 inns, at Chichi-jima and Haha-jima. The biggest inns include Ogasawara Kanko Hotel and Green Villa.

Palau (Belau)

Palau, a republic associated with the United States in a compact of free association, is comprised of a group of islands in the western Carolines, lying approximately between 6 deg 50 min and 8 deg 15 min N latitude and 133 deg 50 min and 134 deg 45 min E longitude. There are about 340 islands in the group, with a total land area of about 500 sq. km. A reef about 181 km long surrounds the main group of islands and encloses a large lagoon on the western side.

All the larger islands of the group are high. Babeldaop, Arakabesan, Koror and Malakal are volcanic. Babeldaop is the second largest island in Micronesia (after Guam). The remainder are of raised coral limestone, except for Kayangel in the north, which is an atoll comprising four small islets. The distance from Kayangel to Angaur in the south is about 160 km, but Palau's southernmost islands are closer to Indonesia than to Babeldaop. The administrative centre of the republic is Koror, which contains more than half the country's estimated population of 12,250 (1985) giving it the highest population density in Micronesia, apart from Ebeye in the Marshall Islands. Local time in Palau is 10 hours ahead of GMT.

Public holidays include New Year's Day, Youth Day (15 March), Senior Citizens' Day (15 May), Constitution Day (9 July), Labor Day (First Monday in September), United Nations Day (24 October), Thanksgiving (fourth Thursday in November) and Christmas Day.

THE PEOPLE. Palauans are Micronesians in the broad sense and Caroline Islanders in a narrower sense, having considerable ethnic affinity with the people of the Federated States of Micronesia. Within Palau itself, however, there are apparent ethnic and certainly linguistic distinctions; the people of the extreme southern islands — Tobi, etc. — speak a language different to that of the rest of the population. Archaeological evidence has indicated that Palau was populated as far back as 1000 BC. Its people, like other Pacific Islanders, are thought to have originated in South-East Asia.

Estimated population in 1985 was 12,250, of whom 7585 lived on Koror. There are at least 5000 Palauans living outside the country, most of them in Guam. Only eight islands in the group are permanently inhabited and fewer than 160 people live in the southernmost islands. Palauans, like other Micronesian people, have witnessed waves of colonialism by the Spanish, Germans, Japanese and, finally, Americans. Each wave has left its mark but the last is likely to be the most far-reaching. Palauans are sometimes said to be the most Americanised of all Micronesians.

Language. Like the other indigenous languages of Micronesia, those spoken in Palau are part of the vast Malayo–Polynesian language family, and like the others there are dialectical differences between islands. The people of Palau's southern islands, for instance, speak a language more closely related to that of Woleai in Yap State than to the rest of Palau. Literacy is high — said to be about 80 per cent — and because of the American presence English is widely spoken. Many older people can also converse in Japanese.

Religion. Palau's people have been influenced by Christian missionaries since the earliest days of Spanish contact. For all that,

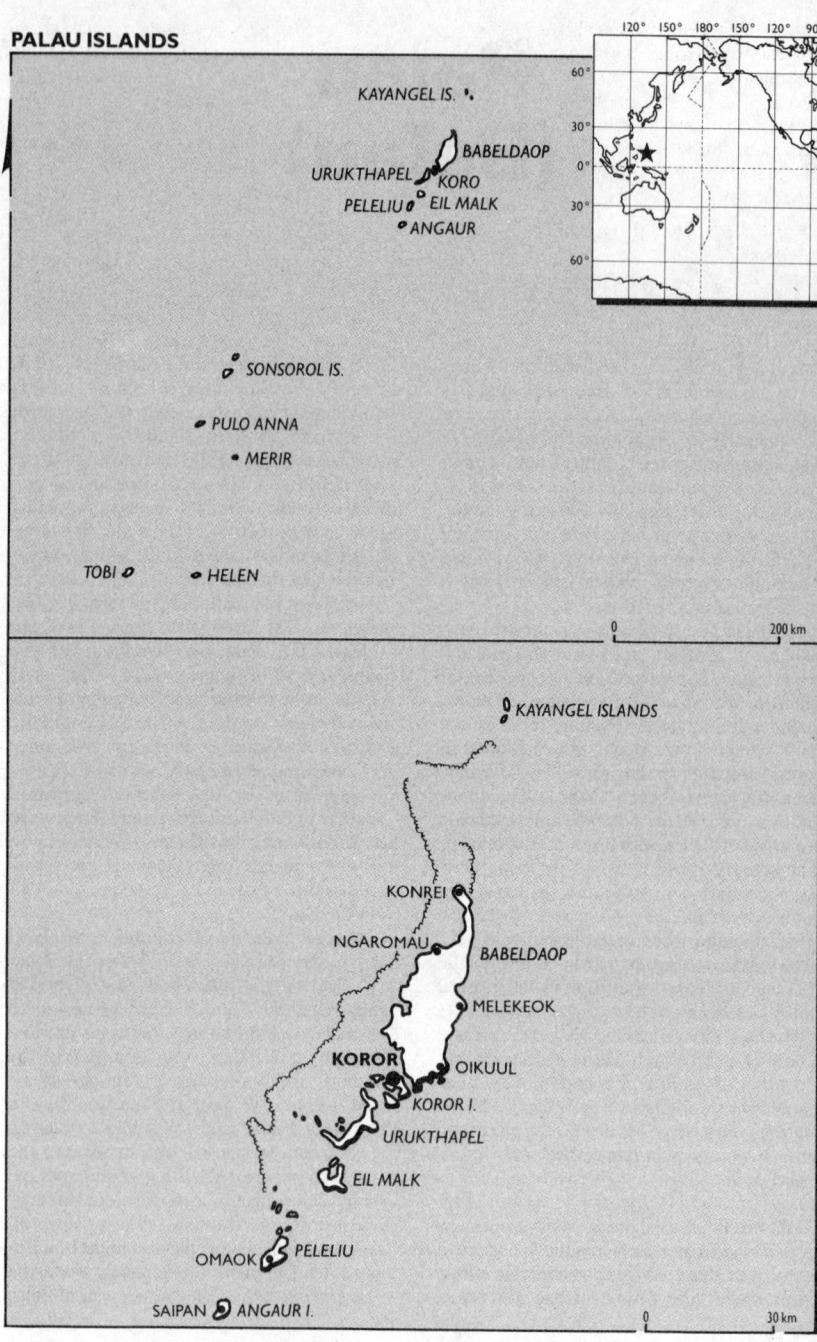

PALAU ISLANDS

KAYANGEL IS.

BABELDAOP

URUKTHAPEL KORO
PELELIU EIL MALK
ANGAUR

120° 150° 180° 150° 120° 90°
60°
30°
0°
30°
60°

SONSOROL IS.

PULO ANNA

MERIR

TOBI HELEN

0   200 km

KAYANGEL ISLANDS

KONREI

NGAROMAU

BABELDAOP

MELEKEOK

KOROR OIKUUL

KOROR I.

URUKTHAPEL

EIL MALK

OMAOK PELELIU

SAIPAN ANGAUR I.

0   30 km

in the last census only about 73 per cent of the population identified themselves as Christians, 40.7 per cent Roman Catholic, 24.7 per cent Protestant and 7.5 per cent 'other'. Almost 25 per cent described their religious beliefs as 'traditional', a much higher percentage than anywhere else in the Pacific Islands.

GOVERNMENT. The republic is formed under a constitution which gives it a President and Vice-President elected for a four-year term by popular vote. The executive branch of the republic is of the ministerial type, with the President choosing his cabinet. The national legislature is bi-cameral; a House of Delegates comprising one delegate from each of the 16 states (formerly municipalities of the Palau district), and a Senate consisting of 14 senators. There is also a council of chiefs. Under the separate state constitutions, each state has a governor, some elected by popular vote, others chosen because of their traditional status. The national legislature is termed the Olbiil Era Kelulau. The highest chief in the land is the Ibedul, whose prestige, if not power, is at least as high as that of the President.

JUSTICE. The Minister of Justice is charged with the basic functions of domestic security and law enforcement. The functional organisation of the Ministry of Justice comprises two bureaus, the Bureau of Legal Affairs and the Bureau of Public Safety. The Bureau of Legal Affairs consists of: (1) legal and civil law divisions; (2) registrar of corporations; and (3) immigration and customs. This bureau is headed by the Attorney-General and serves also as a legal consulting agency to the executive branch of the National Government. The office of the Attorney-General consists of three attorneys, two trial assistants, two secretaries and an investigator. There are also four immigration officers and a secretary within the division of customs and immigration.

The Bureau of Public Safety consists of: (1) the criminal investigation division; (2) the patrol division; (3) the fire protection division; and (4) the corrections and rehabilitation division. The bureau is headed by a director and is responsible for the protection and security of life and property throughout the nation. Its enforcement functions extend to the state levels, since the states are not empowered to create their own police forces.

The Micronesian Occupational College Police Academy is based in Palau. In September 1985 it graduated 36 police officers.

DEFENCE. Defence in Palau, as in the other Micronesian countries which were once part of the US Trust Territory, is the prerogative of the US. The Statement of Agreed Principles for Free Association (Hilo, Hawaii, 1978) declares that 'the United States will have full authority and responsibility for security and defense matters in or relating to Micronesia, including the establishment of necessary military facilities and the exercise of appropriate operating rights ... The authority and responsibility will be assured for 15 years, and thereafter as mutually agreed'. In the case of the Republic of Palau, however, the period of responsibility is 50 years, a difference thought by the US to be justified by the extremely strategic nature of Palau's geographical location.

The Compact of Free Association and its subsidiary agreements allow the US to exercise contingency land-use rights in Palau for military purposes. Specifically, these rights are a small exclusive use area and a larger, adjacent non-exclusive use area for military training on the island of Babeldaop; joint use of two existing airfields; and use of part of Malakal harbour in Koror, Palau's capital.

The US has claimed that it has no present intention to establish military facilities in Palau or in any other way to exercise these contingency rights.

The Government of Palau (together with those of the Marshall Islands and the Federated States of Micronesia) agrees to refrain from actions which the US considers to be incompatible with its responsibility to defend the areas. Similarly, the three 'freely associated' countries agree that their territories will be foreclosed to the military forces or the military purposes of any third nation unless otherwise agreed by the US.

The great stumbling block to US strategic aspirations, however, has been the clause in the Palauan constitution which prohibits the entry into the country of nuclear and other harmful substances (such as might be carried on a US warship). This can only be changed by a majority of at least 75 per cent of Palau's voters, something that numerous US inspired referendums on the subject had — up to mid-1987 — failed to produce. This has led, both inside and outside the country, to a certain amount of confusion on the precise legal status of the Compact. It has also apparently delayed US funding of a number of projects within the country and placed the Government of Palau in an economically precarious position. Independent studies have concluded that the prevailing feeling on Palau is 'pro-American' but 'anti-nuclear', attitudes evidently regarded by the US as mutually exclusive.

EDUCATION. All children between six and 14 years are required by law to be enrolled in school. There are 25 elementary schools and one high school in the public education system. During 1985 enrolment in primary schools totalled 2565. Enrolment in the Palau High School totalled 780. Remedial programmes are applied to those students who do not pass the high school entrance examinations.

Bureau of Education reports state that about 90 per cent of primary school structures are badly deteriorating and several need major renovations. Schools also lack adequate furniture and other basic equipment. Parents and community groups have in recent years donated several thousands of dollars towards the improvement of the high school.

Curriculum in both primary and secondary schools includes Palauan and English language, science, social studies and mathematics. Vocational courses offered at secondary level include construction and auto mechanics.

A Special Education division provides education and related services to handicapped children, serving 95 children in 1985, most in the Koror area. The Special Education programme has five centres and a service personnel of 21. A series of community education workshops in nutrition, health and sanitation reaches about 37 adults annually.

Funding for education has to date come from the US Department of the Interior and from other federal grants provided by the US Office of Education.

LABOUR. The Republic's Labour Division is funded by a Department of Interior grant which amounted to $54,394.19 in financial year 1986. Its functions include determining wages and conditions for both resident and non-resident workers, establishing appropriate occupational categories and minimum standards or qualification procedures, and issuing permits to non-resident workers. In 1985 530 such permits were issued, most involved with small business constructions.

In 1985 the breakdown of workers by nationality was as follows: 1062 residents, 325 Filipinos, 93 Americans, 42 Japanese, 38 Koreans, 15 Chinese, and 17 others including six Swiss and one New Zealander. These are presumably government employees, since labour figures also show another 1910 people in the private sector. Figures on unemployment are unavailable.

Incomes. Approximate total incomes per fortnight are: resident workers, $171,755.84 and non-resident workers, $113,608. On an annual basis resident workers receive a total of $4,122,140, and non-residents $2,726,592.

HEALTH. Health services are co-ordinated by the Bureau of Health Services within the Ministry of Social Services. Palau in 1984 had 148 physicians, 132 nurses of various grades and 43 certified midwives. There are also some traditional midwives, most of whom have had some general hospital training. The general hospital in Koror is supplemented by 13 field dispensaries in the more remote parts of the country.

Hospital outpatient clinics in 1985 treated more cases of diseases of the respiratory system then any other, although ear, skin and eye problems provided significant numbers of outpatients. Complaints of the digestive system and intestinal tract were also frequently reported. Accidents of various types were the major cause of reported death, followed by cancer, heart disease and suicide. In 1984 there were no deaths from homicide, and only one from cirrhosis of the liver.

The crude birth rate in 1984 was 19.7 per 1000 and the crude death rate 4.5 per 1000. The infant mortality rate was 32.7 per 1000 live births.

THE LAND. The total land area of the Republic of Palau is about 500 sq. km. Babeldaop, the largest island in the group, accounts for 397 sq. km of this, though it is second in population size to Koror, the capital. The two are connected by a concrete span bridge. Palau's main airport is on the southern end of Babeldaop.

The facilities, especially industrial ones, of the capital spill over onto the islands of Malakal and Arakabesan, the latter a Japanese military base during WW II.

Babeldaop's size (397 sq. km) and thickly forested, relatively rugged interior make it fairly clear why the US seeks to use almost half the island for jungle warfare training. Its eastern coastlands are comprised mainly of raised coral reefs. Babeldaop contains the second largest population group in the country.

Other islands of Palau are quite small, though not without significance. South of Koror they include Auluptagel and Urukthapel, both of raised coral limestone and reaching maximum elevations of over 200 metres. The latter is the second largest island in the Palau group. Eil Malk (also known as Amototi) is immediately south of Urukthapel and separated from it by the Sar Passage. Its crescent-shaped bay encloses many small islets. About 16 km south of Urukthapel is Peleliu, the southernmost island on Palau's main reef system, about 9.6 km in length, also of limestone formation and once exploited for its phosphate resources.

Situated some 10 km apart from the main reef complex is Angaur, a raised limestone island about 10.4 sq. km in area and rising in the west to heights of 70 metres. After Angaur, several small islands extend south as far as 2 deg 52 min N latitude. They include Sonsorol, Banna, Pulo Anna, Merir, Tobi and Helen Reef, the latter very low and enclosing an atoll about 21 km long.

The islands north of Babeldaop are those of the Kayangel group, four small low-lying islets on an atoll about 7.5 km long. There is only one small village.

Natural features. Babeldaop, Arakabesan, Malakal and the west of Koror are of volcanic formation and contain areas of great fertility and reasonable elevations above sea level. Babeldaob has several mostly small rivers, although one of them — the Ngardorok — is navigable by small boats in its lower reaches. It also boasts a small lake in the interior. The rivers drain into mangrove swamps.

Most of the remaining islands are of coral limestone formation, raised to considerable heights in some places (207 metres in the case of Urukthapel). Despite the often infertile nature of coralline limestone these islands are densely forested. Coastlines are very steep in many places.

The outstanding natural feature of the Palau group is probably the vast reef-enclosed lagoon on the western side of the main islands. The reef is over 100 km from north to south and the lagoon about 20 km at its widest point. Within the reef near Koror are hundreds of small raised coral outcrops known as the Rock Islands.

Soil. Soil on the coral islands is of variable fertility, but where the limestone has broken down over centuries and mixed with natural compost dense vegetation has resulted. On the 'high' or volcanic islands soil fertility is much greater, but the physical character of the largest islands makes crop farming difficult. Under the Japanese administration of the 1920s and 1930s a greater variety of crops were farmed than at present.

Climate. Palau's proximity to the equator means constant temperatures, the monthly mean hovering at 27°C. Two heavy rainfall periods occur: July–August and December–January. Some 750 mm to 800 mm of rain in July alone is not uncommon, but hardly a month passes without at least 100 mm falling. North-east trade winds predominate from November to April, tending easterly during May and June.

Flora and fauna. Vegetation in the volcanic islands of Palau is reasonably varied, from the mangrove swamps of the coast, with trees often from 10 to 16 metres high, to the savannah type grasslands of the near interior which support palms and pandanus, to the densely forested valleys further inland. Common trees are *Calophyllum inophyllum*, *Barringtonia* and *Serianthes grandiflora*, the latter once used for the manufacture of large canoes.

Neither land animals nor land birds are numerous, except for pigs, bats and rats and some pigeons, doves and kingfishers. There is, however, a greater variety of reptiles than in most Pacific Islands outside of Western Melanesia, including lizards, skinks, snakes and crocodiles. The latter occur in the rivers of Babeldaop and reach lengths of five metres. There are eels in many of the mangrove swamps.

Marine fauna are much more prolific and include an estimated 1500 species of tropical fish, together with other marine life such as turtles, abundant crustaceans and a declining number of dugongs.

Land tenure. In traditional Palau land belonged to the *blai*, a group larger than a family but smaller than a clan. Land was administered by the head of the group, whose own rank and prestige depended upon his individual ownership of a small portion of land which could be sold or given away. This action caused the rank attaching to the land to be transferred to the new owner. Attitudes to traditional ownership of land have suffered some erosion in Palau ever since the time of the Japanese regime. Land on Babeldaop sought for military use by the US Government is to be leased from the Palau government and not directly from the traditional owners.

PRIMARY PRODUCTION. Agricultural production in 1985 amounted to a value of $124,581 made up of 260,528 kilos of assorted agricultural produce. A small fishing industry exports fresh fish to Saipan, Guam and Honolulu and there are facilities for fish storage in Malakal. No details of fisheries or other production figures are available. Gross domestic product in 1985 was estimated at $31.58 m.

TOURISM. Palau regards tourism as being of great importance to its economy. The future of the industry is apparently promising and visitor arrivals are increasing.

The country's first luxury hotel, the Palau Pacific Resort, opened for guests in December 1984. Owned by the Tokyu Land Corporation of Japan and operated by the Pacific Islands Development Corporation, this is a $20 million, 100 room structure. Some 90 per cent of resort employees are locals.

There are an estimated 286 people directly employed in the visitor industry, of whom Palauans account for 243. There are 47 Palauans and eight non-Palauans in jobs indirectly related to tourism.

With the opening of the Palau Pacific Resort, 11 hotels or motels are in operation, with a combined total of 254 rooms. Some of these facilities are quite small, comprising only four units.

Visitor numbers in 1984 were 7975. A 52 per cent increase in 1985 raised the total to 12,092.

Tourism is co-ordinated by the Palau Tourism Authority which admits to a lack of funding for promotional and marketing activities. However, a regional non-profit organisation made up of government and industry representatives from the Northern Marianas, Guam, the FSM and Palau and called the Micronesian Regional Tourism Council serves as a co-ordinating agency for promotional activities related to Micronesia.

An October 1984 tax law requires the payment of a 10 per cent hotel room tax, a $3 airport departure tax and other tourist business taxes. In fiscal year 1985 direct revenues of $166,642.87 were obtained from tourism related taxes. Estimates of tourist expenditure of $85 per visitor per day indicate that income generated from tourism amounted to $3.8 million in 1985.

OVERSEAS TRADE. Foodstuffs and consumer goods are imported from the US, Japan, Australia and East Asia. There is no evidence that the country exports anything of significance.

FINANCE. Funding for government operational support and capital improvement programmes in Palau as in other one time members of the Trust Territory is derived from three major sources: (1) an annual grant provided from funding appropriated to the Secretary of the Interior of the US; (2) federal categorical grants provided on a matching or outright grant basis; and (3) tax revenues levied by the Government of Palau.

In fiscal year 1985 Department of Interior funding amounted to $10.5 m, federal grant funds to $2.07 m, CIP funds to $3.7 m and locally raised revenues to $7.5 m. In 1986 the Department of the Interior grant was $10.08 m. Government expenditures in 1985 amounted to $26.828 m.

Banking. Palau residents have access to banking institutions in Guam, Hawaii and mainland US as well as branch banks within the country. There are, in addition, a Bank of Palau which provides various kinds of banking services and a Palau National Development Bank. US currency is legal tender and used for all monetary transactions.

Foreign investment. In 1983 there were 38 foreign investment companies, with aggregated foreign capital of $7 m, permitted to do business in Palau. In 1984 the number increased to 42, with capital of $10 m. In 1985 14 such companies were operating with capital of $10.7 m. Details of requirements and business permits for foreign investors may be obtained from the Palau Foreign Investment Board, PO Box 100, Koror, Palau. Foreign companies are taxed in the same manner as local ones.

Credit Unions. The credit union concept was first attempted in 1959, the year that Palau played host to the first credit union seminar for Micronesia. By 1980 Palau had 20 chartered credit unions with total assets of $1 m. In 1985 there were 23 credit unions with total assets of $2 m. Specialists from the United Nations Development Programme (UNDP) assist in planning and general management.

TRANSPORT. There are 22.5 km of primary roads in the country, with the greater part of the road network being in the area in and around Koror. The islands of Peleliu and Angaur also have extensive road networks for their size. In 1985 there were 1700 registered motor vehicles in Palau.

Airlines. Palau is served by Japan Airlines (Tokyo–Koror), Air Micronesia (Koror–Guam), Air Nauru (from Manila, Hong Kong and Nauru), and Continental/Air Micronesia (from Guam, Yap and Manila). Inter-island services are provided by Emerald Air and Palau Paradise Airways, the latter a Seventh-day Adventist enterprise which does not fly on Saturdays. Palau's main airport is Airai on Babeldaop, 16 km from Koror.

Shipping. Palau's large natural harbours have made it attractive to shipping almost since the time of its discovery by Europeans. Germans, Japanese and Americans alike have sought to exploit these waterways for trade and military purposes — the latter still a formidable possibility.

The central part of the group, generally referred to as Palau or Koror harbour, actually comprises several anchorages, of which Malakal is the most important. Malakal is effectively Koror's industrial and shipping suburb, from which overseas and inter-island vessels depart.

COMMUNICATIONS. Palau has television each day from 3 pm. Programmes are from Honolulu. A Government owned radio station broadcasts news and music. The *Palau Gazette* is a weekly newspaper, also Government-owned. The country's internal telephone service is poor, but international telecommunications are connected with the COMSAT system and all facilities are available.

MAJOR OFFICE HOLDERS

President:
   His Excellency Ngiratkel Etpison
Vice President:
   Honorable Thomas O. Remengesau
Chief Justice:
   Honorable Mamoru Nakamura
President of Senate:
   Honorable Joshua Koshiba
Speaker of House of Delegates:
   Santos Olikong

GOVERNMENT OFFICES

President, PO Box 100, Tel.: 403/828 Divisions: Planning and Statistics, Federal Programs, Public Information, and Postal Service
Vice President and Minister of Justice, PO Box 100, Tel.: 702 Divisions: Legal Affairs, Public Safety, and Prisons
Minister of Administration, PO Box 100, Tel.: 561/545 Divisions: National Treasury, Program and Budget and Public Service System
Minister of National Resources, PO Box 100, Tel.: 701 Divisions: Commerce, Public Works, and Resources and Development
Minister of Social Services, PO Box 100, Tel.: 464 Divisions: Education, Health Services, and Community Service
Minister of State, PO Box 100, Tel.: 509 Divisions: Foreign Affairs, Domestic Affairs, and Palau Maritime Authority
Palau National Congress (Olbiil Era Kelulau), PO Box 8, Tel.: 507/526 (House of Delegates) and 521/522 (Senate)
Judiciary, PO Box 248, Tel.: 461 (Supreme Court) and 482 (Court of Common Pleas)

STATUTORY BODIES

Belau National Museum, PO Box 666, Tel.: 265/841
Foreign Investment Board, PO Box 100, Tel.: 490/828

Micronesian Legal Services Corporation,
PO Box 57, Tel.: 473
Micronesian Mariculture Demonstration Center, PO Box 100, Tel.: 266
Micronesian Occupational College,
PO Box 9, Tel.: 471/357
National Service Board, PO Box 100,
Tel.: 652/806
Palau Community Action, PO Box 3000,
Tel.: 469
Palau Fishing Authority, PO Box 586,
Tel.: 502/352
Palau Housing Authority, PO Box 197,
Tel.: 422
Palau Maritime Authority, PO Box 100,
Tel.: 490
Palau National Development Bank,
PO Box 816, Tel.: 578/9
Palau Visitors Authority, PO Box 100,
Tel.: 489
Private Industry Council, PO Box 100,
Tel.: 513
Public Defender, PO Box 248, Koror,
Palau
Social Security Administration,
PO Box 679, Tel.: 45
US National Weather Service,
PO Box 520, Tel.: 488
US Officer in Charge of Construction,
PO Box 497, Tel.: 410
US Peace Corps Micronesia, PO Box 158,
Tel.: 548

HISTORY. The early history of Palau is inseparable from that of the Caroline Islands generally, while its development from 1947 to the 1980s is closely associated with the rest of the Trust Territory of the Pacific Islands. The account which follows, therefore, makes extensive reference to islands in Micronesia other than Palau.

From the little that is yet known of the prehistory of the Caroline Islands, it appears that some parts of the archipelago have been inhabited for more than 4000 years. The chief archaeological work carried out so far has been in Palau, Yap, Pohnpei and the Polynesian outlier, Nukuoro, but there has been considerably more work done in the last 10 years. Not all the results have been published and some are still at the preliminary stage. Excavations in Palau have revealed extensive agricultural terraces, trade beads, pottery and shell artifacts resembling those of the Marianas. The trade beads indicate links with South-East Asia dating back some 200 years before the Christian era. On Yap two types of pottery have been discovered, the earlier of which is thought to have been in use from at least the second century to 847. On Pohnpei, stone structures with walled and unwalled burial sites have been investigated as well as stone and coral platforms. The chief artifacts found have been of shell. Radiocarbon dates obtained have ranged from AD 1180 to 1430. At Nukuoro, excavations have suggested human occupation since about AD 1300. Early in 1979, an ancient living site was found on Mt Tonachau overlooking Truk Airport on Moen. Tradition has it that the great leaders Soukachaw and Souwooniiras had a meeting-house on the mountain.

The history of European contact with the Carolines has much in common with that of the Marshalls. After some of the islands had been discovered by the first European navigators to cross the Pacific in the 16th century, the archipelago remained largely unvisited until the end of the 18th century. Ulithi and Fais, in the north-western corner of the group, are thought to have been the first islands to be discovered, as their description seems to match that of the Spanish explorer Villalobos in 1543. On his way from Mexico to the Philippines, Villalobos called at two islands which he named Matelotes (Sailors) and Arrecifes (Reefs).

Galleon trade. After the galleon trade between Acapulco and Manila began in the mid-1560s, the captains of the galleons were instructed to cross the Pacific from east to west in the latitude of the Mariana Islands and they thus avoided both the Marshalls and Carolines. However, occasionally a galleon would be driven out of its way and some new island would be discovered. Thus, in 1686, Francisco Lazeano, commanding a westbound galleon, chanced on the high island of Yap, which he called La Carolina, after Charles II, the Spanish king of the time. The name was later applied to the archipelago as a whole. Another island, Faraulep, was discovered by a Manila ship in 1696. It was at about that time that the Spaniards were also made aware of the existence of the Carolines by the arrival of islanders in the Philippines and Guam who had drifted from there in storms. In 1710, the Spaniards made an exploratory voyage to the archipelago which resulted in the discovery of Palau and Sonsorol. Two years later, a second ship went to Palau and Ulithi; and in 1731 yet another Spanish ship went to Ulithi with a party of missionaries headed by Juan Antonio Cantova. Although Cantova had taken a close interest in the welfare of some Carolinians who had drifted to Guam several years earlier, he and his party were murdered within three months, apparently in retaliation for some imagined misdeeds. This setback dissuaded the Spaniards from any further efforts to Christianise the Carolines for the time being.

Wreck of the *Antelope*. In 1783, an event occurred which was to bring the Palau islands to the notice of people in Europe for the first time. This was the wreck of the East India Company ship *Antelope* at Palau, and the subsequent escape of the crew to the Philippines in a much smaller vessel which they built there. The crew took with them the second son of the island's principal chief — a young man of 20 who eventually reached London where he was much feted as Prince Lee Boo of the Pelew Islands. A book compiled by George Keate from a journal kept by the *Antelope*'s commander, Captain Henry Wilson, was one of the most popular books on the Pacific of the late 18th century.

A few British ships sailing to China from New South Wales began passing through the Carolines in the 1790s. At about the same time, an occasional Spanish ship also ventured there en route from the Philippines to Peru. Almost every voyage resulted in the discovery of new islands. Captain James Wilson of the *Duff* discovered Satawal, Lamotrek, Elato, Ifaluk and Woleai in 1797. Juan Ibargoitia discovered Pulusuk, Pulawat and Oran in 1800, and his countryman, Juan Baptiste Monteverde, added Nukuoro to the charts in 1806. Meanwhile, in 1804, Luis de Torres, vice-governor of Guam, paid a visit to several of the Carolines in the American ship *Maria* of Boston.

Trading posts. A surveying voyage by the French exploring vessel *Coquille* under Captain L. I. Duperrey in 1824 greatly increased European knowledge of the Carolines; and the Russian explorer Lutke in the ship *Seniavine* added further details to the charts in 1828. At about this time, American whalers

and traders began frequenting the archipelago; and by the middle of the century the high islands of Palau, Yap, Pohnpei and Kusaie (now Kosrae) were all known. However, evangelists' visits to Truk were uncommon until the 1880s. Protestant missions were established on Pohnpei and Kosrae by American evangelists in 1852; and in the next few years British, American and German companies established trading posts there and elsewhere and became rivals in the copra trade. One of the leading figures was David O'Keefe, an American, who built up a trading empire on Yap.

In 1869, Germany acquired 1215 ha on Yap for use as a way station between Samoa and Cochin to serve as a centre for her Caroline-Marshalls-Marianas trade. Later, Germany's increased presence in the area was seen by Spain as a threat to her interests in the Philippines. In 1873, Spain demanded that all merchant ships bound for the Carolines should stop in the Philippines to receive permission to trade there and to pay customs and licensing fees for the privilege. The Germans refused to comply, and Britain later took Germany's side. Both nations declared that they did not recognise Spanish sovereignty over the Carolines because the islands had never been occupied by Spain.

Spanish sovereignty. In 1885, Spain sent a warship to take possession of Yap. But the Germans anticipated it and ran up the flag first. When the Germans also occupied Truk, Pohnpei, Kosrae and some of the lesser islands, Spain protested, but later agreed that Pope Leo XIII should arbitrate in the matter. On 22 October 1885, the Pope declared in favour of Spain; but Germany was given liberty to trade and fish in the area, and to establish settlements and coaling stations. Spain thus gained sovereignty over the archipelago with all the attendant expenses and responsibilities, while Germany was given the privileges without responsibilities.

In 1886, Spain sent two warships to the Carolines to raise the flag and bring the islands under the control of the Philippines government. Pohnpei was made the administrative centre and an agency of the administration was opened at Yap. At the same time, Capuchin priests established missions and schools in Yap, Pohnpei and Palau. The arrival of the Spaniards at Yap produced little change; but difficulties arose on Pohnpei. A Protestant missionary, E. T. Doane, was arrested and sent to Manila in June 1887; native Protestant teachers were removed; and the islanders generally were forced to work like convicts. In an uprising against the Spaniards, the governor and some of his men were killed and the priests fled. Three Spanish warships later called at Pohnpei and arrested a few islanders, but on being tried in Manila they were acquitted. Another party of Spaniards was killed on Pohnpei in 1890. When news of this reached Madrid, a punitive expedition was sent to the island. But the transport vessel carrying the Spanish troops ran aground on a reef and the Pohnpeians killed 1500 men.

During the Spanish–American war in 1898, Germany made a secret provisional agreement with Spain whereby it secured a lien on Kosrae, Pohnpei and Yap in any future disposal of Spain's insular possessions. Later that year, Spain agreed to give Germany the right to purchase all the Caroline and Mariana Islands, other than Guam, which the Americans had captured. A German–Spanish treaty of 12 February 1899 transferred the Carolines and Marianas to Germany for 25 million pesetas.

German administration. With the establishment of German administration in the Carolines, German Catholic missionaries arrived to replace the Spanish Capuchins, and German Protestants moved into the islands where the American Protestants had been working. The Germans governed the eastern Carolines from Pohnpei and the western Carolines including Palau, from Yap. The Germans introduced strict sanitary measures to control epidemics of diseases the islanders had no immunity to. By 1900 the pre-contact population of Palau of perhaps 40,000 had dropped to 4000. Relations between the islanders and the German administration were mainly peaceful. However, in 1910, a German overseer was killed after striking an islander with a whip, and when the governor hastened out to restore order he was shot dead. The ringleaders in this incident were later executed and 200 islanders were deported to Angaur to work in the phosphate deposits.

Japanese administration. The Japanese, who had had commercial interests in the Carolines, from 1893 onwards, were quick to occupy the islands in World War I. Having declared war on Germany on 23 August 1914, the Japanese captured Yap on 7 October, and less than three weeks later all islands in the Carolines were under their control. The islands were mandated to Japan by the League of Nations in 1921 and administered from 1922 as an integral part of the Japanese empire. Administrative headquarters were at Koror, a small island off Babelthuap, and there were district offices at Yap, Truk and Pohnpei. Following the arrival of the Japanese civilian administrators, Spanish Jesuit missionaries replaced the German Catholics and pastors from the Congregational Church of Japan replaced the German Protestants.

As in the other islands of its Micronesian territory, Japanese policy was to develop the resources of the Carolines to the full. Japanese immigration was encouraged. In Palau, the biggest centre of Japanese interest, there were more than 25,000 Japanese civilians in 1935, four times as many as the local population of the group. The Japanese introduced modern conveniences such as electricity, sewerage and good roads, and improved the standard of living. Harbour facilities were developed in Palau; production was stepped up from the Angaur phosphate deposits; the copra industry was expanded; and the growing of tapioca, rice and oil palms was introduced to some islands. After Japan withdrew from the League of Nations in 1935, Palau and Truk were developed for military purposes and other islands were fortified. The islands became a closed military area. When Japan entered World War II, Palau was used as a base to attack the Philippines and the Netherlands East Indies, and Truk was a key to the Japanese thrust into the South Pacific.

World War II. American fleet aircraft attacked Truk early in 1944 and destroyed 23 ships and 201 planes at a cost of 17 American planes. However, Ulithi Atoll was the only island in the Carolines to be occupied by the Americans before the Japanese surrendered in September 1945. After the Caroline Islands became part of the United States Trust Territory of the Pacific Islands in 1947, the archipelago was divided into four districts — Palau, Yap, Truk and Pohnpei — with headquarters for each district on the islands named. Kosrae, which was a sub-district of Pohnpei, became a separate district in 1977. The five districts developed into the separate entities of today through the constitutional developments described below.

Trust Territory. The Caroline Islands, like the rest of Micronesia, remained under US military occupation for two years after the war. In 1947 the United Nations, responding to considerable pressure from the US, agreed to create the only Trusteeship based on strategic factors. Thus was born the United Nations Trust Territory of the Pacific Islands, to be administered by the US. The legal status of the Territory was based on the Trusteeship Agreement between the US and the UN Security Council which came into force on 18 July 1947. In the view of the Trusteeship's many critics, Micronesia became little more than a colony of the United States for a period of over 30 years.

The US President delegated authority for the civil administration of the territory to the Secretary of the Navy on an interim basis. Subsequently, Admiral Louis E. Denfeld was commissioned as the first US High Commissioner of the Trust Territory (with headquarters in Hawaii) and Rear-Admiral Carleton H. Wright was appointed Deputy High Commissioner (with headquarters in Guam). On 1 July 1951, administration of the territory passed from the Navy to the US Department of the Interior and Mr Elbert D. Thomas became the first civilian high commissioner. But in 1953 all islands in the Marianas, except Rota, were returned to the control of the Navy Department for a special security purpose. This situation prevailed until mid-1962 when control reverted to the Department of the Interior and the northern Marianas became the Mariana Islands District of the Trust Territory. At the same time headquarters for the entire territory were transferred from Guam to Saipan. Beside the Mariana Islands, five other districts were established — Palau, Yap, Truk and Pohnpei (Carolines) and the Marshall Islands.

Congress of Micronesia. The Micronesians were given a voice in their own government in January 1965 when the first elections were held for a bicameral Congress of Micronesia, consisting of a House of Representatives and a Senate. The Congress held its first meeting in the following July. In 1967, the Congress established a Future Political Status Commission, comprising six of its members (later increased to 10), to investigate ways in which

the territory might develop politically. The commission visited Washington and Puerto Rico in 1968 and American and Western Samoa, Fiji and Papua New Guinea in 1969, besides studying the political systems in the Cook Islands and Okinawa. When it eventually reported to the Congress of Micronesia, the commission recommended that the territory should either become a self-governing state in free association with the US, or it should have complete independence. The US, for its part, offered the territory commonwealth status, like that of Puerto Rico. Talks between US representatives and the commission in 1970 and 1971 resulted in impasse. But in 1972 there was a breakthough when the US agreed to guarantee the four basic requirements of the Micronesians. These were: the right of self-determination; the right to decide their own constitution and laws; the right to control their own land; and the right, unilaterally, to terminate any compact with the US. However, the 1972 negotiations did not cover the future status of the Marianas which, it was agreed, should be decided through direct dialogue between Marianas leaders and the US.

Northern Marianas opts out. From the beginning of the negotiations the people of the Northern Mariana Islands had made known their longstanding desire to permanently integrate with the US and become US citizens. In 1972, after it became obvious that the different future political status aspirations of the people of the Northern Marianas and the peoples of the remaining areas of the Trust Territory were irreconcilable, the elected representatives of the Northern Marianas and the US began separate negotiations for territorial status.

Those negotiations were completed in 1975 and resulted in the 'Covenant to Establish a Commonwealth of the Northern Mariana Islands in Political Union with the United States'. The Covenant was approved by the people of the Northern Marianas in a United Nations-observed plebiscite on 17 June 1975 by a margin of 79 per cent and was subsequently approved by the United States Congress. A separate constitution and government were proclaimed on 9 January 1978.

Separate states emerge. The negotiations for free association continued throughout the 1970s under three American administrations and were based on principles put forward by the Micronesian negotiators. In 1978, as the result of action by the remaining districts of the Trust Territory on a draft constitution for a unified Micronesia, three separate political groupings emerged: Palau, the Marshall Islands, and the Federated States of Micronesia (FSM).

The US had agreed to respect the outcome of the constitutional referendum and therefore negotiated with each of them for a free association relationship, the provisions of which would be set forth in a single Compact of Free Association.

Meanwhile the Congress of Micronesia, which had been elected in July 1965, fell apart when it became obvious that there would be no unified Micronesia.

The Compact and several of its related agreements were initialled, but not signed, by the Government of the United States and by the Governments of Palau, the Marshall Islands and the Federated States of Micronesia in October and November 1980.

By this time, each of the three groups had approved a locally enacted constitution. Constitutional governments were installed in the Marshall Islands and the Federated States of Micronesia on 1 and 10 May 1979 respectively and in Palau on 1 January 1981.

The thirteen years of negotiations were concluded with the signature of the Compact and its related documents by the US and the Marshall Islands on 30 May 1982, Palau on 26 August 1982 and the Federated States of Micronesia on 1 October 1982.

A plebiscite held in the Federated States the following year gave the Compact overwhelming approval, although the Trusteeship was not terminated in the Federated States until 1986. In Palau it dragged on still longer as a result of both US and Palauan intransigence over constitutional and nuclear issues.

What the Compact provides. The Compact of Free Association has no precedent in US constitutional practice and few precedents in international law. Essentially, it recognises three sovereign states as having emerged from the Trust Territory. They each have full self-government; their capacity in the field of foreign affairs is recognised; and they will vest in the US full responsibility for their

defence for minimum periods of 15 years (in the cases of the Marshall Islands and the FSM) and 50 years in the case of Palau.

The period of free association is indefinite but may be terminated at any time by mutual agreement or by the unilateral action of any of the governments. The economic and defence provisions are subject to renegotiation and renewal at the end of their specified minimum periods.

The US will provide agreed amounts of grant economic assistance and certain US Government services for the same minimum periods. Forty per cent of the grant funding will be earmarked for economic development with projected uses including new infrastructure programmes, major maintenance activities and revenue generating projects.

The assistance funds will be spent in accordance with jointly developed programmes which will establish goals for the various sectors of the economies in an effort to lessen the freely associated states' dependence on outside resources, and to help achieve economic self-reliance.

Funding. The Compact's funding scheme provides for the diminution of US grant-assistance in stages after the fifth and tenth years, although an integrated system of partial adjustment for inflation which is tied to the performance of the US economy would help to maintain the value of the funding over the years.

The estimated cost to the US over the initial 15-year period is approximately $2.2 billion before adjustment for inflation. Funding for Palau during the 16th through 50th years will be provided entirely out of an initial investment made during the first year.

The Compact and its subsidiary agreements commit the US to continue to provide, at no cost to the Governments of Palau, the Marshall Islands and the Federated States of Micronesia, airline and airport safety services, economic regulation of commercial air service, weather prediction, and assistance in the event of natural disasters. The United States Postal Service will continue to provide international postal service, although each of the three governments assumes responsibility for its domestic postal operations.

Defence provisions. With respect to defence and security matters, the Compact and its subsidiary agreements allow the US to continue to operate the Kwajalein Missile Range in the Marshall Islands for a period of up to 30 years and would allow the US to exercise contingency land-use rights in Palau for military purposes.

Specifically, these rights in Palau are a small exclusive-use area and a larger, adjacent non-exclusive use area for military training on the main Palauan island of Babeldaop; joint use of two existing airfields; and use of a portion of Malakal harbour in Koror, the capital of Palau. These are contingency rights; the US has said it has no present intention to establish military facilities in Palau or in any other way to exercise these contingency rights. There is no reservation of military use rights in any of the four groups of the FSM.

In addition, the US undertakes in the Compact to defend the freely associated states as the US and its citizens are defended, for the minimum periods mentioned — that is, 15 years in the cases of the Marshall Islands and the FSM, and 50 years in the case of Palau. For the same minimum periods the Governments of Palau, the Marshall Islands and the Federated States of Micronesia agree to refrain from actions which the US determines to be incompatible with its responsibility to defend the areas.

In order 'to assist one another in the areas of mutual security and the maintenance of peace and stability in the region', the US and the Governments of Palau, the Marshall Islands and the Federated States of Micronesia have agreed that the territory of the freely associated states will be foreclosed to the military forces or the military purposes of any third nation unless otherwise agreed by the US. This arrangement prevails with respect to each jurisdiction until otherwise mutually agreed.

Other agreements subsidiary to the Compact of Free Association deal with such matters as telecommunications, extradition, the transfer of Federal property, the status of such US forces as may be stationed in the freely associated states (including personnel at Kwajalein and military civic action teams), and other technical matters.

Nuclear claims. As a result of special negotiations the Compact requires the Government of the US and the Government of the Marshall Islands to set forth in a separate agreement provisions for the comprehensive settlement of all claims arising out of the nuclear testing programme which the US conducted at Bikini and Enewetak atolls in the northern Marshalls from 1946 to 1958, as well as to provide for the medical treatment, care and supplementary feeding of persons affected by the testing programme. The separate agreement on this topic provides about $150 million in payments and programmes and for the settlement of all related claims.

Compact approval process. The Compact provides that it must be approved by the Governments of Palau, the Marshall Islands and the Federated States of Micronesia in accordance with their constitutional processes (which includes approval by their legislatures) and by their voters in plebiscites.

The plebiscites constitute acts of self-determination and the expression of free choice as referred to in the Trusteeship Agreement. The US, with the concurrence of the Governments of Palau, the Marshall Islands and the Federated States of Micronesia, presented to a special session of the UN Trusteeship Council on 16 December 1982, a formal request for the dispatch of observer missions representing the international community to all three plebiscites after suitable dates for them were decided.

Events in Palau since the Compact was signed have been characterised by uncertainty arising from the apparent incompatibility of Palau's 'nuclear-free' constitution (the world's first) with the strategic aims of the US. That section of the constitution which bans the use, testing, storage or disposal of nuclear weapons and the transit of nuclear-powered ships can only be removed by a vote of at least three-quarters of the country's voting population.

Although Palauan voters had approved the Compact in several plebiscites up to December 1986, the Supreme Court of Palau had ruled in three separate decisions that the Compact, in the form proposed by the US, was inconsistent with the Palauan constitution, and that the Compact should be approved by a majority of at least 75 per cent of the electorate.

The stalemate in the implementation of the Compact, during which Palau's economy disintegrated almost entirely and an increasing amount of violence took place between supporters and opponents of the Compact, was thought to have been resolved in August 1987, when a constitutional amendment provided for the approval of the Compact by a simple majority. On 21 August 1987 yet another plebiscite recorded a 73 per cent approval. The result was challenged again in the Supreme Court, but the suits brought against it were subsequently dismissed in circumstances which were dubious and which provoked further outbreaks of violence.

In the meantime an apparent reconciliation between supporters of the Compact, led by Palau's President Lazarus Salii, and former opponents led by Chief Yutaka Gibbons, had been effected, to the dismay of numbers of Palauans claiming that coercive tactics had been used to bring about the amendment of the constitution and the result of the latest plebiscite.

Palau's problems during the early 1980s were compounded by the assassination in 1985 of its first President, Haruo Remiliik, although it was later claimed that the murder was not politically motivated. The economy of the country, based almost entirely on grants from the US, and the expectations of funds flowing from implementation of the Compact, became increasingly precarious as the Government defaulted on a $35 million loan for a power station and President Salii threatened to retrench 90 per cent of the public service. In August 1988 President Salii was found dead of an apparently self-inflicted gunshot wound. In late 1988 acceptance of the Compact and the amount of US money it provides seemed to be becoming a desperate necessity, nuclear-free clauses notwithstanding.

FURTHER INFORMATION. Books specifically on Palau are not numerous and their circulation has not been extensive. These titles are probably the most useful: H. G. Barnett, *Being a Palauan*, (New York, 1960). D. R. Smith, *Palauan Social Structure*, (New Brunswick, 1983). F. X. Hezel, SJ, *The First Taint of Civilization: A History of the Caroline and Marshall Islands in Pre-Colonial Days, 1521–1885*, (Honolulu, 1983). D. J. Peacock, *Lee Boo of Palau: A Prince in London*, (Honolulu, 1987).

FOR THE TOURIST. Palau is placing increasing emphasis on tourism to generate income for the country and employment for its people, and facilities for visitors are improving rapidly. Visitors need not spend all their time on Koror, as air and boat services to outer islands are reasonably frequent. Accommodation on them still remains a problem, however. The Rock Islands, a group of raised limestone formations between Koror and Peleliu, are probably the republic's most outstanding scenic feature, but diving, fishing and water activities generally are among the best in the Pacific.

Entry formalities. Palau has its own immigration and customs procedures. Citizens of the US need only show proof of citizenship, but nationals of other countries must possess a valid passport and proof of onward travel. A tourist visa valid for 30 days is obtainable on entry.

Airport tax. An airport departure tax of $3 is levied. Tipping in Palau is an 'optional' 10 per cent.

Sightseeing. Taxis are widely available at most times of the day and fares are reasonable. Rental cars may be obtained from a number of companies. Driving is, of course, on the right side of the road. Diving excursions to the Rock Islands and other locations may be arranged through several operators or at hotel tour desks. Palau's National Museum is worth a visit, both for its exhibits and the handicrafts sold there. These include the famous Palau 'storyboards', an apparently indigenous art form that displays much affinity with that of Papua New Guinea but which was actually introduced and promoted in the 1930s by Japanese anthropologist Hisakatsu Hijikata. Among the most skilful practitioners of the craft are several of the inmates of Koror's jail, who will carve to order. Palau's annual fair is held in May. For travellers seeking islands as close to unspoiled as one can find nowadays in the Pacific, a 'field trip' boat leaves Malakal Harbour every three months or so for the distant southern islands. Closer to Koror, the islands of Peleliu and Angaur contain many relics left over from World War II and earlier periods of Palau's history.

ACCOMMODATION

Palau Pacific Resort: PO Box 308, Koror, Palau, Tel.: 600.

Hotel Nikko Palau: PO Box 310, Koror,

Palau, Tel.: 878.
New Koror Hotel: PO Box 64, Koror, Palau, Tel.: 231.
Palau Hotel: PO Box 457, Koror, Palau,

Tel.: 935.
West Motel: PO Box 280, Koror, Palau, Tel.: 218.

Papua New Guinea

Papua New Guinea is an independent state and a member of the Commonwealth. It consists of the eastern half of the island of New Guinea and many offshore islands including New Britain, New Ireland and Bougainville.

The nation extends from the equator to 12 deg S latitude and from 141 to 160 deg E longitude. Port Moresby, the national capital, is 3900 km north of Sydney. Local time is 10 hours ahead of GMT.

The estimated population in July 1987 was 3,483,360.

The national flag is divided diagonally with a red upper right triangle on which is superimposed a yellow bird of paradise. The lower left is black with five white stars representing the Southern Cross. The national song is *Oh arise, all you sons*.

Currency is the kina, which is divided into 100 toea. There have been suggestions that Papua New Guinea should become a republic while remaining a member of the Commonwealth, to keep in line with the other Melanesian countries.

THE PEOPLE. The inhabitants include a large diversity of types although some ethnologists make a distinction between the Papuan-type people, who are believed to have been the first arrivals and who now tend to inhabit the interiors of the mainland and big islands; and the Melanesians who are the people of the coasts and offshore islands.

But there had been much mixing of people long before Europeans made their first contacts, and the indigenous people of PNG can be considered to be related to those other Melanesians who occupy the greater part of the Western Pacific.

There are a few groups of people in the Central Province and on the Upper Ramu, around Aiome in Madang, who have sometimes been described as pygmies or Negritos but this is probably incorrect. Although of very short stature they are similar in other respects to other local people and it could be that they are not the remnants of a separate migration at all but a development from people similar to neighbouring stock.

The people of the North-Western Islands of the Manus Province (which are closest to the Caroline Islands) are basically Micronesian although they now have been subjected to incursions of Melanesian blood. The people of Takau (Mortlock) and the Nukumanu (Tasman) Islands, are predominantly Polynesian but mixed now with New Britain, Manus and Caroline Islands blood. The people on the Nukumanu Islands are practically pure Polynesian and there is occasional immigration from Polynesian Ontong Java, a Solomon Islands outlier.

However, the above people are very tiny minorities in the predominantly Melanesian scene, which also contains such diverse types as the black-skinned people of Buka and the tallish, light-skinned people of the Trobriand Islands and the coast near Port Moresby.

Europeans who work in PNG usually have short-term contracts and stay only a few years. Current Public Service contracts are for a maximum of 3 years. The Asian population in PNG established itself because the German New Guinea Company which administered New Guinea under charter for the first 15 years after German annexation in 1884 found New Guinea labour initially

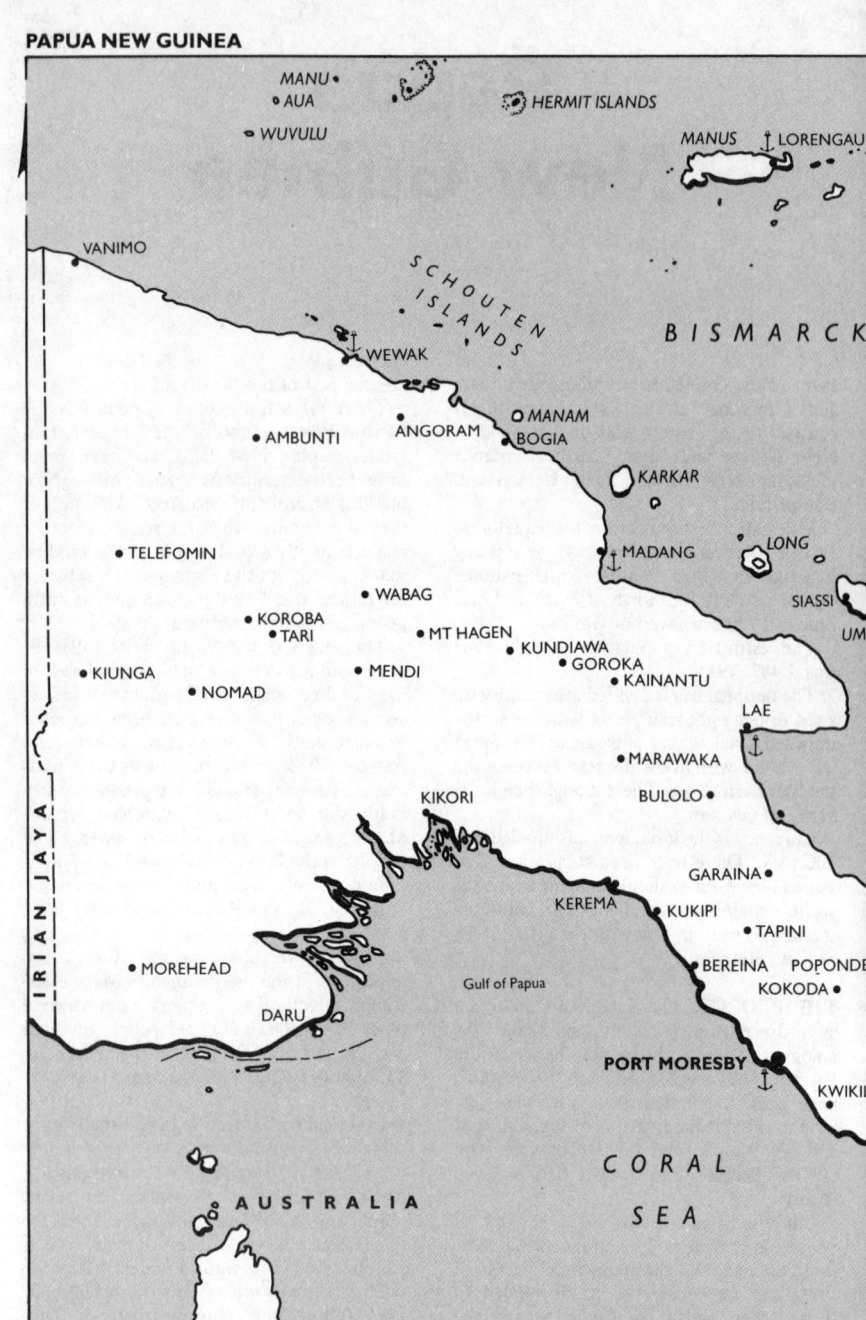

unsatisfactory and introduced Chinese, Malays and Ambonese. By the time Germany took over administration from the company the Asian population was between 300 and 400. Thenceforth labour was brought mostly from Hong Kong. At the time Australia began civil administration in 1921 there were 1424 Chinese and 163 Ambonese and Malays. The Chinese ultimately became the small shopkeepers and artisans of Papua New Guinea.

In 1987 the population estimate was 3,483,360–3,452,360 citizens and 31,000 'others'.

The number of non-citizens is decreasing annually but the figure depends on the success of the educational system in producing the necessary quantities of skilled citizens who can replace non-citizens in employment.

The population is scattered widely throughout the country, but the greatest concentrations are in the Highlands provinces. Population of the Central Province, including the National Capital District of Port Moresby, was estimated at 265,600 in 1985, of these 136,210 being in Port Moresby. The other provinces had the following population estimates in 1985: Western (headquarters at Daru) 89,010; Gulf (Kerema) 69,990; Milne Bay (Alotau) 145,940; Northern (Popondetta) 87,630; Southern Highlands (Mendi) 254,090; Enga (Wabag) 175,330; Western Highlands (Mount Hagen) 292,990; Chimbu (Kundiawa) 184,440; Eastern Highland (Goroka) 299,580; Morobe (Lae) 346,810; Madang (Madang) 238,390; East Sepik (Wewak) 247,910; West Sepik (Vanimo) 125,250; Manus (Lorengau) 28,950; New Ireland (Kavieng) 74,830; East New Britain (Rabaul) 149,350; West New Britain (Kimbe) 103,840; North Solomons (Arawa) 148,790.

Citizenship. At the time of independence, 16 September 1975, anyone who had two Papua New Guinean grandparents and did not hold foreign citizenship automatically became a citizen of Papua New Guinea. Others who had lived for over eight years in the country could apply for naturalisation but had to do it within two months after independence day. If the eight years falls after independence day, application must be

made within two months of the date it falls due. One of the qualifications for naturalisation is that the applicant must be able to speak and understand Pidgin or Motu. The citizens of Papua New Guinea are known as Papua New Guineans.

Languages. There is a great multiplicity of languages, in all there are probably 700–800. Various attempts to cope with the language problem have been tried, including the use of Police Motu as a lingua franca in Papua before World War II, and the use of Pidgin English in New Guinea from the German era onwards. Pidgin has tended to supplant Motu in recent years.

Religion. The people had their own religions strongly influenced by a belief in magic, spells and sorcery. Although many now claim to be Christian, superstition is still prevalent. Religious beliefs that embrace magic are an integral part of all Papua New Guinea native cultures. These beliefs and practices differ in detail from area to area but they are based largely on a form of ancestor and spirit worship. Most of the emphasis is on pleasing and propitiating spirits — some of relatives who are still remembered, some from the remote past.

Lifestyle. Changes in the social structure have come as a result of contact with outside influences but the social set-up in native life is still as varied as the people themselves. In some communities there is a form of matrilineal inheritance of land and other property; others follow a patrilineal system.

The community unit is the village (which is generally from 50 to 300 people but may be either larger or smaller) although in some communities people live in smaller hamlets or even individual homesteads.

Dwellings are often made of local materials and therefore vary in type, size and material according to environment, although this, like everything else, is being modified by European contact.

There was not, as in Fiji and Polynesia, any system of hereditary leadership. Men in their own lifetime rose to be leaders because they had more energy than their fellow men and generally they acquired status by giving feasts and through a complex sequence of gift exchanges.

The life was completely communal, the economy subsistence, and allegiance never extended beyond the village or the collection of hamlets that made up the community unit. This exclusiveness is breaking down slowly but is an obstacle to the concept of a national identity of the country as a whole.

In the cities, such as Port Morseby and Lae, the lifestyle is quickly becoming Westernised, with the people living in Western style housing, driving their own cars and shopping at supermarkets. There is increasing migration from rural areas to the cities. In 1987 a UNDP/World Bank project was approved to concentrate on low-cost housing for low-income families. A pilot scheme will prepare 3000 housing plots on 400 ha in four priority towns. The World Banks allocation was $US8 million and UNDP $US462,100. The Government contributed a further K160,000.

Recreations. Papua New Guinea is very sports minded, and most sports are played by all races. Football is a national enthusiasm. There are some excellent playing fields, sports grounds and golf courses, probably the finest golf course being the one at Lae. Bowling clubs flourish, as do clubs for yachting and power-boating.

GOVERNMENT. Papua New Guinea is an independent state within the Commonwealth with Queen Elizabeth II as Head of State. She is represented in PNG by a Governor-General who is appointed by the Queen acting with the National Executive Council. In practice, the person to be Governor-General, whose term of office is six years, is nominated by parliament after a secret ballot.

The first Governor-General was Sir John Guise. He resigned to return to politics on 28 February 1977 and was replaced by Sir Tore Lokololo. Sir Tore was succeeded on 1 March 1983 by Sir Kingsford Dibela, who presently holds office.

National parliament. During the transition period before and after independence, the National Parliament elected in 1972 remained in office until June–July 1977. At the 1977 election, the National Parliament was enlarged to 109 members — 20 representing Provincial seats and 89 representing Open electorates. The voting system was also changed to 'first-past-the-post' in place of the previous modified preferential system.

Seven parties contested the 1977 election, the major ones being the Pangu Pati, the People's Progress Party and the United Party.

Mr Michael Somare was re-elected Prime Minister when the new National Parliament met. As leader of the Pangu Pati, he formed a coalition government mainly with the support of the People's Progress Party.

Parliament elected Mr Kingsford Dibela as Speaker and Sir Tei Abal, leader of the United Party, became Leader of the Opposition. He was replaced in May 1978 by Mr Iambakey Okuk.

After three unsuccessful attempts the Okuk opposition finally won a 'no-confidence' motion which unseated the Somare government in March 1980. Mr Okuk deferred to the popularity of Sir Julius Chan (Peoples Progress Party) who became Prime Minister in a five-party coalition. The coalition made Mr Okuk Deputy Prime Minister and Parliament elected Mr Sevese Morea as Speaker. Mr Somare became Leader of the Opposition.

Mr Somare was returned as Prime Minister in the general elections of July 1982. The Pangu Pati won 52 seats and formed a coalition with the United Party. Mr Paias Wingti was appointed Deputy Prime Minister and Mr Timothy Bonga was elected Speaker.

The Pangu Pati was splintered in 1985 when Paias Wingti defected to the opposition to lead a 'no-confidence' motion. He formed a new party, the Peoples' Democratic Movement (PDP), while other former Pangu Pati supporters founded the League for National Advancement (LNA). In November 1985 Somare was ousted by a vote of 'no-confidence' and Paias Wingti became Prime Minister with Sir Julius Chan as his deputy.

In January 1987 Sir Iambakey Okuk, Leader of the Opposition, who had replaced Ted Diro in August 1983, died. His position of Leader was taken by Somare for the campaign up to the general election in July 1987. Paias Wingti remained Prime Minister following the election heading a seven party alliance. Early in 1988, the opposition, led by Somare, introduced a motion of 'no confidence' in the Government. In an attempt to defeat this motion, Wingti asked Ted Diro, leader of the Papuan bloc, to return to the Cabinet. However, this move divided his own alliance and in a further attempt to get enough support to change the 'no confidence' vote constitutionally, Wingti asked Somare to form a 'grand coalition'. To the amazement of observers, the bitter rivals publicly shook hands, but within days, Somare had resigned from both the 'grand coalition' and from politics.

The Prime Minister in late 1988 was Rabbie Namaliu.

The National Executive Council consists of all the Ministers with the Prime Minister acting as chairman. This council is responsible for the executive government of PNG.

Local government. There is a developing system of local government. The system, introduced in 1950, provided for indigenous local government bodies with authority to keep law and order; financing, organising or engaging in any business enterprise for the good of the community; carrying out works or providing any public or social service for the good of the community.

Later legislation provided for multi-racial councils with wider scope in the fields of health, education, commercial enterprises and in the collection of local taxes. The first multi-racial council was elected in 1965 and in the next four years most councils became multi-racial.

City and town councils came into operation in 1971 and in 1980 there were city councils for Port Moresby and Lae and urban councils at Madang, Rabaul and Arawa. However, these may be changed from their present form and replaced by 'community governments' established under the aegis of provincial governments.

Council members are elected from wards; there are Lord Mayors in Port Moresby and Lae; the others usually have presidents.

These urban councils raise revenue by various means including head taxes, rates on alienated land, entertainment taxes and grants from central government.

Provincial government. There are 19 fully-elected provincial governments, formed to decentralise administration. There is one national Public Service. The provincial governments receive revenue grants, and may apply provincial taxes. All local and provincial government is the responsibility of the Department of Provincial Affairs.

Public Service. The Papua New Guinea Public Service is under the control of the Department of the Public Services Commission. The department also recruits overseas officers needed to meet the shortage of some specialised manpower.

In 1986, total public service strength was 50,014, which included 1927 officers from overseas. The figure does not include the Defence Force.

Ombudsman commission. This is provided for in the constitution. A Chief Ombudsman and two Ombudsmen were appointed in December 1975.

Justice. The source of the laws of Papua New Guinea is the PNG constitution. A unified Criminal Code came into force on 1 November 1975. The code has been brought up to date, doing away with the death penalty except for treason, introducing among other items, crimes involving aircraft (e.g. hijacking) and increasing fines in line with present-day economic realities.

The Chief Justice is appointed by the Head of State acting with the National Executive Council. The other judges are appointed by the Judicial and Legal Services Commission.

The courts. It is likely that, as time goes on, there will be considerable reorganisation in the instrumentalities concerned with legal matters, which prior to independence were set up in traditional Australian fashion. But in 1987 the courts that exercised jurisdiction in Papua New Guinea were: (a) National Court; (b) District Courts; (c) Local Courts; (d) Village Courts; (e) Children's Courts; and (f) Warden's Courts. There is also a Court of Appeal called the Supreme Court.

Village Court decisions can be reviewed by Local or District Courts. Appeals from Local and District Courts go to the National Court and then to the Supreme Court, which is the last court of appeal.

Only the National Court has unlimited jurisdiction. It is presided over by the Chief Justice, or other judges, who also comprise the full bench of the Supreme Court for appeals.

PNG does not, as yet, have a jury system but it is planned that assessors will sit with judges to give an opinion on fact and traditional PNG customs.

There is a scheme to train local magistrates

for work in lower courts. They graduate as Assistant Magistrates and after a year, during which they sit with the court and perform other functions ancillary to the administration of justice, become full magistrates.

Legal aid. This is available to people irrespective of race who do not have the money to assist themselves.

Legal practitioners are both barristers and solicitors in Papua New Guinea, instead of practising as one or the other as in some Australian States and in Britain.

Policy. Law and order are maintained by the Royal Papua New Guinea Constabulary, divided into two branches: Regular Constabulary and Field Constabulary, of the Department of Police.

The Regular Constabulary carries out general and specialised police duties within the country. They Field Constabulary consists of delegated officers of the Department of the Prime Minister with ex-officio police powers in areas where there are no commissioned officers of the Regular Constabulary.

Local police officers are graduates of the Police College, at Bomana, outside Port Moresby. The initial year of the 2-year course is conducted at the Joint Services College, Lae. For police recruited as other ranks there is no set period of service but policemen may retire on pension after 20 years.

At the head of the Constabulary is the Commissioner of Police with headquarters at Port Moresby. The Constabulary is responsible direct to the Minister for Police.

In 1987 there were 4814 members of the PNG Police. There is a distribution of 0.9 operational policemen per 1000 population.

Between 1987 and 1992 Australia will spend K13 million in tied aid to upgrade the Royal Papua New Guinea Constabulary. Specialised training will be given in Australia and capital works projects are to include a new central police station in Lae and other stations in Mount Hagen, Madang and on the Okuk Highway.

Gaols. Prisons in PNG are called corrective institutions. The main institution for long-term prisoners is at Bomana, near Port Moresby. There are subsidiary institutions near Lae, Wewak, Rabaul and Mount Hagen, plus smaller institutions in other provincial centres.

Liquor laws. Control of liquor licensing is through the Liquor Licensing Commission, which has power to grant the following 12 classes of licence: publicans; tavern; limited hotel licence; dealers; storekeepers; booth; bottle shop; restaurant; packet; club; occasional; or canteen.

Hours for hotels, taverns and clubs are: 11 am to 2 pm and 4 pm to 8 pm, Monday to Thursday; on Friday the sale of liquor in hotels, taverns and clubs is permitted only between the hours of 12−1 pm and 6.30−9.30 pm; 10 am to 2 pm and 4 pm to 8 pm Saturday; and 11 am to 1 pm and 5 pm to 7 pm on Sundays. In 1988 new regulations banned sale of liquor in retail outlets on Fridays, Saturdays and Sundays in an attempt to curb drunkenness and related problems which have been widespread in recent years. Foreign owned companies holding retail licences also had their licences revoked in 1988 in a move designed to support localisation.

Licensed stores must close at 6 pm or one hour before hotels, whichever is earlier. Bottle shops close two hours before hotels.

Customers must be off licensed premises 15 minutes after closing time; club members and guests may stay after trading hours although they cannot drink liquor.

There are restrictions on what type of liquor may be sold in public bars. Liquor cannot be consumed in a bottle shop, store, in a moving vehicle, or in a street, road or any public place. All advertising of spirits and wines is banned except in licensed premises or the vehicles owned by the licensee.

Gambling. No poker machines or gambling devices are permitted. However, playing cards is allowed. There are licensed bookmakers operating with a turnover in 1987 of K40 million. The tax rate of two per cent will yield an estimated K800,000 to government revenue.

DEFENCE. Papua New Guinea assumed responsibility for defence from the Australian Government on 6 March 1975. At the end of 1986 the PNG Defence Force numbered 3592. The fully integrated units consist of a land element with three battalions (two of the Pacific Islands Regiment at Wewak and one Pacific Islands Regiment at Port Moresby; and an Engineer Battalion). The Maritime element is equipped with five Attack class patrol boats based at Lombrum, Manus Island, and with heavy landing craft based at Port Moresby. In 1987 the Defence Force decided to sell its six DC-3 aircraft which would enable it to concentrate its personnel on flying the three Nomad and three Arava aircraft.

The PNG Defence Force priorities as set down in a 1983 White Paper are first national development and internal security; second defence against external threats; and third, upholding PNG's international obligations. Priority actions include fisheries and maritime surveillance, border patrols and external security, civil emergency coordination, civic action and maintenance of internal security.

Civic actions include the use of servicemen for road and bridge building, airstrip construction, mapping, medical and health projects, fisheries surveillance, help in civil disasters and in search-and-rescue operations. Australia also provides practical assistance of this nature, in national aerial mapping, engineering works in the Southern Highlands Province, and advice to the Police. Australia continues to provide technical expertise and training under the Defence Co-operation Program.

PNG pilots and loadmasters begin training at Port Moresby. Other officers are trained at the Joint Services college at Lae while specialists, such as legal officers, medical orderlies and dentists receive their training in Australia.

Under the PNG Constitution, the Defence Force is an arm of the government and is controlled, through its headquarters at Murray Barracks, Port Moresby, as part of the Ministry for Defence.

It is under the control of the Minister for Defence through the Secretary for Defence at Waigani and the Commander of the Defence Force at Murray Barracks.

EDUCATION. Education is controlled through the Department of Education, with the missions and churches playing an important part, especially at primary level. The total amount spent by Government on education in 1986 was estimated at K166.9 million. In February 1976, a Five-Year Education Plan was adopted, providing for six years of primary and four to six years of secondary education. Targets have been only partly met.

The education system includes government schools and schools nominated by other education agencies which meet prescribed conditions. There is a National Education Board, consisting of the Director of Education and members representing the government, churches and missions, local government, teachers, commercial interests and tertiary institutions. A Papua New Guinea Teaching Service includes teachers in government schools and those teachers in agency schools which have been brought within the education system; and there is a Teaching Service Commission which determines service conditions for teachers. In 1986 the commission employed 13,237 teachers, 264 being non-citizens.

All government schools are full members of the education system. Other education agencies, virtually all of them church or mission bodies, may nominate their schools as member schools, associate member schools or affiliated schools, if they meet the prescribed conditions. Only the Seventh-day Adventists have elected to stay outside the system while co-operating and remaining consistent with it in some respects. The majority of non-government schools have been accepted as full members of the education system. The Government pays the salaries of qualified teachers in agency schools which have been accepted into the system; these schools also receive classroom materials; there is a subsidy for approved building programmes for high schools, technical colleges and teachers' colleges, maintenance and boarding grants for secondary school boarders, and grants for some other agency education personnel in secondary schools.

Expatriate education. There is a marked division between general schooling in PNG and schooling for expatriates. The system is geared to concentrate resources on schools for Papua New Guineans, but the government has agreed to continue to provide a metropolitan type education for children of expatriates who need to be equipped for their eventual departure, provided they pay an economic fee. These schools are administered by the International Education Agency of Papua New Guinea Ltd.

In 1987 the total enrolment in this expatriate education system was 7574. There were 18 preschools, 29 primary schools and seven high schools. PNG children can attend these schools if the parents can afford the relatively high fees charged: K784 to K1568 for preschool annually, K1660 to K1880 for primary schools and K2930 to K3030 for high schools. In 1987, 41 per cent of enrolments were indigenous students.

Primary education. Primary schools on a PNG curriculum are called community schools. The government's aim is to provide primary, or community, education for all children and it plans that 100 per cent of all seven-year-olds will be enrolled by 2000. In 1986 there were 2358 community schools. Total community school enrolment in 1986 was 382,112 with a staff of 11,475. This is 76 per cent of all school age children.

Secondary education. There are national high schools at Sogeri, Keravat and Aiyura, and at Passam. Students are selected from all provinces.

In 1986 there were 113 high schools in PNG, with a total student enrolment of 46,317 and a staff of 1762. The Government aims to correct the imbalance and put more high schools in disadvantaged provinces.

School fees. Originally tuition for all pupils and students was free. However, in recent years charges have crept into the system, including charges for equipment. Charges at high schools are also made and vary from area to area. The maximum community or primary school fee in 1986 was K200. Conclusions of an education finance study will be used to set up a formula for future fees.

Technical education. Technical education and training is provided for in technical colleges and schools, commercial training centres and vocational training centres. Continuous training courses are offered to students who have successfully completed Form II at a high school.

People who enter apprenticeships straight from high school at Form II level, attend technical courses on a block release system, i.e. they spend up to 10 full weeks at a technical college during the year and supplement this with training on the job, night classes or correspondence courses.

Commercial and secretarial training is available at Port Moresby, Lae and Rabaul and vocational training centres have been developed in many areas to provide full-time basic training for students who have completed primary school.

There are ten technical colleges including the secretarial colleges, with a total enrolment in 1986 of 1687 students, and 243 teachers.

Teacher training. The training of local community school teachers is undertaken in nine teachers' colleges. Two are run by the government and seven by church organisations. Secondary school teachers are trained locally at the Goroka Secondary Teachers' College which is part of the University of Papua New Guinea.

In 1986 there was a total of 1887 student places in all teachers' colleges.

In the past, teachers at all levels have also been recruited in Australia, but by 1973 teachers' colleges in PNG were training sufficient primary school teachers to staff existing primary schools.

Grants, scholarships. Although the Government provides secondary education for children of all races through the multi-racial high schools, subsidies are being paid to expatriate parents who wish their children to go to secondary schools in Australia.

A bursary system also operates, subject to a means test. Expatriate public servants are entitled to an education allowance in lieu of a subsidy.

Tertiary education. The University of Papua New Guinea was established in mid-1965 and enrolled its first students in February 1966.

The faculties are medicine, arts, science, agriculture, education and law. The degrees of MB, BA, BSc, LL.B, BAgr, BEc, BMedSc, BS and BEd are offered. In the post-graduate field the degrees offered are Diploma of Teaching English as a Second Language, Child Health, Obstetrics and Gynaecology, and Education in Developing Countries; BA(Hons), BEc(Hons), MA (Qualifying), MEcQ, MLQ, MScQ, LL.MQ, MA, MEc, MEd, MSc, LL.M, PhD.

There are a number of sub-graduate courses, including Mass Communication and Land Administration.

University entrance is a minimum of five credit passes in the School Certificate, after which students do a preliminary year at the university before starting degree courses. The first students graduated at the end of 1970.

In 1986 there were 2604 students enrolled at UPNG. Approximately 450 students were enrolled at the Goroka campus of UPNG. Most were Papua New Guineans with others from neighbouring Pacific countries. All full-time students live on campus. The university has its own buildings, in landscaped gardens at Waigani, Port Moresby.

What began as the Institute of Higher Technical Education, at Lae, later renamed the Institute of Technology and, since September 1973, the University of Technology, gave its first courses in 1967 with an enrolment of 31 students. It has an elaborate establishment close to Lae. It includes halls of residence for students, all of whom live on campus.

Students, who numbered 585 in degree courses and 281 in diploma courses in 1986, are offered degree courses in engineering, business administration, commerce, architecture, building economics, surveying, forestry and chemical technology. Diploma courses are offered in cartography, communications, fisheries technology and valuation; and certificate courses in surveying and drafting.

Students are usually sponsored by a company organisation or attend on government scholarships.

Other institutions of higher learning in PNG are the Vudal Agricultural College at Keravat, East New Britain, where there is a three-year course leading to a Diploma of Agriculture; (one year of the course is spent at a field station in the Western Highlands), and the Bulolo Forestry College at Bulolo, in Morobe.

Vocational education. There are various vocational, adult education and correspondence courses in operation. Vocational centres offer a wide range of short term courses open to village groups. There are adult education officers at most provincial headquarters.

LABOUR. Regulations fix minimum wage rates in various centres, and there are a number of awards in industry also setting minimum rates. Since 1 September 1977, wages have been subject to half-yearly adjustments based on movements of the Consumer Price Index. Urban rates are not binding on employers of domestic servants. In 1986 the average weekly wage was K47 per week, at the same time the wages for rural primary workers was K18.

Social security. A National Provident Fund was started in mid-1981 covering most private sector firms. Firms with more than 25 workers are required to match employee contributions at a rate of 7 per cent to 5 per cent.

The plantation sector engaged in the growing and processing of cocoa, copra, oil palm, rubber and tea are exempt from the NPF. Total membership exceeds 70,000. In 1984 the amount standing in credit to the members of the fund grew to K36.4 million. Total net assets, including land and buildings, were K38.5 million.

HEALTH. The Department of Health provides hospitals, dispensaries and public health facilities for all Papua New Guinea. In addition, dental and ancillary services are provided and the department undertakes the training of nursing, some medical and other public health personnel.

The various Christian church bodies operating in Papua New Guinea all undertake health services, providing hospitals, nursing staff and medical officers. The PHD maintains close contact with the church missions in order to co-ordinate activities.

Hospitals. Hospital charges are based on ability to pay. Most people are treated free or for a nominal sum. Higher fees are charged in the intermediate wards found in major hospitals.

There are four base hospitals which provide specialist services for the four geographical regions of Papua New Guinea. They are at Port Moresby, Lae, Rabaul and Goroka. In addition there are district hospitals in those provinces which do not have a base hospital. The big copper project in Bougainville is served by a hospital at Arawa which replaced the old Kieta district hospital in 1972. The Lutheran Mission hospital at Mambisanda serves as district hospital for Enga Province.

Health Facilities 1985

Health centres 190
Health sub-centres 269
Urban clinics 23
Aid posts 2231
Hospitals 19

Specialist hospitals include the Laloki Psychiatric Hospital, near Port Moresby. The four base hospitals have either psychiatric wards or clinics. A new Port Moresby General Hospital costing K22 million is to be built on the site of the present hospital. It is being financed by the Japanese Government and will be in operation by mid-1989.

The Health Department is responsible for training staff other than medical officers. The trainees include health inspectors, health extension officers, medical technologists, radiologists, nurses, and nursing aides, the latter being trained in most of the larger hospitals.

The PNG Institute of Medical Research, at Goroka, under the control of the Health Minister, undertakes research into PNG's health problems. The Papuan Medical College was established in 1959 and became the Faculty of Medicine at the University of Papua New Guinea in 1971. This institution awards the degree of MB. Minimum education requirement for entrance is matriculation.

Although all members of the community may avail themselves of government medical services, there are also medical practitioners and dentists in private practice throughout Papua New Guinea.

Health Staff Numbers 1985

PNG hospital staff 2459
Gvt. health staff outside hospitals 4428
Church health services staff 1353

The budget allocation for health services in 1987 was K33,567,900. It is anticipated that this will increase annually until 1991 when the allocation will be K38,154,600.

Diseases. Malaria control is one of the prime aims of the Department of Health. This disease is now regarded as entirely preventable, but it is still the major health problem among the indigenous population, mostly because of its secondary debilitating effects, and accounts for approximately 10 per cent of the national health budget.

It is calculated that populations would double in a few years if malaria could be eradicated. To this end, special malaria-control areas have been established where mass treatment and preventive measures have been carried out including complete spraying, usually with DDT, of the inside of houses. The complete eradication of this disease will require the co-operation of the people, and this has not always been forthcoming. The malaria control programme reaches about 58 per cent of the people of PNG.

Pneumonia, usually a secondary result of some other disease, is the greatest cause of death in PNG hospitals and also the greatest cause of hospitalisation.

Tropical ulcers are prevalent.

Child mortality rate is high and to combat this Maternity and Child Health Clinics (including mobile clinics) have been set up and special efforts are made to educate people in these matters.

Venereal disease is on the increase, but cases of TB and leprosy under treatment are decreasing.

Dental health. In 1984, 30.6 per cent of all children enrolled at school received dental examinations. A third of this number received actual treatment. In 1984, 227 people worked in the field of dental health.

THE LAND. Papua New Guinea lies wholly within the southern tropics. Its territorial boundaries stretch from the equator, in the north, to 12 deg S latitude in the south; from 141 deg E longitude in the west to 160 deg E longitude in the east. However the boundaries are irregular — for example, they exclude the Torres Strait Islands which go right up to the coast of western Papua New Guinea, but include the bulge of the Fly River into Irian Jaya in the west, and the islands of Bougainville, Buka and other smaller groups, which geographically are part of the Solomon Islands.

The total land area is 461,690.33 sq. km. The land area includes the eastern half of the New Guinea mainland (Indonesia's province of Irian Jaya occupying the western half); the Bismarck Archipelago, the main islands of which are Manus, New Ireland and New Britain; the northernmost Solomon Islands of Bougainville and Buka; and the groups of islands of the easternmost part of the mainland (Trobriands, D'Entrecasteaux, etc.).

All the above groupings include their innumerable offshore islands which range in size from small islets to islands as large as Lavongai (New Hanover, which is 1544 sq. km in area).

Natural features. The central core of the main island of New Guinea is a massive cordillera 2500 km long that stretches from one end of the big island to the other. It is one of the world's great mountain systems and forms a drainage divide between rivers that, so far as Papua New Guinea is concerned, flow north into the sea off the north coast and those that flow south into the Gulf of Papua.

The mountains do not, however, consist of a single chain but rather a complex of ranges interspersed by wide valleys.

The principal units of the main mountain system in PNG, from west to east, are the Star Mountains (which extend across the Irian Jaya border), the Hindenburg, Muller, Kubor, Schrader and Bismarck Ranges each of which has peaks of over 3280 m, and the Owen Stanley Range with peaks of over 4265 m. Some of the highest peaks in PNG are: Mt Wilhelm (4697 m), Mt Hagen (3778 m); Mt Michael (3750 m); Mt Bangeta (4425 m); Mt Giluwe (4361 m); Mt Victoria (4037 m); and Mt Albert Edward (3990 m).

The islands of New Britain, New Ireland and Bougainville are also characterised by the typical central chain of mountains.

In New Britain, they reach a height of 2295 m, in Bougainville of over 2630 m, but in New Ireland the highest range is the Rossel Mountains in the south, the highest peak of which is 2108 m.

West of the head of the Gulf of Papua, there are large areas of foothills between the central mountain chain and the swampy coastline. The foothill country has some ancient volcanic peaks which, though worn, still attain considerable heights — the Bosavi Mountains over 2600 m, Mt Murray, 2432 m and Mt Sisa, 2902 m.

Volcanoes. A line of volcanoes stretches along the northern coast of the mainland, crosses Vitiaz Strait, goes along the north coast of New Britain into the Gazelle Peninsula where Rabaul is situated, and then on through Bougainville. On the mainland south of this line there is little volcanic activity although there are many signs that there have been eruptions in the past. There was a serious eruption in what was regarded as an extinct volcano, at Mt Lamington, near Popondetta, in 1951.

In 1984 volcanic activity around Rabaul threatened to become a major eruption but after several months the activity subsided. The area is closely monitored.

Most of the islands of the D'Entrecasteaux and Louisiade Archipelago are of volcanic origin and represent the peaks of a submerged mountain range. There are hot springs and other signs of volcanic activity at Fergusson Island.

A distinctive feature of the mainland is that within the interior there is a vast series of wide, well-watered valleys, stretching from the headwaters of the Markham River to the Irian Jaya border, and on both sides of the mountain divide. These valleys, with an average elevation of 1640 m, are clear of jungle, have a cool climate and support large native populations.

As this is a region of high rainfall there are a number of very large rivers on the mainland, notably the Fly, Purari, Kikori, Markham, Ramu and Sepik. The Sepik, Ramu and Markham drain the NE side of the mainland, and the others the southern side. There are hundreds of rivers of lesser size. There are no comparable rivers in the big islands of New Britain, New Ireland or Bougainville. The drainage of these is taken care of by innumerable, small, rapid rivers flowing down from the mountains.

The north-eastern coastal areas of the mainland are believed to be rising while those of the south-east are continually sinking. For this reason coral reefs are not continuous along the coasts. Raised reefs do extend from the Sepik River mouth to Cape Cretin but from Salamaua, on the Morobe coast, to Goodenough Bay in Milne Bay Province, the coast is of drowned littoral type and there are no reefs.

Coral reefs are, however, an outstanding feature of the islands off the eastern tip of the mainland, and the coasts of New Britain, New Ireland and east and south coasts of Bougainville have fringing or barrier reefs.

Because of the character of the whole region, there are very few deep landlocked harbours — exceptions being Port Moresby, Rabaul and Madang.

Climate. Apart from the Port Moresby area, which is in the 'rain shadow' of the Owen Stanley Range and consequently has a dry climate, there is a regular and generally high annual rainfall in Papua New Guinea. The average is about 2000 mm per year but there are wide variations — from 1195 mm per annum in Port Moresby to 5080 mm at Kikori on the Gulf of Papua.

There are two seasons — the south-east, or trade winds season, which lasts from May to October; and the monsoon, or north-west season which lasts from December through March. In the intervening periods the winds are variable, or there can be periods of unpleasant doldrums.

Although rain tends to be heavier in the monsoon season, rain can occur at any time in most places. Port Moresby is the only place in the country where the weather can be reasonably predicted into wet and dry seasons.

Because of the configuration of the mountains behind Huon Gulf, Lae city has its wettest season during the period of south-east trades.

Temperatures vary little through the year, the average coastal readings being between 21.1°C min. and 32.2°C max.

Temperature varies with altitude and the highland areas can be cool to miserably cold.

The country is not subject to hurricanes but is subject to earthquakes, which are much more frequent north of the Sepik River and in New Britain.

Flora and fauna. Dense jungles are a striking characteristic of a large part of Papua New Guinea. In most areas from sea level to 980 m the rainforests grow in profusion.

Various types of indigenous sugarcane have been found for example, and some of them have enriched the world's sugar plantations.

The fauna of Papua New Guinea is closely related to that of Australia. Of the 100 species of mammals found, marsupials predominate and only a native cat is carnivorous.

There are wallabies, several species of the phalanger family (sometimes called gliding possums in Australia), the cuscus and the red bandicoot. There are spiny anteaters, bats, rats and mice and the southern coast has a native dog, now very rare, apparently related to the Australian dingo.

There are 70 species of snakes some of which are not venomous (such as the python and some water snakes) but the majority are. Lizards of all sizes including the giant monitor are present; tortoises and crocodiles are found in the rivers and sea and there are 1400 species of fish which contribute largely to the diet of coastal people.

There are over 650 species of birds that inhabit the mainland alone, including the glorious Birds of Paradise and the cassowary which are indigenous.

The most harmful of the insects are the malarial-carrying mosquito and the scrub typhus (or Japanese River fever) carrying tick or mite. The most beautiful of the insects are the huge and often vividly coloured moths and butterflies.

Land tenure: The total area of Papua New Guinea is 46,169,033 hectares. According to the latest figures available, 43,966,077 ha of this is unalienated land; 216,628 ha freehold land owned by non-indigenes; 3747 ha are held under tenure conversion; 1,982,581 ha are government land (407,167 ha of which are under leases; 38,070 ha are native reserve; and 1,537,344 ha designated 'other', including land held for public purposes, for leasing, etc.).

Of the 407,167 ha of land let out by the government under lease, 256,900 ha are used for agriculture, 814 ha for dairying, 81,433 ha for pastoral, 16,287 ha for residential and business purposes, 40,717 ha for other leases, 10,179 ha for missions and 837 ha for town subdivisions.

The ownership of land and the use of available land are subjects of much importance in Papua New Guinea and widespread changes in tenure are planned.

All unalienated land is deemed to be native-owned until proved otherwise. This protects the interests of the indigenous people until the ownership position is clarified by the Lands Titles Commission.

Customary land is land possessed or owned by an indigenous person or community by virtue of rights of a proprietary or possessory kind which arise from and are regulated by native custom.

Freehold land is of two kinds: (a) that which originated during the German administration, prior to 1914, in New Guinea and prior to 1906 in Papua; and (b) that which has, in recent years, been tenure converted by individual indigenes from customary ownership.

After Papua became an Australian territory and when New Guinea became a mandated territory after World War I, the principle was accepted that no further freehold land was to be granted to non-indigenes. Freehold land that existed at that time continued to be freely bought, sold or leased. However, since World War II ownership of some of the permanently alienated land has been challenged by national groups. In other cases freehold land held by Europeans has been purchased back by government and restored to local groups or cut up for small holdings.

The 1973 Land Commission Report made many recommendations including:

All freehold and leasehold titles should be statutorily converted into government-guaranteed leaseholds. No compensation should be paid to freeholders and the government should be protected from compensation claims; however, freeholders who have their titles changed to leaseholds should have a five year 'holiday' before rents are charged and in the case where the property is mortgaged they should be able to appeal to the Minister for special consideration.

Freeholds now held by Papua New Guineans should be converted into group titles, conditional freeholds used for unregistered customary land, or into government leases.

Government leases should be for 60 years with right of renewal, for PNG citizens; but for 40 years, with no automatic right of renewal, for non-citizens. (Non-citizens who involve substantial citizen ownership in their leases to have leases of 60 years duration.)

Present government leases which have less than 40 years to run (for 60 years for citizens) should continue to expiry; where the leases are for more than 40 years (or 60 years for citizens) they should be reduced to the appropriate term.

A government lease should be the only way a non-citizen can hold land, although a citizen should be able to grant or take a small area of land on direct lease, subject to certain conditions.

In areas where most of the rural land has been alienated and people are seriously short of land and where the return of undeveloped alienated land does not sufficiently relieve the shortage of land for cash cropping as well as subsistence, the Government should take steps to recover developed land nearby, by compulsory process if necessary, and return it to the land-short people. Compensation paid to the holders of the former developed land should be limited to the unexhausted improvements on the land.

In line with these recommendations, the government has passed legislation to help transfer expatriate-owned plantations to Papua New Guinean groups. A special fund to help in the purchase of these plantations has been set up and is administered by the Department of Natural Resources.

So far more than 70 European plantations have been bought for redistribution under the Plantation Redistribution Scheme. However, redistribution has been slower than acquisition and further outright purchases were suspended for a time. The government is also arranging to have part equity in some of the larger company-owned plantations.

The Government will continue working on the proposals for legislation to provide for the registration of national land, the conversion of freehold to leaseholds, and for legislation to enable the registration of customary land.

Government land is land that has come into the hands of government through purchase or as successor to the German administration through mandatory powers after World War I, or through acquisition for public purposes.

Only the Government, through the Department of Lands, has power to purchase land from the indigenes and this it does only after all the present and future needs of the owners and the best economic use of the land are taken into consideration.

Apart from the comparatively small areas of land acquired for public purposes such as roads, airports, defence, and public safety, the land purchased from indigenous owners by the Government is for the purpose of leasing to individuals or organisations of all races in line with the planned economic development of the country.

Native land systems. There is considerable variation in indigenous inheritance systems of land or use of land. Rights of ownership are normally acquired through birth but acquisition by purchase, once unknown is now an established custom in some places. Land use must also be distinguished from land ownership. Some communities still practise a system of shifting cultivation and they may, for a time, use the land of one or two individuals for gardens and then move on to land owned by some other individual or group.

This type of customary land tenure is not considered satisfactory for economic progress as it lacks flexibility.

Many of the proposals of the 1973 report of the Commission of Inquiry are being put into effect in stages.

The commission stated that four main aims were to return land to land-short New Guineans; to provide a system of land holding that would promote good race relations; to treat land as a national resource and emphasise the need to use it properly; and to discourage speculation in land.

A considerable part of the report dealt with customary land. The commission recommended that there should only be cautious alteration of some features of the customary system, which accounts for about 97 per cent of all PNG land; and that individualism in native land matters should not be encouraged. However, it believed that registration of some customary land is required and that provision should be made for various kinds of title, but only where the people understand and want it.

The commission suggested four kinds of titles for customary land: (a) group titles; (b) customary rights — under which clan leaders declare a named member of the clan has sole rights to any given portion of land for commercial purposes for a given time; (c) subsidiary rights, which individuals or groups may hold in land over which another group has the main rights (such as right to gather fruit, or basic materials for building); and (d) conditional freeholds which are suitable for groups, such as a family, to hold land in common.

One of the more important recommendations of the Land Commission Report was that all land laws in force in PNG be repealed and replaced by new legislation enacted by the National Parliament.

PRIMARY PRODUCTION. Until 1972 Papua New Guinea's most important industries were agricultural. However, Bougainville Copper Ltd began producing in 1972 and by 1973–74 was responsible for approximately 64 per cent of the total value of PNG exports. This had fallen to 51 per cent in the year ended December 1982 due to weaker mineral prices on world markets.

In 1981 work began at the Ok Tedi mining site in the Western province. Copper yield here is 0.7 per cent higher than Panguna. Ok Tedi now accounts for more than a third of the total mineral production and this is expected to increase significantly by 1987. Mineral exports continue to account for more than 50 per cent of PNG's total exports. In 1985 mineral sector export receipts increased by 49 per cent to K487 million.

Primary industries are still, however, the largest market for labour. Since 1972 palm oil has also entered the export field and exports from this industry were valued at K61.5 million for 1985.

Apart from copper and concentrates Papua New Guinea's main export industries now are coconut planting (copra and coconut oil, animal foodstuffs); cocoa; coffee; palm oil and palm kernels; rubber; timber milling; plywood and veneer manufacture; tea planting; gold mining, pyrethrum (producing an extract used in insecticide), and also tuna, prawns and crayfish.

Primary industries that produce for local consumption are vegetable growing, cattle raising, dairying and sawmilling.

The total value of agricultural exports in 1985 was K330.2 million. See Table 4 for export earning in all major areas.

A project estimated at K8 million has been implemented by the Department of Primary Industry with the aim of assisting more than 4000 smallholders to restock with high-yielding hybrid copra and cocoa plantings. This will ultimately increase production of copra by 1000 tonnes annually and cocoa by 5000 tonnes.

Copra: Papua New Guinea is the biggest producer of copra and coconut oil in the

South Pacific. The most important coconut plantation areas are the Gazelle Peninsula in New Britain, New Ireland, NE coast of Bougainville, Madang coast, parts of West New Britain and Manus, and the Milne Bay and Central provinces. Most of the country's export copra is dried in modern hot-air mechanical driers that produce a better quality product than the old village sun-dried or smoke-dried copra.

Part of PNG's coconut products is now exported in the form of coconut oil.

About 50 per cent of all copra is produced from village groves and plantations; the rest from large scale plantations owned by individuals or companies, many of which have been resumed by government for redistribution to Papua New Guineans under a scheme which is designed to place the whole coconut industry in indigenous hands.

Prices for copra (and hence coconut oil and other coconut products) fluctuate widely.

The Copra Stabilisation Fund has ensured that producers get around K200 per tonne. In 1984 prices reached a peak at K633 per tonne export price, however since then they have dropped steadily and in June 1986 it was K104 per tonne. Copra's continuing difficulties are principally attributed to a general glut on the world market of edible oils.

All copra is marketed by the PNG Copra Marketing Board, which is a corporate body with power of succession and a common seal. The board consists of a chairman and members representing producers, and the Department of Primary Industry.

Copra is purchased by the board under a system of grade and ownership markings. A modified pool principle is employed, tentative purchase prices being declared and then, after the end of the trading period, final prices are determined in the light of actual trading results, and final payments made.

Palm oil: In 1967 the Papua New Guinea Government and a British firm, Harrisons and Crossfield, set up New Britain Oil Palm Development Ltd, on a 50/50 ownership basis. The idea was for a balance between a company plantation and adjacent local smallholders, who would have their crop processed in a factory built by the company; the Government would be responsible for roads, and an overseas wharf at Kimbe.

Smallholders from all over Papua New Guinea were assisted to establish themselves by loans from the PNG Development Bank, and this has grown into a large development.

Palm oil prices have continued to remain depressed since mid-1985 when they reached K599 per tonne. In June 1986 the price was K244 per tonne. In 1985 growers produced 123,800 tonnes but the depressed prices have resulted in a fall in production, reflecting partly the sensitivity of the smallholder to price falls. The Stabilisation Fund pays K19.12 per tonne per month to growers.

Cocoa was planted as an alternative to copra before the Pacific War but plantations were all wiped out during the Japanese occupation 1942–45. After the war high prices for cocoa gave the industry a boost and there was vigorous planting either interplanted between coconuts, or on its own, especially in New Britain.

By the mid-1960s there were about 64,800 ha under cocoa in Papua New Guinea and the economic development plan called for an increase to 91,125 ha and a production of 35,560 tonnes. However this target was not achieved. Exports for 1985 were 30,900 tonnes, somewhat under the 34,100 tonnes exported in 1984. About 50 per cent of the production comes from plantings by Papua New Guineans.

Most provinces produce some cocoa but the most important production areas are in East New Britain, North Solomons, New Ireland and Madang.

PNG cocoa is of good quality and finds markets in West Germany, Netherlands, US, UK etc., as well as Australia. Value of exports for 1985 was K62.5 million.

A Cocoa Industry Board was established in Rabaul in 1974. In 1976–77 it began to compile a register of fermentaries and it established a stabilisation fund in 1977.

Coffee. A little Arabica coffee was grown near Wau before World War II and some Robusta in New Britain and Bougainville, but the big increase in coffee production came after the New Guinea Highlands were opened for settlement in the early 1950s. It is now one of the country's largest agricultural export earners and there are in excess of 200,000 smallholder growers who produce 70 per cent of the total crop.

In the year ended December 1985 about

40,600 tonnes of coffee beans valued at K117.5 million were exported.

Although coffee was originally grown by European planters, most production is now in the hands of Papua New Guineans.

The most important Arabica coffee growing areas in Papua New Guinea are Eastern and Western Highlands and Chimbu provinces and the high elevation areas of Morobe province. However, Robusta coffee is grown in Central, Milne Bay and Northern provinces and to a more limited degree in most of the other provinces. PNG coffee is exported to Germany, Netherlands, Australia, South Africa, UK and elsewhere.

During 1985 PNG's coffee export quota varied as the global International Coffee Organisation's quota varied. At the start of the year it was 657,000 bags, in July it fell to 633,222 bags, but by December, because of the drought in Brazil, it had risen to 690,700 bags. Under the terms of the International Coffee Agreement the global quota system was suspended when prices exceeded US150 cents per pound. In 1986 there was an outbreak of coffee rust in five highland areas. Quick measures taken by the industry controlled the outbreak but results will not really be known until after the 1987 crop yield.

Sugar. Although PNG has always had indigenous cane, commercial production is a recent development. Ramu Sugar Ltd, with canefields and a sugar mill on Yusap Downs in the Morobe Province, made its first export shipment of about 5000 tonnes of sugar in late 1983. Its first crop, in 1982, yielded 1700 tonnes of sugar from 118,000 tonnes of cane. It also supplies sugar for the local market.

Rubber. This is mostly confined to the Port Moresby side of Papua New Guinea. The Australian Government made substantial grants to encourage rubber planting and the industry was well established by the 1920s. In the 1950s special marketing arrangements were made by the Australian Government for an assured market for PNG rubber in Australia which now takes the whole production. Production was 5400 tonnes in 1985.

Indigenous production is still negligible although smallholder interest has been fostered in Western Province at Cape Rodney and Bailebo in Central Province and at Gav-

ien, East Sepik.

The sale of rubber in Australia has been through a rubber pool since the 1950s and this has been continued since PNG independence. Towards the end of each year the rubber pool negotiates with Australian manufacturers for the sale of all PNG rubber in the following year. Prices are tied to world price for RSS No.1 grade. For this concession the manufacturers are able to import all their other rubber requirements from non-PNG sources duty free. The export value of rubber for 1985 was K3.7 million.

Tea The possibilities of tea growing were discussed in New Guinea in the late 1930s but only a few experimental plots were grown until the late 1940s when the government selected Garaina in the Morobe district, at an elevation of 600 m, for large scale experiments. It was not until late 1962 that a tea factory was built at Garaina. Although Garaina tea was mid-level it was of good quality; moreover the yield per acre was about 80 per cent more than expected, and New Guinea labour, especially the women of the Waria valley in which the plantation is situated, took to picking easily.

Tea growing did not extend in that area but all commercial plantations were subsequently established in the Highlands, notably the Western Highlands and to a minor degree in Southern Highlands. From 1966 all production from Garaina was used as seed tea for the Highlands plantations, and Garaina was later closed.

The first private tea estates were established in 1963–64 when several lots averaging 400 ha each were put up for tender in the Wahgi Valley near Mount Hagen. By 1973 there were eight major non-indigenous estates in Western Highlands and four tea factories have been built. Two tea estates were then developed in Southern Highlands.

In 1985 the export of 6600 tonnes of tea was worth K11.5 million.

Exports of spices including chillies and cardamom fluctuate according to demand. Chillies worth K56,000 were exported in 1985. Cardamom exports were worth K2,360,000.

Spices are mostly grown in the Highlands and Morobe Province.

Pyrethrum. Pyrethrum, an ingredient of some insecticides, is extracted from a daisylike plant, *Chrysanthemum cinerariaefolium*, which grows in the tropics at altitudes over 1800 m. Varieties that would grow well in the PNG highlands were selected in the 1950s but the industry did not progress until a British firm established an extraction factory near Mount Hagen.

Some thousands of hectares were planted by New Guineans in the Highlands provinces. In 1973 the factory was taken over by the government as the Kagamuga Natural Products Co. Pyrethrum is now obtained from 830 ha in Enga province where there are some 30,000 smallholder growers. Exports of pyrethrum extract were worth K704,000 in 1985 — a large increase on the previous year's level of K441,000.

Other Agricultural Industries. Vegetable growing is very important to the economy. The rural population in 1985 was 2.9 million, of which an estimated 725,000 people were engaged in subsistence farming, mainly vegetable growing. It has been estimated that probably four or five million tonnes of vegetables and fruit are produced each year from some 250,000 ha.

The greatest output is of sweet potatoes which may represent 40 per cent of total vegetable production. Other important food crops include bananas, taro, yams, sugar cane and coconuts. Up to 175,000 people who live near the great rivers and swamps, rely on the sago palm to provide the major part of their diets.

The people use an estimated 500 species of native fruits, vegetables and leaves. They also plant introduced varieties including tomatoes, maize, citrus fruit, pawpaw and peanuts. Cold climate vegetables including cabbage and potatoes are grown in some Highland areas.

All major vegetables are sold in town and country markets. The quantities are not recorded but may amount to 250,000 tonnes worth, perhaps K30 million. Despite the large quantities of vegetables produced, a large and growing amount of food is imported.

The Government is encouraging increased production of vegetables in an attempt to reduce the imports. It is providing advice and assistance to smallholders and is building or improving roads to enable crops to be taken to sales outlets. Miscellaneous cash crops include peanuts for processing into roasted peanuts and peanut butter; tobacco for blending with imported leaf; and rice. However, all are produced only in small quantities.

Rice is grown in Central, Gulf, Madang, Milne Bay, Morobe and East and West Sepik provinces but on a small scale. Production rose from 1133 tonnes in year ended June 1974 to 1610 tonnes by June 1976.

In 1985/86 a record 115,822 tonnes of rice were sold locally but Rice Industries of Papua New Guinea, the company which until the end of 1986 had a monopoly on rice distribution, warned that supplies of subsidised imported rice could become a threat to local production. A new rice mill opened in Lae in 1988.

FOOD MARKETING CORPORATION. The Food Marketing Corporation Pty Ltd, a registered company fully owned by the PNG government, operates from headquarters in Port Moresby to handle distribution of fruit and vegetables throughout Papua New Guinea. It was established in 1976. The corporation is also interested in exporting produce, although its main objective is to increase local production and distribution so that fruit and vegetable imports may be reduced.

The corporation is undertaking research into improved processing methods and is developing a number of new products. The corporation has branches in Lae, Kainantu, Goroka and Mt Hagen but plans to be represented eventually in every province.

Cattle raising and dairying. The long-range plan of the Government is to make Papua New Guinea self-sufficient in meat. However this has not been achieved although the progress in the last decade has been considerable.

In most localities, crosses with tropical breeds have proved superior to pure British breeds, and the majority of cattle in PNG would now be crossbreeds.

There were about 108,440 cattle in PNG in 1985. Morobe province is still the most important cattle area. After Morobe, in order of cattle importance, come the Central Province and Madang and Western Highlands although all provinces have some cattle.

Indigenous farmers, especially in the Highlands areas, are being encouraged to develop an interest in cattle raising, by having a nucleus of 15 breeding cows and a bull. These smallholder cattle ventures are being financed by a World Bank loan of $US5 million and administered through the PNG Development Bank.

In 1985, the number of cattle owned by smallholders was appoximately 14,470.

About 42 per cent of fresh, chilled or frozen beef is supplied locally but when canned and other meat are taken into consideration local supplies amount to only one-sixth of requirements.

Dairy cattle number less than 3000 and dairying is carried on notably at Port Moresby, Lae, Goroka, Mount Hagen, Minj and Banz only in proximity to towns. Production of milk does not meet demand.

There is a central abattoir controlled by the government in Lae and there are smaller abattoirs in other cattle producing districts.

Other livestock. Experiments have been made from time to time with sheep, notably the Nondugl experiment with Romney Marsh sheep immediately after the war. But in large herds they have been unsuccessful. Some success is being achieved with experimental flocks in the Highlands which are partly financed with New Zealand aid.

The most important animal in the native economy is the pig. Pigs in most communities are primarily an indication of individual or village wealth, used for ceremonial purposes. In native life, pig meat contributes little to the diet of the people. However, efforts are being made by the Government to improve the quality of local pigs through extension work. Commercial piggeries operate near the towns and local supplies to these areas are adequate and of good quality.

Poultry are also a part of village life. Some 60 per cent of poultry meat consumed is locally produced, and almost all the eggs.

Donkeys, goats and horses are also kept in Papua New Guinea but not in sufficient numbers to be economically important.

Marine industries. Traditionally coastal villagers have always fished for food and this has remained largely unchanged except for the introduction of modern aids such as outboard motors and imported nets. In recent years villages have been encouraged to preserve their surplus catch either by drying, smoking, or by the use of small freezers that have been established in strategic localities and from

which fish are distributed to local markets.

Local fishermen have also participated in some commercial fishing, for example, in the Western Province where barramundi is caught in season in the estuaries of the large rivers. In 1985, barramundi worth K445,000 was exported, or 154 tonnes.

A fleet of 47 tuna boats based at Kavieng, Rabaul and Manus caught tuna worth K5.1 million in 1985, or 11,700 tonnes.

A fleet of 15 trawlers was working the Gulf of Papua for prawns. The catch of prawns and crayfish was valued at K9.8 million, or 1448 tonnes.

The PNG Government has reorganised fishing activities under the Division of Fisheries with the aim of promoting local fishing and controlling resources.

Training of inspecting officers was through the Fisheries School, Madang. In mid-1977, training in fisheries skills was provided by the new National Fisheries College of Kavieng, with one, two and three-year courses in commercial fisheries techniques. Up to 100 residential students per annum can be trained at the college which was funded with a grant of K1.65 million provided by Japan.

PNG reefs abound in trochus and green snail shell, bêche-de-mer and pearl shell and all three products are exported.

The South Pacific Regional Fisheries Treaty, a five-year agreement which allows American tuna boats to fish within the 200-mile fisheries zones of member countries of the South Pacific Forum, was signed in Port Moresby on 2 April 1987. Papua New Guinea expects to earn more than K3 million a year as its share of the catch fees.

Cultured pearls. Samarai Pearls Ltd produces half-pearls from local MOP near Samarai.

Forestry and timber industry. Forestry products are one of the country's main export commodities. The country has 36 million sq. ha of enclosed forest, of which 8 million are considered suitable for immediate development. Current timber operators have rights over 900,000 ha.

Export of forest products in the form of logs, sawn timber, plywood, veneer, woodchips, chopsticks and sandalwood realised a value of K114 million in 1987.

Some 17,870 ha of forest have been replanted, two thirds of it in pine at Wau-

Bulolo where natural hoop and klinkii pines are being cut for the manufacture of plywood at PNG Forest Products Pty Ltd's factory at Bulolo.

Currently about 680 ha are being replanted per annum. Policy now favours big timber companies who can utilise the total produce of forests — timber, wood chips and pulp — and who can create a permanent industry through reafforestation. Small operators who worked timber leases for export logs, the land then being used for agriculture, are being phased out.

The oldest established timber enterprise in PNG is that of Commonwealth New Guinea Timbers which was set up in 1954 as a joint effort on behalf of the Australian Government and what was then Bulolo Gold Dredging. (Since 1973 the BGD share was owned by Japanese interests and in 1979 the PNG Government bought control. The name has been changed.) By reafforestation the klinkii and hoop pine forests have been maintained while the trees that are cut are turned into plywood and veneer at the factory at Bulolo.

Another important timber area, the Madang forest, is located about 40 km from Madang town and, including the Gogol forest, has a total area of 83,000 ha. Right to exploit this forest is held by Jant Pty Ltd, a Japanese company. The company produces woodchips and Quila logs. A sawmill at Binnen Harbour, Madang, with a chip mill to take care of waste, are in operation. Total investment is K10 million.

In 1973 rights to a 183,000 ha forest at Open Bay, East New Britain, were let to the Open Bay Timber Co. Ltd. Another important development in New Britain, in the Kapuluk area, is the sawmill and woodchip mill of Nam Yam timbers; and in the Kimbe area the Stettin Bay Lumber Co.

A large development on the Port Moresby side of the country is ANG Timbers, which operates in the Marshall Lagoon–Cape Rodney area of Central Province.

During 1985 Vanimo Timber Products began producing and exporting with a five year logging permit which allows logging at an annual rate of 120,000 cubic metres.

In 1988 the American Scott Paper Company was invited to establish a pulp paper mill and to assist with a reafforestation project. The Government said the invitation was in line with Government policy of promoting local processing of timber.

MANUFACTURING AND MINING.

Excluding the Panguna copper mining activities and Ok Tedi, the main secondary industries producing for export are the copra crushing mill at Rabaul, owned by a W. R. Carpenter and Co. Ltd subsidiary, the plywood factory at Bulolo, and the oil-palm processing factory near Kimbe, West New Britain and the factory at Higaturu. They are not labour intensive.

There are several large tea factories in the Wahgi Valley, but these are processing units rather than secondary industries in the usual sense.

Apart from secondary export industries there are a large number that produce for the local market with a minor export to neighbouring territories.

Gold mining. Papua New Guinea has a long and lucrative history of gold mining. It has been the subject of heavy investment since the 1970s and output has increased steadily until a record 32.1 tonnes were exported in 1985. Panguna has been joined by Ok Tedi since 1984 as the major gold mines. Ok Tedi has been producing an average of 16,000 kg per annum but after 1987 this is expected to drop back to 14,000 kg per annum as copper production rises. It is anticipated that by 1989 this will decline even further to 7000 kg. Ok Tedi is estimated to have an estimated 34 million tonnes of gold ore with a grading of 2.86 g per tonne.

Across the Star Mountains from Ok Tedi is the Frieda River Valley. Prospectors have

TABLE 1 GOLD EXPORTS 1980–85

Year	K million	Tonnes
1980	172.9	14.5
1981	158.9	17.6
1982	171.8	19.1
1983	200.9	19.1
1984	183.3	19.4
1985	319.6	32.1

estimated even larger gold reserves here than Ok Tedi and an international company is performing feasibility studies and carrying out further prospecting in the area. Other significant finds have been made, particularly in the mountains near Madang. A significant gold prospect on Lihir Island, New Ireland Province, is being appraised. Capital expenditure for the development of the Misima Island project is also expected to begin in 1987.

Copper mining. The biggest copper development on the PNG mainland is at Ok Tedi in the Star Mountains area of Western Province where Kennecott Explorations (Aust.) Pty Ltd completed preliminary drilling in 1973 at a cost of $16 million.

In late 1973 Kennecott asked the PNG government for certain concessions before it proceeded further. Negotiations broke down, and the PNG government decided to pay for the final exploration itself and in 1975 set up the government-owned Ok Tedi Development Company to do the work.

A K10.6 million feasibility study completed in 1979, assessed mineable ore reserves at 410 million tonnes, including 34 million tonnes of gold-bearing ore and 351 million tonnes of porphyry copper ore. The BHP Company of Australia and a consortium of overseas miners formed a public company in 1981 with the PNG Government to undertake the venture.

Open-cut methods are used and a working life of 25 to 30 years is anticipated. Ok Tedi Mining Ltd's authorised share capital is K200 million.

The copper success story has been at Panguna, Bougainville, in the Crown Prince Range behind Kieta, where Bougainville Copper Ltd went into production in 1972. The parent company, Conzinc Riotinto, had begun prospecting the area in 1964 following a government examination in 1960. Reserves are at least 944 million tonnes of ore with a copper content of 0.48 per cent, and 15.83 g of gold to the tonne. Markets are assured for many years.

The value of the Bougainville copper project is thus a vital part of Papua New Guinea's economy. In addition the company provides job opportunities on a larger scale than any other enterprise in PNG (except the Government).

In addition to the mine site and town of Panguna up in the ranges, a coastal satellite town, Arawa, has been established on the coast. Arawa was built by the company and the PNG government on the site of a former plantation. Population of the Kieta/Arawa/Panguna region in 1984 was 22,900. Over the headland at Loloho, on Anewa Bay, is the port for the whole project, with wharf, power station, bulk loading equipment and ore driers.

The copper, gold and silver is mined at Panguna about 25 km from the coast by all-weather road that goes over the Crown Prince Range at an altitude of 1037 m. The mine is worked by open cut methods, the ore being crushed, ground and piped down to Loloho in the form of slurry where it is filtered and dried and exported as dry concentrate. It is shipped abroad for refining.

It cost over $A400 million to establish the Panguna-Arawa-Loloho complex.

Estimates of the reserves at the Ok Tedi site are 350 million tonnes with a considerably higher yield than Panguna. Copper mining from under the extensive gold cap began in late 1986 at a predicted rate of 59,000 tonnes per annum. It is anticipated that this production rate will rise to 117,000 tonnes by 1989. In 1985 the state closed the mine over doubts about the commitment of the private shareholders to develop the copper. From that event emerged the Ok Tedi Fifth and Sixth Supplemental Agreements in which the capital expenditure over the next five years will be largely devoted to the construction of the copper processing plant, with the construction of the copper tailings dam deferred until at least 1990.

TABLE 2 COPPER EXPORTS 1980–85

	K million	'1000 tonnes
1980	139.3	142.2
1981	134.6	164.0
1982	122.8	173.2
1983	161.0	181.1
1984	135.5	163.3
1985	160.5	168.6

Capital expenditure of around K390 million will be involved.

Apart from Bougainville and Ok Tedi, other deposits are being investigated at Frieda in West Sepik and at Yandera in Madang Province.

Petroleum policy continues to be a major area of Government interest. In the 1987 Budget 10.3 per cent of the allocation to the Department of Minerals and Energy was targeted for the Petroleum Development Expenditure Programme. This allocation will continue until 1991. Exploration continues offshore in the Papuan Gulf and in 1985 major discoveries were reported in the Southern Highlands field of Juha and Mananda. It was anticipated that the first full year of production would be 1991.

TOURISM. PNG has had casual visitors for almost a century but only in recent years has it become interested in organised tourism and even now, with so many other important industries, this still has a minor place in the economy.

The Office of Tourism was a victim of expenditure cuts in the November 1981 Budget. A National Tourist Authority with an eight-member board headed by Sir John Guise was set up in 1983.

In 1986 Mrs Nahau Rooney, Minister for Civil Aviation and Tourism, announced that tourism would be given greater priority in the country's economic development. The National Tourist Authority was given a budget of K328,500 in 1987.

In the last few years there has been an improvement in the standard of facilities provided for travellers, both in hotels and air transport.

There were 30,391 short-term arrivals in Papua New Guinea in 1985. Of these, 6873 stated on arrival that they were on holiday. This represents a 1241 decrease on 1984 arrivals, although the current statistics do not include cruise ship passengers who have not been required to complete customs documents as their visit does not extend beyond 24 hours. American tourists visit parts of the country as part of Pacific circle tours and there has been increasing interest from Japanese tour groups.

OVERSEAS TRADE. For many years Papua New Guinea had an imbalance of trade, with imports being considerably higher than exports, but this has changed somewhat since 1973 when exports of copper from Panguna and increased agricultural returns considerably improved the economy.

TABLE 3

	Exports K million	Imports K million
1980	691.8	684.2
1981	565.9	738.2
1982	570.4	751.7
1983	687.4	821.7
1984	822.0	866.9
1985	883.3	743.7 (to Oct.)

The accompanying tables show the main exports and imports and their destination or origin.

TABLE 4 QUANTITIES OF MAIN EXPORTS

	1984 '000 tonnes	1985 '000 tonnes
Cocoa beans	34.1	30.9
Coffee	49.4	40.6
Copper ore	163.3	168.6
Copper concentrate	550.8	560.0
Copra	93.5	103.5
Copra oil	40.7	41.4
Fish (inc. barramundi, crayfish and prawns)	2.7	1.5
Gold (tonnes)	19.4	32.1
Palm oil	129.9	123.8
Rubber	3.4	5.4
Tea	7.3	6.6
Tuna	0.9	11.7
Timber, logs (000 m³)	1278	1158

TABLE 5 VALUE OF MAIN COMMODITIES EXPORTED FROM 1983–85
(K million)

	1983	1984	1985
Cocoa	41.4	67.0	62.5
Coffee	94.7	110.7	117.5
Copper ore & concentrate	116.0	135.5	160.5
Copra	24.0	49.1	33.4
Copra oil	20.0	39.4	23.7
Fish products	9.1	10.0	12.1
Gold	200.9	183.3	319.6
Palm oil	23.7	75.8	61.5
Rubber	2.2	2.4	3.9
Tea	10.4	17.1	11.5
Timber, logs	43.2	69.9	58.4
Timber, lumber	11.5	11.8	8.9

TABLE 6 EXPORTS — MAIN COUNTRIES OF DESTINATION 1985

	K million	per cent
West Germany	264.5	30.0
Japan	199.0	22.5
Australia	91.4	10.3
United Kingdom	66.0	7.5
Spain	41.3	4.7
Netherlands	38.0	4.3
All others	183.1	20.7
Total	883.3	

Note: Copper/gold concentrate is exported to Japan and West Germany for refining. This accounts for the high value of exports to these countries.

TABLE 7 IMPORTS — MAIN COUNTRIES OF ORIGIN (to Nov. 1985)

	K million	per cent
Autralia	324.1	40.5
Japan	140.4	17.5
Singapore	80.6	10.1
USA	74.8	9.4
New Zealand	45.8	5.7
United Kingdom	24.3	3.0
All others	110.3	13.8
Total	800.3	

Customs tariff. Import duties are levied on a wide range of goods, and there is in addition a 3½ per cent general import levy imposed on the fob value of all goods except for some basic items such as rice, sugar, flour, tinned fish and tinned meat.

Australian project aid is being used to provide high level training to increase the effectiveness of customs collection. In 1985 K171.700 was raised through customs. The 1987 budget predicted this figure would rise to K240.000.

TABLE 8 VALUE OF MAIN IMPORT CATEGORIES (K'000)

	1983	*1984*	*1985 (to Oct.)*
Food and live animals	135,459	154,767	133,355
Beverages & tobacco	8232	11,248	8209
Inedible crude materials, except fuel	4627	6289	5952
Mineral fuels, lubricants, etc.	167,280	156,278	134,966
Animal & vegetable oils, fats	2522	3927	2853
Chemicals & chemical products	60,522	68,171	55,732
Manufactured goods, classified by material	128,536	140,064	112,920
Machinery & transport equipment	222,552	243,538	199,212
Misc. manufactured articles	57,592	70,064	60,964
Miscellaneous transactions	34,318	12,485	29,504
TOTAL	821,640	866,831	743,667

There are export duties on a wide range of items, mostly agricultural, including logs and minerals.

FINANCE. Papua New Guinea derives its public revenue mainly from three sources — locally raised revenue, grants from the Australian Government, and public loans. Before Papua New Guinea independence Australian grants provided about two-thirds of total revenue, but the proportion has gradually diminished as local revenues have increased. Main sources of internal revenue are from customs (mainly import and excise duties), personal and company income tax.
Budget. As from 1 January 1978, PNG moved to a financial year of 1 January to 31 December. The first budget under this scheme was announced on 21 February 1978.

Estimated budget receipts for 1987 are,

Foreign grants (mostly
  Australian) .... 186.0 K million
Internal revenue .... 650.0 K million
TOTAL .... 836.0 K million

The budget deficit for 1987 is estimated at K124 million, K16.6 million lower than for 1986. The deficit will be financed by concessional borrowing K86.1 million and commercial borrowing K37.9 million.
Internal revenue. For 1987 internal revenue

FIGURE 1 SOURCES OF BORROWING (K million)

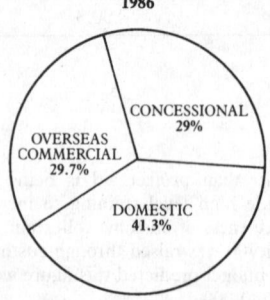

1986

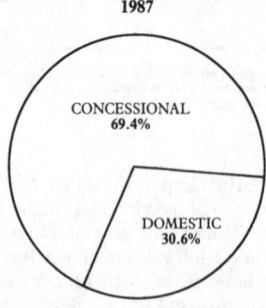

1987

will come from customs K240 m, taxation K260 m, revenue from assets K85 m, other K65 m. Import duties will account for 65 per cent of customs revenue.

Expenditure. In 1987 main areas of expenditure were:

Economic sector	(K'000)	94,649.6
Infrastructure sector	"	135,372.0
Social services	"	109.391.3
Law and order	"	100,628.3
Administrative sector	"	85,932.2
Others	"	434,026.6
Total	"	960,000.0

Under an agreement negotiated in 1985, aid from Australia will decline by three per cent in real terms with untied budget support component declining by five per cent annually. The decline in the value of the Australian dollar further reduced the value of aid in 1986. The 1987 budget estimated the Australian aid contribution would be K176 million.

Tax system. Papua New Guinea has a pay-as-you-earn income tax system. Wage earners have their taxes deducted at source and they are required to submit income tax returns only if they earn money other than by salary and wages. In 1987 the tax threshold was lifted to K2080.

Company taxation is at the rate of 35 per cent on taxable income, and 48 per cent on foreign companies not incorporated in Papua New Guinea and operating through branches within the country.

There is a dividend withholding tax of 17 per cent, which applies to non-resident shareholders in local companies. The 1987 Budget introduced many new tax measures designed to shift the emphasis from direct to indirect taxation. Comprehensive information on all aspects of taxation in Papua New Guinea, especially that pertaining to investment, is available from Coopers and Lybrand, Papua New Guinea, PO Box 484.

Foreign aid. A major part of PNG's Government revenue is aid from abroad. In 1987 aid totalled K186 million; aid from Australia forms the largest part of this form of revenue.

The World Bank and Asian Development Bank provide loans which are usually used for road construction, telecommunications development and other schemes requiring large capital sums.

Currency. Until 19 April 1975 Papua New Guinea used Australian currency, but since then it has used its own currency, which is not tied to the Australian dollar. The main unit is the kina, made up of 100 toea. Kina notes are issued in denominations of K2, K5, K10 and K20. Coins are in denominations of K1, 20t, 10t, 5t, 2t and 1t.

Banks and financial institutions. The Bank of Papua New Guinea is the central bank and its activities include administering the currency and foreign exchange, managing the country's international reserves and supervising the banking system. The Papua New Guinea Banking Corporation is a commercial bank wholly owned by the Government. There are also several other commercial banks including Westpac Banking Corp. (PNG) Ltd, Australia and New Zealand Banking Group (PNG) Ltd, Bank of the South Pacific Ltd, Niugini-Lloyds International Bank Ltd, and Indosuez-Niugini Bank Ltd. The Agricultural Bank of Papua New Guinea provides finance for primary production or the establishment, development or acquisition of industrial or commercial projects by Papua New Guineans.

Other financial institutions include finance companies, some of which are subsidiaries of commercial banks, and savings and loans societies.

Investment controls. The National Investment and Development Authority (NIDA) is a government agency responsible for collecting information on foreign investment within PNG, and for controlling investment activities. All foreign businesses must register with NIDA, and provide information on their foreign exchange arrangements. Foreign nationals must notify NIDA before they take up shares in established business, or otherwise become involved. NIDA seeks to identify businesses which will make best use of PNG resources and/or will give Papua New Guinea participation.

The government has set guidelines for

foreign investment, and publishes lists of activities reserved for Papua New Guinean investment, and others in which overseas investment is encouraged. These vary from time to time and inquiries should be made to NIDA, Port Moresby.

The Investment Corporation of Papua New Guinea is a government corporation which buys shares in operating companies and sells them to Papua New Guineans either directly or indirectly through a mutual fund. From 1987 the corporation actively developed and packaged new projects. In 1986 it made a net profit of K8.8 million, an increase of 186 per cent over the 1985 profit.

TRANSPORT. Since the end of the Pacific war, Papua New Guinea has known a period of active road-building. There are good roads around towns, extending along the coasts and a developing system of interior roads.

Total length of roads in all provinces at the last formal listing was 17,241 km, but the actual total is certainly higher — the shortest length being in Manus (147 km) and the longest in the Central Province (1753 km). The major highways extend from Lae to Mt Hagen and on to Mendi in the Southern Highlands; from Wewak to Nuku in the Sepik; and between Kieta-Arawa-Panguna, on Bougainville. There is an important network of roads in the Gazelle Peninsula and, since 1975, a link between Lae and Madang. Roadbuilding is proceeding in the Western Province, associated with the Ok Tedi mine.

A sum of K138 million was provided for roads and bridges maintenance in the 1987 budget.

In 1984 newly registered vehicles included 1356 cars, 724 station wagons, 728 buses, 651 motor cycles, 283 tractors and 6269 commercial vehicles (total 9283).

Overseas airlines. Air Niugini and Qantas operate international services to Port Moresby from several cities on the Australian eastcoast, including Cairns. Air Nuigini also has flights from Port Moresby to Jayapura, Honiara, Manila, and Singapore. Solomon Islands Airlines flies into Kieta.

Domestic airlines. Papua New Guinea registers three types of operators. 1st and 2nd level operators can run international routes

(1st level) and main trunk routes (2nd level). Third level operators run feeder services. First, second and third level operators all must run regular services, although they may also run charters. All other operators have charter licences, which restricts them as to passengers and freight.

There is a very wide network of internal air services. Because of the comparatively poor development of highways, air transport is an important method of travel.

Airports. The main airport in Papua New Guinea is Jackson's, Port Moresby, which has a runway 2750 metres long, and able to take wide-bodied aircraft such as the 747. Jackson's is used as the main terminus for the country's air services, with feeder services operating from it. The Government hopes to build a new international airport by 1992 to overcome the lack of facilities and international standards at Jackson's. There are six other airports in PNG suitable for international operations, but on a more modest scale.

Lae airport was once an important feeder airport, but development of the city of Lae has restricted its extension.

Important airports are at Wewak, Madang, Mt Hagen, Goroka, Rabaul, Kieta, Alatau, Hoskins, Kavieng, Kundiawa, Manus Island, Mendi, Popondetta, Tari and Vanimo.

There are hundreds of aerodromes in PNG, many owned by private interests.

Ports. The Papua New Guinea Harbours Board is responsible for the ports of Aitape, Alotau, Lorengau, Vanimo, Port Moresby, Samarai, Rabaul, Lae, Madang, Kavieng, Kieta, Wewak, Oro Bay and Kimbe. The board has a full-time chairman and a full-time secretary. Main ports are in charge of port managers. The board is financed by port and harbour charges and in addition can raise loans.

In 1987 the ports at Port Moresby, Kimbe, Bialla and Oro Bay, were further developed at a cost of K14 million.

Ports of entry. Ports of entry are Port Moresby, Samarai, Lae, Rabaul, Madang, Wewak, Lorengau, Oro Bay, Kavieng, Kieta, Alotau and Kimbe.

Customs officers are stationed at main ports but for others notice of arrival is necessary so that a customs officer can be sent.

Wharves. The following are the main wharves in use:

	Length m	Depth alongside m
Aitape	18.3	4.3
Alotau	93	10
Buka	31.4	3.65
Daru	29.6	2.4
Kavieng	93.8	7
Kieta	122	7.5
Kimbe	60.9	10.7
Lae — old section	246	11
new section	184	11
Lorengau (Nabu)	15.2	5.1
Madang	137.1	10.1
Oro Bay	60.3	11.4
Port Moresby	213.3	7.6
NE berth	118	4.6
SW berth	67	3.8
Rabaul Bay Rd.	152.4	10.2
Blanche St.	121.9	7.9
Samarai	93.2	7.8
Vanimo	18.7	4.9
Wewak	73.1	6.7

The overseas wharf at Loloho, Anewa Bay, is privately owned by Bougainville Copper Ltd. In addition to the above main wharves, there are small ship or coastal wharves at Alotau, Kieta, Lae, Lorengau, Madang, Port Moresby, Rabaul, Samarai and Wewak. Pilots are stationed at Kieta, Lae, Madang, Port Moresby, Rabaul and Kimbe. Pilotage can be arranged in advance at other ports.

Shipping services. Papua New Guinea has a great variety of shipping services connecting the islands with world markets. Most ships are cargo carrying, although there are some passenger opportunities apart from the occasional cruise vessel.

The most frequent services are between PNG and Australia because of the importance of Australia in the supply of goods. There are a number of operators, but the most frequent services are supplied in a joint operation by New Guinea Express Lines, Chief Container Service, and Karlander Asia Pacific Lines, which run four ships between PNG ports and the Australian east coast. Chief Container Service comprises PNG Line-PNG Shipping Corp, New Guinea Australia Line and Containers Pacific Express.

Among the services to the East are New Guinea Pacific Line, with container services to Singapore, Hongkong and PNG ports; the Forum Line connects with New Zealand, and there are cargo services to the US, Britain and Europe, as well as with other Pacific groups.

PNG Shipping Corporation. The PNG Shipping Corporation has been in operation since 1977. It is government-owned, and as well as operating overseas services it has coastal cargo vessels servicing PNG main ports.

Local shipping. Over 100 coastal vessels ranging in size from five tonnes to 1000 tonnes provide cargo and limited passenger services between PNG main ports, outports, plantations and missions.

COMMUNICATIONS. Papua New Guinea is linked via the Seacom coaxial international cable to Guam, Kota Kinabalu in Sabah State, Hong Kong and Singapore in the northern hemisphere and to Australia in the south. Further connections can be made to New Zealand, Canada and Britain via the Compac cable. This is effected at the Sydney terminal.

Transmission levels are of a high quality.

International telecommunications are part of the services provided by the PNG Department of Public Utilities. The Coastal Radio Service, with two stations (Port Moresby and Rabaul), which provides communication with ships at sea, is also administered by the Department of Public Utilities.

Internal links from the Seacom cable are by very high frequency (VHF) and microwave radio circuits between Madang and Lae and between Lae and Port Moresby and other centres.

PNG subscribers connected to all automatic exchanges except Alotau and Samarai can dial their own calls to subscribers in most Australian States through International Subscriber Dialling (ISD) and Australian Subscriber Trunk Dialling (STD).

Within Papua New Guinea, STD calls may be made between subscribers in most areas.

A large section of the trunk telecommunications system has its electricity provided from solar power. This makes PNG the first country in the world to power its trunk system in this way.

In 1987 an Australian company was awarded a multi-million dollar contract to install a microwave communication system to improve and expand telephone communications between Port Moresby, Lae, Goroka and Mount Hagen. Microwave repeater stations will be installed along a 700 km route.

PNG telex subscribers are connected to telex services throughout the world via the automatic exchanges in Port Moresby and Lae.

Internal radio network. Internal radio communication is provided by the Public Utilities Department through a system of zone centres which are linked to government by privately operated HF outstations. Communication between the outstations and the zone centre to which each is attached is by radio telephone. There are well over 1000 of these outstations on isolated missions, timber camps, mineral survey camps, plantations and goverment posts.

Radio. The National Broadcasting Commission came into operation on 1 December 1973. The commission combines the functions of the Australian Broadcasting Commission which had operated in PNG since the end of World War II, and the 17 regional radio stations which had previously been run by the PNG Government. It now operates 19 provincial stations and three networks: the Kundu (provincial), the Karai (national), and Kalang (commercial) services. The latter is the only service to accept advertising and operates on the FM band.

Generally the national stations are designed to serve the better educated Papua New Guineans, expatriates and the schools. The provincial short wave stations are designed exclusively for the local people they serve in the areas where they are located.

NBC medium wave stations are located at Port Moresby, Rabaul, Madang, Goroka, and Wewak although the national programmes originate in Port Moresby. NBC short wave stations which also carry the national programme are located in Port Moresby, Rabaul and Wewak.

Provincial short wave stations that cater only for their immediate areas are located at Kimbe, Kundiawa, Goroka, Kavieng, Mount Hagen, Popondetta, Lae, Kerema, Madang, Mendi, Port Moresby, Daru, Wewak, Kieta, Alotau, Vanimo, Rabaul, Corengais and Wabag.

Under an agreement signed in 1987, Japan will give PNG nearly $A5 million for the upgrading of 11 provincial radio stations.
Newspapers. Papua New Guinea has two national dailies, the mass circulation *Papua New Post-Courier* which is produced Monday to Friday and the *Niugini Nius* which is produced Monday to Saturday. Both are produced in Port Moresby and are air-freighted to other areas of the country. *The Times of Papua New Guinea* is a weekly paper.

Numerous smaller newspapers and newssheets, covering regional areas, are produced. Churches, educational and professional bodies produce various periodicals.

Television. The first television transmission in the country was on 21 January 1987. The Niugini Television Network (NTN) is majority-owned by Australian Kevin Parry. There are an estimated 7000 television sets in Port Moresby. A second channel began broadcasting in August 1987. Media Niugini's EMTV serves Port Moresby, Rabaul, Lae, Goroko, Mt Hagen and their surrounding districts.

WATER. Port Moresby and suburbs have a fully reticulated water supply which is filtered and treated to be safe for drinking. Some other towns have a partially reticulated supply and where reticulated water is available there are usually sewerage works. Some towns — such as Rabaul — are in a difficult position because there are no adequate rivers in the vicinity. In villages, people draw their water from adjacent streams except where villages have become part of towns.

ELECTRICITY. The Papua New Guinea Electricity Commission operates generating stations in the main centres and maintains numerous small stations on behalf of the government. In some industrial areas, notably the copper mining operations in Bougainville, town supplies are made available by private enterprise. All PNG centres have some electricity supply, although in the remoter areas the supply is restricted to certain hours. Distribution voltages are 240/415 volts 50 cycles alternating current.

MAJOR OFFICE HOLDERS

Governor-General:
  Sir Kingsford Dibela GCMG
Prime Minister:
  Rabbie Namaliu
Deputy Prime Minister:
  Akoka Doi
Chief Justice:
  Mari Kapi

GOVERNMENT DEPARTMENTS

Auditor-General, PO Box 42, Konedobu, Tel.: 214388, 214470
Bank of Papua New Guinea, PO Box 121, Port Moresby, Tel: 212999
Business Groups Registry, PO Box 1281, Port Moresby, Tel.: 212733
Commerce Department, PO Box Wards Strip, Waigani, Tel.: 271150
Community & Family Services Department, PO Box 130, Port Moresby, Tel.: 214144
Consumer Affairs Bureau, PO Box 694, Boroko, Tel.: 254389
Corrective Institution Services, PO Box 6889, Boroko, Tel.: 281007
Culture & Tourism Office, PO Box 7144, Boroko, Tel.: 272065
Customs Bureau, PO Box 923, Port Moresby, Tel.: 212844
Decentralization Department, PO Box 1287, Boroko, Tel.: 271731
Defence Department, PO Box Wards Strip, Waigani, Tel.: 242165
Department of Labour, PO Box 5644, Boroko, Tel.: 272034
Department of Lands, Surveys &

Environment, PO Box 5665, Boroko, Tel.: 272562
Department of Primary Industry, PO Box 417, Konedobu, Tel.: 214699
Education Department, PO Box Wards Strip, Waigani, Tel.: 272340
Environment & Conservation Office, PO Box Wards Strip, Waigani, Tel.: 271788
Finance Department, PO Box Wards Strip, Waigani, Tel.: 271812
Foreign Affairs Department & Trade, PO Box Wards Strip, Waigani, Tel.: 276111
Forests Office, PO Box 5055, Boroko, Tel.: 254022
Governor General, PO Box 79, Port Moresby, Tel.: 214466
Health Department PO Box 84, Konedobu, Tel.: 211700
High Education Office, PO Box 5117, Boroko, Tel.: 272090
Information Office, PO Box 313, Konedobu, Tel.: 211677
Institute of Applied Social and Economic Research, PO Box 1432, Boroko, Tel.: 254644
Institute of Medical Research, PO Box 60, Goroka, Tel.: 712200
Institute of Papua New Guinea Studies, PO Box 1432, Boroko, Tel.: 254644
Insurance Commissioners, PO Box 122, Port Moresby, Tel.: 214801
Justice Department, PO Box Wards Strip, Waigani, Tel.: 271013
Law Reform Commission, PO Box Wards Strip, Waigani, Tel.: 258755
Legal Training Institute, PO Box 9084, Hohola, Tel.: 257522
Legislative Counsel, PO Box Wards Strip, Waigani, Tel.: 271541
Liquor Licensing Commission, PO Box 6976, Boroko, Tel.: 271565
Medical Board of Papua New Guinea, PO Box 841, Port Moresby, Tel.: 211814
Minerals & Energy Department, PO Box 352, Konedobu, Tel.: 214011
Minimum Wage & Industrial Arbritration Board, PO Box 5644, Boroko, Tel.: 272274
National Archives & Public Records, PO Box 1089, Boroko, Tel.: 254332
National Museum & Art Gallery, PO Box 5560, Boroko, Tel.: 252422

National Parks Service, PO Box 5749, Boroko, Tel.: 254956

National Parliament, PO Box 596, Port Moresby, Tel.: 212677

National Planning Office, PO Box Wards Strip, Waigani, Tel.: 276111

National Statistical Office, PO Box Wards Strip, Waigani, Tel.: 271705

Nursing Council for Papua New Guinea, PO Box 841, Port Moresby, Tel.: 211395

Papua New Guinea Harbours Board, PO Box 671, Port Moresby, Tel.: 211400

Papua New Guinea Constabulary, PO Box 85, Konedobu, Tel.: 211222

Prime Minister's Department, PO Box 6695, Boroko, Tel.: 271764, 272557

Public Service Commission, PO Box Wards Strip, Waigani, Tel.: 276111

Public Solicitors Office, PO Box 5812, Boroko, Tel.: 421092

Registrar General's Office, PO Box 1281, Port Moresby, Tel.: 212733

Religion, Youth & Recreation Office, PO Box 9097, Hohola, Tel.: 255425

Security & Intelligence Organization, PO Box 333, Konedobu, Tel.: 251415

Supreme & National Courts, PO Box 7018, Boroko, Tel.: 257099

Transport & Civil Aviation, PO Box 457, Konedobu, Tel.: 211860

Urban Development Department, PO Box 5245, Boroko Tel.: 524500 Boroko

STATUTORY BODIES

Air Niugini, PO Box 7186, Boroko, Tel.: 259000

Cocoa Industry Board of Papua New Guinea, PO Box 532, Rabaul, Tel.: 921354, 922218

Copra Marketing Board of Papua New Guinea, PO Box 81, Port Moresby, Tel.: 211133, 211513

Electricity Commission of Papua New Guinea, PO Box 1105, Boroko, Tel.: 822531, 822967

Forestry Industries Council of Papua New Guinea, PO Box 3498, Port Moresby, Tel.: 214003

Investment Corporation of Papua New Guinea, PO Box 155, Port Moresby, Tel.: 212855, 212921

National Broadcasting Commission, PO Box 1359, Boroko, Tel.: 255233

National Housing Commission, PO Box 1550, Boroko, Tel.: 253255

National Insurance Corporation, PO Box 124, Arawa, Tel.: 971106

National Investment & Development Authority, PO Box 5053, Boroko, Tel.: 258777

Papua New Guinea Banking Corporation, PO Box 78, Port Moresby, Tel.: 211999

Papua New Guinea Coffee Industry Board, PO Box 137, Goroka, Tel.: 721207

Papua New Guinea Development Bank, PO Box 6310, Boroko, Tel.: 259255

Papua New Guinea Postal & Telecommunications, PO Box 6666, Boroko, Tel.: 276000

Papua New Guinea Technology University, PO Box 793, Lae, Tel.: 424999

University of Papua New Guinea, PO Box 4820, Waigani, Tel.: 245200

PROVINCIAL GOVERNMENTS

Central Province Government, PO Box Wards Strip, Waigani, Tel.: 214727

East New Britain Government, PO Box 714, Rabaul, Tel.: 921198

East Sepik Government, Wewak, Tel.: 862200

Eastern Highlands Government, PO Box 348, Goroka, Tel.: 711265

Enga Province Government, PO Box 157, Wabag, Tel.: 571077

Gulf Province Government, PO Box 87, Kerema, Tel.: 681044

Madang Province Government, PO Box 2108, Yomba. Tel.: 822966

Manus Province Government, PO Box 190, Lorengau, Tel.: 409088

Milne Bay Province Government, PO Box 104, Alotau, Tel.: 611256

Morobe Province Government, PO Box 572, Lae, Tel.: 431600

New Ireland Province Government, PO Box 103, Kavieng, Tel.: 942336

North Solomons Province Government, PO Box 120, Arawa, Tel.: 971101

Northern Province Government, Popondetta, Tel.: 297010

Simbu Province Government, PO Box 192, Kundiawa, Tel.: 751155

Southern Highlands Province, Government, PO Box 220, Mendi, Tel.: 591096
West New Britain Province Government, PO Box 287, Kimbe, Tel.: 935260
West Sepik Province Government, PO Box 42, Vanimo, Tel.: 871001
Western Highlands Province Government, PO Box 17, Mt Hagen, Tel.: 521211
Western Province Government, PO Box 24, Daru, Tel.: 659008

PNG OVERSEAS REPRESENTATIVES

PNG High Commission, PO Box 572, Manuka, ACT 2603, Australia Tel.: (3062) 953477, Telex: (71) 62592 KUNDU CANBERRA
PNG Consulate, GPO Box 4201, Sydney NSW 2001, Australia, Tel.: (302) 295151, Telex: (71) 202263 KUNDU SYDNEY
PNG Consulate, GPO Box 220, Brisbane Qld 4001, Australia, Tel.: (307) 2217915, (307) 2218067, Telex: (71) 40897 KUNDU BRISBANE
PNG Embassy to the EEC, Avenue des Ombrages, 11 Bis, Brussels 1200, Belgium, Tel.: 771 0150, 771 0159 Telex: (46) 62249 KUNDU BRUSSELS
PNG High Commission, PO Box 2447, Suva, Fiji, Tel.: 24939, Telex: (701) 2113 KUNDU SUVA
PNG Embassy, Level 4 Wisma Metropolitan, Jalan Sudirman Kav 9, Jakarta, Indonesia, Tel.: 584 604/5, Telex: (73) 46122 KUNDU JAKARTA
PNG Embassy, Mita Kokusai Building 3F 313, 4-28 Mira 1-Chome Minato-Ku, Tokyo 108, Japan, Tel.: 4547801/2/3/4, Telex: (72) 25488 KUNDU TOKYO
PNG High Commission, PO Box 9746, Courtenay Place, Wellington, New Zealand, Tel.: 849893/4, Telex: (74) 31353 KUNDU WELLINGTON
PNG Embassy, Pacific Bank Mataki Building, Ayala Avenue, Makati, Manila, Republic of the Philippines.
High Commission, 14 Waterloo Place, London SW1R4AR, United Kingdom, Tel.: (01) 930 0922/7, Telex: (51) 25827 KUNDU LONDON
PNG Mission to the UN, 801 Second Avenue, 12th Floor, New York 10017, United States, Tel.: (212) 6826447, Telex: (23) 666603 KUNDU NEW YORK

PNG Embassy, 1800 K Street NW, Suite 631, Washington DC 20006, United States of America, Tel.: (202) 6590859, Telex: (23) 64440 KUNDU

FOREIGN MISSIONS

American Embassy, PO Box 3492, Port Moresby, Tel.: 211511
Australian High Commission, PO Box 9129, Hohola, Tel.: 259333
British High Commission, PO Box 739, Port Moresby, Tel.: 212500
Indonesian Embassy, PO Box 7165, Boroko, Tel.: 253116
Japanese Embassy, PO Box 3040, Port Moresby, Tel.: 211800
New Zealand High Commission, PO Box 1144, Boroko, Tel.: 259444
Philippine Embassy, PO Box 5916, Boroko, Tel.: 256577

NON-GOVERNMENTAL BODIES

Association of Consulting Engineers of Papua New Guinea, PO Box 1720, Boroko, Tel.: 214918
Association of Licensed Stevedores, PO Box 1463, Port Moresby
Association of Surveyors of Papua New Guinea, PO Box 1422, Boroko
Coastal Shipowners Association, PO Box 698, Port Moresby
Crocodile Industry Association, PO Box 3387, Port Moresby, Tel.: 211623, Telex: 22267 CIA
Drilling Association of Papua New Guinea, PO Box 108, Madang
Employers Federation of Papua New Guinea, PO Box 490, Port Moresby, Tel.: 214772
Forest Industries Association, PO Box 1829, Port Moresby, Tel.: 256399
Goroka Chamber of Commerce, PO Box 949, Goroka Tel.: 721888
Highlands Farmers and Settlers Association, PO Box 18, Banz
Institute of National Affairs, PO Box 1530, Port Moresby, Tel.: 211044
Insurance Underwriters Association of PNG, PO Box 1270, Port Moresby, Tel.: 212612
Kimbe Chamber of Commerce, PO Box 222, Kimbe
Lae Chamber of Commerce, PO Box 265, Lae, Tel.: 422340, Telex: NE 44217 CHACOM

Liquor Trades Association, PO Box 2091, Konedobu

Madang Chamber of Commerce, PO Box 512, Madang, Tel.: 822355

Manus Chamber of Commerce, PO Box 38, Lorengau, Telex: NE 40806 EANDW

Milne Bay Chamber of Commerce, PO Box 252, Alotau

New Ireland Chamber of Commerce, PO Box 64, Kavieng, Tel.: 942180

Papua New Guinea Association of Accountants, PO Box 5831, Boroko, Tel.: 258734

Papua New Guinea Institute of Architects, PO Box 1278, Port Moresby, Tel.: 217041

Papua New Guinea Institute of Management, PO Box 1060, Port Moresby, Tel.: 213275

Papua New Guinea Palm Oil Producers' Association, PO Box 586, Lae, Tel.: 421755

Papua New Guinea Real Estate Institute, PO Box 1188, Boroko

Papua New Guinea Shipping Association, PO Box 145, Port Moresby, Telex: NE22139 SWIRE

Papua New Guinea Society of National Managers, PO Box 2632, Lae, Tel.: 421318

Petrol Retailers Association, PO Box 6868, Boroko

Planters Association of Papua New Guinea, PO Box 14, Rabaul, Tel.: 921377, Telex: NE 92910(TROSS)

Port Moresby Chamber of Commerce, PO Box 1764, Port Moresby, Tel.: 213077, Telex: NE 22246 CHACOM

Rabaul Chamber of Commerce, PO Box 1335, Rabaul

Road Transport Association of Papua New Guinea Inc., PO Box 2257, Lae, Tel.: 423647, Telex: NE 42522(PABRAM)

Sepik Chamber of Commerce, PO Box 35, Wewak

Society of Professional Engineers, PO Box 793, Lae

Travel Association of Papua New Guinea, PO Box 118, Port Moresby, Tel.: 255922, Telex: NE23360

Western Highlands Chamber of Commerce, PO Box 523, Mount Hagen

Western Highlands Tea Manufacturers'

Association, PO Box 1184, Mount Hagen

HISTORY. Until recently, little was known about the pre-history of Papua New Guinea, and a great deal has yet to be discovered. But modern scientific methods have established that man was in the New Guinea highlands at least by 8000 BC, and it is probable that the first arrival of man in New Guinea was as early as 30,000 years ago.

There appear to have been several migrations from Asia by way of Indonesia over a great length of time — the first ones at a time when sea levels were considerably lower than they are today, and New Guinea and Australia were joined.

The eastward movement from Asia and Indonesia continued on to other islands, including the Solomons, Vanuatu, New Caledonia and Fiji.

The early people were hunters, not agriculturalists, who used bone and stone tools and weapons. Later migrations introduced agriculture, plants such as yams, taro, green vegetables and fruit, pigs and dogs. Along the coast the sago palm and the coconut were bountiful providers, together with seafood.

There was no central government. Each community was virtually its own government, with little contact with other areas except through certain trade links.

The island of New Guinea, especially the part now known as Irian Jaya, was known to seamen and adventurers from Indonesia and the Asian mainland centuries before the first documented sightings. Antonio d'Abreu of Portugal sailed as far east as the Aru islands on the south coast of what is now Irian Jaya, in 1511, but the first definite recorded landing of a European was in 1526, when another Portuguese, Jorge de Meneses, made a landing on the north-west coast and named it Ilhas dos Papuas. Papuas came from the Malay word Papuwah, meaning frizzy-haired, and Meneses is generally credited with being the actual European discoverer of New Guinea.

New Guinea named. The name New Guinea was coined in 1545 by the Spaniard Ortiz Retes, who while attempting to return from the Moluccas to Mexico, sailed along the north coast. The name appeared for the first time in print on Mercator's world map of 1569. The people reminded Retes of those of the Guinea coast of Africa.

Torres arrived in 1606, examined the Louisiade Archipelago and the entire southern coast of Papua and Irian Jaya, passing through Torres Strait and sighting Cape York, in the course of his discoveries.

Dutch vessels also made visits about this time, followed by the English and French up to the 19th century. Among the visitors were Willem Jansz, Le Maire and Schouten, Carstenz, Tasman, Dampier, Carteret, Bougainville (who left his name on Bougainville Island), Cook, and Captains Owen Stanley, John Moresby and Blackwood (in the *Fly*, in which he discovered the mouth of the great river that now bears the ship's name).

The first Englishman to claim any part of New Guinea for Britain was Captain Philip Carteret at New Ireland in 1767. The next was Lieut. Yule in the *Bramble* in 1846 at Cape Possession. Captain Moresby, who named Port Moresby, did so again in 1873 — but no action was taken by Britain, although in the Australian colonies there was considerable interest developing in the political future of the islands.

In 1828, when the Dutch had annexed the Western half of New Guinea (now Irian Jaya), Australia was still a penal settlement but within the next 50 years Australia went a long way towards nationhood and was more closely concerned with events in the area.

Germany, after the end of the Franco-Prussian war of 1870–71, precipitated a scramble by the big powers in the South Pacific and caused considerable alarm in Australia and New Zealand, in regard to her intentions in New Guinea. They were concerned about their own security.

The Australian colonies became so agitated in 1883 that the Premier of the day in Queensland sent the police magistrate at Thursday Island, Henry M. Chester, to Port Moresby, to take possession of south-east New Guinea in the name of Queen Victoria. Chester raised the flag at Port Moresby, then the headquarters of the London Missionary Society and one European trader, on 4 April 1883. It was hoped that Britian, presented with a fait accompli, would ratify Chester's act, but Britain decided against this.

Australia and New Zealand continued to urge Britain to annex that part of New Guinea not already claimed by the Dutch,

and finally, in September 1884, Britain officially informed Germany that she planned to establish a protectorate.

Germany urgently asked that no further action be taken pending clarification of certain points, and while these discussions were continuing, Germany formally hoisted the German flag at three points in north-east New Guinea and the Bismarck Archipelago, and proclaimed a protectorate on 3 November 1884.

Britain, on 6 November 1884, proclaimed a protectorate over the south-east coast and the islands to the east, with an expedition by Commodore Erskine. This area became known as British New Guinea. The borders between British and German New Guinea were officially defined in 1885.

German administration. The German Government exercised authority in its new possession through the South Seas syndicate, which on 15 May 1885, became the New Guinea Company. The company was controlled by a board in Berlin, and head of administration in New Guinea was a governor.

It sought to operate plantations and trading stations, but it was unsuccessful, and after 15 years of muddle and heavy loss the charter of the New Guinea Company was cancelled, and, in 1889, the administration of the colony was taken over directly by the German Government. Earlier, the company had administered the colony's affairs from Finschhafen, then had moved to Stephansort (Bogadjim) and finally to Madang.

The new Governor, Rudolph von Benningsen, shifted headquarters to Herbertshohe, now Kokopo, near Rabaul, and arrangements were much better as the Germans began building up a system of village administration.

Queen Emma. Among the planters and traders who lived under the German administration in those days was Mrs Emma Forsayth, known as 'Queen Emma', who had arrived from Samoa in the late 1870s to become New Guinea's first planter. She and others were established around the Gazelle Peninsula and the Duke of York Islands nearby.

In October 1899, the Germans incorporated the Marianas, Carolines and Marshall Islands (the three groups of Micronesia) into the administration, and on November 8, Bougainville and Buka were included as a result of an agreement with the US and Britain. Nauru was included later.

With the New Guinea Company concentrating on commerce, and a final shift of headquarters from Herbertshohe to Rabaul in 1910, the German colony began to make progress.

Britain and Germany at war. When World War I began in August, 1914, an Australian Expeditionary Force was sent to German New Guinea. It landed near Kokopo on 11 September 1914, and on the following day, after a brief battle with German forces, seized the German radio station at Bita Paka. The German administration surrendered on 14 September and for the next seven years German New Guinea was under an Australian military administration. Few changes were made in the German administrative system.

At the end of the war, all German properties were 'expropriated', and control was vested in the New Guinea Expropriation Board. The properties, mostly plantations, were later put up for tender to private individuals.

The arrangement was that Germany would later repay the value of the properties to those who lost them and returned to Germany. This was done, but acute inflation in Germany made the payments virtually worthless and the former owners were ruined.

League of Nations mandate. On 17 December 1920 the council of the League of Nations gave Australia a 'C' class mandate to govern the former German colony (but not Nauru or Micronesia) and to report regularly. This administration under the mandate remained in force until the Japanese invaded Rabaul on 21 January 1942. The whole of the Mandated Territory of New Guinea thereafter became a theatre of war.

British New Guinea. Meanwhile the protectorate over British New Guinea of 1884 made little progress until 1888, when Dr (later Sir) William MacGregor headed a new administration with greater powers, the responsibility being shared by Britain and Queensland (acting on behalf of the other Australian colonies). The protectorate gave way to annexation the same year.

Administrator MacGregor was an explorer who did much to establish government influence through his travels. He also set up a Legislative Council and established a police force and a system of administration controlled by Resident Magistrates and village constables in various districts.

He wrote a series of reports during his 10 years in office in an effort to prove the country fit for commercial development. But the only outstanding development until 1900 was the discovery of several godfields — Misima and adjacent islands proclaimed in 1889; Woodlark Island proclaimed in 1895; Gira, 1889, and Yodda, 1900. Neither these nor others proclaimed later were very rich and they did little to promote Britiish New Guinea.

The title of Administrator was changed to that of Lieutenant-Governor in March 1895, and MacGregor retired from his post in 1898.

Papua created. The Australian States federated in 1901. The new Federal Government of the Commonwealth of Australia agreed to take responsibility for British New Guinea. But it was several years before it formally did so, through the Papua Act of 1905, which also changed the name of the new Australian possession to the Territory of Papua. The Papua Act came into force on 1 September 1906, and provided a constitution under which Papua would be governed by a Lieutenant-Governor, Executive Council and Legislative Council.

But meanwhile on 18 March 1902, the authority exercised by the Governor of Queensland on behalf of the other former colonies had been transferred to the Governor-General and the new Australian Commonwealth, so there was a period of administrative inactivity and confusion.

The constitutional machinery established by the Papua Act continued right up to 1949, although because of the Japanese invasion of New Guinea in 1942, a military government took over in Port Moresby on 12 February 1942, and civil administration was suspended.

Pacific War. A Japanese force landed at Rabaul on 23 January 1942. It soon overwhelmed the small Australian garrison and volunteers. About 300 civilians and 900 soldiers were captured and later lost their lives when their prison ship, *Montevideo Maru*, was torpedoed en route to Japan.

The Japanese made Rabaul their forward base but went on to establish themselves in the mainland of New Guinea and on the coast of Papua. From there they pushed inland to Kokoda and across the Owen Stanley mountains with the idea of taking Port Moresby from the rear. This plan did not succeed, and by September 1942, the Japanese advance had been halted by American and Australian forces under the command of General Douglas MacArthur; and thenceforward north-eastern Papua, and all of New Guinea, were recovered from the Japanese, district by district.

The Australian New Guinea Administrative Unit was formed in 1942, staffed mostly by experienced former officers of the Papua and New Guinea administrations. Its job was to take over administration of the districts as they were progressively cleared, and by 1944 the Allies were in control of both territories, although some Japanese forces did not surrender until 1945.

ANGAU administered all that part of Papua and New Guinea south of the Markham River until 31 October 1945, when civil administration took over. ANGAU continued to administer the rest until 24 June 1946, when all of the country was put under civil administration.

Administrative union. By this time it had become apparent that it was possible to administer both Papua and New Guinea jointly, and not as separate administrations as happened before the war. By means of the Papua-New Guinea Provisional Administration Act of 1945–46, and the Papua New Guinea Act 1949, and other legislation, the governments of the Australian Territory of Papua and the Trust Territory of New Guinea were gradually integrated, and the new structure functioned as the Administration of Papua and New Guinea.

The League of Nations had meanwhile been replaced by the United Nations Organisation, and Australia's mandate to continue to administer New Guinea under trusteeship was approved by the UN in December 1946.

First Administrator of the combined territories was Colonel J. K. Murray, who remained in office until June 1952.

The decades of the 1950s and 1960s saw great commercial and agricultural development in the combined territory, a similar increase in the numbers in the public service and an eight-fold increase in the non-indigenous population of Papua and New Guinea

in comparison with the pre-war figures.

A great deal of the development and increased activity was from the non-indigenous sector, but from the resumption of civil administration it was made clear that the New Guineans were to be encouraged to take an increasing part in the development of the country.

Parliamentary development. Before the war, both Papua and New Guinea had separate Legislative Councils. In 1951, the first Legislative Council for the combined territories was inaugurated. It had 16 official members, three elected Europeans, and nine nominated members. The Administrator was the president. The council had little authority.

An enlarged council came into being in 1960, but the first big constitutional step did not come until 1964 when a House of Assembly of 64 members was established. It consisted of 10 official members, 44 members elected from open electorates, and 10 members from reserved electorates for which only non-indigenes could stand. Everyone over 21 was entitled to a vote and for the first time the legislative body had a preponderance of indigenous members.

The House of Assembly was enlarged to 94 in 1968 and a Ministerial member system introduced. It was further enlarged for the elections of 1972 to a House of 100 elected members, 82 from open electorates and 18 from regional electorates where candidates were required to have certain educational qualifications. Voting age was reduced to 18.

Self-government and independence. This House of Assembly had the task of preparing the country for self-government, which was declared on 1 December 1973, and for full independence, which came into effect on 16 September 1975. PNG then became a sovereign state within the Commonwealth, with the Queen as Head of State.

The National Identity Bill which was promulgated on 1 July 1971, established the name of the country as Papua New Guinea — thus doing away with the old title of 'Territory' and the 'and' that linked the two names.

At independence, the House of Assembly became the National Parliament, and at the 1977 election it was enlarged to 109 members.

Papua New Guinea's recent history has

been characterised by a number of controversial developments, including a rising crime rate and frequent charges of corruption made against leading political or public figures. Former Commander of the PNG Defence Force and one-time Minister for Forests, Ted Diro, is one of the more recent and significant casualties of inquiries into corruption.

In foreign affairs, the country has begun to pursue a more independent line, relaxing slightly the long reliance and close association with Australia and seeking closer ties with both Pacific Melanesian nations and the nations of South-East Asia, especially Malaysia and Indonesia, the latter once widely regarded as implacably hostile to Papua New Guinea.

Further information. There is a wealth of material on Papua New Guinea, covering many aspects of the country. Among the most useful are Gavin Souter, *New Guinea: The Last Unknown* (Sydney, 1963); C.D. Rowley, *The New Guinea Villager* (Melbourne, 1965); Albert Maori Kiki, *Kiki: Ten Thousand Years in a Lifetime* (Melbourne, 1968); Peter Hastings, *New Guinea: Problems and Prospects* (Melbourne, 1969); Paul Hasluck, *A Time for Building* (Melbourne, 1976). Recent works have concentrated mainly on anthropological or political subjects.

PAPUA NEW GUINEA ISLANDS IN DETAIL

Islands of Milne Bay Province

This area includes Woodlark Island, Louisiade Archipelago and the Trobriand, Laughlan, D'Entrecasteaux and Conflict groups.

Trobriand Islands. The Trobriand Group lies to the north of the D'Entrecasteaux Islands. There are four main islands, and several islets. The islands are all of coral. Some rise abruptly from the shore to a height of 30 m, forming coral cliffs. Others are only just above the surface of the water. They are named after Denis de Trobriand, an officer of the D'Entrecasteaux expedition. The people are more like Polynesians than Melanesians, both in appearance and disposition, and are hospitable. They were made famous to the rest of the world through the work of the anthropologist Malinowski, between 1915–18. Trobriand carvings are exported to centres like Port Moresby and Lae where they

are much sought after by tourists. The people practise a trade and exchange system called Kula. The Trobrianders are considered some of the best gardeners in Papua New Guinea. The soil on some of the coral islands is very rich. This area was the most important in the old Territory of Papua for mother-of-pearl and bêche-de-mer fishing but there is little exported these days. Administative headquarters is at Losuia, on the main island, Kiriwina, where there is also a hospital. There is an airstrip and on Kiriwina lagoon, a hotel which is popular with tourists and weekending Port Moresby residents. The population of the Trobriands is approximately 17,000.

Woodlark. Woodlark Island — or Murua, to give it its native name — was at one time the chief goldfield of Papua. It was here that the first payable goldfield was worked. It received its name from Captain Grimes of the *Woodlark*, of Sydney, around 1836. The island, which is situated north of the Louisiade Archipelago, is about 60 km in length from east to west. There are good anchorages on the south coast, including Guasopa Harbour and Suloga Harbour. The main centre was Kulumadau on the south coast. There is a sub-district office at Guasopa where there is an airstrip. The island comprises a succession of hills and valleys and is covered in parts by dense tropical jungle. The people are Melanesians like those on the east coast of the mainland. The island has been thoroughly prospected. It produced over $1,400,000 worth of gold in the days when the price of gold was far below the present price. From Woodlark Island was obtained so-called 'greenstone' for axes, adzes, chisels and ceremonial stones. The stone is an impure serpentine, almost as hard as the nephrite (jade or greenstone) of New Zealand. For administrative purposes, Woodlark is included in the Losuia district and estimated population is 3,800

Laughlan Group. The Laughlan Group consists of five islands and several islets and rocks, and is some 64 km to the east of Woodlark. Population is about 160. The largest island, Abomat, is located at latitude 9 deg 17 min S and longitude 153 deg 17 min E. The lagoon of this is from 12 to 21 metres deep and is a secure anchorage. There is a plentiful supply of fresh water. The group is composed of coral and sand and only coconuts grow there, with the exception of small patches of sweet potatoes and bananas. There is generally a strong sea running between this group and Woodlark, but provided the weather is favourable they are in constant communication with each other. At present there is a small export trade in ebony.

D'Entrecasteaux Group

Fergusson Island. Fergusson Island is the central island of the D'Entrecasteaux group, with Normanby Island to the southward and Goodenough to the north-west.

Fergusson Is. is 60 km long in a NW and SE direction, with an average width of 25 km and an area of 1345 sq. km. There are three groups of mountains — Mt Kilkerran, 1375 m; Mt Euagwaba, 1220 m to 1525 m and Mt Maybole, 760 m.

From these mountains flow many small rivers and creeks, the principal being the Salamo River, running southerly into Dawson Strait, the Auwopal River, easterly into Hygeia Bay, and the Nuitala River into Hughes Bay, on the north coast. Good anchorages may be obtained at all times at the head of Dawson Strait, Hygeia Bay, and usually along the western coastline.

There is a large population distributed over Fergusson Island, particularly along the southern coastline, where numerous gardens cover a large area of the steep mountain slopes. There are several lakes, the largest of which is Lake Lavu. They are saline, and where evaporation has taken place a white deposit of soluble salts is often seen.

The most interesting features on Fergusson Island are the numbers of extinct volcanoes, hot springs, geysers, fumaroles, and the magnificent deposits of sulphur and geyserite. The geyserite, in parts, has formed beautiful white terraces. Thermal springs occur at Iamalele (Yamalele) and Deidei. Many of these contain sulphur, carbonic acid, gas, iron, alkalis, lithium, etc.

Population is an estimated 15,000, all nationals.

Normanby Island. Normanby Island is about 72 km in length and from 19 km to 24 km at its greatest breadth. It has an area of 1036 sq. km. There is a range of mountains

(Prevost) whose highest peak is 1098 m.

The island is surrounded by deep water and there are some safe harbours — Sewa being the best on the west coast. It was used during World War II by Allied naval vessels. It is a port of call for inter-island small ships.

There is also good anchorage at Maiobari Bay, north of Sewa, where the bay is sheltered by Duchess Island. There is an excellent anchorage just north again where at Ubuia, the United Church has a Hansenide settlement.

Rock carvings in Sewa Bay are of unknown origin but are said to resemble others in Irian Jaya.

The population of Normanby is approximately 12,186.

Goodenough Is. — Dobu Passage. Goodenough Island is separated from the western end of Fergusson Island by Moresby Strait. A mountain range, extending through almost the whole length of the island, culminates in two rugged peaks of about 2440 m. The range is flanked by an extensive plain, which is studded with native groves. Part of the mountain slopes are occupied by terraced gardens, planted with yams. Limestone caves exist on the mountain spurs. Indications of gold have been found in several of the creeks.

Population is 12,681, all nationals.

In the interior of Goodenough Island is a large rock, covered with paintings in black and white. It is regarded by the people with veneration because of its supposed mystical powers over the yam crops. An anthropologist has remarked that the nearest parallel to this rock is found in Central Australia.

Vivigani airstrip on the east coast of Goodenough Island was an Allied airfield developed during the war with Japan. It is used by a scheduled service.

There is a road from Wailagi to Nuatutu to Vivigani and on to Wataluma on the North Coast.

Dobu is a very fertile islet between Normanby and Fergusson Islands, and was originally the headquarters of the Methodist Mission. There is beautiful scenery in the little known Dobu Passage, with ranges rising to 1653 m and 1830 m. Behind these are mountains of 2440 m.

Welle, or Samaroa Island, lies to the east

of Fergusson Island, and is of volcanic origin. It contains an area of about 64 sq. km. It is low-lying, its height in any place not exceeding 90 m.

Louisiade Archipelago

Louis Vaez de Torres is credited with being the European discoverer of this archipelago in August 1606. He also spent 14 days in a bay on the south coast of Sideia Island just east of Samarai. In 1793 Joseph D'Entrecasteaux passed through these waters, and the northern group received his name.

It has been suggested that the Malays and the Chinese knew of the existence of these islands and visited them prior to Europeans.

The archipelago was rich in gold, and up to the Pacific War produced about 4500 kg. Sudest, or Tagula Island. Sudest is the largest island in the group. It is about 80 km in length and 24 km at its greatest breadth. The island is formed by a succession of irregular hills and mountains. The highest point is Mt Rattlesnake, 915 m. Gold has been found in nearly all the watercourses. The rush was at its height in 1889, when many diggers worked the island quite profitably.

Sudest is known also as Tagula. It has an area of 802 sq. km and an approximate population of 2173. There is a provincial office at Tagula on the NW coast.

Rossel Island and others nearby. Rossel Island, situated 25 km to the east of Sudest, is 39 km in length and possesses a most irregular and tortuous coastline. This terminates in the east in Rossel Spit, which has been made famous by the many tales of shipwreck and danger emanating from there. There are traces of gold on the island.

Around Rossel Island are High Heron and Adele (the most easterly island in PNG). Estimated population is 3060. Joannet, about 40 km north of Sudest, contains an area of about 65 sq. km. It is well watered and there are indications of gold.

Misima Island. Misima (or St Aignan) is situated in the NW extreme of the Louisiade Archipelago and has an area of between 223 sq. km and 259 sq. km. The island extends about 40 km in an east and west direction, being irregular in width, varying from 10 km to 11 km, in the eastern portion and tapering suddenly from near the centre of the island to a narrow strip about two or three km wide in the western portion. Bwagaoia is the largest harbour, situated on the south-eastern extreme, and is sheltered by a fringing coral reef, adjacent to a shallow lagoon with an extremely small entrance, but quite suitable for craft up to 500 tonnes. The island is very mountainous, particularly in the western narrow portions.

Mount Oiatau 1037 m, is the highest point to a steep range trending parallel with the island.

There is little swampy country on the island, and consequently few mosquitoes. Gold has been found in many parts of the island, the main fields being near Bwagaoia, in the vicinity of Mt Sisa, with which it was connected by an old steam tramway and at present a ring road servicing the eastern half of the island approximately 65 kilometres in length, linking Bwagaoia with Liak on the north coast and Eiavs on the south coast.

An important gold mining industry was established on Misima between the World Wars and two companies were operating there. There was a township and port at Bwagaoia. The evacuation of these islands by the Europeans when the Japanese invaded in 1942 caused the abandonment of these gold mines, and the industry was not re-established after the war. The most valuable property, Cuthbert's Misima Goldmines Ltd, which had earned fantastic profits in the thirties, liquidated. A new company, Pacific Island Mines Ltd, was successfully floated in Australia in 1959 but by 1969 its interest on Misima had turned from gold to copper. In the 1980s there has been renewed investment in gold prospecting. The estimated population is 8088.

Calvados Chain. Included in the Louisiade Archipelago is the long string of islands known as the Calvados Chain, comprising Mabui, Panasagusagu, Utian (Brooker), Rara, No Ina, Moturina, Basses, Panaroa, Panasia (Real), Vanariwa, Bushy, Leiga, Sabari (Owen Stanley), Laiwan, Bobo Ema, Bonawan, Bagaman (Stanton), Mabneian, Pananumara, Panakrusima (Earle), Abaga Gaheia, Hemenahei, Wanim, Nimoa (Pig), Iyin (Garden), and Ululina. The estimated Calvados population is 2175.

Population of the Louisiades is approximately 16,478, about half of it on Misima.

Conflict

The Conflict Group is about 113 km eastward of Samarai, and is well planted with coconuts. The group consists of more than 20 small islands on a large oval atoll and was named after HMS *Conflict* in 1880. Largest island is Irai, about 5 km long. To the west is the Engineer Group, comprising three main islands.

Samarai. A small island of about 24 ha is a port of entry. As a commercial centre it is being superseded by Alotau, on the mainland. It was until only recent times an important commercial and shipping centre, but it has been eclipsed by Alotau, on the mainland. The island is situated 5 km from the mainland. Captain Moresby in 1873 named it Dinner Island, and in 1878 it was made chief missionary station in south-east Papua for the LMS.

Gurney airstrip, at the head of Milne Bay, is the nearest airport. There are regular air services from Port Moresby to Gurney, and a connecting launch to Samarai from the mainland for passengers, mail and freight.

Samarai, one of the most attractive settlements in Papua pre-war, was burned out by Japanese air raids in 1942. The township and wharf were rebuilt.

The islet is picturesque and beautifully situated, with views up and down China Strait out along the Eastern Passage and across the water to the mountains of the mainland. Post-war growth made it crowded — hence the decision to establish headquarters on the mainland at Alotau. There is a roadway round Samarai and it can be walked in 20 minutes. Population is approximately 864, and the population of Alotau, on the mainland, approximately 4311.

Among the islands within sight of Samarai are Logeia, Sariba, Doini and Kwato. Stretching south-east from the Samarai group of islands lie the following: Dumoulin, Wari, Imbert, Stuers, Quessant, Sable, Kosmann, Lejeune, Duperre, Jomard, Pana Waipona, Montemount and Duchateau.

Islands off New Britain

Witu Islands. These are a group of volcanic origin about 80 km off the north coast, opposite the Talasea Peninsula. The largest are Garove (or Deslacs) about 67 sq. km in area;

Unea (or Merite) 28 sq. km; Mundua, three sq. km; and there are five other smaller islands. There are several extinct volcanoes, all densely forested. The highest is on Unea, 783 m. There are a number of very good coconut and cocoa plantations in this group, and an excellent harbour in Garove — a beautiful, landlocked bay apparently formed when the sea broke into a crater. There once was a very large population in this group but it was decimated by a smallpox epidemic in the first decade of the century. The population has increased steadily in recent years, and now numbers 6750. There are airstrips for light aircraft on Unea and Garove.

Duke of Yorks. The Duke of York group consists of Duke of York Island (8 km by 8 km) and a number of small islands — notably Makada, Ulu (or Mouke, or Pig), Kabakon, Kerawara and Mioko. This group is low, thickly wooded, well populated, contains several plantations, and has a total area of 60 sq. km. Population is approximately 6100. The group is situated in St George's Channel, near Rabaul. The Duke of York group had an important part in the first colonisation of New Guinea. The first Methodist Mission station was located here, at 'Port Hunter', in 1875. Various traders and planters established themselves there about the same time (including Mrs Forsayth, or 'Queen Emma'); and from here they gradually colonised the adjoining Kokopo area of New Britain, then inhabited by formidable tribes. The beginnings of the later powerful German firms of Godeffroy and Hernsheim were here. Kabakon, in 1903, was selected by a man named Engelhardt as the scene of a notable — but vain — attempt to establish a sun-worshipping cult. Other offshore islands of New Britain (East and West Province) are:

Off north coast, west to east — Jamalaure, Galimaruhe, Poi, Nusasi, Talangonai, Kautagi, Tuare, Garua, Banban, Lolobau, Tiwongo, Kakolan, Talele, Lolonakuka.

Off south coast, west to east — Arawe Group (Kaptimati, Marklo, Kumbum, Arawe, Angup, Ablaugi, Pileto), Ganglo, Bugi, Geglep, Aweleng, Amge, Alago, Abungi, Ampul, Lakei, Melinglo, Ayet, Ablingi, Agur, Gasmata, Dililo, Awrin, Amerer, Kiwok, Siwot, Walanguo, Lue,

Lilum, Baronga, Kaskas, Mangrove, Kawauwu, Mockton.

Off Gazelle Peninsula — Watom, Urara.

New Britain itself, a narrow, crescent-shaped island, is the largest and most important unit of the archipelago. It is about 600 km long. The most important town, Rabaul, is situated on the north-east coast. Rabaul's population is approximately 14,954.

The total area of the island is estimated at 37,736 sq. km and as the main breadth is only 80 km, its extreme narrowness can be easily realised. A high and very rugged range of mountains runs along its length.

The highest peak in New Britain is an active volcano, The Father, 2284 m high, on the north-west coast, near which are the two mountains, the North and South Son. Close to Rabaul are three peaks, the Mother and the South and North Daughter, the first named being an extinct volcano.

Volcanic action is very evident throughout New Britain.

New Ireland and its islands

New Ireland, like Manus, is also a province. It consists of the long narrow island of New Ireland, the fairly large island of Lavongal, which is better known as New Hanover, and which has its own offshore islands and islets; the Saint Matthias Group, which is NNW of New Hanover, and groups of small islands that lie east of New Ireland — Tabar, Lihir, Tanga and Feni. Some other islands off the south coast are described under Bougainville. The offshore islands of Lavongai include Mussau, Emirau, Tingwon, and Tench.

New Ireland itself lies at right-angles to the northern end of New Britain. It is 320 km long with an average width of 11 km except in the south where it expands to 50 km and is very mountainous without any rivers of size. Its coastline is fairly broken and its best harbours are at Kavieng (the chief town), Namatanai, Muliana and Kalili. There are more than 400 km of roads down the east coast, and 300 km along the west coast. A large part of the island is under cultivation, particularly on the east coast. Kavieng's population is approximately 4633.

The southern tip of New Ireland was the scene of a French 'South Sea Bubble', when a Frenchman, Marquis de Rays set up a colony at Port Breton, which failed.

Islands off Bougainville

Because of over-population and land shortage the North Solomons Provincial Government is encouraging resettlement on the mainland for some of its offshore population. Land has been selected for them near Kieta. **Nukumanu (Tasman) Islands** lie about 400 km to the north-east of Bougainville, in 4 deg 35 min S latitude and 159 deg 25 min E longitude, on a reef measuring 11 km by 18 km, and on which there are some 40 small islands. The largest is Nukumanu with an area of 2.6 sq. km. The population is almost pure Polynesian stock. There is immigration and inter-marriage from Ontong Java just to the south in the Solomon Islands.

Takau (Marqueen or Mortlock) group is about 195 km north-east of Bougainville, in 4 deg 50 min S latitude, and 157 deg E longitude. This group also is a ring-shaped reef, on which there are about 20 islands with a total area of 85 ha. The largest is Takau. The population is about 500, the main strain being Polynesian, with an admixture of New Britain, Manus and Caroline Islands natives.

Kilinailau (Carteret) Group is about 70 km north-east of Buka, in 4 deg 45 min S latitude and 155 deg 20 min E longitude. There are about six islands which form an almost circular atoll about 16 km in diameter. There is a trading station. The population consists of about 1011 people from Buka, who have apparently displaced a Polynesian population. The islands are planted with coconuts.

Nissan or Green Islands (Sir Charles Hardy) are coral islands in 4 deg 30 min S latitude and 154 deg 15 min E longitude. The atoll is elliptical, and measures about 16 km by 8 km and contains three islands. The greatest height does not exceed 60 metres. Coconuts, native fruit trees and ivory nuts are grown. The population is about 3100. Nissan is the chief island. The other islands are Barahun and Sirot. Within the centre of the atoll is Han Island.

Pinpill, a coral island a little to the north-west of the Nissan Group, is included with the latter for administration purposes. It is planted with coconuts. One of the most important landings of the war in the Southwest Pacific took place on Nissan, which is also known as Green Is. There is an airstrip.

Nuguria (or Fead) Group is about 200 km east of New Ireland and the same distance north of Bougainville, in 3 deg 15 min S latitude and 154 deg 45 min E longitude. It consists of two atolls with some 50 islands, the total of which is only about 5 sq. km. There are coconut plantations on the group. The population, which is mostly Polynesian, numbers about 300.

Bougainville Island itself is about 204 km long (excluding Buka, which is 32 km × 82 km) and varies in width from 65 km to 97 km. The Emperor Range (highest point Mount Balbi, 2745 m), occupies the northern half, and the Crown Prince Range (200 m), the southern half. The interior is wild and broken, jungle clad and inaccessible. Balbi and Bagana (2000 m) are active volcanoes and well-known landmarks. There are numerous small islands along the NE coast and off the NW coast.

There are a few good harbours, the best being at Kieta, Anewa Bay, Tonolei and Buka Passage. Other harbours on the east coast suitable for small craft are Raua, Tinputz, Tiop, Inus, Numa Numa.

On the west coast there is a safe anchorage for small ships at Banoni, and a fair anchorage for small craft at Mamaregu in Gazelle Harbour (Empress Augusta Bay).

Buka Island, to Bougainville's north, is hilly in the southern portion, the highest point reaching to about 400 m. In the south-west there is a mountain range of volcanic origin, and to the north and east the island is of raised coral rock. The interior, except in the south-west, is a lowland of level and undulating country.

Buka is separated from Bougainville by the very narrow Buka Passage.

Along the coast there are large areas of mangroves, and in the interior of Buka, dense forest, with some areas of grass. A great number of low coral islands lie off the south and west coast, and on them, and on the west coast, there are several plantations. The principal harbour is Queen Carola harbour on the west coast.

Buka and its adjacent islands have a population of about 20,000 nationals.

Islands off Morobe

The main islands included in the Morobe Province are the large island of Umboi (Rooke) and the smaller islands of Tolokiwa and Sakar. All are in Vitiaz Strait between the mainland and New Britain. Umboi, 43 km by 24 km, is of volcanic origin, is up to 1370 m high, has an area of 777 sq. km, cultivated, populated in parts and has two good anchorages — Marien Harbour and Luther. Sakar is volcanic and very high, is 34 sq. km in area and has at times been in violent eruption. Tolokiwa, wooded and inhabited, is 39 sq. km in area, and has a conical volcanic peak 1377 m high.

Islands off Madang

Off the coast of Madang Province are three large islands, each running up to a high peak — Manam Island (1800 m), Karbar Island (1835 m) and Long Island (1305 m). Manam or Vulcan Is. is 83 sq. km in area and 15 km offshore. It is inhabited but the volcano that forms practically the whole island is frequently in eruption and at times the whole population has had to be evacuated. Aris is a small island off its western end.

Karkar or Dampier, 362 sq. km in area, is thickly wooded and fertile. It is extensively planted in coconuts.

Bagabag an outlier of Karkar, is a sunken crater with an area of 36 sq. km. It is wooded and inhabited. Long Is. is 48 km from the mainland coast, 414 sq. km in area and has two cone-shaped active craters, in one of which is a lake.

Islands off the Sepik

Off the coast of the East Sepik Province are the islands of Kairiru, Mushu, Schouten Group, Tendayne, Valif and a number of small islets of little consequence. The islands of Aua and Wuvulu are also administered from Wewak. These islands, on the extreme north-western ocean fringe of Papua New Guinea, are officially part of Manus Province.

The islands off the East Sepik coast range from upthrust coral islands to volcanic islands, some with active and others with dormant craters. They are all thickly populated and some support coconut plantations.

Manus and its islands

Manus consists of a scattered province

stretching between the equator and 3 deg S latitude and between 143 deg E longitude and 149 deg E longitude. The islands consist of Admiralty, Hermit, Ninigo, Anchorite, Pelleluhu and Nauma groups. Manus, the largest in the group, is 96 km long by 32 km wide. Most of the population lives on Manus Island. It is heavily timbered and has a poor agricultural potential due to the broken nature of the region and generally low fertility of the soil. A central range of hills rises to 720 m.

Lou Island, some 32 km due south of Los Negros Island, is notably more fertile; this is due to its volcanic origin.

Nearly all of the small islands are low-lying atolls. They are covered with a very shallow topsoil in which coconuts but little else will grow.

The Hermits and Ninigo atolls, about 320 km north-west of Manus Island, have a population of about 700.

At the eastern end of Manus is Los Negros Island, separated from the main island by the extremely narrow Loniu Passage, the northern end of which runs into Seeadler Harbour. Lorengau is on the western side of Seeadler Harbour. Lorengau, Seeadler Harbour, Loniu Passage and Los Negros Island together provided the site for the huge Manus naval and air base built by the Americans at great cost during the Pacific war, and later abandoned.

Manus is closest to Micronesia and the old names of the many small islands that surround Manus Island within a radius of 60 km are all that remain to indicate that the Spanish saw some of them several centuries ago. Their official names and those by which they were originally known are: Sabben; Alim (Elizabeth); Baluan (St Patrick); Sivesa (Fedarb, Seppressa); Horno; Los Reyes; Pak (San Gabriel); Mbuke (Sugarloaf); St Andrew; Lou (St George); Rambutyo (Jesu Maria); Johnston; Pam (Maitland); Lambutin (San Miguel); Ton (San Rafael).

The North Western Islands lie from 290 to 320 km north-west of Lorengau and are atolls. The islands of Wuvulu and Aua are much closer to Wewak, in East Sepik Province.

The main atolls in this North Western group are Anchorites or Kaniet — five large islets scattered along the reef, at 0 deg 55

min S latitude 145 deg 30 min E longitude. Sae or Commerson, a large atoll with two islets, is at 0 deg 45 min S latitude 145 deg 15 min E longitude.

The Hermits is a large atoll supporting four large islets. Djalon, Maron, Akib and Luf, and a number of small islets. There was a famous plantation and home established at Maron in German times but the home has been demolished. Ninigo Group consists of large islets scattered over half a dozen atolls.

There has been much settlement and planting of these atolls from earliest European times and they also supported a healthy Micronesian population, but contact with Europeans almost depopulated the group in the early years of this century. Population is now increasing, although the people are no longer pure Micronesian.

Manu or Allison, Aua or Durour, and Wuvulu or Maty, are about 50 to 65 km west of the Ninigos, and are now administered from Wewak, for convenience.

In recent years there were plans for developing Wuvulu, which has an indigenous population, as a tourist resort. It has an airstrip.

FOR THE TOURIST. Papua New Guinea is no Pacific atoll. With its mainland, archipelagoes and offshore islands it is continental in scope and presents vast contrasts in climate, scenery and terrain. Every province has its own attractions. Publicity and travel information is mostly in the hands of the airlines and travel agents, particularly Air Nuigini, which produces regular tourist brochures dealing with all aspects of the country.

Entry formalities. All visitors must have a passport, but those from many areas, including Australia, New Zealand and the US, if bona fide tourists, are granted a visa upon arrival in Port Moresby provided their stay in PNG does not exceed 30 days, and they have return air fares and sufficient funds for their support while in PNG. Vaccinations and inoculations are optional for travellers arriving in PNG from Australia. Visitors are advised to take anti-malarial tablets before arriving in the country and during their stay, as a precautionary measure.

Airport tax. Departing travellers pay an airport tax of K10.

Duty free facilities. A limited range of duty free goods is available at Jackson's Airport, Port Moresby.

Places to see. Most visitors arrive in the national capital, which is the main gateway to Papua New Guinea, and from there make their plans to visit other areas. Organised package tours usually turn out to be best value for the average visitor, because of the comparatively high cost of air fares in PNG where the aircraft is often the only means of getting anywhere, and package tours can usually hold down the cost of hotel accommodation. Air travel is the best way to see the most of Papua New Guinea.

Port Moresby, and the National Capital District have come a long way since the end of World War II, when the town was a sleepy little tropical port. It has long since sprawled into a busy city across the hills and far out beyond the airport. The area known as Waigani is where the Government offices and embassies are found. The imposing Parliament building here is well worth a visit.

The old town area around the harbour has lost much of the bustle and significance it had for many years, although it is unlikely to lose its commercial importance because of the port.

With its good climate, splendid harbour and blue water on both sides, Port Moresby is attractive, except at the end of the dry season when it can be dusty, brown and parched. Port Moresby is a growing city with where there are department stores, hotels, cinemas, clubs and adequate taxi services.

A number of firms run full or half day tours in Port Moresby, around the city itself or to points of interest in the surrounding countryside. Alternatively, visitors can hire rental cars from several firms in Port Moresby and suburbs.

Outside National Capital limits, longer trips can be taken to Bomana War Cemetery, about 16 km out of Port Moresby, or to Rouna Falls, the Sogeri Tableland, and Variarata National Park. Rouna Falls are large and spectacular in the wetter times of the year, and accessible. They occur where the Laloki River plunges off the tableland that forms the foothills of the Owen Stanley Range, and a steep road winds up above the falls to the monument that marks the start of the wartime Kokoda Trail and from there on, the area is devoted to rubber plantations.

The national park is splendid, with long views of the coast from the top of the ranges. A good park road makes it easily accessible.

There are several travel agencies in Port Moresby plus the travel departments of the big firms, shipping companies, airline offices and hotels.

Shows. Most of the provinces of Papua New Guinea have an occasional 'show'. These were originally designed to exhibit the local produce of primary and secondary industry, however, they also have all the elements of a country fair where thousands of Papua New Guineans gather to dance, sing and feast and hundreds of visitors arrive to watch and to photograph.

The shows that attract the biggest attendances are those held at Goroka, Eastern Highlands, and Mount Hagen, Western Highlands.

Other dancing and feasts, generally known as 'sing-sings' are organised for special local occasions; or smaller versions can be arranged for large groups of tourists or cruise ships.

War cemeteries. Three war cemeteries in Papua New Guinea are much visited by touring parties.

The cemeteries are at Bomana, near Port Moresby; at Lae; and at Bita Paka not far from Rabaul.

Each of the three cemeteries is of individual plan, designed to make best use of local surroundings, and all are, in fact, beautifully kept parks, characterised by dignified stonework — in gateways, entrances, memorials and pavilions — and by green lawns and brilliant flowers, shrubs and trees.

Cruises and 'adventures'. Of growing importance are 'adventure tours' and island cruises. The adventure tours can be sophisticated or designed for the back-packers, with camping out and canoeing down fairly savage rivers, and are now run by a number of operators.

On an adventure tour you can climb to the top of Mt Wilhelm, PNG's highest peak at 4800 m, dive in the clear waters off Madang, raft down the Watut River, trek across the famous wartime Kokoda Trail, or retrace the steps of the early goldminers. These are a good way of seeing the 'real' Papua New Guinea, because despite the big populations of the urban areas, most Papua New Guineans still live in the mountain valleys.

Cruising, whether down the Sepik River or among the small and beautiful coral islands off the east coast of the mainland, is the way to see a different side of PNG. Off the east coast there is a Polynesian strain among the islanders, and certainly life there can be the typical fish and coconuts style of the traditional South Sea Islander.

There are several fairly large touring vessels operating, and it is possible to choose a cruise that will show you a large part of the PNG coastline and the offshore islands, with all accommodation abroad.

Melanesian Explorer. Melanesian Tourist Services in Madang have a very comfortable, small cruise ship which takes seven day trips through the islands of Milne Bay or along the Sepik River. The company has tried to ensure that passengers see as much traditional culture as possible as well as providing onboard facilities including a library, films and a very well informed 'cruise director', to give background information on the area. Villages are visited, dugouts are used for side transport, the flora and fauna are examined and explained (including crocodiles!) and access is gained to a variety of fine handicrafts from the region. The capacity passenger complement is only 30, thus avoiding the feeling of being part of a herd of foreigners. This trip is highly recommended. Contact Melanesian Tourist Services, PO Box 707, Madang. Tel. 82 2766.

Highlands life is entirely different. A tour from, say, Lae on the nouth coast by road along the famous Highlands Highway to its farthest ends, is still a unique travelling experience. It is not a trip that should be rushed through, with at least a week being allocated. Similarly, a holiday at the Bensbach wildlife lodge in Western PNG, is an experience which is different.

There is plenty of history to be found, particularly of the old German times in Rabaul, on New Britain, where there are also many relics of the long wartime Japanese occupation of that area.

It is impossible to list all the attractions of Papua New Guinea, because there is such a variety of experience available to the tourist.

To date tourism has not been given high priority by the Government, as PNG's economy is based on agriculture and mining, and is likely to continue to be.

ACCOMMODATION. Accommodation is generally expensive and price is not a reliable indication of quality. This list has been made alphabetically and is not meant to be a guide to standards. Because tourism has had a low priority in PNG many accommodations have not been successful and have been allowed to deteriorate, although prices have not been lowered accordingly. Many of the small places in more remote areas are built of traditional Melanesian materials and facilities are very basic indeed. It is very difficult to get any detailed lists of accommodations from the authorities; good travel agents should be able to supply information on the few facilities which are rated at the top of the market. Many of the small guest houses and lodges are left over from the days of colonial administration and were used by government officers as they moved through their territories. Many of the church guest houses were originally built to house their workers but will take in travellers as required and if room is available.

The term 'restaurant' listed in many of the outlying accommodations must be taken very lightly. Meals are likely to be of the most basic kind and probably only available if requested early in the day.

NATIONAL CAPITAL DISTRICT

Boroko Hotel: 36 rooms, aircon, restaurant, bar. PO Box 1033, Boroko. Tel.: 25 6677.

Civic Guest House: 22 rooms, shared facilities, bed and breakfast tariff. PO Box 1139, Boroko. Tel.: 25 5091

Country Women's Association: 4 rooms, shared facilities including kitchen. PO Box 1222, Boroko. Tel.: 25 3646.

Davara Hotel: 80 rooms, pools, restaurant, bar, close to Ela Beach. PO Box 799, Port Moresby. Tel.: 21 2100.

Gateway Motel: 35 rooms, some aircon, bar, restaurant, close to airport. PO Box 1215, Boroko. Tel.: 25 3855.

Islander Hotel: 96 rooms, restaurant and bar, close to government offices. PO Box 1981, Boroko. Tel.: 25 5955.

Kokoda Trail Motel: 16 rooms, restaurant, pool, bar, approximately 40 km from Port

Moresby. PO Box 5014, Boroko.
Tel.: 21 7422.

Kone Hotel: 10 rooms, PO Box 407,
Boroko. Tel.: 21 1879.

Loloata Island Resort. 9 rooms, all
inclusive tariff. PO Box 5290, Boroko.
Tel.: 25 8590.

Mapang Guest House: 9 rooms, bed and
breakfast tariff. Lahara Road, Boroko.
Tel.: 25 5251.

Papua Hotel: 46 rooms, some aircon,
restaurant and bar, in central Port Moresby.
PO Box 92, Port Moresby. Tel.: 21 2622.

Port Moresby Travelodge: 188 rooms,
aircon, restaurants, bars, pool, shops,
conference facilities, centrally located.
PO Box 3661, Port Moresby. Tel.: 21 2266.

Owen Stanley Lodge: 6 rooms, share
facilities, tariff includes all meals, at
Woitape. PO Box 6036, Boroko.

Rabao Mareana Hotel: 10 people, tariff
includes all meals. Coral Sea Travel Service,
Port Moresby. Tel.: 21 4474.

Red Shield Holiday House: 1 cottage
sleeping 5 people, close to start of Kokoda
Walking Trail. PO Box 1323, Boroko.
Tel.: 25 5507.

Rouna Hotel: 6 rooms, shared facilities,
restaurant and bar, close to Rouna Falls.
PO Box 67, Port Moreby. Tel.: 28 1146.

Salvation Army Hostel: 15 rooms, share
facilities including kitchen facilities, near
Koki markets. PO Box 245, Port Moresby.
Tel.: 21 7683.

Tapini Hotel: 7 rooms, tariff includes all
meals, at Tapini. PO Box 19, Tapini.
Tel.: Tapini 28.

YMCA Hostel: 4 rooms, bed and breakfast
tariff, restaurant, share facilities, women and
couples only. PO Box 1883, Boroko.
Tel.: 25 6604.

LAE AND MOROBE

Dregerhafen Lodge: 3 units, share cooking
facilities. PO Box 126, Finschhafen, Morobe.
Tel.: 44 7050.

Finschhafen Community Hostel: 4 rooms,
share facilities. PO Box 196, Finschhafen,
Morobe. Tel.: 44 7046.

Huon Gulf Motel: 30 rooms, aircon pool,
restaurant and bar. PO Box 612, Lae.
Tel.: 42 4844.

Hotel Cecil: 30 rooms, tariff includes
breakfast. PO Box 12, Lae. Tel.: 42 3674.

Klinkii Lodge: 20 rooms, share facilities,
meals available. PO Box 192, Lae.
Tel.: 42 1281.

Lae Lodge: 75 rooms, some share facilities,
restaurant, bar, pool, tennis courts.
PO Box 2774, Lae. Tel.: 42 2000.

Lutheran Mission: Small guest house, share
facilities, tariff includes breakfast. c/- Post
Office, Lae.

Melanesian Hotel: 67 rooms, restaurant,
bar, pool. PO Box 756, Lae. Tel.: 42 3744.

Pine Lodge Hotel: Bulolo, 16 rooms, share
facilities, restaurant, pool. PO Box 26,
Bulolo. Tel.: 44 5220.

Salvation Army Hostel: 5 rooms, share
facilities, cooking facilities. PO Box 259,
Lae. Tel.: 42 2487.

Wau Ecology Institute: 5 houses plus
10 room hostel, share facilities, cooking
equipment. PO Box 77, Wau. Tel.: 44 6207.

WESTERN HIGHLANDS PROVINCE

Baiyer River Bird Sanctuary Lodge:
7 rooms, share facilities, cooking
equipment. PO Box 490, Mt Hagen.
Tel.: 52 1482.

Hagen Park Hotel: 32 rooms, restaurant,
bar. PO Box 81, Mt Hagen. Tel.: 52 1388.

Highlander Hotel: 38 rooms, tariff includes
breakfast. PO Box 34, Mt Hagen.
Tel.: 52 1355.

Kimininga Hostel: 37 rooms, share
facilities, restaurant, tariff includes
breakfast. PO Box 408, Mt Hagen.
Tel.: 52 1865.

Kunguma Haus Poroman: sleeps 6, cooking
facilities provided. PO Box 1182, Mt Hagen.
Tel.: 52 1957.

Kundiawa Hotel: 10 rooms, share facilities,
bar. PO Box 12, Kundiawa. Tel.: 75 1033.

Mt Hagen Missionary Home: small guest
house, share facilities, tariff includes
breakfast. PO Box 394, Mt Hagen.
Tel.: 52 1041.

Plumes and Arrows Inn: 16 rooms,
restaurant, bar, pool. PO Box 86, Mt
Hagen. Tel.: 55 1555.

EASTERN HIGHLANDS PROVINCE

Bird of Paradise Motel: 55 rooms, pool,
restaurant, bar. PO Box 12, Goroka.
Tel.: 72 1144.

Kainantu Lodge: 17 rooms, meals available.
PO Box 31, Kainantu. Tel.: 77 1021.

Lantern Lodge: Restaurant, bar.
PO Box 769, Goroka. Tel.: 72 1776.
Minogere Lodge: 57 rooms, share facilities,
restaurant, bar, tariff includes breakfast.
PO Box 450, Goroka. Tel.: 72 1009.
National Sports Institute: Large
accommodation block, share facilities,
sports facilities, restaurant. PO Box 3377,
Goroka.

SIMBU PROVINCE
Chimbu Lodge: 20 rooms, restaurant, bar.
PO Box 191, Kundiawa. Tel.: 72 1144.

ENGA PROVINCE
Kaiap Orchid Lodge: 10 rooms, share
facilities, tariff includes meals. PO Box 193,
Enga Province. Tel.: 52 2087.
Wabag Lodge: 14 rooms, share facilities.
PO Box 2, Enga Province. Tel.: 57 1069.

SOUTHERN HIGHLANDS PROVINCE
Mendi Hotel: 24 rooms, share facilities,
restaurant, bar. PO Box 108, Mendi.
Tel.: 59 1188.

MADANG AND ENVIRONS
Coastwatchers Motel: 14 rooms, aircon,
pool, restaurant. PO Box 324, Madang.
Tel.: 82 2684.
CWA Cottage: 4 rooms, share facilities,
cooking equipment. PO Box 154, Madang.
Tel.: 82 2216.
Jais Aben Resort: 16 rooms, some units
contain cooking facilities, restaurant, bar,
pool. PO Box 105, Madang. Tel.: 82 3311.
Lutheran Guest House: 4 rooms, tariff
includes meals. PO Box 211, Madang.
Tel.: 82 2589.
Madang Resort Hotel: 40 rooms,
restaurant, bar, beachside. PO Box 111,
Madang. Tel.: 82 2655.
Plantation Hotel: 7 units, restaurant, bar,
diving equipment available. PO Box 302,
Madang. Tel.: 82 3176.
Saimon Tewa's Guest House: share
facilities, located on Siar Island, meals
available. PO Box 887, Madang.
Smith Keenan's Guest House: share
facilities, located on Siar Island, meals
available. PO Box 792, Madang.
Smugglers' Inn: 50 rooms, variety of
accommodations, restaurant, bar,
waterfront location. PO Box 303, Madang.
Tel.: 82 2744.

THE SEPIK REGION
Angoram Hotel: 40 rooms, aircon,
restaurant, bar. PO Box 35, Angoram.
Tel.: 52 1589.
Narimo Hotel: Tariff includes breakfast.
PO Box 42, West Sepik Province.
Tel.: 98 1102.
Sepik Motel: 16 rooms, aircon.
PO Box 51, Wewak. Tel.: 86 2422.
Sepik International Beach Resort:
33 rooms, some aircon, restaurant, bar.
PO Box 20, Wewak. Tel.: 86 2155.
Tamara Hotel: All inclusive tariff.
PO Box 72, Aitape. Tel.: 87 2060.
Windjammer Motel: 35 rooms, variety of
accommodations, restaurant, bar, beach
location. PO Box 152, Wewak.
Tel.: 86 2548.
Vanimo Guest House: PO Box 35,
Vanimo. Tel.: 87 1113.

THE GULF REGION AND
WESTERN REGION
Bensbach Wildlife Lodge: 12 rooms, share
facilities, restaurant, bar, located in wildlife
sanctuary, tariff all inclusive, PO Box 371,
Mt. Hagen. Tel.: 52 1483.
Daru Guest House: 6 rooms, share
facilities, tariff includes breakfast.
PO Box 62, Daru. Tel.: 65 9016.
Daru Hotel: 14 rooms, some aircon,
restaurant. PO Box 6, Daru. Tel.: 65 9120.
Hotel Kerema: 8 rooms, share facilities,
restaurant, bar. PO Box 25, Kerema.
Tel.: 68 1041.
Ihu Guest House: 3 rooms, share facilities,
tariff all inclusive. c/- Post Office, Ihu.

ORO PROVINCE
Christian Training Centre: Share facilities,
tariff includes all meals. PO Box 126,
Popondetta.
Kofure Village Guest House: 18 rooms,
share facilities, tariff includes all meals. c/-
Post Office, Tufi.
Konambu Lodge: 7 rooms, share facilities,
tariff includes all meals. c/- Post Office,
Tufi.
Lamington Hotel: 18 rooms, some aircon,
restaurant, bar. PO Box 27, Popondetta.
Tel.: 29 7152.
Mirigina Lodge: 7 rooms, share facilities,
tariff includes all meals. c/- Post Office,
Tufi.

Waijuga Park Guest House: 14 rooms, share facilities, tariff includes all meals. c/- Wanigela Post Office.

MANUS PROVINCE
Lorengau Hotel: 6 rooms, bar. PO Box 86, Lorengau. Tel.: 40 9093.
Lorengau Kohai Lodge: 12 rooms, restaurant, bar, diving facilities. PO Box 100, Lorengau. Tel.: 40 9004.
Campbell's Inn: all inclusive tariff. PO Box 37, Lorengau. Tel.: 40 9008.

NEW IRELAND PROVINCE
Kavieng Hotel: 34 rooms, some aircon, bar, restaurant. PO Box 4, Kavieng. Tel.: 94 2199
Kavieng Club: 8 rooms, some aircon, restaurant, bar. PO Box 62, Kavieng. Tel.: 94 2027.
Namatanai Hotel: 4 rooms, meals, bar. PO Box 48, Namatanai. Tel.: 94 3057.

NEW BRITAIN
Hoskins Hotel: 15 rooms, meals, bar. c/- Post Office, Hoskins. Tel.: 93 5113.
Kaivuna Motel: PO Box 395, Rabaul. Tel.: 92 1766.
Kulau Lodge: PO Box 359, Rabaul. Tel.: 92 2115.
New Britain Lodge: PO Box 296, Rabaul. Tel.: 92 2247.

New Guinea Club: PO Box 40, Rabaul. Tel.: 92 1801.
Palm Lodge Hotel: 35 rooms, bar, restaurant. PO Box 32, Kimbe. Tel.: 93 5001.

NORTH SOLOMONS PROVINCE
Arovo Holiday Island: 16 rooms, some aircon, restaurant, bar, tennis. PO Box 44, Kieta. Tel.: 95 1855.
Buka Luman Guest House: 10 rooms, all inclusive tariff, bar. PO Box 251, Buka Passage. Tel.: 96 6057.
Davara Motel: 43 rooms, restaurant, bar. PO Box 241, Kieta. Tel.: 95 6175.
Hotel Kieta: 27 rooms, aircon, bar, restaurant. PO Box 22, Kieta. Tel.: 95 6277.

MILNE BAY PROVINCE
Kainakwau Lodge: tariff all inclusive. PO Box 36, Losuia.
Kinale Guest House: PO Box 88, Samarai. PO Box 62 1239.
Kiriwina Lodge: 18 rooms, meals, bar. PO Box 2, Losuia. Tel.: 61 1250.
Masurina Lodge: 28 rooms, some aircon, tariff includes all meals. PO Box 5, Alotau. Tel.: 61 1098.
Provincial Government Hostel: All inclusive tariff. PO Box 104, Alotau. Tel.: 61 2095.

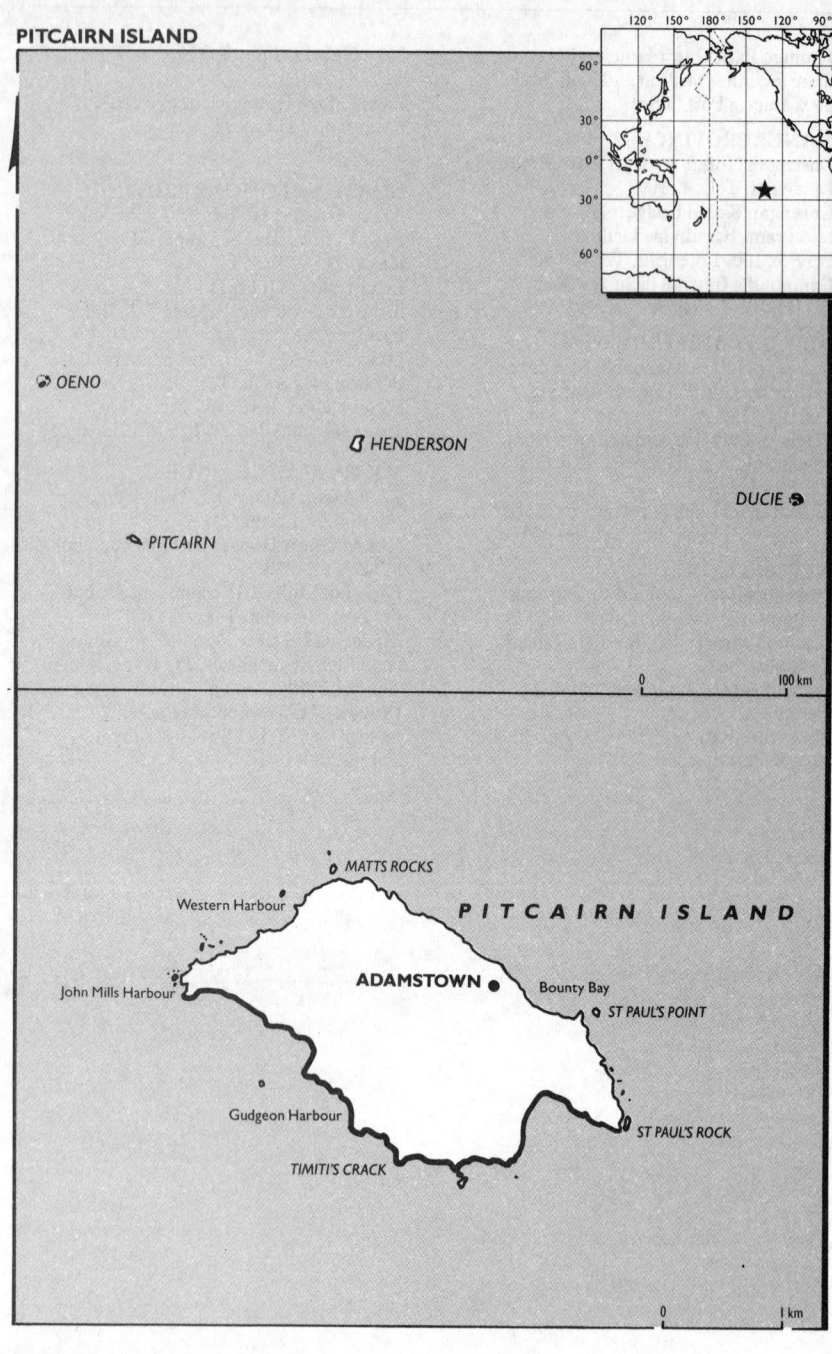

OENO

HENDERSON

DUCIE

PITCAIRN

0   100 km

MATTS ROCKS

Western Harbour

PITCAIRN ISLAND

John Mills Harbour

ADAMSTOWN ●   Bounty Bay

ST PAUL'S POINT

Gudgeon Harbour

ST PAUL'S ROCK

TIMITI'S CRACK

0   1 km

Pitcairn Islands

This is a British dependency, Pitcairn Island itself being a small irregular-shaped island only 3 km long by 1.5 km wide, with a total land area of about 450 ha. Included in the district are three uninhabited islands, Oeno, Ducie and Henderson, which is why the group is called Pitcairn Islands. Pitcairn is about 2160 km south-east of Tahiti, at 25.04 deg S latitude and 130.06 deg W longitude.

Population is about 58. An Island Council manages local affairs and there is also a Governor, who is the British High Commissioner based in Wellington, New Zealand. New Zealand dollars and cents are official currency.

THE PEOPLE. Today's inhabitants are mostly the descendants of the *Bounty* mutineers. Of the 48 local people and 11 'non-Pitcairners' in the islands in mid-1988, most were in the 16–55 age group. Many of the community have migrated over the years, particularly to New Zealand, and the population has been steadily dropping. Of the Pitcairner residents there were 25 Christians, 13 Warrens, 7 Youngs and 3 Browns. A century ago, McCoy was the most common name on Pitcairn, but there is none there now.

Adamstown is the only settlement, consisting of a scattering of houses, many of them now abandoned, and some public buildings, including a school. The settlement, original home of the mutineers, is situated on a northerly slope about 130 m above sea level, and covers about 25 ha of parklike land. There are many paths and lanes.

Language. English is the official language and is taught in the school, but the dialect of Pitcairn is a mixture of English and Tahitian, with the former predominating. Visitors may hear a softly-slurred English which is perfectly comprehensible, but among themselves the islanders may lapse into speech which is hard to understand. They also use unusual local place names in conversation, such as John Catch a Cow, Where Tom off, Timiti's Crack, Up in Ti, Down Cask, Up the Beans.

Religion. The islanders are firm adherents of the Seventh-day Adventist faith. An SDA pastor is permanently stationed on the island.

Lifestyle. One of the highlights of community life is the ringing of different peals of bells to mark such events as times of worship, public entertainment, participation in public work, or occasionally to signal the approach of a ship, when everybody hastens to the landing.

The public square is the heart of Pitcairn. Here there are buildings which serve as courthouse, Island Magistrate's office, community hall, church, dispensary, library and post office. Outside the court house stands one of the anchors from the *Bounty*. In the church is kept the famous Bible from the *Bounty*, on permanent loan to Pitcairn from the Connecticut Historical Society.

Community recreation is not deeply rooted in the island, but there are occasional picnics, frequent birthday parties, fishing and goat hunting, basket-weaving, swimming or children's games around the landing at Bounty Bay, video watching or community cricket games with local rules and many players a side.

Citizenship. Pitcairners have British Dependent Territories citizenship.

GOVERNMENT. Management of internal affairs is in the charge of an Island Council, normally meeting monthly under the chairmanship of the Island Magistrate, in whom are vested executive as well as judicial powers.

The council is composed of the Magistrate, two elected councillors, the Chairman of the Internal Committee, the Island Secretary, three nominated members (one appointed by the Governor and two by the elected members), and two advisory members (one appointed by the Governor and one by the council). The Island Education Officer also acts as Government Adviser but has no vote on the council.

Elections for the Island Council are held annually on Christmas Day, but the Island Magistrate is elected on a three-year term. Residents aged 18 or over, and who have lived three years on the island, are entitled to vote. Candidates for the post of Magistrate must have had 21 years' residence, and councillors five years.

Posts of Island Secretary and other local government officials, such as Postmaster, Radio Officer and Police Officer, are appointed by the Governor after consultation with the council. They are part-time posts which include modest cash allowances.

The council is empowered to enact regulations, but the Governor may revoke or alter them. In practice, there is rarely alteration to council decisions.

The Internal Committee of the council comprises a chairman and other members, which the council may appoint, and its principal task is directing the local work programme.

Justice. There is an Island Court consisting of the Island Magistrate and two assessors. Its jurisdiction is limited to offences under the island code, really local by-laws and to civil actions. Its ability to jail or fine is limited. The Island Magistrate also has summary jurisdiction of his own, which is further limited.

There is provision for a Supreme Court of Pitcairn, and for another court subordinate to the Supreme Court but distinct from the Island Court. But these are provisions only, for the Island Court itself is rarely required to sit.

Liquor and gambling. There are no liquor regulations, or liquor sales on the island, which is traditionally 'dry'. Nor is there any gambling. The importation of liquor without a licence is prohibited.

EDUCATION. Education is free and compulsory. Schooling for children between 6 and 15 was in the hands of the SDA church until 1948, when a school teacher was seconded from the New Zealand Department of Education, teaching to the NZ syllabus. There have been education officers appointed on the same basis ever since. The teacher also acts as Government Adviser. Secondary education for those over the age of 15 is available in New Zealand. It is free, with passage, boarding fees and holiday travel paid for. Management of the Pitcairn School is in the hands of the Education Officer and a local maintenance team.

LABOUR. The manufacturer of carvings and other artefacts for sale to passengers on passing ships or through mail orders provides many people with an income.

The law requires all men between 16 and 65 to make themselves available for public work. This is directed by the Island Council and might necessitate building repairs, road work or the maintenance of the all-important boats at Bounty Bay.

HEALTH. There is no permanent doctor. There is a well-stocked dispensary and by tradition the pastor's wife must be a trained nurse. Occasionally medical help is received from passing ships, and medical advice in an emergency has also been received from overseas via the two-way radio. Surgical cases have sometimes been evacuated to New Zealand or Tahiti, although there is no prompt or reliable means for doing this. Specialist treatment is free to pensioners, but for others, two-thirds of the cost including travel, accommodation and hospital fees are met from Pitcairn funds. Visits to Pitcairn by dental and medical teams are also funded locally.

THE LAND. Pitcairn is a steep island, with a rugged coastline. Highest point is about 350 m above sea level. There are no streams, but abundant rainfall ensures fresh water, and the island is most productive. Soil is volcanic and very fertile. The islanders grow many fruits and vegetables, including citrus, sugarcane, watermelons, bananas, yams, taro, beans, pumpkin and coconuts. The fruit trees usually have large crops. The island is well stocked with wild goats and poultry. Fish are plentiful and fishing is a popular pursuit.

Most of the gardens lie on the more gentle slopes to the south and west of Adamstown, although fruit trees are everywhere.

When Carteret sighted the island in 1767 he reported it was mostly entirely covered with trees, but clearing and burning which followed settlement has resulted in there being only a remnant of the original forest at the western tip of the island. Some steps towards forest regeneration have been taken. Miro (*Thespesia populnea*) is one of the most sought after timbers; it is used for woodcarving. It is taken from Henderson Island or the council's plantations on Pitcairn.

Climate. Mean monthly temperatures vary from 18°C in August to 24°C in February, the absolute range being from about 11 to 33°C. Average rainfall is about 1680 mm annually, fairly evenly spread through the year. July and August are the driest months and November the wettest. Rainfall for 1983 was 1830 mm, with rain recorded on 178 days.

Fauna and flora. There is no especially distinctive flora on the island, and the only native mammal is the Polynesian rat. Other animals, such as cats and goats, have been introduced but there are no pigs or cattle and in 1982 there was only one dog. Most of Pitcairn's birds are oceanic and migrant, and of the land birds most are to be found on the outlying islands of Henderson, Oeno and Ducie. Henderson has a unique flightless chicken bird. Of the birds breeding on Pitcairn the best known are the Fairy Tern and the Common Noddy.

Land tenure. Land is held under a system of family ownership based on the original division of the island by Fletcher Christian but modified over the years. There were new divisions, perhaps better described as acquisitions, following the return of some few families to Pitcairn after the wholesale move to Norfolk Island in 1856 (see History).

Under a system of bilateral inheritance, a wife's land passes to her husband, and ownership of land on the island is thus something of a patchwork quilt, with many scattered small holdings by families. The falling population has further complicated the situation, with plots of land owned by former residents who may never return. In 1985 a cadastral survey of Adamstown and surrounding areas was undertaken by a surveyor from the UK. This helped to clear up some

of the confusion over land boundaries.

Any temporary scarcity of good land (premium is placed on flattish land near Adamstown) is taken care of by a system of 'borrowing', under which an owner grants rights to a borrower for food gardens or housing for as long as he remains on Pitcairn. There is no legislation to prevent land alienation to foreigners, but in fact this does not happen.

TRADE AND FINANCE. Pitcairn's revenue is derived mainly from the sale of postage stamps overseas, interest from investments, and from irregular British development grants. Government expenditure is on administration services, such as radio communications and agriculture, and on education, health, works and the post office. Postal expenses for many years have been the largest single expenditure. Total Government expenditure for the 1985/86 financial year was $NZ773,400.

There are no records of the total income earned by Islanders from curio sales. Bartering is an important part of life, either among individuals or on behalf of the whole community when fruit and vegetables are exchanged for other goods with visiting ships or yachts. The regular supply ships carry Pitcairn cargo freight free with the exception of fuel and motor vehicles. This keeps prices down at the Pitcairn Co-operative store.

In 1987 five Japanese fishing boats agreed to pay $50,000 for a one-year agreement with the Pitcairn Islanders which would allow them to operate within the 200-mile fishing zone. The fishermen will not be able to fish within the 12-mile limit but will be able to land to purchase supplies.

Postage stamps. Pitcairn went without stamps, and finally used New Zealand postage stamps until October 1940, when it established its most important revenue-earner.

Taxes. There are no income taxes, tariffs or duties. There are some minor licence fees.

TRANSPORT. There is no airstrip on the island and the number of visiting ships has declined in recent years. In 1985 30 ships called, compared with 38 in 1984 and 11 yachts. Ten years earlier there were 50 ships a year. There are about four scheduled supply vessels calling each year from New Zealand, and other vessels call occasionally.

Some of these visiting ships may fail to make contact with the shore if the weather is bad, for Pitcairn has no wharf and overseas ships must wait in the open sea. Bad weather can prevent the islanders from launching their boats from the jetty at Bounty Bay and getting out through the surf. There have been delays as long as eight months between supply ships.

The facilities at the jetty include boat repair sheds, a slipway, a winch and an unsealed roadway up the steep slope above the bay to what is called The Edge. Harbour improvements have been made twice in the last 10 years with UK aid — the last in 1985 at a cost of £303,000. In March 1987 the Islanders also received a new 10-metre aluminium launch valued at $210,000 to replace the old vessel.

Dirt roads link Adamstown with most frequented parts of the island. These are used by the motorcycles, including some three wheelers, and tractors, but one special feature is still the low-slung, wooden Pitcairn wheelbarrow, used to carry firewood and supplies.

COMMUNICATIONS. Pitcairn keeps regular radio schedules with the outside world through its radio station on a high location known as 'Taro Ground'. The island radio and electrical technician is Mr Kay Brown. There are now four licensed amateur radio operators. VR6TC, the call sign of Tom Christian, MBE, is known by enthusiasts throughout the world. The other call signs are VR6KY, VR6YL and VR6KB. In June 1985 a new radio telephone service was established with New Zealand. There is a partyline telephone service on the island.

A roneoed news sheet called *Pitcairn Miscellany* is published monthly by the Pitcairn Islands education officer, sponsored by the school. There are video TV sets on the island.

WATER, ELECTRICITY. Tank water is used on the island and there are storage wells. Electric power is provided in Adamstown by a diesel generator that operates each morning and evening. Home appliances including freezers are common. Electricity charges are subsidised.

MAJOR OFFICE HOLDERS
Governor:

T. D. O'Leary, British High
Commission, Wellington, New Zealand
Commissioner:
G. D. Harraway, British Consulate-
General, Auckland
Island Magistrate:
Brian Young
Education Officer:
Leon Satt
Radio Operator:
Tom Christian
Internal Committee Chairman:
Jay Warren

HISTORY. Pitcairn Island was inhabited long before Europeans discovered it. Evidence of this has been found in the form of burial sites containing human skeletons, petroglyphs, earth ovens, stone adzes, gouges and other artefacts as well as breadfruit and coconut trees that were almost certainly planted by man. However, archaeologists have not determined where the first Pitcairners came from or when.

The European discoverer of Pitcairn was Captain Philip Carteret who passed it an HMS *Swallow* in 1767 and named it after the midshipman who first sighted it. An account of the *Swallow's* voyage, with a description of Pitcairn, was among the books on board HMS *Bounty* when she sailed from England in 1787 to obtain a cargo of breadfruit in Tahiti. Under the command of Lieutenant William Bligh, the *Bounty* was to transport the breadfruit to the West Indies for replanting in the hope that it would become a staple diet for slaves employed on British plantations.

Bligh had to stay at Tahiti for about five months before he could complete his cargo. This long sojourn resulted in loss of discipline among his crew and the formation of some amorous attachments with the Tahitian women. These two factors undoubtedly contributed to the mutiny which occurred on the *Bounty* on 28 April 1789, three weeks after her departure from Tahiti.

Bligh and 18 others were cast adrift in an open boat near the Tongan Island of Tofua, while the *Bounty*, under Fletcher Christian, was put about to sail back towards Tahiti. Bligh and his companions succeeded in reaching Timor, from where they returned to England. Meanwhile, Christian and his fellow mutineers had tried to form a settlement on Tubuai, an island about 480 km south of Tahiti. When this failed, Christian returned to Tahiti, left 16 of his companions there, then sailed in search of a more suitable place to live. He had with him eight mutineers, six Polynesian men, 12 Polynesian women, and a small girl.

Christian's search for a home occupied about four months. He first sailed, via Rarotonga, probably Mangaia, and Tongatapu to the eastern outliers of Fiji. Then, because he had been impressed by Carteret's description of Pitcairn, he resolved to seek out that isolated island, which was sighted on 15 January 1790. The *Bounty* anchored in what is now called Bounty Bay.

The *Bounty* was stripped of her contents and everyone moved ashore. On the 23rd the ship was burned to the waterline so that no clue to the mutineers' whereabouts would be visible from the sea. The mutineers were not heard of again for 18 years.

There was much violence in the meantime. About a month after their arrival, the Polynesian wife of one of the mutineers (John Williams) was killed while searching for birds' eggs. After about two years, Williams demanded the wife of one of the Polynesian men. This demand outraged the Polynesians and led to orgies of slaughter in which five mutineers, including Christian, and all the Polynesian men, were killed. The last massacre took place on 2 October 1793, when the mutineers left alive were Edward Young (a midshipman), William McCoy, Matthew Quintal and Alexander Smith, alias John Adams (seamen). There were also 10 women and a number of children.

In 1796, McCoy threw himself off a cliff in a delirious fit after producing an intoxicating liquor from the ti-root. Several years later, another woman, Quintal's wife, was killed while searching for birds' eggs, and Quintal went mad and threatened to kill both Adams and Young. The latter therefore felt justified in doing away with him before he could kill them, and did so with an axe. After Young died of asthma in 1800, Adams, the only man left alive, became a community husband to the nine remaining women. With the help of books taken from the *Bounty*, he set about educating the mutineers' 19 children and bringing them up according to

strict moral standards.

Hideout discovered. When Captain Mayhew Folger of the American sealing vessel *Topaz* put into Pitcairn in February 1808, he was surprised to see smoke ascending from an island that he thought was uninhabited. His surprise turned to astonishment when some of the mutineers' part-Polynesian sons rowed out to his ship and greeted him in English.

Although a report from Folger reached the British Admiralty, few people learned of the Pitcairn community until after the island was visited by two warships, HMS *Tagus* and *Briton*, in 1814. From then until Adams died in 1829, about three dozen ships are known to have called there. Accounts which they carried back to Europe, India and the United States attracted the interest and benevolence of missionary societies and others.

As a result, Pitcairn received many gifts of Bibles, prayer books, spelling books, seeds, tools, crockery, cutlery, etc. Meanwhile, three new settlers arrived on the island — John Buffett, John Evans and George Hunn Nobbs, who became pastor to the little community.

Moved to Tahiti. Concern over the Pitcairners' increasing numbers prompted the British Government to transfer them to Tahiti in March 1831. Although the Tahitians welcomed them and provided land for them, the Pitcairners were unhappy in their new environment. After 12 had died of unfamiliar diseases, a fund was raised to send the remaining 65 back to Pitcairn. They returned in the American brig *Charles Doggett* (Captain William Driver) in September 1831.

In 1832, a strange, domineering, half-mad man called Joshua Hill settled on Pitcairn, claiming to represent the British Government. Before long he had assumed the role of dictator, had expelled Nobbs and others, and had instituted a repressive regime. His rule lasted until 1838 when he was forcibly removed from the island. At the same time, Captain Russell Eliott of HMS *Fly* drew up a simple constitution and code of laws for the Pitcairners. The constitution was dated 30 November 1838. It provided for the annual election by universal suffrage of a native-born magistrate to govern the island with a council of two, and for compulsory schooling.

Apart from a devastating storm in 1845,

the next 18 years were fairly uneventful. As American whalers were now calling at the island in substantial numbers, the islanders developed a profitable trade in island produce. Meanwhile, their numbers grew apace and fears were again expressed that they would outstrip their island's resources. Finally, in 1856, the Pitcairners agreed to a British Government proposal that the entire community — then numbering 193 — should be transferred to uninhabited Norfolk Island. A baby was born en route.

The transfer was carried out in the British merchant ship *Morayshire*. Most of the islanders soon settled down in the new and much larger home. But some pined for Pitcairn. Two families named Young, 16 people in all, seized an opportunity to return in 1858, and four more families followed in 1864. This brought Pitcairn's population to 43. They shared five surnames — Christian, Young, McCoy, Buffett and Warren (that of an American newcomer). The male lines of the McCoys and Buffetts have since died out.

In March 1883, the Pitcairners adopted a resolution which has affected their lives ever since. Abandoning the Church of England, they became Seventh-day Adventists. This meant that Saturday became their day of rest; they became teetotallers, and gave up eating pork (they killed all the pigs). An SDA pastor has generally resided on the island since then.

In 1893, Captain Rooke of HMS *Champion*, introduced parliamentary government to Pitcairn — and an elected council of seven with a president at its head. This, however, proved too cumbersome, and a magisterial form of government was reintroduced after the British High Commissioner for the Western Pacific became responsible for Pitcairn's administration in 1898.

The change was made in 1904 by the British consul in Tahiti. R. T. Simons, acting on the High Commissioner's behalf. With some amendments, Simons' constitution remained in force until 1940 when H. E. Maude, also representing the High Commissioners, introduced the present system of government.

In 1938, two American philanthropists gave Pitcairn its first radio transmitting and receiving station. This was superseded during World War II when much improved facilities were introduced and a small team of New Zealand radio operators was stationed on the island. The wartime radio station has since been rebuilt.

Modern developments. There have been many innovations on Pitcairn since the war. In 1948, a prefabricated school was erected, with electric light and modern equipment; and a schoolmaster, on loan from the New Zealand Education Department, was sent to the island. New Zealand has supplied Pitcairn's teaching needs ever since. In 1959, the teacher and the SDA pastor began a monthly newsheet, *Pitcairn Miscellany*, which is now distributed to many people throughout the world. In 1965, earth roads were constructed between Adamstown and the most frequented parts of the island with two tractors provided by the British Government. Subsequently, bicycles, light motor cycles and even Mini-Mokes were introduced. Other public works projects included the improvement of shore facilities, the erection of a prefabricated hostel for official visitors, and the introduction of a diesel generating plant to provide light and power to Adamstown.

However, the quality of life on Pitcairn has also regressed. In 1968, Shaw Savill passenger ships stopped calling at Pitcairn on voyages between Panama and New Zealand. This meant that the Pitcairners had less opportunity to sell their curios, and so personal incomes dropped. As a result, many of the young people left the island. The population of 47 in 1985 compares with 136 people 20 years earlier and a peak of 233 in 1937.

In early 1975 one of the islanders, Tom Christian, appealed to Pitcairners abroad to come and 'repopulate a dying land'. Later in the year, six young Pitcairners returned from New Zealand where five of them had been receiving medical treatment. This averted the immediate possibility that Pitcairn would have to be abandoned as a *Bounty* settlement for lack of viable numbers.

The question of Pitcairn's future is still a matter of concern among Pitcairners, and in 1982 they asked the Governor to try to arrange more shipping services, possibly through French Polynesia, to make the island a more attractive place to live. The possibility of a small airstrip is also occasionally raised.

When Fiji became independent in 1970, Pitcairn and its dependencies were put under the administrative control of the British High Commissioner in New Zealand. Previously, the Islands had been the responsibility of the Governor of Fiji who took over from the British High Commissioner for the Western Pacific after the posts of Governor and High Commissioner were separated in 1952. The British High Commissioner in New Zealand has the title of Governor of Pitcairn.

Further information. Numerous books and articles covering Pitcairn's history or aspects of it have been published. The most reliable is H. E. Maude's *The History of Pitcairn Island* in *The Pitcairnese Language*, A. S. C. Ross and A. W. Moverley (eds), London, 1964. David Silverman's *Pitcairn Island*, Cleveland, 1967, covers the island's history by topic.

PITCAIRN'S DEPENDENCIES. Oeno, Henderson and Ducie Islands, all of which are uninhabited, are Pitcairn Island's nearest neighbours. They were annexed by the British Crown in 1902 when the British consul in Tahiti sent Captain G. F. Jones to visit them. Jones placed a board on each inscribed with the words: 'This island is a dependency of Pitcairn and is the property of the British Government'. In 1937 when the Pacific islands attained new values as aviation stations, the three islands were visited by HMS *Leander* and new signboards were erected to reaffirm British sovereignty. They were made part of the Pitcairn Island colony in 1938. Since 1940, the island's stamps have borne the words 'Pitcairn Islands' to cover its three dependencies.

Oeno Island. Oeno Island, about 120 km NW of Pitcairn, is a low atoll some 3.5 km in diameter. On the reef, which completely surrounds the lagoon, is a substantial sandy islet on which coconut trees, pandanus and other vegetation grow well. Water may be had by scooping sand from a depression in the centre of the islet. A boat passage on the northern side gives access to the lagoon.

Oeno was discovered by Captain James Henderson of the *Hercules* in 1819, but it takes it name from the American whaler *Oeno* (Captain George Worth) which was in the

area in 1822. About once every two years the Pitcairners visit Oeno for a working holiday when they fish, collect shells and coral for curios and pandanus leaves for basket-making.

Henderson Island. Henderson Island, lying about 168 km ENE of Pitcairn, is formed of upraised coral limestone. It is roughly rectangular in shape, some 7 km long by 5 km wide. Except in the north where a fringing reef runs into a sandy beach, it is bounded on all sides by perpendicular cliffs considerably undermined by the sea. The island as a whole is about 30 m high, flat-topped, and covered with dense bush, and prickly vines, almost impenetrable. There is very little fresh water.

The island is a natural bird sanctuary, and 13 species have been observed there, including two land birds believed to be unique to the island — the flightless rail (or Henderson chicken) and a green fruit pigeon.

Quiros discovered Henderson Island in 1606 and named it San Juan Bautista. Its present name is that of the captain of the British merchant ship *Hercules* who rediscovered it in January 1819. It was also known as Elizabeth Island last century from a ship of that name, Captain Henry King, which visited it in February 1819.

In 1820–21, some sailors from the American whaleship *Essex*, which was stove in by a whale, lived on Henderson for several months after reaching it in an open boat from the vicinity of the Marquesas. The *Essex* men found eight skeletons in a cave, others have been found there since. It is not known whether the skeletons were those of islanders or Europeans. It is likely they were of shipwrecked mariners of last century.

The Pitcairners visit Henderson Island occasionally to collect miro wood for curio-making. The island received considerable publicity in 1957 when an American citizen at his own request was put ashore there for three weeks with a chimpanzee, and again in 1982 when a wealthy American proposed colonising Henderson and establishing a light-aircraft link with Pitcairn and Tahiti.

Ducie Island. This island, an atoll, is the most easterly of the Pitcairn group. It lies about 300 km east of Henderson and some 470 km east of Pitcairn. There is a low islet covered with trees on the northern and NE part of the reef and several smaller ones on the southern side. The lagoon has no entrance and landing on the island can be difficult. Sharks are said to be dangerous.

Quiros, who discovered the atoll in 1606, named it Encarnacion. Its present name was bestowed on it by Captain Edwards of HMS *Pandora* who passed it in 1791.

Revilla Gigedo

Revilla Gigedo consists of three islands and a large rock. The group lies at 18 deg 29 min – 19 deg 20 min N latitude and 110 deg 45 min – 114 deg 50 min W longitude, about 550 km from the coast of Mexico. It is a Mexican possession.

Socorro, or Santo Tomas, the largest island, is 107 sq. km in area, and about 13 km long by 10 km wide. Its single volcanic peak is 1051 m above sea level.

Clarion, or Santa Rosa Island, which is about 8 km long by 3 km wide, is 345 km to the west of Socorro, and is about 335 m at its highest point, Cerro Gallegos.

San Benedicto, which is about 5 km long and 1 km wide, is 50 km to the north of Socorro. About 297 m at its highest point, the island's surface is marked by cinder cones and deep ravines.

Roca Partida, a rock about 90 m long and 45 m wide, is 33.5 m high and lies about 11 km west of Socorro.

From sea level to 500 m, rainfall is less than 600 mm, and the temperature has a mean of 25 deg C.

From 600 m to 1000 m, rainfall averages from 600 to 1000 mm.

REVILLA GIGEDO ISLANDS

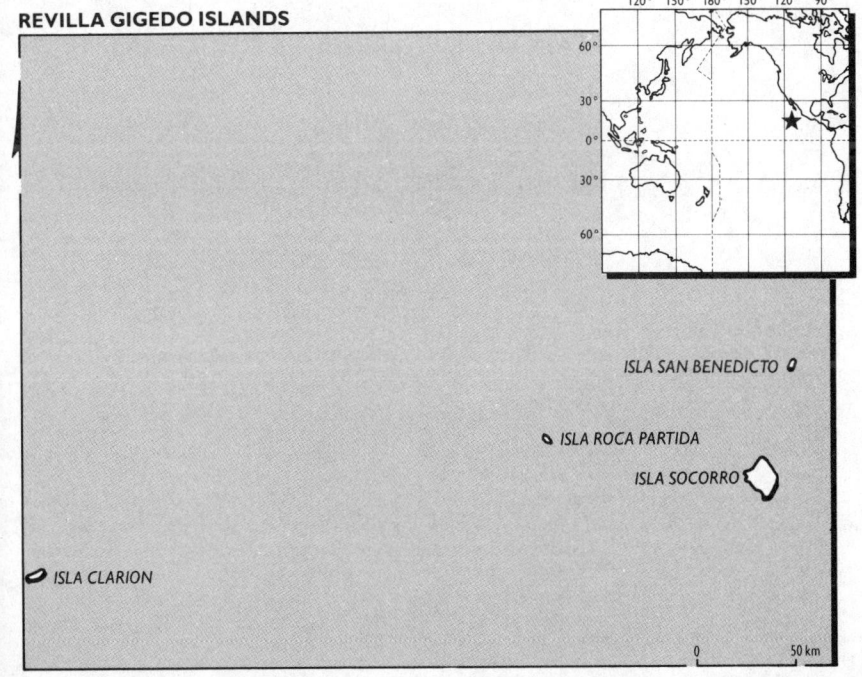

ISLA SAN BENEDICTO

ISLA ROCA PARTIDA

ISLA SOCORRO

ISLA CLARION

0   50 km

Solomon Islands

The Solomon Islands, which became an independent member of the British Commonwealth on 7 July 1978, consist of a double chain of six large islands and many smaller ones including those of the Lord Howe, Santa Cruz, Duff and Reef groups. The total land area is 29,785 sq. km and the islands are located between 5 and 12 deg S latitude and 155 and 170 deg E longitude.

The major island is Guadalcanal (pop. 50,327), with the capital Honiara (pop. 30,499) which is about 2575 km north-east of Sydney and 1600 km east of Port Moresby.

The 1986 census showed the population figures for other provinces as: Choiseul and New Georgia (Western Province) 55,372, Santa Isabel (Isabel Province) 14,564, San Cristobal (Makira Province) 21,646, Malaita (Malaita Province) 80,183, Santa Cruz (Temotu Province) 14,683, and Rennell (Central Province) 18,522. These main islands are mountainous, and heavily wooded.

Local time is 11 hours ahead of GMT.

Solomon Islands has it own currency, introduced in 1977 before independence and circulating alongside Australian currency until 1979 when the latter was withdrawn. The dollar rate is floated and related to a trade-weighted basket of other currencies. Currency consists of 1c, 2c, 5c, 10c, 20c, $1 in coins and $2, $5, $10 and $20 in notes. The Solomon Islands Monetary Authority issued two special coins in 1982 to commemorate the 40th anniversary of the US Marines' landing on Guadalcanal, one $100 coin of gold and the other $5 in sterling silver.

The flag is green and blue halved diagonally by a thin, gold stripe and has five white stars clustered at the hoist representing the four districts and the outliers. The coat of arms includes a crocodile, shark, two frigate birds, and eagle, spears with shield and a turtle. The birds, spears and turtle represent the four districts. The motto is 'To Lead is to Serve'. The National Anthem is *God Save Our Solomon Islands*. The Constitutional Review Committee recommended that the country become a republic on the tenth anniversary of its independence.

THE PEOPLE. The census taken in February 1970 showed a total population of 160,998, of whom 94 per cent were Melanesians. The next largest group are the Polynesians who have mainly settled on small offshore islands or atolls such as Ontong Java, Sikaiana, Rennell, Bellona, the Reef Islands and Tikopia. The population at the end of 1986 was 285,796 and the national projection is for a population of 318,693 by 1990.

The 1986 census indicated that the population growth had been at the rate of 3.5 per cent annually since 1976, compared with a 2.6 per cent annual growth rate between 1959–70. The overall increase since 1976 has been 45 per cent. This increase has resulted from a falling mortality rate and an increase in fertility.

The population of the Solomons is predominantly young. In 1986 more than 50 per cent of the total population were under the age of 15. Females have increased in number somewhat faster than males. The 1986 figures were females 137,866 and males 147,930, compared to 1976 figures of females 94,015 and males 102,808.

The average number of persons per household increased from 5.6 in 1976 to 6.4 in 1986. Increases were particularly evident in Honiara, the capital of the Solomon Islands which was built at the end of the Pacific War.

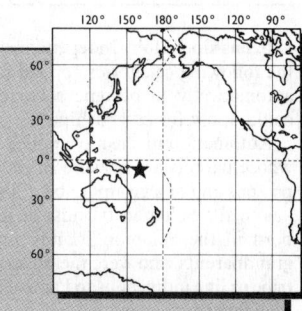

E

VA

E SISTERS IS.

AKIRA

•

• DUFF ISLANDS

• REEF IS.

S A N T A   C R U Z   I S L A N D S

NDENDE

UTUPUA

VANIKORO

ANUTA •

FATAKA •

• TIKOPIA

0   200 km

Citizenship. After Independence in 1978, the following categories applied for a person automatically to become a citizen, or who could apply for citizenship:

Automatic citizenship applied to anyone whose parents are or were British protected persons and of a group, tribe or line indigenous to the Solomon Islands; or if they were born in the Solomon Islands and had two grandparents who were members of a group, tribe or line indigenous to Papua New Guinea or Vanuatu.

Citizenship was also granted on application to all others who had been resident in the Solomon Islands for seven years during which any periods of absence had not totalled more than 18 months.

Further information is available from: The Citizenship Committee, PO Box CL, Honiara, Guadalcanal, Solomon Islands.

Language. The official language is English, although the most effective lingua franca is Pidgin. In addition about 87 different vernacular forms of speech are used, with Melanesians living in villages only a few miles apart frequently unable to understand each other. There is no vernacular common to the whole country.

Religion. More than 95 per cent of the inhabitants are Christian. More than a third of the population belongs to the Anglican Diocese of Melanesia, while 19 per cent belong to the Roman Catholic Church; 17 per cent to the South Sea Evangelical Church; 11 per cent to the United Church; 10 per cent to the Seventh-day Adventist; other churches 8 per cent; and those who choose to categorise themselves as pagan, 3 per cent.

Lifestyle. Most islanders follow the traditional village life where every family produces its own food and builds its own house.

Recreation. A major source of recreation for the islanders is the sea, where big, black, canoes may still be seen among motorised boats. The traditional canoe is made of bent planks with stern and sometimes bow carried high and decorative. There is often much inlay work done with mother-of-pearl. The people also take their soccer, rugby, tennis, cricket, athletics and basketball competitions seriously.

GOVERNMENT. The Solomons is a constitutional monarchy with the British monarch as Head of State and represented in the Solomons by a Governor-General appointed, on the recommendation of the legislature, every five years.

Legislature. It is a single-chamber National Parliament composed of 38 elected members. The normal life of parliament is four years.

Executive. The executive arm of government is the National Cabinet headed by the Prime Minister who chooses his ministers, limited to 15 including the Prime Minister.

Elections. Voting for the Legislative Assembly is by universal suffrage on the English model of 'first past the post'. Everybody over the age of 18 is entitled to vote.

The political parties in 1986 were the United Party (UP), Solomone Ano Sagufenua (SAS), the Nationalist Front for Progress (NFP), the Peoples' Alliance Party (PAP) and the National Democratic Party (NADEPA). There are also several independent members of Parliament.

Local government. Since 1974 local government reform has aimed at increasing responsibility at the local level, with the financial support of the central government. The Solomons are administered through four districts, divided into eight local councils. The four districts are Malaita, Eastern, Western and Central districts.

The local councils, elected by universal adult suffrage, operate a wide range of facilities including communications, rural health services and schools. Many such projects, including roads, bridges and road transport are wholly subsidised by the Government. Education and health facilities co-ordinate with the churches and central government.

Public service. Independence has seen a rapid replacement of expatriate public servants by Solomon Islanders wherever possible, although a number of overseas officers have remained on contract. The total employed in the Public Service in 1985 was 6094, of which 109 were expatriates.

Justice. The judiciary has been organised on the English system. The High Court of the Solomon Islands is composed of the Chief Justice and two puisne judges. The court is a Superior Court of Record and possesses all the jurisdiction which is invested in Her Majesty's High Court in England. It hears appeals from magistrates' courts, customary land appeal courts and various tribunals.

The Solomon Islands Court of Appeal was established on 8 May 1978, and is composed of six senior Commonwealth judges, three of whom sit at a time to hear appeals from the High Court. Magistrates' courts are held by principal magistrates who have professional legal qualifications, and by magistrates of the first and second class who are required to pass the Solomon Islands Law Examination. They hear all but the most serious criminal and civil cases and appeals from local courts. Customary land appeal courts are located in each province and are composed of at least four local men learned in custom, and one clerk/magistrate. They hear appeals in land cases from the local courts. There are local courts established throughout the island group by warrant. They are composed of a lay president and members who use the language of the area, with a salaried clerk keeping records in English.

In 1987 a law reform commission was established to examine existing legislation and make recommendations for improvement. It will also propose legislation to meet the changing needs of the people. It is expected that these changes will be implemented in the 1988–89 period.

Police. The Royal Solomon Islands Police Force, headed by the Commissioner of Police, has its headquarters in Honiara, together with the Police Training School and the HQ of the Police Mobile unit.

A radio network connects Honiara to 23 police stations in the islands. Training courses at home and abroad are held in co-operation with the police of Vanuatu, Kiribati, Papua New Guinea and Britain. The RSIP is also responsible for policing the 200-mile EEZ and the 12-mile Territorial Sea and Archipelago Zone. For this purpose the SIPV *Savo* is used.

There are six prisons but only the largest, in Honiara, has separate facilities for men and women.

Liquor laws. Liquor is sold in hotel bars, clubs and licensed stores. Hotel hours are from 10 am to 10.30 pm weekdays, and on Sundays 12 midday to 10 pm, but restricted to hotel residents from 2 pm to 7 pm.

EDUCATION. Organised schools provide for about two-thirds of the school-age children. Government expenditure on education in 1984 was $4,260,000. Capital expenditure in 1984 was $3,126,000. The national system is wholly financed by central government. Private educational agencies like the churches can operate outside the national system but get only limited financial help.

Responsibility for running primary and certain secondary schools is in the hands of provincial assemblies. The Government gives grants to primary schools for equipment and pays teachers' salaries. Secondary schools controlled by local authorities receive grants for boarding, equipment, building maintenance and pupils' travel costs. Capital aid is available for primary and secondary schools.

In 1984 a preparatory grade was introduced prior to entry into grade one and this enrols pupils from five to eight. There are 423 primary schools operated by the provincial assemblies and about 54 primary schools run by the churches. Provincial Education Boards employ 1536 teachers for the primary schools.

The secondary system is composed of National and Provincial Secondary schools. The National Secondary Schools (NSS) provide an academic oriented education over a five-year period which leads to the Solomon Islands School Certificate. The Primary Aptitude Test is used to select pupils from grade six for form one at either the NSS or PSS. Two NSS provide a form six year in preparation for overseas tertiary education.

The Provincial Secondary Schools (PSS) provide a free vocational oriented education catering mainly for those students who would return to village life rather than go into paid employment or further education. The schools are also based on the lifestyle and cultures of the Solomon Islands in both their location and curriculum. A small number of students in form three are selected for form four in the NSS. There are eight national secondary schools — one administered by a voluntary agency — and 12 provincial secondary schools.

Another move to introduce the 'Island' environment into education has been the replacement of the Cambridge School Certificate examination (established in 1950) by the Solomon Islands School Certificate examination introduced with the help of the universities of Papua New Guinea and the South Pacific (Suva).

TABLE 1 PRIMARY ENROLMENT
BY PROVINCE AND ANNUAL GROWTH (per cent)

	1982	1983	1984
Western	7639	8588	8745
%	1.87	12.42	1.83
Isabel	1709	2162	2554
%	4.72	26.51	18.13
Central	2429	2554	2687
%	9.17	5.15	5.21
Guadalcanal	4608	5260	5580
%	6.86	14.15	6.08
Honiara	2468	2664	3047
%	10.97	7.94	14.38
Malaita	7506	8530	9219
%	2.33	13.64	8.08
Makira	2168	2971	3280
%	−3.77	37.04	10.40
Temotu	2089	2224	2410
%	17.82	6.46	8.36
Total	30,616	34,953	37,522
%	4.66	14.17	7.35

The Solomon Islands College of Higher Education in Honiara provides teacher training courses, particularly for primary teachers. In 1984 there were 340 enrolled in the certificate course and 32 in the diploma course.

In 1984, there were 34,522 pupils at primary schools, 2369 at national secondary schools and 2716 at provincial secondary schools. The national secondary schools are King George VI (Honiara), Betikama, Selwyn and St Joseph's Tenaru, all on Guadalcanal, Goldie (Western) and Su'u (Malaita) and Waima. Students at the Honiara Technical Institute in 1983 totalled 770 on full-time courses and 120 on part-time courses. There were 36 overseas students at the full-time courses. In 1984 there were 262 staff teaching in the secondary school system — 73 expatriates and 189 Solomon Islanders.

The Ministry of Education, Training and Cultural Affairs is responsible for the library, museum and fostering of National Archives and local custom. On 4 November 1977 the Pro-Chancellor of the University of the South Pacific, Dr S. Langi Kavaliku, formally opened the first permanent buildings of the Solomons Islands' Centre of the university at Honiara. They new complex cost more than $A100,000 and was funded by grants from the Australian and New Zealand governments.

The Government does not, at present, possess the capacity or resources to provide universal primary, secondary, or tertiary education for all children aged between five and 15, and it hopes to rectify this situation by encouraging the participation of community and non-government organisations in education. Enrolment into primary schools had the greatest growth rate in 1983 but this has declined recently due to a rapidly increasing school age population and the slower rate of providing additional school places.

LABOUR. In 1985 the active labour force was 23,996, an increase of 5.8 per cent over the 1984 figure and a general increase of 17 per cent over the preceding five-year period. Honiara had 8424 workers, 35 per cent of the total work force.

The labour force consists largely of unskilled men, with an acute shortage of skilld islanders for supervisory posts. Employers engaging overseas workers are urged to train locals at the same time. Efforts at localisation have led to the number of employed expatriates falling. Total number of non-Solomon Islanders in the workforce in 1985 was 935. There is always a number of volunteers from agencies in Australia, New Zealand and Britain who work in the Solomons.

Most work with the malaria eradication programme, public health, library, fisheries, engineering, women's interest, small business, co-operative development and rural secondary school teaching.

Few workers are able to bring their families to their area of work although employers are improving this situation, especially in urban areas.

In 1985, 3876 island women were registered as employed. Of the total workforce of 23,996 in 1985, agriculture, forestry and

TABLE 2 EMPLOYMENT BY TYPE OF EMPLOYER AT 30 JUNE 1985

Province	Government Central govt	Local govt	Total	Non profit bodies	Co-operatives	Statutory authorities	Private business	Grant total
Western	1294	316	1610	321	47	160	2351	4489
Isabel	278	82	360	27	57	9	242	695
Central	380	108	488	33	4	1	2279	2805
Guadalcanal	664	167	831	147	147	135	3262	4522
Honiara	3195	255	3450	205	86	856	3827	8424
Malaita	799	303	1102	162	205	30	273	1772
Makira	355	136	491	17	25	14	219	776
Temotu	335	130	465	4	39	9	6	523
Total	7300	1497	8797	916	610	1214	12,459	23,996

TABLE 3 TOTAL WAGE BILL NON-GOVERNMENT SECTOR, JUNE 1985

Province	Total no. of employees	Total reported wage bill ($000)	Average monthly wage/salary ($)
Western	2879	508	176
Isabel	335	20	59
Central	2317	243	105
Guadalcanal	3691	592	169
Honiara	4974	1610	324
Malaita	670	103	156
Makira	275	61	220
Temotu	58	6	96
Total	15,199	3142	207

fisheries employed 8039; construction, manufacturing and mining employed 3281; services such as utilities, commerce, transport and finance employed 12,676.

Most of the growth has taken place in the agriculture, forests and fisheries sector. This reflects the development of large-scale primary industries and increased investment in forestry activities by both Government and private sector. There has also been a healthy investment in manufacturing and light industry over the last five years. It is predicted that the demand for employment by school leavers will exceed the estimated creation of 1000 new jobs per annum over the next five years. Only a small portion of these new positions will require secondary education.

Wages. The Wages Advisory Board regulates minimum wages and housing facilities for workers. Unskilled daily-paid workers employed by the Government in 1985 received a basic wage of $5.76 per day for a five-day week of 40 hours. Skilled, daily-paid Government workers received up to $9.68 a day. Annual salaries of public service established staff ranged from $2298 to $17,172 in 1985.

The average monthly salary is $207 in the non-government sector with workers in Honiara receiving approximately $324 per month while workers in Isabel Province receive approximately $59 per month. Those employed in financial services average $602 per month, then there is a considerable drop to $346 for electricity and water employees, $341 for mine workers, $267 for transport and communication employees, $270 for construction workers and $135 for agriculture, forestry and fishing employees.

Unions. There are 14 trade unions, the largest being the Solomon Islands Public Employees Union, the S.I. National Workers Union, the S.I. National Teachers Association and the S.I. Post and Telecommunications Association. A National Centre for Trade Unions is affiliated with the S.I. Council of Trade Unions. There are three active employer associations — the Chinese Association, the Chamber of Commerce and the Federation of Employers.

Social security. Social security legislation provides for the payment of workers' compensation for accidents at work. There is a

National Provident Fund to which contributions for the year ended 30 June 1984 totalled $6.8 million.

HEALTH. The Ministry of Health and Welfare is responsible for government health programmes. Hospitals maintained by the government include the Central Hospital in Honiara with 256 beds, as well as provincial hospitals in Western 12 hospitals, 96 beds), Isabel (1; 36) and Malaita (2; 219), Makira (1; 72), and Temotu (1;34). Roman Catholic nursing sisters staff the Government leprosarium on Guadalcanal; extra beds are provided by three church hospitals maintained by the Church of Melanesia (Anglican), United Church (Methodist) and the Seventh-day Adventist Church. Many other church centres provide a variety of medical services. In 1984 there were eight hospitals (six Government, two church-owned), 124 clinics, and 78 health and village aid posts. There were 38 doctors and 1076 nurses and aides.

The School of Nursing at Central Hospital had 70 students in 1984, while 60 islanders were studying at the Fiji School of Medicine and elsewhere. This figure included students of dentistry, entomology, laboratory skills, medicine, physiotherapy, radiography and pharmacy.

The government health budget for 1984 was $4.17 million. Existing facilities are being upgraded and gradually new facilities are being constructed to cope with the rapidly growing population. There is an urgent need to expand the operations of the School of Nursing to increase the output of qualified nurses and to increase the number of nationals working within the system as fully trained doctors. At present only 14 of the 38 doctors are Solomon Islanders.

Diseases. Problems include malaria, tuberculosis and leprosy. The Malaria Eradication Programme has been intensified in recent years, with frequent DDT sprayings to eliminate mosquitoes from dwellings. There were 84,343 cases treated in 1983 and 72,108 in 1984, Guadalcanal, with 35,418 cases in 1983 and 17,513 in 1984 being the main problem area. Among tuberculosis sufferers, 302 cases were treated in 1983 and 337 in 1984. BCG vaccination appears to have reduced pulmonary cases while the apparent increase in non-pulmonary forms probably reflects better public awareness and detection techniques.

Concerning leprosy, 26 cases were treated in 1984, maintaining the success of the eradication efforts. Surveys of the disease have been made by the WHO and the NZ Lepers Trust Board.

THE LAND. The Solomon Islands extend over some 600,000 sq. km of sea, lying as a scattered archipelago in a south-easterly direction from off Bougainville to Santa Cruz Is. The group has a total land area of 29,785 sq. km.

The six major islands are Choiseul, New Georgia, Santa Isabel, Guadalcanal, Malaita and San Cristobal. They vary in length between 145 and 200 km and in width between 30 and 50 km. The largest, Guadalcanal, has an area of approx. 5650 sq. km. The group is stretched over 1400 km from one extremity to the other.

The main islands are rugged and mountainous, the highest named peak Mt Makarakombou (2447 m) on Guadalcanal. Most islands are of igneous and metamorphic rocks, overlaid with considerable layers of marine sediments. The only extensive coastal plains are on the north-east coast of Guadalcanal. Many outer islands are coral atolls and raised coral reefs.

Climate. The tropical climate is modified by the surrounding sea. Late April to November is the season of south-east trade winds. The highest temperature and rainfall are usually recorded from November to April, when cyclones may also occur. On 18 May 1986 Cyclone Namu struck the east coast of the Solomon Islands causing $100 million worth of damage. Over 100 people were killed and 90,000 left homeless.

Rainfall generally averages 3000–3500 mm a year, while reaching as high as 8000 mm in some parts and averaging 2250 mm in Honiara. Mean daily temperatures range from 21 to 30°C.

All the larger islands are well watered by rivers, with steep courses over most of their length and many have a significant energy potential.

There are four volcanoes: one on the island of Savo 30 km off Honiara, which has hot springs but has not erupted since 1840; Tinakula, in the far east of the Solomons, which

has been active from time to time; one on the island of Simbo near the New Georgia group, together with Kavachi, a submarine volcano in the same area.

Flora and fauna. Vegetation on the large islands is mainly dense rain forest. There are few endemic animals — phalangers and bush mice, as well as a large skink, equipped with a prehensile tail and believed to be unique to the Solomons. There is a great variety of bird life while crocodiles are also present.

Resources. Many regard the seas as the most reliable area of future development, although mineral prospecting continues and bauxite exists in large deposits on Rennell Island. Good agricultural land is limited, except on the Guadalcanal coastal plains. Main resources comprise the coconut and oil palms, forests, minerals and fisheries.

Land tenure. The registration of land titles was introduced in 1963, under the Land and Titles Ordinance 1959.

Land in the country can be classified into two categories according to the system of tenure governing ownership of rights and interest in land. Customary land is owned and used according to traditionally unwritten rules that vary across the country. All such land is usually owned in a lineage group. Registered land has its ownership and boundaries recorded in the land registry in Honiara. This land is also known as alienated land. Titles to 97 per cent of such land are registered, while title to three per cent is pending registration. Registered rights and boundaries are guaranteed by law rather than by custom. The Government and non-Solomon Islanders are not permitted to own interests in customary land. Perpetual estate owned by Solomon Islanders or the Government may be leased, such a lease being known as a fixed term lease. Such land is attractive to investors, both indigenous and expatriate. Approximately 88 per cent of the land area is held under the indigenous customary land tenure system whilst the remaining 12 per cent has been alienated. Nearly all this land has been registered under the 'Torrens System' following the introduction of land registration in 1963. Approximately half of this alienated land is owned by Solomon Islanders though some of this is leased out to companies and churches. Land legislation is comprehensive and provides for perpetual estates, fixed term estates, leases etc guaranteed by the State, but non-Solomon Islanders cannot hold an interest in land in excess of 75 years.

Customary land can become registered after a process of explanation, investigation, adjudication and survey by the Lands Division of the Ministry of Lands, Energy and Natural Resources. The process must in law take at least six months but in practice normally takes several years. Customary land owners then become registered as the owners of the 'perpetual estate' in the land. Land owned by groups is registered in the name of trustees chosen by the group. Most of the customary land which has been registered has been for lease to foreign investors. Of the registered land owned by Solomon Islanders, 67 per cent is accounted for on Santa Isabel. Registration aims to provide the local farmers with long-term security, including the right to pass on their land as they wish so as to encourage investment in cash crop production. Maintenance of the Land Registry is carried out by the Registrar General's office.

PRIMARY PRODUCTION. Copra was the chief primary industry up to 1979 but it has been overtaken by the fishing industry which is managed by Japanese experts. Copra production has been climbing since 1984 although the effects of Cyclone Namu in 1986 were evident in the production figures of 1986/87. In 1985 the total production of copra was 43,557 tonnes, with 75 per cent of that coming from the smallholders, the remaining 25 per cent from large plantations. World copra prices escalated in 1984 to $871 per tonne after 1982 and 1983 prices of $301 and $568 per tonne respectively, but declined again in 1985. The Government is encouraging the production of high quality copra and the planting of improved seed which will increase yields.

All copra is marketed through the Solomon Islands Copra Board which operates buying points at Noro (Western Province), Yandina (Central Islands), Lala (Temotu Province) and Honiara on Guadalcanal.

Cocoa. Cocoa, which has been cultivated in Solomon Islands for more than 30 years, is grown by smallholders and plantations but, unlike copra, there is no central marketing authority and a number of individuals and organisations export the crop. By law, however, all cocoa must be graded before export. Production has risen steadily in the last 10 years. Total production for 1984 was 1709 tonnes 1610 tonnes from smallholders and 1099 tonnes from plantations). This was an

TABLE 4 COPRA PRODUCTION 1981–84

Year	Small holder (tonnes)	Plantation (tonnes)	Total (tonnes)	World price av ($/tonne)
1981	23,701	9970	33,673	323.77
1982	22,429	9723	32,173	301.58
1983	19,555	8864	28,421	568.69
1984	31,587	10,999	42,586	871.34

TABLE 5 COCOA PRODUCTION 1981–84

Year	Small holder (tonnes)	Plantation (tonnes)	Total (tonnes)	Value ($000)
1981	208.0	382.6	590.6	893
1982	155.6	512.4	668.0	895
1983	399.7	769.6	1169.3	2259
1984	610.1	1099.2	1709.3	3366

TABLE 6 RICE PRODUCTION 1981–84

Year	Area cultivated (ha)	Rice harvested (tonnes)	Local sales polished (tonnes)	Export polished (tonnes)	Import (tonnes)
1981	1637	13,866	5375	1081	1530
1982	1010	10,538	5312	248	3107
1983	1010	9481	5215	0	2021
1984	1010	7137	8114	0	5106

80 per cent increase in total production since 1980. Government projects include the provision of some cocoa drier parts, production of fermentary, provision of fertilisers and the distribution of cocoa seeds. Cocoa production is seen as a significant cash crop for smallholders. Most cocoa is exported to Europe.

Rice. A private company began large-scale rice growing on Guadalcanal Plains in the late 1960s but the industry has been bedevilled by problems of finance and competition on overseas markets. One of Hawaii's 'Big Five' companies, C. Brewer & Co. Ltd, formed a joint venture with Solomon Islands Government in the 1970s, Brewer Solomons Associates, and took over the Guadalcanal Plains rice plantation, but in 1982, there were more problems caused by over-expansion and a vanished overseas market. The Government Shareholding Agency, which had a 45 per cent holding in Brewer Solomons worth $1.35 million, bought out the Hawaiian partner and halved the size of the company, the Brewer Solomon Agriculture Company. Conditions are now more stable but production is mainly for the local market. In 1981 1637 ha were under cultivation

but by the end of 1982 this had fallen to 1009 ha, and has remained at this level.

Palm oil. The first palm oil mill began operating in 1976. It is operated by Solomon Islands Plantations Ltd, which is a joint venture between the Commonwealth Development Corporation and the Government. Partners in the extensive oil palm plantation on Guadalcanal Plains are the Commonwealth Development Corporation (70 per cent), the Government (26 per cent) and Solomon Islands landowners (4 per cent). The first commercial palms were planted in 1971. The oil is exported to Britain and Europe where it benefits from the European Economic Community preferential tariff, and kernels are exported to Europe and Japan.

Production continued to increase until 1984 but declined again in 1985 when world prices began to decline. Government policy is to further develop and expand oil palm production, particularly through an outgrowers pilot scheme with a view to involving smallholders and communal agriculture ventures. Holdings of 60 to 100 ha are envisaged within easy access of the Solomon Islands Plantation Limited estates.

TABLE 7 OIL PALM PRODUCTION AND EXPORT 1981–84

Year	Palm oil (tonnes)	Palm kernels (tonnes)	Palm oil export ($000)	Palm kernel export ($000)	Per cent of all exports
1981	18,081	3163	7093	7436	25.24
1982	19,238	3603	6880	6485	23.52
1983	19,654	4004	7789	7815	21.91
1984	19,666	3979	17,134	1963	16.11

TABLE 8 DISTRIBUTION OF CATTLE BY OWNERSHIP 1981–84

Year	Plantations	Missions	Solomon Islanders	Government	Total
1981	8279	1075	9014	4968	23,336
1982	7279	1018	9761	5613	23,671
1983	7255	1103	8562	5986	22,906
1984	7262	788	7941	6731	22,722

Other crops. In areas not dealing in copra, cocoa or cattle, production continues in spices such as turmeric, ginger, cinnamon, tabasco and all-spice. However, they do not appear in any statistical tables. Investigations have also been made into butterfly and crocodile farming.

Cattle. A cattle industry has been growing steadily since 1978 aided by funds from Britain, Australia and New Zealand. Slaughterhouses are at Azuki, Gizo and Kira Kira. The Government supports programmes which aim to improve the generally low fertility level of indigenous cattle, encourage the tethering of cattle for fattening, reduce the high incidence of disease among livestock and develop the integration of cattle farming with other cash crops with the aim of increasing returns for the smallholder.

Over 56 per cent of the cattle are in the Central district, 20 per cent in the Western district, 16 per cent in Malaita and eight per cent in the Eastern district. In 1987 a dairy cow known as the Australian Milking Zebu, specially developed for tropical climates, was introduced to encourage milk production. The AMZ has a high milk capacity, high heat tolerance and is tick resistant. It is anticipated that, with artificial insemination, the AMZ will be crossbred with Friesians already in the islands.

Fisheries. The fishing industry is now Solomon Islands' largest export earner. The introduction of the 200-mile fisheries and economic zones stretching over more than 600,000 sq. km of sea has greatly enlarged the potential. A skipjack survey and assessment programme of Solomon Islands waters by the South Pacific Commission, published early in 1983, revealed that the present pole-and-line fishery was only harvesting a fraction of the available resources in the survey

area, which was only 10 per cent of the total area of the Solomon Islands' fishery zone. The survey also reported that bait fish stocks were the highest in the region with the possible exception of Papua New Guinea waters. Skipjack tuna constitutes most of the catch of Solomon Taiyo Ltd, which is jointly owned by the government and Japanese interests. The company has a shore base and canning factory at Tulagi, the old capital, and one at Noro in the Western Province, comprising a cold store and fish smoking plant. In 1988 work began on a new canning factory at Noro at an estimated cost of $23.5 m with the Government and the Western Provincial Government as partners. In 1977, a second commercial tuna fishing company, National Fisheries Development Ltd, was established, again as a joint venture between the Solomon Island Government (owning 75 per cent of its equity) and Solomon Taiyo (owning 25 per cent). This company was formed to stimulate local involvement in the industry, by building its own fishing vessels and manning them with Solomon Island crews. By the end of 1985 the company had built 10 ferrocement pole-and-line vessels.

In 1986 the Government signed a contract with a West Australian firm to build two purse seiner tuna vessels, with construction costs to be met by the Australian Government. The contract was worth $28 million. The vessels, delivered in 1987, are very similar to the American purse seiner *Jeanette Diana* which was confiscated by the Solomon Islands Government in 1984 for illegal fishing in territorial waters. The vessel was eventually retrieved by her owners after they paid approximately US$770,000 to the Government. The US had retaliated to the confiscation by placing a ban on all fish imports from the Solomons but they eventually

TABLE 9 CATCH UTILISATION SUMMARY (in metric tonnes)

Year	Frozen exports	Frozen local sales	Canned	Smoked
1981	23,721	291	2060	843
1982	15,261	194	2680	1324
1983	30,750	309	2824	1576
1984	33,227	149	3205	859

lifted the ban in mid-1985 when the Government of the Solomons agreed to enter into negotiations with the American Tuna Association for a bilateral fishing agreement. The South Pacific Forum, of which the Solomon Islands is a member, signed an agreement with the ATA in Tonga in 1986 regarding fishing rights. In 1988 the Government passed the Fisheries (USA Treaty) Bill, which governs the licensing and activities of US vessels in the Solomon Islands Exclusive Economic and Fisheries Zone. The Bill limits US operations to 10 per cent of the zone and imposes penalties, including seizure of vessels and contents, for captains contravening provisions of their licence. The new vessels are owned by the Government but operated by the National Fisheries Development and Solomon Taiyo.

Since 1975, attention has been directed increasingly at the rural sector, which ultimately resulted in the establishment, in 1982, of a separate management and advisory body, the Provincial Fisheries Development Division, within the Ministry of Home Affairs and National Development. Under the first joint venture agreement, Solomon Taiyo Ltd was limited to pole-and-line fishing to exploit the tuna resources. Provision, however, was made that surveys using other fishing techniques could be carried out, upon approval from the Solomon Island Government. As a result, in 1976, Solomon Taiyo initiated a pilot longline survey to assess the commercial viability of the technique in Solomon Island waters. This was concluded in 1981, and led to the acquisition of two longliners by National Fisheries Development Ltd. In 1980, a payao purse seine survey was also undertaken which was successfully concluded in July 1982. In 1981 a second joint venture agreement was signed between Solomon

Islands Government and Taiyo Fishing Company which is current until 1992.

Until the formation of the Fisheries Division in 1973, rural fishing activities were almost exclusively for subsistence but since a successful fish collection and marketing scheme was launched in 1975, a co-ordinated development programme has been pursued to provide ice and insulated containers to rural fishing groups, to develop fish marketing centres with a guaranteed price scheme and implement training programmes in fishing techniques and fish-handling. In 1977, the commercial company of Siaco Ltd was formed to provide improved marketing and retailing in Honiara and to ensure the effective operation of the fish pricing policy.

Total fish production from the rural fisheries sector is difficult to assess owing to the largely subsistence nature of the fishery. However, it is estimated to be about 6000 tonnes a year. Government sources estimate that only about 15 per cent of the fish caught in the rural subsistence sector is actually traded for cash. There are eight Provincial Fisheries Training and Marketing Centres scattered throughout the country to assist with administration, fish collection and marketing. The main commercial species are skipjack tuna, yellowfin, albacore and other tuna types suitable for the raw fish market in Japan.

Timber. This is the second largest export earner. Forests cover about 2.4 million hectares with about 250,000 hectares of exploitable land and 10.4 million m^3 of commercial timber. Logs form the bulk of the exports with 95 per cent going to Japan and the rest to Korea, France and Germany. Sawn timber goes to Australia, United Kingdom, New Zealand and some of the South Pacific Islands.

TABLE 10 TIMBER AND LOG:
PRODUCTION UTILISATION AND EXPORT 1981–84

Year	Total log production (000 m³)	Log exports	Sawn timber total	Export	D/Sales	Total export ($000)
1981	364.50	315.20	49.38	7.23	11.69	16,071
1982	388.30	330.00	58.67	7.11	7.94	22,850
1983	394.80	336.70	49.46	5.76	9.62	19,976
1984	422.94	391.54	31.46	6.21	7.09	30,058

As it is estimated that timber resources will last only about another 11 years, reafforestation programmes are operating in association with local and overseas interests. Logging will be reduced, especially of species which are, commercially, more viable as sawn timber and veneer, and provide more employment.

The logging industry is dominated by some nine or ten companies, most of which are foreign owned. These companies operate mainly in Western Province and on Guadalcanal. Total production and export of logs has been rising steadily over the last five years to 423,000 cubic metres in 1984. Work began in 1983 on a $1.3 million reafforestation project in the Viru Harbour area of New Georgia. The project, to last four years, forms part of the National Development Programme to be grant-aided by the Commission of the European Communities. Reafforestation of commercially-acceptable timber species will follow after the logging of 875 ha in the Viru area. Two similar projects, in the Shortlands and Santa Cruz islands, also financed by the EEC, also operate.

The Government, so far, has planted about 20,101 ha, mostly on Government land. However, it is planned to begin reafforestation of custom land with a pilot programme beginning on 500 ha in Malaita, to be undertaken over a five-year period from 1985 to 1989. It is hoped that this programme will encourage custom owners to practise reafforestation. Logging is far outstripping replanting and this, coupled with devastation to timber stands caused by cyclones, has forced the Government to make a comprehensive study of the industry. In 1984 timber exports were worth 25 per cent of the total exports.

In November 1986, Lever's Pacific Timbers Ltd, the oldest foreign owned logging operator in the Solomons, closed its mills on Kolomangara Island, in the New Georgia group. This was done as part of the Government's attempt to localise companies. Buyers attended the auction of the entire plant in one of the biggest sales ever held in the South Pacific. The closure affected several thousand families who relied on the logging operation for employment.

MINING. Chief interest lies in the bauxite deposits of about 30 million tonnes contained in some 65,000 ha on Rennell Island which the Mitsui Mining and Smelting Co. of Japan is keen to work in conjunction with Conzinc Riotinto of Australia, which has deposits of about 28 million tonnes on Wagina (or Vaghena) Island. After an agreement between the Government and the two mining companies, a feasibility study was conducted in 1975. However, Mitsui withdrew in 1977, although the company stated that it was still interested in the project.

On the neighbouring atoll of Bellona, a tentative interest has been shown in an estimated 10 million tonnes of phosphate-bearing material, spread over about 115 ha.

There has been mineral prospecting on each main island group except Malaita. CRA Exploration has worked especially in the Gold Ridge area, and Amoco Minerals in the Poha River region.

Gold and silver production is low. It is operated by islanders using hand-panning methods. Gold exports amounted to $715,000 in 1983. Alluvial gold deposits at Gold Ridge and on Guadalcanal are estimated to contain 10,000 ounces.

Geological mapping has continued, together with geohydrological, seismological and geothermal work. Mining activity has been regulated since 1969 by the Mining Ordinance, which is administered by the Director of Geological Surveys. Monthly maps show the holdings of mining tenements.

In August 1982 the Government called for tenders from international mining companies for the detailed evaluation and prospecting of the Gold Ridge primary deposit which ranks as one of the most attractive underdeveloped gold prospects in the region. Work, under a three-year prospecting licence, was begun by Amoco Minerals Australia Company in mid-1983.

Interest in other gold prospects, notably in the New Georgia area, has been prompted by the work of the Western Solomons Mapping Project. This project, funded by the UK Ministry of Overseas Development and staffed by geologists of the Institute of Geological Sciences is aimed at producing regional geological and geochemical maps.

A major offshore regional seismic survey was completed under the auspices of CCOP/SOPAC in 1982. The data from this survey plus that from several speculative surveys undertaken over the last 10 years or so are beginning to reveal the presence of four deep sedimentary basins on which more detailed surveys are justified. New petroleum legislation was enacted in anticipation of such follow-up surveys.

MANUFACTURING. Established industries include the Solomon Taiyo fish freezing and canning facilities at Tulagi. Other production includes rattan and other furniture, fibreglass articles, clothing, boat building, batteries and spices. Hand crafted articles of wood and decoration with mother-of-pearl shell inlay, mats, baskets and shell jewellery are produced for local and overseas markets. Biscuits, tobacco, soft drinks etc. are also processed.

Overseas interest seeking to promote new industries need to assure that there will be Solomon Islanders participation. The Industrial Development Unit was established in 1985 to promote development, particularly of small scale, indigenous enterprises. In 1985 only seven per cent of the workforce was employed in manufacturing industries.

TOURISM. In 1987 visitor figures were 12,555, 60 per cent of whom were tourists. Visitors came mainly from Australia, Papua New Guinea, the US and New Zealand. Many Americans come as members of the Guadalcanal Veterans Association to see battlefields of the Pacific. The Japanese also come with the same purpose. The 1985–89 National Development Plan has set a target of 13,000 visitor arrivals, increasing over the period to 18,000.

Cruise ships also bring tourists. In 1982 cruise ship arrivals reached an all time low of only two, however the number has begun to increase again as cruise lines design some schedules around wartime memories. In 1987 11 cruise ships brought 5814 visitors.

The average length of stay for visitors arriving by air is 11 days, a marked increase on the average stay in the 1970s which was only about six days. July, August and September are the most popular months. Tourist accommodation facilities are few. There are only 21 officially recognised establishments.

The Solomon Islands have direct airlinks with Brisbane, Nadi, Port Vila, Auckland, Kieta and Port Moresby in Papua New Guinea and Nauru. The Solomon Islands Tourist Authority is financed by the Government.

LOCAL COMMERCE. More than one quarter of the population is involved in the co-operative movement. In 1986 the 145 societies had a reported turnover of $24 m and provided jobs for 704 people.

In 1984, there were 452 private companies and three public companies incorporated locally with authorised capital of $86,345 million and $42,925 million of paid-up capital. Companies incorporated overseas totalled 38, the majority (21) in Australia.

Gross domestic product. Estimates for GDP in 1984 show a total value of all goods and services of $227.4 million, a rise of 25 per cent above the 1983 estimate of $178.3 million. Included in this is the estimated value of non-cash production of $76 million, making 33 per cent of the total. Production for cash is estimated to have risen from $113 million to $152 million, a rise of 34 per cent.

TABLE 11 PRINCIPAL SOURCES OF IMPORTS 1982–84 ($000)

	1982	*1983*	*1984*
Australia	19,448	23,307	30,394
Japan	8012	13,738	12,588
Singapore	10,089	13,231	12,135
United Kingdom	2537	2121	2734

TABLE 12 PRINCIPAL DESTINATIONS OF EXPORTS 1982–84 ($000)

	1982	*1983*	*1984*
Japan	33,239	30,971	39,385
United Kingdom	8153	8157	14,700
Netherlands	2012	1792	13,307
West Germany	1014	3033	5740

TABLE 13 EXPORTS BY PRODUCTS 1984–MID 1986 ($000)

	1984	*1985*	*Mid 1986*
Fish, fresh & frozen	25,088	27,662	11,126
Fish, smoked	610	212	168
Fish, canned	3102	3566	1318
Timber, logs	28,742	23,709	8750
Timber, sawn	1316	1035	536
Copra	32,199	23,417	1337
Palm Oil	17,135	12,382	1650
Rice & rice products	68	24	2
Cocoa beans	3366	5009	1930
Gold	715	800	435
Palm kernels	1963	1365	128
Marine shells	691	877	285
Tobacco	105	88	0

Domestic prices rose on average by 11 per cent between 1983 and 1984, and the population is estimated to have increased by 3.5 per cent.

OVERSEAS TRADE. Trading results for 1984 continued the upward trend started in 1983 with exports of $118.6 million exceeding imports by $34.7 million. The years

TABLE 14 MAJOR IMPORTS BY PRODUCTS — ($000)

	1984	1985	Mid 1986
Food	13,146	15,660	4148
Beverages & tobacco	3746	3946	1030
Crude materials (inedible)	1236	887	247
Mineral fuels, lubricants	19,061	20,892	5055
Animal & vegetable oils & fats	788	1806	169
Chemicals	5043	6120	1347
Manufactured goods	13,554	16,181	4220
Machinery & transport equipment	20,051	27,002	7316
Misc. manufactured articles	6735	9792	2700
Misc. transactions & commodities	499	442	129

1980, 1981 and 1982 all registered a trade deficit. The situation changed in 1983 with exports of $71.2 million, exceeding imports by $592,000. Exports for the first nine months of 1987 totalled $93.5 m and imports were $92.7 m.

Customs tariff. In 1988 tariffs moved from f.o.b. to c.i.f. A 3 per cent levy was placed on all imports except petroleum products. Copies of the tariffs are available from the Government Printer, Honiara.

FINANCE. The Solomon's recurrent budget until 1983 was balanced by a grant-in-aid from Britain, however since 1984 other bilateral aid has been a factor in the balance. Aid is provided by Japan, Australia and New Zealand with multilateral aid coming from the Asian Development Bank, the European Development Fund, the United Nations and its various agencies and the Monetary Fund. There has been a marked increase in the supplement of revenue from both domestic and overseas borrowings.

Revenue. The main sources of local revenue were: 1984, direct taxation (company, personal, estate duty) $14.2 million; indirect taxation (import/export, excise, stamp duties, licences, etc.) $28.2 million; other (timber royalty, rents, stamp sales, aircraft landing fees, etc.) $11.5 million; loan repayments $524,000.

Aid. Under the independence settlement (1978) Britain made grants in aid of about $40 million for the following four years made up of $7.75 million for joint venture projects

TABLE 15 REVENUE AND EXPENDITURE ($000)

Year	Total revenue	Total expenditure	UK aid	Borrowing
1981	50,479	50,963	5680	6671
1982	69,367	55,312	2976	22,079
1983	56,207	59,381	2208	11,038
1984	65,504	66,397	320	7578

Note: all aid figures take account of cash grants only; some aid is given directly in goods and services and does not appear in statistics.

promoted through the Government Share-holding Agency, $4.65 million in special assistance on a gradually reduced scale for the recurrent budget and the remainder for development aid. A further allocation was made of nearly $4 million from the European Development Fund in addition to more than $10 million previously allocated from the same fund.

In 1986 the Asian Development Bank gave aid of $4.5 million towards power generating plants and port development. Japanese aid of $10.5 million went toward the building of a malaria research complex at the Solomon Islands College of Higher Education and general road improvements. British aid of $8 million was to be directed to education and health projects. The EEC, under Lome II Convention, agreed to give aid of $US47.5 m between 1987 and 1992 to be divided among projects of rural transport, agriculture, village fisheries development and cyclone rehabilitation. In 1988, under Lome III Convention, the country received a further $US3.6 m in aid.

The UNDP allocated $2.2 million to assist in reconstruction of sanitation services and special anti-malarial compaign as special aid in the aftermath of Cyclone Namu in 1986.

In the 1985–89 National Development Plan, it is estimated that grants from foreign aid sources will amount to $70 million in real terms. Foreign aid grants cover both capital projects and technical assistance.

Australian aid through its Australian Development Assistance Bureau (ADAB) was at the level of $7.4 million in 1984/85. In 1985/86 ADAB aid was $6.4 million.

Loans. There are two sources from which Solomon Islands obtains its loan money. International agencies such as the Asian Development Bank, the World Bank, the EEC's European Development Fund and others advance loans for specific projects on highly concessional terms with, usually, a period of grace before interest becomes due, followed by a long repayment period and very low interest rates. The Government's overseas debts at the end of 1984, most incurred through concessionary loans, totalled about $4.5 million. The other loans source is a group of international banks who lend in US dollars, called Eurodollars outside the US, on commercial terms, for eight years at interest rates

slightly above the London market rate with a four-year grace period.

Postage stamps. Postage stamps contribute to local revenue and, by adopting a wise policy of limiting the number of issues, Solomon's stamps are recognised as a good 'buy' and a sound hedge against inflation as their value steadily appreciates. Total stamps sales in 1984 were $658,000.

Income tax. The PAYE (pay as you earn) system operates for wages earners with employers having the responsibility of deducting the tax each pay day and remitting it to the taxation authorities.

The Government, in 1986, engaged an IMF expert to review the overall tax structure of the country. Fundamental changes are expected to be an increase in the company tax from 35 per cent to at least 40 per cent, the possible reduction of non-resident corporation tax (currently 50 per cent); an adjustment of the rate structure imposed on PAYE tax payers according to inflation; and a review of tax concessions currently available to new companies. These are regarded as overly generous and are to be formulated in accordance with similar concessions offered by neighbouring countries. The Government also agreed in principle to the introduction of sales tax on selected goods and services.

Income tax inquiries may be addressed to the Commissioner of Income Tax, Inland Revenue Division, Ministry of Finance, Honiara.

Banks. There are six banks, four operated by private corporations, the Australia and New Zealand Banking Group Ltd (ANZ), the Hong Kong and Shanghai Banking Corporation, Westpac Banking Corporation, and the National Bank of Solomon Islands Ltd. The last-named is a joint venture between the government, which has an initial investment of $500,000 contributed by Australia, and the Commonwealth Banking Corporation of Australia. There are also two Government-owned banking institutions, the Solomon Islands Development Bank, previously the Loans Board, and the Central Bank of Solomon Islands, previously the Solomon Islands Monetary Authority, which began operation in 1983. The three trading banks provide a full range of services with a number of savings bank agencies throughout the country. In 1988 Westpac Banking Corporation was expected to take over the Solomon Islands' branch of the Hong Kong and Shanghai Banking Corporation.

The Development Bank makes loans for a wide range of projects in all sectors, aiming particularly at increasing the participation of nationals in the cash economy and developing rural areas.

The Central Bank issues and manages international exchange of Solomon Islands' currency and provides overall banking and lending facilities, particularly in the sphere of major commerce. At the end of 1984 the trading banks had assets of $63.5 million and the Central Bank $77.1 million. The Development Bank had current assets of $38,000, fixed assets accounting for $826,000, and total assets of $9.9 million. During 1984 it made net loans and advances of $8.7 million. Of this 47 per cent went to agriculture, fishing and forestry, 24 per cent to commerce, 23 per cent to service and transportation, 5.5 per cent to industry and .5 per cent to construction. Savings accounts held by commercial banks in June 1984 totalled $9.3 million.

Overseas investment. The Prime Minister at the time, Mr Solomon Mamaloni, announced new economic policies in January 1982, and the Government issued a new investment guide, a booklet entitled *National Economic Development Policy* intended to encourage private enterprise and attract foreign and local investment in priority areas. The policy aimed at increasing production and raising the level of the islanders' participation in all areas of commerce and industry.

Special emphasis was given to the full and best use of the country's human and natural resources and called for investment in agriculture, particularly in pigs and poultry, forestry, mining, mineral processing and manufacturing industries.

Mr Mamaloni stressed that his government would 'strongly encourage' foreign investment on a long-term basis for fair reward. The overall policy aimed at increasing production, improving productivity and reducing waste, encouraging agricultural and market diversion, greater participation of Solomon Islanders in development, new centres of economic activity, import sub-

stitution in food and increased domestic processing and manufacture for export.

Mr Mamaloni announced that, although the government recognised the danger of interfering with free market forces they would monitor to protect the public from monopolistic price-fixing. The Government would set maximum prices.

Projects approved by the government may receive assistance over site negotiations, tax relief, import duty concessions, infrastructure, staff training and purchase contracts for outputs. The guidelines indicate preference for investment in agriculture, livestock, forestry, mining, fisheries, small manufactures, food processing, tourism and transport.

Two amendments to the Income Tax Act in 1982 provided new incentives to encourage investment in the timber industry and in development. The cost of reafforestation can be offset by timber investors and developers against taxable profits in the year the reafforestation expenses are incurred. There is also an option to spread the tax relief over 15 years.

The special development asset order permits the minister, in the national interest, to declare the activity of any investor to be a special development activity for a period of up to five years during which time the investor can offset the cost of development activity assets against taxable profits in the year the asset is purchased or spread the relief forward by claiming standard depreciation. Factors to be taken into account by the minister when considering applications for inclusion in the category of special development activity will include the contribution the new investment activity will make towards increased exports, import substitution, increased employment and rural development.

Foreign investment is governed by the Foreign Investment Act which can be obtained from the Government Printer, PO Box G14, Honiara.

The Government has also established the Foreign Investment Board to decide on all foreign investment proposals. The board is served by a technical secretariat and the Foreign Investment Division.

Provincial taxation. Provinces have a wide range of rating powers including basic rates and rates on possessions and property. Basic rates vary between $1 and $90 a year and are generally at a uniform amount per capita, although some provinces have introduced graduated rates according to the occupation or assessed income of the ratepayer. Basic rates are payable by all persons of or above the age of 18 and resident within the area of a province's authority unless generally or specifically exempted. The Honiara Municipal Authority has introduced general property rates based on the unimproved value of rateable land in the town. Business licence fees paid to provinces are treated as prepayments of income tax.

Development Plans. The National Development Plan 1985–89 is directing its attentions to the wellbeing of the people. The aims are to promote an equitable distribution of the benefits of resources, a greater self-reliance and local control of the national economy, to strengthen diversity and productive base and the capacity of the national economy, preserve the values, traditions and integrity of Solomon Islands society and to promote national unity within the diversity of the nation.

TRANSPORT. Hire cars are available in Honiara; taxis and taxi trucks are available in Honiara and in Auki. Scheduled bus services operate along the coast road through Honiara and the suburbs.

Roads. There are 1900 km of roads in the Solomons including 100 km of bitumen roads, mainly around Honiara, with small sections in Auki and Gizo. Major roads are on Guadalcanal, Malaita and at Munda in the New Georgia group.

In the rural areas there are some 1770 km of secondary roads of varying standard. Gurkhas and Royal Engineers have assisted in road and wharf construction.

Vehicles. Vehicle registration figures are only kept for the area around Honiara, around Auki on Malaita and for Gizo. The number of vehicles is insignificant elsewhere. The following figures show total registrations in 1984: motor cars, 974; goods vans, etc. 1016; motor cycles, 354; public service vehicles, 413; taxis, 202; motor vehicles registered were 3400.

Overseas airlines. Overseas services are provided by Air Niugini flying in from PNG, Air Pacific operating from Fiji and Vanuatu

and Australia and Air Nauru. The national airline, Solomon Islands Airlines, flies to PNG and Vanuatu. The airport departure tax is $10.

Domestic airline. Internal services are provided by Solomon Islands Airlines which operates Beechcraft Barons and Britten Norman Islander. The Seventh-day Adventist Mission and the United and South Sea Evangelical Churches are also authorised to operate non-scheduled services.

Airports. Four aerodromes are open to international traffic: Honiara (Henderson) for regional services up to BAC 1-11 and Boeing 737 standard, Munda for regional services up to F27 standard, Gizo (Nusatupe) and Santa Cruz (Graciosa) for aircraft up to HS748 standard. Henderson Airfield has been extended by 2200 metres to accommodate large jets.

There are 28 airfields throughout the islands including four privately owned which are not open for public use.

Domestic aerodromes are Yandina (Russell Is.), Auki (Malaita), Barakoma (Vella Lavella), Kira Kira (San Cristobal), Mono (Stirling Is.), Seghe (New Georgia), Avuavu, Marau and Babanakira (Guadalcanal), Paraxi (Small Malaita), Rennell, Choiseul Bay, Ballalae I. (Shortland group), Graciosa Bay (Santa Cruz), Fera, Kukudu, Ringicove, Koli, Bellona and Atoifi. This list excludes the international airports.

Port facilities. Overseas shipping uses the ports at Honiara, Yandina and Noro. There are also 44 provincial wharves, 31 of them in the Western Province. Allardyce Harbour is no longer in use and log exports have been transferred from there to Graciosa Bay in Santa Cruz. Wharfage at Auki is now available for local vessels of 36.6 m with a draught of 3 m and a council wharf has been built in Santa Cruz.

The main port of Honiara has two wharves, the larger capable of taking container vessels up to 15,000 tonnes. Three small jetties cater for local shipping. Noro and Honiara operations are controlled by the Ports Authority. The Yandina port is operated by Lever's Pacific Plantations Ltd., with a wharf length of 53.5 m. The Government operates Tulagi Marine Base which is responsible for the repair and maintenance of the Government marine fleet. It also provides services on a commercial basis and is capable of slipping vessels up to 300 tonnes.

Island shipping also uses wharves built at various trading centres. Inter-island transport is by a fleet of about 140 craft, including private and mission vessels and about 26 operated by the government. Lagoon transport is popular, with an increasing use of outboard motors around the islands of New Georgia, Santa Isabel and parts of Malaita.

Shipping services. Various shipping services link Honiara with other countries. A consortium of Conpac/NGAL/PNGL has four container vessels operating on a 28-day turn-around from Australian ports to Honiara via Papua New Guinea ports. The Pacific Forum Line runs a containerised and general cargo service from New Zealand ports to Honiara, PNG and Brisbane and New Guinea Express Lines has a weekly container service from Australia to Honiara via PNG ports. The China Navigation's New Guinea Pacific Line (NGPL) operates a regular cargo service from Hong Kong, Taiwan, Manila, Port Kelang and Singapore to Honiara via PNG ports, and Kyowa Shipping Ltd has a monthly service from Japan to Honiara through Micronesia.

The Bank Line has a regular service from Honiara to Hull (UK) and European ports while Sofrana Unilines has three ships servicing Honiara via Vanuatu. Polish Ocean Lines has regular monthly sailings for containerised and breakbulk cargo and reefer space, conventional and in reefer containers from Europe to Honiara via Tahiti, New Caledonia and New Zealand. Regular services are also operated by Columbus Line Reederei GMBH from Europe to Honiara after calling at Tahiti, Apia, Suva, Lautoka, Port Moresby and Lae, and Star Shipping Associates operate a monthly service originating in Honolulu. Several cruise lines call occasionally at Honiara including Royal Viking, Sitmar and Princess Cruises.

TELECOMMUNICATIONS. Telecommunications have been upgraded and expanded extensively over the last five years. Improved services have meant an increase in telephone connections by 30 per cent per annum. In 1983 revenue collected from installation, rental and call charges totalled $30,000. In 1984 it had increased to $80,000

and in 1985 it was expected to reach $1.2 million. New exchanges using digital SPC switching equipment have been installed at Honiara, Auki, Gizo, Kira Kira, Tenakara and Tulagi. Honiara, Auki, Tulagi and Tenekara are linked by high quality multi-channel UHF radio systems which allow direct dialling between these exchanges. These centres also have access to ISD and telex services. The EEC has been funding the new system at a cost of $6 million.

In 1986 a new company, a joint venture between the Government and British Telecom, obtained a licence to operate the national and international telecommunications service. This agreement provides for the construction of a domestic satellite system of five earth stations in the provinces linking them with the main centre. The changeover from the old operators took place at the beginning of 1987.

In addition to the General Post Office in Honiara, post offices are established at Gizo, Munda, Yandina, Tulagi, Auki, Kira Kira, Lata and Taro. There are also 98 postal agencies operating throughout the country and 126 licensed stamp dealers.

Radio. The Solomon Islands Broadcasting Corporation, an independent statutory body, produces radio programmes every morning, noon and evening, Monday–Saturday and noon and evening on Sundays. Transmission during the week includes programmes for schools during term time. News programmes include local and relayed overseas broadcasts, some in Pidgin.

All transmitters have an aerial power of 5 kilowatts but plans are being made, through the Australian Aid Development Bureau, to substantially increase the broadcasting range. The work will be carried out in stages. The first phase is for higher powered transmitters to be installed near Honiara, together with two omni-directional aerials 100 metres in height, with another transmitter at Gizo, in the Western part of the country. These transmitters will be of 10 kW capacity.

Later stages involve building new studios and offices for the corporation in Honiara. A studio and offices will also be built at Auki on Malaita Island. It is planned to erect a 10kW transmitter at Kira Kira to relay the Honiara signal on MF.

Films. There are two commercial cinemas

in Honiara and one in Gizo.

Public information. The Government's Information Service produces a monthly official magazine which carries news of government activities and policies and generally acts as a link between the Government and the people. The department also distributes news items free of charge to local media and representatives of other Governments stationed in the country.

Newspapers are the *Solomon Star*, a weekly established in 1982 by former members of the Government Information Service staff when the Government stopped publishing the *Solomon News Drum* on 7 May 1982, and *Solomon Tok Tok*, a weekly owned by the local firm of Atkins Limited. Some of the local churches produce regular periodicals.

WATER AND ELECTRICITY. Electricity is in continuous supply at Honiara, Auki, Gizo, Kira Kira, Munda, Santa Cruz, Buala and Tulagi, operated by the Solomon Islands Electricity Authority. Wiring rules of the Standards Association of Australia are used. Plans have been made for eventual electricity supplies at Mali'u (Malaita). The supply is 230/415V at 50 Hz.

Generally good drinking water is abundant throughout the country, except in some outlying areas during extreme drought conditions. A reticulated water supply is provided in Honiara, Gizo, Auki, Malu'u, Munda, Dodo Creek, Kira Kira, Santa Cruz and Tulagi.

A number of hydro-electric projects are being studied including a large scheme to supply electricity to Honiara and North Guadalcanal by harnessing the River Lungga. In 1986 solar power was used in the installation of a water heating system, a desalination plant and a copra dryer. Their success is being monitored.

MAJOR OFFICE HOLDERS

Governor-General:
  Sir George Lepping, K St J.
Prime Minister:
  Solomen Mamaloni
Speaker of National Parliament:
  Maepeza Gina
Chief Justice:
  Gordon Ward

GOVERNMENT MINISTRIES AND DEPARTMENTS

Office of the Prime Minister, PO Box G1, Honiara, Tel.: 23018 Tlx: 66311
Ministry of Agriculture and Lands, PO Box G13, PO Box G13, Honiara, Tel.: 21430 Tlx: 66311
Ministry of Economic Planning, PO Box G1, Honiara, Tel.: 23111 Tlx: 66311
Ministry of Education and Training, PO Box 584, Honiara, Tel.: 23900 Tlx: 66311
Ministry of Foreign Affairs, PO Box G10, Honiara, Tel.: 22223 Tlx: 66311
Ministry of Finance, PO Box G26, Honiara, Tel.: 22535 Tlx: 66337
Ministry of Health and Medical Services, PO Box 349, Honiara, Tel.: 23600 Tlx: 66432
Ministry of Home Affairs and Provisional Government, PO Box G11, Honiara, Tel.: 22262 Tlx: 66311
Ministry of Immigration and Labour, PO Box G20, Honiara, Tel.: 22761 Tlx: 66358
Ministry of Natural Resources, PO Box G24, Honiara, Tel.: 22944 Tlx: 66306
Ministry of Police and Justice, PO Box G3, Honiara, Tel.: 22915 Tlx: 66358
Ministry of Posts and Communications, PO Box G25, Honiara, Tel.: 21281 Tlx: 66310
Ministry of Public Service, PO Box G1, Honiara, Tel.: 23111 Tlx: 66311
Ministry of Transport, Works and Utilities, PO Box G8, Honiara, Tel.: 21141 Tlx: 66352
Ministry of Trade, Commerce and Industry, PO Box G26, Honiara, Tel.: 22274 Tlx: 66311

STATUTORY BODIES

Central Bank of Solomon Islands, PO Box 634, Honiara, Tel.: 21791 Tlx: 66320
Development Bank of Solomon Islands, PO Box 760, Honiara, Tel.: 21595/6/7 Tlx: 66427
Government Shareholding Agency, PO Box 570, Honiara, Tel.: 22511 Tlx: 66337
Livestock Development Authority, PO Box 525, Honiara, Tel.: 21650
National Fisheries Development Ltd, PO Box 717, Honiara, Tel.: 30358 Tlx: 66341
Solomon Islands Airways, PO Box 23 , Honiara, Tel.: 20031 Tlx: 66312
Solomon Islands Broadcasting

Corporation, PO Box 654, Honiara,
Tel.: 20051 Tlx: 66406
**Solomon Islands Commodity Export
Marketing Authority,** PO Box 54, Honiara,
Tel.: 22529 Tlx: 66313
Solomon Islands Copra Board, PO Box 54,
Tel.: 22017 Tlx: 66313
Solomon Islands Electricity Authority, PO
Box 6, Honiara, Tel.: 23029 Tlx: 66353
Solomon Islands Housing Authority, PO
Box 291, Honiara, Tel.: 21845 Tlx: 66362
**Solomon Islands International
Telecommunications Ltd,** PO Box 148,
Honiara, Tel.: 21576 Tlx: 66301
**Solomon Islands National Provident
Fund,** PO Box 619, Honiara, Tel.: 21659
Tlx: 66311
Solomon Islands Ports Authority,
PO Box 307, Honiara, Tel.: 22646
Tlx: 66348
Solomon Islands Tourist Authority,
PO Box 321, Honiara, Tel.: 22442
Tlx: 66436

PROVINCIAL GOVERNMENTS
Central Islands Provincial Assembly,
Tulagi, Central Islands Province Tlx: 66311
Guadalcanal Provincial Assembly,
PO Box G7, Honiara, Tel.: 20041
Tlx: 66311
Makiara Provincial Assembly, Kirakira,
Makira Province, Tlx: 66311
Malaita Provincial Assembly, Auki,
Malaita Province, Tlx: 66311
Temotu Provincial Assembly, Lata,
Temotu Province, Tlx: 66311
Western Provincial Assembly,
PO Box 36, Gizo, Western Province,
Tlx: 66311

FOREIGN MISSIONS
Australian High Commission, PO Box 589,
Honiara, Tel.: 23109 Tlx: 66325
British High Commission, PO Box 676,
Honiara, Tel.: 21705 Tlx: 66360
**European Economic Commission
Delegation,** PO Box 844, Honiara,
Tel.: 22765 Tlx: 66370
Japanese Embassy, PO Box 842, Honiara,
Tel.: 22953 Tlx: 66385
**Japanese Overseas Cooperation
Volunteers,** PO Box 793, Honiara,
Tel.: 22615
New Zealand High Commission, PO Box
697, Honiara, Tel.: 21502 Tlx: 55322

Papua New Guinea High Commission,
PO Box 626, Honiara, Tel.: 21591
Tlx: 66344
Republic of China Embassy, PO Box 50,
Honiara, Tel.: 22590
South Pacific Forum Fisheries Agency,
PO Box 629, Honiara, Tel.: 21124
Tlx: 66336
U.S. Peace Corps, PO Box 547, Honiara,
Tel.: 21612 Tlx: 66354

HISTORY. Archaeological research has
revealed that the Solomon Islands have been
occupied by man for at least 3000 years.
Material excavated on Santa Ana, Guadalcanal and on Gawa in the Reef Islands has all
been radiocarbon-dated to about 1000 BC.
Red pottery, though to be related to Lapita
ware, has also been found on Santa Ana,
where it is estimated to have been used between 140 and 670 AD. Similar pottery has
been found in the Reef Islands. The European discoverer of the Solomons was the
Spanish explorer Alvaro de Mendana, who
set out from Peru with two ships in 1567 to
seek the legendary Isles of Solomon, believed
to lie to the west of South America, and said
to have been visited by the Incas. In February
1568, after sighting Nui in the Tuvalu group,
he came upon a large, mountainous island
which he named Santa Isabel.

Other large islands, including Guadalcanal, Malaita and San Cristobal, were discovered over the next six months, as well as
several smaller ones. Although miners from
Spain were carried in the ships to seek reef or
alluvial gold, it has not been revealed whether
or not any gold was located on Guadalcanal.
King Solomon's 'riches'. The Spaniards in
Peru and Chile were told of islands to the west
which they assumed were the lost islands of
Solomon, and the name was mentioned in
some documents between 1531 and 1539.
Again, in 1565 and 1566, the Governor of
Peru, Lope Garcia de Castro mentioned 'yslas
que llaman de Salomon' in regard to projected
voyages of discovery. In 1566 the governor
described the projected voyage of Mendana
and said he would be seeking the 'Islands of
Salomon'. This name was subsequently applied to the islands that Mendana found in
1567 and added to the attraction of potential
settlers being recruited in 1595.

Mendana himself does not seem to have

had any part in spreading these rumours. But he did succeed in persuading officialdom to provide him with the necessary ships to go on a colonising expedition to the same parts of the Pacific.

For a variety of reasons, Mendana's second expedition did not leave Peru until 1595. There were four ships and a large number of prospective colonists. After discovering the southern Marquesas Islands and losing one ship in a fog near the volcanic island of Tinakula, Mendana reached Ndeni (Ndende) Island, which he named Santa Cruz. Here a vain attempt was made to found a colony. Mendana himself and many other Spaniards died; dissension broke out among the others; and there were difficulties with the islanders. Finally, the remnants of the expedition made for the Philippines; the flagship's remaining two consorts became lost on the way although one later reached Mindanao. The *Almiranta*, which was lost at night in poor visibility just as the fleet reached Santa Cruz, is now known to have called at San Cristobal, where the remains of a settlement have been found.

In 1606, Pedro Fernandez de Quiros, Mendana's chief pilot in 1595, commanded a second colonising expedition to the Western Pacific. The expedition touched at Taumako Island in the Duff group, and then went on to the northern New Hebrides. It, too, was a failure, and the Spaniards thereafter lost interest in Pacific exploration.

Two Dutch expeditions were the next to visit the Solomons area. In 1616, Schouten and Le Maire discovered some low islands which seem to have been part of the atoll of Ontong Java; and in 1643 Tasman bestowed the name Ontong Java on that atoll because of the resemblance of its islands to islands of that name near Batavia.

Carteret, Bougainville. Most than 120 years passed before Captain Philip Carteret rediscoverd the Santa Cruz group, including Utupua and Vanikoro, and the northern coast of Malaita in 1767. He also added the small island of Ndai, north of Malaita, to the map. About a year later, the French explorer Bougainville, coming north from the New Hebrides, passed through the waters now known as Bougainville Strait and so came upon Choiseul, which he named after a French minister. He also passed the Treasury Islands, Vella Lavella, Bougainville and Buka.

In 1769 Surville, another Frenchman, rediscovered several of the islands seen by Mendana, Carteret and Bougainville and named them Terres des Arsacides (Lands of the Assassins). Mourelle, a Spaniard, rediscovered Roncador Reef in 1781 and so named it for its 'frightful roaring'. Six years later, the American ship *Alliance* (Captain Thomas Read) sailed along the western fringe of the islands of Tetipari and Rendova, then northwards to Bougainville.

In 1788, Lt John Shortland, in command of the *Alexander* and *Friendship*, two transport vessels of the First Fleet to Botany Bay, sailed along the coast of San Cristobal and Guadalcanal. From there, he coasted the largish islands in the central part of the archipelago, which he named New Georgia. Two smaller groups to the northward were given their present names, Treasury and Shortland Islands.

Accounts of the voyages of Shortland, Surville, Bougainville and Carteret led the French geographer M. Bauche to the realisation in 1781 that their discoveries had been made in the same area as those of Mendana, and that they were all part of the Solomon Islands. But just over a century passed before all the islands were reasonably well charted.

Some important details were added to the charts in the 1790s. In 1791, Captain John Hunter discovered Sikaiana, and Captain Edward Edwards of HMS *Pandora* became the first European to sight Anuta and Fataka. In 1792, Captain Edward Manning discovered the passage between Santa Isabel and Choiseul now known as Manning Strait. In 1793, Captain Matthew Boyd of the *Bellona* became the discoverer of Bellona Island and probably its neighbour, Rennell Island. In 1794, Captain Wilkinson of the *Indispensable* discovered Indispensable Strait between San Cristobal and Guadalcanal. And in 1799, Captain James Wilson of the missionary ship *Duff*, rediscovered Quiros' Taumako and other islands in the same group and gave them the name of his ship.

La Perouse episode. The most celebrated episode in the early history of the Solomons concerned the French explorer La Perouse. In January 1788, in the ships *Boussole* and *Astrolabe*, La Perouse had arrived in Botany Bay in the course of an extensive voyage of exploration in the Pacific. He sailed again in the following month — and was never seen again. Despite many rumours and an official search by the d'Entrecasteaux expedition, no positive clue to La Perouse's fate was found for almost 40 years.

The man who unveiled the mystery was an Irishman, Captain Peter Dillon, who chanced on some articles of European origin during a visit to Tikopia in 1826. The islanders told him the articles had come from the neighbouring island of Vanikoro. Dillon visited Vanikoro in the following year and recovered numerous articles that had been washed ashore or salvaged by the islanders. He was told that La Perouse's two ships had been wrecked in a storm, one in shallow water inside the reef and one in deep water outside. The survivors had lived on shore for a time and had built a boat from local timber. They had eventually sailed away in their boat, never to be heard of again.

Several months after Dillon's visit to Vanikoro, the French explorer Dumont d'Urville recovered several cannon and other relics from the inner wreck, which was identified as the *Astrolabe*. Numerous other relics were recovered from Vanikoro in subsequent years. However, it was not until 1962 that the remains of the *Boussole* were found by Mr Reece Discombe, of Vila, New Hebrides, after many hours of swimming over the outer edge of the reef. The *Boussole* had come to grief in a deep, wedge-shaped chasm, about 1 km from where the *Astrolabe* was wrecked. Several coral-encrusted anchors and cannon, many iron and lead ingots, and a number of other items were subsequently recovered.

Missionaries rebuffed. The discoveries of Dillon and d'Urville at Vanikoro focussed some European attention on the Solomon Islands. But apart from occasional visits by whalers, there was little European contact with the area until the mid-19th century. The first Europeans to try to establish themselves were seven priests and six lay brothers of the French Marist order, under the direction of Bishop Epalle. They landed on the south coast of San Cristobal in 1845. But the bishop was murdered on Isabel within a few days, and the mission, which they established at Makira Bay, never really got going. After three more of its members had been murdered and one had died of malaria,

the mission was abandoned in 1848.

Another person to lose his life in the Solomons at this time was Benjamin Boyd from New South Wales. In 1851, he visited San Cristobal and Guadalcanal in his yacht *Wanderer* with the idea of forming an independent government there under his own control. However, this idea came to nothing, for Boyd was murdered by islanders when he landed to shoot birds at a place still known as Wanderer Bay on the south-west coast of Guadalcanal.

Boyd's murder and the grim experiences of the Marists may have prompted the cautious methods of the Melanesian Mission of the Church of England, which extended its work to the Solomons in the early 1850s. Instead of establishing missionaries in the group, the Anglicans persuaded young islanders to go with them for training either in New Zealand or Norfolk Island. The idea was that, on being returned to their home islands, these novices would start converting their own people. The mission ship *Southern Cross* made regular visits to the Solomons each year. But the Anglicans made little progress until they themselves began to settle in the group in the late 1870s.

The labour recruiters. Meanwhile, labour recruiters had moved into the Solomons seeking labour for plantations in Fiji, Queensland and occasionally New Caledonia and Samoa. The first recruiting vessel appeared in 1870. Recruiting for Queensland continued until 1904 and for Fiji until 1911. Nearly 19,000 islanders are estimated to have been taken to Queensland and more than 10,000 to Fiji. Less than half of those indentured for Fiji were returned to their homes, but 14,105 are estimated to have been returned from Queensland. Descendants of those who went to Fiji live in the village of Wailoku near Suva, Fiji's capital.

Abuses committed by the labour recruiters, known as blackbirders, frequently led to the murder of innocent people, particularly in the early days. Two prominent Europeans who lost their lives were Bishop J. C. Patteson, the second bishop of Melanesia, who was clubbed to death at Nukapu, Reef Islands, in 1871, and Commodore J. G. Goodenough of HMS *Pearl*, who died from a poisoned arrow wound sustained at Carlisle Bay, Santa Cruz, in 1875.

Protectorate declared. The evils of the labour trade and its consequences prompted Great Britain to declare a protectorate over the southern Solomon Islands (Guadalcanal, Savo, Malaita, San Cristobal, and the New Georgia group) in 1893. In 1898 and 1899, the islands of the Santa Cruz group, including Utupua, Tikopia, Vanikoro, and the outlying islands of Anuta, Fataka, Sikaiana, Rennell and Bellona were added to the protectorate.

There were further additions in 1900. By a treaty with Germany, and in exchange for Britain's withdrawal from Western Samoa, several islands in the north of the group that had previously come within the German sphere of influence were transferred to British administration. These islands were Isabel, Choiseul, the islands south and south-east of the main island of Bougainville, and the atoll of Ontong Java.

When the British protectorate was established, approximately four dozen European traders were resident in the group. Twelve years later, in 1905, there was a move to open up the Solomons commercially. Lever's Pacific Plantations Ltd chartered the steam yacht *Victoria* to visit the protectorate, and representatives of the company took up land on a large scale. Planting began almost immediately, and by 1940 the company had more than 8000 hectares under cultivation. Two other companies that acquired interests in the Solomons early in the 20th century were Burns, Philp & Co., of Sydney, and the Malaita Co. The latter sold out to W. R. Carpenter & Co. Ltd in the 1930s.

Pacific War. The economic development of the Solomons progressed only sluggishly before World War II. After the Japanese entered the war in 1941, most of the planters and traders in the group were evacuated to Australia. Soon afterwards, the Japanese occupied the main islands. From May 1942, when the Battle of the Coral Sea was fought, until December 1943, the Solomons were almost constantly a scene of combat.

One of the most furious sea battles ever fought took place off Savo Island, near Guadalcanal, in August 1942. Heavy losses were inflicted on both sides, but more crushingly on the Allies. Many fierce naval engagements followed before the Japanese withdrew completely from Guadalcanal in February 1943. The Allied forces later drove them from other islands, and by December 1943 they were in command of the Northern Solomons.

When civil administration of the Solomons resumed after the war, the authorities found that Tulagi, the former capital, on an islet off Florida, had been destroyed. It was decided to establish a new capital at Honiara on the north coast of Guadalcanal. This was the site of an important American wartime campaign against the Japanese, situated about 16 km west of Henderson Field, a major wartime air base. Originally, many of the buildings in use in Honiara were relics of the war, but few of these are now to be seen.

Marching Rule. Between 1946 and 1950, a good deal of official attention was devoted to a native movement known as Marching Rule, believed to be an Anglicised version of 'masina' (brotherhood). Some people thought it had its origin in the close wartime contacts between islanders and American soldiers with their seemingly limitless wealth; others looked on it as a nationalist movement that followed naturally on the profoundly disturbing effects of the war.

In a general way, the movement took the form of adherence to some chief who assumed dictatorial power, was strongly anti-European, and who led his people in a sullen defiance of governmental authority. Large numbers of people on Malaita and in other islands were affected, and there was much disorder until some of the leaders were gaoled in late 1948.

Other indigenous movements that developed later were breakaway movements from the Christian missions. In 1959–60, followers of Silas Eto, later called Holy Mama, broke away from the Methodist Mission on New Georgia. They lived in a model village called Paradise and engaged in bursts of agricultural development. Silas Eto died in January, 1983. In the early 1960s, the adherents of a cult called Moro collected about $8000 to buy their freedom from the government.

Gradual changes in the system of governing the Solomons were made from the end of World War II until the early 1970s, after which changes came much more rapidly as Britain prepared to give the islanders their independence.

When civil administration was resumed after the war, an advisory council, first created in 1921, was re-established. This had originally consisted of the resident commissioner as president and four nominated members, but membership was now increased. In 1960, the advisory council was superseded by a legislative council, and an executive council was created as the policy-making body for the protectorate. Progressively the council was given more authority.

In 1970, under a new constitution, both the legislative council and the executive council were replaced by a single governing council. The constitution provided for 17 elected members and up to nine public service members, with the high commissioner holding reserve powers of disallowing legislation. The new council sat for the first time in July 1971, and five committees were subsequently set up in an interesting experiment in consensus. These committees covered Finance: Natural Resources; Communications and Works; Education and Social Welfare; and Health and Internal Affairs. Legislation was initiated by these committees, except in respect of some reserved subjects such as defence and internal security; and as every elected member belonged to one of the committees, he therefore had a direct say in framing policy.

After the governing council, with its committee system, had been in operation about 18 months, its members generally agreed that a cabinet system, under a chief minister, would be more practical.

A new constitution was adopted in April 1974. Under this, the high commissioner became governor, the chief secretary became deputy governor, the governing council became the legislative council with 24 elected members and three ex-officio, and the leader of government business became chief minister with the right to select his own cabinet. Solomon Mamaloni was appointed the first chief minister. In mid-1975, the name Solomon Islands was officially adopted in place of British Solomon Islands Protectorate. And on 2 January 1976 the Solomon Islands became an internally self-governing state. Independence followed on 7 July 1978.

Since Independence politics in the Solomon Islands have been generally stable, although there have been frequent changes of Prime Ministership. The two main contenders for the office have been Sir Peter Kenilorea and Solomon Mamaloni. The present Prime Minister, Ezekiel Alebua, gained office when Sir Peter Kenilorea stepped down after being faced with charges of misuse of French relief funds, following the disastrous cyclone Namu in early 1986.

Further reading. Janet Kent, *The Solomon Islands*, Newton Abbot, 1972. Colin Jack-Hinton, *The Search for the Islands of Solomon*, Oxford, 1969. Hugh Laracy, *Marists and Melanesians*, Canberra, 1973. R. M. Keesing (ed.), *Elota's Story*, St Lucia, 1978.

ISLANDS OF THE SOLOMONS IN DETAIL.

The Solomon Islands are divided into seven provinces, each headed by a premier with a secretary as overall supervisor of the administration of the province. Headquarters are: Honiara — Guadalcanal Province; Tulagi — Central Islands; Auki — Malaita; Kirakira — Makira Temotu; Lata — Eastern Outer Islands; Gizo — Western; and Buala — Isabel.

Guadalcanal. Guadalcanal, the largest of the Solomon Islands, is about 150 km long from west to east, by 48 km wide. The interior is high and rugged, with many razorback mountains. Mt Makarakombou (2447 m) and Mt Popomaniasu (2440 m) are the highest points. On the northern coast, foothills descend in many places to a coastal plain of varying width. There are many coconut plantations in this area. Timber and rice are also produced, and oil palms have been planted in recent years. Most of the southern coast falls in precipitous cliffs to the sea. Strong currents, tide rips and a heavy surf make it dangerous for small ships even in moderate weather. Both the northern and southern coasts are cut by many rivers. During the rainy season, those in the south are likely to become raging torrents.

Honiara, the capital of the Solomons and main port of entry, is situated on the northern coast, about 40 km from the north-west point. It is built on both sides of Point Cruz where Mendana anchored in 1568. In mid-1983, Honiara was officially designated Capital Territory. Point Cruz has a deep-water wharf which can accommodate vessels of nearly 200 m length. There are also facilities for small ships. Sheltered anchorages, except in the NW region, exist at

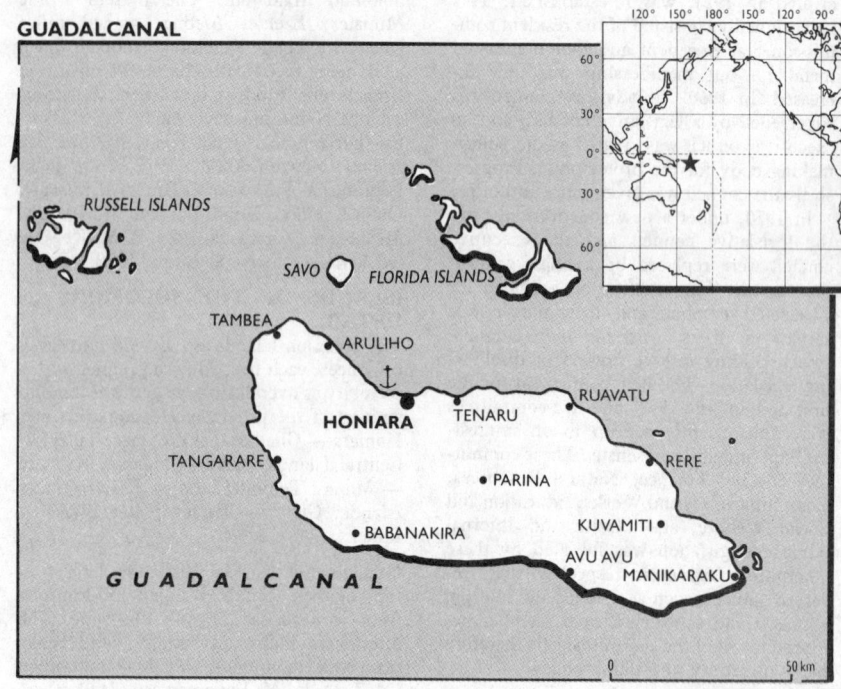

GUADALCANAL

RUSSELL ISLANDS

SAVO   FLORIDA ISLANDS

TAMBEA

ARULIHO

HONIARA   TENARU

RUAVATU

TANGARARE

RERE

PARINA

BABANAKIRA

KUVAMITI

AVU AVU

MANIKARAKU

G U A D A L C A N A L

0   50 km

many points along the north coast. About 16 km east of Honiara is Henderson Field, an international airport, which links the Solomons with Australia, Papua New Guinea, Nauru, Vanuatu, New Caledonia and Fiji. It is also the hub for internal air services in the Solomons.

Other airstrips on Guadalcanal are at Avuavu on the north-west coast, at Marau Sound at the eastern end of the island, and Bababanakira.

A road about 117 km long runs along the northern coast from Lambi Bay in the west to Bokokimbo, east of Henderson Field.

Honiara is a post-war town which stands on the site of a former coconut plantation. Its name is derived from Naghoniara, meaning 'place of the east wind'. The Japanese had a small base on the site in 1942. Later the Americans built a much larger one after defeating the Japanese in a bitter struggle.

The post-war civil administration of the Solomons used many of the wartime army buildings as offices and quarters until the

late 1950s and early 1960s when both the Government and private enterprise carried out a vigorous building programme. In 1969, the reconstruction of Government House was completed at a cost of $270,000.

Recreations available in Honiara include golf, tennis, bush walking and swimming, although there is a serious shark danger on the coast.

A picturesque suburb of Honiara is Chinatown with its double row of Chinese-owned shops which, along with a number of European stores, cater for most needs.

Honiara has an elected town council, a public bus service, adequate taxis, and electricity and water supplies.

Several places on or near Guadalcanal figured in the early history of European penetration of the Solomons. The small island of Rua Sua off the NE coast was the site of a Roman Catholic mission station in the 1840s.

Wanderer Bay on the SW coast is the spot where Benjamin Boyd, who had plans to create a private kingdom in the Solomons, went ashore from his yacht *Wanderer* in 1851 and was never seen again.

Tetere, about 32 km east of Honiara, was the scene of the murder of five Austrian gold-seekers who landed there in 1896 and expressed a desire to climb Mt Tatuve, despite local opposition to their plan. There is a stone memorial to them at Tetere.

Savo. Savo, a quiescent volcano, rises abruptly from the sea about 32 km NW of Honiara. Its last known eruption took place in 1840 with considerable loss of life. Areas of boiling mud and ground temperatures of up to 84°C (215°F) are constant reminders that the volcano is far from dead. The volcano has two craters, one inside the other, at the western end of the island. Waterfalls of almost boiling water and sulphur vents issue from the inner crater.

Savo has several peaks, the highest being 510 m. The shores of the island are steep and there is little shelter for vessels. There is a large Melanesian population in 12 villages scattered around the coast. Coconuts thrive as do fruit and vegetables. Near the village of Pamueli, the islanders maintain hatcheries of megapode eggs in the warm volcanic sands.

The waters between Savo and Guadalcanal were the scene of a disastrous naval battle for the Allies in August 1942, with many ships sunk. The sea between Savo and Honiara is now known as Ironbottom Sound as a result of the battles in that area.

Florida. Florida is the name given by the Mendana expedition to a group of volcanic islands lying northward of Guadalcanal and clearly visible from Honiara. There are two large islands, Gela and Small Gela, separated by the narrow Utaha Passage.

Olevugha, Vatilau, Hanesavo and several other small islands lie off the western extremity of Gela. Another, Tulagi, which is about 5 km in circumference, lies off the south coast. Before World War II, this was the capital of the British Solomon Islands Protectorate. Nearby is the islet of Makambo, the pre-war head station of Burns Philp (SS) Co. Ltd in the Solomons. Taroaniara on Gela and Siota on Small Gela figure prominently in the history of the Melanesian Mission in the Solomons.

Iron and nickelliferous laterites occur near Siota. Manganese has been found on Olevugha and Hanesavo. Gavutu, about 3 km south of Tulagi, has been leased to Lever's Pacific Plantations Pty Ltd. Mandoliana Island, south of Small Gela, was the scene of the murder of Lieut J. St C. Bower and several seamen of HMS *Sandfly* in 1880.

Rennell and Bellona. Rennell Island (Mu Gava) and Bellona Island (Mu Giki) are two upraised coral limestone islands lying about 190 km SW of San Cristobal. They are about 24 km apart. Rennell, by far the larger, is SW of Bellona. It is about 80 km long by 16 km wide, and 150 m high. It has an extensive lake, Tinggoa, at its SE end, the largest in the South Pacific. The water of the lake is at sea level, but is surrounded by lofty cliffs. Bellona is only about 11.5 km by 3 km at its widest. Both islands are thought to be raised atolls. Rennell is the finest example of its kind in the world.

Bellona is named after the merchant ship *Bellona* (Captain Matthew Boyd) which passed it in 1793. But historians have yet to discover why Rennell was so named, and by whom. The significance of the two native names, Mu Gava and Mu Giki is also unknown.

Because both islands are difficult of access, the Rennell and Bellona people, who are Polynesians, were little visited by Europeans until after the turn of the century. It was not until 1939 that the islanders adopted Christianity. They have since been studied intensively by the Danish scholars Kaj Birket-Smith and Torben Monberg, and by an American linguist, Samuel H. Elbert.

Rennell Island has extensive bauxite deposits. Bellona is also of interest to the mining world because of valuable deposits of phosphatic rock — some 10 million tonnes of it. An airstrip was opened for service on Rennell in 1970.

Russell Islands. The Russell Islands comprise two large islands, Pavuvu and Banika, with a fringe of small ones, including Money. They lie about 40 km NW of the NW tip of Guadalcanal. Pavuvu is about 16 km from east to west, and rises to about 488 m. It is extensively planted with coconuts, as is Banika. At Yandina on the eastern side of Banika is a wharf capable of accommodating overseas copra vessels, and also Renard Airfield.

Santa Isabel. Santa Isabel (formerly Ysabel) is a long, narrow island some 80 km north-westward of Guadalcanal. It is about 145 km long by 30 km at its greatest width. It is made up of a single chain of volcanic mountains which generally dip to a lowlying coastal strip. A complex of small islands extends off the NW end of Santa Isabel; and at the SE corner is San Jorge, about 24 km long by 14 km wide.

The leeward side of Santa Isabel is largely under coconuts, plantations having been established there from a very early date. Meringe Lagoon, formerly a port of call for ships from Sydney, extends about 13 km along the NE coast. It is formed by five islets in a semi-circle, and is a favourite watering place for inter-island vessels. Allardyce Harbour in the south-west was used until recent years for the export of timber.

There is an airstrip on Fera Island, off the NE coast.

San Jorge, which is separated from the mainland by Thousand Ships Bay, has been thoroughly investigated for minerals.

New Georgia Islands. The New Georgia Islands, a group of 11 islands of moderate size and a number of smaller ones, lies to the south and SW of Choiseul and Santa Isabel. The group is separated from those islands by New Georgia Sound, otherwise known as The Slot. The islands extend in a double chain from NW to SE over a distance of about 200 km. Those on the inner side (facing The Slot) are: Vella Lavella, Kolombangara, New Georgia, Vangunu and Gatokae. Those on the outer side are: Ranongga, Gizo, Vonavona, Arundel, Rendova and Tetepare.

The group was the scene of some fierce fighting during World War II. But it is still little known to Europeans, and some of its coasts have never been thoroughly surveyed. Gizo (see below), the smallest of the 11 principal islands of the group, is the administrative centre and port of entry for the Western District. The group is noted for its copra plantations.

DETAILS OF THE INNER ISLANDS, FROM WEST TO EAST:
Vella Lavella, at the western end of the group, is mountainous and forest-covered,

with several dormant volcanoes, fumaroles and hot springs. There are numerous trading stations on the island visited regularly by local small ships. An airstrip is situated at Barakoma (Mbarakoma) on the SE side.

Kolombangara, 21 km SE of Vella Lavella, is roughly circular in shape. It is an extinct volcano rising directly from the sea to a series of peaks up to 1661 m high.

Both logging and reafforestation work is carried out. There is an airstrip at Kukudu on the western side.

New Georgia, the largest island in the group, lies to the eastward of Kolombangara. It is separated from it by the deep waters of Kula Gulf. It was named by Lieut. John Shortland who coasted its southern side in 1788. The island is about 80 km long from NW to SE and from eight to 48 km wide. The most populated part is around the Roviana Lagoon on the SW side. The lagoon is about 40 km long by 6.5 km wide, and is sheltered by a series of flat-topped islands about 60 m high.

Roviana was one of the first places in the Solomons to attract European traders. One such pioneer, Norman Wheatley, established Lambete Plantation at the western end of the lagoon in an area known as Munda. Munda is the site of the second busiest airfield in the Solomons — after Guadalcanal's Henderson Field. It was originally built by the Japanese in 1942. A rest house at Munda provides limited accommodation for travellers. Another airfield is situated at Seghe at the SE end of New Georgia. This serves the people of Marovo Lagoon, a large expanse of water extending from the NE side of New Georgia to the northern side of the adjacent Vangunu Island. Marovo is entered through an opening in a high cliff which separates the lagoon from the sea.

Vangunu Island, roughly circular with an extremely indented coastline, is about 26 km in diameter. Besides the Marovo Lagoon on its north coast, it has another, Kolo Lagoon, on its eastern side. The island is probably the remains of a single volcanic cone whose summit reaches a height of 1123 m and is usually lost in cloud.

Gatokae Island, about 6 km SE of Vangunu and about one-fourth of its size, is another volcanic cone. The highest point is 887 m.

Mbulo Island, with steep coral cliffs, lies about 3 km NE. In 1952, a submarine volcano erupted 29 km SSW of Gatokae.

OTHER ISLANDS, FROM WEST TO EAST:

Rangonga (or Ghanongga) Island is the westernmost of the outer chain of New Georgia Islands. It is about 25 km long by eight broad. About eight km due south is Simbo Island, formerly known as the Eddystone. Simbo is about 6.5 km from north to south, and is formed of two volcanic hills joined by a low coral isthmus. In the 19th century Simbo was a popular calling place for ships sailing northwards from Sydney to China and the Philippines. An 1863 sailing directory recommended captains to call there for pilots and interpreters, as the islanders, unlike their neighbours, were 'on friendly terms with Europeans'.

Gizo, lying about midway between Ranongga to the west and Kolombangara to the NE, is an island of coral formation. It is about 13 km long by five km wide, rising to a height of about 180 m. There are no prominent features. A chain of small islands extends for about eight km off the SE extremity, from near Gizo harbour. The township of Gizo, badly damaged during the war, is on the southern side of the harbour. It has been headquarters for the Western District since 1949. In 1955, the first Gilbertese to be resettled in the Solomons were landed at Gizo. Since then some have gone to the Shortland Islands. An airfield for Gizo is situated on Nusatupe Island to the east.

Vonavona (Wana Wana) and **Arundel** (or **Kohinggo**) Islands lie to the southward of Kolombangara. Arundel is separated from the western end of New Georgia Island by Hathorn Sound and the Diamond Narrows, Vonavona lies to the SW of Arundel. Both are flat and of coral formation.

Rendova, the largest of the outer islands, lies to the southward of Roviana Lagoon. It is roughly rectangular, about 26 km long and with a long peninsula extending from its SE corner. Rendova Peak, a volcanic cone with an extinct crater, is 1063 m high. The US capture of a Japanese base on Rondova in 1943 was a preliminary to the recapture of the important Munda airfield.

Tetepare, SE of Rondova, is about 26 km long by 14.5 km wide. It is separated from New Georgia Island by the Blanche Channel.

Choiseul. This is a long, mountainous island, extending about 144 km from NW to SE, and with a maximum width of 32 km. It is on the eastern side of Bougainville Strait and northward of New Georgia Sound. Mt Maitambe (1006 m) near the middle of the island is its highest point. Much of the interior has never been explored, and only the SW and NW sides of the island have been surveyed. Most of the people live round the coast.

Choiseul Bay, near the NW tip of the island, is the site of several coconut plantations. Taro Airfield is nearby. There are mission stations at Sasamungga on the central western coast and on Mole Islet further north.

Off the eastern end of Choiseul are a number of islands, the largest of which are Rob Roy (Vealaviru), Susuku and Vaghena (Wagina). Vaghena is the site of a Gilbertese resettlement scheme dating back to 1963. The name Choiseul was given to the island by the French explorer Bougainville in 1768. The local name of Choiseul is Lauru.

Shortland and Treasury Islands.

The Shortland and Treasury Islands lie only a few kilometres eastward and southward of the large island of Bougainville, and are at the border of Papua New Guinea. They are westward of Bougainville Strait. The main islands in the Shortland group are Shortland and Fauro. The Treasury group consists of Mono and Stirling.

Shortland Island (local name: Alu) is the largest in the two groups. It is about 30 km by 24 km, rising to a height of nearly 200 m. Korovou, at the SE end, is the main settlement and headquarters for the district. Logging is carried on nearby.

Faisi, a small island NE of Korovou, was formerly the government station. It encloses a sheltered harbour where overseas ships can be accommodated. Faisi and surrounding foreshores are planted with coconuts. Other islands off the coast include: Magusaiai, Pirumeri, Poporang, Onua, Olofi and Aloataghala.

Fauro, about 18 km NE of Shortland, is an

irregularly shaped island of volcanic origin. It is about 22 km long. Numerous small islands lie nearby. To the north are Ovau and Oema (island and atoll); to the west are Asie, Ilina, Nusave, Nielal, Nusakova, Beniana and Nuhahana; to the south is Mania; and to the NE, Piru (Piedu), Obeani (Cyprian Bridge) and Masamasa.

Mono in the Treasury group lies about 32 km SSW of Shortland Island. It is oval in shape, densely wooded, and about 14.5 km long by eight broad. Its highest point is 355 m. Falamae village stands on a promontory near the island's southern extremity.

Stirling Island, off the south coast of Mono, is separated from it by Blanche Harbour. Several small islands in the harbour are planted with coconuts.

Two airfields serve these groups — one on Mono and one on Ballalae Island between Shortland and Fauro. Both were built during the war.

Malaita. Malaita, lying NE of Florida and Guadalcanal and SE of Santa Isabel, is separated from them by the deep waters of Indispensable Strait. It is a mountainous, densely wooded island, running roughly from NNW to SSE. It is about 165 km long by 37 km at its greatest width, with an area of about 3840 sq. km. The land rises gradually from the coast to a maximum elevation at Mt Kolovrat of 1303 m.

There are many indentations along the coast affording shelter for coastal shipping. These are often at the mouths of fast-flowing rivers, which, together with many precipitous hills, kept tribes apart in ancient times, fostered suspicion, and favoured the survival or development of many languages and dialects. Today, however, there is a unity of purpose among the Malaita people and they are most progressive.

Because Malaita had a large population when European contact began, it was a popular rendezvous for labour recruiters from the 1870s onwards. Abuses committed by the labour traders made the establishment of law and order difficult after the Solomons became a British protectorate in 1893.

However, by the 1920s, a good start had been made from the government station at Auki on the west coast, while Catholic missionaries had made some progress from a station at Bina, south of Auki. The murder

of District Commissioner Bell and some members of a police detachment in 1927 was a serious setback.

When World War II came, many Malaita men volunteered to serve with the Americans on Guadalcanal as guides, scouts and labourers. Their sudden contact with the ships, aeroplanes, bulldozers, canned food and other marvels of the Americans had an unsettling effect after the war. The Marching Rule movement, a cargo cult, was one manifestation of it. Later there was a Federal Council. Although neither Marching Rule nor the Federal Council achieved much materially, they did help bring about the unification of the Malaita people. In 1953, the first Malaita Council was formed. This and its successors have been responsible for a great deal of economic development on the island — copra, rice and cocoa growing; road-building; the establishment of schools, etc.

Auki, now the seat of administration of the Malaita District (which includes the atolls of Ontong Java and Sikaiana), is a township with modern offices and housing, a district hospital, schools, a shopping centre, harbour facilities for coastal ships, yards for boat-building, etc. There is an airfield about 2.25 km northward of the town. The longest road in the Solomons runs through Auki. Beginning at Bina, 27 km south of Auki, it extends to the northern most point of the island and continues down the east coast to Fouia, a distance of 147 km.

Many Malaita people live on artificial islands off the coast. These are built up with coral and frequently have the appearance of forts. Sharks, which are numerous, are held to be sacred.

Maramsike, sometimes called **Small Malaita** lies off the SE end of Malaita. The two islands are separated by a narrow and tortuous passage. The local council maintains an airfield at Parasi on the SW side. Maana'oba (Manaoba) is an island off the NE coast.

The population of Malaita, including Maramsike, was 80,183 at the 1986 census, the largest for any island in the group. The native name for Malaita is Mala. It was once known to Europeans as Malanta.

Ndai, Ramos. These are two islands off Cape Astrolabe, the NW point of Malaita.

Ndai, about 40 km northward, is some 8 km long by 3 km wide. It was called Gower Island by Captain Carteret in 1767.

Ramos, about 2.5 km long, is 33 km west of Cape Astrolabe. Ramos, Spanish for 'palms' as in Palm Sunday, was the name that Mendana gave to Malaita in 1568. It was mistakenly applied to the present Ramos Island by the Russian hydrographer Krusenstern in 1824.

Sikaiana. Sikaiana, sometimes written Sikayana, is a triangular atoll lying about 177 km NE of Malaita. It takes its name from the largest of four islets on its reef, which is the site of the principal settlment. The other islets are called Matuavi, Matuiloto and Tehaolei. The inhabitants are Polynesians, probably of Tuvalu origin.

Sikaiana's reef is steep with tremendous depths a few metres out. This makes it dangerous to approach by night or in poor visibility as no warning is given by soundings. Moreover, lack of anchorages and a continual heavy swell make it very difficult of access. A few small trading vessels visit it occasionally to collect copra and bêche-de-mer. They make use of two boat landings at either end of Sikaiana islet. The islanders are adept at building canoes and in handling them in the surf.

The atoll was formerly known as Stewart Island. The first European to report it was Captain John Hunter, who passed it in the ship *Waaksamheyd* in 1791. One of the best early accounts of it was given by Dr Karl Scherzer of the Austrian frigate *Novara* which called there in 1859. It became a British protectorate on 18 August 1889.

Ontong Java. Ontong Java, the northernmost island in the Solomons, lies 5 deg south of the Equator, some 250 km north of Santa Isabel. It is an atoll shaped like a boot, the toe being in the SE. It is about 72 km long from north to SE, and about 48 km at its greatest width.

There are about 100 islets on the reef, mainly on the southern and eastern sides. Luangiua, the largest, and site of the principal settlement, is at the SE end. Other sizeable islets are Pelau (site of the only other village), Avaha and Keila. All the islets are well planted with coconuts and copra production is large. There are 23 passages through the reef. Kaveiko pass, to the south

of Luangiua, leads to the main anchorage.

The first Europeans to see Ontong Java were probably the Dutch explorers Schouten and Le Maire in 1616. But the name Ontong Java was applied to the atoll by Tasman in 1643. Captain Hunter named it Lord Howe's Group in 1791, and it was commonly known as Lord Howe Atoll until recent times (it is not to be confused with Lord Howe Island, off Australia's east coast). Because of its isolated position, few whalers or traders appear to have visited it before about 1875 when labour recruiters sought men there. In 1895, the E. E. Forsayth Company of New Guinea's so-called 'Queen' Emma, established a trading station on the atoll and visitors became more frequent. The population was then about 2000. Introduced diseases caused it to drop to a record low of 588 by 1939, when the atoll was declared a closed district. Since then the numbers have gradually increased again. The islanders are Polynesians. They have the unusual burial custom of marking graves with large upright coral stones.

Further information. Article by T. Bayliss-Smith in *Pacific Atoll Populations* (Vern Carroll, ed.), Honolulu, 1975.

San Cristobal. San Cristobal, known locally as Makira, is about 112 km from NW to SE, with a maximum width of about 38 km. It lies about 53 km SE of Guadalcanal. A series of mountain ranges run parallel to the main axis of the island, which is densely wooded. The highest point is 1250 m. There is a strip of level land along the north coast, but the south coast falls precipitously to the sea. Star Harbour, near the eastern end, is the best anchorage on the north coast. Others are Wanione (Wanoni) Bay, Kirakira Bay and Wango Bay. Makira and Marunga Harbours afford the best shelter on the south coast. Makira is the site of a Catholic mission.

Kirakira, headquarters for the Eastern District, is situated on the north coast on the bay of the same name. It is a short distance eastward of Wanione Bay. It has a small hospital and an airstrip, Ngora Ngora, which links San Cristobal with Honiara.

There are several islands off the coast of San Cristobal. Santa Ana (Owa Raha) and Santa Catalina (Owa Riki) lie off the eastern end. Uki (formerly written Ugi), Bio and the Three Sisters (or Olu Malau) lie from 7 to

32 km to the northward. About 27 km northward of the Three Sisters is Ulawa. Ulawa, the largest of these islands, is about 20 km long.

All the islands produce copra. Santa Ana, a raised atoll, is particularly well planted. Both Santa Ana and Santa Catalina have been investigated for phosphates. Santa Ana was one of the first islands in the Solomons to have a resident European trader.

Pamua, on the north coast of San Cristobal, is now known to have been the site of a camp established in 1595 by the passengers and crew of the Spanish ship *Santa Isabel*. The *Santa Isabel* was one of the four vessels of Mendana's second expedition to the Solomons. She became separated from her companions near the volcano island of Tinakula, and was never seen again. Evidently she continued due westward to Pamua, a distance of about 440 km. Pieces of pottery from the Spanish camp were first found at Pamua in 1923, but it was not until 1970 that archaeologists identified these and other pieces, plus an iron nail, as being of Spanish-American origin and undoubtedly from the *Santa Isabel*. The ultimate fate of the *Santa Isabel* and her complement is unknown.

Santa Cruz Group.

The Santa Cruz Group, lying some 450 km eastward of San Cristobal, consists of four main islands: Ndende (Ndeni or Santa Cruz), Utupua, Vanikoro and Tinakula.

The name Santa Cruz dates back to 1595 when the Spanish explorer Mendana tried to form a colony at Graciosa Bay. Although Peter Dillon found relics of the La Perouse expedition at Vanikoro in 1827 (see under History), the group had little continuous contact with Europeans until quite recent times.

Early this century, a trader, Captain Oscar Svensen, established a store at Graciosa Bay, and Lever's had a station there for about 16 years until just after World War I. But it was not until 1923 when the Kauri Timber Co. of Melbourne took up rights to export kauri from Vanikoro that direct British administration was extended to the group. From a district office on Vanikoro, it took about 10 years to bring law and order to all the islands.

During World War II, the Americans had an observation post on Ndende and a major naval battle was fought in Santa Cruz waters against the Japanese. The extraction of kauri from Vanikoro ended in 1964. Since then copra has been the main source of income in the group.

Ndende, by far the largest of the Santa Cruz group, is roughly rectangular in shape, about 25 km from west to east, and 17 km across. Its densely wooded hills rise to a height of about 550 m. Graciosa Bay is the principal harbour. There is an airfield nearby. Byron and Carlisle Bays on the north coast also give good shelter. Offshore islands are Temotu, at the entrance to Graciosa Bay, and Lord Howe (Tomotu Noi) on the SE side.

Utupua lies about 70 km SE of Ndende. It is roughly circular, about 11 km in diameter and with a fringing reef about 3 km wide. A passage through the reef leads into Basilisk Harbour.

Vanikoro, about 32 km SE of Utupua and somewhat larger, is ruggedly volcanic, with traces of recent lava flows still visible. A small island, Tevai, lies off the east coast. Both islands are densely wooded. The highest point on Vanikoro is 923 m. Peu is the principal harbour.

Tinakula, or Tenakula, lies about 30 km north of Ndende. It has been an active volcano for most of its recorded history. But during a lull in 1958, people from Nupani, one of the Reef Islands, planted gardens there, and in 1960 some of those islanders occupied it.

Further information. Articles by William Davenport in *Baessler-Archiv*, 1986, 1969 and 1972, and that cited under Reef Islands.

Reef Islands. The Reef Islands, also known as the Swallow Islands, comprise about a dozen small islands lying 60 km and more northward of Ndende. They are spread over an area of about 70 km and appear to be the remnants of a raised atoll. They are generally surrounded by fringing reefs. The men have a reputation as daring navigators.

The other islands from Ndende, called the Outer Reef Islands, are only a few metres above sea level. They are from west to east: Nupani, Naloko, Nukapu, Makolobu and Pileni. They are inhabited by Polynesians. Nukapu was the scene of the murder of Bishop J. C. Patteson in 1871.

The other islands, known as the Main Reef Islands, are as much as 50 metres high.

They are: Nifiloll, Fenualoa, Ngabelipa, Ngagaue, Nananiebulel, Nibane Tema (or Pangani), Nibange Nede (or Pokoli) and Matema. The inhabitants are Melanesian, except on Nifiloli, the northernmost island, where they are Polynesians. The islands of Ngabelipa, Ngagaue and Nananiebulei are known collectively as Ngailo, Nevelo or Lomlom.

Further information. Article by William Davenport in *Pacific Atoll Populations* (Vern Carroll, ed.), Honolulu, 1975.

Duff Islands. The Duff Islands, a chain of 10 small volcanic islands and pinnacles, lie about 110 km NE of the Reef Islands. The principal island, Taumako, is 365 m high. Others are Bass, Obelisk and Treasurers. They are inhabited by Polynesian-speaking people who maintain close ties with the Reef Islanders. Quiros, in 1606, discovered the group. Captain James Wilson of the *Duff* visited it in 1797 and gave the name Disappointment Island to Taumako.

Further information. Article by William Davenport in *Baessler-Archiv*, 1968.

Anuta, Fataka, Tikopia. These three islands are the easternmost outliers of the Solomons. Anuta is about 320 km due east of Vanikoro and 120 km NE of Tikopia. Fataka is 42 km SE of Anuta. Only Anuta and Tikopia are inhabited, their people being Polynesians.

Anuta is little more than 1 km from north to south. Fataka, steep and rocky, is somewhat larger. Tikopia, the largest of the three, is about 5 km by 3 km, being roughly oval in shape. It is an ancient volcano and heavily wooded. The old crater rim, which rises to a height of 366 m, encloses a lake of fresh, but murky water.

The original settlers of Anuta are said to have come from Tonga and Uvea (Wallis Island) about 14 generations ago. They maintain contact with the Tikopians, and some are inter-related.

Anuta and Fataka were 'discovered' in 1791 by Captain Edwards of HMS *Pandora* while searching for the *Bounty* mutineers. He named them Cherry and Mitre, respectively.

Tikopia acquired some celebrity early last century as the place where Captain Peter Dillon acquired a silver sword guard engraved with a fleur-de-lis, which led him to discover the fate of La Perouse at Vanikoro in 1827. The Tikopians have been intensely studied since the 1930s by the anthropologist Raymond Firth. Because of overcrowding, some Tikopians have been resettled on San Cristobal and in the Russell Islands.

FOR THE TOURIST. The chief interest of visitors to the Solomons in recent years has been to see this major theatre of US operations in World War II. Improved air links are bringing greater numbers of Japanese back to visit this area. The scene of the fiercest battles was Guadalcanal.

Entry formalities. All visitors must carry a valid passport. Entry visas are not required from British subjects or certain others such as US citizens.

Transit visas are not required by persons who have confirmed onward bookings by air or sea, except for nationals of certain countries. Visitors entering Solomon Islands may normally obtain a permit on arrival allowing a stay for a period of two months. Residency permits must be obtained from the Chief Immigration Officer before entry.

Yellow fever vaccinations are required if entry has been made from an infected area within the previous fourteen days. Health authorities strongly recommend that antimalarial medication be taken during and after a visit to Solomon Islands. The antimalarial should be appropriate to the area and advice on latest developments should be obtained from doctors or government health offices *before* arrival.

Airport tax. There is an airport tax of $10.00. Tipping in the Solomons is not encouraged.

Duty free shopping. Several ships in Honiara offer duty free goods with delivery to plane or ship. Also on sale are local carvings, handicrafts, etc.

Sightseeing. Drive-yourself cars can be hired in Honiara and there are several travel agencies that arrange tours. Half-day tours from Honiara include Honiara and environs, with residential ridges, museum, botanical gardens, etc.; World War II battlefields inc. Henderson Field; Melanesian villages and dancing. Full day tours inc. car tour to Tambea village; boat tours to Savo Island with its megapode bird sanctuary and hot springs; boat tours to Tulagi, Marau Sound, etc.

There are war relics in and adjacent to Honiara and boards may be seen indicating major battles and incidents in the World

War II Guadalcanal campaign. There is a National Museum at Honiara, and Solomon Islander Fred Kona, at Vilu Village 24 km from Honiara, has war relics in his museum. Tours of the surrounding battlefields or excursions to the other islands by boat or aircraft can be arranged.

Apart from the war debris, there are several Japanese monuments to World War II dead.

ACCOMMODATION
HONIARA

Hotel Mendana: on Honiara waterfront, 90 a/c rooms, refrig., tea and coffee-making facilities, bar, coffee shop, restaurant, swimming pool, gift shop, tour desk, hairdresser. PO Box 384, Honiara, Solomon Islands. Tel.: 20071, Telex HQ 66315.
Hibiscus Hotel: near town centre, budget rooms, bar, restaurant. PO Box 268, Honiara, Solomon Islands. Tel.: 21205.
Honiara Hotel: near Chinatown area, a/c and non-a/c rooms, bar, restaurant, swimming pool. PO Box 4, Honiara, Solomon Islands. Tel.: 21737.

OUTSIDE HONIARA
ON GUADALCANAL

Tambea Village Resort: 45 km by road from Honiara, 24 bungalows, licensed restaurant, scuba dive service. PO Box 506, Honiara, Solomon Islands, Tel.: 23639, Telex HQ6 6338.
Tavanipupu Island Resort: on Marau

Sound 100 km from Honiara, accessible by air or trading ship, 2 bungalows, cooking facilities.
Velelua Resort: 45 km east of Honiara, no other details available.

MALAITA

Auki Lodge: 8 rooms, fan, bathroom, licensed dining room, tours arranged. PO Box 9, Honiara, Solomon Islands, Tel.: 40131.
Malu'u Rest House: 6 beds, one self-contained unit, meals by arrangement.

WESTERN PROVINCE

Gizo Hotel: in Gizo town, 6 a/c rooms, others with fan, some with refrig, and tea/coffee-making facilities, bar, restaurant.
Munda Rest House: near airfield and government wharf at Lambete, some rooms with shared bathroom, some with private facilities, licensed dining room.
Other rest houses, intended mainly for the use of Government officials, who are given priority, may be found at Gizo, Kira Kira (San Cristobal), Buala (Santa Isabel), and Ngarando (Reef Islands). Locations are sometimes spectacular, facilities are usually basic.

FLORIDA ISLANDS

Anuha Island Resort: 150 acre island in Gela Group. International standard. This resort was burned down in 1988; it may be rebuilt.

Tokelau

Tokelau (formerly known as the Tokelau Islands) is a non-self-governing territory under New Zealand's administration. The group consists of three atolls located between 8 and 10 deg S latitude and 171 and 173 deg W longitude, and about 483 km north of Western Samoa. Local time is 11 hours behind GMT.

The three atolls are Fakaofo, Nukunonu, and Atafu. Fakaofo, the southernmost atoll, is 64 km from Nukunonu, which, in turn, is 92 km south of Atafu. Each atoll has its own administrative centre.

In November 1981 the census population was 1572. A 1985 estimate was 1703. The census showed each atoll's population as Atafu 554, Nukunonu 368 and Fakaofo 650.

New Zealand currency and the Tokelau souvenir coin are the legal tender. The Western Samoan tala and sene are also commonly used.

The national anthem is *God Save the Queen*

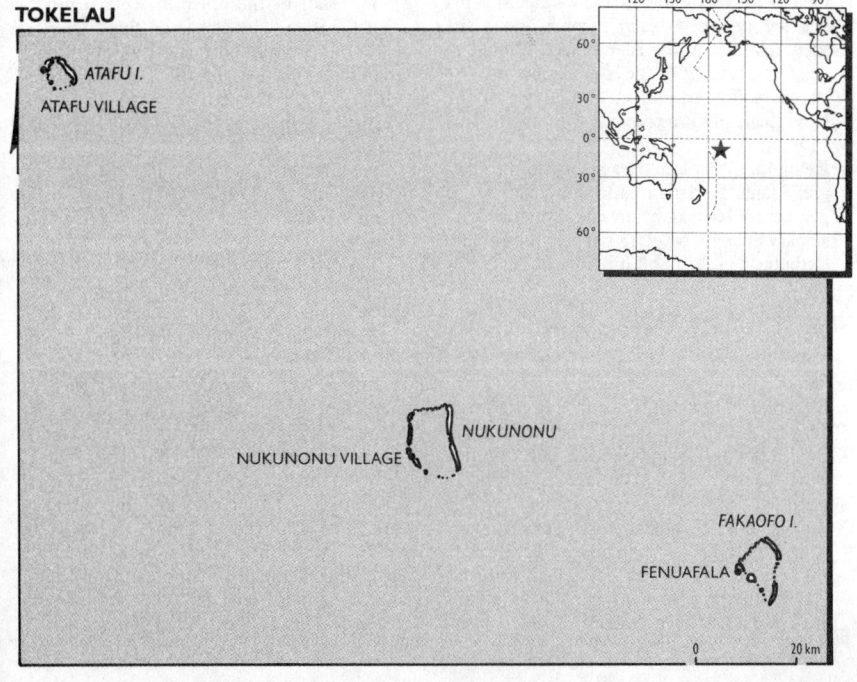

TOKELAU

ATAFU I.
ATAFU VILLAGE

NUKUNONU
NUKUNONU VILLAGE

FAKAOFO I.
FENUAFALA

0   20 km

and the New Zealand flag is used. Public holidays are New Year, Waitangi Day, Good Friday, Easter Monday, ANZAC Day, Queen's Birthday, Labour Day, Tokehega Day, Christmas Day and two other village holidays to be chosen by the three island councils.

THE PEOPLE. The people are Polynesians. They have family, linguistic and cultural links with Western Samoa through contacts by radio broadcasts, church ties and between their administrations.

Nationality. Tokelauans are British subjects and New Zealand citizens.

Language. Tokelauan speech has similarities with Samoan and Tuvaluan. English is sometimes spoken and is taught as a second language.

Migration. In the early 1960s overcrowding was seen as a serious problem. As a result, the New Zealand Government instituted a Tokelau Resettlement Scheme, to ease overcrowding and to allow people to earn income instead of depending on the meagre resources available. The scheme resulted in the movement of a lot of families to New Zealand. This enabled people to earn income and assist their relatives in the islands who wanted to emigrate. In 1976 the population on the islands stabilised and on the advice of the New Zealand Government, the scheme was suspended.

Religion. Most islanders belong to the Congregational Christian Church of Samoa (70 per cent) deriving from the London Missionary Society, while 28 per cent are Roman Catholic. On Atafu all inhabitants belong to the Congregational Church; on Nukunonu all are Roman Catholics, while both faiths are represented on Fakaofo. The work of both missions is directed from Western Samoa.

Lifestyle. The islands are in a border area between Micronesia and Polynesia. To some extent the inhabitants retain cultural ties with Samoa but the culture is distinctly moulded by the atoll environment, which has its closest parallel with Tuvalu, with which there are also linguistic, family and cultural affinities. The lifestyle is centred mainly on the family group. Village affairs are conducted by a council of elders consisting of representatives of the families.

GOVERNMENT. The basis of Tokelau's legislative, administrative and judicial systems is the Tokelau Islands Act, 1948, and amendments enacted by the NZ Parliament. In November 1974, the administration of Tokelau was transferred from the Maori and Island Affairs Department to the Ministry of Foreign Affairs. From then until 25 September 1980, the Secretary of Foreign Affairs was the Administrator of Tokelau. New regulations then came into force whereby the Minister of Foreign Affairs was empowered to appoint a suitable person to be the Administrator of Tokelau, who continues to be responsible to the Minister. The first Administrator, Frank Corner, was appointed on 25 September 1980, for a term of three years. The current Administrator is H. H. Francis, who is the New Zealand Deputy Secretary of Foreign Affairs.

The powers of the Administrator are delegated to an Official Secretary (in 1986 Adrian Macey) in Apia. By agreement with the Government of Western Samoa, the Office of Tokelau Affairs continues to be based in Apia.

The staff of the office in Apia regularly visit the islands by chartered ship. There is close co-operation between the Government of Western Samoa and the Tokelau Office. Officers of the Western Samoa Government, particularly medical officers, visit the island on request.

Six directors, also based in Apia, are responsible to the Official Secretary. Five of these are Tokelauans and one is a Western Samoan.

Tokelau is included in the South Pacific Commission area and benefits from the results of the commission's work. Delegates from Tokelau attend the annual South Pacific Conference.

Elections. The faipule (commissioner or headman) and pulenuku (village mayor) are democratically elected for three-year terms.

Local government. The dominant village political institution is the Council of Elders (Taupulega). Differences in composition of the three Councils of Elders do exist. In Atafu, the Council is made up of all family heads together with the faipule and pulenuku. The Nukunonu one is comprised of both elders and heads of extended families as well as the faipule and pulenuku. The Fakaofo

Council is essentially made up of the elders only. The heads of families are only consulted when the Council requires their advice. A faipule (who is also a Commissioner of the Court), a village mayor (pulenuku) and a village clerk (failautuhi) are responsible for the day-to-day administration on each island. An administrative officer acts in a supervisory capacity over public servants on his island. The faipule administers the law and presides over the court. The village mayor is responsible for the maintenance of good order, sanitation, cleanliness, water supplies and the inspection of plantations. The village clerk keeps the records of deaths, births and marriages.

Public service. There is a Tokelau Public Service under the control of the New Zealand State Services Commission. In 1986 the number of employees in the Tokelau Public Service was 168. They included doctors, nurses, teachers, administrative personnel, tradesmen and agricultural field workers. Tokelau public servants receive in-service training in other countries under the sponsorship of the administration's training scheme, South Pacific Commission, Bureau for Economic Cooperation, United Nations Development Programme FAO, Commonwealth Fund for Technical Co-operation, the University of the South Pacific and the World Health Organisation. All senior positions in the service are filled by Tokelauans, except the Director of Finance's position and one doctor's position. The Administration is continuing a policy of attracting Tokelauans with suitable skills from New Zealand into the service. There are currently three New Zealand-based recruits and a fourth will be appointed.

About twice a year, delegates meet at one of the islands in the group to decide on issues relating to the overall development of Tokelau. this is the General Fono of Tokelau and in recent years it has essentially decided on budgetary priorities and other developmental issues.

Self-government. New Zealand is committed to assisting Tokelau towards a greater degree of self-government and economic self-sufficiency. There is no timetable for this; it is the Administering Power's stated intention to be guided by the wishes of the Tokelauan people and to introduce greater self-determination at the pace they desire.

Two visits have now been made to Tokelau by visiting missions from the United Nations Special Committee on Decolonisation. In both 1976 and 1981 the missions noted that the people of Tokelau had no wish to review the nature of the existing relationship between Tokelau and New Zealand. At the March 1985 General Fono, it was decided to ask the New Zealand Government to invite another mission from the United Nations Special Committee on Decolonisation to visit Tokelau.

Justice. The Tokelau Amendment Act 1970 gave the High Court of Niue civil and criminal jurisdiction in Tokelau as if that court had been established as a separate court of justice in Tokelau. This arrangement is, however, inoperative. The law reform project was expected to result in a transfer of High Court jurisdiction to Tokelau from Niue to New Zealand in mid-1986. The local commissioner on each island has jurisdiction to deal with certain civil proceedings and criminal offences.

Police. The police force consist of seven Tokelauan officers — three in Fakaofo, two in Atafu and two in Nukunonu. A chief policeman is in charge of each atoll. Apart from petty offences there is little crime. There are no prisons. Punishment takes the form of public rebukes, fines or labour, which is directed to assist with public work, but there is little restraint on personal conduct during the sentence.

EDUCATION. Primary education is available for all children. The NZ Education Department gives the administration advisory assistance. It also provides material and equipment for the schools and carries out periodic inspections.

Since the departure of the last New Zealand education officer in 1976, education advisers have been recruited from New Zealand on two-year term contracts. The first one was Mr Eddie McKersey who completed his term in 1980. Mr McKersey was succeeded by Mr Brian Healey, 1981 to September 1983. A third one, Mr Barry Clarkson, was recruited in February 1983 to ensure a continuity in curriculum development programmes.

Apart from these expatriate advisers the teaching staff are Tokelauans numbering 42 qualified teachers and 18 teacher aides.

All the primary schools cater for children from five to 15 years of age. Schooling is free and attendance is close to 100 per cent. There are also pre-school classes in each village. School equipment includes radio sets, tape recorders and slide and movie projectors. Each island has a parent's committee which raises funds and helps to organise school activities. The schools have a dual aim — to prepare the children for life in Tolelau or for a career in New Zealand.

LABOUR. Copra production and the manufacture of plaited ware and woodwork are the only industries of significance. No supervision of employment conditions in these industries is necessary.

Members of the communities who are not permanent members of the public servies devote their labour to procuring food from lagoons, ocean, or plantation, to village maintenance, and to the production of woven mats, fans and curios.

The various public works and agriculture programmes and projects also provide casual employment, rotating all wage worker positions in order to distribute the money available from public service incomes more widely throughout the communities. Some work is now carried out under contract by village labour forces.

Social security. There is an accepted family responsibility to provide food and accommodation for the aged and impoverished. Village women's committees, constituted mainly of married women, help the nursing staff in infant care and child welfare.

HEALTH. The health care system is operated by the Health Section, a part of the Tokelau Public Service. Each of the three rural general hospitals is serviced by a team of one Fiji-trained medical officer, Fiji or Western Samoa-trained staff nurses and local aides. Much of the work involves public health preventive services, including an ongoing water supply and sanitation programme, and a Vector Control Programme. The dental service is provided by a dentist, a New Zealand qualified dental nurse and a dental assistant.

The Women's Committee of each atoll community, in conjunction with health personnel, is involved with maternal and child-health activities and with cleanliness of the village environment and homes.

The Health Section operates a referral service to Western Samoa and to New Zealand. The Director of Health, who is based at the Office for Tokelau Affairs, Apia, travels to Tokelau periodically to screen patients for whom the local doctor has requested transferral to Apia.

In 1984 a Health Committee was formed by the General Fono. Its goals and objectives call for an increased emphasis on prevention of diseases, health promotion and community health programmes. The role of traditional medicine in the Tokelauan community has been taken into account in the drawing up of health regulations which support these goals.

HOUSING. Most Tokelau houses are constructed of native materials, kanava and pandanus timbers with walls and roofs of plaited pandanus leaves, but the use of imported building materials is steadily increasing. The Atafu people live in one village which occupies part of a motu (islet), while at Nukunonu the village occupies about half a motu, which is connected by a bridge to a neighbouring motu, where some families have settled. The village at Fakaofo is on a small but comparatively high and well-shaded motu. There are overcrowding problems at Fakaofo, although emigration to New Zealand has been a partial solution. A new village has been established on a larger motu nearby, Fenuafala, and has school, hospital and other facilities. Housing policy is based on the self-help principle. Materials are bought through the co-operative stores and the Public Works assists with design and construction.

THE LAND. Each atoll consists of a number of reef-bound islets (motus) encircling a lagoon. The islets vary in size from 90 m to 6 km in length. The largest atoll is Nukunonu, 4.7 sq. km. Fakaofo and Atafu are 4 sq. km and 3.5 sq. km respectively. From Atafu in the north to Fakaofo in the south, the group extends for just under 200 km. The atolls are three to five metres above sea level.

Climate. The mean average temperature is 28°C. July is the coolest month and May the warmest. Rainfall is heavy but inconsistent. A daily fall of 80 mm or more can be expected at any time of the year. Severe tropical storms are rare.

Land tenure. The shortage of natural resources has been the major factor encouraging migration. Practically all their land is held by customary title in accordance with the customs. The Tokelau Islands Amendment Act 1967 provides that islanders may dispose of land by custom among themselves, but may not alienate land to non-indigenes. Land holdings pass from generation to generation within families, being held by the head of a closely-related family group, although some land is held in common.

PRIMARY PRODUCTION. The physical charactistics of the atolls allow very little scope for economic development and the few natural resources are sufficient only to meet the needs of the simple pattern of life followed by the people. Until recent years, there had been little demand for the material standards of more developed countries, but increasing contact with Western Samoa and New Zealand has stimulated a desire for wider opportunities.

The economy is based mainly on the resources of the sea, and the coconut and pandanus palms. Most families get part of their cash income from relatives working in New Zealand. Funds are also sent by the Tokelau communities in New Zealand for village and church projects.

Crop production. Apart from the manufacture of copra, agricultural products are of a basic subsistence nature. Food crops consist of coconuts, pulaka, breadfruit, taamu, papaw, the fruit of the edible pandanus and bananas. Many other seeds have been tested but because of the poverty of the soil very poor results were achieved. UNDP and USP School of Agriculture assisted the setting up of a vegetable trial using alternative growing media and so far the results are promising. On the many uninhabited islands where food plantations are located an attempt is made to replant and rehabilitate the coconut groves. The coconut palm, which is predominant in the atolls, provides the staple export crop of copra.

Crop protection. The Polynesian rat and rhinoceros beetle are the two key pests of the coconut palm. The former, which is present on all the islands, is controlled by chemicals whereas the latter, found only on Nukunonu, is suppressed by regular release of beetles infected with *Baculovirus oryctes*.

Livestock. This consists of pigs, poultry and goats. Attempts to improve the local swine stock have achived only fair results as the introduced breed has not adapted adequately to the rather harsh conditions. Recently introduced goats have adapted well.

Fisheries. Ocean and lagoon fish and shellfish are available in quantity and form a staple constituent of the diet. The most common species of fish caught are tuna, bonito, trevally and mullet. Fisheries experts from UNDP/FAO and the SPC have visited Tokelau, and UNDP donated one fishing alia (boat) to each island for the purpose of improving catches for local consumption. These have hardly served their intended purpose. One fish aggregating device was deployed on a trial basis with very good results. Deployment of more devices is under consideration. Trochus from Fiji have recently been transplanted to Fakaofo.

Timber. Local timber is used for canoe-making, house-building and domestic utensils. The kanava (*Cordia subcordata*), a short, stubby tree, is the main timber used for the above purposes.

MANUFACTURING. Local industries are copra production, woodwork and finely plaited goods, such as hats, mats and bags. The office of Tokelau Affairs in Apia, Western Samoa, maintains a range of handicraft for sale. In other Pacific countries the very fine work of the Tokelaus stands out amongst collections of craft.

LOCAL COMMERCE. Each village has its own co-operative store run by a village management committee and supplied by the Office of Tokelau Affairs.

FINANCE. For total revenue and expenditure for financial years ending 31 March see Table 1.

Revenue is derived mainly from an export tax of 10 per cent on handicrafts, from shipping and copra, freight charges, the sale of postage stamps and coins, from customs duties, the return from radio and telegram services and service charges on remittances. Budgetary estimates are initially prepared by a budgetary advisory committee. These are then discussed in the General Fono, and, if agreed to by the Fono, are passed on to the Minister of Foreign Affairs for approval.

TABLE 1

Expediture	1984–85 WS$	1985–86 NZ$
Administration services and supplies	218,457	218,054
Capital works	149,706	114,279
International relations	46,080	45,619
Land and building upkeep	77,892	87,119
Agriculture	31,149	72,288
Education	592,844	583,184
Health	94,546	128,224
Public works	111,389	183,736
Transport and communication	643,211	656,427
Publicity and economic development	180,194	166,722
Salaries and employment costs	1,026,481	1,063,945
Staff recruitment and support	149,355	132,138
Total expenditure	3,321,304	3,451,735
Revenue	$ WS	$ NZ
Local revenue	530,288	441,256
Miscellaneous grants		11,384
New Zealand aid grant	3,005,905	3,100,000
Total revenue	3,536,193	3,552,640
Excess revenue over expediture	214,889	100,905

The budget for 1988–89 is $US 2.3 m, a seven per cent increase on that of the previous year.

UNDP Aid. The United Nations Development Programme (UNDP) has given aid worth $US 1.15 million, to be used over a five-year period from 1987. Special projects include water supply development including rainwater tanks ($150,000); energy development ($145,000); manpower development ($240,000); improvement of transport and communications ($315,000); and agriculture development ($100,000).

Currency. The New Zealand currency and the Tokelau souvenir coin are legal tender in Tokelau, but for convenience, Western Samoan currency is also used. There are no banks in the territory but savings facilities have been set up on each island since February 1977 and are under the control of the respective administration officers.

Tokelau released its first coin, a souvenir dollar, in 1978. Since then, four other issues have been minted. The obverse of all show the effigy of Queen Elizabeth II by Arnold Machin, RA, of London. The designs on the reverse were all done by a Tokelauan artist, Faraimo Paulo, of Atafu.

TRANSPORT. The islands were without a regular shipping service after the withdrawal of the Pacific Navigation Company's *Aoniu* from charter in 1974. The administration then arranged to charter the Nauru Pacific

Line's *Cenpac Rounder* for regular calls, generally about five times a year. This link was severed when the *Cenpac Rounder* went aground in March 1979. Charters were organised on an ad hoc basis, while a search for a suitable vessel for long-term charters continued. In mid-1981 the MV *Frysna* belonging to Warner Pacific Line of Tonga began a four-year charter arrangement. From January 1986 Interports Shipping of Suva has provided a monthly service to Tokelau with the MV *Wairua* under a contract with the New Zealand Government which should last at least until 1988.

Port facilities. There are no ports. Landing conditions at the main settlements of all three atolls have required blasting of the coral at various times to provide adequate small-boat channels through the reef. Aluminium whaleboats powered by 35 hp outboard motors are used for loading and unloading of cargoes. Vessels are normally anchored about 360 metres from the channel entrances during cargo operations.

An air-link became operational towards the end of 1981, using an amphibian aircraft chartered from Tuvalu. The agreement expired in September 1983. A few weeks earlier, Tuvalu decided to close down its domestic airline operations because it could no longer bear the cost. Islanders have, to date, opposed the construction of an airstrip, despite recommendations by visiting missions and delegations.

COMMUNICATIONS. Radio stations at Atafu, Nukunonu and Fakaofo transmit traffic and weather reports every four hours, apart from schedules for official and commercial traffic. Radio telephones are available at all three stations. Single sideband tele-radio equipment is installed at all stations, including Apia. In August 1983 the United Nations Development Program (UNDP) sanctioned a $US695,000 telecommunications project linking the three atolls with each other and, through Western Samoa, with the outside world. There is a quarterly newsletter called *Te Vako.*

HISTORY. Nothing is known for certain about the origins of the Tokelau people. Samoa, Rarotonga and Nanumanga in the Tuvalu group are all described in the islanders' traditions as homelands, and the pro-

bability is that early settlers of the three islands came from each of those places. Atafu was the first island seen by Europeans, on 24 July 1765, by Commodore John Byron in HMS *Dolphin,* and named Duke of York's Island. Captain Edward Edwards of HMS *Pandora* sighted the same island in June 1791 while searching for the *Bounty* mutineers. A few days later he discovered Nukunonu, which he called Duke of Clarence's Island. Atafu was uninhabited at that time.

Although islanders were seen on the beach at Nukunonu, Edwards had no contact with them. Several whalers were in the vicinity of Tokelau in the late 1820s. But Fakaofo, the most populated island, appears to have remained unknown to Europeans until 14 February 1835, when Captain Smith of the whaler *General Jackson* of Bristol, Rhode Island, sighted it. Smith called his discovery De Wolf's Island after the owner of the ship.

First European knowledge. The first detailed knowledge of Tokelau was obtained in 1841 when the USS *Peacock* and *Flying Fish* of the United States Exploring Expedition spent several days among the islands. Horatio Hale, the expedition's ethnologist, wrote an account of the islands and recorded something of the local language. As Smith's discovery of Fakaofo was unknown to the *Peacock*'s commander, he named it Bowditch Island. This name remained in use for many years. Fakaofo's population in 1841 was estimated at between 500 and 600 while about 120 people were thought to live on Atafu.

Christian conversion. French Catholic missionaries on Wallis Island (Uvea) and missionaries of the London Missionary Society in Samoa used native teachers in various attempts to convert the Tokelauans between 1845 and 1863. By the latter year, Atafu had been entirely Christianised by the LMS. Nukunonu was entirely Catholic. Catholic teachers later established themselves on Fakaofo. As a result, that island now has both Protestant and Catholic adherents, while Atafu and Nukunonu have remained Protestant and Catholic respectively.

Slave raids. In 1863, several Peruvian slave raiders removed about 140 people from the three islands. A dysentery outbreak at about the same time reduced the total population to barely 200. During the next few years, several beachcombers — American

Portuguese, Scottish, French and German — settled in the islands and intermarried with the local women. Some Polynesian immigrants did likewise. The present-day Tokelauans are thus 'an improbably bizarre genetic mixture', according to a recent description. One of the Portuguese settlers, a Cape Verde Islander of African descent, obtained control over large areas of land and dominated the local copra-based commerce.

British jurisdiction. In 1877, the British High Commissioner for the Western Pacific in Fiji was given jurisdiction over British subjects in the Tokelaus, as those islands had not come within the jurisdiction of any foreign power. Twelve years later, when Britain thought the islands might prove useful as staging points for the then-proposed trans-Pacific cable, the commander of HMS *Egeria* visited each of them and formally placed them under British protection.

During the next 20 years, Britain nominally administered the islands through her representative in Western Samoa, then Tonga, and finally Ocean Island, then headquarters of the Gilbert and Ellice Islands Protectorate. In 1916 the three islands, then known as the Union Group, became part of the newly proclaimed Gilbert and Ellice Islands Colony. Administration from Ocean Island resulted in some improvement in medical care, and some Tokelauans were recruited to work that island's phosphate deposits.

Samoan administration. However, the long distance from Ocean Island — 2200 km — made administration difficult. In 1925, the New Zealand Government undertook to administer the islands from Western Samoa, then a mandated territory. This arrangement still persists even though Western Samoa became independent on 1 January 1962.

In 1946, the group was officially designated the Tokelau Islands under the Tokelau No-menclature Ordinance, and the islands were included within the territorial boundaries of New Zealand by the Tokelau Islands Act of 1948. For 10 years after Western Samoa became independent, New Zealand's high commissioner in Apia held the office of administrator of the Tokelau Islands. In 1976, the territory was officially re-designated Tokelau, the name used by the inhabitants.

Administration of Tokelau from Western Samoa has fostered ancient Tokelauan linguistic and cultural links with that country. Before 1962, it also encouraged immigration. In 1951, for example, 220 Tokelau-born islanders were living in Western Samoa, and by 1956 the number was 297. Meanwhile, the population was also growing apace. It reached its highest known figure, nearly 2000, in the 1960s.

FOR THE TOURIST. There are no hotels as yet in Tokelau, although from time to time tourists are accommodated by private individuals on each of the three atolls. All tourists are required to contact the Office of Tokelau Affairs in Apia to supply information concerning their intended arrival and departure in the territory as well as accommodation arrangements. This information is then passed on to the relevant atoll council for approval. Custom life is very strong in these islands and respect and courtesy is expected from visitors. Access to Tokelau is via Apia on the supply ship *Wairua*. Allocation of space on this vessel is entirely at the discretion of the Office of Tokelau Affairs; visitors have low priority. There are no airstrips in the group although there has been discussion concerning the construction of one on Fakaofa.

Further information. Official Secretary, Office for Tokelau Affairs, PO Box 865, Apia, Western Samoa.

Tonga

The independent kingdom of Tonga, a member of the Commonwealth, consists of three main island groups and many smaller islands located between 15 and 23 deg 30 min S latitude and 173 and 177 deg W longitude. Total area is 696.71 sq. km. There are about 150 islands of which about 36 are inhabited. The capital is Nuku'alofa, on Tongatapu, which is about 170 km north-east of Auckland. Local time is 13 hours ahead of GMT.

The national anthem is *E' 'Otua Mafimafi* (*O Almighty God above*); the flag is light red with a white upper left quarter which encloses a light red cross.

Public holidays are: 1 January; Good Friday; Easter Monday; 25 April (ANZAC Day); 4 May (Crown Prince's birthday); 4 June (Emancipation Day): 4 July (King's birthday); 4 November (Constitution Day); 4 December (King Tupou I Day); Christmas Day and 26 December (Boxing Day).

THE PEOPLE. The Tongans are Polynesians. The census of 1986 recorded a population of 94,535, of which 47,589 were male and 46,946 were female. The 1976 population was 90,085, therefore the annual average growth rate over the decade was 0.48 per cent, considerably down on the 1966–76 census period of 1.5 per cent. Considerable internal migration from outlying areas to urban areas was evident in the 1986 census.

Individual district figures are; Tongatapu, 63,614; 'Eua, 4393; Ha'apai, 8979; Vava'u, 15,170; Niuas, 2379. The population of the capital, Nuku'alofa, is 28,899.

Of the total population, more than 52,000 are under the age of 20.

Language. The islanders speak their own dialect of Polynesian and, usually, English.

Migration. Many Tongans migrate, attracted by better opportunities for employment. The US and New Zealand are the most popular destinations, and money sent home to relatives is an important part of Tonga's economy.

Between 1 December 1986 and 18 February 1987, New Zealand allowed visa-free entry for a stay of three months, with the opportunity of extension for a further 12 months with the support of a New Zealand sponsor. In the two and a half month period, 5000 Tongans left for New Zealand, many on special flights arranged by Tongans already resident in New Zealand. The scheme was supposed to last six months as a trial period but was terminated early because the New Zealand Government felt that the large influx of people from Tonga, Samoa and Fiji strained the resources of the island communities in Auckland, already regarded as the largest Polynesian community in the world.

Religion. The Free Wesleyan Church has the largest number of adherents and has had a profound influence in Tonga. In 1986 the Constitutional Free Church of Tonga was officially founded, the fourth in a series of breakaway churches from the original Free Wesleyan Church. Other churches include the Free Church of Tonga, the Anglican, the Roman Catholic, Seventh-day Adventist, Pentecostal, Worldwide Church of God, Baha'i, Gospel Fellowship and Mormon. In 1984 the Tongan Muslim League was established. Strict observance of the Sabbath precludes all work, trade, sport, transport services, etc. on Sunday but the requirements of a developing tourist industry mean that exceptions are made. Bakeries are also exempt.

Recreation. The main recreations are imported: rugby, boxing, soccer, cricket and

TONGA

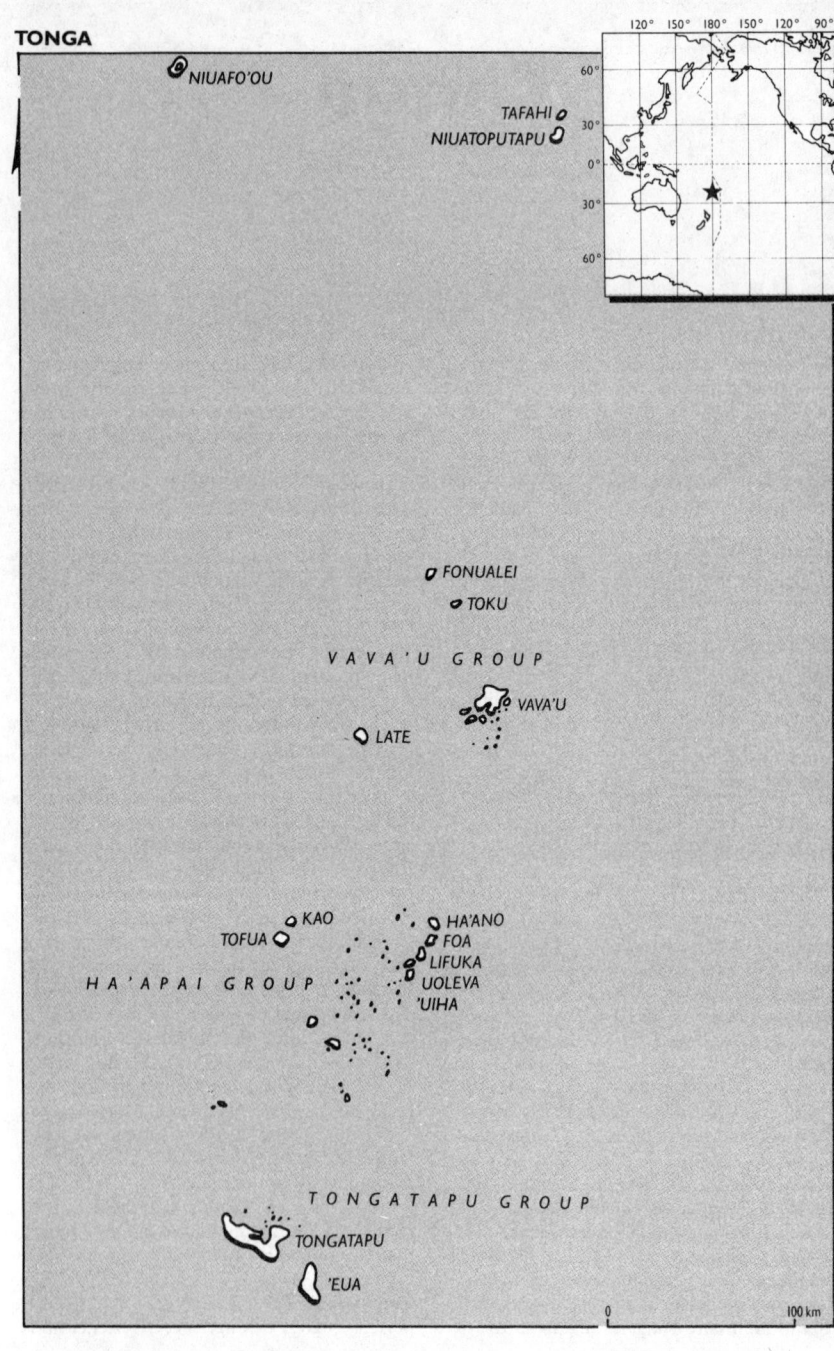

NIUAFO'OU

TAFAHI
NIUATOPUTAPU

FONUALEI
TOKU

V A V A ' U   G R O U P

LATE   VAVA'U

KAO   HA'ANO
TOFUA   FOA
                LIFUKA
H A ' A P A I   G R O U P   UOLEVA
                'UIHA

T O N G A T A P U   G R O U P

TONGATAPU

'EUA

0   100 km

basketball. However, indigenous games and sports survive. Lafo is a game similar to carpet bowls, except that round wooden discs made from coconut shells are used instead of bowls. Hiko is a juggling game played by young girls — they juggle up to six candlenuts or oranges at a time, while they sing or recite special rhymes, using archaic words which are no longer understood. Another local recreation is 'Ilo'ito', a dance in which girls sit on their heels facing each other in two rows. To the accompaniment of a chant and hand movements they hop and skip, and in their singing they refer to flowers and the names of unmarried chiefs. Every time a girl begins to tire and has to drop out, the others make fun of her, telling her she will never win a young chief. Finally, only one or two are left and they are reputedly the ones who will win a handsome chief.

GOVERNMENT. Although a constitutional monarchy on the British model, the King in fact exercises wide influence. The government consists of the King, the Privy Council, Cabinet, the Legislative Assembly and the judiciary, The constitution was handed down by King Tupou I on 4 November 1875. The King voluntarily limited his own powers after emancipating his people from the semi-serfdom in which they had lived for centuries.
Legislature. The members of the Legislative Assembly are the Speaker, members of the Cabinet, seven nobles elected by the 33 nobles of Tonga, and seven representatives of the people elected by universal suffrage of all Tongans over 21. Three of those representatives are from Tongatapu and the two Niuas, and two each from Ha'apai and Vava'u. The seven nobles are elected to represent similar areas.

The Prime Minister is head of the Government and administers several departments. He also controls district and town officers. Parliament meets about the end of May or early June to pass the estimates before 1 July, the beginning of the financial year.
Executive. The King appoints a Speaker and Cabinet which includes Ministers of the Crown and the Governors of Ha'apai and Vava'u, presided over by the Prime Minister. All the Ministers are permanently appointed by the King and retain office until retiring age. The Cabinet becomes the Privy Council when presided over by the King.

The Privy Council also sits as the Court of Appeal, with the addition of the Chief Justice of Tonga.
Local government. The only form of local government is through town and district officers. Town officers represent the government in a village. District officers have authority over a group of villages. In addition, Ha'apai and Vava'u have their own governors.
Justice. The judicial system is based on the British model. At the top is the Court of Appeal (the Privy Council), then the Supreme Court, the Land Court and magistrates' courts. In criminal cases before the Supreme Court an accused person has the right to elect for trial by jury or by judge alone. Appeals from the Supreme Court lie with the Privy Council. The Chief Justice is also the judge of the Land Court, on which he sits with an assessor, who acts in an advisory capacity. A number of magistrates preside over the magistrates' courts throughout the group.
Police. The Police Force had a strength of 318 in 1985 including the police band. The Minister of Police is the principal Immigration Officer and is also responsible for all prisons and prisoners. Prison policy is administered by the Superintendent of Prisons. There are seven prisons — in Tongatapu, Ha'apai, Vava'u, Niuatoputapu, 'Eua, Nomukeiki and 'Ata.

In 1985 reported crimes and offences showed an 11.1 per cent increase over the 1984 figures. Traffic offences had increased by 27.9 per cent. Theft and assault accounted for over 60 per cent of reported criminal offences. The increase is attributed to the rapid growth in the Nuku'alofa urban area coupled with unemployment and the break-down of traditional closely structured, family units.
Liquor laws. Liquor is sold in bars, clubs, and in restaurants and night clubs. Bottled liquor is available in the larger supermarkets.

DEFENCE. Tonga has had various defence systems. In 1954 a military training scheme, headed by a New Zealand Army officer, was instituted to train a defence force, known as the Tonga Defence Force. It was composed of Tongan officers and NCOs and a seconded NZ commanding officer. In 1974 the force was renamed the Tongan Defence

Services. The four divisions include the Land Force, the Infantry and the Royal Guards. Total strength of the Land Force is 49 and Royal Guard 37. The Logistic Support Division totals 52, and the Maritime Division totals 62. In 1987 a national Computer Training Centre was established at headquarters in Nuku'alofa and in July 1987 training commenced for a newly organised Air Wing of the Tongan Defence Services.

EDUCATION. Primary education has been compulsory since 1876. The 1974 Act provides free education for children aged between six and 14. The Tongan School Certificate is attained after six years of secondary school and is the major leaving certificate.
Schools. There are 111 primary schools, 100 of them administered by the Government and 11 by the churches. Total enrolment in 1986 was 17,072 (15,886 Government pupils and 1186 church). At secondary level there were 15,673 students; 2612 attended the five Government secondary schools including Tonga High School, Vava'u High School, Tonga College and Niuatoputapu Secondary School. At the one private secondary school there were 462 students. In the 45 church secondary schools there were 12,599 students. Atenisi Institute now has university status within the Kingdom of Tonga and now confers degrees. In 1986 there were 65 students. There is a USP Extension Centre in Tonga with a new $500,000 building which opened in 1987.

The largest church schools include: Free Wesleyan Church — Queen Salote College for girls (888 students), Tupou College for boys (686), Mailefihi Siu'ilikutapu (746), and Nuku'alofa College (299); Roman Catholic — St John's High School (581), Takuilau (602) and St Mary's High School (500); Anglican — St Andrew's School (769, coeducational); Church of the Latter Day Saints — Liahona High School (1078); Seventhday Adventists — Beulah College (363); and Free Church of Tonga — three Tailulu Colleges (852) (1985 figures).
Training. The Fourth Development Plan (1980–85) made provisions for the establishment of an Institute for Vocational Education and Training. Teacher training, agricultural, maritime and technical training are to be incorporated into the syllabus. In 1985 the

Tonga Maritime Polytechnical Institute — 'Fokololo 'O E Hau' — was established and six Tongans were sent to Germany for training as instructors. Teacher training is undertaken by the Government Teachers' College with a two-year course followed by a one-year probationary period. In 1986 there were 115 students. The first Tongan-trained secondary teachers graduated in 1987 as a part of the STEP training programme.

The Government provides apprenticeship training at the Ministry of Works; training of nurses at the Queen Salote School of Nursing; and police training at the Tonga Police Training School. Some of these programmes will be under the umbrella of the proposed Community Development, Training and Research Centre.

The Free Wesleyan Church of Tonga trains young men as farmers at Mango Agricultural College on 'Eua Island, Toafa on Vava'u Island and Mahinae'a on Tongatapu, and trains both men and women at Sia'atoutai Theological College. The Roman Catholic Church trains young men as farmers at Fualu Rural Training Centre, and women are trained at the 'Ahopanilolo Technical College. The Piarson Theological College is a training institute for the Seventh-day Adventist Church.
Overseas studies. In 1985, 201 Tongans were studying overseas, mostly in New Zealand, Fiji, Australia and the United Kingdom.

LABOUR. The labour force numbers 37,800. Of these 14,400 (43.3 per cent) were employed in agriculture, 1900 (5.7 per cent) in manufacturing and 17,000 (51 per cent) in 'other' employment. Unemployment in 1984 was 4400 (11.7 per cent).

There were 31,700 people considered to be dependent entirely upon subsistence agriculture and traditional methods of livelihood. The economy is gradually being diversified through industrial development and an attempt to expand exports. Tourism is also slowly expanding. However, agriculture still constitutes the back-bone of the economy.
Wages. Daily wage earnings of workmen range from $4 for the unskilled to $6 for skilled workers. A maximum wage control is enforced.
Social security. Legislation for provision of social security benefits to to the workforce was planned by the Government in 1983,

which included workmen's compensation in the event of injury or death and retirement benefits. The legislative coverage also included conditions governing terms of employment, minimum wages and health, safety and welfare at work regulations. However by 1986 no further progress had been made. Some of the statutory organisations, as well as the Government, already have some form of retirement benefits.

Trade unions. Legislation exists in Tonga for registration of trade unions, though none have been formed and registered.

HEALTH. Health services are provided through four general hospitals, 14 health centres and 33 public health nurse clinics. The hospitals are Vaiola (Tongatapu), Ngu (Vava'u), Niu'ui (Ha'apai) and Niu'eiki ('Eua) with a total capacity of 307 beds. In 1985 there were 7603 admissions which gave a ratio of 24.8 admissions per bed. All four hospitals showed decreases in admission.

The health centres provide both clinical and community health services. Expansion of these facilities greatly relieves the pressure of outpatient consultations in the hospitals. The public health nurse clinics deal mainly with maternal and child health as well as family planning services.

In 1985 the Ministry of Health personnel included 55 medical officers, 24 dental staff, 281 nursing staff and 62 technical staff.

Diseases. The general health of the population is good; there are no serious endemic diseases. The predominant illnesses encountered are those related to poor sanitation and hygiene, such as gastroenteritis, infantile diarrhoea, and acute respiratory infections such as bronchopneumonia. Tuberculosis and typhoid are on the decline.

Family planning. A programme funded by UNFPA with support from WHO has been promoting and encouraging family planning since 1972. The acceptance rate has been good. The birth rate has dropped from 32 per 1000 in 1964 to 27.4 per 1000 population in 1985. Crude death rate in 1985 was 5.1 per 1000.

THE LAND. The land area of 697 sq. km is in an ocean area of 259,000 sq. km. There are about 150 islands, but only 36 are permanently inhabited. The largest is Tonga-tapu, 260 sq. km in the south of the group. From north to south, the kingdom extends 560 km from Niuatoputapu to 'Eua, but there is an isolated uninhabited island, Ata, 136 km SSW of Tongatapu.

The islands fall into three main groups — the southern or Tongatapu group, the central Ha'apai group and the northern Vava'u group. The highest point in the islands is an extinct volcano, Kao, of 1030 m. Apart from 'Eua, the islands have no distinct mountains. Vava'u has hills of between 150 and 300 m.

Most of the islands are of raised coral, with an overlying soil developed from volcanic ash, which is fertile. The remainder of the islands, generally forming a western chain, are volcanic. These are relatively young islands, and soil development is still progressing.

Climate. The climate varies, becoming cooler and drier in the south: Niuatoputapu has an average rainfall of 2500 mm, Vava'u has 2000 mm, while Tongatapu and Ha'apai have 1500 mm. The average temperature also varies from 23.5°C on Vava'u to 21°C at Tongatapu (Nuku'alofa). Mean humidity is about 77 per cent. Hurricanes are more frequent in the northern islands.

Land tenure. The Tongan land system is, in many respects, unique. All land is the property of the Crown, but large estates have been divided among the nobles. Every Tongan, when he attains the age of 16, and thereby becomes a taxpayer, is entitled to a bush allotment of about 3 ha and a town site of about 0.16 ha. He pays an annual rental of $T0.80 for his allotment and no rent for his town site. The Minister of Lands registers the allotment from the estate of the noble where the applicant lives, and subject to agreement by the noble. Otherwise the grant may be made from government land if available.

Provision is made in the law for eviction for non-payment of rent or for failing to comply with the planting laws. The interest of Tongans in land, whether they are the holders of hereditary estates or of tax allotments, is lifelong and alienation is expressly forbidden. Leasing, whether to Tongans or to aliens, is subject to the consent of Cabinet. A tax allotment can be transferred to widow or heirs, on death of the holder.

The law provides that a Tongan instead of applying for a tax allotment, with its definite area, may apply for an ordinary lease. An allotment holder may also be granted a lease, and a condition precedent to any grant is a well-cultivated allotment.

Shortage of land is a major problem and a large number of male taxpayers are without tax allotments. The nobles may retain a portion of their holding for their own use, although the law does not specify the area. Since 1945, they have been able to lease out only 5 per cent of their land, the remaining 95 per cent being reserved for Tongans.

This system does not apply to Crown land, but all leases are subject to Cabinet approval and rentals are reviewed every five years. Government surveyors are constantly employed — mostly in defining hereditary estates and in demarcating tax allotments.

Although the rental of allotments is very low, every year some holders are taken to court for non-payment of rent (292 were prosecuted in 1985).

Of the total land area of 697 sq. km, ownership in 1985 was as follows — tax and town attotments 63 per cent; government leases 1.0 per cent; leased by Tongans 1.5 per cent; leased by commodity boards 0.2 per cent; government land (uninhabited islands, forest reserves, etc.) 11 per cent; estates of hereditary nobles 7 per cent; foreign leases 2.7 per cent; charitable leases (church) 3 per cent; lakes and internal waters 4 per cent; Telekitonga and Telekitokelau Islands 6.5 per cent.

By law, every holder of an allotment is required to plant 200 coconuts within 12 months of acquisition and maintain it in a weed-free condition.

There have been moves to set up a Royal Land Commission to review provisions of the Land Act, particularly the right to land use.

Flora and fauna. There is a variety of land birds — doves, rails, starlings, kingfishers, owls, cuckoos, shrikes, bulbuls, whistlers, honey-eaters, purple swamp hens and swiftlets. Two of the most beautiful birds in the Pacific — the red-breasted musk parrot and the blue-crowned lory, are to be found on the island of 'Eua, near Tongatapu. Red-tailed and white-tailed tropic birds make their homes in the cliffs there.

Niuafo'ou, in the north ('Tin Can Island'), has endemic birds, including the incubator bird.

Apart from the common reef heron, found everywhere in the islands, the shore birds in Tonga are transient. These include the golden plover, wandering tattler, long-billed curlew and bar-tailed godwit. Seabirds include varieties of noddies and other terns, the frigate bird and the mutton bird.

Flying foxes make an extraordinary sight as they cling by day to large trees in the village of Kolovai, outside of Nuku'alofa (they go foraging by night).

The waters around Tonga are renowned for their variety of gamefish. They include barracuda, tuna, marlin and sailfish. Sea turtles, once difficult to catch, are being killed in greater numbers because of the increasing use of spear guns. They are allowed to be hunted only during season, but they are nevertheless being threatened as a species.

Many bird species are also under threat because of unnecessary clearing of land, the haphazard use of weedkillers and other poisons that destroy insects that birds feed on, and the use of guns and slingshots, and the introduction of new birds and animals.

One example is the Fiji shrikebill (fuiva), formerly found in all area of Tonga but now restricted to Niuatoputapu, Tafahi and possibly Tofua. The red-breasted musk parrot was prevalent on Tongatapu as well as 'Eua, as was the blue-crowned lory (henga), but with the deforestations that took place on Tongatapu neither species is now found there.

Other birds which are reduced in numbers with the defoliation of the native flora are the Pacific (lupe) pigeons and many coloured fruit doves.

The red-vented bulbul (manu fo'ou) and the European starling (ngutuenga) are two of the species of birds introduced in recent years which have proven to be pests, destroying both planted crops and natural growing fruits. But the parrots of 'Eua appear to be both abundant and widespread over the island and the government's forest replanting scheme has helped that situation.

The bird most susceptible to extinction is the incubator bird (malau). The Niuafo'ou incubator bird is endemic to that one island, but its egg-laying sites are scattered around the island's crater lake shore, and the regular collection of its eggs by the people is threatening its existence.

Tonga's other endemic species, the Tonga whistler (hengehenga) of Vava'u, is also abundant throughout the island group, but only remains in its habitat (dense woodland) if it is left intact. It could be endangered as well as those species which are hunted for food and not particularly abundant, such as the Pacific pigeons and the Australian gray duck.

Indigenous plants are declining in numbers but more and more exotic ones are being introduced, hence indigenous birds are mostly found in the last remaining forests, which are themselves being threatened as the increase in Tonga's population requires the clearing of more land for agriculture and settlement.

The Tonga Office of National Parks and Reserves has put forward proposals to reserve certain natural forests such as those of the eastern side of 'Eua, the last remaining forests of Tongatapu at Vaomapa, Pelehake, and the forest of Toloa.

Marine park. In 1977, Tonga became the first Pacific country to officially create marine parks and sanctuaries. There are now marine parks at Pangaimotu, Monuafe Reef, Malinoa Island and Reef and Ha'atafu Beach.

The Pangaimotu Park is on the western perimeter of the island. The reef flat has been heavily exploited and is almost devoid of shell fish. Some attractive coral may be seen on the Piha Channel side. The area is rich in tropical fish, such as the clown fish.

The reef at Monuafe is off the Piha Channel, about 6.5 km from Nuku'alofa. Many species of corals and their faunas are found there. The reef is dangerous as it is at the confluence of channel tides. The sand flats adjoining the reef are unique as they are inhabited by sand-living univalve shells of many different families.

Malinoa Island, 14.5 km north of Nuku'-alofa, is of historical interest as it was there that the attempted assassins of the second prime minister of Tonga were taken in 1835 to be summarily shot. The graves are still tended. The reefs around the islands have large fish populations.

Ha'atafu Beach is on the south-west side of Tongatapu, about 22.5 km from Nuku'-alofa. There are still healthy outcrops of coral despite some damage from starfish and indiscriminate coral and shell collectors. The reefs are the habitat of a variety of wrasses, butterfly fish and the clown fish.

PRIMARY PRODUCTION. Copra and bananas provide the basis of the economy. Both are subject to the vagaries of overseas markets.

Copra. Tonga ceased to export copra in November 1978, since then all copra has gone to Oil Mills of Tonga Ltd at Ma'ufanga where the oil is extracted and exported. The resultant coconut meal is used for stockfeed. The mill has crushing capacity of between 12,000 and 15,000 tonnes annually. Tonga also produces desiccated coconut.

The coconut palms have been subject to the depredations of the rhinoceros beetle for many years. It has been cleared from Niuatoputapu but is now on Ha'apai. It does considerable damage in Tongatapu and Vava'u.

In 1985 two hurricanes caused a great deal of damage to coconut tree stands and a concentrated effort has been put into replanting schemes on all major island areas. In 1985 Tonga exported 370,700 whole coconuts.

Bananas. Banana production and earnings, except in a few isolated cases, have been declining slowly for several years. A number of catastrophes, such as hurricanes and plant disease, disheartened growers, who turned to other crops. New Zealand, the biggest market for island bananas, is looking at other suppliers.

Banana growers were also badly affected by cyclones and drought in 1985 and exports dropped accordingly. In 1985, 134,714 cartons were exported, a drop of 8 per cent over 1984.

Vanilla. Both the Department of Agriculture and smallholders cure vanilla beans. Tougher standards were introduced in 1985 which resulted in improved harvests. Kolonga and Fua'motu produce the greatest quantities but other areas are improving their yield. In 1985 1608.4 kg of beans were exported.

Vegetables. Other crops produced for export, mainly to New Zealand and Australia, include ginger, watermelons, taros and capsicum. A new enterprise has been the processing of passionfruit into pulp. Other produce being experimented with includes black pepper and coffee beans.

Commodities Board. Marketing of local produce is handled by the Commodities Board.

Livestock. Cattle farmers in Tonga receive a subsidy for pasture development as incentive to increase production. Brahmin, Santa Gertrudis and Herefords are the main breeds.

Tonga is now self-sufficient in eggs and is nearly so with poultry meat. However, feed and day old stock are still imported. The subsidy for the pig industry has been phased out. Predominantly, pigs are still free ranging, although interest in semi-intensive and intensive pig keeping is increasing.

Pigs are probably the most important livestock in Tonga. As a sucker, the pig is a traditional dish. It is estimated that 2000–3000 sucklings pigs are slaughtered each Sunday to provide the weekly feast. On national festive occasions as many as 8000 pigs will be cooked for a single feast.

The horse is important for transport although it is rarely used for cultivation, most of which is by long handled hoe.

In 1985 three horse-drawn cultivators were designed and built by the Advisory Section of the Department. After demonstrations around the country, several were ordered by farmers and it is hoped that their use will increase.

The rearing of goats is being encouraged particularly on 'Eua and Ha'apai. They are seen as a useful source of protein for families and as a means of controlling weeds.

A national agricultural census was conducted in 1985/86, the first of its kind.

Fisheries. The Fisheries Development Programme contained within the kingdom's 4th Five-year Development Plan 1980–85 aimed at lessening dependency on meat and tinned fish imports and establishing a fish export industry.

The programme has been directed towards developing a deep-sea tuna fishery and modernising the traditional small scale fishing industry in order to exploit surface and bottom fish resources further offshore.

Extensive aid from Japan, Australia, the UN agencies, the Asian Development Bank and others has provided Fisheries Development Extension Centres in Tongatapu, Ha'apai and Vava'u. These centres contain boatbuilding yards and marine engineering repair shops as well as ice-making/cold storage facilities.

The Artisanal Fisheries Project provides for the construction of 60 fishing vessels which will be purchased by individuals who will also receive training in small business management, boat operation and maintenance. Fishermen actually pay for only half the total cost of the vessel, the remainder being funded by Japanese aid. By 1986 a total of 21 vessels, each approximately 28 feet in length, had been built and distributed.

The kingdom would also like to develop its own deep sea fishing industry and purse seine bait fishing trials continue to be run.

In June 1987 the new Fua Fisheries Harbour was opened. The project was funded entirely by the EEC under Lome 11 and facilities include a new fish market to replace the Vuna Wharf market, blast freezers and storage for 10 tonnes of fish, a main wharf of 350 metres and secondary wharf of 150 metres which can be used in all tides by vessels drawing less than 3 metres, mooring jetties, slipway and boatlift and passenger landing facilities. This development is expected to provide a sound infrastructure for the continued development of the fisheries industry.

Forestry. The Forestry Division has its headquarters on Tongatapu. Several small mills have operated on 'Eua, Ha'apai and Tongatapu, processing coconut and some hardwoods. However, in 1985 the Mataliku Mill was fully electrified which enabled increased production. A joinery shop was also opened to manufacture block flooring and roof shingles on a commercial basis. Afforestation projects, particularly on 'Eua, are proving successful.

ECONOMIC DEVELOPMENT. Diversification of the economy through industrial development has received active encouragement by the Government. An industrial development policy backed by legislation was formulated in 1979. Among its more important fiscal incentives is a five-year tax holiday that can be extended another five years; duty free importation of plant and machinery for up to two years; concessional port and service tax on such imports, and exemption from duty and tax on raw materials if the final products are re-exported.

Industries also benefit from financial schemes supported by the New Zealand and Australian Governments. Local finance is available from the Tonga Development

Bank and the Bank of Tonga.

Industries are encouraged that would bring clear benefits to Tonga, and a growing number of business licences have been introduced.

The Industrial Development Incentives Policy and Act was reviewed in 1985. Detailed information may be obtained from the Department of Labour, Commerce and Industries, Nuku'alofa, although the wait for a reply could be a lengthy one.

Among the products manufactured for export are knitted garments, desiccated coconut, light machinery, sports goods, black coral jewellery and fibreglass products. The value of exports of industrial products has been many times that of primary products. Tonga's total exports are in the order of $8 million against imports of $59 million. Both import substitution, and export oriented industries which bring technology transfer and employment, are being encouraged by the Government.

Industrial estate. A Small Industries Centre has been established close to the port area and there are 24 companies operating, producing an output of over $2 million. In 1985 the value of exports from the SIC was $900,000. The Government has an investment of $1.4 million in the SIC and currently receives a return of $44,000 per annum. In 1986 the Asian Development Bank approved finance to undertake the development of a further 8 acres of the SIC.

A similar development has been approved for Vava'u with funding also from the Asian Development Bank. The 13-acre site is expected to cost $300,000 to supply the infrastructure for the types of service industries expected to establish there.

Natural resources. A search for oil was initiated after oil seepages were found in 1968. The seepages occurred in coral limestone in the sea off 'Ohonua harbour in 'Eua. Samples of the oil were analysed by several oil companies, and the results showed it to be weathered crude oil. A consortium of major oil companies was set up in 1968, with Tonga Shell NV appointed as operator.

Shell undertook a geological field survey in 1970 concentrating on 'Eua, but extending to most of the islands. From the results of the survey, two drilling locations were proposed in August 1971, and two 'wild cat' wells were spudded in at Ma'ufanga and at Hofoa. They were abandoned at 1684 m and 1685 m respectively.

These disappointing but inconclusive results caused Shell to withdraw from the petroleum agreement in 1972. The remaining participants attempted unsuccessfully several 'farm out' proposals in 1973, but the agreement terminated in 1974.

In February 1976, a new petroleum agreement was signed between the Tonga Government and Webb Tonga Inc. Webb Tonga re-evaluated all the available data and reprocessed the Shell seismic lines. Three well sites were chosen.

The first of the Webb Tonga wells, Kumimonu No. 1 on the Malapo prospect in February 1978 reached a depth of 2555 m, a dry hole. Kumimonu No. 2 was drilled in April 1978 on the Fua'amotu prospect. It was proved also to be a dry hole, at a depth of 2295 m. The final hole, Kumimonu No. 3, was drilled in Nuku'alofa in May–July 1978, and reached a depth of 2635 m. All three wells were plugged and abandoned.

In July 1980 Samuel Gary Oil Producers Inc. took over the petroleum agreement from Webb Tonga.

In recent years several international companies have again expressed interest in drilling offshore and they have taken the data available for research purposes.

Studies continue to be made by universities and CCOP/SOPAC to locate possible oilfields but to date no major findings have taken place. The Department of Lands, Survey and Natural Resources, with the support of His Majesty, has sought to interest Malaysian oil companies in the promotion of oil exploration in Tonga. Two geologists from CCOP/SOPAC arrived in Tonga in June 1987 to analyse and reinterpret all the data collected since 1968.

Gold. Because of recent theories regarding the origin of gold in the Pacific region, there has been an upsurge of interest by mining companies in mineral exploration in the Kingdom. Several have lodged applications for prospecting licences.

TOURISM. The tourist industry is a major contributor to the economy. Foreign exchange earnings were $10.1 million in 1985, $12 million in 1986 and $14.6 million in

1987. Cruise ships go into both Nuku'alofa and Vava'u in the north but since 1985 cruise ships berthing in Tonga have become fewer and fewer. The explanation given is that the trend is for shorter cruises from Sydney therefore eliminating the more distant island groups. The majority of accommodations available are in guest houses. There are no hotels of international standard. Most visitors come from New Zealand, US, or Australia.

TABLE 1 VISITOR ARRIVALS IN TONGA

	1986	1987
Air	16,088	17,239
Yacht	1659	1982
Cruise ship	14,510	9055
Cargo ship Passengers	59	428
Ships' crew	12,361	10,866
Total	44,677	39,550

LOCAL COMMERCE. There were 82 societies on the Register of Co-operative Societies at the end of 1985, the 15th year of the movement. The most recent project has been the establishment of a Family Life Improvement unit which aims to increase awareness of nutrition, budgeting, health matters and community resources. Societies are involved in copra and vanilla production, limited manufacturing, and handicraft. The Federation is also involved in merchandising of imported goods as well as fish marketing.

In 1985 there were 42 credit unions.

DUTY FREE SALES. A small range of duty free goods are sold, available to residents as well as travellers. Most international visitors would find the prospect of duty free shopping in Tonga a non event. There is a duty free shop at the International Dateline Hotel and one at the airport which is open for all departing flights. Other shops in Nuku'alofa and Vava'u advertise duty free goods also. Some electrical goods, watches and liquor are the major components of the range.

OVERSEAS TRADE. Tonga regularly has an adverse balance of trade, offset to some extent by invisible earnings from such sources are remittances from overseas, tourism, donations, gifts, etc.

In 1985 the adverse balance of trade moved up to to $51.7 million. The total value of imports and exports in recent years is shown in Table 2.

TABLE 2 TONGA — OVERSEAS TRADE (in $T millions)

	1981	1982	1983	1984	1985
Imports	35.1	41.2	41.7	46.6	58.9
Exports	6.3	3.6	5.8	10.0	7.2

New Zealand was Tonga's best customer, taking 48.4 per cent of total exports in 1985. Australia was next with 34.8 per cent, and Fiji with 5.1 per cent.

Tonga's main imports are flour, fresh and canned meat, canned fish, dairy products, tobacco, cotton piece goods, drapery, motor cars, motor cycles and petroleum products. Australia and New Zealand, are the biggest suppliers, chiefly of food.

The values of main export commodities in recent years are shown in Table 3.

The invisible earnings have played a key role over the years to compensate for a merchandise trade deficit. In 1984/5, these earnings included $2.7 million from tourism, $18.5 million in remittances from overseas, $2.9 million in gifts and donations and $13.2 million in grants, aid and transfers. There was a net increase of $4 million over the 1983/4 figures.

CUSTOMS TARIFF. There have been some changes made to tariffs by recent legislation. A detailed list is available from the Collector of Customs, Fakafanua Building, Nuku'alofa. Merchandise particularly affected by the changes are liquor, cigarettes and tobacco (tariff to be increased from 15 to 18 per cent), petroleum, motor spirit, diesel and benzine (increased 2 seniti per litre) and luxury goods (tariff increases ranging from 15 to 25 per cent).

FINANCE. Since 1983 the direction of fiscal policy has been towards freeing up the economy to enable the private sector to develop. Policies have included deregulation and changes to taxes and customs duties and

TABLE 3 TONGA — EXPORT COMMODITIES (T$ million)

	1981	1982	1983	1984	1985
Coconut oil	1.2	1.3	2.1	5.0	2.8
Copra	1.8	—	—	—	—
Desiccated coconut	0.8	0.2	0.5	0.8	0.5
Bananas	0.5	0.1	0.3	0.9	0.9
Vanilla beans	0.3	0.6	0.6	1.1	0.4
Agricultural n.e.s.	1.3	0.9	1.4	1.6	2.0
Manufactures	0.4	0.5	0.9	0.6	0.7
TOTALS	$6.3 m	$3.6 m	$5.8 m	$10.0 m	$7.3 m

the improvement of economic infrastructure which will encourage investment and economic growth. In spite of the considerable deficit on merchandise trade, revenue derived from tourism, remittances, taxes, rents, interest and postal and philatelic sales have kept the balance of payments position in the surplus.

Budget. Recurrent revenue and expenditure in recent years are as shown in Table 4.

TABLE 4 TONGA — REVENUE AND EXPENDITURE (in $ million)

	Revenue	Expenditure
1980/81	12.6	11.8
1981/82	15.7	16.3
1982/83	18.3	17.0
1983/84	18.0	17.8
1984/85	22.6	21.3

The main areas of expenditure are public works (14 per cent), education (13 per cent) and health (12 per cent). This distribution reflects the kingdom's commitment to social services, administration and the development of infrastructure.

In 1987 the recurrent expenditure was set at $29.8 million while development expenditure was expected to be the same as the 1986 level — $31.2 million. The Government increased its contribution to the Development Fund to $2 million while the balance was to come from grant aid, soft loans and other miscellaneous sources.

External aid. In the 1984/5 financial period Tonga received a total of $15.4 million in foreign aid, an increase of $3 million over the previous year. In bilateral aid, (worth approximately $12 million) Australia was the principal donor ($5.4 million), New Zealand gave $4.7 million, while Japan gave $.9 million. Other aid donors included the UK, Canada, France, the Federal Republic of Germany, US Aid and India. Multilateral aid totalled $3.3 million in 1985, with the greatest amount coming from the Asian Development Bank ($1.4 million).

Major projects over the 1985/86 period included the development of the Queen Salote Wharf using Australian assistance, the Nuku'alofa foreshore redevelopment using German assistance, the Fuau Fisheries Harbour project supported by EEC finance and, most recently, the construction of a cultural centre, financed by Japan and expected to cost over $7 million when completed in 1988.

Treasury investments. On 30 June 1985 the Treasury held investments in overseas government securities of a nominal value of $4.2 m. Government shareholdings are shown in Table 5 (over page).

Currency. Tonga's currency consists of pa'anga ($T banknotes) and seniti (cents). The banknotes are in denominations of 20, 10, 5, 2 and 1 pa'anga. The coins are for 1 pa'anga, 50, 20, 10, 5, 2 and 1 seniti. Tonga converted to decimal currency in 1967.

Numismatics. An issue of regular and proof

TABLE 5 GOVERNMENT INVESTMENTS, 1985

Air Pacific Co. Ltd	$88,465
Kintail Honey (Tonga) Ltd	$4000
Bank of Tonga	$400,000
Shipping Corporation of Polynesia Ltd	$6000
Pacific Forum Line Ltd	$757,500
Tonga Development Bank	$2,935,120
Coast Biologicals (Tonga) Ltd	$16,000

gold and silver coins was made in 1981 with the theme of Food for All, under the auspices of FAO. Also 10 coins consisting of six coins in cup nickel, two in bronze and two in pure silver were minted in 1981 featuring new FAO motifs of Food for All, but because of technical and minting delays these coins were not issued until 28 January 1982.

The New Zealand firm of Pacific Commemoratives produced, through the UK Royal Mint, gold and silver coins to commemorate the centenary of the Treaty of Friendship between Tonga and Great Britain which was signed by Queen Victoria and King George I of Tonga, and ratified on 8 September 1981. The coins also commemorated the wedding of Prince Charles and Lady Diana Spencer. The gold coins were in 5 Hau (100 proof and 25 uncircu-

lated) and 1 Hau (2500 proof and 500 uncirculated) and the silver coins of half a Hau (15,000 proof and 1000 uncirculated).

In 1985 the company produced a Christmas 1 pa'anga coin. They also issued two other commemorative coins: the first a set of five coins for the Queen Mother's 85th birthday, the second a set of four coins for the Centenary of the Motor Car.

Stamps. Tonga has been of considerable interest for philatelists because of its unusual stamps. In 1985 sales to overseas collectors were worth $240,173, despite the recession suffered by most major stamp markets in that year. Ten sets of commemorative stamps were issued that year.

Banks. The Bank of Tonga was established in 1974 to meet the demand for commercial banking services, and took over the functions previously undertaken by the Treasury. The bank provides all the services of a trading and savings bank and is the holder of the country's foreign exchange reserves.

The Bank of Tonga is owned 40 per cent by the Government of Tonga, with the remaining shares being held by the Bank of New Zealand, Bank of Hawaii and Westpac, Australia. In 1986 the Legislative Assembly passed the Bank of Tonga (Amendment) Act, increasing the authorised capital of the bank from $1 million to $3 million. The paid up capital at the end of 1986 was $3 million.

The Tonga Development Bank was set up in September 1977, supported by the Government. In April 1983 the Asian Development Bank approved a $US2.2 million concessional loan and technical assistance, with $1.2 million to go for Cyclone Isaac rehabilitation projects and $1 million for the Tonga Development Bank. The loan was

TABLE 6 THE NUMBER OF DEVELOPMENT BANK LOANS

	1984		1985	
Sector	No.	Amount ($000)	No.	Amount ($000)
Agriculture	2544	1967	2488	1880
Industry & commerce	370	1462	303	1690
Others	180	98	270	128
Total	3094	3527	3061	3698

estimated to have provided about 800 jobs through subloans.

The declines in agricultural lending can be attributed to the effects of cyclone damage and the loss of the New Zealand market for watermelons because of fruit fly. A prolonged drought in 1985 also affected agricultural development. There was a drop in applications for industrial/commercial loans but those approved were, on the whole, for larger amounts, particularly to several tourism projects. A main objective of the TDB is to assist small farmers, fishermen and businessmen.

Investment incentives. The Tonga Government has approved legislative amendments to allow Privy Council discretion in offering incentives for the development of new industries with overseas capital. These are in the form of a tax holiday for up to five years with a possible extension of another five years, tax exemptions on dividends and withholding taxes, export duties exemptions and repatriation of funds are included. Joint ventures are favoured but there is no limit to foreign equity. A detailed guide to investment incentives is available from the Department of Labour, Industries and Commerce.

TRANSPORT. There are approximately 300 km of formed roads: 190 in Tongatapu, 74 in Vava'u, 20 in Ha'apai and 16 in 'Eua; 155 km are classed as main road — 52 km with bitumen surface and 103 with a coral surface. Forty km are classed as either secondary road or town bitumen and are sealed, and the remaining roads are unsealed secondary coral or earth.

Vehicles. The number of vehicles licensed as at December 1985 was 3394, including 624 cars, 392 motor cycles and 1794 trucks and vans. The rapid growth rate of registered vehicles, mainly imported secondhand, reconditioned and ageing vehicles with their attendant problems, has created problems not foreseen when the road system was constructed. The driving abilities of the over 5000 licence holders are also of indifferent quality coupled with the thousands of pedestrians, cyclists and the condition of the roads 'make up the ingredients of the kingdom's traffic lottery: a rather complex game in which the stakes are life, death, social and economic loss' according to a recent Police Department report.

Overseas airlines. Tonga is serviced by: Air New Zealand (weekly from Auckland to Tonga and Tonga to Apia); Air Pacific (flies from both Suva and Nadi to Tonga several times a week); Polynesian Airlines (flies from Apia to Tonga and on to Auckland); and Hawaiian Air (flies from Pago Pago to Tonga and return on a weekly basis). These flight schedules change regularly and intending travellers should confirm the latest timetable.

Domestic airlines. 1985 was a year of changes for internal flights in Tonga. A number of operators provide services on a short-term basis, including Talair, operating under the name of Velegair, Tongair, SPIA and Tonga Air Services. The national airlines, Friendly Islands Airways, began its domestic services in December and continues to run regular services between the major islands of the group, and occasionally to Pago Pago. FIA is the sole internal operator in 1988.

Airports. There are six airfields — Fua'amotu (Tongatapu), Lupepau'u (Vava'u), Salote Pilolevu (Ha'apai), Kaufana ('Eua), Mata'aho (Niuatoputapu), Lavinia (Niuafo'ou). Fua'amotu International Airport (the main air gateway into the kingdom) has a sealed runway 2071 × 45 m and a grass runway 1828 × 152 m, Lupepau'u and Salote Pilolevu airports have coral-base runways 1763 × 30 m and 1201 × 30 m respectively. Kaufana and Lavinia airfields have grass runways 731 × 30 m. Mata'aho has a 867 × 27 m coral-base runway.

Fua'amotu, Lupepau'u and Mata'aho airports are the customs entry points by air. In 1988 Australian grants worth nearly $10 million were to be directed at upgrading the airport to international standards and lengthening the runway by 3000 metres to accommodate 747s and other wide bodied aircraft. Lupepau Airport, Vava'u is expected to be enlarged to handle medium jet aircraft.

Port facilities. Points of entry are Nuku'alofa, Pangai, Neiafu and Niuatoputapu.

Tonga has two good harbours at Nuku'alofa and Neiafu (Vava'u). Both handle overseas ships. Nuku'alofa is enclosed by coral reefs and islands.

Extensions to the Queen Salote Wharf

were completed in 1986. Facilities now include two cargo transit sheds, fumigation facilities, police post, forklift storage shed, administration buildings and amenities block. The first berth is 100 m long with an apron of 10 m while the new berth is 110 m long with 10 m of water alongside. Touliki Harbour nearby is maintained by the Tonga Defence Services as a patrol boat base.

At Neiafu, ships drawing less than 7 m and no longer than 120 m may berth. The wharf is in the inner harbour, which is enclosed. Ships of unlimited tonnage and draught may anchor in the sheltered harbour anchorage off 'Utulei Point, which is about 2 km from the wharf. At Lifuka, Ha'apai, large ships anchor about 1 km from the jetty.

Shipping services. Shipping Corporation of Polynesia operates the internal shipping of the group. The Forum Pacific Line operates services between Sydney, Fiji, the Samoas and Tonga as well as a New Zealand service to Fiji, the Samoas and Tonga. Warner Pacific Line operates on the same services as the Forum Line. Bali Hai Line operates between Japanese ports and the islands including Tonga.

COMMUNICATIONS. Internal communications using telephone, telex, telegraph and data are carried by satellite circuits, with an Earth Station operated by Cable and Wireless Ltd in Nuku'alofa. A troposcatter system is installed for trunk calls between the main islands. Other projects being implemented are digital electronic exchanges for the three major centres, an automatic telex centre and a marine radio system. International calls are directed through either Suva or Pago Pago.

Radio. Broadcasting is administered by the Tonga Broadcasting Commission. The studio is in Nuku'alofa. The station, A3Z, is known throughout the South Pacific as the 'Call of the Friendly Islands'. It may be heard in New Zealand and the nearer island groups.

Programmes are devoted to the work of local artists, and include traditional Tongan music, stories and legends, public events, interviews with visiting personalities, etc. The service runs advertising in Tongan, English and Samoan. It broadcasts personal messages to areas not covered by the Telegraph and Telephone Department. Regular bulletins covering overseas and local news are broadcast in Tongan and English.

Newspapers. There is one weekly newspaper, the *Chronicle*, published each Thursday, in Tongan and English. It covers items of local and overseas interest. There is also an independent Tongan-language news sheet, *Ko'e' Kele'a*. In 1986 a bimonthly magazine appeared called *Matangi Tonga*. In June 1987 a second magazine appeared, a monthly called *Tonga Today*.

Television. Services are only available to members of a private club. ASTL–TV3 is the second privately owned television club to be licensed, the first having folded after only a few months of operation. For a $75 membership fee, $100 installation charge and $15 per month, club members receive approximately nine hours of broadcasts a day, mainly imported news programmes and American comedies. Several religious organisations from the US have proposed building a television station but no definite plans have yet eventuated.

WATER AND ELECTRICITY. The electrical system is 230 V AC 50 cycles, generated by diesel motors.

The water in Nuku'alofa is safe to drink. Elsewhere it should be boiled, unless advised otherwise.

The Tonga Electric Power Board and the Tonga Water Board are responsible for these two services.

A major electrification project was completed in 1987, funded entirely by the Kingdom of Tonga; the foreshore reclamation area from the royal palace to the Queen Salote Wharf was illuminated to complete the redevelopment project. This lighting is gradually being extended along the western side of the harbour as the sea wall project proceeds.

MAJOR OFFICE HOLDERS
Head of State:
    His Majesty King Taufa'ahau Tupou IV
Prime Minister:
    Prince Fatefehi Tu'ipelehake
Speaker of Legislative Assembly:
    Honorable Malupo
Secretary to Cabinet:
    Taniela H. Tufui
Crown Solicitor:

T. Tupou
Solicitor General:
  Pohiva Tui'onetoa

GOVERNMENT MINISTRIES
AND DEPARTMENTS
Cabinet, Hala Taufa'ahau, Tel.: 21300.
Divisions: Prime Minister, Minister of
Agriculture, Fisheries & Forestry, Minister
of Marine; Deputy Prime Minister, Minister
of Lands, Surveys & Natural Resources;
Minister of Police & Prisons; Minister of
Health; Minister of Labour, Commerce &
Industries; Minister of Foreign Affairs &
Defence; Minister of Finance,
Commissioner of Island Revenue, Controller
of Customs, Controller of Post Office;
Governor of Vava'u; Governor of Ha'apai;
Chief Secretary & Secretary to Cabinet
Parliament House, Tel.: 21525. Divisions:
Nobles' Representatives, People's
Representatives
**Agriculture, Fisheries & Forestry
Ministry,** Hala Vuna, Tel.: 21511.
Divisions: Agriculture Service Division,
Forestry, Fisheries, Marketing Services
Civil Aviation Ministry, Hala Salote, Tel.:
21744. Divisions: Civil Aviation, Fua'amotu
Airport, Meteorological Service
Education Ministry, Hala Vuna, Tel.:
21511. Divisions: Curriculum Development
Unit, Scholarship, Technical Services,
Vocational Guidance, GPS Nuku'alofa, FPS
Ngele'ia, GPS Ma'ufanga, Teacher's
Training College, Tonga College, Tonga
High School
Finance Ministry, Hala Vuna, Tel.: 21666.
Divisions: Treasury Department, Customs
Department, Harbour & Wharves
Department, Post Office, Statistics
Department, Island Revenue Department
Foreign Affairs & Defence Ministry, Hala
Taufa'ahau, Tel.: 21300. Divisions: Tonga
Defence Services
Health Ministry, Hala Taufa'ahau, Vaiola
Hospital, Tel.: 21200. Divisions:
Administration, Dental Services,
Laboratory & X-Ray Service, Public Health
Service, Training Services, Catering
Services, Pharmacy & Medical Store, Health
Centres
**Labour, Commerce & Industries
Ministry,** Hala Salote, Tel.: 21888.
Divisions: Price Control Section, Labour

Scheme, Co-operative Office, Industrial
Promotion & Evaluation Unit, Small
Industries Centre
**Lands, Survey & Natural Resources
Ministry,** Hala Vuna, Tel.: 21511.
Divisions: Land Valuer, Town Planning,
Survey Division, National Park Rangers
Police & Prisons Ministry, Hala
Vaha'akolo, Tel.: 21233. Divisions: Police
Training School, Central Police Station,
Bailiff Section, Charge Section, Immigration
Section, Traffic Section, Prosecution
Section, District Police Station, Fire
Services, Prisons Department, Hu'atolitoli
Prisons
Prime Minister's Office, Hala Taufa'ahau,
Tel.: 21300 Divisions: Secretary to Cabinet,
Establishment Division, Audio Visual Aid
Centre, Audit Department, Central
Planning Department, Chronicle Office,
Crown Law Department, Justice
Department, Printing Department, Tonga
Visitors Bureau
Public Works Ministry, Hala Lavinia,
Tel.: 21100. Divisions: Works, Transport,
Government Store
Tonga Broadcasting Commission, Hala
Tungi, Tel.: 21555. Divisions: News
Current Affairs & Sports, Technical
Services, Programmes, Sales & Marketing
Tonga Commodities Board, Hala
Vaha'akolo, Tel: 21555. Divisions:
Processing & Researching Division,
Desiccated Coconut Factory, Construction
Division, Primary Produce Division
Tonga Electric Power Board, Hala
Taufa'ahau, Tel.: 21311
Tonga Telecommunications Commission,
Hala Takaunove, Tel.: 21255. Divisions:
Engineering Branch. Planning &
Development Branch, Radio Branch,
Traffic Branch, External Plant, Training
School
Tonga Visitors Bureau, Hala Vuna,
Tel.: 21773
Tonga Water Board, Hala Taufa'ahau,
Tel.: 21299. Divisions: Accounts Section,
Pumping Station

FOREIGN MISSIONS
Australian High Commission, Hala Salote,
Tel.: 21244
British High Commssion, Hala Vuna,
Tel.: 21021

Chinese Embassy, Hala Holomui,
Tel.: 21766
France (Honorary Consulate), Hala
Taufa'ahau, Tel.: 21831
Germany (Honorary Consulate), Hala
Taufa'ahau, Tel.: 21477
Korea (Honorary Consulate), Hala
Uelingatoni, Tel.: 21633
Nauru (Honorary Consulate), Hala
Taufa'ahau, Tel.: 22109
New Zealand High Commission, Hala
Taufa'ahau, Tel.: 21122

HISTORY. Recent archaeological research has revealed that the Tongan archipelago was inhabited at least 3000 years ago. The earliest radiocarbon date so far established is 1140 BC.

The Tongans of those days were makers of elaborately decorated Lapita pottery, like that also found in Fiji. But a few centuries later they were making only plain ware. A small amount of pottery was still in use when the first European explorers visited Tonga.

Tonga had a highly developed social system long before the arrival of Europeans. Originally, the paramount ruler was called the Tu'i Tonga. The first such leader, who is estimated to have reigned about AD 950, was considered to be the son of the sun god Tangaloa. He and his successors for about 500 years had both spiritual and temporal power. But a series of murders is said to have caused the 24th Tu'i Tonga to hand over his temporal powers to his brother, and a new dynasty was created under the title of Tu'i Ha'atakalaua.

About the beginning of the 17th century, a third dynasty, with the title of Tu'i Kanokupolul indicating a link with Upolu, Samoa), was created. Thereafter, some historians say, the position of Tu'i Ha'atakalaua gradually became redundant, while the office of Tu'i Tonga, became increasingly ceremonial. When the first Europeans arrived, the most powerful person was the Tu'i Kanokupolu.

Eventually, when the religious functions of the Tu'i Tonga were rendered obsolete by the adoption of Chirstianity, all the remaining functions of the three most important titles were merged into one, that of Tu'i Kanokupolu; and the holder of that title was the sovereign of all Tonga, as is the case today.

European discovery. The first Europeans to sight any of the islands of the Tongan archipelago were members of the Dutch expedition of Schouten and Le Maire. They came upon the northern outliers of Tafahi and Niuatoputapu in 1616 while crossing the Pacific to the East Indies. In 1643 their countryman, Abel Janszoon Tasman, approached the archipelago from the south. Sailing with the ships *Heemskerck* and *Zeehaan*, he sighted the southernmost island, Ata, before coming upon 'Eua and Tongatapu, which he named Middelburgh and Amsterdam respectively. Tasman spent thress days at Tongatapu, and a week at Nomuka to the northward, taking in provisions. Nomuka was named Rotterdam.

In 1767, Captain Samuel Wallis, the discoverer of Tahiti, came upon the two northern islands seen by Schouten and Le Maire. Unaware of their prior discovery, he gave the name Boscawen to Tafahi and Keppel to Niuatoputapu — names they bore on European charts for the next century or so.

Cook's voyages. In October 1773 Captain James Cook made the first of three visits to Tonga. Approaching the group from the Society Islands, he anchored briefly at 'Eua (which he recognised as Tasman's Middleburgh) before going on to Tongatapu. Five days at Tongatapu gave him and some of his companions the first opportunity to write detailed descriptions of Tongan life.

In the following June, Cook returned to Tonga and spent several days trading amicably at Nomuka.

Cook's third visit was made on his final voyage in 1777. He then spent two and a half months at Nomuka, Lifuka, Tongatapu and 'Eua, during which much valuable information was obtained about the inhabitants. He named the Lifuka (Ha'apai) group the Friendly Islands although, ironically, there was a plot by the Tongans to kill Cook during his sojourn at Lifuka.

In 1781 a Spaniard, Francisco Antonio Mourelle, chanced upon some of the northern islands in attempting to sail from the Philippines to Mexico during the wrong season of the year. His landfalls included Fonu'lei. Late and Vava'u, of which he was the European discoverer. Cook had heard about Vava'u but did not see it. Mourelle spent a fortnight trading for supplies at Vava'u before picking his way through the more southerly islands in the hope of finding a favourable wind.

About six years later, in 1787, the French explorer, La Perouse, reached Tonga from Samoa and touched briefly at Niuatoputapu, Vava'u and Tongatapu.

In April 1789 the mutiny on the *Bounty* took place off the volcano island of Tofua, a few weeks after the *Bounty* had arrived from Tahiti with a cargo of breadfruit. Her captain, William Bligh, and 18 other men were cast adrift in an open boat. They landed on Tofua in the hope of obtaining provisions. But the Tongans attacked them killing one man, and Bligh had to head for Timor in his open boat empty-handed.

In 1791, Captain Edward Edwards of HMS *Pandora*, sent from England to find and arrest the *Bounty* mutineers, passed through the Tongan archipelago twice in the course of his search. Two years later, the French explorer, d'Entrecasteaux, visited Tongatapu seeking traces of his countryman, La Perouse, who had disappeared after leaving Botany Bay in January 1788.

Malaspina's arrival. Barely two months after the departure of the d'Entrecasteaux expedition, two Spanish ships, *Descubierta* and *Atrevida*, anchored at Vava'u under the command of Captain Alessandro Malaspina. As Vava'u was considered a Spanish possession by virtue of Mourelle's discovery, Malaspina formally annexed it and buried a message in a bottle to attest the fact. Although Malaspina and some of his officers wrote exceptionally interesting accounts of what they saw and learned at Vava'u, these have never been translated from Spanish.

Malaspina was the last European explorer to visit Tonga before the arrival of the first permanent European settlers. These were six deserters from the American ship *Otter* who went ashore at Ha'apai and 'Eua in 1796. A year later, the first European missionaries — 10 lay members of the London Missionary Society — landed at Tongatapu from the ship *Duff*. Three of them were murdered in 1799 during a civil war between followers and opponents of the Tu'i Kanokupolu of the time. Six of the others eventually escaped to Sydney. The tenth man. George Vason, abandoned his faith and lived among the Tongans until 1804. He later published a

book about his experiences.

Fighting was incessant in one or another of the Tongan islands until 1809. During this time an unscrupulous chief called Finau Ulukalala gained control over Vava'u and Ha'apai, and sometimes ascendancy in Tongatapu as well.

In 1806, the Tongans cut off the English privateer *Port-au-Prince* at Ha'apai and killed many of her crew. One of the survivors, a youth called William Mariner, lived in Tonga under Finau's protection for the next four years. His record of Tongan lifes, *An Account of the Natives of the Tonga Islands*, first published in 1817, is a classic of South Seas literature.

After Finau's death in 1809, most of the fighting stopped in Vava'u and Ha'apai, although it went on spasmodically in Tongatapu. Meanwhile, the three royal titles had fallen into abeyance, and the islands were ruled by a variety of lesser chiefs.

The title of Tu'i Ha'atakalaua became vacant in 1799 after the murder of the incumbent. No Tu'i Tonga was appointed between 1800 and 1827. And even the office of Tu'i Kanokupolu was vacant for much of that period.

However, in 1820, a man appeared who was to acquire all three royal titles and create the modern kingdom of Tonga. This was Taufa'ahau, whose father, the Tu'i Kanokupolu, died in 1820. Taufa'ahau thereupon became chief of Ha'apai.

First missionaries. While Taufa'ahau was consolidating his position in Ha'apai, several new missionaries arrived in Tonga. The first, a Wesleyan, was the Rev. William Lawry, who settled on Tongatapu in 1822 and stayed for 16 months. He was followed in 1826 by two Tahitian missionaries; then came two more Wesleyans, the Revs. John Thomas and John Hutchison.

Although all the early evangelists found much to discourage them, they and others who came later gradually persuaded some of the Tongans to take heed of their teachings. Among these was Taufa'ahau, who was baptised in 1834, a year after he had defeated and expelled from Ha'apai several chiefs, including the Tu'i Tonga, who had opposed his rule. Under Taufa'ahau's influence, the whole of Ha'apai became Christian. And when Taufa'ahau succeeded soon afterwards to the chieftainship of Vava'u, the people of that archipelago followed his example also. Meanwhile, although some of the Tongatapu chiefs had adopted Christianity, there were several who were still resolute heathens. These included Taufa'ahau's grand-uncle, the Tu'i Kanokupolu.

During the next few years, war went on almost constantly between the Christian and heathen parties. Twice Taufa'ahau successfully intervened on his grand-uncle's side, but the state of war continued. In 1840, Captain Croker of HMS *Favourite* was killed when he tried to mediate between the two parties. However, two years later, when a party of French Roman Catholic priests established themselves on Tongatapu, many of the remaining heathens adopted Christianity — as Roman Catholics. One such convert was the Tu'i Tonga.

Rise of Tupou. In 1845, after his grand-uncle's death, Taufa'ahau was elected to the title of Tu'i Kanokupolu under the name Siaosi (George) Tupou. However, not all the chiefs were willing to accept him, and there was further fighting until August 1852. When Tupou (as he is called henceforth) finally emerged the victor, he was indisputably the most powerful chief in Tonga.

In 1862, Tupou introduced a code of laws for the whole of Tonga. Features of the code were that the chiefs and commoners were to be treated equally before the law; the commoners were freed from forced labour for, and compulsory contributions to, the chiefs; and the commoners were given control over their own property. In addition, a parliament was set up, with representatives of both the chiefs and the commoners. Another significant event occurred three years later. The incumbent Tu'i Tonga died, and Tupou was invested with all the dignities of his office, although the office itself was of little significance because of the universal adoption of Christianity.

At a meeting of Parliament in 1895, Tupou declared that the title of Tu'i Ha'atakalaua had also been conferred upon him. This meant that he was now the possessor of all three ancient titles. He was thus in a position to introduce a constitution for Tonga, making it a limited monarchy.

Constitution effected. The constitution became effective on 4 November 1875. It guaranteed rights to life, property and worship, it defined the form of government; and it declared that all land belonged to the king, that he could grant estates to the nobles, and that key, in turn, could lease portions of their estates to the people.

The Rev. Shirley Baker, a Wesleyan missionary, was conspicuous in advising the king about the constitution and other acts of government during this period. In the next few years, Tonga signed treaties with Germany (1876), Great Britiain (1879) and the United States (1888), in all of which the kingdom's independence was recognised. A treaty of a similar character had been signed with France 30 years earlier.

After Tonga's first Premier, Tevita Uga, died in 1879, Baker resigned from the Wesleyan ministry and became Premier himself, as well as Minister of Foreign Affairs and Minister of Lands. With the king well into his eighties, Baker was soon wielding considerable influence. He quickly moved to have hereditary estates conferred on 30 nobles and six matapules, and the government took over all the primary schools from the missions, besides establishing a government college. Later, in 1885, Baker persuaded the king to establish a Free Wesleyan Church of Tonga.

Baker's great influence was resented by many Tongans, and in 1886 four escaped prisoners attempted to assassinate him, but only succeeded in wounding his son and daughter. In retaliation, Baker arranged for armies of men from Ha'apai and Vava'u to attack the Wesleyans on Tongatapu; and several hundred Wesleyans were eventually exiled to uninhabited islands in Tonga. Later, Baker interfered to such an extent in the administration of justice in the Tongan courts that the British High Commissioner for the Western Pacific visited Tonga and ordered him to be deported.

As Tonga's affairs generally were in an intolerable mess, a British official, Basil Thomson, was sent from Fiji for nine months as Assistant Premier. Thomson described his sojourn in *The Diversions of a Prime Minister* (London 1894).

King George I dies. A year after Thomson left Tonga, King George Tupou died at the age of 96. He was succeeded by his great-grandson, as George Tupou II, who inherited an empty treasury and many other problems. As Britain feared that some other power might attempt to annex the kingdom at this stage, Basil Thomson was again sent to Tonga to negotiate a treaty of friendship with Britain. Under the treaty Tonga agreed not to make agreements with any other nation, and to transact her foreign affairs through the British Agent and Consul. The treaty was signed on 18 May 1900, and ratified on 16 February 1901. But in 1905 it was amended to give the British Consul the power of veto over Tonga's foreign affairs.

When King George Tupou II died in 1918, he was succeeded by his daughter Salote as Queen Salote Tupou III. She had married a Tongan noble, Uiliame Tungi, in 1917, and he became Premier in 1923. In the following years, a schism that had existed in church circles since Baker's time was healed when the Queen, who occupied the position of chief member of the Free Wesleyan Church, persuaded 12,000 members of that church to unite with 4000 Wesleyans who formed the old parent church. However, some 6000 Tongans who were unwilling to join the Wesleyans either abstained from church attendance or joined the body calling itself the Free Church of Tonga.

The Queen's consort, Tungi, remained Premier of Tonga until his death in 1941. His successor was Ata, a high chief, who was in office until his retirement in 1949. During Ata's premiership, Tonga, in close collaboration with New Zealand, formed a local defence force of 2000 men. Some of these saw action in the Solomons against the Japanese. Meanwhile, New Zealand and American troops were stationed on Tongatapu, which became a staging point for shipping. An airfield was also built at Fua'amotu.

Ata was succeeded as Premier by Queen Salote's eldest son, Crown Prince Tungi (the present king), who had succeeded to his father's title of Tungi in 1945. As Prince Tupouto'a, he had matriculated from Newington College, Sydney, and in 1943 had taken an honours degree in jurisprudence at Sydney University. Meanwhile, his brother, Prince Sione Ngu, studied agriculture at Gatton College, Queensland, and returned to Tonga in 1944. He was later given the title of Tu'ipelehake and was made Minister of Lands and Health. The two royal brothers

were married in a double wedding, an occasion for great celebration in Nuku'alofa on 10 June, 1947. Crown Prince Tungi married Princess Halaevalu Mata'aho, and Prince Tu'ipelehake married Princess Melenaite Tupou Moheofo. A son, Prince Taufa'ahau Manumataongo Tukuaho, was born to Crown Prince Tungi and his wife in May 1948, and there were three subsequent children. The eldest is now Crown Prince under the name Tupouto'a.

Two events in 1953 brought Tonga into the world spotlight as never before. In June, Queen Salote attended the coronation in London of Queen Elizabeth II, and spent about two months in Britain during which she endeared herself to all who saw and met her. In December, Queen Elizabeth and the Duke of Edinburgh visited Tonga.

In 1958, a new treaty of friendship was signed between Tonga and Great Britian. It was ratified in May 1959. It provided for the appointment of a British Commissioner and Consul (in place of the former British Agent and Consul) to be responsible to the Governor of Fiji, who held the office of British Chief Commissioner for Tonga. In 1965, the British Commissioner and Consul of Tonga became directly responsible to the British Secretary of State for the Colonies.

On the death of Queen Salote in December 1965, Prince Tungi acceded to the throne as King Taufa'ahau Tupou IV, and his brother Prince Tu'ipelehake became Premier, Minister for Foreign Affairs, Minister of Education, and Minister of Agriculture and Works. When Tonga became completely independent of Britain on 4 June 1970, the title of Prime Minister was substituted for that of Premier. Other consequences of this development were that Britain appointed a high commissioner and a deputy high commissioner to Tonga, and Tonga joined the Commonwealth and appointed a high commissioner in London.

Notable developments in Tonga's recent history have been government encouragement for the growth of tourism and industry and the temporary migration of large numbers of Tongan men to New Zealand as 'guest workers'. Over the last few years many Tongans have adopted a more critical attitude towards the present political system.

Tonga signed treaties of friendship with

Germany (1979) and France (1980).

Further reading. Noel Rutherford, *Shirley Baker and the King of Tonga*, Melbourne, 1971; Sione Latukefu, *Church and State in Tonga*, Canberra, 1974; Noel Rutherford (ed.), *Friendly Islands: A History of Tonga*, Melbourne, 1977.

TONGAN ISLANDS IN DETAIL

Tongatapu group. The Tongatapu group is the most southerly of the Tongan islands. Tongatapu Island ('Sacred Tonga') is the largest in the group, with an area of 257 sq. km. Nuku'alofa, on the northern side of the triangular island, is the capital and chief port. Population in 1986 was 34,715. The harbour is protected by reefs. Just to the east of Nuku'alofa is the reefstrewn entrance to a large central lagoon that runs back behind Nuku'alofa and also towards the eastern end of the island.

The town stretches along the harbourside, most of which has a verge of green grass bordering Vuna Road. At one end of it is the Royal Palace and Chapel, set in lawns. The International Dateline Hotel is about a kilometre away from the palace and faces the harbour. The Government offices, business houses, park, hospital, etc., are in streets that run back from the harbour. An increasing number of modern buildings have been built in recent years. The population in 1986 was 28,899.

Tongatapu is of coral formation, quite flat and without running streams. It has many roads and all of the tourist sites and ancient monuments are easily accessible.

Rainfall on Tongatapu is from 1500–1700 mm per annum.

'Eua lies south and east of Tongatapu and with an area of 87 sq. km is the second largest of the group. It is well timbered and the source of most of the sawn local timber used in the kingdom.

Unlike Tongatapu it is hilly and rises to about 330 m. Sheep were established there because of its cool climate but they died out due to disease. The population of Niuafo'ou were settled there after an eruption on their northerly island in 1946 but many returned to their home island.

Tests have shown that the purest water in Tonga is in the village of Houma, on 'Eua. It comes from a spring inside Kaha Cave in the second terrace on the northern side of 'Eua, and supplies 26,000 litres of water every 24 hours.

'Ata. Tasman sighted 'Ata in 1683 as he sailed from New Zealand and he gave it the name of Pylstart. The island is 136 km SSW of Tongatapu. There are two peaks, the higher being 382 m, but the volcano is extinct. Ata contains deposits of guano, suitable for manure, but the lack of a harbour renders these useless commercially. The island was formerly inhabited, but in the 1860s King George Tupou I ordered the 200 inhabitants to move to 'Eua because the islanders were being taken away by kidnapping ships to work in the mines of Chile.

The other islands of this group are Atata, Euaiki, Kala'au and Kanatea. Together they are about 1 sq. km in area and the last two are uninhabited. Population of the whole Tongatapu group in 1986 was 63,614.

Ha'apai group. The Ha'apai group is about 144 km north of Nuku'alofa by sea.

Lifuka. is a low sickle-shaped island, so narrow that it can be crossed in ten minutes. The main anchorage is on the west side of the island, opposite the township of Pangai.

The site of the old palace of the chiefs of Ha'apai, the last of whom was the first constitutional King of all Tonga, George Tupou I, is a short distance from the landing place of Lifuka. The present Royal family has a summer residence there. Three kilometres along the shore from the jetty is the point where Captain Cook landed in 1777.

Lifuka has an area of 11.8 sq. km. It has a strip for light aircraft.

The Governor of Ha'apai resides at Pangai. It was here that the Rev. Dr Shirley Baker, a former Premier of Tonga, died. A large monument has been erected to his memory.

The total area of the 36 islands of the Ha'apai Group is 118 sq. km.

In the group an extinct volcano, Kao, has a perfect cone. The summit is 1030 m high, the highest point in the Tongan group. It is easily visible from Lifuka, which is 56 km to the eastward. The island is uninhabited. It is 12.5 sq. km in area.

Tofua is a large island 558 m high, over 8 km long, and about 6 km wide. Its area is 46.6 sq. km, of which over 7 sq. km is the lake in the crater of the active volcano, Lofia. There is no record of damage in recent years. The island was once inhabited. When Captain Bligh and his loyal sailors called there for water in 1789, after the *Bounty* mutiny, they were attacked and the quartermaster, Norton, was killed.

Nomuka, south of the main Ha'apai group, was visited by more voyagers than any other island in Tonga. The large pond of fresh water from which Tasman, Cook, Bligh and others took supplies is still there. Nomuka has an area of 5 sq. km.

Hunga Tonga and Hunga Ha'apai are sister islands north-west of Tongatapu. Both possess deposits of guano, but no anchorages. Volcanic activity has long ceased. The former is 161 m high and Hunga Ha'apai 131 m high.

In addition to the islands mentioned above, the group has the following inhabited islands: Mango, Oua, Tungua, Matuku, Ha'afeva, Uiha, Fotuha'a, Lofanga, Foa, Ha'ano, and Mo'unga'oneo. Fao is connected to Lifuka by a cause way. The other uninhabited islands are: Noumuaiki, Kelefesia, Tonumea, Telekitonga, Lalonna, Telekivava'u, Teaupa, Fetoa, Uanukuhihifo, Uanukuhahake, Tofanga, Tatafa, Niniva, Uoleva, Ofolonga, Nukuamu and Lekalega. Total population of the group in 1986 was 8979.

Vava'u group. There are, in all, 34 islands in the Vava'u group with a total land area of 115 sq. km and a population of 15,170 (1986). The main concentration of people is around Neiafu, the town on Vava'u. Population here in 1986 was 5273.

The island of Vava'u is the largest (89 sq. km) and is famous for its harbour. The port of Vava'u, Neiafu, is reached after steaming some kilometres up a sound of great beauty.

Vava'u was the last part of Tonga to be discovered by Europeans — by the Spaniard, Mourelle, in 1781. Twelve years later Vava'u was visited by Captain Alessandro Malaspina, Italian-born officer of the Spanish Navy.

He arrived in Vava'u in May 1793 and established friendly relations with the Tongans, especially with a chief named Tupau, an ancestor of the present King of Tonga. On 30 May Malaspina buried a document proclaiming annexation at a secret 'observation point' and had the Spanish flag raised. The Tongans raised no objection — doubtless only because they did not know what was going on. Spain never followed up the gesture.

It is believed that the document proclaiming annexation was contained in a bottle

which was buried on an islet in the habour. It has never been found but one view is that the Tongans on the islet probably unearthed the bottle as soon as Malaspina's ships had sailed.

A great attraction of Vava'u is the caves, which are reached in a short launch journey from Neiafu. The most interesting, 'Mariner's Cave' — first described by William Mariner in his *Tonga Islands* (1817) and woven by Byron into his poem 'The Island' — is only reached by diving through an underwater passage. The Swallows' Cave, which is nearer Neiafu, can be entered by boat. It is a fine cathedral-like chamber, nearly 32 m high and 65 m in circumference. The sunlight at the entrance sometimes lights up the cave in multi-colours. The 'Bell Rock', nearby, is famous for an obvious reason — when struck it rings like a bell.

There are several types of accommodation at Neiafu. The settlement also has stores, a hospital and other amenities. In 1987 the Tonga Development Bank opened a branch in Neiafu. There is also a modern building housing the Bank of Tonga. There is a good airstrip.

There is a dormant volcano on late which has not erupted since 1854. The island's height is 557 m and the island has an area of 15 sq. km. The peak is plainly visible for 80 km on clear days and has always been a landmark for mariners. The island, now uninhabited, is very fertile and densely wooded.

Lateiki. In May 1979 Metis Shoal, lying between the volcanic cones of Kao and Late in the Vava'u Group, erupted and a small volcanic island appeared for the third time in the last 100 years. The island, named by the King Lateiki ('It lies beside Late'), was 320 metres long and 120 metres wide, rising to a height of 16 metres. On 7 July 1979, the King sailed in the MV *Sami* to the new island, and, while His Majesty watched from the boat lying off the island, His Royal Highness Prince 'Aho'eitu raised the Tongan flag on the island and the King named it. Scientists believe that the new island, through erosion by the sea, will disappear once again.

Fonualei is 64 km north-west of Vava'u, and is 197 m high. The Spaniard, Mourelle, discovered it in 1781, and he named it Amargura, or 'Bitterness', because of his disappointment at not getting food and water there. In 1846 the volcano threw ashes over such a large area that the gardens in Vava'u were spoilt. Fonualei is uninhabited.

Other populated islands in the group are Taunga, Ovaka, Hunga, Lape, Nuapapu, 'Otea, Kapa, Pangaimotu, Ofu, Olo'ua, Koloa and Okoa. Unpopulated islands not mentioned above are 'Euakafa, 'Ovalau, Foilifuka, Luamoko, A'A, Tapana, 'Utungake, Mafana, Kenutu, 'Umuna, Fai'oa, Sisia, Tu'ungasika, Foeata, 'Oto, 'Euaiki, Fonua-'One'one, Fua'amotu and Toku.

Niuatoputapu. Niuatoputapu, or Keppel Island, lies 240 km north of Vava'u. The anchorage on the west of the island is not good and is not a regular port of entry. Nonetheless, it is a convenient calling point for Tonga's own vessels on voyages to and from Pago Pago and Apia, in the Samoas. There is an 867 m coral base airstrip on the island.

Tafahi. Tafahi, or Boscawen, is about 10 km from Keppel, and reaches a height of 656 m. It is of volcanic origin. It is 3.4 sq. km in area. Tafahi was the first part of the group seen by Europeans — the Dutchmen, Schouten and Lemaire, in 1616.

Niuafo'ou. Niuafo'ou, which is on the outskirts of the Tongan group, is nearly 640 km from Tongatapu and west and slightly north of Niuatoputapu; it is 34.7 sq. m in area and of volcanic origin, and has a long record of serious eruptions, in which parts of the island were devastated. Following a violent eruption in September, 1946, which wiped out practically the whole of the government headquarters and the villagers' homes and property, the 1300 inhabitants were removed and eventually resettled at 'Eua Island, south of Tongatapu. However, many later returned.

Pre-war, its interest to tourists was its unique method of mail delivery, instituted by a European resident named C. S. Ramsay and; because of this the island has been nicknamed 'Tin Can Island'. The mail from the steamer was sealer by the ship's carpenter in large biscuit tins. The outward mail was made up ashore into several parcels and tied to the ends of sticks about one metre long. Two or three islanders usually swam out, each with a stick topped by its parcel of mail supported by poles of fau wood, of 2 m in length.

A large lake, which lies in the old crater of the island, contains islets, which themselves have craters. Hot springs are found in various parts of the lake. There is now a 731 m grass airstrip on the island.

Falcon Island. To the westward of Ha'apai, and between the two ports of Nuku'alofa and Lifuka, is Falcon Island. Several times in the 19th century, the island was above water; other times a shoal marked its location. Mourelle, in 1781, and La Perouse, both observed a reef there; so did HMS *Falcon* in 1865. The warship *Sappho* in 1865 saw smoke issuing from it. In October 1885 it appeared as an island 2 km long and 50 m high but by 1894 it had 'washed away'. Early in 1896, the shoal suddenly erupted and cast up an island of pumice more than 320 m high. This subsided too.

In October 1927, violent volcanic eruptions again began. As a result of this disturbance, a pumice island 118 m high and 2.4 km long was formed, but as on previous occasions the sea again gradually eroded the pumice to below sea level. It has appeared and disappeared several times since 1927.

FOR THE TOURIST. The Tonga Visitors Bureau produces excellent literature on all aspects of tourist accommodations, other facilities and Tongan culture. It is available from the Information Officer, Tonga Visitors Bureau, PO Box 37, Nuku'alofa.

Entry formalities. Visitors staying for not more than 30 days require a valid passport, onward sea or air ticket, and proof that they have adequate funds. If they wish to extend their stay they must apply to the Principal Immigration Officer.

Valid smallpox vaccination certificates are required by all travellers, except children under six months, who have been in infected areas within 14 days of arrival in Tonga. Valid certificates showing inoculation against yellow fever are required by all travellers over one year of age who have been in an infected area before arrival in Tonga.

Airport tax. An airport tax of $T5 is payable by all departing passengers.

Shopping. Tonga produces some of the best handicrafts in the Pacific. The quality and range of woven articles — from place mats to large 'Ali Baba' baskets, the black coral jewellery and the magnificent tapa — is second to none. Several co-operatives specialise in handicraft sales, both in Nuku'alofa and on Vava'u. The Langa Fonua in the main street, sharing premises with the offices of Friendly Island Airways, was founded by the late Queen Salote to promote handicraft skills. The Friendly Islands Marketing Co-operative on Taufa'ahau Road has an excellent range of top quality handicraft in two shops, while Kato's on Wellington Road and the small shop at the Bascilica also have a small quantity. All shops will pack and post purchases. There are also branches of the first two shops in Neiafu.

Sightseeing. In Nuku'alofa there is the Victorian white-framed royal palace and chapel, surrounded by tall Norfolk pines; the royal tombs, the burial place of Tongan royalty since 1893; Talamahu market, the major fruit and vegetable market, open every day except Sunday, as well as the town centre itself.

Some distance from Nuku'alofa, at Houma, are the famous blow holes, where the waves send water spouting 20 m into the air though coral rock. This stretch of coastline is called Mapu'a Vaea (the Chief's Whistle) by the Tongans.

Hufangalupe (the Pigeon's Doorway) is one of the scenic areas of Tongatapu. It has three main attractions: a huge natural coral bridge under which sea water churns, towering cliffs overlooking the sea, and a beautiful beach at the bottom of a steep downhill trail.

The Ha'amonga trilithon is an ancient construction built to enable the early people to identify the seasons. It consists of two upright coral stones, each about 5 m high, topped by a horizontal connecting stone 6 m long. Each stone weighs an estimated 40 tonnes. Ten kilometres from the Ha'amonga are the terraced tombs, or 'langi', built for an ancient dynasty of kings. They form quadrilateral mounds faced by huge blocks of stone rising in terraces to 4 m. The stones are of coral and are extremely heavy.

At Captain Cook's landing place near Mu'a is an 'ovava tree, descendant of one under which the navigator is said to have rested while visiting that area for Tongan ceremonies.

Near the coastal village of Haveluliku, about 21 km from Nuku'alofa, are impressive underground stalactite and stalagmite caves of unknown length through which

flows a deep underground river. They can be visited on a guided tour.

In the Vava'u islands, the Port of Refuge, named by the Spanish navigator Malaspina, is one of the most picturesque harbours in the Pacific.

Swallow's Cave, which may be entered by launches, is a sanctuary for thousands of swallows in autumn. The fluorescent blue water, in which stalagmites grow, make the cave an excellent swimming pool.

Not far away is Mariner's Cave, a submerged grotto, about which there is a legend of a young chief and his sweetheart who used it in ancient times when feuds raged between noble Tongan families.

The entrance is below water at all times, but it may be entered with the aid of local guides if the wind is in the right direction, otherwise the sea becomes too choppy.

At the southern end of 'Eua Island is Matalanga'a-Maui, a high natural stone bridge. Less than 1 km away are the 115 m sheer cliffs of Lakufa'anga, at the base of which turtles can usually be seen.

Also on 'Eua, the clear Heike stream rushes from the hills to form a natural pool at Hafu.

Pangai, in Ha'apai, is worth a visit. It is accessible by air or boat. The royal family keeps a residence there for holidays and there is much of historic interest in the area, where the Rev. Shirley Baker, former Premier of Tonga, is buried. 'Uiha island, in the group, is the burial place of the old kings.

Tonga's primary attraction is its culture and associated lifestyle. Traditional dress is still very common; older people and those in mourning often wear all black, their ample girths swathed in large mats (ta'ovala); the younger generation wear smaller versions (kie kie for women and ta'ovala for men) over their modern jeans and t-shirts. The wearing of this special 'garment' shows respect for the royal family and elders. Sunday observance is very important and it is only very recently that the people have been allowed to perform manual tasks on this day. Tourism and its seven-day demands have had a lot to do with this change of attitude. Even the seemingly harmless occupation of swimming on a Sunday is only tolerated for tourists. Sunday is the day for church and family feasting. A large Tongan feast means the killing of many pigs and the cooking of up to 30 different dishes in the 'umu' (earth oven). Family feasts are smaller affairs but an invitation to a Tongan home to share the Sunday meal is a cultural and culinary experience.

The presence of a reigning royal family also adds interest for the visitor to Tonga. King Taufa'ahau Tupou IV and his family live in the white, wooden two-storey palace on the seafront in Nuku'alofa. Their privacy is respected within their home but the king is often seen at many functions as, are the other members of the royal family. On special occasions the Tongan people present their monarch with many finely woven mats and huge pieces of tapa.

In 1988 an elaborate show place for Tonga's cultural heritage was opened. The Tonga National Centre, on the shore of Fanga'uta Lagoon, near Nuku'alofa was financed by Japanese aid at a cost of $T6 m. The complex contains an educational centre for training in ancient crafts and skills, exhibition hall, amphitheatre and handicraft displays. Cultural tours are available on Tuesday and Thursday afternoons.

Dining and nightlife. Apart from the restaurant at the main hotel, there is the Seaview which serves freshly prepared dishes from a small menu, Chez Alisi and Andre on Wellington Road which serves good basic French food Fred's àla carte restaurant on salote Road and Lazelo's Italian restaurant on Vuna Road. The Fale Fakalato on Wellington Road is a good lunch venue. Akiko's underneath the Bascilica is a recommended place for cheap eating but the last orders are taken at 8 pm. There are also several Chinese restaurants including the Arcade Gallery, the Hua Hua, close to the International Dateline Hotel, and the Tong Hua which started life as a Mormon church until the king reclaimed it. Finally, there are a number of small cafes which serve local foods, most of which are not open during the evening. The small resorts out of Nuku'alofa have their own dining rooms.

In Nuku'alofa itself, the nightlife consists mainly of discos at the Ramanlal Hotel or at the Friendly Islander Motel. Friday night is the biggest (and loudest) night while on Saturday night everything ends at midnight when Sunday observance takes over. The infiltration of videos has affected nightlife in Pacific countries as much as it has elsewhere and there is a movie theatre in Wellington Road which screens nightly films, mainly of violent content.

Transport. Avis, Budget and several local firms supply rental cars at reasonable cost and there are always plenty of taxis available for short- or long-term hire. Taxis have meters but long distance hiring should always be negotiated and a price settled upon before starting out. All buses leave from the market area and on weekdays services are quite frequent to most parts of Tongatapu but on Saturday afternoons and Sundays services virtually cease. There are also bikes for hire — both push and motor — but the casual attitude to driving regulations make self-propelled transport hazardous at times. The very flat terrain, however, more than compensates. A Tongan driving licence is necessary for hiring cars. It is available at the police station on production of a current overseas licence and an $8 fee.

Nuku'alofa has nothing to offer in the way of good beaches. For sea activities it is best to go out to the small offshore islands such as Pangaimotu or Atata or go to the other side of Tongatapu to Keleti, Ha'atafu or Oholei.

ACCOMMODATION.

Accommodation in Tonga is of medium standard, but generally comfortable and clean. There are several quite large hotels with bar and restaurant facilities and a number of small guest houses where bathroom facilities are shared and whose rates can include three meals a day. This type of accommodation is quite distinctly Tongan and is rarely found in other Pacific destinations. The Tourist Bureau publishes a detailed guide of accommodations available and the visitor would be advised to write for this pamphlet before making any decisions. One drawback with this publication is that the proprietors write their own descriptions and tend to elaborate somewhat. The list is alphabetical by island.

TONGATAPU

Baby Blue Guest House: 6 rooms, share facilities, meals available. PO Box 249, Nuku'alofa, Tel.: 22 349

Beach House: 10 rooms, share facilities, tariff includes breakfast. PO Box 18, Nuku'alofa. Tel.: 21 060

Captain Cook's Apartments: 6 self-contained units with 2 bedrooms.
PO Box 838, Nuku'alofa. Tel.: 21 615,
Telex 66231 VITAL TS
Fafa Island Resort: 11 Tongan fales some deluxe, water sports, restaurant, bar. PO Box 42, Nuku'alofa. Tel.: 22 800
Fasi-Moe-Afi Guest House: 7 rooms, share facilities. PO Box 316, Nuku'alofa. Tel.: 22 829
Friendly Islander Hotel: 12 self-contained units, 1 and 2 bedrooms, pool, restaurant, bar, disco. PO Box 142, Nuku'alofa. Tel.: 21 900, Telex 66280 FRIEND
Good Samaritan Inn: 24 Tongan fales, share facilities, restaurant, bar, beach. PO Box 36, Nuku'alofa. Tel.: 41 022, Cable, GOOD SAMARITAN
International Dateline Hotel: 76 rooms, airon, restaurant, bar, pool, entertainment, duty free shop, credit cards. PO Box 39, Nuku'alofa. Tel.: 21 411. Telex 66223 DATELINE TS
Keleti Beach Resort: 8 units with private facilities, restaurant, bar, beach, entertainment. PO Box 192, Nuku'alofa. Tel.: 21 179, Cables SO SONS
Joe's Kahana Beach Resort: 4 self-contained fales. PO Box 137, Nuku'alofa. Tel.: 21 144
Kimiko's Guest House: 8 rooms, share facilities, meals available PO Box 693, Nuku'alofa. Tel.: 22 170
Nukuma'anu Motel: 4 self-contained fales with 1, 2 or 3 bedrooms. Usually on long term lease only. PO Box 390, Nuku'alofa. Tel.: 21 491, Telex 66232 TSUNAK TS
Pacific Apartment: 2 self-contained two bedroom units or available as single rooms with use of all facilities. Contact through Tonga Visitors Bureau, P.O. Box 37, Nuku'alofa. Tel.: 21 733.
Pangaimotu Island Resort: 6 fales, meals and bar, beach. PO Box 740, Nuku'alofa. Tel.: 22 588
Ramanlal Hotel: 53 rooms, aircon, restaurant, bar, disco, pool, credit cards. PO Box 74, Nuku'alofa. Tel.: 21 344, Telex 66205
Royal Sunset Resort: 24 units with private facilities, restaurant, bar, pool, beach, water

sports, entertainment, shop, credit cards.
PO Box 960, Nuku'alofa. Tel.: 21 254,
Telex 66284
Sela's Guest House: 14 rooms, share facilities, dining room, tariff can include meals. PO Box 24, Nuku'alofa. Tel.: 21 430, Cables SELA'S GUEST HOUSE
Sunrise Guest House: 6 rooms, share facilities, tariff includes meals. PO Box 132, Nuku'alofa. Tel.: 22 141
Phoenix Hotel: 10 rooms with facilities, restaurant, (to reopen 1989). Private Bag, Nuku'alofa. Tel.: 21 834

'EUA ISLAND
Fungafonua Motel: 10 rooms with facilities. PO Box 1, 'Ohonua, 'Eua
Haukinima Guest House: share facilities. c/-Futu, 'Eua

VAVA'U ISLAND
Paradise International Hotel: 43 rooms, restaurant, bar, pool, beach, shop.
PO Box 11, Neiafu, Vava'u.
Tel.: 111, Cable PARADISE
Tongan Beach Resort: on beach at 'Utungake Island. 12 self-contained units. PO Box 104, 'Utungake, Vava'u
Stowaway Village Motel: 6 fales, bar, restaurant. PO Box 102, Neiafu, Vava'u. Tel.: 70 137.
Vava'u Guest House: 8 rooms and 4 self-contained fales, restaurant, share facilities. PO Box 148, Neiafu, Vava'u

HA'APAI GROUP
Fonongava'inga Guest House: 5 rooms, share facilities, meals available. c/- Pangai, Ha'apai
Seletute Guest House: 6 rooms, share facilities, meals available, c/- Pangai, Ha'apai

NIUATOPUTAPU ISLAND
Fita Motel: 4 fales, share facilities, dining room. c/- Hihifo, Niuatoputapu. Cable FITA MOTEL
Niuatoputapu Guest House: 5 rooms, share facilities, dining rooms. c/- Hihifo, Niuatoputapu. Cable NTT GHOOSE

TORRES STRAIT ISLANDS

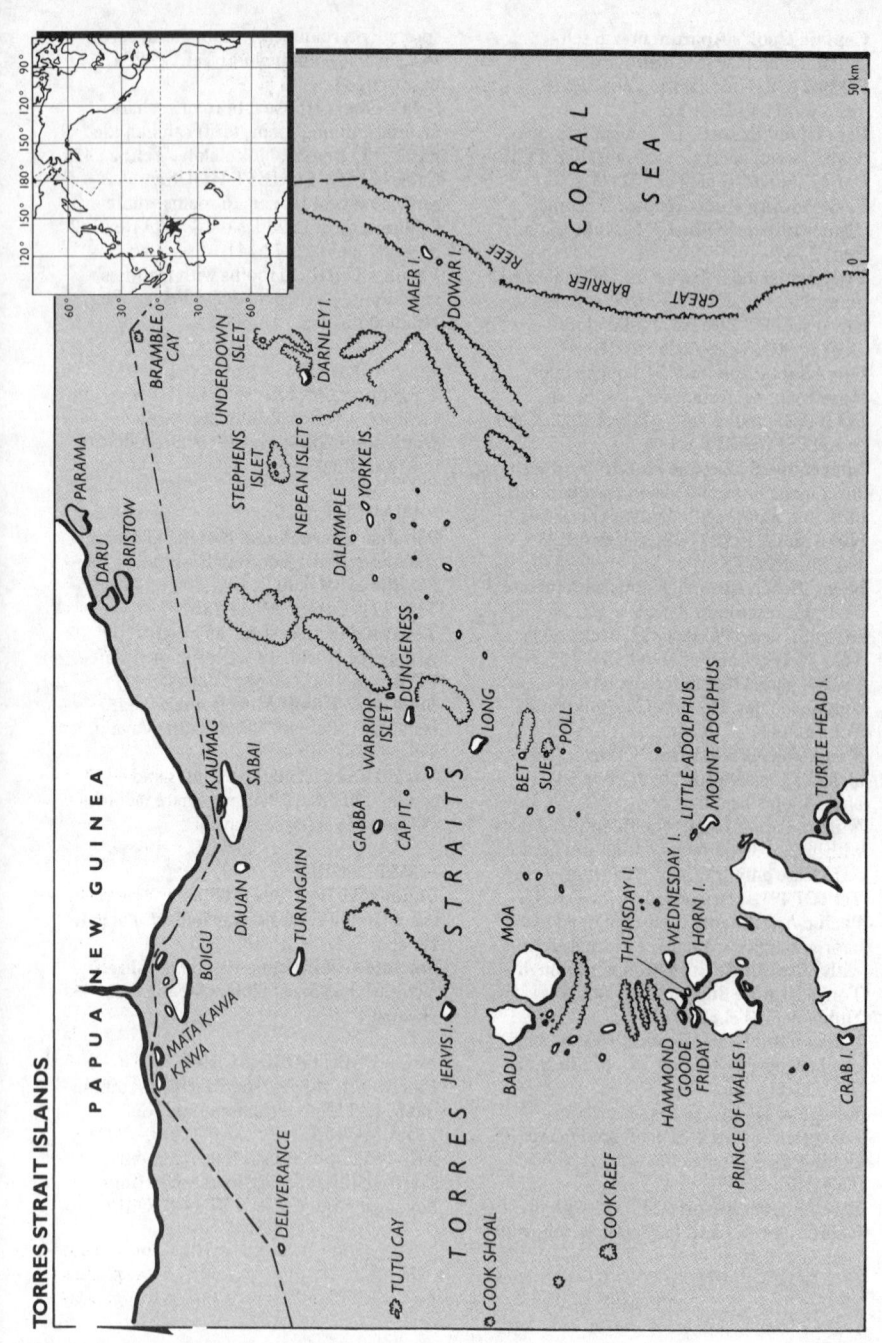

Torres Strait Islands

The Torres Strait Islands are an Australian possession administered as part of Queensland. There are more than 70 islands and islets between 11 deg S latitude and the Papua New Guinea mainland. They extend from 141–144 deg E longitude. The administrative centre is on Thursday Island and local time is 10 hours ahead of GMT.

According to the 1986 census there are 21,541 Torres Strait Islanders living in Queensland and in the islands, 4837 of them living in the Torres Strait area including 1570 on Thursday Island, and the rest elsewhere in Queensland.

The flag, national anthem and currency are those of Australia.

THE PEOPLE. The most heavily populated island in the group is Thursday Island, which offers some employment because it is the administrative centre and has some industry, based on marine resources, and a ship repair facility.

There is a serious sexual imbalance in the population with more women than men on every island. On Saibai, women outnumber men by as much as 80 per cent. There is a big concentration on all islands in the under-15 age group. Many of these children belong to single mothers or to parents in Australia who have sent their children home to be cared for by grandparents.

The people fall roughly into three categories. Those of the eastern group have Polynesian blood and characteristics; those in the western group tend more to be Melanesian; and in the central group there are Melanesians with an infusion of European blood. Malay, Chinese and Japanese intermingling is also evident. However, the Torres Strait Islanders are a unified people, proud of their identity.

Language. There has been a revival of traditional languages. Two distinct languages are spoken. One commonly spoken in the eastern group is known as Meriam, the other is more generally spoken throughout the islands and is known as Mabuiag. English and Torres Kreole are the usual languages spoken on Thursday Island.

Nationality. The Torres Strait Islands are part of the state of Queensland, and the inhabitants are citizens of Australia. Of the inhabited islands, 14 are held by Councils through a Deed of Grant in Trust. Three are non-reserve and are open to visitors or intending residents without any need for permits from the Department of Aboriginal and Islanders' Advancement. Some of the reserve islands are administered by missions. Christian missions are operated by the Church of England, which succeeded the London Missionary Society in 1914, and the Roman Catholic Church.

Lifestyle. The lifestyle of the islanders is changing as more 'Western' type amenities are introduced. Diesel generated electricity powers freezer units to store fish and other seafood awaiting transport to Thursday Island have been installed on Yorke, Coconut, Badu, Mabuiag and Stephen Islands. Eventually the freezer unit system will be extended to cover Warraber, Boigu and Dauan islands and the village of Kubin on Moa Island. An experimental solar power generating unit is to be installed on Coconut Island.

The Department of Community Services is building houses of various types on several of the islands. Between 1981 and 1985 161 module-type houses were delivered to the Torres area.

A junior youth council on Hammond Island organises recreation, sports, dances, picnics and special film showings during school holidays. The young people are encouraged to give half a day a week during holidays to community work. The islanders' custom of accepting care of children other than their own is being practised now more than ever with the advent of legal adoption. Adoption procedures usually take about five months.

GOVERNMENT. An Executive Officer and Assistant Executive Officer of the Department of Community Services are based on Thursday Island with subsidiary staff. They are responsible to the Departmental Under Secretary in Brisbane. There are four administrative divisions, each electing its own council.

Elections. Islander Community Councils are usually elected every three years by people of 18 years and over. These councils, which meet monthly, have complete control of the domestic affairs of their own islands. They frame their own laws, and their policemen are responsible for enforcing them. The powers of the councils are very wide. They include control of the islands' revenue, the flow of non-island visitors, and exclusion of some islanders for various reasons.

Each island has its own Chairperson and one, two or three Councillors. Chairpersons and Councillors in turn act as advisers to the Group Representative. They undertake a major and increasing role in relation to planning, budgeting and general community development. Various workshops and conferences have been held at Thursday Island in recent years to assist Councillors to interpret education and legislative changes.

The Chairperson of each island becomes a member of the Island Co-ordinating Council which meets regularly to discuss matters of importance to the region.

In May 1987 at the South Pacific Forum meeting in Western Samoa, the Island Coordinating Council suggested that the group would consider breaking away from Queensland because of what it considered to be neglect in welfare and development by the administration. The demands gained strength in early 1988, causing some embarrassment to the Federal Government of Australia.

The Torres Strait Islanders' Act 1971 provides for the conduct of island reserves and the admission of those who want to live there.

Justice. Law-breakers are brought before the courts, where the councillors act as judges.

Liquor laws. Torres Strait Islanders generally enjoy all rights available to Europeans on Thursday Island. There are beer canteens on some of the islands. Island councils provide tables and chairs for the canteens. Alcohol is usually consumed within a couple of days after the fortnightly shipment's arrival. It has caused some minor problems.

International border. Part of the Australian international border with Papua New Guinea passes through the Torres Strait region, and a border agreement between the two countries was signed late in 1978. The border recognises cultural affinities on both sides by establishing a marine reserve in which traditional freedom of movement and sharing of economic resources is recognised. At the wish of the Islanders, three islands close to the PNG coast — Boigu, Dauan and Saibai — remain part of Australia but they are effectively island enclaves within a PNG sea.

EDUCATION. The education system caters for children at preschool, primary and secondary levels, with provision for secondary education also at Bamaga on nearby Cape York Peninsula, and at secondary schools in other parts of Queensland. Most schools are state schools but the Roman Catholic Mission has a primary school on Thursday Island.

The Queensland Department of Education administers the state primary schools and one state high school in the region. There are also 14 preschools now established. In 1986 there were 72 fully qualified teachers, 38 primary, 32 secondary and two special. The preschool teachers have all been Kindercraft certified or primary trained. These teachers are also supported by two itinerant advisers and one preschool officer. In 1985 there were 985 primary school students and 370 secondary students in the area.

A number of students, after completing Grade 7 in their island schools, now go to mainland schools and are generally able to cope with the demands of secondary education. High schools on Thursday Island and at Bamaga on Cape York Peninsula cater for most secondary school needs. The courses are designed to teach technical skills and crafts, and academic, commercial and industrial subjects. Children from other islands attending the Thursday Island High School either board on the island, or travel there daily by barge. Bamaga has a residential college for island students.

Supervised evening study is a feature on Hammond Island. It is done with the assistance of the sisters and teachers' aides from the Sacred Heart School and teachers from both the high and primary schools on Thursday Island.

A redevelopment programme involving the improvement of school facilities on the islands is under way and will extend until 1989. Preschool facilities are also being extended. A campaign is well under way to encourage Aboriginal and Islanders education workers within the State education departments, as well as Aboriginal and Islander school leavers and adults to undertake teacher education and other tertiary courses. One effect of this campaign will be to increase the number of fully qualified Aboriginal and Islander teachers employed in community schools. By 1986, 19 people from Torres Strait had undertaken the Community Teachers Course at the TAFE College, Cairns.

LABOUR. As the Torres Strait area is more than 90 per cent open sea, the islands do not lend themselves to widespread agricultural or pastoral activities. Employment centres mainly on marine industries. Some islanders are employed as crew and divers on pearling and fishing ships. A number of Torres Strait men have developed technical skills in carpentry and marine and mechanical engineering which have helped them to find lucrative employment.

Social services. The social services section of the Department of Community Services acts as an agent for Queensland Government departments not represented. The section advises and assists the islanders on all aspects of social security and repatriation benefits. It is also responsible for the administration of estates of deceased islanders. The section's liaison officers actively participate in education, employment, housing, health and many other activities, including community and group affairs.

The people, under the Community Services (Torres Strait) Act 1984, are eligible for Commonwealth social services, pensions,

etc., and have a vote in Australian Federal and State elections.

A savings bank, operated by the Department of Community Services, and the commercial banks at Thursday Island offer banking services.

HEALTH. Health services are maintained by the department in conjunction with the Thursday Island Hospital authorities and the Royal Flying Doctor Service. There are medical aid posts on all 13 populated outer islands. Each is staffed by nursing assistants employed by the department on the recommendation of the Islands Councils. Most of the posts are staffed by two assistants, however, the islands with large populations have three. These assistants are supervised by qualified nursing sisters based on Badu, Saibai and Yorke Islands. The Sisters are responsible for the training of the assistants as well as for the planning of regular clinics on the outer islands, the organisation of monthly doctors' clinics and immunisation programmes. They are on call at all times for emergencies. There is daily radio contact between sisters and assistants at all smaller centres.

The Base Hospital is at Thursday Island and is under control of the Hospital Board. There are four doctors on the staff. Dental, X-ray, physiotherapy and pathology services are provided along with specialist clinics conducted by specialists from Australia. Emergencies are evacuated to Thursday Island by air. The Royal Flying Doctor Service is also available if patients require further treatment in Cairns. Persons requiring specialist treatment in Cairns. Persons requiring specialist treatment in Cairns can call on benefits provided by the Isolated Patients' Travel and Accommodation Assistance Scheme. They can be accommodated at the 'Abigail Bann' hostel.

The area is generally free from many diseases common to tropical areas. The incidence of tuberculosis is quite high and venereal diseases are common. Generally, however, the health of the Torres Strait people is good.

THE LAND. The islands range in size from a few sq. km to 180 sq. km. Prince of Wales Island is the largest. Some peaks on this island are about 250 m high. The land area ranges from small cays, barely visible above sea level, to coral and volcanic islands, and high rocky islands, sparsely covered with vegetation.

The islands' tropical climate is modified by trade winds. The annual rainfall on Thursday Island is 1500 mm. Rainfall is restricted for much of the year, leading to water shortages at various time on some islands. A natural rock well on Booby Island holds more than 30,000 litres of water and never runs dry.

PRIMARY PRODUCTION. Most industry is based on marine resources such as pearl culture, barramundi, trochus, turtle, skipjack, sardines, mackerel and crustaceans. Prawns are processed on Thursday Island.

The pearl culture industry flourished in the early 1960s, employing about 200 men. But in 1970, the live shell was attacked by disease and most farms closed. Employment fell to less than 40. Although the situation has improved, it is too early yet to predict if the industry will fully recover.

A pilot fishing scheme for Yorke Island was launched in 1979. The fish processing and freezing plant, developed at a cost of $175,000, was designed to handle fish fillets and lobster tails caught by island fishermen for the commercial market. Production commenced in March 1979, with catches exceeding expected levels and returning Islander fishermen approximately $1000 net per week. The plant has two blast freezers with a storage freezer of approximately 8000 kg capacity. There are also three ex-Taiwanese dories attached to this operation. In 1985 catches increased from 7035 tonnes to 12,624 tonnes with a value of $55,176.

Island fishermen are paid for their catch on the spot. Marketing is handled through the Island Industries Board and various wholesalers.

Apart from providing a basis for an expanding fishing industry in Torres Strait, the project has generated a local source of income for residents on Yorke and neighbouring islands.

TRANSPORT. There are many roads sealed with bitumen on Thursday Island. Vehicles are also used on several of the other islands.

Airfields. The airport for Thursday Island is on nearby Horn Island. Connections are made by launch. Air Queensland maintains a daily Fokker Friendship service from Weipa and Cairns except for Saturday and Sunday. The flight time between Horn Island and Cairns is two hours and between Horn Island and Weipa is 45 minutes. Badu, Boigu, Murray, Saibai, Warraber, Yam, Coconut, Yorke, Moa and Mabuiag all have airstrips. Darnley Island acquired an airstrip in 1986 and all other islands are serviced by helicopter.

Local vessels. Two ships, the *Dogai II* and *Melbidir* deliver food and building materials, and carry people who travel for medical and dental checks and school interviews.

The Queensland Coast and Torres Strait Pilot Service consisted (in 1986) of 42 master mariners who provide a pilotage service from the western approaches of the Torres Strait to ports on the east coast of Australia, as far south as Sydney, and to Papua New Guinea by the Great North-East Channel. None of the pilots has his home on Thursday Island. Most live in Brisbane, Sydney and Cairns and commute by air to the islands as required. There is a Transit Station with resident manager on Thursday Island which provides accommodation for the pilots when required.

The recommended safe working limit for the Torres Strait is 12.2 metres. The service, established in 1884, now handles 80 million tonnes of shipping annually. The service also provides a shipping mail exchange, medical aid and stores and police services, if required by ships. Thursday Island has the best anchorage between the Australian mainland and PNG.

COMMUNICATIONS. Each island has a radio transmitting and receiving set. These operate in conjunction with a 'mother' station at Port Kennedy (Thursday Island). This gives most islands quick communication with the outside world. Equipment for the VHF radio used for Thursday Island harbour is housed in one of the underground chambers of a large old fort high on the island.

Several communities have been brought onto the new FSK Digital Codan Selcall system, thus making for more reliable alerting procedures. This is an ongoing programme requiring modification of equipment on

Thursday Island, installation of equipment at the site concerned and instruction of the operators in use of the equipment. Telephones are available on the islands and provide a link to the mainland. Reception of radio broadcasts from the mainland is generally poor. There is a weekly news sheet produced by a local resident.

HISTORY. Because it is a navigable passage, though perilous, between Australia and New Guinea, the discovery, exploration and history of Torres Strait is overwhelmingly a maritime story. All information about the natives of the islands and their way of life came from navigators and the survivors of shipwrecks, until the arrival of missionaries in 1871. All communication between the islands was by sea until the recent building of airstrips, and most economic activity has been pearl-shelling and other maritime occupations.

The first European knowledge of Torres Strait dates from 1606, when Captain Luis Vaez de Torres took a month to work his way through the maze of islands and reefs, finally passing through Endeavour Strait into the open waters of the Arafura Sea. An imaginary strait had been shown on some charts before 1600, drawn at about 21 deg S latitude (instead of between 9 and 11 deg S) in order to separate the known land of New Guinea from the mythical and undiscovered continent of Terra Australis Incognita.

Torres' report. Torres' report to the King of Spain lay buried in the archives until 10 years after the strait had been rediscovered by Cook in 1770. The story that a copy of the report was found in Manila in 1764 by Dalrymple is quite untrue, though it has been repeated by writers from Flinders in 1814 to the most recent history books. Dalrymple was sent a copy from Spain in 1780, and translated it himself for publication in 1806, just 200 years after the voyage of Torres.

The report was very brief, but a much fuller account came to light in 1929, written by a noble passenger who travelled with Torres, Captain Don Diego de Prado y Tovar, who also drew the charts of their discoveries. From Prado's narrative we can work out that they anchored off at least 10 islands, though they did not land on them all, and often

when they did land the natives had taken off to other islands, or had hidden in the bush. The islands involved were Parama, Bristow, Dungeness, Turtlebacked, Cap, Gabba, Long, Mount Ernest, Twin and Prince of Wales. The last anchorage, in Endeavour Strait, was two miles south of Cape Cornwall, and here Torres' ship, *San Pedro*, bumped on the bottom during the night on a five-metre shoal. His consort, the launch *Los tres Reyes*, though anchored closer to the shore, did not bump, and next day, 4 October, Torres made the latitude 11 deg at noon, before leaving the strait.

He had been in sight of the Australian coast for about two days, but did not know it was the continent he had been searching for. He thought it was just an extensive group of islands.

Jansz's voyage. He was actually preceded in the sighting of this part of Australia by the Dutchman Willem Jansz in the small vessel *Duyfken*, who landed near the present port of Weipa, followed the coast south to Cape Keer-Weer, and then returned northwards. He passed up the western side of Torres Strait, and landed on Prince of Wales Island, which he named Hoogh Eylandt (High Island), and returned to Banda in the East Indies.

A fine chart of his discoveries was made, but no journal or log-book of the voyage exists, so we do not know the details or dates of his contact with Australia, which were probably in March or April 1606, and therefore six months before Torres. To Jansz the strait appeared to be a large shallow bay or bight, so he and his successors, including Tasman, assumed that Cape York Peninsula was a part of New Guinea, despite the vague reports that Torres had sailed through a strait in the area.

Although Prado's charts of the southern coast of New Guinea were sent to Spain, they were later lost, and we only have a few rare hand-drawn copies which vary widely in details and place names. To navigators using the strait, the islands and their warlike and cannibal natives were regarded as of no particular importance.

The islands. The islands of Torres Strait are of all sizes and of two kinds, high and rocky and low and coralline. There are about 100 of each, if you count the smallest rocks and sand-cays, but only about 30 are inhabited.

Australia and New Guinea are joined over hundreds of kilometres by the continental shelf, and in Torres Strait this becomes a shallow bank of less than 17 m depth. There is no doubt that in prehistoric times there was a land bridge right across the strait, especially during the Ice Ages. The last of these was at its height about 50,000 years ago when man first came into the area, and the strait would have been dry for thousands of years after that, possibly until 10,000 years ago.

To the east the shallow waters of the strait are flanked by the Great Barrier Reef, which extends to the edge of the continental shelf. To the west the shallows merge gently into the Arafura Sea, though the shoal water follows the coast of Irian Jaya for hundreds of kilometres further.

From the earliest days of contact the natives of the strait were known as fierce warriors, with fleets of large canoes for raiding neighbouring islands and the adjacent coast of New Guinea. In spite of a brisk trade for canoes, bows and arrows with villages near the Fly River, the islanders regarded the New Guineans as permanent enemies.

After 1606 there were several Dutch expeditions to the western side of the strait, including Tasman's in 1644, but no one approached the eastern side until Cook left himself with no choice but to find a way through the strait in August 1770. He had no contact with the natives, but sighted a few with bows and arrows while he was taking possession of 'the east coast of New Holland' on Possession Island, a few kilometres west of Cape York.

Bligh's visits. The next visitor to the strait was Captain William Bligh in the *Bounty* launch in June 1789. He also passed close to Cape York but missed Endeavour Strait, thinking it was a bay, and made his way through Prince of Wales Channel, which is today the main shipping channel. Bligh named Wednesday Island, setting the fashion for later navigators to name Tuesday Islets and Thursday and Friday Islands, all in the Prince of Wales group.

During 1791 a boatload of escaped convicts from Sydney, including Mary Bryant, worked their way right up the east coast, through

Torres Strait and on to Timor, but the long arm of the law was not far astern. In August HMS *Pandora* was wrecked trying to enter Torres Strait near Raine Island; many lives were lost, including some of the mutineers of the *Bounty*, who had been arrested in Tahiti.

Captain Edwards sailed the ship's boats through the strait to Timor, where he was able to add the escaped convicts to his prisoners. On reaching Java, Captain Edwards met the *Resolution*, a small vessel built by the mutineers at Tahiti, but manned by some of the *Pandora* crew before leaving Tahiti. They had also sailed through the strait in 1791.

The next visitor was again Captain Bligh, in 1792, this time with two ships carrying breadfruit plants from Tahiti to the West Indies, HMS *Providence* and *Assistant*. This time Bligh avoided the Barrier Reef by entering the strait near the coast of New Guinea, believing that Torres had taken a northerly track in better waters. He sailed down what is now called the Great North-east Channel, then through Basilisk Pass, and passed Gabba Island before being blocked by extensive coral reefs, as Torres had been in the same area. Bligh worked his ships down towards Banks Island, and then escaped to the open sea through Bligh Channel.

In 1793 two ships, the *Shah Hormuzeer*, under Captain Bampton, and the whaler *Chesterfield*, under Captain Alt, also looked for a passage in the northern part of the strait and after following the tracks of Torres and Bligh, pushed on through the shoals, keeping close to the New Guinea coast. The two ships took turns in running aground and in helping each other off, and it was a whole month before they finally cleared the shoals near Deliverance Islet.

Flinders' charts. The strait remained largely uncharted, despite these perilous passages by different ships, and Flinders made a chart of all the tracks followed for his book in 1814. He had passed through the strait three times himself, first as a midshipman under Bligh in 1792, then in command of HMS *Investigator* in October 1802, and finally in the smaller HMS *Cumberland* in October 1804. On the two latter occasions he used Prince of Wales Channel, and so did not add much to our knowledge of the rest of the strait.

There is no foundation for the many reports of Spanish galleons being wrecked in the strait. The finding of stray Spanish dollars on the islands would be due to the fact that these were common currency in Sydney in the early years, being imported by Governors Macquarie and Brisbane to overcome the shortage of coinage in the colony. Many ships were wrecked in the strait and in the approaches through the Barrier Reef, and many boats' crews were attacked by natives. The warriors of Turtlebacked Island (Yam or Yama), tried to capture Torres' launch, but were repelled. Torres named the island 'Caribes' or 'Cannibals', being impressed by the collection of skulls and bones found in the village where he landed. He also saw masks and figures made from turtle-shell, similar to those seen in museums today. Their canoes were later reported to be over 18 m in length.

Naval surveyors. The fullest accounts of the natives of the Torres Strait Islands were written by various naval surveyors who charted the area between 1819 and 1875. Their ships included the *Fly*, *Rattlesnake*, *Bramble* and *Basilisk*. In 1844 a beacon, almost 20 m high, was erected on Raine Island to mark an entrance through the Barrier Reef for ships making for Torres Strait.

An unofficial 'post office' came into use at Booby Island, and here a supply of provisions was left for wrecked crews making their way towards Timor. The post office was unmanned, and consisted of a cave in which bundles of letters were left for other ships to pick up and deliver. The cave is also an archive of inscriptions made by passing ships and survivors of wrecks and massacres.

In October 1849 men from HMS *Rattlesnake* picked up a white woman, Mrs Barbara Thomson, on Prince of Wales Island. She was the sole survivor of the cutter *America*, wrecked nearby about four years before. She had been taken to wife by the chief, Boroto, and renamed Gi'Om after a dead girl of the tribe. During her stay she had met the infamous runaway convict named Wini, who had become the war chief of Badu, or Mulgrave Island, where he led the locals into killing all white men who came near their island. He was finally shot by a punitive expedition from the settlement founded at Somerset in Albany Passage in 1864, only

nine kilometres south-east of Cape York. It was under the charge of John Jardine, with a garrison of 25 marines, and formed a harbour of refuge for castaways. During the next 11 years there were 14 wrecks recorded, and it was an important port for ships working in Torres Strait.

Modern period. The year 1871 marked the beginning of modern history in the strait, with the arrival of the first missionaries, and the development of fishing for bêche-de-mer, pearl shell and trochus shell. By 1877, when the settlement was moved to Thursday Island, there were 16 firms in the trade employing 109 vessels, 50 Europeans and about 700 natives. The area being worked covered 800 sq. km, and the value of pearl shell was £200 a ton. The value of pearls found in the shells amounted to only a third of the value of the shell. The trade went through many vicissitudes through the following decades, and finally stopped about 1940, when the settlement at Thursday Island fell into decline.

Thursday Island's native name was Wyben; it used to be referred to as Port Kennedy. The island was fortified about 1880 to defend the navigational passage. The first nine official pilots were licensed in 1884 by the Queensland Government, and the service still flourishes as the Queensland Coast and Torres Strait Pilot Service, and numbers 42 pilots, all experienced master mariners. Their services are not compulsory to passing ships, but most large ships use them to pass safely through the dangerous waters of the strait and of the Great Barrier Reef.

The Anglican Cathedral at Thursday Island was originally built as a memorial to the 173 people lost in the steamer *Quetta*, which struck an uncharted pinnacle of coral near the Albany Passage on 28 February 1890. The 109 people saved included an unidentified baby girl, later named Quetta Brown. Perhaps the luckiest survivor was a teenager named Emily Lacy, who was picked up nearly 36 hours after the wreck; she was later married in London and her son, Dyson Hore-Lacy, was well known in New Guinea.

Bathurst Bay disaster. Another disaster occurred in 1899, when the pearling fleet from Thursday Island was struck by a hurricane in Bathurst Bay: about 50 vessels were lost, and about 300 lives, with only three pearling luggers left afloat.

Perhaps the best-known massacre of castaways occurred on Aureed Island in 1834, after the wreck of the barque *Charles Eaton*. Five survivors reached Timorlaut, and four young boys were spared by the natives. Two survived, to be picked up by a punitive party in the schooner *Isabella* in 1839, and the skulls of the victims were brought to Sydney for burial.

The pearling firms at Thursday Island employed divers of many races, so the population of Thursday Island came to include Aborigines, Melanesians, Polynesians, Malays and Japanese, the last-named in overwhelming numbers in the last 70 years of the industry. The other islands often had a white resident of unknown origin, some being escaped convicts from New Caledonia, and others escaping from the world or from the laws of various countries.

The last 100 years have seen a steady spread of administration and education throughout the islands of Torres Strait, and the Islanders have become citizens of Queensland, gained access to social benefit payments and freedom to travel and work in Australia. Hundreds of them now live on the mainland, including a settlement at Bamaga in the north, which was first peopled by natives from Saibai I. who needed more land for development.

The history of Torres Strait has continued to be mostly maritime, and the developments of the last 100 years belong to the subjects of administration, missions and education, communications, and finally navigation, which can be taken to cover the improvements in charts of the area, and the provision of navigational lights and facilities. The recent development of aviation between the islands has lessened dependence on launches and luggers for inter-island services, though they will continue to be used for all forms of exploitation of the waters in the strait.

ISLANDS IN DETAIL

The individual islands have often had more than one name, even in the native languages, and although none of the names given to them by Europeans in 1606 has survived, some given in 1770 and later are still in use. In 1977 the Queensland Department of Lands tried to establish the preferred names of the islands, whether native or European, to form an official list for general use and or mapping purposes.

A list of past and present names for 124 of the islands is given at the end of this section. Only 17 have permanent inhabitants. Islands which are official reserves are divided into four groups.

EASTERN. Stephen, Darnley, Murray. These are small and steep with rich volcanic soil and dense tropical vegetation. Surrounding waters are deep, and fish are plentiful.

CENTRAL. Warraber or Sue, Coconut, Yorke. Small and flat, with coral base and less tropical vegetation. Waters are shallower, fish are plentiful.

WESTERN. Badu, Mabuiag, Moa, Dauan, Yam, Larger and elevated, rocky soil with only bush and scrub. Water shallow, suitable for pearl diving.

NORTH-WESTERN. Saibai, Boigu. Large and low lying swamps and mangroves. Little marine life. In the southern part is the island of Hammond, administered as a reserve by the Catholic Mission, and the three non-reserve islands of Prince of Wales, Thursday and Friday. Some other islands in this Prince of Wales Group are inhabited sporadically by fishing parties.

Thursday Island. The administrative and business centre of Torres Strait, has a harbour and a wharf, and is surrounded by seven islands of the Prince of Wales Group. It measures 2.4 km by 1.2 km, and has the main radio station, hospital and hotels. It is nearly surrounded by seven other islands — Horn, Tuesday, Wednesday, Goode, Hammond, Friday and Prince of Wales. Ships pass through a passage with Friday and Prince of Wales on one side, and Goode and Hammond islands on the other to reach Thursday Island's harbour.

Friday Island. About 1.6 km long and 3.2 km south-west of Thursday Island is a resort area for Thursday Islanders. It has attractive beaches and low sand dunes, and the beaches are a natural breeding ground for green turtles. There are some pearl-culture enterprises.

Prince of Wales is the largest of the Torres Strait islands with an area of 180 sq. km and peaks up to 250 m high. It has a number of permanent families, and weekend cottages cater for many visitors. The island has never been exploited to any extent, as it lacks a good anchorage on the northern side, is very rugged, except for a small area of cultivable land, and has no permanent fresh water supply. It is little more than 1 km from Thursday Island at the nearest point.

Tuesday, Wednesday, Goode. Tuesday islets, named by Flinders in 1802, are small and rocky. Wednesday, named by Bligh in 1789, has some weekend cottages. Goode Island, with a lighthouse, is 2.5 km wide. It was actually named Good's Island by Flinders in 1802.

Moa, originally called Banks by Bligh in 1792, is about 48 km north of Thursday Island. The native community, with a few European missionaries, live at Kubin village, a government reserve, and at St Paul's Anglican Mission reserve. Both communities are interested in the possible mining of wolfram (tungsten).

Badu, is just north-west of Moa, and is a fertile island. It is also known as Mulgrave.

Mabuiag, just north of Badu, is small, but has traditionally provided the best sailors for pearling luggers, as well as one of the two main languages for the Strait. The natives are largely engaged in the crayfish trade. Also known as Jervis Island.

Murray. This is near the northern end of the Great Barrier Reef, and with Darnley and Stephen, has supplied many men for work on the mainland. They mostly return to the islands in their old age.

Darnley is noted for its unusual fish traps, which completely encircle the island. They are made of huge boulders, and their origin is a mystery.

Yorke is known best for its colourful history. Many early ships frequented the area, some sailing past, and others coming to grief on reefs in the area. Relics of these wrecks, in the form of cannon, guns, swords and old coins, are still being found today.

Yankee Ned was an American sailor who deserted his ship, settled on Yorke Island, amassed a fortune in pearls and reputedly married eight wives, leaving many descendants. He was nearly 90 when he died about 1920.

Saibai, Dauan, Boigu. These are the islands mainly affected by the bid to move the Australian border further away from the New Guinea coastline. In addition to the islands in the Strait, many islanders have moved to the mainland to the west of Cape York, where they live with some Aborigines on reserves called Bamaga, Cowal Creek, New Mapoon, Umagico and Red Island Point. The area has a water supply used for domestic purposes and irrigation. The community is self sufficient in meat, grows fruit and vegetables, and operates a timber mill. There is also a small airstrip. Most of the islanders came from Saibai, owing to shortage of cultivable land there.

TORRES STRAIT ISLANDS

Alphabetical list of names, including alternative and obsolete names from old charts. Current official names are given in capitals, but are liable to change in accord with custom. Names of very small islands close to the coasts of New Guinea and Australia are omitted. To help in locating an island on a map the Strait is here divided into six areas, and each name is followed by initials representing the area in which it may be found: CY for Cape York area north of 11 deg S latitude; E for eastern islands; C for those in the centre of the Strait; B-M for the Badu-Moa group; POW for Prince of Wales Group area; N for the northernmost islands.

Aada — HAMMOND ROCK POW
AKONE ISLAND CY
ALBANY I. CY
AUKANE I. E
AURID — Aureed I. E
BADU — Mulgrave I. B-M
Banks I. — MOA B-M
Barn I. — Tarrau CY
BARNEY I. — B-M
BELLE VUE Islands B-M
BET Islet — Burrar C
BOIGU — Talbot's I. N
BOND I. B-M
BOOBY I. POW
BOURKE I. E
BRAMBLE Cay — Massaramcoer E
Brothers I. — GABBA C
BROWN I. B-M
Burke I. — SUARJI, Suaraji C
Burrar — BET Islet C
BUSH Islet CY
CAMPBELL I. — Tappoear E
CANOE ISLET E
CAP ISLET — Muquar, Moquar C
Caribes — YAM, Yama, Turtlebacked
CASTLE I. B-M
CLARKE I. B-M
COCONUT I. — Parremar E

CRAB I. CY
Cuddalug — TUESDAY Islets POW
DALRYMPLE I. — Damuth E
DARNLEY I. — Errub E
DAUAN I. — Cornwallis N
DAYMAN I. CY
DELIVERANCE I. N
Djuna — ENTRANCE I. POW
Double I. — TWIN I., Nelgee POW
DOVE I. — Utta E
DOGONG I. E
DUNCAN I. B-M
Dungeness I. — Jeaka, ZAGAI C
DUMARALUG Islet POW
EAST STRAIT I. POW
EBORAC I. CY
Eegarba — MARSDEN I. E
Eet — western side of MOA B-M
ENTRANCE I. — Djuna POW
Mt. ERNEST I. — Nagheer C
Errub — DARNLEY I. E
FAREWELL Islets B-M
FLAT I. B-M
FRIDAY I. — Jealug POW
GABBA — Brothers I. C
Garboy — ARDEN Islet E
GETULLAI — Pole I. C
GOODE I. — Good's I. POW
GREAT WOODY I. POW
GREEN I. B-M
HALFWAY I. E
HAMMOND I. — Kerriri POW
HAMMOND ROCK — Aada POW
HAWKESBURY I. B-M
HIGH I. CY
HIGH I. B-M
Hogar — STEPHENS I. E
Homogar — KEATS I. E
Hoogh Eylandt — POW
HORN I. — Laforey, Narupai POW
IDA I. CY
Jeaka — Dungeness, ZAGAI C
Jealug — FRIDAY I. POW
KABBIKANE I. E
KAPUDU I. POW
KAUMAG I. N
KEATS I. — Homogar E
KEATINGE I. CY
Kei Cuddalug — No. 3 of the TUESDAY
Islets, POW
Keriri — FRIDAY I. POW
KERR I. N
Kodal in YORKE Islets E
KUNAI I. POW

LACEY I. CY
Laforey's I. — HORN I., POW
LITTLE ADOLPHUS I. CY
LITTLE WOODY I. POW
Long I. — SASSIE C
LOWRY I. C
MABUIAG — Jervis I. B-M
Maer, Mer — MURRAY I. E
MAI Islet CY
MARSDEN I. — Eegarba E
Masig, Massig — YORKE Is. E
Massaramcoer — BRAMBLE Cay E
Mauar — RENNEL I. E
Maururra — WEDNESDAY I. POW
MEDDLER I. CY
MEIPA I. near Jervis I. B-M
Mer, Maer — MURRAY I. E
Moquar — CAP Islet C
MOA — Mua, Banks I. B-M
Monserrat I. — Mt. ERNEST I. C
MORILUG Islet CY
Mt. ADOLPHUS I. CY
Mt. ERNEST I. — Nagheer C
Mt. Cornwallis — DAUAN E
Mua — MOA, Banks I. B-M
Muggi Cuddalug — No. 2 of the
TUESDAY Islets POW
Muralug — PRINCE OF WALES I.
MURRAY I. — Maer, Mer E
Muquar — Moquar, CAP Islet
Nagheer — Mt. ERNEST I. C
Narupai — HORN I. POW
Nelgee — TWIN I., Double I. POW
NEPEAN I. — Attogoy E
NICKLIN Islet POW
NORTH I. B-M
NORTH POSSESSION I. B-M
PACKE I. POW
Parilug — GOODE I. POW
Parremar — COCONUT I. C
PASSAGE I. — B-W
PEENECAR C
Perros — Dungeness, ZAGAI C
PHIPPS I. B-M
Pole I. — GETULLAI C
POLL Islet C
PORTLOCK I. B-M
POSSESSION I. — Bedanug CY
PRINCE OF WALES I. — Muralug POW
QUOIN I. CY
RAINE I. (on edge of Barrier Reef)
RED I. CY
RED WALLIS I. CY
RENNEL I. — Mauar E

ROBERTS I. E
ROUND I. POW
ROUND I. B-M
SADDLE I. C
SAIBAI I. N
SALTER I. CY
SASSIE — Long I. C
Six Sisters, sand cays, E
SOUTH I. B-M
SPENCER I. B-M
SAURJI — Suaraji, Burke I. C
SUE Islet — Warraber C
Talbot's I. — BOIGU N
Tappoear — CAMPBELL I. E
Tarrau — BARN I. CY
Three Sisters — BET, SUE, POLL C
TERN I. CY
THURSDAY I. — Wai-ben, Wyben POW
TOBIN Cay E
TOBIN Islet B-M
TRAVERS I. B-M
TREE Islet B-M
TREE Islet CY
TROCHUS I. CY
TUDU I. — Warrior I. C
TUESDAY Islets (4) C
TURNAGAIN I. N
TURTLE I. near ENTRANCE I. POW
TURTLE I. & TURTLEHEAD I. CY
Turtle-backed I. — YAM, Yama C
TWIN I. — Double I., Nelgee POW
UNDERDOWN I. E
Uttu — DOVE I. E
Wai-ben — THURSDAY I. POW
WAI-WEER I. POW
Warrior I. — TUDU, Tutte C

WEDNESDAY I. — Maururra POW
WEST I. B-M
WHALE I. B-M
WILSON Is. (2) B-M
WOODY WALLIS I. POW
Wyben — THURSDAY I. POW
YAM — Yama, Turtle-backed I. C
YORK I. CY
YORKE Islets, Kodal & Masig E
ZAGAI — Dungeness, Jeaka C

The three main islands belonging to Papua-New Guinea are not given above, but are Parama or Bampton, Bobo or Bristow and Daru, the last-named being a government station.

FOR THE TOURIST. The islands with their beaches offer a fascination for a particular type of tourist who enjoys getting away into a rugged and remote environment.

Accommodation facilities on Thursday Island include the Rainbow Motel with about a dozen units and a restaurant, and hotels such as the Federal, the Grand and the Royal.

Thursday Island has a bowling club with a licensed bar, plus a tennis court. The island also offers water sports. A guest house on Yorke Island caters for the increasing number of people requiring accommodation while en route to other islands.

Apart from flying, it is possible to travel to Thursday Island by boat from Cairns. For further information contact the Queensland Government Travel Centre, cnr Adelaide and Edward Streets, Brisbane 4000. Tel. (07) 312211.

TUVALU

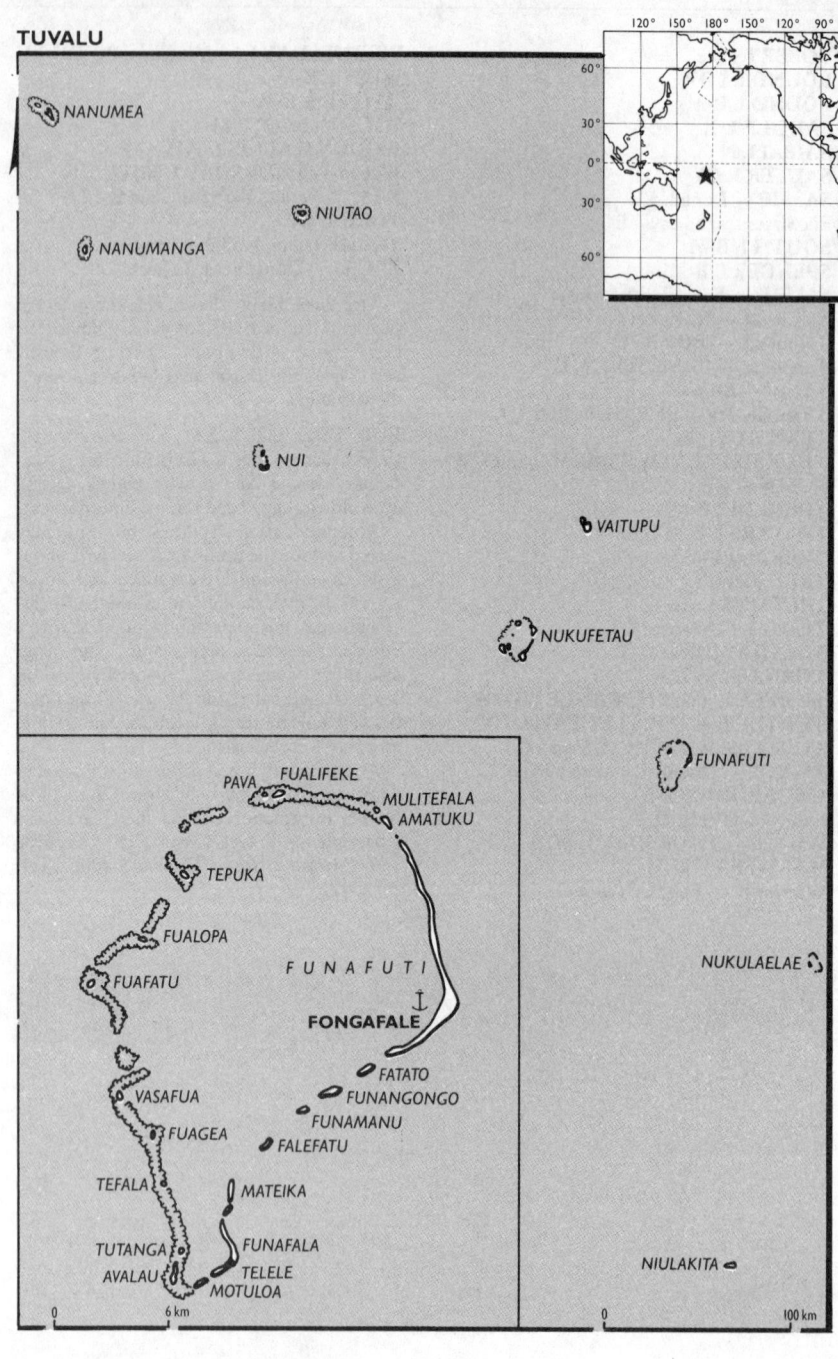

Tuvalu

Tuvalu has been an independent state, with Britain's reigning monarch as its head, since 1 October 1978. Until October 1975, when it became separated from the Gilbert Islands (now Kiribati) and adopted the name Tuvalu (meaning Eight Standing Together), the group was known as the Ellice Islands and was part of the British Colony of the Gilbert and Ellice Islands. There are nine atolls or coral islands, only eight of which are permanently inhabited. They are located between 5 and 10 deg S latitude and 176 and 179 deg E longitude. The capital and main island is Funafuti about 1100 km north of Suva, capital of Fiji. Local time is 12 hours ahead of GMT.

The flag is the Blue Ensign with a light blue field. Nine gold stars show the positions of the main islands. Local public holidays are: New Year's Day; Commonwealth Day (second Monday in March); Good Friday and Easter Monday; Queen's Birthday (early June); National Children's Day (August); Tuvalu Days (early October); Prince Charles' Birthday (November); Christmas Day and Boxing Day.

THE PEOPLE. The islanders of Tuvalu are Polynesians, unlike their former partners, Kiribati, who are Micronesians. In 1983 the total population was 8364. This figure does not include those islanders who work overseas, mainly in Nauru and Kiribati. The population is continuing to grow at a rate of two per cent per annum and it is estimated that if this growth continues, the population will double every 35 years. Females outnumber males (100 to 89); this difference is due to migration of working males. Of the population, 58 per cent is aged between 15 and 54.

Nationality. Almost all the inhabitants are Tuvaluans. The 1979 Citizenship Ordinance lays down the registration qualifications for Tuvalu citizenship which say that the applicant must have been ordinarily resident in Tuvalu for the seven years immediately prior to the date of his application for naturalisation; that he intends to make Tuvalu his permanent home; that he will remain financially self-supporting now and in the years to come; that he is familiar with the laws and customs of Tuvalu; that he is of good character and free from communicable disease; that he qualifies in accordance with any such other matters as the Citizenship Committee may consider material.

TABLE 1 POPULATION DISTRIBUTION BY ISLAND (1983)

Funafuti	2620
Vaitupu	1320
Niutao	917
Nanumea	906
Nanumaga	762
Nukufetau	739
Nui	650
Nukulaelae	355
Niulakita	195

Language. This is a Polynesian tongue, closely related to Samoan. A Gilbertese dialect, introduced by invaders several hundred years ago, is spoken on Nui. English is also used throughout the islands.

Migration. Tuvaluans move out of their islands to find employment. Most of those living overseas do so because of their own or their families' employment. One source of employment, Banaba (Ocean Island) where more than 600 Tuvaluans were employed in the phosphate industry, is now closed, the phosphate petering out late in 1979.

Religion. The Church of Tuvalu, derived from the Congregationalist foundation of the London Missionary Society, embraces about 97 per cent of the population and small communities from the Seventh-day Adventists, Baha'i and others comprise the remainder. The Church of Tuvalu is headed by a president. With the aid of the Bible Society in the South Pacific, it was responsible for the publication, in 1977, of the first book in the Tuvalu language — a translation of the New Testament. The complete Tuvaluan Bible was consecrated in June 1987.

Lifestyle. Although many Tuvaluans earn wages or receive income from the sale of copra, the cultivation of gardens in the sparse soil and fishing are still fundamental to the Tuvaluan way of life.

Recreation. The islanders' favourite recreations are singing and dancing at the 'feast of fatele'. The Tuvalu Amateur Sports Association plays an important part in organising other sporting activities, including volleyball (played by both men and women) and cricket.

GOVERNMENT. Tuvalu is an independent state, the 38th member of the Commonwealth, with the Queen as Head of State, represented in the islands by a Tuvaluan Governor-General. In July 1986 Tuvalu announced that it intended to modify its constitution to restrict the powers of the Governor-General. The Queen will still remain head of state but her representative, the Governor-General, will no longer be able to reject the advice of the government in power.

Previously known as the Ellice Islands, from 1916 to 1975 it formed part of the British Gilbert and Ellice Islands Colony. Following overwhelming support for separation in a referendum among Tuvaluans in 1974, the territory was legally separated from the Gilbert Islands on 1 October 1975, and formal separation took effect from 1 January 1976.

Legislature. The Tuvalu Parliament consists of a single chamber with 12 members. Four islands (Nanumea, Niutao, Vaitupu and Funafuti) each return two members (for electoral purposes Niulakita is regarded as part of Niutao) and the others one each. A speaker, elected by members of Parliament, presides at sittings. The normal life of Parliament is four years, the first General Election being held in August 1977. The Attorney-General attends the sessions.

Executive. The Cabinet consists of Prime Minister and four other ministers. The Attorney-General attends Cabinet meetings. The power to summon, prorogue and dissolve Parliament rests wih the Governor-General, acting on the advice of the Prime Minister.

Elected Chief Minister in October 1975 and confirmed in that office following the general election in 1977, Mr Toaripi Lauti became the country's first Prime Minister at Independence. Mr, later Sir, Fiatau Penitala Teo was chosen to be the country's first Governor-General. Mr Lauti was defeated in the general elections of September 1981, by Doctor Tomasi Puapua.

Overseas relations. Apart from its ties with other members of the Commonwealth Tuvalu has established diplomatic relations with the following countries: Belgium, Chile, Netherlands, Republic of China, France, West Germany, Japan, South Korea, Turkey and the United States. It is represented in Suva by a High Commissioner, who also acts as Tuvalu's High Commissioner to Papua New Guinea. There are Honorary Consuls in New Zealand and Australia and Hong Kong. A special Treaty of Friendship was signed in 1979 between Tuvalu and the US wherein the latter relinquished its claim to the four southern islands of Tuvalu. The Treaty was ratified in June 1983.

Tuvalu was the 10th country to join the South Pacific Commission and among other organisations belongs to the SPEC and WHO.

Electoral system. Voting is on a common roll, restricted to citizens of Tuvalu aged 18 or over. A person must be 21 before being eligible to stand for Parliament.

Local government. There is a Town Council on Funafuti and Island Councils on the seven other main islands, each consisting of six elected members including a president.

These councils are designed to accept responsibility for and to finance local services required at the island level.

Members of Parliament and medical officers are ex-officio members of Island Councils. The Minister responsible for local government, after consultation with a council, may appoint additional persons, but the number of nominated and ex-officio members shall in no case exceed two-thirds of the number of elected members.

Justice. There is a High Court of Tuvalu provided for in the Constitution, with a judge appointed from among judges in neighbouring countries. The office of Chief Justice is, at present, held by the Chief Justice of Fiji. Appeals from the High Court lie with the Court of Appeal which, until resolved otherwise, is the Fiji Court of Appeal, from which there is a right of further appeal to the British Privy Council. The High Court is governed by the same law which applied immediately before Independence, subject to any changes necessary to make that law comply with the Constitution.

Serious crime is rare in the islands. The majority of offences are minor, being of assault or infringements of the traffic laws or drinking laws. Civil litigation is limited, apart from land and other customary laws and rights and divorce cases.

Island courts, presided over by Tuvaluans, operate on the eight islands with limited jurisdiction in criminal and civil matters. There is also a Tuvaluan magistrate who presides over the Magistrate's Court, which is a Court of Appeal from the Island Courts, with some original jurisdiction. A Senior Magistrate sits, approximately, three times a year to review magistrates' decisions and hear more serious or complex matters.

The Chief of Police and 30 officers and constables are all Tuvaluans. There is also a part-time force of 16 Special Policemen. The police force is also responsible for manning the fire-fighting service. Their main duty is for airport standby. The Chief of Police is also the principal Immigration officer and is responsible to the office of the Prime Minister.

Liquor laws. There are several public bars and a government-owned hotel on Funafuti. Except for Niutao, Nukufetau and Vaitupu, all other islands are 'dry'. There are no discriminatory liquor laws in force and licensing hours for a public bar are normally from 11 am to 3 pm and 6.30 pm to 10 pm.

EDUCATION. All children in Tuvalu go to primary schools, of which there are 12 in the country. Primary school enrolments in 1986 were 1064 (1021 at the nine government schools and 43 at the three church schools). There were 13 kindergartens attended by 614 children and 40 teachers. The primary school system had 44 teachers and four students in training. For students who fail to qualfy for academic training, there are eight Community Training Centres with 18 teachers and 276 pupils. Attendance at either primary school or a CTC is compulsory and in 1984 regulations were drawn up to allow for enforcement of this policy. The CTC schools are equipped to train students in skills which will suit their life within small island communities as well as basic skills in English, mathematics, environmental studies and first aid. Secondary education is provided at Motufoua School on Vaitupu Island to School Certificate level. Students attending in 1986 numbered 280 with 11 teachers. A number of secondary students also attend school in Fiji, Tonga or Samoa, although this programme is being reduced because of the high cost to the Government.

Maritime training school. Tuvalu has its own maritime training school. Built with finance from the Australian Government, the school was opened in 1979 on the Funafuti islet of Amatuku. However it experienced severe staffing problems and budget constraints during its first four years and it was not fully operational until 1983. Courses last for 12 months and include specialist training in one of three areas — deck, engine room or steward — as well as four months sea-time experience on the country's inter island vessel H.V. *Nivaga*. In 1986 there were 52 students and nine teachers. Approximately 70 per cent of students complete their courses, many gaining employment with major shipping companies who have associations with the school.

Tertiary education. There is a USP Extension centre in Funafuti, which plays a vital role in overall education development in Tuvalu. The Government also sponsors some students to gain technical training at the Fiji Institute of Technology and the Telecommunications Training Centre in Suva.

LABOUR. The active workforce is estimated to be 4838 (1983). However Tuvalu is still heavily dependent on the subsistence sector and this makes classifications of employment and related figures difficult to assess. Most employment in the cash economy is on Funafuti. The last official survey of employment showed that 72 per cent of cash employees lived on Funafuti while 92 per cent of people engaged in village life were found on the outer islands. Figures for 1986 show 230 employed in the government sector, 140 in the private sector, 320 with the Nauru Phosphate Company and 166 as seamen overseas. On Funafuti, 400 people were classified as unemployed (i.e. people aged between 17 and 55). No official figures are available for any of the other islands because of the nature of the village economy.

Wages. In 1986 classified workers' wage rates began at 38 cents per hour for people under 18, rising to 96 cents an hour for the top group. There are no trade unions in Tuvalu.

HEALTH. The Princess Margaret Hospital at Funafuti was opened in 1978. It has 30 general beds in two wards, 4 maternity beds and 2 private wards. There is an operating theatre, a dental centre, X-ray unit, a laboratory and a rapidly-expanding family planning unit. Each island has a resident dresser, a state-registered nurse and a maternity–child health nurse. The hospital advocates both modern and traditional medicine and, encouraged by the WHO, is assessing the effectiveness of local plants and customary health skills. Preventative health services are increasing with the sanitation programme being the major part. Family planning is also an important programme, particularly in light of the unacceptably high annual growth rate of the population. Main diseases are tuberculosis, leprosy, filariasis and parasitic diseases. Hypertension is also on the increase as the western lifestyle and diet are increasingly adopted.

THE LAND. The total land area of the islands is 25.9 sq. km. The largest island is Vaitupu of 5.6 sq. km. The main island, Funafuti, has an area of 2.8 sq. km; the smallest of the nine atolls, Niulakita, is only 41 ha. The other islands are Nanumea, Nanumanga, Niutao, Nui, Nukufetau and Nukulaelae. The territory encompasses 1.3 million sq. km of sea. The atolls extend over 560 km in a winding line from Nanumea in the north to Niulakita in the south. They are no more than 5 metres above sea level.

Climate. The climate is not unduly trying, particularly during the season of the north-easterly trade winds (March–October) but becomes enervating during the season of rains and westerly gales (November to February). The temperature varies from 22–38°C in the shade, but usually between 26 and 32°C.

Rainfall varies considerably, not only between the islands but also from year to year. In an average year, the annual rainfall extends to 3000 mm in the islands farthest to the south.

Because of the atoll terrain, there are no rivers. Nanumaga, Niutao, Vaitupu and Niulakita are reef islands. Vaitupu has a closed-off lagoon, and there is a brackish lake on Niutao.

Fauna and flora. Local vegetation is limited to plants such as coconuts, bananas, breadfruit etc. The only animal wildlife is the Polynesian rat. There are only 22 known species of moths and butterflies (Australia has 12,000).

Land tenure. Most land is owned by islanders in small holdings. Land is also held communally and jointly. With the limited resources available, one problem is the repeated splitting of holdings for next-of-kin upon the death of a land owner.

A cadastral survey of all islands is being undertaken.

PRIMARY PRODUCTION. The position of agriculture within the general economy is important mainly as the provider of subsistence for the majority of the population. Copra is the only export but even that is a limited commodity; in 1985 only 300 tonnes were exported. A small scale coconut oil extraction plant on Vaitupu makes soap but domestic production of copra in 1985 was only 333 tonnes. Pork and poultry processing is for local consumption only, and a small number of goats are kept, mainly for grazing. General policy of the Agricultural Division of the Government is to encourage the planting of improved hybrid crops by the

TABLE 2 COPRA PRODUCTION
(tonnes)

1980	212
1981	294
1982	243
1983	254
1985	333

smallholder, particularly crops of indigenous vegetables which will assist in improving the diet of the population. The Government would also like to develop the processing of timber, and assessment is being made of the viability of coconut trees being processed for timber. A feasibility study was also done in 1985 into beekeeping and the production of honey.

Fisheries. A fisheries development station was established on Funafuti in 1970 but it was seriously hampered by hurricane Bebe which sank two deep sea fishing boats and damaged the mother ship. The South Pacific Commission, however, carried out a skipjack tuna survey in Tuvalu waters from 25 June to 4 July 1978 and later reported that bait fish was plentiful, that an average of one school of tuna was sighted for every hour of searching time and that 'the location of Tuvalu close to the equator would suggest that skipjack should be abundant year-round and the excellent seasonal catches taken by the Japanese distant water fleet in this area endorse optimism for the establishment of some type of skipjack fishery in Tuvalu'.

Early in 1982, a fishing vessel, *Te Tautai*, was given to Tuvalu as part of the Japanese aid programme. Crewed mainly by Tuvaluans, the vessel operates commercially, both inside and outside Tuvalu's territorial waters. Vessels from South Korea and Taiwan are allowed to fish under licence within Tuvalu's 200-mile economic and fisheries zone.

Licensing fees from foreign fishing vessels have generally increased.

The Government is also seeking to persuade other distant fishing nations to take out licences. Bêche-de-mer exports from Nanumea, Nukufetau, Funafuti and Nukulaelae used to provide a useful source of revenue through markets in Fiji and Hong

LICENSING FEE REVENUE FROM FOREIGN FISHING VESSELS

	Revenue (A$)
1980	35,346
1981	46,206
1982	146,800
1983	206,000
1984	170,000
1985	516,617
1986	384,000

Kong but this activity has now declined. The Government sees the development of the commercial tuna fishery, focused on the pole and line vessel, *Te Tautai*, and the licensing of foreign fishing vessels as the major sources of economic growth, the latter continuing to have high priority.

LOCAL COMMERCE. A co-operative wholesale society is established on Funafuti to carry out importation for the co-operative societies, one of which is retail trading on each island. There are a number of small businesses on Funafuti including grocery, baking and building. The Tuvalu Co-operative Society has branches on each of the islands as well as a warehouse which sells bulk items to small businesses which then resell them.

TABLE 3 TUVALU CO-OPERATIVE SOCIETY BRANCH SALES 1982/83 FINANCIAL YEAR

Funafuti	A$1,175,002
Warehouse	A$ 305,544
Vaitupu	A$ 260,233
Nanumea	A$ 121,257
Nukufetau	A$ 116,570
Niutao	A$ 113,962
Nui	A$ 95,127
Nanumaga	A$ 73,773
Nukulaelae	A$ 71,923
Total	A$2,333,391

Advisory bureau. The Business Development Advisory Bureau (BUDAB) was established in 1982 to help the growth and improvement of all forms of commercial enterprise. It grew from the original idea of a National Loans Board which was repealed by government as there is already a National Bank. BUDAB, therefore, has a more general function than merely lending money. It can provide support services for the small businesses it assists with establishment. These include secretarial services and, as demand and budget allow, bookkeeping and a customs clearance agency. BUDAB have helped finance a wide variety of businesses including cinemas, ice-cream parlours, poultry farms, a mobile disco and a bus service. It is particularly interested in businesses which will assist in the country's goal of self-sufficiency and is always eager to evaluate proposals particularly from the agricultural sector.

TOURISM. In the generally accepted sense tourism does not exist at present. The country receives a number of visitors but the majority come for specific reasons and not for vacations. The principal constraints on the development of a tourist industry are the infrequency of air services, the high costs of air travel to the country (rated among the highest in the world per route mile), the relative isolation of Tuvalu from other major Pacific destinations and the limited facilities available.

The Government operates the only small hotel in Funafuti. The Vaiaku Lagi Hotel has only seven rooms. The outer islands have small rest houses but these are primarily for the use of Government officials, and are of very basic standards. In 1985–86 a feasibility study was conducted into the possibility of building a new hotel but results have not yet been decided.

Handicraft. The development of a handicraft industry is seen as an important contribution to the economy. In 1982 a handicraft retail outlet was opened in Funafuti and visited by Her Majesty the Queen during her official visit to Tuvalu. The Tuvalu Women's Council has been very active in promoting the sales of local craft, particularly within Tuvalu itself, but with increasing interest in establishing regular markets internationally. The Community Training Centres include instruction in these traditional skills and primary schools encourage active participation of the pupils in any handicraft production which takes place in the home. Income generated by handicraft sales is a valuable contribution to the family's resources. In 1987 $10,000 was allocated nationally for craft development.

OVERSEAS TRADE. Copra exports, the licence fees from foreign fishing vessels and the sales of stamps to overseas philatelists are the main earners of foreign exchange. Significantly, a 20c surcharge on Tuvalu's 45c special stamp commemorating the 1982 wedding of the Prince of Wales and Princess Diana raised $A44,781 which was given to Tonga for relief of those who suffered loss in the March (1982) hurricane.

Between 1981 and 1983 export earnings were: (in A$000)

	1981	1982	1983
Philatelic sales	2107	1077	587
Copra	19	17	61
Fish	—	191	250
Handicrafts	1	—	2
Total	2127	1285	900

Philatelic sales. The Philatelic Bureau is a statutory body (1982) utilising the management skills and advice of a specialist British firm, Philatelists (1980) Ltd, of Bristol. The company provides a European adviser and European bureau manager. The Government's share of stamp sales through the bureau came to $120,177 in 1985, and $160,589 in 1986.

Apart from the Co-operative Society, the bureau is the largest employer of labour outside the civil service, with a local staff of 51.

Customs tariff. A new tariff, based on the Customs Corporation Council Nomenclature, came into effect on 1 January 1980.

Imports. Tuvalu's import bill in the first half of 1986 was $2,212,184 compared to $1,884,653 in the same period in 1985. It was almost twice the amount it had been in 1977 ($1,246,862). Australia, Fiji and New Zealand were the major suppliers with 35.8

TABLE 4 IMPORTS TO TUVALU 1982–1984 BY CATEGORY

	1982 Value ($A)	%	1983 Value ($A)	%	1984 Value ($A)	%
Food and live animals chiefly for food	647,848	22.4	815,732	27.5	965,027	24.4
Beverages and tobacco	130,620	04.5	157,387	05.3	164,551	04.2
Crude materials, inedible, except fuels	97,376	03.4	116,512	03.9	54,722	01.4
Mineral fuels, lubricants and related materials	484,525	16.8	415,071	14.0	461,758	11.7
Animal and vegetable oils, fats and waxes	6882	00.2	7744	00.3	14,753	00.4
Chemicals and related products, n.e.s	187,818	06.5	205,157	06.9	198,990	05.0
Manufactured goods classified chiefly by material	553,348	19.1	502,285	16.9	870,741	22.0
Machinery and transport equipment	464,299	16.1	365,019	12.3	588,033	14.9
Miscellaneous manufactured articles	263,237	09.1	303,453	10.2	554,407	14.0
Other commodities and transactions	54,424	01.9	75,949	02.6	76,245	01.9
TOTAL IMPORTS	2,890,377	100.0	2,964,309	100.0	3,949,227	100.0

per cent, 40.5 per cent and 10.4 per cent respectively. Japan, Nauru and the UK supplied most of the remainder.

FINANCE. Estimates of revenue and expenditure for 1984 provided for a Budget of A$3,598,000, of whch $2,673,000 was to be raised locally and $925,000 was a grant-in-aid from the British Government. Direct taxes were to raise $145,000, customs duties $539,000 and philatelic sales $300,000.

The main expenditure heads are shown in Table 5.

Budget figures for 1986 and 1987 were: revenue $3,925,920 and $4,120,766, and expenditure $3,933,624 and $4,194,830.

The Third Development Plan 1984–87 anticipated funding for capital development is shown in Table 6.

In 1987 Tuvalu set up a trust fund which generates income that can, in turn, be used

TABLE 5 MAIN EXPENDITURE

	A$(000)
Commerce and natural resources	182
Works and communications	1106
Social services	970
Finance	665
Pensions and gratuities	21
Office of Governor-General	31
Office of Prime Minister	413
Office of Principal Auditor	26
Police, prisons and immigration	132
Parliament	52
Total	3598

TABLE 6 ANTICIPATED FUNDING FOR CAPITAL DEVELOPMENT

Country	Estimated aid $A million
Australia	4.50
Canada	0.30
European Development Fund	3.85
Japan	2.50
New Zealand	2.50
United Kingdom	9.85
UNDP	1.00
Others	2.00
Not yet identified	2.70
Total	29.20

to pay its recurrent budget costs. It is aiming for $A27 million and by February 1987 New Zealand had already committed $1 million and Australia had promised $8 million provided Britain would also contribute and providing a satisfactory trust arrangement could be made.

Britain followed with a contribution of $8.5 million and the Government of Tuvalu itself added $2 million which it had derived from licence fees paid by US tuna fishermen. The Government also hopes to encourage Japan and Canada and any other interested country to contribute.

Tuvalu was also added to the United Nations list of least-developed countries in 1987. This allows Tuvalu access to concessional loans from the World Bank and the International Monetary Fund while her exports qualify for special tariff concessions under the General Agreement on Tariffs and Trade.

Banks. The National Bank of Tuvalu is a joint venture between the Tuvalu Government (60%) and Westpac Banking Corporation (40%).

Currency. Australian currency is legal tender but Tuvalu also has its own coins in circulation.

TRANSPORT. All islands have tracks or feeder roads to give access to cultivated areas but Funafuti alone has a network of roads of compacted coral to serve the capital.

Vehicles. Vehicles in Funafuti are increasing as the capital grows. On the outer islands motor cycles are the most common form of transport.

Airlines. Fiji Air, a domestic operator in Fiji, flies between Suva and Funafuti three times a week. The Airline of the Marshall Islands connects Tuvalu with Nadi, Fiji and Tarawa in Kiribati once a week. The Government attaches high priority to the Fiji–Funafuti connection because of the number of tourists which could possibly come from that direction. In 1986 the EEC approved a grant of $US5 million to assist in the development of air communications in the South Pacific. Part of this grant went towards upgrading Funafuti Airfield.

Between 1980 and 1983 a domestic seaplane service was given a trial connecting most of the outer islands with Funafuti; however, the service was terminated when examination of running costs found that the level of subsidies either from overseas aid or the Government would have to be maintained at an excessively high level. The Government would like to have a land-based internal service and it maintains the basic infrastructure already established for the seaplane service (hangar facilities and outer island non-directional navigation beacons) until the time when airstrips can be constructed on the outer islands.

Port facilities. Port of entry is Funafuti, which has a deep-water lagoon 20 km by 16 km with three entrance passages. A deepwater wharf, provided with Australian aid of nearly $2.7 million, allows ships drawing up to 5 m to come alongside. In can handle vessels up to 18,000 tons.

Shipping. A replacement vessel for the elderly *Nivaga* was expected to be launched in late 1988. The Pacific Forum Line operates a service to Tuvalu out of Suva, Fiji. The service is every six weeks and is underwritten by Australia and New Zealand. Kalander (Asia–Pacific) operates between Australia and Funafuti approximately every three months.

COMMUNICATIONS. A duplex HF network operates to all islands with separate links to specific population centres such as the Maritime School on Ainatuku Islet and the Motufoua High School at Vaiatupu. The network is solar-powered on the outer islands. There is also an HF link with Fiji which connects Tuvalu internationally. There is a limited telephone system on Funafuti and telex services are available.

It is anticipated that Tuvalu will have to join in the regional approach towards satellite circuits which will mean the establishment of an earth station on Funafuti. Long-term plans will look at the use of satellite circuits for improving domestic telecommunications. In 1987 A$1.5 million was allocated to the construction of this earth station.

Radio. Radio Tuvalu (621 kHz) broadcasts approximately 45 hours of programmes per week. These are principally in Tuvaluan but news and announcements are made in English.

Newspapers. Two newspapers are published fortnightly by the Government. The *Tuvalu Echoes* is an English paper and *Sikuleo o Tuvalu* is Tuvaluan.

ELECTRICITY AND WATER.

Four 150 kVA generators supply electricity on Funafuti while on the outer islands councils and individuals have installed their own generators. Electricity is 240 volt. By 1987 90 per cent of all households in Funafuti had been connected to the extended cable system provided by the authorities. For future development of electricity supplies on outer islands, solar cells are seen as the answer.

Ground water on Funafuti is not potable and there are no strems. Therefore, all water must be collected and stored. A priority of the Government is to improve catchment and storage facilities in order to avoid shortages. This policy applies to all islands in the country.

MAJOR OFFICE HOLDERS

Governor-General:
  His Excellency Sir Tupua Leupena
  GCMG, MBE
Prime Minister:
  The Right Honourable Dr Tomasi
  Puapua PC
Secretary to Government:
  Gregory Polson
Attorney-General:
  Robin Webster
Chief Justice:

  Sir Gaven Donne
Speaker of the Legislature:
  Hon. Vasa Founuku Vave

GOVERNMENT MINISTRIES AND DEPARTMENTS

Office of the Cabinet, Vaiaku, Funafuti, Tuvalu. Departments include: Office of the Prime Minister, Minister of Finance, Minister of Commerce and Natural Resources, Minister of Works and Communications, Minister of Social Services, Speaker of the Legislature.

Government Departments, Vaiaku, Funafuti, Tuvalu. Including: Attorney-General, Foreign Affairs, Local Government, Philatelic Bureau, Business Development Advisory Bureau, Cooperative Society.

HISTORY.

Although the name Tuvalu is a local word meaning 'eight standing together', there are nine islands. The southernmost of the nine in the group, Niulakita, stands apart from the others and is not permanently inhabited. The old name Ellice commemorates a 19th century English politician, Edward Ellice, MP for Coventry and owner of the ship *Rebecca* in which Captain Arent De Peyster discovered Funafuti atoll in 1819. De Peyster named Funafuti in Ellice's honour, and this name was later applied to the whole group by the English hydrographer A. G. Findlay.

The people of Tuvalu are of Polynesian origin, but many now have some European blood, derived from beachcombers and traders who settled in the group in the 19th century. On Nui there is a strong Gilbertese component. The local language has affinities with Samoan and Tongan. Most traditions refer to Samoa as the islanders' original home. But there are also stories of marauders from the Gilberts and Tonga. Many of the early settlers were no doubt castaways who drifted northwards and westwards before the south-east trade wind.

First Europeans. The first of the Tuvalu Islands to become known to Europeans was Nui. This was sighted by the Spanish explorer Mendana on his first voyage to the Pacific in 1568. He sighted another island, Niulakita, on his second voyage in 1595.

However, Mendana's discoveries had been forgotten by the time the next European was in Tuvalu waters almost two centuries later.

This was the Spaniard Francisco Mourelle who came upon the northern atolls of Nanumaga and Nanumea in the frigate *Princesa* in 1781.

The other islands were not discovered, or rediscovered, until the end of the first quarter of the 19th century. Captain De Peyster discovered two — Nukufetau and Funafuti — in 1819. Captain George Barrett, of the Nantucket whaler *Independence II*, discovered Nukulaelae and rediscovered Niulakita in 1821. Four years later another whaler, Captain Obed Starbuck of the *Loper*, came upon Niutao and Vaitupu, while Captain Eeg of the Dutch ship *Pollux* rediscovered Nui after a lapse of more than 250 years.

From the date of Captain Barrett's voyage in 1821 until about 1870, the waters in the vicinity of Tuvalu were frequented by whalers operating in what became known as the 'on-the-line-grounds'. Seamen from these ships occasionally deserted and settled ashore, while some of the more adventurous islanders shipped as crewmen. Some of the European beachcombers became traders and agents for firms in Australia, Germany and the US. They organised the export of coconut oil and later copra.

In the early 1860s, 'blackbirders' carried off about 400 islanders from Funafuti and Nukulaelae to work in Peru. None of them returned. Others were later recruited for plantations in Fiji, Samoa and Hawaii. European diseases introduced at this time caused many deaths among the islanders.

Christianity was first adopted in 1861 after some adherents of the London Missionary Society on Manihiki, Cook Islands, drifted to Nukulaelae in a canoe. In May 1865, the Rev. A. W. Murray visited the group from Samoa and placed Samoan pastors on the various islands. The pastors were soon exercising considerable sway; the new faith was universally adopted, and all aspects of island life that did not conform with it were abandoned.

In 1877, British subjects in Tuvalu were brought formally within the jurisdiction of the High Commissioner for the Western Pacific in Fiji. Fifteen years later, following the establishment of a protectorate over the Gilbert Islands, Captain E. H. M. Davis of HMS *Royalist* visited the group to ascertain whether the inhabitants also wished to come under the British flag. They said 'yes' and Captain H. W. S. Gibson of HMS *Curacao* was sent to Tuvalu to raise the flag at each island. This was the origin of the Gilbert and Ellice Islands Protectorate. It became the Gilbert and Ellice Islands Colony in 1916.

For most of the colonial period, the Ellice Islands consisted of a single administrative district with its headquarters at Funafuti which was also a port of entry. During World War II, Tuvalu remained outside the immediate war zone. However, the Americans established a base on Funafuti in 1942, and it was from there that the colony was administered until the Japanese were driven from the Gilberts in November 1943. The Americans cut down coconut trees to build airstrips on Funafuti, Nukufetau and Nanumea. All areas were replanted after the war but in the early 1960s the Funafuti runway was again cleared when a commercial airstrip was required. A Fiji Airways aircraft used the strip for the first time in July 1964.

Migration. After World War II, many Tuvaluans migrated to Tarawa, capital of the Gilbert and Ellice Islands Colony, because it offered better opportunities for education and employment.

Partly because of the pre-war standards attained at the Ellice Islands School, partly because Ellice schools had continued during the War, and partly because the Ellice Islanders capitalised more quickly on the opportunities available, these Islanders soon found employment opportunities far exceeding their numbers. This led to rivalries within the civil service and an assertion of Gilbertese rights. In an attempt to protect their identity, as well as their future well-being against a perceived Gilbertese threat, the Ellice Islanders sought secession when Britain began to prepare the colony for self-government.

A British commissioner, Sir Leslie Monson, held an inquiry into Tuvaluan attitudes in 1973. This was followed in 1974 by a referendum in which the Tuvaluans could opt to remain with the Gilberts or secede from them. They were told beforehand that, if they voted to separate, they could expect no share in the colony's royalties from Ocean Island phosphate or other assets apart from one ship. Despite this, 3799 islanders voted to secede, only 293 voted against secession, and there were 40 spoilt papers.

Separation. A year later, on 1 October 1975, the Gilbert and Ellice Islands were legally separated, the latter became Tuvalu, and a new constitution was proclaimed for the group. Toaripi Lauti was elected the first Chief Minister. However, to make the changeover smooth, Tuvalu continued to be administered from Tarawa until 1 January 1976 when Funafuti became the administrative centre. Efforts were then directed to establishing an administration in Tuvalu by people who, in some cases, had spent a lifetime in Tarawa. All this became necessary because it was decided that Tuvalu would gain independence on 1 October 1978.

Independence. Tuvalu formally achieved independence on 1 October 1978, but ceremonies were marred by the illness of the Queen's sister, Princess Margaret, who was confined to bed on the New Zealand frigate, HMNZS *Otago*, at Funafuti, with a high temperature. The official "handing over" of independence from Britain was performed by Lord Napier.

Early in 1979 Tuvalu signed a treaty of friendship with the United States. Under the treaty, the US agreed to drop its claims, based on the Guano Act of 1856, to four of Tuvalu's nine islands, Funafuti, Nukufetau, Nukulaelae and Niulakita. The treaty calls for consultations between the two partners to the agreement on security and marine resources matters. The treaty was ratified in the US in 1983.

Further information: Gerd Koch, *The Material Culture of Tuvalu*, reprinted Suva, 1983 is a standard work. Hugh Laracy (ed.) *Tuvalu, A History*, Suva, 1983, has contributions from Tuvaluans.

ISLANDS IN DETAIL

Nanumea. Nanumea, the most northerly and most populous of the Tuvalu group, has two main islets, Lakena and Nanumea. They are 5–6 km apart. There is an unsheltered anchorage off the NW end of Lakena, and landing is made on the western side of the other islet. It was occupied by American armed forces during World War II as is attested by landing craft still visible on the reef. The population in 1983 was 906.

Nanumaga. This island is only 2.5 by 1.5 km. It has three lagoons; two small ones (Hapai lagoon in the south, Te Ava Tahi lagoon in the north) and a much larger (600 m by 400 m) one near the centre, called Vaiatoa lagoon. Landing is difficult. In 1781, Mourelle named the island Isla del Cocal because it was covered with coconut trees. This was later converted to Gran Cocal. Captain William Hudson of the United States Exploring Expedition surveyed the island in 1841 and it was subsequently known as Hudson Island. The author Louis Becke lived for about a year on Nanumaga in

TABLE 7 THE ISLANDS OF TUVALU — AREAS AND DISTANCES

Area (ha)					*Distances (Nautical Miles)*				
361	Nanumea								
310	40	Nanumaga							
226	77	63	Niutao						
337	144	77	73	Nui					
509	188	160	118	93	Vaitupu				
307	197	164	132	90	36	Nukufetau			
254	254	220	188	151	74	64	Funafuti		
166	317	283	248	208	124	120	70	Nukulaelae	
41	367	329	308	254	204	180	137	85	Niulakita
2511									

the 1880s. Population in 1983 was 765.

Niutao. Niutao is roughly triangular in shape and a little over 1.5 km at its widest. It is heavily wooded with coconuts, and has a tiny lagoon in its centre. Its European discoverer, Captain Obed Starbuck, named it Loper's Island after his ship in 1825. It has also been called Lynx and Sepper. In 1973, this was the most densely populated island and residents were given the right to occupy and exploit Niulakita. Present population is 917.

Nui. Nui is a crescent-shaped island running north and south, 16 km long with two islets, one at each of its horns. New Zealand engineers completed work, in September 1979, on blasting the reef to widen the 122 m boat passage into the lagoon. Attempts have been made to construct a safe anchorage and also to clear a lagoon site for the amphibious aircraft which links most of Tuvalu's islands. The people, numbering 650 in 1983, are I-Kiribati in appearance and are closely affiliated with them in language and culture.

Mendana sighted Nui in 1568 and called it "Isla de Jesus". When Captain Eeg of the Dutch ship *Pollux* rediscovered it in 1825, he called it "Nederlandsch Eiland" (Netherlands Islands).

Vaitupu. This is a pear-shaped island, about 5.5 km long by 3.25 km at its greatest width. It is completely surrounded by a fringing reef, much of which is dry at low water. There are two lagoons, but only one practicable entrance for boats, and then only at high tide. There is an anchorage in seven fathoms off the village.

Vaitupu has rather better soil than most coral islands and, although small, it is the second most populous island in the group with 1320 residents. Fearing overcrowding, its inhabitants bought Kioa Island, Fiji, in the 1940s, and about 150 islanders went to live there.

The writings on the culture of Vaitupu by D. G. Kennedy, one-time headmaster of the local school, have made the island better known than most of the other Tuvalu islands. He originally established it on Funafuti but after a brief period, moved his Ellice Islands School to Vaitupu in the 1920s. It is now at Motufoua on Vaitupu.

Vaitupu is shown on some maps as Oaitapu or Tracy Islands. The latter was the name given to it by Captain Obed Starbuck, its European discoverer, in 1825.

Nukufetau. This is an oval-shaped atoll, about 38 km in circuit, with 37 islets on its reef. Ships may enter its larger lagoon through a channel on the western side. The lagoon was once suggested as a base for flying boats. The island was previously known as De Peyster's Group, after the captain of the ship *Rebecca* who discovered it in 1819. A wartime strip is a reminder of US occupation. In 1983 its population was 739.

Funafuti. Funafuti is a pear-shaped atoll enclosing a lagoon about 18 km long by 20 km wide at its widest. There are about 30 islets on the reef. On the eastern (windward) side, the islets form an almost continuous line, but on the western side there are many gaps. Only three entrances into the lagoon can be safely used, and then only with local knowledge. They are Te Ava i Mateika, Te Ava i Te Puapua and Te Ave i te Lape.

Funafuti is the capital of Tuvalu. The administration offices, a hotel, gaol and hospital are all located at Fongafale on the largest and easternmost islet, Funafuti, which gives its name to the whole atoll. The airstrip is also situated on that islet. The atoll is the only port of entry for Tuvalu.

The population was 300 in the 1860s but in 1866, Murray found only 100 people after the island had been raided by Peruvian slavers. Recovery was assisted by migration from other Ellice Islands and from Samoa, Tokelau and Manihiki. There were 200 people on the island by the 1880s and 250 by 1900. In 1983 there were 2620.

Captain De Peyster who discovered Funafuti in 1819 named it Ellice's Group. In 1897–98, Professor (later Sir) Edgeworth David, of Sydney University, bored through the coral to a depth of about 330 metres to substantiate Darwin's theory on the origin of coral reefs. Edgeworth David made another expedition about 1911, as he had sunk his bore on one of the islands at the edge of the atoll, which did not satisfy some scientific critics of Darwin's theory. So the second time David had to sink his bore in the centre of the atoll, where the critics claimed he would find a rocky volcanic peak. He found only sand and coral as before. David's wife published a book, *Funafuti, or Three Months on a Coral Island: An Unscientific Account of a Scientific Expedition*, which remains a popular account of life in Tuvalu.

Nukulaelae. This is an atoll with about two dozen islets, of which the two largest are on the eastern side. The reef on the western side is largely submerged. There is no entrance into the lagoon.

The atoll was discovered by Captain George Barrett of Nantucket in 1821 and named Mitchell's Group. The native name is shown on some maps as Nukulailai.

About 200 of the atoll's 300 inhabitants were kidnapped by Peruvian slavers in the 1860s. None returned. The population numbered 355 in 1983.

Niulakita. This island, sometimes called Nurakita, is slightly higher than the others in the group. It is about 5.5 km in circumference and thickly wooded with coconut palms. Landing is difficult except in canoes. There is an anchorage off the SW side.

Mendana in 1595 called it La Solitaria. Captain George Bennett, a Nantucket whaler who rediscovered it in 1821, named it Independence Island after his ship. It has also been called Sophia and Rocky.

The American trader Harry S. Moors, of Samoa, exploited its guano deposits late last century. It later passed into the control of Burns, Philp & Co. Ltd., of Sydney, who sold it during World War II to the Western Pacific High Commission on behalf of the Ellice Islanders. It is now occupied and worked by people from Niutao. The population in 1983 totalled 95.

FOR THE TOURIST. The small number of tourists who get to Tuvalu usually only see the island of Funafuti, the capital. Accommodation is very limited. Several cafes provide food. The one hotel has a restaurant. There is a cooperative store and a number of small shops.

There are rest houses on the outer islands but they are usually occupied by visiting government officials. Their standard is very basic and they are often in a poor state of repair. Small craft leave Funafuti for the outer islands at infrequent intervals and it is possible to get a passage on one of these by negotiating with the owner. It is also possible to get passage on the government inter-island trader.

The government wishes to encourage tourism — but with considerable caution and control. While it recognizes the employment potential tourism can offer, it is also aware of the dangers that uncontrolled tourist development can bring to what is still very much a traditional society with a subsistence economy.

The tourist who makes it to Tuvalu will find beautiful lagoons, a traditional Pacific society and very few other tourists. Modesty in dress, particularly for women visitors, is expected. No visa is required for a maximum stay of four months as long as sufficient funds and an onward ticket are evident. There is a $A5 departure tax.

ACCOMMODATION
Vaiaku Lagi Hotel. 7 rooms, restaurant, bar, close to lagoon and airstrip.
Church of Tuvalu Guesthouse. Accommodates four people, cooking facilities.

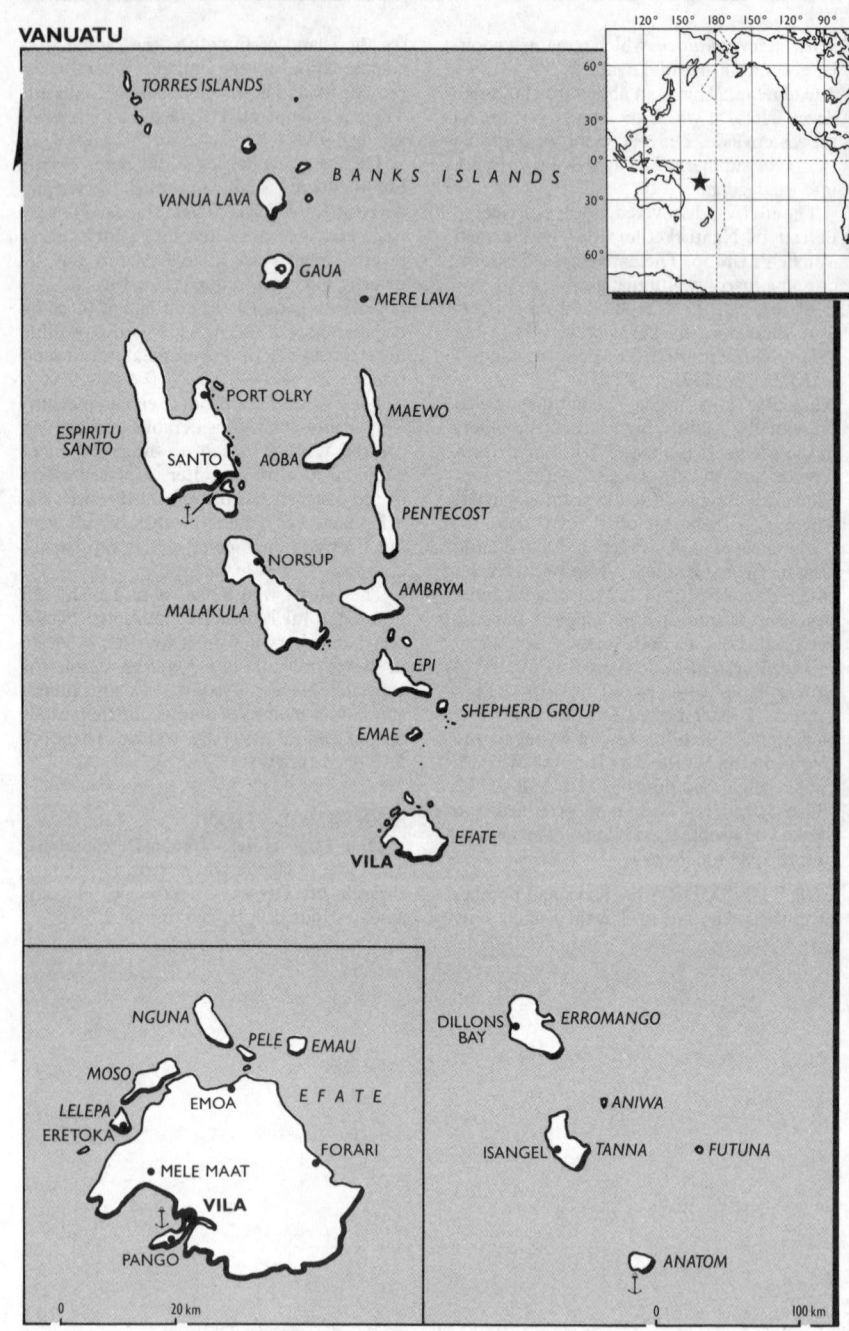

VANUATU

TORRES ISLANDS

BANKS ISLANDS

VANUA LAVA

GAUA   • MERE LAVA

ESPIRITU
SANTO   • PORT OLRY   MAEWO

SANTO   AOBA

PENTECOST

NORSUP

MALAKULA   AMBRYM

EPI

SHEPHERD GROUP

EMAE

EFATE

VILA

NGUNA   ERROMANGO
PELE EMAU   DILLONS
MOSO   BAY
LELEPA   EMOA   E F A T E   ANIWA
ERETOKA   FORARI   ISANGEL   TANNA   FUTUNA
• MELE MAAT
VILA
PANGO

0   20 km   0   100 km

ANATOM

120° 150° 180° 150° 120° 90°
60°
30°
0°
30°
60°

Vanuatu

Vanuatu, known until attainment of independence on 30 July 1980, as the New Hebrides, is a double chain of 80 islands located between 12 and 21 deg S latitude and 166 and 171 E longitude. It was jointly administered by France and Britain as a condominium from 1906 until independence. Its new name of Vanuatu, meaning Our Land, was given to the group by the Vanua-aku Party (formerly the New Hebrides National Party) which became the government on independence. The new state has a president and is a full member of the Commonwealth of Nations and of the French cultural organisation, the Association de Co-operation Culturelle et Technique.

The main island, Efate, with the administrative centre Port Vila, is about 2250 km north-east of Sydney, Australia.

The mid-year 1986 estimate gave the population as 140,154, an increase of 28,903 over the total of 111,251 calculated in the January 1979 census, the previous census held in the country. The average annual rate of growth between 1979 and 1986 was 3.1 per cent, and, for Ni-Vanuatu only, 3.2 per cent. The urban census of January 1986, the first census conducted since Independence, showed that growth was more rapid in Port Vila than the national average. The capital showed an average growth per annum of 4.2 per cent from 1979 to 1986.

Local time is 11 hours ahead of GMT, but Summertime has been introduced with the time advanced by one hour in summer. The currency is the Vatu, a national currency which came into circulation in March 1982.

THE PEOPLE. The indigenous people are of Melanesian stock, speaking more than 100 Melanesian languages with Bislama as the lingua franca. They are now known as Ni-Vanuatu.

Population estimates at the end of various years have shown the urban–rural distributions, in Table 1. Of the total estimated population (1986) of 140,154, Efate region had the greatest number (27,239), followed by Santo/Malo (25,313), Tafea (including Tanna and Erromango) (21,727), and Malakula (18,363). In Port Vila Ni-Vanuatu comprised 84 per cent of the population, Europeans 8.2 per cent and others 7.8 per cent. Luganville comprised 92.5 per cent Ni-Vanuatu, and 2.3 per cent Europeans. French citizens make up the largest group of

TABLE 1 VANUATU — POPULATION DISTRIBUTION

	1967 census	1972	1975	1979 census	1986 census
Urban Vila	7738	12,700	16,604	14,598	14,184*
Urban Santo	2564	3900	4954	5183	5621
Rural	67,686	72,400	74,974	91,470	120,349
Total	77,988	89,000	96,532	111,251	140,154

*Port Vila urban area defined differently in 1986 urban census.

non-Ni-Vanuatu in the country accounting for about one-third of all non-nationals.

The full national census of 1979 recorded 53 per cent males and 47 per cent females in the total population, while the ethnic breakdown showed that 93.8 per cent of the population was Ni-Vanuatu, followed by European, Micronesian/Polynesian, other Melanesian, Chinese and Vietnamese.

Nationality. The Constitution, adopted at independence, frames the regulations for citizenship. Automatic citizenship is bestowed on all persons with four grandparents belonging to a tribe or community indigenous to Vanuatu; on a person of Ni-Vanuatu ancestry who has no citizenship, nationality or the status of an optant. Anyone born after Independence Day may become a citizen if at least one parent is a citizen. Nationals of a foreign state or stateless persons can apply for naturalisation after 10 years residence in Vanuatu. Dual nationality is banned.

Language. The Constitution declares the national language of the republic to be Bislama, the Vanuatu pidgin (Bichelamar in French). The 'official' languages are Bislama, English and French and the principal languages of education are English and French. The Constitution also lays it down that 'The Republic shall protect the different local languages which are part of the national heritage and may declare one of them as a national language.' About 115 languages are spoken.

Migration. Until fairly recently, the only movement of Ni-Vanuatu in and out of the country was to work in the nearby French overseas territory of New Caledonia, but an increasing number of students are entering the University of the South Pacific in Fiji and French universities. However, with the downturn of prosperity in the New Caledonian nickel industry, the steady stream of Ni-Vanuatu into New Caledonia became only a trickle.

Religion. According to the 1979 census, 90,713 persons (81.5 per cent) declared themselves to be Christians and 8460 (7.6 per cent) to be adherents of Custom religion with the remainder of 'no religion' or unspecified. The largest Christian group was Presbyterian 40,843 (36.7 per cent), followed by Anglican 16,778 (15.1 per cent), Roman Catholic 16,502 (14.83 per cent) with Seventh-

day Adventist, Church of Christ, Assemblies of God, Apostle Church and French Protestant also represented.

Public holidays. Since independence, public holidays have been established as follows: New Year's Day; National Chief's Day, 5 March; Good Friday; Easter Monday; Labour Day, 1 May; Independence Day, 30 July; Assumption Day, 15 August; Constitution Day, 5 October; Unity Day, 29 November; Christmas Day, 25 December; Family Day, 26 December.

Lifestyle. About 80 per cent of the islanders live in rural communities. Chief activity for rural dwellers is their traditional subsistence agriculture, while those in the towns have greater opportunities to share in the diversions of a cash economy.

Recreation. Soccer is the main sport, although there is a thriving cricket league on Efate, including school teams. Other activities are golf, yachting, boxing, netball, tennis, basketball and rugby union.

GOVERNMENT

Head of State. The President of the Republic is elected by secret ballot by an electoral college of Parliament and the Presidents of the Regional Councils, and the office, which has a term of five years, is open to any indigenous Vanuatu citizen qualified to be elected to Parliament. The President can only be removed from office for gross misconduct or incapacity on a motion introduced by at least one-third of the members of the electoral college and approved by at least two-thirds of the members when at least three-fourths of the members including at least three-fourths of the Presidents of the Regional Councils are present. In the absence overseas of the President or his incapacity, his duties will be taken over by the Speaker of Parliament. The President can refer to the Supreme Court any regulation which he considers to be inconsistent with the Constitution.

The Executive. Executive power is vested in the Prime Minister and Council of Ministers which consists of the Prime Minister and other ministers, the number of which, including the Prime Minister, does not exceed a quarter of the number of parliamentary members. Parliament elects the Prime Minister by secret ballot from among its members. The Prime Minister and the Council of Ministers cease to hold office if Parliament passes a motion of 'no confidence' in the Prime Minister. The motion must be signed by at least one-sixth of the MPs and supported by an absolute majority. The Prime Minister chooses his own ministers.

Legislature. Voting for the first Representative Assembly by universal suffrage took place in November 1975. Prior to this there had been an Advisory Council, established in 1957 and enlarged in 1969 to 30 members of whom 14 were elected.

The new Representative Assembly provided 42 seats, of which 29 were for members elected in Vila, Santo and rural electorates while 4 were reserved for indigenous chiefs and 9 represented economic interests.

The 1975 elections led to victory for the National Party, which sought independence within two years. In February 1977, the Vanuaaku Party (formerly the National Party) members refused to sit again while the House included special members representing the Chamber of Commerce which, the party claimed, was undemocratic. The Assembly was then dissolved and a seven-man provisional council was formed to advise the Resident Commissioners until new elections were held based entirely on universal suffrage.

After subsequent elections, boycotted by the Vanuaaku Party, and eventual constitutional changes, the size of the Representative Assembly was settled at 39 members, elected by universal adult suffrage. In the general election of November 1979 the Vanuaaku Party won 26 of the 39 seats. They have remained in power ever since.

The National Council. The Constitution also provides for a National Council of Chiefs composed of custom chiefs elected by their peers sitting in District Councils of Chiefs. The National Council meets at least once a year and further meetings may be held at the request of the National Council, Parliament or the government. The council, which elects its own president, discusses all matters relating to custom and tradition and can make recommendations for the preservation and promotion of Ni-Vanuatu culture and languages. It can also be consulted on any question relating to tradition and custom in connection with any bill before

Parliament. The organisation of the National Council and, in particular, for the role of chiefs at the village, island and district levels is determined by Parliament.

Members of the National Council, like Members of Parliament, are protected against arrest or prosecution in respect of opinions given or votes cast by a member in the council in exercise of his office. No member, like MPs, can be arrested or prosecuted for any offence during a council session without the council's authorisation. Chairman of the National Council of Chiefs is Chief Willie Bongmatur.

Island government councils. The Constitution provides for the establishment of regional councils as a means of decentralising government to enable the people to participate in the government of their regions, but island government councils were proposed in the place of regional councils. Vanuatu has now established all its 11 island government councils.

Local government. Though there was no mention of municipal councils in the Constitution, Vila and Luganville (Santo) have each a municipal council headed by a mayor. These councils replace the municipal councils established on the French 'commune' principle in August 1975 as part of the political evolution agreed on by France and Britain.

The Ombudsman. The Constitution provides for an Ombudsman, who has a five-year tenure and is appointed by the President after consultation with the Prime Minister, the Speaker, leaders of parliamentary parties, President of the National Council of Chiefs, Presidents of the Regional Councils, Chairmen of the Public Service and Judicial Service Commissions.

Public service. In condominium days there were two separate public services, one with the British Administration, the other with the French, but employees from both services were integrated after independence into the Vanuatu Government Public Service. In 1983 there were approximately 2751 Ni-Vanuatu employees and about 419 expatriates serving as contract officers.

Justice. The Chief Justice is appointed by the President after consultation with the Prime Minister and the Leader of the Opposition. The puisne judges (limited to 3)

are appointed by the President, one being nominated by the Speaker of Parliament, one by the President of the National Council of Chiefs and one by the Presidents of the Regional Councils.

The Judicial Service Commission consists of the minister responsible for justice, as Chairman, the Chief Justice, the President of the Public Service Commission, a judge appointed for three years by the President of the Republic, and a representative of the National Council of Chiefs appointed by the Council.

The Judicial Service Commission is not subject to the direction or control of any other person or body in the exercise of its functions.

Parliament provides for appeals from the original jurisdiction of the Supreme Court and may provide for appeals from such appellate jurisdiction as it may have to a Court of Appeal constituted by two or more judges of the Supreme Court sitting together.

Parliament may provide for the manner of the ascertainment of relevant rules of custom, and may, in particular, provide for persons knowledgeable in custom to sit with the judges of the Supreme Court or the Court of Appeal and take part in its proceedings. Parliament also provides for the establishment of village or island courts with jurisdiction over customary and other matters and defines the role of chiefs in such courts.

Acting on the advice of the Judicial Service Commission, the President appoints the Public Prosecutor and the Public Solicitor, who provides legal assistance for needy persons.

Public Service Commission. The Public Service Commission controls the Public Service and appointments to it, and only citizens of Vanuatu can hold the appointments. Membership of the commission is limited to five who are appointed for a three-year term by the President after consultation with the Prime Minister. The commission has no authority over the judiciary, the armed forces, police and the teaching service.

Police. The Vanuatu Police Force, under the command of the Commissioner of Police, has an establishment of 270, including gazetted officers, inspectors, other ranks and clerical staff. The force maintains a fleet of about 40 automobiles and 15 motorcycles in six stations.

Prior to independence there were two separate forces which functioned under different philosophies, enforced different laws and spoke different languages.

In November 1980, a three-man survey team of high-ranking police officers from the Solomon Islands Police Force, the New Zealand Police Force and the Australian Federal Police Force carried out a detailed study of the Vanuatu Police and as a result of the report, experienced expatriate officers were seconded to the positions of Commissioner of Police and Commanding Officer of the Vanuatu Mobile Force (VMF), to assist in the administration, operations and development of the force. Within the re-organised structure, the Vanuatu Police Force provides the following services: General Duties Police, Prison Service, Immigration Department and Vanuatu Mobile force.

Specialist branches in the General Duties Police include traffic, criminal records, criminal investigation (CID), police training school, state prosecutors, radio section, a Special Branch (security intelligence), and security officers for the Prime Minister and visiting VIPs.

There are five prisons, two in Port Vila and the others at Santo, Malakula and Tanna and about 20 officers are attached to the prisons service.

The Vanuatu Mobile Force is a 250 strong paramilitary force with headquarters at Port Vila and detachments permanently based on Santo and Tanna.

EDUCATION. Originally, the main initiative was taken by the various church missions. In 1959, the British Administration co-ordinated facilities for English-medium education, eventually leading to a six-year primary course. Secondary courses were developed in the 1960s. The French Administration took charge of French-medium, non-denominational schools in 1968 and assumed full responsibility for all schools, including Catholic and some Protestant institutions from 1973. Since independence the Goverment has assumed responsibility for education and is working towards a unified Vanuatu system.

Schools. In 1984 there were 140 English-medium primary schools with 12,671 pupils and 104 French-medium primary schools with 10,678 pupils. There were ten secondary schools, seven of them with English as the medium with 1074 pupils and three French medium secondary schools with 955 pupils. A secondary school, Matevulu College, financed by the Australian Government, opened in 1983 on Santo. Secondary schools are planned for Tanna and Malakula.

Tertiary. The Vanuatu Technical Institute, formerly the Lycée d'Enseignement Professional (French medium mainly), has 300 students.

Responsibility for primary teacher education rests with the Teachers' Education Centre within the Vanuatu Institute of Education. A common programme for both Anglophone and Francophone student teachers has been developed and commenced in 1983. The course leading to a certificate in primary education is expected to maintain a balanced intake of 15 French-speaking and 15 English-speaking students per year.

Training for secondary teachers is at present only available abroad, with a considerable imbalance in the number of Anglophone teachers compared to Francophone. In 1984 there were 46 Anglophone trainees and only one Francophone. Pupil to teacher ratios are about 23 to one in primary and 16 to one in secondary schools.

Other neo-tertiary opportunities exist at the nursing school (run by the Ministry of Health), the Tagabe Agricultural College (under the Ministry of Agriculture) and at the University of the South Pacific, which maintains an extension centre in Port Vila.

The Vanuatu centre of this Suva, Fiji-based university was established at its present location in 1981. An average of 120 students enrol each semester in the university's correspondence course programme, leading to full-time study at USP. The majority of students (100 in 1985) study social sciences. The university also offers courses in French, and established a Pacific Languages Unit in Vanuatu in 1983.

Overseas studies. Technical education and commercial training (in addition to the Vanuatu Technical Institute) is provided in regional institutions in English, mainly at the Honiara Technical Institute in Solomon Islands, the Fiji Institute of Technology, and in apprentice training in Australia and

New Zealand. Some places are available in New Caledonia for French-medium students. Places are also available in the University of Papua New Guinea, the Fiji School of Medicine and other tertiary institutions in Australia, New Zealand and the United Kingdom. There is also some provision for tertiary education for Ni-Vanuatu in Tahiti and France.

The National Development Plan of 1982–86 provided for the expenditure of VT4,974 million on education. A revised estimate in 1984 put the figure at VT3,504.7 million. In 1987 projected expenditure on education was VT832.9 million.

LABOUR. The labour force according to the 1979 census, totalled 51,130 persons (28,953 males and 22,177 females) of whom 39,145 were engaged in agriculture, fisheries and forestry, 2470 in professional and technical pursuits, 1558 in clerical work, 1015 in the distributive trades, 2234 in services and 4320 in production, transport and labouring work.

The 1986 urban survey revealed 8242 economically active people in the two urban areas, Port Vila and Luganville, the majority (3464) engaged in services. There were 1580 in trade, restaurants and hotels and 850 in transport and communication.

Unions. There are 16 registered trade unions and six employers' associations. These cater for most sectors of industry.

Foreign labour. The French authorities, prior to World War II, introduced into Vanuatu over 1000 Tonkinese labourers from French Indo-China to work French plantations, on five-year contracts. After the war diplomatic difficulties prevented their repatriation to their homeland — Vietnam — until mid-1963 when all but a few left.

This left a temporary shortage of skilled building workmen in the group, partly made up by the introduction of a limited number of tradesmen from Fiji. This led to the introduction of Wallis Islanders, Tahitians and I Kiribati (Gilbertese) for agricultural work. However, there are not more than a few hundred of them at any one time. Labour shortages and the high costs of what labour exists contribute to the decline in skills of all sorts. The situation was made even worse in the early 1970s when

Ni-Vanuatu were in demand as labourers in the nickel industry in New Caledonia where wages were high. However, with the recession, New Caledonia nickel does not promise the same rewards.

In 1986 there were 28 Vietnamese living in urban areas, 22 of them in Port Vila where the majority are in small businesses.

Work permits. Non-citizens and expatriates need work permits before being allowed to work in Vanuatu. In 1986 a total of 762 work permits were issued to expatriate workers, compared with 148 in 1982 and 605 in 1984, making it fairly obvious that the number of expatriate workers is not diminishing as is often claimed. Management and administration accounted for the greatest number, followed by professional and technical occupations.

National provident fund. Founded in 1986, the fund had contributions from 1500 employers and 12,000 employees in 1988.

HEALTH. Health conditions are considered satisfactory and without major problems. Authorities acknowledge, however, that inadequacies in health management and infrastructure development have created difficulties which require resolution soon if health standards are not to deteriorate.

Facilities in Vanuatu consist of two referral hospitals (on Efate and Santo), two district hospitals, three rural hospitals, 17 health centres and 52 dispensaries. Total bed capacity in 1986 was 428.

There were 23 doctors in the Public Health service in 1986, five of whom were specialists. These were supported by 237 registered nurses and 49 nursing aides. There was one Ni-Vanuatu and two French dentists, with three dental assistants.

Private facilities include three dentists, three doctors and three opticians, all in Port Vila.

Diseases. Most common diseases are those of the skin and the upper respiratory tract. Gastro-intestinal parasites are endemic and account for failure to thrive in many children.

Malaria is the most serious public health problem. In 1983 there were 19,119 confirmed cases, with 16 deaths. Malaria control funded by the WHO and other bodies is ongoing.

Health statistics have been inadequately kept, both before and after independence. The first Hospitals Report was not published until 1984. Recently, however, much progress has been made in the recording and collating of statistical information.

Infant mortality is estimated at 70 to 75 per 1000 but is probably under-reported. Life expectancy at birth is 56 for men and 54 for women. The crude birth and death rates are 43 and 9 per 1000 respectively.

THE LAND. The total land area of the group is 11,880 square kilometres with the largest single island being Santo, 3947 sq. km, while Efate, with the capital Vila, is 915 sq. km. Some 80 islands and islets in the group are spread in the shape of a Y extending about 800 km from north to south. Santo is 145 km from north to south and 65 km from east to west. The island of Efate extends about 45 km from east to west and 30 km from north to south.

Largest islands of the group are: Santo, Malakula, Maewo, Pentecost, Ambrym, Epi, Efate, Erromango, Malo, Tanna and Anatom (formerly Aneityum). Vanuatu also includes the Banks group, due north of the main islands, and the Torres group, 60 km northwest of the Banks group.

The highest peak in the group is Mt Tabwemasana of 1877 m, on Santo, while Mt Lairiri or Santo Peak reaches 1652 m. While half the islands are simply islets and rocky volcanic outcrops, the other half are also punctuated by numerous peaks in a terrain dominated by mountains and plateaus with only limited coastal plains.

Two small islands, Matthew and Hunter, south of Anatom, which are uninhabited and little more than rocky outcrops, are claimed by Vanuatu and also by France on behalf of New Caledonia.

Natural features. Within the Vanuatu Group there are a number of active volcanoes. Yasur (Yahuwei) crater on Tanna continues to produce periodic ash showers. Two volcanoes on Ambrym emit showers of ash also and occasionally this is accompanied by lava. Lopevi (Ulveah), south of Ambrym, has erupted intermittently, and Mt Garet, on Santa Maria, in the Banks Group, and Suretimeat on Vanua Lava, both erupted in August 1965. Sometimes lakes are maintained in volcanic depressions as on Santa Maria and Ambae.

Soil. Besides the timber it supports, the soil contains mineral deposits such as the manganese at Forari on the island of Efate. Prospecting has been conducted for nickel, copper and bauxite.

Climate. The south-east trade winds prevail, with frequent calms which are often followed by winds from the north and east which bring rain.

At Vila the average year-round humidity is 83 per cent. Average rainfall is about 2300 mm; the average at Luganville is 3100 mm.

In the southern hemisphere winter the southern Vanuatu islands, including Efate, can experience quite cool weather; and in the summer, December–April, all islands of the group can experience cyclones. Major ones occured in 1985 and 1987.

Flora and fauna. The tropical rain forests abound with a thick undergrowth of ferns and vines as well as tall trees, common also to the Solomons, such as Barringtonia and Eugenia.

The discovery of sandalwood in the 19th century helped to change the history of these islands. There are limited supplies remaining. Several bird species are found in Vanuatu, but numbers vary considerably from one island to another. Reptiles, except for skinks, are increasingly few in number, as are land-based animals, apart from rats and bats. Pigs and dogs are usually domesticated, but have feral cousins. Some wild horses are to be found on Tanna.

Land tenure. Land rights generated considerable controversy before independence but the Constitution killed controversy by ruling that 'all land belongs to the indigenous custom owners and their descendants'. Only indigenous citizens, who have acquired their land in accordance with a recognised system of land tenure, shall have perpetual ownership. All alienated land has been repossessed but a leasing system, under government control, is working satisfactorily and, in many cases, expatriates who were landowners have been able to remain in control of the property as leaseholders. In some cases, the signing of a lease has been the occasion of rejoicing with feasting in which the custom owners and the former owner, now the lessee, have taken part.

However, as the Mid-term Review of Vanuatu's First Development Plan points out, in a number of cases the negotiation of agricultural leases with custom landowners has taken a considerable time. As a result redevelopment of the plantation/estate sector has been slower than expected. In addition, in some cases the true custom landowners of potential leases have not been ascertained.

Legal machinery for registering leases under the independent government did not become organised until 1984. Thus registration of leases can now be facilitated, but other constraints — in custom rather than legal matters — still exist.

PRIMARY PRODUCTION. Copra, fish and beef are still the main exports of Vanuatu. The coconut is the source of the major export and, between 1979 and 1983, copra provided about 73 per cent of the country's export earnings. The total area under coconuts is about 70,000 ha but about 82 per cent of the copra produced comes from small holders rather than large plantations. Production is concentrated in the central and northern islands, particularly Malakula, Espiritu Santo, Ambae and Ambrym.

The Copra Quality Improvement Programme began in 1982 and was designed to encourage copra producers to dry copra by hot air driers or sun-drying rather than the smoke-curing method. Great improvement in quality has resulted. Most of Vanuatu's copra is sent to French, Dutch and Belgian markets. In 1986 copra exports totalled 40,612 tonnes, worth only VT443 million because of depressed world prices. World price for copra fell from a high of $US792 per tonne during 1984 to a record low of $US154 per tonne during 1986.

Little crushing of copra is now done in Vanuatu. The only mill, at Luganville on Espiritu Santo, was burned down during the rebellion of 1980.

Cocoa. Cocoa has long been the second most important cash crop in the country. By 1935 the area planted under cocoa — entirely on plantations — was 5260 hectares producing 2700 tonnes of cocoa beans annually. Over the past 20 years, annual production has fluctuated between 300 tonnes and 1000 tonnes of beans, due mainly to climate but also to price fluctuations.

Cocoa exports in 1983 were the highest since 1945 and earned three times more foreign exchange than in 1982. In 1983, 1297 tonnes were produced, three-quarters of it coming from smallholders. More recently smallholder production has accounted for 81 per cent of production.

Under the Cocoa Development Project (1983–85) smallholders were encouraged to use new improved seedlings, rehabilitate existing cocoa and improve quality by better processing. As a result, cocoa production reached the second highest post-war level in 1986 with 1282 tonnes, 66 per cent of which was graded export quality.

An estimated 100 ha of cocoa is being planted each year and averages indicate a generally upward trend in production.

Metenesel Estates was launched in 1983, a joint venture involving custom landowners, the Government of Vanuatu and the Commonwealth Development Fund. The company was set up to develop a 1700-ha cocoa project at Lambubu on Malakula. By mid-1985 130 ha had been planted, but difficulties arose with both rate of growth and the labour supply. As a result the project was divided into two phases, the first to run to mid-1988 and involve the planting of 500 ha, and the second to complete most of the original area planned, if reviews of performance were satisfactory. Present indications are that the first phase is on target.

Equity in Metenesel is as follows: custom landowners 3.88 per cent; Government of Vanuatu 36.65 per cent; Commonwealth Development Corporation 59.47 per cent. Funding has also been provided by the Caisse Centrale de Co-operation Economique. Production from the estates is projected to reach over 2000 tonnes by the year 2000.

Coffee. Coffee production has been undertaken for many years. The level of output and exports have varied considerably reaching, in the peak year of 1939, a record level of 932 tonnes. Present production rarely exceeds 100 tonnes per year.

Arabica coffee is grown in the upland villages in Tanna. In the past there was no systematic development of the crop, or any assistance given to growers in the processing

and marketing of the beans. As a result production varied, with much mature planting being either partly or totally abandoned. It is estimated that there are 45,000 coffee bushes scattered over some 100 smallholdings in Tanna, but few are productive. Elsewhere smallholder production of coffee is limited to the islands of Malakula (South West Bay) and Pentecost (Melsisi).

There was an increase in production from 49 tonnes in 1985 to 57 tonnes in 1986, the greater part of it robusta coffee from the northern islands.

Arabica coffee from Tanna, however, is expected to increase in importance as a result of the establishment of the Tanna Coffee Development Co. in 1984. By mid-1986, 57 ha had been planted and by the end of the project's fifth year it is expected that a 475 ha estate will have been established. It is hoped that smallholders in the Middle Bush area of Tanna will also plant a further 250 ha. Forecasts are for 90–95 per cent of production being exported, but at present exports only amount to about 35 tonnes annually.

Other vegetables and fruits. Market gardening is developing in the peri-urban area of Port Vila, and, with the use of varieties developed for the tropics and improved pest and disease control techniques and hydroponics, is now able to supply the market with some vegetables throughout the year. The capacity for production during the cool season exceeds the local demand.

Production of European-type vegetables for the Port Vila market was formerly encouraged in Tanna, but production is handicapped by the lack of regular inter-island transport and by the absence of production planning by the farmers. Farmers are now encouraged to produce less-perishable vegetables such as cabbages, onions, garlic and potatoes. They are encouraged to aim for year-round supply as the more temperate climate in Tanna makes this possible without heavy investment in sophisticated production systems.

Bananas, breadfruit, mangoes, guavas, etc. are a regular part of the diet in rural areas, but there is no nation-wide marketing network for these products. The Port Vila market for fruit is supplied by Efate farmers, but suffers from periods when there is little variety of locally-grown fruit. There is more fruit available during the summer. Growers near Port Vila are trying to produce pineapple throughout the year. Cool season fruits such as strawberries are also being grown. A major need is to provide a regular supply of fruits to hotels, which still rely on imports. Oranges from between 2000 and 3000 trees are produced in Aniwa and are sent to the Port Vila market. Imports of fruit and vegetables have been reduced through a policy of import substitution, from VT35.6 million in 1983 to VT33.2 million in 1986.

Rice. Apart from a few hectares of dryland rice grown in Espiritu Santo and Tanna, there is no local production of this crop. Rice is becoming an increasingly popular component of local diet and subject to a high and increasing level of imports.

Livestock. Conditions are suitable for cattle grazing as the country is free of most cattle diseases. Cattle, introduced by early missionaries for milk, were increasingly grazed under the coconuts in the plantation sector. Unlike other states in the region, the republic is self-sufficient in beef production and beef is an established export. The present cattle population is estimated at about 108,300 head, 35.5 per cent of which are in smallholdings.

The remainder of the national herd is grazed on coconut plantations and some large cattle ranches, but the number of cattle owned by smallholders and grazed under coconuts is increasing in areas where technical support is available. Much of this increase is attributable to the success of the Smallholder Cattle Development Project, which began in 1982 and has seen significant improvements in marketing services, training courses and general awareness. The second phase of the VT26 million project will run to 1989.

Cattle on Vanuatu are a mixture of a number of imported breeds including Hereford, Illawarra and Jersey. More recently cattle more suited to the tropics such as Charolais, Limousin and Brahman have been brought in for breeding purposes. Cattle diseases are limited mainly to brucellosis, bovine tuberculosis having been brought under control. A brucellosis eradication scheme, begun in 1982, is also having some success, although the situation on the outer islands was worse than had been originally thought.

On Espiritu Santo a joint venture between the Government and Australian partners has been established. The project covers an area of 8400 ha south-west of Luganville. ADAB funds are to be the source of the Government's contribution. The aim is to establish a herd of at least 5500 breeding cows, and to provide a market for weaners from local smallholders. At full development the project is expected to produce over 5000 head each year for slaughter. The project will employ about 108 labourers, plus technical staff.

The development of the livestock industry has been supported by the establishment of meat preparation and processing facilities. There are abattoirs at Port Vila and Luganville and canneries. The abattoirs have depended largely on a Japanese export market. Both have recently experienced difficulties, with declining local demand. After a temporary closure of the Luganville facility, it was bought by Sun Japan Vanuatu Livestock Co. and will be brought up to EEC standard.

Over 7000 cattle were slaughtered in 1987, most at Luganville. In 1986 supply of tinned meat to the domestic market amounted to VT22 million. Exports of tinned beef were 13 tonnes, chilled and frozen 489 tonnes, to a total of VT130 million.

Milk production on Efate, serving the Vila market, was 153,333 litres in 1986, but sales were lower than the previous year as a result of a decline in the hotel and restaurant trades.

Pigs and poultry. Smallholders have traditionally raised pigs for customary celebrations. They scavenge or are fed on food wastes and coconuts. There were six commercial piggeries which supplied the urban markets with approximately 57 tonnes of carcass meat in 1984, most of it through the abattoir in Port Vila. Little emphasis has been given to village poultry production by the extension services but commercial broiler and egg production now supply most of the local demand. In 1986 85 per cent of egg supplies and practically all poultry needs were met by local production.

Both commercial pig and poultry industries use imported stockfeed. As the costs of these products are rising fast, the enterprises are turning increasingly to self-reliance as far as stockfeed is concerned.

Sheep and goats. The agricultural sector supports a small number of sheep and goats. The national consumption of goat meat and milk is low. There is a regular demand in the urban areas for lamb, most of which is imported.

Diversification. Besides increasing cocoa and beef production and to lessen reliance on copra, the agricultural sector is investigating such crops as pepper, vanilla, ginger, garlic and kava. The latter is thought to have great export potential, for social and medicinal uses.

Fisheries. Fishing falls into three categories: traditional fishing within the reef, for domestic consumption; artisanal fishing, organised at the village level for local and urban market sales; industrial oceanic fishing, primarily for the export market.

Projects in operation under the Village Fisheries Development Programme rose from 54 in 1985 to 60 in 1986. However, production under these projects remained the same at about 107,628 kilos, valued at VT14,302. Value of sales by the Government-owned Port Vila Fisheries Ltd (Natai) also declined from about VT29.2 million in 1985 to VT20.4 million in 1986. Imports of tinned fish, however, rose from a value of VT96 million to VT104 million.

The South Pacific Fishing Company, operated at Palikulo on Espiritu Santo since 1957 and in recent years declining in the size of its fleet and the quantity and value of its catch, closed in 1986. In that year it had a fleet of 12 boats, landed 1186 tonnes of fish and had re-exports valued at $US3.8 million.

Towards the end of 1986 the Vanuatu Government signed a fishing agreement with the USSR. This provides for Vanuatu to license eight Soviet fishing vessels, registered by the Forum Fisheries Agency in Honiara, to fish within Vanuatu's 200-mile exclusive economic zone. Only purse seine and long line methods will be used. Fishing will not be undertaken within Vanuatu's territorial waters. The Soviet vessels will have access to Vanuatu ports for buying bait, supplies, or for undergoing repairs, all of which are expected to generate additional commercial activity in the country. The USSR will pay a fee of $US1.5 million for the fishing rights, which will be for one year with a possibility of extension if agreed upon by both parties.

A small export trade in trochus, green snail, bêche-de-mer and shark fins also exists. These amounted to only VT13 million in 1986.

Forestry. The Ministry of Land and Natural Resources is responsible for the management of Vanuatu's forest resources through the forestry service of the Department of Agriculture, Livestock and Forestry.

Government involvement in the forestry sector began in 1970, and in the first five years forest resources were identified and 40 plantation species from worldwide sources were tested. About 75 per cent of the nation's land area is under natural vegetation, but much of it is too steep to be logged or contains little timber of value. Forest resources are poor compared with those of neighbouring countries, due to geological youth, geographical isolation, shifting cultivation and previous hurricanes.

Local Supply Plantation Programmes were established on a number of islands but the planned rate of expansion is now thought to have been over-ambitious. Several plantations have therefore been placed on a care-and-maintenance basis only. Industrial Forestry Plantations were commenced on Anatom, Erromango and Pentecost in 1982–83 and four more were projected. The target has since been reduced to two — on Vanua Lava and on Espiritu Santo. These are expected to produce high quality saw and veneer logs for export. Plantings include *Pinus caribaea* and *Cordia alliodora*.

However, in 1983 the Government imposed a ban on log exports, with the exception of milk tree (*Antiaris toxicaria*) for which there was no local demand. A review of policy in 1986 resulted in an extension of the ban and the establishment of a quota on milk tree log exports.

Total log production in 1986 was 18,300 cubic metres, 6600 cubic metres of which were exported. Total value of timber exports in 1985 (the most recent figures) was VT140.2 million.

There was an increase in the export of sandalwood in 1986 with 126 tonnes leaving the country, valued at VT15.2 million. Government concern over the extent of this resource has prompted a moratorium on exports until an inventory is carried out.

Cyclone Uma in early 1987 put one sawmill in Port Vila out of commission and created an additional domestic demand for timber.

MANUFACTURING AND MINING.

Secondary industry is on a small scale, catering almost exclusively for local consumption. The only exceptions are the small meat canneries and fish freezing works and sawmills, which have a limited export trade. Other industries include a soft drinks plant, printeries, furniture manufacturing, cement works, building materials and accessories, and boat building. Still smaller enterprises include soap manufacture (from coconut oil milled on Tanna) and garment manufacture.

The nation's First Development Plan (1982–86) identified six objectives for the growth of industry including those relating to the use of raw materials, local control, foreign exchange, employment creation and the establishment of a sound industrial infrastructure. Some of these, such as local participation leading to control, have been accorded a higher priority. The Government, however, recognises that certain constraints exist, such as the scarcity of skilled and semi-skilled workers, small domestic markets and lack of knowledge of credit availability.

Investment guidelines indicating Government policy towards local and foreign investments are contained in the publication *Vanuatu's Investment Incentives*, available from the Ministry of Finance, Commerce, Industry and Tourism.

In 1986 the manufacturing sector employed 976, about one-third of them in food and beverage manufacturing, compared with 816 in 1983 and 896 in 1985. Real GDP in the sector is estimated to have grown by 41.8 per cent in 1984, by 9.4 per cent in 1985 and by 10 per cent in 1986. Increases in gross value added in manufacturing were from VT 813.6 million in 1985 to VT958.4 million in 1986, a rise of 17.8 per cent.

Mineral resources. There is only small-scale quarrying to meet local demand taking place at present. The exploitation of manganese at Forari on Efate island ceased in 1978 when the mining became uneconomic, though its evidence remains in the form of rusting structures and cantilevers which have some value as a tourist attraction. The quarrying of pozzolana to supply a local cement works ceased in 1985.

Nine companies, however, have taken out gold prospecting licences, a result of the renewed interest in gold prospecting activity throughout the Southwest Pacific, especially in Papua New Guinea. Exploration in Vanuatu is still at the preliminary stage and very little drilling has been undertaken, but initial prospects on Espiritu Santo, Malakula and Efate are thought to be of sufficient interest to warrant further detailed investigation.

Evaluation of manganese deposits on Erromango is being carried out at a modest level, as is investigation of black sand deposits on other islands.

TOURISM.

After an initial period of ambivalence concerning the role of tourism in the economic development of the country, the Government indicated its intention of taking a positive part in the future of tourism policy by creating in 1981 the post of Director of Tourism within the Ministry of Finance, Commerce, Industry and Tourism. Subsequently the structure was changed with the creation of the National Tourism Office and the appointment of Peter Taurakoto as General Manager. The Government is also involved in the retail sector of tourism through Tour Vanuatu.

The Government established a national airline in 1981 in conjunction with Ansett Airlines of Australia. Disagreement between the parties, however, led to the withdrawal of Ansett in early 1986, and a consequent decline in visitor numbers. Negotiations have been under way ever since for a new national airline, and in early 1988 the flag-carrier, Air Vanuatu, took to the skies again with the managerial co-operation of Australian Airlines.

In 1986 there were 11 hotels in the Greater Port Vila area, offering 469 rooms and 1042 beds. There were over 100 beds elsewhere in the country, most of these in Luganville. In early 1987 Cyclone Uma demolished most of them, leaving Vanuatu's tourism plant in a sorry condition. But in late 1987 it was expected that most hotels would be operating at full capacity again by Christmas that year.

As a result of Cyclone Uma, visitor numbers, already affected by airline problems, the decline in Australian dollar values, unfavourable publicity on Vanuatu in the international press and a curious confusion in travellers' minds between Vanuatu and troubled New Caledonia, fell drastically in the first part of 1987. Visitor numbers for previous years were: 1983, 32,374 visitors; 1984, 31,615; 1985, 24,521; 1986, 17,515. An average of 60 per cent of Vanuatu's visitors come from Australia. New Caledonia provides the next largest number, followed by New Zealand and Japan. Cruise ship passengers, numbered 75,742 in 1985 and 56,090 in 1986. The occupancy rate for hotels in 1985 was 45.3 per cent in 1985 but declined by 25 per cent to average 30.4 per cent in 1986 (measured by bed rather than room occupancy). 'Tourist' arrivals are usually 4–5000 less annually than 'visitor' arrivals.

LOCAL COMMERCE. Economically the French were dominant in Vanuatu until the British instituted liberal legislation for company registration in 1971 which led to the country being regarded as a 'tax haven'. This attracted the setting up of many new banks, trust funds, etc. But local trade is still dominated by two large companies, Ballande Vanuatu and Burns, Philp (Vanuatu) Ltd, a subsidiary of the Australian firm. **Co-operative societies.** The Co-operative Movement was formally established by Joint Regulation in 1962, but a number of unregistered co-operative-type organisations had been operating during the previous decade. The movement proved popular, especially in the British Administration's sector where, in 1967, there were 46 registered societies against only 10 French-registered societies. In 1981, when the two sections of the movement were unified, there were 287 co-operative societies. Most of the societies are consumer/marketing, i.e. selling copra and running a trade-store. Co-operatives sell copra from their members to the Vanuatu Commodities Marketing Board, via private distributors and shippers. Other societies are organising and selling local artifacts and garden produce.

Membership of the 206 primary co-operative societies in 1985 totalled 13,500. Consumer sales totalled VT756,583,000 and produce sales VT271,378,000. Total assets were VT363,202,000.

The French-administered Syndicat des Co-operatives Autochtones sous control Français (SCAF) went into liquidation following the withdrawal of French financial and technical assistance at Independence, and in 1981 the British-administered New Hebrides Co-operative Federation became the Vanuatu Co-operative Federation Ltd (VCF), the chief organisation for co-operative trading activities which now include the provision of shipping, wholesale and banking services. It has a 51 per cent shareholding in the Vanua Navigation Shipping Company which enables it to charter ships throughout the year for co-operative trading between the islands. The Vanuatu Co-operative Savings Bank is part of the VCF.

OVERSEAS TRADE. Until 1969 Vanuatu enjoyed a favourable trade balance, because of the fishing and manganese industries. However the decline in manganese exports, coupled with increased imports due to development projects, produced the trade deficit of recent years.

Export markets are still dominated by Europe, largely as a result of exports of copra under the STABEX arrangements, but the direction of exports from Vanuatu has shown a significant change in the past few years. This had been due to the emergence of Japan, Korea, Hong Kong and Taiwan as important buyers of goods. Japan, in particular, became a major buyer of beef.

While copra dominates exports, however, Holland, Belgium and France remain significant, the former accounting for just over one-third of the value of exports, followed by France with just over one-quarter. Other export markets include Australia, Singapore, New Caledonia, New Zealand and Papua New Guinea.

Despite the widening of markets, 1986 was not a good year for exports generally. Domestic exports, which had risen to VT3221 million in 1984, fell to VT1981 million in 1985 and to VT935 million in 1986. The closure of the South Pacific Fishing Co., which had operated since the late 1950s, resulted in a severe drop in re-exports also, although the output of the

TABLE 2 VANUATU — OVERSEAS TRADE (VT000,000)

Year	Exports (including re-exports)	Total Imports	Balance
1981	2833	5116	− 2283
1982	2201	5663	− 3462
1983	2940	6292	− 3352
1984	4395	6811	− 2416
1985	3263	7537	− 4274
1986	1518	6105	− 4587

TABLE 3 VANUATU — IMPORTS FOR DOMESTIC CONSUMPTION (VT000,000) ORIGIN

Year	Australia	Japan	New Zealand	Fiji	France	New Caledonia	Singapore	Hong Kong	Others	Total
1981	1342	475	329	423	424	167	190	169	386	3905
1982	1546	591	483	420	431	275	212	202	471	4631
1983	1766	620	597	387	478	178	252	232	719	5229
1984	2022	758	562	428	542	249	260	270	734	5825
1985	2344	787	697	440	528	256	253	283	882	6470
1986	2151	768	568	288	443	345	233	221	886	5906

TABLE 4 VANUATU — DOMESTIC EXPORTS DIRECTION (VT000,000)

Year	Belgium	Holland	France	New Cale.	Singa.	Japan	F. Poly.	Taiwan	Others	Total
1981	472	354	385	91	20	31	6	—	43	1402
1982	349	337	123	134	20	17	4	1	37	1027
1983	548	614	196	90	143	105	30	23	32	1781
1984	746	1299	327	44	164	428	163	43	7	3221
1985	337	946	200	25	19	316	2	4	132	1981
1986	39	321	249	24	22	163	—	18	99	935

company had been declining for some years. Re-exports of fish dropped from an annual average of over VT700 million since 1981 to VT126 million in 1986. But the most obvious reason for the decline in export income was the slump in copra prices — from peak earnings of VT2734 million in 1984 to VT443 million in 1986, despite the fact that there was only a 16 per cent fall in the quantity exported in these years. The only commodity to show an increase in export volume and value during 1986 was cocoa, which increased in both value and quantity by 47 per cent, bringing VT196 million.

Major suppliers. Australia takes only 4.2 per cent of Vanuatu's exports but provides 36.4 per cent of its imports. This percentage has remained more or less constant since 1980. Japan is the second major supplier, providing an annual average of 12 per cent, followed by New Zealand (10 per cent), France (7.5), New Caledonia (5.9) and Fiji (4.9) in 1986.

Financial sources attribute the high propensity towards imports mainly to the demands of the tourism and expatriate sectors. In 1986 the country had an unfavourable trade balance of VT4587 million, despite a reduction in imports as a consequence of the slump in tourism. See Tables 2–4.

Tariffs. Imported goods are classified according to the local tariff classification which contains 21 sections, 99 chapters and 1300 items. It is based on the Customs Council Nomenclature as amended to January 1981. Exports are restricted to a small number of commodities which can be identified with the Brussels Tariff Nomenclature.

FINANCE. Since independence in 1980. Vanuatu has had to rely, mainly, on France and Britain for budgetary aid. Its recurrent budget expenditure is financed from local revenue, mostly from import and export duties which make up almost 70 per cent of revenue plus some aid from France and Britain, but development expenditure is financed almost completely by overseas aid.

There are three types of foreign aid from donor countries and agencies, grant aid, technical assistane and recurrent budgetary aid. The First National Development Plan (1982/86) explains it as follows:

Grant aid. This aid consists of direct cash grants which can be used in various areas of development. Some donors (e.g. France and Britain) specify that grant aid must be used for capital projects whereas other donors (e.g. Australia, New Zealand and the European Development Fund (EDF)) make grants which can be used for a variety of purposes. The policy which all donors follow is that grant aid is not to be allocated to supplement recurrent budgetary requirements. During the Plan period, Australia will become the major donor of grant aid while the commitments of France and Britain will decline relatively.

Technical assistance. Technical assistance consists of the provision of personnel by donors to fill both staff positions in government and advisory positions, with partial or full payment of salaries, benefits and relo-

cation expenses of such personnel, and in addition short term aid in the form of consultancies. Such aid offsets to some extent higher recurrent expenditure which would have to be borne by government. Throughout the Plan period, France and Britain will remain the major donors of such aid.

Recurrent budgetary aid. This aid is provided by the ex-metropolitan powers to enable the Government to cover part of its recurrent budgetary requirement. While Britain has made a definite commitment to reduce such aid over the Plan period, the future amounts of the French Government's contribution are less certain. It may as indicated be reduced at a similar rate to Britain's contribution or it may be open to negotiation. In summary, France and Britain will remain the major aid donors during the Plan period. However their aid will continue to be concentrated more in technical assistance while Australia becomes the major donor of grant aid. The economy will remain reliant on foreign aid throughout the Plan period for the implementation both of developmental programmes and for the provision of existing government services. Budgetary aid is due to be phased out and this could require radical rationalisation of government services unless new revenue sources develop. Britain's last contribution to budgetary aid was $A200,000 in 1986.

According to Central Bank of Vanuatu figures, foreign development aid grants in 1985 totalled VT524.4 million, with the country's major donors Britain, France, Australia and New Zealand, accounting for VT385.7 million of this figure. In 1986 the total was VT410.1 million, with a decline in the contribution made by Britain offset to some extent by increased contributions from Australia and France.

Tax system. Vanuatu has neither personal income tax nor tax on company profits. Main tax revenue is derived from duty imposed on imports and exports. In the 1987 recurrent budget revenue, these were expected to account for 59.5 per cent of the total. There are also company registration fees, taxes on goods and services (providing 15.7 per cent of revenues), shipping registration fees, licences, airport and wharfage taxes and a 10 per cent tourist tax on hotel and restaurant charges.

Banks. A Finance Centre (tax haven) was created by British legislation and resulted in an influx of banks between 1971 and 1973. The banks are Westpac Banking Corporation (Vila), Australia and New Zealand Bank (Vila and Santo), Bank Gutzwiller, Kurz, Bungener (Overseas) Ltd (Vila), Hong Kong and Shanghai Banking Corporation (Vila), Vanuatu Savings Bank (Vila), Central Bank of Vanuatu (Vila), Development Bank of Vanuatu (Vila and Santo). In mid 1988 Westpac Banking Corporation was expected to take over the Vanuatu Branch of the Hong Kong and Shanghai Banking Corporation. Banking hours are generally 0800–1100; 1330–1500 Monday to Friday.

Trust companies. Seven trust companies maintain offices in Vanuatu offering a full range of trustee services.

Finance centre. A Finance Centre Association exists, composed of international banks, trust companies, international affiliated chartered accountants and solicitors. The association has effectively promoted Vanuatu as an international finance centre. The tax haven legislation has been designed specifically to encourage the use of its income-tax-free environment, using as a basis British laws and adapting them to meet the special requirements of an international finance centre. Like the Bahamas, Bermuda, Cayman Islands and Nauru, Vanuatu's finance centre is known as a "pure tax haven", having no company or personal income tax, no capital gains or profits tax and no estate or death duties.

Company registration. The total number of companies, including local, overseas and exempt, registered at the end of 1984 was 1039. This had increased to 1109 at the end of 1985, but declined slightly to 1105 at the end of 1986. New registrations during 1986 for exempt companies totalled 109.

Of considerable importance to the finance centre was the enactment in 1986 of the new Companies Act No. 12 which helped to consolidate the dual system of company laws and regulations inherited from the days of the Condominium. Several changes were brought about by the Act, including the need for companies registered under French law to reregister as Vanuatu companies. French law relating to companies in Vanuatu is ex-

pected to be repealed at a date to be determined. Details of other changes brought about by the Act may be obtained from the Registrar, PO Box 92, Port Vila.

Finance centre employment and performance. The finance centre is seen to occupy a significant position in the economy of Vanuatu, not the least reason for which is the amount of employment created by the institutions within the centre, and the degree of indigenisation which is taking place. In 1981, total local employment in the finance centre was 322, of whom 210 were expatriate and 112 Ni-Vanuatu. The Ni-Vanuatu component has grown quickly. The respective figures in 1984 were 123 expatriate and 257 Ni-Vanuatu, and by the end of 1986, 98 expatriate and 272 Ni-Vanuatu.

In 1985 earnings of banks on non-resident assets amounted to VT2625.7 million and in 1986 VT4155.8 million. Gross income of trust companies was VT332.6 million in 1985 and VT271.1 million, a decline of 18.5 per cent, but gross income of accounting firms was respectively VT222.8 million and VT261.5 million, a rise of 17.4 per cent. Legal firms increased their gross income from VT54 million in 1985 to VT67.1 million in 1986, a rise of 24.3 per cent.

Currency. A national currency called the Vatu came into circulation in March 1982 and was issued by the Central Bank of Vanuatu.

Investment incentives. Certain tax exemptions covering import duties and export duties may be granted to new enterprises. Encouragement is given to industries involving fishing, processing of agricultural or marine products, tourist industries and other spheres, with minimum levels of investment stipulated. Information of a detailed nature on investment incentives may be obtained from any member of the Finance Centre Association in Port Vila. In addition the Government publishes a comprehensive guide entitled *Investing in Vanuatu: a guide to entrepreneurs*. This is available from the Ministry of Finance, Commerce, Industry and Tourism, PO Box 31, Port Vila.

Development plans. Vanuatu's First National Development Plan covered the period 1982–86, and was designed to achieve six main objectives: balanced rural and regional growth; increasing natural resource utilisation; realisation of the nation's human resource potential; private sector contribution; preservation of cultural and environmental heritage; and economic self-reliance. In his preface to the mid-term review of the plan, Prime Minister Father Walter Lini said that great strides were being made towards achieving the goals set. The 1984 review, however, pointed out that there were still a number of constraints to such objectives as balanced rural and regional development, with most development tending to occur in the urban areas and thus benefiting only 20 per cent of the population. In addition, the legacies of the dual administration in such areas as education, with its divided system, were more difficult to overcome than had been thought. Economic self-sufficiency for the country, once thought to be a feasible goal by 1990, is now thought to be a long-term objective which will be achieved upon completion of the third Plan period, i.e. 1996 or later.

The Second National Development Plan was still in preparation in late 1987.

TRANSPORT. The island of Efate has about 246 km of all-weather roads, and Espiritu Santo about 253 km. There are also roads on Tanna (150 km), Pentecost (144 km), Ambrym (50 km), Ambae (70 km), Malakula (201 km) and Epi/Lamen (58 km). Total road kilometres in 1986 were 1353.

Vehicles. New motor registrations have shown a steady increase in recent years. In 1981 there were 3821 registered vehicles in the country, in 1983, 4157 and in 1985, 4234. In 1986, 281 new registrations were recorded.

Overseas airlines. Vanuatu acquired its own international airline in 1983, Air Vanuatu, co-owned and managed by Ansett Airlines of Australia. The agreement was terminated in early 1986 when the partners disagreed on the terms of the contract. The result was an immediate drop in Vanuatu's tourism figures. Although Ansett maintained a weekly service from Australia to Vanuatu, it tended to advertise its aircraft rather than the destination. In mid-1987 negotiations for Vanuatu's flag carrrier to take to the air again under different management were proceeding, and the nation had a fully-staffed operation and new offices in Port Vila but no aeroplane. In early 1988 an agreement was reached with Australian Airlines.

Air Pacific connects Fiji with Brisbane via Port Vila twice a week. Air Caledonie International links Noumea with Vila four times a week. Air Nauru provides a weekly service from Nauru to Vila via Honiara. Air Nauru also flies between Auckland and Vila once a week, as does UTA. Ansett's Vila service flies from Melbourne to Vila via Sydney once a week and from Melbourne via Sydney and Brisbane once a week. Australian Airlines flying as Air-Vanuatu provides a weekly service between Sydney and Port Vila.

Domestic airlines. Domestic services are provided by Air Melanesiae, formed in 1966 by the amalgamation of New Hebrides Airways Ltd (British) and Hebridair (French). Air Melanesiae uses Britten-Norman Islanders, Twin Otter 300 turbo-props and Banderantie aircraft to provide services to 27 ports within Vanuatu and also Magenta airport near Noumea in New Caledonia. Air Tropicana, which has provided charter and taxi services for a number of years, is soon to withdraw from service and re-emerge as Dovair (Domestic Airline of Vanuatu), a collaboration between Tropicana's founder Keith Barlow, and another local businessman. ,

Airfields. The main international airport is near Vila, several kilometres out of town and called Bauerfield, after a US Air Force commander in World War II. A new terminal building was opened in 1971, run by the Vila Chamber of Commerce. The strip is 2231 m long. Upgrading is planned at a cost of VT615.6 million.

Santo's airport is at Pekoa, a reconditioned wartime strip. The runway was sealed in 1976 to take F-27 and B-737 aircraft in all-weather conditions.

Other airfields are at Torres, Sola and Mota Lava in the Banks, Maewo Island, Longana, and Walaha on Ambae, West Coast on Santo, Norsup, South West Bay and Lamap on Malakula, Craig Cove and Ulei on Ambrym, Lonorore on Pentecost, Valesdir and Lamen Bay on Epi, Emae and Tongoa in the Shepherds, Dillon's Bay and Ipota on Erromango, Lenakel on Tanna and Anelghowat on Anatom.

Lenakel airstrip on Tanna receives infrequent international flights of a tourist nature from Magenta in New Caledonia. A customs officer is flown from Port Vila to attend to formalities. On Efate the wartime strip at Quoin Hill is occasionally used for domestic services.

International aircraft arrivals in Vanuatu in 1985 totalled 999. Of these, 833 were at Port Vila and one at Tanna. Domestic arrivals in 1985 numbered 12,953, 2813 at Vila, 2674 at Santo and 7466 at other islands.

Port facilities. Ports of entry are Port Vila and Luganville (Santo), plus Forari with prior radio permission. The deep sea wharf at Pontoon Bay was completed in 1972 and is 228 metres long with 11 metres alongside. The wharf at Santo can accommodate vessels of 156 metres with a draught of 10 metres. There are 12 wharves in all and 150 anchorages regularly used to load and unload cargo by lighter. Cruise ships call at Champagne Bay in Espiritu Santo, Anatom Island, and Havannah Harbour on Efate, the latter renamed Paradise Bay for tourist purposes. None of these, however, constitutes an official port of entry. About 75 per cent of Vanuatu's exports go out over the Luganville wharf, while approximately 73 per cent of the country's imports come in over the wharf at Port Vila.

Shipping services. International cargo services are operated by the French companies Sofrana Unilines and Compagnie Generale Maritime. Other companies are the Bank Line, Swire/NYK, Kyowa Line and a consortium comprised of NGAL/PGL and CONPAC/NEL. The domestic inter-island shipping fleet consists of four largish vessels and a considerable number of smaller freight–passenger vessels. In addition to the commercial vessels, the Government has a fleet of 12 vessels for administrative purposes.

In June 1987 the Government took delivery of its first patrol boat, the *Tukoro*, at a ceremony in Jervoise Bay, Western Australia. The occasion made Vanuatu the first country in the region to accept an Australian-sponsored patrol boat.

SHIPPING REGISTRY. The Vanuatu Maritime Law and the Vanuatu Maritime Regulations, closely resembling those of Liberia, were gazetted in 1981, establishing the Vanuatu flag of convenience. The Marine Administrator is Investors' Trust Limited, a Vanuatu trust company, but the actual registration is handled in New York by the Deputy Commissioner of Maritime Affairs. Coopers and Lybrand, international accountants, act in various ports in the world as agent for the Commissioner of Maritime Affairs.

Surveys. All ships must be surveyed and classification societies recognised by Vanuatu are Lloyds' Register of Shipping, London; American Bureau of Shipping, New York; Norske Veritas, Oslo; Bureau Veritas, Paris; Germanischer Lloyd, Hamburg; Nippon Kaiji Kyokai, Tokyo.

Competency certificates. Crew members of Vanuatu ships must be qualified and hold valid licences issued by a recognised maritime nation appropriate to their station on the ships. The Commissioner or Deputy Commissioner has a discretion as to the suitability of the licence.

International conventions. International conventions relating to shipping and ratified by Vanuatu are: International Convention on Load Lines, 1966; International Convention for the Safety of Life at Sea, 1974; Convention on the International Regulations for Preventing Collisions at Sea, 1972; International Convention on Civil Liability for Oil Pollution Damage, 1969; International Convention for the Prevention of Pollution of the Sea by Oil, 1954; protocol of 1978 relating to the International Convention for the Safety of Life at Sea, 1974.

Registration of ships under the Vanuatu Shipping Registry is thought to be showing dynamic growth. The number of ships registered annually rose from two in 1981, the first year of the registry, to 22 in 1985, to 53 in 1986. At the end of 1986 there were 117 ships on the register. Revenues collected rose from VT18.5 million in 1985 to VT 29.1 million in 1986. Vanuatu's maritime law is to be amended in order to bring it more up-to-date and to make the country competitive with other flag of convenience centres.

COMMUNICATIONS. There are automatic telephone exchanges in Vila and Santo. There is internal radiophone between Vila, Santo and district headquarters, and a teleradio network of more than 100 stations, including plantations, missions, etc.

Overseas telephone links, boosted by the activities of the finance centre, are handled through Vanitel (Vanuatu International Telecommunications). Once a 50/50 partnership between Cable and Wireless (UK) Ltd and Cables et Radio (France), Vanitel in July 1987 became a three-way arrangement, with the Vanuatu Government taking a one-third share. Vanitel operates an Intelsat standard B earth station. There is no automatic gateway exchange. Semi-automatic working is provided from switchboards at the Telecommunications Department.

A Government Coast Station at Vila provides public telephone and telegraph services to ships; there is also a privately operated service at Palikulo.

The Meteorological Department provides weather information from six reporting stations and transmits to Fiji as part of the Western Pacific meteorological network.

Telex. Telex services were introduced in 1973. There are direct links to Sydney, Noumea and Hong Kong and these may be extended to most countries. Telex services are confined to Port Vila and Luganville. Full postal services and telegraph (radio telephone only) operate at Lolowai on Ambae, Norsup on Malakula, Isangel on Tanna and at Tongoa airfield. There are postal agents at Lonorore and Melsisi on Pentecost, Toak (Ambrym), Sola (Vanua Lava) and Liro (Paama). The volume of domestic mail rose from 300,000 items in 1981 to 500,000 items in 1984. Incoming international mail increased from 1.7 million items in 1981 to more than two million items in 1984.

Philatelic sales have been an important source of revenue for many years, representing over half of all stamp sales. In 1983 philatelic sales amounted in value to VT19.64 million and the following year to VT23 million.

Broadcasting. Radio Vanuatu now broadcasts seven days a week and offers programmes in Bislama (Vanuatu pidgin), English and French. Morning programmes begin at 6.00 am and end at 1.00 pm — Monday to Friday. Programmes for Saturday begin at 4.00 pm and end at 10.00 pm. Sundays' programmes begin at 4.00 pm and end at 9.00 pm. Weekday evening programmes, from 4.00 pm to 10.00 pm, include a variety of music and information. There is no local television. Video is popular in urban areas, with at least six video libraries in Vila alone.

Newspaper. A weekly newspaper, *Vanuatu Weekly/Hebdomadaire* is published by the Office of Information and Public Relations. It is tri-lingual, with content in French, English and Bislama.

A tourist-oriented publication, *What to do in Vanuatu*, is produced irregularly by the tourism industry.

WATER AND ELECTRICITY. A private undertaking, Union Electrique d'Outre Mer (UNELCO) has a contract for the generation and supply of electricity in Vila. Voltage is 240. A private company in Santo supplies a limited area of the town. Cost of electricity from both systems is high.

The Public Works Department provides reticulated water supplies to Vila, Santo, Isangel (Tanna), Lakatora and Norsup (Malakula). Vila's water supply comes from a semiartesian aquifer at Tagabe, 3 km from the centre. According to the 1979 census, 56 per cent of the population have a running water supply within 100 metres of their dwellings, but it is believed that this includes unprotected streams and open dry wells. It is estimated that about 25 per cent of the rural population has access to a relatively safe and reliable water supply.

Rural sanitation. It was reported in the census statements that 74 per cent of the population had access to sanitary facilities, mainly pit latrines, but most were regarded as inadequate and, according to the plan, 103,000 people would have to be provided with sanitary latrines before the end of the decade. It was estimated that VT463.5 million would be spent on the plan's rural water supply programme and VT41,200,000 on latrine construction. The plan's mid-term review admitted that a manpower shortage was delaying the schemes.

MAJOR OFFICE HOLDERS

President and Head of State:
   Fred Timakata
Prime Minister, Minister of Public Service, Justice, Information and Civil Aviation:
   Father Walter Hadye Lini
Attorney-General:
   Silas Hakwa

Chairman of National Council of Chiefs (Malvatumauri):
  Chief Willie Bongmatur

GOVERNMENT MINISTRIES AND DEPARTMENTS
Agriculture, Fisheries & Forestry Ministry, PO Box 129, Port Vila, Tel.: 3406
Divisions: Department of Agriculture & Forestry, Fisheries Department
Auditor General's Office, PO Box 757, Port Vila, Tel.: 3232
Finance, Commerce, Industry & Tourism Ministry, PO Box 31, Port Vila, Tel.: 2951
Divisions: Accountant General's Department, Budget Control Section, Co-operative Department, Customs Department, Development/Enterprises, Industries Price Control, Registrar & Receiver General, National Tourism Office
Transport, Communications & Public Works Ministry, PO Box 381, Port Vila, Tel.: 2790 Divisions: Meteorological Department, Ports & Marine Department, Posts & Telecommunications Department, Postal Services, Radio Services, Telephone Service, Commercial Section, Public Works Department
Education, Youth & Sports Ministry, PO Box 153, Port Vila, Tel.: 2309
Divisions: Primary Education, Secondary Education, Tertiary Education, District Education Office, Social Development Service, Teaching Service Commission.
Lands, Energy & Rural Water Supply Ministry, PO Box 151, Port Vila, Tel.: 3105 Divisions: Department of Geology, Mines & Rural Water Supply, Department of Land Surveys, Department of Land Records, Department of Lands, Lands Referee Office, Vila Urban Land Corporation
Foreign Affairs & External Trade Ministry, PO Box 124, Port Vila, Tel.: 2413.
Health Ministry, PO Box 102, Port Vila, Tel.: 2545 Divisions: Central Hospital, Rural Health Service, Vanuatu Nursing School, Public Health, Malaria Control, Dentistry
Home Affairs Ministry, PO Box 157, Port Vila, Tel.: 2252 Divisions: Civil Status Office, Electoral Office, Labour Headquarters, District Labour Office,

Vanuatu National Trade Testing Scheme,. Local Government Department, National Council of Chiefs (Malvatumauri), Vanuatu Police Force, Vanuatu Mobile Force
Parliament, Parliament Building, Port Vila, Tel.: 2951
President's Office, State House, Port Vila, Tel.: 3055
Prime Minister, Minister of Justice & Public Service, PO Box Box 110, Port Vila, Tel.: 2413 Divisions: Attorney General's Office, Council of Ministers, Information and Public Relations Office, Judiciary, Public Solicitor, Language Services, National Planning & Statistics Office, Public Service Department, Radio Vanuatu, Civil Aviation.
National Tourism Office, PO Box 31, Port Vila, Tel.: 2813
Radio Vanuatu, PO Box 49, Port Vila, Tel.: 2999
National Planning and Statistics Office, PO Box 741, Port Vila Tel.: 2605
Vanuatu Weekly-Hebdomadaire, PO Box 927, Port Vila, Tel.: 2999

FOREIGN MISSIONS
Australian High Commission, PO Box 111, Port Vila, Tel.: 2777
British High Commission, PO Box 567, Port Vila, Tel.: 3100
French Embassy, PO Box 60, Port Vila, Tel.: 2353
ESCAP Pacific Operations Centre, PO Box 503, Port Vila, Tel.: 3458
New Zealand High Commission, PO Box 161, Port Vila, Tel.: 2933

HISTORY. The islands have been inhabited for several thousand years. Archaeology in the group is still in its infancy, but some useful clues to the past have already been obtained. Pottery has been found on many of the northern and central islands, namely Espiritu Santo, Malo, Aore, Ambae, Malakula, Makura, Tongoa and Efate. However, little has been found on the southern islands of Erromango, Tanna, Anatom (Aneityum), Aniwa and Futuna (Erronan).

The making of pottery appears to have died out in all islands except Espiritu Santo (where it is still made on the west coast) between AD 1300 and 1400. A French archaeologist, Jose Garanger, believes this may have been due to the arrival of conquerors from the south, headed by a chief known in tradition as Roymata. At Eretoka (Hat) Island off the coast of Efate, Garanger has excavated Roymata's elaborate burial site, complete with human sacrifices. The site has been dated at AD 1265.

A feature of archaeological research is the similarity from island to island of shell and stone artefacts. The earliest radiocarbon date so far established for settlement in the southern islands is 420 BC on Tanna. A site on Aore in the northern part of the group yielded a date of 1300 BC.

First European. The first European to see Vanuatu was the Spanish explorer Pedro Fernandez de Quiros. He sighted several islands in the Banks Group and Maewo on 25 April, 1606. About a week later, he anchored in a large bay at an island which he called Austrialia del Espiritu Santo, now known simply as Espiritu Santo or Santo. To the large bay, he gave the name of St Philip and St James, and in its south-eastern corner he planned a future city to be known as La Nueva Jerusalem and located on the banks of the River Jordan. Officials with high-sounding titles were appointed as civic dignitaries but as there were no women aboard the expedition ships, the proposed settlement remained a dream. A stockade fortified with 'sturdy stakes and earthworks with loopholes' was built there. There were fireworks, religious processions, high masses, and much beating of drums. After two vain attempts to explore the eastern coast of the island, which Quiros believed to be the Southern Continent, the strong easterly winds which prevented exploration also negated attempts by the mariners to regain their former anchorage near the Jordan River. On the stormy night of 11 June Quiros in his flagship was forced from his anchorage and sailed northward, deserting his two consorts. They finally left the bay on 26 June under command of Torres, after a total stay of 55 days.

Bougainville and Cook. Nothing more was heard of the group until 1768 when the French navigator Bougainville passed between Maewo and Pentecost, landed on Ambae, and continued on between Santo and Malakula. It remained for Captain Cook to discover and chart the greater part of the group. In 1774, he entered the area from the north, and, in sailing southward, he discovered most of the southern islands. It was he who gave the name New Hebrides to the islands.

In 1789, William Bligh sighted several of the islands of what he called the Banks Group during his open boat voyage following the mutiny in the *Bounty*. The Torres Islands, north-west of the Banks Group, were among the last islands in the Pacific to be discovered by Europeans, the first positive report of them coming from Captain J. E. Erskine of HMS *Havannah* in 1850.

Sandalwooders. The Irish seaman Peter Dillon found sandalwood at Port Resolution, Tanna, in 1825. This led to the development of a trade in sandalwood on both Tanna and Erromango. The unscrupulous methods of the sandalwooders resulted in numerous bloody affrays with the islanders. These, in turn, led to the massacre at Erromango in 1839 of the first European missionaries to try to land in the group — the Revs John Williams and James Harris, of the London Missionary Society.

However, in the following year, the Rev. T. Heath, of the LMS, sailed from Samoa with several Samoan teachers, of whom he left two at Tanna, two at Aniwa and two at Erromango. Futuna and Anatom each got two Samoan teachers in 1841, and in the same year the LMS sent the Revs George Turner and Henry Nisbet to Tanna. All these early missionaries had little success, and by 1845 only the two Samoans at Anatom remained.

In 1848, the Samoans at Anatom were joined by the Rev. John Geddie, of the Presbyterian Church of Nova Scotia. Another Presbyterian, the Rev. John Inglis, arrived in 1852. By 1856, all but 200 of the 3000 to 4000 Anatomese were under Christian instruction. During the next few years, Anatom was a base from which Presbyterian missionary influence spread to the islands as far north as Espiritu Santo.

Meanwhile, the Church of England (Melanesian Mission) had entered Vanuatu through New Zealand with visits to the northern islands of the group by Bishop George Augustus Selwyn. In 1859, after many setbacks, Selwyn established headquarters for the Melanesian Mission at Mota in the Banks Group. Selwyn had a great colleague in John Coleridge Patteson. Patteson reduced the Mota language to writing, made it the lingua franca of the mission, and used it as a medium for training native teachers.

In 1860, the Presbyterians in the southern islands suffered a severe setback when a measles epidemic killed thousands of islanders. The survivors blamed the missionaries for the epidemic and revolted against them. Two European missionaries were killed on Erromango and two attacked on Tanna. The two islands were then abandoned. However, new recruits arrived in 1863 and the station at Erromango was reopened. Other missionaries were sent to Efate, Futuna (Erronan) and Aniwa.

Blackbirding. The first recruitment of native labour was made by whaling ships from Twofold Bay, NSW, in 1847. They were used as shepherds on Ben Boyd's sheep properties in the Monaro district. Captain Kirsopp obtained 65 men from Tanna and Erromango and landed them at Twofold Bay on 9 April 1847. The natives found the Monaro far too cold and the experiment was not a success. Then some sandalwood cutters began to recruit native labour for the cotton plantations in Fiji and the cotton and sugar plantations of Queensland. The first shipload of islanders left Tanna for Fiji in 1864. Others soon followed. At first, this labour trade was orderly and humane. But within a few years there were abuses.

Protests, particularly from missionaries, about 'blackbirding' from Vanuatu and other islands forced the British Parliament to pass the Pacific Islanders Protection Bill in 1872.

Under this law, cases of actual kidnapping became rare in Vanuatu. But a Royal Commission in 1883 found that misrepresentation and cajolery by recruiters were virtually universal. By 1876, Vanuatu had provided over 7200 labourers for Queensland; about 4500 went to Fiji between 1868 and 1878; and about 2000 were taken to New Caledonia around the same time. Mortality among them was heavy. For instance, of 600 Erromangans recuited between 1868 and 1878, only 200 returned to their homes. Those who did return frequently brought diseases with them that killed many who had stayed at home. European traders also brought decimating diseases.

Against this sombre background of de-

population, the missionaries continued to extend their work of teaching, preaching and pacification. By 1885, most of the islands had their missions. Meanwhile, the number of European traders and planters in the islands was increasing, particularly on Ambrym, Ambae and Efate.

Most of the settlers were either British or French, who bought large areas of land from the islanders. One of the biggest landbuyers, however, was not a settler but a speculator. This was John Higginson, a British-born naturalised Frenchman of New Caledonia, who asked the French to annex Vanuatu. His request was refused. About the same time, a French plan was put forward to allow liberated convicts from New Caledonia to settle in the group. The Presbyterian missionary J. G. Paton organised a protest movement in Australia against this plan, and so began an Australian agitation for annexation. The French Government countered in 1878, suggesting to the British Government an agreement to respect the independence of Vanuatu.

Birth of the condominium. Eight years of proposals, counter-proposals, gunboat diplomacy and alarms in Australia followed, during which Higginson formed a company in Noumea which claimed to buy almost all the land in the group.

In 1886, Britain and France agreed to set up a Joint Naval Commission for safeguarding order in Vanuatu. A convention to this effect was signed a year later — on 16 November 1887. A declaration, signed in Paris on 26 January 1888, settled the details of the Joint Naval Commission.

The commission was charged with the protection of the lives and property of the subjects of Britain and France. It was composed of two French and two British naval officers from warships in Western Pacific waters, and was presided over alternately by the British and French commanders. But the commission did not work, as there was no civil law to enforce any kind of contract. Finally, in 1906, while German interests were trying to gain a foothold, the British and French Governments agreed to establish a condominium in the group.

In Queensland, economic pressure for repatriation of Islands labour went on for many years and the first Australian Federal

Government accelerated it by imposing an excise duty of £3 per ton on all sugar produced, with a rebate of £2 per ton on sugar produced by all-white labour. By 1906 virtually all islanders had been returned home, but recruiting of labour for New Caledonia went on for several years.

After World War I, the continuing depopulation of the group created a serious labour shortage. The French met this by introducing labourers from Tonkin (now Vietnam) on five-year indentures. Later, during the depression of the thirties, the French planters received bounties which kept them out of financial difficulties.

British planters, on the other hand, could not import Asian labour and were not allowed to employ indentured Tonkinese until the late thirties. Also, they received no financial help during the depression. Thus they either lost their copra trade to the French or were forced to take French nationality to stay in business.

World War II. In July 1940, after France fell, the Frenchmen in Vanuatu, under Resident Commissioner Henri Sautot, were the first of their nation in overseas territories to rally to the Free French flag of General de Gaulle.

After Japan entered the war at the end of 1941, Vila and Santo became huge forward bases for the Americans. The country enjoyed a brief period of dollar prosperity, which, with the end of the war, petered out.

Many of the roads, bridges, wharves and airstrips built by the Americans became overgrown or fell down. A few wartime relics still survive. But much of the American war material, including trucks, bulldozers and other mechanical equipment, was dumped in the Segond Channel before the Americans withdrew.

Jon Frum Movement. A native movement that began on Tanna in 1940–41 became more firmly entrenched after the arrival of the Americans and their obvious material possessions. Its followers believed that a figure known as Jon Frum would deliver them from the influence of missionaries and Europeans generally, and that he would bring with him great wealth in the form of refrigerators, trucks, canned food, cigarettes and so forth. The appearance of these goods along with the openhanded Americans convinced the Tannese that these things were freely available in the outside world and that they had been kept from them by the Europeans for ulterior motives.

At one period during the war it appeared that the movement would erupt into violence, but this was averted when the leaders were gaoled. The movement has had a number of crises since then — usually when some man has announced that the mantle of Jon Frum has fallen on him. At its most extreme periods, the movement has been anti-missionary, anti-government and anti-white. In 1987 many Tannese were still adherents, but they are generally no longer hostile.

Nagriamel. A movement of another kind, the first political organisation in Vanuatu, came into being in the late 1960s. Called Nagriamel, it was said in 1969 to have about 10,000 followers, mainly in the northern islands. Its leader was a man of mixed ethnic origins, Jimmy Tupou Patuntun Stevens, also known as Chief President Moses. The organisation had a settlement on French company land at Vanafo, near Luganville.

Originally, Nagriamel's aim was confined to obtaining rights over what its followers described as 'dark bush' — land owned by Europeans but never developed by them. But more recently, Nagriamel became increasingly involved in politics. In 1971, Nagriamel presented a petition to the United Nations asking for 'an act of free choice' on the issue of independence in Vanuatu. Britain and France refused to discuss the matter at the time. But the French subsequently set out to influence Stevens. In 1975, for example, he was taken to Paris and presented to President Giscard d'Estaing. Later that year, Stevens demanded independence for the island of Santo and an end to the British presence in the territory. This resulted in a declaration by the British and French Resident Commissioners that, under the 1914 Protocol, neither power would withdraw from the territory without the other.

The existence of Nagriamel, the establishment of three or four other political parties from 1971 onwards, and the disruptive tactics by the Advisory Council were among the factors that led the British and French Governments to agree on some constitutional reforms in 1974–75. These included the establishment of municipal councils in Vila and Santo, and the replacement of the Advisory Council with a Representative Assembly.

Representative Assembly. Elections for the municipal councils were held in August 1975. A pro-French alliance of three parties won 15 of the 16 seats in Santo, while the pro-French UCNH (Union des Communautes des Nouvelles Hebrides) won 18 of the 24 seats in Vila. The remaining six seats in Vila went to members of the New Hebrides National Party, a strongly pro-New Hebridean movement now called the Vanuaaku Party, which aimed for independence in 1977. By contrast, elections for the Representative Assembly in November 1975 resulted in a triumph for the National Party. It won 17 of the 29 'people's' seats, against 10 for the UCNH and two for an alliance of Nagriamel and the Mouvement Autonomiste des Nouvelles Herbrides. The Assembly elections were accompanied by demonstrations and accusations of bribery and corruption. Thirteen other seats in the Assembly were filled from the Chamber of Commerce (six seats), Co-operative Federations (three) and customary chiefs (four).

When elections were held on 29 November 1977, there was a boycott by the majority of the Vanuaaku Party. This resulted in the Assembly being representative mainly of pro-French groups, and to be lacking moral and political authority.

Agreement was reached between all parties in 1978 and a Government of National Unity was formed with the Vanuaaku Party holding five of the 10 seats, including that of Deputy Chief Minister (Walter Lini), the Chief Minister being Fr. Gerard Leymang, who had the casting vote.

A general election followed on 14 November 1979, and resulted in the Vanuaaku Party winning 26 of the 39 seats. Fr. Lini was elected Chief Minister by the new Representative Assembly on 29 November 1979.

'Moderate' party representatives on the northern island of Santo and the southern island of Tanna refused to accept the results, alleging Vanuaaku Party irregularities in the polling. They declared 'independence' of the two islands in February 1980, with Santo being renamed 'Vemarana' and Tanna 'Tafea', an acronym now used for all the Southern Islands.

A second declaration of secession by 'Vemarana' was made on 28 May but, despite attempts by the secessionists to delay the granting of independence to Vanuatu, including attacks on police posts and some looting, independence was declared on 30 July. There were further outbreaks of violence, which resulted in the death on Tanna of a Member of the Assembly, Alexis Yolou, and the death on Santo of a son of Nagriamel's leader, Jimmy Stevens. Asserting its authority in the face of inaction by the British and French forces, the newly-independent Government applied for help to the Papua New Guinea Government, which sent troops to Santo. All resistance by the secessionists collapsed when the PNG troops captured the secessionists' headquarters at Fanafo outside Santo town on 31 August.

More than 200 rebels, including Jimmy Stevens, were sentenced to imprisonment. The Vanuaaku Party has continued in government. The first National Parliament was dissolved on 5 September 1983, and the first general election since independence was held on 2 November 1983. The Vanuaaku Party retained power, winning 24 seats, two less than in the previous election, and the Opposition parties (Union of Moderate Parties, Namaki Aute, Nagriamel and Fren Melanesian Parties) winning 15 seats.

Vanuatu's determination to take an independent stance in foreign policy, and its resulting membership of the association of non-aligned nations together with its diplomatic recognition of such countries as Cuba, Vietnam and Libya, brought criticism from the major powers of the Pacific rim, particularly the US. By late 1987, however, much of the controversy had subsided.

The second general election since independence, in November 1987, resulted in the return of the Vanuaaku Party presided over by long-serving Prime Minister Father Walter Lini. His authority, however, continued to be challenged regularly.

Further information. Jeremy MacClancy's *To Kill a Bird with Two Stones*, Vila, 1981, is a short but comprehensive history of Vanuatu until independence. Dorothy Shineberg's *They Came for Sandalwood*, Melbourne, 1967, gives an account of the trade which helped change the pattern of Melanesian economies. Roger Thomson examines the Australian historical connection in *Australian Imperialism in the Pacific: The Expansionist Era*, Melbourne, 1980. Various Ni-Vanuatu contributors describe many aspects of their country in *Vanuatu*, Suva, 1980. Norman Douglas's *Vanuatu–a guide*, Sydney, 1986, contains much historical background as well as detailed descriptions of islands and towns in Vanuatu.

VANUATU ISLANDS IN DETAIL
BANKS GROUP. The Banks Islands are a scattered group lying 80 km north-east of Vanuatu proper. They include Vanua Lava, Gaua, Mere Lava (or Star Peak), Ureparapara, Mota (or Sugarloaf), Mota Lava (or Valuwa), Vatganai (Vatu Rhandi), Merig and the Reef Islets. Vanua Lava and Gaua are each about 24 km long and 20 km across. The group is of volcanic origin, and extremely fertile. It enjoys a good annual rainfall and vegetation is luxuriant.

Vanua Lava. It was first explored by Bishop Selwyn, who located the excellent harbour of Port Patteson and named it after the man who became the first Bishop of Melanesia. There is good anchorage also at Vuras Bay. The Melanesian Mission has a school at Pt Patteson. Mt Suretimeat is an active volcano. It is also the highest peak on the island, 950 metres, and has extensive deposits of sulphur which were worked at one time by a French company.

Gau. Gaua is very broken. Mt Garet is an active volcano. Highest point on the island is 700 metres. There is a crater lake about 6 km long.

Ureparapara. It appears to be the top of an old volcano, one side of which has disappeared. Thus a fine harbour has been created, which can accommodate large ships. The island lies 12 km north-west of the Reef Islets (three low, wooded islands on a reef about eight km north of Vanua Lava) and rises to a height of 742 metres.

THE TORRES GROUP, which lie to the northwest of the Banks Group, consist of a chain of small, high islands — Hiu, Metoma, Tegua, Loh and Toga. Hiu is the largest, about 16 km long by three km across. A once considerable population has dwindled now to a little more than 200.

Espiritu Santo. Known as Santo, this is the biggest island, being 145 km long and 65 km wide. It has a mountain range along the western division, with a peak, Mt Tabwemasana, rising to 1877 metres. It is heavily wooded, and there are many streams. There are some good harbours, and in the north is the great Bay of St Philip and St James.

At the southern extremity, between Santo and Aore island, is the Segond Channel where most of the European population of the island is congregated, with Luganville the next biggest European settlement to Vila. (There is some confusion in the use of 'Luganville' and 'Santo'; both usually refer to the settlement that has developed out of the former US base on the Segond Channel, although Santo can also refer to the whole island of Espiritu Santo.)

The population of Santo and Malo according to a 1986 estimate was 25,313, and of Luganville 5621.

Santo was where, at the head of St Philip and St James Bay, known locally as Big Bay, the Spanish navigator Quiros built a short-lived settlement in 1606. A low wall, containing two embrasures and the remains of a third, was found at the site of the settlement in January 1967.

As well as a plantation industry, Santo has a growing interest in cattle raising. A small meat cannery in Luganville takes care of surplus beef. An abattoir built to conform to international standards was constructed in 1977.

A tuna fishing industry, based at Palikulo, south-east Santo, was established in 1957, but closed in 1986, after some years of declining production.

There is a hotel and one 'motel' at Luganville, a remarkable number of multipurpose Chinese stores, several churches and most of the other amenities of a small tropical town. Pekoa airport, a few kilometres out of town, is an improved WW II airstrip, but the country's second port of international entry.

Other reminders of WW II linger in Luganville: the number of Quonset huts doing service as cinemas, garages, churches and houses, the number of bunkers dotting the rural landscape and the amount of rusty, congealing metal in the bush or on the reef are constant evidence that during the Pacific conflict there were up to 100,000 servicemen and up to 100 warships here at any one time.

The most obvious reminder of the excess of the war is Million Dollar Point, where the debris of vehicles, weapons and other war technology is still clearly visible at low tide.

Vanafo village, a short distance form Luganville, was the headquarters of Jimmy Stevens' Nagriamel movement (described in the History section). It is possible for visitors to Santo to take a tour which includes Stevens' village, where many of his family still live. They are generally quiet and reserved people, however, and not always anxious to receive visitors.

Santo's economy, depressed in the years immediately following the 'rebellion', shows evidence of picking up again with large-scale projects. Cruise ships call occasionally at Champagne Bay on Santo's east coast, once the scene of American land speculation.

Aore, 24 km in circumference, lies in the narrow strait between Santo and Malo, forming one side of the Segond Channel.

Small islands off the east coast of Santo are Lathi (Sakeo), Dolphin, Elephant, Pilot, Pilotine, Mavea and Aese. Off the south coast are Araki, Tangoa, Aore, Tutuba and Malo. Tangoa should not be confused with Tongoa, south-east of Epi. The Presbyterian Church of Vanuatu has a Bible college at Tangoa, South Santo.

Malo. This is 55 km in circumference, is very fertile and almost all cultivable, as there is only one high point (Mt Mbwelinmbwevu, 346 metres) on the island. There were several European planters on Malo and some of the plantations were up to 2000 hectares.

Malokilikili, Malotina, Maloveleo, Amalo Vorivori, Asuleka and Ratua are small islets off Malo.

Ambae. This island is 38 km long by 14 km across, and rises in places to about 1220 metres. There are lakes in the interior. The Melanesian, Roman Catholic and Church of Christ churches are established on the island. The Melanesian Church has its headquarters for the group at Lolowai (the only good harbour, at the eastern end of Ambae). There are three airstrips on the island.

Maewo (or Aurora) is 46 km long and six km broad. It has a 610 metre central range, which probably accounts for the fact that it has the highest rainfall in the group. There are numerous streams — a large one (north-west coast) that falls over the cliffs at Laka-

rare, was for many years known as a favourite place at which wandering vessels obtained fresh water supplies. The island is well wooded and fertile, but the Melanesian population has dwindled considerably. The combined population of Maewo and Ambae, according to a 1986 estimate is 11,518, with more than four-fifths of that number on Ambae.

Pentecost is 61 km long and 12 km wide. There is a central range, with numerous fertile valleys and many permanent streams on the western side. The islanders on the northern part are expert in various handicrafts, particularly in the braiding of mats and in carving. The Anglican Diocese of Vanuatu, the Churches of Christ and the Roman Catholic Church have stations on this island. Population (est. 1986) is 11,452.

The native name for the island is Raga. A central peak rises to a height of 934 metres.

The islanders were once noted for their large canoes. Since the 1950s they have been better known for their so-called land-diving ceremonies. In these, men leap head-first from towers built of bush timber and vines up to 25 metres high. Bush vines are tied to their ankles and tethered to the tops of the towers. The vines are just short enough and springy enough to break their fall. The ceremony has legendary associations and is generally held shortly before the important yam harvest. In recent years it has become a significant tourist attraction, with hundreds of people travelling to Pentecost to witness the spectacle. Cruising yachts also converge on the island at the time of the dive. Pentecost has basic visitor accommodations.

The island's airstrip is at Lonorore on the east coast. The most highly regarded land-diving ceremony takes place at Bunlap on the south-west coast.

Malakula is the next largest island after Santo, being 88 km long and in parts, 24 km across. A broken range runs the length of the island, rising in one place to form Mount Penot, 892 metres. The western portion is somewhat inaccessible, but the long eastern coast is broken by numerous harbours and bays, with fair-sized streams running through undulating well-wooded country — a fertile region, where many settlers once made their homes.

There is a fine, land-locked harbour, Port

Sandwich, on the south-eastern corner, and along the coast are Bushman Bay and Port Stanley, both well sheltered. The interior is still not very well known, and the islanders may sometimes be unfriendly — it is the home of the people called Big Nambas. The coastal islanders, however, have long been in contact with Europeans. The native population of the island, 18,363 (est. 1986), makes it one of the most heavily populated islands in Vanuatu.

Vanuatu's largest copra plantation was established at Norsup on Malakula during the time of the Condominium. Norsup, while still little more than workers' quarters and copra driers, is the nation's third largest town.

Other projects on Malakula include the very large Metenesel cocoa estate. The island is considered to have vast economic potential.

Off the north-east coast of Malakula are the islands of Vao, Atchin, Wala, Rano, Norsup and Uripiv. Off the south coast are Tomman, Lanur, Akhamb, and the Maskelyne Islands, the chief of which are Vulay, Khuneveo and Sakao.

There are airstrips at Norsup, Lamap and South-West Bay.

Ambrym, 38 km long by 25 km broad, is notable as the scene of more than one eruption by Mt Marum (1336 metres), an active volcano which dominates the island. There was a severe eruption on 6 December 1913, accompanied by a great earthquake, and much of the fertile island was laid waste. Streams of lava ran down into the sea, wiping out numerous coconut plantations. Hundreds of the islanders were rendered homeless, but there was little loss of life.

Mount Benbow, near Mount Marum, erupted in 1929, wiping out several mission stations. There was an eruption in 1946 which considerably altered the landscape. In 1950 after another eruption, 300–400 islanders were resettled on Efate at Mele Maat. The two volcanoes still emit periodic ash-showers and occasionally lava. Population in 1986 was 7828.

Paama. A densely wooded, volcanic island with peaks up to 550 metres high, Paama lies between the south coast of Ambrym and the north coast of Epi. The nearest parts of Ambrym and Epi are about 6 km away. There is a good anchorage on the western side of Paama. The Presbyterian Church has

a station at the village of Liro.

Lopevi. About 5 km east of Paama, is a volcanic cone rising to 1456 metres with a small crater at its summit. An eruption of some magnitude occurred in 1883 and there have been many lesser eruptions since. The Anglican Diocese of Vanuatu has a station on the island.

Epi is a very fertile, well-watered island, about 43 km long and 17 km wide, on which there were once some fine plantations which since have deteriorated. It is mountainous — its highest peak is 851 metres. The main port is Ringdove Bay. Formerly the island was called Tasiko, also Volcano. There are two airstrips. A Presbyterian Church hospital is situated at Vaemali on the north coast. There is also a Presbyterian Church station at Lamen, a small island off the north-west coast. Namuka is a small island off the southern coast. Tafala and Tefala Kiki are islands off the east coast.

Shepherd Islands, so named by Captain Cook, are a volcanic group consisting of seven islands and several islets off the south-eastern extremity of Epi. Tongoa is the largest in the group. It is about 12 km in circumference, with several cone-shaped peaks up to 510 metres high. The island is heavily wooded and densely populated. There is a Presbyterian Church station on the island, and an airstrip. Other islands in the Shepherd Group are Buninga, Tongariki, Falea, Ewose, Laika and Tevala.

Emae. This island is about 16 km in circumference and lies about 22 km due south of Epi. It has three thickly-wooded mountains, the highest of which is 662 metres. The Presbyterian Church has a station and sub-station on the island. About 8 km south of Emae is a small, steep island, Makura; and 9 km south of Makura is Mataso Island, which has a sharp peak 510 metres high. Population of the Shepherds and Emae is 5076 (1986 est.)

Efate Island, 41 km by 22 km, possesses the two finest harbours in the group — Vila and Havannah. Vila is the administrative and commercial centre of Vanuatu. It has hotels, shops, transport facilities and all the amenities of a small but growing tropical town. Population is 14,184 in Vila (1986 census) and 27,239 for Efate (est.).

Vila Harbour is picturesque and within it

are two islets — Fila (Ifira) inhabited by local Ni-Vanuatu and Iririki, once the site of the British Residency, and now the site of a luxury tourist resort. A French administration block was built in 1963 high on the mainland overlooking the harbour. It now contains the Office of the Prime Minister and other government offices.

New buildings constructed in recent years include banks; private office blocks; the government office block on the main street, Kumul Highway; hotels; a post office; stores. Reclamation work has extended and beautified the waterfront area, and there have been extensive housing developments, particularly near Erakor lagoon.

On the waterfront is the Cultural Centre, erected with funds provided by the British and French Governments to mark the jubilee of the condominium in 1956. The centre houses a free library of English and French books and magazines, and a fine museum of native artifacts, fine stuffed birds of the group, geological specimens, etc. Archives contain video and audio tapes.

The influence of the condominium and the mixed population of French, British, Ni-Vanuatu, Vietnamese and Chinese, has made Vila a multi-cultural town in appearance and habits.

There are a number of large plantations on Efate and a growing interest in beef breeding with stud herds of Charolais and Limousin cattle.

Bauerfield, the country's main international airport, is a few kilometres out of Vila. It can take medium jet aircraft. Extensions are planned.

The island of Efate is rugged and covered with tropical rain forest. There are some useful stands of commercial timber and sawmills cut for local consumption.

There are about 246 km of all-weather roads on Efate, the only island in Vanuatu to have a road right around it. Forari is the site of a manganese mine which has now closed.

Hat, Lelepa, Moso (Verao), Nguna (9 by 6 km), Pele, Kakula and Emao are small islands off the northern coast of Efate. Emao should not be confused with Emae south of Epi.

Erromango, 56 km long by 40 km broad, is well watered and fertile. There are various interior ranges, rising to Traitor's Head, 915

metres high. There are no good harbours, but various bays provide safe anchorages — notably, Dillon's Bay, in the north-west; Elizabeth Bay, in the north; Narevin and Cook Bay, in the east.

Europeans were first attracted to Erromango by the extensive stands of sandalwood. Small quantities were still being cut in recent years, although the Government has now placed a ban until December 1991 on further cutting, fearing that the limited supplies may be exhausted.

Many missionaries were killed in the early days by the islanders. The Martyrs' Memorial Church at Dillon's Bay has tablets to the memory of missionaries who died on the island.

Sheep were once successfully raised on Erromango, and good prices obtained for their wool, but the station has been abandoned for many years.

There is an airstrip on the east coast, and another on the west coast.

Goat Island is a small island off the northeast coast. Population of Erromango (1986 est.) is 1000.

Aniwa is 11 km by 3 km, mostly coral, and has no harbour. There is good anchorage, however. It is a fertile place. Dr John G. Paton, a notable Presbyterian missionary, settled there in 1866. The island is sometimes referred to as Nina (or Immer). It is noted for its oranges. It has a small airstrip. Aniwa rises to 40 metres and it lies 20 km northeast of Tanna.

Tanna, 51 km long by 24 km across, is probably the most fertile island in the group. Its southerly position gives it an equable climate. It is exceedingly well watered and well wooded. There are various ranges, and the highest rises to Mount Melen, 1043 metres. The rainfall is heavy but there are dry periods, sometimes lasting two to four months. The soil will grow most tropical produce. The 1979 census showed a population of 15,593.

One of the most accessible active volcanoes in the world is situated 4 km from Port Resolution and 1.5 km from Sulphur Bay. This is Mt Yasur. The crater may be reached by an hour's walking. The volcano is constantly active, and the caldera may be viewed from the crater rim.

There has been no serious eruption on

Tanna since 1878 when the south-eastern end of the island was raised and Port Resolution became inaccessible to deepwater ships. It also lifted 20 metres into the air an isolated pinnacle with a flat top known as 'Cook's Pyramid'. It is said that it was originally at water level, and that Cook used it as a point for taking observations when he was charting the group on his second voyage.

Custom in belief and behaviour is still strong on Tanna and staunch adherents to traditional ways may be found in several villages, the best known of which is Iohnanen, home of Chief Chiak (Jack) Naiva and his people, who regard the Duke of Edinburgh as being of particular significance. Elsewhere on the island, belief in Jon Frum as saviour of the people still exists.

There is a Government station at Isangel; at White Sands there is a former French hospital and a mission station. The former British Hospital is at Lenakel.

There is a regular air service between Vila and Tanna. There is a store and tourist cabins near Lenakel airfield and other tourist bungalows at White Grass.

Anatom, formerly Aneityum, 56 km in circumference, is the most southerly of the group. Mountains rise in the interior to 850 metres, but the valleys and the flat lands along the shore contain much fertile land, which easily supports a small population. All forms of tropical and subtropical fruits and vegetables grow luxuriantly and there is abundant timber including some kauri pine. This has not been exploited in recent years. There are some permanent streams and a fine harbour, Anelghowhat, on the south coast. An airstrip has been built on Inyeug, a small island opposite Anelghowhat and once thought to be haunted.

The climate at Anatom is very pleasant, the mean shade temperature being 24.5°C, and ranging between 15 and 26°C.

About 120 years ago, the native population was estimated at between 3000 and 4000 but a disastrous measles epidemic in 1860, followed by an outbreak of dysentery, wiped out more than 1000 people. Since then the native population has declined and in the 1979 census was only 516.

For many years, Anatom was a base for sandalwooders and whalers. It was also the centre from which missionary influence

spread throughout Vanuatu. Cruise ships call at Anatom occasionally.

Futuna (which should not be confused with the Futuna near Wallis Island) is a small island which lies about 72 km east of Tanna. It runs up to a 388 metre peak in the centre. It is a fertile, well-watered, attractive island, and its native population call the island Erronan. The total population of the southern islands (TAFEA) is 21,727 (1986 est.)

FOR THE TOURIST. The official body concerned with tourism promotion is the National Tourism Office (Peter Taurakoto, General Manager). The office is located on the Kumul Highway in Port Vila, opposite Burns Philp, and there is a branch of the office in Sydney at 17/37 Alexander St, Crows Nest.

Vanuatu has a great deal to offer the visitor looking for an unusual destination: the interesting racial and cultural mix; the evidence of colonial institutions both French and British; a delightful climate and unique attractions such as the land-divers of Pentecost and the volcanoes of Tanna and Ambrym.

Travel arrangements within Vanuatu can be made by the Vila offices of Air Melanesia, Tour Vanuatu, Frank King Tours, Air Caledonie and other smaller or more specialised operators.

Entry formalities. All visitors must be in possession of a valid passport. Vanuatu requires visas from nationals of only a few countries. Visitors must produce an onward ticket and proof may be required of sufficient funds for maintenance while in Vanuatu. A temporary visa may be obtained for a maximum of three months (in stages of a month at a time) upon application to the Immigration Department. Inoculations are not required unless entering from a designated infected area.

Airport tax. There is an airport departure tax of VT1000 payable in Vatu.

Duty free facilities. Shops in Vila offer tourist-orientated goods such as electronics, photographic equipment, jewellery, perfume, precious stones and metals, ornaments at duty free prices. The Vietnamese and Chinese shops are well worth exploring for textiles and oriental-style artifacts. Local handicrafts are in wood, stone, mother-of-pearl and woven materials.

Customs. The following items can be brought into Vanuatu duty free: 200 cigarettes or 100 cigarillos or 50 cigars or 250 g of tobacco; 2 litres of wine and two bottles (max. 1.5 litres) of spirits; 25 centilitres of eau-de-toilette and 10 centilitres of perfume; other dutiable goods not exceeding VT4000. These allowances are per person over the age of 15.

Dogs and cats may enter Vanuatu from New Zealand and Australia providing necessary requirements, including an import permit, are first approved by the Ministry of Agriculture and Fisheries. No other animals may be brought into the country. Meat, dairy products, plants, seeds and flowers are prohibited, without necessary licences from the Ministry of Agriculture.

Motoring. Overseas driving licences and international permits are recognised for a period of 6 months after arrival. Driving is on the right-hand side of the road and though the roads through both Port Vila and Santo are sealed those outside the urban areas are not.

Car rental companies in Port Vila include Avis — tel. 2533; Budget — tel. 3170; Hertz — tel. 2244; National Car Rentals — tel. 2997.

By ship. Visiting the outer islands of the group aboard the small inter-island cutters is an experience for the adventurous. Regular schedules may be obtained from the shipping companies such as David Edson and Co. — tel. 2569; Issachar Dennis and Co. — tel. 3097; Vanua Navigation — tel. 2929.

Yachts. Yachts visiting Vanuatu must first be cleared at Port Vila. Once in the harbour, the yachts are boarded by customs officers and yachtsmen then proceed to the Immigration Department for clearance. Yachts wishing to visit the outer islands should first obtain clearance from Port Vila.

Public transport. Buses are scheduled only in the town areas. Taxis are plentiful in both Port Vila and Santo. The tourist office suggests using a metered taxi. Fares are relatively inexpensive around the town. For longer journeys prices should be agreed upon beforehand.

Sightseeing. Each island has somethig different, with Tanna offering volcanoes, Efate and Santo modern facilities and Pentecost and Malakula the fascination of a people with a living culture and customs. Vila, the administration centre, has some excellent restaurants, interesting shops, an attractive waterfront, a cultural centre, library, museum, musicians' club, the Vila Amateur Theatre, the Natural Science Association and the Michoutouchkine and Pilioko Foundation art gallery.

For divers there is a rare combination of tropical fish, corals and spectacular wrecks in the clear, calm waters of the lagoon. One of the most interesting wrecks is the *President Coolidge*, sunk during World War II and now lying on her side 30 m from the shore of Santo Island at a depth of 20 to 80 m. Spear fishing is discouraged by tour operators, as is the souveniring of fragments of wreckage from either the *Coolidge* or Million Dollar Point. The latter has been designated a national park and removal of pieces of the congealing wreckage will attract fines of up to VT1,000,000.

Visitors are requested *not* to tip or bargain as both practices are at odds with Melanesian custom. This applies to open markets as well as stores.

ACCOMMODATION. Cyclone Uma caused havoc in Vanuatu in early 1987 resulting in damage estimated at $A200 million. Much of this was in the area of Port Vila, and much of it to the country's tourism facilities. By late 1987 it was evident that, although clean-up and restoration had progressed very satisfactorily, Vanuatu's tourism plant would not be fully operational until at least early 1988. Visitor accommodations and, therefore, visitor numbers would continue to be constrained. In late 1987 only one tourist hotel in Port Vila, the Intercontinental, was functioning at full capacity. Others, like the Solaise and Le Lagon, had suffered so much damage that they had chosen to rebuild from the ground up, and recommenced operations in early 1988. Iririki Island resort, in Vila harbour, was also taking guests in early 1988 but still rebuilding much of its plant. Other smaller facilities such as the Marina Motel and the Hotel Rossi were gradually resuming normal operations.

PORT VILA AND ENVIRONS
Intercontinental Island Inn: 3 km from Port Vila on lagoon, 166 rooms, 2 suites, all a/c, restaurants and bars, conference

facilities, swimming pool and water sports, golf and tennis, shops, tour desk, credit cards. PO Box 205, Port Vila. Tel.: 2040, Telex 1042 NH.

Le Lagon Pacific Resort: 4 km from Port Vila on Erakor Lagoon, totally rebuilt following the cyclone of early 1987 at a cost of $US13.4 million, new accommodation units including bungalows, duplexes etc., conference rooms, coffee shop and restaurants, bars, swimming pool, golf and tennis, water sports, credit cards. PO Box 86, Port Vila. Tel.: 2313, Telex 1032 NH.

Solaise Hotel: short distance out of town on Kumul Highway, 32 studio apartments in first stage (80 on completion), restaurant, bar, barbecue, swimming pool, 24-hour office service, some credit cards. PO Box 810, Port Vila. Tel.: 2150, Telex 1065 NH.

Marina Motel: just outside of town on Kumul Highway, 12 self-contained apartments, swimming pool, barbecue, some credit cards. PO Box 681, Port Vila. Tel.: 2566, Telex 1111 VANTEX MARINA VILA.

Iririki Island Resort: on Iririki Island in Vila Harbour, 72 bungalows, bar, restaurants, swimming pool, gift shop, some credit cards. PO Box 230, Port Vila. Tel.: 3388, Telex 1080.

Olympic Hotel: situated in business centre of Port Vila, studio or double apartments, self-contained and a/c, business facilities, telex and direct-dial telephones, some credit cards. PO Box 709, Port Vila. Tel.: 2464, Telex 1090 OLYMPH NH.

Rossi Hotel: on waterfront in Port Vila, 25 rooms, some a/c, restaurant, bar, some credit cards. PO Box 11, Port Vila. Tel.: 2528.

Teouma Village Resort: 5 km from Port Vila, 15 self-contained units, kiosk, swimming pool, recreation area, some credit cards. PO Box 651, Port Vila. Tel.: 3241, Telex 1072 NH.

Vila Chaumieres: 6 km from Port Vila, 4 self-contained bungalows, bar, some credit cards. PO Box 400, Port Vila. Tel.: 2866.

Erakor Island Resort: on island in Erakor Lagoon, 11 bungalows, 1 longhouse, restaurant, bar, gift shop, water sports, some credit cards. PO Box 24, Port Vila. Tel.: 2983, Telex 1010 COLYBR.

Hideaway Island Resort: 9 km from Port Vila on Mele Bay, 10 bungalows, restaurant,

bar, gift shop, water sports, some credit cards. PO Box 875, Port Vila. Tel.: 2963.

Manuro Paradise Resort: 55 km from Port Vila on east coast of Efate, bungalows, rooms in longhouse, restaurant, bar. PO Box 1009, Port Vila. Tel.: 2378.

Takara Lodge Resort: 60 km from Port Vila at North Efate, Melanesian-style waterfront bungalows, bar, restaurant, accessible by air from Port Vila. PO BOX 947, Port Vila. Tel.: 3576.

Kalfabun Guest House: 1.5 km from Port Vila at Tebakor, 3 rooms, cooking facilities. PO Box 494, Port Vila. Tel.: 2930.

Coral Apartments: outskirts of Port Vila, self-contained serviced apartments, some credit cards. PO Box 810, Port Vila. Tel.: 3569, Telex 1065 NH.

ESPIRITU SANTO

Hotel Santo: Main street, Luganville, 22 rooms, a/c, restaurant, bar, sometimes swimming pool, Tour Vanuatu office in building, some credit cards. PO Box 178, Luganville, Vanuatu. Tel.: 250.

New Look Motel: Main street, Luganville, 6 rooms, share cooking facilities and lounge. PO Box 114, Luganville, Vanuatu. Tel.: 440.

Asia Motel: Main street, Luganville, 11 rooms. PO Box 323, Luganville, Vanuatu. Tel.: 323.

TANNA

White Grass Bungalows: 8 km from Lenakel, 3 bungalows and 1 family unit, solar power, restaurant, bar. PO Box 5, Tanna, Vanuatu.

Tanna Beach Resort: 4 km from Lenakel on Ebul Bay, 11 Melanesian-style bungalows with private facilities, restaurant, bar, swimming pool, some credit cards. PO Box 27, Tanna, Vanuatu. Tel.: 3510, Telex 1011 NH BPVILA.

ERROMANGO

Dillon's Bay Bungalow: 1 bungalow sleeping two persons comfortably, meals included in tariff. PO Box 973, Port Vila. Tel.: 2219 (Port Vila).

PENTECOST

Bay Barrier Bungalows: 1 longhouse sleeping up to 18 persons, meals available.

Maru Motel: Near Wali village, 1 longhouse sleeping up to 8 persons, meals available.

Wake Island

Wake Island, located in 19 deg 18 min N latitude and 166 deg 35 E longitude, is midway between Hawaii and Guam. It is an atoll with a land area of about 650 hectares. There are three islets — Wake, Peale and Wilkes. Mendana is credited with discovering the island in 1568. It received its name from Captain William Wake of the British schooner *Prince William Henry* who rediscovered it in 1796. The United States Exploring Expedition under Commodore Wilkes fixed its position in 1840. Mariners of the 19th century also knew the island as Halcyon or Helsion.

It was uninhabited, but Marshallese tradition holds that it was used by them in the past as a place to collect birds and turtles. It is known by the Marshallese as Enen-Kio.

Today it is an American possession. The US annexed Wake Island for a cable station in 1899. It established an important naval and air base there in 1939–41. However, on

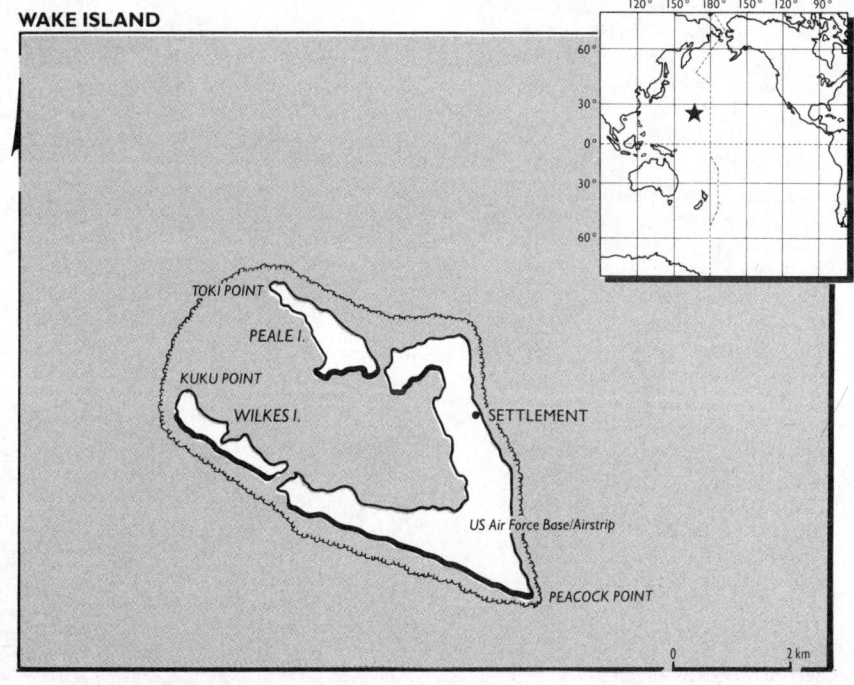

WAKE ISLAND

TOKI POINT
PEALE I.
KUKU POINT
WILKES I.
SETTLEMENT
US Air Force Base/Airstrip
PEACOCK POINT

0   2 km

24 December 1941, having bombed Pearl Harbor and seized Guam, the Japanese captured and occupied it. The Americans did not return until 4 September 1945, following the Japanese surrender.

In the post-war years, Wake was developed to provide commercial and military aircraft with a stopover and fuelling station between Honolulu and Tokyo and Honolulu and Guam. Since 1974 the island has been used mainly as en emergency stopover. The US National Weather Service has a weather station on Wake. For a time the US Federal Aviation Administration had administrative jurisdiction over the island, but this is now the responsibility of the US Air Force, which administers it under an agreement with the Department of Interior, which has overall jurisdiction. Wake is a contingency base and, except for emergency landings, prior permission must be obtained from US Air Force headquarters on Hawaii before landing.

Bridges and roads connect the three islets but most of the development has been on Wake. Peale is used as a recreation area. Wake is linked to Honolulu and Guam by an underwater cable completed in 1964.

Rainwater is caught in two huge water catchments and is supplemented by a distillation plant capable of producing 680,000 litres a day. The population consists of a number of US Air Force personnel who manage the base and several hundred civilians who operate the various functions of the base and a branch of the National Oceanographic and Atmospheric Administration.

In 1975, some 15,000 Vietnames refugees stayed at Wake for four months while awaiting transportation to the US.

Wake is one of the islands which has been investigated in recent years by the US Government as a possible home for the people of Bikini Atoll, which cannot be occupied for another 50 years as a result of the effects of radiation there.

Wake occasionally experiences typhoons.

Wallis and Futuna

Wallis and Futuna, an overseas territory of France, consists of two main islands about 200 km apart, extending from 13 deg 20 min S to 14 deg 21 min S latitude and from 176 deg 10 min to 178 deg 10 min W longitude. Futuna is about 240 km northeast of Vanua Levu, Fiji. The capital is Mata Utu on Wallis Is.

The national anthem and flag are those of France and currency is the French Pacific franc (CFP).

Public holidays are New Year's Day; Easter Monday; 1 May (Labour Day); Ascension (39 days after Easter Sunday); Monday after Pentecost (about 10 days after Ascension); 14 July (Bastille Day); 15 August (Assumption); 1 November (All Saints); 11 November (Armistice Day); and Christmas Day.

THE PEOPLE. The islanders are Polynesians. At the census in March 1983, the territory had a population of 12,391 (including 200 Europeans). This compared with 9113 in 1976. The total Wallisian population in New Caledonia was 13,000 in 1983 compared to 6000 in 1970.

In recent years, due to the continuing crisis in New Caledonia's nickel industry, an increasing number of Wallisians who had emigrated to work in the territory have returned to their homeland. About 1000 Wallisians were living in Vanuatu, mainly on Santo, at the time of Vanuatu's independence in 1980. There is now a community of approximately 200 still in Vanuatu. The Wallis population of 8072 is distributed between the central district of Hahake, Hihifo in the north, and Mua in the south. The 4319 inhabitants of Futuna are divided between the western district of Sigave and Alo in the east.

The population of the territory is increasing rapidly, with a birthrate of 32 per 1000

and a mortality rate of eight per 1000. There are 57 per cent under 20 years of age. If present trends continue, the population will have doubled by the year 2007.

The islanders have French nationality. The local language belongs to the Malayo–Polynesian family. Linguists refer to it as East Uvean to distinguish it from the language of Ouvea in the Loyalty Islands, which is called West Uvean. The Wallisian language is closely related to Tongan.

The language spoken on Futuna — East Futunan, as distinct from West Futunan, which is spoken on the island of Futuna in Vanuata — is distinct from Wallisian. Futunan shares many linguistic properties with Samoan. French is the official language in the administrative services.

Schooling was made compulsory only in 1961. Many people over 45 don't speak French. Meetings of the Territorial Assembly are conducted in French and Wallisian, with the aid of an interpreter. Teaching of Wallisian is restricted to one hour a week at junior high school level.

Through the work of French missionaries of the Marist order, the islanders are all Roman Catholics. Until 1935 Wallis and Futuna were part of the Vicariate Apostolic of Central Oceania, with headquarters in Tonga. However, unreliable transport and communication links led the Vatican in that year to establish a separate Vicariate Apostolic 'Wallis and Futuna'. Now a diocese, Wallis and Futuna is administered by a native bishop, Monsignor Lolesio Fuahea.

GOVERNMENT. For administrative purposes, the territory is divided into three districts, corresponding to the three ancient kingdoms Wallis, Alo (Futuna), and Sigave (Futuna).

WALLIS AND FUTUNA

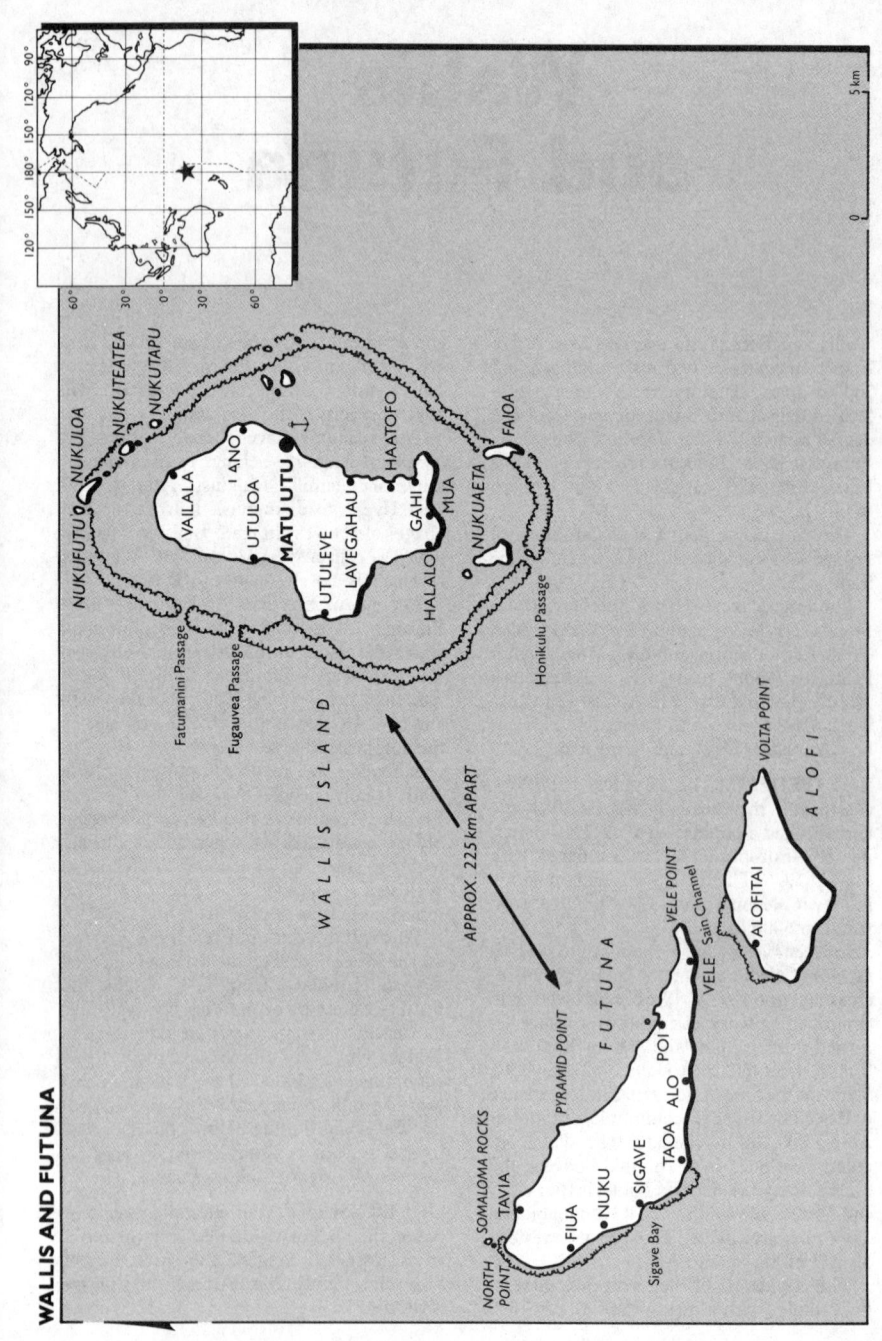

A French administrator (*administrateur supérieur*) is the head of the territory. He is ex-officio the president of the Territorial Council, which includes the Lavelua (King of Wallis), Tuiagaifo (King of Alo), Tuisigave (King of Sigave), and three members appointed by himself with the approval of the Territorial Assembly. The council decides on matters of general policy.

Legislative power lies with the Territorial Assembly, whose members (13 from Wallis, seven from Futuna) are elected for terms of five years by universal suffrage.

The administrator can veto decisions taken by the Territorial Assembly, with the exception of matters concerning social and economic programmes, and customs and excise duties.

Wallis and Futuna is represented in the National Parliament in Paris by a deputy and a senator. The deputy is elected for a five-year term by general suffrage, while the senator is elected by members of the Territorial Assembly, by simple majority vote, for a term of nine years.

An economic and social counsellor appointed by France's Secretary of State for Overseas Departments and Territories represents Wallis and Futuna on the State's Economic and Social Council.

There are two political parties in the territory, corresponding roughly to the Gaullists (RPR) and the Giscardians (PR/RDF) in metropolitan France. The Giscardians, known locally as *Lua Kae Tahi*, with their programme of socio-economic change and active participation in local government, attract the younger generation. The RPR is more conservative and traditionalist, and appeals to those who believe in the monarchy and the inherited pattern of social organisation. The sitting deputy and senator belong to the RPR.

EDUCATION. All children of school age attend school (3500 students in 134 classes in 1982). The primary school system developed from the mission schools. When Wallis and Futuna became an overseas territory in 1961, the French Education Ministry took over the responsibility for funding and co-ordinating educational policies. The Catholic Church retains a certain influence with regard to staffing and curricula.

The secondary school system is entirely run by the metropolitan Education Ministry, represented by a Vice-Rector in Mata Utu. There are only junior high schools in the territory, one at Salauniul (Futuna) and one at Alofivai (Wallis). The Catholic Church provides boarding facilities at Lano. Students qualifying for further education are sent to senior high schools or technical schools in Noumea with a scholarship provided by the territory (150 students in 1982). Those who meet metropolitan entrance requirements receive a government scholarship to study at tertiary institutions in France.

LABOUR. At the end of 1986 an estimated 80 per cent of the active population was engaged in agriculture and fishing. There were 656 people working in the public service, while 134 received regular cash incomes from employment in the private sector.

Wages. The minimum hourly rate was set at CFP 3.30, (1982).

HEALTH. The French Government provides free health services. Facilities include dispensaries at Hihifo, Mua and Alo, and a modern hospital at Sia (Wallis), staffed by three doctors and a dentist. There is one doctor on Futuna.

The principal local diseases — filariasis, tuberculosis, and leprosy — have been virtually eradicated. Ailments related to inadequate hygiene are on the decline as sanitation services improve.

THE LAND. Wallis and Futuna consist of two separate groups about 200 km apart. They are west of Samoa and north-east of Fiji.

Wallis Island (native name Uvea) is located at 13 deg 20 min S latitude and 176 deg 10 min W longitude.

Futuna, and its smaller neighbour, Alofi, are between 14 deg 11 min and 14 deg 21 min S latitude and between 177 deg 55 min and 178 deg 10 min W longitude.

Wallis consists of one major island surrounded by a barrier reef with 19 uninhabited islets. Together, they extend for 21 km and are 16 km at the greatest width. The main island, Uvea (not to be confused with Ouvea in the Loyalty Islands), has an area of 6000 hectares. It is of volcanic origin, but its highest point, Mt Lulu, is only 145 metres above sea level. Its chief islets are Nukuatea, Nukuafo, Nukufetao, Faioa, Fenuafoou, on the south; Nukulufala, Luaniva, Fugalei, on the east; and Nukuteatea, Nukuloa, Nukutapu, on the north.

Futuna and Alofi are both of volcanic origin. Each is surrounded by a fringing reef. The only anchorage for Futuna is Sigave Bay on the south-west side. Futuna is 13 km long and 8 km at its widest. It has an area of about 6400 hectares. Mountains run the length of the island, reaching a height of 760 metres (Mt Puke).

Alofi is about 9.5 km long east and west and about 5 km at its widest. Its area is 2954 hectares. Alofi's highest point is about 365 metres above sea level. Alofi is separated from Futuna by the Sain Channel, about 3 km wide. There are no permanent settlements on the island due to the lack of fresh water.

Futuna and Alofi were formerly known as the Hoorn Islands.

Futuna should not be confused with an island of the same name in Vanuatu, which, together with Sikaiana in the Solomons, is said to have been settled from Futuna.

PRIMARY PRODUCTION. The island population lives in a subsistence economy. The main means of obtaining cash is through government work, and funds sent home by relatives working in New Caledonia.

The agricultural production meets local consumption needs. A small amount of foodstuffs is sent to family members abroad.

There is little prospect for agricultural development because of a shortage of fertile soil (only a quarter of the land is suitable), the inherited land tenure system (tiny parcels of land belonging to various members of the clan are scattered all over the island), adherence to traditional ways of cultivation (two or three years of cropping are followed by long periods of fallow), and progressive soil deterioration through lack of proper fertilisation.

In 1980 the territory produced:

Bananas	4300 tonnes
Breadfruit	4400 tonnes
Taro	1750 tonnes
Kape	1000 tonnes
Manioc	2400 tonnes
Yams	560 tonnes
Mangoes	12 tonnes
Pineapples	4 tonnes
Coconuts	2,500,000 units

No more recent figures are available, but it is unlikely that much change will have occurred.

Copra. The coconut groves on Wallis were destroyed by an infestation of the coconut bettle in the 1930s. Since then copra production has ceased. Futuna escaped the pest, but the last recorded export of copra amounted to a negligible 100 tonnes in 1979. Today the yields of the 4000 ha of coconut trees are used to feed livestock.

Livestock. There are about 60 head of cattle at the Catholic Mission at Lano (Wallis), and the experimental station on Matalaa Peninsula. Lack of suitable pasture is the main obstacle to developing a cattle industry.

Pigs still play an important role in traditional ceremonies, and on festive occasions, reflecting the status and wealth of the family or the village. There are about 17,000 pigs (10,000 on Wallis, 6000 on Futuna) living in semi-freedom in the territory.

In 1981 two piggeries were opened by the State *Service de l'Economie Rurale*. There are an estimated 150 horses in the territory. The relatively small number of fowls — an estimated 8000 — cannot meet the local demand for eggs. On private initiative, a poultry farm was established in Mua in 1981.

Imports of frozen and canned meat continue to rise.

Fisheries. Fish remains the principal source of animal protein for the islanders. In the lagoon, traditional methods of fishing are still practised — nets, spears, angling, trolling, weirs, poisoning. To prevent depletion of stock the Government is encouraging people to fish beyond the reef.

Since its establishment in 1970, the Government shipyard at Mata Uta has built over 250 canoe-type fishing boats equipped with outboard motors. A catamaran especially suited for deep sea fishing is now being produced. In 1981 a larger fishing vessel, with a freezing room capacity of four tonnes, was acquired by the territory. In the same year a shipyard was opened on Futuna.

The French Government signed treaties with the governments of Japan and South Korea for fishing quotas of 3000 tonnes in the territory's waters. Revenue derived from these contracts amounted to CFP20 million in 1981.

Forestry. On Wallis, with the exception of a thin strip stretching from east to west, the natural forest has completely disappeared. The same holds for Futuna, where the mountainous terrain is particularly prone to erosion. Only on the island of Alofi is there an undisturbed area of natural forest.

Reafforestation programmes began in 1962. By 1982, 160 ha of Caribbean pine, and 20 ha of a local tree, *toafa*, had been planted on the northern plains of Wallis.

Timber products are used for the construction of the traditional *fale* — pandanus leaves for the thatched roof, breadfruit tree for the superstructure, and xylosma for the supporting posts.

Wood is still the main source of energy for home cooking and heating.

A wood-based product which is eagerly sought by visitors is tapa cloth made from the bark of the young *tutu* tree. Decorated with traditional designs, it is sold by the Sisters of the Catholic Mission at Sofala, and by a local co-operative sponsored by the *Service de l'Economie Rurale*.

TOURISM. Tourism is undeveloped in the territory. Although generally recognised as a promising source of revenue, it has met with the resistance of the local chiefs.

At present four hotels operate on Wallis, including the Lomipeau at Mata Utu, and the Grigri at Hihifo. The total number of rooms is 28, including 25 which are airconditioned. On Futuna accommodation is available at Poi for pilgrims visiting the shrine of St Peter Chanel.

LOCAL COMMERCE. There are several stores, petrol stations and garages on Wallis Island.

OVERSEAS TRADE. Due to the near absence of exports, the territory's trade deficit each year tends to equal the imports. No figures as to the quantity and value of agricultural products and handicrafts sent to family members in New Caledonia are available. The only known export is trochus shell of which 58 tonnes were exported in 1980 — 40 tonnes to New Caledonia, and 18 tonnes to Vanuatu. In 1981, 43 tonnes were exported (New Caledonia seven tonnes, Vanuatu 36). Trochus exports for the two years were valued at CFP2 million, and CFP2.3 million respectively. The trade deficit in 1983 amounted to CFP951 m, precisely the value of imports.

Customs tariffs and taxation. Duty and indirect taxes on imported goods are the main source of fiscal revenue. Various categories of duty and tax apply: (a) customs duty of 3 per cent on foreign goods except basic essentials. Products from member countries of the European Economic Community are exempt. (b) General import tax on all goods entering the territory, usually at 6 per cent.

TABLE 1 IMPORTS IN TONNES, AND CFP MILLIONS (IN BRACKETS)

	1977*	1978	1979	1980	1981**
Food	1421 (79)	2008 (120)	1343 (99)	1628 (143)	2076 (160)
Textiles, clothing	17 (14)	29 (19)	24 (21)	21 (18)	23 (28)
Petrol products	1156 (22)	1555 (32)	1359 (23)	3913 (84)	3333 (113)
Raw and industrial materials	2172 (55)	4256 (128)	1729 (103)	2576 (123)	4496 (163)
Machines, transport	133 (42)	286 (81)	650 (201)	289 (136)	257 (102)
Others	194 (45)	388 (121)	93 (54)	102 (36)	142 (60)
Total	5093 (257)	8522 (501)	5198 (501)	8529 (540)	10,327 (626)

* The 1977 figures do not include imports coming in by air.
** The 1981 figures are estimates only. No later figures are obtainable.
(The dramatic increase in imported foodstuffs reflects changes in eating habits, with more and more processed European-type foods being consumed.)

Luxury items such as tobacco, alcohol, cameras, radios, etc., attract a higher rate, between 15 and 30 per cent. (c) A special tax of 62.5 per cent on alcohol imported for commercial purposes, and a levy on petrol of CFP1.5 a litre. (d) A levy on hydrocarbons to repay the loan on the oil storage depot (tank capacity 1614 cubic metres) built by Total in 1979 at Halalo (CFP5 to CFP9 per litre). (e) A levy of CFP40 to CFP48 per hectolitre to compensate for movements in the retail price of hydrocarbons.

There is no income tax, and business licence fees are low.

FINANCE. Revenue for the territorial budget is derived from import taxes, the licensing of fishing rights to Japan and South Korea, and French Government subsidies.

Banking, currency. The first bank, a branch of the Banque de l'Indochine et de Suez, BIS, opened in mid-1977. Local currency is the Course du franc Pacifique (CFP), with notes and coins from New Caledonia.

External aid. Total external aid, including grants from France and the EEC, amounted to CFP956 million in 1981.

Expenditures on health services, education and general administration (including salaries), are met by the relevant metropolitan ministries.

Construction of roads and maintenance of the shoreline are financed through grants from FIDES (*Fonds d'Investissement pour le Développement Economique et Social*).

TRANSPORT. Through its international airport at Hihifo, Wallis is linked to Fiji (Nadi).

Previously operated by UTA French Airlines, the service was taken over in 1984 by Air Calédonie International. Like UTA, ACI uses a Boeing 737 on lease from Air Nauru for the service.

An eight-seater Britten Norman Islander is used to connect Wallis and Futuna three times a week. Flights are always booked out weeks in advance. The 700 m grass airstrip at Point Vele (Futuna) cannot be used in adverse weather conditions.

Flight time between the islands is about one hour.

Shipping. The islands are serviced by the Wallisian navigation company Sofrana, which owns the vessel *Moana II* (1000 tonnes). The *Moana II* makes 10–12 round trips a year through Noumea. There is a wharf at Mata Utu on Wallis. A jetty ending in a slipway at the village of Halalo permits the unloading of heavy machinery. Berthing facilities exist at Sigave on Futuna. Yachts find suitable anchorage in the Bay of Gahi on the east coast of Wallis.

About 8400 tonnes of merchandise was landed on the territory in 1980. An additional 130 tonnes arrived by air. The capacity of the *Moana II* is insufficient to meet the growing demand. As a result, long waiting times and shortages of commodities are experienced on both islands.

COMMUNICATIONS. There are no local newspapers, but the *Fetu'u Aho*, a Wallisian weekly paper published in New Caledonia, is available on Wallis. The Government gazette, the *Journal Officiel*, is published monthly.

The overseas branch of French Government radio opened a transmission station for public broadcasting in 1979. Radio Wallis broadcasts six hours a day, from 12–2 pm and from 6–10 pm. Part of its transmission

TABLE 2 WALLIS AND FUTUNA TERRITORIAL BUDGET (in CFP millions)

	Local revenue*	Expenditure
1977	176	157
1978	216	184
1979	272	249
1980*	289	263

* *Including government subsidies*
** *No later figures obtainable.*

is in Wallisian. There are direct radio links with Nadi airport and Noumea, which connects the territory with the international telephone network.

WATER AND ELECTRICITY. Good quality tap water is available almost everywhere on Wallis Island. On Futuna there is no lack of water, either from tap supplies or numerous streams and wells. All villages on Wallis have electricity. There is an ongoing electrification programme on Futuna, for which the French company UNELCO has a 25-year servicing licence.

MAJOR OFFICE HOLDERS
Administrator:
  M. Robert Thil
King of Wallis:
  the Lavelua, M. Tomasi Kulimoetoke
King of Alo, Futuna:
  the Tuiagaifo Lopeleto Tuikalepa
King of Sigave, Futuna:
  the Sau, Sagato Keltaona
President, Territorial Assembly:
  M. Manuele Lisiahi

HISTORY. Tradition suggests that Wallis Island was colonised from Tonga about AD 1450 or 1550 and that contact with Tonga was maintained at fairly frequent intervals thereafter. Until the early nineteenth century, there were constant struggles between rival chiefs for supremacy over the whole island.

The island's European name is that of its discoverer, Captain Samuel Wallis, who came upon it in HMS *Dolphin* in 1767 following his discovery of Tahiti. Apart from Mourelle (1781) and HMS *Pandora* (1791), there seem to have been no other European visitors until the mid-1820s. In 1837, French Marist priests visited the island, and one of them, Father (later Bishop) Pierre Bataillon, remained. After many difficulties, Bataillon converted the native king and all the islanders adopted Christianity. In 1842, the king petitioned France for protection. However, Wallis did not become a French protectorate until 1887.

In 1909, Wallis was given an autonomous budget in conjunction with Futuna. It was declared to be a colony of France in 1913, but this declaration was not ratified. During World War II, Wallis was an American military base, although it was outside the area of active hostilities. Airfields were built at Hihifo in the north and Uvea and at Lavegahau in the south.

Following a referendum in 1959, Wallis and Futuna together became an overseas territory of France on 29 July, 1961.

Futuna and Alofi. The early history of Futuna and Alofi is obscure. The first settlers in the Tua district of Futuna are said to have come from Samoa. There is also a well-known tradition about the arrival of a 'Chinese' ship — possibly a vessel from the Marshall Islands — whose crew left numerous descendants. And there are traditions about Tongan invaders who were generally repelled.

The first European record of the two islands dates back to 1616 when the Dutchmen van Schouten and Le Maire discovered them. They named them the Hoorn Islands, after a town in Holland. Whalers put into the island for provisions and refreshment from the 1820s onwards.

Father Pierre Chanel, a Marist, was the first European missionary to settle in the group. He was murdered in 1841 at the instance of the native king, but many of the people accepted Christianity soon afterwards. The chief asked for French protection in 1842. Thereafter, the political history of the group ran parallel with that of Wallis Island.

In 1976 the relics of the canonised St Pierre Chanel were flown from France to be enshrined at Poi on Futuna.

Voters on Wallis and Futuna have consistently opposed Socialist governments in France and any proposal for a change in their dependent status.

Further information. Edwin G. Burrows, *Ethnology of Uvea* (Wallis Island), Bernice P. Bishop Museum Bulletin 145, Honolulu, 1937 (Kraus Reprint, New York, 1971). Edwin G. Burrows, *Ethnology of Futuna*, Bernice P. Bishop Museum Bulletin 138, Honolulu, 1936 (Kraus Reprint, New York, 1971). Journal de la Société des Océanistes, vol. 19, 1963, Paris. Alexandre Poncet, *Histoire de l'île Wallis*, vol. 2, Paris, 1972, (vol. 1 has never been published). Karl H. Rensch, *Te Lea Faka'uvea: Introduction à la langue de Wallis (Uvea)*, Archipelago Press, Canberra 1982. Ron Crocombe and Ahmed Ali (eds), *Politics in Polynesia* (Chap. 1), Suva, 1983.

Western Samoa

Western Samoa consists of two large islands and several small ones with an area exceeding 2900 sq. km located between 13 and 15 deg S latitude and 168 and 173 deg W longitude. Western Samoa is an independent state and a member of the Commonwealth. The capital is Apia on Upolu where local time is 11 hours behind GMT. The islands are about 3700 km south-west of Hawaii and 2900 km north-east of Auckland. Its closest neighbours are American Samoa, Tonga, Wallis and Tokelau.

Western Samoa gained its independence from New Zealand in 1962, being the first South Pacific island nation to become independent, to be a member of the United Nations and to be considered a Third World non-aligned state. An estimated 162,200 people live in Western Samoa, the overwhelming percentage of them being pure-blood Samoans. The national flag is red with five white stars representing the Southern Cross on a blue background in the top, left quarter. Currency is the tala ($) composed of 100 sene.

Holidays include New Year, Easter and Christmas; Anzac Day (April); White Sunday (early October, the Monday being a holiday); Arbor Day (November); and Independence (the first three days of June). The national anthem is *The Banner of Freedom*.

THE PEOPLE. In 1981, Western Samoa had a population of 156,350, 107,350 on the main island of Upolu and 49,000 on Savai'i. Estimates for 1987 are 162,200. In addition there are an estimated 40,000 Samoans in New Zealand, about half being New Zealand born. Population breakdown shows 40.7 per cent of the population under the age of 15, 56.0 per cent between 15 and 64 and 3.3 per cent 65 and over.

Nationality. The people are Western Samoan Citizens. The prerequisites for citizenship are (a) to be born in the country; or (b) to have five years residence, land to live on and a job. Citizenship is not automatic for non-Samoans, and can only be granted at the discretion of the Minister of Immigration.

Language. The Samoan language is a Polynesian tongue, but English is widely spoken although rural Samoans do not always speak it well, and, generally, older Samoans cannot speak English. English is the language used in conducting business in government departments and the commercial sector. Samoan is used for conducting the proceedings in the Fono (parliament) with simultaneous translation into English over an internal headphone system.

Migration. In past years, large numbers of Western Samoans have migrated to New Zealand providing an outlet for the surplus workforce but recently New Zealand has insisted on a severe reduction in the numbers of migrants. This has added to rising unemployment in Western Samoa.

An undetermined number of Western Samoans are migrating to American Samoa and from there to Hawaii and California. The remittances received at home from New Zealand and the US form an important source of revenue for the nation.

Religion. 'Fa'avae i le Atua Samoa' ('Samoa is Founded on God') is part of the crest of Western Samoa, and indicates the strength of the Christian Church. Religion is today embodied into the traditional life of Samoa, and is very much part of daily life. The population is more than 60 per cent Protestant. Sunday is reserved for church services, and little else. There are a great many locally funded churches and all important villages have one or more.

White Sunday, 'Lotu Tamaiti', which is on the second Sunday in October, is probably the most important religious and social day in Samoa, even including Christmas. It is a day in honour of children and features church services where the children are in all white, and feasts where the children are served by the adults, a reverse of the normal order.

Religion arrived in Samoa in July 1830, when the ship *Messenger of Peace* carrying Reverend John Williams of the London Missionary Society arrived off Sapapali'ie in Savai'i. In a relatively short time the church became established and later became known as the Congregational Christian Church of Samoa. It now sends missionaries to other parts of the Pacific and Africa. It has the largest number of adherents in the country.

The capital, Apia, gives its name to the Roman Catholic See, the Bishopric of Apia established in the 1960s when the Pope set up a hierarchy among the South Pacific Islands. The present incumbent is also a Cardinal. Other groups include the Church of Jesus Christ of Latter Day Saints (Mormon), the Seventh-day Adventist Church and the Methodist Church in Samoa.

Lifestyle. The 'faa Samoa' or traditional Samoan way, remains the central force. The 'aiga' or extended family is the critical unit. The head of the 'aiga', which may include several Western-style families, is the 'matai'. The 'matai' has 'pule', or authority, over the traditional lands associated with that 'aiga'.

The clan, whose head is called the 'matai', owns all the lands, and parcels it out to the members as necessity arises. All produce of the soil is theoretically the property of the 'matai' in trust for the community, but in modern days it is becoming increasingly common to allow the actual cultivator to retain for his own use the fruits of his labour.

Each 'matai' has his place in the village council, or 'fono', the governing authority in each 'nu'u' or parish. The village council

WESTERN SAMOA

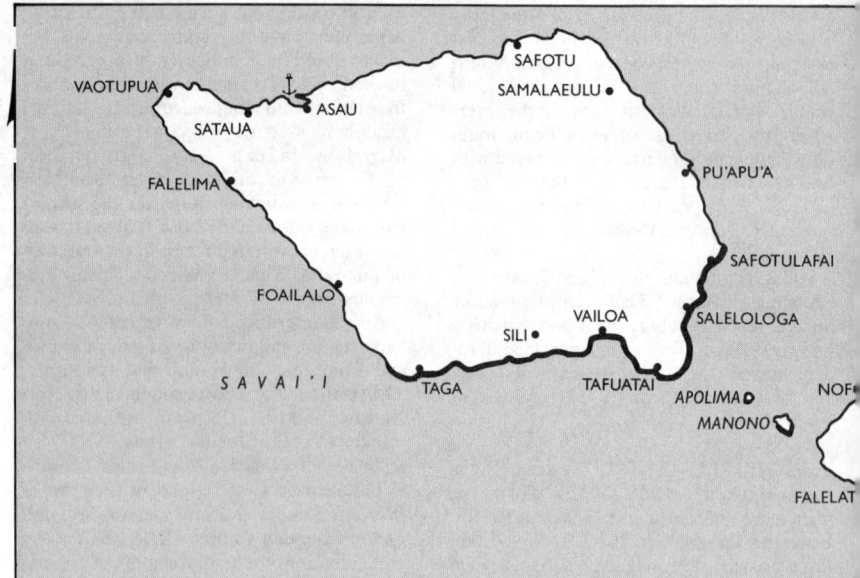

has wider powers than Western style local government.

There are two main forms of 'matai' title. One is the 'ali'i' or high chief title, the other is the 'tulafale' or orator title. Some titles are more important than others, and each title ranking and history is containing in the 'fa'alupega', which is the spoken history of the titles in that district, and is repeated at significant occasions.

The delivery of the 'fa'alupega' is considered important, and in recent times chiefs, orators and scholars have been helped by the regular publication of *O le Tusi Fa'alupega o Samoa*, a publication listing titles.

The four highest titles are known as the 'tama aiga'. They are Malietoa, Tupua Tamasese, Mata'afa and Tuimaleli'fano. Each 'aiga' decides on its own 'matai', usually by talking until a consensus is reached. Titles do not automatically go from father to son. Occasionally, a title becomes the subject of a dispute, a frequent event with 'tama aiga' titles. Families then have recourse to the

Lands and Titles Court. This court, which is headed by the Chief Justice, usually defines who may be involved in deciding on a title. It then instructs that group to consider the issue within a certain time to select a holder, and if it fails to do so, the court then selects a holder.

Factors taken into consideration are many and varied, but the wishes of the previous holder, the candidate's knowledge of 'fa'a Samoa', his contribution to village welfare, whether he is resident in the village and his acceptability to the aiga are factors. All titles are registered by the court, and the court can void any appointment made by a 'saofai', traditional ceremony of bestowal.

It is unconstitutional for foreigners to be given titles, although in recent times the practice of giving 'honorary' titles has arisen. Such titles have no significance. Only 'matai' can vote in general elections with the exception of two seats elected by an individual voters' roll that are outside the 'matai' system.

Samoan etiquette. The 'matai' are held in

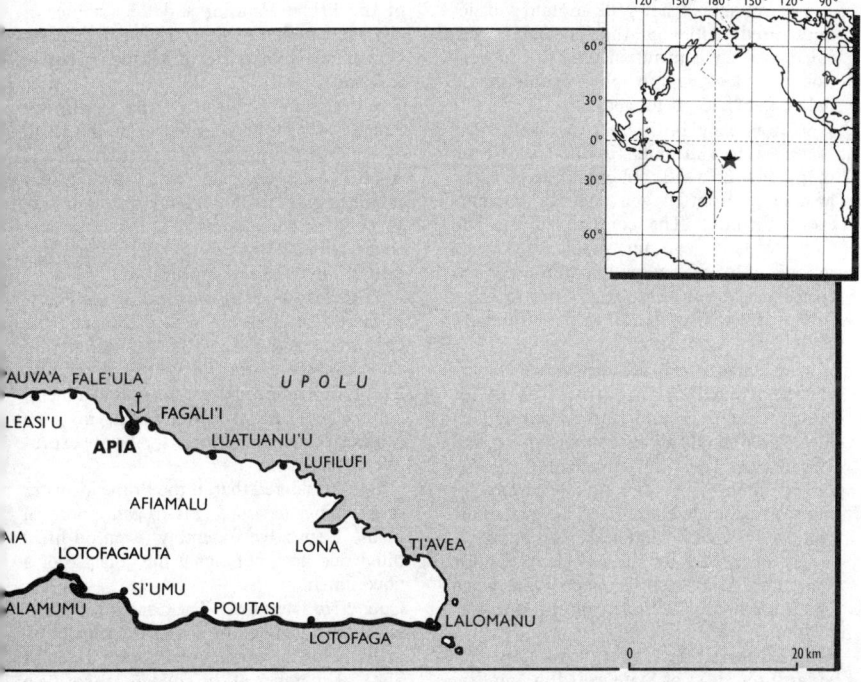

high respect. A 'matai' is addressed by his title name, and only if a person is on close and familiar terms can a person use the Christian name of a person.

Mr is not necessary in Samoa. There are Samoan honorifics and these are Afioga, Susuga, Tofa and Masiofo. Each applies for certain titles, for example Susuga Malietoa Tanumafili (the Head of State) or Afioga Faumuina Fiame Mata'afa Mulinu'u (late Prime Minister). Masiofo is reserved for the wives of 'tama aiga'. Samoan children usually have a Christian name, and a surname that is the Christian name of their father.

For the visitor the ritual of Samoa can appear complex, and it can be relatively easy to break conventions without knowing it. For example it is impolite to address hosts in their 'fale' (houses) while standing. All important conversations, both in business and at home, are carried out sitting. In the 'fale' it is usual to sit cross-legged on the floor. It is rude to stretch one's legs out, unless they are covered by a mat. Sympathetic hosts usually understand the plight of stiff-legged foreigners and provide mats for this purpose.

Visitors should not walk around villages unescorted. Although the 'fale' are open-sided, privacy is maintained by the convention of not looking into 'fales'. People should only enter 'fales' if invited.

Visitors may be invited to drink ''ava' (kava). When drinking in the ''ava' ceremony, first tip a little out of the cup on to the ground in front of you and say 'Manuia' (good fortune). The contents of the cup (made of half a coconut) should be downed in one gulp. For very important persons (usually heads of states or governments and high titles) a village will host the impressive Royal ''ava' ceremony.

Most villages impose 'curfews.' A vespers curfew is held in the early evening for prayers, and at around 10 pm. During curfew people should avoid making a noise, and stay in the 'fale'. Curfew customs are observed in some parts of Apia. Flowers are not worn inside a church and heavy manual work should not be undertaken on Sundays.

Out of respect for the elders, passers-by should walk quietly past an open 'fale' when chiefs are holding a 'fono' (meeting) inside.

GOVERNMENT. The Constitution provides for a Head of State called in Samoan,

O le Ao O le Malo, to be elected by the Legislative Assembly for a term of five years. However, in the first instance, it was decided that the two High Chiefs, who had been titled the Fautua (Tupua Tamasese and Malietoa Tanumafili II), should become joint Head of State and have a lifetime tenure of office unless they resigned or were removed from office by the Assembly. Moreover, if one predeceased the other, the survivor continued as sole Head of State during his lifetime — subject to resignation or removal from office. (On 5 April 1963, the death occurred of Tupua Tamasese; the sole Head of State thereafter was Malietoa Tanumafili II.)

There is nothing in the Constitution to prevent others being elected to office but it was recommended at the time of the Constitutional Convention that the Head of State always be chosen from the 'Tam-a-aiga' or Four Royal Sons, or families.

EXECUTIVE. The function of the Head of State is similar to that of a Constitutional Monarchy as in Britain — rules but does not govern. The Head of State acts on the advice of the Prime Minister and the Cabinet of eight and, with the Prime Minister and members of the Cabinet, constitutes the Executive Council.

All legislation passed by the Legislative Assembly must be assented to by the Head of State who must act on the advice of the Executive Council. The Head of State has power to grant pardons and reprieves or may suspend or commute any sentence by any court, tribunal or authority. He can use this power only with the approval of Cabinet.

The Head of State appoints as the Prime Minister the member who commands the confidence and support of the majority of the members of the Legislative Assembly. This is determined by a secret ballot of members. The Prime Minister selects his own cabinet, which is considered to be the executive government.

It is considered that, if the Prime Minister or a cabinet measure fails to gain approval in the Legislative Assembly (even on fiscal bills) this does not signal the collapse of a government.

Council of Deputies. The Constitution provides for a Council of Deputies, which virtually holds the powers of a deputy Head of State. A member of the council cannot be a member of the Legislative Assembly, and its function is to act in place of the Head of State if a vacancy exists in that office, or the holder is overseas or incapacitated. The council also performs useful ceremonial functions for the government.

Legislature. The 'fono', or Legislative Assembly is composed of 47 members, including a Speaker elected by the members. Of these, 45 members are elected by 'matai' suffrage. There are 12,958 (1983) people on the 'matai' roll. The other two members are elected by universal suffrage from an individual voters' roll of 1600 people. Entry to that roll is open to citizens of European blood who are not members of a 'matai' family. Elections are held every three years.

The proceedings are broadcast by the Samoan Broadcasting Service in Samoan on one channel, and English on another.

The 'Maota Fono', or Parliament Buildings, a modern building of traditional design opened in June 1972, is at historic Mulinu'u, a piece of land that juts out from Apia.

DIPLOMATIC. Western Samoa maintains a High Commission office in Wellington, New Zealand, and a Consul-General in Auckland, New Zealand. Western Samoa's Permanent Representative to the United Nations in New York is also the country's Ambassador to the United States, and High Commissioner to Canada.

Western Samoa has diplomatic relations with Great Britain, France, the Federal Republic of Germany, Yugoslavia, the Soviet Union, China, Israel, Egypt, India, Thailand, North and South Korea, Japan, the Philippines, Indonesia, Australia, Chile, Canada, the Netherlands, Sweden, Fiji and Nauru. Most representation is handled through embassies and high commissions in Wellington, New Zealand, but see the end of the main section for a list of missions in Apia.

Western Samoa is a member of the South Pacific Forum and the South Pacific Commission and is an associate member of the European Economic Community.

LOCAL GOVERNMENT. On the island of Savai'i there are representatives of the Prime Minister's and other departments, a police station, court house, hospital, school, etc. Administrative districts, based mainly on geographical regions, were established at the end of 1956, and are used in the operation of government services such as health, education, police, agriculture, etc. However, the Samoans have mainly kept local government in its traditional form based on the 'matai' system, and the meeting together of these family heads in the village 'fono'.

In 1977, the 'pulenu'u system was reorganised to improve government technical help to villages.

Public service. There are almost 4500 permanent and temporary officers in the Public Service, with a Public Service Commission responsible for appointments and transfers.

Volunteers. There are about 20 US Peace Corps volunteers in Samoa, about 15 members of Australian Volunteers Abroad, and 20 members of the Japanese Overseas Volunteer corps. Most volunteers fill secondary teaching posts.

Courts. There are four types of court: Magistrate's Court, Supreme Court, Appeal Court and Lands and Titles Court.

The Magistrate's Court is presided over by the senior magistrate, who is a qualified lawyer; or by the three Senior Samoan Judges/ Fa'amasino Fesoasoani; or by the seven other Samoan magistrates.

The Senior Magistrate/Fa'amasino Fesoasoani sit alone on the bench; the other Samoan magistrates sit in pairs.

The three grades of cases that they can hear are as follows: the magistrate can hear any criminal case involving imprisonment up to five years or any case involving a fine only. The Senior Samoan Judges/FF can hear cases involving imprisonment for one year (although they cannot imprison anyone for more than 6 months). The other Samoan magistrates hear cases where imprisonment is not involved and can impose lesser fines.

Appeals from the Magistrate's Court go to the Supreme Court. The Constitution provides for a Chief Justice of the Supreme Court and any other judges as become necessary. It has full jurisdiction in both criminal and civil cases. Appeals go to the Court of Appeal.

Provision is also made for a Judicial Service Commission consisting of the Chief Justice as President, the Attorney-General (or, if he is unable to act, the Chairman of the Public Service Commission); and some other person nominated by the Minister of Justice.

A Court of Appeal was also set up after independence (appeals previously going to the Supreme Court of NZ). It must consist of three judges, who can be the Chief Justice or Judges of the Supreme Court; any other active or retired British judge; or a person possessing the qualifications required for appointment as a Judge of the Western Samoa Supreme Court.

English is the official language of the court but both Samoan and English are used. Interpreters have to be fluent in both languages. Court procedure in the Supreme Court is that followed in most British courts; Samoan custom is taken into consideration in certain cases.

The only other legally constituted judicial body is the Land and Titles Court which has jurisdiction in respect of disputes over Samoan land and succession to Samoan titles. The Chief Justice presides over this court or he can appoint a Deputy President from either the Puisne Judge or the two senior Samoan magistrates to act in his place.

Major crimes are rare — the principal offences brought before the courts are petty theft, assault, disorderly conduct, trespass and traffic violations.

Police. Most crime is confined to Apia and its environs. There are three police outposts on Upolu and three on Savai'i and they have little to do because the 'matai' system keeps its own order. Average daily prison population in 1985 was 139, with theft and burglary the most common offences.

The Department of Police and Prisons, headed by a Commissioner, with a Police Force of about 200, maintains law and order.

Liquor laws. The sale of liquor in clubs and hotels is prohibited on Sundays. Hotel guests, however, are allowed drinks on a discreet service basis. In recent years liquor laws have been relaxed considerably and liquor is now freely available. Both beer and fruit wine are produced locally.

DEFENCE. The Treaty of Friendship signed by Western Samoa and New Zealand in August 1962 symbolises a high degree of co-operation and association. In particular, New Zealand has agreed to 'consider sympathetically requests from the Government

of Western Samoa for technical, administrative and other asistance', and, on request, to act as the agent of Western Samoa in its dealings with other countries and international agencies.

Samoa is not aligned to any of the existing defence pacts in the region. Samoa does not maintain any military force, and security of nationhood is based on the universal and uncontested right or sovereignty, and the notable lack of any perceived threat.

In civil emergencies, such as search and rescue, previous experience has shown that Samoa can call on the assistance of regional powers such as Australia and New Zealand, and even the US.

The port of Apia has been host to military vessels of many nations on the basis of 'goodwill visits', and not as part of military exercises. Military aircraft from any nation are usually granted diplomatic clearance to use Faleolo Airport if necessary.

EDUCATION. Education is the responsibility of the Department of Education, but several missions also operate schools and, though they are not grant-aided, the mission schools work in close co-operation with the government schools. The education system is in three divisions: primary, intermediate and secondary. There is also vocational training through a technical institute, a primary teachers' college and a secondary teachers' college.

Primary schools take children from the primer classes to Standard IV, from the ages of 5½–7 to 12 on the average. Instruction is in Samoan, but there is a strong program of English to prepare children for the intermediate stage.

In the intermediate schools the instruction is in English with the vernacular taught as a leading subject to preserve the importance and value of the native tongue. Children attend these schools for two or three years i.e. from 12 or 13 to 14 or 15.

The secondary school is entered at 15 and a pupil may then continue to 19 or 20, though there is election at the end of the second and fourth year for continued attendance in accordance with ability.

In 1983 there were 51,851 pupils at Samoan schools, or 32.6 per cent of the total population. Of these, 26,857 were males and 24,787 female. There were 26,589 at government primary schools and 4858 at mission primary schools; 7208 at government intermediate level and 1435 at the missions; 6527 at government secondary schools and 5234 at mission secondary schools, and 200 at vocational schools. There were 1288 primary and intermediate teachers, 267 secondary teachers and 30 vocational teachers.

UNIVERSITY OF THE SOUTH PACIFIC. In 1975 the former Alafua Agricultural College became the Samoa campus of the University of the South Pacific, specialising in agriculture and offering a degree course in agriculture.

The independent National University of Western Samoa was established by government legislation in 1984. The investiture of the first Chancellor, Western Samoa's Head of State, H. H. Malietoa Tanumafili II, took place in October 1986. The appointment of the first Vice-Chancellor took place in September 1987, when Le Afioga Tauili'ili Uili, hitherto co-ordinator at the university, was appointed.

In 1987, the university was offering a preparatory year programme and a Bachelor of Education degree, the latter intended mainly to raise the qualifications of teachers already in the educational service. It was intended to offer BA and BSc degrees as well as Certificates of Commerce and Diplomas in Accountancy in courses commencing in 1988. Student enrolments in 1987 totalled 141. Academic staff numbers were 12 full- and five part-time staff.

LABOUR. With changing emphasis in Samoa from village agriculture to migration to Apia and overseas, the demand for employment has increased. Unemployment has become a serious factor in Apia. The government has attempted to overcome the problem by making farming a more profitable activity for villagers, and by providing increasing employment opportunities. The labour force is estimated at 42,000, or 26 per cent of the total population. Just over half of this is engaged in the subsistence sector as unpaid family labour and the balance in the cash sector. Government and public enterprises account for the bulk of employment in the latter sector and transport, trade and related services dominate in the private sector. Em-

ployment in manufacturing numbers 1500.

Wages. There is a surplus of unskilled and semi-skilled labour. Wages are low, and the minimum adult basic wage by law is 40 sene per hour.

Overseas work. Until the reduction in the number of migrants permitted to enter New Zealand, many semi-skilled Samoans went there. They felt that there were better opportunities for advancement and education. However, the trend has changed and there is more movement to American Samoa, Hawaii and California.

Social security. The National Provident Fund was introduced as a source of social benefit to workers but the funds are also lent out to finance development projects. Contributions to the Fund come from employers who pay out about five per cent on top of their wages and salaries bill. Part of this contribution can be recouped from employees earning over a minimum rate. The sums paid are placed at the credit of each individual as the basis of lump sum payments and pensions payable on his reaching retirement age.

In 1977, an Accident Compensation Bill was introduced to the 'fono'. This provided for payment on a 'no fault' basis for all people injured in motor and industrial accidents. It also provided for payments to dependants where death occurs. The legislation called for establishment of an Accident Compensation Board designed to calculate a system of payments, and to promote safety in industry and on the roads. The scheme is financed by a one per cent payroll tax on employers and a tax on petrol.

HEALTH. In 1986 Western Samoa had 32 qualified doctors and 8 specialists; 5 doctors worked within the public health system. There were also 283 nurses, 130 of whom were public health nurses, 24 health inspectors and 35 dental staff. There was one major national hospital in Apia with 339 beds, and seven district hospitals — three in rural Upolu with 199 beds and four on Savai'i with 148 beds. There were also nine health centres (seven on Upolu and two on Savai'i) as well as 16 sub-health centres (12 on Upolu and four on Savai'i).

The 1986 Budget for public health services was $1,568,445. Services provided include maternal and child health, family planning, immunisation programmes, health education, support services for TB and leprosy victims and the provision of sanitary inspections. There is also an extensive schools health programme which includes routine checks of skin problems, oral health services, immunisation to new entrants and school leavers, provision of dressings for open wounds, sores, etc. as well as general health education.

Main diseases in Western Samoa are influenza, gastroenteritis, diarrhoea, measles, conjunctivitis, gonorrhoea, pulmonary tuberculosis and fish poisoning. The main causes of death are heart diseases, diseases of the cardiovascular system, cerebrovascular diseases and intestinal poisoning. Western Samoa has a high suicide rate particularly among the nation's youth. Paraquat poison is the common pesticide used.

The birth rate in 1985 was 22.5 per 1000 population while the death rate was 1.7 per 1000 population. Family planning methods have been accepted by 25 per cent of the population in the Apia region, 8.4 per cent of the population in the rural area of Upolu and 11 per cent in Savai'i. Overall there has been acceptance by 14 per cent of the population. Average life expectancy is 60 for males and 65 for females.

THE LAND. Western Samoa has a land area of 2934 sq. km. The two main islands are the most densely populated; Upolu (1100 sq. km) and Savai'i (1820 sq. km). The island of Upolu extends about 72 km from east to west and up to 24 km from north to south. Savai'i is also about 72 km across but is 35 km wide. The islands have numerous volcanic peaks, the highest being Mt Mata'aga, of 1850 m, on Savai'i, and Mt Fito, of 1100 m, on Upolu.

Savai'i has a central core of volcanic peaks surrounded by a ring of lava-based plateaux, then lower hills and coastal plains. Upolu has a chain of volcanic peaks running from one end of the island to the other, with hills and coastal plains on either side.

Climate. The south and south-east windward areas receive from 5000 to 7000 mm of rain annually. On the leeward side, the islands receive from 2500 to 3000 mm of rain. There is, however, a marked dry season, from May to August. The average rainfall for Apia is 3072 mm a year.

The islands' volcanic origins have produced a terrain with abundant streams and waterfalls. At sea, the coral reef is broken in many places, thus exposing the lagoon.

Flora. The rain forests produce dense growth with Barringtonia and other tall trees as well as luxuriant ferns and vines. The volcanic soil is rich and fertile.

Land reclamation. The most important land reclamation scheme in recent years has changed the face of Apia harbour. About 15 hectares of land was reclaimed in the central waterfront area, for recreational use, when over 600,000 cubic metres of material was dredged out of the harbour in a project to ensure adequate depth for ships.

Land tenure. All land in Western Samoa since the end of 1961 is legally: (a) customary land, held from the State in accordance with Samoan custom, i.e. land traditionally vested in 'matai' (chiefs) who hold the land in trust for their aiga (family group). Customary land can be leased but not purchased. The Lands and Titles Court settles land disputes arising mainly out of badly defined boundaries and from conflicting claims of individual matai; (b) freehold land (meaning alienated land) which is held from the State of Western Samoa in fee simple; and (c) Government land which is free from customary title and from any estate in fee simple.

In earlier times, the Berlin Act of 1889 provided for a commission to settle all alien land titles, with instructions that there should be disallowed all claims to land based upon 'the consideration of a sale of firearms or munitions of war, or upon the consideration of intoxicating liquors' — a hint of the origin of some of the claims put forward. This was the first attempt to examine and record in a central registry the European lands in Samoa, and the decisions then made are still the root of the titles to such land.

The intervening years saw some modifications to the registration system under German and New Zealand administration.

There were no changes in land tenure after Independence except that land formerly called Crown Land, and vested in Queen Elizabeth, became vested in the Sovereign State of Western Samoa.

Samoan land is divided as follows: customary land (almost 80 per cent), Government land (just over 10 per cent), Western Samoa

Trust Estates Corporation and freehold land (held by persons of European status and by missions), both about 4 per cent each.

Trust Estates Corporation. After World War I, New Zealand Trust Estates took over former German plantations and worked them. In all these, total land involved amounted to about 36,800 ha. All but 12,800 ha of this was subsequently passed back to the Crown. In 1957 the New Zealand Government passed over to the Samoan people all the land and assets of reparation estates. They became known as Western Samoa Trust Estates Corporation (WSTEC). The corporation is run by a board of directors.

PRIMARY PRODUCTION. Western Samoa is dependent largely on three crops — coconuts, cocoa and taro — for exports and for its internal needs. In order to diversify output, the country is developing other produce such as timber and cattle. Banana exports, once the country's main export, are now only minor.

Copra. A major element of development plans has been the upgrading of old coconut plantations. In 1970, about 22,000 ha of coconuts were in full bearing but the majority of these trees were 60 years old or more and had a low or declining yield. By 1975, the replanting programme was left only 2800 ha short of the planned target of 35,120 ha. In 1976, 259,300 seedlings were planted in 2097 ha. By the end of 1987 another 2667 ha of coconuts will be replanted. Production of copra rises and falls according to prevailing price. When the price is high more people are encouraged to cut it; when it is low they don't bother.

Recent copra export figures have been as follows:

	Copra (000 tons)	Value ($000)
1982	11.82	2760
1983	4.78	1398
1984	N/A	N/A
1985	2.75	954
1986	3.29	1049
1987	.56	65

The estimates in any year do not tell the full story as a large proportion of the crop is consumed locally. The export pattern may change, however, as Western Samoa moves away from the export of unprocessed copra to that of coconut oil.

Coconut oil exports rose from a value of $11,085 m in 1983 to $20,725 m in 1984, but fell to $8.7 m in 1987 because of a drop in commodity price. Copra meal exports rose from nil in 1981 to $757,000 in 1987. Coconut cream also showed a big increase in value, from $635,600 in 1981 to $3.1 m in 1987.

The WSTEC Mulifanua coconut plantation is 40 km west of Apia and is the base for a joint WSTEC and Department of Agriculture 'cattle under coconuts' project designed to make more intensive use of plantation lands.

Cocoa. Although cocoa was originally grown on the big private plantations, Samoan smallholders now grow a large proportion of it. Total area planted is about 5000 ha. Samoan cocoa is much in demand as a high-grade product: it is used particularly for blending. The locally-developed hybrid 'Lafi-7' was first grown at the Central Group Cocoa Plantation of the WSTEC, which is five km inland from Apia.

Marketing of the beans is handled by the Cocoa Board which is endeavouring to establish new sales outlets through membership of the International Cocoa Organisation. A new cocoa development project estimated to increase production to 8000 tonnes a year by 1990 was opened at Nuu in 1979. Australia financed the buildings, vehicles and equipment.

	1983	1984	1985	1987
Cocoa (tons)	2123	709	581	839

Cocoa exports in 1983 were valued at $4.616 m, in 1985, $2.36 m and in 1987 $2.62 m.

Bananas. Once the country's main export, bananas are no longer of major significance in the country's export industry. Disease, hurricane damage, intense competition from South America and poor shipping put the industry into serious decline. A growing population and the popularity of bananas as a staple food means that growers can obtain satisfactory prices at local markets without the fuss of exporting them, but some shipments are made to American Samoa. New

Zealand was the biggest market for Samoan bananas but the market has been taken over by Ecuador.

In 1958, Western Samoa shipped 884,000 cases, but by 1978 the figure was down to 12,900 cases. Exports are now minimal.

		1985	1986	1987
Bananas	Value ($'000)	28	39	40

Livestock. Efforts are being made to build up the cattle industry with aid received from such bodies as the Asian Development Bank. The country is estimated to have about 30,000 head of cattle, about 40 per cent of which are kept by the Trust Estates.

The WSTEC actually supplies most of the cattle killed locally for meat. Besides their beef value, the cattle keep down grass that grows on plantations.

Other livestock in the country are estimated to include 40,000 pigs and 500,000 fowls. Horses are used as pack animals for transporting produce.

Fishing. With Japanese assistance, commercial fishing has undergone considerable development. A fisheries training centre has been built in Apia, and a fisheries training boat provides training in long line techniques. A Food and Agriculture Organisation boat building project has provided almost 400 twin-hulled fishing boats to villages around the country. Refrigeration and regular collection has meant that any surplus fish in the villages can be sold in Apia. A Japanese-financed fish market was opened in Apia in 1983.

In 1983 fish production totalled 3193 tonnes, an estimated value of $4.0 m. Of canned fish and fish products $1.524 m worth were imported. Several fisheries projects have been declared unviable.

Timber. There are very valuable stands of timber, particularly on Savai'i. Timber has assumed greater importance in the Samoan economy since a timber industry began on Savai'i when the US company, Potlatch Forests Inc., obtained extensive timber leases in 1968. The company has now pulled out and the Government and Standard Sawmilling of Australia are partners in the operation, with the government holding 80 per cent of the shares.

Exports of tropical hardboard and other timber earned more than $403,000 in 1974 but the value of shipments has since been erratic. Timber exports for 1981 were worth $288,500, for 1982 $1.207 m, for 1983 $540,600, for 1985 $817,000 and for 1987 $396,000.

MANUFACTURING. Most light industries are concerned with supplying the local market and thus contribute to import substitution. Local plants produce concrete products, industrial and household gases, paints, and sundry building materials. Goods for export include clothing, canned fruit, processed food and handicrafts marketed by the Western Samoa Handicrafts Corporation.

Western Samoa Breweries Ltd, a company owned by the Government of Western Samoa, the DEG (German Development Corporation), Brauhausse (the brewers) and Breckwoldt (a trading company) was registered in Apia in 1976. The brewery produce beer sold under the 'Vailima' label. Exports alone were worth $841,400 in 1983 and $815,900 in 1984, but fell to $469,000 in 1987.

TOURISM. Enthusiasm to encourage tourism was only aroused about 1965 and then with emphasis placed on preserving Samoan traditions. This has resulted in a slow increase of visitors.

Western Samoa — Tourists

1983	1984	1985	1986
36,720	40,430	43,920	49,280

In 1986 most visitors came from American Samoa, followed by New Zealand and the US. More than two thirds of all visitors arrived by air. Tourism and hotels come under the portfolio of the Minister of Economic Affairs, who is also responsible for Broadcasting and Transport and Telecommunications.

LOCAL COMMERCE. There is a growing range of businesses and services supplying the local market, in addition to those manufacturers who are export-oriented. Nearly all are based in Apia, which has an extensive shopping area where most local goods are obtainable. Where once the big stores such as Burns Philp and Nelson's supplied most requirements, there are now a variety of stores including boutiques, gift and handicraft shops, snack bars and restaurants, beauty parlours, etc. There are several car rental firms, tour and travel agencies, taxi services, movie theatres and nightclubs. There is a big sale in handicrafts, sold at the produce markets, in a number of local stores and at the Government-run Western Samoa Handicraft Corporation store. Just outside of the Apia town area, past Vailima, is the Island Styles textile printing factory, run by Bob and Sophia Rankin, which specialises in tapa designs and is open for inspection. The company also bottles wines made from local fruits.

OVERSEAS TRADE. Western Samoa has faced significant trade deficits over recent years, and only foreign aid, and remittances sent home to Samoan families from islanders in New Zealand and the US have kept it afloat. As the accompanying table shows, imports have been considerably higher than exports, and the gap has been widening. There has been a serious drop in copra and cocoa exports due to a world downturn in produce prices, although export in coconut oil, husked coconuts and various manufactured coconut creams has replaced much of this loss. Coconut oil exports accounted for

only $11.07 m in 1983 but in 1984 they jumped in value to $20.8 m. There have also been important increases in exports of copra meal, soap, fruit juice, cigarettes, and beer. Value of non-food exports in 1985 increased to $30.65 m.

These improvements resulted in Western Samoa's exports in 1985 rising to $36.2 m, an increase of $2 m on the previous 12 months.

Some recent export/import figures are shown in the table.

In August 1983 the Government announced there had been a very strong surge in exports for the first six months of 1983, with values being twice those of the same period in 1982. Improvements were recorded in almost all export categories, in both volume and prices. The trend continued into 1984–85, but 1986–87 saw a decline.

Imports. Of the country's import bill of $75.1 million in 1983, manufactured goods accounted for $15.243 million, followed closely by food and live animals $15.197 million, machinery and transport equipment $14.968 million, petroleum products $13.074

TABLE 1 WESTERN SAMOA — EXPORTS AND IMPORTS (in $ million)

	1982	1983	1984	1985	1986	1987
Imports	60.1	75.1	93.3	115.0	105.4	N/A
Exports	16.2	27.4	34.2	36.2	23.5	25.0

TABLE 2 WESTERN SAMOA — MAJOR EXPORTS (in $000)

	1982	1983	1984	1985	1986	1987
Copra	2760.4	1397.5	N/A	950.7	1057.5	65
Cocoa	985.4	4616.8	2414.2	2357.9	3186.0	2622.0
Bananas	596.7	407.1	158.5	29.5	39.5	40.0
Taro	2126.1	2371.3	4223.4	5284.3	4335.0	5077.0
Timber	1207.7	540.6	1478.2	754.6	780.2	396.0
Coconut cream	936.9	1197.5	1582.6	2959.4	2822.0	3109.0
Coconut oil	3640.3	11,075.0	20,809.5	16,306.6	6542.1	8730.0
Beverages and tobacco	1176.1	1943.3	2302.9	2134.1	1321.3	1087.0

million, beverages and tobacco $1.913 million and vegetable oils and fats $392,400. The cost of imports has increased substantially since then, but a detailed breakdown is not available.

Customers. New Zealand represents the major market with a consistent 30–31 per cent of Western Samoa's products, followed by Australia, West Germany and the US with about 18 per cent each.

Suppliers. New Zealand also represents the major source of imports, providing a little over 30 per cent of Western Samoa's needs regularly, followed by Australia with 20 per cent and Fiji and Japan with 15 per cent. Imports from the US amount to only five per cent of the total.

Balance of trade. There was a trade deficit of $43.9 million in 1982, $59.1 million in 1984, $81.9 million in 1986, and $106 million in 1987, figures which make the claims of economic recovery seem a little hollow.

Customs tariff. The country has been struggling over the past decade to reduce its trade deficit. One method has been to raise customs duties. Since 1980 increases of up to 100 per cent have been applied to alcohol and tobacco imports, and heavier taxes were also imposed on electric-powered stoves, turbines and air-conditioners. Since then increases on an even wider range of goods have been applied.

FINANCE. Since independence the financial infrastructure has developed steadily. Originally it comprised only one commercial bank, which also performed some functions of a central bank, whereas now two commercial banks and several non-bank financial institutions play a significant role in the mobilisation of financial resources.

The establishment of the Central Bank of Samoa in May 1984 was another important advance in the development of the country's financial infrastructure. Although the Central Bank's responsibilities are similar at first to those of the Monetary Board, the bank will gradually assume wider responsibilities, i.e. control and regulate the money supply; administer the country's foreign exchange reserves; promote and foster credit and exchange conditions conducive to orderly and balanced economic development; pro-

mote a sound banking and financial structure for the country, and be an important adviser to the Government in the formation of economic policy.

During the early 1980s Western Samoa witnessed a period of monetary instability, reflected in high inflation rates (33 per cent in 1980 and 20.5 per cent in 1981), and an excessive growth in liquidity. Mounting budget deficits, poor performance of major public sector enterprises, both induced by internal and external factors, caused a sharp acceleration in credit to the public sector.

Balance of payments deficits from 1980 to 1982 were financed through the accumulation of arrears both on account of imports and debt-servicing. This resulted in a drastic reduction of the country's foreign assets, and corresponding foreign exchange claims on the Government. Net credit to the Government increased from $0.8 m at the end of 1979 to $34.1 m at the end of 1983, resulting from both foreign exchange claims on the Government and growing budget deficits.

Credit to the private sector, channelled through the commercial banks, grew modestly at a rate of 10.5 per cent, from $10.7 m at the end of 1979 to $15.94 m at the end of 1983. At the end of 1980 non-bank financial institutions provided the private sector with $16.6 m credit which rose to $27.6 m at the end of 1983.

With the advent of the worldwide recession in 1980–81, terms of trade turned against Western Samoa; prices for leading exports dropped dramatically, but import prices continued to rise rapidly. During 1979–82 the export unit price per ton of copra fell from $473 to $248 and for cocoa from $2355 to $1519. Export earnings fell from $15.6 m in 1979 to $11.6 m in 1981, reflecting, in large measure, lower prices for those two products.

The weakened export position combined with high import demand led to a severe balance of payments problem and a subsequent depletion of international reserves. Economic decline and balance of payments instability were accompanied by rapid inflation which averaged 20 per cent annually for the first few years of the decade. This reflected the influence of 'imported' inflation but it was also influenced by domestic forces, particularly by a rapid expansion of the money supply and later by shortages of domestic produce brought on by drought. From 1983 the effects of several currency devaluations were also contributing factors.

To restore economic growth and achieve external viability in the immediate term, the Government embarked on a stabilisation programme in 1983, supported by an International Monetary Fund (IMF) standby agreement. Various fiscal, monetary and exchange rate measures were introduced in early 1983 and followed by supplementary measures later that year. Among specific corrective measures were: import control through a new foreign exchange allocation system; concessionary loans for export promotion; a flexible exchange rate policy; increased rate levels; reduced government borrowing from the commercial banks; strict guidelines on bank lending to the private sector; and careful monitoring of public enterprise activity. Limits were also set on the size of the deficit of government accounts, mainly by restraint on development expenditure, economy in administrative expenditure and by introducing a range of new measures to bolster revenue.

The measures appear to have largely succeeded in restoring external balance, including a considerable reduction of payment arrears, and have strengthened the international reserve position. Significant price increases in 1982–83 for copra, coconut oil and cocoa also assisted in this recovery.

By 1986, however, there had been a drop in the value of exports, a trend which appeared to be continuing well into 1987.

Nonetheless, the General Manager of the Central Bank of Western Samoa, John Howard, could point in early 1987 to a number of economic achievements observable in the previous year: a declining inflation rate; a government budget surplus (in 1986); a balance of payments surplus (in 1986); a significant increase in gross international reserves and an economic growth rate of about 2 per cent in real terms.

In mid-1987 Finance Minister, Faasootauloa S. P. Saili, admitted that while recovery had been effected the country was still heavily dependent upon overseas remittances and foreign aid.

Revenues. Government revenues are raised from: taxes on income; excise taxes (levied on both domestically produced and imported goods); taxes on international trade (including import duties and foreign exchange levies); fees and service charges; rents and royalties; and a number of lesser means. Foreign cash grants and project grants account for about 25 per cent of government revenues.

The 1985 budget breakdown of receipts included: tax revenues of $52.3 m (including $12.5 m from income tax, $7.8 m from excise tax, and $30.7 m from various taxes on international trade). Non-tax revenues amounted to $11.3 m (including $3.0 m from fees and service charges, $5.5 m from operating surplus of departmental enterprises, and $2.5 m from rents, royalties and interest). Foreign cash grants amounted to $2.0 m, and project grants to $20.0 m. By 1987 the main categories of revenue were projected to increase as follows: tax revenue $57.6 m, non-tax revenue $12.4 m, foreign cash grants $1.5 m, and project grants $23.5 m.

Expenditures for 1985 for major government departments were: education $7.765 m, health $5.797 m, treasury $3.979 m, public works $7.636 m including $5.12 m fully recoverable, police and prisons $1.604 m, agriculture $1.441 m, transport $1.268 m, Prime Minister's Department $1.071 m.

External aid. Western Samoa receives considerable external financial and technical assistance from various sources, bilateral and multilateral. Apart from the traditional sources, namely, New Zealand and Australia, other friendly countries such as West Germany, Japan, and the Netherlands have been supporting the country's development efforts.

On the multilateral side, in addition to United Nations related bodies like the Asian Development Bank, the World Bank and the United Nations Development Programme, other inter-governmental bodies that provide assistance to Samoa include the European Economic Community, Commonwealth Fund for Technical Co-operation and the OPEC Fund. New aid donors include Kuwait and Saudi Arabia.

Project grants in 1987 amounted to $26.5 million, with Japan contributing $6.3 million of this, New Zealand $5 million and Australia

$8.8 million. New Zealand's assistance has been used mainly in forestry, agriculture and education, Japan's in fisheries and Australia's in imports grants schemes.

Another important source of funds is in the form of remittances from Samoans working outside the country. This flow of private transfers was estimated at $62 million in 1986 and $77 million in 1987.

Currency. Western Samoa uses the tala (dollar) divided into 100 sene (cents). A new set of coins was introduced in 1975, depicting the country's agricultural projects. These are for 1, 5, 10, 20 and 50 sene and one tala. Bank notes are in denominations of 1, 2, 10 and 20 tala. Western Samoa issued its own coinage for the first time in July 1967.

Western Samoa's gross international reserves amounted to $3.5 million as at 30 December 1980, a drop of 31 per cent on the previous year. But a recovery saw reserves standing at $58.5 million by early 1987.

Banks. The Bank of Western Samoa was established on 1 April 1959 with 55 per cent of capital provided by the Bank of New Zealand which conducted former operations, and 45 per cent from the Government of Western Samoa. The bank has a board of directors appointed by the Bank of NZ and the Samoan Government.

The Pacific Commercial Bank, in Apia, is a joint operation between the Bank of Hawaii and Westpac, Australia. It was founded in 1977 as Samoa's first independent bank.

The Development Bank of Western Samoa became independent in October 1974, evolving out of what was until then the Development Department of the former bank. Agricultural loans account for over 90 per cent of all loans. In 1984, 2919 loans totalling $8.081 m were approved. Half of these were for taro growing projects.

The Central Bank of Samoa was set up in May 1984 and is assumming the responsibilities of controlling and regulating the money supply, administering the country's foreign exchange reserves and promoting and fostering sound exchange and credit conditions.

Investment policy. Priority areas for investment are regarded as those which use locally produced raw materials and create local employment opportunities. Rigid rules are not laid down concerning the proportion of foreign shareholding in any enterprise, but participation by local shareholders is encouraged in the interests of sound economic growth.

Conditions for investment were changed in 1984 with the introduction of the Enterprises Incentives Act (1984), which replaced an earlier act of 1965 and modified the tariff system. Under the new tariff system a uniform rate of protection of 80 per cent is provided for all import-competing industries.

The Income Tax Act (1974) provides income tax incentives for primary production. Primary producers are entitled to an incentive allowance which may be deducted from assessable income.

The Industrial Free Zone Act (1974) provides incentives to new enterprises established with the principal objective of manufacturing, processing or assembling products for export.

Additional details on investment policies may be obtained from the Director, Department of Economic Development, PO Box 862, Apia, Western Samoa.

TRANSPORT. There are about 2042 km of roads on the two large Samoan islands of which 1234 km are access roads and 300 km are sealed. To enable more areas of Samoa to be cultivated, large-scale road-building projects have been initiated under the Rural Development Programme.

In Apia, rental cars and taxis are available as well as public buses. There is a timetable for buses serving the villages and districts but visitors are advised to consult the traffic policeman on duty at the old market bus stand for full particulars.

Vehicles. There were 4537 vehicles registered in 1985. Of that total, 1406 were private cars 1969 pick-ups, 432 trucks, 192 buses, 351 taxis, 165 motor cycles, 8 tractors and 14 'other vehicles'.

Air services. Western Samoa is served by a number of airlines. Besides Polynesian Airlines, its own flag-carrier, services are operated by Air Pacific, Air New Zealand, Air Nauru and Hawaiian Air. These airlines connect Apia with Auckland, Nadi (Fiji), Honolulu, Papeete, Rarotonga (Cook Islands), Nauru, Pago Pago and Sydney. The most frequent long-distance connections are with Fiji, Tonga and New Zealand, usually several times a week. Polynesian Airlines operates several services a day between Apia and Pago airports, and thus additional international connecting flights can easily be made through Pago. Internally, Polynesian Airlines runs services connecting the two main Western Samoan islands of Upolu and Savai'i.

Airports. The country's international airport is at Faleolo, about 32 km from Apia. The new runway and terminal opened in mid-1972, and work began in 1983 to upgrade and extend it to take larger jets, a project largely funded by Australian aid. The completion of the runway in 1986 allows Polynesian Airlines to fly a service directly from Sydney via Noumea.

There is also a 623 m strip for light planes at Fagali'i, about 4 km east of Apia wharf. The airstrips on the island of Savai'i are located at Asau on the north coast and near Salelologa in the south-east. The Savai'i airstrips take planes of the Britten–Norman Islander class.

Port facilities. Ports in Western Samoa are administered by the Marine Department. At Apia there is a deepwater wharf, 198 m in length, with a low water depth of 12 m alongside. Facilities include large goods sheds, a mobile crane, forklifts and other modern cargo-handling equipment. The Vacuum Oil Co. Pty Ltd has a bulk oil terminal at Sogi, near Apia.

At Asau, on the north coast of Savai'i, a deepwater wharf was completed in late 1966. However it was not until five years later that the necessary access channel was blasted through the coral reef to allow shipment of timber exports.

Outport harbour facilities are usually jetties adjacent to convenient reef passages. Ferry terminals at Mulifanua and Salelologa link Savai'i and Upolu.

Shipping services. The Pacific Forum Line is headquartered in Apia, and the line has regular services between Samoa, other Pacific islands and Australia and New Zealand.

Cruise liners call at Apia very occasionally but most regular transport is for the purpose of freight.

China Navigation Co. vessels operate a regular cargo service from Hong Kong and Asian ports via Pacific ports including Apia.

Bali Hai also operates a service between Japan and Apia. Pacific Islands Transport operates a cargo service from North American west coast ports. Kyowa Line runs a service from Japan and Asian ports to those in the Pacific including Apia. Warner Pacific Line operates from New Zealand and Australia. Nedlloyd operates a service from Europe, as do Bank Line and Columbus Line jointly. Marshall Is. Maritime Co. operates a service connecting with Honolulu. The Western Samoa Shipping Corporation operates weekly services using a vehicular ferry between American and Western Samoa, as well as between Savai'i and Upolu. Inter-Island Shipping Company runs similar motor launch services.

In 1983, 209 overseas vessels called at Apia and the port landed 105,144 tonnes of cargo.

COMMUNICATIONS. The Postal and Radio Department looks after all internal and external communications, maintaining sub-post offices under the control of the Director of Post Office and Radio at Apia. Radio out-stations staffed by trained Samoan operators serve Upolu and Savai'i.

In mid-1986 a fire destroyed the main post office in Apia, resulting in a permanent change of location. The new facilities were completed in late 1987. The fire was aided by the fact that Apia's fire brigade, barely half a mile from the post office, was without an engine for its fire-fighting vehicle at the time.

In the last few years Western Samoa has seen considerable improvements to internal and international communications. Apia is served by an automatic telephone exchange, while the telephone services operated by a manual exchange are being extended to villages in Savai'i and Upolu.

Under the Lome Convention, the EEC in 1979 granted a loan of $2.5 million to Western Samoa for the supply and installation of an Intelsat standard B earth station plus a spur system from the satellite earth station to the Samoan central telephone exchange as well as gateway telephone exchange facilities.

The installation has allowed direct dialling telephone services to other countries by satellite, and improved telex services. Marine Radio services have been upgraded. All services are operated 24 hours.

Apia Radio is the main connecting link for overseas communications. The out-stations communicate with Apia Radio by radio-telephone and telegraph in daily schedules. There is overseas radio-telephone to most overseas countries. Most local ships are now fitted with radio.

A continuous watch is kept on the international distress frequencies for ships at sea. A continuous radio link is also maintained with Faleolo airport.

Western Samoa updated ship-to-shore radio communications in 1979. Apia Radio's coast station 5WA was completely re-equipped, new HF and VHF transmitting and receiving stations being built with remote control exercised from the communications centre in Apia.

Ship-to-shore telegrams are accepted from any vessel. For radio telegraphy, Apia Radio keeps a 24-hour watch on 500 kHz. The working frequency is 483 kHz and 512 kHz is also available. For HF radio telephony, Apia Radio maintains a 24-hour watch on 2182 kHz and 621 kHz. Vessels calling on these frequencies are replied to on the same frequency as that on which they call. These frequencies are for distress and calling purposes only and may not be used for passing traffic or radio-telephone calls. Apia Radio is equipped to connect radio-telephone calls into the local telephone network. A station for VHF radio-telephone has been built on Mount Fiamoe in the centre of Upolu Island at about 914 m from which height the estimated range is about 129 km.

For navigation, the HF transmitting station is at 13 deg 40'55" S and 171 deg 49'46" W. The Fiamoe VHF station is at 13 deg 55' S and 171 deg 47'45" W. Antennas at both stations are fitted with red aircraft obstruction lights and should be visible for a considerable distance.

Radio. Known widely throughout the Pacific as 2AP, the Voice of Western Samoa, the local broadcast station began operations in 1948 and is government owned.

Broadcasts are in Samoan and English and consist mainly of entertainment, news, news reviews, farm and rural broadcasts, schools programmes and Legislative Assembly meetings.

The station accepts advertising and also broadcasts telegrams for the Post Office to listeners not served by telephones and in isolated villages where broadcasting is the only source of daily information. The broadcasting service operates from 6 am to 11 pm. About 80 per cent of all households possess at least the radio.

The American Samoan station WVUV and the American television station, KVZK-TV are well received in Western Samoa. Radio Australia is the best received of the shortwave stations, with the BBC and Voice of America being clear at certain times. Reception of 2AP is fair in neighbouring islands such as Fiji and the Cook Islands.

Newspapers. Western Samoa has several low-budget newspapers, the two main weekly newspapers being *The Samoa Times*, which was established in 1967 (as an amalgamation of a long-established weekly *Samoa Bulletin*, *Samoana* and a third newspaper the *Samoa Times* of Pago Pago), and *The Observer*, which was established in 1978. Others include *The Samoa Weekly*, and *O le Tusitala Samoa*.

The Prime Minister's Department produces two editions, one Samoan and one in English, of *Savali*, a fortnightly which carries government notices and news, much of it dealing with the progress of government schemes. The Samoan language edition is delivered free to the villages. Churches also publish small newspapers.

WATER AND ELECTRICITY. An area exceeding 50 sq. km around Apia is served by combined hydro-electric and diesel-electric installations.

About 49 per cent of the country's electricity was supplied by hydro following the opening of the Samasoni hydro scheme in February 1983, and this increased to 70 per cent with the opening of another project, Fale ole Fee, not far from Samasoni, in mid-1983. Samasoni has a capacity of 1650 kW, and Fale ole Fee, 1560 kW. Another new hydro project, the Sauniatu hydro, about 20 km east of Apia, with a capacity of 3500 kW, was completed in 1985. Other projects are planned to provide all of Upolu's power needs through hydro.

Rural electrification commenced in 1967 with the construction of a 22,000 volt distribution line from Apia. A number of small private and village-owned electrical schemes using diesel generators operate, somewhat erratically, in the outlying districts.

About 95 per cent of the population receive water from a piped supply, the rest from springs or roof catchment, but the authority admits these figures to be misleading since water supply is not continuous in many rural areas due to frequent breakdowns and vandalism. As much as 50 per cent of piped water is lost through wastage and leakage.

Water storage facilities have been constructed in several areas including a 4500 cubic metre reservoir at Mt Vaea near Apia. A water supply project for Apia, at present under construction with the assistance of Australian aid, is expected to cost over $9.0 m by 1988 and will almost completely replace the existing system which dates back to 1920. Rural supplies are also being upgraded to meet WHO standards and overcome the high incidence of infantile diarrhoea and other intestinal problems.

MAJOR OFFICE HOLDERS

Head of State:
His Highness Malietoa Tanumafili II
Prime Minister:
Tofilau Eti Alesana
Chief Justice:
Trevor Maxwell
Attorney-General:
Misa Foni Retzlaff

GOVERNMENT MINISTRIES AND DEPARTMENTS

Agriculture Ministry, Apia, Tel.: 22 561. Divisions: Forestry, Fisheries, Produce Marketing, Cocoa Board, Copra Board, Banana Board, Agricultural Store and Samoa Coconut Products
Economic Affairs Ministry, Apia, Tel.: 20 471. Divisions: Post Office and Telecommunications, Transport, Broadcasting and Tourism
Education Ministry, Apia, Tel.: 21 911. Divisions: Labour, Youth, Sports and Culture
Finance Ministry, Apia, Tel.: 22 822/ 21 682. Divisions: Inland Revenue, Customs, Audit, Statistics, Development Bank, National Provident Fund, Western Samoa Trust Estates Corporation, Samoa

Forest Products, Control of Foreign Exchange, National Pacific Insurance, Western Samoa Life Assurance, Accident Compensation and Public Trust
Health Ministry, Apia, Tel.: 21 212. Divisions: National Hospital, Public Health, Maternity Ward
Justice Ministry, Apia, Tel.: 22 671. Divisions: Land and Titles, Deaths and Marriages, Land Registry
Lands and Survey Ministry, Apia, Tel.: 22 481. Divisions: Parks and Recreation, Water Conservation
Prime Minister, Apia, Tel.: 21 500. Divisions: Foreign Affairs, Legislative, Attorney General, Cabinet, Police and Prison, Internal Affairs, Immigration, Public Service Commission and Fire Brigade
Works Ministry, Apia, Tel.: 21 611. Divisions: Special Project Development Corporation, Electric Power Corporation and Transport Pool
Broadcasting Department, Apia, Tel.: 21 420
Central Bank of Samoa, Apia, Tel.: 24 100
Economic Development Department, Apia, Tel.: 20 471
Immigration Department, Apia, Tel.: 20 291
Visitors Bureau, Apia, Tel.: 20 471

OVERSEAS OFFICES
New Zealand
Western Samoa High Commission, PO Box 1430, 1A Wesley Road, Kelburn, Wellington, New Zealand
Western Samoa Consulate, 3rd Floor, Maota Samoa, 283–293 Karanghape Road, Auckland 1, New Zealand
United States
Samoa Mission to the United Nations, 820 Second Avenue, Room 800, New York, NY 10017 Also accredited to: United States and Canada

FOREIGN MISSIONS
Australian High Commission, Beach Rd., Apia, Tel.: 23 411
Britain, Honorary Representative, PO Box 498, Apia, Tel.: 21 777
New Zealand High Commission, Beach Rd., Apia, Tel.: 21 711
People's Republic of China Embassy, Vailima, Tel.: 22 474

United States Consular Agent, Apia, Tel.: 21 631

Federal Republic of Germany Honorary Consul, Vaigaga, Tel.: 23 699

France, Honorary Consul, Vailima, Tel.: 21 246

Nauru Consulate, Sogi, Tel.: 23 320, 23 744

Japan Overseas Volunteers, Motootua, Tel.: 22 572

Peace Corps, Matautu-Tai, Tel.: 22 345

United Nations Development Programme, Matautu-Uta, Tel.: 23 670, 23 038

Unesco Office, Matautu-Uta, Tel.: 24 276

HISTORY. The history of Western Samoa concerns the history of the Samoan Islands as a whole. Little is known of the group in pre-European times. Fijian conquerors are said to have established themselves in Manu'a in the dawn of known Samoan history, and to have received tribute from all Samoa. There are many Samoan legends which have as heroes and heroines, princes and princesses of Fiji — legends which show ancient knowledge of the Fijian people and customs and indicate intercourse between Samoa and Fiji.

Later, the Tongans established themselves on Savai'i, crossed to Upolu, and were eventually beaten from the group by the first Malietoa, who arranged between Tonga and Samoa a treaty of peace.

Early visitors. The first European navigator to visit Samoa was Jacob Roggeveen in 1721–1722. He located the group somewhat inaccurately, called several of the islands by names now unused, and sailed away without landing. More than 40 years later, in May 1768, Bougainville passed through the group. Seeing many canoes moving along the shores of the islands, he named the group Navigators' Archipelago. He did not land either.

La Perouse was the next visitor. He called there in 1787 and fixed the position of the various islands. During his stay, a shore party for water from both of his ships was attacked near Asu, on Tutuila (American Samoa), and Commandant Vicomte de Langle and 11 others were killed.

The first British ship to visit the group was HMS *Pandora*, in 1791. It was not, however, until 1830 when the pioneer missionary, John Williams, of the London Missionary Society, landed at Sapapali'i, on Savai'i, that much was learned about the group. John Williams mentions several white men whom he found living among the Samoans. Two important events around this time were that in 1834 the Samoan language was reduced to print in tracts compiled by the missionaries, and that in 1838 the captain of HMS *Conway* concluded a commercial treaty with the leading chiefs. The agreement, between Captain Bethune and the chiefs, established a code of 'Commercial Regulations' by which, in consideration of the ships paying harbour dues when using the ports, foreign interests should be protected.

The following year there arrived the United States Exploring Expedition, under Commander Charles Wilkes, specially equipped for the expedition and survey of the then little-known islands of Polynesia. This American expedition did useful work in a number of Pacific groups, and in its published records are the first descriptions of the flora and fauna of Samoa, while its Samoan surveys are the foundation of practically all Samoan land measurements. Wilkes made an agreement with the chiefs similar to that made by Captain Bethune, and these two sets of regulations represented the first formal recognition of the Europeans by the Samoans.

Consuls appointed. White immigration and settlement proceeded steadily. In 1847, G. Pritchard (a former LMS missionary, who had been British Consul in Tahiti) was appointed first British Consul in Samoa. His son, W. T. Pritchard, in 1847, established the first permanent European store in Samoa, and succeeded his father as consul in 1856; and, in 1853, the first United States Commercial Agent was appointed.

Between 1840 and 1880, the Europeans settled in Apia formed a sort of protective society, and administered a code of laws, with the approval and consent of the native chiefs. It was based on the Conway–Wilkes 'Commercial Regulations', added to and amended as required.

The old system of native government continued in the districts beyond Apia. The consuls had supreme authority within Apia districts, but in the districts outside the Samoans did not always accept European orders, and there were occasional 'incidents'

— especially as inter-tribal wars were frequent, and European adventurers often became advisers to the various contending chiefs.

There was an important commercial-political development when, in 1856, August Unshelm arrived in Apia. Unshelm came from Valparaiso as the representative of Johann Cesar Godeffroy und Sohn, of Hamburg. Unshelm was immensely impressed by the possibilities of trade in Polynesia, and decided to remain in Apia and extend the operations of his firm. Within five years he had greatly extended operations, and opened trading stations in Fiji, and at Vava'u in Tonga. Thus was born German commercial activity in the Pacific Islands — the actual and direct forerunner of the German colonies and protectorates established during the ensuing 50 years.

Theodor Weber, a Godeffroy man, was appointed German Consul in Apia in 1861, and when in 1864 August Unshelm was drowned, Weber took control of the company and in a few years he had extended the trading business all over the Central and Western Pacific.

He had traders on hundreds of islands, each a centre of the spreading German influence. He had agencies in Fiji, Tonga, Niue, Futuna and Wallis Islands, the Tokelaus, Ellice and Gilbert Groups, Northern Solomons, New Hebrides (Vanuatu), New Britain, New Ireland and Nauru; and they were so firmly established in the Caroline-Marshall-Mariana Archipelagoes that they bought 1200 ha of land at Yap and established a great station, to be the centre of their activities in the north-west Pacific, and a half-way place between Samoa and Cochin.

Weber acquired some 30,000 ha of the best land on Samoa's best island, Upolu; and he had prepared a gigantic colonisation plan, to be operated by Germany in the Pacific Islands. Between 1850 and 1870, Germany was being swept by a fever for world colonisation and Weber's Pacific Islands plan was welcomed and supported by many influential people in Germany. In 1870, the Pacific islands belonged to anyone who cared to raise a flag.

The Franco-Prussian War in 1870 ruined Weber's plans. Godeffroy's home port,

Hamburg, was blockaded and the economic dislocation, plus unwise speculation in some countries, brought Godeffroy und Sohn to bankruptcy. The colonisation plan was put aside. When it was revived, 10 years later, the same chances for German settlement did not exist. Nonetheless, large German colonies were formed in the Pacific Islands.

Godeffroy's place was taken by 'Deutsche Handels und Plantagen Gesellschaft der Sudsee Inseln zu Hamburg', known for the next 40 years as 'D.H. & P.G.', or, more simply, 'the Long-Handle Firm'.

International rivalries. By 1870–80, conditions in Samoa were becoming more settled, but an international rivalry, between Britain, the US and Germany, was beginning to arise. This rivalry became entangled with native disputes.

Samoa was divided into four districts, ruled by five chiefly families. These five great names, or titles, either ruled alone, or made unions to rule over combined districts, or became completely united in one family, in which event Samoa had an overlord or king, Tupu-o-Samoa. After bitter wars, Malietoa Vaiinupo of Savai'i became king in 1830, and held office until his death in 1841.

There followed 25 years of squabbling and fighting between the chiefly families. In 1867, thousands of men were under arms — half, in support of one 'king', to the east of Apia, and the other half, urging the claims of another 'king', in the west. Thus, they remained for nearly two years, getting poorer and poorer, bartering their possessions, and selling their lands to the whites, to get food and arms.

In 1872, when USS *Narragansett* visited Pago Pago, the high chief of Tutuila sought US protection, and offered in return the exclusive right of establishing a naval station in Pago Pago. The US took no action.

At this stage, in the early seventies, Britain and the US were using all their influence to secure a peace in Samoa; and there then entered the picture Colonel A. B. Steinberger, special agent of the US Government.

The consuls, aided by Steinberger, arranged a formal peace, in April 1873. Malietopa Laupepa became king, and a constitution for Samoa, functioning as an independent state on the European model, was drafted, and finalised in 1875.

Steinberger then severed all official connection with the US and settled among the Samoans at Samoan headquarters, at Mulin'u (in Apia). He was instrumental in drafting a Declaration of Rights', in the name of the people of Samoa, and in finalising a constitution of 32 sections, providing for a limited monarchy and two Houses of Parliament. He soon became Premier of Samoa, under King Malietoa; but he was the virtual dictator of Samoa. His influence was so great that he prevented a developing war by inducing the Samoans to accept another claimant to the kingship — Tupua Pulepule. Malietoa and Tupua were to reign alternately, each for four years.

The consuls did not like Steinberger — neither his methods nor his growing power. The US Consul finally acted. At his request, conveyed through the British Consul, Captain Stevens, of HMS *Barracouta*, arrested Steinberger in February, 1876, and deported him to Fiji. Steinberger returned to America, and sued the British Government for damages in an action which was settled by compromise. Britain reprimanded Captain Stevens, and the US recalled the American Consul.

The elaborate Samoan Government collapsed after Steinberger departed; and, as the position deteriorated into factional fighting, the consuls of the three powers seemed to be always engaged in intrigue, supporting this or the other chief, in the hope of getting a political or commercial advantage.

A delegation of Samoans went to Fiji (now a British colony) early in 1877, to seek British protection. Britain declined. The delegation then visited the US seeking American protection; but Washington did nothing but accept the right to establish a naval station at Pago Pago in Tutuila. Next year, 1879, Samoa gave Germany and Britain similar permission to establish naval stations.

The Municipality of Apia was established in 1879 by the British High Commissioner for the Western Pacific (Sir Arthur Gordon) — an international settlement where European law was supreme, and where native fighting must not take place. It was governed by a board consisting of the three consuls, each appointing one assessor.

Every year of the next 30 years was noted for 'incidents' arising out of the ceaseless struggle of the high chiefs for power, out of trade rivalries, and the jealousies of the consuls. The latter, in the eighties, were supported by the warships of their respective nations.

Hurricane disaster. Just when the situation was particularly tense, there came the hurricane of 16 March 1889, and seven warships were trapped in Apia Harbour because they were watching each other so closely they were reluctant to leave when the storm warnings flew.

The Germans lost the *Adler*, *Eber* and *Olga*; the Americans the *Vandalia*, *Trenton* and *Nipsic*; but the only British warship there, the *Calliope*, under Captain Kane, fought her way out in the teeth of the hurricane, and was undamaged. Two of the ships were later refloated. The Germans lost 92 men and the Americans 54.

This effectively dampened the powers' inclination towards war over their interests in Samoa, and there was a temporary settlement in the Berlin Treaty of 1889. This treaty was between Britain, the US and Germany, under which an independent government was set up in Samoa under King Malietoa Laupepa, and the three consuls given authority to supervise the Apia Municipal Council.

This treaty marked the end of German intrigue and aggressiveness in Samoa, which had caused friction and difficulties there for 30 years. But, within five years, Mataafa was challenging the kingship of Maleitoa, the powers again were taking sides, and again the Samoans were fighting.

In 1890, Robert Louis Stevenson arrived in Samoa and settled in Vailima. His stay was brief, however, for he died suddenly on 3 December 1894. He was buried on Mount Vaea, overlooking Apia, where his tomb is still to be seen above his old home, which is now a State house.

Stevenson was very interested in the Samoan wars and the reasons for them, and in 1892 published an account called *A Footnote to History: Eight Years of Trouble in Samoa*. It includes a dramatic account by eye-witnesses of the hurricane of 1889, and the loss of the ships.

In 1899, treaties were drawn between the three powers, under which the Berlin Treaty was annulled; Germany was permitted to annex Western Samoa; the US was permitted to exercise sovereignty over Eastern Samoa as a territory under naval control; Britain renounced all claims in relation to Western Samoa. In return for British withdrawal Germany surrendered all her rights in the Tongan Islands (including Vava'u), in Niue (Savage Island), and all the Solomon Islands east and south-east of Bougainville.

German control. Thus, in 1899, Western Samoa became a German colony. In February 1900, Dr Solf, who was at the time President of the Municipality of Apia, was appointed Governor.

In 1908, Samoans saw the beginning of a long history of resistance to colonial overlords. The Mau of Pule was established, a movement based in Savai'i and resistant to German rule. Then, in March 1909, tensions grew so intense the Germans had to exile the movement leaders to the Marianas, and take punitive measures against their supporters.

On 29 August 1914, with the outbreak of World War I, a force of New Zealanders annexed Western Samoa without a shot being fired. The New Zealand military occupation continued under Colonel Logan until 30 April 1920. Logan's rule was marked by an appalling error which saw the deaths of 8500 people, or 22 per cent of Western Samoa's population. Through carelessness Logan had allowed a ship into Apia, known to be carrying Spanish influenza. And even when the disease was causing many deaths and illness, Logan refused much needed medical assistance from American Samoa. The disease was never introduced into American Samoa because of tough quarantine regulations.

By the Treaty of Versailles, Western Samoa became a 'C' class mandate of New Zealand.

The Mau. New Zealand's early years were marked by endless political trouble. Basically, the Samoan traditional leadership did not accept the need for foreign overlords, and the New Zealand administration was unprepared and ill-suited for running other people's countries. The epidemic had caused considerable discontent. Furthermore the New Zealand administration was led by military officers who had no understanding of Samoa's national feeling or pride. To them, the Samoans were simply natives led by agitators.

By the 1920s, the Mau movement had grown. The word 'mau' means testimony and was used to indicate that the movement represented a particular body of opinion critical of the New Zealand authorities.

The Mau was a non-violent passive resistance movement, which included leading Europeans, especially Mr O. F. Nelson, a wealthy and influential man. Judge Gurr, an American, and Mr A. G. Smyth, a leading merchant, were also active. The New Zealand administrators feared the growth of the Mau, and on various occasions had the three Europeans exiled.

The Samoans abandoned any hope of receiving any consideration from New Zealand. They became unco-operative — they would not in any way assist the administration and they refused to pay taxes.

One of the deported Europeans, Mr Smyth, returned to Samoa after three years banishment on 28 December 1929. Members of the Mau marched through Apia, in procession, to greet Smyth. Outside the administration building a group of armed policemen attempted to grab some men known to be wanted by the police. A fight ensued and several shots were fired by the police. This was followed by the firing of a police machine gun directly into the unarmed Mau.

Eleven people died that day, including a Mau leader, Tupua Tamasese Lealofi III who was hit as he tried to calm his followers.

New Zealand sent a warship to Samoa and banned the Mau. Most of the nation's men went into the bush to resist arrest. The time was extremely tense and the Mau remained a movement engaged in non co-operation and hostility. New Zealand responded with raids on Samoan houses in attempts to find the men.

In 1936, New Zealand elected a new Labour Government which cancelled the order of banishment against the leaders, and sent them back to Samoa. Relations between the Samoans and the New Zealand administration improved slowly, but the obvious incompetency of the administrators resulted in continued frustration and bad feeling.

By World War II, Samoa reached a turning point. US Marines were stationed on Upolu and constructed roads and an airport. Today their influence is felt to have been considerable, and a watershed between an old Samoa, and a developing Samoa. After the war Samoa became a trustee of the United Nations, administered by New Zealand. But by this time, New Zealand had begun to prepare Samoa for self-government, which was to come in 1962.

Preparation for self-government. A Council of State was established in 1947, consisting of the NZ High Commissioner (president) and the two Samoans holding office as Fautua (leading chief). Under the Samoan Amendment Act 1947, the High Commissioner had to consult the Council of State in the exercise of those powers about which he was not bound to consult the Executive Council. A Legislative Assembly was also set up.

New Zealand suggested in 1953 that a Constitutional Convention, representing all sections of the West Samoan population, be set up to consider proposals for future political progress. The Convention met at the end of 1954.

The New Zealand Parliament in October 1957 passed the Samoa Amendment Act 1957. The most important provisions of this were to redefine the functions of the High Commissioner, redefine and enlarge the membership of the Executive Council, provide for the appointment of a Leader of Government Business, reconstitute official and increased Samoan membership, provide for a Speaker, redefine the Assembly's privileges and powers and abolish the Fono of Faipule, which was a Samoan advisory body.

The Executive Council became 'the principal instrument of policy'. The 1957 Act provided that members, other than the High Commissioner and the Fautua, should be designated Ministers.

A Prime Minister, in place of the Leader of Government Business, was appointed in September 1959, and by the end of 1960 the Samoan Constitutional Convention had approved a draft constitution for an Independent State of Western Samoa. Prime Minister Fiame Mataafa took the proposals to the United Nations in January 1961. This led to a UN supervised plebiscite on 9 May 1961, wherein all adult citizens of Samoa were asked whether (a) they approved the Constitution; and (b) whether they wanted independence on 1 January 1962.

The affirmative vote on both clauses was

a foregone conclusion — the only unique feature about the plebiscite was that it was the first time that people of Samoan domestic status voted according to adult universal suffrage and not on the 'matai' system.

The Constitution of Western Samoa became 'the supreme law of Western Samoa' at independence on 1 January 1962. The Constitution provides for a Head of State, called in Samoan, O le Ao O le Malo, to be elected by the Legislative Assembly for a term of five years.

However, in the first instance, it was decided that the two High Chiefs, who had been titled the Fautua (Tupua Tamasese and Malietoa Tanumafili II), should become joint Heads of State and have a lifetime tenure of office unless they resigned or were removed from office by the Assembly. If one predeceased the other, the survivor continued as sole Head of State during his lifetime — subject to resignation or removal from office. On 5 April 1963 Tupua Tamasese died; the sole Head of State thereafter was Malietoa Tanumafili II. Western Samoa joined the United Nations in 1976.

Western Samoa had a constitutional crisis in 1982 which resulted in the country having three Prime Ministers that year. The year began under Prime Minister Tupuola Efi, who had been in office for six years. He lost power following the February elections to Va'ai Kolone, leader of the Human Rights Protection Party. Va'ai lost his seat in September following a successful court petition on electoral irregularities. The Head of State empowered Tupuola to form a new government, but he was later defeated in the House when he sought to table the 1983 budget. The new leader of the HRPP, Tofilau Eti, was sworn in as Prime Minister on 30 December. The difficulties of the year were compounded by a legal challenge to the system of 'matai' voting, which the then Chief Justice held to be unconstitutional. By-elections could not be held until the results of an appeal were known. The Court of Appeal ruled against the Chief Justice. Also during 1982 the Privy Council, in London, held that all Western Samoans born between 1928 and 1949, or their children, were New Zealand citizens with full rights in New Zealand. There was much controversy and confusion when an agreement between New Zealand and the Va'ai Kolone government effectively cancelled this situation in August 1982.

Since the elections of 1985, the political rivalries and constitutional difficulties which racked the country earlier had been largely overcome by a government which appeared to be based on the concept of national unity and co-operation rather than confrontation. The political opponents of 1982–83, Va'ai Kolone and Tupuola Efi, served as Prime Minister and Deputy Prime Minister respectively. The elections of February 1988, however, were vigorously contested and at first returned a tied result, an almost peculiarly Samoan situation. The subsequent defection of one member of the former government to the opposition party, saw eventual victory go to the Human Rights Protection Party led by Tofilau Eti Alesana.

Further reading. For a discussion of the emergence of Western Samoa as an independent state, particularly the making of the constitution, see J. W. Davidson, *Samoa mo Samoa*, Melbourne, 1967. David Pitt's *Tradition and Economic Progress in Samoa*, Oxford, 1970, and Brian Lockwood's *Samoan Village Economy*, Melbourne, 1971, are also detailed, but technical works on the grass roots of Samoa. Margaret Mead's *Coming of Age in Samoa*, researched in American Samoa in 1927, still has relevance, as does Derek Freeman's *Margaret Mead and Samoa* ..., Melbourne, 1979.

FOR THE TOURIST. General visitor information is provided by the Western Samoa Visitors Bureau, PO Box 862, Apia, phone 20471. The bureau is on the Beach Road near the markets.

Entry formalities. No entry permit is required if stay does not exceed 30 days. For a longer stay, apply direct to the Immigration Division, Prime Minister's Department, Apia, or through a New Zealand diplomatic post or British Consular office. Visitors staying more than three months require an exit permit from the Immigration Office before departure.

Airport tax. There is an airport departure tax of 20 tala ($WS20) for non-residents and 5 tala for residents. There is also a hotel room tax of 10 per cent.

Sightseeing. Numerous scenic drives can be made by tourist coach or rental car. These include plantations, lush rainforests, waterfalls and freshwater bathing pools of the inland or coastal villages and their fine sandy beaches.

Apia itself has much of interest. Set on the water's edge, the town straggles casually along the beach, and its architecture no less than its disposition embodies its history.

Perhaps the feature of Apia first to catch the eye is the series of denominational churches along the shore line. On the western horn of the half-moon bay stands the observatory at Mulinu'u; at the eastern end is Matautu and the main wharf. Recent building development along Beach Road has begun to alter the well-known sky-line of Apia, although none of the development so far is exactly high-rise. The buildings owned by the Congregational Church, the Commercial Bank, and the Post Office are the most outstanding of the developments.

Apia now has two hotels and a number of restaurants, clubs, bars and honky-tonks where the visitor can spend a varied hour or two on most evenings. Entertainment of a traditional or modern kind is offered at most of them. The ex-services club in the centre of town welcomes visitors and offers some recreational facilities in addition to its bar.

Visitors who arrive by air get their first introduction to Western Samoa coming in from the airport, which is 40 km from Apia. The road skirts the shore and meanders through Samoan villages — usually situated near a freshwater creek. Each village has a church and some have more than one — some very modern in design, some massive with cupolas and turrets, some whitewashed, some picked out in multi-colours. The number of churches is the first surprise for visitors.

Many village houses are of European materials but traditional Samoan is still the style in the majority of cases. Round or oval shaped, thatched roof supported by closely spaced posts and walls of mat blinds that are pulled up except when it rains, these houses are cool but also give the passerby an unexpected close-up view of village life.

Some recommended excursions: to Falefa Falls, about 30 km east of Apia, then over the Mafa Pass and another 35 km to the Aleipata District on the south-east corner of Upolu. On the way you see the Fuipisia Falls which have a drop of nearly 60 m.

About 40 km west of Apia (beyond the airport) is the West Samoan Trust Estate's coconut plantation of Mulifanua, said to be the largest single coconut plantation in the Southern Hemisphere. At the extreme point of this west coast road is Lefatu Cape. There are some delightful beachside picnic spots here — and a view of the small islands of Manono and Apolima which lie between the big islands of Upolu and Savai'i. Manono can be visited on a day tour by boat from Manono-uta, near Cape Lefatu.

A scenic drive round the island of Upolu can be made as a day excursion. The cross-island road at the western end of Upolu branches off some miles from Faleolo, on the north coast, and connects with Lefaga on the south coast.

Closer to Apia is Papaseea, or sliding rock, where the visitor can slide down a natural rock slide into a freshwater pool. This is about 8 km out and can be reached by car.

For the vigorous there is Lake Lanoto which is 17 km from Apia and at an elevation of 600 m. A car can get half way there, after which it is a matter of walking or riding a horse.

Directly above Apia is Mt Vaea, at the top of which is Robert Louis Stevenson's grave. The trail that leads to the summit begins at Vailima, the final home of RLS, now the residence of the Western Samoan Head of State. The house is about 7 km from the waterfront. It can be visited with permission from the Prime Minister's office or through visitor information centres in Apia. The climb to the tomb can be strenuous and best done before heat builds up. Average walking time is 45 minutes.

At Mulinu'u, a 20 minute walk from the centre of Apia, are the traditional burial grounds of Samoan royalty and the Legislative Assembly building, styled after a Samoan 'fale'. Adjacent are the 'malae' grounds for national celebrations. Also at Mulinu'u, along the road leading to it, are a number of monuments dating from the 19th century when the Samoans were engaged in civil wars and Britain, Germany and the United States were rivals for power in the area.

The larger island of Savai'i remains large-ly untouched by outside influence. Here are old man-made rock formations including an old Samoan fort and other historical relics. Savai'i can be reached by daily air flights from Faleolo airport or from the domestic airstrip at Apia to Asau (in about 25 minutes) and Salelologa (in eight minutes). A visit of at least two days is recommended if the visitor wants to see anything of the big island at leisure. Regular overnight visits are arranged by Apia travel agents, but the independent traveller can reach Savai'i by passenger/vehicular ferry from Mulifanua, although the crowds are often formidable, and can get around the island economically, if not particularly comfortably, by the buses which meet every ferry.

ACCOMMODATION
APIA AND ENVIRONS

Aggie Grey's Hotel: at eastern end of Apia, probably the best-known hotel in the South Seas, 120 rooms and several VIP fales, a/c, coffee-making facilities, restaurant, bars, function rooms, large swimming pool, laundry/dry cleaning service, live music nightly, traditional entertainment regularly, credit cards. PO Box 67, Apia, Western Samoa. Tel. 22880, Telex SX 257

Tusitala Hotel: at western end of Apia, 96 rooms, a/c, restaurant and snack bar, bars, swimming pool, conference facilities, guest laundry, regular entertainment, credit cards accepted from guests only. PO Box 101, Apia, Western Samoa. Tel. 21122, Telex 226 Tusitala SX

Harbour Light Hotel: near main wharf at eastern end of Apia, 30 rooms, a/c, restaurant, bar, regular entertainment. PO Box 8, Apia, Western Samoa. Tel. 21103, 21933

Vaiala Beach Cottages: at Vaiala Beach, 1.5 km from Apia, several self-contained motel style units, close to Palolo Deep marine reserve. PO Box 1157, Apia, Western Samoa. Tel. 22202

Seaside Inn: near main wharf at eastern end of Apia, single and double rooms with toilet and shower, share kitchen facilities, private bar, laundry facilities, tariff includes breakfast. PO Box 325, Apia, Western Samoa. Tel. 22578

Betty Moor's Tourist Accommodation: 100 metres from Vaiala Beach, 5 single, 4 twin and 2 double rooms, share shower and toilet facilities, share kitchen facilities. PO Box 18, Apia, Western Samoa. Tel. 21085

Valentine Parker Accommodations: ten minutes from Apia at Fugalei, rooms can sleep two, kitchen facilities and refrigerator available, shop on premises. PO Box 395, Apia, Western Samoa. Tel. 22158

Olivia Yandall's Casual and Tourist Accommodation: adjacent to Apia Park, one fully self-contained unit sleeping up to four, small fale, 4 double rooms in large bungalow, meals or kitchen facilities available. PO Box 4089, Apia, Western Samoa. Tel. 22110

Hideaway Beach Resort: on South Coast of Upolu, about 21 km from Apia, 30 units, undergoing extensive renovations in late 1987, restaurant, bar, regular entertainment. PO Box 1191, Apia, Western Samoa. Tel. 23800, Telex 213 HIDETOURS SX

SAVAI'I ISLAND

Safua Hotel: on coast near Salelologa, 9 fales with private shower/toilet, meals included in tariff, restaurant, bar, tours by arrangement. PO Box 5002, Salelologa, Savai'i, Western Samoa. Tel. 24262, 24202

Salafai Inn: in Salelologa, 7 double rooms and 4 self-contained flats, meals by arrangement. PO Box 1193, Salelologa, Savai'i, Western Samoa. Tel. 22536

Savai'ian Guest Fale: at Lalomalava, short distance from Salelologa, traditional large Samoan fale, sleeping an apparently unlimited number of people if required, meals available. Bookings through Apia travel agents or direct.

Vaisala Hotel: at Vaisala Bay near Asau at western end of Savai'i, 18 units, private shower/toilet, coffee-making facilities, restaurant, bars, recreational facilities, tours and rental vehicles by arrangement. PO Box 570, Apia, Western Samoa. Tel. 22027, 21842, Telex 202 UNITEDCO SX

South Pacific Forum

The South Pacific Forum, an organisation of Heads of Governments of independent and self-governing countries of the South Pacific, was formed at a meeting in Wellington, New Zealand, in August 1971, attended by the President of Nauru (Hammer DeRoburt), the Prime Ministers of New Zealand (Sir Keith Holyoake), Tonga (Prince Tu'ipelehake), Fiji (Ratu Sir Kamisese Mara) and Western Samoa (Tupua Tamasese Lealofi IV), the Premier of the Cook Islands (Mr Albert Henry) and the Australian Minister for External Territories (Mr C. E. Barnes).

The forum was created out of a need by the then newly-independent Island countries of the South Pacific for an organisation through which to voice their joint political views, denied to them by the South Pacific Conference which proscribed political expression.

Principal architect of the forum, which meets annually, was Fiji Prime Minister Ratu Sir Kamisese Mara, who was also creator of the forum's forerunner, the Pacific Islands Producers' Secretariat (PIPS), later the Pacific Islands Producers' Association (PIPA). The first meeting of PIPS was at Apia in 1965, with Fiji, Tonga and Western Samoa taking part. The Cook Islands and Niue joined later. With the change in name to PIPA, a full-time executive secretary was employed with headquarters in Suva and Ratu Mara as its first president.

Originally a commerical pressure group aiming to find markets for the Islands' exports, it began to assume a political tinge by the beginning of the 1970s. Its sixth meeting, at Nuku'alofa in April 1971, when the Gilbert and Ellice Islands Colony was admitted as a member, and 60 delegates and observers attended, saw an unofficial, private meeting between Ratu Mara, Prince Tu'ipelehake, Tamasese Lealofi and Mr Albert Henry. The four leaders discussed the formation of the forum. The result was a request to New Zealand to host a meeting of the independent South Pacific countries to form the South Pacific Forum. The meeting was followed, in February 1972, by a second meeting at Canberra. The South Pacific Bureau for Economic Co-operation (SPEC) was established at the 1973 Apia Forum and subsequently became the forum's secretariat in 1976. In late 1988 SPEC's name became, simply, the forum secretariat. PIPA was still in existence but it voted for its own dissolution in 1974.

The forum has continued to meet every year and, through it, the Secretariat has co-operated on several projects with the South Pacific Commission. The forum's most important decision was made at the 1977 meeting in Port Moresby when it moved to establish a South Pacific Regional Fisheries Agency with a broad membership and urged forum members to claim a 200-mile economic and fishing zone in their national waters.

The 1978 Niue Forum established the South Pacific Forum Fisheries Agency with members confined to the forum. The headquarters of the Agency is at Honiara, capital of the Solomon Islands.

The forum has continued as a Heads of Government organisation with plenary powers and membership confined to independent and self-governing countries in the South Pacific including Australia and New Zealand. As its meetings are attended, in most cases, by government leaders, the forum can make decisions on the spot whereas, in the South Pacific Conference, most matters have to be referred by delegates to their governments.

The forum has given membership 'in an observer capacity' to governments in the region on the verge of independence and has also placed the services of the Secretariat at the disposal of those governments.

The Secretariat has its headquarters in Suva, built with funds from Australia and New Zealand. The formal agreement establishing the Secretariat was signed in Apia on 17 April 1973 by the Governments of Australia, Cook Islands, Fiji, Nauru, New Zealand, Tonga and Western Samoa. These member countries have since been joined by Niue, Papua New Guinea, Kiribati, Solomon Islands, Tuvalu, Federated States of Micronesia, Republic of the Marshall Islands and Vanuatu. Membership now totals 15. While the Secretariat does have a formal membership, it was not designed to create exclusive benefits for those members alone. It has always been the wish of the forum that the Secretariat should be available to help other Pacific Island territories, and thus promote the interests of the region as a whole.

Organisation. The Secretariat's activities are co-ordinated at the inter-governmental level. Apart from the annual meetings of the forum, there are consultations through the 'Secretariat Committee', the Bureau's executive board comprising representatives — usually at senior official level — from all member countries. This provides an opportunity for detailed discussion of the Secretariat's work programme and the ideas that political leaders wish to promote. Meetings on specific topics are also convened from time to time.

Work Programme. The Secretariat's trade activities have covered trade promotion, the identification and development of export-oriented industries, and the negotiation of export opportunities. Following a study of trade relations and industrial development in the South Pacific, the Secretariat assisted Island countries in the negotiation of the South Pacific Regional Trade and Economic Co-operation Agreement (SPARTECA), a major step in the expansion of export markets and impetus to the development of Island export-based industry.

To promote the flow of Island products to Australian markets, the **South Pacific Trade Commission** was established in May 1979,

in Sydney under Secretariat auspices, with the financial backing of the Australian Government. The South Pacific Trade Commission now has a showroom available for the use of Pacific Island exporters or potential exporters for trade displays. All inquiries should be directed to SPTC, Sydney.

Regional Transport is an important part of the Secretariat's activities. The Regional Shipping Council and its Advisory Board was formed in 1974 and in 1976 the forum endorsed the formation of the Pacific Forum Line as a regional shipping venture. The Secretariat is also involved in other shipping matters including wage rates and working conditions for Island seamen and uniform maritime standards for the region.

Following a decision by the Rotorua Forum meeting in 1976, a Regional Civil Aviation Council and Advisory Committee were established.

Telecommunications has constituted another major field of the Secretariat's activity, following the decision of the 1973 Forum that it should act as the co-ordinating agency for telecommunications work being undertaken in the South Pacific by the United Nations and other agencies. Technical support has been provided for the Secretariat by the International Telecommunications Union (ITU).

Energy, including alternative energy sources, has emerged as a top priority of Secretariat member governments. Following a study on appropriate regional institutional arrangements for energy matters, the forum decided in 1981 that the Secretariat should assume the role of overall regional energy co-ordinator. An Energy Unit was established in 1982 to carry out this responsibility.

Aid co-ordination and, in particular, the development and implementation of regional aid projects funded by the EEC under the Lome Convention is another activity for which the Secretariat is responsible. Since 1981 the Secretariat has also acted as the administrative office to the ACP Pacific Group Council which meets annually.

In 1981, forum leaders decided that a **Pacific Regional Advisory Service** (PRAS) should be established under the auspices of the Secretariat. The main functions of PRAS are to maintain a systematic register of skilled personnel in Pacific Island countries which would be available to meet requests from governments in the region, and to facilitate transfers of such personnel.

A UN funded programme to assist member countries through **Short Term Advisory Services** in a wide range of fields is administered by the Secretariat which also administers a **Fellowship Scheme** funded by Australia and New Zealand and the Commonwealth Fund for Technical Co-operation (CFTC). The fellowship scheme provides in-service training in Island member countries for two candidates per country per year.

The Secretariat also manages a **Regional Disaster Relief Fund** which provides monetary assistance to countries in the region suffering from the effects of natural disasters. It also provides assistance in disaster preparedness for member governments.

The Secretariat also participates in the **South Pacific Regional Environment Programme** (SPREP) which is a co-operative effort between it and SPC along with other UN agencies working in the region. The programme is aimed at co-ordinating and assisting Pacific Island countries with the proper management of their environment and natural resources.

Forum Secretariat Director, Mr Henry Naisali, Deputy Director, Mr Rene Wilson, Ratu Sukuna Road, Box 856, GPO, Suva, Fiji. Telephone: Suva 312600. Telex: 2229FJ. Cables: SPECSUVA.

South Pacific Trade Commission, Trade Commissioner, Mr Bill McCabe, South Pacific Trade Commission, 9th Floor, Somare Haus, 225 Clarence Street, Sydney, NSW 2000, Australia.

The South Pacific Commission

The South Pacific Commission is an international organisation which provides technical advice, training, assistance and dissemination of information in social, economic and cultural fields to 22 governments and administrations of the region. Altogether, the countries contain approximately five million people scattered over some 30 million square kilometres. Less than two per cent of this area is land.

HISTORY
Membership. The South Pacific Commission was founded on 6 February 1947, when representatives from six governments signed the Agreement Establishing the South Pacific Commission. The agreement, usually known as the Canberra Agreement, was signed in Canberra, Australia, by the Governments of Australia, France, the Netherlands, New Zealand, the United Kingdom and the United States of America.

Since the signing, the Netherlands has withdrawn from the Commission (in 1962, when it ceased to administer the former colony of Dutch New Guinea, now known as Irian Jaya), and the following independent and self-governing Pacific states were later admitted to membership: Western Samoa (October 1965), Nauru (July 1969), Fiji (May 1971), Papua New Guinea (September 1975), Solomon Islands and Tuvalu (November 1978), and Niue and Cook Islands (October 1980).

Following recommendations in the Secretary-General's internal review of the South Pacific Commission, the 23rd South Pacific Conference in Saipan, Northern Mariana Islands, in October 1983, adopted by consensus a resolution that the conference's 27 governments and administrations should have full and equal membership, thus admitting to the commission: American Samoa, Federated States of Micronesia, French Polynesia, Guam, Kiribati, Marshall Islands, New Caledonia, Northern Mariana Islands, Palau, Pitcairn Islands, Tokelau, Tonga, Vanuatu, and Wallis and Futuna.

South Pacific Conference. Until 1974, commissioners from the participating governments met in the annual session. The South Pacific Conference, attended by delegates from the Pacific territories, originally met only once every three years. It provided an opportunity for representatives from the Pacific Islands to make known to the participating governments their territories' special needs and problems. The first South Pacific Conference met in 1950. In 1967, the conference became an annual event; it met immediately before the Session of Commissioners and made recommendations to it.

Proposals for changes in the functioning of the commission were incorporated in a Memorandum of Understanding which was formally signed by representatives of the eight participating governments in Rarotonga, Cook Islands, on 2 October 1974, during the 14th South Pacific Conference. The Memorandum provides for the former Session of Commissioners and South Pacific Conference to meet annually as a single body, known as the South Pacific Conference.

The South Pacific Conference examines and adopts the commission's work programme and budget for the coming year, and discusses any other matters within the commission's competence. Each government and administration has the right to send to the conference a representative and alternate. Each representative, or in his absence an alternate, has the right to cast one vote on behalf of the government or administration which he represents.

To assist the conference in its work, the Memorandum signed in 1974 also provided for a Planning and Evaluation Committee and a Committe of Representatives of Participating Governments. The South Pacific Conference resolution adopted in October 1983 replaced these two committees by providing for a Committee of Representatives of Governments and Administrations (CRGA) to operate as a Committee of the Whole. This committee meets at least four months prior to, and immediately before, the annual conference to consider and recommend the administrative budget and other administrative matters, evaluate the draft work programme and budget presented by the secretary-general, nominate the principal officers of the commission, and report thereon to the conference.

Members of the South Pacific Conference (27).
American Samoa
Australia
Cook Islands
Federated States of Micronesia
Fiji
France
French Polynesia
Guam
Kiribati
Marshall Islands
Nauru
New Caledonia
New Zealand
Niue
Northern Mariana Islands
Palau
Papua New Guinea
Pitcairn Islands
Solomon Islands
Tokelau
Tonga
Tuvalu
United Kingdom
United States of America
Vanuatu
Wallis and Futuna
Western Samoa

Countries in which programmes of the South Pacific Commission are implemented (22).
American Samoa
Cook Islands
Federated States of Micronesia
Fiji
French Polynesia
Guam
Kiribati
Marshall Islands
Nauru
New Caledonia
Niue
Northern Mariana Islands
Palau
Papua New Guinea
Pitcairn Islands
Solomon Islands
Tokelau
Tonga
Tuvalu
Vanuatu
Wallis and Futuna
Western Samoa

South Pacific Commission Emblem. The SPC emblem, designed in New Caledonia, was officially adopted on 6 February 1970 on the occassion of the 23rd anniversary of the South Pacific Commission. Each star represents a member government and administration of the Commission, which at present number 27.

ROLE OF THE COMMISSION
The commission's role is advisory and consultative. Its programmes are closely coordinated with those of the countries of the Pacific for which it works. The commission does not wish to concern itself with the politics, nor does it attempt to control development programmes, of governments or administrations within the region.

The 16th South Pacific Conference, which met in October 1976, adopted a recommendation made by a review committee that met earlier in the year, which reads as follows:

The South Pacific Commission, with the objective of encouraging and promoting the economic and social welfare and advancement of Pacific peoples in accordance with the Canberra Agreement as amended, should undertake the following functions:

(a) to provide a common forum within which the Island peoples and their governments can express themselves on issues, problems, needs and ideas common to the region, with a view to maintaining the opportunity for all Islands to be heard, viewed, considered and assisted on equal terms with one another;

(b) to be a vehicle for the development and implementation of the concept of regionalism;

(c) to assist in meeting the basic needs of the peoples of the region;

(d) to foster and develop means to facilitate the flow of indigenous products, technical know-how and people among the islands;

(e) to serve as a catalyst for development of regional resources that are beyond the capability of individual Island governments to develop;

(f) to serve as an aid-organising machine for Islands which are otherwise unable to reach aid sources outside the Islands or outside the region itself;

(g) to act as a centre for collection and dissemination of information on the needs of the region and also as a depository for such information;

(h) to undertake such other appropriate activities as may be determined by the South Pacific Conference.

Languages. The official working languages of the commission are English and French.

Finances. Contributions are made to the regular budget of the commission by all members on an agreed formula:

Australia	33.26%
USA	16.83%
New Zealand	16.14%
France	13.86%
United Kingdom	12.18%
American Samoa, Fiji, French Polynesia, Guam, Nauru, New Caledonia	0.55% each;
Federated States of Micronesia, Marshall Islands, Northern Mariana Islands, Palau, Papua New Guinea	0.393% each;

Cook Islands, Kiribati, Niue, Solomon Islands, Tokelau, Tonga, Tuvalu, Vanuatu, Wallis and Futuna, Western Samoa	0.247% each.

A unanimity rule requires the agreement of all 27 member countries to any increase in their annual contribution levels.

Voluntary contributions are also made to the commission's regular budget by some members. The total regular budget for 1984 was 404,242,700 CFP francs. In addition to projects funded from the regular budget, the commission also carries out a number of activities funded by governments, international organisations and other external sources. In 1983, the largest projects of this kind were the Tuna and Billfish Assessment Programme, funded by voluntary contributions from the governments of Australia, France, New Zealand, the United Kingdom and the United States; a project for technical assistance and training for census, demography and population statistics, funded by the United Nations Fund for Population Activities; a rural water supply and sanitation programme, funded by a voluntary contribution from the United States Government; a South Pacific Regional Environment Programme, carried out in collaboration with other organisations and funded by the United Nations Environment Programme; a project on migration, employment and development in the Pacific, funded by the United Nations Fund for Population Activities; a project to increase self-sufficiency on atolls, funded by the United Nations Development Programme; an infectious diseases project in Vanuatu, funded by the Australian Development Assistance Bureau; and the Pacific Women's Resource Bureau, funded by voluntary contributions from the Australian Government, the French Government, and the Commonwealth Foundation. Altogether, projects funded from external sources in 1983 were worth 266,170,800 CFP francs. In 1986 half of the commission's projects were funded from external sources.

Publications. Technical publications are published as the need arises, and include the following series: technical papers, handbooks; information documents; information circulars, reports of meetings; statistical bulletins; newsletters on various topics. These publications disseminate information on recent developments in the commission's field of work.

Other publications include: *Monthly News of Activities*; *Report of the South Pacific Conference*; and *Annual Report*.

These publications can be obtained from the commission's Noumea office.

Management Committee. Since November 1976, the secretariat has had a management committee which has a supervisory and advisory role over all commission activities. Committee members are the principal officers of the commission: Secretary-General Mr Palauni M. Tuiasosopo; Director of Programmes Mr Jon Jonassen; Deputy Director of Programmes Mrs Hélène Courte. The Secretary-General is the chief executive officer of the Commission.

Secretariat. *Permanent secretariat headquarters:* Anse Vata, Noumea, New Caledonia. Telephone: 26.20.00 and 26.20.11. Telex: 139 NM SOPACOM. Cables: SOUTH-PACOM. Postal address: B.P. D5, NOUMEA CEDEX, New Caledonia. Office hours: Monday–Friday, 7.30 a.m.–12 noon, then 1.00 p.m.–4.00 p.m. Holidays: 6 February: SPC Anniversary; Good Friday; all official New Caledonia holidays.

Branches. *Fiji:* SPC Community Education Training Centre, Private Mail Bag, Suva, Fiji, or SPC Regional Media Centre, Private Mail Bag, Suva, Fiji. *Australia:* SPC Publications Bureau, PO Box A245, Sydney South, NSW, Australia 2000.

Staff. One hundred and three based in Noumea, 29 in Fiji, 12 in various countries within the region for training programmes, and two in Sydney.

ACTIVITIES

The 16th South Pacific Conference adopted a recommendation by the 1976 Review Committee that the commission should carry out the following specific activities:

(a) rural development;

(b) youth and community development;

(c) *ad hoc* expert consultancies;

(d) cultural exchanges (in arts, sports and education);

(e) training facilitation; and

(f) assessment and development of marine resources and research

and that special consideration should be given to projects and grants-in-aid which do not necessarily fall within these specific activities, but which respond to pressing regional or sub-regional needs or to the expressed needs of the Pacific countries.

The review committee also recommended that the three main sectors (health, social development, economic development) into which the commission's work programme was formerly divided be abolished, and an integrated work programme, incorporating all activities, be established.

Within the framework of this integrated work programme, the 23rd South Pacific Conference accorded top priority to the following items, projects and programmes: **Food and materials.** *Agriculture:* Family-level food crops and home economics projects; sub-regional training course on beef cattle; agricultural clearing-house and advisory services. *Plant Protection:* South Pacific Commission regional plant protection service; UNDP FAO-SPC project for strengthening plant protection and root crops development in the South Pacific (Suva, Fiji); sub-regional training courses and workshops on plant protection; regional technical meeting on plant protection; special plant protection publications and training aids; plant protection clearing-house and advisory services.

Professional staff: Tropical Agriculturalist; Plant Protection Officer. Two more scientists and an information officer were added in 1987.

Marine resources. *Marine resources:* Regional technical meeting on fisheries; tuna and billfish assessment programme; deep sea fisheries development project; awards for fisheries training. Eighty-one students from 19 countries have attended the six month Fisheries Officers Training Course held in Nelson, New Zealand.

Professional staff: Tuna and Billfish Programme Co-ordinator; Senior Fisheries Scientists (3); Fisheries Research Scientists (3); Systems Manager; Fisheries Statisticians (2); Fisheries Adviser; Assistant Fisheries Officer; Master Fishermen (3).

Rural management and technology. *Conservation and environment management:* South Pacific Regional Environment Programme (SPREP); environmental education; environmental research and monitoring activities; clearing-house and advisory services. *Rural health, sanitation and water supply:* Rural water supply and sanitation projects; regional training course in drug identification and drug concealment methods. *Rural employment:* Rural employment and development project. *Rural technology:* Rural technology projects; project to increase self-sufficiency on atolls.

Professional staff: Regional Co-ordinator (SPREP); Project Officer (SPREP); Information Officer (SPREP); Adviser in Environmental Health and Food Hygiene; Volunteer water supply technicians (3); Assistant Economist; Rural Technology Officer.

Community services. *Community education training:* Community Education Training Centre; development of resource materials for community education and training programmes. *Youth and adult education:* Mobile Training Unit for Youth and Community Workers; awards for youth work training within the region; Pacific youth council (Youthlink); clearing house and advisory services (out-of-school youth and adult education). *Women's programmes and activities:* Pacific women's resource bureau; women and child health and nutrition; regional health survey — health status of women; Pacific pre-school development programme; Pacific women's newsletter. *Family and community health services:* Regional workshop on health education nutrition strategies and techniques; health education materials; clearing house and advisory services (health education). *Public health:* In-country training course in dental health; pilot demonstration dental projects; clearing-house service (dental public health); project on dengue fever and other insect-borne diseases; strengthening of prevention and control programmes against non-communicable disease in Pacific Islands; prevention of respiratory diseases; regional conference on social effects of alcohol; infantile gastroenteritis project; South Pacific Epidemiological Information Service; cancer registry; hepatitis prevention and control.

Professional staff: Principal/CETC; Instructors/CETC (5); Specialist in Out-of-School Youth Education; Mobile Training Unit Instructors (2); Women's Programmes Development Officers (2); Health Education

Officer; Dental Public Health Officer; Epidemiologist; Nutritionist; Medical Technologist; Health Surveys Technician.

Socio-economic statistical services. *Statistics section:* Generalised statistical training; specialised statistical training; statistical co-ordination and advisory services. *Economic section: information, research, advisory services and training:* Regional conference of senior development planners; sub-regional training course in project analysis and evaluation; sub-regional training course in farm management and economics. *Services in Population Data and Data Utilisation:* UNFPA/SPC project on technical assistance and training in census, demography, and population statistics; ILO/SPC project on migration, employment and development in the South Pacific; in-country introductory courses on programming and operating micro-computers.

Professional staff: Statistician; Statistical Training Officer; Statistical Research Officer; Economist; Demographer; Population Adviser; Population Data Utilisation Specialist; Population Data Processing Officer; Migration and Employment Specialist; Calculating Assistant.

Education services. *English language programme:* Consultant services (English as a Second Language); major revision of core materials for the 1980s; production of core materials by the Sydney Publications Bureau. *Media unit:* Regional media centre; subregional radio and video production courses; subregional audio-visual training courses.

Professional staff: Language Teaching Specialist (English); Manager Publications Bureau; Educational Broadcasts Officer; Audio-Visual Officer.

Information services. Library; headquarters publications printing section; Sydney publications bureau; operation and maintenance of PEACESAT terminal; computer processing services; conference interpretation and translation services.

Professional staff: Librarian; Cataloguer; Publications Officer; Assistant Publications Officer; Program Systems Manager; Conference Interpreters and Translators (6).

Regional consultation. South Pacific Conference; Committee of Representatives of Governments and Administrations; inter-organisation consultations for funding of programmes; regional conference of permanent heads of agricultural and livestock production services.

Awards and grants. *Short-term experts' and specialists' services; Assistance to applied research, experiments and field work; Inter-country study visits and travel grants:* Inter-country study visits; travel grants — SPC meetings and courses; funds for regional travel — student training.

Cultural conservation and exchange. Festival of Pacific Arts: grants-in-aid; grants for emoluments and travel of festival director; meeting of council of Pacific arts; grants-in-aid of cultural development and the conservation of traditional practices; regional programme for the safeguard of the cultural heritage of the Pacific Region.

SECRETARIES-GENERAL — SOUTH PACIFIC COMMISSION

Mr William D. Forsyth (Australia)
1 November 1948–30 June 1951;
Sir Leslie Brian Freeston (United Kingdom)
12 November 1951–12 November 1954;
Dr Ralph Clairon Bedell (United States of America)
1 March 1955–28 February 1958;

Mr Thomas R. Smith (New Zealand)
1 March 1958–21 March 1963;
Mr William D. Forsyth (Australia)
24 March 1963–31 December 1966;
Sir Gawain Bell (United Kingdom)
1 January 1967–11 December 1969;
Afioga Afoafouvale Misimoa (Western Samoa) (died while on official tour in Tarawa, Kiribati)
1 January 1970–18 February 1971;
Mr John E. Deyoung (United States of America) (Programme Director (Social))
Acted in the interim period from 18 February 1971–31 October 1971;
Hon. Gustav F. D. Betham (Western Samoa)
1 November 1971–30 November 1975;
Dr E. Macu Salato (Fiji)
9 December 1975–30 June 1979;
Hon. M. Young Vivian (Niue)
1 July 1979–30 June 1982;
Mr Francis Bugotu (Solomon Islands)
1 July 1982–30 November 1986;
Mr Palauni M. Tuiasosopo (American Samoa)
5 December 1986–.

Churches Conference

The Pacific Conference of Churches (PCC) embraces almost all the Christian denominations in an area which is, coincidentally, the same as that covered by the South Pacific Commission, not including Australia and New Zealand.

The conference was inaugurated at a Pacific-wide Conference of Churches and Missions at Lifou in the Loyalty Islands (New Caledonia) in 1966, and was a merger of Pacific ecumenical bodies.

Member churches in mid-1987 were: Anglican Diocese of Vanuatu; Melanesian Council of Churches; Anglican Diocese of Polynesia; Church of Christ in Vanuatu; Cook Islands Christian Church; Kiribati Protestant Church; Nauru Protestant Church; Ekalesia Niue; Congregational Christian Church in Samoa; Tuvalu Church; Evangelical Church of New Caledonia and the Loyalty Islands; Evangelical Church of French Polynesia; Methodist Church in Fiji; Methodist Church of Samoa; Free Wesleyan Church of Tonga; Presbyterian Church of Vanuatu; United Church of Christ in Pohnpei; United Church of Christ in the Marshall Islands; United Church of Papua New Guinea and Solomon Islands; Samoa Council of Churches (hitherto Fellowship of Christian Churches in Samoa); Tonga National Council of Churches; Congregational Christian Church in American Samoa; Solomon Islands Christian Association; and the Episcopal Conference of the Pacific (Roman Catholic) which includes the Archdioceses of Suva, Noumea and Papeete, and the Dioceses of Samoa and Tokelau, Guam, Saipan, Rarotonga, Tarawa, Tonga, American Samoa, Port Vila, Taiohae (Marquesas) and Wallis and Futuna.

The conference describes itself as 'an organ of cooperation among the Churches and their associated mission boards in the Pacific within the framework of the wider ecumenical movement'.

Office bearers, elected in September 1986 for a five-year term, are: Chairman Bishop Leslie Boseto, United Church of Papua New Guinea and Solomon Islands; General Secretary Mr Sione K. Motu'ahala of Tonga; and Financial Secretary Mr Tulanga Manuella of Tuvalu. Bishop Boseto resides at Munda in Solomon Islands; the other two officers reside in Suva and work at the Secretariat, which is located at 4 Thurston Street, Suva, Fiji.

Asian Development Bank

The Asian Development Bank (ADB), of which eight South Pacific Island countries were members at the end of 1986, is an international development finance institution owned by its member countries. Its main role is to promote the economic and social progress of its developing member countries (DMCs) by lending funds and providing technical assistance.

The ADB began operations in December 1966, with its headquarters in Manila, Philippines. By the end of 1986 it had 47 members, 32 from the region of Asia, including the South Pacific, and 15 from outside the region, the 15 'outsiders' being the developed countries like the United Kingdom, the United States, Canada, Belgium, Federal Republic of Germany and others, 13 of the 15 coming from Western Europe.

The ADB's regional membership consists of 29 DMCs, with individual populations ranging from 64,000 (Kiribati) to 1.04 billion (People's Republic of China), and per capita incomes ranging from $150 (Bangladesh) to more than $7400 (Singapore), and three developed countries.

The bank is organised and funded mainly on the basis of regional self-reliance. About 64 per cent of the capital subscribed, the President, eight out of 12 members of the board of directors, and about 63 per cent of the professional staff, are all from the region. At the same time, the foresight of the bank's founders in departing from precedent and establishing the bank as an international partnership has paid large dividends. The bank has greatly benefited from the infusion of non-regional capital and talent in its organisation and activities.

Membership in the bank is open to members and associated members of the United Nations Economic and Social Commission for Asia and the Pacific (ESCAP), and other regional countries and non-regional developed countries which are members of the UN or any of its specialised agencies.

The bank's principal functions in utilising the resources at its disposal are:

- to provide technical assistance for the preparation, financing and execution of development projects and programmes;
- to promote investment of public and private capital for development purposes, and
- to respond to requests for assistance in co-ordinating development policies and plans of member countries.

In its operations, the bank is required to give special attention to the needs of the smaller or less developed countries and give priority to regional, sub-regional and national projects and programmes which will contribute to the harmonious economic growth of the region as a whole.

The ADB's loans from its Ordinary Capital Resources have a variable lending rate which is adjusted every six months, taking into account the cost of the bank's borrowings, a maturity period varying between 10 and 30 years and a grace period from two to seven years.

For less developed countries there are concessional loans from the Asian Development Fund, the ADB's soft loan window. These carry only a service charge of one per cent per annum with repayments extending over 40 years including a grace period of 10 years.

About 59 per cent of the bank's capital is owned by its developed member countries which include the 13 Western Europe countries, the United States and Canada and, in the region, Japan, Australia and New Zealand.

The South Pacific Island members and their subscriptions in US$ (at 31 December 1986) were:

Cook Islands,	$US0.575 million
Fiji	$14.715 m
Kiribati	$0.868 m
Papua New Guinea	$20.305 m
Solomon Islands	$1.443 m
Tonga	$0.868 m
Vanuatu	$1.443 m
Western Samoa	$0.710 m

ADB headquarters are at 2300 Roxas Boulevard, Metropolitan Manila, Philippines.

AIDAB
in the South Pacific

To many developing and underdeveloped countries the Australian International Development Assistance Bureau, an arm of the Australian Department of Foreign Affairs, has assumed great importance, representing the efforts of Australia to play its part in raising living standards in those countries, especially the South Pacific Islands. Today, aid is an important element in the diplomatic programme of the developed countries, representing in financial terms in the Pacific region alone a total of about $A300 million over the five-year period 1983–84 to 1987–88. AIDAB's Pacific regional program involves aid for nine countries: Cook Islands, Fiji, Kiribati, Niue, Solomon Islands, Tonga, Tuvalu, Vanuatu and Western Samoa. Papua New Guinea is in a separate category of its own, Australia, as its former administrator, having a special, long-term commitment to it.

The altered scene. As all these countries were, until comparatively recently, colonies, little aid flowed to them from other than their respective colonial masters. As independence came, the scene altered. An independent Fiji or an independent Western Samoa was free to choose its own friends. Western Samoa which, in 1962, became the first South Pacific island nation to achieve independence, made that quite clear soon afterwards. It asked its former colonial master, New Zealand, and then other Western nations for some extra aid and was turned down. 'Then we'll ask Russia,' said Western Samoa Prime Minister, the late Fiame Mataafa. Russia responded immediately. Mr Khrushchev sent his son-in-law to Western Samoa and followed up with two economists, but Mataafa changed his mind as the Western nations changed theirs and agreed to help the Samoans.

Reasons for giving aid. Today, Australian aid is motivated by reasons other than political ones as the Joint Committee on Foreign Affairs and Defence, considering the Jackson Report on Australia's Overseas Aid Program, commented: 'The Committee endorses the basic concepts put forward by Jackson that, firstly, the primary reason for giving aid is humanitarian; that, secondly, the goal of the aid program is development; and that, at a third level and without compromising the integrity of the aid program, there can be a coincidence of humanitarian, foreign policy and economic objectives, "a plurality of mandates", and that humanitarian concerns must be paramount. These mandates have to be taken into account in the Government's decisions on the direction of the aid program in order to ensure continuing broad-based community support.'

The Jackson Report stemmed from a committee of inquiry chaired by Sir Gordon Jackson which reviewed the development assistance programme in 1983–84.

The Pacific Regional Team. For its South Pacific aid program, AIDAB established a Pacific Regional Team now located at the AIDAB centre for Pacific Development and Training, Middle Head Road, Mosman NSW. (Phone 02 960 9500)

Meeting three clients' needs. The team's work programme has evolved to meet the needs of three 'clients'. First, the team serves AIDAB's requirements at any stage of programme identification, development and monitoring. Second, the team provides professional advice in response to requests from Heads of Missions and AIDAB staff in the field. Third, the team provides professional services directly to national planning offices and to senior members of governments in the Pacific Island countries. For example, national planning offices have asked for assistance in macro-economic analysis and with the identification of strategy options for the development of outer islands. Departments of Agriculture have requested assistance with issues such as research planning and livestock sector planning. Departments of Education have asked for assistance with curriculum development for primary and secondary schools and with their planning for post-secondary institutions.

During the course of these assignments, many existing projects have been monitored and recommendations concerning their implementation and future developments made. Advice has also been given on new project proposals and training programmes.

Co-operation with other donors. The team has established close working relationships on technical matters with the External Aid Division of the New Zealand Government and with the British Development Division based in Suva, and also the EEC offices in Suva and Port Moresby and the UNDP office in Suva. They have also been in touch with the ESCAP Pacific Operations Center (EPOC) and the ADB office in Vila. Likewise, they have established working relationships with the South Pacific Bureau for Economic Co-operation (SPEC), now the Forum Secretariat. They have already participated with New Zealand and with the British in joint examinations of sectoral issues at the request of some governments in the Pacific.

Forms of Australian aid. The forms of Australian aid available to the South Pacific are:

Project aid: projects implemented by island governments through joint management arrangements with Australian consultants, government departments, statutory authorities and academic institutions as agents of AIDAB include specific requirements for these agents to maximise the transfer of skills and technologies.

Accountable cash grants: cash grants to island governments to enable them to meet local costs comprising labour and locally produced goods or services thereby mobilising local resources and stimulating the growth of local development capacity. Many of these grants are directed to national rural development funds.

Development import grants: cash grants to island governments to enable the direct purchase of goods and services for developmental purposes thereby allowing domestic budget resources to be applied to local employment.

Staffing assistance: grants to island governments for salary supplementation of skilled Australians recruited for in-line government positions where there is a local skills deficiency.

Joint venture schemes: the provision of funds to help finance South Pacific equity in joint ventures with Australian business is designed to stimulate growth of the productive sector and facilitate flow of managerial and technological skills.

Development bank grants: grants to official local development finance institutions were introduced in 1976 with the specific aim of equity extension, on-lending subsidisation of rural lending programmes.

Human resource development: apart from training provided through projects there is a continuing programme of assistance to the South Pacific in the form of awards for training in Australia on specialised short courses and for undergraduate and postgraduate degrees.

Support for USP. In addition to budget and special purpose support for multilateral and regional institutions such as the Forum Secretariat, SPC and the Forum Fisheries Agency, Australia has a large programme of ongoing support for the University of the South Pacific (USP) including staffing assistance, research and extension programmes and capital works. Australia wishes to promote continued and growing interest by other donors in this important regional tertiary institution particularly with forms of aid which do not put undue strain on the university's recurrent budgetary resources. Australia also has ongoing programs of assistance to the Regional Telecommunications Centre based in Suva and announced at the 1983 South Pacific Forum assistance for a major regional communications programme.

South Pacific aid recipients:

Below is a list of recipients of bilateral development assistance under AIDAB-administered programmes:

	1984–85 actual	1985–86 estimate
	expenditure ($000)	
Papua New Guinea	$315,359	$320,918
Fiji	16,715	16,162
Vanuatu	4,261	6,643
Solomon Islands	7,397	6,344
Tonga	6,799	5,622
Western Samoa	4,693	5,365
Niue	449*	386
Cook Islands	579*	620
Tuvalu	845*	1,176
Kiribati	2,095*	2,630

* *Estimated.*

To take account of the special needs of small island nations, Australia's aid to the South Pacific exhibits features different from other parts of the aid programme. In the 1985–86 programme Australia funded the local costs of some small-scale development projects through accountable cash grants. The total amount of bilateral aid devoted to the South Pacific in 1985–86, the third year of the current five year programme of assistance to the region, was $55.7 million. This did not include aid to Papua New Guinea.

Aid for Papua New Guinea: In 1985–86 Papua New Guinea received $326.4 million in assistance, of which $302.8 million was a budget support grant provided under the five-year aid agreement between Australia and Papua New Guinea that expired in financial year 1986. A new agreement finalised during the next financial year continued Australia's long-term commitment to co-operation with Papua New Guinea in order to assist the economic development of that country. Australia's support for Papua New Guinea is the largest single component of the overseas aid programme, accounting for about 31.8 per cent of total official development assistance during 1985–86. Aid to Papua New Guinea over the five-year life of the current agreement will have totalled $1477.3 million.

In 1985–86 Australia provided $3.1 million for the Papua New Guinea–Australia Tech-

nical Co-operation Program (PATCOP). Under this programme Australia provides training in a wide variety of fields, as well as providing expert services and related equipment.

Small island states. The Jackson Report underlines the problems associated with aid planning for the islands of the South Pacific region. It states:

> In developmental terms, the South Pacific is a region of contradictions. Population is minute, but population growth is a major obstacle to development. Land areas are very small, but sea areas and distances are enormous. The region receives the most aid, per capita, in the world although compared with other regions the need for aid is marginal. Even where poverty exists in statistical terms, the quality of life is high. Economically, the islands are not of major significance although they will provide increasing, albeit modest, commercial and trading opportunities for Australia. Strategically, the location of these island nations gives them special significance.
>
> Australia's aid policy must take account of these factors in its contribution to regional development. Despite the present prosperity, there is a danger that 'subsistence affluence' could become 'subsistence poverty', at least in some of these island countries. The economic prosperity and political stability of the region reflects Australian interests as well as those of the island states themselves. The island nations are small, and the very small states, such as Kiribati and Tuvalu, face a difficult future. Some other states have better economic prospects. In the longer term the islands may also benefit from closer association, a freer movement of goods, capital and labour, and some rationalisation of resources on a regional basis.

Development and Training. One of AIDAB's successes is the Centre for Pacific Development and Training at Middle Head Road, Mosman, on Sydney Harbour foreshore, about 10 kilometres from the city centre. It is one of the oldest of Australia's aid institutions, starting life in 1946 as the Australian School of Pacific Administration

(ASOPA) for the training of teachers and patrol officers for service in Papua New Guinea. With self-government and, later, full independence looming for Papua New Guinea — then called Papua and New Guinea — training of Australians for PNG service was phased out in the early 1970s, their places being taken by Papua New Guineans who were trained for jobs in their country's public service. But the establishment took on a global perspective with training opportunities being offered to people from a wide variety of nations, mostly developing countries, from the South Pacific Islands, from Africa, Asia, including remote Nepal, China and others, which is why, in December 1973, ASOPA was renamed the International Training Institute. In January 1988, the institute was renamed the AIDAB Centre for Pacific Development and Training.

Described as a centre for the development of human resources, it specialises in the following areas of development activity: development and educational administration; financial management; industrial relations;

local government; management development; mass media; personnel management; rural development; and training of trainers. The centre can offer to client governments and organisations the following services: design, planning and implementation of conferences, seminars, workshops and courses; consultancy services; advice and assistance to training institutions; high-level vocational training for senior professionals; design, planning and implementation of in-country training; assessment of training needs; evaluation of the effectiveness of training; production of learning materials and co-ordination of briefing and debriefing programmes.

Since 1973, more than 3000 people from 60 countries have been awarded certificates. Most are middle to senior level professionals or managers working in a variety of development fields.

In early 1988 Australia decided to replace its five-year aid programme with a three-year programme.

Adapted from *The South Seas Digest Fact Sheet*, No. 20, Vol. 5, January 1986.

The Law of the Sea

The main provisions of the Treaty of the Law of the Sea were signed in Montego Bay, Jamaica. Fiji was among the first to sign and when 60 other nations signed it came into force one year later. The United States is among the nations which have not signed.

Territorial waters. Each coastal nation's territorial waters extend for 12 nautical miles beyond its coast. The territorial limit was previously three miles. The zone is open to all foreign vessels on 'innocent passage', that is, passage which does not threaten the nation's security. Beyond the 12-mile limit, all ships and aircraft, commercial, military and private, can move freely.

Exclusive Economic Zone. Each coastal nation has exclusive rights to the fish and other marine life in the waters extending for 200 nautical miles beyond its coast. This provision in the treaty is opposed by the United States of America which holds that migratory fish, such as tuna, are part of the common heritage. When the body of water separating nations is less than 400 nautical miles, those nations must agree on dividing lines for the zones.

Straits. Straits or 'choke points' 24 nautical miles wide or less, of which there are more than 100, do not become territorial waters and all traffic has the right of 'transit passage' through them. Examples are the Straits of Gibraltar and the Straits of Hormuz.

Continental shelf. This is the most critical economic portion of the treaty. It deals with the continental shelf extending from a nation's shores. Each nation is given exclusive rights to all resources, including oil and gas, in the shelf for 350 nautical miles beyond the coast.

Seabed mining. The mineral wealth of the sea, almost unheard of 20 years ago, and consisting of nodules of nickel, copper, cobalt, zinc and other minerals, is regarded as the 'heritage of mankind'. To mine these metals on the ocean floor, a complex global authority has been established. Priority contracts will be awarded to four groups of companies led by American mining interests, a French consortium, a Japanese group, the Soviet Union and India. A global mining enterprise will be given one site, equal in size or value to any mined by a national or private company. The treaty fixes a production ceiling to support ruling prices of the metals and ensure that they are not reduced by a glut. Private mining companies must sell their technical knowledge to the global enterprise. The whole arrangement can be amended by agreement of three-quarters of the treaty signatories.

Disputes. A new international tribunal has been established to settle disputes over Law of the Sea matters involving nations or individuals. Arbitration will also be employed and litigation will also be referred to the International Court of Justice at The Hague.

Treaty of Rarotonga

(SOUTH PACIFIC NUCLEAR FREE ZONE TREATY)

The Treaty of Rarotonga, presented at the South Pacific Forum in Rarotonga, Cook Islands, in August 1985 is, notwithstanding its critics, a document of considerable significance to a region bordered by nuclear-capable powers and in which nuclear weapons testing is still carried out. Despite the amount of comment it has occasioned, however, the text of the Treaty is not well known.

The treaty was signed at the forum in Rarotonga by eight of the forum countries; Australia (the driving force behind the treaty), Cook Islands, Fiji, Kiribati, New Zealand, Niue, Tuvalu and Western Samoa. The following month Papua New Guinea signed, followed by Naúru in July 1986 and Solomon Islands in May 1987. By early 1988 nine of the signatories had ratified, although the treaty entered into force with the deposit of the eighth instrument of ratification on 11 December 1986.

By early 1988, two members of the South Pacific Forum, Vanuatu and Tonga, had not signed; the former claiming that the treaty did not go far enough in preventing nuclear activity, the latter claiming that its terms left small states vulnerable.

Protocols 2 and 3 to the treaty, to be signed by regional powers with nuclear weapons capabilities, the United Kingdom, France, the Republic of China, the USSR and the USA, had, by early 1988, been signed but not ratified by the USSR, which signed Protocols 2 and 3 on 15 December 1986, and the People's Republic of China, which signed Protocols 2 and 3 on 10 February 1987. Protocol 1, relating to the manufacture, stationing and testing of nuclear weapons within the South Pacific Territories of France, the United Kingdom and the USA, had not

been signed by early 1988.

The full text of the treaty and its annexes is reproduced below. The wording of the protocols has been reduced to their most significant articles.

SOUTH PACIFIC NUCLEAR FREE ZONE TREATY.

The Parties to this Treaty

United in their commitment to a world at peace;

Gravely concerned that the continuing nuclear arms race presents the risk of nuclear war which would have devastating consequences for all people;

Convinced that all countries have an obligation to make every effort to achieve the goal of eliminating nuclear weapons, the terror which they hold for humankind and the threat which they pose to life on earth;

Believing that regional arms control measures can contribute to global efforts to reverse the nuclear arms race and promote the national security of each country in the region and the common security of all;

Determined to ensure, so far as lies within their power, that the bounty and beauty of the land and sea in their region shall remain the heritage of their peoples and their descendants in perpetuity to be enjoyed by all in peace;

Reaffirming the importance of the Treaty on the Non-Proliferation of Nuclear Weapons (NPT) in preventing the proliferation of nuclear weapons and in contributing to world security;

Noting in particular, that Article VII of the NPT recognises the right of any group of States to conclude regional treaties in order to assure the total absence of nuclear weapons in their respective territories;

Noting that the prohibitions of emplantation and emplacement of nuclear weapons on the seabed and the ocean floor and in the subsoil thereof contained in the Treaty on the Prohibition of the Emplacement of Nuclear Weapons and Other Weapons of Mass Destruction on the Seabed and the Ocean Floor and in the Subsoil Thereof apply in the South Pacific;

Noting also that the prohibition of testing of nuclear weapons in the atmosphere or under water, including territorial waters or high seas, contained in the Treaty Banning Nuclear Weapon Tests in the Atmosphere, in Outer Space and Under Water applies in the South Pacific;

Determined to keep the region free of environmental pollution by radioactive wastes and other radioactive matter.

Guided by the decision of the Fifteenth South Pacific Forum at Tuvalu that a nuclear free zone should be established in the region at the earliest possible opportunity in accordance with the principles set out in the communique of that meeting; have agreed as follows:

ARTICLE 1
Usage of terms
For the purposes of this Treaty and its Protocols:

(a) 'South Pacific Nuclear Free Zone' means the areas described in Annex 1.

(b) 'territory' means internal waters, territorial sea and archipelagic waters, the seabed and subsoil beneath, the land territory and the airspace above them;

(c) 'nuclear explosive device' means any nuclear weapon or other explosive device capable of releasing nuclear energy, irrespective of the purpose for which it could be used. The term includes such a weapon or device in unassembled and partly assembled forms, but does not include the means of transport or delivery of such a weapon or device if separable from and not an indivisible part of it;

(d) 'stationing' means emplantation, emplacement, transportation on land or inland waters, stockpiling, storage, installation and deployment.

ARTICLE 2
Application of the Treaty
1. Except where otherwise specified, this Treaty and its Protocols shall apply to territory within the South Pacific Nuclear Free Zone.

2. Nothing in this Treaty shall prejudice or in any way affect the rights, or the exercise of the rights, of any State under international law with regard to freedom of the seas.

ARTICLE 3
Renunciation of Nuclear Explosive Devices
Each Party undertakes:

(a) not to manufacture or otherwise acquire, possess or have control over any nuclear explosive device by any means anywhere inside or outside the South Pacific Nuclear Free Zone;

(b) not to seek or receive any assistance in the manufacture or acquisition of any nuclear explosive device;

(c) not to take any action to assist or encourage the manufacture or acquisition of any nuclear explosive device by any State.

ARTICLE 4
Peaceful Nuclear Activities
Each Party undertakes:

(a) not to provide source or special fissionable material, or equipment or material especially designed or prepared for the processing, use or production of special fissionable material for peaceful purposes to:

(i) any non-nuclear-weapon State unless subject to the safeguards required by Article III.1 of the NPT, or

(ii) any nuclear-weapon State unless subject to applicable safeguards agreements with the International Atomic Energy Agency (IAEA).

Any such provision shall be in accordance with strict non-proliferation measures to provide assurance of exclusively peaceful non-explosive use;

(b) to support the continued effectiveness of the international non-proliferation system based on the NPT and the IAEA safeguards system.

ARTICLE 5
Prevention of Stationing of Nuclear Explosive Devices

1. Each Party undertakes to prevent in its territory the stationing of any nuclear explosive device.
2. Each Party in the exercise of its sovereign rights remains free to decide for itself whether to allow visits by foreign ships and aircraft to its ports and airfields, transit of its airspace by foreign aircraft, and navigation by foreign ships in its territorial sea or archipelagic waters in a manner not covered by the rights of innocent passage, archipelagic sea lane passage or transit passage of straits.

ARTICLE 6
Prevention of Testing of Nuclear Explosive Devices

Each Party undertakes:

(a) to prevent in its territory the testing of any nuclear explosive device;
(b) not to take any action to assist or encourage the testing of any nuclear explosive device by any State.

ARTICLE 7
Prevention of Dumping

1. Each Party undertakes:

   (a) not to dump radioactive wastes and other radioactive matter at sea anywhere within the South Pacific Nuclear Free Zone;
   (b) to prevent the dumping of radioactive wastes and other radioactive matter by anyone in its territorial sea;
   (c) not to take any action to assist or encourage the dumping by anyone of radioactive wastes and other radioactive matter at sea anywhere within the South Pacific Nuclear Free Zone;
   (d) to support the conclusion as soon as possible of the proposed Convention relating to the protection of the natural resources and environment of the South Pacific region and its Protocol for the prevention of pollution of the South Pacific region by dumping, with the aim of precluding dumping at sea of radioactive wastes and other radioactive matter by anyone anywhere in the region.

2. Paragraphs 1(a) and 1(b) of this Article shall not apply to areas of the South Pacific Nuclear Free Zone in respect of which such a Convention and Protocol have entered into force.

ARTICLE 8
Control System

1. The Parties hereby establish a control system for the purpose of verifying compliance with their obligations under this Treaty.
2. The control system shall comprise:

   (a) reports and exchange of information as provided for in Article 9;
   (b) consultations as provided for in Article 10 and Annex 4(1);
   (c) the application to peaceful nuclear activities of safeguards by the IAEA as provided for in Annex 2;
   (d) a complaints procedure as provided for in Annex 4.

ARTICLE 9
Reports and Exchanges of Information

1. Each Party shall report to the Director of the South Pacific Bureau for Economic Co-operation (the Director) as soon as possible any significant event within its jurisdiction affecting the implementation of this Treaty. The Director shall circulate such reports promptly to all Parties.
2. The Parties shall endeavour to keep each other informed on matters arising under or in relation to this Treaty. They may exchange information by communicating it to the Director, who shall circulate it to all Parties.
3. The Director shall report annually to the South Pacific Forum on the status of this Treaty and matters arising under or in relation to it, incorporating reports and communications made under paragraphs 1 and 2 of this Article and matters arising under Articles 8(2)(d) and 10 and Annex 2(4).

ARTICLE 10
Consultations and Review

Without prejudice to the conduct of consultations among Parties by other means, the Director, at the request of any Party, shall convene a meeting of the Consultative Committee established by Annex 3 for consultation and co-operation on any matter arising in relation to this Treaty or for reviewing its operation.

ARTICLE 11
Amendment

The Consultative Committee shall consider proposals for amendment of the provisions of this Treaty proposed by any Party and circulated by the Director to all Parties not less than three months prior to the convening of the Consultative Committee for this purpose. Any proposal agreed upon by consensus by the Consultative Committee shall be communicated to the Director who shall circulate it for acceptance to all Parties. An amendment shall enter into force thirty days after receipt by the depositary of acceptances from all Parties.

ARTICLE 12
Signature and Ratification

1. This Treaty shall be open for signature by any Member of the South Pacific Forum.
2. This Treaty shall be subject to ratification. Instruments of ratification shall be deposited with the Director who is hereby designated depositary of this Treaty and its Protocols.
3. If a Member of the South Pacific Forum whose territory is outside the South Pacific Nuclear Free Zone becomes a Party to this Treaty, Annex 1 shall be deemed to be amended so far as is required to enclose at least the territory of that Party within the boundaries of the South Pacific Nuclear Free Zone. The delineation of any area added pursuant to this paragraph shall be approved by the South Pacific Forum.

ARTICLE 13
Withdrawal

1. This Treaty is of a permanent nature and shall remain in force indefinitely, provided that in the event of a violation by any Party of a provision of this Treaty essential to the achievement of the objectives of the Treaty or of the spirit of the Treaty, every other Party shall have the right to withdraw from the Treaty.
2. Withdrawal shall be effected by giving notice twelve months in advance to the Director who shall circulate such notice to all other Parties.

ARTICLE 14
Reservations

This Treaty shall not be subject to reservations.

ARTICLE 15
Entry into Force

1. This Treaty shall enter into force on the date of deposit of the eighth instrument of ratification.
2. For a signatory which ratifies this Treaty after the date of deposit of the eighth instrument of ratification, the Treaty shall enter into force on the date of deposit of its instrument of ratification.

ARTICLE 16
Depositary Functions

The depositary shall register this Treaty and its Protocols pursuant to Article 102 of the Charter of the United Nations and shall transmit certified copies of the Treaty and its Protocols to all Members of the South Pacific Forum and all States eligible to become Party to the Protocols to the Treaty and shall notify them of signatures and ratifications of the Treaty and its Protocols.

ANNEX 1
South Pacific Nuclear Free Zone

A. The area bounded by a line —

(1) Commencing at the point of intersection of the Equator by the maritime boundary between Indonesia and Papua New Guinea;

(2) running thence northerly along that maritime boundary to its intersection by the outer limit of the exclusive economic zone of Papua New Guinea;

(3) thence generally north-easterly, easterly and south-easterly along that outer limit to its intersection by the Equator;

(4) thence east along the Equator to its intersection by the meridian of Longitude 163 degrees East;

(5) thence north along that meridian to its intersection by the parallel of Latitude 3 degrees North;

(6) thence east along that parallel to its intersection by the meridian of Longitude 171 degrees East;

(7) thence north along that meridian to its intersection by the parallel of

Latitude 4 degrees North;

(8) thence east along that parallel to its intersection by the meridian of Longitude 180 degrees East;

(9) thence south along that meridian to its intersection by the Equator;

(10) thence east along the Equator to its intersection by the meridian of Longitude 165 degrees West;

(11) thence north along that meridian to its intersection by the parallel of Latitude 5 degrees 30 minutes North;

(12) thence east along that parallel to its intersection by the meridian of Longitude 154 degrees West;

(13) thence south along that meridian to its intersection by the Equator;

(14) thence east along the Equator to its intersection by the meridian of Longitude 115 degrees West;

(15) thence south along that meridian to its intersection by the parallel of Latitude 60 degrees South;

(16) thence west along that parallel to its intersection by the meridian of Longitude 115 degrees East;

(17) thence north along that meridian to its southernmost intersection by the outer limit of the territorial sea of Australia;

(18) thence generally northerly and easterly along the outer limit of the territorial sea of Australia to its intersection by the meridian of Longitude 136 degrees 45 minutes East;

(19) thence north-easterly along the geodesic to the point of Latitude 10 degrees 50 minutes South, Longitude 139 degrees 12 minutes East;

(20) thence north-easterly along the maritime boundary between Indonesia and Papua New Guinea to where it joins the land border between those two countries;

(21) thence generally northerly along that land border to where it joins the maritime boundary between Indonesia and Papua New Guinea, on the northern coastline of Papua New Guinea; and

(22) thence generally northerly along that boundary to the point of commencement.

B. The areas within the outer limits of the territorial seas of all Australian islands lying westward of the area described in paragraph A and north of Latitude 60 degrees South, provided that any such areas shall cease to be part of the South Pacific Nuclear Free Zone upon receipt by the depositary of written notice from the Government of Australia stating that the areas have become subject to another treaty having an object and purpose substantially the same as that of this Treaty.

ANNEX 2
IAEA Safeguards

1. The safeguards referred to in Article 8 shall in respect of each Party be applied by the IAEA as set forth in an agreement negotiated and concluded with the IAEA on all source or special fissionable material in all peaceful nuclear activities within the territory of the Party, under its jurisdiction or carried out under its control anywhere.

2. The agreement referred to in paragraph 1 shall be, or shall be equivalent in its scope and effect to, an agreement required in connection with the NPT on the basis of the material reproduced in document INFCIRC/153 (Corrected) of the IAEA. Each Party shall take all appropriate steps to ensure that such an agreement is in force for it not later than eighteen months after the date of entry into force for that Party of this Treaty.

3. For the purposes of this Treaty, the safeguards referred to in paragraph 1 shall have as their purpose the verification of the non-diversion of nuclear material from peaceful nuclear activities to nuclear explosive devices.

4. Each Party agrees upon the request of any other Party to transmit to that Party and to the Director for the information of all Parties a copy of the overall conclusions of the most recent report by the IAEA on its inspection activities in the territory of the Party concerned, and to advise the Director promptly of any subsequent findings of the Board of Governors of the IAEA in relation to those conclusions for the information of all Parties.

ANNEX 3
Consultative Committee

1. There is hereby established a Consultative Committee which shall be convered by the Director from time to time pursuant to Articles 10 and 11 and Annex 4 (2). The Consultative Committee shall be constituted of representatives of the Parties, each Party being entitled to appoint one representative who may be accompanied by advisers. Unless otherwise agreed, the Consultative Committee shall be chaired at any given meeting by the representative of the Party which last hosted the meeting of Heads of Government of Members of the South Pacific Forum. A quorum shall be constituted by representatives of half the Parties. Subject to the provisions of Article 11, decisions of the Consultative Committee shall be taken by consensus or, failing consensus, by a two-thirds majority of those present and voting. The Consultative Committee shall adopt such other rules of procedure as it sees fit.

2. The costs of the Consultative Committee, including the costs of special inspections pursuant to Annex 4, shall be borne by the South Pacific Bureau for Economic Co-operation. It may seek special funding should this be required.

ANNEX 4
Complaints Procedure

1. A Party which considers that there are grounds for a complaint that another Party is in breach of its obligations under this Treaty shall, before bringing such a complaint to the Director, bring the subject matter of the complaint to the attention of the Party complained of and shall allow the latter reasonable opportunity to provide it with an explanation and to resolve the matter.

2. If the matter is not so resolved, the complainant Party may bring the complaint to the Director with a request that the Consultative Committee be convened to consider it. Complaints shall be supported by an account of evidence of breach of obligations known to the complainant Party. Upon receipt of a complaint the Director shall convene the Consultative Committee as quickly as possible to consider it.

3. The Consultative Committee, taking account of efforts made under paragraph 1, shall afford the Party complained of a reasonable opportunity to provide it with an explanation of the matter.

4. If, after considering any explanation given to it by the representatives of the Party complained of, the Consultative Committee decides that there is sufficient substance in the complaint to warrant a special inspection in the territory of that Party or elsewhere, the Consultative Committee shall direct that such special inspection be made as quickly as possible by a special inspection team of three suitably qualified special inspectors appointed by the Consultative Committee in consultation with the complained of and complainant Parties, provided that no national of either Party shall serve on the special inspection team. If so requested by the Party complained of, the special inspection team shall be accompanied by representatives of that Party. Neither the right of consultation on the appointment of special inspectors, nor the right to accompany special inspectors, shall delay the work of the special inspection team.

5. In making a special inspection, special inspectors shall be subject to the direction only of the Consultative Committee and shall comply with such directives concerning tasks, objectives, confidentiality and procedures as may be decided upon by it. Directives shall take account of the legitimate interests of the Party complained of in complying with its other international obligations and commitments and shall not duplicate safeguards procedures to be undertaken by the IAEA pursuant to agreements referred to in Annex 2(1). The special inspectors shall discharge their duties with due respect for the laws of the Party complained of.

6. Each Party shall give to special inspectors full and free access to all information and places within its territory which may be relevant to enable the special inspectors to implement the directives given to them by the Consultative Committee.

7. The Party complained of shall take all appropriate steps to facilitate the special

inspection, and shall grant to special inspectors privileges and immunities necessary for the performance of their functions, including inviolability for all papers and documents and immunity from arrest, detention and legal process for acts done and words spoken and written, for the purpose of the special inspection.

8. The special inspectors shall report in writing as quickly as possible to the Consultative Committee, outlining their activities, setting out relevant facts and information as ascertained by them, with supporting evidence and documentation as appropriate, and stating their conclusions. The Consultative Committee shall report fully to all Members of the South Pacific Forum, giving its decision as to whether the Party complained of is in breach of its obligations under this Treaty.

9. If the Consultative Committee has decided that the Party complained of is in breach of its obligations under this Treaty, or that the above provisions have not been complied with, or at any time at the request of either the complainant or complained of Party, the Parties shall meet promptly at a meeting of the South Pacific Forum.

PROTOCOL 1
Article 1

Each Party undertakes to apply, in respect of the territories for which it is internationally responsible situated within the South Pacific Nuclear Free Zone, the prohibitions contained in Articles 3, 5 and 6, insofar as they related to the manufacture, stationing and testing of any nuclear explosive device within those territories, and the safeguards specified in Article 8(2)(c) and Annex 2 of the Treaty.

PROTOCOL 2
Article 1

Each Party undertakes not to use or threaten to use any nuclear explosive device against:

(a) Parties to the Treaty; or
(b) any territory within the South Pacific Nuclear Free Zone for which a State that has become a Party to Protocol 1 is internationally responsible.

PROTOCOL 3
Article 1

Each Party undertakes not to test any nuclear explosive device anywhere within the South Pacific Nuclear Free Zone.

The Pacific War

The Pacific War began on 7 December 1941 with attacks by Japan on British, American and Dutch territory and ended on 14 August 1945 with Japan's unconditional surrender. Following is a summary of the main actions of the war. During this time Japan was still fighting in China, which she had attacked in 1937, and had also kept large numbers of troops in Manchuria to protect her borders with Russia, with whom she had signed a neutrality pact in April 1941.

Japanese attack forces prepare. On 26 November 1941 Japan's Pearl Harbor Striking Force of 28 ships under Vice Admiral Chuichi Nagumo assembled in the Kurile Islands and headed south-east, blacked out and under strict radio silence. On 2 December Nagumo received confirmation from Admiral Isoroku Yamamoto, Commander-in-Chief of the Japanese Combined Fleet, that the Striking Force would attack the US base at Pearl Harbor on 8 December (Tokyo time, 7 December Hawaii time). Japanese forces meanwhile were being moved into attack positions in widely-scattered areas of the North Pacific and Asia, as Japan prepared for a seven-point simultaneous assault on British, American and Thai territory.

Japan strikes in seven places. In less than 14 hours from 7 December, the Japanese struck Malaya, Hawaii, Thailand, the Philippines, Guam, Hong Kong and Wake Island, in that order. The first Allied shots were fired near Kota Bharu, a small village on the east coast of Malaya, when an invasion force of Japanese transports with 5500 men and naval escorts anchored offshore at 2200 hours on 7 December local time, and British shore batteries fired on them. The Japanese escorts replied and Japanese troops began landing at 0030 on the 8th. Hudson aircraft of the Royal Australian Air Force No. 1 Squadron attacked the force, thus striking the first air blows against Japan in the war. When the Japanese began their landing

there was still an hour and a quarter to go before the Japanese attack began on Pearl Harbor. That same night the Japanese had landed in Thailand as a stepping stone to northern Malaya.

Pearl Harbor debacle. Japan's air attack, from Nagumo's carrier-based force, began on 0755 on 7 December, achieving complete surprise. Total US losses were 2341 servicemen killed and 1143 wounded, and 68 civilians killed and 35 wounded. Of the service dead, more than 1000 men were in the battleship *Arizona* sunk at its moorings. Of eight battleships in port, four were sunk or capsized and four damaged. Of the 97 ships in port, 18 were sunk or damaged, and 188 aircraft destroyed. Japanese casualties were fewer than 100 killed or wounded, 29 aircraft and five midget submarines destroyed.

Guam falls quickly. Guam was attacked by air at 0830 on 8 December and invaded on 10 December, surrendering the same day. It was the first US territory to be captured by the Japanese.

Wake Island surrenders. Japanese bombers began attacking US Wake Island, 2092 km east of Guam, on 8 December. A small invasion fleet was repelled on 11 December, but arrival of a second invasion fleet on 23 December resulted in Wake's surrender that day.

Philippines attacked. Air attacks began on US airfields and installations in the Philippines on 8 December and within one week US air power there was rendered impotent and the harbour at Manila made untenable for shipping. Japanese landings also began on 8 December.

Hong Kong falls. Japan had concentrated forces on the frontier opposite the New Territories by 8 December and immediately began attacking British territory by air and by land, advancing swiftly into Kowloon and assaulting Hong Kong island, which surrendered on 25 December 1941.

The fight for Singapore. The Japanese advanced swiftly down both coasts of Malaya, overcoming ground resistance and being little inconvenienced by an Allied air force which was seriously under strength with fewer than 160 first-line aircraft. British naval strength was decimated with the sinking by the Japanese of the battleship *Prince of Wales* (35,700 tonnes) and battle-cruiser *Repulse* (33,900 tonnes) off Malaya on 10 December, with the loss of 840 men from both ships. Allied troops were forced to withdraw to Singapore, which surrendered on 15 February 1942, after a Japanese Malayan campaign totalling 70 days, one month less than the Japanese had estimated. British losses totalled 138,708, of whom over 130,000 were taken prisoner. Japanese casualties were 9824 dead.

Netherlands East Indies invaded. Attacks had earlier been made at Borneo, and stepping stones to Java — Amboina, Sumatra, Bali and Timor — were seized. The Japanese came ashore on the night of 28 February 1942, simultaneously in eastern and western Java, and Dutch and other Allied forces surrendered on 12 March.

The Philippines fall. Meanwhile, the defence of the Philippines, under the control of Lieutenant-General Douglas MacArthur, was going as badly for the Allies as had the campaign in Malaya. The Japanese made main landings at Davao in the south, and at several points in northern and southern Luzon, the main island. The Davao landings were meant to facilitate the invasion of Borneo and the Netherlands East Indies and played no part in the Luzon conquest. When MacArthur's plan to defeat the Japanese on the beaches failed, he withdrew to the Bataan Peninsula for a last ditch stand, with headquarters on Corregidor. Manila had been declared an open city on 26 December 1941. There was fierce fighting for the peninsula, and on 12 March 1942 MacArthur, with some of his officers, escaped from the Philippines under US Presidential order from Roosevelt, and reached Australia on the 17th. The Bataan defenders were defeated in April. On 6 May the Luzon force surrendered, and the US defenders of the Philippines were finally overcome.

Bataan death march. With the surrender of Bataan, about 64,000 Filipinos and about 12,000 Americans became Japanese prisoners, and on 10 April they were forced to begin an 88 km march from Mariveles to San Fernando, then by crowded rail truck to Capas, and a further 12 km march to POW compounds at Camp O'Donnell. This became known as the Bataan Death March, during which 7000 to 10,000 men, including 2330 Americans, died from disease, exhaustion or brutality.

The fall of Burma. The British regarded Burma as a bastion against Japan's invasion of India's eastern frontiers. Through Burma also ran the Burma Road, by which China's armies were supplied and US air bases in China were maintained. If Burma were captured, China would be isolated and might collapse, thus releasing Japanese armies for use in the Pacific. Japan assigned its XV Army for the conquest of Burma. Small forces attacked as early as 11 December 1941, but the Japanese began to move into Burma in strength on 20 January 1942, and the capital, Rangoon, fell on 8 March. By the end of May, Allied forces were in full retreat, although many Burmese personnel took to the hills and continued to wage war against the Japanese

Further attacks on the Pacific Islands. After repeatedly bombing Rabaul, capital of Australia's mandated territory of New Guinea, Japanese forces landed in Rabaul on 22–23 January 1942, and soon overcame Australian resistance. New Ireland to the north was successfully occupied at the same time, and this was followed by heavy air raids on various New Guinea towns and on Port Moresby, capital of the Australian territory of Papua. Landings were also made on the New Guinea mainland. Rabaul was soon being developed as a Japanese naval base. The Japanese now laid plans to capture Port Moresby in May, Midway Island and the Aleutians in June and in July to move against Fiji, Samoa and New Caledonia. Meanwhile Nauru and Ocean Island were left undefended and were eventually occupied by the Japanese on 26 August 1942.

Australia reinforced. Australia was now quickly being built up as a base for Allied offensive operations in the South-West Pacific. Between January and mid-March 1942, 90,000 US Army men were sent to the Pacific, 57,000 of them to Australia. To secure supply lines from the US to Australia, the

US garrisoned Palmyra, Christmas Island, Canton Island, Bora Bora, the Samoas, Fiji, Tonga, New Caledonia and the New Hebrides and smaller garrisons appeared on many other islands. In Australia the Japanese made nuisance air raids on Darwin, Townsville and Sydney. Following General MacArthur's arrival in Australia in March from the Philippines, he was appointed Supreme Commander of the South-West Pacific, which was henceforth an Army responsibility. Admiral Chester Nimitz, Commander-in-Chief. US Pacific Fleet, was appointed Commander-in-Chief Pacific Ocean area, which became Navy responsibility. They were required to co-operate with one another. Allied forces operated under their direction. General MacArthur elected to call himself Commander-in-Chief rather than Supreme Commander.

Doolittle raid on Tokyo. During this period of Allied reverses, Allied morale was temporarily lifted through a daring raid on 18 April 1942, by 16 US Army Air Force B-25s, on the Japanese mainland cities of Tokyo, Nagoya, Osaka and Kobe. The flight took off from the aircraft carrier *Hornet*, then 1011 km east of the Japanese coast, and was led by Lt.-Col. J. H. Doolittle. The raids inflicted little material damage, but convinced Japan that it needed to seize Midway Island as a forward base from which to attack the US Pacific Fleet.

Tulagi captured. Japanese forces assigned to capture Tulagi, capital of the British Solomons, and Port Moresby in Papua, had assembled in Truk, in the Japanese mandated islands of the Carolines, and sailed south on 30 April, one of its groups occupying Tulagi without opposition on 3 May. On 4 May the force directed to land in Port Moresby sailed from Rabaul, and other Japanese naval groups planned to rendezvous with it in the Coral Sea for this attack. But the Allied navies now moved to meet them.

Battle of the Coral Sea. This took place on 7 May 1942, when US and Australian land-based aircraft sighted some of the Japanese ships and reported them to a combined US and Australian naval force nearby. In the subsequent attacks on each other's ships, only aircraft were used, and the Coral Sea battle was the first naval battle in history in which opposing ships never came within sight of one another. The Allies lost more

ships than the Japanese, but fewer aircraft than the Japanese and had only half as many casualties, and they succeeded in turning back the Port Moresby invasion force. The Japanese had planned to seize Port Moresby to safeguard their flanks and provide a base for attacking Australia; this was the first check on Japan's advance towards Australia.

Battle of Midway. Large opposing naval forces under the commands of Admiral Yamamoto and Admiral Nimitz met off Midway on 4 June 1942, after the Japanese had made a carrier-borne airstrike on the American-held island, unaware that US naval forces were in the vicinity. The Japanese fleet suffered losses so severe that it never recovered, and Midway became a turning point in the war.

Aleutians occupied. As a by-product of their attempted occupation of Midway, Japanese forces successfully occupied Attu and Kiska, in the American-owned Aleutian Islands, on 7 June.

Papua fighting. The Japanese made an overland bid to capture Port Moresby, having failed by sea in the Coral Sea battle. Landing at Buna on 21 July 1942, they fought their way across the Kokoda track to within 48 km of Port Moresby before being forced back, mainly by Australian forces, who also repulsed landings at Milne Bay. The Allies then began to fight their way up the north coast of Papua in a long campaign that did not end until January 1943 with the fall of Buna.

Guadalcanal offensive. While the Papua campaign waged and began extending into New Guinea, a large, mostly American force launched the first big Allied offensive in the Pacific by landing more than 17,000 troops on Guadalcanal and the Tulagi area on 7 August 1942, taking the enemy by surprise. The battle for Guadalcanal soon developed into a struggle for possession of the partly built Japanese airfield, near Honiara, which the Americans named Henderson Field for a Marine Corps hero of the Battle of Midway. It was a war of supply, with the Allies bringing in supplies and reinforcements during the day, and the Japanese bringing them in at night aboard destroyer-transports which ran down 'The Slot' to Savo Sound with such regularity that the Americans called the operation the 'Tokyo Express'. Within two months there was especially bitter fighting as the Japanese developed an all-out offensive to recapture Guadalcanal. The tide was finally turned against the Japanese in November in a fierce three-day naval battle. By February 1943 the 'Tokyo Express' was running in reverse.

Battle of Savo. Two days after the Allied Guadalcanal landing in August 1942, Japanese and Allied naval forces met off Guadalcanal in what became known as the Battle of Savo Island. This resulted in the worst defeat ever suffered by a predominantly American force in a surface action, with the loss of 1023 men, with 709 wounded. Among the ships lost was the Australian cruiser *Canberra*.

Coastwatchers. During the Guadalcanal and Papua New Guinea campaigns the Allies were assisted by men, mostly Australians supported by Islanders, operating in Japanese-held territory and supplying valuable information on Japanese movements by portable radio. These men were directed by the Coast Watching Organisation, which had been developed and was administered by the Royal Australian Navy through the Naval Intelligence Division. Most Coastwatchers had lived in the islands before the war as planters, or plantation workers, government officers and small businessmen and were given naval rank for their operations. Many were killed or were posted missing during service.

Allied Pacific drive. Allied forces by mid-1943 had gone on the offensive everywhere in the Pacific against what had been developed as a purely defensive Japanese island perimeter. American aircraft struck an important blow to Japanese morale and planning capacity by ambushing and shooting down an aircraft carrying Admiral Yamamoto (Commander-in-Chief of the Japanese Combined Fleet) over Buin, Bougainville, on 18 April, killing Yamamoto. The Americans had earlier cracked the Japanese naval code and knew his movements and many other Japanese key moves in the Pacific. The Allies occupied Papuan offshore islands and captured Salamaua and Lae, and continued to fight up the New Guinea coast. In the Solomons, they pushed the Japanese out of New Georgia, and began air attacks aimed at neutralising the vital Japanese base at Rabaul, New Guinea, in preparation for an island-hopping campaign.

Ellice Islands occupied. The Americans occupied the Ellice Islands, establishing a base at Funafuti, and developed other islands, including Baker Island.

Bougainville campaign. The Allies launched a campaign to recapture Bougainville on 27 October 1943, with the seizure of the nearby Treasury Islands, followed on 1 November by troop landings at Cape Torokina, in Emperor Augusta bay. They were soon firmly established at Torokina. Important work was done here by the 1st Battalion of the Fiji Infantry Regiment.

Rabaul neutralised. A prolonged and crippling series of air raids on Rabaul in November finally resulted in the withdrawal to Truk of major Japanese naval forces that had been stationed there. Rabaul ceased from that time to be an offensive threat to the Allies, remaining only as a strong defensive position.

Central Pacific island-hopping. The Americans attacked the Gilbert Islands on 20 November, the invasion of Betio, on Tarawa, being especially hard fought with the loss of 1090 US Marines and 2311 wounded, and the loss of the entire Japanese garrison of 4690 except for 17 Japanese and 129 Korean labourers taken prisoner. Most of the US losses were due to the beach landing being made at unusually low tide, which stranded landing barges on the reef. Kwajalein, Japanese headquarters in the Marshalls, was attacked and in American hands by 4 February 1944, comparatively cheaply in US lives but not in Japanese, and Majuro and other Marshall Islands were also captured. This was followed by the capture of Enewetak, and air attacks on Truk, where on 18 February American carrier-based aircraft sank most of the Japanese naval fleet in the lagoon. Truk was not invaded.

Two-pronged drive for the Philippines. Allied strategy was for a two-pronged drive against the Philippines, and to Japan itself, through the Central Pacific islands and the South-west Pacific via the north coast of New Guinea and former Dutch territories. It was decided to by-pass a number of Japanese-held areas including Rabaul, Kavieng, Truk and Yap. The main Allied effort was to be made through the Central Pacific under Admiral Nimitz. With extended supply lines and a growing shortage of ships and aircraft, Japanese defences were now beginning to crumble. American submarines, which hitherto had had comparatively little effect, were beginning to sink an increasing number of Japanese warships and transports attempting to reinforce scattered, hard-pressed garrisons in many areas.

Dutch New Guinea campaign opens. In December 1943 the Allied South-West Pacific forces under General MacArthur landed in west New Britain, and in the first few months of 1944 the Allies fought up the north coast of New Guinea, capturing Madang and Aitape, and Hollandia in Dutch New Guinea. The landings at Aitape and Hollandia cut off 180,000 Japanese troops and 20,000 civilians, many of whom were later killed or died of starvation or disease. The New Guinea Admiralty Islands and Emirau Island were captured, and the Americans quickly developed Manus, in the Admiralties, into one of the largest naval bases in the Pacific.

Burma offensive. In early 1944 Allied forces went on the offensive in Burma at several points, and Japanese forces began to lose ground.

Fight for Biak. Airfields at Biak, Dutch New Guinea, were required to give support to the Central Pacific operations, but General MacArthur's forces met stiff resistance in the invasion of Biak on 27 May 1944, as the Japanese had dug into caves and cliffs. Not until mid-August were the last pockets overcome, with Japanese losses more than 4700.

Saipan invaded. Meanwhile, Admiral Nimitz's Central Pacific forces had invaded Saipan on 15 June, but not until 10 August was the island secured after some of the most bitter fighting of the war. More than 57,000 American troops were employed, of whom 3426 were killed and 13,099 wounded. The Americans killed 23,811 Japanese, but many others died in the jungle. More than 14,000 civilians were captured, most of them Japanese. The nearby island of Tinian also fell. Admiral Chuichi Nagumo, who had led the Pearl Harbor Striking Force in 1941, committed suicide on Saipan.

Guam falls. American forces invaded Guam on 21 July 1944, after the most prolonged air and naval bombardment yet delivered in the Pacific. Guam was secured by 12 August, but mopping up of Japanese guerillas continued until the end of the war. Almost 18,000 Japanese died in the fighting.

Morotai, Palaus, captured. Forces under General MacArthur secured Morotai Island, in the Dutch Halmaheras, on 15 September 1944, meeting no opposition on the beaches. In the Carolines, American forces assaulted the southern Palaus — Peleliu, Angaur and Ngesebus — at the same time. From the south and the east the Allies were now closing in on the Philippines. The Americans planned to take Peleliu in four days, but it did not fall until 26 November, after one of the war's bloodiest encounters. The Americans lost 1792 killed or missing and 8011 wounded in the Palau operations, most of them on Peleliu; of 13,600 Japanese who died, about 11,000 died on Peleliu.

Assault on the Philippines. The Allied invasion of the Philippines was preceded by an intensive air campaign, begun in September 1944, to reduce Japanese air defences there. The largest convoy ever seen in Pacific waters — totalling 701 vessels — invaded the Leyte Gulf on 20 October, and 200,000 men of the US Sixth Army were put ashore on beaches of Leyte's east coast, with only minor casualties. Japanese forces numbering 387,000 troops were distributed throughout the Philippines, under the command of General Yamashita, conqueror of Malaya and Singapore, but only some 22,000 were on Leyte. Japanese reinforcements were soon pressed into Leyte, which became the crucial battleground for possession of the Philippines. Outside the gulf there was fierce naval action — the Battle of Leyte Gulf — which virtually destroyed Japan's faded naval strength.

Kamikaze units formed. At Clark Field, Luzon, on 20 October 1944, the Japanese 1st Air Fleet formed the first unit of the Kamikaze Special Attack Corps, whose suicide pilots were to crash their bomb-laden Zeke aircraft on enemy installations or warships. The corps was sponsored by Vice-Admiral Takijiro Ohnishi and the first unit was commanded by Lieutenant Yukio Seki. The first Kamikaze attack, on the Australian cruiser *Australia* off the Leyte beaches on 21 October, killed 20 crew members and the captain and so badly damaged the cruiser that she was forced to withdraw to Manus. Kamikaze attacks soon became commonplace, and probably more than 34 ships were sunk and 300 damaged by suicide pilots in different areas of the Pacific. Casualties from them in the US Navy alone exceeded 4400 killed and 5400 wounded.

Final Philippines operations. After heavy fighting, Leyte was finally secured by Christmas 1944, and Luzon was assaulted in January 1945, with the immense amphibious fleet the target of many Kamikaze attacks. The repaired Australian cruiser *Australia* was crashed into by no less than five aircraft in three days with a further loss of 44 crew members. The Allied land forces captured Clark Field on 1 February, but the fight for Manila was street by street and the capital was reduced to rubble, the Japanese garrison dead almost to a man, before the city was taken on 4 March 1945. The Bataan Peninsula and Corregidor had meanwhile been attacked and subdued, but northern areas under the control of General Yamashita had still not been controlled by the time the war ended in August. A total of 114,011 Japanese in the Philippines surrendered on Japan's defeat, but in the fighting another 300,000 had died.

Iwo Jima won. Bombing of Tokyo from Saipan by B-29s had begun in November 1944, but the range was regarded as too great for effective attacks, and the Allies decided to secure closer bases by occupying Iwo Jima, in the Bonin Islands only 1062 km south of Tokyo, and Okinawa, one of the Japanese home islands, which also could be used as a naval base if Japan had to be invaded. Iwo Jima, powerfully fortified and defended, was given the heaviest pre-invasion pounding of any island in the Pacific and invaded on 19 February 1945. Iwo Jima had to be won yard by yard over a month, with the loss of 6812 Americans killed and 19,189 wounded and virtually the entire Japanese garrison of 22,000 killed.

Okinawa operation. Okinawa was attacked with an invasion fleet of 1300 vessels and 183,000 assault troops on 1 April, but was not secured until 2 July after more fierce fighting. Supporting naval forces were under continual attack by Kamikaze planes, 355 Kamikaze missions having set out on one single day, 6 April. Okinawa was the costliest operation in the Central Pacific. American losses were 12,520 killed and 36,631 wounded; Japanese losses were 110,000 killed and 7400 taken prisoner. The Allies

had 36 ships sunk and 368 damaged at Okinawa.

Borneo, Burma operations. Allied forces captured Tarakan Island and other points on Borneo beginning in April and continuing through to July. The Japanese in Burma, exposed to increasing attack because of the fall of the Philippines, were driven back and the Allies re-occupied the capital, Rangoon, on 3 May.

Japan bombed and blockaded. Tokyo and other Japanese cities came under increasing air attack from February 1945. On 10 March, over 300 B-29s in the most destructive raid of either the European or Pacific wars razed a quarter of Tokyo's buildings and killed more than 83,000 people, leaving more than 1,000,000 homeless. In the following months, about 66 cities were systematically burned out, with a paralysing effect on war production and civilian morale. Japan's depleted merchant shipping was further reduced by increased Allied air and sea attacks including extensive mining of Japanese home waters, thus effectively blockading her. Japan's imports of bulk commodities dropped from 22,039,000 metric tons in 1940 to 2,743,200 in 1945.

Peace-feelers. In February and March, and again in July, Japan put out peace-feelers through Russia in the hope of finding a face-saving formula to stop the war. Russia ignored these moves.

Atom bombs dropped. In July 1945, the United States successfully tested the atom bomb, and on 6 August the first such bomb to be dropped was loaded into a B-29 in secrecy at Tinian in the Marianas and exploded that morning over the Japanese city of Hiroshima, burning out the city in extensive fires which burned for days, killing an estimated 71,379 people and injuring 68,023 others. On 9 August a second atom bomb was dropped on Nagasaki, causing less damage and killing, by Japanese estimates, 25,680 people and injuring 23,345. The bombs provided the face-saving pretext needed by the Japanese leaders for surrender, and Japan surrendered unconditionally on 14 August.

Russia declares war. Russia, which had hitherto not intervened in the Pacific War, declared war on Japan on 8 August and on the 9th invaded Manchuria, Korea and southern Sakhalin, and later the Kuriles. She crushed the Japanese forces and continued the fighting for some days after Japan's formal surrender, capturing, among other material, 600 tanks.

Surrender signed. The formal instrument of surrender was signed aboard the US battleship *Missouri* on 2 September 1945. Other ceremonies in other areas followed and for several years Japanese servicemen were still being repatriated.

Obsolete and Alternative Names for Pacific Islands

Most of the islands of the Pacific have been known by at least two names, and sometimes by as many as six, during the past two centuries or so. There are simple historical reasons for this. First, the European explorers were wont to bestow their own names on the islands regardless of the indigenous names, and sometimes the same islands were 'discovered' by more than one explorer. Later, the native names tended to supersede those of the explorers, but because many years elapsed before the spelling of such names became standardised, Europeans frequently spelt the names in a variety of ways. As a result, modern readers of Pacific literature of the 18th and 19th centuries are apt to be confused by such antique names as Todos Santos, Cherry and Bligh's Lagoon, or by obsolete spellings such as Niaur, Aborima and Ticumbia. The gazetteers appearing in this chapter and the next should help to alleviate these difficulties.

The gazetteers were compiled by the Pacific Manuscripts Bureau, Research School of Pacific Studies, Australian National University, Canberra. The principal reference works used in their compilation were: Alexander G. Findlay, *A Directory for the Navigation of the North Pacific Ocean*, 2nd edn (London, 1870); Alexander G. Findlay, *A Directory for the Navigation of the South Pacific Ocean*, 3rd edn (London, 1871); Edwin H. Bryan, Jr., *American Polynesia and the Hawaiian Chain* (Honolulu, 1942); Naval Intelligence Division, *Pacific Islands*, 4 vols (Cambridge, 1943–45); Andrew Sharp, *The Discovery of the Pacific Islands* (Oxford, 1960); H. E. Maude, *Of Islands and Men* (Melbourne, 1969); and Judy Tudor (ed.), *Pacific Islands Year Book*, 11th edn (Sydney, 1972).

The gazetteer in this chapter lists obsolete/alternative names for the islands with their current equivalents; the one in the next chapter lists the current names with their obsolete/alternative equivalents.

No attempt has been made to list all known alternative spellings — merely to give enough clues to enable a researcher to establish an island's most commonly used current name in the English-speaking world. The current name is not necessarily that used by islanders themselves. For example, one of the islands of the northern Cook Group is still better known to outsiders by its European name, Penrhyn, than by its local name, Tongareva. In some cases, arbitrary decisions had to be made on which of a pair of names is now the more current one.

Users of the gazetteers should bear in mind that some islands discovered by 16th-century explorers were not correctly identified by 19th-century hydrographers. Thus, for example, the 16th-century Spanish name Arrecifes seems, correctly, to belong to Ulithi Atoll in the Carolines whereas 19th-century hydrographers identified it as Ujelang Atoll in the Marshalls. Because such connections as Arrecifes/Ujelang became accepted, these cases of mistaken identity have been perpetuated in the gazetteers. It should also be borne in mind that:

• In current *Fijian* orthography, *b* is pronounced *mb* as in member; *c* is *th* as in than; *d* is *nd* as in friend; *g* is *ng* as in hang; *q* is *ng* as in finger.

• In *Samoan* orthography the *g* is sometimes used to represent *ng* as in singer and sometimes the *ng* spelling is used. Thus, an island in the Manua group is sometimes spelt Olosega and sometimes Olose*ng*a.

• In *Tongan* orthography *b* and *p*, and *g* and *ng* were used indiscriminately until about 30 years ago when the use of *p* and *ng* became official.

• In a number of Islands languages, the *t* and *k*, and the *l* and *r* are, or were, frequently confused.

Abbreviations used in the gazetteers, with 'I' standing for Islands, are:

AI	Austral
BI	Bonin
Car.	Caroline
CI	Cook
Gal.	Galapagos
GI	Gilbert
Haw.	Hawaii
JF	Juan Fernandez
Kir.	Kiribati (formerly Gilberts)
KI	Kermadec
LI	Line
MI	Mariana
Marq.	Marquesas
Marsh.	Marshall
NC	New Caledonia
NH	New Hebrides
PNG	Papua New Guinea
PI	Phoenix
RI	Ryuk
SI	Society
Sol.	Solomon
TA	Tuamotu Archipelago
Tok.	Tokelau
Tuv.	Tuvalu (formerly Ellice I.)
Van.	Vanuatu (formerly New Hebrides)
VI	Volcano
W & F	Wallis and Futuna

Abgarris	Nuguria *PNG*
Abingdon	Pinta *Gal.*
Aborima	Apolima *Samoa*
Adams	Nukuhiva *Marq.*
Adams	Uapou *Marq.*
Admiral Chichagov	Faaite *TA*
Adventure	Motutunga *TA*
Agrigan	Agrihan *MI*
Ailinglabelab	Ailinglapelap *Marsh.*
Aimeo	Moorea *SI*
Alamaguan	Alamagan *MI*
Albemarle	Isabela *Gal.*
Alice Thorndike	Kingman *LI*

Allen	Butaritari *Kir.*
Amargura	Fonualei *Tonga*
Amat	Tahiti *SI*
Ambow	Bau *Fiji*
Ambrim	Ambrym *Van.*
Amota	Mota *Van.*
Amsterdam	Tongatapu *Tonga*
Anamooka	Nomuka *Tonga*
Anatajan ⎫	Anatahan *MI*
Anataxan ⎭	
Andema	Ant *Car.*
Aneiteum	Anatom *Van.*
Angatau	Fangatau *TA*
Animas	Amanu *TA*
Anir	Feni *PNG*
Annatom	Anatom *Van.*
Anne	Vostok *SI*
Anonima	Namonuito *Car.*
Anonima	Onon *Car.*
Anthcaen ⎫	Tanga *PNG*
Anthony Kaan ⎭	
Apaiang	Abaiang *Kir.*
Apamama	Abemama *Kir.*
Api	Epi *Van.*
Apia	Abaiang *Kir.*
Apoucaroua	Pukarua *TA*
Appallo	Kabara *Fiji*
Arakcheev	Fangatau *TA*
Araktcheeff	Maloelap *Marsh.*
Arhno	Arno *Marsh.*
Armstrong	Rarotonga *CI*
Arore	Arorae *Kir.*
Arossi	San Cristobal *Sol.*
Arragh	Pentecost *Van.*
Arrecifes	Ujelang *Marsh.*
Arrowsmith	Majuro *Marsh.*
Arthur	Enewetak *Marsh.*
Arzobispo	Bonin *BI*
Asaua	Yasawa *Fiji*
Ascension	Ponape *Car.*
Assumption	Asuncion *MI*
Atooi	Kauai *Haw.*
Augier	Tatakoto *TA*
Aura	Kaukura *TA*
Aurh	Aur *Marsh.*
Aurora	Maewo *Van.*
Aurora	Makatea *TA*
Auura	Kaukura *TA*
Avondstond	Apataki *TA*

Barclay de Tolly	Raroia *TA*
Baring	Namorik *Marsh.*
Barren	Starbuck *LI*
Barrington	Sante Fe *Gal.*

Barrow	Vanavana *TA*
Barstow	Morane *TA*
Bartholomew	Malo *Van.*
Bartolome	Pulusuk *Car.*
Barwell	Tikopia *Sol.*
Bass	Marotiri *AI*
Bass Reef-tied	Maloelap *Marsh.*
Basse des Fregates Françaises	French Frigate Shoal *Haw.*
Batou-bara	Vatuvara *Fiji*
Baux	Nukuhiva *Marq.*
Bedford	Vahanga *TA*
Bedrieglyke	Tikei *TA*
Benga	Beqa *Fiji*
Bertero	Maria *TA*
Bigar	Bikar *Marsh.*
Bigini	Rongelap *Marsh.*
Bindloe	Marchena *Gal.*
Bird	Farallon de Medinilla *MI*
Bird	Nihoa *Haw.*
Bird	Reitoru *TA*
Bishop	Tabiteuea *Kir.*
Bishop Junction	Erikub *Marsh.*
Bishop of Osnaburg	Moruroa *TA*
Biva	Viwa *Fiji*
Blake	Moturiti *Marq.*
Bligh	Ureparapara *Van.*
Bligh's Lagoon	Tematangi *TA*
Bolabola	Borabora *SI*
Bona Vista	Tinian *MI*
Bonham	Jaluit *Marsh.*
Bonin	Ogasawara *BI*
Bordelaise	Oroluk *Car.*
Boscawen	Niuatoputapu *Tonga*
Boston	Ebon *Marsh.*
Boucher	Tiga *NC*
Boudoir	Mehetia *SI*
Bouka	Buka *PNG*
Bow	Hao *TA*
Bowditch	Fakaofo *Tok.*
Brattle	Tortuga *Gal.*
Britannia	Mare *NC*
Britomart	Hereheretue *TA*
Brooke	Jarvis *LI*
Brooks	Midway
Brown	Enewetak *Marsh.*
Brown	Lae *Marsh.*
Buen Viaje	Butaritari *Kir.*
Buena Vista	Tinian *MI*
Buga Buga	Toga *Van.*
Buka	Toga *Van.*
Bulloo	Ovalau *Fiji*

Bunker	Jarvis *LI*
Button	Utirik *Marsh.*
Byam Martin	Ahunui *TA*
Byron	Nikunau *Kir.*
Cadmus	Morane *TA*
Cainga	Taenga *TA*
Calvert	Maloelap *Marsh.*
Cantab	Kadavu *Fiji*
Carlshoff	Aratika *TA*
Carteret	Kilinailau *PNG*
Carteret	Malaita *Sol.*
Carysfort	Tureia *TA*
Casbokas	Ujelang *Marsh.*
Casobos	Ujelang *Marsh.*
Catharine	Kwajalein *Marsh.*
Cavahi	Kauehi *TA*
Chabrol	Lifou *NC*
Chain	Anaa *TA*
Chanal	Hatutu *Marq.*
Charles	Floreana *Gal.*
Charlotte	Abaiang *Kir.*
Chatham	Erikub *Marsh.*
Chatham	San Cristobal *Gal.*
Chatham	Savaii *Samoa*
Chaves	Santa Cruz *Gal.*
Cherry	Anuta *Sol.*
Chichagov	Faaite, Tahanea *TA*
Chichia	Cicia *Fiji*
Chicobea	Cikobia *Fiji*
Christiana	Tahuata *Marq.*
Clark	Caroline *LI*
Clarke	Butaritari *Kir.*
Clarke	Tatakoto *TA*
Clerk	Onotoa *Kir.*
Clermont de Tonnere	Reao *TA*
Cockburn	Fangataufa *TA*
Cocos	Niuatoputapu *Tonga*
Consolacion	Niuafo'ou *Tonga*
Constantin	Kapingamarangi *Car.*
Contrariete	Ulawa *Sol.*
Conversion de San Pablo	Hao *TA*
Cook	Tarawa *Kir.*
Coquille	Jaluit *Marsh.*
Coquille	Pikelot *Car.*
Coral Queen	Starbuck *LI*
Count Arakcheev	Fangatau *TA*
Count Heiden	Likiep *Marsh.*
Count Wittgenstein	Fakarava, Toau *TA*
Covell	Ebon *Marsh.*
Crescent	Temoe *TA*

Croker	Haraiki *TA*
Cuatro	Actaeon *TA*
Coronados	
Cumberland	Manuhangi *TA*
Dagenraad	Ahe, Manihi *TA*
Danger	Pukapuka *CI*
Dangerous	Tuamotu *TA*
Daniel	Arno *Marsh.*
Daugier	Tatakoto *TA*
David Clark	Tatakoto *TA*
Dawahaidy	Ravahere *TA*
Dawson	Bikar *Marsh.*
Dean	Rangiroa *TA*
Deception	Moso *Van.*
De Peyster	Nukufetau *Tuv.*
Disappointment	Napuka, Tepoto *TA*
Disappointment	Taumako *Sol.*
Dog	Pukapuka *TA*
Dominica ⎤	Hivaoa *Marq.*
Dominique ⎦	
Doubtful	Tekokoto *TA*
Douglas	Parece Vela *Japan*
Drummond	McKean *PI*
Drummond	Tabiteuea *Kir.*
Duke of Clarence	Nukunono *Tok.*
Duke of	Manuhangi *TA*
Cumberland	
Duke of	Paraoa *TA*
Gloucester	
Duke of York	Moorea *SI*
Duncan	Pinzon *Gal.*
Duperrey	Mokil *Car.*
D'Urville	Losap *Car.*
Eap	Yap *Car.*
East Danger	Enewetak *Marsh.*
Ebrill	Fakahina *TA*
Eddystone	Simbo *Sol.*
Edgecumbe	Utupua *Sol.*
Egerup	Erikub *Marsh.*
Egmont	Vairaatea *TA*
Eimeo	Moorea *SI*
Eliza	Beru *Kir.*
Eliza	Hiti *TA*
Eliza	Onotoa *Kir.*
Elizabeth	Henderson *Pitcairn*
Elizabeth	Jaluit *Marsh.*
Elizabeth	Toau *TA*
Ellice	Funafuti *Tuv.*
Ellice	Tuvalu *Tuv.*
Enderby	Enderbury *PI*
Enderby	Puluwat *Car.*
Eooa	Eua *Tonga*

Eourypyg	Eauripik *Car.*
Eromango	Erromango *Van.*
Erronan	Futuna *Van.*
Eschscholtz	Bikini *Marsh.*
Faarava	Fakarava *TA*
Fagatau	Fangatau *TA*
Faite	Faaite *TA*
Falcon	Fonuafo'ou *Tonga*
Fangahina	Fakahina *TA*
Fanoualie	Fonualei *Tonga*
Farewell	Cikobia *Fiji*
Farroilep ⎤	Faraulep *Car.*
Fattoilap ⎦	
Fatuuhu	Hatutu *Marq.*
Fead	Nuguria *PNG*
Federal	Nukuhiva *Marq.*
Feejee	Fiji *Fiji*
Fetuku	Fatuhuku *Marq.*
Flora	Florida *Sol.*
Foraulep	Faraulep *Car.*
Fortuna	Futuna *Van.*
Fotuna	Erronan *Van.*
Four Crowns	Actaeon *TA*
Fourteen	Ebon *Marsh.*
Francis	Beru *Kir.*
Franklin	Motuiti, Nukuhiva *Marq.*
Fraser	Ant *Car.*
Freemantle	Eiao *Marq.*
Friendly	Tonga *Tonga*
Furneaux	Marutea *TA*
Gallipagoes	Galapagos *Gal.*
Gambier	Mangareva *TA*
Gardner	Faraulep *Car.*
Gardner	Maria *AI*
Gardner	Tabar *PNG*
Gaspar Rico	Taongi *Marsh.*
Gela	Florida *Sol.*
General	Katiu *TA*
Osten-Saken	
Gente Hermosa	Swain *Samoa*
Georgian	Society Islands *SI*
	(*W'ward Group*)
Gerrit de Nijs ⎤	Lihir *PNG*
Gerrit Denys ⎦	
Gillespie	Butaritari *Kir.*
Gillet	Rabi *Fiji*
Gloucester	Paraoa *TA*
Goede Hope	Niuafo'ou *Tonga*
Goede	Rangiroa *TA*
Verwaghting	
Good Hope	Rekareka *TA*
Goro	Koro *Fiji*

Goulou .... Ngulu *Car.*
Gow .... Gaua *Van.*
Gower .... Ndai *Sol.*
Graf .... Katiu *TA*
  Osten-Sacken
Gran Cocal .... Nanumanga *Tuv.*
Grand Duke .... Rakahanga *CI*
  Alexander
Great Ganges .... Manihiki *CI*
Greenwich .... Kapingamarangi *Car.*
Greig .... Niau *TA*
Grenville .... Rotuma *Fiji*
Grigan .... Agrihan *MI*
Groene .... Green *PNG*
Guahan ⎫.............. Guam *MI*
Guajan ⎭

Habai .... Haapai *Tonga*
Hadow .... Munia *Fiji*
Hagemeister .... Apataki *TA*
Halcyon .... Wake
Halgan .... Ouvea *NC*
Hall .... Maiana *Kir.*
Hancock .... Hatutu *Marg.*
Harpe .... Hao *TA*
Harvest .... Namoluk *Car.*
Hashmy .... Namoluk *Car.*
Hat .... Eretoka *Van.*
Henderville .... Aranuka *Kir.*
Hergest .... Motu-iti *Marq.*
Hero .... Starbuck *LI*
Hervey .... Cook *CI*
Hiau .... Eiao *Marq.*
High .... Raivavae *AI*
Hinchinbrook .... Emau *Van.*
Hirst .... Caroline *LI*
Hogoleu .... Truk *Car.*
Holland .... Howland *PI*
Holt .... Taenga *TA*
Hood .... Espanola *Gal.*
Hood .... Fatuhuku *Marq.*
Honden- .... Pukapuka *TA*
Hoorn .... Futuna *W&F*
Hopper .... Aranuka *Kir.*
Horn .... Futuna *W&F*
Hudson .... Nanumanga *Tuv.*
Hull .... Maria *AI*
Humphrey .... Manihiki *CI*
Hunter .... Kili *Marsh.*
Hurd .... Arorae *Kir.*

Ibargoitia .... Pulusuk *Car.*
Ibbetson .... Aur *Marsh.*
Ifalik .... Ifaluk *Car.*

Ile De Pins .... Isle of Pines *NC*
Immer .... Aniwa *Van.*
Inattendue .... Ndai *Sol.*
Indefatigable .... Santa Cruz *Gal.*
Independence .... Caroline *LI*
Independence .... Malden *LI*
Independence .... Niulakita *Tuv.*
Industriel .... Vairaatea *TA*
Ireland .... Raraka *TA*
Isla Del Cocal .... Nanumanga *Tuv.*

Jabwat .... Jabwot *Marsh.*
James .... San Salvador *Gal.*
Jefferson .... Uapou *Marq.*
Jervis .... Rabida *Gal.*
Jesus .... Nui *Tuv.*

Kadoolawe ⎫......... Kahoolawe *Haw.*
Kadulaui ⎭
Kandavu .... Kadavu *Fiji*
Kantavu .... Kadavu *Fiji*
Karlshoff .... Aratika *TA*
Kata .... Puluwat *Car.*
Kaven .... Maloelap *Marsh.*
Kawahe .... Kauehi *TA*
Kemin .... Gardner *PI*
Keppel .... Tafahi *Tonga*
Kili .... Hunter *Marsh.*
King .... Taiaro *TA*
King George .... Takapoto, Takaroa *TA*
King George III ...... Tahiti *SI*
Kingsmill .... Southern Gilberts *Kir.*
Knox .... Eiao *Marq.*
Knox .... Tarawa *Kir.*
Kongelab .... Rongelap *Marsh.*
Kordiukoff .... Rose *Samoa.*
Koutousoff .... Makemo *TA*
Krusenstern .... Ailuk *Marsh.*
Krusentstern .... Tikehau *TA*
Kunie .... Isle of Pines *NC*
Kutusoff .... Utirik *Marsh.*
Kutusov- .... Makemo *TA*
  Smolenski
Kwadelen .... Kwajalein *Marsh.*
Kyli .... Jaluit *Marsh.*

Lacona .... Gaua *Van.*
Ladrones .... Mariana *MI*
Lagoon .... Vahitahi *TA*
Lagoon (Bligh's) .... Tematangi *TA*
Lakoon .... Gaua *Van.*
Lambert .... Ailingalapalap *Marsh.*
Lamoliork .... Ngulu *Car.*
Lamuliur .... Ngulu *Car.*

Lanciers	Akiaki *TA*
Langdon	Hatutu *Marq.*
Latte	Late *Tonga*
Lauru	Choiseul *Sol.*
Lazarev	Matahiva *TA*
Legiep	Likiep *Marsh.*
Leopoldi	Nukutavake *TA*
Lepers	Aoba *Van.*
Lette	Late *Tonga*
Lieutenant-General Yermolov	Taenga *TA*
Lifu	Lifou *NC*
Lincoln	Onotoa *Kir.*
Linnez	Ebon *Marsh.*
Little Ganges	Rakahanga *CI*
Lomo-Lomo	Lomaloma *Fiji*
Loo-Choo	Ryuku *RI*
Loper	Niutao *Tuv.*
Lord Egmont	Vairaatea *TA*
Lord Hood	South Marutea *TA*
Lord Howe	Ontong Java *Sol.*
Lord Howe	Mopelia *SI*
Lord Howe	Vavau *Tonga*
Lord North	Tobi *Car.*
Lostange	Nengonengo *TA*
Louasappe	Losap *Car.*
Lougounor	Lukunor *Car.*
Low	Starbuck *LI*
Luaniua	Ontong Java *SI*
Lu-Chu	Ryukyu *RI*
Lugunor	Lukunor *Car.*
Lutke	East Fayu *Car.*
Lydia	Ujae *Marsh.*
Lynx	Niutao *Tuv.*
Maataah	Makatea *TA*
Macaskill	Pingelap *Car.*
Mackenzie	Ulithi *Car.*
Macquemo	Makemo *TA*
Madison	Nukuhiva *Marq.*
Mae	Emae *Van.*
Maeteea	Makatea *TA*
Magdalena	Fatuhiva *Marq.*
Mai	Emae *Van.*
Maitea ⎱ Maitia ⎰	Mehetia *SI*
Maiwo	Maewo *Van.*
Makin	Little Makin *Kir.*
Makira	San Cristobal *Sol.*
Mala	Malaita *Sol.*
Malanta	Malaita *Sol.*
Malayette	Malaita *Sol.*
Mallicollo	Malakula *Van.*

Maloelab	Maloelap *Marsh.*
Mandeghughsu	Simbo *Sol.*
Mangea	Mangaia *CI*
Mannicolo	Vanikoro *Sol.*
Man-of-war Rock	Gardner Pinnacles *Haw.*
Manuae	Fenua-Ura *SI*
Maraki	Marakei *Kir.*
Maralaba	Mera Lava *Van.*
Marchand	Uapou *Marq.*
Margaret	Nukutipipi *TA*
Margaretta	Namu *Marsh.*
Maria	Beru *Kir.*
Marina	Espiritu Santo *Van.*
Marque(e)n	Tauu *PNG*
Martin de Mayorga	Vavau *Tonga*
Martires	Tekokoto *TA*
Marua	Maupiti *SI*
Mary	Kanton *PI*
Mary Balcout	Kanton *PI*
Massachusetts	Eiao *Marq.*
Masse	Eiao *Marq.*
Masuna	Tutuila *Samoa*
Mataa ⎫ Matea ⎪ Mathea ⎬ Matia ⎭	Makatea *TA*
Matilda	Moruroa *TA*
Matoriki	Moturiki *Fiji*
Matthew	Abaiang *Kir.*
Matthew	Marakei *Kir.*
Maty	Woodlark *PNG*
Mau	Emau *Van.*
Mauiti	Maiao *SI*
Maura	Maupiti *SI*
Mauti	Mauke *CI*
Mbau	Bau *Fiji*
Mbenga	Beqa *Fiji*
Meduro	Majuro *Marsh.*
Meerderzorg	Arutua *TA*
Melbourne	Maturei, Vavao *TA*
Melville	Hikueru *TA*
Merlav	Mera Lava *Van.*
Miadi	Mejit *Marsh.*
Middle	Tegua *Van.*
Middleburgh	Eua *Tonga*
Middleton	Rose *Samoa*
Mille	Mili *Marsh.*
Miloradovich	Faaite *TA*
Minerva	Reao *TA*
Minto	Tenarunga *Ta*
Mitchell	Nassau *CI*
Mitchell	Nukulaelae *Tuv.*

Mitiero	Mitiaro *CI*
Mitre	Fataka *Sol.*
Moerenhout	Maria *TA*
Mokogai ⎫	Makogai *Fiji*
Mokungai ⎭	
Moller	Amanu *TA*
Mollet	Laysañ *Haw.*
Montagu	Nguna *Van.*
Monteverde	Nukuoro *Car.*
Mopihaa	Mopelia *SI*
Morotoi	Molokai *Haw.*
Mortlock	Nomoi *Car.*
Mortlock	Tauu *PNG*
Mururoa	Moruroa *TA*
Mota Lava	Valua *Van.*
Motane	Mohotani *Marq.*
Motuiti	Tupai *SI*
Moumolu-Naunitu	San Jorge *Sol.*
Mourileu	Murilo *Car.*
Mowee	Maui *Haw.*
Mulgrave	Mili *Marsh.*
Munggava	Rennell *Sol.*
Mungiki	Bellona *Sol.*
Murua	Woodlark *PNG*
Musgrave	Pingelap *Car.*
Muskillo	Namu *Marsh.*
Musquillo	Ailinglapelap *Marsh.*
Nairsa	Rangiroa *TA*
Namarik	Namorik *Marsh.*
Namo	Namu *Marsh.*
Namuka	Nomuka *Tonga*
Nanouki ⎫	Nonouti *Kir.*
Nanouti ⎭	
Narciso	Takakoto *TA*
Narik	Knox *Marsh.*
Natlop	Valua *Van.*
Navigators	Samoa *Samoa*
Nawodo	Nauru
Ndeni	Ndende *Sol.*
Nduke	Kolombangara *Sol.*
Nederlandsch	Nui *Tuv.*
Neow	Gau *Fiji*
Neu Mecklenburg	New Ireland *PNG*
Neupommern	New Britain *PNG*
Neville	Tobi *Car.*
New Hanover	Lavongai *PNG*
New Nantucket	Phoenix *PI*
New Year	Mejit *Marsh.*
New York	Eiao *Marq.*
New York	Washington *LI*
Nexsen	Hatutu *Marq.*
Ngaryk	Ngatik *Car.*
Nggela	Florida *Sol.*

Nhow	Gau *Fiji*
Niau	Greig *TA*
Niaur	Angaur *Car.*
Nieue	Niue
Niguria	Nuguria *PNG*
Nihera	Nihiru *TA*
Nine	Kilinailau *PNG*
Ningoningo	Nengonengo *TA*
Nissan	Green *PNG*
Nitendi	Ndende *Sol.*
Niua	Aniwa *Van.*
Niuafu	Niuato'ou *Tonga*
Niuatabutabu	Niuatoputapu *Tonga*
Nooaheevah	Nukuhiva *Marq.*
Norbarbar	Ureparapara *Van.*
North	Hiu *Van.*
North	San Alessandro *VI*
Nougouore	Nukuoro *Car.*
Nouvelle Cythere	Tahiti *SI*
Nukulailai	Nukulaelae *Tuv.*
Nukunau	Nikunau *Kir.*
Nukunonu	Nukunonu
Nurakita	Niulakita *Tuv.*
Nurorutu	Maria *AI*
Nusi	Tench *PNG*
Nutloff	Valua *Van.*
Oahtooha	Upolu *Samoa*
Oaitupu	Vaitupu *Tuv.*
Oba	Aoba *Van.*
Obalauo	Ovalau *Fiji*
Obelisk	Elina *Sol.*
Ocean	Banaba *Kir.*
Ogasawara	Bonin *BI*
Oheteroah	Rurutu *AI*
Ojalava	Upolu *Samoa*
Olosenga	Swain *Samoa*
Olosinga	Olosenga *Samoa*
	(*Manua Group*)
Omba	Aoba *Van.*
Onalau	Ovalau *Fiji*
Onavero ⎫	Nauru
Oneeheow ⎭	
Oneeow	Niihau *Haw.*
Onutu	Onotoa *Kir.*
Oparo	Rapa *AI*
Opoloo	Upolu *Samoa*
Opoun	Manua, Manua-Tele *Samoa*
Oraison	Tanga *PNG*
Orisega ⎫	Olosenga *Samoa*
Orosenga ⎭	
Orona	Hull *PI*
Osnaburg	Moruroa *TA*
Osnaburgh	Mehetia *SI*

Osten-Saken	Katiu *TA*
Otaha	Tahaa *SI*
Otaheite	Tahiti *SI*
Otdia	Wotje *Marsh.*
Otooho	Tepoto *TA*
Ouahouka	Uahuka *Marq.*
Oumaitia	Makatea *TA*
Ovolau	Ovalau *Fiji*
Owahi	Hawaii *Haw.*
Owa Rafa }	Santa Ana *Sol.*
Owa Raha }	
Owa Riki	Santa Catalina *Sol.*
Owhyhee }	Hawaii *Haw.*
Owhyhi }	
Paanopa	Banaba *Kir.*
Pagon	Pagan *MI*
Palaos	Palau group *Car.*
Palliser	Apataki, Arutua,
Islands	Kaukura, Toau *TA*
Parry	Enewetak *Marsh.*
Parry	Mauke *CI*
Pascua	Easter
Paterson	Namu *Marsh.*
Paum	Paama *Van.*
Paumotu	Tuamotu *TA*
Peacock	Ahe *TA*
Pedder	Arno *Marsh.*
Peguenema	Pakin *Car.*
Pelew	Palau *Car.*
Pentecote	Pentecost *Van.*
Peroat	Beru *Kir.*
Peru	Beru *Kir.*
Pescadore	Rongelap *Marsh.*
Philip	Makemo *TA*
Philip	Soroi *Car.*
Phillip	Makemo *TA*
Phoebe	Phoenix *PI*
Pic de la	Mehetia *SI*
Boudeuse	
Pitt	Little Makin *Kir.*
Pitt	Vanikoro *Sol.*
Platte	Manono *Samoa*
Pleasant	Nauru
Pollard Is. }	Gardner Pinnacles *Haw.*
Pollard Rock }	
Poloat	Pulawat *Car.*
Pomotu	Tuamotu *TA*
Poreemo	Apolima *Samoa*
Portland	Tingwon *PNG*
Poulousouk	Pulusuk *Car.*
Predpriatie	Fakahina *TA*
Prince de	Taenga *TA*
Joinville	

Prince	Makemo *TA*
Golenitschev-	
Kutuzov-	
Smolenski	
Prince of Wales	Manihi *TA*
Princess	Lib *Marsh.*
Princessa	Jabwot *Marsh.*
Prince	Takume *TA*
Volkhonski	
Prince William	Nengonengo *TA*
Henry	
Proby	Niuafo'ou *Tonga*
Prospect	Washington *LI*
Providence	Ujelang *Marsh.*
Pukararo }	Vairaatea *TA*
Purarunga }	
Puynipet	Ponape *Car.*
Pylstaart	Ata *Tonga*
Quatre Facardins	Vahitahi *TA*
Queen Charlotte	Nukutavake *TA*
Quiros	Swain *Samoa*
Radokala	Rongerik *Marsh.*
Raevski	Eliza, Tepoto *TA*
Raga	Pentecost *Van.*
Rairoa	Rangiroa *TA*
Rambi	Rabi *Fiji*
Ranai	Lanai *Haw*
Ranbe	Rabi *Fiji*
Rapa-iti	Rapa *AI*
Rapa-nui	Easter
Ratak	Radak *Marsh.*
Recherche	Vanikoro *Sol.*
Recreation	Makatea *TA*
Reef	Rowa *Van.*
Reid	Tuanake *TA*
Reine Louise	Pinaki *TA*
Reirson	Rakahanga *CI*
Resolution	Tauere *TA*
Rimatera	Rimatara *AI*
Rimski-Korsakoff	Rongerik *Marsh.*
Riou	Uahuka *Marq.*
Roahouga	Uahuka *Marq.*
Roberts	Eiao *Marq.*
Rocky	Niulakita *Tuv.*
Roger Simpson	Abemama *Kir.*
Romanzoff	Wotje *Marsh.*
Romanzoff	Tikei *TA*
Rooahooga	Uahuka *Marq.*
Rook(e)	Umboi *PNG*
Ross	Namu *Marsh.*
Rotch	Tamana *Kir.*
Roxburgh	Rarotonga *CI*

Ruk	Truk *Car.*
Rumanzoff	Tikei *TA*
Sacken	Katiu *TA*
Saddle	Valua *Van.*
St Andrew	Sonsorol *Car.*
St Bartholomew	Malo *Van.*
St Claire	Merig *Van.*
St Jans	Emirau *PNG*
St John	
St Matthias	Mussau *PNG*
St Paul	Hereheretue *TA*
Saken	Katiu *TA*
Salt	Lo *Van.*
San Agustin	Nanumea *Tuv.*
San Agustino	Oroluk *Car.*
San Christoval	San Cristobal *Sol.*
San Cristobal	Mehetia *SI*
San Dionisio	San Augustino *VI*
Sands	Maria *AI*
Sandwich	Efate *Van.*
Sandwich	Hawaiian Is. *Haw.*
San Juan	Hikueru *TA*
San Julian	Tahanea *TA*
San Marcos	Mera Lava *Van.*
San Miguel	Vairaatea *TA*
San Narciso	Tatakoto *TA*
San Pablo	Hereheretue *TA*
San Pablo	Pukapuka *TA*
San Pedro	Mohotani *Marq.*
San Quintin	Haraiki *TA*
San Simon y Judas	Tauere *TA*
Sansoral	Sonsorol *Car.*
Santa Cristina	Tahuata *Marq.*
Santa Cruz	Ndende *Sol.*
Santa Gertrudis	Isabela *Gal.*
Santa Magdalena	Fatuhiva *Marq.*
Santa Maria	Floreana *Gal.*
Santa Maria	Gaua *Van.*
Santa Polonia	Vairaatea *TA*
Santa Rosa	Raivavae *AI*
Santa Ysabel	Santa Isabel *Sol.*
Santiago	San Salvador *Gal.*
Santo	Espiritu Santo *Van.*
Sariguan	Sarigan *MI*
Sarpan	Rota *MI*
Satouwan	Satawan *Car.*
Savage	Niue
Schadelyk	Takapoto *TA*
Schantz	Wotho *Marsh.*
Scilly	Fenua-ura *SI*
Seagull	Raevski *TA*
Seniavine	Ponape *Car.*
Sepper	Niutao *Tuv.*
Serle	Pukarua *TA*
Setuahal	Satawal *Car.*
Seu	Hiu *Van.*
Seypan	Saipan *MI*
Shanz	Wotho *Marsh.*
Siew	Hiu *Van.*
Sir Charles Hardy	Green *PNG*
Sir Charles Middleton	Lomaloma *Fiji*
Sir Charles Saunders	Maiao *SI*
Sir Henry Martin	Nukuhiva *Marq.*
Small Malaita	Maramsike *Sol.*
Smith	Butaritari *Kir.*
Smyth	Taongi *Marsh.*
Sola	Ata *Tonga*
Solitaria	Niulakita *Tuv.*
Sondergront	Takapoto, Takaroa *TA*
Sooughe	Pulusuk *Car.*
Sophia	Niulakita *Tuv.*
Souworoff	Suwarrow *CI*
Souworoff	Taka *Marsh.*
Spencer Keys	Ngulu *Car.*
Spiridoff	Takapoto *TA*
Squally	Emirau *PNG*
Star Peak	Mera Lava *Van.*
Starve	Starbuck *LI*
Stavers	Vostok *LI*
Steep-to	Jemo *Marsh.*
Stewart	Sikaiana *Sol.*
Storm	Emirau *PNG*
Strong	Kosrae *Car.*
Sugar-loaf	Mota *Van.*
Suk	Pulusuk *Car.*
Sulphur	Volcano *VI*
Sunday	Raoul *KI*
Surry	Hereheretue *TA*
Suvarov	Suwarrow *CI*
Swallow	Kanton *PI*
Swallow	Reef *Sol.*
Sydenham	Nonouti *Kir.*
Sydney	Manra *PI*
Taapoto	Takapoto *TA*
Taaroa	Takaroa *TA*
Tabutha	Tuvuca *Fiji*
Tacume	Takume *TA*
Tagai	Taka *Marsh.*
Tahaurawee	Kahoolawe *Haw.*
Tahoora	Kaula *Haw.*
Tahoorowa	Kahoolawe *Haw.*
Takoto	Tatakoto *TA*
Tana	Tanna *Van.*
Tannoa	Tongoa *Van.*
Tapamanoa	Maiao *SI*

Taputeouea	Tabiteuea *Kir.*
Taritari	Butaritari *Kir.*
Tchitchagoff	Tahanea *TA*
Teapy	Easter
Tebut	Jabwot *Marsh.*
Tehuata	Rekareka *TA*
Temo	Jemo *Marsh.*
Tethuroa ⎫ Tetuaroa ⎭	Tetiaroa *SI*
Thornton	Caroline *LI*
Three Hills	Emae *Van.*
Thrum Cap	Akiaki *TA*
Ticumbia	Cikobia *Fiji*
Tika	Tiga *NC*
Timoe	Temoe *TA*
Tin Can	Niuafo'ou *Tonga*
Tindal & Watts	Ailuk *Marsh.*
Tiokea	Takaroa *TA*
Todos Santos	Anaa *TA*
Tongareva	Penrhyn *CI*
Tootooilah	Tutuila *Samoa*
Torga	Toga *Van.*
Touching	Butaritari *Kir.*
Tower	Genovesa *Gal.*
Tracy	Vaitupu *Tuv.*
Traitors	Tafahi *Tonga*
Traversey	Aur *Marsh.*
Trevenen	Uapou *Marq.*
Tromelin	Fais *Car.*
Tschitschagoff	Erikub *Marsh.*
Tubai	Tupai *SI*
Tubuai Manu	Maiao *SI*
Tucker	Satawal *Car.*
Tucopia	Tikopia *Sol.*
Tuga	Tegua *Van.*
Tupuaemanu	Maiao *SI*
Turtle	Vatoa *Fiji*
Tuscan	Hikueru *TA*
Two Brothers	Motuiti *Marq.*
Two Groups	Marokau, Ravahere *TA*
Two Hills	Mataso *Van.*
Ualan	Kusaie *Car.*
Udia-Milai	Bikini *Marsh.*
Udirick	Utirik *Marsh.*
Uea	Uvea *NC*
Uea	Wallis *W & F*
Ugi	Uki *Sol.*
Ujilong	Ujelang *Marsh.*
Uliatea	Raiatea *SI*
Ulie	Woleai *Car.*
Ulietea	Raiatea *SI*
Union	Tokelau

Uracus	Farallon de Pajaros *MI*
Uvea	Ouvea *NC*
Uvea	Wallis *W & F*
Vaghena	Wagina *Sol.*
Valientes	Ngatik *Car.*
Vanikolo	Vanikoro *Sol.*
Van Shirnding	Cikobia *Fiji*
Vanua-Valavo	Vanuabalavu *Fiji*
Vate	Efate *Van.*
Vatiu	Atiu *CI*
Vatu-Rera	Vatuvara *Fiji*
Vatu Rhandi	Vatganai *Van.*
Vavitao	Raivavae *AI*
Verkwikking	Makatea *TA*
Verraders	Tafahi *Tonga*
Vincennes	Kauehi *TA*
Viti	Fiji *Fiji*
Vlieghen	Rangiroa *TA*
Waihu	Easter
Warren Hastings	Meru *Car.*
Washington	Uahuka, Uapou *Marq*
Wateeoo	Atiu *CI*
Waterlandt	Ahe, Manihi *TA*
Wellington	Mokil *Car.*
Wenooaete	Takutea *CI*
West Danger	Enewetak *Marsh.*
Whitsun	Pentecost *Van.*
Whitsun ⎫ Whitsunday ⎭	Pinaki *TA*
Whytootackee	Aitutaki *CI*
William The Fourth	Ant *Car.*
Wilson	Ifaluk *Car.*
Wilson	Manihi *TA*
Woahoo	Oahu *Haw.*
Wolea	Woleai *Car.*
Wolkonsky	Takume *TA*
Woodle	Kuria *Kir.*
Worth	Howland *PI*
Wottho	Wotho *Marsh.*
Wright's Lagoon	Maria *TA*
Wytoohee	Napuka *TA*
Yermoeloff	Taenga *TA*
Ysabel	Santa Isabel *Sol.*
Zarpane	Rota *MI*
Zealandia Rocks	Farallon de Torres *MI*
Zondergrondt	Takaroa, Takapoto *TA*

Current Names for Pacific Islands

This gazetteer lists current names of Pacific Islands with obsolete/alternative equivalents. Refer to the notes at the beginning of the preceding chapter for further details.

Abaiang .... Apaiang *Kir.*
Apia
Charlotte
Matthew
Abemama .... Apamama *Kir.*
Roger Simpson
Actaeon .... Cuatro Coronados *TA*
Four Crowns
Agrihan .... Agrigan *MI*
Grigan
Aguijan .... *MI*
Ahe .... Dagenraad *TA*
Peacock
Waterlandt
Ahunui .... Byam Martin *TA*
Ailinginae .... *Marsh.*
Ailinglapalap ...... Ailinglabelab *Marsh.*
Lambert
Musquillo
Ailuk .... Krusenstern *Marsh.*
Tindal & Watts
Aitutaki .... Whytootakee *CI*
Akiaki .... Lanciers *TA*
Thrum Cap
Alamagan .... Alamaguan *MI*
Alofi .... *W & F*
Amanu .... Animas *TA*
Moller
Ambrym .... Ambrim *Van.*
Anna .... Chain *TA*
Todos Santos
Anatahan .... Anatajan *MI*
Anataxan
Anatom .... Aneiteum *Van.*
Annatom
Angaur .... Niaur *Car.*

Aniwa .... Immer *Van.*
Niua
Ant .... Andena *Car.*
Fraser
William the Fourth
Anuanuraro ..... Duke of Gloucester *TA*
Anuanurunga
Anuta .... Cherry *Sol.*
Aoba .... Lepers *Van.*
Oba
Omba
Apataki .... Avondstond *TA*
Hagemeister
Apolima .... Aborima *Samoa*
Poreemo
Aranuka .... Henderville *Kir.*
Hopper
Aratika .... Carlshoff *TA*
Karlshoff
Arno .... Arhno *Marsh.*
Daniel
Pedder
Arorae .... Arore *Kir.*
Hurd
Arutua .... Meerder Zorg *TA*
Asuncion .... Assumption *MI*
Ata .... Pylstaart *Tonga*
Sola
Atafu .... Duke of York *Tok.*
Atiu .... Vatiu *CI*
Wateeoo
Aur .... Aurh *Marsh.*
Ibbetson
Traversey

Babeldaob .... Babelthuap *Car.*
Baker .... New Nantucket *PI*
Phoebe
Baltra .... *Gal.*
Banaba .... Ocean *Kir.*
Paanopa

Banks .... *Van.*	
Bau .... Ambow *Fiji*	
Mbau	
Belep .... *NC*	
Bellona .... Mu Ngiki *Sol.*	
Beqa .... Benga *Fiji*	
Mbenga	
Beru .... Eliza *Kir.*	
Francis	
Maria	
Peroat	
Peru	
Bikar .... Bigar *Marsh.*	
Dawson	
Bikini .... Eschscholtz *Marsh.*	
Udia-Milai	
Birnie .... *PI*	
Bonin .... Arzobispo *BI*	
Ogasawara	
Borabora .... Bolabola *SI*	
Bougainville .... *PNG*	
Buka .... Bouka *PNG*	
Buninga .... *Van.*	
Butaritari .... Allen *Kir.*	
Buen Viaje	
Clarke	
Gillespie	
Smith	
Taritari	
Touching	
Canton .... Mary *PI*	
Mary Balcout	
Swallow	
Caroline .... *Car.*	
Caroline .... Clark *LI*	
Hirst	
Independence	
Thornton	
Chesterfield .... *NC*	
Choiseul .... Lauru *Sol.*	
Christmas .... *LI*	
Cicia .... Chichia *Fiji*	
Cikobia .... Chicobea *Fiji*	
Farewell	
Ticumbia	
Van Shirnding	
Clipperton	
Cook .... Hervey *CI*	
Culpepper .... *Gal.*	
Duff .... *Sol.*	

Easter .... Pascua	
Rapa-Nui	
Teapy	
Waihu	
East Fayu .... Lutke *Car.*	
Eauripik .... Eaurypyg *Car.*	
Ebon .... Boston *Marsh.*	
Covell	
Fourteen	
Linnez	
Efate .... Sandwich *Van.*	
Vate	
Eiao .... Freemantle *Marq.*	
Hiau	
Knox	
Masse	
New York	
Roberts	
Elato .... *Car.*	
Elina .... Obelisk *Sol.*	
Emae .... Mae *Van.*	
Mai	
Three Hills	
Emau .... Hinchinbrook *Van.*	
Mau	
Emirau .... Squally *PNG*	
Storm	
Enderbury .... Enderby *PI*	
Enewetak .... Arthur *Marsh.*	
Brown	
East Danger	
Parry	
West Danger	
Epi .... Api *Van.*	
Tasiko	
Eretoka .... Hat *Van.*	
Erikub .... Bishop Junction *Marsh.*	
Chatham	
Egerup	
Tschitschagoff	
Erromango .... Erromanga *Van.*	
Espanola .... Hood *Gal.*	
Espiritu Santo .... Marina *Van.*	
Santo	
Etal .... Mortlock *Car.*	
Eua .... Eooa *Tonga*	
Middleburgh	
Ewose .... *Van.*	
Faaite .... Admiral Chichagov *TA*	
Faite	
Miloradovich	
Fais .... Tromelin *Car.*	

Fakahina .... Ebrill *TA*
    Fangahina
    Predpriatie
Fakaofu .... Bowditch *Tok.*
Fakarava .... Count Wittgenstein *TA*
    Faarava
Fangatau .... Angatau *TA*
    Arakcheef
    Count Arakcheev
    Fagatau
Fangataufa .... Cockburn TA
    Grimwood
Farallon de Medinilla .... Bird *MI*
Farallon de Pajaros .... Uracas *MI*
Farallon de Torres .. Zealandia Rocks *MI*
Faraulep .... Farroilep *Car.*
    Fattoilep
    Foraulep
    Gardner
Fataka .... Mitre *Sol.*
Fatuhiva .... Magdalena *Marq.*
    Santa Magdalena
Fatuhuku .... Fetuku *Marq.*
    Hood
Feni .... Anir *PNG*
    St Jans
    St John
Fenua-Ura .... Manuae *SI*
    Scilly
Fernandina .... Narborough *Gal.*
Fiji .... Feejee, *Fiji*
    Viti
Flint .... Flint *LI*
Floreana .... Charles *Gal.*
    Santa Maria
Florida .... Flora *Sol.*
    Gela
    Nggela
Fonuafo'ou .... Falcon *Tonga*
Fonualei .... Amargura *Tonga*
    Fanoualie
French Frigate .... Basse des *Haw.*
  Shoal   Fregates
    Francaises
Funafuti .... Ellice *Tuv.*
Futuna .... Erronan *Van.*
    Fotuna
Futuna .... Hoorn *W & F*
    Horn

Gaferut .... *Car.*
Galapagos .... Gallipagoes *Gal.*
Gardner .... Kemin *PI*
Gardner .... Man-of-War Rock *Haw.*

Pinnacles   Pollard Is
    Pollard Rock
Gau .... Neow *Fiji*
    Nhow
Gaua .... Gow *Van.*
    Lacona
    Lakoon
    Santa Maria
Genovesa .... Tower *Gal.*
Gilbert .... Kingsmill (Sthn Gilberts) *Kir.*
Green .... Groene *PNG*
    Nissan
    Sir Charles Hardy
Guadalcanal .... *Sol.*
Guam .... Guahan *MI*
    Guajan
Guguan .... *MI*
Haapai .... Habai *Tonga*
Hall .... *Car.*
Hao .... Bow *TA*
    Conversion de San Pablo
    Harpe
Haraiki .... Croker *TA*
    San Quintin
Hatutu .... Chanal *Marq.*
    Fatuuhu
    Hancock
    Langdon
    Nexsen
Hawaii .... Owahi *Haw.*
    Owhyhee
    Owhyhi
Hawaiian Islands ...... Sandwich *Haw.*
Henderson .... Elizabeth *Pitcairn*
Hereheretue .... Britomart *TA*
    St Paul
    San Pablo
    Surry
Hikueru .... Melville *TA*
    San Juan
    Tuscan
Hiti .... Clute *TA*
    Eliza
Hiu .... North *Van.*
    Seu
    Siew
Hivaoa .... Dominica *Marq.*
    Dominique
Howland .... Holland *PI*
    Worth
Huahine .... *SI*
Hull .... Orona *PI*
Hunter .... *Van.*

Huon .... *NC*

Ifaluk .... Italik *Car.*
Wilson
Isabela .... Albermarle *Gal.*
Santa Gertrudis
Isle of Pines .... Ile des Pins *NC*
Kunie

Jabwat .... Jabwot *Marsh.*
Princessa
Tebut
Jaluit .... Bonham *Marsh.*
Coquille
Elizabeth
Jarvis .... Bunker *LI*
Brooke
Jemo .... Steep-to *Marsh.*
Temo
Johnston .... *near Haw.*
Juan Fernandez .... *JF*

Kabara .... Appallo *Fiji*
Kadavu .... Cantab *Fiji*
Kandavu
Kantavu
Kahoolawe .... Kadoolawee *Haw.*
Kahulaui
Tahaurawe
Tahoorowa
Kapingamarangi ...... Constantin *Car.*
Greenwich
Katiu .... Gen. Osten-Saken *TA*
Sacken
Saken
Kauai .... Atooi *Haw.*
Kauehi .... Cavahi *TA*
Kawahe
Vincennes
Kaukura .... Aura *TA*
Auura
Kaula .... Tahoora *Haw.*
Kermadec .... *KI*
Kili .... Hunter *Marsh.*
Kilinailau .... Carteret *PNG*
Nine
Kingman .... Alice Thorndike *LI*
Kioa .... *Fiji*
Knox .... Narik *Marsh.*
Kolombangara .... Nduke *Sol.*
Koro .... Goro *Fiji*
Kuria .... Woodle *Kir.*
Kosrae .... Strong *Car.*
Ualan

Kwajalein .... Catherine *Marsh.*
Kwadelen
Lae .... Brown *Marsh.*
Lakeba .... *Fiji*
Lamen .... *Van.*
Lamenu .... *Van.*
Lamotrek .... *Car.*
Lanai .... Ranai *Haw.*
Late .... Latte *Tonga*
Lette
Lau .... *Fiji*
Lavongai .... New Hanover *PNG*
Laysan .... Moller *Haw.*
Lelepa .... *Van.*
Lib .... Princess *Marsh.*
Lifou .... Chabrol *NC*
Lifu
Lihir .... Gerrit de Nijs *PNG*
Gerrit Denys
Likiep .... Count Heiden *Marsh.*
Legiep
Line .... *LI*
Lisiansky .... *Haw.*
Lo .... Salt *Van*
Lomaloma .... Lomo-Lomo *Fiji*
Sir Charles Middleton
Lopevi .... *Van.*
Lord Howe .... *Aust.*
Losop .... D'Urville *Car.*
Louasappe
Loyalty .... Loyaute *NC*
Lukunor .... Lougounor *Car.*
Lugunor
Mortlock
McKean .... Drummond *PI*
Maewo .... Aurora *Van.*
Maiwo
Maiana .... Hall *Kir.*
Maiao .... Mauiti *SI*
Sir Charles Saunders
Tapamanoa
Tubuai Manu
Tupuaemanu
Majuro .... Arrowsmith *Marsh.*
Meduro
Makatea .... Aurora *TA*
Maataah
Maeteea
Mataa
Matea
Mathea
Matia
Oumaitia

Makemo .... Koutousoff *TA*
                        Macquemo
                        Philip
                        Phillip
                        Prince Golenitschev-
                        Kutuzov-Smolenski
Makin .... Makin *Kir.*
                        Pitt
                        Recreation
                        Verkwikking
Makogai .... Mokogai *Fiji*
                        Mokungai
Makura .... *Van.*
Malaita .... Carteret *Sol.*
                        Mala
                        Malanta
                        Malayette
Malden .... Independence *LI*
Malakula .... Mallicollo *Van.*
Malo .... Bartholomew *Van.*
                        St Bartholomew
Maloelap .... Araktcheef *Marsh.*
                        Bass Reef-tied
                        Calvert
                        Kaven
                        Maloelab
Malolo .... *Fiji*
Mangaia .... Mangea *CI*
Mangareva .... Gambier *TA*
Manihi .... Dagenraad *TA*
                        Prince of Wales
                        Waterlandt
                        Wilson
Manihiki .... Great Ganges *CI*
                        Humphrey
Manono .... Platte *Samoa*
Manra .... Sydney *PI*
Manua
Manua-Tele .... Opoun *Samoa*
Manuae .... Hervey *CI*
Manuhangi .... Cumberland *TA*
                        Duke of Cumberland
Marakei .... Maraki *Kir.*
                        Matthew
Maramsike .... Small Malaita *Sol.*
Marchena .... Bindloe *Gal.*
Marcus .... *near BI*
Mare .... Britannia *NC*
Maria .... Gardner *AI*
                        Huli
                        Nurorutu
                        Sands

Maria .... Bertero *TA*
                        Moerenhout
                        Wright's Lagoon
Mariana .... Ladrones *MI*
Marokau .... Two Groups *TA*
Marotiri .... Bass *AI*
Marquesas .... *Marq.*
Marshall .... *Marsh.*
Marutea .... Furneaux *TA*
Marutea (Sth) .... Lord Hood *TA*
Mas-A-Fuera .... *JF*
Mas-A-Tierra .... *JF*
Maskelyne .... *Van.*
Matahiva .... Lazarev *TA*
Mataso .... Two Hills *Van.*
Matthew .... *Van.*
Maturei Vavao .... Melbourne *TA*
Maug .... *MI*
Maui .... Mowee *Haw.*
Mauke .... Mauti *CI*
                        Parry
Maupiti .... Marua *SI*
                        Maura
Mehetia .... Boudoir *SI*
                        Maitea
                        Osnaburg
                        Pic de la Boudeuse
                        San Cristobal
Mejit .... Miadi *Marsh.*
                        New Year
Mera Lava .... Maralaba *Van.*
                        Merlav
                        San Marcos
                        Star Peak
Merig .... St Claire *Van.*
Merir .... Warren Hastings *Car.*
Midway .... Brooks
Mili .... Mille *Marsh.*
                        Mulgrave
Mitiaro .... Mitiero *CI*
Mohotani .... Motane *Marq.*
                        San Pedro
Mokil .... Duperrey *Car.*
                        Wellington
Molokai .... Morotoi *Haw.*
Moorea .... Aimeo *SI*
                        Duke of York
                        Eimeo
Mopelia .... Lord Howe *SI*
                        Mopihaa
Morane .... Barstow *TA*
                        Cadmus
Mortlock .... *Car.*

Moruroa	Bishop of Osnaburg *TA*	
	Matilda's Rocks	
	Mururoa	
	Osnaburg	
Moso	Deception *Van.*	
Mota	Amota *Van.*	
	Sugar-loaf	
Motuiti	Blake *Marq.*	
	Franklin	
	Hergest	
	Two Brothers	
Motu-Oa	Lincoln *Marq.*	
Moturiki	Matoriki *Fiji*	
Motutunga	Adventure *TA*	
Munia	Hadow *Fiji*	
Murilo	Mourileu *Car.*	
Mussau	St Matthias *PNG*	
Nama	*Car.*	
Namoluk	Harvest *Car.*	
	Hashmy	
Namonuito	Anonima *Car.*	
	Onon	
Namorik	Baring *Marsh.*	
	Namarik	
Namu	Margaretta *Marsh.*	
	Muskillo	
	Namo	
	Paterson	
	Ross	
Nanumanga	Gran Cocal *Tuv.*	
	Hudson	
	Isla del Cocal	
Nanumea	San Agustin *Tuv.*	
Napuka	Disappointment *TA*	
	Wytoohee	
Nassau	Mitchell *CI*	
Nauru	Nawodo	
	Onavero	
	Pleasant	
Ndai	Gower *Sol.*	
	Inattendue	
Ndende	Ndeni *Sol.*	
	Nitendi	
	Santa Cruz	
Necker	*Haw.*	
Nendo	see Ndende above	
Nengonengo	Lostange *TA*	
	Ningoningo	
	Prince William Henry	
New Britain	Neu Pommern *PNG*	
New Caledonia	*NC*	
New Georgia	*Sol.*	
New Guinea	*PNG*	

New Ireland ...	Neu Mecklenburg *PNG*	
Ngatik	Ngaryk *Car.*	
	Valientes	
Ngulu	Goulou *Car.*	
	Lamoliork	
	Lamuliur	
	Spencer Keys	
Nguna	Montagu *Van.*	
Nihiru	Nihera *TA*	
Nihoa	Bird *Haw.*	
Niihau	Oneeheow *Haw.*	
	Oneeow	
Nikunau	Byron *Kir.*	
	Nukunau	
Niuafo'ou	Consolacion *Tonga*	
	Goede Hope	
	Niuafu	
	Proby	
	Tin Can	
Niuatoputapu	Boscawen *Tonga*	
	Cocos	
	Niuatabutabu	
Niue	Nieue	
	Savage	
Niulakita	Independence *Tuv.*	
	Nurakita	
	Rocky	
	Solitaria	
	Saphia	
Niutao	Loper *Tuv.*	
	Lynx	
	Sepper	
Nomoi	Mortlock *Car.*	
Nomuka	Anamooka *Tonga*	
	Namuka	
Nomwin	*Car.*	
Nonouti	Nanouki *Kir.*	
	Nanouti	
	Sydenham	
Norfolk	*Aust.*	
Nuguria	Abgarris *PNG*	
	Fead	
	Niguria	
Nui	Jesus *Tuv.*	
	Nederlandsch	
Nukufetau	De Peyster *Tuv.*	
Nukuhiva	Adams *Marq.*	
	Baux	
	Federal	
	Franklin	
	Madison	
	Nooaheevah	
	Sir Henry Martin	

Nukulaelae .... Mitchell *Tuv.*
    Nukulailai
Nukumanu .... *PNG*
Nukunono .... Duke of Clarence *Tok.*
Nukuoro .... Monteverde *Car.*
    Nougoure
Nukutavake .... Leopold I *TA*
    Queen Charlotte
Nukutipipi ...... Duke of Gloucester *TA*
    Margaret

Oahu .... Woahoo *Haw.*
Oeno .... *Pitcairn*
Ofu .... *Samoa*
Olimarao .... *Car.*
Olosenga .... Olisinga *Samoa*
    Orisega
Onon .... Anonima *Car.*
    Namonuito
Onotoa .... Clerk *Kir.*
    Eliza
    Lincoln
    Onutu
Ontong Java .... Lord Howe *Sol.*
Oroluk .... Bordelaise *Car.*
    San Agustino
Ouvea .... Halgan *NC*
    Uea
    Uvea
Ovalau .... Bulloo *Fiji*
    Obalauo
    Onalau
    Ovolau

Paama .... Paum *Van.*
Pagan .... Pagon *MI*
Pakin .... Peguenema *Car.*
Palau .... Palaos *Car.*
    Pelew
Palmerston .... *CI*
Palmyra .... *LI*
Paraoa .... Duke of Gloucester *TA*
    Gloucester
Parece Vela .... Douglas Reef *Japan*
Pearl & Hermes .... *Haw.*
  Reef
Penrhyn .... Tongareva *CI*
Pentecost .... Arragh *Van.*
    Pentecote
    Raga
    Whitsun
Phoenix .... *PI*
Pikelot .... Coquille *Car.*

Pinaki .... Reine Louise *TA*
    Whitsun
    Whitsunday
Pingelap .... MacAskill *Car.*
    Musgrave
Pinta .... Abingdon *Gal.*
Pinzon .... Duncan *Gal.*
Pitcairn .... *Pitcairn*
Pohnpei .... Ponape *Car.*
    Ascension
    Puynipet
    Seniavine
Pukapuka .... Danger *CI*
Pukapuka .... Dog *TA*
    Honden
    San Pablo
Pukarua .... Apoucaroua *TA*
    Serle
Pulo Anna .... *Car.*
Pulusuk .... Bartolome *Car.*
    Ibargoitia
    Poulousouk
    Sooughe
    Suk
Puluwat .... Enderby *Car.*
    Kata
    Poloat

Rabi .... Gillet *Fiji*
    Rambi
    Ranbe
Rabida .... Jervis *Gal.*
Ratak .... Radak *Marsh.*
Raevski .... Hiti *TA*
    Tepoto
    Tuanake
Raiatea .... Uliatea *SI*
    Ulietea
Raivavae .... High *AI*
    Santa Rosa
    Vavitao
Rakahanga .... Gente Hermosa *CI*
  Grand Duke Alexander
    Little Ganges
    Reirson
Ralik .... *Marsh.*
Rangiroa .... Dean *TA*
  Goede Verwaghting
    Nairsa
    Rairoa
    Vlieghen
Raoul .... Sunday *KI*
Rapa .... Oparo *AI*
    Rapa-iti

Raraka .... Ireland *TA*
Rarotonga .... Armstrong *CI*
                    Roxburgh
Raroia .... Barclay de Tolly *TA*
Ravahere .... Dawahaidy *TA*
                   Two Groups
Reao .... Clermont de Tonnere *TA*
                   Minerva
Reef .... Matema *Sol.*
                   Swallow
Reitoru .... Bird *TA*
Rekareka .... Good Hope *TA*
                   Tehuata
Rennell .... Mu Nggava *Sol.*
Rimatara .... Rimatera *AI*
Rongelap .... Bigini *Marsh.*
                   Kongelab
                   Pescadore
Rongerik .... Radokala *Marsh.*
               Rimski-Korsakoff
Rose .... Kordiukoff *Samoa*
                   Middleton
Rota .... Sarpan *MI*
                   Zarpan
Rotuma .... Grenville *Fiji*
Rowa .... Reef *Van.*
Rurutu .... Oheteroah *AI*
Russell .... *Sol.*
Ryukyu .... Loo-choo *RI*
                   Lu-chu

Saipan .... Seypan *MI*
Sala-y-Gomez .... *Chile*
Samoa .... Navigators *Samoa*
San Alessandro .... North *VI*
San Ambrosio .... *Chile*
San Augustino .... San Dionisio *VI*
San Cristobal .... Chatham *Gal.*
San Cristobal .... Arossi *Sol.*
                   Makira
              San Christoval
San Felix .... *Chile*
San Jorge .... Moumolu-Naunitu *Sol.*
San Salvador .... Santiago *Gal.*
                   James
Santa Ana .... Owa Rafa *Sol.*
                   Owa Raha
Santa Catalina .... Owa Riki *Sol.*
Santa Cruz .... Chaves *Gal.*
               Indefatigable
Santa Fe .... Barrington *Gal.*
Santa Isabel .... Santa Ysabel *Sol.*
                   Ysabel

Sarigan .... Sariguan *MI*
Satawal .... Setuahal *Car.*
                   Tucker
Satawan .... Satouwan *Car.*
Savaii .... Chatham *Samoa*
Seymour .... *Gal.*
Shepherd .... *Van.*
Shortland .... *Sol.*
Sikaiana .... Stewart *Sol.*
Simbo .... Eddystone *Sol.*
              Mandeghughusu
Society .... *SI*
Sonsorol .... St Andrew *Car.*
                   Sansoral
Sorol .... Philip *Car.*
Sotoan .... Mortlock *Car.*
South Marutea .... Lord Hood *TA*
Starbuck .... Barren *LI*
                 Coral Queen
                   Hero
                   Low
                   Starve
Surprise .... *NC*
Suwarrow .... Souworoff *CI*
                   Suvarov
Swain .... Olosenga *Samoa*
                   Quiros

Tabar .... Gardner *PNG*
Tabiteuea .... Bishop *GI*
                   Drummond
                   Taputeouea
Taenga .... Cainga *TA*
                   Holt
        Lieutenant-General Yermalov
       Prince de Joinville Yermoeloff
Tafahi .... Keppel *Tonga*
                   Traitors
                   Verraders
Tahaa .... Otaha *SI*
Tahanea .... Chichagov *TA*
                   San Julian
                   Tchitchagoff
Tahiti .... Amat *SI*
                 King George III
               Nouvelle Cythere
                   Otahiti
Tahuata .... Christiana *Marq.*
                 Santa Cristina
Taiaro .... King *TA*
Taka .... Souworoff *Marsh.*
                   Tagai

Takapoto	King George *TA*
	Schadelijk
	Sondergrondt
	Spiridoff
	Taapoto
	Zondergrondt
Takaroa	King George *TA*
	Sondergrondt
	Taaroa
	Tiokea
	Zondergrondt
Takume	Prince Volkhonski *TA*
	Tacume
	Wolkonsky
Takutea	Wenoaette *CI*
Tamana	Rotch *Kir.*
Tangoa	Anthony Caen *PNG*
	Anthony Kaan
	Oraison
Tongoa	Tannoa *Van.*
Tanna	Tana *Van.*
Taongi	Gaspar Rico *Marsh.*
	Smyth
Tarawa	Cook *Kir.*
	Knox
Tatakoto	Augier *TA*
	Clarke
	Daugier
	David Clark
	Narciso
	San Narciso
	Takoto
Tauere	Resolution *TA*
	San Simon y Judas
Taumako	Disappointment *Sol.*
Tauu	Marque(e)n *PNG*
	Mortlock
Te Au-O-Tu	*CI*
Tegua	Middle *Van.*
	Tuga
Tekokoto	Doubtful *TA*
	Martires
Tematangi	Bligh's Lagoon *TA*
	Lagoon
Temoe	Crescent *TA*
	Timoe
Tenararo	*TA*
Tenarunga	Minto *TA*
Tench	Nusi *PNG*
Tepoto	Disappointment *TA*
	Otooho
Tepoto	Eliza *TA*
	Raevski
Tetiaroa	Tethuroa *SI*
	Tetuaroa

Tiga	Boucher *NC*
	Tika
Tikehau	Krusenstern *TA*
Tikei	Bedrieglyke *TA*
	Romanzoff
	Rumanzoff
Tikopia	Barwell *Sol.*
	Tucopia
Tingwon	Portland *PNG*
Tinian	Buena Vista *MI*
Toau	Count Wittgenstein *TA*
	Elizabeth
Tobi	Lord North *Car.*
	Neville
Toga	Buga Buga *Van.*
	Buka
	Torga
Tokelau	Union *Tok.*
Tonga	Friendly *Tonga*
Tongatapu	Amsterdam *Tonga*
Torres	*Van.*
Tortuga	Brattle *Gal.*
Truk	Hogoleu *Car.*
	Ruk
Tuamotu	Dangerous *TA*
	Paumotu
	Pomotu
Tuanake	Reid *TA*
Tupai	Motu-iti *SI*
	Tubai
Tureia	Carysfort *TA*
Tutuila	Masuna *Samoa*
	Tootooilah
Tuvalu	Ellice *Tuv.*
Tuvuca	Tabutha *Fiji*
Uahuka	Massachusetts *Marq.*
	Ouahouka
	Riou
	Roahouga
	Rooahooga
	Washington
Uapou	Adams *Marq.*
	Jefferson
	Marchand
	Trevenen
	Washington
Ujae	Lydia *Marsh.*
Ujelang	Arrecifes *Marsh.*
	Casbobas
	Casobos
	Providence
	Ujilong
Uki	Ugi *Sol.*
Ulawa	Contrariete *Sol.*

Ulithi .... Mackenzie *Car.*
Umboi .... Rook(e) *PNG*
Upolu .... Oahtooha *Samoa*
                     Ojalava
                     Opoloo
Ureparapara .... Bligh *Van.*
                     Norbarbar
Utirik .... Button *Marsh.*
                     Kutusoff
                     Udirick
Utupua .... Edgecumbe *Sol.*

Vahanga .... Bedford *TA*
Vahitahi .... Lagoon *TA*
                     Quatre Facardins
Vairaatea .... Egmont *TA*
                     Industriel
                     Lord Egmont
                     Pukararo
                     Pukarunga
                     San Miguel
                     Santa Polonia
Vaitupu .... Oaitupu *Tuv.*
                     Tracy
Valua .... Mota Lava *Van.*
                     Mottlap
                     Natlop
                     Nutloff
                     Saddle
Vanavana .... Barrow *TA*
Vanikoro .... Mannicolo *Sol.*
                     Pitt
                     Recherche
                     Vanikolo

Vanuabalavu .... Vanua-Valavo *Fiji*
Vanua Lava .... *Van.*
Vatganai .... Vatu Rhandi *Van.*
Vatoa .... Turtle *Fiji*
Vatuvara .... Batou-Bara *Fiji*
                     Vatu-rera
Vavau .... Lord Howe *Tonga*
                     Martin de Mayorga
Viwa .... Biva *Fiji*
Volcano .... Sulphur *VI*
Vostok .... Anne *LI*
                     Stavers

Wake .... Halcyon
Wallis .... Uea *W&F*
                     Uvea
Washington .... Prospect *LI*
                     New York
Wenman .... *Gal.*
West Fayu .... *Car.*
Woleai .... Ulie *Car.*
                     Wolea
Woodlark .... Murua *PNG*
Wotho .... Schantz *Marsh.*
                     Shanz
                     Wottho
Wotje .... Otdia *Marsh.*
                     Romanzoff
Wuvulu .... Maty *PNG*

Yap .... Eap *Car.*
Yasawa .... Asava *Fiji*

Index of Islands
Atolls and Islets

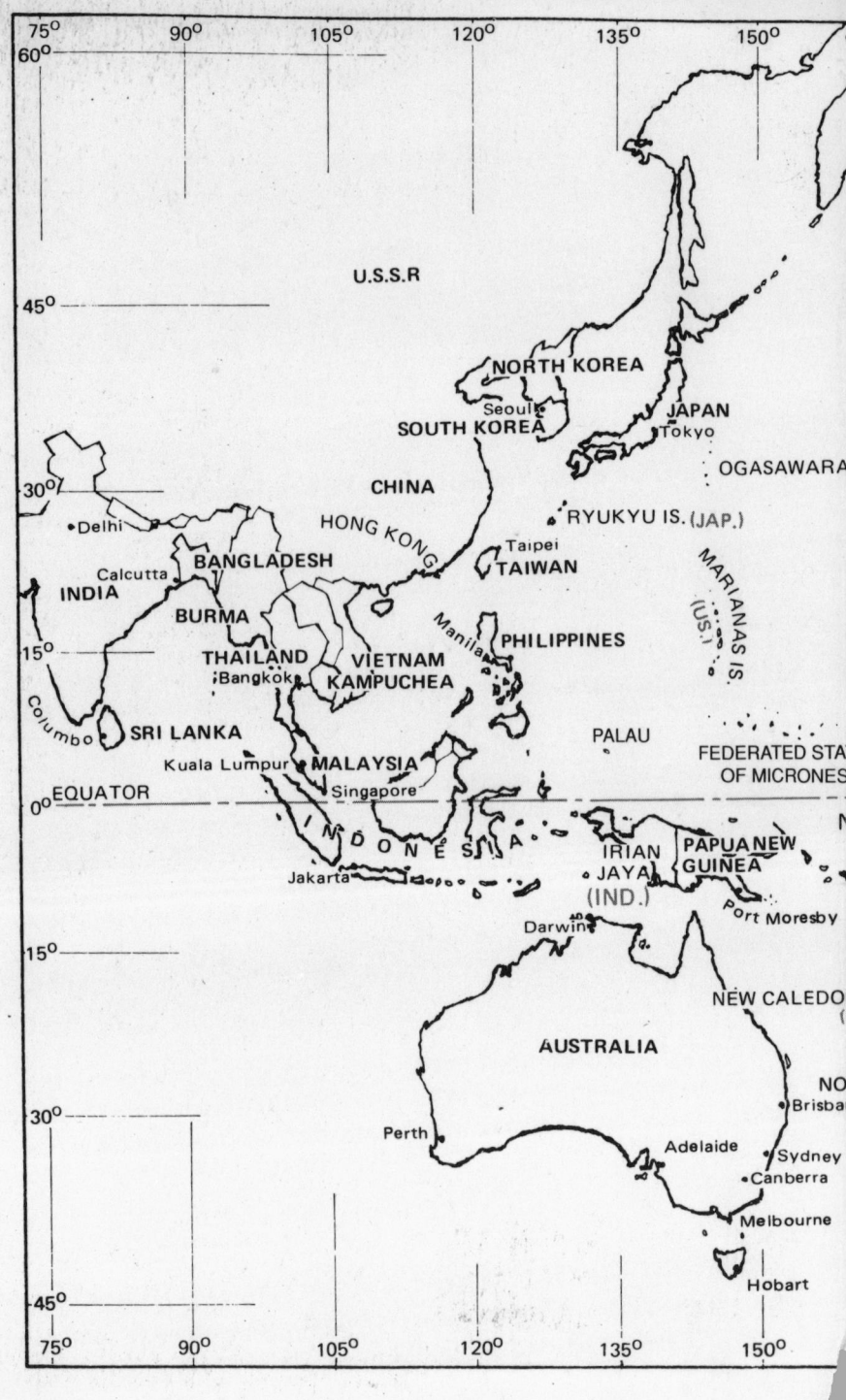